For Students

©Shutterstock/wavebreakmedia

Effective, efficient studying.

Connect helps you be more productive with your study time and get better grades using tools like SmartBook, which highlights key concepts and creates a personalized study plan. Connect sets you up for success, so you walk into class with confidence and walk out with better grades.

"I really liked this app—it made it easy to study when you don't have your textbook in front of you."

- Jordan Cunningham, Eastern Washington University

Study anytime, anywhere.

Download the free ReadAnywhere app and access your online eBook when it's convenient, even if you're offline. And since the app automatically syncs with your eBook in Connect, all of your notes are available every time you open it. Find out more at **www.mheducation.com/readanywhere**

No surprises.

The Connect Calendar and Reports tools keep you on track with the work you need to get done and your assignment scores. Life gets busy; Connect tools help you keep learning through it all.

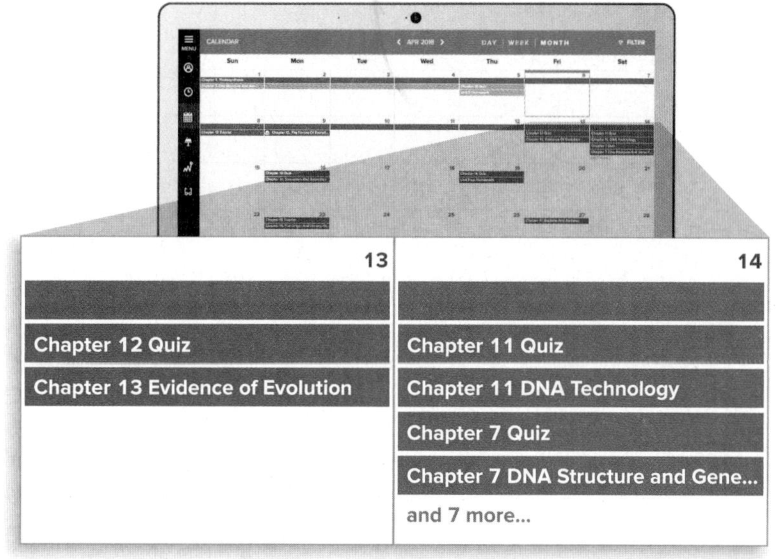

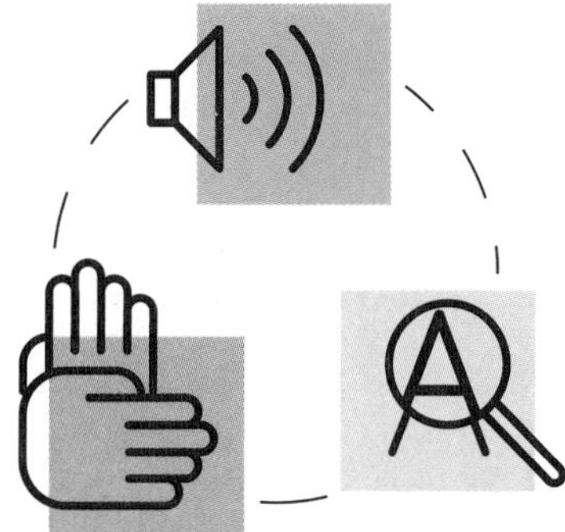

Learning for everyone.

McGraw-Hill works directly with Accessibility Services Departments and faculty to meet the learning needs of all students. Please contact your Accessibility Services office and ask them to email accessibility@mheducation.com, or visit **www.mheducation.com/accessibility** for more information.

EXPERIENCE

SOCIOLOGY

FOURTH EDITION

DAVID CROTEAU

WILLIAM HOYNES

EXPERIENCE SOCIOLOGY

Some ancillaries, including electronic and print components, may not be available to customers outside the United States.

This book is printed on acid-free paper.

1 2 3 4 5 6 7 8 9 LWI 21 20 19

ISBN: 978-1-260-54786-3
MHID: 1-260-54786-8

mheducation.com/highered

About the AUTHORS

©David R. Croteau

DAVID R. CROTEAU earned a BA in sociology from Brandeis University and a PhD in sociology from Boston College. Over the years he has taught a diverse range of students at Boston College, Clark University, Keene State College, and the University of Mary Washington. He is an Associate Professor Emeritus in the Sociology Department at Virginia Commonwealth University, where he taught introductory sociology as well as both undergraduate and graduate courses on theory, methods, stratification, social movements, and media. He also worked as an online learning specialist in VCU's Academic Learning Transformation Lab (ALT Lab) helping faculty to develop online courses. In addition to various journal articles and book chapters, David Croteau is the author of *Politics and the Class Divide*, a finalist for both the C. Wright Mills Award from the Society for the Study of Social Problems and the Transformational Politics Book Award from the American Political Science Association.

©William Hoynes

WILLIAM HOYNES earned a BA in history and political science from Tufts University and a PhD in sociology from Boston College. He is Professor of Sociology at Vassar College, where he teaches introductory sociology as well as courses on media, culture, research methods, and social theory. During his more than 25 years at Vassar, Professor Hoynes has served as chair of the Sociology Department and director of both the Media Studies Program and the American Studies Program.

In addition to various journal articles and book chapters on public broadcasting in the United States, Professor Hoynes is the author of *Public Television for Sale: Media, the Market, and the Public Sphere,* which was awarded the Goldsmith Book Prize from the Shorenstein Center on Media, Politics and Public Policy at Harvard University's John F. Kennedy School of Government.

CROTEAU and HOYNES are coauthors of *Media/Society*, which was published in a revised sixth edition in 2019; *The Business of Media: Corporate Media and the Public Interest*, which won the Robert Picard Award for best new book in media economics by the Association for Education in Journalism and Mass Communication; and *By Invitation Only: How the Media Limit Political Debate*. They are also coeditors, with Charlotte Ryan, of *Rhyming Hope and History: Activists, Academics, and Social Movement Scholarship*.

Dear Colleagues

Now more than ever, we want to help a diverse range of students grasp the basic concepts of the discipline, see the relevance of those concepts to their everyday lives, and apply what they learn to the world around them. We want students to see the familiar in a new way and realize that sociology's tools can help them better understand their rapidly changing social world. In other words, we want students to see the world from a sociological perspective and to actively use their sociological imagination. We want them to experience sociology.

What's unique about *Experience Sociology*?

CULTURE. STRUCTURE. POWER. *Experience Sociology* engages students with a clear framework for understanding their world based on three familiar terms at the heart of sociology: culture, structure, and power. Through the lenses of these three concepts, students learn from their first class to see the world from a sociological perspective and to grasp the significance of sociology for their own lives. For every topic in the book–from the family to the economy to the environment–they learn to recognize the effects of the culture they have been taught, see the structures that constrain or empower them, and notice how power operates at every level of society.

How is theory covered?

Theory has a role in every chapter in *Experience Sociology*. We know how important it is for students not only to be able to apply concepts to their lives, but also to understand and be able to apply sociological theory. With its innovative organization around primary sociological concepts, *Experience Sociology* emphasizes the common ground that informs a basic sociological perspective. But every chapter also addresses the way differing theoretical perspectives illuminate various facets of these key sociological concepts, letting instructors and students go beyond conventional theoretical boundaries and the either-or framing of theoretical perspectives to see how each can contribute to our understanding of the social world.

What's the full Experience?

The fourth edition of *Experience Sociology* is much more than this text alone. Incorporating the work of many sociology instructors, it is instead a comprehensive instructional program that combines digital and print resources to promote student learning. Integrated with McGraw-Hill's Connect Sociology, including SmartBook's adaptive technology and learning resources, *Experience Sociology* helps you manage assignments and makes learning and studying more engaging and efficient for your students.

We wrote *Experience Sociology* because we want students to be able to experience their world differently through the insights of sociology. We hope these resources will help you in introducing your students to the excitement of sociology.

Sincerely,

BRIEF CONTENTS

CONTENTS

PART 2

SOCIOLOGY'S CORE CONCEPTS: TOOLS FOR ANALYSIS AND UNDERSTANDING

3

©Eric Nathan/Alamy Stock Photo

CULTURE 50

4

©Imageplus/Corbis

SOCIAL STRUCTURE 76

5

©Jabin Botsford/The Washington Post/Getty Images

POWER 98

PART 3
THE SOCIAL SELF

©Creatas Images/Getty Images

©Karl Weatherly/Photographer's Choice/Getty Images

©Jenner Images/Moment/Getty Images

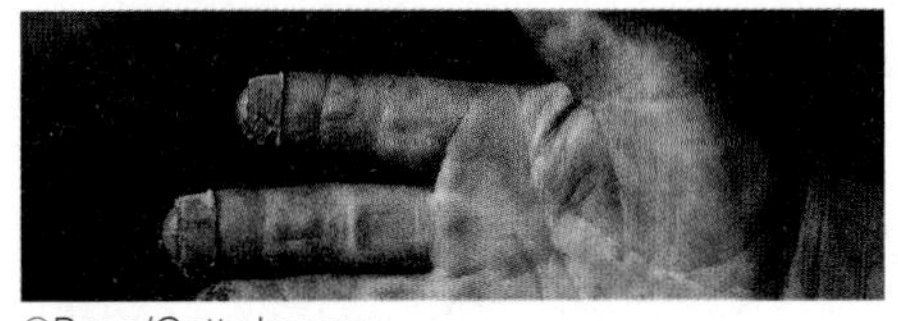
©Reza/Getty Images

10

©Jim West/Alamy Stock Photo

11

©MoMo Productions/DigitalVision/Getty Images

PART 5
SOCIAL INSTITUTIONS AND SOCIAL ISSUES

12

©P. Deliss/Corbis Documentary/Getty Images

13

©Sturti/E+/Getty Images

14

©Damien Meyer/AFP/Getty Images

15

©John Seaton Callahan/Getty Images

16 
©Drew Angerer/Getty Images

POLITICS AND THE ECONOMY 410

17 
©Matt McClain/The Washington Post/Getty Images

SOCIAL CHANGE: GLOBALIZATION, POPULATION, AND SOCIAL MOVEMENTS 440

Give your students a clearer picture of their world

WHY THE GLASSES?

We want students to see their familiar world in a clearer and deeper way. *Experience Sociology,* Fourth Edition, uses the lenses of culture, structure, and power to encourage students to move beyond an individual perspective while developing their own sociological imagination.

How were you socialized into your society's **culture**?

How do agents of socialization reproduce social **structure**?

How does **power** shape your daily life and your sense of self?

Using the lenses of **CULTURE**, **STRUCTURE**, and **POWER**, *Experience Sociology* shows students the significance of sociology for their own lives.

CULTURE, **STRUCTURE**, and **POWER** help students explore sociological theory in ways that go beyond conventional theoretical boundaries.

EXPERIENCE SOCIOLOGY includes a variety of boxed features and in-text learning aids to help students appreciate the range of sociology's insights and their relevance to today's fast-changing social world, and to apply sociology's concepts and theories to their own lives.

BOXED FEATURES

Sociology in Action boxes highlight the contributions of sociological research to public policy and to the efforts of public interest organizations, social movements, and others to effect social change.

Sociology Works boxes profile people who studied sociology in college and are now using sociology's insights in diverse work settings. These high-interest stories feature people working in fields such as health care, criminal justice, social work, labor unions, business, mass media, government, and the military.

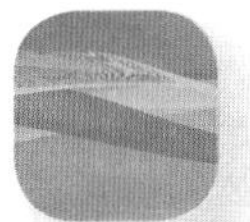

Through a Sociological Lens boxes demonstrate how sociology can provide distinctive insights into contemporary social issues. Students can see how sociological research reveals information that can both surprise and empower them in their everyday lives.

FF

Fast-Forward boxes illuminate the ever-evolving nature of our social world. These brief, engaging features—illustrated with photographs, advertisements, or other images—show students how change has been a constant feature of social life.

A Changing World sections conclude each chapter with a look at the influence of changing social conditions on some aspect of the chapter topic. Examples include culture and globalization, increasing inequality in the United States, social structure and privacy, and convergence in gender and sexuality.

IN-TEXT LEARNING AIDS

think

Thinking About notes help students connect chapter content to their own experience. These brief notes, found at the bottom of text pages, prompt students to consider how the three core concepts of **culture, structure,** and **power** apply to their own lives and views on issues, thus encouraging students to think sociologically.

CCC

Core Concepts Challenge questions encourage students to apply their sociological imagination to what they are learning. Appearing with selected figures, tables, and photographs, these questions prompt students to apply **culture, structure,** and **power** in thinking about an issue as well as to think critically about the graphic, table, or image.

Spotlight notes prompt students to consider social theories that are discussed within the text. These notes help students use the three concepts to apply theory to their own lives.

Help Your Students Succeed with *Connect*

McGraw-Hill Education Connect® is an integrated educational platform that includes assignable and assessable quizzes, exercises, and interactive activities, all associated with learning objectives for *Experience Sociology,* Fourth Edition. Videos, interactive assessments, links to news articles about current issues with accompanying questions ("NewsFlash"), and scenario-based activities engage students and add real-world perspective to the introductory sociology course. In addition, printable, exportable reports show how well each student or section is performing on each course segment.

Here are some of the media-rich activities that will help your students succeed in the introductory sociology course:

In Their Shoes. In Their Shoes develops students' sociological imagination by walking them through the situation, challenges, and crises in the character's life. Covering topics such as "Deviance and Social Control," "Racial and Ethnic Inequality," and "Socialization and the Life Course," these activities prompt students to explore and navigate life choices in another's shoes.

Applying the Perspectives. In Applying Their Perspectives, students examine a problem—global inequality, gender stratification, or family and intimate relationships—from three sociological perspectives and apply their critical-thinking skills to align theories with the appropriate perspective.

Concept Clips. Concept Clips are animations designed to engage students and walk them through some of the more complex concepts in the course. Each clip concludes with assessment questions to test student understanding. Topics include research variables, functions of religion, and power and authority.

Put students first with Connect's intuitive mobile interface, which gives students and instructors flexible, convenient, anytime-anywhere access to all components of the Connect platform. It provides seamless integration of learning tools and places the most important priorities up front in a new "to-do" list with a calendar view across all Connect courses. Enjoy on-the-go access with the new mobile interface designed for optimal use of tablet functionality.

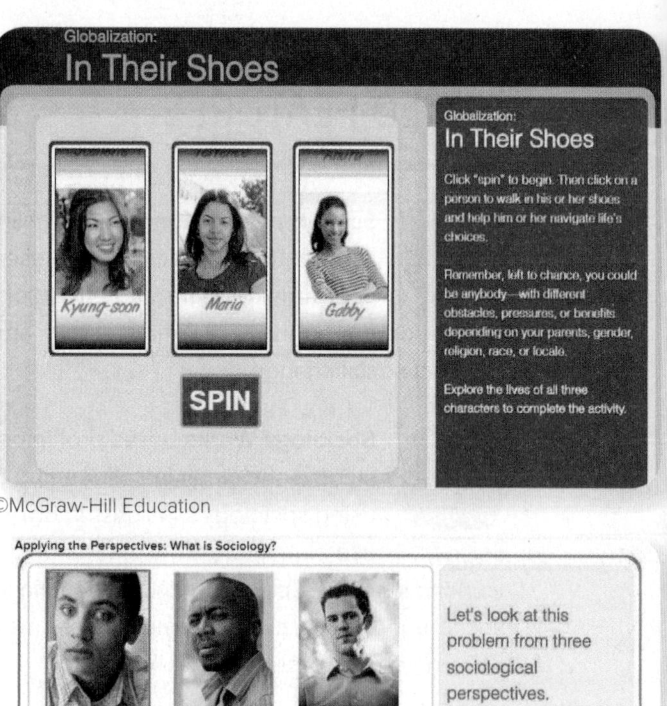

©McGraw-Hill Education

©McGraw-Hill Education

Concept Clip: Sociology as a Science

Watch the Concept Clip and then respond to the following questions.

©McGraw-Hill Education

Provide a Smarter Text and Better Value with *SmartBook*

SMARTBOOK®

Available within Connect, **SmartBook** makes study time as productive and efficient as possible by identifying and closing knowledge gaps. SmartBook is powered by the proven LearnSmart® engine, which identifies what an individual student knows and doesn't know based on the student's confidence level, responses to questions, and other factors. It then provides focused help through targeted learning resources (including videos, animations, and other interactive activities).

SmartBook builds an optimal, personalized learning path for each student, so students spend less time on concepts they already understand and more time on those they don't. As a student engages with SmartBook, the reading experience continuously adapts by highlighting the most impactful content a student needs to learn at that moment in time. This ensures that every minute spent with SmartBook is returned to the student as the most value-added minute possible. The result? More confidence, better grades, and greater success.

New to this edition, SmartBook is now optimized for phones and tablets and accessible for students with disabilities using interactive features. Just like our new ebook and ReadAnywhere app, SmartBook is available both online and offline.

Prepare Students for Higher-Level Thinking

Aimed at the higher level of Bloom's taxonomy, **Power of Process for Sociology** helps students improve critical thinking skills and allows instructors to assess these skills efficiently and effectively in an online environment. Available through Connect, preloaded readings are available for instructors to assign. Using a scaffolded framework that includes synthesizing and analyzing, Power of Process moves students toward higher-level thinking.

Access Performance Data Just in Time

Mc Graw Hill Education connect INSIGHT

Connect Insight® is Connect's one-of-a-kind visual analytics dashboard, now available for both instructors and students, that provides at-a-glance information regarding student performance, which is immediately actionable. By presenting assignment, assessment, and topical performance results, together with a time metric that is easily visible for aggregate or individual results, Connect Insight gives the user the ability to take a just-in-time approach to teaching and learning, which was never before available. Connect Insight presents data that empowers students and helps instructors improve class performance in a way that is efficient and effective.

A Revision Informed by Student Data

Ever since students began using it, Connect Sociology's SmartBook for *Experience Sociology*, has been collecting anonymous data on students' performance on specific learning objectives. This aggregated data, displayed in the form of **heat maps,** graphically identifies challenging "hot spots" in the text, helping guide the revision of both core content and assessment activities for the Fourth Edition. This heat-map-directed revision is reflected primarily in Chapters 5, 14, and 16.

Highlights of the Fourth Edition

The text has been refreshed throughout with references to recent scholarship, and figures, maps, and tables have been updated throughout with the most recent available data. Revisions in response to heat-map data are indicated by ✓.

CHAPTER 1

- New chapter-opening vignette on bilingual education
- Clearer explanation of the concept of sociological theory
- Revised discussion of postmodern society, with updates reflecting current events, such as the Trump presidency and the global economy
- Significantly updated Sociology in Action box, "Working to Reduce Homelessness"

CHAPTER 2

- New chapter-opening vignette on research into urban violence "hot spots"
- New data on voting rates in the 2016 election
- Revised discussion of qualitative research methods, utilizing new study on homeless young adults
- Revised discussion on explaining data, referencing new study on "tagging" ✓
- Up-to-date analysis of Pew Research Center's 2017 American Trends Panel survey
- Revised discussions of focus groups and research utilizing existing sources, including new examples ✓
- Updated Sociology in Action box, "The U.S. Census Bureau," addressing proposal to include citizenship question on 2020 questionnaire
- Updated Changing World feature, "Technology and Social Research," discussing research into massively multiplayer online games

CHAPTER 3

- Updated discussion of the means through which values change over time ✓
- New Map 3.1, "The 2016 Election: Red and Blue or Purple?"
- New example of attempts to preserve culture by revitalizing dying languages
- Updated Fast Forward feature, incorporating a new graphic antismoking ad
- Updated coverage of the criticisms of multiculturalism ✓

CHAPTER 4

- Revised introduction to social structure, utilizing the aftermath of Hurricane Maria as an example ✓
- New example of parent-teacher conferences in discussion of conversation analysis
- Updated Through a Sociological Lens box on organizational structure and school violence
- Updated section "Globalization and the Structure of Work" to reflect current events ✓
- Updated Sociology in Action box featuring Ruth Milkman
- Updated discussion of mobile phones in Africa
- Revised Changing World section on loneliness and the changing structure of friendship ✓

CHAPTER 5

- New chapter-opening vignette on the power struggle between the movement for gun control and the National Rifle Association
- Expanded discussions of feminist approach to understanding power and intersectionality ✓
- Revised discussion of class in capitalist systems ✓
- Rewritten Fast Forward feature, "Social Change and Class Segregation" ✓
- New Sociology Works box, "Leveraging Power for Economic Justice"
- New Changing World feature, "Algorithms and the Power of Tech Companies" ✓

CHAPTER 6

- Updated chapter-opening vignette on Melanie Matchett Wood and the gender gap in mathematics
- Revised discussion of "media" as an agent of socialization ✓
- Updated discussion of adolescence and adulthood ✓
- New information in epigenetics section ✓

CHAPTER 7

- Discussion of the Thomas Theorem revised for clarity ✓
- Discussion of the partisan divide as an example of an in-group/out-group dynamic
- Revised section on social network analysis ✓
- Revised and updated discussion of networks and groups in the digital age
- Updated and revised "A Changing World" section on privacy and social media

CHAPTER 8

- Updated material on the impact of contact with the police on middle school students

- Significantly rewritten section on "Surveillance and Social Control in the Digital Age," addressing current topics such as digital tracking on Facebook and through GPS, the use of "scraping" to link data about online and offline activities, the 2018 revelations regarding Cambridge Analytica's use of Facebook data, government use of digital surveillance, and recent discussions regarding privacy concerns ✓
- New figure, "Personal Data Likely Collected and Stored about You (a partial list)"
- Updated data on crime rates, incarceration rates, and capital punishment in the United States
- New coverage of the popularity and impact of "deviant leisure" ✓

CHAPTER 9

- Updated statistics on social classes In the United States
- Updated data and new figure on the distribution of income and wealth in the United States
- Updated list of occupations with the largest projected job growth
- Revised Through a Sociological Lens box on growing inequality among African Americans
- Comprehensively revised and updated discussion of the relationship between class and education ✓
- Updated discussion of U.S. poverty rates, including new statistics ✓
- Revised and updated discussion of wages, labor laws, and labor union decline, including a new figure ✓

CHAPTER 10

- New chapter-opening vignette on the Trump presidency and race relations in the United States
- Updated data on racial and ethnic diversity in the U.S. population
- Updated data on the foreign-born population in the United States
- Revised discussion of unauthorized immigration ✓
- Revised and updated coverage of racial and ethnic inequality today ✓
- Expanded discussion of implicit bias
- Significantly revised section on multiracial and multiethnic identities

CHAPTER 11

- Updated data on gender stratification in leadership positions in the United States, college graduation rates by gender, and women in the workforce
- New coverage of #MeToo movement
- Updated coverage of human trafficking and globalization
- Updated coverage of same-sex relationships, including new map, "Sexual Orientation Laws around the World"

CHAPTER 12

- New chapter-opening vignette on a minister who left his religion
- Updated data on marriage and cohabitation rates, the average age of first marriage, and the U.S. divorce rate
- Revised discussion of unmarried and single parents ✓
- New figure, "U.S. Fertility Rate (Total Births Per Woman)"
- Updated data on the religious composition of the United States
- Updated discussion of secularism in the United States

CHAPTER 13

- Updated data on global literacy rates, educational attainment and median income, graduation rates, and college cost and student debt
- Revised discussion of the effects of cultural capital ✓
- Updated discussion of the increasing segregation of U.S. schools ✓
- Updated coverage of standardized testing, including new map, "Common Core in the United States"
- Updated discussions of charter schools, online learning, for-profit colleges, and cyberbullying
- New coverage of 2018 teacher strikes in various states
- Updated coverage of emotional labor in the U.S. workplace
- Updated discussions of outsourcing, the sharing economy, and precarious work

CHAPTER 14

- New chapter-opening vignette on the data Facebook gathers from its users
- Significant revisions for clarity throughout, including new organizational structure, clearer and more logical headings, and new figures and tables ✓
- New figures include "Daily Time Spent with Select Media by Generation," "Racial and Ethnic Representation on Prime-Time Broadcast TV Networks by Season," "Digital Divide: U.S. Adults Who Do Not Use the Internet, 2018," and "Global Internet Usage, 2018" ✓
- New tables include "Types of Media and Their Usual Characteristics" and "Select Media-Related Companies by Revenue, 2017" ✓
- Updated discussion of college students' credit card debt

- Expanded and updated coverage of product integration and stealth advertising ✓
- Significantly revised and updated Changing World section, "Targeting Consumers in the Digital Age" ✓

CHAPTER 15

- Clarifying revisions made to the sections on nomadic life and rural life
- New material on the "urban renaissance"
- Updated material in the sections on suburban and rural life ✓
- Updated material on environmental threats

CHAPTER 16

- New chapter-opening vignette on filling low-paid teaching jobs with foreign workers
- Clarified explanation of what sociologists mean when they use the terms *politics* and *power* ✓
- Updated coverage of the Democracy Index, including updated map and discussion of falling ratings worldwide
- Updated and clarified explanation of the "spiral of silence," including discussion of its relation to the 2016 presidential election ✓
- New section, "Cultural Values and Political Ideologies" ✓
- Updated coverage of campaign contributions to the 2016 presidential election
- New coverage of 2017 tax cut, including new figure "Average Annual Federal Tax Savings by Income Group, 2017 Tax Cuts and Job Act"
- New material on the effects of cynicism and alienation on a democracy ✓
- Updated coverage of U.S. military spending and military engagements around the world
- New Through a Sociological Lens box on what motivated people to vote for Trump
- New "A Changing World" section on populism ✓

CHAPTER 17

- New data on world population structures and international migration
- Updated coverage of changing U.S. demographics, including the effects of immigration and an aging population
- New material on the documented decline in internet freedom

Teaching and Learning with *Experience Sociology*

TEACHING RESOURCES

Instructor's Manual. The Instructor's Manual includes detailed chapter outlines and chapter summaries, learning objectives, a chapter-by-chapter bulleted list of new content, key terms, essay questions, and critical-thinking questions.

PowerPoint Slides. The PowerPoint Slides include bulleted lecture points, figures, and maps. They can be used as is or modified to meet the instructor's individual needs. Now WCAG compliant.

Test Bank. The Test Bank includes multiple-choice, true-false, and essay questions for every chapter. TestGen software allows the instructor to create customized exams using either publisher-supplied test items or the instructor's own questions.

Guide to Connect Resources. The Guide details the resources available to instructors in Connect and correlates them with chapter-by-chapter content.

These instructor resources can be accessed through the Library tab in Connect.

McGraw-Hill Education Create® is a self-service website that allows you to create customized course materials using McGraw-Hill Education's comprehensive, cross-disciplinary content and digital products. You can even access third-party content such as readings, articles, cases, videos, and more.

- Select and arrange content to fit your course scope and sequence.
- Upload your own course materials.
- Select the best format for your students—print or eBook.
- Select and personalize your cover.
- Edit and update your materials as often as you'd like.

Experience how McGraw-Hill Education's Create empowers you to teach your students your way: http://create.mheducation.com.

McGraw-Hill Education Campus® is a groundbreaking service that puts world-class digital learning resources just a click away for all faculty and students. All faculty—whether or not they use a McGraw-Hill title—can instantly browse, search, and access the entire library of McGraw-Hill Education instructional resources and services, including eBooks, test banks, PowerPoint slides, animations, and learning objects—from any Learning Management System (LMS), at no additional cost to an institution. Users also have single sign-on access to McGraw-Hill Education digital platforms, including Connect, Create, and Tegrity, a fully automated lecture capture solution.

ACKNOWLEDGMENTS

Writing and revising *Experience Sociology* has been an ongoing journey for us, a journey we could not have undertaken without the support of many people along the way. We would like to thank Sherith Pankratz, our initial editor at McGraw-Hill, for encouraging us to begin the project in the first place. And thanks to the many folks at McGraw-Hill Education who have helped us complete this Fourth Edition.

Many thanks to our colleagues who have helped us think about teaching sociology, including Mike Malec and William Gamson at Boston College; Joe Marolla at Virginia Commonwealth University; Steve Lyng at Carthage College; and Carlos Alamo, Eileen Leonard, Bob McAulay, and Marque Miringoff at Vassar College. We appreciate the contributions of our various research assistants, including Meg Burns, Kelly Capehart, Rachel Cerlen, Clara Howell, Nick Hoynes, Zak Leazer, Corrina Regnier, Mollie Sandberg, Jacinthe Sasson-Yenor, Shawna Seth, and Tali Shapiro. More generally, we are grateful to our students, from whom we have learned a great deal about sociology and pedagogy over the past two decades.

Finally, David would like to thank Cecelia Kirkman—again—for everything. William would like to thank his family, Deirdre, Ben, and Nick, for their support, encouragement, and patience throughout the years required to produce this book.

ACADEMIC REVIEWERS

Thanks to the following for their thorough and thoughtful evaluations of various portions and drafts of *Experience Sociology*.

Cawo Abdi, University of Minnesota–Minneapolis
Wesley Abercrombie, Midlands Technical College
Donna Abrams, Georgia Gwinnett College
Doug Adams, University of Arkansas–Fayetteville
Isaac Addai, Lansing Community College
Adansi Amankwaa, Albany State University
Trudy Anderson, Texas A&M–Kingsville
Robert Aponte, Indiana University–Purdue University Indianapolis
David Arizmendi, South Texas College
Bryan Auld, Indiana University—Purdue University Fort Wayne
Robert Baker, Sandhills Community College
Sergio Banda, Fullerton College
Baishakhi Banerjee Taylor, University of Kentucky–Lexington
Carlin Barmada, Burlington County College–Pemberton
Nadine Barrett, University of Central Florida
Joshua Bass, Portland State University
Lance Basting, Chippewa Valley Technical College
John Batsie, Parkland College
James Bazan, Central Piedmont Community College
Eric Beasley, Oakland University
James Becker, Pulaski Tech College
Joseph Beczak, San Diego City College
Janice Bending, University of Cincinnati–Cincinnati
Claudette Bennett, Howard University
Todd E. Bernhardt, Broward College–Central
Terry Besser, Iowa State University
Gary Bittner, York College of Pennsylvania
Amy Blackstone, University of Maine
Michelle Blake, University of Evansville
Adriana Bohm, Delaware County Community College
Carolyn Bond, Boston University
Christine Borden-King, Minot State University
Karyn Boutin, Massasoit Community College
Christopher Bradley, Indiana University–Purdue University Fort Wayne
Judith Brake, Ozarks Technical Community College
John Brenner, York College of Pennsylvania
Helen Brethauer-Gay, Florida A&M University
Daniel Brewster, West Virginia University–Morgantown
David L. Briscoe, University of Arkansas–Little Rock
Rebeca Brittenham, College of Southern Nevada–West Charles
Scott Brooks, University of California–Riverside
Richard Bucher, Baltimore City Community College
Jonathan Bullinger, Camden County College
Mary L. Burns, Michigan State University–East Lansing
Andrew Butz, Portland Community College
Paul Calarco, Hudson Valley Community College
Farrah Cambrice, Prairie View A&M University
Allison Camelot, Saddleback College
Roberta Campbell, Miami University
Elaine Cannon, El Camino College
Gina Carreno-Lukasik, Florida Atlantic University
Marketa Cawood, Hopkinsville Community College
Edwin Chambless, El Paso Community College–Valle Verde
Gina Chance, Central New Mexico Community College
Nina Chapman, Golden West College
Adrian Cheatwood, University of Texas–San Antonio
Adrian Chevraux-FitzHugh, Sacramento City College
Andrew Cho, Tacoma Community College
Margaret Choka, Pellissippi State Technical Community College
Bridget Christensen, Southeast Community College
Sue Ciriello, Naugatuck Valley Community College
Rodney Clayton, Central Community College–Hastings
Susan Cody, Georgia Perimeter College–Dunwoody
Charles Combs, Sinclair Community College
Ida Cook, University of Central Florida
Lisa Coole, Massasoit Community College
Mary Kay Cordill, Cape Cod Community College
Linda Cornwell, Bowling Green State University
Carolyn Corrado, State University of New York at Albany
Mary Croissant, Front Range Community College–Fort Collins
April Cubbage, Saddleback College
Larry Curiel, Cypress College
Cloyis Daughhetee, Arkansas State University
Robert Scott Davis, Treasure Valley Community College

Rhett Davy, North Central Texas College
Susan Day, Texas State University
Rohan De Silva, Milwaukee Area Technical College–Milwaukee
Kelly Dever, University of Florida at Gainesville
Aimee Dickinson, Lorain County Community College
Nancy Dimonte, Farmingdale State College
Wendy Dishman, Santa Monica College
Greg Donnenwerth, University of Memphis
Joe Donnermeyer, Ohio State University–Columbus
Brian Donovan, University of Kansas–Lawrence
Sue Dowden, El Camino College
Lilli Downes, Polk State College
Michael Dreiling, University of Oregon
Adam Driscoll, University of North Carolina–Charlotte
Susan Dumais, Louisiana State University
Gianna Durso-Finley, Mercer County Community College
Shelly Dutchin, Western Tech College
Isaac W. Eberstein, Florida State University
Samuel Echevarria-Cruz, Austin Community College–Riverside
Martin Edelstein, Baruch College
Sherwood Edwards, College of Dupage
John Ehle, Jr., NOVA Community College–Annandale
Susan Eichenberger, Seton Hill University
Richard Ellefritz, Oklahoma State University–Oklahoma City
Jim Elliott, University of Oregon
David Embrick, Loyola University–Chicago
Graves Enck, University of Memphis
Kevin Ervin, Northern Illinois University
Nora Fellag, Rowan College at Burlington County
Kathryn Feltey, University of Akron
Catherine Felton, Central Piedmont Community College
Leticia Fernandez, University of Texas at El Paso
Richard Fey, Arizona State University
Lauralee Finley, Florida Atlantic University
Kevin Fitzpatrick, University of Alabama at Birmingham
Dona Fletcher, Sinclair Community College
Martha Flores, El Paso Community College–Valle Verde
Tammie Foltz, Des Moines Area Community College–Boone
Murray Fortner, Tarrant County College Northeast
Tony Foster, Lone Star College–Kingwood
John Gannon, College of Southern Nevada–North Las Vegas
Beverly Gartland, Youngstown State University
David Gay, University of Central Florida
Marie L. Germain, City College–Miami
Steve Glennon, Iowa Western Community College–Council Bluffs
Sergio Gomez, Chaffey College
Natasha Gouge, Cape Fear Community College
Kyra Greene, San Diego State University
Mike Greenhouse, Middlesex County College
Sara Grineski, University of Texas at El Paso
Elke Grogg, Ivy Tech Community College of Indiana
Heather Guevara, Portland Community College–Sylvania
Jeffrey Hall, University of Alabama at Birmingham
Bram Hamovitch, Lakeland Community College
Carl Hand, Valdosta State University
Sara Hanna, Oakland Community College–Highland Lakes
Peggy Hargis, Georgia Southern University
Terri Hardy, Indiana University East
Kalynn Heald, Northwest Arkansas Community College
Nina Heckler, University of Alabama at Tuscaloosa
Garrison Henderson, Tarrant County College Southeast
Kimberly Hennessee, Ball State University
Marta T. Henriksen, Central New Mexico Community College
Pablo Hernandez, Lansing Community College
Teresa Hibbert, University of Texas at El Paso
Carmon Weaver Hicks, Ivy Tech Community College of Indiana
Tonya Hilligoss, Sacramento City College
Candace Hinson, Tallahassee Community College
Caroll Hodgson, Rowan-Cabarrus Community College
Donna Holland, Indiana University–Purdue University
Kathleen Holmes, Darton College
Mark Horowitz, University of Texas at Brownsville
Nils Hovik, Lehigh Carbon Community College
Erica Hunter, State University of New York at Albany
Ronald Huskin, Del Mar College
Creed Hyatt, Lehigh Carbon Community College
Peter Iadicola, Indiana University–Purdue University Fort Wayne
Denise Ingram, Mercer County Community College
Michael Itagaki, Fullerton College
Jennifer Jackson, Cincinnati State Technical & Community College
Ron Jacobs, State University of New York at Albany
Timothy Jacobs, Naugatuck Valley Community College
Jennifer Jacobson, Yavapai College
Laura Jamison, Parkland College
Randy Jarvis, South Texas College
J. Craig Jenkins, Ohio State University–Columbus
Mark Jepson, University of California–Los Angeles
Dennis Johnson, Craven Community College
Jim Jones, Mississippi State University
Ali Kamali, Missouri Western State University
Irwin Kantor, Middlesex County College
Michael Kaune, Saint Francis College
Henry Keith, Delaware Technical Community College
Margaret Kelly, University of Minnesota–Minneapolis
Paul Ketchum, University of Oklahoma–Norman
Steve Keto, Kent State University
William Kimberlin, Laini County Community College
Brian Klocke, State University of New York at Plattsburgh
James Knapp, Southeastern Oklahoma State University
Michelle Knoles, Cowley County Community College
Jamee Kristen, University of Nebraska–Lincoln
Lorien Lake, University of Arizona
Judy Lasker, Lehigh University
Terina Lathe, Central Piedmont Community College
Jodie Lawston, DePaul University
Rebecca Leichtfuss, Moraine Park Tech College
Jason Leiker, Utah State University
Joe Lengermann, University of Maryland–College Park
Troy Lepper, Colorado State University
David Liu, Harrisburg Area Community College
David Locher, Missouri Southern State University
William Lockhart, McLennan Community College
Nicole Loftus, Saddleback College
Royal Loresco, South Texas College
Joleen Loucks, Kutztown University of Pennsylvania
Michael Loukinen, Northern Michigan University
Gregory Lukasik, Florida Atlantic University–Boca Raton

Bradford Lyman, Baltimore City Community College
Jean Lynch-Brandon, Lansing Community College
Joanna Maata, Pennsylvania State University
Anne MacLellan, Community College of Baltimore County–Catonsville
I. Ross Macmillan, University of Minnesota–Minneapolis
Sherry Mader, Western Technical College
M. Wilbrod Madzura, Normandale Community College
Cheryl Maes, University of Nevado–Reno
Lori Maida, Westchester Community College
Farshad Malek-Ahmadi, Naugatuck Valley Community College
Susan Mann, University of New Orleans
Nick Maroules, Illinois State University
Ronald Matson, Wichita State University
Deborah McCarthy, College of Charleston
Dorothy McCawley, University of Florida
Karen McCue, Central New Mexico Community College
Victor McCullum, Triton College
Marian McWhorter, Houston Community College–Central College
Ronald Meneses, University of Florida
Chadwick L. Menning, Ball State University
Melinda Messineo, Ball State University
Janet Michello, LaGuardia Community College
Harvest Moon, University of Texas at Arlington
Mel Moore, University of Northern Colorado
Marcillino Morales, East Los Angeles College
John Morra, Quinnipiac University
Edward Morris, University of Kentucky–Lexington
Kelly Mosel-Talavera, Texas State University–San Marcos
Brian Moss, Oakland Community College–Highland Lakes
Sepandar Mossadeghi, Palm Beach State College–Eissey Campus
Dan Muhwezi, Bulter Community College
Lynn Newhart, Rockford College
Bruce Nicometo, Northwest Arkansas Community College
Claire Nivens-Blower, Cape Cod Community College
Nelda Nix, Community College of Baltimore County–Essex
Cheryl North, Tarrant County College Northeast
Kwaku Obosu-Mensah, Lorain County Community College
Patricia O'Brien, Elgin Community College
Bob O'Neil, Louisiana State University–Baton Rouge
Jacob Oni, Cape Cod Community College
Takamitsu Ono, Anne Arundel Community College
Robert Orrange, Eastern Michigan University
Diane Owsley, Elizabethtown Community College
Bruce Pabian, Delaware Technical Community College–Stanton
Frank Page, University of Utah–Salt Lake City
Chris Papaleonardos, Ohio State University–Columbus
Elizabeth Pare, Oakland University
Caroline Parham, Craven Community College
Kathrin Parks, Loras College
Kevin Payne, Park University–Parkville
Douglas Peck, Stark State
Lisa Pellerin, Ball State University
Jane Penney, Eastfield College
Narayan Persaud, Florida A&M University
Nancy Pietroforte, Rockland Community College
Peggy Preble, Thomas Nelson Community College
Paul C. Price, Pasadena City College
William Price, North Country Community College
Ariane Prohaska, University of Alabama at Tuscaloosa
Adrian Rapp, Lone Star College–North Harris
Todd Rasner, Hudson Valley Community College
Roblyn Rawlins, College of New Rochelle
Kent Redding, University of Wisconsin–Milwaukee
Nancy Reeves, Gloucester County College
John Rice, University of North Carolina–Wilmington
Ray Rich, College of Southern Nevada–West Charles
Cecelia Rivers, Northwest Florida State College
Gregg Robinson, Grossmont College
Christine Rodriguez, East Los Angeles College
Fatima Rodriguez, Rutgers University
Robyn Rodriguez, Reedley College
Luis Rodriguez-Abad, University of Texas at Brownsville
Richard Rosell, Westchester Community College
Olga Rowe, Oregon State University
Alan Rudy, Central Michigan University
Amy Ruedisueli, Tidewater Community College
Igor Ryabov, Ohio University–Athens
Charlotte Ryan, University of Massachusetts–Lowell
Christina Ryder, Missouri State University
Ivanka Sabolich, Kent State University
George Saunders, Ball State University
Peter Sawyer, Hudson Valley Community College
David Schall, Milwaukee Area Technical College
Jon Schlenker, University of Maine–Augusta
Andreas Schneider, Texas Tech University
Rachel Schneider, University of Akron
David Schjott, Northwest Florida State College
Sarah Bill Schott, North Central College–Naperville
Terri Schrantz, Tarrant County College
Ron Schultz, Gateway Technical College
Jeff Schulz, Central Community College–Grand Island
Megan Seely, Sierra College
Lystra Seenath, Palm Beach State College–Lake Worth
Barbara Seiter, Raritan Valley Community College
Patricia Seitz, Central New Mexico Community College
Charles Selengut, County College of Morris
Monissa Shackleford, Pensacola Junior College
Robert Shelly, Ohio University–Athens
Marie Sheneman, Marshalltown Community College
Anson Shupe, Indiana University–Purdue University Fort Wayne
Denise Shuster, Owens Community College
Mike Sickels, Winthrop University
Edward Silva, El Paso Community College–Valle Verde
Toni Sims, University of Southwestern Louisiana
Amy Slater, MCC–Blue River Community College
Steven Sloan, Gateway Technical College
Michael Smith, Lakeland Community College
Michelle Smith, Southwestern Illinois College
Karrie Snyder, Northwestern University
Tomecia Sobers, Fayetteville Technical Community College
Stephanie Southworth, Clemson University
Ryan Spohn, Kansas State University
Johnnie Spraggins, University of Texas at San Antonio
Dan Stalder, University of Wisconsin–Whitewater
Barbara Stauffer, Lehigh Carbon Community College
Rachael Stehle, Cuyahoga Community College Western–Parma

Lawrence Stern, Collin County Community College–Plano
Terrence Stewart, Mott College
Michelle Stewart Thomas, Mt. San Antonio College
Jill Stiemsma, Moraine Park Tech College
Beverly Stiles, Midwestern State University
Randolph Ston, Oakland Community College–Auburn Hills
Michael Stupak, Milwaukee Area Technical College
Holly Suarez, University of North Carolina–Charlotte
Rose Suggett, Southeast Community College
Deborah Sullivan, Arizona State University–Tempe
Richard Sweeny, Modesto Junior College
Diana Sweigert, Lehigh Carbon Community College
John Szivos, Mount Wachusett Community College
Margaret Taylor, Greenville Technical College
Sara Thompson, Laredo Community College
Ruth Thompson-Miller, Texas A&M University
Lorna Timmerman, Indiana University East
Gary Titchener, Des Moines Area Community College
Bob Transon, Milwaukee Area Technical College
Timothy Tuinstra, Kalamazoo Valley Community College
Toby Vance, El Paso Community College–Valle Verde
Melinda Vandervis, Orange Coast College
Steven Vassar, Minnesota State University–Mankato
Ray Von Robertson, Lamar University
Vu-Duc Vuong, De Anza College
Sally Vyain, Ivy Tech Community College of Indiana
Florence Wakoko, Columbus State University
Glenda D. Walden, University of Colorado–Boulder
Marie L. Wallace, Pima Community College–West
Suzan Waller, Franklin University
Gina Walls, Parkland College
Sheryl Walz, Citrus College
Martha Warburton, University of Texas at Brownsville
Elizabeth Watts Warren, Gordon College
Sandra Way, New Mexico State University–Las Cruces
Sharon Wettengel, Tarrant County College Southeast
Shonda Whetstone, Blinn College
Amanda White, St. Louis Community College–Meramec
Debbie White, Citrus College
Gailynn White, Citrus College
Gordon Whitman, Tidewater Community College–Norfolk
Cindy Whitney, Kansas State University, College of Technology & Aviation
Linda Wicks, Stony Brook University
Cleon Wiggins, Kansas City Kansas Community College
Marion Willetts, Illinois State University
Gerald Williams, Camden County College
L. Sue Williams, Kansas State University
Bryan Williamson, Lorain County Community College
Beate Wilson, Western Illinois University
Charles Wilson, Kansas City Kansas Community College
Rowan Wolf, Portland Community College–Sylvania
Amy Wong, San Diego State University
Peter Wood, Eastern Michigan University
Robert E. Wood, Rutgers University
Timothy Woods, Manchester Community College
Diane Wysocki, University of Nebraska–Kearney
Marik Xavier-Brier, Houston Community College
Erica Yeager, Anne Arundel Community College
Pat Yeager, Ivy Tech Community College of Indiana–Evansville
Andrew Ziner, Kutztown University of Pennsylvania
John F. Zipp, University of Akron

©Buena Vista Images/DigitalVision/Getty Images

1 Sociology in a Changing World

looking AHEAD

How can sociology and the sociological perspective help us understand society and our place in it?

How can three of sociology's core concepts—culture, structure, and power—and its diverse theories help us understand ourselves and our world?

How can sociology, which emerged in a period of revolutionary change, help us understand our own rapidly changing world?

©Blend Images/123RF

As a child growing up in Van Nuys, California, Daniel Miramontez spoke Spanish at home, like most of his older relatives. However, the 19-year-old sociology student notes, "When I started going to school, I started losing my Spanish and speaking more English" (Castanada 2017).

His is a common experience. Families that emigrate to the United States bring with them the culture and customs of their homeland, including their language. One in five U.S. residents speaks a language other than English at home (U.S. Census Bureau 2017). However, for each succeeding generation in the United States, English proficiency increases while proficiency in their parents' language declines. This pattern is as old as immigration itself. A century ago, the immigrants' language was more likely to be Italian, German, or Russian; today it might be Tagalog, Urdu, or Mandarin. Regardless of the era, though, the children of immigrants have always adopted English, the dominant language of their society.

There are practical reasons for this. English is the primary language of schooling and employment, so succeeding fully in these social arenas requires being able to speak the language well. Often, a lack of English skills has hampered immigrant parents in the labor market. They understand the importance of English for their children's future success and insist their children learn it. However, this can be a bittersweet process. Immigrant children may lose the ability to fluently speak the language of their parents and grandparents, and thus be cut off from a part of their heritage. That is one reason why bilingual education is highly prized in many communities. Bilingual education enables students to become proficient in English while simultaneously cultivating their native language skills, helping them to embrace their bicultural identities.

You do not have to be sentimental about culture, though, to appreciate the value of a second language. Research shows that knowing multiple languages can be a major asset on the job market. A wide range of employers are looking for people who can speak Chinese, French, Korean, Arabic, and, most of all, Spanish (New American Economy 2017).

Growing up, Daniel and other children of immigrants learn one of the basic insights of sociology: to understand the lives of individuals, we need to understand the broader social context in which they live. Growing up in a different society than your parents or grandparents means you become a different person. A different language takes priority, a different worldview develops from your experiences, and different opportunities present themselves because of where you live. In short, the society in which you live helps shape your life, while your actions—like those of millions of recent immigrants—can help change society.

Change—and its effects on people's lives—has long been one of sociology's major concerns. Indeed, sociology was born during a period of breathtaking change—the late 1800s—when Europe and the United States were shifting from a rural agricultural economy to an urban industrial economy. Early sociologists grappled with the impact of those changes on people's

families, their living conditions, and the way they supported themselves.

Sociologists today are grappling with a similar period of rapid change arising from many sources, including a global economy, the expansion of media and technology, a fast-changing population, and enduring cultural conflicts, to name just a few. *Experience Sociology* introduces you to sociology's insights into this shifting social landscape. This chapter introduces you to sociology itself, its unique perspective, and its early development as a discipline. It examines some of sociology's diverse theories and the core concepts that unite the field, along with a number of key concerns of sociology—indeed, of all of us today. We will see how sociology offers insight into the forces that are shaping our lives and, at the same time, how it helps us recognize our own capacity to bring about change.

©Fritz Goro/The LIFE Picture Collection/Getty Images

C. Wright Mills wrote a classic description of the sociological perspective called *The Sociological Imagination* (1959) and a series of books focused on social class and power in the United States (1948, 1952, 1956). He taught at Columbia University from 1946 until 1962, when he died of a heart attack at age 45. Mills's critique of the concentration of power in the United States inspired a generation of activists in the 1960s to promote a more inclusive and democratic society, themes that continue to resonate today.

What Is Sociology?

Sociology is *the systematic study of the relationship between individuals and society.* The approach used in sociology can be thought of as a perspective, a way of looking at the world. To take a **sociological perspective** is *to see and understand the connections between individuals and the broader social contexts in which they live.* You can understand your own life—including the forces that have shaped your current daily routines and the options you have in your future—only by considering the broader social contexts within which you live. Your identity (including your race, ethnicity, class, gender, and nationality) as well as the social environment in which you live (including your family, neighborhood, country, culture, and historical period) influence who you are and who you can be. Understanding those connections is at the heart of a sociological perspective.

The Sociological Perspective

Writing in 1959, U.S. sociologist C. Wright Mills provided the best-known description of the sociological perspective (or, as he called it, the *sociological imagination*). According to Mills, "The sociological imagination enables us to grasp history and biography and the relations between the two within a society" (6). In other words, our individual condition (what Mills calls "biography") depends, in part, upon larger forces in society ("history").

Do you live in a prosperous, peaceful society with democratic freedoms or in one where survival is a challenge, violence is a constant threat, and people's basic civil rights are suppressed? Is your mother or father a retail clerk, an auto worker, a schoolteacher, an engineer, in the military, a business executive, or unemployed? Are you African American, Latino, Asian, white? Are you male, female, or transgender? Are you gay or straight? Are you from a rural community, the suburbs, or a major city? Were you raised as a Christian, a Jew, a Muslim, a Hindu, or a nonbeliever? Although we often like to think of ourselves as rugged individuals responsible for our own lives, characteristics and circumstances like these influence who we are and the options we have. And as Mills (1959) points out (using "man" instead of "person" in the convention of his day), as social conditions change, so do the lives of individuals:

> When a society is industrialized, a peasant becomes a worker; a feudal lord is liquidated or becomes a businessman. When classes rise or fall a man is employed or unemployed; when the rate of investment goes up or down, a man takes new heart or goes broke. When wars happen, an insurance salesman becomes a rocket launcher; a store clerk, a radar man; a wife lives alone; a child grows up without a father. Neither the life of an individual nor the history of a society can be understood without understanding both. (3)

We need only consider the 2007–2009 economic recession, the wars in Iraq and Afghanistan, the rapid growth of technology, and accompanying social developments to see that Mills's observations are as relevant today as they were more than half a century ago.

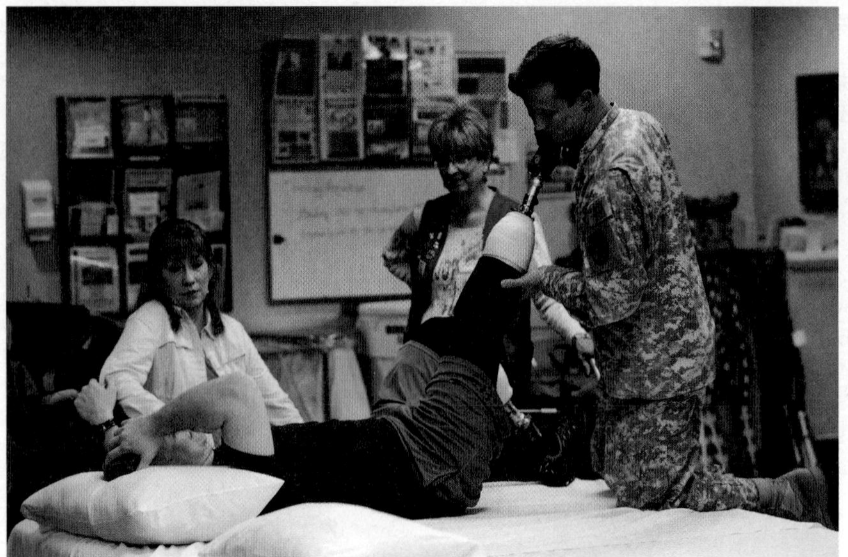

©Kevin Lamarque-Pool/Getty Images

Personal choices—especially deciding to volunteer for the armed forces—contributed to this veteran's current situation. But those decisions were made in the context of broader social conditions, including economic pressures to earn a living, a culture of popular patriotism, key decisions made by those with political power, and events that transformed international relations. The connections between individual lives and larger social processes are rarely so explicit or so poignant.

However, Mills and other sociologists do not argue that people are simply the passive victims of their social circumstances. Rather, as the sociological perspective reveals, interaction exists between the social conditions that shape our lives and the actions we take as individuals. We don't get to choose the conditions under which we live, the opportunities we enjoy, or the barriers we face, but we do have choices about how we respond to those circumstances, both individually and collectively. Deciding to join the military, have children, attend college, or move to another city are among the many individual decisions a person can make that have a major impact on his or her future. Mills himself was a strong advocate for collective action to strengthen democracy and help change the difficult and often unequal conditions that people face in society. That idea, too, is as relevant today as ever.

Sociology and Common Sense

You do not have to be a professional sociologist to look at the world from a sociological perspective. Indeed, many popular expressions reflect a kind of commonsense folk wisdom that assumes a sociological perspective. You have probably heard some version of the expression "You've got to play the cards you're dealt in life." The card game metaphor makes the point that from the beginning, our options in life have been shaped by social conditions that we did not get to pick ourselves. Such factors can heavily influence the opportunity people have for good health, education, material comfort, and overall well-being.

You don't get to choose the cards you are dealt, but you do get to decide how you will play them. For example, you no doubt decided to go to college with the hope that doing so could positively influence your future. Others may have had the option of attending college but chose not to exercise it. Many more people, of course, never had the option of attending college in the first place; they were dealt a very different hand in life.

The idea that people must play the cards they are dealt in life is consistent with a sociological perspective. But the problem with relying on commonsense folk wisdom to understand the world is that, however insightful it may sometimes be, it can produce a bewildering array of contradictory claims. One popular saying, "Life is what you make of it," suggests that individuals have total control over their fate. In contrast, "The apple doesn't fall far from the tree" suggests that our social origins largely predetermine our character and fate. Without some way of gauging their accuracy, such wildly contradictory claims provide no insight at all.

In addition, an understanding of the world based only on our own individual experience may not be helpful in unfamiliar circumstances. This is especially true in a world in which communications, media, immigration, and international travel are bringing together people of vastly different backgrounds as never before. To operate in such a diverse society we need to understand not only how *we* make sense of the world, but how other people do so as well.

If we are to understand our connection to the social world beyond our own limited experience and be able to sort through competing claims about that world, we need a more systematic way to comprehend the patterns of behavior and the processes that make up social life. We need the discipline of sociology.

Sociology as a Discipline

Sociologists combine the sociological perspective with a variety of research methods (discussed in Chapter 2) to study in a systematic way how our actions shape, and are shaped by, broader social forces. Because the sociological perspective can apply to any aspect of people's lives and any social issue, the discipline of sociology addresses an especially broad array of topics, as we will see throughout this book.

Sociology is one of the *social sciences,* a group of research-based disciplines that gather and evaluate evidence to study human society. This focus on human society distinguishes the social sciences from the *natural sciences,* which focus on the physical aspects of nature.

In addition to sociology, the social sciences include political science, economics, psychology, and anthropology. Each of these disciplines highlights different aspects of social life. Take crime, for example.

- *Political scientists* might study how politicians use the issue of crime in their campaigns.
- *Economists* might examine the financial impact of crime on society.

©Andrew Holbrooke/Corbis/Getty Images

©Moodboard/Alamy Stock Photo

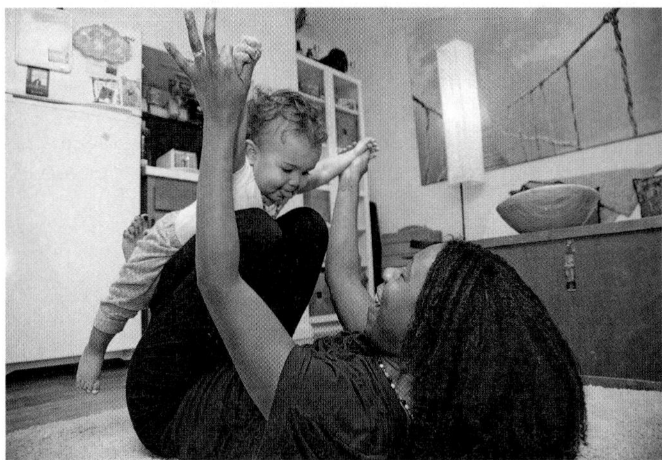

©Ashley Corbin-Teich/Cultura RM/Alamy Stock Photo

©John Miles/The Image Bank/Getty Images

These children's life chances—their opportunities for good health, education, material comfort, and overall well-being—are significantly influenced by the social environment into which they were born. What differences are evident from these photographs? What elements of your social environment influenced your development?

- *Psychologists* might look at the individual features of criminals, perhaps suggesting personality traits associated with certain types of criminal behavior.
- *Anthropologists* might compare how different societies define crime and respond to it.

Sociologists, in contrast, emphasize the interrelationship between individuals and larger social forces, as well as the interactions between various social institutions such as government, economy, media, schools, and family. The result is a broad range of research interests. Sociologists, for example, might

- explore why crime rates vary over time and are often linked to social trends such as changes in the age of the population (since younger people commit crimes at a higher rate than older ones).
- examine the role of media in helping shape people's perception of crime and the criminal justice system through both news coverage and entertainment dramas.
- examine the effectiveness of government efforts to reduce crime.

Sociologists have many interests, and the discipline as a whole has many areas of specialization, including medical sociology, sociology of the family, sociology of religion, political sociology, the sociology of race and ethnicity, the sociology of work, the sociology of gender, the sociology of media, and the sociology of social movements. As a result, sociology courses can provide a foundation for further study in any of these fields. As the Sociology Works box suggests, the study of sociology can also provide valuable skills for many careers, including some that may seem completely unrelated to sociology itself.

Sociology's Historical and Social Context

Imagine a time in which scientific discoveries alter our understanding of the world, political unrest sparks calls for social change, and economic crises and new technologies transform daily life. You might suspect this was a description of the world today, but similar upheavals disturbed Europe leading up to the 1800s, which is where and when the formal discipline of

SOCIOLOGY WORKS

The Sociology Major and the Job Market

People, culture, social problems, social change—these fascinating topics help explain why students often enjoy sociology. However, practical concern about the future might lead some to ask, "What can I *do* with a degree in sociology?"

The answer is, "Plenty." By majoring in sociology you not only learn to better understand yourself and your world, but you also develop important skills that can prepare you for entry-level positions in a variety of employment settings, including business, education, social services, health care, government, media, and criminal justice. Sociology can also be an excellent choice for students who plan to go on to graduate school.

Here are four key advantages of majoring in sociology:

1. *A sociology degree is flexible.* Because sociology can be applied to virtually any aspect of social life, you can major in sociology with an eye toward your own particular interests. For example, if you are interested in health and medicine, you can take a course in medical sociology; if you are interested in social work, you can take courses related to the social problems you wish to address or the populations you wish to serve. Sociology can help you understand the issues related to your field of interest.
2. *Sociology focuses on the critical use of information.* As part of a liberal arts education, a sociology degree prepares you to find, understand, analyze, use, and communicate information. These fundamental critical-thinking skills apply to an array of work settings and will not become obsolete; they are highly valuable in today's rapidly changing, information-based job market. Since most people change jobs—and even careers—during their lives, mastering such information-based skills is crucial for success. The ability to work with social science data found in government reports, marketing surveys, and other information sources is particularly important.
3. *Sociology provides insights into diversity.* Success in many fields of employment requires understanding people from different backgrounds. Sociology majors have an advantage in understanding diversity. As a result, they are more likely to work effectively in multicultural workplaces such as schools, hospitals, and businesses as well as in any field in which the players may be from diverse social backgrounds.
4. *Sociology explores the source of social problems.* Are you interested in a field that addresses social problems, such as social work, criminal justice, or health care? Do you plan to work with community organizations, international aid agencies, or social movements to bring about social change? If so, studying sociology can be particularly relevant. By focusing on the relationship between individuals and their social context, sociology helps you understand the roots of social problems.

Majoring in sociology allows you to study a subject area that interests you *and* helps you prepare for your future.

The Sociology Works boxes throughout this book highlight how former sociology students are using the insights of sociology in a variety of fields. If you are considering majoring in sociology, talk with your instructor, who can tell you about the programs available at your school.

think about it

1. *Do you have any tentative ideas about the kind of work you'd like to do when you complete school? What kinds of classes do you think will help you prepare for the future? Why?*
2. *Take a look at your school's course listings. Do you see any sociology courses that you think you may want to take? What interests you about the topics covered in these courses?*

©WDC Photos/Alamy Stock Photo

©Bettmann/Getty Images

©Olivier Douliery-Pool/Getty Images

©Robin Marchant/NYCWFF/Getty Images

©Jamie McCarthy/WireImage/Getty Images

Sociology majors in many occupations have made contributions to their professional fields. A few well-known majors have had an impact across society. Pictured here, from left to right, are former U.S. president Ronald Reagan, civil rights leader Martin Luther King Jr., former First Lady Michelle Obama, celebrity chef Stephanie Izard, and actor Kal Penn.

TABLE 1.1 SOCIOLOGY AND REVOLUTION

Sociology Arose in the Context of Revolutionary Change

Cultural Revolution	Political Revolution	Economic and Social Revolution
The declining influence of religion	Declining power of monarchies; American and French revolutions	Decline of agricultural life; industrialization and rise of consumer society
The rise of scientific thought	Uprisings of 1848	Capitalism
The Age of Enlightenment	Growth in democracy and individual rights	Urbanization

sociology first emerged. To better understand the origins of the discipline, we need to consider that historical and social context.

In the eighteenth and nineteenth centuries, European society entered a new historical era marked by revolutionary cultural, political, economic, and social change (Table 1.1). This period, known as **modernity,** was *characterized by the growth of democracy and personal freedom, increased reliance on reason and science to explain the natural and social worlds, and a shift toward an urban industrial economy.* Early sociologists sought to understand these dramatic changes and to suggest what might be done to deal with the social problems that resulted from them.

©DeAgostini/Getty Images

©Prisma/UIG/Getty Images

The rise of modernity introduced rapid social change. Work life shifted from fields to factories. Home and community life was transformed as people moved from small rural villages to rapidly expanding urban centers. What effect do you think the shift from rural village life based on farming to urban life based on wage labor had on family life?

Cultural Revolution: Science and the Enlightenment

During the Middle Ages the Church and its clergy dominated European intellectual life, controlling the era's limited number of books, libraries, and schools. Because religious doctrine formed the basis for acceptable social thought, heretics–those who held beliefs contrary to Church teaching–were often persecuted and even killed for questioning the accepted order. This intellectual climate was not hospitable to the open and free inquiry required for **science,** which *uses logic and the systematic collection of evidence to support its claims about the world.*

The Church slowly lost its dominance, however, as scientific research exposed the shortcomings of religious explanations of the natural world. For example, proof that the earth orbited the sun contradicted Church doctrine that the earth was at the center of the universe. Writers and philosophers seized on these advances in the natural sciences to promote the *Enlightenment,* an eighteenth-century intellectual movement that combined a belief in individual freedom and respect for individual rights with the logic of the natural sciences. These Enlightenment thinkers, who were among the first intellectuals independent of the Church, argued that neither the physical nor the social world should be taken on faith. Instead, both should be open to questioning and examined through reason; claims to knowledge should be subject to testing through the collection of evidence, and explanations should be based in natural causes and events. German philosopher Immanuel Kant summed up this revolutionary way of thinking in the motto "Dare to know" ([1784] 1999). This new emphasis on reason and science created the cultural conditions needed for the emergence of sociology.

Political Revolution: The Rise of Democracy

Enlightenment thinkers believed that the open debate of ideas and the application of reason and science to questions of social significance would promote tolerance, freedom, individual rights, equality, and democracy. Enlightenment ideas provided the intellectual basis for both the American (1775–1783) and French (1789–1799) revolutions, as well as for a series of uprisings that swept through Europe in 1848, challenging traditional rulers and promoting democratic ideals. These revolutions stimulated much interest in achieving a more equal society and improved living conditions, but they provoked condemnation from conservatives who saw them as a threat to stability, traditional values, and social order. Thus controversies about the nature and desirability of social order versus social change were among the first topics addressed by early sociologists.

Economic and Social Revolution: Industrial Capitalism and Urbanization

The term *Industrial Revolution* refers to a collection of major developments that transformed rural agricultural societies into urban industrial societies. This process began in Great Britain and spread through Europe and the United States in the nineteenth century.

The practical application of scientific developments, such as the creation of the steam engine, paved the way for **industrialization,** *the use of large-scale machinery for the mass manufacture of consumer goods.* Industrialization required a major investment in factories and mills with complex machinery—such as mechanized looms—at a cost that was often beyond the reach of a single owner. Thus industrialization became linked to the rise of *capitalists,* people who pursued profits by investing in and owning businesses. Mass manufacturing relied on a new type of relationship between workers and owners in which the workers sold their labor for a wage. They used their wages to buy food, clothing, and shelter, unlike rural peasants who produced many of their own material goods and met their basic needs by farming. The result was the birth of both wage labor and *consumerism,* a way of life that depends on the purchase and use of commercial goods and services. These developments fueled the rapid expansion of *capitalism,* an economic system in which the machinery used for production is owned privately, workers are paid a wage, and markets facilitate the exchange of goods and services.

Economic changes fueled changes in social life. In the agricultural economy of the Middle Ages, peasants worked the fields and were spread out in tiny rural villages among people mostly like themselves. Children could expect to grow up and live in the village they were born in and to do the same sort of work their parents and grandparents did.

In contrast, an industrial economy requires many workers to live close to each other near large factories and mills. As the Industrial Revolution took hold, many people left their rural homes and traveled to newly emerging cities for entirely new types of jobs they hoped would mean a better life.

This migration contributed to **urbanization,** *the growth of cities.* Before 1800, more than 90 percent of Europeans lived in rural areas; by the 1890s, more than half lived in cities. These bustling cities featured considerable diversity and rapid social change, some of which contributed to growing social problems.

Early industrial capitalism was highly productive, but it also created great inequalities, generating tremendous profits for a few wealthy owners from the labor of many overworked and underpaid workers. Disease (linked to poor sanitation), overcrowded and unsafe housing, inadequate transportation, and crime plagued the rapidly growing cities. Staggering inequality and growing social problems caused great concern among political and social thinkers, inspiring calls for reform and igniting revolutionary movements.

The rise of modernity produced rapid and immediately visible changes that showed traditional ways of life were not inevitable; the fate of individuals was tied to broader social changes beyond their control; and human action could transform the world through new ideas, political reform, and technological innovation. Faced with the challenge of understanding these dramatic transformations, social thinkers began applying reason and scientific techniques to study social life systematically and to suggest ways that society might be improved. The resulting ideas became the foundation of sociology.

Foundations of Sociological Thought

Sociology today has its roots in the ideas developed by early sociologists more than a century ago. Some of these thinkers asked profound questions of enduring relevance and are still widely read (Calhoun et al. 2012; Ritzer and Stepnisky 2014). Their work on the rapidly changing world of the late eighteenth and early nineteenth centuries continues to provide insight into our own social world today.

Defining the Terrain of Sociology: Comte and Spencer

Auguste Comte (1798–1857) and Herbert Spencer (1820–1903) helped establish the idea that the social world could be the subject of systematic, scientific investigation.

EARLY SOCIOLOGICAL THINKERS

	 ©Popperfoto/Getty Images	 ©Bettmann/Getty Images	 ©AKG Images/Newscom
	Karl Marx	**Emile Durkheim**	**Max Weber**
Biography	1818–1883	1858–1917	1864–1920
	German	French	German
	Writer and activist	Academic	Academic
Key issues and key work	The nature of capitalism	The nature of social solidarity	Decline of tradition
	Conflict and inequality	Shared values and morals	Rationalization of society
	Capital	*Suicide*	*The Protestant Ethic and the Spirit of Capitalism*

Auguste Comte: Stability and Change

Auguste Comte, a French intellectual with wide-ranging interests, coined the term *sociology* in the early nineteenth century. Comte sought to establish sociology as a rigorous science of society—modeled on the natural sciences—that would identify the laws that govern human behavior.

At the core of Comte's new field of study were two fundamental questions about social life: "How and why do societies change?" (social dynamics) and "What is the basis of social stability at a specific historical moment?" (social statics). Comte was interested in how society had developed from humanity's earliest small-scale bands of hunters and gatherers to his own nineteenth-century European society. He theorized that throughout history societies progressed through several stages: the theological (ruled by religion), the metaphysical (ruled by philosophy), and the positivist (ruled by science). For Comte, **positivism,** *a belief that accurate knowledge must be based on the scientific method,* enabled a deeper understanding of human life and was the key to solving persistent social problems.

Herbert Spencer: Society as a Social Organism

The British intellectual Herbert Spencer was another early adopter of the term *sociology.* Taking a cue from the biological sciences, Spencer argued that society is a "social organism," much like a human organism. He theorized that, like its biological equivalent, society is made up of separate parts, each with a unique function, that work together to sustain the entire organism. Thus Spencer's theory emphasized the overall structure of society, the functions served by the various elements of society, and the interactions among these elements. Spencer also theorized that when societies evolve, their component parts—and the functions they serve—change as well.

Spencer believed that society progresses as it evolves. Therefore, evolution should be allowed to take place without interference from government. Rather than intervene with reforms in the face of the growing inequality created by unregulated industrial capitalism, Spencer believed in the "survival of the fittest," a phrase he devised before Charles Darwin's work on natural selection and the theory of evolution was published. Spencer's application of the survival of the fittest to human society is today known as *social Darwinism.* Spencer later recanted some of his more extreme views, but in recent years, those who wish to minimize the role of government in social and economic affairs have revived some of Spencer's ideas.

The Key Founders: Marx, Durkheim, and Weber

Spencer and Comte helped define the terrain of sociology in its earliest years. But the thinkers who are widely seen as the founders of sociology and who set the agenda for the next century of sociological theory were Karl Marx, Emile Durkheim, and Max Weber.

Karl Marx: The Effects of Capitalism

The German-born Karl Marx (1818-1883) is best known as a revolutionary thinker who advocated radical change to advance the interests of workers. Marx combined writing with political activism, and much of his life was spent escaping political repression. Because of his writings, Marx was expelled from France (twice!) and Belgium. In Germany he was arrested, tried, acquitted, and also expelled. Finally, in 1849 he went to London, where he spent the rest of his life in exile. He lived in poverty while he wrote his greatest works, including *Capital,* his comprehensive analysis of the history and dynamics of capitalism.

Marx recognized that industrial capitalism was remarkably productive and thus capable of doing away with hunger and poverty for all. But instead, industrial capitalism was used to produce huge fortunes for a few owners, while leaving workers to labor in dangerous conditions and often live in poverty. In much of his work, Marx sought to explain how and why so much wealth and productivity could coexist with such widespread poverty and misery.

For Marx, the answer could be found in the relationship between capitalists, who owned the means of production, and workers (the proletariat), who sold their labor to the capitalists. The dynamics of capitalism, said Marx, encouraged owners to pay the lowest wages possible because lower labor costs mean higher profits. This dynamic explained the simultaneous creation of enormous fortunes and devastating poverty. Capitalists accumulated great wealth precisely because they were able to exploit the workers who toiled in their factories. This wealth gave owners great power, which they used to control governments and cultural institutions (Marx [1867] 1976).

To Marx, conflict between owners and workers was an inevitable feature of capitalism. As a result, he argued that capitalism—like earlier economic forms based on inequality—had within it the seeds of its own destruction. He theorized that the exploitation of workers would eventually become so extreme, wage laborers would rise up and overthrow the capitalist system. In its place, they would adopt *socialism,* a system in which ownership of the major means of production—such as factories, utilities, and railways—is in public, rather than private, hands, and government directs the use of the productive forces of industry for the public good. The goal of socialism would be a society without the extreme inequalities that characterized capitalism. (We explore the nature of capitalism and socialism more closely in Chapter 16.)

Marx's analysis of industrial capitalism was insightful in specifying the connection between wealth and poverty. He accurately predicted that the search for cheap labor would lead to the expansion of capitalism around the globe. He also correctly predicted the growth of labor movements demanding an end to unregulated capitalism. But he failed to appreciate the ability of capitalism to accommodate reform or the important role markets play in stimulating innovation and efficiency. The revolutionary worker movements Marx supported in recently industrialized countries like Great Britain, France, and Germany ultimately reformed, rather than overthrew, capitalism. Meanwhile, the socialist revolutions that did occur, most notably in Russia and China, took place in primarily agricultural societies that did not have the capacity to produce an abundance of material goods. Even though the brutal totalitarian states that emerged after these revolutions invoked Marx's name in their official ideology, they bore almost no resemblance to the humanist egalitarian vision that Marx had promoted.

Beyond his specific analysis of capitalism, Marx highlighted what became a core concept in sociology: power. Economic power, he argued, could be used to influence other aspects of social life, including government and cultural institutions such as schools and the media. Marx also stressed how people both create the societies they live in and are in turn influenced by them, an insight that is at the heart of the sociological perspective. "Men make their own history," he wrote, "but they do not make it just as they please; they do not make it under circumstances chosen by themselves, but under circumstances directly found, given and transmitted from the past" (Marx [1852] 1978, 595).

The issues Marx explored continue to be important today. Questions about the nature and direction of our economy are among the most significant ones addressed by sociologists. Examples include

- How has globalization changed our economy?
- How is extreme economic inequality linked to the dynamics of capitalism?
- How has the nature of work been changing?
- How have the labor movement and social welfare programs—both examples of attempts to moderate the excesses of capitalism—affected the lives of workers?

Emile Durkheim: Social Solidarity Emile Durkheim (1858–1917), who lived a generation after Marx, was also concerned with understanding social change in the modern world, but Durkheim's life could hardly have been more different from Marx's. The descendant of a long line of rabbinical scholars in France, Durkheim studied to be a rabbi but rejected religion in his teens, believing there was no way to know whether or not God existed. However, he retained a lifelong interest both in the role of religion in social life and in the scientific study of morality.

Durkheim is perhaps the single individual most responsible for establishing sociology as an academic discipline. He held the first academic position in sociology; wrote a book laying out the methods of the discipline, *The Rules of Sociological Method* (Durkheim [1895] 1982); and established a well-respected academic journal devoted to the new field.

Like many social thinkers who witness dramatic change, Durkheim was concerned with how to maintain social order. He was particularly interested in the question of **social solidarity,** *the collective bonds that connect individuals.* At the core of his theory was the proposition that society is held together by shared cultural values, promoted informally through custom and tradition, and spelled out more systematically in laws. When internalized by individuals, shared values and morals become the foundation for social solidarity.

Durkheim observed that traditional agricultural societies were often tight-knit communities. They shared social bonds across generations because people did the same sort of work, shared a common religion, and followed similar customs. These similar experiences resulted in *mechanical solidarity*—social cohesion based on shared experience and a common identity with limited individuality. As societies grew and became urbanized and industrialized, however, people increasingly differed from one another. A more complex economy required an increasing **division of labor,** in which *people specialize in different tasks, each requiring specific skills.* As cities developed, a diverse array

THROUGH A SOCIOLOGICAL LENS

Explaining the Social Basis of Suicide

Why do people intentionally kill themselves? At first glance, suicide seems to be the ultimate example of a private individual act, best explained by psychologists, not sociologists. But sociologist Emile Durkheim broke new ground when he made suicide the subject of the first sociological study to use large-scale data analysis. After examining official government records of suicide cases, Durkheim found that people committed suicide at higher rates in some groups than in others. Suicide, he theorized, was therefore not a purely individual act, but rather people were more or less likely to commit suicide because of the nature of their relationship to society within those groups.

Durkheim's study, *Suicide,* showed that a sociological perspective could help explain how individuals are affected by the quality of their relationship with larger social groups, even to the extent of taking their own lives. His research revealed, for example, that unmarried adults had higher rates of suicide than married adults, and Protestants had higher rates than Catholics or Jews. Durkheim explained these differences through an analysis of social *integration,* the strength of social ties that allow people to feel they belong to a group, and social *regulation,* the strength of social norms that control people's behavior. Too much or too little of either would increase the likelihood of suicide. Thus Durkheim identified four types of suicide—egoistic, anomic, altruistic, and fatalistic.

Egoistic suicides result from too little social integration and are committed by people who feel isolated and detached from society. For example, married couples are likely to have a strong bond with one another, whereas divorced, widowed, and unmarried people are more likely to lack a strong social connection; thus suicide rates among these latter groups are higher. Protestants lack the intense communal rituals associated with Catholicism and Judaism, which helps explain their higher rates of suicide. At the other extreme, *altruistic* suicides result from too much social integration, leading individuals to sacrifice themselves for the sake of the collective. Examples might include today's Islamic extremist suicide bombers or the Japanese kamikaze pilots who volunteered to fly suicide missions for their country during World War II.

The absence of regulation in the form of social norms and boundaries is also associated with higher suicide rates. *Anomic* suicide often results from a sudden and dramatic change in the level of social regulation, which leaves the individual without clear rules about how to adapt. These changes can be negative, such as those that occur after a natural disaster or the loss of a job. Ironically, the changes can also be positive, as when entertainers become "overnight successes" and suddenly have access to endless amounts of money and attention. The self-destructive behavior and suicides of many celebrities, such as musician Kurt Cobain and actor and reality television star Gia Marie Allemand, fit into this category. Conversely, too much regulation can result in *fatalistic* suicide, as in the case of slaves, prisoners, or those with terminal diseases who see no hope or way to escape their desperate conditions.

Today, the issue of suicide remains a poignant one, and Durkheim's work remains a touchstone. News outlets have been filled with stories about the alarmingly high suicide rate among returning U.S. veterans. In 2013, medical researchers launched a suicide prevention study that monitors Facebook profile content and Twitter posts of veterans who have volunteered to share their social media activity, with the aim of providing clinicians with real-time assessments of risk factors for suicide and other dangerous behaviors. The study's name? The Durkheim Project.

Suicide and Social Integration

	TOO LITTLE	TOO MUCH
Integration	Egoistic	Altruistic
Regulation	Anomic	Fatalistic

think about it

1. *The suicide rate among whites in the United States is more than double that of blacks or Hispanics. Using Durkheim's insights, speculate about why this might be so.*
2. *Based on Durkheim's analysis, what positive steps could be taken to help reduce the risk of suicide for any particular individual?*

of people coexisted, often with different religions and cultural traditions. Given this increasing social complexity and diversity, how could social solidarity be maintained?

Durkheim's answer was *organic solidarity,* a new form of social cohesion, characteristic of modern industrial societies, that is based on interdependence. In the tradition of Spencer's "social organism," Durkheim argued that the social glue that holds together modern societies mirrors the way living organisms depend on multiple, specialized components operating in unison. Social cohesion is possible because we are different from and dependent on one another. With its increased division of labor, modern urban industrialized society requires doctors, construction workers, salesclerks, police officers, factory workers, janitors, and thousands of other specialists to keep operating. Durkheim's theory helped explain why rapid growth and social differentiation in European societies did not lead to the breakdown of social solidarity, but instead produced a new and, Durkheim thought, even stronger form of solidarity that would permit a balance between individuality and a commitment to the group. In short, mechanical solidarity is based on the similarity found in small communities, while organic solidarity is based on the diversity and differentiation found in larger communities.

Much of Durkheim's sociological work builds upon his central concern with social solidarity. Indeed in *Suicide,* one of his most influential works and one of the first to show the potential of the sociological perspective combined with systematic research, Durkheim argued that suicide rates could be explained by the strength of the social ties people have with larger social groups (Durkheim [1897] 1951). (See the Through a Sociological Lens box.)

Durkheim also argued that crime and punishment are fundamentally about solidarity (see Chapter 8). Crimes, for Durkheim, are acts that offend the **collective conscience,** or *the shared norms, beliefs, and values in a community.* Punishment serves as a means to reinforce social solidarity in the face of such antisocial actions. Without the moral constraints provided by the collective conscience, Durkheim argued, people—and society as a whole—would descend into a chaotic state of **anomie,** or *social normlessness, without moral guidance or standards.*

Today, close to a century later, people are still debating the proper role of values and religion in public and private life, and Durkheim's theories continue to be relevant to such twenty-first-century questions as these:

- What explains the resurgence of traditional religious belief?
- Can the increasing diversity of our society serve as a source of strength rather than division?
- How can people maintain healthy social ties in a world where they regularly move from one community to another?
- How can we affirm people's individuality while maintaining a sense of common identity?

Max Weber: The Protestant Ethic and the Rationalization of Modern Life Like Durkheim, German theorist Max Weber (pronounced "VAY-ber") (1864–1920) was also trying to make sense of the shift from traditional to modern society. The son of a high-ranking government bureaucrat, Weber took a series of university positions as a young man, carried out major research projects, and served as a consultant for government agencies. By his mid-thirties, Weber was in a state of exhaustion and suffered a nervous breakdown that left him incapacitated for nearly seven years. When he was able to return to his writing full time, Weber produced his best-known work, *The Protestant Ethic and the Spirit of Capitalism* (Weber [1905] 1958).

In *The Protestant Ethic,* Weber argued that culture—in the form of Protestantism—had helped promote the early development of capitalism in northern Europe. Traditionally, the Catholic Church had encouraged the rejection of worldly affairs and wealth, promising everlasting life to those who were faithful and participated in the Church's defining rituals such as baptism and communion. However, after the Protestant Reformation, some sects—particularly Calvinists—rejected this approach to salvation and instead maintained that people's fate in the afterlife was predetermined before birth and could not be changed by actions they took on earth. But how could a person know whether he or she was going to heaven or hell? Some believers thought that wealth, accumulated through diligent work, was a sign of God's favor, indicating likely salvation. This cultural belief encouraged hard work, investment, and the accumulation of wealth—the essential requirements for success in a capitalist economy. Marx had focused on the economy's role in influencing other aspects of social life—including culture. With *The Protestant Ethic and the Spirit of Capitalism,* Weber argued that cultural beliefs could influence economic development.

As *The Protestant Ethic* illustrates, Weber sometimes tried to understand social action by viewing it from the perspective of the actor, an approach known by the German word *verstehen,* which means "understanding." Understanding why someone behaves the way he or she does also provides insight into the broader culture in which the action is taking place. As we will see, this approach was an important precursor to later sociological theory that focused precisely on how people make meaning of the social world.

Weber also contributed to sociological theory through his effort to explain the shift from traditional to rational action. One of his central theoretical propositions was that, in earlier societies, *tradition*—beliefs and customs often charged with emotional significance that are passed on from generation to generation—primarily influenced the actions of people. However, in newly industrialized capitalist societies, *rationality*—the use of reason and logical calculation to achieve a goal as efficiently as possible—was much more likely to influence people's actions.

Weber argued that the **rationalization of society**—*the long-term historical process by which rationality replaced tradition as the basis for organizing social and economic life*—propelled the social change of his day. The influence of rationalization went beyond individual human action to include broader social institutions. For example, Weber argued that whereas rulers had previously claimed authority based solely on their claim to descent from previous rulers, the authority of government officials now rests increasingly on such rational-legal foundations as elections or specific training and certification. In addition, Weber argued that the principle of rationality was responsible for the formation of bureaucracies within large organizations—government agencies, political parties, industrial companies—that manage economic and political life.

Weber could see that rationalization might be productive for society, since it focused on specifying procedures, training officials, and pursuing efficiency. But he also saw that as rationalization permeated all aspects of social life it would create cold and impersonal societies. Weber believed that bureaucracy was self-perpetuating and becoming the dominant type of social organization. He worried it would constrain human action and imprison us in an "iron cage of bureaucracy."

Ultimately, Weber feared that in modern society humans could engage in meaningful action only in large organizations, in which they were allotted narrowly defined tasks and sacrificed their personal goals to the impersonal goals of the whole. And although he agreed with much of Marx's critique of industrial capitalism, Weber's theory of rationalization led him to predict that postcapitalist societies would not produce the kind of egalitarian future that Marx predicted, but would instead be even more highly rationalized, with more layers of bureaucracy. In this way, Weber was perhaps the most prophetic of the three major founders of sociology. He did not share in the pure optimism for science and rational thought that emerged from the Enlightenment. Instead, he saw the early signs of a dark side to rationality that has now become a cautionary element of contemporary sociological thought.

Weber's sociological theory applies to a wide range of contemporary concerns. Rationalization continues to pervade our lives at home, school, and work in a variety of ways. For example:

- Do large university lecture courses and the even larger online courses represent the rationalization of higher education?
- How do the bureaucracies of governments and corporations assist in—and interfere with—the work of those organizations?
- Are such bureaucracies a threat to our privacy and freedom?

©Thomas Imo/Alamy Stock Photo

Weber gives us valuable tools for analyzing the role of rational thought and practice in many areas of our lives.

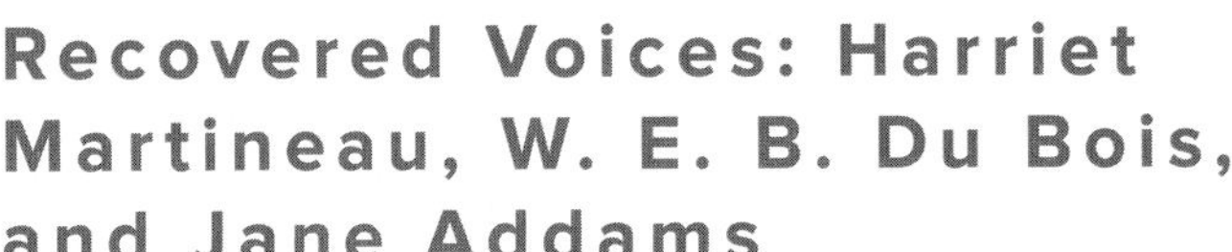

Recovered Voices: Harriet Martineau, W. E. B. Du Bois, and Jane Addams

Because of the prevailing racism and sexism during the early years of sociology, a variety of social thinkers were excluded from or marginalized in the academic world. Instead of writing for a strictly academic audience, they wrote for popular publications, authored novels, and spoke out as activists advocating social change. In many ways, they were ahead of their time. Although often at the margins of academic sociology while they were alive, these thinkers are now appreciated more widely for the contributions they made to our understanding of social life. Among these voices are Harriet Martineau, W. E. B. Du Bois, and Jane Addams.

Harriet Martineau: Gender Discrimination

Many consider Harriet Martineau (1802–1876), born into an affluent English family, to be the first female sociologist. Her work delved into issues of gender discrimination and slavery that many of the white male sociologists of her time had largely ignored. She also agitated for women's suffrage and the expansion of women's rights in England.

Self-taught and—like other women at the time—excluded from an academic appointment, Martineau began by writing magazine articles and then a series of books on economics and politics that were geared toward the general public rather than an academic audience. Her books were highly successful, making her wealthy as well as a literary celebrity. After traveling in the United States for two years, she wrote two books based on her observations, most notably *Society in America* (Martineau [1837] 2009), a forceful critique of the failure of the United States to live up to its democratic promise in its treatment of both enslaved people and women. At this time, she also wrote about the methods of social research in *How to Observe Morals and Manners* ([1838] 2009). Finally, Martineau made an important contribution to sociology by translating the work of Auguste Comte for English-speaking audiences.

W. E. B. Du Bois: Racial Inequality

W. E. B. Du Bois (pronounced "doo-BOYS") (1868–1963) made important contributions to sociology with his groundbreaking research on race in America as well as with his efforts to promote racial justice. Du Bois, a descendant of African, French, and Dutch ancestors, came from a comfortable middle-class Massachusetts family that provided him with a solid early education and insulated him from the worst effects of racism. When he traveled south to Nashville to study at Fisk University in the 1880s, however, he encountered a rigidly segregated world in which African Americans were frequently the targets of beatings and lynchings. This injustice strengthened his interest in race as a subject of sociological study. In 1895, Du Bois became the first African American to obtain a PhD from Harvard University. He went on to teach sociology and to write a series of studies that elevated race to a place of prominence in sociology. Du Bois published the first sociological study of a black community, *The Philadelphia Negro* ([1899] 1996), followed by the widely read *The Souls of Black Folk* ([1903] 2005). Both works explored the complexity of race relations in turn-of-the-century American society.

Throughout his life, Du Bois combined scholarship with activism. He played an important role in the founding of the National Association for the Advancement of Colored People (NAACP), arguably the leading civil rights organization of the twentieth century. He founded—and for a quarter century edited—the NAACP's influential magazine, *The Crisis,* which is still published today (thecrisismagazine.com). He also nurtured efforts to promote unity among people of African descent worldwide.

RECOVERED VOICES: MARTINEAU, DU BOIS, AND ADDAMS

	 ©Spencer Arnold/Getty Images	 Source: Library of Congress Prints and Photographs Division [LC-USZ62-16767]	 Source: Library of Congress Prints and Photographs Division [LC-DIG-ggbain-12065]
	Harriet Martineau	**W. E. B. Du Bois**	**Jane Addams**
Biography	1802–1876 English Writer and activist	1868–1963 American Scholar and activist	1860–1935 American Scholar and activist
Key issues and work	Gender, slavery, and discrimination *Society in America*	Race and discrimination NAACP cofounder *The Philadelphia Negro; The Souls of Black Folk*	Urban social problems Hull House founder *Hull House Maps and Papers*

As an agent of change, he faced opposition from powerful forces. During the Cold War anticommunist hysteria of the 1950s, the U.S. Justice Department accused Du Bois of being an agent of the Soviet Union because of his peace activism and promotion of nuclear disarmament. Although he was acquitted, the FBI continued to harass him and the government revoked his passport. Eventually, he was allowed to travel abroad and he moved to Ghana, where he became a citizen. He died there at the age of 95 on August 27, 1963, the day before the civil rights march on Washington, D.C., where Martin Luther King Jr. gave his famous "I Have a Dream" speech.

Jane Addams: Urban Social Problems

Jane Addams (1860–1935) is best known as a social reformer and the founder of Hull House, which provided a wide range of social services in the poor immigrant communities of Chicago and served as a model for later similar establishments, known as settlement houses, in other cities. Addams was the first American woman to win the Nobel Peace Prize, awarded to her in 1931 for her longstanding work in building an international women's coalition to promote peace and prevent war. But Addams also made an important contribution to the development of sociology. Her social reform work and her research on social life on Chicago's South Side had a significant influence on the development of urban sociology at the University of Chicago, the home of the first sociology department in the United States.

However, unlike some University of Chicago sociologists, who limited their work to understanding urban life, Addams believed that social theory and research should be linked to action promoting social change. Working to address social problems enabled her to contribute to social reform while developing and testing theories about how society worked. In doing so, she often challenged those in power, advocating for the poor and others at the margins of society.

In *Hull House Maps and Papers* ([1895] 2007), Addams chronicled life in the immigrant communities around Hull House, producing data that were used to promote reform. In *Democracy and Social Ethics* ([1902] 2002), she linked democracy with diversity, explaining that a well-functioning democratic society requires an understanding of a wide range of experiences and perspectives, something that early sociology was well equipped to provide. In addition, Addams foreshadowed the development of feminist social theory by critiquing the way male sociologists often based their generalizations about society on men's experiences only. She argued that for researchers to fully understand social problems, they needed to have a sympathetic connection with the people affected by those problems. Her collaboration with poor immigrants informed her sociological understanding that people actively seek to improve their conditions, even when facing great odds in extremely difficult situations.

Although the works of Martineau, Du Bois, Addams, and others may have been underappreciated when they wrote them, those works have since had a significant impact on sociology, encouraging sociologists to pay careful attention to the social complexities of gender, race, class, and power.

Sociology's Diverse Theories

The work of early sociologists served as the source for the development of later sociological theory. In the chapters to come, we consider different theories regarding specific social phenomena. In this section, we examine some of the general approaches to theory that have developed over the years. First, though, we consider what theory is and examine some basic ways that sociological theories vary.

Understanding Theory

A national survey of adults in the United States conducted in 2015 by the Pew Research Center found that more than two-thirds of young respondents—those between 18 and 34, known as millennials—favored the legalization of marijuana. In contrast, only about half of respondents 35 or older favored marijuana legalization (Pew Research Center 2015a).

Why do you think young adults are more supportive of marijuana legalization than their older counterparts? Perhaps it's because young people in any era are typically more open to change than older adults. Alternately, perhaps there was something unique about the historical period in which millennials grew up that encouraged their favorable attitude toward marijuana legalization.

Each of these explanations is, in effect, a *theory* because it tries to explain an observation. Attributing the observed difference in attitudes toward marijuana legalization to the characteristics of age groups generally reflects a life-course theory. Attributing it to the experience of growing up in a particular historical period, in contrast, reflects a generational theory.

Accurate data—such as a national survey showing that younger adults are more supportive of marijuana legalization than are older adults—describes the world and helps us see "what" has occurred. Theories answer "why?" questions and help explain the data: "Why is this so?" "Why did this happen?" More formally, a **social theory** is *a set of principles and propositions that explains the relationships among social phenomena.* Through their explanations, theories also alert us to the sorts of questions we should be asking in future research.

Sociological theories address broad questions, such as "Why don't complex societies fall apart?" and "Why do wealth and poverty coexist?" as well as more narrowly defined questions, such as "Why do some schools succeed while others fail?" or even "Why do students who sit in the back of the class tend to have lower grades than those who sit up front?" When we speak of approaches to sociological theory, therefore, we are referring to broad explanations sociologists have for why society operates the way it does. Although thinking about theory can seem intimidating at first, it actually is fairly straightforward and involves answering the most interesting question of all: Why?

A few other characteristics of theories are important to remember:

- ***A theory is not just a hunch or personal opinion.*** It may start off that way, but to be useful, theories have to be put to the test to see if they are consistent with the evidence; that's the nature of science. Sociological theory is linked to research and evidence in ways that we explore in Chapter 2.
- ***Theories evolve and are sometimes rejected, leaving the most useful to survive.*** When evidence repeatedly contradicts a theory, the theory is either revised or discarded. The most useful theories are those that endure, some of which we discuss later in this chapter.
- ***Multiple theories often give us a more complete picture than any single one.*** Many factors contribute to most aspects of social life. Considering different theories can alert us to a variety of possible explanations for a social phenomenon and to a range of factors that can contribute to it.

Finally, theories tend to vary along a few key dimensions, which we now consider.

Key Dimensions of Theory

How do professional football teams vary? Some focus on offense, others on defense. Some rely on skilled veteran players, whereas others groom the abilities of younger team members. Some teams get most of their points by running the ball, whereas others generate most of their offense by passing. These are among the key dimensions on which teams vary.

Sociological theories, too, vary along key dimensions, including consensus and conflict, subjective and objective reality, and micro-level and macro-level analyses (see Figure 1.1). Think of each dimension as a continuum rather than an either-or division. Knowing where a theory lies on each continuum can help you understand how it fits into the larger picture of sociological thought.

Consensus and Conflict

Conflict refers to tensions and disputes in society, often resulting from the unequal distribution of scarce resources, which can contribute to social change. *Consensus* refers to solidarity and cooperative interaction, often due to shared values and interests, which can contribute to social stability. Although different theories focus more on one or the other, both consensus and conflict coexist in every society, institution, and organization—indeed, in all social life.

In some instances, conflict can produce certain kinds of consensus (Coser 1956). When countries go to war, a dramatic example of conflict, citizens in each nation often feel a renewed sense of solidarity, which they express through increased patriotism and nationalism. On the other hand, sometimes apparent consensus masks simmering tensions that become evident only when they erupt into full-blown conflict. For example, the ordinary daily routines of some cities have sometimes concealed underlying racial tensions, such as longstanding conflict between local police and the African American community in Ferguson, Missouri; Baltimore, Maryland; and other cities that exploded after high-profile cases of police shootings.

Objective and Subjective Reality

Objective conditions are the material aspects of social life, including the physical environment, social networks, and social institutions. All of these exist outside of us, and collectively they make up the

FIGURE 1.1 | DIMENSIONS OF SOCIOLOGICAL THEORY

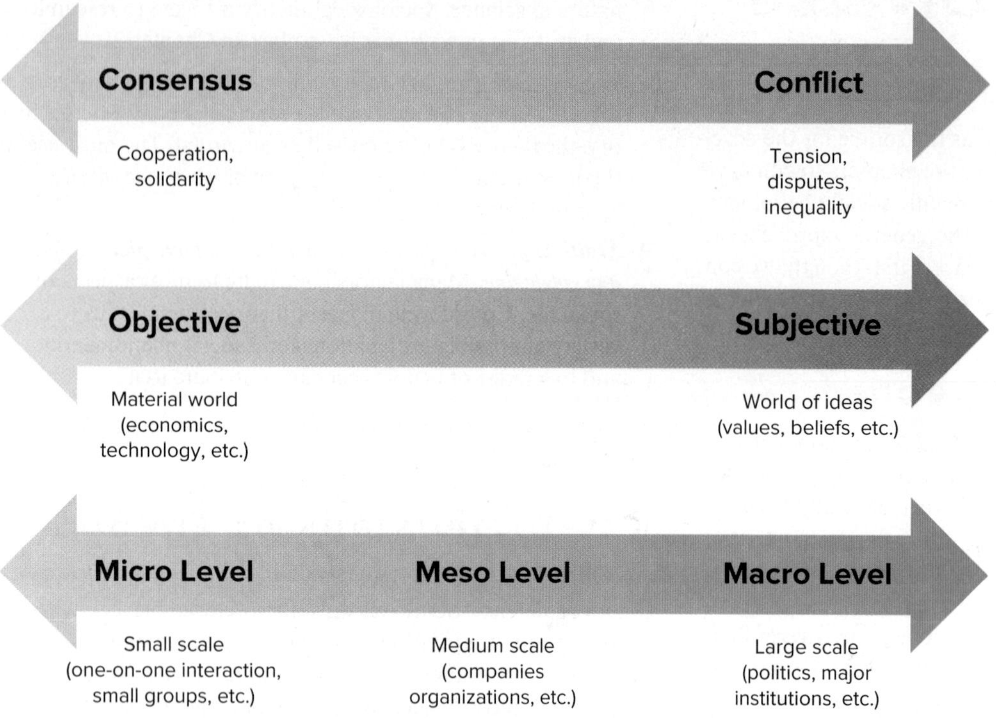

Different sociological theories focus on various dimensions of social life.

objective dimension of social life. In contrast, the *subjective dimension* of social life involves the world of ideas, including our sense of self, social norms, values, and belief systems. These all exist "in our head," so to speak, and are part of the cultural aspect of social life.

Both the objective physical world we live in and our subjective interpretations of that world have a significant impact on our lives and our society. For example, we have seen that Marx emphasized the impact of economic life (an objective factor) whereas Weber's theory regarding the Protestant ethic highlighted the role of cultural beliefs (a subjective factor).

Micro-Level and Macro-Level Analyses

The third dimension of sociological theory relates to different levels of analysis—as well as to different levels of society itself. Theories that focus on small-scale, usually face-to-face, social interaction are operating at the **micro level of analysis.** (*Micro* means "small.") Theories that focus on large-scale social systems and processes such as the economy, politics, and population trends operate at the **macro level of analysis.** (*Macro* means "large.") Theories that focus somewhere between very large and very small social phenomena—on organizations or companies, for example—are using a **meso level of analysis.** (*Meso* means "middle.") Often, sociological work focuses on the interaction between these various levels of social life.

Now that you are equipped with a better understanding of what theory is and how theories vary, let's take a closer look at some major theoretical traditions. Since the mid-twentieth century, sociologists have sometimes grouped varied sociological theories into three broad categories: *structural-functionalist theories, conflict theories,* and *symbolic interactionist theories.*

Structural-Functionalist Theories

Structural-functionalist theories *focus on consensus and cooperative interaction in social life, emphasizing how the different parts of a society contribute to its overall operation.* The roots of this tradition can be found in the work of Spencer and Durkheim. Structural-functionalist theories—often referred to simply as **functionalist theories**—were dominant in the United States in the middle of the twentieth century, when their leading proponent was Talcott Parsons (1902–1979). Parsons saw societies as complex systems made up of interdependent parts—for example, families, courts, schools, the economy—that work together to produce social stability. Because the systems are balanced, they tend to move toward normal states of equilibrium; a change in one part of the system results in a change in another part to compensate. Individuals are integrated into the social structure through culture, especially in the form of shared values. These shared values in turn promote a moral commitment to the society among its members that contributes to the society's smooth functioning.

To endure, a social institution must meet a need of the system as a whole; institutions that do not contribute either adapt or disappear. Parsons argued that any social organization—whether a small group or a large and diverse society—must perform several key functions to survive, including teaching group members core community values, integrating members into productive participation in social life, defining and attaining community goals, and adapting to a changing environment.

In an important contribution to functionalist theory, Robert K. Merton (1910–2003) distinguished between **manifest functions,**

©Jean Catuffe/Getty Images

Individuals are embedded within larger social structures that correspond to different levels of sociological analysis. For example, these Swedish gold medal-winning athletes brought their individual talents to the competition (micro level), but their curling matches were coordinated by the organization behind the 2018 PyeongChang Olympics in South Korea (meso level), which was, in turn, one project of the global International Olympic Committee (macro level).

the recognized and intended consequences of social phenomena, and **latent functions,** *their largely unrecognized and unintended consequences.* A manifest function of schools, for example, is to help prepare people for future employment, whereas a latent function is to serve as a dating pool or marriage market. Merton also reminds us that even though some phenomena are long-standing and seem permanent, they can be **dysfunctional,** *inhibiting or disrupting the working of a system as a whole.* For example, persistent classroom overcrowding is dysfunctional and can undermine the educational effectiveness of schools.

Consider how one might study the family as a social institution using functionalist theories. Families serve a number of functions, including the raising of children (though some societies raise children communally outside of the family and many families do not include children). In recent decades, a changing economy (another part of the social system) and changes in cultural values have contributed to changes in the family, including the rise of two-wage-earner families, single-parent families, blended families, and families with same-sex parents. Despite such changes, shared values continue to tell us how to raise children and maintain family life. Families can be dysfunctional, too—for example, by harboring child abuse or domestic violence.

Conflict Theories

Conflict theories *focus on issues of contention, power, and inequality, highlighting the competition for scarce resources.* This approach has its roots in the work of Marx and Weber. And through the work of others, such as Martineau, Du Bois, and Addams, it often finds expression in studies of class, race, gender, and other forms of inequality. The conflict approach emphasizes that, to meet common needs, people attempt to acquire scarce and valuable resources. These include material goods—such as food, housing, and good jobs—as well as less tangible resources, such as social respect and freedom. Because these resources are often limited, people compete for them, bringing different groups into conflict. Even when conflict is not visible, it is often present but repressed by the dominance of the powerful over the less powerful.

Conflict theories, then, see power at the core of social life. Power enables some people to gain an advantage over others and acquire more resources; more resources, in turn, give them more power. In this ongoing struggle, different groups use culture's values and ideas as weapons to advance their own positions. The dominant culture supports and justifies existing inequalities. Various countercultures articulate different values in their challenge to the existing condition.

How would one study the family with conflict theory? Conflict theories explain that tension and disagreement within families are routine and ordinary. Some of this discord emerges because of differences in power between women and men. Historically, the extensive legal, economic, and social inequalities between women and men reflected the different amounts of power each possessed. This inequality had been justified by a dominant culture that viewed men as naturally superior to women. Such cultural beliefs traditionally kept women in restricted family roles and prevented them from pursuing ambitions they might have had for themselves, topics we explore in Chapter 12. Inequalities continue to exist around family life today, both within families, where power may not be shared evenly, and within broader society, where some forms of family such as gay and lesbian couples, continue to face discrimination, even though same-sex marriage is legally recognized in the United States.

Symbolic Interactionist Theories

Symbolic interactionist theories *focus on how society emerges from people's use of shared symbols in the course of their everyday interactions.* Weber's approach of *verstehen,* in which the researcher tries to understand action from the perspective of the actor, laid some groundwork for these theories, as did early work by Georg Simmel (1858–1918), who wrote insightful essays on the dynamics of daily life. However, symbolic interactionist theories were fully developed in the United States, building on work by social psychologists in the early and mid-twentieth century. George Herbert Mead (1863–1931), for example, wrote about how we develop a sense of self through our interaction with others and by self-reflection (see Chapter 6). In his dramaturgical theory, Erving Goffman (1922–1982) showed how social life was very much like a play, with people adopting roles, complete with props and scripts (see Chapter 7).

Symbolic interactionist theories are strongly associated with the subjective and micro-level dimensions of social life. They explain social life by highlighting that the social world is based on interaction between people using cultural symbols, such as words and nonverbal body language. Through interaction, individuals develop a sense of self and create a shared understanding of reality with others. People with more power are typically better able to influence this interpretation of reality. This common interpretation of reality leads to patterns of social interaction within groups that form the basis of social structure. But everyday interaction is also constantly re-creating or changing these patterns, so society itself is inherently unstable and constantly in flux. Always under construction, the social world is therefore always capable of change. In this way, the symbolic interactionist theories explain social life by highlighting the active role people take in constructing shared understandings of social reality and creating society.

Applied to the family, the symbolic interactionist approach directs our attention to micro-level interactions between family members. As they interact, they develop an understanding of who they are and what their role is within the family. What does it mean to be a "good parent" today? Who will work to earn money? Who will care for children? What responsibility does a child have for an aging parent? Family members must come to some mutual understanding about what is expected from each of them. This shared interpretation of reality produces patterns of behavior that provide a routine structure to family life. But these interpretations and arrangements are not static; they are continuously reexamined and thus subject to change. The changes in family structure over the past half century illustrate the cumulative effect of individual-level decisions. People in different types of family—including two-parent families, one-parent families, childless couples, families with same-sex parents, and step-families—actively interpret the meaning of "family" and act accordingly.

Feminist Theories and Theoretical Diversity

As we see throughout this book, sociological theory has developed considerably since the mid-twentieth century, when some sociologists grouped the field's varied theories into the categories of functionalist, conflict, and symbolic interactionist perspectives. Newer perspectives often do not fit neatly into these older categories. Among the most important contemporary perspectives is feminist theory. Feminist theories focus on inequality between women and men and could be considered in the tradition of conflict theories. But feminist theories also provide insight into how those inequalities are created and reinforced in daily interactions, placing these insights squarely in the tradition of symbolic interactionism (see Chapter 11).

As with other theoretical traditions, there is no single feminist theory. Instead, a variety of feminist theories emphasize the importance of women's experience, analyze gender inequality, and advocate gender equality (Anderson 2015; Taylor, Rupp, and Whittier 2012). As we saw earlier in the chapter, feminist ideas from Harriet Martineau, Jane Addams, and others were present during the early years of sociology but were often marginalized in the male-dominated world of academia. The women's movement of the 1960s and 1970s, however, helped create a space for the emergence of feminist scholars who transformed many academic fields, including sociology. Often working across disciplinary boundaries and in newly established women's studies departments, feminist theorists challenged male assumptions about the world and about how social research should be done (Harding 1991; Reinharz 1992).

Historically, men had dominated the analyses of social life and often assumed that their understanding and perspective applied to everyone. Feminist "standpoint theory" rejected this notion, instead emphasizing that all knowledge is constructed from a particular perspective and that women's different experiences need to be included to produce an accurate understanding of social life (Harding 2004; Smith 1974, 1989). In the years that followed, this basic insight was extended to include the recognition that women's experiences vary depending on their class, race, and sexual orientation (Collins 2009; hooks 2000). This understanding has contributed to a wider recognition of "intersectionality"—that the effects of gender, class, race, and sexual orientation intersect in shaping social life (Anderson and Collins 2013; Collins and Bilge 2016; Rothenberg 2014) and that women's lives vary across different societies (Mohanty 2003). Feminist theory has also contributed to a focus on women's bodies as a site of social struggles involving sexuality, beauty norms, violence, reproductive rights, and health (Lorber and Moore 2010). Finally, feminist theory has informed work on men, gender, and sexuality, revealing how our ideas about masculinity are socially constructed (Kimmel and Messner 2013; Pascoe 2011).

In addition, various recent theories—under the umbrella term *postmodernism*—have highlighted how shared meanings and assumptions about the world have fragmented, as different groups in society come to understand social reality differently (Dasgupta and Kivisto 2014). Meanwhile, rational choice theories have introduced a sort of economic analysis, suggesting that social interaction be understood as exchanges between rational individuals. And queer theory challenges the stability of basic identity categories—such as straight or gay, male or female—highlighting the fluidity and complexity of identity in contemporary society.

One of the great strengths of sociology is that it contains a variety of theories about the workings of social life that reach well beyond the three traditional approaches. But what unites sociology? What is the common ground that enables people using such disparate theories to identify as sociologists? That common ground is the sociological perspective and the core concepts that are at its heart.

Sociology's Common Ground: Culture, Structure, and Power

Diverse sociological theories are united by the core concepts that are central to a sociological perspective, including culture, structure, and power. As we have already seen, these concepts

TABLE 1.2 CORE CONCEPTS AND APPROACHES TO SOCIOLOGICAL THEORY

	Functionalist Theories	Conflict Theories	Symbolic Interactionist Theories
Key questions	How is society held together? What function do the parts of society serve?	How is inequality structured in society? How are power relations maintained; how can they be changed?	How do people interpret and understand the social world in their interactions? How do they help shape the reality they experience?
Culture	Culture represents the consensus values and norms of a society into which individuals are socialized.	Conflicting parties use culture to advance their interests. Those in power perpetuate their privilege by socializing people into dominant values and norms. Those who are oppressed develop countercultures that challenge the dominant worldview.	Through the use of symbols, people create culture based on their interpretation of social reality. They pass on these ideas and values in the socialization process.
Structure	Society is a stable system made up of interconnected structures. People act within structural constraints so that change is typically gradual and temporary, returning societies to a stable equilibrium.	Structure is the social order maintained by dominant groups primarily through coercion and the threat of force. Collective action challenging the existing order is often the source of structural change.	Social structure is produced through recurring individual actions that create a pattern. Structure is inherently unstable and changeable since it must be reproduced continually through individual action.
Power	Power is the ability of a social system to achieve its collective goals. Inequalities between groups serve a positive function in society by motivating the most qualified to fill the most important positions.	Power is often concentrated in the hands of a dominant group that uses it to exploit or oppress others. Inequality is the result of struggle between groups for scarce resources.	Power is rooted in the social relationships between people. Inequality results from the actions of individuals and therefore can be changed.

were used extensively by sociology's early thinkers and they have been at the heart of sociology ever since.

To varying degrees, all theoretical approaches rely on sociology's core concepts. For example, functionalism highlights culture's role in providing society with common values, such as love of family. Conflict theory emphasizes how competing groups can manipulate cultural ideas and symbols to their advantage, as when politicians attach the idea of "family values" to their legislative initiatives and suggest opponents are antifamily. Symbolic interactionism emphasizes the process by which individuals create culture, as when people redefine "family" to incorporate a broader range of relationships. Although these approaches differ in their interpretations and emphases, they all agree that culture is a significant feature of social life worthy of close attention. Similarly, structure and power are important to all sociological theories. Table 1.2 summarizes how these core concepts provide the common ground that links the major approaches to sociological theory.

This section presents a brief overview of sociology's three core concepts. Each concept is later covered in depth in a separate chapter. By learning to use these three concepts to analyze and understand social life, you will succeed in developing a sociological perspective.

Culture

Culture is *the collection of values, beliefs, knowledge, norms, language, behaviors, and material objects shared by a people and socially transmitted from generation to generation.* Culture operates at all levels of society: through everyday interactions between individuals; through organizational norms in schools, businesses, and other groups; and through society-wide mechanisms such as the media and religion. At its broadest, culture is a way of life.

We tend to take our own culture for granted since we have internalized its basic customs and assumptions. For example, most of us, most of the time, have a fairly good understanding of what to expect from routine social interactions and what is considered appropriate behavior in those settings. We know when we are expected to be more formal and polite (perhaps with authority figures) and when we can relax and be casual (perhaps with close friends and family). We know that raising a hand to speak when hanging out with friends is unnecessary and that cracking open a beer in class is unwise. These unwritten "rules"—and the ideas about courtesy and respect that inform them—are part of our culture that we have learned.

Consider, for example, the simple matter of where to look when speaking with someone. Most Americans look people in the eye since in American culture direct eye contact signals honesty and forthrightness, whereas avoiding eye contact suggests that one has something to hide. But in some Asian societies, extended direct eye contact is often considered rude and impertinent, whereas averting one's gaze is a sign of deference and respect. Imagine the potential miscommunication if, say, an Asian and an American business executive, unaware of these cultural differences, were assessing each other as potential business partners. The American might think her Asian colleague had something to hide, whereas the Asian executive might think his American colleague was being rude and disrespectful. Understanding the concept of culture helps us interact in a world of diversity and allows us to critically examine beliefs and behaviors we might otherwise view as "natural."

Culture is not "natural" or biologically based because it must be taught and learned through the process of socialization (see Chapter 6). Since people must reproduce culture for it to survive, people can also change culture by adopting new values, beliefs, and behaviors and abandoning older ones. This process of cultural evolution can create conflict as some people seek to hold on to more traditional values and ways of life, while others embrace new ideas and behaviors. As a result, cultural conflicts are common. Clashes in values, beliefs, and ways of life help fuel conflict, sometimes even contributing to warfare. On the other hand, culture is often something to celebrate, and our identity comes, in part, from the elements of culture that we choose to embrace. Our tastes in music, our dress and appearance, our religious beliefs or nonbeliefs, our language, our family's ancestry, among other things, are all cultural features that help make us who we are.

Structure

Structure refers to *the recurring patterns of behavior in social life.* These patterns occur at all levels of society, from our daily interactions with others to the global economy. Structures range from highly informal patterns, such as where and when we routinely meet up with friends, to much more formal organizations and institutions, such as schools and government.

People create structures to help them accomplish their goals, but, in turn, structures come to constrain what they can do (see Figure 1.2). For example, imagine that you and your friends decide to form a new group to advocate for better student life, including more parking spaces on campus. In establishing your group, you have to decide things like: Will there be formal leadership positions, such as president and secretary? If so, how will those be chosen? How do you become a member? How will decisions be made? How you answer such questions will determine the structure for your organization. You would hope that the structure you create will help the group function smoothly and promote its goal effectively. But the rules that define the structure will also constrain the behavior of group members because they regulate how members are supposed to behave. As new members join your group, they will experience the rules as an already-existing reality that constrains their actions. They may choose to comply with the rules, thereby reproducing the structure of your group, or work to change them in some way, thereby modifying the structure.

FIGURE 1.2 | THE INTERPLAY BETWEEN PEOPLE AND SOCIAL STRUCTURE

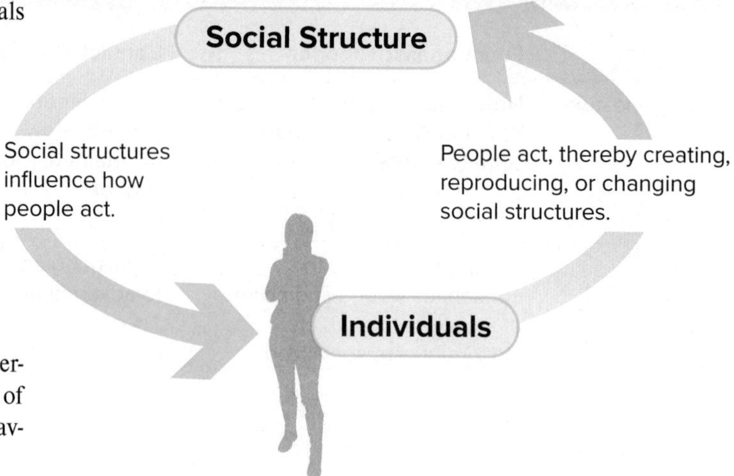

Daily life tends to be ordered by various informal patterns of behavior, or *social structures.* We can talk about "family structure," for example, even though there are no formal organizational by-laws that regulate the behavior of such groups. There are, however, legal standards, social norms, and common practices that establish the "rules" of family life, something we explore later in the book.

Similar to how culture must be reproduced—and can be changed—structures must be reproduced through continuing patterns of behavior or they can be changed through changes in that behavior. History provides examples of how people can act collectively to change social structure. In the nineteenth century, six-day workweeks were the norm in industrial societies, and workers usually labored for 10 or 12 hours a day. By the early twentieth century, however, a growing number of people joined the labor movement, which promoted the then-radical ideas of an eight-hour workday and a five-day workweek. With great difficulty, labor unions struggled successfully to establish this new standard, thus creating the much-beloved weekend with its two-day reprieve from work. This resulted in a fundamental change in the social structuring of time in our society. (See the Sociology in Action box for an example of the role sociology can play in helping address the structures that contribute to a persistent social problem.)

thinking about the core concepts

Review the description of sociology's early thinkers. What roles did culture, structure, and power play in their work?

SOCIOLOGY in ACTION

Working to Reduce Homelessness

In 2017, more than half a million people were homeless in the United States—an enduring, but solvable, social problem. Compared to other states, Rhode Island has done well in both reducing homelessness and sheltering those who are homeless. The rate of homelessness in the state ticked down by 8 percent between 2010 and the 2017, and only 5.8 percent of those who were homeless in Rhode Island in 2017 were without shelter, the fifth lowest rate in the country (U.S. Department of Housing and Urban Development 2017). But major challenges remain—homelessness went up in 2017, for example—and a broad coalition of researchers and advocates continues to work together to fight homelessness and protect the rights of those who are homeless.

For many years, Providence College sociologist Eric Hirsch has been an important figure in that effort, applying his sociological insight and research skills. Hirsch has coordinated data collection for an annual point-in-time "homeless census" that gives advocates important data to help them better serve homeless people. The census data are distributed to state and local government officials and then compiled with other state data in a national report, which informs policymakers about the issue.

Hirsch also serves on the board of the Rhode Island Coalition for the Homeless, a group that played a key role in passing a 2012 Homeless Bill of Rights in Rhode Island. The first statewide legislation of its kind in the United States, it protects those without a permanent address from discrimination in areas such as employment and voting.

As a sociologist, Hirsch is well aware that homelessness results from social forces more than individual shortcomings. While mental health issues and substance abuse have long been a reality among the homeless, Hirsch (2016) writes, "Rates of homelessness in the United States were quite low in the post–World War II period until a dramatic rise in income inequality in the late 1970s. With a lot of income and wealth concentrated at the top, developers began to build only expensive suburban homes and luxury downtown apartments and condos. Restricting the supply of low- and moderate-income housing has meant higher and higher rents for poor households."

Hirsch and his colleagues (Glasser, Hirsch, and Chan 2014) argue that the increase in the United States homelessness was caused by (1) the reduction in affordable housing, (2) policy changes that reduced or eliminated financial assistance for single unemployed individuals, and (3) long-term stagnant or falling incomes for low-wage workers. In responding, though, many municipalities have taken an individualistic "out-of-sight out-of-mind" approach, for example, making it illegal to panhandle. Hirsch warns that, too often, "We have criminalized extreme poverty and homelessness. We refuse to address the root causes" (Carini 2016).

In recognition of his many years of scholarship and advocacy in support of Rhode Island's homeless, the political blog *RI Future* named Hirsch a winner of its annual award given to people who "work to improve the human condition." Because of his efforts "on the streets, in the classroom, and in the statehouse," they described Hirsch as "a tireless advocate for the poor and homeless" (Plain 2015).

think about it

1. *How do you think regular data collection on a community's homeless population can help advocates and policymakers address homelessness?*
2. *How does taking a sociological perspective help us to understand homelessness as a social problem?*

Power

Power is *the ability to bring about an intended outcome, even when opposed by others.* Power, too, operates at all levels of society, including in families (parents have power over their children), in organizations (managers have power over the people who report to them), and in national and international relations (leaders exercise military and economic power to achieve national goals). Sometimes people *empower* themselves to achieve a goal (as when a student completes a degree to qualify for a particular career). Other times power is used to influence the thinking and behavior of others and even to dominate others. For example, an employer can dictate the rules that employees must follow during work hours.

Power is commonly used to allocate resources (economic power), make rules and decisions (political power), and help define reality (cultural power). It is thus closely tied to *inequality,* the systematic and unequal distribution of resources among various groups of people. All societies have some form of inequality; it just varies by type and degree. Those who have more economic, political, and cultural resources have a better chance to achieve their goals and overcome hurdles and opposition. In other words, they have more power.

Paying attention to power allows us to see connections and similarities between different forms of inequality, which coexist and interact. Considering the intersections of race, class, gender, and sexuality has proven to be especially important in understanding power and inequality.

©Carlos Barria/Stringer/Reuters

©Xinzheng/Moment/Getty Images

FAST-FORWARD

Social Change and Urbanization

Social change influences the lives of individuals and communities alike. These photos show the rapid development that has occurred in a portion of Shanghai, China, between 1987 (*top*) and 2017 (*bottom*). Just as the fast growth of industrial cities more than a century ago prompted early sociologists to study urbanization, the incredibly fast growth of Shanghai directs contemporary sociologists to examine the impact of such rapid change on the lives of local residents.

Culture, structure, and power are not unchanging features of social life; they are part of ongoing social processes. Culture is reproduced and changed through socialization. Structures are created and altered through action. Power can be used to produce or reduce inequalities, which in turn can alter the distribution of power. These dynamics are at the heart of a sociological analysis that recognizes the ever-changing nature of social life.

A Changing World

FROM MODERN TO POSTMODERN SOCIETY

Sociology arose over a century and a half ago during a period of transition that marked the emergence of modernity in the eighteenth and nineteenth centuries. Early sociologists, drawing on the core concepts of culture, structure, and power, sought to explain that transition and the social turmoil that often accompanied it. Today, we are living through another period of transition, this time from modernity to an as-yet-uncertain postmodernity, and sociologists are studying the nature and consequences of these changes.

Modernity was a period associated with the rise of industrialization, democracy, and science. In contrast, **postmodernity** is *a historical period beginning in the mid-twentieth century characterized by the rise of information-based economies and the fragmentation of political beliefs and ways of knowing.* Because we are in the midst of this transition, it is difficult to summarize neatly what postmodernity will look like or what long-term impact it will have. Nonetheless, we can point to certain features of this transition to the postmodern world (see Table 1.3).

Classical theorists were concerned with the rise of an industrial economy; today's sociologists are interested in the relationship between so-called postindustrial economies, in which information-based and service-sector jobs predominate, and the developing industrial economies that now produce the bulk of the world's manufactured goods. Classical sociologists studied the rise of urban life that accompanied industrialization; contemporary sociologists have examined the emergence of suburban life as a new social reality in advanced economies while documenting continued urbanization in the developing world and the growth of "mega-cities." The modern era was marked by a great faith in democratic governments as a means to human progress; in postmodern times, distrust of government and a loss of faith in political ideologies have often led to stalemated conflicts, political disengagement, and widespread cynicism. Finally, classical theorists highlighted the declining influence of religion, the rise of science, and the rationalization of modern life. Contemporary sociologists have studied our highly fragmented culture, which includes everything from the rise of multiculturalism and rejection of universal truths to a resurgence of fundamentalist religions and reaffirmation of universal truths.

Ten Features of Postmodern Society

Beyond such broad changes, a number of significant developments are transforming our way of life. These changes tend to affect the wealthier societies of the world most. Throughout this book, we use a sociological perspective to better understand these aspects of postmodern society. As you read the list try to

TABLE 1.3 KEY FEATURES OF PREMODERN, MODERN, AND POSTMODERN SOCIETIES

	Premodern	Modern	Postmodern
Economy	Agricultural	Industrial	Information based Service oriented
Social life	Rural	Urban	Suburban Mega-cities
Politics	Religiously sanctioned leaders	Democracy	Disengagement Cynicism
Dominant culture	Religion	Rationality and science	Fragmented Multicultural

use a sociological perspective to imagine how your individual life might be affected by these broader social changes. Consider, too, how you might work with others to effect change in one or more of these areas:

1. ***The expansion of media and commercial culture.*** In postmodern society, media technologies have dramatically expanded into all aspects of social life, creating new opportunities for communication and new dilemmas. The boundaries between the internet, television, smartphones, video games, and other media continue to blur, resulting in the all-encompassing and commercialized media environment in which we live. Closely connected to this expansion has been unprecedented growth in advertising and the promotion of consumption. How is the saturation of society by the media influencing social life? How often do you check or send texts or check Facebook? How many advertisements have you seen today? (See especially Chapter 14.)
2. ***The threat to the natural environment.*** The ever-increasing production and consumption of consumer goods have taken a serious toll on the environment in the form of resource depletion, pollution, climate change, and an ever-growing accumulation of waste. How can we balance the desire for material comfort with the need to protect diminishing resources? How are environmental changes potentially affecting our health and our way of life? (See Chapter 15.)
3. ***The decline of U.S. cities and the rise of suburbs.*** In the postmodern era, corporations have moved many industrialized manufacturing jobs to developing nations with lower-wage workers. As industrial jobs in U.S. cities disappeared, the economic base of major urban areas crumbled, leaving behind unemployment, poverty, and crime in many inner cities. Meanwhile, a lengthy period of suburban growth permitted people to own homes in relatively safe and tranquil surroundings. But suburban life can leave people feeling socially isolated and require lengthy commutes to work in heavy traffic. The recent resurgence of some cities has produced new challenges associated with gentrification. How can U.S. cities remain vital in postmodernity? How have the suburbs changed the rhythms of daily life, and what is their effect on people's sense of community? How will the expansion of urban life in developing nations affect those societies? (See Chapter 15.)
4. ***The global economy.*** You need only consider the route traveled by the components of your smartphone—from its designers at a high-tech company in Silicon Valley in the United States to mineral mining in Africa, to parts suppliers in Japan, South Korea, and Europe to production in China and distribution all around the world—to realize that we are inextricably part of a global system of production and consumption. The global economy is transforming societies around the world, and the debate over the nature of this change has been an important topic in sociology. How does a global economy affect the inequality between rich and poor nations? How has the growth of a global economy impacted employment patterns, educational requirements, and family life? (See Chapters 9, 16, and 17.)
5. ***The aging population.*** We are living longer and healthier lives thanks to advances in health information and medical technology. Now society must adjust to the new reality of an aging population. The U.S. Census Bureau reports that the number of Americans aged 90 and over increased from 720,000 in 1980 to 1.9 million in 2010, and projects the 90+ population to grow to more than 10 million by 2050 (He and Muenchrath 2011). How will the need to care for aging parents and grandparents affect future American families? How will social services and the health care system cope with an aging population? (See Chapter 17.)
6. ***The changing family.*** Effective contraception, divorce, blended families, two-wage-earner families, single-parent families, same-sex marriage, and surrogate parenting, among other developments, have changed the definition of the family and its role in society. How does today's family differ from yesterday's? How have recent social changes affected the nature and function of the family? What is in store for the family in the future? (See Chapter 12.)
7. ***Troubled political institutions.*** In many parts of the world the prospect of democracy holds great promise as a substitute for repressive political regimes. But long-established democracies often seem to have their own troubles with declining trust in government, growing public cynicism, and partisan gridlock. Why do some well-established democracies stagnate? What threats challenge the vitality of our democratic institutions? (See Chapter 16.)
8. ***Increased diversity and multiculturalism.*** A recent influx of immigrants has been a catalyst for change as well as conflict in the United States, just as was a previous wave of immigrants who arrived in the early twentieth century. In addition, the global economy and the relative ease of modern travel have begun to erode the significance of national boundaries. However, President Trump's calls for

"America First," border walls, travel bans, and reduced immigration reflect a very different—and controversial—direction. Do the fragmentation and juxtaposition of cultural experiences—in music, food, film, and more—point to a new cultural mash-up? Does the presence of such cultural diversity threaten societies with fragmentation? How can the distinct contributions of different cultures be preserved in a world in which cultural traits are increasingly blended? (See Chapters 3, 10, and 14.)

9. ***The changing nature of violence and warfare.*** Powerful and wealthy countries, including the United States, possess advanced weapons that can destroy humanity many times over. Some smaller nations and various nonstate actors have developed low-tech but deadly weapons and tactics. The result is a world bristling with arms, threatened by violence, and locked in political and military stalemates. How can societies reduce violence? What factors contribute to the recent rise in terrorist activity? Why is the United States locked in seemingly endless wars it can't seem to win? What is the future of warfare? (See Chapter 16.)
10. ***The changing role of religion.*** To varying degrees, the world's wealthy industrialized nations have become increasingly secular—that is, religion plays a much less significant role in public and daily life in those nations than it once did. But in other parts of the world, religious beliefs continue to inform and drive many aspects of social life. Because of the increased contact among cultures, differences in religious beliefs now fuel some of the world's major conflicts, as well as divisive political issues at home. Will secularization continue to expand, or will religious revivals spread? Can different cultures coexist even with fundamental religious differences? (See Chapter 12.)

The Challenge and Hope of Sociology

Sociology holds great promise. As C. Wright Mills pointed out, it can help us understand the connections between ourselves and the larger social world. In studying society, we learn more about who we are as individuals, why we face the conditions that we do, and how we are connected to others. At its best, sociology promotes an understanding of the social world and our place in it and suggests ways that we might act to improve our lives, our community, and our world.

But sociology comes with some challenges, too. Because it addresses serious problems that face society, sociology can lead us to some disturbing discoveries about society and ourselves. Issues such as how to care for an aging population, how to balance human needs with environmental concerns, how to address persistent poverty, how to combat racism and sexism, and how to respond to extremist violence are not easy to think about, but they are important and must be faced. Also, looking at our experiences in a broader social context sometimes reveals disconcerting insights about our relative privilege, or lack of it, due to the effects of class, race, gender, sexual orientation, or nationality. Achieving a better understanding of our place in the world's hierarchy of privilege can be enlightening, but also unsettling.

As you will see throughout this book, sociology can force us to move outside our comfort zone and challenge us to think in new ways about things that we take for granted. If we live in relative comfort and freedom, we might find it easy to ignore difficult issues that face society, and hope they won't affect us personally. If we are struggling to get by, we might prefer to focus solely on taking care of our private lives, hoping that eventually we can insulate ourselves from economic upheaval, crime, and other social problems. But sociology reminds us that in taking either position we are, by default, helping reproduce the society in which we live, with all its problems. Whether we realize it or not, whether we like it or not, we are part of the broader social world.

In the face of our changing world, sociology offers hope. It is not a fearful hope that we can somehow manage individually to escape the world's problems. Instead, it is the hopeful realization that societies—and the issues that confront them—are largely created by human beings. That means people working together also have the capacity to change and improve those societies, as well as their own lives. We invite you to take up the challenge to use sociology to better understand the world and your place in it. And we hope that from this understanding, you'll be inspired and better equipped to act—in whatever way you see fit—to make a positive difference in your life and in our rapidly changing world.

REVIEW, REFLECT, AND APPLY

Looking Back

1. The sociological perspective is a way of looking at the world that focuses on the relationships between individuals and larger forces in society. Sociology as a discipline couples this perspective with systematic study and research using the methods of social science.
2. The discipline of sociology emerged in the late 1800s, in part as a response to the dramatic economic, political, cultural, and social changes taking place in the modern world.
3. Karl Marx, Emile Durkheim, and Max Weber were the three most influential classical sociological thinkers. Marx is best known for his work on capitalism and on the role of conflict in society. Durkheim's work focused on social solidarity. Weber is best known for his work on the rationalization of society, including the rise of bureaucracy.
4. Because of the sexism and racism of the day, the contributions of other social thinkers such as Harriet Martineau, W. E. B. Du Bois, and Jane Addams were not fully recognized or accepted within the discipline of sociology in their time. However, they made a major contribution, especially in spotlighting issues of gender- and race-based inequality.
5. Sociological theories seek to explain the workings of society by explaining why things happen as they do. These theories vary along three key dimensions: consensus and conflict, subjective and objective reality, and micro-level and macro-level analyses. Diverse theories are sometimes grouped into the functionalist, conflict, and symbolic interactionist approaches.
6. The foundational work in sociology highlighted a number of core concepts that still serve as sociology's common ground. Among these enduring concepts are culture, structure, and power. These concepts are used throughout the book to help analyze social issues and phenomena.
7. Today, sociologists continue to study the social changes taking place as modernity gives way to the postmodern era. In many respects, the postmodern world is distinctly different from the one studied by the classical sociologists. But the enduring core concepts and theoretical insights of those early sociological thinkers—combined with new ideas and theories—can help us better understand our contemporary society. That is the focus of this book.

Critical Thinking: Questions and Activities

1. What is sociology and what is the sociological perspective? How does the sociological perspective apply to your own life?
2. The use of indiscriminate deadly violence against civilians, often referred to as terrorism, is a topic of intense interest to social scientists. What sorts of issues and questions would someone using a sociological perspective focus on in addressing this topic? What sorts of questions might researchers in other social science disciplines—such as economics, psychology, anthropology, and political science—focus on when considering this phenomenon?
3. What do you see as some of the advantages and disadvantages of the rise of modernity?
4. Of the 10 changes in contemporary society listed on pages 23–24, which one do you think is the most significant? Why? What important changes, if any, would you add to the list? Why do you feel they should be included?
5. What cards have you been dealt? Consider, for example, these questions about your childhood: Did you regularly have access to adequate food and clean drinking water? Did you live in a neighborhood that was relatively safe and free of crime? Did you have access to a good education? If you answered no to one or more of these questions, you no doubt had to overcome some hurdles while growing up. If you answered yes to these questions, you have enjoyed privileges that are unavailable to others. Using your sociological imagination, list 10 more questions that could help determine whether people have enjoyed access to privileges in their lives.

Key Terms

anomie (p. 12) social normlessness, without moral guidance or standards.

collective conscience (p. 12) the shared norms, beliefs, and values in a community.

conflict theories (p. 17) social theories that focus on issues of contention, power, and inequality, highlighting the competition for scarce resources.

culture (p. 19) the collection of values, beliefs, knowledge, norms, language, behaviors, and material objects shared by a people and socially transmitted from generation to generation.

division of labor (p. 10) the way people specialize in different tasks, each requiring specific skills.

dysfunctional (p. 17) inhibiting or disrupting the working of a system as a whole.

functionalist theories (p. 16) see "structural-functionalist theories."

industrialization (p. 8) the use of large-scale machinery for the mass manufacture of consumer goods.

latent functions (p. 17) the largely unrecognized and unintended consequences of social phenomena.

macro level of analysis (p. 16) a focus on large-scale social systems and processes such as the economy, politics, and population trends.

manifest functions (p. 16) the recognized and intended consequences of social phenomena.

meso level of analysis (p. 16) a focus somewhere between very large and very small social phenomena—on organizations or institutions, for example.

micro level of analysis (p. 16) a focus on small-scale, usually face-to-face social interaction.

modernity (p. 7) a historical era in the eighteenth and nineteenth centuries characterized by the growth of democracy and personal freedom, increased reliance on reason and science to explain the natural and social worlds, and a shift toward an urban industrial economy.

positivism (p. 9) a belief that accurate knowledge must be based on the scientific method.

postmodernity (p. 22) a historical period beginning in the mid-twentieth century characterized by the rise of information-based economies and the fragmentation of political beliefs and ways of knowing.

power (p. 21) the ability to bring about an intended outcome, even when opposed by others.

rationalization of society (p. 12) the long-term historical process by which rationality replaced tradition as the basis for organizing social and economic life.

science (p. 7) a method of inquiry that uses logic and the systematic collection of evidence to support claims about the world.

social solidarity (p. 10) the collective bonds that connect individuals.

social theory (p. 15) a set of principles and propositions that explains the relationships among social phenomena.

sociological perspective (p. 3) a view of the social world that focuses on discovering and understanding the connections between individuals and the broader social contexts in which they live; what C. Wright Mills called the "sociological imagination."

sociology (p. 3) the systematic study of the relationship between individuals and society.

structural-functionalist theories (p. 16) theories that focus on consensus and cooperative interaction in social life, emphasizing how the different parts of a society contribute to its overall operation. Often referred to simply as "functionalist theories," or "functionalism."

structure (p. 20) the recurring patterns of behavior in social life.

symbolic interactionist theories (p. 17) social theories that focus on how society emerges from people's use of shared symbols in the course of their everyday interactions.

urbanization (p. 8) the growth of cities.

©Spencer Grant/agefotostock/Newscom

2 Understanding the Research Process

looking AHEAD

How do social science researchers know what they claim to know?

What special challenges might confront you as a social science researcher?

How can you become a more informed consumer of social science research?

©Bilgin S. Sasmaz/Anadolu Agency/Getty Images

What are the sources of violence within poor urban neighborhoods? Why are some neighborhoods "bad" or "dangerous" places that outsiders typically fear and avoid? These are the kinds of questions that sociologist Robert Vargas (2016) had when he began talking to people in Chicago's Little Village neighborhood for a study that became his book, *Wounded City*.

One of the first things Vargas learned was that the very idea of a "neighborhood" was inadequate for analyzing violence. Little Village was widely labeled a dangerous neighborhood, but Vargas found large sections of it to be full of life, with neighbors talking on front stoops and children playing outside; there was little sign of the fear that is so common in violent neighborhoods. Just a few blocks away, however, Vargas experienced a very different scene: few people outside, lots of wrought iron fences blocking access to front doors, and a palpable fear among the residents.

After spending time in Little Village, Vargas learned that defining violence as a "neighborhood" problem was a mistake because it did not take into account the diversity of experiences within the neighborhood. Vargas realized that a smaller geographic unit would be a more appropriate level of analysis, so he focused on block-level crime statistics. He discovered that violence was concentrated in "clusters of blocks" within the neighborhood, raising a new question: Why do some blocks experience far more violence than other blocks in the same neighborhood?

Vargas found that the blocks where violence was most common—the "hot spots"—were sites of highly localized "turf wars" involving gangs, the police, and even politicians. Specific blocks were sites of competition among four street gangs, generating high levels of violence. Clashes between police and gangs for control of these blocks intensified conflict among the different gangs and undermined public trust in local police. Turf wars even extended to political life; election district gerrymandering had split Little Village into five election wards, making it difficult to have the unified political leadership needed to address violent crime. Focusing on the neighborhood level obscured these block-level dynamics that, Vargas argued, are key to understanding—and eventually reducing—urban violence.

Vargas's study reminds us that how researchers collect and analyze their data matters. If you read his study carefully, you can examine how he collected his multiple sources of data and how he analyzed those data to answer his research questions. This transparency is a central element of the scientific method, enabling you to decide for yourself whether the conclusions he reached seem reasonable and valid.

Sociology is not just a perspective and a discipline. It is also an *activity* that uses the framework of science to ask questions, gather data, and seek answers about the phenomena of the social world (Babbie 2016). This activity of sociology can involve not only doing research, but also addressing practical problems and communicating with a broad public.

To look at social science research critically and better understand its claims, however, we need to know something about the research process–the focus of this chapter. In particular, this chapter examines the elements of social scientific thinking; explores the role of theory in research; sketches out the major data-gathering techniques; reviews various types of research; provides some critical questions to ask about any social research; and concludes with a glimpse of how research methods are evolving in the twenty-first century.

This chapter gives you critical-thinking tools with which to become a more informed consumer of social science research. Reading this chapter might also be a first step toward conducting a research study of your own.

Social Science as a Way of Knowing

As we saw in Chapter 1, for most of human history, people relied on religious doctrine to interpret both the natural and social worlds. But as the explanatory power of science proved its usefulness, systematic investigation and evaluation of evidence supplanted religion as a way of learning about the natural, or physical, world. Many of us still turn to religion for spiritual guidance, but nearly all of us rely on meteorologists for a weather forecast, medical doctors for health care, and a host of scientists and engineers for everything from repairs to our cars and computers to safe bridges and clean water.

For insights into the social world, we turn today to social scientists. They examine such social phenomena as homelessness, health care, violence against women, public opinion, trends in crime, hiring discrimination, and images of masculinity and femininity in the media and in society. Much of the work sociologists do is **basic research,** *the primary goal of which is to describe some aspect of society and advance our understanding of it.* Some work is **applied research,** *the primary goal of which is to directly address some social problem or need.*

Academics typically conduct basic research and publish their findings in journals and books addressed to a scholarly audience. Applied research often takes place outside academia—in social service agencies, businesses, nonprofits, and social change groups, for example—and its results tend to be distributed within the organizations commissioning the study. Each day educators, government officials, business managers, social service providers, health care workers, urban planners, and others rely on the findings of social science research to do their jobs.

The term **public sociology** refers to *efforts to reach beyond an academic audience to make the results of sociological research, both basic and applied, known to the broader public.* Sociologists often use the mass media in this effort, writing magazine articles or blogs or contributing op-ed columns to newspapers (Burawoy 2014; Sternheimer 2018).

Social science research may not provide us with all the answers we would like, but it can illuminate aspects of society that would otherwise remain unnoticed, and it can help us avoid common pitfalls in everyday thinking.

The Limits of Everyday Thinking

Growing up, many children are taught to believe in the existence of Santa Claus, a mysterious but jovial character who delivers gifts to good boys and girls during the Christmas holiday. For many of those who celebrate Christmas, Santa plays a central role in the holiday festivities. At some point in childhood, however, believers in Santa have to face the harsh reality that their understanding of this particular part of the social world has been tragically flawed. How could Santa have seemed so real? And how did they go so wrong in sizing up the situation?

These tough lessons of childhood can teach something about the common pitfalls of everyday thinking and the usefulness of scientific investigation. Let's take a look at the series of errors children make in evaluating the truth of the Santa story, errors that we adults need to guard against in our everyday thinking:

- ***Unquestioned trust in authorities.*** A child who believes in Santa relies on the truth claims of authority figures—parents and other adults. Although we adults are not naïve enough to believe everything we are told, the claims of some authorities can be persuasive. Blindly believing an "authoritative" person or institution (including social scientists!), however, is never a good idea. Intentionally or not, authority figures can be—and often are—wrong. To obtain the most accurate understanding of the world possible, we have to be skeptical about knowledge claims based solely on someone's status as an authority.
- ***Unquestioned acceptance of "common sense."*** Children inhabit a world in which Santa's existence is reinforced by other believers—their peers. In such a world, the existence of Santa may seem to be common sense since so many others share the belief. But history is full of false ideas that were considered common sense by many people in their time, such as the idea that the world was flat. Common knowledge claims need to be considered with a questioning mind.

" I'm feeling a bit cynical this year.Just bring me cash."

A belief in Santa Claus can have benefits for children, but it involves some common errors in everyday thinking.

- ***Unquestioned acceptance of traditional beliefs.*** Santa has long been a part of U.S. culture, providing further evidence to a child that he must be real. What else would account for all those Santa decorations, greeting cards, and television specials? Ideas that have withstood the test of time deserve our attention. But beware: just because a belief has been around for a long time doesn't make it true. As with our approach to authorities, we need to temper our respect for tradition with a healthy skepticism that demands knowledge claims be backed by evidence.
- ***Generalizations based on personal experience.*** Some children have the ultimate evidence: personal experience. They have seen, heard, touched, and even talked to Santa at the local mall. After all, "Seeing is believing." Well, maybe not. In some cases, personal experience can be very useful, but relying on it can also be misleading. We may misunderstand or misinterpret an experience. Or our experiences may not be typical; we may overgeneralize from them. We need broader sources of evidence, especially when we are talking about the social world.
- ***Reliance on selective observation.*** Using *selective observation,* anyone can find evidence that might appear to confirm the existence of Santa. For example, the milk and cookies left for Santa disappear. A more accurate picture of the world requires us to remain open-minded, however, willing to take seriously evidence that contradicts our initial inclinations and to consider alternative explanations for the evidence we have. In other words, we must gather and evaluate evidence systematically to increase the chances that we will reach an accurate conclusion.
- ***Biased observation and interpretation.*** One final barrier to clear thinking about Santa may be *bias*: a child has a vested interest in believing the story. Who wants to mess with a legend that delivers such generous benefits? In assessing what someone believes, it is helpful to keep in mind the potential interests that this person has in promoting certain ideas. By itself, a person's bias is not a reason to reject a claim, but if someone benefits substantially from interpreting evidence one way or another, we certainly should pay especially close attention to how he or she has gathered and explained the evidence.

Our Santa example may seem trivial, but the problems it illustrates are serious. When adults reach conclusions based solely on a belief in authority, common sense, tradition, personal experience, or selective observation—or when they allow their personal bias to influence their conclusions—they are likely to wind up with a distorted and inaccurate picture of the world. Acting on the basis of such misjudgments can be disastrous for people, public policy, and societies. People can avoid these mistakes by using an approach to knowledge based on social scientific principles, which we discuss next.

The Elements of Social Science Research

Four key elements distinguish social science research: identifying and understanding patterns in social life, gathering empirical evidence, explaining how the evidence was collected and analyzed, and viewing the resulting research claims as provisional knowledge (see Table 2.1).

Patterns in Social Life

Social science focuses on the patterns in social life—identifiable, repeating patterns in human thought and action. Of course, each human being makes independent decisions, and as a result an individual's behavior is not entirely predictable. On the other hand, social life is not merely a chaotic series of random events. Research shows that there *are* recurring patterns to human perception, behavior, and experience. Social science research largely consists of identifying and understanding these patterns in social life.

For example, social science research can tell us the probability that certain categories of people will or will not vote. Figure 2.1 provides some data from the U.S. Census Bureau on the percentage of U.S. citizens aged 18 years or older who said they voted in the 2016 presidential election.

Do you see the pattern? The older the age group, the more likely its members were to vote. Although there is a slight drop in turnout for those aged 75 or older, the overall pattern is clear.

Social scientists use a variety of techniques to describe and measure the patterns in social life. Some of these efforts involve the use of sophisticated statistical techniques. But even a straightforward analysis of the simplest data, such as those presented in Figure 2.1, can provide us with insight about the social world.

Empirical Evidence

To describe patterns in social life, sociologists depend on gathering relevant **empirical evidence**—*evidence that can be observed or documented using the human senses.* Empirical evidence can be categorized broadly as

TABLE 2.1 THE ELEMENTS OF SOCIAL SCIENCE RESEARCH

Identifying and understanding patterns in social life	Social scientists seek to identify recurrent patterns in human thought and action.
Gathering empirical evidence	Patterns are identified based on evidence that can be observed or documented using human senses.
Using transparent methods	Researchers need to disclose how they collect and analyze their evidence.
Viewing knowledge as provisional	Social science is based on the idea that truth claims are tentative and open to revision if new evidence is discovered.

FIGURE 2.1 | VOTING IN THE 2016 ELECTION, BY AGE

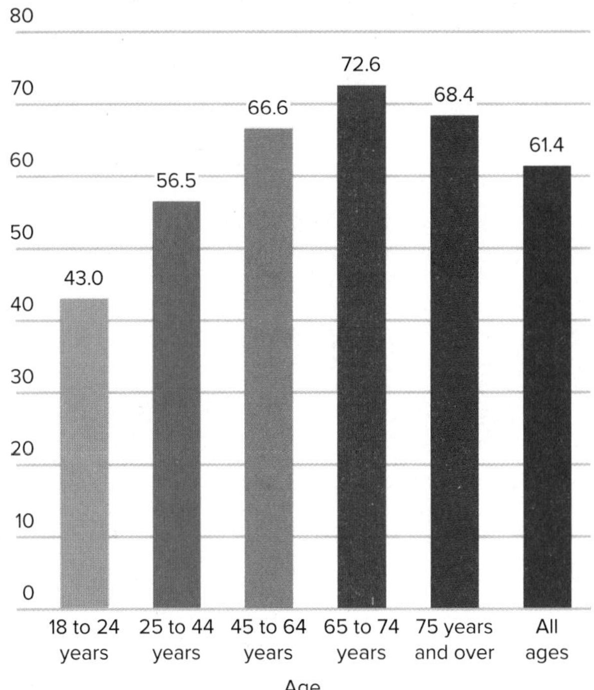

Source: U.S. Census Bureau, Current Population Survey, November 2016.

quantitative or qualitative. **Quantitative data** are simply *evidence that can be summarized numerically.* Quantitative data are presented in the form of **variables,** *measures that can change (or vary) and thus have different values.* To assign values to their variables, researchers must **operationalize** them, that is, *define them clearly so that they can be measured.* Figure 2.1 includes data for two variables—age and voting. Age is measured in terms of years, and voting is measured in terms of how people responded—yes or no—when asked whether or not they voted.

Variables are often categorized as independent or dependent. The **independent variable** is *associated with and/or causes change in the value of the dependent variable.* The **dependent variable** *changes in response to the independent variable.* In our example, age is the independent variable (because its value is independent of voting), whereas voting is the dependent variable (because it varies with age). Thus our data show that people are more likely to vote as they get older; voting doesn't make them grow old.

A **correlation** is *a relationship in which change in one variable is connected to change in another.* The variables age and voting are correlated because changes in voting behavior are connected to changes in age in a systematic way. Correlation, however, is not the same as causation. (See the Through a Sociological Lens box.) Age is *correlated* with voting, but age doesn't *cause* voting. Instead, age is associated with a variety of factors that influence the likelihood of voting, such as living in a community longer. In 2016, 76 percent of eligible voters who had lived in the same location for five or more years said they had voted compared to only 55 percent of those who had been in their residence less than a year (U.S. Census Bureau 2016a).

As a starting point for quantitative research, researchers often pose a **hypothesis,** *a statement about the relationship between variables that is to be investigated.* In addition to age, for example, we might hypothesize that the more education people have, the more likely they are to vote. Researchers would have to investigate this relationship to either confirm or reject the hypothesis.

Qualitative data are *any kind of evidence that is not numerical in nature, including evidence gathered from interviews, direct observation, and written or visual documents.* Whereas researchers using quantitative data focus on measuring variables, those who use qualitative data usually focus on describing social processes. In presenting qualitative data, researchers often organize their evidence around central themes that have emerged in their study and use direct quotations or vivid descriptions to illustrate their points. For example, to understand why a smaller percentage of people between the ages of 18 and 24 tend to vote than do people in older age groups, you might interview segments of this population. A qualitative approach can provide valuable insights into the specific experiences and attitudes of this group.

To take another example, one study used qualitative data as a tool to examine how homeless young adults perceive housing and employment prospects in their community and how they view local social services for homeless and at-risk young people. Researchers conducted interviews with 30 homeless 18- to 24-year-olds in Buffalo, New York (Bowen et al. 2017). One common theme in the interviews was frustration with how difficult

©RichLegg/E+/Getty Images

Correlation, Causation, and Spuriousness

Imagine you visit your favorite online news site and are greeted by this headline: "Ice Cream Can Kill You!" In this hypothetical example a reporter investigating why people drown accidentally has made the startling discovery that when ice-cream sales go up, accidental drowning increases.

This reporter has found a relationship, or *correlation*, between two variables: ice-cream sales (A) and the rate of accidental drowning (B). When one value goes up (or down), so does the other.

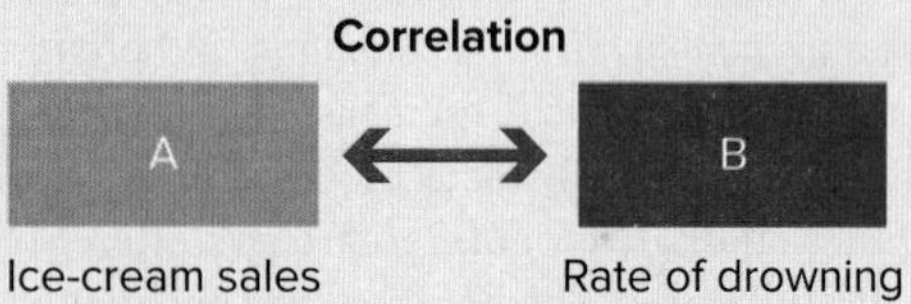

Because ice cream isn't typically served at funerals, the reporter had no reason to believe that drowning leads to ice-cream sales. So the reporter concluded that eating ice cream (the independent variable) must somehow contribute to accidental drowning (the dependent variable). Ice cream can kill you, she reasoned.

However, this proposed *causal relationship* is *not* supported by the evidence. Instead, the reporter has stumbled upon a *spurious* relationship between A and B, a correlation that does not result from any direct relationship between the two variables, but rather from their relationship to another variable (C).

To establish causality, three conditions must be met typically (Babbie 2016):

1. The variables must be correlated.
2. Cause must precede effect. In other words, change in the independent variable must occur before the change in the dependent variable.
3. The causal relationship must not be explainable by some third variable.

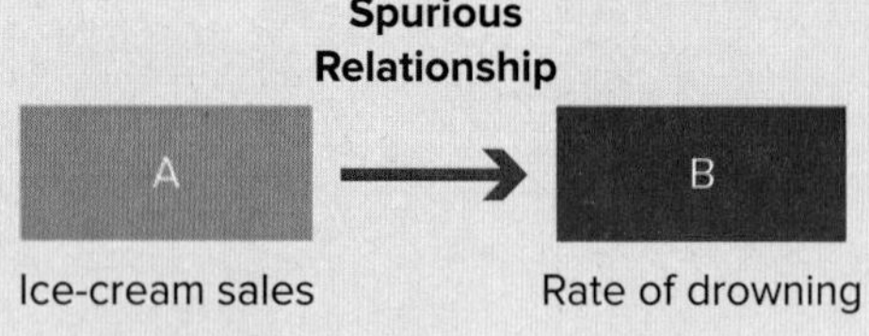

Although a correlation exists in the case of the reporter's story, both ice-cream sales and drowning can be explained by a third variable, weather temperature. People are more likely to eat ice cream and to go swimming when the weather is warm. An increase in temperature, therefore, produces an increase in both ice-cream sales and drowning accidents.

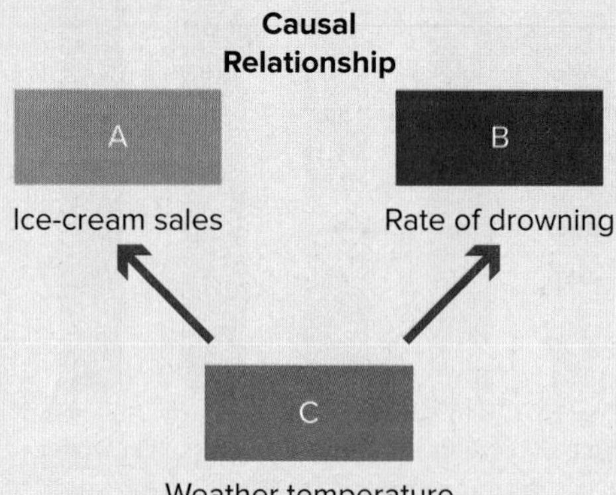

This example is simple, but sociologists encounter complex questions about the relative influence of different variables all the time. Does gender, work experience, or discrimination best explain the pay gap between women and men? Is it race, class, or some other factor that influences educational attainment most? What factors are most important in explaining disparities in health? Sociological researchers use a variety of advanced statistical techniques to help sort out these sorts of questions, assess the influence of many variables, and avoid errors in logic like the one shown here.

So relax; you can eat that ice cream (in moderation) without worrying about lethal consequences.

think about it

1. *As children's shoe size increases, so does their level of academic knowledge. What third variable likely explains this correlation?*
2. *The overall mortality rate in the United States varies by season, with the highest rate of deaths occurring in the winter and the lowest in the summer. Why do you think this might be the case? How might you go about investigating the correlation between season and mortality?*

it is to apply for services. One African American young woman explained: "They think because I'm young, I'm young-minded, I don't know what I want . . . they don't treat me like an adult" (217).

Personal stories of this sort, as well as other types of qualitative data, allow researchers to see *how* people experience the social world and how they understand their own experiences. This kind of qualitative data can be extremely important, revealing complexities that statistical data cannot capture. In the study of homelessness, for example, the authors make a compelling case that these personal stories can help us understand the often-hidden experience of homeless youth: "With many homeless young adults relying on couch-surfing and the winter climate restricting the viability of sleeping outdoors, emerging adult homelessness is rendered largely invisible in cities like Buffalo" (Bowen et al. 2017, 218). These findings highlight the importance of educating local officials and social service agencies about the distinct needs and experiences of homeless young adults.

Usually a quantitative study allows a researcher to gather information on many different cases but provides a limited amount of information on each case. In contrast, qualitative studies provide a wealth of detail on a relatively small number of cases. Sometimes a sociologist will use a combination of quantitative and qualitative data to get the best of both worlds.

Transparency of Methods

Social science depends on **transparency,** *the requirement that researchers explain how they collected and analyzed their evidence and how they reached their conclusions.* Transparency allows others to "see" how the research was done by reading a description of the process used in the study. Readers, including scholars, can then critically assess the research and its findings and replicate the study if they wish.

Provisional Knowledge

Social science is based on **provisional knowledge**—that is, on *truth claims that are tentative and open to revision in the face of new evidence.* According to this approach, we can never be 100 percent certain about our understanding of social phenomena, but we can use systematic analyses to rule out certain claims and identify explanations that are probably true.

The goal of social scientists is to reach tentative conclusions that they can act on, while remaining open to new insights that might be generated by more research. In this sense, social science research is an ongoing process: new studies respond to and build on prior research.

The Special Challenges of Social Science

Because social scientists study people and not the physical or natural world, they face a number of challenges that do not generally confront natural scientists:

- ***Social researchers are unlikely to be able to control conditions.*** In a lab experiment a chemist can control the environment and manipulate a variable such as heat to study its impact on a chemical reaction. But for ethical, legal, and practical reasons, human beings cannot be manipulated at will by a sociological researcher. For example, a sociologist can't set up an experiment in which children are subject to varying levels of abuse to observe the effects. Some sociologists conduct lab experiments on small-group interactions, but the vast majority of research on large-scale social phenomena takes place through the use of other methods, such as surveys and observation.
- ***Social life cannot be predicted with the certainty of natural laws.*** At sea level, raising the temperature of water to 212 degrees Fahrenheit causes it to boil. Assuming the conditions remain the same, the water responds exactly the same way every time the temperature increases. We can never be certain how different people will perceive, interpret, or react to a given situation, however. As a result, in social science there are always exceptions to any rule. We must talk in terms of *rates* of behavior, for example, or the *probability* of something happening. Still, as we have seen, sociologists can describe and explain the *patterns* of perception, behavior, and experience that characterize social life and predict the *likelihood* that certain social phenomena will occur.
- ***Human beings are conscious of being studied, which may change their behavior.*** In a classic example, researchers in the 1930s tested various ways to improve the productivity of workers at Western Electric's Hawthorne plant outside of Chicago (Roethlisberger 1939). No matter what changes the researchers initiated—whether they increased or decreased the lighting or lengthened or shortened break times—they discovered that productivity went up. They concluded that the very fact that workers were being observed, rather than the particular changes being tested, contributed to higher productivity. *This tendency of humans to react differently than they otherwise would when they know they are in a study has since come to be known* as the **Hawthorne effect.** Although researchers have ways of dealing with it, the Hawthorne effect is nonetheless a constant challenge.

©Marmaduke St. John/Alamy Stock Photo

One of the ongoing challenges of sociological research is that those who participate in studies know they are being observed. This awareness can alter their behavior or responses accordingly.

©Randy Faris/Corbis

In the early 1930s, researchers seeking to enhance productivity studied workers at Western Electric's Hawthorne Works plant outside Chicago. They found that no matter what various small changes in working conditions they made, productivity at the plant improved. They concluded that workers were responding not to the changed conditions but to being the focus of attention, a phenomenon now known as the Hawthorne effect. Here, a supervisor monitors the performance of workers.

The important elements and special challenges of social science research are best seen by examining the actual work of research, a subject to which we now turn.

Doing Research

Two key components, theory and data, act together in social science research. Theory helps us identify key research questions and interpret the data that are collected. Data provide the evidence that can support existing theory, lead to changes in theory, contradict a theory, or result in the development of a new theory (Merton 1968a). In this section we explore the role of theory as well as the various types of research techniques used to collect data.

The Theory–Research Dynamic

Theory plays several vital roles in social research:

- It highlights key questions that can help direct research.
- It helps explain data collected by research.
- It can reveal connections among social phenomena that are not otherwise apparent.

Researchers reason *deductively* from a general theory when they use it to inform the gathering of specific data. They reason *inductively* when they develop a theory based on data they already have.

To illustrate the roles theory plays in social science research, let's consider a classic theory proposed by Arnold van Gennep ([1909] 1961) in the early twentieth century regarding rituals—repeated patterns of behavior performed at specific times, often involving symbols. Van Gennep proposed that the function of some rituals was to mark a change of social status; he called such rituals *rites of passage.*

Highlighting Key Questions

Van Gennep's theory suggests that rites of passage help encourage or reinforce certain behavior, affirm common ties through their use of cultural symbols, serve as a communal acknowledgment of the change of status, and provide an outlet for emotions related to the status change. A researcher can draw from van Gennep's theory about rites of passage to ask questions about the contemporary social world. What are the significant rites of passage today? Are these rites of passage different from those experienced by previous generations? If so, how and why? How do such rituals mark changes in social status? In our diverse society, how, if at all, do different communities experience distinct rites of passage?

Explaining Collected Data Van Gennep's theory can likewise help explain data collected by research. For example, when Brown, Brunelle, and Malhotra (2017) analyzed "tagging," a form of graffiti involving the marking of physical space with one's stylized signature—or tag—they found that inexperienced taggers typically participate in daring activities, writing graffiti in dangerous places. They argue that such "tagging in dangerous places offers a powerful emotional experience to the writer similar to a perilous rite of passage trial providing a sense of empowerment" (492). This rite of passage is an act of separation from mainstream culture, a public statement of one's identity as a tagger, and a key moment in one's entry into a new subculture. Understanding the theory associated with rites of passage helps make sense of this risky behavior.

on social theory

Functionalism suggests that long-lasting social phenomena serve a useful purpose for society, and van Gennep's theory suggests several useful purposes for rituals. What rituals have been important in your life, and, in retrospect, what purposes did they serve?

Seeing Connections By moving beyond description and analysis of specific phenomena to a general or abstract level, theory can help us see patterns and connections between phenomena that are not immediately apparent. For example, through the theory of rituals as rites of passage we can see the

common features of graduations, funerals, and high-risk tagging. With a little sociological imagination, you can begin to recognize rites of passage in a wide range of social settings and expand your insights into the various roles they play in social life.

A Hypothetical Example

We've noted that theory helps us interpret research and research helps us build theory. To better understand this interactive relationship, let's look at a hypothetical example from the world of sports.

What makes a sports team successful? Of course, different levels of talent and experience are important, but some teams seem to perform better than expected, whereas other teams with highly talented players don't live up to expectations. Emile Durkheim's theory of social solidarity (see Chapter 1) could provide a starting point for an investigation into the question of the causes of team success. Durkheim proposed that any well-functioning social group is held together by a sense of social solidarity. So, if player talent doesn't offer a complete explanation of team success, we may want to examine whether team solidarity is related to team success. You may have observed that winning teams generally are a tight-knit group. Durkheim's theory could help us articulate hypotheses for explaining the potential relationship between solidarity and success. Perhaps winning builds team solidarity. Alternately, winning may result from already-existing team solidarity. Theory has helped us to identify a useful concept—social solidarity—and suggest two competing hypotheses about the relationship between solidarity and success in sports.

on social theory

Symbolic interactionism focuses on how people use shared symbols and construct society through everyday interactions. If you were to use this perspective, how would you approach the question of the relationship between solidarity and success in sports?

To assess these hypotheses, we would need to design a study that will examine the relationship between solidarity and success. Perhaps we could survey the members of various teams about their group solidarity before a season begins and again after the season concludes. Coupled with the team's performance record, a survey would give us data to assess our competing hypotheses. We hope that our results will elaborate and clarify our theory, which will lead us (and perhaps other researchers) to conduct further research about the relationship between success and solidarity in any number of organizations, including businesses, schools, and military units. One study will not provide a final answer to the broader theoretical question about success and solidarity, but each study will provide additional insight into this relationship.

Theory, then, suggests areas of possible research by highlighting key questions, and it helps explain the data collected. In turn, we need data to assess the accuracy of theory. In some cases, research findings support a specific theory; in others, the data contradict the theory. Either way, we gain a better understanding of the social world when we consider theory and data together.

Research Methods

There is no single correct way to gather evidence for a research study. Instead, sociologists use a variety of **research methods,** *procedures for collecting and analyzing data*. Sociological research methods fall into five general categories (see Table 2.2):

- Surveys
- Interviews and focus groups
- Field research
- Analysis of existing sources
- Experiments

Generally, researchers choose whatever method allows them to collect the most appropriate type of data needed to address the questions they are asking. Researchers who are interested in, say, what percentage of students at a particular school voted in the last presidential election might collect quantitative data from a survey and from the analysis of existing sources, such as official poll results. Researchers who want to know why the students voted the way they did, though, might be more likely to collect qualitative data from interviews and use focus groups. Other topics might require the researcher to do field research or conduct experiments.

Survey Research

Probably the most commonly used technique in sociology is the **survey,** *a data collection technique that involves asking someone a series of questions.* Surveys are popular in part because they are versatile, are useful for a wide variety of issues, and effectively describe large populations, if appropriate sampling techniques are used (Blair, Czaja, and Blair 2014).

Survey researchers can use different kinds of questions. Some survey questions are constructed in a *closed-ended* or fixed-response format, which means a respondent must choose from a given set of responses. For example, the Pew Research Center (2017a) gathers data regularly on which media outlets people in the United States rely upon for news. The center's 2017 American Trends Panel survey asked more than 4,900 adults a series of questions about where they turn for news. One question was "Thinking about your general news habits, how often do you get news from a social media site (such as Facebook, Twitter, or Snapchat)?" and asked respondents to check one of the following: Often, Sometimes, Hardly ever, Never. The advantage of such closed-ended questions is that the researcher can easily code them for quantitative analysis. According to the Pew Center's 2017 report on news audiences, 20 percent of adults in the United States get news "often" from social media sites, while 33 percent report that they "never" get news from social media.

However, if you have ever filled out a survey consisting of nothing but closed-ended questions, you might have noticed that sometimes the preselected answers didn't fit what you really wanted to say. Moreover, these types of answers may encourage people to respond in ways that they might not have otherwise. To address such problems, some surveys include *open-ended* questions that do not provide predetermined response categories. The Pew Center's (2017b) survey of online harassment asked

TABLE 2.2 MAJOR RESEARCH METHODS

	Features	Strengths	Weaknesses
Surveys	A series of questions is administered in writing (on paper or online) or verbally (by telephone or in person).	Cost-effective way to get information on a wide range of issues. Results, especially from large random samples, can be generalized.	Closed-response options can be limiting. Data are broad but often not particularly deep.
Interviews and focus groups	Open-ended questions and improvised follow-up questions are asked in relatively lengthy face-to-face interviews that are typically recorded for later analysis.	Allow subjects the freedom to develop detailed responses in their own words; researchers can immediately ask follow-up questions.	Time and labor intensive. Data are rich and deep, but small, nonrandom sample limits generalizability.
Field research	Researchers work in natural settings observing social interactions and ongoing nature of social life.	Less intrusive than direct questioning, resulting in more natural data. Goes beyond what people say to observing what they do.	Very time and labor intensive. Data are rich and deep, but small, nonrandom sample limits generalizability. Researcher presence can affect results.
Analysis of existing sources	Quantitative data are reanalyzed or existing materials, such as media content or historical records, are used.	Convenient and cost-effective. Existing content not affected by researcher's presence.	Data specific to the researcher's question may not be available.
Experiments	Researchers use controlled manipulation of social conditions to test hypotheses.	Can isolate specific variable to study and establish causality.	Typically limited to micro-level questions. Ethical considerations restrict their applicability.

respondents who answered yes to questions about whether they had ever witnessed various forms of bad behavior online: "Can you describe what you have witnessed in your experience of this kind?" This allowed people to use their own words to describe an incident rather than fit their experience into a preexisting category. Such open-ended questions allow for a wider, and perhaps more accurate, range of responses. However, the wide array of answers can be time-consuming to record and difficult to summarize and analyze.

Researchers also need to pay careful attention to the way the questions in a survey are worded because even small variations in wording can influence results significantly. The following are just a few of the many problems that can arise when researchers write survey questions:

- ***Lack of clarity.*** An unclear question can produce inaccurate results. In one infamous example, the well-known Roper polling firm found that 22 percent of people in the United States believed it was possible that the Holocaust never happened, while another 12 percent said they weren't sure (Morin 1994). This startling finding was later revealed to be the result of a poorly worded question: "Does it seem possible or does it seem impossible to you that the Nazi extermination of the Jews never happened?" This awkwardly phrased question required a person affirming the existence of the Holocaust to agree with a double negative: that it was impossible it never happened. The percentage of people expressing doubt dropped to the single digits when the question was later rephrased to read, "Do you doubt that the Holocaust actually happened, or not?"
- ***Validity.*** A survey's *validity* refers to its ability to successfully measure what researchers intend it to measure. For example, if respondents aren't familiar with a question's terminology, their responses will likely lack validity, or so discovered the designers of a national survey on sexual identity (Miller and Ryan 2011). Many respondents, particularly those with lower levels of education, misclassified themselves when asked to identify as "heterosexual," "homosexual," or "bisexual" because they weren't familiar with those abstract, scientific-sounding labels or didn't think of themselves in terms of them. Replacing those words with everyday words like "straight," "lesbian," and "gay" improved respondents' accuracy and increased the survey's validity.
- ***Lack of reliability.*** *Reliability* refers to a measure's ability to yield consistent results over time. In the case of a survey, reliable questions are those that will produce consistent results from the same respondents. For example, a survey seeking to measure health problems in a community would likely face reliability problems if questions asked how respondents were feeling at a specific moment (Are you experiencing severe anxiety right now?), since daily feelings of well-being will

SOCIOLOGY WORKS

Sydney Hessel and User Experience Research

When Sydney Hessel started college, she was interested in questions of design and planned to major in studio art. She quickly shifted gears to sociology, however, when she realized that for her, the concept of design extended beyond art to broader issues such as how the design of social programs and public policies affects the way people experience those programs and policies.

As an undergraduate student of sociology, Sydney had hands-on practice with a range of quantitative and qualitative research methods, including surveys, interviews, and direct observation. Reflecting on her college years, Sydney notes that studying research methods helped her "immensely with skills like study design and data analysis in social science contexts."

In addition to sharpening her research skills, sociology offered Sydney new insights that helped to focus her interest in design. She explains that she became fascinated "with the idea that studying human experiences of products, policies, and services could lead to improvements in the way that those experiences were designed."

When Sydney graduated with a degree in sociology, her social science research skills helped her secure a job with an audience research firm that conducted studies on the impact of the arts for nonprofit arts organizations. Her training in statistical analysis was particularly important in preparing her for this first postcollege job. "It was a wonderful first job," she notes, that "allowed me to conduct social research in industry settings, including presenting research findings to nonprofit stakeholders."

> "Sociology provided me with a critical foundation in theory and methods that continues to inspire my work."

Sydney has since been working in the rapidly growing field of UX (user experience) research for a major global media and technology company. UX research involves studying the way people ("users") experience a wide range of products and services to better design new products or rethink the design of existing products. As Sydney explains, at the core of UX research is a deep interest in putting "human perspectives and needs" at the center of the design process.

Courtesy of Sydney Hessel
Sydney Hessel

In her role as a user experience researcher, Sydney engages in a wide range of research-based activities. "In a typical workweek, I might be planning research studies to address product team questions, conducting research using a range of methods (everything from surveys and in-depth interviews to diaries kept by users of their experience with a product), and presenting findings and recommendations to shape the design of digital products such as apps and websites in a human-centered way."

Sociology, however, taught Sydney more than just how to conduct research. It also nurtured in her a deep respect for how people make sense of their own lives, giving her a "framework for understanding human beings as authorities on their experiences." Sociology was vital in the development of what she describes as her most valuable job skills—her "empathetic approach to research and belief that study participants are truly the experts on their lives." These skills—and her sociological imagination—help make Sydney Hessel a UX research innovator who is helping to pioneer ways to involve users actively in the design and making of new digital products.

likely fluctuate, potentially masking stable patterns. That's why such health-related surveys typically ask respondents to consider a broader time frame (Have you experienced severe anxiety in the past month?) or ask about the frequency of such health problems (How often do you experience anxiety?), with clear and specific response categories.

- ***Loaded language.*** Some emotionally charged words and expressions have positive or negative connotations that can influence a survey's results. For example, one widely cited study (Rasinski 1989) found that only 23 percent of respondents said too little money was spent on "welfare," but 63 percent said too little money was spent on "assistance to the poor"—essentially the same thing. Clearly, the word *welfare* had a negative connotation. Trained survey researchers are aware of the pitfalls of such "hot-button" terms and generally avoid questions with loaded language. However, novice survey researchers and those seeking to use survey data for political purposes may, wittingly or not, ask questions with language that steers respondents toward a particular response. A loaded question like "Do you support legislation that will violate your constitutionally protected right to bear firearms?," for example, stands in stark contrast to "Would you favor or oppose a law that would require a person to obtain a police permit before he or she could buy a gun?"—a question the National Opinion Research Center's General Social Survey has been asking regularly for more than 45 years.

- ***Double-barreled questions.*** Each question should be about one topic only. Questions that cover more than one topic are called "double-barreled." A question intended to measure trust and widely used by pollsters for decades reads, "Generally speaking, would you say that most people can be trusted or that you can't be too careful in dealing with people?" Researchers (Miller and Mitamura 2003) showed, however, that this question is really double-barreled: it asks whether or not people can be trusted *and* whether or not you should be careful. It's quite possible to trust people in general but still feel you should be careful in dealing with them. Trust and caution are not the same thing, and the question as originally worded conflates the two concepts.

When you are considering the results from survey research, examine the questions to see if their wording might have influenced the results.

When you interpret survey results, it is also important to know two factors. What is the *population,* the target group a researcher is interested in studying? And who participated in the survey? Researchers refer to this group as the **sample,** or *part of the population that represents the whole.*

Depending on what is being studied, a population might be made up of individual people, institutions, newspaper articles, or a host of other things. Let's say you want to study how students on your campus get news about current events. In this case, you would be interested in the entire student population on your campus. It would be virtually impossible for you to gather data on all the cases in that population—all the students who attend your college. Instead, to conduct high-quality research, you need a good sample that accurately represents the larger population you are studying.

There are many different types of samples. (See Table 2.3.) One way to obtain a high-quality sample is to choose it randomly. In a **random sample,** *every element of the population has an equal chance of being chosen.* To draw a random sample, you need a complete list of all the members of the population you want to study. Putting the names of all the students enrolled at your college in a (very large) hat and choosing some of the names would be a random sample, since every student from that population (your college) would have an equal chance of being chosen.

Random samples of adequate size allow researchers to accurately **generalize,** or *describe patterns of behavior of a larger population based on findings from a sample.* Pollsters, for example, are able to make good predictions about the outcome of national elections in the United States by sampling only about 1,200 people. Such polls are not perfect—most polls were wrong in predicting that Hillary Clinton would beat Donald Trump in what turned out to be a very close 2016 presidential election—but they generally give a close approximation of the views of the target population as a whole.

For many research projects, however, it is not possible to gather a totally random sample. For your hypothetical study of how students on your campus get news about current events, you might decide to walk across campus and give your survey to people you meet "at random." This method will *not* yield a random sample of the students at your college, though, because your selections will be influenced by the area of campus you choose, the time of day you go out, and so forth. In other words, every student at the college will *not* have an equal chance of being chosen. This method is called a *convenience sample,* a way of choosing study participants based simply on the fact that it is convenient for the researcher. In this case, because you do not know if your sample is representative of all students at the college, you cannot generalize your findings to the population of the campus as a whole.

In between a random sample and a convenience sample is the *quota sample,* in which the researcher tries to achieve a generalizable sample by making sure various groups within the target population are present in representative proportions. The groups typically targeted in a quota sample are those that are relevant for the research question at hand and those that have proven to be significant in other research. For example, if you were studying whether or not students at your school were satisfied with their college experience, you would want your sample to match key features of the student population as a whole, including gender and full- or part-time status. If 60 percent of the students at your college are women, and 25 percent of students attend part time, then your quota sample should match these characteristics. Even though a quota sample is not a true random sample, the more specific your quota system, the more confident you can be that the sample can be generalized to the larger population.

TABLE 2.3 THREE TYPES OF SAMPLES

	Convenience Sample	Quota Sample	Random Sample
Key feature	Data are not representative, in a statistical sense, of a broader target population.	Specific groups in the broader target population are included in representative proportions.	Every element of the population has a known and equal chance of being chosen.
Strengths	Simple and often inexpensive.	Balances generalizability with practicality.	Generalizable to a broader population.
Weaknesses	Not generalizable to a broader population.	More difficult to achieve than a convenience sample.	Often not practical; most difficult and expensive sample to achieve.

There is one final critical factor in using samples: research studies should report how a sample was generated so that readers can make their own assessment of how well the sample represents the population as a whole.

Intensive Interviews and Focus Groups

An **intensive interview** (sometimes known as a "qualitative interview" or "in-depth interview") is *a data-gathering technique that uses open-ended questions during somewhat lengthy face-to-face sessions.* These interviews are semistructured, with the interviewer usually using a combination of preplanned questions along with follow-up and clarifying questions that he or she improvises as the session progresses (Rubin and Rubin 2012). Intensive interviews produce more in-depth information from a respondent than a survey provides, but they are very time consuming to conduct. As a result, intensive interview studies generally include a far smaller number of respondents than surveys, commonly fewer than 100 participants, making it more difficult to generalize a researcher's findings to larger populations. One way to expand the number of people involved is to interview them in a *focus group,* made up usually of 6 to 12 people (Stewart, Shamdasani, and Rook 2015). A moderator asks preplanned and follow-up questions, encourages participation, and helps ensure that no one participant dominates the discussion.

When sociologist Arlie Hochschild (2016) set out to explore the foundations of deepening political polarization in the United States, she designed a study that used intensive interviews as the primary source of data. In her interviews with a core group of 40 Tea Party supporters in Louisiana, Hochschild learned what she calls the "deep story"—a story that "tells us how things feel"—of the men and women she came to know very well over a period of five years. Central to their deep story is an experience of persistent economic hardship; a sense of betrayal by the government, as other people "cut the line" to get ahead of them; and a feeling that other Americans, especially people in Washington and Hollywood, look down on them. As Hochschild's research was coming to a close in 2016, she found the deep story helped her to understand the rise of then-presidential candidate Donald Trump. In particular, Hochschild recognized how Trump's campaign connected with the deep story of the folks she met in Louisiana, and made them feel good about themselves. "While economic self-interest is never entirely absent," Hochschild explains, "what I discovered was the profound importance of emotional self-interest—a giddy release from the feeling of being a stranger in one's own land" (228). The interview format allowed Hochschild to learn the nuances of the deep story in a way that a closed-ended set of questions would not have revealed.

Field Research As the name suggests, **field research** (sometimes called *ethnography* or *fieldwork*) is *a data collection technique in which the researcher systematically observes some aspect of social life in its natural setting.* In some cases, the researcher tries to remain separate from the activities he or she is studying. In other cases, the researcher engages in *participant observation,* a type of field research in which the researcher both observes and actively takes part in the setting or community being studied. Field researchers talk to the people they observe and develop detailed field notes about what they see and hear—notes that form the foundation of the researcher's analysis (Bailey 2018). One of the key challenges for observational field researchers is gaining access to the setting and being accepted by those they are studying.

As field researchers immerse themselves in the environment they are studying, they become aware of significant questions or issues that deserve closer attention. Mark Fishman worked as a newspaper reporter for seven months in his investigation of how news is made. In a now-classic study, *Manufacturing the News,* Fishman (1980) drew on his field notes from his participant observation as an apprentice reporter to explore how reporters' daily routines—where they look for news and whom they talk to each day—define the stories that become news.

More recently, a field study of Twitter use among journalists covering the New York State legislature in Albany (Revers 2014) found that journalists who most enthusiastically integrated Twitter into their reporting had a different view of news than did the Twitter skeptics. The tweeting journalists believe that the ability to instantly share and briefly comment on political developments as they unfold is journalistically valuable. In contrast, the Twitter skeptics stress the traditional journalistic values of fact checking and the presentation of conflicting viewpoints, which are impractical in the context of Twitter's constant updating. Ultimately these differences reflect a broader shift within journalism toward a style of reporting that is both less detached and less definitive and to forms of news that are more of a developing discussion among peers than a conclusive report by an ostensibly objective reporter.

Existing Sources Researchers frequently rely on existing sources, making use of available data and documents rather than collecting new data and evidence. A researcher who conducts **secondary data analysis** *uses data previously collected by other researchers.* Government and private agencies such as the U.S. Census Bureau, the National Opinion Research Center, and Statistics Canada maintain and continually update major data sets, which are made available to researchers wishing to address a variety of research questions. Since such ready-made data sets

Source: U.S. Census Bureau Fact Finder

SOCIOLOGY in ACTION

The U.S. Census Bureau

Sociology has made its way into almost every U.S. home—literally. That's because many sociologists work on the census that is mailed to every U.S. household. Sociologists help create the census questions, design the collection methods, and analyze the results. In these ways, sociological insights shape one of the best-known sources of data on population trends and countless other topics.

Administered by the U.S. Census Bureau, which employs many sociologists, the census is conducted every 10 years. Unlike a survey, in which information is gathered from a population sample, a census aims to reach every resident. The U.S. Constitution mandates this population count to determine the number of seats each state is allotted in the House of Representatives. Thus the census has been conducted every decade since 1790.

Over the years, the purpose of the census and the work of the U.S. Census Bureau have expanded significantly. Census data are now used to inform the allocation of billions of dollars in federal funds to local communities. The Census Bureau has many other data collection efforts that occur between the decennial census, including the annual American Community Survey. The information citizens provide is not traceable to individuals and cannot be used by law enforcement, the Internal Revenue Service, or immigration authorities.

Sociology has affected the range of topics the Census Bureau studies. In 2010, data on household size, age, sex, race, and ethnicity were collected through the census short form's 10 basic questions. Census Bureau questionnaires also explore income levels, employment patterns, household characteristics, business information, and education levels. The influence of sociology can be seen, too, in the bureau's methods. In the 1940s, Census Bureau sociologists were involved in developing the basic sampling and statistical analysis techniques that are now a routine part of political polling, consumer satisfaction surveys, and biomedical research. Ever since, sociologists have helped design and refine the Census Bureau's sampling techniques and data collection methods. Sociologists also analyze the data the bureau collects, writing issue briefs for the bureau, presenting scholarly papers at the American Sociological Association's annual meetings, and publishing findings in sociological journals.

The impact of sociology on the Census Bureau is perhaps best symbolized by sociologist Robert Groves, bureau director from 2009 to 2012. A sociologist who specializes in surveys and statistical analysis, Groves was a transitional figure, nudging the Census Bureau to adopt new technologies and techniques. He helped make the bureau's data and analyses more readily accessible through the internet, set up the bureau to begin collecting data via the internet instead of only paper surveys, and was the first director to maintain a blog to discuss his work and a range of data-related topics. Groves also stirred controversy by advocating that the Census Bureau supplement the traditional census count with sampling techniques that might more accurately capture the number of hard-to-reach populations such as the homeless and the poor. He argued that the Census Bureau needs to make better use of existing statistics already gathered by private industry and other government agencies, to promote cost efficiency. In the end, said Groves, "I don't think this is a job for political animals. . . . The most important thing to get right in this role is to make sure you're serving in a nonpartisan, objective nature" (Morello 2012). A new debate emerged in 2018, as the Census Bureau finalized its questionnaire for Census 2020. The Trump administration called for a new question on the short form distributed to every resident asking whether or not they are a U.S. citizen, arguing that information on citizenship status is necessary to draw election districts. Critics, including the American Sociological Association, expressed concern that a new citizenship question "is likely to keep some people from responding to the questionnaire and others from responding truthfully, thereby undermining the accuracy of the data" (American Sociological Association 2018). Visit census.gov to explore a treasure trove of information about the country, which was designed, collected, and analyzed with the help of sociologists.

think about it

1. *Have you ever filled out a census form? If so, did you know what the data would be used for?*
2. *Why do you think Congress might oppose using sampling techniques as part of the census?*

enable them to skip the time, cost, and effort of gathering original data, many researchers find them an attractive option. (The Sociology in Action box examines the role of sociologists at the Census Bureau.)

For example, one researcher used data from the U.S. Census Bureau's 1990 through 2010 American Community Survey and publicly available data on home sales to compare how five small riverfront cities in New York's Hudson Valley have adapted to post-9/11 population changes in the New York City metropolitan area (Nevarez 2018). His analysis shows that what he calls "Brooklynization"–the influx of young, highly-educated professionals as weekend visitors and, increasingly, part-time residents–has produced substantial change in three small cities. Beacon, Hudson, and Kingston have experienced economic revitalization linked to a growing arts scene and vibrant nightlife; such economic change, however, has also driven up the cost of housing, threatening to push out longtime working-class residents of these newly-hip cities. In contrast, Newburgh and Poughkeepsie have not experienced the same growth in economic activity, cultural amenities, or home values. Nevarez notes that these are the two largest cities in the region, suggesting that city size may be a key to understanding different small-city adaptations. However, he also finds that the two least-Brooklynized cities are the two with the largest populations of color in the region. "Insofar as the urban in-migration of so-called Brooklyners has a racialized aspect–involving mostly white faces, perhaps seeking mostly white faces–Poughkeepsie and Newburgh may not be favored destinations" (20).

Researchers can also analyze various other kinds of existing sources. Historical documents found in libraries and archives are essential to a researcher who is creating a social history. Similarly, mass media content such as a TV reality series or a video game can be an important source of sociological information. **Content analysis** refers to *a variety of techniques that enable researchers to systematically summarize and analyze the content of various forms of communication–written, spoken, or pictorial* (Holsti 1968).

One content analysis examined gender portrayals in the world of video games (Summers and Miller 2014). Drawing on a sample of images from popular video game magazines–a total of 223 images of game characters in 175 articles appearing in *Xbox, PlayStation,* and *Nintendo Power* magazines over a 20-year period–the authors found that images of female characters had changed substantially over time. For example, early in the period, women were far more likely to be portrayed as helpless and in need of rescuing than they were later in the period. In the newer games, in contrast, female characters were far more likely to be portrayed as sexy and revealingly dressed than they had been in earlier games. Summarizing their findings, Summers and Miller note: "There has been a vast change from a benevolent sexism to a hostile sexism portrayal of female characters as represented in video game magazines. This sexist shift may impact attitudes, which have very real consequences outside the game arena" (1037). In other words, the quantitative data the researchers extracted from their content analysis helped them identify a trend in popular culture with potentially broad social significance.

Experiments An **experiment** is *a data-gathering technique in which the researcher manipulates an independent variable under controlled conditions to determine if change in an independent variable produces change in a dependent variable, thereby establishing a cause-and-effect relationship* (Campbell and Stanley 1963). In an experiment a researcher compares two groups of subjects: a *control group* and a group that is exposed to some "stimulus" or "treatment." Afterward, the two groups are compared to evaluate the effects of the treatment. Since researchers need to control the experimental situation, experiments usually must take place in a laboratory setting, rather than in a natural social setting. This requirement greatly limits the types of issues that sociologists can examine using experiments and is one of the reasons experimental research is relatively uncommon in sociology. Still, some sociologists have designed innovative studies that have taken advantage of the benefits of an experimental design in a real-world setting.

For example, in a widely cited experimental study, sociologist Devah Pager (2007) examined the impact of a criminal record on a person's job prospects, making use of job applications submitted to real-world employers. Pager hired and trained two pairs of testers–one pair was white and one pair was African American–and gave them identical backgrounds and resumes, except for one difference. In each pair, one of the testers was given a criminal record and the other was not. She sent the testers out to apply for a total of 350 jobs (the pair of African American testers applied for 200 jobs and the pair of white testers applied for 150 jobs) and waited to see who would be called back for a job interview. The study design was complex, but Pager made sure that the only difference within each pair of job applicants was the criminal record. The independent variable in each pair, then, was a job applicant's criminal record; the dependent variable was whether the applicant would be invited for a job interview. Pager's findings were stark but not unexpected: those applicants with a criminal record were far less likely to get called back for a job interview than their counterparts with no criminal record. Pager's more significant finding was that white job applicants with a criminal record were more likely to get a callback for an interview (17 percent) than were black job applicants with *no* criminal history (14 percent). And black job applicants with a criminal record received a callback only 5 percent of the time. The study's rigorous experimental design applied in a real-world setting, rather than a laboratory, enhances the validity of Pager's research.

A 2014 content analysis of video game characters revealed a shift in the portrayal of female characters over time. Where early on they were more likely to be portrayed as helpless and in need of rescuing, they have increasingly been portrayed sexualized and dressed in suggestive clothing. How might you go about studying gender in video games?

Research Ethics

Regardless of which data-gathering techniques they use, sociologists are expected to adhere to ethical standards in their research activities. Some standards apply to all types of researchers in the natural and social sciences, such as those forbidding the falsification of data or the misrepresentation of findings. All researchers are also expected to take active steps to help ensure the integrity of their work–for example, by disclosing all sources of funding for the research. But other ethical standards apply to the unique situations that arise when scientists study people.

An important summary of ethical standards for social science research can be found in the professional "Code of Ethics" developed by the American Sociological Association (1999). (A revised Code of Ethics was approved by the ASA membership in June 2018.) The code states that the primary goal of ethical guidelines is "the welfare and protection of the individuals and groups with whom sociologists work"–in other words, to ensure that people involved in sociological studies are not harmed in any way. Studies that might be highly stressful or embarrassing, for example, are typically forbidden. In addition, sociologists are obliged to respect the dignity and diversity of all research subjects, to recognize that they and their subjects may not share the same perspectives and values, and to be sensitive to those cultural differences.

Sociologists are also expected to protect the privacy of their research subjects. In studies providing *anonymity,* subjects remain "nameless" even to the researcher, such as when surveys are returned to a researcher without identifying information. Anonymity is very difficult to achieve, however, since in most studies researchers know who the subjects are. It is more common for researchers to ensure *confidentiality:* the researcher knows each subject's identity but will not make it available to the public in any way. Some studies simply report collective data–on opinions, behavior, or demographic characteristics–and never cite any single individual. A study that quotes an individual may use a pseudonym or no name at all or may change some identifying details to ensure confidentiality.

Perhaps the single most important ethical standard in research is the principle of **informed consent,** which means that *subjects in any study must know about the nature of the research project, any potential benefits or risks that they may face, and that they have the right to stop participating at any time, for any reason.* This broad principle goes a long way in protecting human subjects. Because some populations are considered unable to provide informed consent–including those under age 18 and those who are mentally ill–special restrictions limit the sorts of research in which they can be involved.

Any college or university that receives funding from the federal government for research involving people must comply with certain rules and regulations aimed at protecting the subjects of the research. One of the most important is that schools must have an Institutional Review Board (IRB) to review proposed research projects and ensure that they comply with ethical standards, thus providing another layer of protection for research participants.

The Research Process: A Student Example

Perhaps the best way to appreciate all the steps in the research process (Figure 2.2) is to use as an example a project appropriate for a student in an introductory sociology class, like you. Even though this project is simpler in scope than the typical sociological study, the basic research process is the same:

1. ***Choose and explore a general topic.*** A variety of factors, including personal interest, intellectual curiosity, the availability of existing data, and political commitment, could influence the general topic you choose. Perhaps the data on age and voting presented earlier in this chapter piqued your interest, and you find you want to learn more about the behavior of young voters. After selecting this topic, you will want to examine existing research to learn the findings of previous studies of youth voting and to begin to get a handle on broader theories that help explain voting patterns and attitudes among young adults.
2. ***Identify a specific research question.*** "Young people and voting" is too general a topic. You would need to narrow it to a specific question of manageable size. For example, you may have noticed that many of your friends did not vote in the last presidential election. At the same time, in your research you may have read the theory that people who vote are also more

FIGURE 2.2 | THE RESEARCH PROCESS

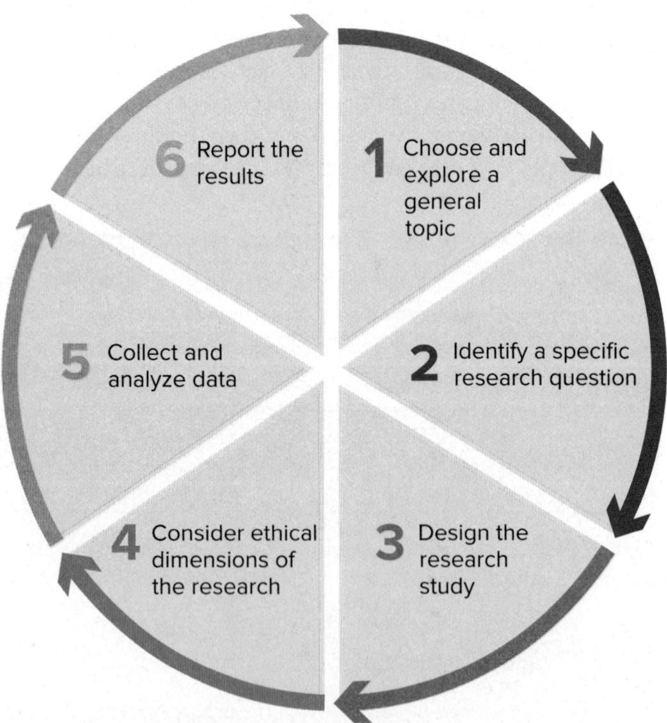

The research process can be thought of as a cycle because existing research is part of the scholarly literature that researchers consult when they develop and design a new study. When findings from a new study are published, they become part of the research literature that future scholars will review as they develop their own research projects.

likely to get involved in other kinds of civic activities. This connection between your own observations and your knowledge of a specific theory might spark a question: What *is* the relationship between voting and volunteer service or charitable work? In posing this research question, you may decide to hypothesize a relationship between two variables: Young people who do service or charitable work are more likely to vote than are young people who do not do such work. This is the hypothesis you would now investigate.

3. ***Design the research study and specify the data to be collected.*** You now have a question that you must translate into a concrete study. Given your limited resources and time (issues that plague all social researchers!), you decide a survey would be the most efficient way to collect the data you need. To create your survey, you must operationalize your terms. For example, what qualifies as service or charitable work? Helping family members? Charity work completed to fulfill a requirement for a course? Do respondents have to be engaged in such work now, or can they have done it in the past? You must be clear about how you will measure these and all other variables in advance of your study. Once you've clarified your key terms, you'll need to create a *questionnaire,* the specific set of questions that you will ask each person you survey.

   At this stage, you must also devise your sampling strategy—that is, determine who will receive your survey. Since this is a small school project, you will likely have to limit your study to students on your own campus. The results of your survey, therefore, will not accurately reflect the voting behavior of all young people, which limits your ability to generalize your findings. Students on your campus are likely to be different from students elsewhere and will certainly be different from young people who do not attend college. But even for your small study, you need to make sampling decisions: How many students will you select for the study? How will you choose them? In addition, you will need to decide how you want to administer the survey—by mail, by phone, over the internet, in face-to-face interviews, or any combination of these methods.

4. ***Consider ethical dimensions of your research and, if necessary, get approval from your school's IRB.*** You should be sensitive to any ethical issues your research raises. In addition, any research project involving people will likely have to be reviewed by your school's IRB, which will want to make sure, for example, that all participants will provide informed consent.

5. ***Collect, analyze, and interpret the data.*** Finally, you are ready to administer your survey. Afterward, you must enter the resulting data in a computer using a software package that will allow you to analyze it. Your analysis could range from simple summaries of the responses (for example, 42 percent of respondents voted in the last election) to comparisons between groups (for example, similarities and differences in the amount of charity work done by voters and nonvoters) or more complex analyses of the relationship between the variables. Once your data analysis is complete, you will need to summarize what you have found. The conclusions to be drawn from data are not self-evident, however; data must be interpreted in light of theoretical or substantive questions. How does your evidence apply to the question you raised originally? What have you learned about the relationship between voting and service or charity work? Has your hypothesis been confirmed? Do your findings have any bearing on theories in this field?

6. ***Report the results.*** The final step involves writing a report of the study. Adhering to the norm of transparency, you will identify your initial research question, explain the process of data collection, present the results, explain what you think these results tell you about your research question, and show how these results fit with previous research and theory on these issues. You might also decide to write a summary of your findings for a broader audience and publish an article in your school's newspaper. Perhaps another researcher will take your study into account when developing his or her own related project, bringing the research process full circle.

Even a simple school project such as this one reveals the complexity of doing research. At every step of the way, you must make decisions that balance the "ideal" project with reality: the limitations under which you are working. Social scientists face similar dilemmas all the time. They do not have unlimited staff, budgets, or time. As a result, research projects always involve compromises. In the best research, though, social scientists find creative ways to gather the data they need to address the question at hand adequately. This process involves both the precision of science and the ingenuity associated with any challenging endeavor.

Now that you have a sense of the general research process, let's take a look at different types of sociological research.

Types of Research

Sociology is a "big tent" discipline that includes a diverse array of approaches to studying the social world. These research approaches can be categorized into three major types summarized in Table 2.4: *positivist, interpretive,* and *critical* social science (Benton 1977; Fletcher 1974; Guba and Lincoln 1994; Ritzer 1975). Because some of the assumptions of these perspectives are mutually exclusive, different researchers tend to emphasize one approach over the other two. However, during their careers, many researchers use two or even all three approaches, depending on the question at hand. Although they vary in some important ways, all three types of research share the basic elements of social science we discussed earlier: their practitioners search for patterns in social life, insist on empirical evidence to support knowledge claims, demand transparency in the methods used to gather and analyze data, and consider knowledge produced by research to be provisional.

In the following sections, we review these three basic approaches—especially with respect to their assumptions about the nature of the social world, their goals, and their view of the role of values in research. We use studies about class and economic inequality to illustrate each type of research.

TABLE 2.4 THREE APPROACHES TO SOCIAL SCIENCE RESEARCH			
	Positivist	**Interpretive**	**Critical**
Areas of agreement	All three are based on the search for patterns in social life, require empirical evidence to support claims, demand transparency in the methods used to gather and analyze data, and consider knowledge produced by research to be provisional.		
Nature of the social world	Composed of discrete elements that interact in recurring patterns, producing usually stable social systems	Composed of evolving definitions of reality formed in the context of human interaction	Structured by power imbalances that produce conflict and result in social change
Goal of the research	Identify laws in social life to enable prediction and control	Better understand the meaning that the social world holds for others	Promote social change by better understanding how society works
The role of values in research	Scientific research should be value-free; researchers should pursue objectivity by maintaining a detached distance from those being studied.	Scientific research should present an accurate portrait of the people being studied, including their values; researchers can gain insight by building relationships with those being studied.	Scientific research inevitably involves a value position that researchers should make explicit; researchers should help promote positive social change.

Positivist Social Science

The most commonly used approach to sociological research is positivism—a term that dates back to Auguste Comte, as you may recall from Chapter 1. **Positivist social science** is *an approach that assumes that the social world, like the natural world, is characterized by laws that can be identified through research and used to predict and control human affairs* (Donovan and Hoover 2014). Researchers using the positivist approach usually look at quantitative data and use the language of variables in their analyses. Positivist social scientists strive for **value-neutrality,** *removing any personal views from the research process.* That is, positivists tend to argue that, with the exception of choosing a topic to study, science should not involve the researcher's values, beliefs, or opinions, and, ideally, social scientists should remain disinterested parties in the research they conduct. To positivist social scientists, a sociologist's job is to study the social world, not try to change it.

One of many examples of positivist research is sociologist Miles Simpson's (1990) examination of the relationship between political democracy and economic inequality. Using existing data from 62 countries, Simpson tried to test various theories about why some countries have greater economic inequality than others. Proponents of some economic theories argue that inequality increases in the early stages of a country's economic development, peaks, and then decreases as the country becomes more developed. These theories explain inequality by focusing on *economic* processes. However, other theories suggest that greater income inequality is the result of greater inequality in the *political* system. Simpson's examination of the data lends support to the latter theory. He finds that more democracy in a society is associated with less income inequality.

Interpretive Social Science

If positivist social science tends to encourage distance between researcher and subject, interpretive social science does just the opposite. Those using this approach suggest that the study of social life cannot be limited to features that are external to individuals, such as economic data. Instead, **interpretive social science** focuses on *an understanding of the* meaning *that people ascribe to their social world.* This focus on meaning makes interpretive social science fundamentally different from the natural sciences in the methods researchers use. In particular, interpretive researchers try to empathize with the people they study to understand the world from their perspective. This method requires close contact with the people in a study, an approach often traced to Max Weber, who argued for using *verstehen*—a German word that means "to understand"—in social research.

Interpretive researchers usually use qualitative data, often in the form of the words and explanations given by the people they are studying. However, interpretive researchers are not interested simply in how individuals understand social life; they seek to uncover patterns in the ways people make meaning of their social worlds and then describe the form and content of such interpretive patterns. This work does not necessarily promote social change, but often it can promote empathy and understanding for the people being studied.

Interpretive studies tend to deal directly with people's values, beliefs, and opinions because those are an integral part of the social world the researcher is studying. To adhere to the requirement of transparency, interpretive researchers often include a substantive discussion in their published research reports of their relationship with their research subjects. Interpretive researchers share the social science norm that their own personal values, feelings, and opinions should not distort their research findings. However, they also believe that their close connections with the people they are studying can enhance, rather than detract from, the accuracy of a study because their rapport with their subjects means there is less chance that they will misinterpret their findings.

For example, in his pioneering study of a poor urban neighborhood, sociologist William Foote Whyte (1914–2000) spent three years living in "Cornerville" (later revealed to be Boston's North End), spending much of his time with members of a gang of young men he called "the Nortons." Whyte was particularly close with the gang's leader, Doc, and the two men regularly discussed the community, the corner gang, even the best way to meet people from different sectors of Cornerville society. Whyte's interpretive field research study, the now-classic *Street Corner Society* ([1943] 1993), is full of lengthy quotes from Doc, who served as an invaluable neighborhood guide, a sounding board for Whyte's still-developing understanding of the community, and a critical reader of the early drafts of what became Whyte's book.

Critical Social Science

Critical social science is *research carried out explicitly to create knowledge that can be used to bring about social change.* Critical researchers do not focus solely on understanding society; rather, they are interested in understanding society to *improve* it in some way. A broad range of sociologists have followed in this tradition. Some invoke a famous line from Karl Marx ([1845] 1978, 145): "The philosophers have only *interpreted* the world, in various ways; the point, however, is to *change* it."

Critical social science rejects the idea of value-neutrality, for which the positivists strive. For the critical researcher, value-neutrality is neither possible nor desirable because all science incorporates some value position. Even advocating value-neutrality is itself a value-laden position. Critical researchers say the issue is not *whether* values will be a part of their work but rather *which* values will inform research. Critical social science is usually associated broadly with values that encourage human freedom and social equality. As a result, this approach often addresses issues of power and inequality in society. The fact that critical researchers embrace such values, they argue, does not undermine the credibility of their research. To the contrary, critical social science researchers want to better understand and reveal the dynamics of power in society in the hope of bringing about social change. If such efforts are to be successful, they must be based on an accurate picture of how society works. Thus, although values are at the core of this approach, critical social scientists seek to understand society *as it is* to help promote society *as it might be.*

One critical social science study involved living wage campaigns, which try to ensure that the wages paid to workers are high enough to keep them and their families out of poverty. These efforts are usually local, and local economic conditions determine the specifics of each campaign. In the early years of this movement, an activist from the Los Angeles Living Wage Coalition turned to Robert Pollin, an economist, to assess the living wage proposal being considered in that city. Pollin teamed up with Stephanie Luce (1998), a sociologist specializing in labor markets, to produce a study of the proposal. Their study concluded that the living wage ordinance would help low-wage workers and would not lead to job losses. The researchers didn't stop there, though. They presented their findings to the Los Angeles City Council and helped get the ordinance passed. The two researchers were then approached by other living wage activists from around the country. Recognizing a need, they decided to produce a book that presented their own research on the issue and also examined other existing work.

As the living wage campaign grew, other sociologists lent their research expertise. For example, scholars working with the National Employment Law Project (Bernhardt, Polson, and DeFilippis 2010) used survey research to document the extent and significance of labor law violations in New York City, including wage theft (failing to give employees money or benefits owed to them). The report included a proposal for how to strengthen worker protections. More recently, researchers at UC Berkeley and UCLA (Koonse, Dietz, and Bernhardt 2015) released a report describing the problem of wage theft in California, the value of local living wage legislation in the state, and best practices for enforcing new municipal minimum wage laws.

These three approaches to social science research share some common ground. At the same time, they allow for multiple approaches to a single issue.

Thinking Critically: How to Assess Research

We can't all be experts on research methodology, so it is helpful to have some authorities who monitor the quality of the research for us. The scientific community does this monitoring through the **peer-review process,** *in which scholars evaluate research manuscripts before they are published in order to ensure their quality.* When a research article is submitted for publication to a peer-reviewed journal, the editors send the article out to be reviewed anonymously by several other scholars in the field. These scholars provide the editors with their analysis of the strengths and weaknesses of the study. The article will be published only if the reviewers and the editors agree that the study is credible and worthy of consideration. The reviewers do not have to agree with the study's findings; they just have to attest that the question being examined is significant, that the data collected are appropriate and adequate, and that the conclusions reached are warranted. University presses often use a similar process when publishing books.

Although far from perfect, the peer-review process does provide the reader with a certain level of confidence about the basic competence of published research. Many research databases available through libraries allow you to limit your search to works that are published in peer-reviewed journals. You need not dismiss research and evidence published elsewhere, but you may want to give such work a more skeptical look since it has not been subjected to this rigorous review process.

After having surveyed some of the basics of social research in this chapter, you too are now equipped to carry out your own review process of the research that you encounter in both scholarly and popular publications. The ability to think critically about research findings is an important skill to develop that will be relevant to whatever field of study you pursue.

To assess a social scientific study, be sure to ask at least these six questions:

1. ***What is the research question?*** This is a simple but fundamentally important issue. Be sure the author has clearly identified the specific research question examined in the study.
2. ***What is the theory informing the research?*** What concepts and perspectives is the researcher emphasizing in this study? What issues might be left out by relying on this theoretical approach?
3. ***How are variables operationalized?*** When different research studies about the same topic reach different conclusions, it is often because of the way variables are defined and operationalized. One study may define "political participation" as "whether or not someone has voted," whereas another study may define it as "whether or not someone has done any of the following: voted, made a campaign contribution, worked on a campaign, joined a social movement organization, volunteered for a political cause, or taken part in a protest or demonstration." Conclusions about political participation in these two studies are likely to differ considerably because their authors have defined variables differently. When you read a study, be sure you understand what the authors mean by the variables they use.
4. ***What is the sample?*** Research is almost always based on a sample of a larger population. Different ways of selecting samples of the same population may lead to different results. When reading research, be sure you understand the sample on which the study is based. Is the study based on a single or a few cases, or on a larger sample? Was the sample chosen randomly? Understanding the dynamics of the sample can help you understand the results of a study.
5. ***What are the data?*** When reading research, be sure you understand what data have been assembled and analyzed. For example, is the research based on a survey that was designed specifically for this study? When and where did the researcher conduct observational fieldwork? What specific materials are the subjects of a content analysis? It is important to ask such questions when assessing how the author reached his or her conclusions.
6. ***Are the conclusions justifiable?*** In the final section of most studies, researchers usually interpret their data and explain the significance of the data for the question under consideration. Be sure you understand the claims the authors are making for their work and try to assess whether these claims are justifiable given the data presented in the report.

Asking these questions can help you think critically about knowledge claims and be an informed consumer of social scientific research.

A Changing World

TECHNOLOGY AND SOCIAL RESEARCH

W. E. B. Du Bois ([1899] 1996) spent more than a year conducting his house-to-house survey of African Americans in Philadelphia's Seventh Ward in 1896 and 1897. Around the same time, Emile Durkheim ([1897] 1951) and his research assistant examined the records of 26,000 suicides to determine each person's age, sex, and marital and parental status. In both cases, the authors completed all their data analysis by hand, painstakingly classifying and calculating everything manually.

Since then, technological changes have helped transform social research. Early sociologists relied mostly on qualitative accounts of social life. After World War II, though, academics quickly adopted the first computers to help them record, store, retrieve, and analyze quantitative data. These efforts were primitive by today's standards, but as increasingly powerful computers became available, a quantitative revolution took place in the social sciences. By the 1960s, much of the best-known and most prestigious research being published in sociology journals used sophisticated quantitative data and statistical techniques that depended on computers. As researchers began to use personal computers throughout the 1980s and 1990s, software packages that can store and analyze quantitative data became a common tool even for those with modest budgets. Computers were also central to the growing popularity of survey research. Researchers use computer-assisted telephone interviewing systems to conduct surveys. A caller reads a prepared script from a computer screen and records respondents' answers directly onto the computer with specially designed software.

Another revolution came about with the development of software programs designed for qualitative data analysis. Data from qualitative interviews and other sources still had to be painstakingly transcribed onto a computer, but a new generation of software allowed researchers to code their transcripts so that they could instantly retrieve relevant portions later on. Other software gave researchers the ability to code digital images and sound recordings as well. Such technology helped raise the profile of qualitative research once again.

Today, by enabling researchers to expand the scale of their work, keep costs down, and manage time efficiently, the internet and related technologies have transformed many aspects of social research (Fielding, Lee, and Blank 2017; Sappleton 2013). For example:

- Rather than relying solely on published articles, researchers use social networks to discuss their preliminary work, get feedback from peers, and learn about the research of others, thus speeding up the process of research innovation. Investigating published research is easier than ever with searchable digital databases of published work.

- Existing data sets on a wide range of topics are publicly available on the internet and thus more accessible than ever for secondary analyses.
- The digitization of newspapers, magazines, and other forms of media makes it easier to conduct content analyses of these traditional cultural artifacts. Meanwhile, the vast content of Twitter, Facebook, YouTube, and other social media offers researchers new opportunities to study current ideas, politics, and popular culture in real time.
- The digital trail we leave in our daily lives has enabled increasingly sophisticated social network analyses that map our connections to media content and one another (Turow 2017).
- Researchers routinely use the internet and even smartphones to collect survey data. Intensive interviews can now be conducted using Skype and other internet-based channels. One researcher (Davis 2013) even studied the online virtual environment Second Life by using her avatar to interview other people through their avatars. Another group of scholars (Snelson et al. 2017) studied the effectiveness of the massively multiplayer online role-playing game *World of Warcraft* as a site for teaching qualitative research methods to graduate students.

As sociologists look for new avenues of research in the twenty-first century, they are certain to take advantage of today's lower-cost digital video cameras and recording devices, no doubt fueling an increase in multimedia research projects. With more academic journals available on the internet, research reports are beginning to include sound, photographs, and video along with the written word. More advanced voice-recognition software that allows digitally recorded interviews to be transcribed automatically will greatly reduce the amount of labor for qualitative researchers. As new research tools continue to develop, researchers will find ingenious and practical ways to put them to use as they investigate the social world.

thinking sociologically about
The Research Process

- Sociology is an activity that uses the framework of science to ask questions, gather data, and seek answers about the phenomena of the social world.
- There are four key elements of social science research: (1) identifying and understanding patterns in social life; (2) gathering empirical evidence; (3) explaining how the evidence was collected and analyzed; and (4) viewing research claims as provisional knowledge, subject to revision.
- Theory and data act together in social science research. Theory helps us identify key research questions and interpret the data that are collected. Data provide the evidence that can support existing theory, lead to changes in theory, contradict a theory, or result in the development of a new theory.
- Sociology includes a diverse array of approaches to studying the social world. These research approaches can be categorized into three major types: *positivist, interpretive,* and *critical* social science.
- Given that we are not all experts on research methodology, it is helpful to have some authorities who monitor the quality of the research, which the scientific community accomplishes through the peer-review process. The ability to think critically about research findings is an important skill to develop that is relevant in a variety of professional fields.

REVIEW, REFLECT, AND APPLY

Looking Back

1. Conclusions based solely on a belief in authority, common sense, tradition, personal experience, or selective observation risk being inaccurate.
2. In addition to being a perspective and a discipline, sociology is an activity that involves basic research aimed at a scholarly audience, applied research often directed to some problem or need, as well as public sociology that tries to communicate the findings of both basic and applied research to a general nonacademic audience.
3. Social science research seeks to investigate patterns in social life systematically through the collection of empirical evidence. In doing their research, social scientists are committed to making their methods transparent, and they recognize that their truth claims are provisional.
4. Social science presents special challenges since the subjects being studied—people—are conscious of being studied and may change their behavior in response. In addition, it is difficult to control social life for experimentation or make predictions with certainty because different people can perceive, interpret, and react to a situation differently.
5. Research involves both theory and data. Theory helps us define research projects and interpret the data we collect. Data provide the evidence that helps us evaluate and build theory.
6. Research methods are the techniques researchers use to systematically collect and analyze data about the social world. The major methods of data collection are surveys, intensive interviews, field research, and experiments. Some research is based on secondary analysis of already-collected data.
7. Especially because people are involved, social scientists must adhere to basic research ethics that protect subjects from any harm caused by a study.
8. Sociological research generally follows a series of steps that includes exploring a general topic, identifying a specific research question, designing a study, considering the ethical dimensions of the study, collecting and analyzing data, and reporting results.
9. The three approaches to sociological research—positivist, interpretive, and critical—each carry distinct assumptions about the nature of social reality, the goals of research, and the role of values in research.
10. Knowledge of research methods helps us critically evaluate sociological research.
11. Rapidly changing technology in the past few decades has enabled researchers to collect and analyze ever-increasing amounts of data.

Critical Thinking: Questions and Activities

1. A friend who is a senior in high school tells you, "I'm not going to college. It doesn't make any sense to start off life by taking on all that debt. I saw some financial expert on TV saying you're better off today skipping college and starting a job right away. Look at my uncle; he never went to college and he manages a hotel and does well. Besides, if I don't go to college I won't have to study for SATs, figure out financial aid, or fill out those applications." Has your friend committed any of the errors in everyday thinking described in this chapter? If so, which ones? Explain.
2. Sometimes two research studies come to different conclusions about the same question. Knowing what you now know about the research process, identify three factors that might explain why two studies of the same issue lead to varying conclusions.
3. Suppose you have agreed to participate in a study of how college students meet potential romantic partners. Would you rather fill out a survey on this topic or participate in an intensive interview? Why? From the perspective of someone participating in a study, what are the advantages and disadvantages of each of these data-gathering techniques?
4. Identify a specific research question having to do with a topic of interest to students at your school. Your question might involve, for example, their satisfaction with their educational experience, their future career plans, their use of media, or their favorite classes. Create an 8- to 12-item questionnaire designed to help you better understand that topic. Remember, all the questions should be related to your specific research topic. Make sure to include both closed-ended and open-ended questions. You'll need to be careful and creative as you consider how to ask questions about your topic. Be as clear as you can in writing the questions and choosing the appropriate response categories for the closed-ended questions. Now give the questionnaire to three students and ask them to fill it out. When they are done, ask them if they were confused by any of the questions or if they have any other feedback on the

questionnaire. Have the respondents brought up issues you didn't anticipate? How would you revise your questionnaire based on their feedback?

5. Advertisements frequently refer to research to demonstrate that a product is popular or effective or recommended by experts. Choose a popular magazine and look through the ads for any research-based claims (for example, "Studies show . . ."). When you have found one, evaluate the claim from a social science perspective. Are data presented to back up any claims? What kind of sample, if any, was used? Is the sample representative of a larger population? Do you agree with the conclusion about the research that the advertisement offers? Can you even evaluate the claim, given the limited information in the ad?

Key Terms

applied research (p. 29) research that has the primary goal of directly addressing some social problem or need.

basic research (p. 29) research that has the primary goal of describing some aspect of society and advancing our understanding of it.

content analysis (p. 41) a variety of techniques that enable researchers to systematically summarize and analyze the content of various forms of communication—written, spoken, or pictorial.

correlation (p. 31) a relationship in which change in one variable is connected to change in another variable.

critical social science (p. 45) research carried out explicitly to create knowledge that can be used to bring about social change.

dependent variable (p. 31) the entity that changes in response to the independent variable.

empirical evidence (p. 30) evidence that can be observed or documented using the human senses.

experiment (p. 41) a data-gathering technique in which the researcher manipulates an independent variable under controlled conditions to determine if change in an independent variable produces change in a dependent variable, thereby establishing a cause-and-effect relationship.

field research (p. 39) a data collection technique in which the researcher systematically observes some aspect of social life in its natural setting.

generalize (p. 38) the ability to describe patterns of behavior of a larger population based on findings from a sample.

Hawthorne effect (p. 33) the tendency of humans to react differently than they otherwise would when they know they are in a study.

hypothesis (p. 31) a statement about the relationship between variables that is to be investigated.

independent variable (p. 31) the entity that is associated with and/or causes change in the value of the dependent variable.

informed consent (p. 42) the principle that subjects in any study must know about the nature of the research project, any potential benefits or risks that they may face, and that they have the right to stop participating at any time, for any reason.

intensive interview (p. 39) a data-gathering technique that uses open-ended questions during somewhat lengthy face-to-face sessions.

interpretive social science (p. 44) an approach that focuses on understanding the meaning that people ascribe to their social world.

operationalize (p. 31) to define clearly the variables to be studied so that they can be measured.

peer-review process (p. 45) the process in which scholars evaluate research manuscripts before they are published in order to ensure their quality.

positivist social science (p. 44) an approach that assumes that the social world, like the natural world, is characterized by laws that can be identified through research and used to predict and control human affairs.

provisional knowledge (p. 32) the idea that truth claims are tentative and open to revision in the face of new evidence.

public sociology (p. 29) efforts to reach beyond an academic audience to make the results of sociological research, both basic and applied, known to the broader public.

qualitative data (p. 31) any kind of evidence that is not numerical in nature, including evidence gathered from interviews, direct observation, and written or visual documents.

quantitative data (p. 31) evidence that can be summarized numerically.

random sample (p. 38) a sample in which every element of the population has an equal chance of being chosen.

research methods (p. 35) the procedures used by sociologists to collect and analyze data.

sample (p. 38) part of the population a researcher is studying that represents the whole.

secondary data analysis (p. 39) a type of research using data previously collected by other researchers.

survey (p. 35) a data collection technique that involves asking someone a series of questions.

transparency (p. 31) the requirement that researchers explain how they collected and analyzed their evidence and how they reached their conclusions.

value-neutrality (p. 44) the goal of removing any personal views from the research process; part of positivist social science.

variables (p. 31) measures that can change (or vary) and thus have different values.

©Eric Nathan/Alamy Stock Photo

3 Culture

looking AHEAD

What is **culture**, and how can you use the sociological perspective to understand its impact on your life?

How can **culture** both promote consensus and create conflict?

Why is **cultural** diversity increasing today?

©Francois Ancellet/Gamma-Rapho/Getty Images

When writer John Wray visited his cousin, an aid worker among the Amazonian Shuar community in a part of Ecuador accessible only by canoe or small plane, he was greeted as an honored guest. His hosts in the village of Pampansa invited him to the home of a local community leader, where they would share a bowl of *chicha*, an alcoholic beverage traditionally offered as a friendly greeting to visitors (Wray 2010).

While Wray was honored by the warm welcome and knew that his hosts were offering him a traditional drink as a gesture of friendship, he reports that he would "have given almost anything to escape." That's because in Pampansa, women prepare *chicha* by chewing on fermented yucca root and spitting into a large barrel, where the beverage accumulates before being transferred into a ceramic bowl for drinking.

After Wray's cousin Martin downed his bowlful of *chicha,* which their hosts described proudly as the best in the region, a newly refilled bowl was placed in front of Wray, who paused, wondering how he had ended up in this situation. After all, a year earlier he had visited Martin in a neighboring village and had managed to take only a sip of ceremonial *chicha.* This time, Wray found the *chicha*'s odor overpowering, likening the smell to "an old man's false teeth." Now, out of respect for his hosts, he was faced with guzzling the entire bowl.

In search of a way forward in this unfamiliar—and, for Wray, very unappetizing—situation, Wray recalled something that made the idea of drinking *chicha* more familiar and eased his sense of anxiety. He thought of all the times he had tasted someone else's saliva: "Hadn't I tasted spit countless times before? What was *chicha* drinking, after all, but French kissing once removed?" With the inspiration of this familiar activity in mind, Wray quietly gulped down his portion of *chicha,* paying respect to his host's generosity.

What we drink and eat, and how we prepare our food, is a familiar—and often vivid—illustration of how culture works. When we are part of a culture, our way of life seems natural, and we take it as a given; we are like fish in water. However, a cultural practice taken for granted by insiders may appear to outside observers as interesting, odd, curious, disturbing, or even threatening.

This chapter explores the central role of culture in social life and its pervasive influence on who we are as human beings. It considers some of the opportunities and challenges posed by our contemporary world, as people of many different cultures interact with increasing frequency and cultural diversity becomes a fact of daily life. As we gain a better understanding of the meaning of culture, we are able not only to analyze its impact on our own lives but also to prepare for a lifetime of interactions with people from cultures other than our own.

Defining Culture

Culture is one of sociology's core concepts. Indeed, it is an essential part of the very definition of **society**—*a group of people who live together in a specific territory and share a culture.* Many people associate the word *culture* with museums and symphonies, a connection that is understandable because one definition of the term does involve the "cultivation" of the mind by studying the "best" a society has to offer. In the West, *culture* in this sense generally refers to such attributes as education and refinement in the arts and such artifacts as great works of literature and classical music. For sociologists and anthropologists, however, culture has a much broader, more inclusive meaning. **Culture** is *the collection of values, beliefs, knowledge, norms, language, behaviors, and material objects shared by a people and socially transmitted from generation to generation.* Sometimes culture is simply referred to as a way of life.

Culture must be learned; it is not biologically based. In fact, we can think of culture as all aspects of society that are transmitted socially rather than biologically. That you may be tall is a biological reality. That you use your height to advantage when you play basketball is a result of cultural influences. The process through which people learn about their culture is called *socialization,* a topic we explore in Chapter 6.

Culture operates at multiple levels, from everyday actions by individuals (micro level), to the norms that operate within an organization such as a school or business (meso level), to the beliefs and practices associated with very large groups of people, including entire societies (macro level). At each level, the elements of culture influence how people live.

At any level, culture can serve as a source of both consensus and conflict in society. Regardless of the size of a particular group, its culture serves as a common ground connecting group members to one another. As we see later in this chapter, however, cultural differences can also contribute to tension and cause clashes among groups within a society and between different societies.

The Elements of Culture

Cultures consist of both material and nonmaterial elements. **Material culture** refers to *the physical objects produced by people in a particular culture, including tools, clothing, toys, works of art, and housing.* **Nonmaterial culture** refers to *the ideas of a culture, including values and beliefs, accumulated knowledge about how to understand and navigate the world, and standards or "norms" about appropriate behavior.* Nonmaterial culture exists in the world of thoughts and ideas; by contrast, material culture is physically real—it can be observed or touched. Collectively, the ideas and practices of a culture make up an entire way of life, affecting how people eat, work, love, think, worship, dress, learn, play, and live.

Because material objects can have symbolic (nonmaterial) meaning, the material and nonmaterial aspects of culture are often interconnected. For example, at the heart of many religions are sacred texts, such as Judaism's Torah, Christianity's Bible, and Islam's Qur'an (or Koran). These writings relate the central beliefs of each faith, thus comprising an essential part of the faith's nonmaterial culture. At the same time, the books themselves are often considered sacred as physical objects, to be treated with great respect as a part of the material culture. The books (Bibles, Qur'ans) are physical objects (material culture), but they also have symbolic (nonmaterial) significance. For example, most U.S. presidents have taken the oath of office with one hand on a Bible.

Let's consider how the various aspects of culture work together by looking at a much less serious topic: the everyday activity of grooming hair. Most people put at least some thought into what their hair looks like. Whether unkempt or coolly styled, our hair often expresses who we are. Hairstyles also reflect cultural values; we learn what is considered attractive and what meaning different hairstyles convey. We may think we are making purely individual statements when we style our hair, but in fact we are likely to be influenced heavily by the ideas and practices of our culture.

Often, we are so familiar with our own culture that we have a hard time recognizing its various elements or their significance. If we take a sociological perspective, however, we can see the often hidden ways that cultural ideas and practices help define our identities and our relationship to various communities. The elements of culture—to which we now turn—are summarized in Table 3.1.

TABLE 3.1 ELEMENTS OF CULTURE

Values: Deeply held principles or standards by which people make judgments about the world, especially in terms of what is desirable or worthwhile (for example, wealth equals success, family is important)
Beliefs: Convictions or opinions that people accept as true (for example, my country is good, God exists, the gods exist)
Knowledge: Information, awareness, and understanding that helps people navigate the world (for example, language, mathematics, sociological insight)
Norms: Rules and expectations for "appropriate" behavior (for example, how to dress, what standards of hygiene to maintain)
Behaviors: The actions associated with a group that help reproduce a distinct way of life (for example, "appropriate" sexual practices, the pursuit of formal education)
Objects and artifacts: The physical items that are created and associated with a culture (for example, food, clothing, music)
Symbols: Anything—a sound, a gesture, an image, an object—that represents something else (for example, a handshake, a corporate logo)
Language: An elaborate system of symbols that allows people to communicate with one another in complex ways (for example, English, Spanish, Chinese, American Sign Language)

©Shanghai Daily/Imagine China/AP Images

©Jeff Morgan/Alamy Stock Photo

Cultures develop different ideas about what constitutes a desirable appearance. These seem perfectly "normal" from the perspective of those inside a culture but can seem odd from the outside. Which hairstyles appear strange to you? Are there appearance norms in your culture that might seem unusual to outsiders?

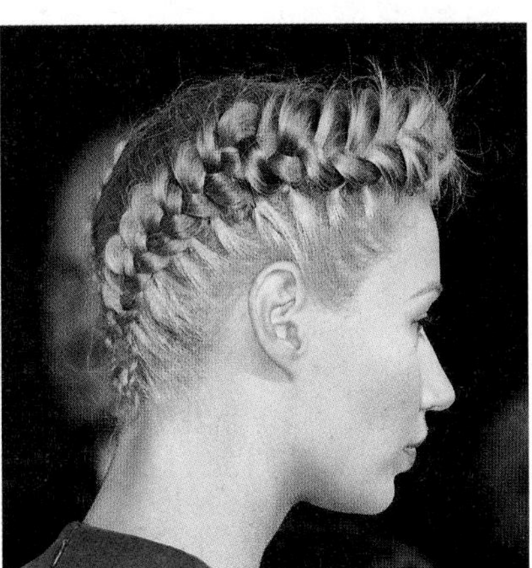

©Jason Merritt/Getty Images

©David Grossman/Alamy Stock Photo

Culture in Our Heads: Values, Beliefs, Knowledge, and Norms

Let's look more closely at the ideas of culture—the particular values, beliefs, knowledge, and norms that lend a culture its unique character. Together, they shape how people think, behave, and view their world.

Values: What Is Desirable?

A **value** is *a deeply held principle or standard that people use to make judgments about the world, especially in deciding what is desirable or worthwhile.* People in the United States, for example, tend to value individual freedom above collective responsibility (Bellah et al. 2007), and they see success as largely a product of a person's own effort rather than a consequence of outside forces. In one global survey, a full 57 percent of people in the United States *disagreed* that "success in life is pretty much determined by forces outside our control," a higher percentage than in all but one country (Venezuela) of the 44 countries surveyed (Pew Research Center 2014b).

Values such as individualism can translate into public policy. Compared to Europeans, people in the United States are more likely to believe individuals are responsible for their own fate, and not surprisingly Americans are less likely to support the kind of social programs that in many European democracies provide citizens with a strong government safety net (Pew Research Center 2011). European social programs, on the other hand, are more consistent with a collective value of mutual responsibility than with the individualism that distinguishes the United States. Global comparisons provide similar results. In one survey, for example, U.S. respondents were the least likely of those in 60 countries (with the exception of Bahrain) to agree that taxing the rich to assist the poor is an essential feature of democracy (Figure 3.1) (World Values Survey 2010–2014a).

Sociologists are often reluctant to label the major values of a given society because they do not want to imply that values are unchanging or universal. The most widely cited sociological description of American values appears in the classic book

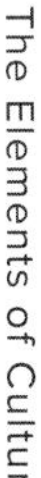

FIGURE 3.1 | SUPPORT IN SELECT COUNTRIES FOR TAXING THE RICH TO ASSIST THE POOR

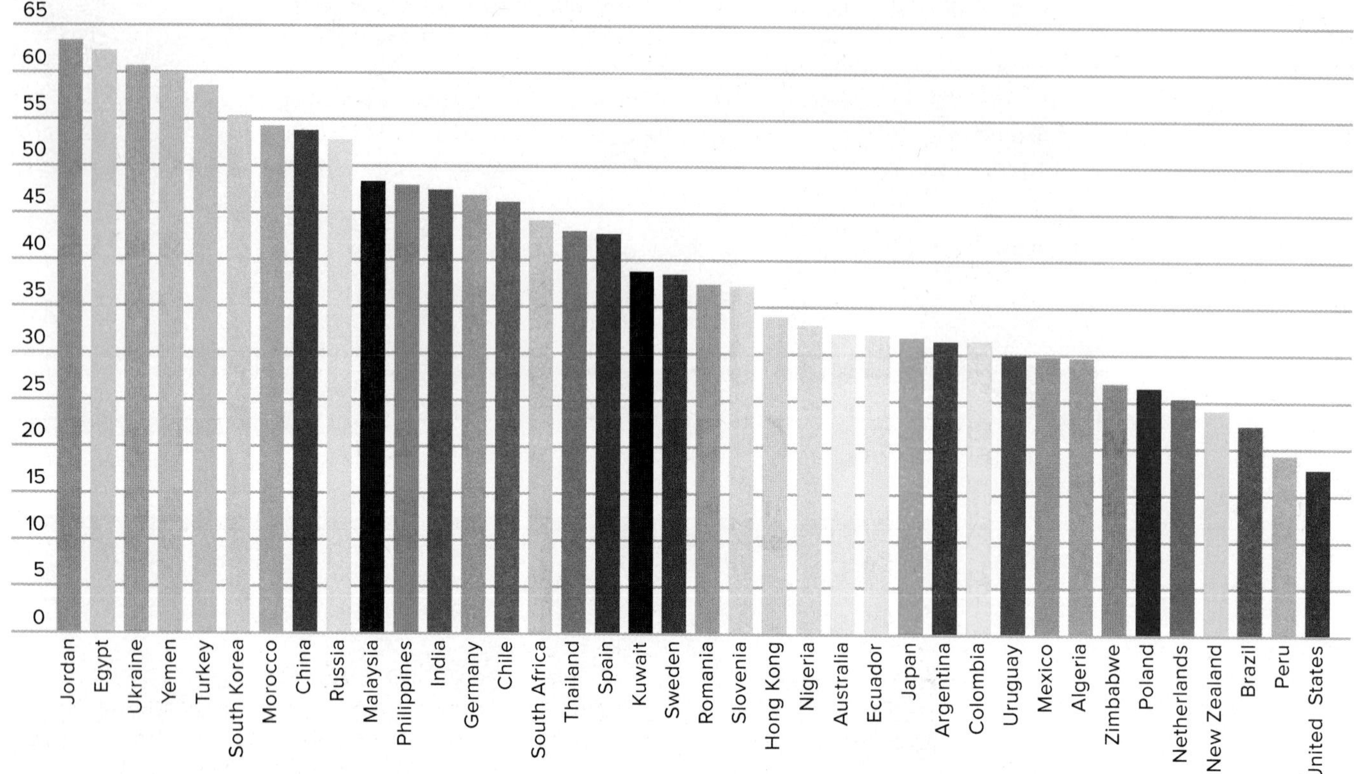

For this survey, respondents in 60 countries were asked to rate—on a scale from 1 to 10—the degree to which they felt taxing the rich to assist the poor was an essential feature of democracy. The graph shows the percentage who responded 8 or higher in 30 of those countries. With the exception of Bahrain, the United States had the lowest percentage for all 60 countries surveyed. ***Source:*** World Values Survey, 2010–2014. Wave 6. OFFICIAL AGGREGATE v.20150418. World Values Survey Association. Aggregate File Producer: Asep/JDS, Madrid SPAIN. Retrieved from: http://www.worldvaluessurvey.org/.

American Society: A Sociological Interpretation by Robin Williams (1970). Williams identified 15 basic value orientations as central to post–World War II society in the United States:

Achievement and success	Freedom
Activity and work	Conformity
Moral orientation	Science and secular rationality
Humanitarian mores	Nationalism-patriotism
Efficiency and practicality	Democracy
Progress	Individual personality
Material comfort	Racism and related-group superiority
Equality	

This wide array of value orientations includes contradictory pairings such as "individual personality" and "conformity" or "equality" and "racism." Acknowledging these contradictions, Williams described his list of values as tendencies, not absolutes and suggested (1970, 453) that we ask questions about each of them rather than taking them as given. He would have us ask, for example, "What groups or subcultures are the main bearers of the value, and what groups or subcultures are indifferent or opposed?" And how do the various value systems "work towards or against the integration of the culture as a whole?"

Like Williams, more recent American sociologists acknowledge both the variety of values that coexist in American society (Cerulo 2008) and their influence on people's lives. As Robert Wuthnow noted in a summary of research on values (2008), "study after study" confirms the important role values continue to play in social life. For example, "people with conservative values voted Republican, people with religious values attended religious services, people with altruistic values did volunteer work, and so on" (337).

But values change over time, and cannot fully account for people's behavior. The economic development of the post–World War II era, for example, created broad economic security that enabled such cultural changes as a shift in values toward more individual autonomy, gender equality, and democracy (Inglehart and Welzel 2005). Conversely, as we will explore in Chapter 16, the recent rise in economic inequality triggered populist and authoritarian movements that call for strong leaders, in-group solidarity, and the rejection of those perceived to be outsiders. Such movements helped elect Donald Trump in the United States, pass the Brexit referendum that led the United Kingdom to leave the European Union, and advance right-wing causes across Europe (Inglehart 2018).

Although values vary a great deal from culture to culture, research shows that some are widespread. A series of studies in dozens of countries over more than two decades by Shalom

Schwartz and his colleagues (Davidov et al. 2008; Schwartz 1992) identified 10 such values that are widely shared and similarly understood across cultures (Schwartz et al. 2001, 2017):

- Power
- Achievement
- Hedonism (the seeking of personal pleasure)
- Stimulation (the seeking of excitement and personal challenge)
- Self-direction
- Universalism (appreciation of and concern for all humanity)
- Benevolence (generosity and compassion)
- Tradition
- Conformity (the desire to blend in)
- Security

Of course, the relative importance of each value on this list differs from culture to culture, and the values do not always coexist easily. People's basic personal values tend to influence the political ideologies and policies they favor. For example, people who value security and power tend to favor policies that promise national strength and security more than do people who value universalism (Schwartz et al. 2010, 2014). Collectively, different cultures prioritize values differently, and these differences can be a major source of conflict between cultures. For example, theocratic societies such as Iran or Saudi Arabia, which are ruled or dominated by religious authorities, value tradition and conformity. They often dislike what they perceive to be the values of secular Western democracies, such as self-direction, stimulation, and relative hedonism as exemplified by popular notions of "rugged individualism," the widespread promotion of consumption, and the prevalence of sexualized media content.

When differences over which values are most important occur *within* a society, conflict emerges. In a classic work from the 1990s, sociologist James Davison Hunter (1991, 1994) argued that the United States was in the midst of an ongoing **culture war,** *an intense disagreement about core values and moral positions.* Debates about gay rights, abortion, prayer in school, gun rights, sex education, immigration, and the role of religion in public life became extraordinarily heated—and even spilled over into violence sometimes—because they were rooted in profound differences in values. Even today, similar debates about social and political issues—from gun rights and immigration policy to transgender rights and antiterrorism policies—continue to dominate political campaigns, cable programs, the internet, and talk radio, and are often seen as part of a political divide that has contributed to gridlock in national politics (Jacoby 2014).

©Emin Menguarslan/Anadolu Agency/Getty Images

Humanitarian efforts reflect the generosity and compassion characteristics of benevolence—one of the values that has similar meaning across cultures. Here, Turkish Coast Guard members help Syrian refugees, whose boat sank as they were trying to reach the Greek islands

But scholars question whether the differences in how various groups prioritize values in the United States are so profound that they warrant the label *culture war.* Some scholars argue that it is the political elites—politicians seeking to mobilize voters and raise money and political commentators trying to attract audiences and sell books—who highlight differences in values and encourage polarization and extremism (Lelkes 2016). Ordinary citizens are actually far more ambivalent about their own views and more tolerant of others (Baker 2005; Fiorina 2011; Koch and Steelman 2009).

Journalists who use the familiar shorthand "red state" and "blue state" to describe differences between conservative and liberal regions of the United States encourage the notion of a culture war. Identifying each state as simply red or blue implies that each state is fundamentally conservative or liberal and that the two types of states have little in common with each other. In reality, however, each state includes communities with differing views and values that reflect varying degrees of conservatism and liberalism. A map reflecting the complexity of value preferences in the United States would consist of various shades of purple rather than stark reds and blues (see Map 3.1).

Key cultural issues remain subject to debate. Observers point out, however, that culture wars—past and present—are largely the product of conservatives lamenting the changes that followed from the turmoil of the 1960s and, more recently, from the increasing diversity of the country's population. These changes resulted in increased tolerance, declining religious orthodoxy, and a reduction in the intensity of cultural conflict (Hartman 2015; Prothero 2016).

Beliefs: What Is True?

Whereas a culture's values are usually a set of broad principles, its **beliefs** are *the specific convictions or opinions that its people generally accept as being true.* Our cultural beliefs encourage us to understand fundamental issues in the world in a particular way. Is democracy the best form of government? Should marriage be based on love, or is it primarily an economic arrangement? What constitutes "success" in life? Is violence justifiable in pursuing an important goal? Are all people created equal? Does God exist? The way people answer these questions depends, in part, on their cultural beliefs. What people believe is, in turn, deeply influenced by the culture of which they are a part.

Belief in a god and concern for religion are widespread but more so in some societies than in others. In general, the

MAP 3.1 | THE 2016 ELECTION: RED AND BLUE OR PURPLE?

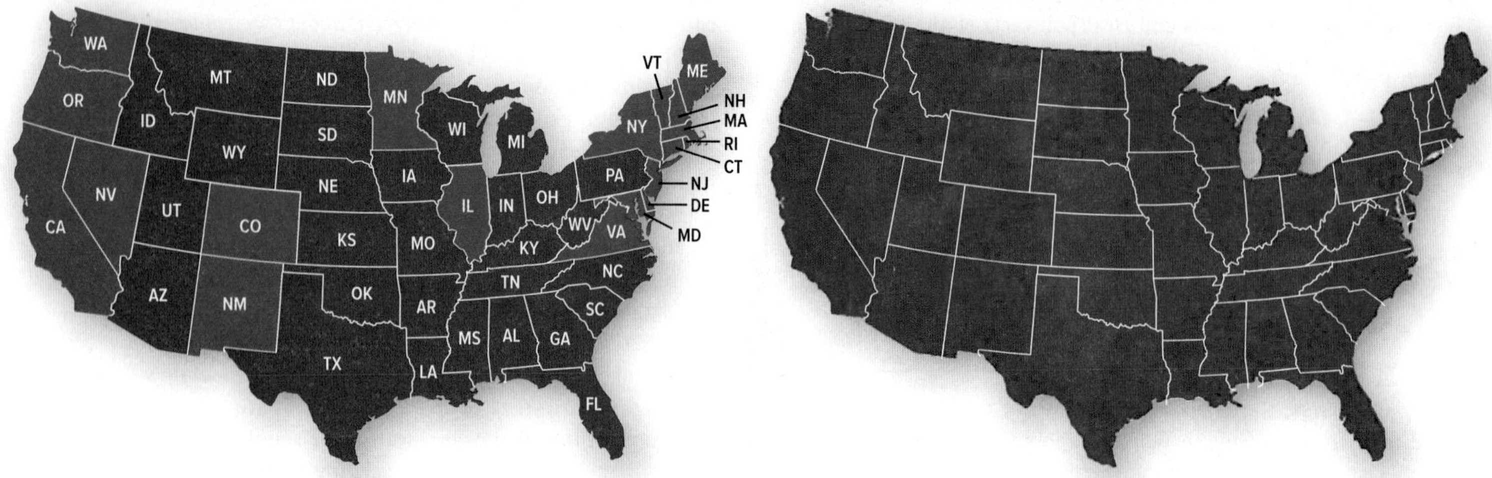

The map on the left shows the results of the 2016 presidential election by state; Donald Trump won the red states and Hillary Clinton won the blue states. The map on the right represents the results of the 2016 election by county and uses red, blue, and shades of purple to indicate percentages of voters for each candidate. ***Source:*** Newman 2016, http://www-personal.umich.edu/~mejn/election/2016/.

CORE CONCEPTS CHALLENGE *Which of these maps do you think is a better representation of the election? What do these maps suggest about how divided the political* **culture** *really is in the United States? Did the media's coverage of the 2016 election suggest a country that was more like the map on the left or the right?*

importance of religion in a culture declines as people become more educated and affluent. As Figure 3.2 shows, however, there is one major exception to this trend: the United States. In a survey of people in more than 30 countries, 53 percent of people in the United States said religion was "very important" in their lives, more than double the figure for other wealthy countries such as the United Kingdom (21 percent) and Germany (21 percent), and more than four times the number for Japan (11 percent) (Pew Global Attitudes Project 2015). Such a relatively high level of religiosity helps explain why debates about abortion, teaching evolution, and LGBT rights are often more vocal and intense in the United States than in many other industrialized societies. A higher percentage of people in the United States tend to believe in God than in other developed countries, and these religious beliefs influence political debates.

In poor countries, though, religion plays an even more important role in people's lives than it does in the United States. An overwhelming percentage of respondents said religion was "very important" in their lives in countries such as Senegal (97 percent), Indonesia (95 percent), and Pakistan (93 percent). Beliefs about God and the importance of religion are central to the culture of these societies.

Knowledge: How Do I Get Things Done?

In the context of culture, **knowledge** is *the range of information, awareness, and understanding that helps us navigate our world.* Sociologists sometimes refer to such knowledge as *cultural capital,* an idea we explore in more detail in Chapter 9, where we consider class-based cultures. People often take for granted the knowledge they have internalized about their own culture. They learn how to speak, read, and write their culture's language; how to dress appropriately for work; and how to behave properly in different situations. To navigate U.S. culture, for example, you have very likely learned how to read a map, how to use a credit card, how to apply to college, how to select items and pay for them in a supermarket, how to practice safe sex, and how to drive a car. In short, you have learned about the sorts of behavior that are rewarded and necessary for success in this culture.

Culture shock is *the experience of being disoriented because of a lack of knowledge about an unfamiliar social situation.* You are most likely to experience culture shock when you are traveling outside your own country, as John Wray did in the Shuar community in our opening example. In describing a research trip to Kenya, anthropologist Rachel Irwin (2007) told of her anxiety about riding in a *matatus*—a minibus typically filled well beyond capacity with people and sometimes goats, driving at "breakneck speeds" on poorly maintained roads. Culture shock can also occur within your own country. When someone raised in a small town visits a big city for the first time, or when a person who is not religious spends time in the home of a devoutly religious family, the visitor may suddenly feel out of place.

Cultural knowledge is essential for survival. People from the United States who are traveling in Australia had better know that motorists in that society drive on the left side of the road—otherwise, they are in for an abrupt case of culture shock! Of course, most cultural knowledge is subtler, involving how to act in order to get something done. When you entered college, you probably had to learn about what makes the culture of higher education different from that of high school.

Norms: What Is Appropriate Behavior?

Norms are *a culture's rules and expectations for "appropriate" behavior.* (Behavior that violates the norms of a culture is often labeled as *deviant,* a topic we explore in Chapter 8.) In a sense, norms serve

FIGURE 3.2 | THE RELATIONSHIP BETWEEN PER CAPITA INCOME AND THE IMPORTANCE OF RELIGION

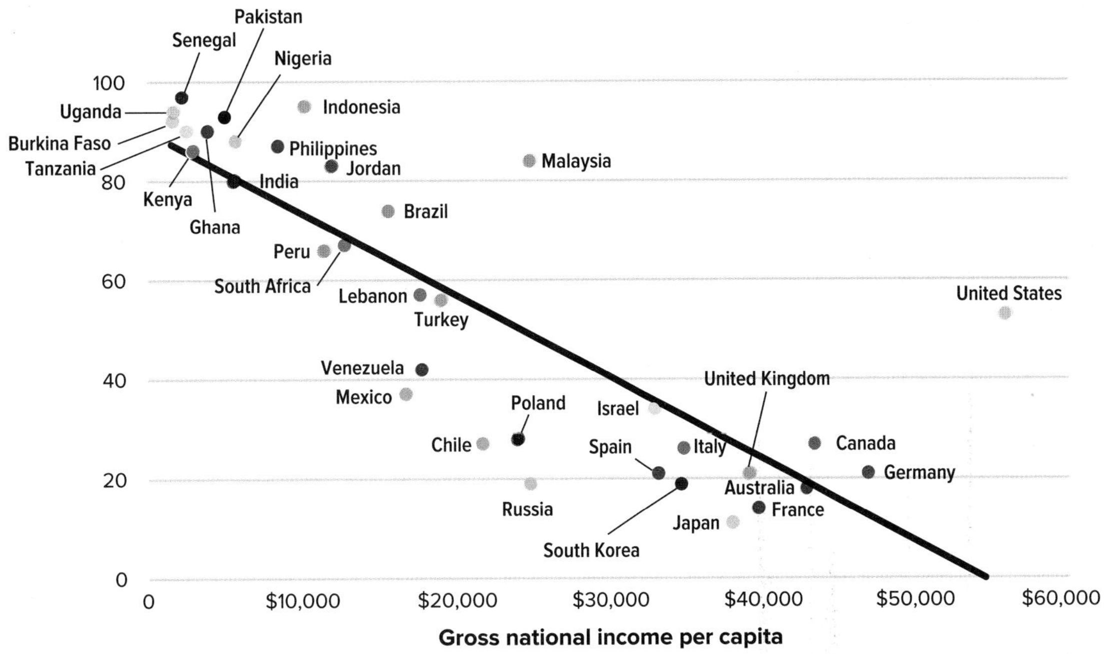

This graph shows the relationship between per capita income (that is, average income per person) and the percentage of people in select countries who said religion was "very important" to them. The trend line is clear: as income increases (left to right), the importance of religion declines. However, the United States is an exception to this trend. It has the highest average per capita income of the countries surveyed ($55,860), but at 53 percent, it is in the middle of the pack for respondents who say religion is "very important" in their lives. ***Source:*** Pew Research Center. 2015. Global Attitudes Project. http://www.pewglobal.org/files/2015/11/Pew-Research-Center-Democracy-Report-FINAL-November-18-2015.pdf; World Bank Database. 2014. http://data.worldbank.org/indicator/NY.GNP.PCAP.PP.CD/countries.

as a bridge between a culture's ideas and its practices since they suggest which practices are appropriate. To think God exists, for example, is to share a cultural belief. To attend weekly religious services, in contrast, is to follow a cultural norm because it reflects expected behavior. Norms can tell people what they *should* do as well as what they should *not* do. However, norms are not fixed or rigid. For example, smoking in public places—once a practice taken for granted in our culture—now increasingly violates informal norms and local laws.

As society changes, culture evolves to address new situations. Users of the internet, for example, created new norms for behavior online—sometimes referred to as "netiquette"—contributing to an emergent culture that is always evolving. Some internet norms are well established. You should never post IN ALL CAPS; that's the online equivalent of shouting. Don't ask a question in a forum until you've read the FAQs (frequently asked questions) page. And don't feed the trolls—people who seek attention by making outrageously provocative posts will not be convinced by your logical argument for why they should stop, so it's usually best to ignore them. If you are a regular internet user, such norms may seem obvious to you now, but they had to be created over time. Like all new users, you had to learn them at some point. If some online norms are clear-cut, however, others may be less so. How many selfies on Snapchat or Instagram is too many? Do emoticons belong in a formal e-mail to your instructor or a prospective employer? These norms are likely fluid or evolving.

Social norms do not always keep up with technological change, In the 1920s, sociologist William Ogburn (1922) coined the term **cultural lag** to describe *the ways that new technological developments often outpace the norms that govern our collective experiences with these new technologies.* For instance, digital photography and high-speed internet access have made it extremely easy to post photos and videos online for wide public viewing. However, the norms that define what is appropriate to make public and what privacy means in this context are still catching up to the technology. Perhaps this concept helps explain the posting of photos of alcohol-fueled high school parties on Facebook or the "sexting" of nude photos among teenagers. As these examples suggest, cultural definitions of what is—or should be—public and private information are lagging behind the development of the internet. New norms and behaviors will undoubtedly emerge and solidify as we advance further into the digital age.

Cultural norms for social interaction vary depending on whether the interaction is face-to-face, over the telephone, via e-mail, on social media platforms, or through text messaging. When we interact face-to-face, we use more than words to communicate; we use our tone of voice, hand gestures, and facial expressions, as well. When we send e-mail and text messages, we do not have these additional means of expression, which is why emoticons or abbreviations like LOL are so useful in online communication. Also, some topics are not appropriate for certain types of communication. Texting a friend to ask her to go out for pizza is fine, but texting to break off a romantic relationship? Maybe not so much.

Society enforces most norms informally. If your cell phone rings during a movie, for example, be prepared for dirty looks from those sitting near you. However, formal regulations, like a university's code of ethics or the legal system, serve to reinforce particularly significant norms. The study of deviance and crime is linked closely to the study of culture since both are largely about violations of a culture's norms.

Norms that are strictly enforced, with potentially severe penalties for violating them, are called **mores** (pronounced "MORE-ays"). Contemporary mores in the United States forbid physical or psychological abuse of one's children, for example. Those who violate such mores face public shame, potential loss of their children, and the possibility of a prison sentence. **Taboos** are *norms with the most severe prohibition or restriction.* For example, the incest taboo restricts sexual activity between certain family members. Cannibalism, too, is a widespread taboo and is considered repugnant in nearly all circumstances.

In contrast, the term **folkways** describes *group habits or customs that are common in a given culture.* Those who violate folkways are not likely to be subject to punishment (Sumner 1906). It may be customary to wear a bathing suit to swim, for example, but those who go swimming in jeans are likely to face only some surprised glances.

Taken together, values, knowledge, beliefs, and norms—the ideas of a culture—help shape people's orientation toward the world, providing an unwritten guidebook on what to think and how to behave. By studying the ideas of a culture, we focus our attention on how people make sense of their experiences. Understanding what people value, believe, and know and what people define as appropriate and deviant reveals a great deal about the complex workings of society—your own, as well as those of other societies. To communicate the ideas of our culture to one another, however, we need symbols and, in particular, language.

Communicating Culture: Symbols and Language

A **symbol** is *anything—a sound, a gesture, an image, an object—that represents something else.* An image of five interlocking rings represents the Olympic Games. A red light means "stop." An upraised forefinger placed on the lips means "quiet." The letters d-o-g together represent the sound "dog," which in English represents a domesticated four-legged creature (which, in turn, represents faithful companionship to many Americans).

The association between a symbol and the thing it represents is arbitrary and culturally defined. The people of Indonesia recognize a banner with a band of red over a band of white as their national flag; turn that banner upside down, however, and you have instead the Polish national flag. In most languages other than English, "dog" is a meaningless sound (and in some cultures the animal itself might more likely represent dinner than companionship).

©Apic/Getty Images

Source: CDC

FAST-FORWARD

Social Change and Norms

Through most of the twentieth century, cigarette smoking was a widespread and socially respectable activity, well within acceptable norms. Tobacco companies marketed their product aggressively, associating it, as in the Camels ad above, with both sex appeal and, ironically, good health. Since confirmation of the health dangers of smoking, an antismoking movement, using public service ads like this one, has gradually but effectively succeeded in changing the norms regarding smoking, making it an activity that now receives widespread social disapproval.

The flags of Indonesia (*left*) and Poland (*right*) are both horizontal blocks of red and white, the same shapes and colors. But they are distinct flags, with specific meanings to their citizens.

CORE CONCEPTS CHALLENGE *Can you think of other* **culturally** *specific symbols that look very similar but have different meanings? Or one symbol that has different meanings to different people?*

Similarly the same symbol can have different meanings in different cultures. In Mexico, raising your hand with a circle formed by the thumb and forefinger is an obscene gesture; in the United States it represents "OK." A "thumbs-up" gesture has a positive connotation in some societies but is an insult ("Up yours!") in Australia, Russia, Greece, Iraq, and much of Western Africa. In many societies, nodding your head up and down means yes, whereas turning it from left to right means no, but in Bulgaria the opposite is true.

Culture is fundamentally symbolic, and it is through symbols that we communicate and reinforce the elements of our culture to one another and pass them on to our children. As the Through a Sociological Lens box makes clear, cultural symbols in many forms can evoke emotionally powerful associations. However, one form of symbolic communication, language, is our primary vehicle for cultural transmission.

Language A **language** is *an elaborate system of symbols that allows people to communicate with one another in complex ways.* Other animals have call systems that allow them to alert each other about their immediate environment—the presence of predators, for example. Human language, in contrast, is unique in its ability to convey information about objects and situations that are not immediately present. With language we can converse about events that happened in the past and plans we are making for the future, and we can even relate stories about imaginary people and occurrences. Language allows us to accumulate and store information, pass it on to one another, and forge a shared history. It is no wonder, then, that efforts to maintain marginalized cultures threatened with extinction often focus on preserving those cultures' languages. Sometimes groups try to revive dying or extinct languages as a form of cultural preservation. For example, the Truth and Reconciliation Commission of Canada (2015) documented how the forced removal of many indigenous children from their families to attend residential schools in the nineteenth and early twentieth centuries was "cultural genocide" (1). It called for government action to preserve and revitalize the Aboriginal languages that children had been discouraged or prohibited from speaking.

Sharing a language, however, does not necessarily mean sharing a culture. English, for example, is spoken in many countries worldwide, in some as a first language and in many others as a nearly universal second language, but the people of these countries do not all share a common culture. They usually do, however, speak a particular dialect of English. A **dialect** is *a variant of a language with its own distinctive accent, vocabulary, and in some cases grammatical characteristics.* For example, what Americans call a "stove," the English call a "cooker." Further, a "truck" and an "elevator" in the United States would be called a "lorry" and a "lift" in England.

The Sapir-Whorf Hypothesis The principle of *linguistic relativity,* developed by Edward Sapir and Benjamin Whorf and popularly known as the **Sapir-Whorf hypothesis,** *suggests that because of their different cultural content and structure, languages affect how their speakers think and behave.* For example, researchers have found that people more easily identify color differences when they have a language to describe different shades of similar colors (Kay and Kempton 1984). That is, having words to differentiate distinct colors in the red spectrum (including scarlet, crimson, rose, magenta, and maroon) helps us see those different colors.

This hypothesis is controversial, however. Many scholars believe it overstates the influence of language on thought (Pinker 2007). They point out that, like other aspects of culture, languages adapt to changing circumstances and that speakers absorb or invent new vocabulary for things as they become culturally important.

Nonetheless, language reflects the broader cultural contexts in which it evolved. As a result, every culture tends to develop unique words, phrases, and expressions that are difficult, if not impossible, to translate into another language. In that sense, language helps shape how we see the world. For example, the Mandarin word *guanxi* (pronounced "gwan-shee") translates literally as something like "connection," but it refers to a sort of social currency in traditional Chinese society. People can accumulate *guanxi* by doing good deeds for others or by giving them gifts, and they can "spend" their *guanxi* by asking for favors owed. In a society in which bonds of obligation form a crucial part of social life, such a word has a significant cultural meaning that cannot be translated easily into English (Moore 2004).

Language and Social Interaction As we saw in Chapter 1, the *symbolic interactionist perspective* emphasizes micro-level interactions—people's everyday behaviors—as the building blocks of society. Rather than focusing on large-scale institutions and processes, symbolic interactionists look at how people make sense of the world through the meanings they attach to their own and others' actions. As a result, sociologists working in this tradition are particularly attuned to the importance of the role of symbols and language in human interaction.

For example, through intensive interviews with clinically depressed adults, sociologist David Karp (2017) found that the specific language that they use helps define their reality. This self-definition in turn shapes the actions people with depression can envision and, ultimately, initiate. Early

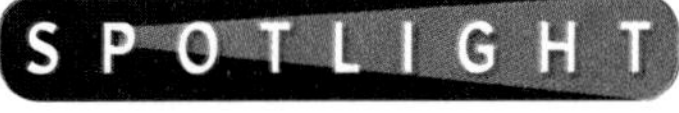

on social theory

Consider the experience of the people Karp interviewed. How have you reached a greater understanding of some situation by finding the right name for it, or finding the best way to describe it? How does this relate to the role of language as emphasized by **symbolic interactionists**?

THROUGH A SOCIOLOGICAL LENS

How We See Powerful Symbols

Symbols can be a powerful means of representing cultural beliefs, especially in the areas of religion and politics. The meaning we give a particular symbol can vary by culture, however. When the symbol is a potent one, the various meanings can be a source of confusion and sometimes conflict.

One of the most controversial symbols in recent American history has been the "Southern Cross." This flag (left) was never the official flag of the Confederacy but rather was one of a number of battle flags used by Confederate forces during the Civil War. In the 1940s the Ku Klux Klan adopted the flag, and in the 1950s supporters of racial segregation used the flag as a prominent symbol of their cause. Today, various white supremacist groups still use the flag as their emblem. As a result, for many in the United States the flag symbolizes the fight to maintain slavery as well as recent and contemporary racist movements. For some Southerners, however, the contemporary use of the flag is not racist. To them it represents "heritage not hate."

Sociologist Lori Holyfield and her colleagues (Holyfield, Moltz, and Bradley 2009) sought to untangle the complex meanings of the Confederate flag. They conducted focus group discussions with white college students at a large southern university. After reading aloud a news article about a controversy involving the Confederate flag in Leesburg, Virginia, groups discussed their views of the controversy and opinions of the flag.

The authors heard only rare instances of overt racism in these focus groups. Instead, they found that white students typically sought to downplay the racial meanings associated with the Confederate flag or became defensive and diverted the discussion away from racial issues. In fact, faced with a highly charged symbol, most of these white students had difficulty explaining their own understanding of southern heritage or the meaning of the flag, even as they denied the implication that the flag is a racist symbol. In analyzing the ways these focus groups largely ignored history and disregarded persistent differences in power and privilege, Holyfield and her colleagues (2009) suggest that, even if unintended, the use of such symbols can convey racist messages. They write, "participants need not approve of uses of the Confederate Flag or racism in order to participate in and perpetuate racist discourses" (525).

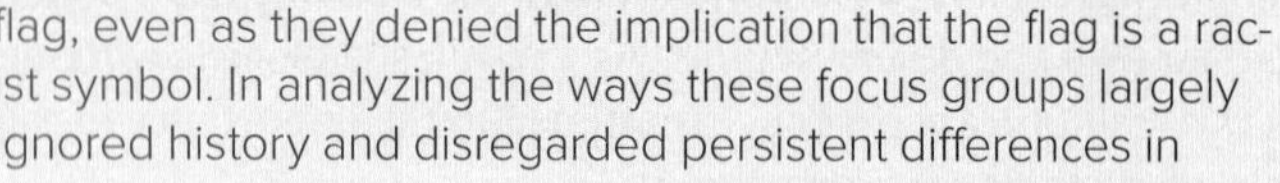

The controversy over the Confederate flag is part of a long history of symbols carrying multiple—and sometimes conflicting—meanings. For example, many Christians use the cross, symbolizing the crucifixion of Jesus (below left), as a sign of their faith. But the cross has been used by other, non-Christian cultures as well. In ancient Egypt the cross (above) was a sign of life. The ancient Greek cross (left)—with vertical and horizontal arms of equal length—represented the four elements: earth, air, fire, and water.

Perhaps the most reviled symbol of the past century is the swastika (right), now forever linked with Nazism. But the swastika is an ancient symbol used in many different cultures. For example, it was a variation on the Christian cross; a Hindu symbol associated with the ferocious goddess Kali; and a Navajo symbol related to healing rituals.

think about it

1. *What symbols do you encounter in daily life? In what other contexts are they used?*
2. *There has been a great deal of debate in recent years about whether statehouses and other government buildings in the South should fly the flag associated with the Confederacy. Where do you stand on this issue? Do you think the flag is simply a symbol of the South's heritage, or do you see it as a symbol of hate?*

in their experiences, respondents often did not have an adequate vocabulary for naming their trouble.

By eventually coming to name their condition as "depression," they began to see it in a new light. In naming their experience depression, Karp's respondents developed a new sense of self, which shaped their response to their pain. Their illness identity also influenced how they interacted with family and friends, and helped break the social isolation that is at the center of the depression experience. They also had to grapple with the exact meaning of this new label, however. One of Karp's interviewees says: "I think of it less as an illness and more something that society defines. That's part of it, but then, it *is* physical. Doesn't that make it an illness? That's a question I ask myself a lot. Depression is a special case because everyone gets depressed. . . . I think that I define it as not an illness. It's a condition. . . . It's something that I can deal with. It's something that I can live with. I don't have to define it as a problem" (Karp 1996, 53). In contrast, other interviewees were comfortable with the definition of depression as "mental illness" and worked to find a "cure"—both distinctly medical ways to define and interpret the situation.

Karp alludes repeatedly to the importance of language throughout his study. He points out that the ideas of "anxiety" and "depression" do not exist in many languages and, therefore, that people who speak those languages cannot use them to define their reality. Even the title of Karp's study—*Speaking of Sadness*—alludes to the importance of language.

Reproducing Culture: Behavior

In the context of culture, **behaviors** are *the actions associated with a group that help reproduce a distinct way of life.* When parents remind their children to tuck in their shirt, greet people with a firm handshake, and say "thank you" in response to a gift or an act of kindness, they are helping encourage a particular set of behaviors considered worthwhile in U.S. culture. These are small matters, but the accumulation of people's many small, everyday actions—at home, at work, at play, at worship—helps distinguish one culture from another.

Behavior also calls attention to the difference between **ideal culture,** *what the members of a culture report to be their values, beliefs, and norms,* and **real culture,** *what they actually do, which may or may not reflect the ideal.* For example, gender equality is an increasingly professed cultural value in American society, but in most two-career households, women do more housework than men (Baxter and Tsui-O 2016; Hook 2010).

Although culture is a social phenomenon, it also permeates our most private and intimate behaviors. Take the case of body hair. Do you shave your legs? Your underarms? Your pubic hair? Your head? Your face? In most cases, your answers to those questions are influenced heavily by cultural norms. Since World War I, for example, most women in the United States have shaved their legs and underarms, a behavior that seems "normal" to them. Yet this practice is less common in many European nations (where in some cases it is associated with prostitution), and it is unheard of in other parts of the world. Similarly, men's shaving their faces (but not their underarms or legs) is the norm in much of contemporary U.S. society but was much less common before the twentieth century.

Even sexual behavior—perhaps the most intimate of all human activity—varies significantly from culture to culture. Cultures differ in their attitudes toward masturbation, premarital sex, homosexuality and bisexuality, prostitution, and other forms of sexual behavior. Even feeling discomfort, awkwardness, or titillation at reading about topics like body hair and sexual practices reflects a culture-laden response. Although advertisers routinely appeal to cultural norms about hair removal to sell products, and sexual imagery permeates the popular media, most people in the United States rarely engage in frank discussion about such topics.

Cultural behavior also encompasses larger-scale, organized phenomena such as religious and political rituals (the president's annual State of the Union address), theatrical entertainment (rock concerts), and sports spectaculars (Super Bowl). Indeed, the widespread popularity of the Super Bowl—and the behaviors surrounding it, including those of viewers as well as the athletes and other participants—likely reflects some unique features of U.S. culture that Americans may take for granted but that may well appear odd to someone from a different culture. Thinking sociologically, what is the meaning of such an event for viewers? What might the popularity of the Super Bowl—even among people who don't like football—tell us about the ideas and values of U.S. culture? In short, understanding culture requires us to examine the complex ways people derive meaning from the cultural behaviors of everyday life. People both create culture and are shaped by it.

Objects: The Artifacts of Culture

Sociologists often refer to the principal elements of material culture as **cultural objects** (also sometimes called "cultural artifacts"), which are *the physical items that are created by and associated with people who share a culture.* Cultural objects are often variations on basic items found in daily life. Consider the many varieties of bread, for instance. Tortillas, baguettes, bagels, and puri bread are cultural objects commonly associated with Mexican, French, Jewish, and Indian cultures, respectively. We live in a culture in which electronic devices of all sorts—such as laptops, smartphones, and tablets—are significant cultural objects, in part because they symbolize a lifestyle and can be linked to our identity. How much of the popularity of iPhones, for example, is due to the brand and what it suggests about the owner, rather than any specific features of the product?

Cultural objects are found not only in your home, however. Highly prized creations such as works of art or religious icons are also cultural objects. Museums are filled with both ordinary and extraordinary objects that help tell the story of a particular culture. And the museums themselves, as well as other public buildings, people's homes, the streets and highways that connect them, gas stations, water reservoirs, and indeed any aspect of the landscape used or modified by humans—are also cultural objects.

Popular media products—such as books and magazines, films and television programs, songs and photographs—are also cultural objects. Analyzing popular media content often reveals a good deal of information about the culture that produced it at a particular moment in history. At the same time, it can be difficult to see the underlying assumptions embedded in the popular media of one's own culture.

Culture, Ideology, and Power

We have seen how culture helps define our world, providing models for appropriate attitudes and behavior. How we dress and speak, whom we admire and despise, and how we mourn

thinking about culture

What is the meaning of World Cup Soccer in U.S. culture? Does this vary by subculture? What do you think its prospects are for becoming a media event comparable to the Super Bowl? Explain.

©Loop Images/Alan Novelli/Getty Images

The National Museum of African American History, near the Washington Monument in Washington, D.C., tells "the American story through the African American lens."

and mark holidays are all shaped by our immersion in a particular culture. Since people are typically deeply embedded within their own culture, they usually find it difficult to see its underlying ideas. Sociologists have long paid attention to the assumptions built into any culture, arguing that what people take for granted is one of the keys to recognizing how culture and power are intertwined. One way to understand the meeting of culture and power is to understand ideology.

Ideology is a tricky term that is used in a variety of ways. Sociologists typically define **ideology** as *a system of meaning that helps define and explain the world and that makes value judgments about that world.* Simply put, an ideology is a comprehensive worldview. When we think sociologically about a culture's ideology, we pay close attention to the most basic assumptions the people living within that culture make, and the consequences of those assumptions.

Within each culture, there is a **dominant ideology,** *a widely held and regularly reinforced set of assumptions that generally support the current social system and serve the interests of authorities.* Even when most people within a culture agree about how the world works, though, most scholars concur that a dominant ideology cannot prevent the emergence of alternative worldviews. Instead, different ideological perspectives, representing different interests with unequal power, engage in a kind of cultural contest.

In considering how culture works through ideology, we need to remember that our commonsense assumptions, the things we take for granted, suggest a particular understanding of the social world, and such assumptions have consequences. In the United States, for example, many people believe that it is simply a matter of common sense that women are better nurturers than men, that education is a route to economic success, and that the United States promotes democracy around the world—although each of these assertions is debatable. When people adopt such commonsense assumptions—as they do with a wide range of ideas—they are also accepting a certain set of beliefs, or an ideology, about the social world.

Similarly, ideology shapes what we define as "natural." We generally think that what is natural is more enduring and stable than what is created by humans. As a result, the structures we define as natural come to be seen as permanent and therefore difficult to challenge. Consider some examples of social relationships that are often seen as natural. Is it natural that some people are rich and others are poor, that most citizens are disconnected from politics, or that people prefer to live in neighborhoods with others of the same racial or ethnic background? If all these situations are simply natural, then we have little reason to be concerned about economic inequality, political apathy, or residential segregation because they are not social problems but the natural order of things. What people think of as natural and normal, then, is fundamentally about ideology.

To effectively wield power, those with power within a culture must continually reinforce the idea that certain assumptions are simply "common sense" and "natural" because people's life experiences are likely to lead them to question these assumptions. (In Chapter 5 we explore this link between culture and power, especially as it relates to justifying inequality.) In recent years, for example, widespread cultural assumptions about the definition of marriage have changed. Gay and lesbian activists demanding the right to same-sex marriage challenged the longstanding belief that marriage is restricted to a relationship between a man and a woman. Now, in the United States and some other countries, same-sex marriage is legally recognized, marking a change from what was once considered "natural."

In addition, even in the most repressive societies, some people will not accept the dominant ideology, some people may resist it, and changing historical conditions will undermine certain aspects of it. Ultimately, when we look at ideology from a sociological point of view, we can see the ways that culture is a contested arena that defines our underlying, and often changing, conceptions of the world.

Cultural Diversity

For much of human history, travel was difficult, expensive, and often dangerous, and only a few people interacted with people from cultures other than their own. Today, widespread mobility, a global economy, large-scale immigration, and technological advances have brought people from diverse cultures into frequent and often sustained contact. Many colleges and universities recognize that students benefit from learning about and working with people from different backgrounds as they prepare for an increasingly diverse social world and the increasingly diverse workplaces into which they will graduate. Many schools have offices devoted to promoting "inclusiveness" and celebrating "multiculturalism," and they strive to achieve a diverse student body. College campuses today often include people from a variety of racial and ethnic groups, from many nations, and from a variety of social class backgrounds. They include people with a variety of life experiences, such as veterans and working adults. They include students with a variety of religious affiliations or none at all. And they include students with a range of sexual preferences and gender identities—gay, straight, lesbian, bisexual, and transgender.

SOCIOLOGY in ACTION

Cultural Competence and Health Care

Lia Lee was a Hmong child living in California. The Hmong are an ethnic group from the Southeast Asian country of Laos whose culture is rooted in a rural way of life. When Lia was born in a California county hospital, her mother spoke no English, and the medical staff spoke no Hmong. At just three months old, Lia experienced fainting episodes, which doctors attributed to epileptic seizures. Over the next four years, Lia's doctors struggled to control her symptoms by prescribing a dozen different drugs in dosages and combinations that changed more than 20 times.

This dizzying array of treatments would have been confusing to anyone, but Lia's family was especially ill-prepared to understand the process. Illiterate even in their own Hmong language, they were able to follow their doctor's advice only intermittently. Instead, they turned for relief to their culture's familiar religious beliefs about illness. According to that tradition, Lia's fainting spells were caused by the temporary departure of her soul from her body, a condition whose name roughly translates as "the spirit catches you and you fall down." Lia's parents sent away to Thailand for sacred charms to protect her and changed the child's name to fool the evil spirits (Underwood and Adler 2005).

As U.S. society becomes ever more culturally diverse, health care workers are increasingly treating people like Lia and her family, whose beliefs about sickness and health differ dramatically from those of mainstream Western medicine. To treat these patients effectively, health care workers need to pay close attention to their cultural beliefs and traditions. Unfortunately, the Western doctors did not understand the Hmong culture, and Lia's family did not understand the doctors' efforts. As a result, the medical treatment was ineffective. Four years after her initial symptoms, Lia experienced a massive seizure that left her in a vegetative state for decades. She died in 2012 at the age of 30.

Lia's story is perhaps an extreme example, but dealing with gaps in communication between patients and health care workers caused by cultural differences is a very real and growing challenge. The federal government, along with several universities, private foundations, and organizations representing health care providers, has launched a variety of public and private initiatives to promote and ensure *cultural competence*—the ability to understand and address the needs of people from different cultures (Rees and Ruiz 2003). For example, some states have enacted regulations that require medical facilities to provide culturally competent care to groups that make up a certain percentage of the community's population. As one key element of this care, facilities are required to make interpreters available who are fluent in the language and cultural traditions of different groups. Organizations such as Resources for Cross Cultural Health Care (diversityrx.org) have stepped up to the challenge. One study found that medical interpreters, those who facilitate bilingual communication in hospitals, often act as an essential part of a medical team, becoming informal co-diagnosticians, even though these interpreters lack formal medical training (Hsieh 2007).

As part of their training, medical students are also learning about the important role of culture in their patients' lives. One book has become required reading in more than 100 medical schools. Titled *The Spirit Catches You and You Fall Down,* it's the tragic story of Lia Lee (Fadiman 2012).

think about it

1. *Have you or your family ever had trouble communicating with a doctor or been uncertain about what is happening at a hospital? If so, do you think cultural differences help explain why?*
2. *How might cultural differences cause problems with communication in school or at work?*

As the college experience reflects, understanding cultural diversity is more important now than ever before. (For a tragic example of what can happen due to a lack of cultural understanding, see the Sociology in Action box.) But to understand cultural diversity, it helps to take a closer look at the various types of cultures within our own and other societies, their positions in relation to one another, and how they interact in what has become an increasingly multicultural world.

Dominant Culture, Subcultures, and Countercultures

When we talk about societies—our own or those of other countries—it is common to speak about them as sharing a single culture (for example, "U.S. culture" or "Afghan culture"). To a degree, this is true; societies share basic cultural features. However, societies are large-scale, complex arrangements that inevitably contain internal differences, as well. Competing cultural systems exist even in what appear to be homogeneous societies.

Rather than consisting of a single culture, most societies contain a **dominant culture,** *a culture that permeates the society and that represents the ideas and practices of those in positions of power,* as well as a number of **subcultures,** *cultures associated with smaller groups in the society that have distinct norms, values, and lifestyles that set them apart from the dominant culture.*

The dominant culture in the United States has long been associated with relatively affluent, white, heterosexual males, often of Protestant Anglo-Saxon (English) ancestry. Disproportionately, these were the people in positions of political, corporate, and military power. They led universities, the media, religious organizations, and major museums. Their accomplishments were taught in classrooms, and their worldview tended to be reflected in popular media. The ideas and views of other segments of society, although rarely excluded entirely by the dominant culture, tended to be marginalized. Evidence of this marginalization can be found in terms like "the black community," "women's history," "gay bar," and "working-class literature" because they call attention to a deviation from the dominant white, male, heterosexual, middle-class norm. In contrast, rarely, if ever, would you come across terms like "the white community," "straight bar," "middle-class literature," or "men's history," because those were the already unspoken standard in the dominant culture.

The makeup of the U.S. population has been changing rapidly, however, and social movements have given previously marginalized groups a greater voice than they had before, helping to displace the traditional white heterosexual male culture—and generating a conservative cultural backlash. There is a long way to go before corporate boardrooms and other institutions of power accurately reflect the diversity of the population as a whole, but the dominant culture has broadened its embrace.

A society's dominant culture coexists with many subcultures. For example, Americans in general are enthusiastic about technological advancements (a feature of the country's dominant culture), but the Amish—an orthodox Protestant sect living primarily in Pennsylvania and Ohio—reject the use of most modern technology, resulting in a distinct way of life. Skateboarders also form a subculture. They define and use public spaces in innovative ways, turning roads and sidewalks, steps and hand railings, into a skating space, while developing a distinctive attitude about risk-taking and authority. Since subcultures often highlight their differences from the mainstream, their members often accept, even celebrate, their nonconformist beliefs or behaviors (Gelder 2005; Haenfler 2014).

Members of a subculture, then, share a common identity, whether they are members of a particular demographic group, extreme-sports enthusiasts, science fiction fans, or Civil War reenactors. Although subcultures typically do not have a formal membership structure, they usually develop a specialized language or style and specific behaviors and objects relevant to their culture. Survivalists, for example, are part of a subculture that emphasizes the need to prepare for extreme emergencies, ranging from natural disasters to widespread social and political upheavals, and even to religiously tinged "doomsday" scenarios. Using specialized language, members share information online and at in-person "prepper shows" about the best tactics, weapons, and equipment needed to survive such disasters. These include preparing a "bug out bag" with portable emergency supplies and planning a strategy for how to deal with "zombies"—people who have not prepared but who will want to "feed off" of the survivalists.

Work and school organizations can develop their own cultural traits, too. Thus we might speak about the corporate culture at Walmart or the organizational culture at a government agency such as NASA. If your school has a significant sports program, take a look around you at the next big game you attend. College athletics—complete with school colors, uniforms, mascots, cheers, and rituals—are part of the distinct cultures of many schools. Special moments in the school's sports history—winning a championship, pulling off a huge upset, a star athlete's choking in a key game—all become part of the lore of that school's culture.

At the micro level, even groups of close friends who live in the same neighborhood can develop a subculture. As they grow up, their common experiences foster similar values and beliefs. They may like the same style of clothing, music, and leisure activities. Over time their shared adventures give them a common history, filled with incidents, terminology, and characters that have little meaning for people outside the group. "Inside" jokes and references help build a sense of solidarity and belonging.

A subculture that organizes itself in opposition to the dominant culture may be categorized as a **counterculture,** which *champions values and lifestyles distinctly opposed to those of the dominant culture.* Members of countercultures challenge widely held values and attitudes and reject mainstream cultural norms.

In the past half century, a series of youth-based countercultures have challenged aspects of the dominant culture in U.S. society. For example, young hippies in the 1960s had a

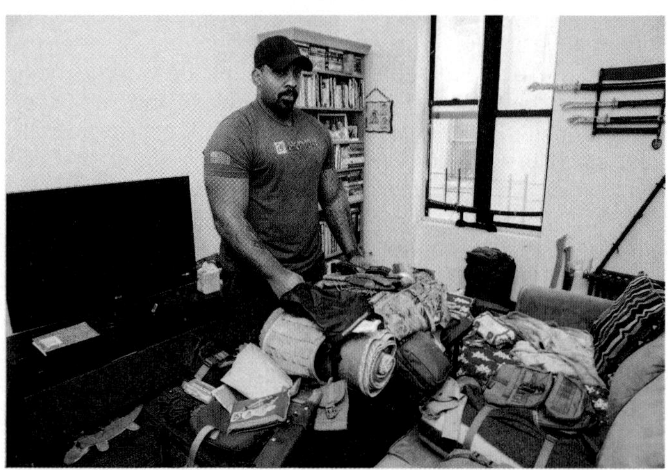

A New York City firefighter poses in his Harlem apartment with some of his "End of the World" supplies he has assembled to enable him and his family to survive for up to 10 months after an emergency. These include combat knives, medicine, tools, water, and much more. Survivalists come in many varieties but they form a subculture with distinctive beliefs, knowledge, and practices. Even the language used by these "preppers" can be unique.

thinking about culture

Do you belong to a particular subculture or know someone who does? If so, what features of this subculture set it apart from the dominant culture? Do you think aspects of this subculture are likely to be incorporated into mainstream culture in your lifetime? Explain.

distinctive lifestyle and language. They challenged traditional authority by experimenting with recreational drugs, practicing communal living, rejecting materialism, espousing "free love," and protesting against the Vietnam War. Punks in the 1970s developed their own particular style, including then-atypical piercings and provocative hairstyles, along with a defiant attitude. In turn, hip-hop introduced new music, language, dance, and fashion while some within hip-hop culture advanced a powerful critique of racism and racial discrimination.

Subcultures—including countercultures—often introduce innovation and change to mainstream culture. Features of a subculture that might appear radical or threatening may over time be incorporated into the dominant culture. Hip-hop—once a provocative subculture—is now firmly a part of mainstream U.S. culture. Similarly, tattoos were once found exclusively among various subcultures such as sailors and bikers but have long since moved into the U.S. mainstream. Access to birth control, racial intermarriage, equal rights for women, and a host of other social reforms began their life as part of the beliefs and values of political subcultures, only to achieve broad mainstream acceptance eventually.

High Culture and Popular Culture

Societies contain not only a dominant culture and various subcultures, but also different cultural expressions that are related to people's position in society. Sociologists have in fact long recognized the relationship between culture and economic inequality. **High culture** refers to *cultural forms associated with—and especially valued by—elites.* Examples of high culture include art galleries, the opera, classical music, and literature. Historically, high culture has been the domain of the wealthy and highly educated. Although others may not be formally excluded from these activities, their expense and the specialized knowledge that is often needed to understand and enjoy them can serve to restrict access to those who are able to afford them.

Proponents of high culture may define these cultural forms as the best and most enduring representations of a society's culture. After all, disciplines that study high culture such as art history and music education are typically part of the high school and college curriculum, and many people associate the very idea of becoming "cultured" with visiting museums or attending the symphony. In contrast, **popular culture** refers to *cultural forms that are widespread and commonly embraced within a society.* Popular culture includes such widely accessible forms as television programs, Hollywood films, rock concerts, spectator sports, and amusement parks. To enjoy popular culture, a person generally does not need a substantial amount of money or specialized knowledge.

©Ted Soqui/Corbis Entertainment/Getty Images

The distinction between high and popular culture was once sharp and reflected a fundamental conflict in worldviews (Gans 1999). Now, though, the line between the two is blurry. More people, including elites, consume a diverse mixture of high and popular culture. Nevertheless, the distinction between high and popular culture remains helpful since the cultural choices people make are still influenced significantly by their social standing.

Culture can also be influenced by people's physical location. The term *folk culture* indicates traditional practices, often passed on orally from generation to generation, that reflect lifestyles in specific—often rural—areas. Unlike pop culture that is widely communicated and easily available in a diverse society, folk culture is produced and consumed locally, often by working-class and poor people. In music, for example, Mississippi Delta blues and the early country and bluegrass of the rural South were distinct folk cultures closely associated with the places and people that produced them. As those examples illustrate, too, folk culture often goes on to influence popular culture.

Battani, Hall, and Neitz (2003, 91) note that, while still vibrant in some isolated rural parts of the world, "in a pluralistic world where every corner has been subjected to the gaze of the mass media and everything has its price, folk culture acquires a narrow meaning. . . . [In the contemporary United States] it is almost a genre of arts and crafts, defined by cultural transmission and learning outside of schools or books." The Smithsonian Institution operates the American Folklife Center (2018), which collects and documents traditional folk culture examples of the "everyday and intimate creativity that all of us share and pass on to the next generation," including recipes, music, stories, ways of speaking, games, crafts, and work traditions. The fact that American folk culture is now showcased in a museum reflects the dominant role that commercial popular culture now holds.

The Commercialization of Culture

A 2010 Lady Gaga and Beyoncé music video for the song "Telephone" is notorious—not for the music or its clichéd women's prison theme but for the sheer number of product placements crammed into it. Shots linger on a pair of Heartbeats headphones, a Virgin Mobile telephone, cans of Diet Coke, a Beats branded HP laptop with the Plenty of Fish dating site open on its screen, a Chevrolet pickup truck, a Polaroid camera, Wonder Bread, and even a jar of Miracle Whip. The video is one example of how cultural creations not only are sold but also are used to sell other products. Not content to insert their products into new music videos, advertisers now even use digital tricks to retroactively insert them into classic music videos (Newman 2014). Similarly, popular music is often used in the background of television commercials, but commercials are also inserted into songs in the hope that the songs will become popular. Rap songs, for example, are loaded with references to brands like Mercedes, Gucci, Glock, Cristal, and Nike, sometimes placed there by companies like Maven Strategies that negotiate deals between major corporate advertisers and hip-hop artists (Williams 2005). And the trend has exploded in recent years. One study found that, between 2000 and 2010, more brand names were mentioned in pop songs than in the prior four decades combined, and many of those mentions were paid for (Gloor 2014). This type of product placement, which continues today, is just one of many ways that *commercialism*—the marketing and sale of products—has become entrenched in contemporary popular culture.

Today, many cultural objects are commodities—products to be bought and sold—produced by corporate conglomerates (Mosco 2009; Noam 2016; Schor 2004). The stories children learn and the music people listen to are produced and marketed by multinational corporations like Disney and Sony. Corporations sponsor a broad range of cultural creations, from rock concerts to museum exhibits (Rectanus 2002). From expensive tickets to major events to streaming video from Netflix, we spend much of our lives—and many of our dollars—buying cultural products. This seems utterly unremarkable to us, but it represents a relatively recent shift in the nature of cultural production, which used to be created noncommercially as part of the traditions of everyday life.

This focus on commerce has meant that the language and images of advertising have increasingly entered public and private space, surrounding us with pictures and symbols whose primary purpose is to get us to buy something. Some communities see this as a problem and are fighting back, however. In 2007, new "Clean City" laws went into effect in São Paulo, Brazil—a city of almost 12 million people—that essentially banned all outdoor advertising. As the president of the city council noted, "What we are aiming for is a complete change of culture [. . .] things were out of hand and the population has made it clear it wants this" (Rohter 2006). Since then, the law has been widely seen as a positive development that has helped beautify the city and encouraged flourishing mural and graffiti art communities.

With the ever-growing influence of commercialism, people increasingly tend to measure the value of most cultural objects by their profitability. How many copies of that book were sold? What were the box office standings for movies released this past weekend? Such concerns reflect a culture in which the dollar sign increasingly denotes "success." As we see throughout this book, especially in Chapter 14, the commercialization of cultural and social life—its packaging, promotion, and sale by major corporations—is an important feature of our changing world, both in the United States and globally.

Multiculturalism

When more than 110 million viewers watched the iconic Super Bowl 50 halftime show in 2016, they got a lesson in multiculturalism. Three musical acts performed—the white musicians of the British group Coldplay; Latino artist Bruno Mars (born Peter Hernández), whose ancestry includes Puerto Ricans and Fillipinos; and pop icon Beyoncé, who has African American and Creole roots. In a nod to the LGBT community, Coldplay's performance featured a multicolored stage set and rainbow flags. Beyoncé sang "Formation," a song that celebrates her multicultural heritage and the video of which includes a reference to the Black Lives Matter movement. She and her dancers wore leather costumes and berets reminiscent of the uniforms of the Black Panthers (who, like the Super Bowl, originated in 1966), while the dancers moved in an X formation (perhaps suggesting Malcolm X) and threw up a Black Power fist pump. The sequence ended with flashback images of diverse musical performances from earlier years, and then all three acts shared the stage while audience members held placards that created a huge rainbow-colored slogan: "Believe in Love." The phrase was likely a reference to the legalization of same-sex marriage in the United States less than a year earlier, as well as to a recent video released by Pope Francis celebrating religious diversity in which people of different faiths all said, "I believe in love." More generally, the entire spectacle was a call for multicultural tolerance. The event would have been unthinkable 50 years earlier at the first Super Bowl, but in the twenty-first-century United States, its multicultural themes were right at home.

Multiculturalism, *the recognition, valuing, and protection of the distinct cultures that make up a society,* has become increasingly relevant in a world of growing cultural diversity and cultural interaction within and among societies. Rather than assume that all people will adopt the ideas and practices of the dominant culture—a process known as *assimilation*—multicultural societies accept, accommodate, and even celebrate differences

©Uschools University Images/E+/Getty Images

A multicultural society accommodates various cultural groups. One way such societies cope is by making voting materials, health care information, signs in public places, and other important information available in the languages spoken in the local community.

thinking about culture

Which policies does your college have that promote multiculturalism? In Chapter 10, we explore how **culture** helps us understand how various racial and ethnic groups have interacted in the United States throughout its history.

©Ezra Shaw/Getty Images

The Super Bowl is a cultural phenomenon that has as much to do with the extravaganza as it does with football. Major corporations unveil new advertising campaigns during the broadcast, international pop stars perform in choreographed halftime shows, and the U.S. Air Force stages a high-profile flyover just before kick-off each year. Watching the Super Bowl has become an annual ritual for millions of Americans—even those who don't necessarily like football very much.

CORE CONCEPTS CHALLENGE *Put yourself in the shoes of someone from a different* **culture** *who watches a football game in the United States for the first time. What would that person make of the game? Might it seem violent, for example? Now, think of how you might react if you were to watch a game you are unfamiliar with, like cricket, a wildly popular sport in much of the rest of the world.*

in language, religion, customs, dress, traditions, and beliefs. Institutions that acknowledge and accommodate different cultures, such as certain businesses and universities, can also be considered multicultural. As the Sociology Works box illustrates, understanding cultural diversity is crucial in today's business world.

Because they live in a multicultural society, many people in the United States are exposed regularly to a number of different cultures. Restaurants, fairs, and festivals celebrate the food, dress, music, and dances of various cultures. More significantly, in communities that are home to a variety of cultural groups, you are also likely to find institutions associated with these groups, such as temples, mosques, churches, and other places of worship. Businesses such as sari shops and halal butchers sell products not available in mainstream dress shops and grocery stores. In addition, today's major cities are home to people who speak dozens of different languages—and their school systems must cope with this linguistic diversity.

Because of the nature of a multicultural society, a significant number of people within it grow up and live their lives defined by more than one culture. If a student speaks English at school but a different language at home, that bilingual capability is a sure sign that he or she lives in two different cultures at the same time. In countries around the world, some immigrant families straddle the society and culture of their birth and those of their new home (Dimitrova, Bender, and van de Vijver 2014). Some travel back and forth to their countries of origin; others send money to aid relatives there. Some are even involved in the political affairs of their native countries (Boruchoff 2013; Levitt 2004). Television and the internet help people stay in touch with the news and entertainment culture of their native countries, even while they live in their newly adopted homes. For example,

SOCIOLOGY WORKS

Dean Foster and the Business of Cultural Diversity

As an undergraduate, Dean Foster didn't have a clue what he would do with sociology, but he thought the subject was fascinating. He found especially appealing the basic premise that "we can understand how we work as cultural and social beings and use this understanding to improve our collective lives." When he looks back today and considers the benefits he gained from sociology, his list is extensive: "my professional career, cross-cultural friendships, life goals, and purpose."

Foster is the founder and president of DFA (Dean Foster Associates) Intercultural Global Solutions. DFA helps organizations and businesses working with other cultures around the globe develop intercultural competencies. Foster spends much of his time traveling to present intercultural seminars, give speeches, and conduct interviews around the world. Describing his work as the "perfect job," Foster notes that "I meet wonderful people from places I only could have dreamed I would visit and work in as a child. I help deal with important cross-cultural challenges in ways that I like to believe change people's lives."

"I work with cross-cultural challenges in ways that I like to believe change people's lives."

When working internationally, businesses must anticipate and address some common differences among cultures. For example, different cultures have various ideas about time. Some value punctuality; in Germany, Austria, and Switzerland being late is considered a sign of disrespect and incompetence. In the countries of Latin America, by contrast, there is more latitude when it comes to meeting times and deadlines.

In addition, norms governing appropriate relationships between employers and their employees can vary a great deal from one culture to another. In some countries, employees are expected to be deferential to their bosses, avoiding eye contact with them and obeying instructions without comment. In other countries, employees are expected to be candid with, although still respectful of, their bosses, giving their input on the task at hand. In all these cases, global businesses must understand the cultural norms within a given society—and convey that understanding to their employees—if they are to communicate and work successfully in international settings.

Courtesy of Dean Foster
Dean Foster

A cottage industry of diversity training specialists such as Dean Foster—often with backgrounds in sociology, anthropology, and psychology—has emerged in response to businesses' need for cultural awareness in today's global economy. Foster notes, however, that when he was a student, "there was no such field as intercultural training, so there were no internships, mentors, or courses of study." By the mid-1980s, though, he had used his sociological knowledge to start one of the first intercultural training consultancies.

Foster says his work forces him "to constantly expect that which cannot be imagined, a testament to the power of culture, and the limits it places on us as cultural beings. I find this is the same kind of challenge that sociology places on us when we try to imagine how is it that we are who we are and behave as we behave. I deal with this question professionally every day."

think about it

1. *What do international businesspeople who come to the United States need to know about culturally specific work routines that people in this country are likely to take for granted?*
2. *In your travels, have you experienced uncertainty about basic cultural norms? If so, what happened? What did you learn as a result?*

the satellite service Dish Network offers a variety of packages with channels based on countries and regions such as Africa, China, South Asia, and Israel, and programming in languages such as French, German, Spanish, Italian, Polish, Portuguese, Russian, Japanese, Filipino, Korean, Farsi, Arabic, and Urdu.

People who live in a multicultural society have an extraordinary opportunity to learn about and appreciate the rich diversity of human cultures. Diversity also brings with it challenges and problems, however, as people with different ways of life attempt to coexist. Unfortunately, cultural difference often leads to inequality and conflict as groups with more power oppress, exploit, or otherwise discriminate against those who are different and who have less power. The long, ugly history of religious conflict, ethnic clashes, racist violence, and warfare between nations is one result of this tendency. Therefore, to understand culture more fully, we must inevitably study conflict, relations of power (a topic explored in Chapter 5), and the domination of some groups by others.

Culture: Consensus and Conflict People from the same culture may share the same language, religion, worldview, history, and traditions. When this happens, cultures nurture and promote consensus, cohesiveness, and solidarity through a shared collective identity. However, just as the common bond of culture creates a sense of "us," it can also create a sense of "them"–those outside the culture who are different in some way. Perhaps the outsiders speak a different language, practice a different religion, dress differently, or are from a different social class. Whatever the distinction, as those who share a culture increase the sense that they have a common bond, they tend to marginalize, belittle, or even demonize "outsiders" who have a different culture.

Cultural conflict is most likely to emerge when values and beliefs differ among different cultures. Contrasting beliefs about religion and clashes over core values have been the source of or justification for many conflicts over the centuries. Unlike questions that can be answered with scientific evidence, disputes about values and beliefs cannot be resolved by appeals to reason. The cultural conflicts that result from these disputes can be intense and ongoing.

One source of cultural conflict is **ethnocentrism,** *the judging of other cultures by the standards of one's own on the assumption that one's own is superior.* Ethnocentrism can have harsh and even violent consequences if members of one culture act upon a conviction that their ideas, values, and way of life are superior to those of another culture. An ethnocentric worldview can be the source of **xenophobia,** *the unreasonable fear or hatred of foreigners or people from other cultures,* which, at its extreme, can result in *genocide*–the deliberate and systematic destruction of a cultural, racial, or political group.

Much of the history of colonialism, in which one country conquers or dominates others, is the story of ethnocentrism in action. The Europeans who conquered much of the world from the sixteenth century into the twentieth were confident that their way of life was superior to that of the people whose lands they colonized. They often sought to "civilize" the native peoples, teaching them their language, and converting them to Christianity. As the native peoples resisted to protect their way of life, the result was centuries of conflict.

SPOTLIGHT on social theory

According to **conflict theorists,** more powerful groups within society dominate less powerful ones. Can you think of an example of a powerful group's demonizing or belittling a less powerful group's culture? Why would the powerful group find it advantageous to do so?

In contrast to ethnocentrism, **cultural relativism** is *the practice of understanding a culture by its own standards.* Cultural relativism does not require adopting or agreeing with the ideas and practices of another culture, but rather making the effort to understand the culture on its own terms and with a willingness to acknowledge it as a viable alternative to one's own. In other words, to practice cultural relativism we need to *understand* a culture, not *judge* it, as, for example, when we seek to learn about religious rituals or family traditions in a different culture.

Studying cultures other than their own (an especially important task in this era of globalization) often requires sociologists to practice cultural relativism so that they can focus their attention on a group's unique values, beliefs, and practices. Such cross-cultural understanding is difficult to achieve; it is hard for any of us to operate outside of the logic of our own culture. At the same time, once we are able to recognize our own values and beliefs–key dimensions of our own culture–we have taken an important first step toward understanding the experiences of people who live in very different societies.

The Critics of Multiculturalism

Less than two weeks after the attacks on the World Trade Center and the Pentagon on September 11, 2001, President George W. Bush framed the assault in cultural terms by telling Congress and the

©Tom Kidd/Alamy Stock Photo

©Fareed Khan/AP Images

The infamously xenophobic Ku Klux Klan, which had several million members during its heyday in the 1920s, appropriated Christian symbolism to promote a white supremacist agenda that asserted the superiority of white Protestants and attacked the supposedly alien influence of blacks and most immigrants, including non-Protestant whites. Today, some Muslim extremists similarly invoke religious symbolism in calling for attacks against perceived threats from the alien cultural influence of nonbelievers. Just as most Christians rejected the Klan, most Muslims reject these extremist views.

people of the United States that the members of Al-Qaeda, the Islamic fundamentalist group that had claimed responsibility, had attacked because "they hate our freedoms: our freedom of religion, our freedom of speech, our freedom to vote and assemble and disagree with each other" (Bush 2001). That quotation came to symbolize one way of thinking about the ongoing conflict between Western secular societies and Islamic societies. It suggested the conflict was based on fundamentally incompatible cultures. President Donald Trump appeared to follow this approach, making numerous statements widely seen as anti-Muslim, re-tweeting a fake anti-Muslim propaganda video, and pursuing a travel ban on visitors from several Muslim-majority countries (Baker and Sullivannov 2017).

One of the best-known discussions of this concept of a "culture clash" came from political scientist Samuel Huntington (1993, 1998), who argued that after the end of the Cold War between the United States and the Soviet Union, most new global conflicts would now take place between cultures rather than countries. He went on to describe what he saw as eight basic cultures (which he termed "civilizations") in the world: Western (United States, Australia, and Western Europe), Eastern Orthodox (Russia), Latin American, Islamic, Japanese, Chinese, Hindu (India), and African. These civilizations, he contended, are based on fundamentally different religious and other cultural beliefs. The Islamic world, for example, has few democratic institutions because it does not have a cultural history of separating religious and secular authority, of valuing social pluralism, and of protecting individual rights and civil liberties from the power of the state. In this way, it differs fundamentally from Western civilization. Huntington maintained that as long as globalization results in more frequent contacts between people living in these civilizations, we are doomed to experience more frequent cultural conflict.

There is no doubt that increased contact between vastly different cultures can result in conflict. However, if we analyze Huntington's thesis from a sociological perspective, we can quickly expose some of its shortcomings. For one thing, it oversimplifies the complex mix of cultures around the world and glosses over the enormous variation *within* each of these cultures (Arnason 2001). None of the so-called civilizations Huntington identifies has a single unified culture. As globalization advances and more people, products, and ideas flow across national borders, cultures continue to blend. Also, by focusing exclusively on culture, Huntington's theory ignores the ways that longstanding inequalities in the distribution of privilege and power have helped fuel global conflict (Evans 1997).

In addition, many different cultures *do* share common values. President Bush recognized these shared values when he told a graduating class at West Point, "The peoples of the Islamic nations want and deserve the same freedoms and opportunities as people in every nation." His earlier quotation about hating our freedoms targeted the Al-Qaeda extremists who attacked the United States. However, violent Islamic extremists do not represent the broader Islamic culture, which encompasses a range of beliefs and values. Indeed, intense debates within Muslim societies regarding democracy, the role of women, and other cultural matters take place every day.

The results of global public opinion surveys show that democracy is widely popular in both Western and Islamic cultures. However, those same surveys show significant differences in the degree of support for gender equality, social tolerance, and freedom of speech (Inglehart and Norris 2003; Pew Research Center 2013e; Welzel and Inglehart 2010), indicating that the reality is complicated, not just a matter of a simple clash of civilizations or an idealized belief that all societies share a unified set of cultural values.

As we have seen, different cultures within a society can also encounter the problem of incompatible values or beliefs. Feminist political philosopher Susan Okin (1999, 117) argued that "many cultures oppress some of their members, in particular women, and . . . they are often able to socialize these oppressed members so that they accept, without question, their designated cultural status." For example, clitoridectomy (the removal of the clitoris) and other forms of genital cutting and the prearranged marriage of children are accepted practices within some cultures. What, if anything, should be done when people from such cultures move to Western societies, where those practices are considered violations of individual rights? Should their adoptive countries accept these practices out of respect for different cultural traditions? Or should Western notions of individual freedom, human rights, and gender equality trump these traditional customs? Such questions are often debated in Europe where, for example, countries have considered policies that prohibit Muslim women from wearing face-covering veils in public places. France and Belgium imposed such bans nationally; other countries allow local jurisdictions to do so, although sometimes only in certain settings such as schools. The reasons given for these bans include concerns that veils undermine gender equality, clash with secular values, and—in the case of full-body burkas—may even be used to hide weapons or explosives for terrorist acts (BBC 2014). This issue raises complex questions about incompatible cultural values and practices and challenges us to consider whether it is legitimate to condemn cultural practices we find offensive and whether we can articulate a universal standard of human rights.

Some U.S. critics of multiculturalism are not concerned with such questions because they reject its value entirely. Instead of encouraging people from diverse cultural traditions to coexist peacefully, these critics argue that new immigrants must assimilate into the dominant culture of their adoptive country; otherwise, they maintain, the common ground that is essential to unite a nation will be lost (Huntington 2005; Schmidt 1997). Some of these critics call for teaching Christian values in schools, the adoption of "English-only" laws, an end to bilingual education, and strict limits on immigration, among other measures, to shore up the dominant culture. Anti-Muslim sentiments are sometimes expressed as fear that "sharia law" will be imposed in the United States. In fact, sharia is a set of guiding principles

on social theory

Emile Durkheim, whose work was influential for the proponents of **functionalism,** focused on social solidarity—on how cultural values serve to unite people. How do you see this process working today in multicultural societies like that of the United States?

based on Muslim teachings—not laws—and its incorporation into the U.S. legal code is a far-fetched proposition, but it still fuels considerable anxiety. Several states have even enacted "foreign law" legislation banning sharia from being used in U.S. courts (Quraishi-Landes 2016). As we will explore in Chapter 10, these arguments are similar to those made a century ago when new Irish, Russian, Italian, Polish, and other European immigrants arrived in the United States in great numbers. Back then these ethnic cultures were seen as a threat to American values.

Societies need common ground—supplied by their cultures—to function successfully, and sociologists since Emile Durkheim have recognized this need. Nevertheless, cultures are also evolving constantly. Think about how global travel, electronic communications, the global economy, and widespread immigration have changed contemporary society. Already contemporary U.S. society has found many ways to accommodate the peaceful coexistence of diverse cultural traditions.

In fact, culture can also be a basis for connection and exchange in ways that help prevent, or even heal, conflicts. Cross-cultural experiences—from reading the novels, studying the art, or learning about the cuisine of another culture to traveling to other countries, studying new languages, or hosting foreign visitors in your home or school—may provide a bridge that promotes greater understanding and improved relationships across national boundaries. Despite the recent backlash, the historical trend has been in the direction of increased tolerance, accommodation, and appreciation among different cultures.

©Saul Loeb/AFP/Getty Images

In one example of cultural misunderstanding, *jihad* has widely come to be associated with violent conflict as a result of extremist actions. However, *jihad* means "struggling in the way of God" and typically implies working for things such as goodness, justice, compassion, and self-improvement. One attempt to educate the public about this misperception was a "My Jihad" media campaign, highlighting the more common meaning of the term as a way to take back Islam "from Muslim and anti-Muslim extremists alike" (myjihad.org).

Cultural Activism

Many people are understandably passionate about cultural issues, which often reflect their deepest concerns. As a result, people from across the political spectrum participate in a wide range of public activities aimed at promoting or contesting culturally specific ideas and practices. In this section, we briefly review three contemporary forms of cultural activism: organizations that promote cultural pride, religious fundamentalism, and anticorporate activism.

Cultural Pride Organizations In communities throughout the United States, a variety of civic organizations maintain and promote particular cultures. They provide children with classes about their cultural heritage and sponsor festivals and other events celebrating their traditions. Because New York City is so ethnically diverse, activities celebrating cultural pride take place throughout the city all year long, including the St. Patrick's Day Parade in March, celebrating the experiences of the Irish and Irish Americans; the Puerto Rican Day Parade in June; the West Indian Carnival in September, which celebrates Caribbean cultures and histories; and the Chinese New Year Parade in January or February. The idea of embracing and celebrating one's cultural heritage has become firmly embedded in U.S. society as well as in many other countries.

Religious Fundamentalism A worldwide resurgence of religious belief among fundamentalists, who believe in the literal interpretation of sacred texts such as the Bible and the Qur'an, represents another form of cultural activism. Whether at home or abroad, religious fundamentalists are using their faith as the basis for their activism. They criticize the cultural values and practices of Western secular society and develop ways to preserve and promote their own cultural values.

Islamic fundamentalists have challenged the export of Western culture to traditionally Muslim societies. They condemn what they perceive as the hedonism and decadent lifestyles promoted in such cultural products, themes that they say contradict Islamic teachings. They are especially angered by what they see as anti-Islamic media content. Pakistan, for example, ordered internet providers to block Facebook in 2010 because one of its pages promoted "Everybody Draw Mohammed Day"—an action that violates Islamic beliefs. The ban was lifted once the page was removed. Islamic fundamentalists have turned to strict religious schooling and mass media, especially the internet, to promote traditional values and defend them against the onslaught of Western media.

Similarly, in the United States, Christian fundamentalists have fought—unsuccessfully—to eliminate from the mainstream media sexual imagery, violence, positive portrayals of homosexuality, and other content they find objectionable and contrary to their religious teachings. At the same time, these activists promote their religious beliefs through homeschooling, religiously based private schools, religious radio and television broadcasting, and religious books, movies, pop music, and other media content. These efforts have had a significant impact on the political culture of the United States, where religious conservatives have been a significant political and cultural force. After his organization, the Faith and Freedom Coalition, hosted a forum for Republican candidates in the 2016 presidential election,

©Nicholas Kamm/AFP/Getty Images

In the past several decades, Christian conservatives played a significant role in U.S. politics, often applying their interpretation of biblical teaching to contemporary social issues, such as abortion, and insisting that the United States should be considered a Christian nation. What are some of the potentially positive and negative consequences of intermingling religious faith with political activity?

activist Timothy Head claimed, "The conservative Christian vote still remains the largest political constituency in all of American politics" (Jackson 2015).

Anticorporate Activism The role corporations play in shaping culture is a source of contention in many countries. Critics of corporate power in the United States and elsewhere, especially on the political left, engage in yet another form of cultural activism, protesting concentrated media ownership and an unregulated global economy. In the United States, anticorporate cultural activists have established small but vibrant independent media outlets for music, art, news, and other cultural products outside of the mainstream commercial corporate system. Groups such as the Media Foundation, with its signature magazine *Adbusters,* promote a form of activism called "culture jamming," which refashions popular brand images to express a critical message about commercial culture, as in the example shown (DeLaure, Fink, and Dery 2017). One group (add-art.org) has taken this battle online with software that replaces ads with artwork.

Whether they are motivated by pride in a culture, by religious belief, or by opposition to corporate power, campaigns by cultural activists often lead to passionate public expression and debate. Although many of the issues taken on by cultural activists receive scant attention in mainstream public policy arenas, this form of activism often produces broad public discussion, testifying to the significance of culture in our everyday lives.

Courtesy of Adbusters Media Foundation, adbusters.org

Culture jamming is a form of activism that attaches new and subversive meanings to well-known corporate brands, often rewriting popular advertising campaigns. This example was produced by Adbusters. Complete with the Nike swoosh, it associates the Nike brand with slave labor—a powerful critique of Nike's labor practices.

A Changing World

CULTURE AND GLOBALIZATION

About 200 million people live in Africa's most populous country, Nigeria, where the largest ethnic groups are the Hausa and Fulani, Yoruba, Igbo, and Ijaw. But in the country's most successful movies, those cultures have been invisible. Indeed, in 2013, the biggest box office hit of the year was the Hollywood film *White House Down*. The previous year, it had been the James Bond film *Skyfall*. Year after year, imported Western–usually U.S.–films have dominated the Nigerian box office. Television, too, is full of Western programs, because importing these shows is cheaper than making TV programs at home.

Much of the rest of the world has been experiencing a similar media-driven globalization of culture (Crothers 2009). One analysis found that U.S. films made up 6 of the top 10 movies of 2012 and 2013 across 51 countries. But this measure varies significantly by region. Up to 8 of the top 10 films in Latin America were from the United States, but in India and South Korea less than half were (UNESCO 2015,129). As in Nigeria, media globalization has primarily meant a massive export of Western television, film, music, and other cultural products to poorer nations that lack the resources or technological infrastructure to support a large media industry of their own. While often popular, these Western products also generate resentment as a kind of foreign invasion that is displacing local cultural practices and challenging traditional values and lifeways. As David Makali, then-director of the Media Institute in Nairobi, put it, "In Kenya, TV has become a major avenue of cultural promotion, and it is really terrible the way Western culture has taken over. The people are being brainwashed, and we are losing out culturally" (Miranda 2003).

The flood of U.S. media inundating foreign markets may have crested, however (Akpabio and Mustapha-Lambe 2008; Flew 2007; UNESCO 2015). India and China, especially, have played an increasingly significant role in exporting cultural products. As new technologies have reduced the cost of media production, local media industries have begun competing for local audiences, though their products are almost never seen in Western cinemas or television. Locally produced programs, finely attuned to local cultures–and now distributed through new digital media platforms–are very popular, offering viewers alternatives to homogenized global content.

In Nigeria, the film industry has exploded, coming to be known as Nollywood. Nigeria is now the world's second-largest movie producer, just behind India and just ahead of the United States. Such projects, often produced on a shoestring budget, are unable to match the slick production values of expensive Western fare, but they are finding an audience. The country's few cinemas are dominated by Western films, so local movies are often shown informally in home theaters and community spaces. In 2011, iROKOtv.com–sometimes referred to as the "Netflix of Africa"–launched, offering a wide variety of African-made films on-demand for home viewing. The project suggests the potential appeal of African films elsewhere: the largest numbers of subscribers come from the United States, the United Kingdom, the Caribbean, and Australia.

©Peter Alexander/Alamy Stock Photo

The opportunities for communication among cultures are greater than ever before. In 2016, Nollywood even had an international hit with the romantic comedy *The Wedding Party*, sparking a 2018 sequel. However, because of the imbalance between wealthy and poor parts of the globe, affluent countries have been doing most of the talking, overwhelming the cultures of other parts of the world. Armed with today's technologies, though, artists in poor countries can feasibly begin to make themselves heard.

©Pius Utomi Ekpei/AFP/Getty Images

The on-demand internet streaming service iROKOtv.com is the "Netflix of Africa," highlighting the work of Nigerian filmmakers and offering viewers around the world an alternative to typical Western fare.

thinking sociologically about
Culture

- Culture must be learned and can be thought of as all aspects of society that are transmitted socially rather than biologically. Culture consists of both nonmaterial and material elements: values, beliefs, knowledge, and norms; symbols and language; behavior and objects.
- Our own culture can be so familiar to us that we often fail to recognize its various elements or even why it matters. A sociological approach illuminates the often-hidden ways that culture helps define our identities and our relationship to our broader communities.
- Sociologists have long paid attention to the assumptions built into any culture, arguing that what we take for granted is one of the keys to recognizing how culture and power are intertwined.
- Culture is highly diverse, varying across time and among different societies as well as within a single society. Humans meet their basic needs by adopting a variety of culture-specific behaviors.
- Most societies contain a dominant culture, as well as a number of subcultures. These subcultures—including countercultures—often introduce innovation and change to mainstream culture.
- Living in a multicultural society gives us an opportunity to learn about and appreciate the rich diversity of human cultures. But diversity also brings challenges and problems; cultural differences are often the basis for inequality and conflict.

REVIEW, REFLECT, AND APPLY

Looking Back

1. Culture is an essential part of social life. It must be taught and learned and exists only in the context of groups.
2. The elements of culture include values, beliefs, knowledge, and norms (the ideas of culture); language and other forms of symbolic communication (for transmitting culture); and behaviors and material objects.
3. Within each culture, there is a dominant ideology that generally supports the current social system and serves the interests of those in authority.
4. Most societies contain a dominant culture as well as a number of subcultures and countercultures.
5. Multiculturalism refers to the willingness to recognize, value, and protect the distinct cultures that make up a society.
6. Ethnocentrism is the practice of judging another culture by the standards of one's own. In contrast, cultural relativism is the practice of understanding a culture by its own standards.
7. Examples of cultural activism include cultural pride organizations, religious fundamentalism, and anticorporate activism.
8. Media globalization has primarily taken the form of the massive export of Western—primarily U.S.—media products to poorer nations. The flood of U.S. media may have crested, however, as local media industries have begun to take advantage of new digital technologies to compete for local audiences.

Critical Thinking: Questions and Activities

1. Why is "culture" a core concept in sociology? How can the concept of culture help us understand social life?
2. Why do changes in today's world make it especially important to understand the concept of culture?
3. Imagine that, because of your sociological training, you have been chosen to select the items to be included in a time capsule for your community that will be opened 100 years from now. Assuming the time capsule is about the size of a large suitcase, what cultural artifacts would you choose to represent your "way of life"? Explain why you believe these items are the most important.
4. Suppose you live in a foreign country and know little about the United States. Watch an hour of prime-time television and take careful notes about what you have learned about U.S. society. Were the media images you saw an accurate representation of U.S. society? Why or why not? What lessons about the United States might the export of such cultural products be teaching people in other societies?

Key Terms

behaviors (p. 61) the actions associated with a group that help reproduce a distinct way of life.

beliefs (p. 55) the specific convictions or opinions that people generally accept as being true.

counterculture (p. 64) a subculture that champions values and lifestyles distinctly opposed to those of the dominant culture.

cultural lag (p. 57) the ways that new technological developments often outpace the norms that govern our collective experiences with these new technologies.

cultural object (p. 61) a physical item that is created by and associated with people who share a culture.

cultural relativism (p. 69) the practice of understanding a culture by its own standards.

culture (p. 52) the collection of values, beliefs, knowledge, norms, language, behaviors, and material objects shared by a people and socially transmitted from generation to generation.

culture shock (p. 56) the experience of being disoriented because of a lack of knowledge about an unfamiliar social situation.

culture war (p. 55) an intense disagreement about core values and moral positions.

dialect (p. 59) a variant of a language with its own distinctive accent, vocabulary, and in some cases grammatical characteristics.

dominant culture (p. 63) a culture that permeates a society and that represents the ideas and practices of those in positions of power.

dominant ideology (p. 62) a widely held and regularly reinforced set of assumptions that generally support the current social system and serve the interests of authorities.

ethnocentrism (p. 69) the judging of other cultures by the standards of one's own on the assumption that one's own is superior.

folkways (p. 58) group habits or customs that are common in a given culture.

high culture (p. 65) cultural forms associated with—and especially valued by—elites.

ideal culture (p. 61) what the members of a culture report to be their values, beliefs, and norms.

ideology (p. 62) a system of meaning that helps define and explain the world and that makes value judgments about that world.

knowledge (cultural) (p. 56) the range of information, awareness, and understanding that helps us navigate our world.

language (p. 59) an elaborate system of symbols that allows people to communicate with one another in complex ways.

material culture (p. 52) the physical objects produced by people in a particular culture, including tools, clothing, toys, works of art, and housing.

mores (p. 58) norms that are strictly enforced, with potentially severe penalties for violating them.

multiculturalism (p. 66) the recognition, valuing, and protection of the distinct cultures that make up a society.

nonmaterial culture (p. 52) the ideas of a culture, including values and beliefs, accumulated knowledge about how to understand and navigate the world, and standards or "norms" about appropriate behavior.

norms (p. 56) a culture's rules and expectations for "appropriate" behavior.

popular culture (p. 65) cultural forms that are widespread and commonly embraced within a society.

real culture (p. 61) what members of a culture actually do, which may or may not reflect the ideal.

Sapir-Whorf hypothesis (p. 59) the idea that because of their different cultural content and structure, languages affect how their speakers think and behave.

society (p. 52) a group of people who live together in a specific territory and share a culture.

subculture (p. 63) a culture associated with a smaller group in society that has distinct norms, values, and lifestyles setting it apart from the dominant culture.

symbol (p. 58) anything—a sound, a gesture, an image, an object—that represents something else.

taboos (p. 58) norms with the most severe prohibition or restriction.

value (p. 53) a deeply held principle or standard that people use to make judgments about the world, especially in deciding what is desirable or worthwhile.

xenophobia (p. 69) an unreasonable fear or hatred of foreigners or people from other cultures.

©Imageplus/Corbis

4 Social Structure

looking AHEAD

How can learning about social structure help you see how it operates in your life?

How can your actions and those of others change social structure?

As you send a text message on your mobile phone or sign an online petition, how does your behavior illustrate the dynamic interplay between structure and action?

©Blend Images - Hill Street Studios/Getty Images

Nobody likes requirements. Students, for example, often experience academic program requirements as restrictive. With mandatory courses often needing to be completed in a particular sequence, students usually have limited choice and flexibility in their education. But the constraints imposed by an academic program's structure have their benefits: they can help students graduate successfully (Baker 2016, 2018).

Research suggests that clear structure in academic programs is particularly beneficial for community college students. The majority of students entering community college will leave without acquiring a degree or credential (Juszkiewicz 2016). The many reasons for this low rate of completion include inadequate academic preparation and insufficient finances. However, one significant factor appears to be the overwhelming number of choices available to students. To flexibly accommodate students with a range of different needs, community colleges often have many more program offerings than their four-year counterparts. Schools with abundant options and choices can be overwhelming for students to navigate successfully, especially students who are the first in their families to attend college and are consequently unfamiliar with the college process.

Students can be paralyzed by indecision as they face so many possible academic routes. In such cases, the absence of constraints can be debilitating. One review of existing research on the factors shaping student success concludes that community college "students will be more likely to succeed in programs that are tightly structured, with relatively little room for individuals to deviate on a whim—or even unintentionally—from paths toward completion" (Scott-Clayton 2015, 103). While this conclusion sounds confining and restrictive, the author asserts that the *lack* of such structure often makes finding the path to degree completion as difficult as "navigating a shapeless river on a dark night." Instead, evidence suggests that enhanced advising, assistance in managing confusing bureaucracies, and fewer curricular choices can help students succeed by balancing the desire for flexibility with the need for structure.

These insights into the effects of academic programs on student success illustrate the ways in which firm patterns of behavior both enable and constrain us. Such *recurring patterns of behavior,* as you'll recall from Chapter 1, are what sociologists refer to as **social structure.** Structure constrains social behavior by putting limits on it, much as course requirements limit what a student can take. But structure also enables social behavior by providing a context within which people can interact, much as college degree programs enable students to pursue an education and achieve a particular degree. Whatever the context, social structures influence our behavior by encouraging or discouraging certain conduct. But we ultimately have the capacity for **action** (or agency), *the ability to behave independent of social constraints.* We can decide to conform to structural expectations, deviate from them, or attempt to change them.

The concepts of structure and action can help us understand the dynamic relationship between well-established patterns of behavior and the human capacity to act in new and sometimes unexpected ways. The concept of structure allows us to analyze the patterns and regularities in social life. At the same time, we are not just pawns playing out predetermined roles within the context of social structure. Although social structure shapes our behavior, expectations, and beliefs, it does not fully determine them.

This chapter begins with a discussion of the important concept of social structure, including the various levels at which we can analyze it. We then turn to a discussion of action, focusing on the ways in which people act in different social contexts. Finally, we conclude the chapter by exploring the changing structure of friendship in the digital age.

Understanding Social Structure

We all know a great deal about the social structure of the various communities in which we live. As we discuss in Chapter 6, we acquire this knowledge as part of the process of socialization through which we learn our culture's basic norms, values, beliefs, and behaviors. For example, you knew what to do on the first day of class; you knew the basic rules and expectations—the patterns—of the classroom. If you think about it, you can probably begin to define the structure of your family, your friendship network, your workplace, or your school. What are the unspoken agreements about people's obligations and responsibilities, who regularly talks with whom, and how are decisions made? When you can identify these kinds of patterns, you are well on your way to understanding social structure.

Seeing Social Structure

Social structure is invisible—we cannot see it with the naked eye. But with a little knowledge of what to look for, we can map its contours at different levels of analysis. At the micro level, we might look at the structure of interaction between two people or within small groups. At the meso level, we might look at the structure of an organization such as a school or a business. At the macro level, we might focus on the structure of inequality between developing and industrialized nations. In all these cases, we have two interconnected goals: to describe underlying patterns and to make connections between these patterns and people's actions and beliefs. Thinking sociologically helps you see both how social structure shapes everyday life and how individual actions help shape social structure.

If we cannot touch it or see it, though, how can we be confident that social structure is real? For one thing, a vast amount of research shows that social life is made up of patterned, routine behaviors. These routines can change, but they tend to be enduring. These more or less predictable routines are the heart of what sociologists call **social institutions,** *the major arenas of social life in which durable routines and patterns of behavior take place.* Social institutions include government, schools, businesses, and organized religions, among others. We explore these social institutions in Chapters 12-17 of this book.

Thinking about what life would be like without it can help us "see" social structure. Daily life would be full of uncertainty: you would not know what to expect or how to meet your ordinary human needs for food, clothing, and shelter. When Hurricane Maria struck Puerto Rico in September 2017, the routine patterns of social life on the island were thrown into disarray. When the storm swept across the island, the high winds and heavy rain brought a trail of devastation; widespread flooding turned streets into rivers littered with the rubble of destroyed homes. The entire island lost electric power, and most residents were without clean water, food, or phone service.

Amidst the hurricane's physical devastation, the social structure of the island seemed to collapse temporarily. Thousands of people lost their homes and had to seek refuge in shelters or with family and friends. Businesses were destroyed and the island-wide blackout meant that most people had no work or income. All of the public schools on the island were closed, so schoolchildren had their studies disrupted. Hospitals, much in need during the crisis, had difficulty operating, so medical treatment was extremely limited. While initial reports indicated 64 deaths from the storm, researchers from George Washington University determined that 2,975 people died as a result of Hurricane Maria (Newkirk 2018), with poor hospital conditions and difficulty accessing medical treatment likely causes. Two months after the storm, half the island was still living in the dark, with no power. People experienced more than a loss of electricity and running water; they also lost phone service and felt completely cut off from the rest of the world, including worried family members on the U.S. mainland. The normal patterns of authority were disrupted because officials—including local authorities and the Federal Emergency Management Agency—did not have a clear plan for how to respond. Social norms were suspended: Was stealing food or batteries from a store allowable in an emergency? Was it all right to break into an empty house for shelter? Even normally mundane patterns of behavior, such as personal hygiene, had to be reinvented as residents struggled to find bathroom facilities, drinking water, and clean clothes.

Let's consider the typical daily routines in a classroom. What would school be like if students and teachers were required to start each class from scratch every day? When would you arrive and where would you sit? Who would speak and when would they speak? How would each person prepare for class, and who would lead it? Would there even be any school? Without set patterns of behavior, each day would involve new negotiations about what to do and how to behave, with little time left to accomplish much. Fortunately, most of our day-to-day interactions follow more or less patterned scripts. The total of all these patterns is what we mean by social structure. As the Sociology Works box shows, the ability to understand social structure can be of great practical value, sometimes in unexpected ways.

Creating and Changing Social Structure

We usually experience social structure as solid and unchanging: patterns of everyday life that seem permanent, natural, and inevitable. As *individuals* we cannot change these patterns—you couldn't simply decide that the correct dress code for a formal dinner is a bathing suit. But sociological insight shows that the patterns that make up social structure are *not* natural, unchanging, or inevitable. Instead, they are the result of human action,

thinking about structure

Can you see patterns associated with economic inequality, racial discrimination, and sexism when you encounter them? In Chapters 9, 10, and 11, we explore the **structure** of inequality in relation to class, race, and gender.

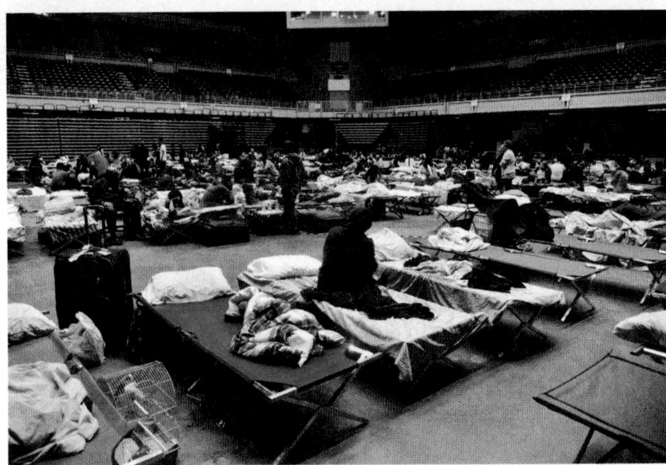

©Hector Retamal/AFP/Getty Images

When social structure is disrupted, we become keenly aware of its existence. In the aftermath of Hurricane Maria in September 2017, residents of Puerto Rico had to grapple with both the physical devastation and the absence of clear norms about how to manage even the most basic activities of social life. When the storm hit, people took refuge in places like the Roberto Clemente Coliseum in San Juan, where temporary residents had to establish norms that govern the routines of daily life.

and humans can therefore change them. People who came before us established these patterns, and by our actions and choices we can help reproduce—or potentially alter—them.

For example, by attending a conventional class as part of your daily routine, you help reproduce the current structure of the college classroom. However, when students and teachers experiment with different classroom structures—with, for example, students as co-teachers, small-group learning exercises, flipped classrooms, or interactive online classes—they are taking part in a process that might create new expectations and different patterns of behavior.

In addition, social structures vary over time and from one culture to another. In fact, one of the best ways to understand the structure of a society is to compare it to other societies or other time periods.

The social structure of child care, for example, differs radically among cultures. Take diapers. Virtually all parents in the United States diaper their newborn babies, changing their diapers several times a day until the children are toilet-trained, commonly between the ages of two and three. Whether they use cloth or disposable diapers, American parents expect babies to wear diapers and consider them to be a necessity. However, most babies in the world do not wear diapers—and they never have. Instead, babies and toddlers commonly go naked from the waist down or wear open-crotch split pants. The structure of parenting in societies where babies do not wear diapers is different from the structure of parenting in the United States. Meredith Small, who studies cross-cultural parenting practices, explains that children in diaperless societies are almost always physically connected to caregiving adults who can sense when their charges need to relieve themselves (King 2013).

To see how social structures vary over time within the same culture, consider gender expectations. The experiences of women and men in the United States in the early twenty-first century are far different from those of the mid-twentieth century. Opportunities for women were significantly more limited at that time than they are today. As recently as the early 1960s, most middle-class American women were expected to marry young, change their last names, have children, and focus their attention on their families and households. Men played a very limited role in childrearing but were expected to support the family. Bank accounts and home deeds were generally issued in the name of the male breadwinner. Child care centers and parental leave from work were virtually nonexistent. Women who did work outside the home were likely to face significant discrimination in the workplace.

Now fast-forward 50 years to the early twenty-first century. Expectations for both men and women have changed substantially. Although many women work at home to care for children, most women in the United States now work outside the home, and men are likely to play an active role in raising children and doing domestic chores. Women who attend college are likely to share the career ambitions of their male classmates.

In short, the expected patterns of beliefs and behavior associated with gender in the United States—that is, the structure of gender—have changed significantly. What seemed natural and inevitable a generation or two ago now seems artificial and outdated, as we discuss further in Chapter 11.

This change occurred through the cumulative actions of many individuals—sometimes acting by themselves and sometimes acting collectively. Once again we see the dynamic relationship between structure and action: human action creates structure, but that structure then shapes subsequent action. Future action will reaffirm, modify, or radically change existing social structures. Understanding this interplay of structure and action is central to the sociological perspective.

Statuses and Roles: Connecting Everyday Life and Social Structure

Social structure is rooted in the everyday activity of individuals in a society. Sociologists use two key concepts—status and role—to help understand what links people to one another and to the patterns that constitute social structure. For sociologists, **status** refers to *a position in a social system that can be occupied by an individual.* We all occupy various statuses, or social positions. For example, you are a student, and you may also be a daughter or son, a classmate, an employee, a roommate, an athlete, or a musician.

A status can be either ascribed or achieved. **Ascribed statuses** are *those that are assigned to us from birth, regardless of our wishes or abilities.* **Achieved statuses** are *those that we attain voluntarily, to a considerable degree, as the result of our own efforts.* For example, in England at the end of the first decade of the twenty-first century, Prince Charles and his son William both occupied the *ascribed* status of member of the royal family and heir to the throne; in the United States, Barack Obama then held the *achieved* status of president. He also occupied the *ascribed* racial status of African American.

SOCIOLOGY WORKS

Brian Reed and the Hunt for Saddam Hussein

Stationed in Iraq from March 2003 to March 2004, where he served as operations officer in the 1st Brigade, 4th Infantry Division, sociologist Brian Reed found a number of ways to apply his sociological training. One of the most dramatic came in December 2003, when Reed used his knowledge of social structure to help plan the military operation that led to the capture of deposed Iraqi leader Saddam Hussein. Reed analyzed the structure of Hussein's social networks, building what he calls "link diagrams" to illustrate the ties among all the people in the network (Hougham 2005; Reed and Segal 2006). Link diagrams are, in essence, visual maps of social structure, emphasizing connections and communications among people. In this case, they led the U.S. military to individuals who ultimately helped them find the former dictator. Intelligence analysts used a similar social network approach in the search for Osama bin Laden. Identifying one of his primary couriers turned out to be the key to locating bin Laden's compound in Abbottabad, Pakistan.

Reed believes that the sociological imagination has valuable military applications, and he advocates training in sociology for all military officers. Social structure is a particularly important sociological concept for soldiers to understand. When American soldiers are stationed abroad, in unfamiliar situations, they have little knowledge of the traditions, assumptions, and daily routines of the local population. What these soldiers need, Reed points out, is training in the social structure of the societies where they are deployed so that they can better understand both allies and enemies.

> "Sociology applies to all facets of my profession. . . . Leadership, relationships, culture, diversity, and social networks are just a handful of relevant topics applicable to me as a professional soldier, and are all areas enhanced by my sociology training."

During the Vietnam War, the U.S. military had a very limited understanding of the routines and patterns—the social structure—of Vietnamese society. Hundreds of thousands of U.S. soldiers fought in Vietnam, but most lacked even a rudimentary understanding of Vietnamese language, culture, or history or of the patterns that structure everyday life in Vietnam. More recently, U.S. soldiers in Afghanistan and Iraq have struggled with a similar lack of familiarity with local society. For example, Reed described the challenges in establishing a joint operation by the U.S. military police and the Iraqi national police. Standard U.S. military procedures do not fit daily routines in Iraq, which include frequent calls to prayer and a generally slower pace of life. In these kinds of joint operations, the ability to understand local social structure, Reed has noted, becomes an essential skill.

Courtesy of Brian Reed
Brian Reed

Knowledge of social structure can also be useful in planning military strategy. During his time in Iraq, Reed used sociological tools to understand the connections among various opposition forces and to determine the social structure of the Iraqi insurgency. In a congressional briefing after his return to the United States, Reed pointed out several ways in which sociological tools were helpful. For example, identifying the structure of insurgent forces gives military commanders practical information on the organization and tendencies of these groups. It also helps commanders make informed predictions about how these forces will respond on the battlefield.

think about it

1. *How might an understanding of social structure be useful in averting war or other types of conflict?*
2. *In what other contexts would the kind of link diagrams Reed describes be useful?*

In contrast, **roles** are *the sets of expected behaviors associated with particular statuses.* For example, the basic role of someone occupying the student status is to attend class, complete assignments, and show a certain measure of respect for teachers and other students. One reason you know what to do on the first day of class is that you are familiar with the student role. After all, by the time you enter college, you've had many years to learn it.

To see how structure shapes your behavior and sense of self, think about how easily you adopt specific roles in different social situations. Figure 4.1 illustrates a few common statuses and the groups and social institutions associated with them. Your status as student and the role you are expected to play in this position connect you to the social institution of schools and education. You occupy a variety of statuses in relation to your family—sibling, son or daughter, perhaps parent—and perform a variety of associated roles. As you perform these and other roles, they embed you within social institutions and social structures. The statuses you occupy and the roles you play are your concrete connections to society.

FIGURE 4.1 | STATUSES AND INSTITUTIONS

©Photodisc/Getty Images

People occupy various statuses that connect them to social groups and larger institutions. What statuses do you occupy, and to what groups or institutions do they connect you?

Roles shape your life by clarifying what is expected of you in different contexts. Members of a social group share similar expectations about each member's role so that as individuals interact, their roles are reinforced. To varying degrees, you internalize the components of your roles. Indeed, some roles become so comfortable that you hardly perceive the ways in which they constrain your actions. In fact, roles become part of your sense of self. You would say, "I am a student," not "I play the role of a student."

When you adopt a new role, however, you can be acutely aware of the pressures it places on you. Think about how it feels to start a job, for example. During the first few days, the expectations associated with your newly occupied status are likely to be unclear or even confusing. Eventually, though, by following instructions, watching other employees, and getting feedback on your own efforts, you learn your role.

The concept of a role explains how an individual's behavior conforms to a general pattern yet is capable of change as a result of social forces. The behaviors associated with a role are not rigid. The student role, for example, permits a range of behavior. You can probably miss a class once in a while. You might be less attentive in class some days and more obviously engaged on other days. Some students ask a lot of questions whereas others tend to remain silent in class. However, there are limits. If you violate basic norms of the student role by, say, neglecting to do assigned readings or not studying before an exam, you will eventually be unable to perform your role adequately. And if you turn in a plagiarized paper or fail to attend class at all, your behavior may temporarily or even permanently remove you from student status.

Roles change over time, as we saw earlier in the case of gender roles. The parent role has also changed significantly during the past 50 years. If you have grandparents or neighbors in their seventies or eighties, they can tell you what it was like to be parents in the 1960s and 1970s, when many mothers did not work outside the home. As the number of single-parent households and two-career families has increased, parents have adapted to the changing structure of work. Many working parents now outsource much of the day-to-day caretaking of small children, either in child care centers, with relatives, or with in-home caregivers. In middle-class families, children's time is often scheduled so heavily that parents find it is part of their role to shuttle their children from one activity to the next. As a result of these changes, the definition of what it means to be a "good parent" and what children, employers, and schools expect from parents has begun to change, as well (Nelson 2010; Pew Research Center 2015e).

Because they connect us to social institutions such as the family, school, and work on a micro level, statuses and roles are key to understanding the way people interact in groups and organizations, and we explore them in more detail in Chapter 7. As the concepts of ascribed and achieved status suggest, however, statuses and roles are also involved in the way structure intersects with power at the micro, meso, and macro levels to produce inequality (for example, compare the status of a corporate CEO to that of a migrant farmworker or the status of a sociology professor to that of a sociology student). For this reason, we visit these concepts again in Chapter 5, on power.

Structure is pervasive throughout social life at the micro, meso, and macro levels. Let's examine each level in turn.

Micro-Level Interaction: Finding Patterns

In Chapter 3 we defined *society* as a group of people who live together in a specific territory and share a culture. As the pioneering German sociologist Georg Simmel (1858–1918) explained, those people regularly interact with each other in ways that form patterns. These patterns of interaction endure over time, becoming so routine that they seem to take on their own existence independent of the individuals who create them. For Simmel (1964), these face-to-face, micro-level interactions are the building blocks that shape a society. Two methods sociologists use to examine micro-level social interactions are ethnomethodology and conversation analysis.

Ethnomethodology

Think of your daily routines. With whom do you interact after you wake up in the morning? How do you get to school or work and with whom do you interact on the way? With whom do you interact during your day and in what way? In the evening?

Sociologists analyze social structure at the micro level by focusing on the patterns and regularities that emerge from such routine daily activities. Some sociologists contend that we construct social structure on a regular basis, working with others collectively to make sense of the chaotic social world that confronts us every day (Garfinkel 1967). **Ethnomethodology,** *an approach that examines the methods people use to make sense of their daily activities, emphasizes the ways in which they collectively create social structure in their everyday activities.* Ethnomethodologists believe that social structure exists precisely because we are constantly creating it as we construct and reconstruct social order in our daily routines.

Harold Garfinkel (1917–2011) and his colleagues sought to reveal these micro-level social structures through **breaching experiments,** *social situations in which the individuals involved intentionally break social rules, violating basic norms and patterns of behavior.* By breaking rules to which we generally don't pay much attention until they are violated, breaching experiments provide creative and often humorous illustrations of micro-level social structure. For example, Garfinkel once had his students act like visitors rather than family members when they returned to their parents' homes during a school vacation. The students quickly identified underlying patterns of behavior between parents and children as their parents reacted to their children's strange—and surprisingly polite—behavior. In another study, Garfinkel had researchers at a grocery store take items out of other people's shopping carts. When puzzled shoppers confronted them, the researchers responded that it was more convenient simply to take items from another shopper's cart than to search the crowded store shelves. Shoppers were surprised by and sometimes angry at this behavior—expecting an apology as well as an explanation for it—revealing a widespread understanding that items "belong" to a shopper once they've been placed in a cart, even though the shopper has not yet purchased them.

SPOTLIGHT

on social theory

Ethnomethodology emphasizes the daily activity through which we construct and reconstruct social structure. Can you identify some of the patterns of behavior that you simply follow without thinking about them? If so, how might you reveal those patterns?

As these examples show, by violating everyday social norms, breaching experiments expose the unstated social rules that structure countless aspects of social life but that are often visible only when they are broken.

Conversation Analysis

Another micro-level approach to social structure focuses on the ways we talk to one another—the structure of talk. **Conversation analysis** is *a method of analyzing the patterns in face-to-face conversation that produce the smooth, back-and-forth turn-taking of such exchanges.* All talk is organized and ordered—from informal conversations among friends to formal types of communication, such as a consultation between a doctor and a patient. In other words, conversation has an underlying structure. Even if you are not consciously aware of how talk is organized, you probably adhere to a set of widely shared assumptions about the give-and-take of conversation—assumptions that may differ from one social setting to another.

For example, think about conversations you may have had recently with a family member, one of your professors, and a manager during a job interview. Each conversation no doubt had a different structure. You are so familiar with the structure of talk in different settings that you can quickly shift gears from freewheeling banter with friends to intimate conversation with a romantic partner to classroom discussion mode. You can do this because talk is not a random activity but is instead rooted in a set of patterns—a structure—that generally do not have to be articulated.

Sociologists use conversation analysis to examine the underlying structure of social interaction. For example, as you approach a classmate on campus, you might ask "How's it going?" Both of you know, however, that you are not asking for a substantive reply about how your classmate is feeling. Your question is more like a polite greeting. Were you to pause to give a

©Eric Raptosh Photography/Blend Images/Getty Images

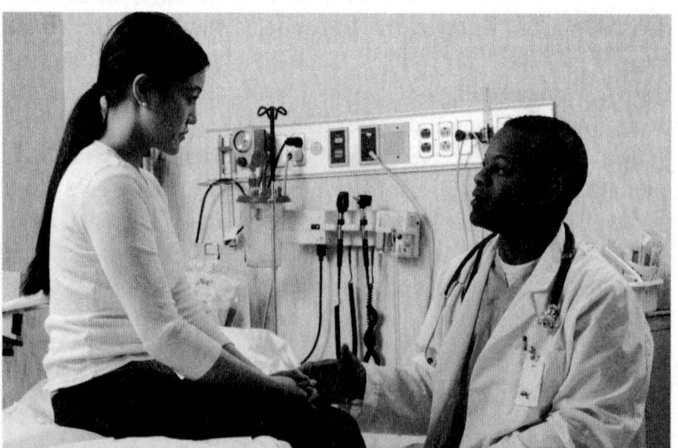

©Rubberball/age fotostock

Patterns of talk are not the same in different social settings. How is the structure of talk different when you are hanging out with your friends compared to when you are conversing with your doctor?

full and honest reply each time an acquaintance asked you, "How's it going?" you would be violating a basic expectation of casual conversation. Of course, in other social settings—at a funeral or in a hospital, for example—the same question becomes a sincere expression of concern, and the questioner expects a full reply. You can navigate these different situations because you and the people you are speaking with know the patterns and expectations of interaction in different social settings. Similarly, in an unfamiliar social setting you may be uncertain how to respond to prolonged silence. Your anxiety—and perhaps your discomfort with such silence—likely results from your lack of familiarity with conversational norms in a different cultural context (Clift 2016; Heritage and Stivers 2013).

In an interesting use of conversation analysis, sociologists Steven Clayman and John Heritage (2002; see also Clayman 2013) showed that news interviews share a similar structure, even though each program has a different host, guests, audience, and set of topics. No matter what the host and guest talk about, the basic routines and patterns are similar. For example, news interviews follow a specific turn-taking process that is different from everyday conversation. The interviewer asks questions, and the guest is expected to respond to those specific questions. In addition, news interviews are produced for what Clayman and Heritage call "an overhearing audience," and the interview is conducted by a host who maintains a neutral position. The structure of the news interview constrains the behavior of both interviewer and interviewee and shapes the expectations of their audience.

Several years ago, however, Jon Stewart of Comedy Central's *The Daily Show* violated these norms. After being introduced, Stewart turned the tables on Tucker Carlson and Paul Begala, the hosts of the CNN interview show *Crossfire,* when he started asking *them* questions about their program, something guests on a news program rarely do:

> STEWART: Thank you very much. That was very kind of you to say. Can I say something very quickly? Why do we have to fight?
>
> . . .
>
> STEWART: Why do you argue, the two of you?
>
> (Laughter)
>
> STEWART: I hate to see it.
>
> CARLSON: We enjoy it.
>
> STEWART: Let me ask you a question.
>
> CARLSON: Well, let me ask you a question first.

Jon Stewart's memorable appearance on *Crossfire* revealed the hidden structure in the conventions of talk-show interviews. In a more recent example, during the presidential primary campaign in 2016, Donald Trump stood out from the rest of a crowded field of candidates by defying the conventions of behavior for televised debates, regularly rolling his eyes, insulting his opponents, and boasting about his wealth. After securing the Republican nomination, Trump continued to defy conventions; during one debate, he threatened to jail his opponent Hillary Clinton when he became president and mockingly uttered "wrong" into the microphone during Clinton's allotted time.

Republican presidential candidate Donald Trump made headlines by violating the conventions of traditional debates during the 2016 presidential campaign. In this photo, Trump offers a "thumbs down" as he makes fun of his rival Ted Cruz at a Republican presidential primary debate in Florida in March 2016. How, if at all, do you think Trump's disregard for debate norms helped or hindered his campaign?

A **convention** is *a practice or technique that is widely used in a particular social setting.* For example, you probably know the conventions associated with a job interview, even if you've never been on one. And you know the conventions associated with standing in a line at a store (even if you find all the waiting frustrating). Conversation analysis helps to reveal the hidden conventions of interaction. One study of parent-teacher conferences, for example, found that teachers are very careful in how they convey negative evaluations of children to parents. Their criticisms typically avoid blaming a child by either obscuring the child's responsibility for misbehavior or suggesting that a student's troubles are routine occurrences (Pillet-Shore 2016). You quickly learn new conventions as you become connected to new social worlds. If, for example, you were to go to a "speed dating" event—where singles meet and talk with a dozen or more potential dates in quick, 5- to 10-minute conversations—or you were called to testify in a courtroom, you would quickly see how the conventions of talk operate in that particular setting.

Meso-Level Social Structure

Shifting now from the micro to the meso level of analysis, let's examine how structure works in organizations.

Organizations and Structure

We all live in and around a vast array of organizations, large and small, from households, schools, and businesses to workplaces, government agencies, and media organizations. The sociological perspective helps us understand how organizational structure shapes our lives and how our daily activities help us negotiate, reaffirm, and sometimes revise this structure. **Organizational structure** refers to *the rules and routines, both formal and informal, that shape daily activity within organizations.* If you think about the structures of the different organizations you deal with or know about, you will probably think of the various statuses people occupy and roles people play in these settings, as well as the norms and expectations of different groups. For example, the structure of your school includes the roles played by administrators, custodial and maintenance staff, professors, and students. Each group has specific norms and expectations associated with a specific status.

Examples of formal rules include codes of conduct and job descriptions. Informal rules and routines include agreements among groups of employees about how best to share office space or computers, the allotment of cooking and cleaning chores among family members, and the regular but unstated ways that students and faculty communicate with one another. As the Through a Sociological Lens box shows, one aspect of organizational structure—the way that information flows within the organization—can sometimes be a matter of life or death.

Structure and Communication within Organizations

By paying attention to organizational structure, we can gain fresh insight into unlikely occurrences. Consider two space shuttle tragedies: the postlaunch explosion of the shuttle *Challenger* in 1986 and the disintegration during reentry into earth's atmosphere of the shuttle *Columbia* in 2003. In each case, NASA engineers were able to pinpoint the specific technical problem that caused the fatal accident: an o-ring failure for *Challenger* and foam debris for *Columbia.* Identifying the source of the problem is only part of the picture, however. That's because, as sociologist Diane Vaughan (1996, 2003) shows in her meticulous research, NASA engineers were well aware of the technical problems that caused the shuttle accidents. What needs explaining, then, is how and why NASA proceeded with the launch of each of these space shuttles, even though the safety problems in both cases were well known.

This issue is far more complex than it may seem initially. Vaughan shows that people in NASA's chain of command adhered to safety rules and followed appropriate procedures as they certified that each shuttle was ready for launch. In both cases, NASA engineers discussed potential hazards and officially defined them as acceptable risks, following standard operating procedure. Instead of looking for rule violations, then, Vaughan explains that we can learn a great deal about the roots of the space shuttle disasters by looking at NASA's organizational structure. In both cases, NASA's complex and hierarchical organization prevented detailed knowledge of the risk from making its way to those ultimately responsible for authorizing the launch.

©Chi Ian Chao/iStock Vectors/Getty Images

Instead of an organization that promoted free-flowing communication between the engineers and managers stationed at various locations, Vaughan describes an organization in which people had limited opportunities to voice their concerns, in which it was difficult to contradict one's senior colleagues in public, and in which hunches or other concerns not supported by scientific evidence were excluded from the flight-readiness review process. These factors add up to a pattern that Vaughan labels "structural secrecy," the result of an organizational structure that undermined communication within NASA and effectively concealed the seriousness of known safety problems. In her written comments on the disintegration of *Columbia,* 17 years after the *Challenger* case she had studied so thoroughly, Vaughan (2003) notes that "the structure of NASA's Shuttle Program blocked the flow of critical information up the hierarchy, so definitions of risk continued unaltered" (197).

More recently, Toyota Motor Corporation made headlines leading to congressional hearings when it ran into difficulty in managing a growing safety problem with the sudden acceleration of some of its car and truck models. As it turned out, this problem was made worse by the company's disjointed organizational structure. Rather than having a single headquarters for all Toyota operations in the United States (the largest market for its vehicles), Toyota required each U.S. subsidiary to report directly to its global headquarters in Japan. This meant that each U.S. division communicated directly with company leaders in Japan—but not with other Toyota officials in the United States. As a result, the subsidiaries did not share information with each other about the extent of the accelerator problem or confer about potential solutions for it. Limited communication between the U.S. subsidiaries hampered efforts to coordinate a unified response to the initial reports of accelerator problems and delayed comprehensive reporting of the developing problem to government safety regulators. According to Robert Bea, a professor of engineering at the University of California, Berkeley, who studied the Toyota case with his graduate students, Toyota's organizational problems "are similar to those that allowed NASA and the Army Corps of Engineers to ignore structural issues leading to the *Columbia* space shuttle and Hurricane Katrina disasters" (Vartabedian and Bensinger 2010). In response to the 2015 revelations that German automaker Volkswagen had installed "defeat devices" that masked the emission of nitrogen oxide pollutants at 40 times the permissible level in the United States, the company pointed to problems of organizational structure as one cause of the fraudulent environmental performance, emphasizing the need to decentralize information flow and decision making to prevent future scandals (Painter and Martins 2017).

THROUGH A SOCIOLOGICAL LENS

Looking at Organizational Structure and School Violence

In February 2018, a 19-year-old former student at Marjory Stoneman Douglas High School in Parkland, Florida, entered school with a semiautomatic rifle and killed 17 students and wounded 14 others before blending in with fleeing students amidst the resulting chaos. The shooter had been expelled from Douglas High the previous year. He was widely known as troubled by teachers and students, and his mother had died just a few months before the shooting. Still, the shooting came as a surprise to school officials. As the Broward County school superintendent put it, "Potentially there could have been signs out there. But we didn't have any warning or phone calls or threats that were made" (Pullen et al. 2018).

This was another tragic example in a long and growing list of school shootings: the 2012 massacre at Sandy Hook Elementary School in Newtown, Connecticut, and the 1999 mass shooting at Columbine High School in Littleton, Colorado, are among the most high profile of the dozens of school shootings in recent years in the United States.

As school officials, survivors, and victims' families struggled to explain such incidents, one question lingered: Why didn't anyone see warning signs? After each incident, community members sought to understand how students could commit such terrible crimes.

The concept of organizational structure can shed light on why those who perpetrate school violence so often escape the notice of school officials until they commit their deadly acts. Sociologist Katherine Newman and her graduate students traveled to two communities that experienced school shootings in the late 1990s—Jonesboro, Arkansas, and West Paducah, Kentucky—where they talked with teachers, parents, and students in the local communities.

In both cases, Newman (2004) found that there were plenty of warning signs that the students who shot their classmates were troubled—including violent writings, threats to classmates, prior disciplinary problems, and mistreatment of animals—but teachers and school officials systematically missed or misread these danger signals. The cause, according to Newman, was a communication problem that she calls "information loss" that resulted from the schools' organizational structure.

As we have noted, *organizational structure* refers to the routines that shape the daily activity within an organization. Standard routines and practices in schools that promote information loss help explain why teachers and school officials often do not recognize troubled students. For example, since school officials commonly believe that students transferring or advancing from one school to another should have the chance to make a fresh start, disciplinary records do not follow students from one school to the next. As a result, a middle school principal usually does not share information about a troubled student with a high school principal. Similarly, strict boundaries between school and community generally prevent school officials from learning of disciplinary or criminal incidents that happen outside of school. In addition, teachers in most middle and high schools see the students for only about 45 minutes each day, and few teachers get to know students outside the classroom. All these factors contribute to a fragmentation of information about troubled students, with any one individual learning only pieces of a larger story.

©Greg Lovett/The Palm Beach Post/ZUMA Wire/Alamy Stock Photo

Given the organizational structure of schools, the depth of a student's alienation and anger often gets lost in the boundaries that limit communication. Therefore, these students commonly go unnoticed until they commit a disruptive and violent act. By determining how the organizational structure of a typical school contributes to information loss about troubled kids, experts can suggest ways to restructure the flow of information so that students with severe emotional problems are less likely to fall through the cracks.

think about it

1. *Do you think the organizational structure of the high school you attended could produce the kind of information loss Newman uncovered in her research? Explain.*
2. *What do you think schools and communities can do to share information more fully in an effort to prevent school violence? Is it possible to restructure the flow of information without encroaching on the privacy of students and families?*

The examples of NASA, Toyota, and Volkswagen demonstrate how organizational structures shape communication patterns and the flow of information. Understanding organizational structure can give us insight into the decision-making process, illuminating the sociological roots of disasters and accidents that we often attribute solely to individual mistakes.

Macro-Level Social Structure

At the macro level, we can see social structure in the broad patterns of behavior in a society. At this level of analysis, sociologists often draw on the functionalist perspective to focus especially on how institutions, such as the family, the economy, government, education, and religion, are interrelated. As explained in Chapter 1, this perspective, which dominated American sociological analysis for much of the twentieth century, views society as a set of interdependent structures, each of which makes a specific contribution–serves a function–in maintaining social order.

Structure, Function, and the Interrelationships among Social Institutions

Sociologists using functional analysis generally assume that social structures have functions that meet the needs of the broader society. For a society to survive, its structures and institutions must continue to meet those needs. At the center of functional analysis is the concept of *equilibrium,* the balance among various structures that maintains social stability. If one part of a society changes, other parts will need to adjust to restore equilibrium.

Functionalists generally focus on broad, macro-level questions, seeking to understand how the various parts of a society work together and what role different structures play in social life (Parsons 1951). Talcott Parsons (1902–1979), one of the leading American sociologists in the middle of the twentieth century and a pioneer of functionalist theory, was particularly interested in questions of **social integration,** that is, *the process by which values and social structures bind people together within a society.*

Consider the functions of work, for example (discussed in detail in Chapter 13). Adults under the age of 65 are generally expected to work, either for pay outside the home or doing housework and caring for children inside the home. The economic functions of work are straightforward: jobs provide people with money to pay their bills; at the same time, the labor force produces valuable goods and services for the society as a whole. But what are the social functions of work? What part does work play in reinforcing social integration? How is the structure of work connected to other social institutions–family or education, for example–and how do changes in family structure or educational structure affect the structure of work? These are the kinds of questions that a functional analysis encourages us to explore.

Perhaps you can begin to answer some of these questions yourself. What are the social functions of work? Jobs provide daily routines that lend stability and predictability to life. A person with a job knows what to expect each day. Work also nurtures a sense of responsibility and the ability to get along with others—connecting workers with others in their community. Further, work helps teach people self-discipline, and working adults are better able to teach their children the values of effort and self-discipline by the example they set than are those who are unemployed. Finally, work helps define leisure: what would *vacation* mean if you did not have work or school from which to take a break?

Analyzing the structure of work can also give us insight into the way people in a given society experience time. For example, the term "rush hour" is meaningful because of its relationship to standard work patterns. City transit authorities schedule more trains and buses at times that are convenient for people whose jobs follow the traditional 9 a.m. to 5 p.m. workday. In Europe, August is vacation time, and many people take a break of up to four weeks from work during that month. Since the August holiday is so common, many Europeans are surprised to learn that U.S. employers commonly permit only two weeks of vacation per year, and often the two weeks cannot be taken consecutively.

on social theory

Functionalists argue that institutions serve specific functions that help maintain social stability. In the text, we explore some of the social functions of work. Consider some other institution important to you—education, religion, or the family, for example—and evaluate its structural role in reinforcing social integration.

Functionalists further point out that because social institutions are interdependent, the equilibrium among them is precarious. As a result, change in one institution will lead to change in others. For example, as the number of jobs that require higher education and training has increased, colleges and universities have expanded to meet the demand. As incomes have stagnated, leaving people struggling to keep up with the cost of living, the number of two-wage-earner families has increased. And because technology has made telecommuting feasible, more and more people work from home rather than travel to an office every day.

Even a brief inventory of how work has changed within the past few decades, then, raises important questions about interrelated institutions such as family and school. For example, how have high school curriculums changed in response to new technology-oriented jobs and the new skills necessary to qualify for them? How has family life adapted to the changing structure of work? What impact does the lack of work–widespread and persistent unemployment–have on social integration?

William Julius Wilson investigates this last question in his classic book *When Work Disappears* (1996), a study of the effect of persistent unemployment on poor, urban communities. Using aspects of a functional perspective, he explores what happens to the hopes and dreams of adults and children, to their family life, and to their schools, when the majority of adults in a neighborhood do not have jobs. Wilson argues that the disappearance of jobs is the root cause of chronic poverty, crime, drugs, and gang violence in poor neighborhoods (Wilson 2017).

Just because a social structure or institution exists, however, doesn't mean that it serves a positive function. Talcott Parsons was criticized widely for his view, typical of the mid-twentieth century, that the traditional separation of gender roles in the family—with the woman as the homemaker and the man as the breadwinner—was functional (Parsons 1949). As feminist theorists have pointed out, rigid gender distinctions constrain both women and men, although in gender-specific ways. For example, traditional gender roles discourage women from contributing to society outside the home and limit men's ability to take time away from work for parenting responsibilities. Parsons's perspective failed to take into account the negative impact of this structure.

©Tor Lindqvist/Getty Images

In some cases, therefore, specific structures have negative functions: they are dysfunctional. Other dysfunctional aspects of American society have included slavery and racial discrimination. The recent #MeToo movement has shined a light on how a rigid workplace gender structure is dysfunctional. To analyze how a structure functions in society, therefore, we need to pay attention to who benefits from it and who might be harmed. This sort of approach, as we see in Chapter 5, involves paying attention to issues of power and inequality.

Globalization and the Structure of Work

For many people in the United States, globalization has changed the structure of their work life and their communities dramatically. Perhaps the most significant change has been the decline in manufacturing in the United States. Over the past 45 years, manufacturing jobs have been exported to other countries, closing factories that once offered good-paying jobs, health insurance, and pensions to workers without college educations. The shift of these jobs to lower-wage countries is part of what some analysts call the deindustrialization of America (Bluestone and Harrison 1982; Strangleman and Rhodes 2014).

The story of the clothing industry is a good example. A half century ago, the vast majority of the clothes Americans wore were made in the United States. However, if you take a look at the label in the T-shirt or blouse you are wearing today, you will see that it almost certainly was made outside the United States—in Honduras or Indonesia, for example—by workers who were paid a fraction of what U.S. workers expect to be paid. Because of low wages, cheap transportation, and improved technology, manufacturers save money by making clothing outside the United States. For similar reasons, many of your possessions—your shoes and accessories, games and electronics, furniture and housewares—were probably made outside the United States.

How has the migration of jobs overseas—a key aspect of globalization—affected the structure of work for U.S. employees? First, of course, it has meant the loss of millions of manufacturing jobs, disrupting longstanding employment patterns. In the late twentieth century, millions of Americans lost their jobs and were forced to find new work, often moving to other cities or states to do so. Unlike many workers in the mid-twentieth century, people could no longer expect to work for the same company or live in the same community that their parents did. Just as important, they could no longer expect to work in the same job or for the same company for their entire adult life. Despite President Trump's campaign promise to bring manufacturing jobs back to the United States, the basic structure of work mobility and uncertainty will almost certainly persist.

Second, the loss of these jobs ended a period of stable, long-term employment with good pay and benefits, the work situation for many Americans in the post–World War II period. In its place are newer types of employment—such as retail sales workers, food and beverage servers, and information and records clerks, the three largest occupations in the United States in 2016 (U.S. Bureau of Labor Statistics 2017a). Many of these jobs tend to pay lower wages and lack many of the benefits of a manufacturing job, such as health insurance and a retirement plan. As a result, an increasing number of Americans need more than one job to make ends meet. (See the Sociology in Action box for a look at efforts to counter the exploitation of low-wage workers.)

Third, the loss of manufacturing jobs can have a devastating impact on an entire community, as the bankruptcy of Detroit in 2013 dramatically illustrated. Kathryn Marie Dudley (1997) documented the impact on another community, Kenosha, Wisconsin, when Chrysler closed its automobile assembly plant there and nearly 6,000 people lost their jobs. In her study, Dudley paid special attention to the dilemma faced by workers who had always labored with their hands but who now had to try to compete for jobs that require other types of skills. She also examined the impact of the shutdown on Kenosha's small businesses, civic associations, schools, and places of worship—all of which depended on a stable and prosperous community for customers, volunteers, and congregation members.

Fourth, when a wage earner shifts to lower-paying work, a family is more likely to need two incomes to pay the bills, producing

thinking about structure

In what ways is your family different from families of earlier generations because of recent changes in the workplace or in another institution?

SOCIOLOGY in ACTION

Ruth Milkman and the Changing Workplace

For more than 30 years, sociologist Ruth Milkman has been studying ongoing changes in the structure of the global economy and the impact of those changes on workers and the workplace. Her books are widely cited and discussed in sociological circles. As president of the American Sociological Association in 2016, Milkman presided over the association's annual meeting with the theme "Rethinking Social Movements: Can Changing the Conversation Change the World?"

With its focus on the structure of work in the United States, particularly as it affects union members, women, and immigrants, Milkman's research has long played a role in public policy debates involving workers' rights. In 2008, for example, Milkman led a research team that produced a series of pioneering studies of wage theft based on surveys of low-wage workers in Chicago, Los Angeles, and New York. *Wage theft* refers to practices that employers use to deprive workers of pay or benefits they are legally entitled to. The project's national report, *Broken Laws, Unprotected Workers: Violations of Employment and Labor Laws in America's Cities* (Bernhardt et al. 2009), documented widespread wage theft and other workplace violations in all three cities. The study found, for example, that more than one-quarter of low-wage workers (26 percent) were paid less than minimum wage. In addition, 19 percent were not paid the proper overtime rate when they had worked more than 40 hours the previous week, and 17 percent were not paid for off-the-clock work.

The light that Milkman and her colleagues' work shone on wage theft attracted media attention to the problem. The *New York Times,* for example, published an editorial praising the study, condemning the "appalling" abuses it documents, and calling for stepped-up enforcement to combat those abuses (2009, A30).

Milkman has also focused substantial attention on work-family policy. Working with economist Eileen Appelbaum, Milkman did pathbreaking research on California's 2004 Paid Family Leave policy, the first such statewide policy of its kind in the United States. The policy, they found, "has substantially benefitted the workers who utilize it, especially workers in low-quality jobs, and has had minimal impact on businesses" (Appelbaum and Milkman 2011, 29).

In a subsequent project, Milkman and Appelbaum examined the effect of Connecticut's first-in-the-nation law, passed in 2011, that requires employers to provide workers with paid sick leave. Based on a survey of 251 businesses and on-site interviews with managers at 15 companies, Milkman and Appelbaum found that "few employers reported abuse of the new law" (that is, by workers falsely calling in sick), "and many noted positive benefits such as improved morale as well as reductions in the spread of illness in the workplace" (Appelbaum et al. 2014, 18). Connecticut's experience with paid sick leave, they suggest, offers valuable lessons for other states.

Milkman teaches at the CUNY Graduate Center in New York City, where she is research director at the Joseph S. Murphy Institute for Worker Education and Labor Studies.

Source: The Murphy Institute, CUNY School of Professional Studies

Each year, Milkman works with her Murphy Institute colleagues to produce a report on "The State of the Unions," a profile of organized labor in New York City, New York State, and the United States. The 2017 report (Milkman and Luce 2017), the eighth annual report Milkman has coauthored, offers a detailed description of the demographics of union members and unionization rates by industry and provides a comparison of public- and private-sector unionization.

In 2013, the American Sociological Association honored Milkman with its prestigious Public Understanding of Sociology award for her longstanding commitment to reaching beyond an academic audience of professional sociologists to engage with the general public on significant public policy issues. As she continues to study the intersection of work, gender, and immigration—and bring her research findings to bear on current policy debates—Ruth Milkman is a model of an engaged public sociologist.

think about it

1. *What kinds of policies do you think could help to remedy wage theft and other workplace abuses of low-wage workers? What role, if any, do you see for continuing research among low-wage workers in this effort?*
2. *What is your view of policy proposals requiring companies to offer paid family leave for new parents or those taking care of a seriously ill family member? How do you understand the costs and benefits of paid family leave?*

significant strain on life at home. With parents working longer hours, their bills will likely include increased child care expenses. Longer hours also leave parents less time to participate in community activities. Adding further to family strain, a growing number of young adults, including many recent college graduates, are living at home as they search for a good-paying job (Fry 2017; Newman 2012).

Beth Rubin (1996, 2012) argues that, in addition to changing the nature of work in the United States, globalization has changed the social norms and expectations associated with our jobs. She characterizes this change as a shift in the social contract, the collective understanding about rights and responsibilities—in this case between companies and employees—within society. In manufacturing plants in the 1950s and 1960s, there was an unwritten understanding that if you did your job well, you would likely be employed for life. Employers were responsible for providing wages and benefits that allowed workers to enjoy a decent standard of living. In turn, workers remained loyal to their employers, with families working at the same plant for multiple generations. These norms and expectations have virtually disappeared in today's new economy. Instead, many of today's employees have a grudging understanding that their employment is fleeting and temporary, that flexibility and change are inevitable, and that they must look out for themselves. Loyalty to a company can seem misguided in such a climate. Thus a change in social norms has accompanied the structural change that has characterized the new global economy (Kwon and Lane 2016; Lane 2011; Sennett 2006).

How Structures Change: Action

So far in this chapter, we have considered the ways in which social structure operates at every level of our social world and how it shapes our social lives at the micro, meso, and macro levels. However, human beings are not simply products of structure. We think, choose, and act, and even if social structure imposes limits, we always have some capacity for action. Structure and action (or *agency*) are in fact two sides of the same coin. As we consider how structure is affected by human action, we need to understand the broader social context as well.

Types of Action

Max Weber, the pioneering German sociologist whom we met in Chapter 1, defined sociology as the science concerned with understanding social action, that is, human action in social context. Weber was particularly interested in understanding what motivates our actions, and he showed that the goals of human action change across time and culture.

Weber identified three basic types of human action:

- **Traditional action** is *motivated by custom.* Guided by the past, traditional action is anchored by a sense that things have always been done in the same way. Perhaps you have family practices that have been passed on for generations, such as how you celebrate a particular holiday.
- **Affective action** is *guided by emotions and feelings.* When fans tear down the goalposts after their team wins a big college football game, they are guided by their feelings.
- **Rational action** is *motivated by calculations of efficiency.* When people determine their goals and decide how to achieve them, their analysis is a form of rational action. Employees who attempt to act efficiently to help achieve a company's financial goals are guided by this type of action.

Of course, as Weber well knew, human action is complex and is often guided by a combination of these different motivations. But Weber's study of human history led him to believe that modern industrial society is increasingly shaped by rational action. Weber recognized the central role of rational action in the development of modern societies and industrial economies. At the same time, he was concerned that rational action had a tendency to squeeze out other ways of living. A society thoroughly saturated by rational action might be very efficient and highly productive, but Weber worried that it would also be cold and impersonal.

©Joe Murphy/Getty Images

Rational Action: McDonaldization

More recently, the sociologist George Ritzer (2019) has argued that a form of rational action he calls McDonaldization is increasingly organizing our everyday lives (see Table 4.1). According to Ritzer, the effect is to impose the standardized, efficient structure of a fast-food restaurant on all aspects of our lives, including school, work, travel, and leisure. For Ritzer, McDonaldization represents an extreme form of rational action. Just as workers respond to the various timed buzzers and "beeps" in a fast-food kitchen, more and more aspects of our lives are organized by the quest for efficiency. For example, in some stores, grocery shopping now requires no contact with other people. You can use a handheld device to scan each item as you put it in the cart, swipe your customer card, place your deli order with a few keystrokes, and pay with your credit card in the self-serve checkout aisle. You can prepare meals by simply pressing a few buttons on your microwave oven. Or you can preplan just about every minute of your vacation, scheduling each activity, tour, meal, and night's sleep as part of a package tour aimed at guaranteeing that you make the most of your time off.

This intense focus on efficiency, however, may lead to unintended consequences. For example, in the name of efficiency we do an increasing amount of unpaid labor—becoming, in effect, our own checkout clerks, bank tellers, gas station attendants, and insurance claims representatives, to name just a few of the tasks we do for ourselves. Simply put, the purpose of a fast-food restaurant is to serve inexpensive, great-tasting food quickly. People who eat in fast-food restaurants, however, sometimes have to wait in long lines, pay more money than they anticipate, and find the food to be unappetizing and unhealthful. Workers in fast-food restaurants do jobs that are so routinized and standardized, they have almost no room for independent action. For Ritzer, this disconnect between the allure and experience of the fast-food restaurant is the puzzle of McDonaldization: how and why highly rational action can produce outcomes that, as Ritzer (2019) puts it, "limit, eventually compromise, and perhaps even undermine their rationality" (167). Put another way, rational action aims to enhance human experience through a commitment to efficiency and progress. Ritzer suggests that the extreme rational action he calls McDonaldization may be both inefficient and, ultimately, dehumanizing.

McDonaldization is an example of the way human action is shaped by the broader structural patterns of society, in this case the commitment to efficiency in business. The history of phone communication, which we look at next, provides another example of this relationship between action and structure.

TABLE 4.1 RITZER'S FOUR DIMENSIONS OF McDONALDIZATION

Efficiency	Seeking the best possible method for completing tasks, often by following a series of highly specified, predesigned steps.
Calculability	Emphasizing the quantitative aspects of products and services (focusing on, for example, product size, cost, and time), often characterized by the notion that "more is better."
Predictability	Striving to make products and services the same, regardless of place or time. This process of standardization can be comforting to customers, who know what to expect, but may produce jobs that offer little room for creative thought.
Control	Exercising control over employees and customers by enforcing rigid rules, limiting options, and using new technologies that monitor and regulate behavior.

Source: Ritzer 2015.

Technology and Action: Telephone to Smartphone

The history of phone communication, from the earliest landline devices to today's smartphones, provides a good example of the way human action interacts with evolving technologies to determine the impact of those technologies on social structures. Whatever potential a new technology has, human action—how people use it—is the key to understanding its social significance.

According to Claude Fischer's study *America Calling* (1992), when telephones first became widely available in the early twentieth century, the leaders of the industry marketed them primarily to businesses and stressed their business uses. When phone companies turned their attention to residential users in the 1920s, they marketed the telephone as a practical tool for managing household affairs and for obtaining help in emergencies. The way people used the home telephone, however, was mostly for regular, informal conversations with family and friends. Nonetheless, until some 40 years after the introduction of the telephone, marketers continued to stress its practical uses, not its social uses.

Some observers feared that the telephone might undermine local communities, since people could ignore their neighbors and instead build relationships with people who lived far away. This and similar concerns reflect an underlying question: Did people use the telephone in ways that changed how they related to their existing friendship structure? The answer, according to Fischer, is no. Instead, people mostly used the telephone in ways that reinforced their existing connections. Telephones made it easier to plan social engagements, though the neighborly practice of "dropping in" unannounced became less common. In addition, telephones certainly made it possible for people to stay in closer contact with their out-of-town relatives.

Mobile phones have seen a similar evolution. We tend to forget that the mobile phone today, like the telephone in the early twentieth century, is a relatively new technology. In 1990, only 5 million Americans had mobile phones; by 2018, 95 percent of U.S. adults owned a mobile phone (Pew Research Center 2018a; U.S. Census Bureau 2012e). During that period, the mobile phone changed from an upscale luxury item to a common accessory. As with early landline telephones, the way people use mobile phones has changed over time. Like telephones, mobile phones were initially promoted as business tools and as useful in case of emergencies. Over time, however, as mobile technology evolved, mobile phones morphed into today's smartphones—powerful, multipurpose computing and communications devices—and people began using them for an increasingly broad array of purposes: talking with friends, sending text messages, checking sports scores, searching the internet, taking pictures, responding to e-mail, listening to music, getting driving directions, reading the daily newspaper, posting to social media sites, playing games, or watching movies or live sporting events. The list continues to grow.

Mobile phones make all of us more accessible to one another (Rainie and Wellman 2014). If you keep a mobile phone on you, your friends and family can reach you just about anytime and anywhere. As a result, frequent mobile phone users probably communicate more regularly with others in their social networks than do those who do not rely on mobile phones for everyday communication (Ling 2008; Ling and Campbell 2012). Mobile phones also make people more available to bosses and coworkers, blurring the distinction between work time and time off (Wajcman 2008, 2015).

Mobile phones have also severed the connection between person and place. When you call a person who has a landline, you are calling a particular place. When you call a mobile phone, however, you are calling a specific person, but you have no idea where that person might be. In fact, it is common for an initial mobile phone greeting to include the question "Where are you?"

Mobile phones, therefore, may be contributing to the loss of private time and space in contemporary society, as well as to the loss of a rooted connection to place. Phones ring all around us, wherever we are, and people carry on conversations on public transportation, in cars, on the street, and in other public settings. We communicate on the go, and the boundaries between our jobs and our personal lives are increasingly permeable. How we choose to use mobile phones contributes to these changes (Ling 2012).

At the same time, people use mobile phones to help arrange traditional face-to-face contact. You can find friends at a crowded concert or make last-minute dinner plans. With networking software, you can use your mobile phone to find out if any of your

©Mary Evans/The Image Works

©Chesnot/Getty Images

FAST-FORWARD

Technology and Change

Over the years, telephone companies changed their marketing approach to reflect how customers were actually using the technology. Originally, companies emphasized the practical and emergency uses of the telephone, as in this ad from the 1930s (*top*) that says: "Remember—a telephone in your home saves you time, money, and worry, and minimizes inconvenience, anxiety, and loneliness . . . in cases of emergency, you can summon the doctor or call the police in a few moments." By the 1970s, ads were stressing the ways talking on the phone could be fun. Today, companies stress the social function of smartphones, including sharing photos with family and friends.

What new uses can you envision for future versions of the smartphone? How might you explain the limited success of the Apple Watch?

thinking about **structure**

Can you think of other examples in which human *action* determined the purpose of a technological advance?

©Ute Grabowsky/Photothek/Getty Images

GPS-based software like the Snap Map feature of Snapchat allow friends to track each other's location on their mobile phones. With this app, you can determine when out-of-town friends are nearby or which local friends are in your neighborhood. Now you can check your phone to see if any of your friends are the local coffee shop.

friends are nearby and leave electronic messages at restaurants or stores that your friends can later retrieve.

Even as people with mobile phones use them to talk casually with their friends and family on a regular basis, the social consequences for those without a mobile phone may be increasing. If you don't have a mobile phone, you are not always accessible, you cannot check in with people on the fly, and you will have a hard time connecting with friends who are delayed by traffic. As mobile phones have proliferated, public pay phones have largely disappeared, so people without mobile phones have an increasingly difficult time staying in touch. Perhaps two separate forms of social structure are evolving, one based on electronic forms of interaction (e-mail, mobile phones, handheld web access) and one that is largely out of the electronic loop.

These two forms of social structure are a global phenomenon, but you may be surprised to learn that Africa is among the world's fastest-growing mobile phone markets. The expected growth rate for mobile phone subscriptions between 2016 and 2020 in sub-Saharan Africa is higher than any other region, and is 50 percent above the global average (GSMA 2017). By late 2017, there were more than 1 billion mobile phone subscriptions in Africa, the equivalent of more than 80 percent of the continent's population (Ericsson 2017). In many African countries, mobile phones have become a standard feature of everyday life in both urban and rural communities. Despite this growth, mobile phones are still less common in Africa than in other regions (see Figure 4.2).

The explosion of mobile phone use in Africa surprised the leaders of the telecommunications industry. Since landline telephones were so rare in Africa, industry leaders expected that there would be little interest in, or few resources to pay for, mobile phones. But it turns out that demand for the mobile phone, even in remote areas, is extraordinary. For most users in Africa, a mobile phone is their first telephone, and people are using this technology in new and unexpected ways. Farmers, for example, are using mobile phones to develop more efficient and effective ways to get their perishable crops to market. Many people who had never had a bank account now use mobile money (mobile-phone-based services for storing and transferring funds) to reduce their reliance on cash for personal and business transactions, thereby reducing their financial risk and increasing their financial security. Medical professionals are taking advantage of the prevalence of mobile phones to distribute public health information through social media and to make it available over call-in help lines. During the Ebola crisis of 2014–15, mobile media helped keep people informed about how to prevent the spread of the disease (Ericsson 2015b, 2016).

©Khalil Senosi/AP Images

The proliferation of mobile phones in Africa has been a boon for farmers and small-business people, like this market woman in Nairobi, Kenya, allowing them to keep up-to-date with one another and with wholesalers about market prices.

Surely, Africans also use the mobile phone to talk with friends and family (Freeman and Mubichi 2017). As these examples suggest, however, mobile phone use is, in many ways, quite different in Africa than it is in the United States.

Mobile phone use in the United States and in other countries, like telephone use before it, shows how actions can lead people to interact with their friends in new ways and to try out new patterns of behavior, which may contribute to the development of new structures. In subsequent chapters, we look at new forms of interaction made possible by recent communication technologies such as peer-to-peer networks, blogs, and virtual reality environments. We turn next, however, to a change on a larger scale: a transformation in the structure of the workplace.

FIGURE 4.2 | MOBILE SUBSCRIPTION PENETRATION RATE BY REGION, 2017

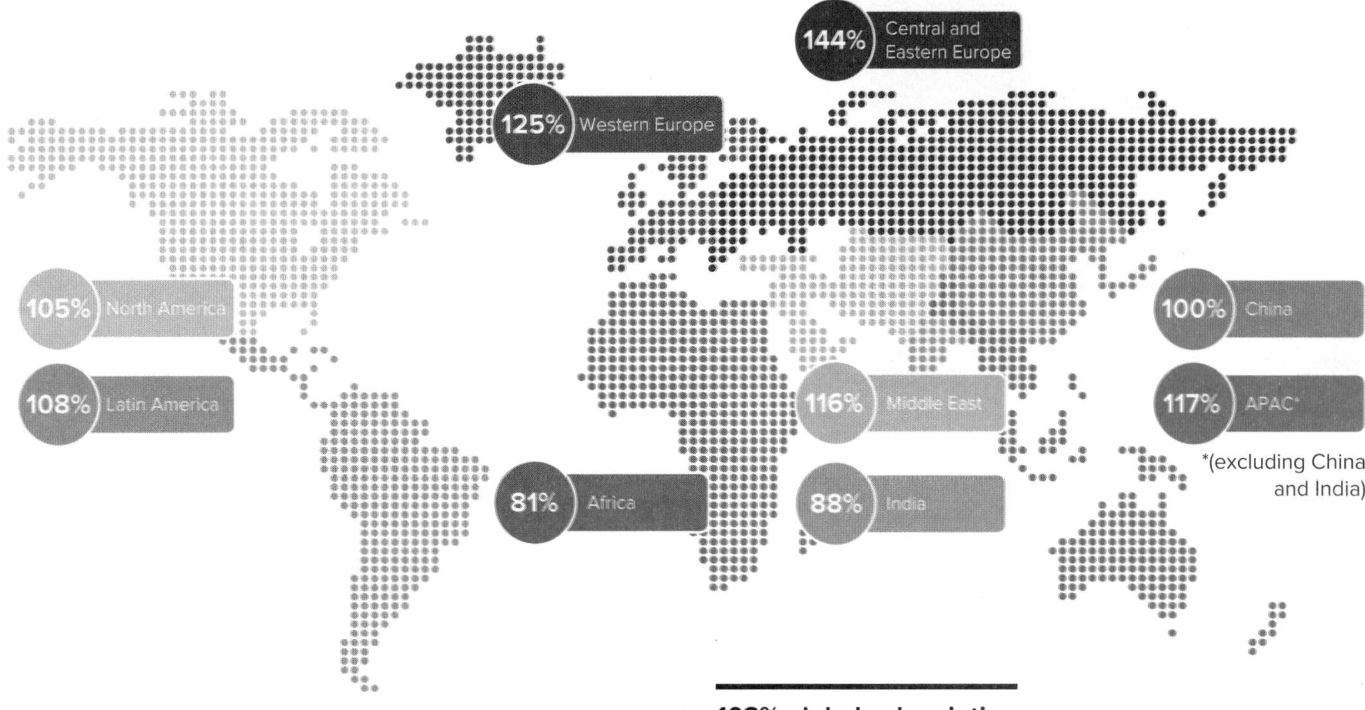

In late 2017, there were a total of 7.8 billion mobile subscriptions, more than one for every person on the planet. But the mobile subscription rate varied significantly by region, from a high of 144 percent of the population in Central and Eastern Europe to a low of 81 percent in Africa. In its November 2017 mobility report, Ericsson anticipates faster growth in mobile subscriptions in sub-Saharan Africa than any other region.

Source: Ericsson Mobility Report, November 2017.

Workers Respond to Globalization

We have seen how the changing structure of work affects employees in the United States, particularly those who work in manufacturing. And as we have learned from studying the dynamic relationship between structure and action, an analysis of structural change reveals only part of the picture. We also need to pay attention to how people respond to structural change, even when their choices are limited.

As the number of manufacturing jobs in the United States declined during the late twentieth century, what choices or opportunities opened up for displaced workers? The lost industrial jobs should not be romanticized. Factory work was often monotonous, difficult, and dangerous. In a 10-year study, Ruth Milkman (1997) examined a General Motors assembly plant in Linden, New Jersey, where, as part of an effort to compete in the new global economy, the company reorganized work and introduced robots and other technological innovations. The union negotiated a buyout package for workers who wanted to leave. According to Milkman, workers who left, it turned out, were happier than those who stayed. Despite their unstable economic future, most were glad to escape the dreary, demanding work of the assembly line. With the exception of skilled workers who learned how to maintain the new robots, most workers who stayed found that new technologies and management programs made life worse for them. Their jobs became even more monotonous. Their relationships with their supervisors grew worse. Despite some economic uncertainty, most of the workers who left were ultimately able to construct better futures for themselves.

Throughout the United States, as workers lost their manufacturing jobs, some fought plant closings and layoffs, working with labor unions and community groups to try to retain jobs, find new factory owners, or buy the factory themselves. Others returned to school to learn new skills or new careers. Still others sought opportunities by moving away. Some tried to start their own businesses. Others retired earlier than they had anticipated. Facing similar structural conditions, different people made different choices.

In the early twenty-first century, new work patterns are emerging as people negotiate the challenges and opportunities of the global economy. With economic uncertainty persisting despite a recovery from the deep recession of 2008–2009, today's workers

©Oscar Wong/Moment/Getty Images

Many people, especially teenagers and young adults, communicate by text message more often than they speak on the phone. People rarely send text messages to strangers; instead, most text messages are directed to friends, family, or others on a person's contact list. New communication patterns associated with texting may be different from those typically facilitated by phone conversations.

CORE CONCEPTS CHALLENGE *Consider* **structure** *and action in regard to the social dynamics of text messaging. Is texting a substitute for the phone? Does texting make communication with friends and family easier, or is it a way of making new social contacts? Are people using text messaging in new or surprising ways?*

are likely to have fewer options than their parents did a generation earlier. The dynamic of structure and action helps us recognize how change shapes people's opportunities and how people in turn respond to change. Equipped with an understanding of social structure, we can see structural change in various arenas of social life, including the structure of friendship in the digital age, to which we now turn.

A Changing World

THE CHANGING STRUCTURE OF FRIENDSHIP

In recent years, the U.S. news media have been full of articles lamenting the rising prevalence—and negative health consequences—of loneliness. For example, the *New York Times* ran a Sunday Review article with the headline "Is Loneliness a Health Epidemic?" (February 9, 2018) and *Forbes* had an article on "Overcoming Loneliness" (March 7, 2018). Sociologists dating back to Durkheim (as we saw in Chapter 1) have long recognized the significance of social solidarity—a sense of connection—for personal and social well-being and the consequent threat to well-being from loneliness. If loneliness is increasing, that would certainly be a matter of concern, but is it?

A greater proportion of U.S. adults are indeed now living alone than in past generations. The U.S. Census Bureau reports that more than 35 million adults lived alone in 2017, representing 28 percent of U.S. households. This is more than double the 13 percent of U.S. one-person households (7 million) back in 1960 (U.S. Census Bureau 2017a). Part of what motivates the rising concern about social isolation is this growth in single-adult households.

Living alone, however, need not signal social isolation. Rather than a weakening of social connections, the growing number of people living alone more likely results from the changing structure of our social ties, including the structure of friendship—the patterns of when, where, and how we interact with friends.

Sociologist Eric Klinenberg refers to adults who live alone as "singletons," to distinguish them from "singles," who, although unmarried, may live with roommates or family members. For some people, especially among the poor and among older men, living alone may be associated with social isolation. Klinenberg (2012), however, offers compelling evidence that many singletons, including young urbanites and older women, have strong social connections with family and neighbors and robust and supportive friendship networks.

In a comprehensive analysis of survey data about connections with family and friends from the 1970s into the 2000s, sociologist Claude Fischer (2011) found that the number of close friends U.S. adults report having—a measure of the size and strength of their friendship networks—has remained relatively stable over time, with very few people (5 percent or fewer in most surveys) reporting that they have no close friends. But if the size of adult friendship networks has remained relatively constant, the way people interact with friends has changed. Fischer reports that although people socialize with friends as often in the 2000s as they did in the 1970s, they are less likely than before to get together in one another's homes. Instead, they are more likely to get together in places like restaurants, bars, and cafes and in shared community, school, or work-based activities.

The growing use of social media and mobile phones has also contributed to change in the structure of friendship. As young people especially connect with peers online, increasingly finding companionship and social support in new online social spaces, the logistics of friendship are evolving (Amichai-Hamburger, Kingsbury, and Schneider 2013; Valkenburg and Piotrowski 2017). According to a national survey of U.S. teenagers (ages 13 to 17) by the Pew Research Center (Lenhart et al. 2015), text messaging is by far the most common way teens "spend time" with their friends. More than half (55 percent) of teens report that they text with their friends daily, far more than the 25 percent who see their friends in person every day or the 23 percent who connect daily on social media. For teens, then, ongoing communication by text is becoming essential for sustaining friendships.

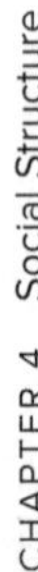

More recently, a national survey found that more than three-quarters of American adults (77 percent) go online every day. Among those with mobile internet access, almost 9 in 10 (89 percent) are online at least once a day. What's more, a full quarter of adults (26 percent) say they are online "almost constantly." Young adults are particularly heavy users of online media, with 39 percent of 18- to 29-year-olds reporting that they are online almost all the time (Perrin and Jiang 2018). Young adults are also the heaviest users of social media, connecting with friends and sharing images. The Pew Research Center's 2018 social media survey found that virtually all 18- to 24-year-olds use social media of some kind: 94 percent use YouTube, 80 percent use Facebook, 78 percent use Snapchat, and 71 percent use Instagram. With the exception of Facebook, 18- to 24-year-old social media use is substantially higher than other age groups, including those in their late twenties (Smith and Anderson 2018).

It appears, then, that despite popular concerns about social isolation and disconnection, most people today are just as socially connected, perhaps even more so, as in previous generations. It is how we connect and to whom—the structure of friendship—that is changing.

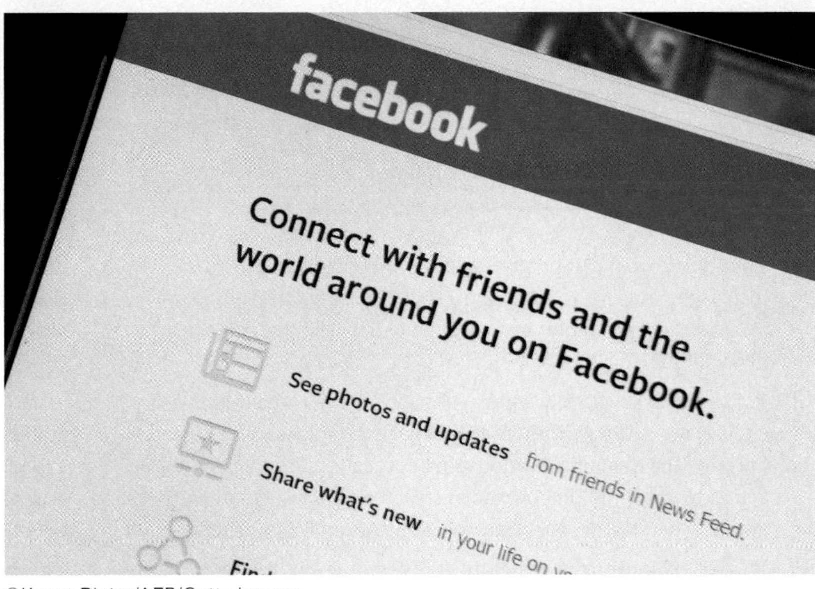

©Karen Bleier/AFP/Getty Images

Social connections among teenagers increasingly rely on regular interaction by text messaging and social media. Friends often spend time together on social media, even when they are socializing in person—taking and sharing photos and communicating with other friends who are not present. How significant is interaction through texting and social media in your friendship networks? How would your friendships change if you only interacted with your friends in-person?

thinking sociologically about
Social Structure

- Social **structure** refers to recurring patterns of behavior that make social life possible. Understanding social structure helps us see connections between these patterns and people's actions and beliefs.
- We can see social **structure** at the micro level (for example, in the structure of talk), the meso level (for example, in organizational structure), or the macro level (for example, in the structure of work).
- **Structure** constrains behavior by putting limits on it, but it can also enable behavior by providing a context for smooth interaction.
- Even when we are limited by social **structure,** we always have at least some capacity for *action.* Structure and action are two sides of the same coin; we always need to consider the two in relation to each other.

REVIEW, REFLECT, AND APPLY

Looking Back

1. The sociological perspective helps us see social structure, the recurring patterns of behavior in social life. Understanding social structure enables us to see the patterns and regularities in social life.
2. People always have the capacity for action, even when their choices are severely limited. Sociology encourages us to examine the dynamic relationship between structure and action by recognizing how social structure shapes, but does not fully determine, our behavior, expectations, and beliefs.
3. We can explore social structure at different levels. At the micro level, we might analyze the structure of daily interactions. For example, our everyday talk and interaction has a structure. We often take for granted our knowledge of this structure of interaction because it seems so natural to us.
4. At the meso level, we might analyze organizational structure. For example, examining organizational structure helps us understand the complex dynamics involved in the space shuttle *Challenger* and *Columbia* disasters.
5. At the macro level, we focus on broad patterns of behavior, especially the interrelationships of various institutions. For example, sociologists using functional analysis seek to understand how various parts of a society work together and the roles that different institutions and cultural components play in maintaining social order.
6. With the growth of the global economy, stable patterns of work in the United States changed for many Americans at the end of the twentieth century. The dynamic of structure and action helps us understand the significance of these changes, how globalization shaped workers' opportunities, and how people responded to these changes.
7. The evolution of phone communication, from the telephone to the smartphone, illustrates people's capacity for action. When the telephone first became available in the United States, it was marketed primarily as a business device. However, most people used the phone for conversation with friends and relatives. Today, the ways in which people choose to use mobile phones and smartphones are once again changing some aspects of social life.
8. The structure of friendship is changing in the digital age. New patterns of making and maintaining social connections in online social spaces highlight changes in how people, particularly young people, practice friendship.

Critical Thinking: Questions and Activities

1. How can the concept of structure and its mirror image, action, help us gain a deeper understanding of social life?
2. Think about the structure of your college classroom. In what ways are the patterns and routines of your classroom similar to those of your high school classes? In what ways are they different? How do the expectations associated with the student or teacher role differ from those you encountered in high school?
3. Identify some of the ways that fast-food restaurants emphasize efficiency, predictability, and an extreme form of rational action. Do you agree with Ritzer's theory of the McDonaldization of society?
4. Turn off your phone for 24 hours. As you go about your day without a phone, pay attention to what, if anything, is different about your daily routines. What do you miss? Is there anything about being away from your phone that you enjoy? How do structure and action help you to understand the role of the mobile phone in your interaction with family and friends?
5. What are the functions of work? Earning a paycheck may be the most obvious answer, but do our jobs serve other functions as well? To answer this question, do some research by conducting short interviews with your family and friends about what they get from their jobs. Did the people you interviewed talk about more than their paychecks? If so, what did they say? Try to interview people who have different kinds of jobs or who are in different age groups. Talk with one or two retired people and ask them what they miss—and don't miss—about their jobs.
6. According to popular wisdom, there is no "I" in "team." Using your knowledge of structure and action, think about the differences between an individual sport like tennis, golf, or high jumping, and a team sport like basketball or soccer. How are the patterns of interaction different? How does the structure of the game shape how participants play, or what they are expected to do, or how fans respond to different sports?

Key Terms

achieved status (p. 79) a position in a social system that a person attains voluntarily, to a considerable degree, as the result of his or her own efforts.

action (p. 77) the ability to behave independent of social constraints.

affective action (p. 89) behavior guided by emotions and feelings.

ascribed status (p. 79) a position in a social system, assigned to a person from birth, regardless of his or her wishes or abilities.

breaching experiments (p. 82) social situations in which the individuals involved intentionally break social rules, violating basic norms and patterns of behavior.

convention (p. 83) a practice or technique that is widely used in a particular social setting.

conversation analysis (p. 82) a method of analyzing the patterns in face-to-face conversation that produce the smooth, back-and-forth turn-taking of such exchanges.

ethnomethodology (p. 82) an approach that examines the methods people use to make sense of their daily activities, emphasizing the ways in which they collectively create social structure in their everyday activities.

organizational structure (p. 84) the rules and routines, both formal and informal, that shape daily activity within organizations.

rational action (p. 89) behavior motivated by calculations of efficiency.

roles (p. 80) the sets of expected behaviors associated with particular statuses.

social institutions (p. 78) the major arenas of social life in which durable routines and patterns of behavior take place.

social integration (p. 86) the process by which values and social structures bind people together within a society.

social structure (p. 77) recurring patterns of behavior.

status (p. 79) a position in a social system that can be occupied by an individual.

traditional action (p. 89) behavior motivated by custom.

©Jabin Botsford/The Washington Post/Getty Images.

5 Power

looking AHEAD

What is **power** and how does it affect your life?

Why do you have more **power** than you might realize?

How is understanding **power** essential for understanding inequality?

©Rhona Wise/AFP/Getty Images

In 2018, a gunman used a semiautomatic weapon to kill 17 people—and injure 17 more—at Marjory Stoneman Douglas High School in Parkland, Florida. This time, students were not content to accept the "thoughts and prayers" that government officials express after every mass shooting. Instead, as student Emma Gonzalez said during a rally speech, "It's time for victims to be the change that we need to see" (CNN 2018). To promote what they saw as sensible gun regulations, students held rallies, gave interviews to news organizations, used social media to spread their message, and lobbied the Florida statehouse. Hundreds of thousands of students marched on Washington and took part in a nationwide 17-minute walkout for gun control—1 minute for each fatal victim. Taylor Maxwell, a Maine participant in the walkout inspired by the students, reflected, "Maybe we have more power than we thought" (Routhier 2018).

The powerful National Rifle Association (NRA) opposes gun regulation. The organization has several million members and spent $5 million in 2017 on lobbying legislators. In the 2016 election, it made $1 million in direct campaign contributions and spent $54 million on "issue ads" that endorse candidates in everything but name (Center for Responsive Politics 2018a). Using its own NRATV channel, NRA president, Wayne LaPierre, referred to the changes endorsed by the Florida students as a "politically motivated agenda that has nothing to do with keeping kids safe" and called some proposals "a road to tyranny." He repeated the NRA's opposition to "any form of a ban on semiautomatic rifles, any form of a magazine capacity ban, and any form of a ban on any firearm accessory." Instead, the NRA called for armed security officers in every school, more mental health services, and better enforcement of existing gun laws. LaPierre vowed that when it came to Second Amendment gun rights "the NRA will never, ever waver" (NRATV 2018).

Nevertheless, following a classic pattern in confrontations between differing forms of power, the Parkland students were taking the long view. Said Emma Gonzalez, "We are going to be the kids you read about in textbooks. . . . [W]e are going to change the law . . . and it's going to be due to the tireless effort of the school board, the faculty members, the family members and, most of all, the students" (CNN 2018).

Power is a fundamental sociological concept, affecting every level of society and influencing our daily lives in countless ways. Because power pervades social life, to understand how society works we must consider its role in various social contexts. As noted political philosopher and social critic Bertrand Russell (2004, 4) put it, "The fundamental concept in social science is Power, in the same way in which Energy is the fundamental concept in physics." Power, like energy, takes many forms and is essential in understanding why things happen as they do in society.

The amount of power that we have heavily influences what we can accomplish in life, whether at home, at work, or in our community. People with more resources typically have more power, and those with power can use it to obtain more resources. Power, therefore, is closely linked to social inequality, another fundamental feature of society. Inequality can be based on many different characteristics, including class, race, gender, ethnicity, nationality, sexual orientation, and religious affiliation. But these different forms of inequality have something in common: power and its influence.

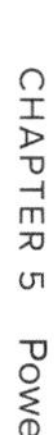

In this chapter, we define and examine power and its various characteristics. We look at examples of power in daily life as well as how differences in power affect inequality, and we explore how different types of inequality interact. We conclude by noting how economic power is increasingly translated into political influence through campaign contributions.

Understanding Forms of Power

You know that the United States is a powerful nation and that your boss has more power than you do. But what is "power," exactly? And how can this concept be applied to such different settings as international relations and the workplace? Different approaches to understanding power highlight different aspects of this important concept (Gaventa 1982; Lukes 2005; Mann 2012; Poggi 2001; Sharp 1973a; Smith 1990; Wrong 1979).

Defining Power

The word *power* is derived from a Latin word, *potere,* which means "to be able." Max Weber ([1922] 1978, 926) viewed **power** as *the ability to bring about an intended outcome, even when opposed by others.* Two key components of this definition are the basis for an important distinction: Some sociologists focus on the "ability to bring about an intended outcome," or the "power to" approach, so called because it highlights the capacity to accomplish something. Others focus on the ability to overcome opposition, or the "power over" approach, so called because it highlights the capacity to dominate others (Göhler 2009). These two aspects of power are not mutually exclusive, and feminist scholars, especially, have worked to integrate both approaches into a comprehensive analysis of power (Allen 2008; Bromley 2012; Hearn 2012). Allen (2008) argues that such a feminist approach is key to "understanding, criticizing, challenging, subverting, and ultimately overturning the multiple axes of stratification" in society, "including (but not limited to) sexism, racism, heterosexism, and class oppression" (2). Let's consider these aspects of power more closely.

Empowerment: "Power To"

As noted, the "power to" approach emphasizes *"the ability to bring about an intended outcome,"* highlighting the positive and constructive aspects of power. **Empowerment,** which *increases people's capacity to bring about an intended outcome,* is the focus of much feminist scholarship on power. Social philosopher Virginia Held (1993), for example, argues that power is the capacity to change and empower oneself and others. According to political scientist Nancy Hartsock (1983, 226), the "feminist theory of power" views power as a competence and ability, rather than a form of dominance. Sociologist Patricia Hill Collins (2000) highlights the use of power to resist oppression.

People often discuss power and empowerment in terms of individual effort and achievement. If your goal is to find an interesting, decent-paying job, then acquiring appropriate education and experience can help give you the "power to" accomplish your objective. Empowerment often involves individual enhancement and self-improvement. Individual self-empowerment is the theme of popular self-help books with titles such as *Empowerment: The Art of Creating Your Life as You Want It.*

SPOTLIGHT

on social theory

Feminist theories point out that power can involve competence and empowerment, rather than just the domination of others. Have you experienced empowerment in your own life in some way without diminishing the power of others?

However, empowerment originally referred to collective political empowerment, involving organizations, communities, and entire categories of people (McLaughlin 2016). For example, the women's movement in the United States has helped empower women, enabling them to gain greater equality in the workplace, more options in their roles at home, better medical care, more equitable access to education, and greater participation in sports. As women have become empowered, they have accomplished these gains without dominating men, making their achievements examples of the "power to" act rather than "power over" others. (Some theorists use the term "power with" to highlight the collective nature of change efforts [Allen 1999].)

The "power to" approach can also apply to social systems such as schools, governments, or even entire societies. American sociologist Talcott Parsons (1960) saw power as the capacity of a social system to achieve collective goals. In the tradition of structural functionalism, Parsons was most interested in the overall operation of societies as social systems. According to his framework, a society is powerful to the extent that it can accomplish its goals. Doing so requires access to resources, among them money and knowledge. Wealthy societies have more resources—and thus are more powerful—than poor societies (one way that power and inequality are often connected). Powerful societies can maintain a high standard of living for their citizens, ensure self-defense, advance scientific and technological frontiers, and achieve other collective goals. By all these measures, the United States and other wealthy nations are powerful societies, whereas impoverished countries are much less powerful.

on social theory

Functionalist theories of power focus on the capacity of social systems to achieve collective goals. What is an example of a social system that you are a part of, and what collective goals does it attempt to achieve?

Strategies of Empowerment: Educate, Organize, Network

The old saying "Give a man a fish and you feed him for a day; teach a man to fish and you feed him for a lifetime" expresses the difference between charity and empowerment. A gift provides only temporary relief and fosters a relationship of dependency; a person who is empowered develops an enduring capacity and independence. Whether adopted by an individual, a small group, or a national or an international organization, strategies to increase empowerment generally involve a combination of education, organization, and networking (Dugan 2003).

- ***Education*** is probably the best-known approach to empowerment. Some teaching philosophies, for example, focus heavily on empowering students rather than simply transmitting facts (Freire 1970; hooks 1994). To achieve their goal, people must understand their situation, have a vision of what needs to be done, and obtain the training and skills they need to reach their goal. College, or other types of education, can help people develop these resources and skills.
- ***Organization*** involves bringing people together to identify common goals and work to achieve them. Smoothly operating workplaces are well organized, for example, with employees and management cooperating to achieve organizational goals. When communities of disempowered people organize, the neighborhood associations, labor unions, and advocacy groups that result can serve as megaphones to amplify the concerns of group members and help them stand up more powerfully to adversaries. As one guide to community organizing notes, "Building a strong, lasting, and staffed organization alters the relations of power. . . . When the organization is strong enough, it will have to be consulted about decisions that affect its members" (Bobo, Kendall, and Max 2010, 12).
- ***Networking*** involves reaching outside your immediate circle of contacts to find allies. Professional associations in many fields hold conferences and social events to facilitate networking to search for employment or to advance careers. Organizations also network by forming coalitions and other collaborative efforts. In this way, they pool their resources to achieve goals they would be unlikely to accomplish on their own.

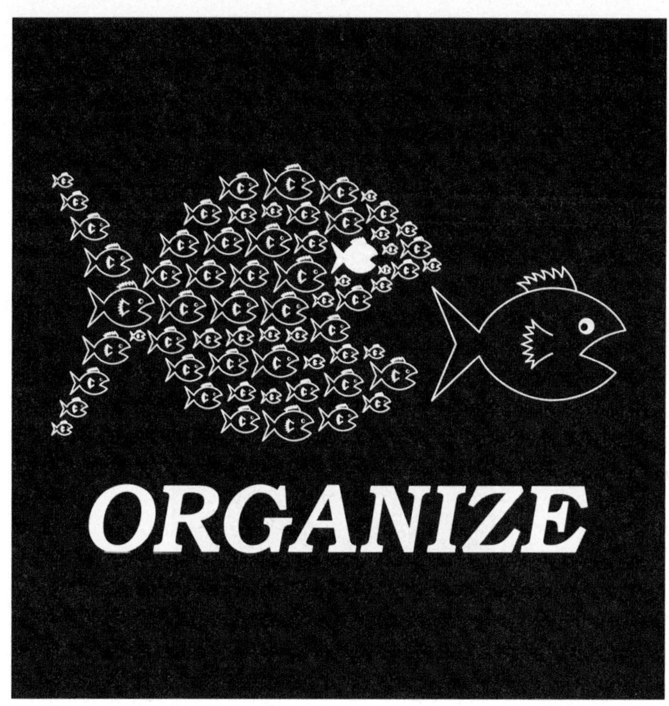

This classic graphic illustrates the idea that through organization weaker parties can join forces to take on a more powerful adversary.

Domination: "Power Over"

At all levels of social life, people disagree. For example, a parent grounds a teenager but the teenager resists; a corporation wants to build a toxic waste incinerator near a neighborhood, but the residents object; or, as we saw at the beginning of this chapter, people disagree about the enactment of legislation. In all these cases, the effort to accomplish something meets opposition and produces conflict. That's why the second part of our definition of power includes the idea of conflict: "the ability to bring about an intended outcome, *even when opposed by others.*" This emphasis is called the "power over" approach, since it focuses on overcoming opposition or dominating others. In one classic definition from political scientist Robert Dahl (1957), power is seen exclusively in terms of domination: "A has power over B to the extent that he can get B to do something that B would not otherwise do" (202).

Domination can occur at any level of society. Forcing children to be brides, as is done in some cultures, reflects both domination at the individual level (the future of a specific young woman is determined by her extended family) as well as inequalities at the societal level (women in such societies lack power in social life). Often macro-level inequalities in power trickle down to affect people's daily lives. At the same time, the personal choices people make have a cumulative impact on broader dynamics of social power, a process captured neatly by the feminist slogan "The personal is political" (Hanisch 1970).

The most obvious use of power as a means of domination is in political and economic conflicts, as powerful elites attempt to maintain their advantages over others. We examine such situations more closely later in the chapter, when we explore systems of social inequality.

Strategies to Overcome Opposition: Persuade, Reward, Coerce

Imagine that someone you live with—your roommate, partner, or spouse—has a much lower standard of cleanliness than you do. He or she leaves the sink full of dirty dishes and leaves clothes, papers, and half-eaten food lying around. If you want this person to be neater, you have three options. First, you could try persuasion, which would involve convincing the person to clean up out of fairness, because of health concerns, or to eliminate the growing stench that is putting a damper on your social life. If persuasion didn't work, you could try offering a reward: "If you do your share of the cleaning for a month, I'll pay for us to go out to see a movie." Finally, if all else fails, you could try a

©Alphabetica, Inc.

Public service announcements, such as this one discouraging texting while driving, illustrate the use of persuasion to influence people's behavior.

©Kevork Djansezian/Getty Images

Rewarding others is one way to achieve compliance. Why are rewards often used to capture criminals? What rewards—other than cash—can be useful in daily life?

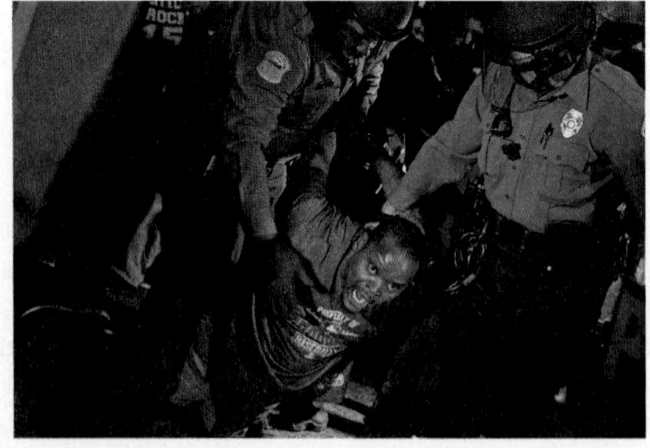

©Michael B. Thomas/Getty Images

Physical force is typically the last resort in obtaining compliance. As a type of coercion, it is expensive, inefficient, and often ineffective in the long run because it generates anger and resentment.

threat: "If you don't keep up with your share of the cleaning, you can't live here anymore."

Participants in any conflict, whether minor or serious, have these same three basic options: persuade, reward, or coerce others to get them to comply (Kriesberg 1982, 115).

- To **persuade** is *to get people's compliance by convincing them of the correctness of your position and goals.* An organization dedicated to combating sexually transmitted diseases, for example, might launch a campaign to educate people about the importance of condoms. Over time, as people hear this message repeatedly, some might begin to alter their behavior. The group has power–it is able to achieve its goals–to the extent that it can reach and influence people through education. However, this type of power is limited, since it usually cannot overcome stubborn opposition. Also, the use of persuasion is not always forthright or honest. Authoritarian governments, for example, may exploit their control of the media to manipulate, distort, or withhold information in order to convince citizens to act in a desired way. The rulers may thus have successfully secured voluntary compliance with their wishes, but they will have done so under false pretenses. Even in open societies, misleading propaganda efforts by governments and powerful corporations can shape the terms of debate about many issues, thereby achieving compliance under false pretenses (Zollmann 2017).
- A second strategy to overcome opposition is to offer a reward. To **reward** is *to encourage people's compliance by offering a positive incentive.* Rewarding a child with words of praise, an athlete with a trophy, or a country with economic or military assistance are all ways to encourage or reinforce desirable behavior.
- To **coerce** is *to force people's compliance by threatening, intimidating, pressuring, or harming them.* Drivers generally obey the speed limit (or something close to it) because they know a speeding ticket can be very expensive. Therefore, the threat of possible punishment has a coercive effect on their behavior. In this case, compliance is a result of *systemic* coercion in which social structures–not just individuals–are in place to deliver a threat.

Reward and coercion are sometimes two sides of the same coin. As a student you may work hard in school, even when you do not enjoy it, because you have been taught that your chances for good employment–with all the accompanying rewards–will be improved significantly if you have a college degree. You also know that receiving failing grades is likely to harm your prospects for graduation and employment–an implicit coercion.

In many cases, coercion is much more sinister, involving threats to people's livelihood, freedom, or physical well-being. In some repressive societies, people who fail to comply with authority can lose their jobs, while those who obey are allowed to pursue successful careers. In the most authoritarian societies, those with power use the most sinister forms of coercion: imprisoning, beating, or killing people who refuse to comply.

Because these techniques are expensive, labor-intensive, and may generate a backlash, they are typically used as a last resort. However, through the force of their example, they can have a coercive effect on large numbers of citizens. (Nations, too, use such coercion against their enemies.) Ultimately, though, people in power cannot rely for long on coercion alone (Camber 2014; Davenport 2007). It is more efficient to have people control their own behavior.

Power in Everyday Life

Power is an essential part of social relationships at every level of social life, including your relationships with your family and friends, your professor, your boss, the police, and the government. Many sociologists, including Max Weber and Karl Marx, focused much of their attention on the operation of power at the macro level of society, examining governmental and economic power. We explore these ideas in more detail later in the chapter.

However, power is also involved in social interactions at the micro level. For example, while rates of intimate partner violence have dropped significantly in recent years, it is still a serious social issue (Black et al. 2011; Catalano 2013). Women, in particular, suffer the consequences of this abuse. Intimate partner violence produces a sense of powerlessness in the victim, often leading to depression. A survey of undergraduate women found that the more violence they experience in their relationships, the less powerful and the more depressed they feel (Filson et al. 2010). Perpetrators use violence to assert control and gain power over their partners.

In between macro- and micro-level interactions are the meso-level organizations to which we all belong. Studying power can also help us understand how such organizations operate.

Power in Small Groups and Organizations

Sociologists who study power in small groups and organizations examine how such groups operate and what roles their leaders play. Many of their insights can be applied to friendship circles, families, and clubs as well as to more formal settings such as schools and workplaces.

In one classic formulation, John French and Bertram Raven identified six bases of power in small groups and organizations (French and Raven [1959] 2001). Notice how these power bases overlap with the broader strategies for overcoming opposition we discussed earlier:

©Simonkr/E+/Getty Images

Power operates in all levels of social life. Many everyday interactions involve power. In this soccer match, a referee uses his authority to intervene in a dispute.

- ***Reward power*** is the control one party has over valued resources that can be used to provide positive incentives. By offering children a weekly allowance, parents can gain power over their behavior.
- ***Coercive power*** is the ability to punish—for example, by withholding valued resources or by inflicting verbal or physical harm. Police officers can usually generate compliance because they can issue citations, arrest people, or even shoot people if necessary.
- ***Legitimate power*** is exercised by those who invoke a feeling of obligation; one "ought" to obey, perhaps as a result of shared cultural values or out of respect for

thinking about power

Think of two examples of people or organizations that have **power** over your actions and decisions. How do they maintain their control?

someone's formal rank or position in the social structure. You are likely to carry out a boss's order to do a routine task at work because you see it as legitimate; you would ignore a similar order about your private home life.

- ***Referent power*** is based on feelings of identification, affection, and respect for another person, even if that person does not seek influence over others. A popular colleague in a workplace might have referent power because others look up to her and view her as a model.
- ***Expert power*** arises from the perception that a person has superior knowledge in a particular area. A lawyer has expert power in legal matters in relation to a client. Expert power is about the perception of knowledge, not necessarily actual knowledge. Someone *seen* as an authority carries expert power whether or not he has actual expertise. Conversely, a real authority on some topic may not have expert power if others do not recognize that expertise.
- ***Informational power*** is based on a person's use of facts, data, or other evidence to argue rationally or persuade. A project manager has informational power when she convinces her boss to approve a new product. Those with information can increase their influence by sharing it, withholding it, organizing it effectively, or even manipulating or falsifying it.

These categories can overlap—a leader can withhold a reward as a type of coercion—but the distinctions help us recognize different sources of power. Also, a person's use of one type of power can affect another. For example, when a manager gives an employee a bad evaluation—a use of coercive power—that action is likely to undermine his or her referent power with that person.

Sociologists and social psychologists have done a great deal of research on the dynamics of small groups, including those associated with power (Forsyth 2019). Researchers have shown that when authorities rely on reward or coercive power, their influence weakens if the amount of resources they control is reduced. However, authorities who have earned respect and are seen as legitimate enjoy group members' loyalty regardless of their ability to reward or coerce. Such loyalty can evaporate, however, if the person in authority acts in ways that group members consider unfair, unethical, or disrespectful (Lammers et al. 2008; Tyler 2005; Tyler and Blader 2003).

Compared to powerful people, those who feel relatively powerless are more likely to use coercion because they think they have no other means of achieving their aims. Some parents and teachers feel relatively powerless when children seem out of control. These adults are more likely to use coercive threats and punishment than are parents and teachers who feel empowered (Bugental and Lewis 1999).

Authorities generally prefer rewards over coercion because they worry about retaliation (Molm 1997). However, group members often tolerate a coercive leader if the group is successful in achieving its goals (Michener and Lawler 1975) or if they trust the leader (Friedland 1976). If a leader lacks referent power, uses coercion, and asks group members to carry out unpleasant tasks, though, group members are more likely to resist his or her authority (Yukl, Kim, and Falbe 1996). People are also more likely to oppose authorities if they perceive their actions as unjust, view fellow group members as comrades, learn to act together as a group, and believe they have group support when speaking out (Gamson, Fireman, and Rytina 1982).

Power Tactics

How do you try to get your way when dealing with your friends or your boss? **Power tactics** are *the specific strategies people use to influence others in everyday life.* These familiar strategies involve power, though we often do not think of them in those terms. (See Table 5.1.) A child who persists in yelling "I want it! I want it!" in a store is using a power tactic. A worker who ridicules his or her colleague is using a power tactic. Power tactics vary along three key dimensions (Forsyth 2019, 243–44):

- ***Hard and soft.*** Hard tactics are forceful, direct, or harsh. People employing them use economic rewards and other tangible outcomes, and even threats. A cash rebate or a threat to repossess your car is a hard tactic. Soft tactics focus on relationships. People employing soft tactics make use of collaboration and friendship to achieve an aim. A friendly reminder that you need to do some task is a soft tactic.
- ***Rational and nonrational.*** Rational tactics appeal to logic and include bargaining and rational persuasion. Many editorials in news outlets use rational tactics. Nonrational tactics include emotional appeals, such as when television commercials imply that driving a particular type of car will make you sexy.
- ***Unilateral and bilateral.*** Unilateral tactics do not require cooperation to initiate; they include demands, orders, or disengagement. Military leaders employ unilateral tactics when they issue orders. Bilateral tactics involve give-and-take, as in negotiations and discussions. When a homeowner and a prospective buyer negotiate a sale price for a house, they use bilateral tactics.

The way power and inequality operate within broader society can influence the dynamics of small groups. For example, studies suggest that women have higher levels of referent power than men do; people typically evaluate women more favorably than men and like them more. But women who use a direct leadership style are judged more harshly than men, and they have to outperform men to be seen as equally competent. Men have more expert power, and because people generally believe men are more competent than women, men can draw upon this perception as a source of influence. Gender differences are affected by a person's position within the social structure, however; people who are relatively powerful—women or men—report using more direct strategies to influence others than do less powerful individuals (Eagly and Karau 2002; Lopez and Ensari 2014). (For a very different take on power, read the Through a Sociological Lens box.)

TABLE 5.1 POWER TACTICS USED TO INFLUENCE OTHERS IN EVERYDAY SITUATIONS

Tactic	Examples
Appeal	Beg for help; plead with someone to play fair
Bully	Yell; push someone around
Collaborate	Invite someone to help; provide assistance as needed
Complain	Protest to a store manager about poor service; grumble to a professor about an assignment
Criticize	Point out the limitations in a plan; find fault with someone's work
Demand	Ask for a refund; insist on speaking to a supervisor
Discuss	Talk over a situation in a group; come up with a plan of action
Disengage	Walk out in the middle of the argument; give someone the cold shoulder
Evade	Change the subject; don't return phone calls
Inform	Point out the advantages of a plan; note the personal benefits someone will receive
Ingratiate	Flatter; compliment
Inspire	Appeal to a person's loyalty; cheer someone on
Join forces	Find allies to help fight an opponent; agree to approach the boss as a group
Joke	Use humor to help others relax; ridicule opponents
Manipulate	Lie; leave out important details in a report
Negotiate	Offer a deal; offer to compromise
Persist	Refuse to take no for an answer; keep trying
Persuade	Convince someone of the wisdom of a position
Promise	Assure someone that you will follow through with a plan
Punish	Fire someone; ground a child for the week
Put down	Insult someone; disparage a person's abilities
Request	Ask for a favor
Reward	Take someone to lunch as thanks; give someone a promotion
Socialize	Ask about the family; make small talk
Threaten	Warn about taking legal action; warn that you will divulge embarrassing information

Source: Adapted from Forsyth (2019).

The Economic, Political, and Cultural Uses of Power

Think of the people and institutions that have power in our society. What do they do with it? Power is used in many ways, but three of the most important purposes to which it is applied are economic, political, and cultural.

Economic Power: Allocating Resources

Within any group or society, power determines who will receive important resources and how those resources will be used. Within a family, the person who controls spending wields considerable power over other family members, deciding in many cases what food or clothes will be bought, how leisure time will be spent, and where the family will live. Business executives have the power to open new stores, offices, or factories in one place and close them in others. They have the power to hire and lay off workers and to

THROUGH A SOCIOLOGICAL LENS

For Foucault, Power Is Everywhere

French sociologist Michel Foucault (1926–1984) introduced a conception of power that doesn't fit neatly into other models described in this chapter. His ideas are complex and evolved over time, but his work has been influential.

Foucault begins his classic *Discipline and Punish* (1995) with a gruesome description of the execution in 1757 of a man who had attempted ineffectively to kill the king of France. The prisoner was first tortured: his legs were crushed, his skin was peeled off with red-hot pincers, he was burned with sulphur, and molten lead and boiling oil were poured into his wounds. Then the executioner took over, tying each of the prisoner's limbs to a different horse to dismember him by pulling him apart. What was left of him was then burned at the stake. All of this took place within view of an assembled crowd.

Eighty years later, as Foucault describes it, the public torture and execution of criminals as models of control and punishment had been replaced by a new model: the modern prison. Here, away from the public's view, prisoners were subjected to a highly structured schedule of daily activities and were the objects of intense observation and evaluation. According to Foucault, this change didn't happen because of concerns about the inhumanity of torture. Rather, prisons emerged primarily because torture and public executions didn't have their desired effect—to encourage obedience to authority. On the contrary, these massive public displays of power made martyrs of their victims and generated resentment against authority. Now, however, hidden behind prison walls, power could be wielded more efficiently. Rather than physical punishment, prisoners were subjected to routines intended to change their minds and their behavior. Through observation, discipline, and evaluation, they were pressured into conforming to expectations about "normal" behavior.

Foucault argues that the prison model of power spread through other social institutions, including psychiatric hospitals, modern schools, and factories. In each case, people's behaviors are closely observed, strictly limited through a disciplinary routine, and evaluated for proper conformity to a standard of normalcy. These standards in turn reflect broader systems of knowledge that "produce reality," as Foucault put it, by organizing, labeling, and measuring the world in distinct ways. As these knowledge systems gain acceptance, they become taken-for-granted assumptions about the world, thereby assuming enormous power and influence. Foucault coined the term *power/knowledge* to identify how the way we understand and interpret the world both enlightens and restricts us. On the one hand, we typically learn to strive to be a "good student" and a "reliable worker," while trying more generally to act "normal," based on the standards created by these systems of knowledge. On the other hand, people who question or challenge the dominant systems of knowledge are marginalized, ostracized, and even punished. Rather than submitting to the power of others, we come to control ourselves.

In this way, Foucault saw power as dispersed throughout society rather than centralized in the hands of small groups or individuals. "Power is everywhere," he wrote (Foucault 1980, 93), "not because it embraces everything but because it comes from everywhere." Power relationships play out in countless local "fields," such as the family, the prison, the workplace, a doctor's office, a classroom, and a place of worship. As a consequence, power is fragmented into many different forms that cause people to change their behavior willingly by monitoring their own actions to conform to expectations. Philosopher and gender studies professor Sandra Lee Bartky (1990) argues that this kind of self-monitoring leads many women, for example, to closely regulate their own bodies through constant dieting, "proper" hair removal, the application of makeup, and the wearing of fashionable clothing. Carried to extremes, the impact of this internalized disciplinary power can produce eating disorders and other unhealthy behaviors—another form of imprisonment (Eagly and Karau 2002; Lopez and Ensari 2014).

think about it

1. *What examples can you think of to illustrate Foucault's idea that we regulate ourselves by conforming to social expectations?*
2. *Do you agree with Foucault that our sense of self is linked to conforming with expectations laid out by various social institutions? Why or why not?*

determine their salaries, decisions that can have a profound impact on employees' lives and communities.

Governments at all levels have the power to allocate resources, generating revenue by collecting taxes and fees and then distributing that money through public projects, social programs, military spending, and other policies. Within particular agencies or departments, officials wield power by exercising control over budgets and supplies.

Political Power: Making Rules and Decisions

Power can also be used for political purposes, enabling some people to set the conditions under which others are expected to live. Parents typically set the rules for how a household will function and how children should behave. In a workplace or school, the managers or administrators establish how the group will operate. Setting the rules for how the entire society will operate is the role of government. Politicians and government officials pass laws and establish regulations that organize many aspects of our daily lives. Those with power set the rules, and those without power are expected to follow them.

©K.M. Chaudary/AP Images

Schools of all sorts shape how children understand the world. Here, boys study in an Islamic religious school or *madrassa*. How did your education help shape your worldview?

Cultural Power: Defining Reality

To prepare others to comply with their agenda, those with power define social reality in a particular way and encourage others to agree with their interpretation. Parents, for example, steer their children toward or away from certain types of books, entertainment, or religious instruction. By doing so, they are trying to shape how their children understand and define social reality by influencing their children's values and worldviews. Children who internalize their parents' beliefs and values are unlikely to violate their parents' rules.

A similar process operates in society at large, as the media and schools shape our worldview. By selecting certain news stories and sources, the news media teach us to view certain topics and people as important and worthy of consideration (local crime stories or celebrities), while marginalizing or ignoring others who are not given routine coverage (advocates for the poor) (Croteau and Hoynes 1994b). Influencing the stories people read, the ideas they consider, and the perspectives to which they are regularly exposed is one way of exercising power in a society (Freedman 2014; Herman and Chomsky 2002).

Schools exert power by including certain topics and excluding others. Until the middle of the twentieth century, American history at all levels—elementary school to college—was taught almost exclusively from the perspective of white, wealthy, straight men. Indeed, U.S. history was virtually equated with this group, since they were the ones who held positions of power in the government, military, and economy. Women of all classes, people of color, the working class, gays and lesbians—the vast majority of the population—were nearly invisible. As these groups have gained power in society, school curriculums have changed, and they now provide a more diverse view of history.

Italian Marxist activist-scholar Antonio Gramsci (1891–1937) argued that the class in power maintains its dominance not simply through the use of force, which is the job of the state's police and military forces, but also through the manipulation of ideas, which it accomplishes primarily through its control of cultural institutions such as the mass media, research and policy institutes ("think tanks"), and universities. Gramsci (1971) applied the word *hegemony* to this situation. **Hegemony** *exists when those in power have successfully spread their ideas—and marginalized alternative viewpoints—so that their perspectives and interests are accepted widely as being universal and true.* By manipulating ideas, those in power can often manufacture the consent of others. For example, political leaders typically demonize foreign enemies in rallying citizen support for a war. Gramsci argued that hegemony is a tenuous condition that must be actively maintained in the face of constant challenges.

As we see later in this chapter, systems of social inequality are also reinforced by a justifying ideology that oppressed people themselves sometimes internalize. Cultural norms, the legal system, schools, the media, and other social institutions may all play a role in creating and maintaining this ideology.

Economic, political, and cultural powers are based in real-world social institutions, including businesses, government, and religions. At different points in history, each of these has been more influential than the other two. In the West, the power of religious institutions was most important in shaping daily life in the medieval period. By the eighteenth and nineteenth centuries, the rise of the secular nation-state signaled the growing influence of military and political power. In recent decades, economic power, in the form of transnational corporations, has become the most influential, in many cases eclipsing the influence of government (Mann 2012; Poggi 2001).

Power and Social Relationships

Power at all levels of society is rooted in social relationships, and it is limited by the relationships on which it is based. In this section we explore various aspects of these social relationships, including the role of compliance in relationships of power and the importance of disobedience as a strategy for resisting power.

Types of Authority: Traditional, Rational-Legal, and Charismatic

Max Weber ([1915] 1946b) made an important distinction between legitimate and illegitimate power. **Legitimate power**—or **authority**—is *voluntarily accepted by those who are subject to it.* A religious congregation, for example, might recognize and accept its spiritual leader's right to issue instructions and therefore voluntarily follow his or her wishes. **Illegitimate power** *relies on force or coercion to generate obedience.* A kidnapper or military dictator may be able to cause others to obey orders, but they do not obey willingly. Instead, they comply only because of the threat of violence if they disobey.

Weber ([1915] 1946b) further specified three types of legitimate power, or authority. The first, **traditional authority,** *has legitimacy because of compliance with well-established cultural practices.* These practices can vary widely, but from Europe's medieval nobility to modern chieftains in countless tribal societies around the globe, traditional leaders are widely perceived as legitimate because they derive their power from longstanding cultural customs that are usually not questioned. The child of a king becomes the next ruler for life because that is the way royalty works; people believe in the tradition. Often religious beliefs help justify and support traditional authority.

By contrast, **rational-legal authority** *has legitimacy because it is based on established laws, rules, and procedures.* A president or prime minister is elected for a set term through an established process. A university president is hired after the school conducts a formal search and a series of interviews. These individuals gain legitimacy because they were selected through an agreed-upon procedure.

In the classic British movie *Monty Python and the Holy Grail,* an amusing scene sums up the difference between traditional and rational-legal authority. (You can find it on YouTube.) In the scene, Britain's legendary King Arthur encounters some peasants who challenge his legitimacy. The king appeals to traditional authority whereas the peasants insist on a rational-legal process for choosing a leader.

ARTHUR: I am your king!

PEASANT WOMAN: Well, I didn't vote for you.

ARTHUR: You don't vote for kings.

PEASANT WOMAN: Well, how did you become king then?

ARTHUR: The Lady of the Lake . . . held aloft [the sword] Excalibur from the bosom of the water signifying by Divine Providence that I, Arthur, was to carry Excalibur. That is why I am your king!

PEASANT MAN: Listen—strange women lying in ponds distributing swords is no basis for a system of government. Supreme executive power derives from a mandate from the masses, not from some farcical aquatic ceremony.

ARTHUR: Be quiet!*

As these peasants recognize, a rational-legal process requires some transparency and logical justification, whereas tradition is, in effect, self-justifying. Weber argued that with the rise of science, industrialization, and democratic processes, rational-legal forms of authority rapidly replaced traditional ones. The contemporary spread of democratic forms of government around the world continues this trend.

Weber also described a third form of legitimate power—**charismatic authority**—which is *power whose legitimacy is derived from the extraordinary personal characteristics of an individual leader, which inspire loyalty and devotion.* Charismatic leadership is usually not transferable. Therefore, this form of authority is typically short lived and episodic. Charismatic leaders can inspire groups of people to act, even though such leaders may possess no formal institutional power. Examples of charismatic leaders include compelling politicians, a motivating team coach or captain, a dynamic celebrity activist, or an inspirational spiritual leader.

The Role of Compliance

Weber based his distinctions between legitimate and illegitimate power on the perceptions of the people obeying the orders, but he did not address *how* those perceptions are created and, therefore, how different types of leaders sustain their power by maintaining their followers' compliance. To take an extreme example, long-term hostages sometimes identify with their captors and voluntarily follow their wishes, an effect called the *Stockholm syndrome* (Reid et al. 2013). This phenomenon, however, does not transform the abductor's power from illegitimate to legitimate. Instead, it shows compliance is more complicated than it may at first appear.

Power is limited by the social relationships on which it is based. The president of the United States, for example, is powerful only as long as others agree to carry out his or her commands. If the president orders a military attack or initiates a relief effort, many other people must carry out the commands for these goals to be accomplished. Authoritarian regimes can collapse when a large enough number of citizens refuse to obey their leaders and demonstrate for change—a situation that has occurred many times in history (Ackerman and Duvall 2000; Chenoweth and Stephan 2011; Sharp 2010).

On a more mundane level, those with power in everyday life also depend on compliance to maintain their position. Students must agree to complete the paper assigned by their teacher, workers usually comply with the boss's rules, and children consent to

*Written by Graham Chapman, John Cleese, Terry Gilliam, Eric Idle, Terry Jones and Michael Palin © 1974 national film trustee company ltd. Krypton international corp. RCA/Columbia Python Pictures in association with Michael White. Reprinted by permission of Python (Monty) Pictures Limited.

thinking about power

How were you socialized to view those who hold **power** in government? Those who wield corporate **power**?

©Franco Origlia/Getty Images

©Scott Olson/Getty Images

©Randall Michelson/WireImage/Getty Images

The three types of authority outlined by Weber can be found in contemporary life. The pope relies on traditional authority to gain the allegiance of the world's Catholics. A police officer relies on rational-legal authority to carry out her duties. Although she is now quite wealthy, Oprah Winfrey's influence on popular culture is due in large part to her charismatic authority. For example, many loyal fans follow her book club recommendations. What other examples of each type of authority can you think of?

their parent's request to finish their chores. In other words, people are not passive objects of the demands of those in power; they can react in a variety of ways, from complying voluntarily to resisting and thereby undermining authority (Sharp 1973b).

The degree of compliance in a social situation is often not apparent at first glance. It takes a sociological understanding of power to see that simmering conflict can lurk just beneath the apparently calm, orderly surface of societies. When compliance is withdrawn, conflict may seem to erupt suddenly and dramatically. For example, beginning in 2014, a series of protests erupted across dozens of U.S. cities under the banner of the Black Lives Matter movement. The immediate trigger for the protests was the killing of black people by police officers, but the protests also addressed a variety of longstanding grievances, including police brutality, racial profiling, and racial inequality in the criminal justice system (Day 2015). This type of protest is itself another form of power: the power of disobedience.

The Power of Disobedience

Since power operates within social relationships, one of the great ironies of social life is that those who think they are powerless often have a great deal of power. History is filled with examples of ordinary people who united and toppled powerful opponents. (The Sociology in Action box discusses several key figures associated with the strategic application of disobedience.)

Workers have united to gain concessions from employers, and women have united to achieve changes in the law and in male-dominated institutions. The nonviolent strategies of the U.S. civil rights movement during the 1950s and 1960s inspired many social movements to fight for the rights of other oppressed groups. The people behind all these movements started out with little or no apparent power to effect change. In the end, however, their collective efforts generated enough power to overcome their oppressors (White et al. 2015).

Everyone has some power. At a minimum, you always have power over your own actions. Political scientist and anthropologist James Scott (1987) found that peasants in a Malaysian community could exert some influence over public policies by using "weapons of the weak," including gossip about those in authority, foot-dragging, noncompliance, pilfering, and sabotage. None of these were organized or formal protests, but they enabled relatively powerless peasants to resist domination.

Though it may appear that college students are another group with little power within the institutions they attend, successful student activism has led to significant changes. During the 1980s, for example, student activism caused many institutions to

©Chip Somodevilla/Getty Images

A 2017 "Unite the Right" rally in Charlottesville, Virginia brought together white power advocates, neo-Nazis, "alt-right" supporters, and other racist and anti-Semitic groups who clashed violently with opponents of white supremacy. One counter-demonstrator was killed. In addition to race, what other issues related to power are likely to produce opposing protests in the coming years?

SOCIOLOGY in ACTION

Promoting the Power of Nonviolence

One of the core sociological insights about power is that it depends on compliance. Consequently, those with little apparent power can use noncompliance, or disobedience, to great effect in bringing about social change. Since this insight comes from sociology, it is no surprise that three of the people most closely associated with the power of disobedience studied sociology in college.

Martin Luther King Jr. (1929–1968) was a sociology major as an undergraduate. His later activism showed his understanding of how power operates in social relationships and how those who appear powerless can organize to effect change. King's well-known role as a charismatic leader in the civil rights movement began during the bus boycott in Montgomery, Alabama, in 1955–1956, a campaign that relied on disobedience. By refusing to ride the city's buses for over a year and setting up an alternative system of transportation, thousands of African Americans helped end segregation on public transportation. King went on to aid other rights campaigns that relied heavily on *civil disobedience:* nonviolent direct action that violates unjust laws. Using this strategy, activists successfully challenged segregation at lunch counters, department stores, public swimming pools, and many other facilities, and their efforts helped achieve access to voting rights that had previously been denied to African Americans throughout the South.

Although not as well known as Dr. King, Saul Alinsky (1909–1972), who studied sociology as a graduate student, was also highly influential. Alinsky transformed his sociological understanding of power into practical applications on behalf of low-income citizens. In "Alinsky-style" community organizing, trained organizers identify and coordinate the efforts of existing neighborhood leaders, who in turn mobilize fellow residents to work on issues they identify as priorities, such as better housing, safer neighborhoods, and stronger schools. In addition to emphasizing the importance of building strong organizations, Alinsky advocated the use of creative confrontational tactics that rely on disobedience to apply pressure on those in power. He emphasized the importance of operating outside of the experience of your opponent: for example, he organized fun public demonstrations, street theater, and other actions in which community residents could participate, rather than closed-door meetings that those in authority could dominate. In 2008, Alinsky-style community organizing received unusual popular attention when one-time community organizer Barack Obama was elected president.

King and Alinksy focused on developing tactics for civil disobedience in the United States, whereas Gene Sharp (1928 –2017) studied and wrote about the power of nonviolent social action to bring about change in the face of dictatorship, war, and oppression around the world. Sharp's academic training included a master's degree in sociology. His classic three-volume work, *The Politics of Nonviolent Action* (1973b), sketches out a theory of power based on sociological principles and describes the strategic uses of disobedience. Volume Two chronicles hundreds of nonviolent protest actions, including many forms of communication (petitions, marches, teach-ins), noncooperation (boycotts and strikes), and nonviolent interventions (sit-ins, land seizures, and disclosure of secret information). One little-known action: in 1942, when the German army occupying Poland posted "For Germans Only" signs at cafes and hotels in Warsaw, Polish youth stole the signs and defiantly placed them on the lampposts and trees where Germans had hanged Polish patriots. Sharp's work, now outlined in *From Dictatorship to Democracy* (2010) and the subject of the 2012 documentary film *How to Start a Revolution,* has been translated into more than 30 languages and made available for free download on the internet.

Sharp irritated authoritarian regimes and influenced activists around the globe. Many democracy movements in Eastern Europe during the 1980s and 1990s used ideas and tactics found in Sharp's work. So did Middle Eastern pro-democracy activists in recent years, leading the *New York Times* to comment, "For the world's despots, [Sharp's] ideas can be fatal" (Stohlberg 2011).

think about it

1. *How does the concept of power relate to the work of the three people featured in this box?*
2. *In what other situations might disobedience be a source of power? If disobedience is so powerful, why isn't it used more often?*

withdraw their investments in apartheid South Africa. Later, student efforts on behalf of living-wage and anti-sweatshop campaigns led to policy changes regarding pay for campus staff and the way in which schools license and acquire athletic wear. In 2015, protests at the University of Missouri against the school's racially hostile environment–including a hunger strike and a threatened strike by black athletes–led to the resignation of the university president and new efforts to promote diversity (Landsbaum and Weber 2015). Even the high school students mentioned at the start of the chapter achieved some success by bringing national attention to an issue that concerned them. The success of these efforts demonstrates that students have more power than they often realize.

The success of efforts on behalf of oppressed groups, as well as student activism, demonstrates two simple truths about power. First, when people work together, they increase their own power as individuals to effect change. Second, disobedience is a powerful weapon for those who struggle to effect change. Since power is a social relationship, people ultimately have the power to refuse to comply. They rarely use this power, often out of fear of coercion or force. But when people unite in an act of civil disobedience, they can instigate enormous change. This insight has been a powerful tool for many social movements, which we explore in Chapter 17. Those in power typically resist change promoted by oppressed groups because it threatens the privileges they hold, a topic we turn to now.

Power and Privilege

As we cautioned in Chapter 1, viewing the world from a sociological perspective can sometimes make people uncomfortable. Nowhere is that more true than in dealing with the issues of power and privilege, topics that cut across race, class, gender, and other social differences (Johnson 2005). Our interests and perspectives—our existing power relations—affect how we think about power (Lukes 2005). When we learn about the unequal power various groups possess, we realize that, compared to many other people in the world, we enjoy a considerable amount of power and privilege. **Privilege** is *a special advantage or benefit that not everyone enjoys.* The fact that most people go about their daily lives unaware of the privileges they enjoy is, in itself, an indicator of that power; they don't have to think about it.

For example, heterosexuals need not concern themselves with their sexual orientation, since our society's norms, laws, and institutional practices have long been organized to accommodate them. Straight people can go about their daily lives without thinking about being heterosexual. But despite the legalization of same-sex marriage, it's still legal in many places for gay or transgender people to be fired from their jobs, denied housing, or refused service in a business simply because of who they are. At the same time, a gay man might be acutely aware of discrimination based on sexual orientation while being unaware of his position of privilege as a white, upper-middle-class male. It is easier to recognize disadvantage than privilege.

The point of recognizing privilege is not to make people feel guilty. Rather, doing so allows us to understand society more accurately by removing the blinders that block our ability to see how power operates. In one way or another, we are all involved in power relations. In our society "race," "gender," "class," and "sexuality" tend to conjure up images of blacks and Latinos, women, working-class and poor people, and lesbians and gays. But studying these topics is not just about studying those with less power. Instead, we study such subjects to determine how *everyone* in a society is connected through relations of power. For example, to understand race in the United States, we need to consider the role of whites throughout history, not just the status of racial minorities, because the two are connected. In addition, understanding privilege can help us identify the resources we have available to empower ourselves, assist others, and perhaps reduce inequality.

To understand dynamics of power and privilege, it is often useful to consider the situation of those with less power. Sociologist Dorothy Smith (1989, 1990) developed **standpoint theory,** which *questions taken-for-granted assumptions about society by looking at it from multiple viewpoints, especially from the perspective of people in subordinate positions.* A "standpoint" is the place from which a person views the world. A person's standpoint is structured by his or her social location, which includes race, class, gender, and sexual orientation.

People with different standpoints see and understand the world differently. For example, in 2013, when a white Latino Florida neighborhood watch volunteer, George Zimmerman, was acquitted of murder after he shot and killed unarmed black teenager Trayvon Martin, public opinion about the verdict varied starkly by race. One poll found that 49 percent of whites were satisfied with the verdict, 30 percent were dissatisfied, and 21 percent did not know. Among blacks, only 5 percent were satisfied, 86 percent were dissatisfied, and 9 percent did not know. A full 78 percent of blacks said they thought the case raised important issues about race that needed to be discussed; only 28 percent of whites agreed. Instead, 60 percent of whites thought race was getting more attention in this case than it deserved; only 13 percent of blacks agreed (Pew Research Center 2013a). To varying degrees, we can find similar differences in the perspectives of different groups (men and women, members of different classes) on a variety of issues.

In societies with deep inequalities, groups have differing perspectives. Each of these perspectives is necessarily partial. As a result, considering multiple standpoints, especially of those who have less power, is crucial to gaining a more complete understanding of social life and potentially addressing inequalities.

Power and Inequality

As we have seen, different groups have varying degrees of power within a society, a situation that produces **inequality,** *the unequal distribution of resources among groups of people.* All societies have some form of inequality, but its nature and extent vary significantly because patterns of unequal distribution are not natural, inevitable, or the product of chance. Instead, inequality is socially constructed; it varies according to the culture and social structure of a society.

Social inequality is multidimensional: in other words, different forms of inequality coexist within a society. Max Weber ([1915] 1946b) argued that society is stratified in terms of class, status, and political power.

Class: Economic Conditions

Everyone has dreamed of winning the lottery at some point because we all know that obtaining a large amount of money can transform a person's life. With it you can buy a beautiful home, a fancy car, premium health care, travel, and other luxury items. You might also use your winnings to buy leisure time, quitting your job and hiring others to cook your meals, clean your home, handle your finances, and so on. Or you might try to help others. Some people have, in effect, already won the lottery simply by being born into wealth. Clearly, one major type of inequality in society is the uneven distribution of money and other economic resources.

A **class** is *a group of people who share a roughly similar economic position and lifestyle.* Karl Marx's analysis of the importance

©Dennis MacDonald/Alamy Stock Photo

©Dennis MacDonald/Alamy Stock Photo

Housing is one of the clearest examples of economic inequality in the United States. Neighborhoods tend to be segregated based on income levels. As children grow up, they tend to accept the economic standards of their neighborhood as the norm.

CORE CONCEPTS CHALLENGE *What did your neighborhood look like when you were growing up? What would pictures of your street suggest about the class composition of your neighborhood and the relative* **power** *of the members of your community?*

SPOTLIGHT on social theory

Marx and Weber both formulated **conflict theories** that address power and economic inequality. Whereas Marx emphasized class differences among workers, Weber focused on lifestyle differences among consumers. Which do you think is more important in understanding inequality today? Why are these approaches compatible?

of class was especially influential. As we discussed in Chapter 1, Marx focused on economic inequality and considered how the different classes in capitalist societies relate to each other as they participate in the process of economic production. Marx highlighted the world of work and analyzed classes as groups of people who share a common relationship to the means of production.

In many ways, Max Weber—whose ideas are also discussed in Chapter 1—agreed with Marx that economics is a key to understanding inequality. However, whereas Marx examined the concept of class in terms of work, Weber looked at class in terms of **life chances,** *the opportunities offered by a person's economic position.* For Weber, a class is a group of people who have a similar capacity to earn money, and who consequently share a similar lifestyle. We consider class-based systems of inequality later in this chapter. In Chapter 9, we explore the importance of class in more detail and examine further the differences between Marx's and Weber's approaches to this topic. For now, it is enough to know that class is one major type of inequality.

Status: Prestige

Although Weber and Marx agreed on the importance of class, Weber differed from Marx by arguing that status and political power—two noneconomic factors—were also key to understanding inequality. To Weber, both status and political power could be sources of power independent of a person's class.

Adherents of traditional Marxist thought treated class as the single most important source of inequality, supported by other types of inequality such as those based on race and gender. Weber, though, argued that a person's status—based on his or her social characteristics, such as race, ethnicity, or gender—could have an impact independent of class and therefore should be considered as a distinct form of inequality, not merely a secondary feature of economic inequality.

As we noted in Chapter 4, *status* refers to a person's position in a social system. Thus people who are paid to play for a team in the National Basketball Association have the status of professional basketball player. That is, they hold a social position based on their occupation, just as accountants do. In a second meaning of the term, however, status also refers to the prestige associated with a particular position. Thus, unlike accountants, NBA players are often held in high esteem and have considerable prestige in our society, giving them high status in the second meaning of the term.

A person has a given status because he or she belongs to a community of people who have the same lifestyle, ethnicity, race, ancestry, gender, sexual orientation, education, or occupation. Often, membership in a status group is not formal. Instead, members define some shared feature as important or valuable. Status groups develop formal and informal rules that designate who belongs. Those who belong may socialize with one another, live in the same neighborhoods, join the same organizations, send their children to the same schools, and marry others within the group.

The members of a status group can sometimes use their membership to gain power over nonmembers by excluding those people. **Social closure** is *the process whereby a status group maximizes its own advantages by restricting access to rewards only to members of the group.* Social closure, therefore, involves excluding outsiders

from the benefits of group membership. This process can involve subtle or blatant **discrimination,** *treating others unequally based on their background or other personal characteristics.* With Jim Crow laws and apartheid, the white populations in the southern states of the United States before the civil rights era and in South Africa before the 1990s both engaged in social closure to exclude other racial groups from access to voting, education, and other rights and opportunities.

In our society, status and class are often linked; people who belong to higher classes disproportionately come from groups with higher status. However, sometimes people of relatively modest means—respected religious leaders, influential politicians, or admired artists—gain access to high-status communities, even though they have relatively modest incomes. Conversely, people with considerable economic resources sometimes face discrimination and other hurdles because of their status. Middle-class African Americans can face both subtle and blatant harassment and discrimination because of their race (Patillo 2013; Roscigno, Williams, and Byron 2012). This situation has improved significantly in recent years, but in many racially diverse communities, high-status organizations and social circles still tend to be all, or nearly all, white (Cornwell and Dokshin 2014; Sherwood 2010).

Ethnicity and religion, too, have long divided status groups in the United States. At one time, people of Irish ancestry, Jews, and Catholics faced discrimination and were excluded, by rule or by custom, from some neighborhoods, jobs, social clubs, civic associations, and schools. In the nineteenth century, for example, employment ads sometimes specified, "No Irish need apply." For the most part, these groups no longer face such discrimination, but Latinos, Muslims, and other ethnic and religious groups continue to experience discrimination today. Gender and sexual orientation, too, continue to present powerful barriers, as we will see in Chapter 11.

Political Power: Strength through Organization

In addition to class and status, Weber argued that society is stratified in terms of political power. Weber saw that by creating organizations to advance particular goals, people working together could influence society. He referred to these organizations as "parties," meaning a broad range of political groups, including what we would today call social movements, advocacy groups, and citizens' organizations, as well as traditional political parties. As we saw earlier, organizing such groups is one form of empowerment.

Weber saw political power as potentially independent of class and status. For example, lesbian and gay people in the United States who faced status-based discrimination due to their sexual orientation have been able to organize themselves into an influential political force over the past few decades. Although not particularly rich and subject to intense social discrimination, this group has been able to develop political power to improve policies and laws affecting its members' lives. Political organization, then, can serve as a source of power independent of class or status and, as we have seen, can accomplish social change through collective action. But like class and status, political power is distributed unequally in society.

The Intersections of Race, Class, and Gender

As we have considered, Weber argued that social inequality involves class, status, and political power. Similarly, in his work analyzing the black community, sociologist W. E. B. Du Bois, writing early in the twentieth century, highlighted issues of race, class, and nationality. These early works suggested that we should consider many aspects of social life when examining power and inequality.

Some feminist scholars (Collins 2000; Collins and Bilge 2016; Hancock 2016) built on this tradition through **intersectionality theory,** which *highlights the connections and interactions between various forms of inequality, especially race, class, and gender.* These theorists recognize the different dimensions of inequality and highlight the interactions that take place between these dimensions. For example, white people as a group enjoy privileges in our society because of their race, but white families trapped in poverty face hurdles because of their class. Meanwhile, within the context of poor white families, men are likely to enjoy privileges not afforded to women. Understanding these cross-cutting forms of inequality is crucial to many social dynamics and helps us to recognize both potential disadvantages and privileges we may have. (The profile in the Sociology Works box notes one example of this.)

Focusing on the interaction between power and inequality can help us gain a deeper understanding of social life in several ways:

- It gives us a more accurate reflection of how we experience the social world. Any person's identity is multifaceted, including his or her race, class, gender, ethnicity, sexual orientation, and nationality. Taking into account all these aspects of identity gives us a better understanding of our own social location.
- Once we recognize that these factors intersect, we can acknowledge that the relative importance of different types of inequality varies depending on the social context and circumstances. Although a Latino man living in poverty may enjoy privileges within his family because of traditional gender inequality, he also faces many disadvantages because he occupies a low position on the class hierarchy and belongs to an ethnic minority.
- We can also see that intersections involve more than simply "adding up" different identities. One aspect of identity can change another. Being wealthy or poor, for example, can change the social significance of being male or female. While

thinking about **power**

What status groups do you belong to? Do the members of those groups use **power** to maximize their advantages over others?

SOCIOLOGY WORKS

Kiya Stokes: Leveraging Power for Economic Justice

When Kiya Stokes enrolled in a sociology course on class and inequality, he had no idea that a few years later he would be on the frontlines of the struggle for economic justice. As he studied the sociological perspective, learned about stratification, and read about the contemporary labor movement, he started thinking that maybe he could become a part of the effort to make a difference.

"As an African-American man, I was well aware of the various forms of racial discrimination and oppression that I witnessed and endured," Stokes notes. "Sociology helped broaden my perspective and showed me that there were other groups within our society that were also victims of various forms of oppression." Learning about the intersections of inequality was not always easy. Stokes admits, "The process was slightly traumatic as I learned not only that there were other oppressed people here but that in different ways I had benefited and participated in their oppression. After I moved past the shame, and empathy, I decided that I needed to do something to make the world a better place."

In the ensuing years, he has done just that. He earned a master's degree in labor studies and went to work with the Service Employees International Union (SEIU), one of the nation's largest labor unions. Stokes eventually became political director for the union in Los Angeles, focusing on frontline healthcare workers. In that position, he helped "support campaigns that are designed to increase worker wages, to improve safety standards, and to eventually stamp out poverty."

After some years, though, Stokes longed to return to his home base of Richmond, Virginia, a city long-marked by its own economic and racial inequality. There, he went to work as a liaison for a City Council member, juggling a wide variety of tasks, including tracking legislative proposals, and helping resolve issues for residents, local businesses, and community organizations. Stokes was in a different institutional environment but he was still working to leverage power to make a difference, especially in promoting affordable housing and antipoverty/community wealth building programs. He notes, "Many of the district residents are poor and low-income residents, which was similar to the low-wage workers that I worked with when I was political director of the union. The difference is that now I am more of an information source or service provider as opposed to building the workers into a force to demand higher wages and benefits. In both jobs, though, I've worked closely with the community."

©Kiya Stokes

Reflecting back, Stokes says, "In sociology class I learned a new way to view the world. I learned that we were not just one big happy family here with a predestined lot in life. I saw that many people do work hard and do not get adequately compensated for that labor. Others do not do a bit of work but have wealth beyond our wildest imagination. I started questioning other premises and assumptions about the state of the world that most people take for granted. In the end I am certain that without the critical thinking and analytical skills that I learned in sociology class I would not be fighting for working people today."

think about it

1. *What are the similarities and differences between leveraging power for economic justice as part of a labor union effort and doing so while working for a local elected official?*
2. *What do you think Stokes meant by saying that seriously considering inequality was "a slightly traumatic experience" for him? Do you feel the same way about your study of power and social inequality? Why or why not?*

straight white men may dominate U.S. society, poor or working-class white men may not feel powerful at all.

- When we recognize that race, class, and gender interact, we are better able to avoid overgeneralizing about any one group of people. Patricia Hill Collins (2000, 5–6) notes, "Theories advanced as being universally applicable to women as a group upon closer examination appear greatly limited by the white, middle-class, and Western origins of their proponents." For example, the idea that the women's movement of the 1960s and 1970s opened the way for women's participation in the paid workforce needs to be qualified, because significant percentages of poor and working-class women in the United States—especially women of color—were already part of the workforce. By viewing women's increased participation in the paid labor force solely through the lens of gender, we miss the important impact of class and race.

Collins (2000) coined the phrase **matrix of domination** to indicate *the interlocking systems of oppression associated with race, class, and gender.* The metaphor of a matrix suggests more than one dimension and allows for the idea that people can be privileged in some ways and oppressed in others. When one group believes it is superior to another, has the right to dominate the

©Bettmann/Corbis

A woman points approvingly to a racist sign in this photograph from the early 1920s. Although this woman faced the disadvantages of gender inequality, her status as a white person afforded privileges not available to Japanese Americans of either gender.

CORE CONCEPTS CHALLENGE *How does this photograph illustrate the fact that inequality is multidimensional? How does a person's* **culture** *teach the kind of attitudes shown in this photo?*

other, and is able to do so, oppression results. Her framework highlights the active domination of weaker groups by those with more power at the individual, group, and institutional levels. Reflecting the core concept of structure, as well as the capacity people have for action, Collins recognizes that these various levels of oppression are also sites for resistance as people use their collective power to achieve autonomy and promote equality.

Collins's matrix approach shows that there are few pure oppressors or victims in society. Most people are privileged on some dimension of inequality and disadvantaged on some other. This is true across different types of stratification systems, which we consider next.

Structured Inequality: Stratification Systems

Societies formalize and institutionalize inequality—including the unequal distribution of power—by developing social structures that perpetuate stratification. **Stratification systems** are made up of *social structures and cultural norms that create and maintain inequality by ranking people into a hierarchy of groups that receive unequal resources.* Over the centuries, various societies have created different types of stratification systems. All stratification systems, however, share three key elements:

1. The unequal distribution of valued *resources*
2. Distinct *groups* that make up society's strata (layers)
3. An *ideology* that explains and justifies inequality

The particular form these elements take in any given society determines the dominant type of stratification system and the distribution of power within the society. We will take a closer look at the elements shared by all stratification systems before we consider some examples.

Unequal Resources

The first element of all stratification systems is the unequal distribution of valued resources. These may include (Grusky and Ku 2008, 6):

- *Economic* resources, including money, property, and land
- *Human* resources, such as education, training, and specialized skills
- *Cultural* resources that aid in achieving success, such as knowledge and skills learned through socialization
- *Social* resources, including access to important networks of people
- *Honorific* resources, involving the acquisition of prestige and status
- *Civil* resources, including legal rights involving property, contracts, voting, and speech
- *Political* resources, involving authority in the home, workplace, political arena, or social life

In any stratification system, some resources are distributed more evenly than others. For example, in the United States all citizens have similar legal rights based on the principle of equality under the law, but there are stark differences between rich and poor in terms of economic and human resources. In addition, if a resource is available more readily to one group than to another, that discrepancy can have an impact on another resource. Because the affluent can afford better legal counsel than the poor, the apparent equality of the legal system can be compromised.

Stratified Groups

The second element of all stratification systems is the groups that make up the various strata in society. Stratification based on class, race, and gender is especially widespread and significant, which is why sociologists pay especially close attention to these factors. However, stratification can also be based on ethnicity, age, religious affiliation, sexual orientation, and disability, among other factors.

The groups within systems of stratification can be based on either an ascribed or an achieved status. As noted in Chapter 4, an *ascribed status* is a position an individual has been assigned in

life, regardless of his or her wishes or abilities. Race and sex are examples of ascribed statuses. Stratification systems based primarily on ascribed statuses are said to be closed: they are rigid and impermeable, making it virtually impossible for an individual to move from one stratum to another.

An *achieved status* is a position an individual attains voluntarily, to a considerable degree, as the result of his or her own effort and abilities. College graduates, for example, attain their status due largely to their own efforts. Stratification systems based primarily on achieved statuses are said to be open: it is possible for an individual within such a system to achieve **social mobility,** *movement from one stratum of a stratification system to another.* In systems of class stratification, for example, a person's class status can change as a result of structural changes in the economy, individual ability, education, effort, luck, or other factors. However, a person's achieved statuses are still influenced to varying degrees by social factors beyond his or her control. For example, the family into which you are born can significantly influence your class status as an adult.

The various social categories associated with inequality—such as races, ethnicities, classes, and genders—are not natural, inevitable, or biologically based. Instead, the meaning and significance of each category is determined by its cultural context and the social structure—in other words, these categories are socially constructed. They change over time, and they are continually contested, revised, and reinvented. We learn the meaning and significance of these categories for our time and our culture through the socialization process, which we discuss in Chapter 6.

Ideologies That Justify Inequality

The third element of all stratification systems is a related *ideology,* a system of beliefs that helps define and explain the world and justifies the existence of inequality. Those in power produce and promote these ideas to maintain the stratification system, but others sometimes internalize them as well. In fact, the most efficient way to maintain a system of inequality is to convince most people that the system is fair, inevitable, or both. If the groups within a society believe in an ideology that justifies a stratification system, or if they are cynical about any possibility of changing the system, they are unlikely to challenge it. Consequently, those who struggle to reduce inequality must often debate the ideology that supports it. For example, women's rights advocates have long had to debunk myths about women's biological inferiority.

The three key elements that all stratification systems have in common—unequal resources, distinct groups, and a justifying ideology—vary within different stratification systems. We now take a brief look at several examples of such systems.

Caste Systems: India, Feudal Estates, and Racial Segregation

A **caste system** features *stratification based on various ascribed characteristics determined at birth.* The social stratum—or caste—into which people are born largely determines their life chances, typically affecting their access to education, their work options, where they can live, and whom they can marry. Many agrarian societies have some type of closed caste system, but the best known, by far, is the one found in India, which was outlawed in 1952 but which continues to be practiced informally.

India's Caste System

India's stratification system is traditionally based on the unequal distribution of social honor or respect associated with four major castes, known as *varnas:*

- ***Brahmins,*** the highest caste, are priests, scholars, and teachers.
- ***Kshatriyas,*** the second caste, are kings, warriors, and political leaders.
- ***Vaisyas,*** the third caste, constitute a broad group that includes landowners, merchants, and skilled craftspeople.
- ***Sudras,*** the fourth caste, includes peasants, servants, and laborers.

Rounding out this complex system are hundreds of subcaste groups, or *jatis,* typically organized around a single occupation, such as carpenters or barbers and often situated in a particular village or region (Natrajan 2012; Rao 2009).

At the lowest stratum of Indian society is a group that exists outside of the *varna* system. Physical contact with members of this lowest grouping is thought to pollute anyone of higher status, so they are often referred to as "Untouchables," but they call themselves *Dalits* ("downtrodden"). *Dalits* are often uneducated and typically perform the lowest and least desirable types of labor, such as cleaning public toilets. In addition, *Dalits* are social outcasts who are banned from worshipping with members of the four *varnas.* Consequently, *Dalits* have little power in society.

©K Asif/India Today Group/Getty Images

Under India's caste system these protesters are *Dalits*—popularly known as "Untouchables—because of the families into which they were born. The man portrayed on the sign in the center is Bhimrao Ramji Ambedkar, a scholar and activist who founded the movement for civil rights for Untouchables, which challenges the ideology underlying this caste system.

Membership in a particular caste is determined at birth and cannot be changed. The justifying ideology, derived from both tradition and Hindu religious doctrine, emphasizes the maintenance of caste purity by restricting social contact to members of one's own caste. People are expected to marry within their own caste.

Throughout India's history, the caste system helped maintain social order by clearly defining the rights and responsibilities of those who belonged to various castes. However, resistance and opposition to this system date back thousands of years. After India gained independence from British rule in the mid-twentieth century, it adopted a constitution that outlawed discrimination based on caste. Today the caste system plays only a limited role in India's modern urban life. However, in the country's more-traditional rural areas and small towns, the influence of castes remains significant.

Feudal Estate Systems

During the Middle Ages, European societies were stratified into a castelike system that regulated economic, political, and social life based primarily on the unequal distribution of land (Martin 1986). Feudalism, as this system is now known, varied but commonly featured three *estates* that comprised a society's major strata:

- ***The nobility.*** The nobility, the dominant estate, owned the vast tracts of land upon which the agricultural economy—and their power—was based. Wealthy and powerful nobles lived lives of relative luxury, reaping the benefits of others' labor. An elaborate system of honorific titles, such as *king, queen, duke, earl,* and *baron,* indicated the relative rank and power of each individual within this estate. A person's rank was inherited, and marriage was typically restricted to other members of the nobility. Typically, only the eldest son of a noble could inherit land, so other male children served as military officers, judges, government administrators, or high-ranking members of the Church.
- ***The Christian clergy.*** As the second estate, the clergy largely served the nobles but had some independence due to their claim of religious authority. They were generally well educated and were themselves divided into an elaborate hierarchy made up of the pope, cardinals, bishops, priests, and other positions. An important role of the clergy was to articulate and enforce the ideology that justified the feudal system. The Church taught that inequality was the will of God and that the poor would receive their reward in heaven rather than on earth. To question inequality, therefore, was to question God's will.
- ***Commoners.*** The commoners made up the bulk of the population. Typically illiterate, they did not own land but instead lived on and worked the land owned by the nobles. The commoners' labor enriched the nobles but left them living in poor and difficult conditions.

Commoners repeatedly challenged the harsh conditions of the estate system by staging peasant uprisings. Eventually, the power of nobles was curbed with the advent of more democratic political systems and less-rigid class-based economic systems in the eighteenth and nineteenth centuries, as we saw in Chapter 1.

Racial Segregation in the United States

The system of racial segregation in the United States, which evolved between the Civil War and the 1960s, can be considered a caste-based stratification system (Massey and Denton 1993). (It influenced South Africa's apartheid, another caste-based stratification system, beginning in 1948.) The division between blacks and whites was based on birth and could not be changed. The ideology that justified racial segregation was racism, which those in power supported by invoking tradition, Christian teachings, and pseudoscience. Racial inequality was said to be the foundation of the traditional "southern way of life." Bible stories and passages were used selectively to justify slavery, including the tale that descendants of Noah's son, Ham, were cursed to be slaves (Genesis 9:18–27) and St. Paul's advice that servants accept their lot and obey their masters (Ephesians 6:5–9). So-called scientific classifications of races, based on racist assumptions, also justified racial inequality, as we examine in Chapter 10.

Though it is primarily associated with the southern states, where it was most comprehensive and brutally enforced, racial segregation existed throughout the United States. Blacks faced the most formal and broadest oppression, dating back to a race-based system of slavery. However, other races, ethnicities, and nationalities—notably Mexican and Chinese Americans—also faced segregation. Whites excluded minorities from many types of employment, and laws restricted their access to education, public transportation, theaters, restaurants, voting, and seats in public office. The legal system supported this unequal treatment. For example, in many communities, deeds to white-owned homes stipulated that they could not be sold to blacks.

Blacks and other minorities long resisted racial discrimination. The civil rights movement of the 1950s and 1960s successfully challenged the legal foundation for racial segregation. Since then, advocates for social justice have reduced the economic and social impact of racial discrimination, though its effects continue, and informal segregation is still a social reality. We examine various aspects of race and ethnicity in more detail in Chapter 10.

Class Systems: Capitalist and Socialist

Unlike a caste system, in which a person's position is determined by birth, a **class system** features *stratification determined by economic position, which results from a combination of individual achievement and family of birth.* Class systems are more flexible than caste systems and offer more opportunities for social mobility. They are still stratification systems, however; they organize the unequal distribution of resources among distinct groups and are supported by a justifying ideology. We examine classes more closely in Chapter 9. This brief preview sketches out some of the features of class systems in the two major types of economies, capitalist and socialist.

Class in Capitalist Systems

In the United States and other contemporary capitalist societies, considerable affluence is accompanied by significant class inequality. Economic resources such as income, stocks, real estate, and other forms of property are distributed unevenly, as are education and training. A small upper class of capitalists owns a substantial amount of the wealth and thereby wields enormous power. A broad middle class of relatively well-educated workers is employed in jobs that require considerable knowledge and skill and that pay well enough to afford a comfortable existence. A large working class is employed in modest-to-low-paying jobs that require less training and formal education. Those working for low wages and those unable to secure steady employment often live in poverty.

The ideology of capitalist class systems emphasizes individualism—the idea that success is based on merit, not inherited advantage. The popular idea that "with hard work and determination, you can accomplish whatever you want" is an implicit explanation for inequality: those at the bottom do not work hard, while those at the top do. Those who do well financially believe they "deserve" their advantages because they have worked hard. Many don't consider that most people struggling economically have also worked hard. Those well off see inequality as good because it motivates people to work hard to achieve economic success, thereby contributing to the overall affluence of society. As we see in Chapter 9, however, structural factors and barriers beyond an individual's control have a considerable impact on economic success or failure.

Throughout modern history, those below the capitalist class have often resisted inequality; in particular, workers in various countries have organized themselves into labor unions to gain more power and improve their working conditions. As a result, today's capitalist societies vary substantially in the degree to which they are unequal, with some offering a much broader social safety net than in the United States.

Class in Socialist Systems The major difference between capitalist and socialist class systems is the nature and degree of government intervention in the economy, a topic we examine in Chapter 16. Capitalist ideology suggests that individuals should compete in the marketplace free of government interference. In contrast, socialist ideology emphasizes the collective good and economic equality as coordinated by the government. In a socialist system, the government typically owns major industries and taxes wealthy citizens heavily to pay for free or subsidized social programs such as education, health care, housing, and day care.

Because the state plays such a central role, economic stratification varies across socialist societies, depending on the type of government. The best-known example of state socialism—often called communism—was in the former Soviet Union, where a totalitarian government downplayed the existence of inequality. In this and other communist systems, political dissent was not tolerated, and those who had access to political positions and resources—especially membership in the Communist Party and authority in the workplace—were at the highest levels of the stratification system. Thus Communist Party officials had the most power. The key divisions in society were between party leaders, workplace managers, and ordinary workers (Holmes 2009).

The politically oppressive nature of state socialism, coupled with its inefficiency as an economic system, helped lead to its demise. Today's major socialist societies are quite different. In China, for example, the Communist Party has adopted flexible economic policies that include aspects of capitalism, but the central authority still rigidly controls the government-owned companies that carry them out. The party also controls government bodies at all levels of society, including the military, the courts, the media, universities, and religious organizations (McGregor 2010). As a result, China continues to suppress political freedom while incorporating aspects of capitalism into its economy and harboring stark inequalities.

In contrast to state socialism, democratic socialism combines a government accountable to the electorate with an economy that includes considerable state intervention. Found most notably in some Scandinavian countries today, democratic socialism has produced some of the world's most affluent and least unequal countries. These societies tend to cultivate an ideology that values equality and the common good, even if it means putting strict limits on the income and wealth of the country's richest citizens.

Perhaps because it was associated with the communist regimes of the Soviet Union and China during the tense standoff of the second half of the twentieth century known as the Cold War, socialism has been decidedly unpopular in the United States, unlike in Europe. Nonetheless, some popular U.S. programs, such as Social Security and the minimum wage, can be understood as socialist, since they involve government intervention in the economy for the public good. More recently, the country's best-known democratic socialist, Senator Bernie Sanders of Vermont, has reframed democratic socialism in a way that appeals particularly to many younger voters. As he put it during his failed bid for the presidency in 2016, "Democratic socialism means that we must create an economy that works for all, not just the very wealthy. Democratic socialism means that we must reform a political system in America today which is not only grossly unfair but, in many respects, corrupt" (Sanders 2015). This reframing, combined with the fading of the communist regimes of the Cold War, may broaden democratic socialism's appeal. One poll found that two-thirds (69 percent) of potential voters under the age of 30 said they would be willing to vote for a socialist for president, which is double the percentage (34 percent) of people 65 and older who said the same (McCarthy 2015a).

Patriarchy

Another type of systemic stratification is based on gender. Women have long been subjected to **patriarchy,** *male domination through social institutions and cultural practices.* Patriarchy can be thought of as a system of stratification since it emphasizes separate and unequal groups (men and women), distributes resources unequally, and justifies this inequality with an ideology that assumes the superiority of men.

thinking about power

Where do you think the greatest inequality in **power** is in U.S. society today?
What would be needed to change this **power** inequality?

Patriarchal arrangements of power are built into many aspects of social life, including the cultural norm that a man should be the "head of household," the idea in some religions that women should play secondary roles, and the continuing underrepresentation of women in positions of political and economic power. Many feminist sociologists focus on understanding women's oppression, how sexism operates, and how women's subordination intersects with other forms of inequality. Consequently, power is an important concept in feminist theory and research.

As we explore further in Chapter 11, feminist scholars have developed a variety of approaches to understanding the relationships among gender, inequality, and power (Allen 1999, 2008; Bryson 2016). Some argue that women's oppression resulted from the power men had over them and that the liberation of women will challenge and break this power (Brownmiller 1975). Socialist-feminists argue that women's oppression was a result of capitalism; women were exploited as cheap labor in the paid labor force and as unpaid labor at home, helping sustain male workers. This argument links class and gender inequality (Eisenstein 1979; Gimenez 2001; S. Smith 2015). Many feminists of color insist on intersectionality, linking gender analyses with race, class, and sexual orientation (Collins and Bilge 2016; hooks 2015a, 2015b; Moraga and Anzaldúa 2015).

These examples of stratification systems illustrate some of the many ways that inequality is structured. Although each form of stratification has distinct features, by viewing all of them through the lens of power, we can see many similarities.

Can Inequality Be Reduced?

If all societies have inequality, can it be reduced? The simple answer is yes, although some forms of inequality are easier to combat than others. Interestingly, equality is a fairly new value in human history. Only since the Enlightenment of the eighteenth century has inequality been seen as undesirable. Before that time, it was considered inevitable and often a part of God's will. However, sociology teaches us that inequality is socially constructed and, thus, its nature and extent are neither inevitable nor foreordained. Human action produces inequality, and people can organize to empower themselves and reduce inequality. Indeed, the levels of inequality in different countries today vary greatly, attesting to the possibility of creating a more just and equitable society.

Source: Library of Congress Prints and Photographs Division [LC-USF3301-006392-M4]

©Christian Heinz/Alamy Stock Photo

FAST-FORWARD

Social Change and Class Segregation

Racist Jim Crow laws in the mid-twentieth century segregated many forms of public accommodations and transportation, giving whites preferred treatment. Today, many forms of segregation exist based on class. Customers who can afford it get preferred treatment with quick check-in lines, luxury seating, and other exclusive accommodations. While the racial segregation that once existed in public facilities appalls most Americans, most people today take class-based segregation for granted. Why do you think that is? Compare the difference between excluding people because of their race and excluding them because of their class.

A Changing World

ALGORITHMS AND THE POWER OF TECH COMPANIES

Some aspects of the internet have helped to empower users to better communicate and gain access to valuable information. However, in our digital world, the algorithms created by technology companies play a surprisingly powerful role in shaping our internet experiences, whether or not we are aware of it. Algorithms are software code created to accomplish various tasks without human intervention. Programmers write guiding rules for how the algorithm should operate and then apply it to vast quantities of data generated by our use of the internet, credit cards, grocery store discount cards, and other tools that record a digital trail. We see the results algorithms produce every day, including in Facebook newsfeeds, Google search results, map routes, "you might like" suggestions about music or movies, and "people you might know" prompts, among countless others. Sometimes, these results can help to reproduce social inequality (Eubanks 2017; Noble 2018; Pasquale 2015).

Most blatantly, programmers—and in some cases hackers—have sometimes worked racist material into the code. For example, during a period in 2015, while Barack Obama was president, entering a racial slur in the search box of Google Maps produced a result pinpointing the White House (see image). More often, the algorithms incorporate the racism of users into results. Until corrected, a Google photo search for "black people" turned up racist memes and images of apes among the top results; a search for "gorillas" turned up images of black people; a search for "black girls" included porn sites among the top results, while a search for "white girls" did not (Noble 2018).

If you Google Map "nigga house," this is what you'll find. America.

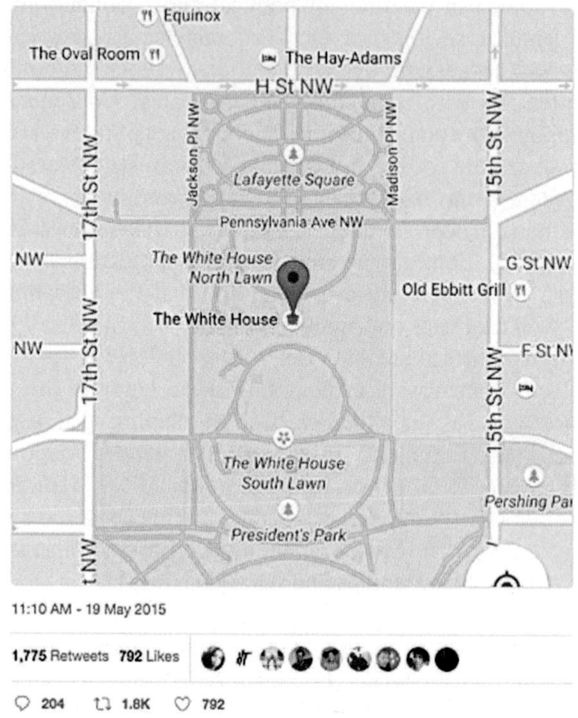

11:10 AM - 19 May 2015

1,775 Retweets 792 Likes

204 1.8K 792

Source: Deray McKesson, Twitter

While Barack Obama was president in 2015, entering a racial slur in the Google Maps search box produced a result pinpointing the White House (Noble 2018). Social media users, including Black Lives Matter activist Deray Mckesson, tweeted the image to get Google to fix the issue.

In addition, algorithms can be misused. For example, Facebook's automated system to purchase advertising relies on algorithms that sort users based on what they read, share, and write on the platform. The result is tens of thousands of categories that enable advertisers to target their message narrowly. Much of this is benign; however, the system operates largely without human involvement, which leaves it vulnerable to abuse. To prove the point, journalists succeeded in taking out ads on Facebook targeting people identified by Facebook's algorithms as being interested in topics such as "Jew hater" and "How to burn Jews." Facebook approved the ads within 15 minutes (Angwin, Varner, and Tobin 2017). Google similarly allows advertisers to target people based on their searches. It accepted ads created to target people based on racist searches such as "Black people ruin everything" and "Jewish parasite" (Kantrowitz 2017). Conversely, journalists also showed that racists could use Facebook's ad system to prevent racial minorities from seeing housing ads, a possible violation of fair housing laws (Angwin and Parris 2016). In all these cases, the companies said they amended their procedures after journalists contacted them.

Less obviously, online stores use algorithms to generate prices based on your buying history and where you live. Judges use them to guide sentencing of convicted defendants. Government agencies use them to assign public housing and to grant or deny food stamps. Insurance companies use them to help set rates and to approve or deny claims. In these cases and many more, users can employ race, class, and gender information in ways that inadvertently reproduce social inequalities.

Because the computations that occur as algorithms churn through big data are massive and involve so many different variables, creators often do not exactly know how they work or how to control them, giving algorithms a degree of autonomy. Because algorithms are usually proprietary, people outside the companies that use them cannot tell how they are written, cloaking them in a degree of secrecy. Because ordinary citizens are often unaware of—or don't think about—algorithms, the companies that create them can have a good deal of power in shaping how we experience the world every day. (We look at related issues in Chapter 14.)

Growing concern about the new power of these companies and their algorithms may trigger use of an older type of power: political regulation. Tim Berners-Lee, the creator of the world wide web—the software that connects content on the internet—argues that "power is concentrated among so few companies" that they can now "control which ideas and opinions are seen and shared." While these companies need to make changes, he says, they "have been built to maximize profit more than to maximize social good" and it may be time for a "legal or regulatory framework that accounts for social objectives" (Berners-Lee 2018).

thinking sociologically about
Power

- **Power** is the capacity to bring about a desired outcome as well as to overcome resistance by others. It operates at all levels of society.
- **Power** can be used to allocate resources (economic), make rules and decisions (political), and help define reality (cultural).
- **Power** is based on social relationships and requires compliance. Disobedience can be a form of power, since it denies the compliance being sought.

REVIEW, REFLECT, AND APPLY

Looking Back

1. Power includes the ability to bring about a desired outcome ("power to"), as well as the capacity to overcome resistance ("power over"). Education, organization, and networking contribute to empowerment. Compliance may be obtained by persuasion, reward, or coercion.
2. Power operates at all levels of society and can be seen in both everyday situations as well as at the macro level. Power is commonly used to allocate resources (economic), make rules and decisions (political), and help define reality (cultural)—and thus is closely tied to inequality.
3. Power can be legitimate, accepted voluntarily by those who are affected by it; or illegitimate, relying on coercion to generate obedience. Legitimate power can be based on traditional, rational-legal, or charismatic authority.
4. Power is based on social relationships and requires compliance from others. Disobedience, or noncompliance, can be a form of power, especially for those without access to other forms of power.
5. Considering power and inequality alerts us to the issue of privilege. Understanding relations of power involves understanding various perspectives, including those of people with little power.
6. Inequality is multidimensional and includes stratification based on class (economic conditions), status (prestige), and power (political organization). Intersectionality theory suggests that to understand inequality, we need to consider the ways in which race, class, and gender interact and form what is sometimes referred to as a matrix of domination.
7. All societies have some system of stratification, featuring unequally distributed resources, distinct groups that make up the strata, and an ideology that explains and justifies inequality. Major types of stratification systems include caste systems, class systems, and patriarchy.
8. Technology companies can exert considerable power over how we see the world through their use of algorithms, sometimes reproducing social inequalities.

Critical Thinking: Questions and Activities

1. What are power and inequality, and how are these two concepts related?
2. Do you consider yourself powerful? If you answer yes, what is the source of your power? If your answer is no, what would have to change to increase your power?
3. Identify and describe a common situation in your daily life where you comply with power. Is this a case of legitimate or illegitimate power? Explain.
4. How do various types of inequality intersect in your life? In what ways are you relatively privileged? In what ways do you face disadvantages?
5. Make a list of three people or organizations that you consider to be powerful. Using what you have learned in this chapter, explain what makes each of them powerful. For each, explain how power is rooted in social relationships. Now do the same with three people or organizations that you think are relatively powerless.

Key Terms

caste system (p. 116) stratification based on various ascribed characteristics determined at birth.

charismatic authority (p. 108) power whose legitimacy is derived from the extraordinary personal characteristics of an individual leader, which inspire loyalty and devotion.

class (p. 111) a group of people who share a roughly similar economic position and lifestyle.

class system (p. 117) stratification determined by economic position, which results from a combination of individual achievement and family of birth.

coerce (p. 102) to force people's compliance by threatening, intimidating, pressuring, or harming them.

discrimination (p. 113) treating others unequally based on their background or other personal characteristics.

empowerment (p. 100) an increase in the capacity of people to bring about an intended outcome.

hegemony (p. 107) a condition that exists when those in power have successfully spread their ideas—and marginalized alternative viewpoints—so that their perspectives and interests are accepted widely as being universal and true.

illegitimate power (p. 108) a form of authority that relies on force or coercion to generate obedience.

inequality (p. 111) the unequal distribution of resources among groups of people.

intersectionality theory (p. 113) a perspective that highlights the connections and interactions between various forms of inequality, especially race, class, and gender.

legitimate power or authority (p. 108) power that is voluntarily accepted by those who are subject to it.

life chances (p. 112) the opportunities offered by a person's economic position.

matrix of domination (p. 114) the interlocking systems of oppression associated with race, class, and gender.

patriarchy (p. 118) male domination through social institutions and cultural practices.

persuade (p. 102) to get people's compliance by convincing them of the correctness of your position and goals.

power (p. 100) the ability to bring about an intended outcome, even when opposed by others.

power tactics (p. 104) the specific strategies people use to influence others in everyday life.

privilege (p. 111) a special advantage or benefit that not everyone enjoys.

rational-legal authority (p. 108) power that has legitimacy because it is based on established laws, rules, and procedures.

reward (p. 102) to encourage people's compliance by offering a positive incentive.

social closure (p. 112) the process whereby a status group maximizes its own advantages by restricting access to rewards only to members of the group.

social mobility (p. 116) movement from one stratum of a stratification system to another.

standpoint theory (p. 111) a theory that questions taken-for-granted assumptions about society by looking at it from multiple viewpoints, especially from the perspective of people in subordinate positions.

stratification systems (p. 115) social structures and cultural norms that create and maintain inequality by ranking people into a hierarchy of groups that receive unequal resources.

traditional authority (p. 108) power that has legitimacy because of compliance with well-established cultural practices.

©Creatas Images/Getty Images

6 Socialization

looking AHEAD

How were you socialized into your society's **culture**?

How do agents of socialization reproduce social **structure**?

How does **power** shape your daily life and your sense of self?

©Laura Pedrick/The New York Times/Redux Pictures

In 1998, 16-year-old Melanie Matchett Wood became the first American woman to make the U.S. International Mathematical Olympiad Team. Wood won a silver medal, went on to earn a PhD in math, and is now a leading scholar in her field. Commenting on her Olympiad victory, Wood recalls, "I thought, 'Why am I so surprised?' And then I realized that it was just that I had this image of the people who won this competition—and that image was of boys." The math world then included few, if any, female role models (Scharf 2003), and little has changed since. Only a few women have been on the U.S. team since Wood won her medal. When the United States competed at the 2017 International Mathematical Olympiad in Rio de Janeiro, Brazil, the team was all-male (MAA 2017).

Wood had to overcome the cultural norms of a society in which girls rarely pursue high-level math, but she had support along her way to prominence. Her father, who died when she was just six weeks old, had been a math teacher, and her mother helped keep his memory alive by teaching Melanie math from early childhood. Later, a seventh-grade teacher encouraged Wood's interest in math, inviting her to join the school's MathCounts team. She also found a role model in Zvezdelina Stankova, a woman mathematician with a Harvard PhD, who had also been an International Mathematical Olympiad medal winner. Wood notes, "Having a role model like that was a big deal in my life" (Gallian 2004). Wood, in her turn, now mentors and supports aspiring women mathematicians.

Culture and socialization contribute to the gender gap in math. Sociologist Maria Charles (2011, 2017) found that the gap is larger in wealthier Western societies, where girls have been encouraged to pursue their own interests. She suspects girls have internalized gender stereotypes at a young age and, when given the choice, tend to stay away from math and other science fields. In contrast, of the 65 countries that have educational systems with a full range of majors, developing countries such as Iran, Oman, and Saudi Arabia have the highest percentage of women in science. (The United States ranks in the middle.) Such countries have a much smaller gender gap between eighth-grade students who say, "I like math." Also, developing countries tend to have education systems that focus on economic development, rather than individual self-fulfillment, socializing students into valuing science-based fields and funneling students with the best skills—female or male—into math and other sciences.

Wood's story illustrates the profound power that the cultural messages we absorb from infancy and throughout our lives have to shape what we believe, how we behave, and how we live. But it also illustrates how those messages–in this case, messages about gender, aspirations, and achievement–are subject to challenge and change.

Socialization is *the process through which people learn their culture's basic norms, values, beliefs, and appropriate behaviors.* Through socialization we learn who we are, what is expected of us, how society operates, and where we stand within our social world. As children we learn the language and symbols of our culture and our social roles as child and, perhaps, sibling. As we grow, we learn new roles, such as friend, student, teammate, employee, lover, spouse, parent, grandparent, and retiree. We also learn and internalize the structure and expectations of the various groups, organizations, and institutions in which we may participate, including families, schools, religious institutions, clubs, sports teams, friendship networks, and workplaces. Through socialization we also forge a sense of self–a sense of who we are as individuals in relation to the people with whom we interact personally as well as to society as a whole. Like Melanie Wood, we can even challenge traditional socialization messages and, in the process, become role models who help open new possibilities for the next generation.

Reproducing Structure: Agents of Socialization

In transmitting fundamental social norms and role expectations from one generation to another, socialization helps reproduce social structure and is a key to social stability. Socialization is a dynamic process, however. As social structure changes, the messages imparted through socialization also change.

Because socialization occurs throughout life, it takes place in different ways and in different social contexts, guided by many different **agents of socialization,** or *people and groups who teach us about our culture.* For children, the family is usually far and away the most important agent of socialization. But as children grow up and are exposed to different people and groups, other socializing agents take on increasingly important roles, including school, media, peer groups, the workplace, religion, and what are known as total institutions. (See the Through a Sociological Lens box for a look at how different agents of socialization—including family, schools, peer groups, and the media—influence people's political identities.)

©Sean Sprague/Alamy Stock Photo

In all cultures, families play a key role in socializing children, especially during the early years. Even while in a refugee camp for internally displaced people, this Timorese mother teaches about hygiene by washing her child. This is just one of the many practices parents teach their children.

CORE CONCEPTS CHALLENGE *What other aspects of their* **culture** *do parents in all societies teach their children?*

Family

Families are the primary agent of early socialization. Within the family most individuals learn basic skills such as how to talk and how to maintain personal hygiene, and they learn important values such as the difference between right and wrong and the proper way to treat other people. "Say 'thank you.'" "Respect your elders." "Don't hit your brother." "Always tell the truth." These kinds of instruction teach children the most basic norms, values, beliefs, expectations, and behaviors of their culture.

Families play a crucial role in the early development of a child's sense of identity. Whether or not children learn to see themselves as loved, smart, creative, and strong depends largely on how their families treat them in their early years. Families also influence what nation, ethnicity, race, religion, and class children identify with as they mature. Families are a child's first teachers about "appropriate" gender roles, which they often signal by the toys and clothing they choose and the chores they assign. Parents—themselves the product of gender socialization—usually assume that gender (culture) should match sex (biology) and sometimes struggle with how much nontraditional gender behavior to accept from their children. As we see in Chapter 11, the process of gender socialization begins at a very young age. Messages full of gender-specific expectations for children about, for example, how to dress and behave are part of a broader process through which girls and boys learn how to act in ways that are promoted as gender appropriate.

Childrearing practices can vary by culture within a society in ways that help reproduce social structure. For example, sociologist Melvin Kohn (1977) found that in the United States, working-class parents tend to teach their children to value obedience, the expected attitude for most working-class jobs, whereas middle-class parents encourage their children to value self-direction, the attitude required for the kind of independent thinking expected in many middle-class occupations. These different values, in turn, increase the likelihood that children will end up with the same educational opportunities and in the same kind of work as their parents, thus reproducing the existing structural inequality from one generation to the next. More recent studies have observed similar class differences across racial lines in the United States (Lareau 2011, 2015).

Similar class differences have also been observed cross-nationally. For example, a study using data from 90 nations found that people in wealthier countries with a highly educated population were more likely to raise their children to be independent than people in poorer countries with a less educated and less urban population, and that people in poorer countries, in contrast, were more likely to emphasize obedience. Likewise, within individual countries those of higher economic status were more likely than those of lower economic status to prioritize independence in parenting (Park and Lau 2016).

THROUGH A SOCIOLOGICAL LENS

Learning Politics

Do you pay attention to politics? Did you vote in the last election and, if so, whom did you vote for? As with other aspects of culture, every society must teach young people what it means to be a good citizen. Democracies base their legitimacy on the active participation of citizens in the political process. So, how do people learn about politics? Research suggests that political socialization involves a complex combination of socializing agents, especially family and media.

Families matter, sometimes in surprising ways. Children of parents who pay attention to politics are more likely to pay attention themselves. But, ironically, young people who pay attention to politics are more likely than those who don't to diverge from their parents' political views. That's because children who don't pay much attention to politics are less likely to question the political ideas they've learned at home (Dinas 2014). Either way, those lessons from home do matter. For example, people who had stay-at-home mothers tend to be more conservative, while people whose mothers work outside the home are more likely to endorse policies that support social equality and the liberal views of feminism. At the same time, compared to child-free adults, parents (whose children get sick, have accidents, and are generally expensive to raise) are more likely to endorse government programs that aim to reduce poverty and assist those who have fallen on hard times (Urbatsch 2014).

Schools, too, can matter—but less than is often supposed. Some research suggests that while education about civic values may raise political awareness, it has minimal impact on actual participation in politics (Manning and Edwards 2014). The influence of peers, too, may be commonly overestimated. Some research suggests that the influence of both schools and peers is indirect. It's the media—especially online media—that turn out to be especially important. Young people use the media to learn about political issues, share information with others, and discuss politics outside the confines of family and school and the influence of their immediate peers (Lee, Shah, and McLeod 2012). In addition, the news media play an especially important role in helping to socialize recent immigrants to the political culture of their new country (Lui and Gastil 2014).

Finally, political socialization varies by society and changes over time. The ideas promoted in democratic societies are different from those in less open societies. And when societies undergo dramatic change—as with the breakup of the Soviet Union in the 1980s and the violent upheavals that some Middle Eastern countries have experienced recently—political socialization, adapting to the larger social environment in which it takes place, likewise changes (Sapiro 2004).

think about it

1. *What socializing agents were important in helping to shape your political views and your level of political participation (or nonparticipation)?*
2. *Do you tend to share the political views of your family? Why or why not?*

School

Day care, preschool, or kindergarten is many children's first extended experience with people and the world outside their home. In these settings children learn to interact with other people and adjust to being part of a group. As the agents of socialization most explicitly focused on teaching cultural knowledge, schools prepare children for their later roles in society, providing instruction in a variety of fields, including advanced language skills, mathematics, history, and science. Schools can also socialize students into the politics of getting ahead in life.

In addition to their formal academic curriculum, schools convey a **hidden curriculum** consisting of *implicit lessons about how children should behave* (Jackson 1968). These lessons vary depending on the school and often change as children advance in grade levels. However, most U.S. schools teach children to be quiet and attentive, to obey authority, to follow rules, to be respectful of others, and to take pride in their country. Schools in the United States also tend to encourage competition and individual achievement by promoting sports, spelling bees, and honor rolls, among other activities. Schools are also the site for lessons about class and gender, topics we explore in Chapters 9 and 11.

Media

Media play a central role in the lives of young people, especially in industrialized nations. On average, U.S. teenagers (13 to 18 years of age) spend nearly nine hours a day with media–*excluding* the time they spend using media for school or homework. So-called tweens–8- to 12-year-olds–spend nearly six hours a day with media . This double counts multitasking; listening to music while using social media for an hour "counts" as two hours of media exposure (Common Sense Media 2015). This is more time than they spend in the classroom and much more time than they spend interacting with their parents. Nearly 40 percent of young adults aged 18 to 29 report being online "almost constantly" (Perrin and Jiang 2018).

Young people's pervasive use of media is due, in part, to the growing pervasiveness of mobile devices, which can provide access to media almost anywhere at any time (Livingstone and Sefton-Green 2016). One study of U.S. teens (13 to 17 years old) found that nearly three-quarters of them (73 percent) had access to a smartphone, 87 percent to a desktop or laptop, 58 percent to a tablet computer, and 81 percent to a gaming console like an Xbox (Lenhart 2015).

As a result, media have arguably become the most influential agents of socialization in contemporary society. For most of human history, in contrast, children learned morals and values from the instructions and stories they heard from their families. The emergence of the earliest mass media—print—in the fifteenth century did little to change the dominant role of family because it required the ability to read and physical access to printed materials. However, with the emergence of broadcast media—radio and, especially, television—children unable yet to read at an adult level for the first time in history had ready access to the world of adult ideas and circumstances. Children could now "see" the battlefields of foreign wars from their living rooms and watch programs that showed the intimate lives of adults (Meyrowitz 1985). Today, the internet, along with mobile devices, provides young people access to a vast array of adult content outside of the supervision of parents, further eroding the boundary between childhood and adulthood that was once a staple of the socialization process.

In addition, often outside of the scrutiny of parents, children are socialized by commercial media companies whose primary interest is selling products and socializing young people to be avid consumers. Thus companies such as Disney (which owns the Disney Channel and Nickelodeon) and Time Warner (which owns the Cartoon Network) play a central part in introducing children to a set of values, beliefs, norms, and behaviors that promote a consumer lifestyle (Buckingham 2011; Pugh 2009; Schor 2004).

Some critics argue that American values are embedded in the media products sold by U.S. corporations abroad and in the social media platforms used across the globe (Boyd-Barrett 2015). Norms of individualism and consumerism, for example, saturate such media and may conflict with traditional values in the nations where such products are consumed. From this perspective, the heavy flow of media from the United States to the rest of the world can erode local cultures and values (Tomlinson 2008). As noted in the discussion of the globalization of culture at the end of Chapter 3, however, the threat may be exaggerated. Some observers argue that the global circulation of U.S.-produced media products does not seem, as some had feared, to be Americanizing global culture. Nor do globally distributed entertainment products seem to be creating a distinctive global consciousness. Even though hundreds of millions of children and teenagers around the world listen to the same music, play the same games, and watch the same movies, they do not appear to be losing their sense of who they are or where they belong (Ugochukwu 2008).

As a powerful socializing agent, media can make positive contributions to society. At their best, children's media can promote positive values such as honesty, compassion, responsibility, self-respect, and standing up for what you believe in. Media also give people access to a much broader range of news, images, and stories than was available in the past. Media thus allow people to learn more about their society and about the cultures of other people.

©ClassicStock/Alamy Stock Photo

©Ariel Skelley/Blend Images/Getty Images

FAST-FORWARD

Social Change and Socialization

Television became a fixture in U.S. households in the 1950s and emerged quickly as a powerful, and sometimes controversial, agent of socialization. Today, online media pervade the daily lives of children in the United States. How have today's ever-present media changed the process of socialization compared to earlier eras?

Peer Groups

Parents often worry about their children's friends, their **peer group,** *a group of people, usually of comparable age, who share similar interests and social status.* Peer groups can significantly influence people's development and behavior. This is especially true of children and adolescents, whose sense of self is not yet firmly developed and is therefore susceptible to influence by others. As they approach adulthood, adolescents usually become increasingly independent of their families, and during this period peer groups can act as a surrogate family. Peer groups provide young people with the opportunity to experiment with

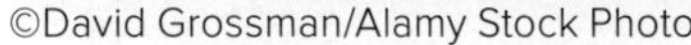

©David Grossman/Alamy Stock Photo

©Paras Griffin/Getty Images

Peer groups can be an important socializing influence on individuals. Members of street gangs, like those pictured on the left, display all the accessories of the subculture they have been taught. They use specialized language, communicate with unique hand gestures, adorn their bodies with gang-related tattoos, often wear special gang colors, and adopt a worldview that places high value on gang membership and loyalty. College fraternities and sororities have similar characteristics. They, too, share special signals and insignia—the Greek letters that identify particular fraternities and sororities—and they encourage group loyalty and mutual assistance.

CORE CONCEPTS CHALLENGE *Peer groups can be powerful socializing agents, strongly influencing the behavior of their members. What is the nature of their* **power,** *and how is it exercised?*

values, beliefs, and behaviors that differ from their parents'. To separate themselves from their families and fit in with peer groups, adolescents commonly change the way they talk, dress, and act, as well as the interests they pursue. This process is not unique to adolescence, however. When adults embark on new jobs and careers or move to new cities or neighborhoods, they often look to members of their new peer groups for clues about social norms and appropriate behaviors. A young couple that moves from the city to the suburbs will have to adopt new norms for social interaction and will probably learn those new norms from a peer group.

There are many different kinds of peer groups. Some are informal, as with groups of friends who choose to spend leisure time together. For teenagers, peer group activities can involve going to the mall or the movies; playing sports or video games; experimenting with cigarettes, alcohol, drug use, and sex; driving around together; or texting and interacting through social media platforms. Other peer groups exist in structured environments, as is the case with classmates, teammates, and colleagues at work.

The Workplace

The workplace is one of the most important social settings in which we experience socialization. **Occupational socialization** is *the process of learning the informal norms associated with a type of employment.* As you study, train, or apprentice in a given job category, you are picking up all sorts of cues, large and small, about how to be successful in a given job. For example, skilled tradespeople such as carpenters, plumbers, and electricians not only have to know the technical details of their craft, but they also typically learn the informal rules about how to work with customers, suppliers, and workers from other trades who share the job site. Understanding the expected norms, values, and behaviors of their position can be vital to success in their field.

Socialization into professional occupations–such as medicine and law–is one of the most significant, if often unrecognized, functions of graduate and professional schools. Of course, these schools provide subject-specific information: medical students study anatomy and law students study contracts. But aspiring professionals also learn the often informal, unstated norms of their profession: how to behave as a doctor or lawyer. Doctors, for example, must learn how to wield authority, behave appropriately, and talk with patients. Similarly, lawyers learn how to talk to judges, relate to clients, and deal with conflicts between their clients' interests and their own beliefs. Although some of this material may be touched upon in formal classroom discussions, students pick up most of it informally through socialization.

A classic study of students at Harvard Law School illustrates the powerful effects of occupational socialization into a profession (Granfield 1992; Granfield and Koenig 1990). The researchers found that many of these elite students entered law school intending to practice public interest law, such as by advocating for nonprofit organizations, representing poor clients, and working to prevent government and corporate fraud and abuse. However, during their three years of professional training at Harvard, they switched course. As they became socialized into their profession, many abandoned their commitment to public interest law and embraced the idea of entering a prestigious, high-paying corporate law firm. There, if their senior partners permitted, they might be able to do some *pro bono* (free-of-charge) work for needy clients.

This kind of professional socialization continues over the course of one's career. As people gain experience in a given field, they learn how to relate to younger or less experienced coworkers. If you are promoted, for example, you will have to learn the norms and expectations of your new position, which may include supervising other employees, attending meetings with senior managers, and participating in long-range planning. Your new position may also require you to dress differently, learn a new style of communication, and perhaps change your own family schedule.

Religion

Religion is the socializing agent most explicitly focused on the teaching of values and beliefs. Religious institutions in the past had enormous influence on all aspects of social life, offering social and educational opportunities as well as indoctrination in morality and values. Overall, that influence declined during the twentieth century, but religion still plays a significant role in many people's lives and the U.S. population is far more involved with religion than are residents of most European countries (Putnam and Campbell 2010). In addition, many parents who are not believers or who do not observe their religion often insist that their children obtain religious instruction.

For believers, religion can be an especially potent socializing agent because it often bases its prescriptions on texts such as the Christian Bible or the Muslim Qur'an that most believers consider sacred and some consider infallible. For people who believe that a divinity advocates or forbids certain values, beliefs, and behaviors, religion can supersede other socializing influences. In a society in which material well-being and consumerism are hallmarks of mainstream culture, religious institutions are among the few that promote the serious discussion of nonmaterial values. For example, in 2013 Pope Francis criticized "big business's idolatry of money over man," arguing instead that "we want a just system, a system that lets all of us get ahead. We don't want this globalized economic system that does us so much harm" (Zaimov 2013).

In recent decades, religious organizations, especially in the United States, have dramatically expanded their use of mass media, spreading their message through religious-themed news, commentary, and entertainment as well as through the traditional broadcast of religious services. In the United States, evangelical Christian groups have been particularly adept at using books, television, radio, and social media to bring together the socializing influences of religion and media (Blake 2005; Ratcliff, McCarty, and Ritter 2017).

Total Institutions

One unique group of socializing agents are what sociologist Erving Goffman (1961) called **total institutions,** *confining social settings in which an authority regulates all aspects of a person's life.* Goffman identifies five general types of total institutions:

1. Institutions that care for people who are defined as incapable and harmless—for example, orphanages and nursing homes.
2. Institutions set up to care for people who cannot care for themselves but who may represent an unintentional threat to the community—for example, psychiatric hospitals.
3. Institutions set up to protect a community from those whom authorities define as posing a significant danger—for example, prisons and jails, and prisoner-of-war camps.
4. Institutions established to pursue a specific task requiring the total commitment of participants—for example, military barracks and boarding schools.
5. Institutions intended as escapes or retreats from the world—for example, monasteries, convents, and some communes.

Total institutions typically share several key features. All aspects of daily life take place in the same setting under the guidance of the same authority. Members live in groups, and all

©Gary Friedman/Los Angeles Times/Getty Images

Prisons are one type of total institution where authorities impose a schedule and regiment activities. Wearing identical clothing, inmates in the California State Prison at Lancaster eat a meal at a designated time.

group members are supposed to be treated the same and complete the same tasks. Authorities impose a specific schedule, monitoring it through the application of formal rules and regimenting all the activities within the institution.

The closed world of a total institution provides an extreme example of **resocialization,** *the process by which individuals replace old norms and behaviors with new ones as they move from one role or life stage to another.* In total institutions people must submit to a strictly controlled regimen and live in a group with other people in the same condition. Such controlled institutions attempt to reprogram people to avoid past problems (substance abuse, for example), accept current realities (as with seniors adapting to residential elder care facilities), or prepare for future commitments. The U.S. Army, for example, requires new recruits to participate in a 10-week Basic Combat Training course that is intended to socialize civilians into soldiers. At their best, as with high-quality mental health facilities, such institutions can be benevolent means of providing care and helping people prepare for new roles in society. At their worst, as with political concentration camps, they can be coercive and oppressive, designed to destroy the individual will and obtain submission. (The Sociology Works box discusses one example of a total institution.)

Total institutions are not always successful at resocializing all their members. For example, although prisons and psychiatric hospitals control the daily lives of their inmates and can compel inmates to behave in specific ways, the inmates don't always internalize the norms and attitudes being promoted and may not behave in ways consistent with these norms when they are released. This is a matter of concern for those who work in fields such as mental health, substance abuse, juvenile delinquency, and criminal justice.

Socialization through the Life Course

Although socialization is most intense in a person's early years, the agents of socialization discussed in the previous section are active throughout a person's entire life span. The **life-course perspective** on socialization *looks at how age, time, and place shape social identities and experiences over a lifetime.* Each stage of life is associated with particular experiences that influence our identity and that require resocialization. Although everyone progresses through various stages of life, those stages and what they mean can differ based on the historical period and culture in which a person lives, as well as on the person's gender, class, and other aspects of personal identity.

The process of change from one life stage to another can involve a shift in a person's responsibilities, living situation, or standing within their community. Moments of transition often involve initiation ceremonies or **rites of passage,** *activities that mark and celebrate a change in a person's social status* (van Gennep [1909] 1961). Some of these ceremonies are rooted in religion, such as a confirmation or bar mitzvah, and follow traditions handed down from generation to generation. In the United States, weddings, graduation ceremonies, quinceañeras, and the Marine Corps' final training exercise known as "the Crucible" all mark the entrance into a new stage of life. Different societies have their own culturally specific rites of passage, and outsiders are likely to find some of these disconcerting. Among the Venda in South Africa, for example, teenage boys and girls go off to separate traditional initiation schools, where older men and women prepare them for sexual relationships with their future spouses. The boys spend up to three months away from their families and undergo male circumcision as the central component of their transition from childhood to adulthood (Lutendo, Maharaj, and Rogan 2008).

on social theory

As part of a broader **symbolic interactionist** approach, Arnold van Gennep theorized that **rites of passage** are a feature of the socialization process in all societies. What events in your own life would you describe as rites of passage? Did your position in your community change after those events? Did you feel different? Did people treat you differently?

Socialization is a never-ending process because people continually adopt new roles and identities. Some of these roles involve advanced preparation. **Anticipatory socialization** is *the process by which individuals practice for a future social role by adopting the norms or behaviors associated with a position they have not yet achieved.* For example, children are engaging in anticipatory socialization when they imitate and practice adult roles, playing with dolls to simulate being parents, or playing school to anticipate becoming students or teachers. In later life, young adults might take on internships to see if they want to pursue employment in a certain field, and couples might live together to find out if they are compatible for marriage.

Childhood

The early stages of life, which we label childhood and adolescence, correspond to the period during which infants gradually mature biologically into adults. However, childhood and adolescence are also social constructs; what it means to be a child or teenager varies over time and from culture to culture. As a result, the way young people experience this particularly intense period of socialization also varies (Handel, Cahill, and Elkin 2007).

thinking about power

Total institutions resocialize people subject to their authority. How does the nature of the **power** they use to do this vary in different kinds of total institutions—for example, military "boot camps" as opposed to prisons?

SOCIOLOGY WORKS

Kate Corrigan, Teaching at a School for Blind Children and Young Adults

When Kate Corrigan graduated from the College of the Holy Cross in 2009, she had a BA in sociology, was fluent in American Sign Language, and was looking for a job that would allow her to combine those two qualifications. She landed a job as a teaching assistant in the Deafblind Program at a school for blind children and young adults, where her sociological background was a valuable asset.

Corrigan worked with 12- to 18-year-olds at the residential school, spending much of her time with students in the cottages where they live, rather than in a traditional classroom. Her teaching stressed developing students' communication proficiency, as well as their social and daily living skills. As part of the program's focus on negotiating everyday life interactions, Corrigan took her students on trips to the local community where they could practice communication in public settings, such as stores and restaurants. Community field trips help students learn independence and how to advocate for themselves in a range of social settings.

Residential schools of this kind have many of the features of a benevolent total institution. As a former sociology student, Corrigan understood the importance of the program's role in the socialization process. At a residential school, Corrigan has noted, "The roles, tasks, and environment typically associated with the home become part of the educational setting." Corrigan found that she often drew upon what she learned in her "Children and Society" class at Holy Cross for insight into the importance of family and school in the lives of children.

> "Sociology expanded my educational horizons while also giving me the freedom to narrow my focus to exactly what I wanted."

Corrigan applied the sociological perspective to the school's sometimes challenging relationship with local residents. She discovered that community expectations about people with special needs, even when well intentioned, could often impose severe limitations on students. Corrigan has noted, however, that in student–community interactions, "we like to pleasantly surprise people." Still, Corrigan recognized that the norms within the school community might not always fit smoothly with the norms of the broader community. This sociological understanding of the complexity of the school–community relationship helped Corrigan navigate her interactions with the school's neighbors.

Courtesy of Kate Corrigan

Kate Corrigan

Corrigan, who now works at a school for deaf and blind teenagers, also appreciates how transferable to everyday life are the skills she learned in her sociology classes. Sociology gave her valuable research tools, for example, that she has brought to bear in studying the impact of assistive devices on communication among the deaf, the benefits of bilingual education for deaf students, and responses to disabilities among athletes in professional sports.

In reflecting on her experience as a sociology student, Corrigan offers some helpful advice: "To anyone taking a sociology course for the first time, let the subject inspire you. There are so many avenues with which the subject can be appreciated and applied. Make it your own."

think about it

1. *Why does a residential school qualify as a kind of total institution?*
2. *What "expectations" do you think the public has about blind and deaf students, and how do you think the students might "pleasantly surprise" people? Does your local community have expectations about how students at your school should look or behave?*

Contemporary Western societies tend to view childhood as a natural condition linked to children's physical immaturity. Children are considered innocent, with limited capacities, and in need of intensive care and protection by adults. However, according to Philippe Aries's classic study of the history of family life in Europe, *Centuries of Childhood* (1965), the idea of a distinct childhood period is really a social construction invented in Western society during the sixteenth and seventeenth centuries. Before then, childhood was not distinguished so clearly from adulthood. European paintings of the fifteenth and early sixteenth centuries, for example, often portray children as miniature adults, complete with adult clothing and adult body proportions. Parents introduced their children to the adult world early and abruptly. Given the cramped living quarters of the day, by necessity parents routinely exposed their children to the full range of adult activity; children were served alcohol and sometimes shared the same room as adults having sex. It was common for parents to apprentice their six-year-old children, sending

©National Galleries of Scotland/Getty Images

This 1626 painting shows a Scottish countess and her two young daughters, both dressed as miniature adults in elaborate clothing similar to that of their mother.

them away from home to live and work. (This practice was imported to colonial America as well.) Peasant parents might exploit their children as a potentially valuable family resource by renting them out as servants in wealthy homes. Children unable to secure such positions would often roam the streets picking through garbage and searching for anything useful to their families. Few ever attended school.

Despite these differences, some aspects of medieval childhood would be recognizable today. For example, medieval children played with toys and engaged in games specifically intended for children (Orme 2003). But scholars agree that the social perception and treatment of children—the meaning of childhood—has evolved over time.

By the eighteenth century, children in Western society were increasingly seen as innocent, weak, and in need of protection rather than as hardy "little adults." Parents socialized their children to behave differently than adults and often punished transgressions with severe beatings. But children's participation in the adult world continued. Child labor—a term that would not have been used at the time—was common throughout the eighteenth century. Children could fit into tight spaces, so they were favored workers for picking coal in tight mine shafts or cleaning the insides of chimneys. As late as 1890 in the United States, about 1.5 million children between the ages of 10 and 15 were working, many in the nation's bustling factories (American Social History Project 2007).

©Victoria Blackie/Photographer's Choice/Getty Images

Only in the early nineteenth century did reformers begin to challenge the idea that children should be employed as laborers. This was part of a broader cultural transformation as, increasingly, Western society defined childhood as a period of life distinct from adulthood. The importance of schooling grew, and the modern-day connection between children and schools was cemented. As a result, children were transformed from being an economic asset—either on the farm or through paid employment in a growing industrial economy—to being an economic burden for whom parents were expected to sacrifice.

In some of the world's poorest nations today, children sometimes continue to live as "little adults." They receive little or no schooling and, by working, begging, or other means, are expected to help support their families.

Adolescence

Adolescence—when youth are nearing physical maturity and are no longer considered children but have not yet taken on the rights or responsibilities of adulthood—was not seen as a distinct period of life until the early twentieth century (see Figure 6.1). Scholars typically tie the rise of adolescence in Western societies to several social developments in the late nineteenth and early twentieth centuries (Chinn 2009):

- Industrialization produced affluence that created a new middle class and enabled middle-class young people to stay out of the full-time workforce, separating them from adult workers.
- Because schooling became an increasingly important requirement for employment, middle-class young people continued their education, completing high school and sometimes even going to college.
- Because they were not working full time, young people had more leisure time and began to be consumers of youth-oriented products, eventually resulting in the formation of a distinct youth subculture.
- In the United States, massive immigration created what we might now call a "generation gap" between young people who were socialized into the culture and customs of the new country and their older immigrant parents who had grown up in the old country.

All these factors helped separate young people from adults and helped make adolescence a distinct period of life.

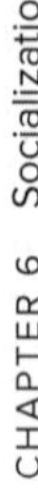

Much of the turbulence we now associate with adolescence results from the contradiction that exists between culture and biology. Adolescence as a social construction is locked in a battle with puberty as a biological reality. Adolescents are capable of sexual activity and of having children—as they did through most of history—but social norms now typically discourage such behavior. Adolescents are maturing physically and mentally and are capable of working in many different jobs—as they did through most of history—but they are now expected to stay in school and delay their entry into the workforce. Cultural inconsistencies exist as well. Sex is glorified in media but discouraged by parents and other authorities. Eighteen-year-olds can serve in the military but are too young to drink alcohol legally. Adolescence, in short, is a period of vexing inconsistencies.

FIGURE 6.1 | THE EMERGENCE OF ADOLESCENCE

Percent usage in English-language books

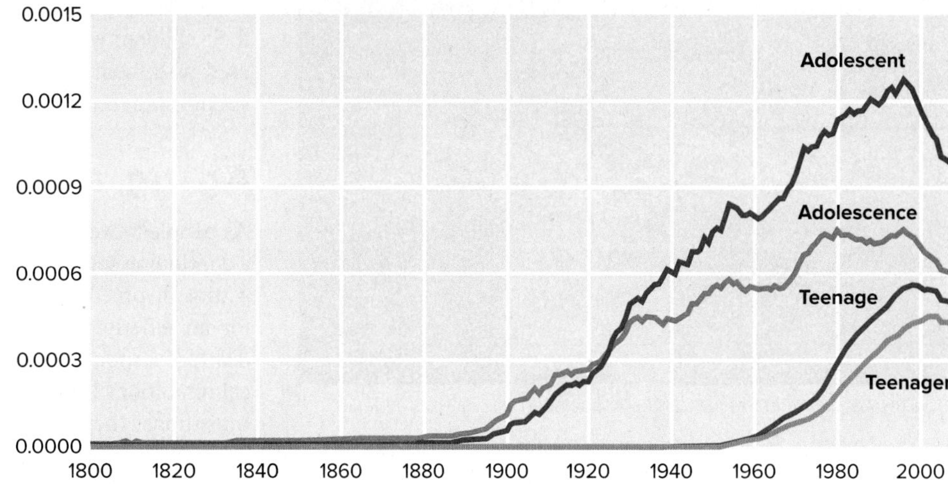

With the emergence of adolescence as a distinct life stage, the terms *adolescent* and *adolescence* became increasingly common in the early twentieth century. As youth subcultures rose in the 1950s and 1960s, the terms *teenage* and *teenager* came into popular use for the first time (In the last two decades, the more informal "teens" has become the commonly used term.) This line graph illustrates the dramatic growth in the use of these terms in books during the twentieth century. The graph was created by a Google tool that calculates the frequency with which any word or phrase appears in the books that have been scanned into the Google Books database so far.

The class differences that played a role in the creation of adolescence continue to play a role in how adolescence unfolds today. Many poor and working-class youth enter the workforce, marry, and start a family at an earlier age than many of their middle-class counterparts (Lundberg and Pollak 2015; Sweeney 2016). In effect, adolescence is a shorter period for them than it is for middle-class youth. In contrast, middle-class youth are more likely to extend adolescence into their twenties by attending college and then returning home and remaining financially dependent on their parents after college. They may delay starting families or experiment with various types of employment before settling down into a more traditional pattern of adult responsibilities. Some researchers suggest that the result is a new life stage in the United States—emerging adulthood—during which people in their twenties experience greater uncertainty and instability in the development of careers and relationships on the road to adulthood than did previous generations (Henig 2010).

Adulthood

As adults enter different stages of life, they take on new roles and responsibilities for which they learn to adopt appropriate ideas and practices (Hunt 2017; Shanahan, Mortimer, and Johnson 2016). For many people, adulthood is marked by a variety of milestones that require resocialization. For example, starting your first full-time job means having to adopt a largely new set of attitudes and responsibilities. Similarly, getting married or living with a romantic partner full time requires taking on the role of spouse or partner, requiring further socialization to a new set of challenges. In these and many other cases, we adjust to new roles and relationships as we accumulate experience.

Adult life-course trajectories in the United States became increasingly standardized in the twentieth century, but they varied by gender (MacMillan 2005; Shanahan 2000). A classic study of men born in the United States between 1907 and 1952 identified a sequence of transitions experienced by roughly half to three-quarters of them—completion of high school, entry into first job, marriage, and parenthood (Hogan 1978; Hogan and Astone 1986). However, this typical sequence could be interrupted by various factors, including military service and college. This life course—finish school, get a job, get married, have children—was never a universal experience, but it became a broad cultural ideal and a widespread aspiration among boys and young men of the twentieth century. The life-course sequence for women of the same generation differed from that of their male counterparts. For example, women in the mid to late twentieth century were far more likely than men to marry before starting their first job (Marini 1984; Ritschard, Burgin, and Schumacher 2017).

Research suggests that the stages of the life course for men and women in recent years are more diverse than they were in

thinking about **structure**

A change in social **structure**—the rise of a new middle class—played a role in the emergence of the currently prevalent view of adolescence as a distinct life stage. How do class differences affect the way different individuals experience adolescence?

Courtesy of National Senior Games Association

The National Senior Games are a multisport event open to athletes aged 50 and older who qualify at state competitions. The 30th anniversary of the games in 2017 featured over 10,000 athletes, from 50 to 103 years old, competing in 19 events including track and field, swimming, and cycling. Divided into five-year age groups, some competitors are serious athletes turning in performances that would be impressive at any age. Others participate more for the fun and friendly competition. Either way, the athletes who compete in these "Senior Olympics" challenge the cultural expectations about "appropriate" behavior for seniors and model new norms for healthy living.

previous generations. Still, the most common life-course pattern for men remains work-marriage-parenthood, which may be followed by divorce or unemployment. Women's life-course trajectories are more varied: although many follow the same stages as men, many others experience a gender-specific trajectory of work-marriage-unemployment-parenthood. That period of unemployment reflects the fact that women are more likely than men to stay home to raise children (García-Manglano 2015; Jackson and Berkowitz 2005).

©Hoby Finn/Getty Images

Becoming a parent, however, is for many adults–men and women alike–one of the most significant life changes they will experience. Our culture encourages new parents to reorient their lives around the socialization of their children, making a priority of their children's needs and taking on the full burden of responsibility for their care and upbringing. As we saw earlier, this expectation is relatively new in Western society. People learn the dominant parenting norms of their culture through socialization. Most new parents have observed friends or family members with their children, they may have cared for younger siblings or babysat their neighbors' children while growing up, and they may have read advice books. A great deal of what new parents know results from their own childhood socialization, when they absorbed parenting lessons from their own parents–knowledge of which they are not always consciously aware. Many parents are surprised to catch themselves talking to their children with the same tone and language their parents had used with them. As this illustrates, one remarkable feature of the socialization process is that it is often invisible to us.

Aging and Retirement

As people move through the stages of adulthood, they experience a continuing set of transitions, including changing or losing a job, getting divorced or remarried, seeing children leave home, caring for an elderly parent, becoming a grandparent, surviving the death of a spouse, and experiencing debilitating mental or physical limitations brought on by aging. As people live through these transitions, they learn the norms and expectations of the new roles they take on.

In the United States, the widespread cultural emphasis on youth can make the social experience of aging a challenge. Although there is no way to stop the aging process, many middle-aged men and women pursue a range of strategies to stay healthy and active as long as possible, including exercising regularly and following a healthy diet. Some pursue the image of youth through cosmetic surgery or other efforts to stave off the effects of aging. In this context, as people continue to grow older, part of the process of aging is negotiating an evolving social identity as someone who is no longer young (Biggs 2018; Moody 2010).

Retirement is a significant life stage, and those who retire need to learn a whole new set of norms and behaviors. Like other life stages, retirement is socially constructed. Until the beginning of Social Security in the 1940s, most people in the United States simply worked as long as they were able. Social Security benefits, Medicare health coverage, and Medicaid long-term care assistance enabled a much broader group of Americans to stop working when they reached the age of 65, which became the standard retirement age. Now, after decades in which the average age at which Americans retire has been declining, that trend has reversed (see Figure 6.2). A restructured Social Security program delays full benefits for those born in 1960 or later until they are 67. Among the other reasons Americans are retiring at a later age are increasing life expectancy, inadequate pensions, the need to accumulate more savings for longer retirement periods, emotional and psychological ties to work, and the social integration and support provided by regular employment.

In a society in which much of our identity comes from what we *do*, leaving the workforce can be traumatic. Some retirees who have waited years to enjoy their leisure time quickly become bored and fall prey to a sense of isolation (Segel-Karpas, Ayalon, and Lachman 2018).

FIGURE 6.2 | LABOR FORCE PARTICIPATION RATE OF WORKERS AGED 65 AND OVER, 1948–2016

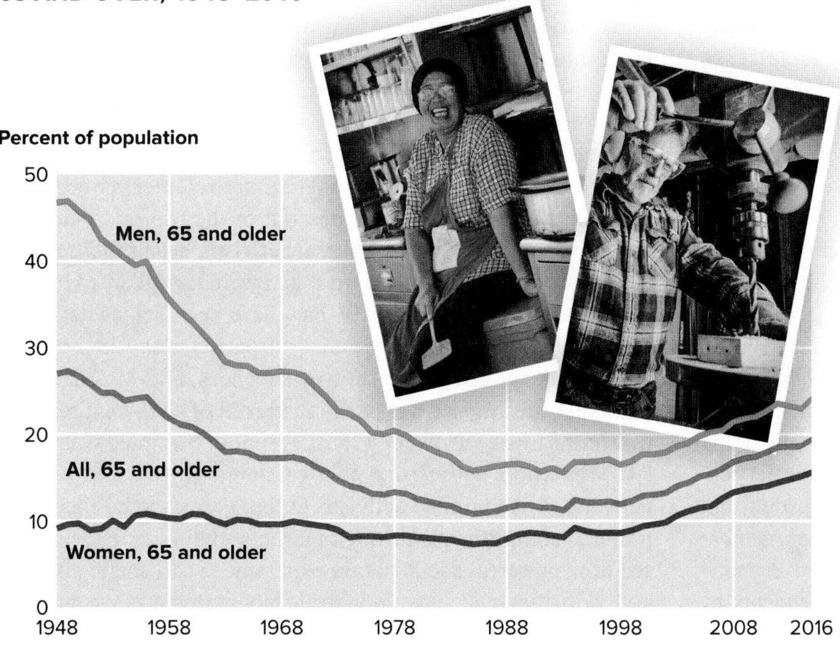

Left: ©Look Die Bildagentur der Fotografen GmbH/Alamy Stock Photo; *Right:* ©Ferrantraite/iStock/Getty Images.

From 1948 until 1985, the percentage of men aged 65 and over who worked dropped significantly; during this period men were retiring at an earlier age. The percentage of women of that age who worked during this period stayed about the same. However, since 1985 an increasing percentage of both women and men have delayed retirement and continued to work past the age of 65.

Source: U.S. Bureau of Labor Statistics, Current Population Survey, 2017.

CORE CONCEPTS CHALLENGE *What does this graph suggest about age, gender, and changes in the* **structure** *of the American workforce since 1948?*

Increasingly, retirement is also a financial challenge as people spend more years outside paid employment because of both longer life spans and the premature loss of employment. Recent practices at many large corporations mean that long-time employees typically have far less job security than did workers in previous generations (Government Accounting Office 2015; Sennett 2006). Employees in their fifties and early sixties may find themselves targeted for job cuts, pressured to retire before they planned to, or simply pushed out by younger, lower-paid employees, making their work experience unpredictable and effective planning for retirement difficult. Such corporate policies produce a population of the involuntarily retired who lose their jobs at an age when they are unlikely to find comparable full-time work. In the competitive economic environment of the twenty-first century, age discrimination for workers aged 50 and over is becoming increasingly common, affecting the quality of the work experience and increasing the likelihood of premature job loss for aging workers (Axelrad and James 2017; Manger 2014; Roscigno et al. 2007).

For workers who have private retirement accounts with stock investments, the stock market downturn in 2008–2009 created new challenges that also meant delays in retiring. Many men and women who had planned carefully for their retirement, accumulating investments that would allow them to retire comfortably in their mid-sixties, absorbed huge losses in the value of their retirement accounts. As a result, some were forced to work longer to recoup their financial losses, leaving fewer jobs for younger people.

As people enter their elder years, many will confront new challenges. Some will experience the prolonged illness or death of a spouse, and others will cope with their own health problems. Still others will remain healthy well into their eighties or nineties but will see their social circles dwindle, as their same-age friends and neighbors move away or die. Among women aged 65 and over in the United States, 32 percent live alone, whereas 18 percent of men in this age group live alone (Stepler 2016). Given the changes associated with one's elder years, aging can lead to social disconnection and a sense of loneliness (Jylha and Saarenheimo 2010).

In the United States, many senior citizens reach a point at which independent living is no longer viable. Some leave their longtime homes to move in with family members; others relocate to specialized elder housing facilities; and still others arrange for in-home elder care, so that they do not have to move out. For those aged 85 and older, 23 percent of women and 10 percent of men live with their children, while 13 percent of women and 8 percent of men live in a nursing home or other long-term care group facility (Stepler 2016). In all these situations, senior citizens must adjust to new living conditions, facing changes to longstanding living patterns. These changes often involve an increased dependency on others for routine household maintenance such as grocery shopping, food preparation, and laundry.

Elder housing patterns vary across cultures. Where multigenerational family living is typical, aging adults can often remain within their homes, relying on their children and grandchildren for care and support. For example, 70 percent of people aged 65 and over in Taiwan live with their adult children, a longstanding pattern of familial caretaking rooted in the Confucian value of respect for elders and a commitment to support one's parents (Chen 2010). Research in various cultural contexts suggests that most elders prefer to "age in place," staying at home as long as they can (Costa-Font, Elvira, and Mascarilla-Miro 2009; Sabia 2008).

Historical Events: Marking Generational Identity

An individual's life course isn't just a matter of passing through a sequence of stages. Lives unfold in particular historical and social contexts, and experiencing major historical events can have a transformative effect. The German sociologist Karl Mannheim (1893–1947) ([1928] 1952) argued that because the shared historical experiences of a group shape its general attitudes and behaviors, the major events that occur during adolescence become key to identifying a specific generation. A summary of the research and theory on the significance of major events suggests that our identity is "stamped by the historically significant events and changes" occurring during adolescence and young adulthood (Griffin 2004, 545). For example, the Vietnam War and political turmoil of the 1960s influenced many baby boomers, who were born in the years following World War II. The succeeding Generation X came of age in the shadow of the 9/11 terrorist attacks. And millennials—those born after 1980—may be marked by the rapid evolution of technology and social media that has accompanied their coming of age.

An early effort to study the relationship between a generation's formative events and adult life experiences was Glen Elder's now-classic study *Children of the Great Depression* (1999), which traced the life histories of 167 men and women born in 1920 and 1921, about eight to nine years before the stock market crash that contributed to the Great Depression. Elder shows how the economic crisis challenged traditional gender roles among adults but strengthened gender roles among the children of the era. As more mothers entered the paid labor force, daughters took over many domestic responsibilities while sons gained more independence by working outside the home to help the family. In general, the harsh experience of unexpected economic hardship hurried both boys and girls of that generation into adult activities and identities.

In another study, sociologist Doug McAdam (1989) explored whether youth involvement in a form of high-risk political activity had lifelong consequences. Mississippi Freedom Summer was a 1964 campaign in which mostly white northern students went south to help with voter registration and to support the growing civil rights movement. The campaign made headlines in June 1964 when white supremacists kidnapped and murdered three of the activists. This event set the tone for the summer project, which became a danger-filled and eye-opening experience for the volunteers.

©Carolyn Cole/Pool/AP Images

Young people who grew up following the attacks of September 11, 2001, are sometimes referred to as the 9/11 generation because the events shaped their long-term attitudes about the world. This is especially true of the victims' children, some of whom, like those pictured here during a commemoration at the 9/11 memorial in New York City, were just infants at the time of the tragedy.

Twenty years after Freedom Summer, McAdam (1989) surveyed more than 200 campaign participants. As a comparison group, he also surveyed more than 100 people who had applied and been accepted to take part in Freedom Summer but had decided not to participate. McAdam found that, in several important respects, the Freedom Summer volunteers were different from those who had dropped out of the project: volunteers were far more involved in political activism, began their careers at a later age, had lower incomes, and were less likely to be married. Although the two groups may have been somewhat different to begin with, the experience of participating in Freedom Summer likely had long-term consequences, and McAdam suggests that this impact was partly the result of a "radical resocialization of those involved" (758). Freedom Summer volunteers left Mississippi with strong political commitments and a strong network of like-minded activists. Often, they pursued their deep political commitments throughout their adult lives. Here we can see how powerful socialization experiences can shape attitudes and priorities and have long-term biographical consequences. Whatever the specifics, historical events provide the context within which our individual socialization takes place.

Culture and Biology: Setting the Stage for Social Life

So far, we have looked at socialization—the way we acquire culture—entirely as a learning process. After all, as Chapter 3 explains, culture is learned, not biologically based. But humans are animals, and like other animals, we have biological constraints and advantages. It is biology that gives us hands capable of making and using our culture's tools; and it is biology that gives us brains capable of developing and learning culture and allowing us to connect with other humans in complex social interactions.

Beyond "Nature versus Nurture"

If biology makes us capable of culture, what other effects does it have on our behavior? In other words, to what extent does biology, rather than culture, influence who we are and how we behave? This question is the crux of the **nature versus nurture debate,** *a disagreement about the relative importance of biology ("nature") and the social environment ("nurture") in influencing human behavior.* Historically, two positions have occupied the extremes of this debate. One of them, **biological determinism,** *contends that biology, specifically our genetic makeup, almost completely shapes human behavior.* Those who hold this perspective argue that biology explains many types of human action, such as crime, violence, or addiction (Byrd and Hughey 2017; Ellison and De Wet 2017). They also sometimes attribute much of the social and economic inequality between

©Clive Bromhall/Oxford Scientific/Getty Images

©Digital Vision/Getty Images

Culture is one of the distinguishing features of humans, although some other animals are capable of culture as well. Chimpanzees learn to place nuts on a stone and break them open using another rock. Humans, however, are capable of vastly more elaborate creativity in the amassing of cultural knowledge, including the invention and use of complicated machinery, such as this combine used to harvest wheat. Both are examples of tools being used to get food, but they are of a radically different order.

groups—especially races, the sexes, and social classes—to innate, biological differences—that is, differences that cannot be changed.

At the opposite extreme, **social determinism** *contends that culture and the social environment almost completely shape human behavior.* Obviously humans have biological differences, but these are insignificant compared to the cultural differences that distinguish societies around the world. Humans, in other words, are the highly malleable product of the social learning that occurs during socialization. According to this perspective, most economic and social inequalities—including, say, the unequal accomplishments of men and women in mathematics—result not from innate differences, but instead from the social systems humans create. As a result, although we may never eliminate such inequalities entirely, we can reduce them dramatically.

Few scholars today subscribe to either of these extremes. Instead, most now understand that biology and the social environment—nature and nurture—interact in complex ways. Our genes—the basic units of hereditary information—represent possibilities; our social environment, acting on those possibilities, makes us who we are. As the editors of the journal *Nature* note, "It has now been proved beyond doubt that although our genes are fixed, their expression is highly dependent on what our environment throws at us" (Nature Editorial Group 2012, 143). (The Sociology in Action box examines the misuse of biology and genetics.)

Epigenetics: Genes and the Environment

Epigenetics is where nature meets nurture. If you imagine genes as a set of lights in a room, epigenetics is the study of the "switches" that turn genes on or off and that can dim or brighten their expression (Stelmach and Nerlich 2015). More formally, **epigenetics** is *the study of changes in gene expression (some of which can be passed on to children) that are produced without changing the underlying genetic code.* Epigenetic influences help explain, for example, why genetically "identical" twins can develop vastly different health profiles.

Gene expression is a complicated and subtle affair (Landecker and Panofsky 2013). In most cases, genes represent the potential for particular traits, but if and how those traits are expressed in a given person depends on the physical and social environment into which the person is born and in which he or she lives. If two children have the same gene for height, but one is born into poverty and malnourished while the other is born into affluence and well fed, the poor child will likely grow up to be shorter than will the affluent child.

The social environment affecting gene expression may involve macro- or micro-level factors. For example, humanity has long harbored genes that predispose people to obesity. Those genes found expression, however, only with the emergence of societies that produced food surpluses—a relatively recent macro-level development in human history. At the micro level, if you have genes that predispose you to obesity, the chance that those genes will be expressed is influenced by your particular social environment, especially that of your family (Classen and Thompson 2016; Martin 2008).

Similarly, some behaviors also reflect the interaction of genes and the social environment. For example, both abuse in childhood and a particular form of a gene have been associated with antisocial behavior in adult men. However, the social condition appears to trigger the gene's effect. That is, boys who both have the gene and have suffered abuse are the most likely to be antisocial as men. In contrast, boys who have the gene but were not abused and boys who were abused but lack the gene tend not to be antisocial as men (Caspi et al. 2002; Guo, Roettger, and Cai 2008). Closeness to a father also appears to decrease the influence of the risky genotype (Roettger et al. 2016).

SOCIOLOGY in ACTION

The Use and Abuse of Biological Explanations of Social Life

Sociologists and other social scientists have long been skeptical of biological explanations of social life, and many continue to be so despite advances in the integration of biological and social research. The source of their suspicion is the ghastly history of abuse that has marked attempts to explain social inequality in biological terms (Gould 1996; Panofsky 2014; Perry 2015). Over time, a preponderance of scientific evidence refuted the false claims behind these attempts, but they live on in popular thinking.

The first phase of abuse involved support for blatantly racist policies. U.S. slavery, for example, was often justified using pseudoscientific assertions of the supposed biological inferiority of African Americans (a topic explored further in Chapter 10). Similarly, claims of biological inferiority often justified opposition to immigrant groups arriving in the United States from the 1880s through the 1920s (Daniels 1997). In the twentieth century, pseudoscience was used to justify social policies aimed at "improving" the human race, including state-level eugenics programs in the United States that sterilized more than 65,000 Americans as late as the 1960s (Bruinius 2006). The most abhorrent of these efforts was the Nazis' use of extermination camps and gas chambers to kill 6 million Jews and millions of other "undesirables" during World War II (Black 2012; Muller-Hill 1988).

In the wake of these horrors, biological theories of human inequality lost credibility among most social scientists. However, a second phase of abuse developed later in the twentieth century with new claims about the biological bases of inequality—albeit framed in less blatantly racist terms than earlier efforts. In *The Bell Curve*, psychologist Richard Herrnstein and political scientist Charles Murray argue that IQ tests accurately measure intelligence and that a great deal of the variation in IQ scores between blacks and whites can be explained by genetic difference (Herrnstein and Murray 1996). Most social scientists regarded these claims as, at best, the result of sloppy science and, at worst, the dressing up of old racist beliefs in new pseudoscientific clothes (Devlin et al. 1997; Fischer et al. 1996; Fraser 1995). Yet, some in the "alt-right" still cite such work to defend racist views (Hawley 2017).

Meanwhile, rapid advances in biological science, particularly progress in genetic screening for susceptibility to particular diseases, have promised significant progress in the treatment of those diseases while at the same time raising familiar concerns about the potential for abuse. Troy Duster, a sociologist with deep roots in the quest for social justice, helped sound the alarm about potential misuses of genetic information (Galliher 2016). Before genetic testing was well known, Duster published *Backdoor to Eugenics* (2003), which explored the potential misuse of genetic screening to discriminate against people in the workplace and in other social settings. His was among the work that informed the Genetic Information Nondiscrimination Act of 2008, which now prevents employers from making hiring, firing, or promotion decisions based on an employee's genetic information. The act also prevents health insurers from denying coverage to a healthy individual or charging that person higher premiums because of a genetic predisposition to developing a disease. However, the act does not apply to life, disability, or long-term care insurance.

Duster argues that we need a broad social discussion about the consequences of improved genetic screening. While recognizing some of the benefits produced by genetic research, Duster cautions that scientists are sometimes too quick to look to genes for answers to what are fundamentally social questions. For example, many diseases, such as cancer and high blood pressure, affect some population groups more than others. The pharmaceutical industry, which funds medical research, focuses on finding genetic sources for these differences that can be treated with drugs—which they sell—often ignoring potential environmental triggers of disease. For example, the rate of prostate cancer is much higher among African American men than white men, and the National Cancer Institute focuses on genetic differences to explain this difference (National Cancer Institute 2016). Duster points out, however, that black men in Africa and the Caribbean, presumably genetically similar to African American men, have lower prostate cancer rates, suggesting that the cause of the difference is as much environmental and social—perhaps the result of diet, stress, or some other factor—as it is genetic (Dreifus 2005; Kheirandish and Chinegwundoh 2011).

The idea that biology—or genetics—is destiny is eroding in the wake of mounting evidence of the importance of epigenetics. But epigenetics opens another door to potential abuse (Meloni 2015). If the social environment is shown to trigger some forms of unhealthy or antisocial behavior, will this knowledge lead to renewed efforts to address environmental disparities? Or will observers conclude that overexposure to toxic environments has so damaged certain social groups that they cannot be salvaged, leading to a new round of science-based discrimination? The answer is not yet certain.

think about it

1. *Why do you think social considerations are deemphasized in a climate that focuses on biological research? What results might this lack of emphasis have?*
2. *How might the misuse of genetic research be avoided or prevented?*

Just as social conditions can trigger a genetically linked effect, they can also help counter it (Shanahan and Hofer 2005). The same gene associated with antisocial behavior in men who were abused as boys is also associated with depression in abused 5- to 15-year-old children (Kaufman et al. 2004). However, access to consistent social support from family and friends reduces the risk of depression among all children, including those who were abused and have the gene. So, a supportive social environment can promote resiliency in children who are otherwise genetically vulnerable to depression. The social environment, in other words, can not only trigger genes, it can also limit their impact.

Factors such as malnutrition, pollution, trauma, and nurturing all appear to produce changes that affect the expression of genes, resulting in long-lasting health and behavioral effects. Environmental conditions to which infants are exposed appear to be especially influential. Perhaps the most startling finding from epigenetics is that some of the changes in a person's genetic expression that are produced by environmental factors can be passed on to the next generation—all without changing the underlying genes (Carey 2012; Francis 2011; Landecker and Panofsky 2013).

Biology matters, but humans are much more than their biology. Rather than determining our fate, biology instead provides us with capacities that allow us to construct our social selves. Virtually all the qualities that make humans distinct—including our sense of self—are a result of social interaction and culture.

In an example powerfully illuminating the effects of insufficient socialization, Romanian orphans, such as those in this photo, were adequately fed, clothed, and housed, but their lack of social interaction and stimulation dramatically stunted their development.

Culture, Power, and the Social Self

In a classic work of anthropology, Clyde Kluckhohn (1968) tells the story of meeting a young man in New York City who was utterly bewildered by the American way of life. He spoke Chinese but not a word of English. His body language—including facial expressions, arm movements, and gait—were all consistent with Chinese norms. His worldview clashed with common American ways of thinking. After a short and alienating time in the United States, he decided to return to China.

This young man was the light-haired, blue-eyed son of American parents from Indiana who had gone to China as missionaries. When they died, the young man was raised by a Chinese family in a remote village. He was socialized into Chinese culture, and his sense of self was inextricably linked to his Chinese upbringing. His social environment was central to his development of a sense of self.

Biology helps set the stage for social life, but our cultural characteristics make us distinct. Our development into fully functioning human beings must be nurtured systematically through ongoing social interaction and socialization.

Humans without Culture

The importance of socialization and culture to becoming human can be illustrated dramatically with the tragic cases of children raised in isolation. One well-documented case from Ohio in the 1930s involved a child who was given the pseudonym "Isabelle" (Davis 1947). Isabelle's mother was a deaf-mute and unmarried. At the time, so-called illegitimate children faced intense social disapproval, and for this reason the child and the mother were kept secluded in a darkened room, shut off from the rest of their family. Isabelle's first six-and-a-half years were spent in this terrible isolation.

When she was discovered, Isabelle seemed to be mentally incapacitated. She could not speak at all and instead made only a "strange croaking sound." She did not respond normally to sights and sounds. She was fearful and hostile toward strangers, behaving like "a wild animal" (Davis 1947, 436). Specialists began to work with Isabelle, and over time they determined that she could hear and see normally. But she scored almost zero on a verbal test, and a test of her social maturity ranked her at the level of a two-and-a-half-year-old.

When given intensive training, Isabelle developed quickly, learning to speak, write, and do basic mathematics. Within two years she had caught up to her peers and had the intellectual development normal for children her age. She went on to function normally in school and took part in activities with children her age. With adequate socialization, the result of systematic training by an expert team that included a speech specialist and a psychologist, Isabelle was able to participate fully in her culture.

A striking large-scale example of the consequences of inadequate socialization emerged during the 1990s. For years, Romania had a state system of poorly run orphanages where more than 100,000 children languished. The children were well fed, clothed, and housed, but they received little stimulation and inadequate attention. After Romania's communist regime fell in late 1989, outside aid agencies took an interest in the orphans and began to promote their placement in foster homes and adoption, though many remained in the orphanages.

Researchers from around the world studied the unfortunate children to learn how inadequate social stimulation had affected their health and to see if they could assist their development. Researchers placed nearly 70 of the children between the ages of 6 and 30 months in high-quality foster care. For five years, they compared the progress of these children to that of a similar-sized group who remained in the orphanages, as well as to a control group of local children growing up with their own families. Studies that are still ongoing as the children enter adulthood (Bick and Nelson 2016; Nelson, Fox, and Zeanah 2013) show that inadequate social stimulation and interaction at an early age produces long-lasting physical and cognitive trauma.

The stress caused by the infants' social deprivation apparently inhibited the production of key growth hormones, an example of how social environment affects biology. The children suffered stunted mental and physical development. Some teenaged orphans had the physical appearance of six-year-olds. They had IQ scores averaging nearly 40 points below normal and high rates of social disorders, including hyperactivity, the inability to form healthy social bonds, and behavior that mimics symptoms of autism, a developmental disorder characterized by impaired social interaction.

When their social environment was improved, the youngest orphans—especially those still less than a year old—made up much of the lost ground in both their physical and mental development, sometimes growing at five times the normal rate while catching up. Stimulation and nurturing support from foster care families, in the form of touching, eye contact, and positive verbal reinforcements (cheers, praise, laughing) encouraged the children to thrive and develop. They developed higher IQs and had fewer social problems, such as anxiety and depression, when compared with children who stayed in the orphanages. However, children who had been in the orphanages for a longer period appear to have missed a crucial window for important brain development. A lack of normal social stimulation early on may have taken a long-term biological toll.

The sad tale of isolated children demonstrates how essential socialization is to making us recognizably human. Through social interaction, we develop our capacities, become healthy adults—physically and socially—and, in the process, develop a sense of self.

Reflexivity: Cooley's "Looking Glass Self"

Your **sense of self** is *the collection of thoughts and feelings you have when considering yourself as an object.* Humans are self-conscious beings: we can make ourselves the object of our own thoughts and attention. This capacity for self-reflection is at the heart of the concept of a self, and as we will see, self-reflection emerges only through social interaction.

We are not born with a sense of self; rather, we develop it over time as a product of the culture in which we are socialized. In particular, we develop a sense of self through our experience of social interaction. An early American sociologist, Charles Horton Cooley (1864–1929), articulated this point with his concept of the **looking glass self,** *the idea that our sense of self develops as a reflection of the way we think others see us* ([1902] 1964). (A looking glass is a mirror.)

According to Cooley, our interactions with others involve three steps that, repeated in all our interactions, forge our sense of self:

1. We imagine our image in the eyes of others.
2. We imagine the others making some judgment about us.
3. We experience a feeling as a result of the imagined judgment.

For example, think of a moment when you were either badly embarrassed or very proud of yourself. Why did you feel this way? Was at least part of your emotion based on your perception of how other people were seeing you, as Cooley suggests?

Cooley wrote long before researchers could probe the workings of the human brain. However, as we see later in this chapter, recent findings in brain science are consistent with Cooley's early sociological insights. Our so-called mind-reading skills (our ability to interpret what other people think or feel) and many of our emotional responses—both central to Cooley's model—are built-in brain functions.

As the looking-glass-self idea implies, people's sense of self is determined in relation to their interaction with others and so varies depending on the people with whom they interact. While hanging out with close friends, you feel confident and comfortable, but during a tough job interview, you feel nervous and uncertain. You haven't changed, but the social context and your interaction with others have. Your confidence or nervousness is linked to your perception of others' judgments of you in each of these situations, as well as to the level of significance you attribute to that judgment.

The extent to which people are attuned to the judgment of others can vary dramatically. Some people feel such an excessive concern about what others think of them that it inhibits their behavior. Others seem to care so little about what others think that they are sometimes unapologetically rude. Navigating smoothly through social life generally requires a balanced reaction: taking into account the reactions of others but not letting them dictate your actions. Acquiring this balance is part of socialization.

SPOTLIGHT on social theory

Cooley's concept of the **looking glass self** is part of a **symbolic interactionist perspective** on social development. Can you think of a "looking glass" moment in your own life when you felt either pride or embarassment about something you had done based on your perception of how other people perceived you?

Spontaneity versus Social Norms: Mead's "I" and "Me"

Another way of expressing the balance required in developing a healthy self comes from the work of American sociologist George Herbert Mead (1863–1931). Mead argued that the self is made up of what he called the "I" and the "me" ([1934] 1962). **Mead's "I"** is *the part of the self that is spontaneous, impulsive, creative, and unpredictable.* It is nonreflective and exists only in the present. The instant you start to think about it, you lose that spontaneous self.

©LWA/Dann Tardif/Blend Images LLC

Have you ever blurted out something you immediately wished you hadn't said? That was the "I" speaking. When people attribute their actions to instinct or reflexes or acting without thinking, they are referring to Mead's "I." The "I" is also the location of what we often refer to as personality. People with a strong "I" tend to be outgoing, spontaneous, and vivacious. The "I" allows for spontaneous action independent of social conventions. In some cases, it can be the source of resistance to social norms and social control.

To create a healthy self, the "I" must be balanced with what Mead calls the "me." **Mead's "me"** is *the sense of self that has been learned from interaction with others.* When you adhere to social norms—such as when you refrain from saying something for fear of offending someone—the "me" is dominating the "I." When you reflect on the "I," it becomes part of the "me." Socialization involves learning to balance the "I" and the "me."

Social Interaction: Developing a Self

The self is constructed through social interaction as a person matures, both biologically and socially. For example, the capacity to take on the perspective of others begins with the biological maturation that takes place between 9 and 14 months, when most children become skilled at "gaze monitoring," the ability to follow someone's gaze to see the same thing that person is looking at (Beier and Spelke 2012). This is a child's early attempt to figure out what's going on in another person's head. Building on this ability, children later learn social interaction skills and construct a robust sense of self.

Mead proposed that children advance through four stages of social development:

1. ***Pre-play stage.*** Through age two children are unable to step fully outside themselves to view themselves. They cannot completely take the perspective of other people. They may imitate behavior they see, but those acts are not meaningful; they do not fully understand what they are doing.

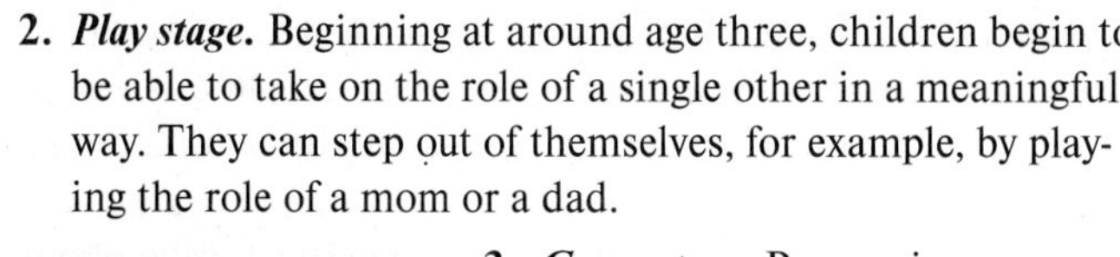

2. ***Play stage.*** Beginning at around age three, children begin to be able to take on the role of a single other in a meaningful way. They can step out of themselves, for example, by playing the role of a mom or a dad.
3. ***Game stage.*** By age six or seven, children learn not only how to play a role but also how to link this role to others' roles. Playing a team sport, for example, involves understanding your role in relation to the roles of others on the team. This in turn involves learning rules and anticipating the actions of others. At this stage, children can fully imagine how the social world appears to others.
4. ***Generalized other.*** Finally, as people mature they develop the capacity to consider the **generalized other,** *the values and orientations of their overall community rather than those of specific individuals.* That is, they internalize the values and beliefs of their culture. Being concerned about "what people would think" and simply "knowing right from wrong" are examples of taking into account the generalized other. The generalized other depends on the social context: it varies greatly from culture to culture.

Neurosociology and the Social Brain

Neuroscience is composed of the various fields that study the nervous system, especially the brain. The emerging study of *neurosociology* integrates findings from neuroscience with a sociological analysis of social behavior (Franks and Turner 2013; Kalkhoff, Thye, and Pollock 2016). From neurosociology we are learning the brain's role in influencing many of the things that make us human, including our unconscious, our emotions, our sense of self, and our ability to interact with others. But we are also learning how social interaction produces physical changes in the brain itself. The brain makes social interaction possible, but it is also itself a product of social interaction. Finally, what we are learning about the way the brain responds to social stimuli is consistent with many of Cooley's and Mead's insights about the importance of social interaction for the development of the self (Mcveigh 2016).

The brain is central to social life because it processes stimuli from outside the body. Much of what the brain does—as much as 97 percent (Gazzaniga 1998)—is automatic. Our breathing and pulse, for example, are maintained by the brain even while we sleep. At any given moment, your brain processes much more information from your senses than you are consciously aware of. When you interact with people face-to-face, you are unconsciously picking up information about them from a variety of nonverbal sources such as their body language and tone of voice (Finnegan 2014; Turner 2000). The facial muscles used in a genuine smile are different from those used in a fake smile, for example, and research shows that most people can recognize the difference and sense a lack of sincerity behind a fake smile (S. Johnson 2004). Such unconsciously perceived signals may account for the "gut feelings" we sometimes have about people we have just met.

The brain helps us "read" people and understand their intentions and behaviors. This task is complex, because social situations are constantly in flux and our assessments must be revised accordingly (Brothers 1997; Franks 2010). For example, on a first date, you probably continually try to read your partner's words, actions, and body language to figure out how she or he feels about you. While still being debated, this ability to read other people—an ability central to Cooley's concept of the looking glass self and Mead's ideas about the stages of child development—is sometimes referred to as "mind reading" by neuroscientists (Borg 2017). It may be partially rooted in the brain through specialized brain cells called mirror neurons that fire whenever you perform an action or experience an emotion. They also fire when you watch someone else perform the same action or convey the same emotion, allowing you to experience what the other person is experiencing.

Emotions are crucial to human communication and behavior, and scientists are beginning to understand how the brain interacts with social cues to control them (Franks 2010). For example, a crying child is often soothed when picked up by a parent. But why? The child's brain produces opioids—morphine-like molecules—that generate feelings of comfort. The emotional change is a result of biology, but the biological change is triggered by a social interaction.

That our biological makeup provides positive reinforcements for attachment to others may be one factor in explaining some social behavior, including bonding and trust (Kosfeld et al. 2005; Nave, Camerer, and McCullough 2015). One type of hormone that generates soothing feelings, oxytocin (not to be confused with the painkiller Oxycontin) is produced in the context of intense social bonding, including breastfeeding, sexual climax, and falling in love. For humans, connecting with others simply feels good.

As Mead suggests with his concepts of the "I" and "me," learning to balance automatic, often emotion-laden, actions and more considered responses is an important part of developing into an adult and being socialized. Youngsters with relatively little socialization have not yet developed such skills. They respond more automatically than adults through laughing, crying, hitting, and acting out in various ways. Part of the socialization process, which varies by culture, is learning to control our emotional responses so that we do not act impulsively. In effect, we train and strengthen a portion of our brains that regulates our feelings and behavior.

Brain plasticity is the ability of the brain to restructure and reorganize itself, especially as a result of social experiences and learning (Kolb and Gibb 2014). When you interact with your environment, you are changing the way your brain is structured or used. Train intensely to become a violinist, and the portion of the brain associated with fingers of the hand that play notes will grow (Schlaug 2015). A person who becomes blind may use the portion of the brain typically devoted to visual information to learn and process Braille (Hannan 2006).

As we are socialized and learn about our culture, we are also shaping our brains. For example, the left side of the brain is associated with language, logic, and linear thinking, whereas the right side is associated with holistic and nonlinear reasoning. In a classic study comparing Australian Aborigine children with Australian children of European descent, sociologist Warren TenHouten (1980, 1999) found that the Aborigine children rely more on the right brain whereas the Euro-Australian children rely more on the left. However, when Aborigine children moved from the Australian outback to Euro-Australian-dominated urban areas, they began to draw more heavily on their left brains. Their need to adapt to a different cultural setting apparently changed the way they used their brains. Since TenHouten's study, many others have demonstrated similar connections between brain development and cultural context (Lende and Downey 2012).

Foucault's Regimes of Power

Social interaction and self-reflection are crucial to creating a sense of self. However, the self develops in a particular historical context under certain social and political conditions. As a result, power relations within a society—who holds power and who does not—are important factors in socialization and in the developing sense of self. Your sense of self would be radically different had you been born, say, a peasant serving a noble in medieval Europe, or a native of a nineteenth-century central African country colonized by a European power, or a member of the Saudi royal family. In other words, your sense of self is partially the product of the power relations in your society.

As we saw in the Through a Sociological Lens box in Chapter 5, Michel Foucault (1979, 1980) maintains that power in the modern world is embodied in various types of knowledge that are connected to particular social sites, such as schools, hospitals, prisons, and the workplace. The connection of power and knowledge in different social settings produces various "regimes of power" (Callero 2003). For example, psychiatry, medicine, personnel management, education, and criminal justice are all fields

on social theory

Michel Foucault focused on the way we internalize our culture's power relationships in developing a sense of self. In what ways do you think power relationships you experienced during socialization may have shaped how you think of yourself?

thinking about culture

Culture shapes our sense of the generalized other. What might be some consequences—large or small—of people with differing views of the generalized other interacting, say, in diplomatic negotiations, business deals, or romantic dating?

in which "experts" use their specialized knowledge in particular settings to monitor, test, categorize, and control others. Thus, Foucault saw power as decentralized within the many social institutions that we encounter in our daily lives. Students, patients, and prisoners, for example, are all monitored by those in power, tested in various ways, and classified so as to fit into a system that categorizes people.

Foucault argued that the very terms and concepts we use to think about who we are do not originate with us but instead are produced and promoted through various regimes of power. Teachers tell us what is good; doctors tell us what is normal and healthy. We are socialized to internalize these definitions. We judge ourselves against these standards and work to comply with these expectations. Over time, through socialization, most of us internalize these various forms of social control by becoming, for example, good students, law-abiding citizens, rational thinkers, hard workers, and avid consumers. By internalizing these standards, we create a self that originates from outside. For Foucault there is no "real" self that struggles against powerful external forces. Instead, the self is the product of these various regimes of power.

Understood in this way, culture is not something outside ourselves that we can choose to ignore. Once we are socialized, culture has become a part of who we are; there is no escaping it. It is embedded in how we think and view the world. Imagine the extreme case of a man who decides he wants nothing to do with society and therefore withdraws to some remote location to live off the land in total isolation. Elated by his newfound independence, he shouts to the stars, "Finally, I am free!"—using words and concepts from his culture! His freedom from society is illusory, since he takes with him all that he has learned through socialization. Like this man, we too have made our culture a part of who we are.

A Changing World

FORMING AN IDENTITY IN A DIGITAL WORLD

As we have seen, our sense of self develops in a social context. This is a lifelong process, but our experiences during adolescence and young adulthood are particularly important (Arnett 2015). However, the way we think about ourselves today is much more fluid and changeable than it was in eras past. As social roles have become less rigid and as global media have exposed people to a broad and sometimes conflicting set of values and lifestyles, developing an identity has become much more of an intentional, self-conscious act. As a result, in contemporary society, young adulthood often involves experimenting with one's identity and monitoring the response of others to these changes.

The internet's growth in the 1990s added a new wrinkle to this process of identity formation. Researchers noticed in particular how early gaming and role-playing sites allowed users to experiment with different identities through their choice of avatars—graphic figures that represented them online. Abandoning the constraints of their biological identity, users could adopt avatars that differed from them in sex, race, age, and appearance (Turkle 1995). One study of virtual sex in the Second Life community found that people saw their online intimate encounters as opportunities to transgress norms and seek out new experiences, even construct secret selves, precisely because they weren't real. Interestingly, however, these transgressions did not extend to the appearance of the avatars—almost all reflected the prevailing real-world standards of beauty and sexiness (Waskul and Martin 2010).

As digital communications became more sophisticated, mobile, and pervasive, they raised new issues about identity formation. Social media, especially, enabled young people to communicate on digital platforms that were often public, visible to potentially millions of people, and sometimes open to responses from friends and strangers alike. Cooley's "looking glass self" had come alive through Facebook pages, YouTube videos, Instagram photos, and Twitter streams. The consequences of these changes are still being studied and debated.

Some researchers worry that digital communication has replaced solitude, self-reflection, and nuanced face-to-face interactions with constant but superficial online interactions that leave us, effectively, "alone together" (Turkle 2011, 2015). This may, however, be an unnecessarily bleak view. Most studies have long shown that people engage with social media not as an alternative to real life, but rather to stay in touch with people they know offline (Quan-Haase and Young 2010). In this way, rather than being pitted against each other, digital and "real" life are more and more integrated into a seamless whole. Location-based social media, such as Foursquare, and dating and mating services like Tinder similarly bridge the digital and "real" worlds (Schwartz and Halegoua 2015).

Social media can also benefit young people developing their identities. Digital engagement can promote the exploration of unfamiliar subjects, provide new learning opportunities and outlets for creative expression, encourage collaboration with peers, teach productive networking, and instill active citizenship and lifelong communication skills. And as for the potential dangers of online life, most teens are relatively adept at managing privacy settings and know how to use social media safely (Madden et al. 2013).

The dangers can be real, however. Bullying, shaming, and harassment can be as damaging online as they are in person (Bonanno and Hymel 2013). And several studies indicate that regular social media participation leaves some people feeling inadequate when they compare their lives to the seemingly more interesting and exciting lives they see described in other people's carefully cultivated self-presentations (Chou and Edge 2012; Vigil and Wu 2015).

Still, for the most part, young people appear to be adept at constructing appropriate identities in digital spaces. One study, for example, found that students in their first semester of college were careful about the way they presented themselves in their Facebook profiles (Yang and Brown 2015). They wanted to make themselves appear socially attractive in their new environment but were unsure how peers would react. They relaxed rather quickly, however, and their self-presentations soon became more open and less stilted. Asked which of the two self-presentations was "authentic," the initial restrained one or the later more-open one, students responded that both were. The change in self-presentation, in other words, did not signal a change in their sense of self but rather an appropriate adjustment based on their evolving assessment of their social environment. Another indicator that young people are sensitive to the effect social media can have on self-presentation can be seen in the popularity of platforms like Snapchat and Telegram that feature online communications that quickly self-destruct, typically leaving no permanent record behind.

Perhaps the most important lesson emerging from the accumulating research into identity formation in the digital world is that it's not that different from identity formation in the offline world. Both require finding a healthy balance between attending to the expectations and responses of others and not being obsessed with or overly sensitive to such judgments.

©PeopleImages.com/DigitalVision/Getty Images

thinking sociologically about
Socialization

culture

- Socialization refers to the process through which we learn the basic norms, values, beliefs, and behaviors of our society's culture. As children we learn the language and symbols of our culture and what is expected of us in such social roles as child and sibling. Once we are socialized, culture becomes a part of who we are. It is embedded in how we think and view the world.
- We are not born with a sense of self; rather, we develop it over time as a product of the culture in which we are socialized. In particular, we develop a sense of self through our experience of social interaction with others.

structure

- In transmitting fundamental social norms and role expectations from one generation to another, socialization helps reproduce social structure.
- Changes in social structure can require new forms of socialization as new roles emerge.

power

- Power relations within a society are important factors in socialization and in the developing sense of self.
- Power shapes our daily life and our sense of self. According to Foucault, our sense of self is produced through various regimes of power connected to particular social sites, such as schools and hospitals. Teachers tell us what is good; doctors tell us what is normal and healthy. We are socialized to internalize these definitions and create a self that originates outside of us.

REVIEW, REFLECT, AND APPLY

Looking Back

1. People learn about their culture through the process of socialization. Various agents of socialization—family, school, media, peer groups, the workplace, and religion—play important roles in socializing individuals. One unique group of socializing agents, total institutions, can have an almost all-encompassing influence over their members' lives as they resocialize people, replacing old norms and behaviors with new ones.
2. The life-course perspective views socialization as a lifelong process of learning and adaptation to the new social contexts we encounter over time as we age and relocate. Powerful youth experiences can shape attitudes and priorities that have long-term biographical consequences.
3. Researchers have moved beyond the longstanding nature versus nurture debate to recognize that both biology and the social environment play important roles in shaping human behavior and that biology and the social environment interact in crucial ways.
4. Cooley's looking glass self and Mead's distinction between the "I" and the "me" provide two ways of understanding how our sense of self develops through social interaction and depends on our ability to reflect on our self as an object.
5. The emerging field of neurosociology explores how our brains process information, help us "read" people, and manage emotions. In turn, brains are changed by the nature of our social environment and social interactions.
6. According to Foucault, the very terms and concepts we use to think about our selves do not originate with us but instead are produced and promoted through various regimes of power.
7. In contemporary society our sense of self is increasingly fluid, or changeable, which is often reflected in our online identity.

Critical Thinking: Questions and Activities

1. One aspect of our identity is gender. As a boy or a girl, how were you socialized into learning what was considered culturally appropriate behavior for your gender? Which agents of socialization taught you these cultural norms, and which was the most significant in shaping your sense of self? Explain.
2. Who are you? How does your sense of self reflect the cultural and historical context in which you live?
3. What event do you think has been the most significant part of your generation's political socialization? Explain.
4. What was the nature versus nurture debate, and why do most researchers now reject this framing of the issue? What common ground has replaced this debate? Do you agree with it? Explain.
5. What sociological lessons are we learning from the case of the isolated Romanian orphans?

Key Terms

agents of socialization (p. 125) people and groups who teach us about our culture.

anticipatory socialization (p. 130) the process by which individuals practice for a future social role by adopting the norms or behaviors associated with a position they have not yet achieved.

biological determinism (p. 136) a theory that contends that biology, specifically our genetic makeup, almost completely shapes human behavior.

epigenetics (p. 137) the study of changes in gene expression (some of which can be passed on to children) that are produced without changing the underlying genetic code.

generalized other (p. 141) the values and orientations of one's overall community rather than those of specific individuals.

hidden curriculum (p. 126) implicit lessons conveyed in school about how children should behave.

life-course perspective (p. 130) an approach that looks at how age, time, and place shape social identities and experiences over a lifetime.

looking glass self (p. 140) the idea that our sense of self develops as a reflection of the way we think others see us.

Mead's "I" (p. 141) the part of the self that is spontaneous, impulsive, creative, and unpredictable.

Mead's "me" (p. 141) the sense of self that has been learned from interaction with others.

nature versus nurture debate (p. 136) a disagreement about the relative importance of biology ("nature") and the social environment ("nurture") in influencing human behavior.

occupational socialization (p. 128) the process of learning the informal norms associated with a type of employment.

peer group (p. 127) a group of people, usually of comparable age, who share similar interests and social status.

resocialization (p. 130) the process by which individuals replace old norms and behaviors with new ones as they move from one role or life stage to another.

rites of passage (p. 130) activities that mark and celebrate a change in a person's social status.

sense of self (p. 140) the collection of thoughts and feelings you have when considering yourself as an object.

social determinism (p. 137) a theory that contends that culture and the social environment almost completely shape human behavior.

socialization (p. 124) the process through which people learn their culture's basic norms, values, beliefs, and appropriate behaviors.

total institution (p. 129) a confining social setting in which an authority regulates all aspects of a person's life.

©Karl Weatherly/Photographer's Choice/Getty Images

7 Interaction, Groups, and Organizations

looking AHEAD

How does the **culture** you have been raised in affect your interactions with your friends and family?

How do your everyday activities and those of your friends help create and sustain complex, large-scale social **structures**?

How are your relationships on campus, at work, or in your family affected by who has and who lacks **power**?

©James Leynse/Corbis News/Getty Images

Zappos, a popular online shoe retailer owned by Amazon, made headlines in March 2015 when it did what many employees have long wished for: it abolished bosses. In place of a pyramidal hierarchy, Zappos introduced Holacracy, a self-management structure based on collaborative "circles" that eliminated job titles and bosses for the 1,600-employee company (Feloni 2016; Gelles 2016; Lam 2016).

The move is part of a mini-trend in corporate life, especially in high-tech firms. Some 300 companies—all smaller than Zappos—were already using Holacracy when Zappos adopted the model. Many others have substantially reduced, if not eliminated, layers of bureaucracy in their organization. One *Harvard Business Review* article discussing some successful cases bore the blunt title "Hierarchy Is Overrated" (Kastelle 2013). Proponents say that the efforts to flatten workplace hierarchies spur innovation and save money. Critics contend that the new approaches are impractical for large companies and that nonhierarchical structures defy what employees expect from organizations: leadership from above and a clear path to advance "up the ladder."

The high-profile move by Zappos took things further than most. Without bosses or managers, employees were asked to use a web-based application called GlassFrog to help make and track strategy decisions. The outcomes of these decisions were measured, and collaboration at every stage was the new expectation.

The experiment won supporters at Zappos who found the changes liberating because they helped break down barriers to honest information sharing and encouraged conflict resolution. But other workers were confused: What were their duties if they had no job title? Whom should they consult on important decisions? How would compensation be structured? Even supporters admitted that the process involved growing pains.

Those pains were too much for some. Within a few weeks of Holocracy's adoption at Zappos, 14 percent of the employees had left. Turnover continued and was 50 percent higher in the first year of Holacracy than it had been in previous years (Zappos 2016). Zappos knew from the start that some employees would have trouble with the new system, and it offered a generous buyout for those who wanted to leave. As the company's CEO noted when he announced the changes, "Self-management and self-organization is not for everyone" (Groth 2015).

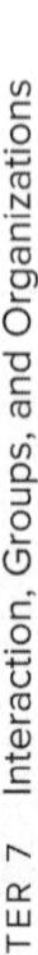

The example of the changes at Zappos illustrates how organizational structures help shape our experiences. What is true in the workplace is also true in social life more broadly. Our daily interactions with others form the basis for our social lives, the topic of this chapter.

We begin at the micro level by examining face-to-face interaction and our shared understanding of social reality (culture) and then by looking more closely at how statuses and roles connect people to one another and to the patterns and routines that are the foundations of social structure. Next we shift to meso- and macro-level phenomena and look at networks, groups, and organizations, the specific social ties that form social institutions and the sites where relations of power occur. Finally, we survey the changes in social interaction and organization brought on by the expansion of the internet.

Culture and Social Interaction

Social life begins with face-to-face interaction. Guided by cultural norms and expectations, we negotiate these micro-level encounters with family members, friends, coworkers, and strangers that are the building blocks of social life. The theoretical tradition of *symbolic interactionism,* introduced in Chapter 1, emphasizes how we make sense of the world by focusing on just these kinds of encounters. As we saw in Chapter 6, two early-twentieth-century sociological thinkers, Charles Horton Cooley and George Herbert Mead, argued that social interactions are crucial in the development of our sense of self.

Through socialization, we become adept at taking the perspectives of others and determining the intent and meaning of their actions, making this process so much a part of our social interaction that we often forget we are engaged in it. Because it is essential to successful social interaction and to the construction of larger social groups, it is worth taking a closer look at how this process works.

Interaction: Arriving at Common Understandings

As humans, we spend our lives producing symbols. Humans have created languages, such as English and Spanish; we constantly use images, such as the emojis in texts and tweets; and we use gestures, such as shaking our head to mean "no." To interact successfully with others, we need to agree with them about the meaning of these symbols. As we communicate, we rely on the language and knowledge that we share with others to get our meaning across (Blumer 1986).

Shared Language Imagine that you are traveling in a foreign country where you do not speak the local language and the locals don't speak yours. You are separated from your travel group and suddenly find yourself lost in an unfamiliar city. You stop strangers, try to explain that you are lost, and ask for directions. Your efforts are met with quizzical looks as people try to understand what you are asking, and their attempts to help bewilder you. Maybe for the first time, you realize how valuable language is. Without the common ground of shared meaning, social interaction becomes confusing, frustrating, inefficient, even frightening.

Even among those who share a language, however, there will always be expressions that some speakers will not understand, depending on the historical period, the country, or the group or subculture from which the expression originates. If you asked an American youngster to "hop the wag," you would likely get a puzzled look, whereas many British teenagers would immediately recognize this slang phrase as an invitation to skip school. Slang is a common part of subcultures, and slang terms such as *groovy* and *da bomb* often evolve rapidly, fall in and out of favor over a short time, and thus lose their ability—across time or even across groups in the same society—to make interactions meaningful.

When we communicate with people we know, our conversation is often rooted in common references and shared understandings, allowing us to rely on unspoken, taken-for-granted assumptions. In the United States, you might greet a friend by saying, "Hey, what's up?" This vague question is understood to mean something like, "Hello, what are you doing now?" Because you understand the slang, you know how to respond.

Shared Knowledge Language is just one example of how shared understanding facilitates social interaction. The smooth functioning of everyday life depends on what sociologists refer to as **intersubjectivity,** *a common understanding between people about knowledge, reality, or an experience.* Successful interaction requires each person to take the perspective of the other to achieve some common understanding. In this way, social interaction constantly constructs our social world.

People within a society share knowledge not just of their common language but also of norms and customs, historical references, and other socially useful information that they have learned through socialization (Schutz 1962). In other words, they have a common perspective that enables them to understand how others see the world and allows society to function smoothly. Daily life is full of unspoken, taken-for-granted, and shared interpretations of reality. For example, you have no doubt learned cultural norms for how to conduct yourself in face-to-face interactions, including whether and when to make eye contact,

©Geert Vanden Wijngaert/AP Images

While trying to capture our attention, advertisements must also convey meaning. By drawing on a common understanding of social reality, ads can leave many things unstated. Recognizing the way this Eurostar high-speed train ad references both Queen Elizabeth II and Marilyn Monroe is what makes this advertisement work.

CORE CONCEPTS CHALLENGE *For this advertisement to make sense, what does the reader need to know that is not explained? Do you think this ad would be effective in all* ***cultures****? Why or why not?*

how much personal space to allow, and if and how to greet a person. Do you use a formal greeting? A casual "Hi"? A handshake? A hug? A kiss? All these cultural norms are part of our routine social interactions.

The smooth functioning of everyday life, therefore, is based partially on people's shared understanding of the nature of reality. For example, when you ride public transportation in your home city, you share a common understanding with your fellow passengers and the conductors or drivers about where and how to board, how to pay your fare, and how and where to get off. In a different city or in a foreign country, you would have to figure out all those things, because you would not share a common framework.

Similarly, your enjoyment of any form of entertainment depends on a shared knowledge base. Television comedies like the long-running *Simpsons* and *The Big Bang Theory* assume their audiences will understand their writers' irreverent references to celebrities and politicians, other television programs, and current events. When you "get"—and laugh at—a joke, your enjoyment is rooted in the unspoken assumptions that you share with others. Advertisers, too, often rely on shared views of what is attractive and desirable. That's why logos and slogans can communicate so much about the meaning and identity of specific brands or products.

Having a common culture facilitates ordinary social interactions. Think of the last time you bought groceries. Now imagine purchasing food from this street vendor in Egypt. How might the two interactions differ? How might they be similar? What explains these similarities and differences?

When you meet and interact with strangers, shared elements of culture form a common ground that facilitates routine interactions. For example, imagine you are purchasing a computer cable at an office products store. As you interact with the checkout clerk, your facial expression, tone of voice, words, and body language all contribute to the brief interaction, during which you and the clerk share basic assumptions about how to proceed (greet each other, exchange money). You don't try to haggle about the price; the clerk doesn't try to give you a hug.

Suppose, however, that you know very little about computer hardware and are trying to find the cable you need to make your printer work. You ask a clerk about the difference between the various cables for sale and—to your shock—she replies by telling you about the differences between HDMI, USB, DVI, and an alphabet soup of cables. The clerk's enthusiasm is blinding her to your perspective—you just want her to pick out an inexpensive cable for you. Exasperated, you leave abruptly without buying anything. In this case, you and the clerk failed to achieve intersubjectivity: you never fully agreed on what was needed for this interaction to be successful.

SPOTLIGHT

on social theory

Symbolic interactionists focus on our day-to-day interactions as the building blocks of social structure. Describe a successful, or unsuccessful, interaction you have recently had with a salesperson, school official, or other stranger. What contributed to its success, or what caused the problem?

Some failed social interactions can have far more serious consequences than a frustrating trip to the computer store. For example, reflecting on an issue that soldiers face in all wars, the U.S. commander in charge of day-to-day military operations in Iraq, Lieutenant General Peter Chiarelli, found that some American troops had been their "own worst enemy" because they didn't understand fundamental aspects of the local culture (Rainey 2006). Chiarelli told the story of how U.S. soldiers arrested a Sunni Arab insurgent in his home. In keeping with the emphasis in Iraqi culture on maintaining a man's honor, the suspect asked to be handcuffed outside, out of view of his family. Instead, U.S. troops forced the man to the floor, handcuffed him, and jerked him out the door—in full view of his family and neighbors. Lieutenant General Chiarelli summed up the incident's consequences in this way: "Every single person in the room, because of this whole concept of honor in this culture, has said, 'To hell with the Americans.'" In this case, an interaction based on fundamental cultural misunderstanding had potentially serious consequences.

People who occupy different social positions often see the world from different perspectives. African Americans living in a city center likely see the world differently not only from their

thinking about culture

How could an understanding of local **culture** help American soldiers in their interactions with citizens abroad? What examples of possible cultural misunderstandings can you think of?

MAPS 7.1 AND 7.2 | MAPPING REALITY

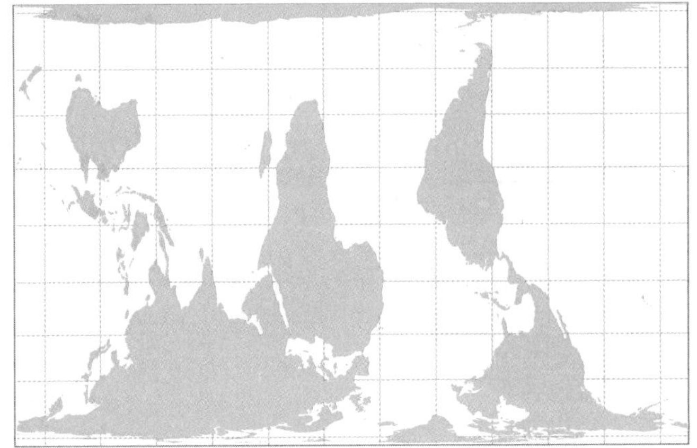

The Mercator projection (Map 7.1, left) and the Peters projection (Map 7.2, right) are two-dimensional representations of the three-dimensional globe, though both maps contain distortions. For example, North America appears to be larger than Africa in Map 7.1. Also, the orientation of the map is completely arbitrary. The Peters projection represents the relative sizes of the continents more accurately. For example, it shows Africa (11.7 million square miles) as being larger than North America (9.4 million square miles), and the inverted presentation is actually as accurate as the Mercator projection. However, the Peters map distorts the shapes of the continents, making them appear stretched out.
Source: Bill Rankin, www.radicalcartography.net.

CORE CONCEPTS CHALLENGE *Which of these maps appears "right" to you? What role do you think* **culture** *played in your choice?*

white urban neighbors but also very likely from African Americans who live in affluent suburbs. The same dynamics operate on a global scale as well: people in France or China often have a different vantage point on world events than do residents of the United States. Each group draws upon different stocks of knowledge and experience to understand the social world.

Defining Situations as "Real": The Thomas Theorem

By being socialized in a particular culture we learn to see our world from a particular perspective, and that viewpoint becomes our reality. Sociologists maintain that what we experience as "reality" is what we learn from our society; in other words, it is socially constructed. Not only does taking our definitions of reality for granted cause us to resist seeing society in all of its complexity, these definitions can also have very real consequences in the actions they lead us to take.

Maps 7.1 and 7.2 show two ways of seeing the world—ideas about geography that have affected the way we view the significance and size of various regions and nations. The traditional Mercator projection (Map 7.1), developed in the 1500s, badly distorts the relative sizes of the continents. Also, the orientation of the map—with South America and Africa on the bottom—is completely arbitrary. The Peters projection (Map 7.2), developed by cartographer Arno Peters in the 1970s, represents the relative sizes of the continents more accurately, though it distorts their shapes, and it is just as accurate to have the North Pole at the bottom as the other way around since the earth has no top or bottom. However, because of how most of us were socialized, the map on the right looks "wrong" to us.

The early-twentieth-century American sociologist W. I. Thomas (1863–1947) noted that before people act, they consider both what they spontaneously understand about the circumstances at hand and what society has taught them about those circumstances. Their resulting interpretation—what Thomas called "the definition of the situation"—influences how they act (see Figure 7.1).

Thomas stated his insight, now known as the **Thomas theorem,** this way: *"If men define situations as real, they are real in their consequences"* (Thomas and Thomas 1928, 572). In other words, subjective interpretations of reality have objective effects. If we are to understand how and why human beings act the way they do, we need to pay attention to how they define reality and how that definition, in turn, influences their behavior.

The Thomas theorem helps us understand how interpretations of a situation shape social interaction on various levels. For example, on the micro level, if a stranger asks for a handout, your definition of the situation is likely to influence whether you give money (see Figure 7.1). Your interpretation may depend on the way you answer some questions: Is this person down on his or her luck? A victim of a weak economy? A veteran? A substance abuser? Someone who is too lazy to hold a job? Or someone with mental illness? The theorem applies to large institutions as well. If the government of one nation sees a neighboring country as a military threat, that government may be more likely to invest substantially in weapons. The neighboring country may then misinterpret this investment as a threat instead of a defensive strategy and increase its own investment in weapons, thereby triggering a dangerous arms race. Whether or not these assessments of threat were accurate, the initial definition of reality can have consequences and shape interpretations of future events.

FIGURE 7.1 | THOMAS THEOREM

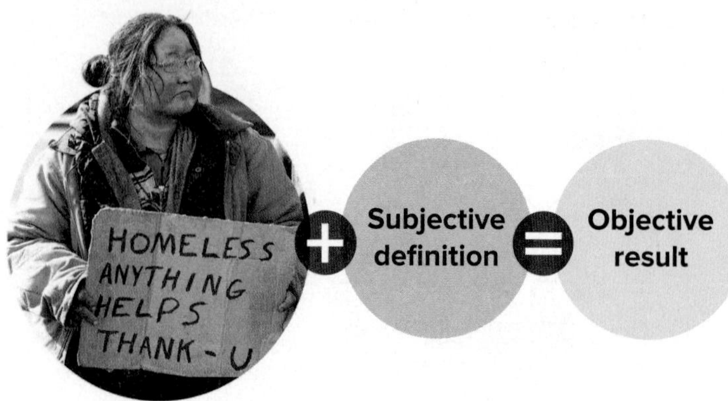

Photo: ©P.A. Lawrence, LLC/Alamy Stock Photo

If a stranger on the street asks you for money, what do you do? Whether accurate or not, your subjective definition of this situation will likely determine whether you give this person any money.

The Thomas theorem can also help us understand stereotypes, which define individuals as typical examples of whole groups of people. **Stereotypes** are *exaggerated, distorted, or untrue generalizations about categories of people that do not acknowledge individual variation.* Stereotypes are often negative; we have all heard stories and jokes or seen memes that belittle various ethnic groups. Indeed, stereotypes typically perpetuate unfair negative images of people and have little relationship to who they are, as individuals or as a group. (Some of the possible interpretations noted earlier for the stranger asking for money—especially that the person is a substance abuser or too lazy to work—are common stereotypes about homeless people.) At the same time, however, you may also be able to think of some "positive" stereotypes, such as the false belief that "all Kenyans are fast runners." Such positive stereotypes also fail to take into account individual variation. Some of the world's best runners are Kenyans, but the vast majority of Kenyans are no more skilled at running than are people from any other society, and top runners come from many parts of the world.

Because they are shared definitions, all stereotypes create a sense of reality, and they can therefore have serious consequences. Television, for example, is full of stereotypes of working-class people, depicting them as unintelligent, lazy, and crude—think of Homer Simpson. Such stereotypes help to justify economic inequality by implying that highly educated professionals are somehow better than working-class folks. The Sociology in Action box examines how using a sociological perspective can challenge stereotypes based on social class and promote social change.

Social scientists often generalize about groups, of course, but these generalizations are usually carefully qualified and based on data. The statement "On average, U.S. citizens have among the highest annual incomes in the world" is not a stereotype because it is qualified appropriately (that is, with the phrases "on average" and "among the highest annual incomes"), and it can be backed up with data about income levels in different countries. By contrast, the statement "All Americans are rich" is a stereotype because it paints with an overly broad brush ("All Americans") and ignores the wide variation in income that exists in the United States. It also employs an undefined term, "rich," which people interpret in a variety of ways.

Three Steps to Constructing Social Reality

In their classic work *The Social Construction of Reality,* Peter Berger and Thomas Luckmann (1966) summarize the process by which people create society through their actions and interactions, thereby highlighting the fact that the social world is neither "natural" nor inevitable. As they put it, "Society is a human product. Society is an objective reality. Man is a social product" (61). That is, (1) we create the social world in which we live, (2) we "forget" that this world is human-made, and (3) this social creation takes on a life of its own, so to speak, and ends up shaping who we are and how we act. They label the steps of constructing social reality as externalization, objectivation, and internalization:

1. *Externalization.* People create society through an ongoing process of physical and mental activity. This complex process helps ensure a stable environment within which we can live. For example, you become friends with another person, spending time together and interacting in ways that create a special relationship.
2. *Objectivation.* Through this process, social arrangements come to seem objectively real; society appears separate from human creation and instead seems "natural," inevitable, and out of people's control. To continue the example of friendship, your newly formed relationship becomes part of your reality. You call each other "friend" and others recognize your relationship as real.
3. *Internalization.* This is the complex process through which we learn our society's culture and establish our view of the world. Through this process humans come to be influenced by their own creations; they are social products. For example, your friendship influences you: you feel obliged to comply with specific expectations associated with this relationship (such as helping your friend move into a new apartment even when you do not feel like doing so).

The same three-step process occurs with larger social structures as with micro-level social interactions. People create various structures and social institutions such as families, schools, and governments. They then treat those socially constructed entities as objectively real. Finally, people are influenced by the society they create. With large social structures, which often take decades to develop and solidify, the influence is often felt by later generations. We didn't create our form of government, but it certainly influences our lives. However, the government—like all social institutions—is continually maintained and reproduced through the actions of participants. Political candidates run for office; citizens vote for their preferred candidates (or choose not to vote); and the winning candidate goes to Washington, D.C. (or the state capital or city hall), to represent his or her constituents.

SOCIOLOGY in ACTION

Overcoming Class Stereotypes

- Jenny was having lunch with a friend. When the server made an error with their order, Jenny's friend commented, "Well, if she was smart, she wouldn't be a waitress."
- Terry received an invitation to attend an annual conference of progressive political activists that cost $100 per day, a significant sum for many working-class people. The invitation noted, "Anybody who does not feel committed enough to pay is not committed enough to participate."
- Gilda was a community organizer. A colleague told Gilda that if she would mobilize working-class residents for a meeting on a local issue, he would then step in and negotiate on their behalf. Gilda noted, "He thought of working-class people as props and their voices as sound bites."

These real examples, from readers of a website called Class Matters, illustrate some of the many ways that poor and working-class people can be stereotyped as unintelligent, uncommitted, or unable to stand up for themselves. The pervasiveness of such stereotypes—sometimes even among middle-class activists who are advocating on behalf of poor and working-class people—makes it difficult for individuals from different classes to work together to accomplish common goals. Sociological insights can be useful in helping people understand and overcome such stereotypes.

"I think the sociological imagination is really essential to making social change happen," says Betsy Leondar-Wright, a sociologist who grew up in a comfortable upper-middle-class family. Leondar-Wright (2005, 2014) has spent years working for a variety of organizations that address issues involving poverty and economic inequality. She held jobs as an organizer in low-income communities and as a coalition builder, working across class, race, and ethnic lines. Her work often involved bringing together people from different backgrounds to address pressing needs such as affordable housing and neighborhood safety. In doing so, she discovered that people had to get past their stereotypes to collaborate successfully.

For example, community organizations based in low-income neighborhoods were frequently staffed by middle-class activists. Too often, activists did not think local residents were capable of leading their own campaigns for neighborhood improvement. "It's easy to fall into stereotypes about people with a particular amount of money or a type of occupation or neighborhood," she writes: "easy and dangerous." Such stereotypes blind people to the complex realities that exist within any group and choke off potentially creative ideas from local residents.

Leondar-Wright argues that what keeps people from being active in their communities is not a stereotypical lack of intelligence or commitment but rather a lack of hope. She notes that "most people can't imagine institutional arrangements" that differ from the ones they know. "[A]t one point my job was to knock on doors of low-income tenants to tell them that their housing was in danger of becoming unaffordable after a certain date [because of changes in ownership]. I saw firsthand how most people in their fear jumped immediately to individual solutions: 'My sister is in Tennessee. Maybe she could take us in for a while if we moved there.' The most valuable thing I brought to them was the information that other tenants in other towns had organized and bought their properties and turned them into permanently affordable housing. Three tenant groups I organized now own and run their apartment complexes. My main contribution to their victories was a sense of informed hope. If we want more people to get active, we need to recognize the critical shortage of hope."

Successful community-based organizing efforts like the one in which Leondar-Wright has been involved directly contradict the stereotypes that poor and working-class people cannot make a difference in their communities. In turn, Leondar-Wright believes that the insights of sociology can themselves be a valuable resource in making a difference.

think about it

1. *Do you ever see stereotypes of poor or working-class people on television or in movies? Explain.*
2. *Have you ever been involved in a group or an organization that included people from different class backgrounds? How do you think class stereotypes influenced the group's dynamics?*

Social order emerges from human action, and it continues to exist only when humans reproduce it through their participation.

Because people are continually constructing society and are, in turn, affected by it, the social world in which we live is always in flux. We may often feel trapped by social institutions and other aspects of society, but anything that humans create they can also change. Thus our definition and understanding of work, families, schooling, and other aspects of society is open to change and evolution.

Social Statuses and Roles

As we have seen, successful social interaction requires some shared understanding through which to create our social reality. But interaction is also shaped by statuses and roles, which provide some of the glue that connects individuals to one another and to the behavioral patterns that constitute social structure. We touched on these ideas in Chapter 4 and examine them in more detail here.

Statuses A **status,** as we saw in Chapter 4, is *a position in a social system that can be occupied by an individual.* (In a different context, the word *status* is used to indicate honor or prestige associated with a position.) A **status set** is *the collection of statuses that an individual holds.* For example, you might be a student, an employee, a parent, a neighbor, a brother or sister, an immigrant, a band member, and a Christian. Each of these positions is a status, and collectively they are your status set. A **status category** refers to *a status that people can hold in common,* such as nurse, father, or New Englander.

Some statuses apply automatically. **Ascribed statuses** are *social positions that are assigned to us from birth or that we assume later in life regardless of our wishes or abilities.* Your nationality, your sex, your race or ethnicity, and your status as someone's cousin are among the ascribed statuses you might have had at birth. Other ascribed statuses may be assigned later in life, such as teenager, person with mental illness, or widow. In most cases, we cannot change an ascribed status, since it is determined by others.

Achieved statuses, in contrast, are *those that we voluntarily attain, to a considerable degree, as the result of our own efforts.* A person might be the mayor of a city, a doctor, a professional athlete, a criminal, or a spouse—all examples of achieved statuses. You must work, in some way, to acquire an achieved status.

©Nycshooter/E+/Getty Images

The line between these two types of status is not always clear-cut. Your family may have influenced some of your achieved statuses, such as your choice of religious affiliation or your decision about whether to attend college. You inherited your class status from your parents as an ascribed status, but that status may change in your adult life. You are assigned a nationality at birth, but you might achieve another nationality by becoming a citizen of a second country.

Some statuses can be achieved only by working through formal structures and meeting certain criteria, whereas other statuses are fairly easy to achieve and are open to most people. Lawyers achieve their status through an arduous process that involves completing college, attending and completing law school, and passing a rigorous bar exam. In contrast, basketball fans can achieve that particular status just by regularly watching games on television.

In addition, not all statuses are equally important. In U.S. society, the status of cousin, say, has much less significance for most people than the status of college graduate. For many Americans, a cousin is often a relatively distant relative they see once a year at holiday gatherings, whereas being a college graduate can be a requirement for a desirable job. In some cultures, though, kinship—even within an extended family—may be an essential status. Extended family ties are typically very strong in Native American communities, for example. In these families, relatives such as cousins often interact on a regular basis and have a sense of mutual obligation to provide economic and social support (Cheshire 2006; Davis, Dionne, and Fortin 2014).

Because statuses are social positions, they exist within hierarchies; as a result, some statuses provide more or less social prestige than others. A **status hierarchy** is *a ranking of social positions according to their perceived prestige or honor.* You can probably recognize the status hierarchy within your college: the president and senior administrators hold the positions with the highest prestige, whereas custodial, food service, and clerical workers—all essential for the smooth operation of the school—occupy less prestigious positions. Status is linked to social inequality because different positions often receive different levels of prestige, power, and, in this case, income. At many college campuses, custodial workers begin their workday before sunrise, receive low pay, and are invisible to many students and faculty. In contrast, college presidents are highly paid and likely to have a formidable presence on campus, with the power to make decisions about college operations.

Many people, regardless of their place in a status hierarchy, have one status that overrides all others. A **master status** is *a social position that is overwhelmingly significant, powerfully influences a person's social experience, and typically overshadows all the other social positions that person may occupy.* Sociologists coined this term to describe the significance of race in the United States in the first half of the twentieth century (Hughes 1945). In the segregated South at that time, race was a master status: it overpowered the importance of other statuses such as education level, religious affiliation, class, gender, and occupation. For example, in the pre–civil rights era, and to a lesser degree today, highly educated African American men were identified primarily by their race, despite their status as skilled professionals or community leaders. For white shopkeepers, police officers, and other people in largely segregated cities, a person's status as a black man was so prominent that it made his other statuses nearly invisible. Even today, as we explore in Chapters 10 and 11, race and gender are among the most visible and most important statuses in U.S. society.

Roles Whereas statuses are positions in a social system, **roles** are *the sets of expected behaviors that are associated with particular statuses.* As a student, you are expected to go to class, turn in assignments on time, and take part in college activities; at the same time, you have the right to choose your own major and courses and to fair treatment from professors, among others. Those general

thinking about **structure**

Humans create, sustain, and change social **structure**. How do your everyday actions and interactions help maintain the structure of your college? How might different actions on your part help to change your school?

expectations regarding behavior, duties, and rights that are associated with that role were defined by our culture before you became a student. You can be somewhat creative in how you carry out a role, but the general rules are well established.

Similarly, the general expectations associated with the parent role in our society are fairly clear. Parents raise their children, are responsible for providing for their basic physical needs, and are expected to give social and emotional support—at least until children leave home as adults. Some parents are unable to fulfill the parent role and are negligent, risking a loss of custody. But there is no single way to fulfill this role effectively, and parents accomplish it in a variety of ways. Some are strict, whereas others emphasize open discussion rather than discipline. Still others try to be friends with their children (and their children's friends) and are a constant presence in their lives. And some parents are so "hands-off" that their children rarely see them.

The roles associated with many statuses are even less formal than that of student or parent. Yet the sets of expectations that come with the role of friend or good neighbor, for example, are still widely recognized. Other roles, such as the one taken on by a person who is ill, are generally understood as well. In a classic essay, Talcott Parsons (1951) argued that physical illness (the "sick role") has a social side that involves four particular expectations. First, being sick exempts an individual from other role expectations, especially if a doctor has certified the illness. Second, people with an illness are often not held responsible for taking care of themselves; a spouse, parent, or health care professional is likely to provide the necessary attention. Third, because illness is socially undesirable, we expect that sick people will want to get better. Fourth, sick people are also expected to make an effort to recover, especially by seeking competent professional help. Sick people who fail to fulfill their role thwart the expectations of others around them. If, for example, you refused to see a doctor after a lengthy ongoing illness, your parents and friends would probably become increasingly frustrated with you and might even attempt to force you to seek medical help.

SPOTLIGHT on social theory

Talcott Parsons was the leading proponent of the **functionalist perspective,** which stresses how the various elements of society work together. How might playing the sick role, in the way Parsons described, help reinforce social stability?

We are all constantly juggling the many roles associated with the various statuses we occupy. **Role conflict** occurs *when the expectations associated with different roles clash.* For example, your boss asks you to work extra hours at the cafe during a particularly busy period, but at the same time, you need to finish a major project for one of your courses. Because there are only so many hours in the day, you must make a choice, and one of your roles—student or worker—is likely to suffer. Parents who must juggle the care of children with the demands of their work are especially prone to such role conflicts. **Role strain,** in contrast, occurs *when the expectations associated with a single role compete with each other.* Teachers experience role strain from the dual responsibility they have both to help and support their students and to evaluate the same students, sometimes with a failing grade (see Figure 7.2).

Roles are crucial in the construction of our everyday lives because they link us to other people. Roles link parents and children, teachers and students, employers and workers, friends, and a host of other statuses. These interconnecting roles form a network of social relationships that are the basis of social structure.

Dramaturgy: Playing at Social Life

If the idea of people playing roles reminds you of actors performing in a film or play, you are not the first to see this analogy. Shakespeare wrote over 400 years ago "All the world's a stage, and all the men and women merely players." Sociologists use this idea as well. **Dramaturgy,** *an approach to the study of social interaction that uses the metaphor of social life as a theater,* is most closely associated with Canadian-born sociologist Erving Goffman. In his well-known work *The Presentation of Self in Everyday Life,* Goffman (1959) drew on some of the elements that make up a theatrical performance to illuminate the nature of social interaction.

Role Expectations In a play, the playwright largely determines the actor's role.

©Daniel Grill/Getty Images

©Jonathan Nackstrand/AFP/Getty Images

Talcott Parsons revealed the widely recognized expectations associated with the "sick role." Like the sick role, other informal roles also involve sets of unstated expectations. Consider, for example, what we might call the "winner role." What expectations exist for this role?

FIGURE 7.2 | ROLE CONFLICT AND ROLE STRAIN

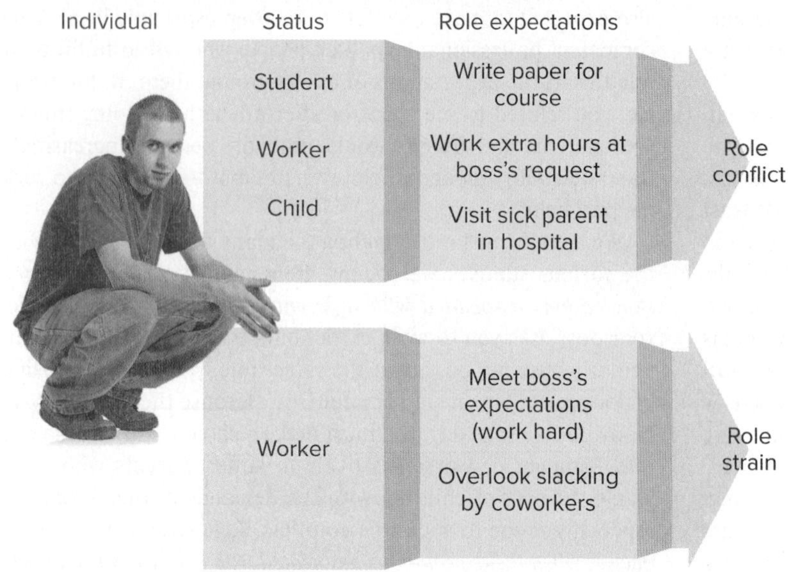

Photo: ©Photodisc/Getty Images

Because individuals hold many statuses simultaneously, they often have trouble meeting associated role expectations successfully. Role conflict occurs when two different roles have incompatible expectations. Role strain occurs when a single role has competing expectations. Have you experienced either role conflict or role strain? Explain.

In real life, cultural expectations establish the content of a social role. For example, imagine a lawyer walking into a courtroom dressed in basketball shorts and a T-shirt and greeting the judge by saying, "Hey, buddy." He pulls his papers out of a knapsack and, as the case proceeds, giggles loudly at the opposing attorney's questions and the witnesses' testimony. Such behavior would be absurd, of course, precisely because it violates our expectations about a lawyer's proper "costume" (formal business attire), "props" (briefcase), language (a respectful "your honor"), and emotion (serious). We often take for granted such expectations, but their significance becomes obvious when they are violated.

Appropriate costumes, props, language, and emotions are among the resources actors use to achieve a convincing performance. But an actor must still interpret a role, and there is considerable room for creativity. The same is true with social roles. The expectations associated with any role are socially defined, but individuals who occupy a particular status must actively "play" the role. A lawyer might be folksy and warm in her summation to the jury, for example, or she might be outraged and impassioned. Either behavior could be appropriate to the role.

on social theory

Dramaturgy is an approach that uses the idea of social life as a kind of theater. Consider a particular role that you play in that theater. What costume, props, language, and emotions are associated with that role? Do you ever feel the need to separate yourself from the role? If so, why?

Impression Management Role playing occurs in the presence of an audience. Actors try to convince the audience that they are "real," that their interpretation of a character is authentic. As social actors, we too engage in *impression management:* we try to control the image others have of us through our performance. (This effort can involve projecting emotion and be done for pay, as the Through a Sociological Lens box explores.) Sometimes people fully embrace a role and see its performance as an integral part of themselves. An aspiring concert pianist might enthusiastically immerse herself in her role, wearing a certain type of clothing and hairstyle and using body language that communicates to her audience that she is already a professional musician. In other situations, though, people attempt to maintain "role distance" by separating themselves from a role as they carry it out. These people want their audience to see the difference between the role they are playing and their "real" selves. A manager who is self-conscious about enforcing discipline, for example, may say, "Look, I hate to do this 'boss' stuff but . . ."

The Front Stage and the Back Stage All actors are familiar with the distinction between the front stage, which the audience can see, and the back stage, which is hidden from view. Actors perform their roles on the front stage, but on the back stage they become themselves again. Social actors also behave differently depending on where they are. The server smiling pleasantly at customers may complain bitterly about poor tips among coworkers in the kitchen. The student feigning interest when discussing a course with a professor may later grumble to friends about how boring the class is. The person posting cheerful pictures of himself on his Facebook page may be deeply unhappy in the privacy of his home.

As we have seen, our social ties are formed through our common culture, our shared interpretation of reality, and the statuses and the roles that we assume as we interact with one another. Our ongoing social interaction results in social networks, groups, and formal organizations that are the backbone of social structure, to which we now turn.

Social Networks

Social networks are *the collections of social ties that connect actors such as individuals and organizations to each other.* Today, the term conjures up images of social media and the web, but people have always formed networks, and sociologists have been studying them since long before the rise of the internet. As we will see, however, the emergence of digital networks has brought about some unique changes to social networks.

As mentioned in Chapter 4, pioneering German sociologist Georg Simmel (1858–1918) argued that the structure of social life is composed of regular, patterned interactions among

THROUGH A SOCIOLOGICAL LENS

Emotions and the Employee Role

"Thank you for choosing our airline!" "Have a great day!" "Would you like to hear our specials for today?" "How may I direct your call?" "I hope your stay with us was a pleasant one!" Health care workers, salespeople, flight attendants, waitstaff, customer service representatives, and workers in many other fields are often required to project an emotion to their customers or clients. Usually these jobs require workers to be exceptionally nice, that is, friendly and helpful. They are expected to greet people with a big smile and cheerful small talk so that the customer or client will feel welcome and relaxed. Bill collectors, on the other hand, need to make people who are delinquent in paying their bills feel uncomfortable; therefore, they are often nastier than natural. Either way, these employees need to express a particular emotion in order to play their role successfully.

©Matthew Staver/Bloomberg/Getty Images

Being a salesclerk can be stressful year-round, as employers expect the clerk to perform "emotional labor" and keep customers satisfied. Holiday "Black Friday" sales, though, can ramp up the pressure of such work significantly.

Sociologist Arlie Hochschild (2012) developed the idea that certain interactions require us to project an emotion we may not feel—to be nicer or nastier than natural. Viewing these interactions through a sociological lens, she called the effort involved *emotion work,* which, in a classic article (Hochschild 1979), she defined as "the act of trying to change in degree or quality an emotion or feeling" (561). We often engage in emotion work, according to Hochschild, because of *emotion rules,* the "social guidelines that direct how we want to try to feel" (563). When people tell you that you "shouldn't feel guilty," or that you "have the right" to feel angry, they are alerting you to these commonly accepted rules. When emotion rules are applied to a workplace, they amount to what Hochschild has called the "commercialization of human feeling."

Emotion work can be stressful (Cottingham, Johnson, and Erickson 2018; Horo 2014). Employees who identify strongly with their jobs, such as social workers, teachers, and nurses, may pour their emotional energy into their work only to experience burnout after a few years. Employees may be required to convey an emotion as genuine even though they do not feel it. As a result, they may struggle to change their emotions to match the feeling they are expected to express. Employees who maintain some distance from their employee role may become exhausted by the constant need to express cheerfulness or enthusiasm, even in the face of rudeness or hostility from customers. Employees who succeed in acting the part may feel like frauds for not genuinely experiencing the emotions they are expected to feel.

The burdens of emotional labor do not fall equally on all workers. Demands to display specific emotions are most common in low-wage working-class service jobs, especially in settings that involve frequent contact with customers. Retail salesclerks, food servers, flight attendants, and child care workers are all required to show deference to customers.

Overwhelmingly, jobs that require "service with a smile" are done by women—who tend to bear the burden of emotional work at home too (Garey and Hansen 2011). Meanwhile, people of color are often expected to perform more emotional labor to contain their feelings in the workplace than are their white counterparts (Evans 2013; Wingfield 2015).

think about it

1. *If you have worked in the labor force, did any of the jobs that you have held involve emotional labor? What was expected of you? Were you comfortable with these expectations?*
2. *Did your emotional labor involve any stress? If so, how did you manage that stress?*

individuals. Simmel ([1903] 1950) observed that in the emerging cities of his day, people gained more freedom and formed more fleeting connections to others than was common in rural village life. Elsewhere he referred to a "network" or "web of group affiliations" ([1922] 1955) that makes up modern life. Simmel, then, was the first sociologist to think systematically about social structure in terms of social networks.

The Nature of Networks and Ties

Who would be willing to lend you a little money in an emergency? Whom would you ask to be a personal reference on a job application? Whom would you invite to your graduation party? These people are part of your social network. Networks connect you to people and resources. Different social networks provide different resources. Some examples identified by Rainie and Wellman (2012, 19) include:

- *Havens* that promote a sense of belonging and fellowship
- *Bandages* that provide emotional and other types of assistance to cope with stress and troubles
- *Safety nets* that lessen the impact of acute crises and chronic troubles
- *Social capital* that helps people find jobs, houses, spouses, and more

Networks come in different sizes, and they vary by the strength of their links, by the characteristics of the people involved, by the physical distance between their members, and by the kind of interaction within them, among other characteristics. Whatever their benefit or form, robust network ties help us navigate social life successfully.

Some of our networks are made up of close friends, family, or others with whom we have strong ties and intimate relationships. Typically, we want to spend time with these people, and the feeling is usually mutual. The stronger our ties are with people, the more likely they are to provide a broad range of support.

Most of our social support comes from a relatively small number of such strong ties (Wellman and Wortley 1990). These close ties can be critical during times of crisis (Aldrich and Meyer 2015). For example, as Hurricane Katrina approached New Orleans in August 2005, residents with strong social networks outside New Orleans were the first to leave the city, relying on family and close friends for food, shelter, and other assistance. In contrast, people without such ties had a more difficult time leaving the city and were typically among the last to evacuate. In the absence of social networks to help with basic necessities such as clothing, food, housing, and transportation, these residents were far more dependent on federal, state, and local government for assistance than were those with strong ties outside the city (Fussell 2006, 2018).

Other networks consist of people who have relatively weak ties with one another: coworkers, neighbors, and casual acquaintances. Though they are made up of weak ties, these networks can be helpful, too, since they connect us to a broader set of social contacts, information, and resources than might otherwise be available to us. In a classic phrase, Granovetter (1973, 1974) argued for "the strength of weak ties." In his review of existing research and in his own study of men in management and the professions, he found that many men were able to obtain better jobs by using their "weak ties" to connect to new opportunities.

Alumni who help college students from their alma mater obtain internships or jobs upon graduation are a good example of this type of "weak tie" network in action. Such contacts are often stratified by class; students from more prestigious schools enjoy the privilege of alumni contacts who wield considerably more power and influence than do alumni from less prestigious colleges. On the other hand, those with less power in society—who are likely to be at less prestigious schools, if they attend college at all—are at a disadvantage because they are largely excluded from powerful social networks. This, too, is a part of the social network phenomenon: access to networks often varies based on how much power a person has; in turn, "who you know" can influence what you can or cannot do in life.

In addition, the more connections people have, the more additional connections they are likely to develop over time (Barabási 2014; Perc 2014). This is an example of what Merton (1968b) called the *Matthew effect*, by which the network-rich get richer and the network-poor get poorer. (The name comes from the biblical verse in Matthew 25:29: "For to all those who have, more will be given . . . but from those who have nothing, even what they have will be taken away.") Those without strong social ties have fewer network resources and are less able to generate social support to meet life's challenges.

Social Network Analysis

The study of social networks can tell us a great deal about patterns of social interaction in a variety of contexts (Borgatti, Everett, and Johnson 2013; Scott 2012). Sociologists, for example, have analyzed networks to study the social dynamics of a neighborhood, to gain insight into communication in a workplace, to analyze how HIV/AIDS is spread, and to better understand online social connections.

Such analysis can reveal that networks matter in unexpected ways. For example, Christakis and Fowler (2007) have shown that people's social network influences the likelihood that they will be overweight (2007) or that they will smoke (2008). Those with networks populated with more people who are overweight or who smoke are more likely themselves to be overweight or smoke. These findings hold even when controlled for self-selection (socializing with similar people) and social environment (being influenced by common environmental factors). Another study (Fowler and Christakis 2008) found that happy people tend to be connected to other happy people, and people at the core of their local networks are happier than those on the periphery. Happiness is "contagious" up to three degrees of separation (to a friend of a friend of a friend), and the characteristics of a person's network can help predict independently which individuals will be happy over time.

Researchers use specialized software to map the linkages among the members of a network and to conduct complex network analyses (Watts 2004). Network diagrams such as the one shown in Figure 7.3 illustrate the connections among members and their pattern of interaction. In this way, they help reveal the hidden ties (indirect connections) that link people to one another and that illuminate some of the structure of social life. Other types of network analysis map interactions among thousands or even millions of people, searching for patterns that can shed light on social life.

Social network analysis reveals that our networks are more likely to include people who are like us than who are unlike us. This pattern is known as **homophily,** *the tendency for social contact to occur at a higher rate among people who are similar than among those who are different* (McPherson, Smith-Lovin, and Cook 2001). Race, age, religion, and class (including education and occupation) are important characteristics that connect or separate people. As a result, most social networks are much more homogeneous than the population as a whole. Homophily influences what we know about our society, since we are apt to share and reinforce our worldview with others who are like us

FIGURE 7.3 | VISUALIZING SOCIAL NETWORKS

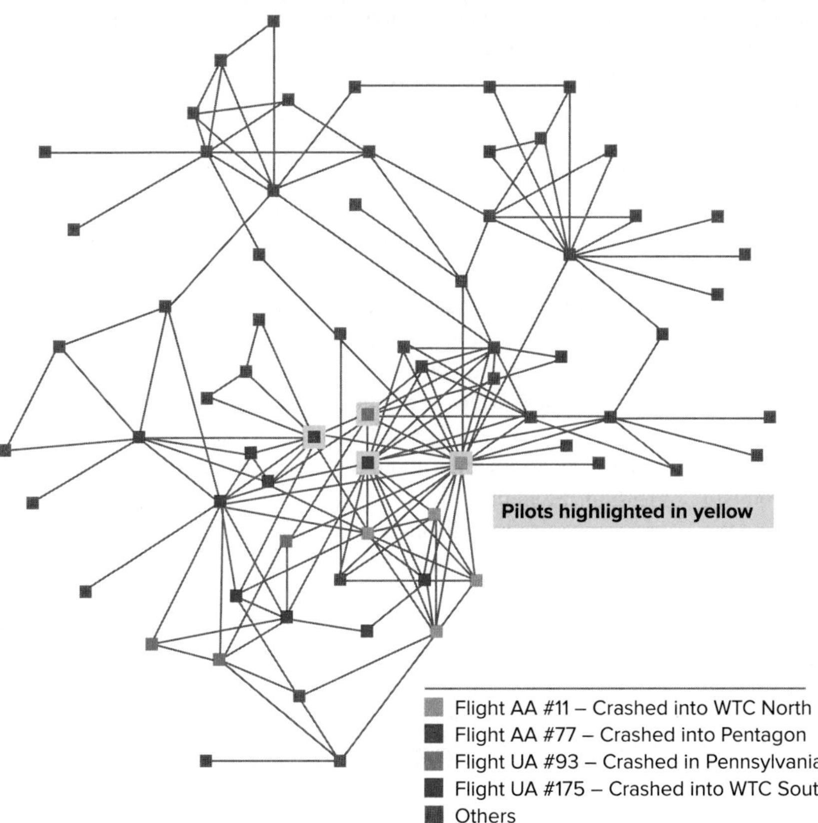

"Small world" social networks that consist of a small number of people (for example, a family, a workplace, a terrorist network, a board of directors) can be mapped out in a simple diagram like this one, which shows the social network connecting the 9/11 hijackers, who are represented by the color-coded nodes indicating the flight they were on. The dark gray nodes are other people who had direct, or indirect, contact with the hijackers, and the gray lines show reported connections.

Source: Valdis Krebs, www.orgnet.com/hijackers.html.

©Cultura Creative/Alamy Stock Photo

Many students inhabit a more racially diverse friendship network during their college years than they did in high school, and this experience can have a significant influence on the diversity of their subsequent networks as adults.

(Smith-Lovin and McPherson 1993). As we will see in Chapter 14, online social networks can contribute to the partisan political divide because they reinforce existing beliefs and often exclude other viewpoints.

Friendship networks in the United States are typically characterized by racial homophily (Mouw and Entwisle 2006; Quillian and Campbell 2003; Wimmer and Lewis 2010). However, students on college campuses may cultivate more robust multiracial and multiethnic friendship networks than is typical off-campus, especially if a school's undergraduate student population is racially diverse (Kim, Park, and Koo 2015). Given the degree to which schools and neighborhoods are segregated by race in the United States, college may be the first opportunity many students have for regular interaction with people of various races. White, non-Hispanic college students who have a black, a Latino, or an Asian roommate are more comfortable interacting in racially diverse settings and are more likely to have interracial friendships than are white students who have white roommates. And although white, non-Hispanic college students have far fewer interracial friendships than do black, Latino, or Asian students during their high school years, their proportion of friends of different races increases during the first year of college (Lee and LaDousa 2015; Sterns, Buchmann, and Bonneau 2009).

Social Groups

Social life involves more than interactions among individuals. Throughout society, people interact in patterns that form the basis of small groups, such as families. **Social groups** are *collections of people who interact regularly with one another and who are aware of their status as a group.* A *crowd* that happens to be in the same place at the same time, such as passengers waiting to board an airplane, is not a group in the sociological sense, since the people are gathered for a onetime event and do not think of themselves as part of some collective entity. Similarly, *categories* of people, such as apartment dwellers or people with blue eyes, also are not social groups in the sociological sense. Some groups can be quite informal and can be created, changed, or dissolved with relatively little fanfare. Nevertheless, unlike a crowd or category of people, members of a group often share common interests, values, norms, and expectations.

Primary and Secondary Social Groups

Sociologists often classify groups according to the nature and intensity of their interaction. **Primary groups** are *made up of people who have regular contact, enduring relationships, and a* *significant emotional attachment to each other.* A family is one example of a primary group; a collection of close friends who regularly hang out together is another. In both cases group members interact regularly, often spending a great deal of time together, and their connection to the primary group endures over time. Primary group members share a sense of both caring and obligation, even if the relationships among them are not equal (for example, parent and child). Primary groups are especially influential agents of socialization and can have a major impact on a person's life, shaping values and priorities. They often provide important social support.

Secondary groups are *made up of people who interact in a relatively impersonal way, usually to carry out some specific task.* Coworkers at your job or members of a neighborhood watch group are examples of secondary groups. Typically, these groups represent shorter-term or temporary associations, without a significant emotional bond between members. Over time, you will probably join and leave many different secondary groups, and the group will usually emphasize a common task or goal—fighting neighborhood crime, for example—over connections among group members. As a result, secondary groups are not nearly as influential in our lives as primary groups.

It is not always easy to distinguish between primary and secondary groups. Is a high school soccer team, whose members train together year-round and see one another more often than their families during the soccer season, a primary group? Sometimes a primary group can form within a larger secondary group, as when a small group of coworkers develops close relationships. The best way to distinguish between primary and secondary groups is to think about the basis and depth of members' attachment to the group, the sense of mutual obligation, and the amount of influence the group has on members' lives.

Reference Groups

We saw in Chapter 6 that we derive our sense of self in part from taking into account how others likely see and judge us—the "looking glass self." **Reference groups** are *the groups against which we choose to measure ourselves.* A reference group can be a family, a circle of friends, an occupational group, or a community of worship—just about any primary or secondary group.

Reference groups matter because they can influence the choices we make. They are the social groups we take into account as we plan and assess our actions. For example, as you were deciding whether to attend college, you may have asked yourself: "What will my friends think? Will my family be disappointed if I don't go to college? Will future employers look at my application more positively if I have a degree?" If the answers were contradictory, you needed to decide which reference group was most important to you.

Reference groups can influence our choices even if we do not yet belong to them. Graduate and professional schools, for example, socialize students about the expectations of their chosen profession. Students who have doctors or businesspeople as their reference group will often adopt new habits, ways of thinking, language, behavior, and dress to conform to that group's likely expectations.

Group Size and Social Relationships: Dyads, Triads, and Beyond

According to sociologist Georg Simmel ([1908] 1964), the size of a group has important effects on internal group dynamics. Consider the characteristics of a *dyad,* a group consisting of just two people (Figure 7.4). Because a dyad can continue to exist only if both participants are committed to it, it is very unstable. Dyads are also the most intense type of social relationships because interaction in a dyad is always between two people. Committed sexual relationships and marriages are classic examples of dyads, but best friends or business partners can also exhibit these characteristics.

Group dynamics fundamentally change when a third person is added, creating a *triad.* In a triad, members' attention is

FIGURE 7.4 | GROUP SIZE AND SOCIAL RELATIONSHIPS

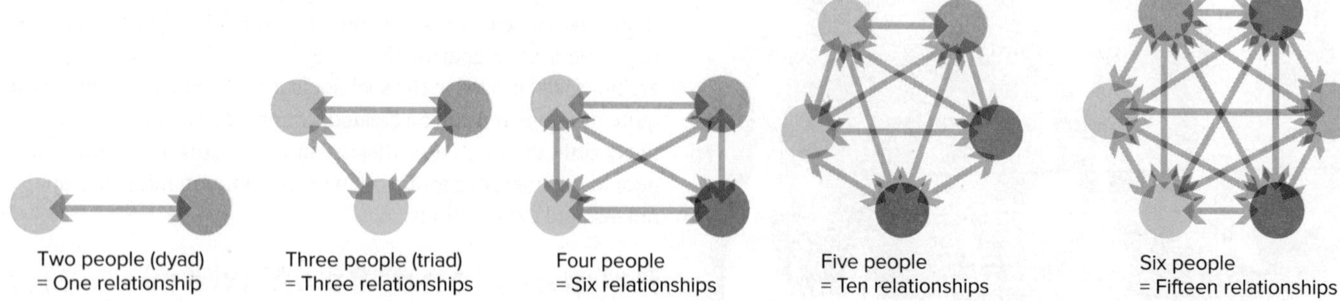

The size of a group affects the social relationships within it. In small groups, members are likely to interact directly with one another and to see themselves as integral members of the group. As groups become larger, there are many more potential relationships, and the connections among group members tend to be less intense. A group of just 20 people can have 190 different relationships. Think of both a small and a large group to which you belong. Do they fit this general pattern?

divided, since the number of possible interactions increases. As a couple adjusts to a first child or a new friend joins a previously existing dyad, difficulties typically emerge. One parent may feel jealous of the bond between the other parent and a new infant, for example. Two members of the triad may form an alliance in opposition to the third person, sparking tension. When a pair of friends becomes a triad, conflict may arise as two members outvote the third when deciding what to do or where to eat.

Group size also influences social interaction within larger groups. Groups generally become more stable as they get larger because the group can withstand the loss of individual members. However, relationships also become less intense as a group gets larger. Because there is less focus and attention on any one person, members of a larger group typically feel less emotional commitment to one another. Therefore, small groups tend to be intense but unstable, whereas larger groups tend to be more stable but less intense.

Large and small groups also differ in the nature of the social interaction among members. To take a familiar example, the size of a class influences the social interaction within the classroom: how the instructor interacts with each student and with the group as a whole, how students interact with each other, and what kinds of in-class activities work best. You can be anonymous and passive in a lecture hall with 200 students. In a seminar with 6 students, however, you must participate actively in the discussion.

Social Networks and Groups in the Digital Age

Teens in the United States are digitally connected. In a 2015 study, 92 percent of teens aged 13 to 17 reported that they are online daily, including 24 percent who said they are online "almost constantly." Teens sent and received an average of 30 texts a day, and 71 percent of this age group said they used more than one social networking site. Teen Facebook users had an average of 145 "friends," and typical Instagram users had 150 followers in their network (Lenhart 2015).

With the explosion of online digital connections, some sociologists argue that contemporary society is now organized by "networked individualism" more than by groups (Rainie and Wellman 2012; see Table 7.1). Three revolutions have propelled this change. First, in a process that has continued since Simmel initially observed it a century ago, the significance of social networks has increased in modern life. Small, densely knit groups that characterized social organization in the past—such as families, villages, and small organizations—have been supplanted by networks. The social networks that characterize contemporary life are more diverse and less constraining than the social groups of the past, even those during Simmel's time. Through networking, we have more leeway in choosing who we want to be, what we want to do, and with whom we want to interact. We have broad opportunities to move well beyond our family and place of birth to explore other places, lifestyles, occupations, and values.

Second, the creation of the internet has given people an unprecedented global communications and information-gathering platform to use in developing their social networks. The introduction of this new technology is what has enabled networks to expand and thrive as never before.

Third, the mobile revolution in communication devices, especially the smartphone, means that people can access their friendship and professional networks whenever and wherever they want. Physical locations that often were the genesis of traditional groups—home/family, neighborhood/neighbors, workplace/coworkers—are less important in contemporary life. Instead, the social and professional circles in which we travel exist increasingly online, supplemented by "real-world" interactions.

Together, Rainie and Wellman (2012, 6) argue, these three revolutions have enabled a major shift in social life: "We have become increasingly networked as individuals, rather than embedded in groups." This does not mean that people are less social or more individualistic. Rather, the nature of our

TABLE 7.1 GROUPS VERSUS NETWORKS: SOME DIFFERENCES

Groups	Networks
1. Contact is within and between groups.	1. Contact is between individuals.
2. Ties are local.	2. Ties are local and distant.
3. Ties are largely homogeneous.	3. Ties can be diverse.
4. Most ties are involuntary (kin, neighbors).	4. Most ties are voluntary.
5. Groups exert strong social control over the individual.	5. Networks exert weak social control over the individual.
6. Groups provide a broad range of resources.	6. Networks provide specialized resources.
7. Groups have tight boundaries.	7. Networks often have permeable boundaries.

Source: Adapted from Rainie and Wellman (2012).

©Sickles Photo Reporting/Getty Images

©David R. Frazier Photolibrary, Inc./ Alamy Stock Photo

FAST-FORWARD

Social Change and Networks

In the internet era, social networks are changing. Until recently, our primary social networks were rooted in a specific place and were based largely on face-to-face interaction. However, online social interaction means that geographic distance is becoming far less significant; people who regularly interact online are building strong friendship networks with people who may live across the country or on the other side of the globe and whom they may never meet face-to-face.

interdependence and the characteristics of our reliance on others have changed in distinct ways:

- We meet a growing portion of our social, emotional, and economic needs by connecting to broad, loosely organized and diverse networks of associates rather than to a small number of tight-knit groups.
- Our work and leisure lives are more intertwined, since the boundaries that used to separate family and friends from work have blurred.
- Similarly, our public and private lives have blurred in a network society.

While being in a network offers some distinct advantages, membership is not automatic; individuals must take the initiative to make and maintain connections. The days of automatically being part of a kinship group, community, or other older, group-based social life are past. Consequently, Rainie and Wellman (2012, 9) note, "Networked individualism is both socially liberating and socially taxing." For example, the expansion of the internet enables people to reach out and find social contacts relatively easily. However, the internet "also made relationships harder to sustain because it brought so many distractions and fleeting interactions." In addition, the digital divide means that differences in the level of internet access and knowledge about how to use it effectively can make social inequalities worse.

Organizations and Bureaucracy

More complex and more formal than most groups, **organizations** are *secondary groups that have a degree of formal structure and are formed to accomplish particular tasks.* This broad definition applies to organizations as diverse as your local chess club, the National Rifle Association, Microsoft Corporation, and the United Nations. Although these examples obviously vary enormously in scale, configuration, and purpose, we can learn a great deal about how they operate, and how people behave within them, by studying the structure and culture of organizations, as well as the environments in which they operate.

Organizational Structure

As with any group, the size of an organization can have a major influence on its structure and operation. Very small organizations can operate with few formal rules, straddling the line between an informal group and a formal organization. But even the smallest organizations require a process for making basic decisions. A small organization such as a neighborhood association may use consensus to reach decisions: all members' views are solicited and every effort is made to reach a general agreement. Such an organization may not need any formal leaders, such as a president or treasurer, but may instead use rotating coordinators to ensure that business gets done.

As organizations grow, however, an informal structure usually proves to be inadequate. A larger organization typically develops a more formal decision-making process and a more elaborate division of labor. As we saw in Chapter 1, Max Weber noted that a shift from traditional to rational action (the *rationalization of society*) was a characteristic of the rise of industrialized society in the nineteenth century. Early industrialists needed to manage ever-larger organizations. Businesses needed to operate factories that employed hundreds or even thousands of workers, producing goods in large quantities that were distributed through a complex transportation network. Paying workers, purchasing raw materials, and shipping goods from the factory—all required the development of complex systems. As new structures and ways of accomplishing tasks became necessary, bureaucracy developed into the dominant organizational structure of the industrial age.

©Chronicle/Alamy Stock Photo

Industrial production required administrative bureaucracies to coordinate huge factories that often employed thousands of workers. In this postcard image, taken around 1916, tens of thousands of workers gather in front of a Ford Motor factory in Detroit, Michigan.

Bureaucracy

A **bureaucracy** is *a hierarchical administrative system with formal rules and procedures used to manage organizations.* Bureaucracies commonly share key features (Weber 1946):

1. ***A division of labor.*** Because of their size, bureaucracies need specialization; not everyone can do everything. In bureaucracies, people are responsible for narrowly defined tasks.
2. ***A hierarchy of authority and accountability.*** Bureaucracies have a pyramidal structure (see Figure 7.5). With power concentrated at the top of the hierarchy and many bureaucrats at the bottom dividing what little influence they have, authority is highly fragmented, and managers' primary job is to enforce rules and monitor other workers.
3. ***Impersonality.*** Power is located within an office, not in the person who happens to hold that position. People are hired, promoted, fired, or retired, but the bureaucratic structure remains.
4. ***Written rules and records.*** The tasks and duties to be carried out within a bureaucracy are usually written out in formal rules and procedures. Written forms for communicating information and for record-keeping help ensure consistency.

These four features allow bureaucracies to coordinate the diverse activities of many people. Without them, organizations, especially large ones—from the national government to your favorite retail outlet—would stop functioning. (Though as we saw in the chapter opening, some organizations are experimenting with less bureaucratic structures.) Your college, for example, undoubtedly has a bureaucracy to schedule classes, coordinate student records, manage housing, pay employees, and keep buildings clean.

As you have probably experienced, however, bureaucracies can have a negative side. If you have ever gotten the "run-around" while trying to figure out who in an organization is responsible for a problem, you have encountered the sometimes maddening results of the division of labor and fragmented authority that characterize most bureaucracies. And, of course, we have all been buried in the avalanche of paperwork—or its digital equivalent—that can be required to accomplish a common task such as visiting a doctor, enrolling in college, applying for financial aid, or opening a bank account. All organizations have some degree of bureaucratization, but too much can be counterproductive, frustrating both employees and the people they are supposed to serve. In addition, because authority is so fragmented in a bureaucracy, these types of organizations tend to be very resistant to change.

Since bureaucracies are governed by rules and regulations that apply to everyone, they can be very impersonal, and it can be difficult to make exceptions to accommodate an individual's specific needs. For example, if the workday at your company begins at 9:00 a.m., you may not be allowed to arrive at 9:15 a.m. so that you can drop your child off at school, even if you would be willing to work an extra 15 minutes at the end of the day. Rules and regulations tend to multiply and become more refined within bureaucracies as new situations arise. As a result, bureaucratic organizations typically have detailed policies that specify not only how to enforce the rules but also how to modify them.

Even though bureaucracies are designed to coordinate activities smoothly, they can be remarkably inefficient, and efforts to maximize efficiency often seem to have the opposite effect. For example, automated customer-service phone lines are designed to manage large volumes of calls. Yet customers complain so frequently about not being able to talk to a live human being that a website has been created that provides frustrated customers of hundreds of companies with guidance on how to get to a live person more quickly (www.gethuman.com).

Although large organizations rely on bureaucratic measures to run smoothly, as the layers of bureaucracy multiply, they often make organizations increasingly unwieldy. Sociologists seek to understand this complexity, recognizing both the mechanisms designed to coordinate large organizations and the dynamics that can make bureaucracies feel like an exasperating maze. Two factors they look at are an organization's culture and its operating environment.

Organizational Culture

Organizations can have distinct cultures that influence how they are organized, the values they espouse, and the way they operate (Hofstede, Hofstede, and Minkov 2010). (For an example of a

FIGURE 7.5 | FORMAL BUREAUCRATIC STRUCTURE

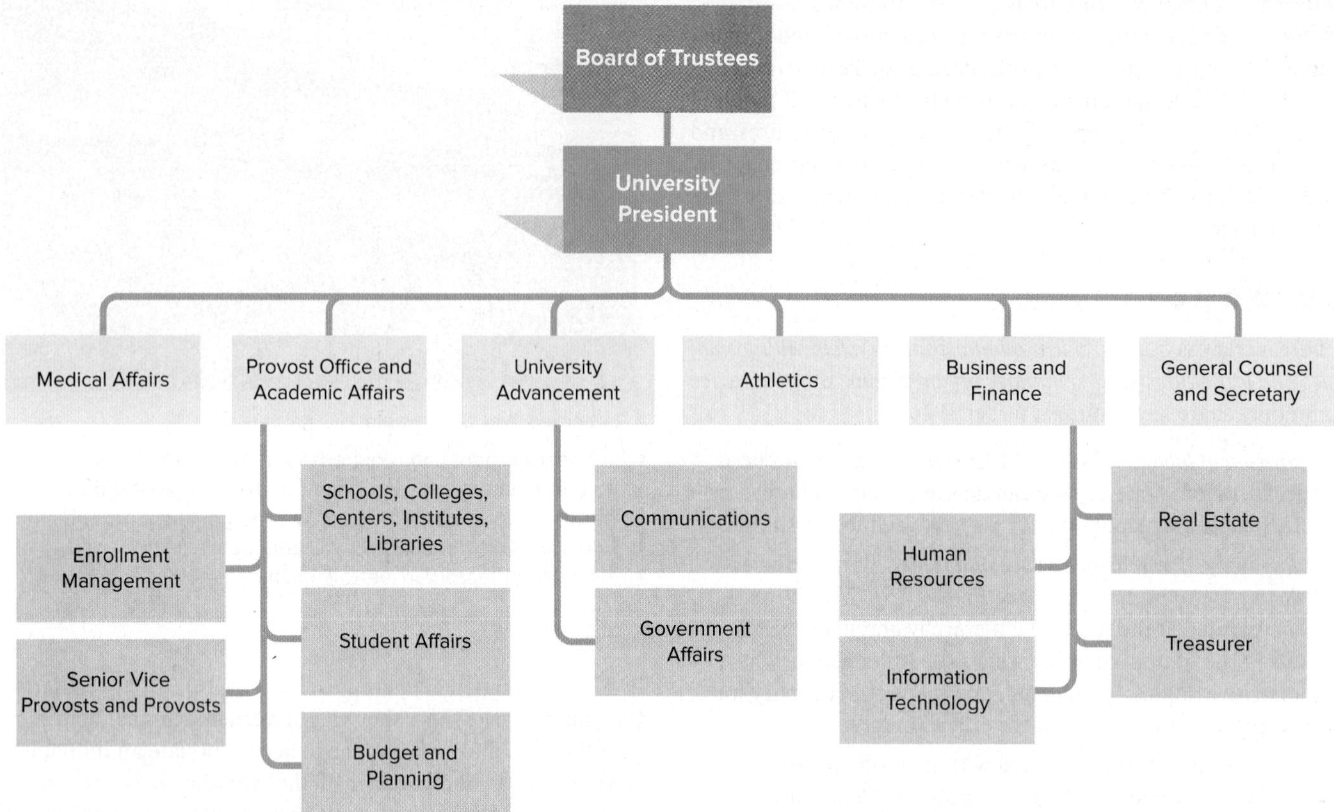

Like all large organizations, the University of Miami has a formal bureaucratic structure, summarized in this chart. Occupying the positions within its bureaucracy (represented by boxes) are particular individuals who can leave the organization without affecting its structure. Positions in such structures usually carry different amounts of power and prestige and command unequal amounts of resources, with those toward the top having more of all three than those toward the bottom. *Source*: University of Miami website.

CORE CONCEPTS CHALLENGE *Locate a copy of your school's organizational* **structure,** *which may be available on its website. How does your school's structure compare with this one? What does this structure tell you about power at your school?*

sociologist who works with different organizational cultures, see the Sociology Works box.) Even organizations involved in very similar activities can have different cultures. One famous example from the business world involved the merger between America Online (AOL) and Time Warner (Klein 2003). AOL, an early successful internet service provider, had a brash, aggressive approach to the business. Its executives were often young, with an informal style, and they viewed their company as the future of the media industry. Time Warner, on the other hand, was the product of an earlier merger between two old-media giants: Time Inc. (print media) and Warner Communications Inc. (film and television). Time Warner's leaders had a reputation for being conservative and straitlaced. At Time Warner, workers saw themselves as potential "lifers" at a stable company with a good retirement plan. In contrast, AOL employees had made quick money and expected that their big payoff would come from selling what they hoped would become valuable AOL stock. Such differences were only the tip of the iceberg; employees at AOL and Time Warner didn't understand and, in some cases, didn't like each other. As a result, combining the two companies proved far more difficult than expected, and the culture clash contributed to the eventual failure of the merger in 2009.

©iStock/360/Getty Images

Organizational Environment

All organizations, whatever their culture may be, operate in a larger environment, which includes other organizations as

SOCIOLOGY WORKS

Mindy Fried and Organizational Change

For more than two decades, sociology has informed Mindy Fried's work as a family policy analyst in state government, a lobbyist for early childhood services, and most recently as an organizational change consultant. Fried was drawn to sociology because it connected her longstanding interest in people to what she calls the "big picture." In sociology, Fried "discovered kindred spirits who asked the same kinds of questions that I had about people and their worlds—questions about how people's experiences are framed by their race, gender, age, and ethnicity, questions about how social structures in our society provide answers to how people behave, the opportunities they have, the barriers they encounter."

Describing herself as an "applied sociologist," Fried works as a consultant specializing in organizational change, drawing upon her sociological perspective to help organizations navigate changing contexts. She works with organizations to solve problems, negotiate conflicts, and respond to new challenges and opportunities, using her sociological understanding of interaction and organizational culture (Fried 2008).

Fried's main clients are nonprofit organizations. In one project, Fried and her colleagues at Arbor Consulting Partners worked with a university–community partnership focused on improving the health of local residents in a low-income neighborhood. Communication problems—the result of two very different organizational cultures—were hampering the partnership. Fried conducted interviews, held focus groups with members of both groups, and used participant observation—research methods that allowed her to help "key players develop a deeper understanding of how power, diversity, and agency affected their organizational dynamic." This shared understanding helped produce more effective communication and a stronger working relationship between the two groups.

Courtesy of Mindy Fried

Mindy Fried

As an organizational change consultant, Fried takes the distinctly sociological approach of an "outsider within," someone who is not emotionally involved with the organization but who makes a commitment to observe, listen, and learn about the various experiences of those who are. Fried explains: "Our status as outsiders within ultimately allows us to interpret multiple perspectives, untangle conflict, and think creatively about how to maximize positive outcomes for an organization." Reflecting on her sociological approach, Fried says sociology gives her both a rich understanding of organizational dynamics and the research skills to help her clients build on their strengths and respond to new challenges.

"Our status as outsiders within ultimately allows us to interpret multiple perspectives, untangle conflict, and think creatively about how to maximize positive outcomes for an organization."

think about it

1. *How might an organization in which you participate (school, community group, extracurricular club) benefit from the assistance of an organizational consultant?*
2. *How do you think the perspective of an "outsider within" differs from that of either an insider or an outsider?*

well as a variety of conditions that are part of the broader context of a society (Hall and Tolbert 2009; Hatch 2018). Collectively, *factors that exist outside of the organization but that potentially affect its operation* constitute the **organizational environment.** The strength of the economy, the stability of political rule, demographic factors, other organizations, the legal context, technology, and the cultural environment can all influence the way organizations operate.

Much like individuals, organizations link to other organizations in a network structure in the course of their normal operations. Your school, for example, interacts with a variety of other organizations. Government agencies and private corporations provide research grants, businesses sell goods and services on campus, and graduate schools and potential employers receive student transcripts.

The organizational environment also includes the legal context within which organizations operate (Edelman and Suchman 1997; Suchman 2015). Laws define the nature of some organizations, such as corporations and nonprofit groups. Laws and law enforcement also provide a stable environment within which organizations can operate. Courts enforce contracts and settle disputes. Legal regulations may also restrict organizational behavior. For example, environmental laws limit pollution and antitrust laws help ensure that companies compete fairly.

Technology is another element of the organizational environment. Computers and the internet have dramatically changed how large organizations function, enabling them to accumulate more data, communicate faster across long distances, and distribute information broadly both internally and externally.

The broader cultural environment also influences how organizations operate. Social norms and role expectations vary across cultures. For example, Chinese managers place a premium on relationships and loyalty, protecting the honor of all members in an organization, and solving problems privately to avoid embarrassing their workers. In addition, Chinese organizations typically feature highly centralized authority, with limited participation in decision making (Nyberg and Jensen 2009). Practicing respect in an organization in the United States might mean treating all organization members equally, whereas in China respect may mean deferring to authority within the organization. Organizations that cross cultural boundaries must accommodate these differing cultural environments, and they must often adapt to the way power is distributed within an organization.

Power in Groups and Organizations

As we have seen, people in groups and organizations have different amounts of power, and this difference both reflects and reinforces inequality. In addition, groups can exert considerable influence over the actions of individual members, gaining obedience or compliance through various means.

In-Groups and Out-Groups

One way that groups exert control is by including or excluding members through the existence of in- and out-groups. An **in-group** is *a social group with which a person identifies and toward which he or she has positive feelings.* Members of an in-group have a collective sense of "us." An **out-group** is *a social group toward which a person has negative feelings, considering its members to be inferiors, or "them."* We feel a sense of loyalty to other members of our in-group, whether they are fellow environmentalists, soccer fans, or Methodists, and this sense of solidarity is essential to the functioning of society. But camaraderie can easily turn into a sense of superiority over those who are not part of the in-group. For example, one study of a diverse group of LGBT youth in Great Britain found that their "in-group" cohesion was enhanced by their use of racist language to position people of South Asian descent as a homophobic "out-group" (Jones 2016). More commonly, people with high-status jobs often build social connections in wealthy neighborhoods and exclusive clubs (Khan 2012). Solidarity within this in-group of the wealthy may be accompanied by negative attitudes toward those less well-off ("they" don't work hard; "they" are not as smart or talented), and may lead the wealthy to exclude others from their neighborhoods and social circles. In- and out-groups cause tension, rivalry, and even overt conflict between social groups, which often struggle for power as in-groups seek to maintain their perceived superiority. The increasing partisan divide in the United States reflects a type of in-group versus out-group dynamic.

Conformity: The Asch Experiments

Sociologists have long been interested in how groups promote conformity and elicit obedience from members. Social psychologists have done important studies that reveal the formidable, and often underappreciated, power dynamics that operate within groups.

Imagine, for example, that you have signed up to take a vision test as part of an experiment. The experimenter introduces himself and explains to you and seven other participants that your task is simple. You will be shown pairs of cards, one with three vertical lines of different lengths on it and the other with a single vertical line (see Figure 7.6). You are to identify which of the three lines is the same length as the line on the comparison card and state your response out loud.

The experimenter shows the first and second pairs of cards, and each participant in turn gives the choice that is obviously correct. When your turn comes, you add your response. With the third set, though, you're surprised to hear all the respondents choose what is obviously the wrong answer. When it's your turn to respond, you wonder if they can all be so obviously wrong. Do you stick with your initial answer, or do you change it to conform to what everyone else has said?

Just such a dilemma faced subjects in the classic experiments carried out by Solomon Asch (1952, 1955). What study participants didn't know was that the other "subjects" in the group were confederates (people working with the experimenter). After providing correct answers for the first two rounds, confederates provided incorrect answers for 12 of the next 18 rounds. Would the "majority effect," as Asch called it, lead the test subject to conform to the group and provide an obviously incorrect response?

FIGURE 7.6 | ASCH EXPERIMENTS

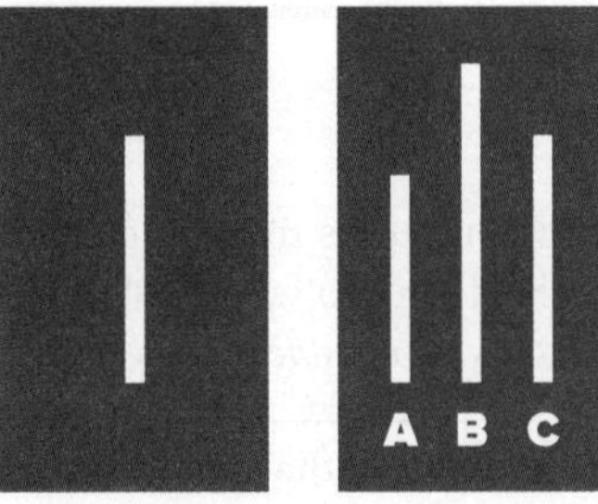

The Asch experiments suggested that group pressure can generate conformity. Experimental subjects were asked which of the three lines on the right was the same length as the comparison line on the left. When group members who had been prompted beforehand by the experimenter gave wrong answers, some subjects agreed with the obviously incorrect response.

Asch found that only a quarter of the respondents gave the correct answer all the time. Three-quarters agreed with at least one wrong answer, though only 5 percent agreed with every incorrect answer. On average, subjects provided an incorrect response about 37 percent of the time. (Subjects in control groups without confederates easily identified the correct answers.) Asch also found that subjects were more likely to give incorrect answers if the confederates were unanimous in their answers and that the size of the group affected the result. Having only one confederate eliminated the "majority effect," and having three or more produced the full effect.

Asch's experiments included only male college students in an artificial setting and involved only a brief, inconsequential activity. Subsequent research, however, has confirmed the findings: the actions of others often promote conformist behavior. For example, eyewitnesses in criminal cases sometimes change their account of what they saw to conform to contrary information about the crime that they receive later (Goodwin et al. 2017; Wright, Self, and Justice 2000).

©Richard Ellis/Alamy Stock Photo

Some cultures are more conformist than others. East Asian cultures, such as in Japan and China, typically define nonconformity in negative terms, whereas Western cultures are more likely to see it in a positive light, viewing nonconformists as unique and their contributions as valuable (Corriveau, Min, and Kurkul 2014; Kim and Markus 1999).

People are more willing to behave in conformist ways when they are anxious about their personal safety and well-being, for example, because of potential terrorism, the threat of natural disasters or infectious diseases, or a perceived menace from the influx of immigrants (Falomir-Pichastor et al. 2013; Murray and Schaller 2012; Renkema, Stapel, and Van Yperen 2008). The 9/11 attacks in the United States and the more recent terrorist attacks in Europe, for example, bred conformity as citizens rallied around public displays of patriotic symbols.

Groups vary considerably in the amount of influence they have over individual behavior. Some research suggests that the results from Asch's experiments were a reflection of the broader conformist culture of the 1950s (Bond and Smith 1996). People in the United States today may be more willing to question authority. Despite often-powerful group influences, individuals still have the capacity to pursue independent action, whether they are operating within an informal group or a formal organization.

Obedience: The Milgram Experiments

In 2010, 80 contestants were recruited for the pilot of a new French reality television game show called *Zone Xtreme.* Contestants signed a contract saying they were willing to administer electrical shocks as part of the game. Each contestant was then paired with another contestant named Jean-Paul, who would be challenged with a series of questions while strapped in an electrically wired chair, which was placed in an isolation booth. If Jean-Paul answered a question incorrectly, his partner was told to push a lever to administer an electric shock. As Jean-Paul continued to answer incorrectly, the voltage increased from 20 to 460 volts—a potentially life-threatening jolt. At the lower levels, Jean-Paul was plainly startled by the mild jolts. As the shocks increased in severity, his cries of pain escalated, and he eventually pleaded, "Get me out of here, please! I don't want to play anymore!" But the game show host—a well-known French television personality—encouraged the contestants to continue administering the shocks, and the studio audience goaded them on. After a series of painful cries, Jean-Paul eventually became silent and stopped responding to the highest shock levels, presumably because he was unconscious or dead. Of the 80 contestants, 64 played the game all the way to the end, administering the highest voltages despite the pain they were clearly causing (Chazan 2010; Keaten 2010).

As you might have guessed, the "game show" was not real; it was staged as part of a documentary called *The Game of Death.* "Jean-Paul" was an actor, but the 80 contestants and the audience believed the situation was real. This demonstration was modeled loosely on experiments conducted in the United States by Stanley Milgram (a former student of Solomon Asch) in the early 1960s. Milgram's experiments—portrayed in the 2015 Hollywood film *Experimenter*—took place in a research lab, where scientists in white lab coats encouraged participants to administer apparently painful—and potentially lethal—electrical shocks, supposedly as part of a study on how punishment affects learning (Milgram 1963, 1965, 1969).

As Milgram's experiments—and the French game show—demonstrate, many of us are socialized to obey authority figures and to comply with social expectations, even when we know such actions are wrong. Although some people in Milgram's experiments did refuse to participate, many others set aside their better judgment and followed orders, ceding power to those in authority. Only when they saw others refusing to take part in the experiment did an overwhelming majority say no—compliance plummeted to just 5 percent when participants were teamed with someone who refused to administer the shocks.

Milgram's experiments were conducted, in part, to better understand why people would go along with atrocities such as the Holocaust, the systematic mass killing of Jews and other people by Nazi Germany during World War II. In the lab, participants often felt uncomfortable, apprehensive, and guilty about the pain they were causing, yet many voluntarily submitted to the man in the white lab coat, whose only power was the perception that he was a legitimate authority figure. A psychologist involved in the updated game show version of the Milgram experiments suggested that it reveals the "terrifying power of TV" (Chazan 2010).

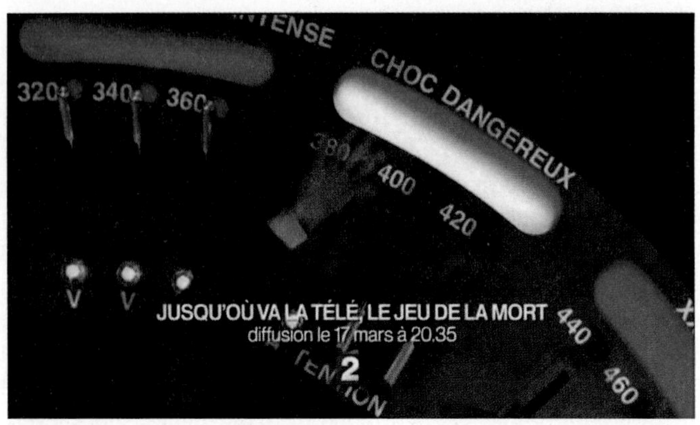

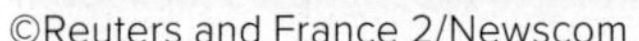

©Reuters and France 2/Newscom

©Reuters and France 2/Newscom

An overhead shot (*left*) shows the "game show" control panel used in *The Game of Death.* Contestants sat in front of the semicircular panel and were told by the celebrity host to push levers that administered increasingly powerful shocks to a contestant-partner seated in an isolation booth (*right*). Much like the Milgram experiments upon which this demonstration was modeled, most participants followed orders and administered what they believed to be painful—and potentially deadly—shocks.

CORE CONCEPTS CHALLENGE *What gave the game show host the* **power** *to get contestants to continue administering the shocks, even when they clearly did not want to do so? What are some real-world situations in which similar power dynamics might operate?*

Because of the potential trauma to participants, Milgram's experiments would not be allowed today. Even the French documentary was highly controversial, with some observers suggesting it manipulated people simply to produce dramatic television—even while it cautioned against the power of television.

Groupthink

Conformity can endanger designated targets of persecution; it can also endanger groups of people working together to achieve a goal. **Groupthink** is *a form of uncritical thinking in which people reinforce a consensus rather than ask serious questions or thoroughly analyze the issue at hand.* The studies that established the importance of groupthink originally focused on elite groups that operated in secrecy as they formulated U.S. foreign policy during the middle of the twentieth century (Janis 1972, 1989). Such groups sometimes produced policy disasters, including the failure to anticipate the Japanese attack on Pearl Harbor at the start of World War II, the failed Bay of Pigs invasion of Cuba in 1961, and the failure to appreciate the capabilities of the North Vietnamese forces during the Vietnam War. In all these cases, U.S. officials made false assumptions about the situation at hand that were reinforced in group discussions until they were eventually exposed as untrue.

People who engage in groupthink ignore evidence or ideas that contradict what they and fellow group members believe. The more group members are alike—the more they share key characteristics such as education, social background, and values—the more likely they are to accept common assumptions about the world rather than ask critical questions about these assumptions. The advisors who developed the Bay of Pigs invasion plan, for example, were the same experts President John F. Kennedy enlisted to assess its likely success. Staunchly opposed to Fidel Castro, Cuba's revolutionary leader, these policymakers ignored his widespread popularity among Cubans and suggested that he could be overthrown by a small army of lightly supplied Cuban exiles who, with limited air cover from the United States, could invade Cuba and trigger a spontaneous uprising. The ill-prepared exiles failed quickly, and the successful Cuban defense against the U.S.-backed invasion became a rallying point for Castro supporters, reinforcing his hold on power. Groupthink likely played a role again in 2003 when U.S. leaders decided to use military forces to invade Iraq in response to a perceived threat of weapons of mass destruction (WMDs), a threat that never existed.

Since they define situations similarly, groupthink participants are more likely to agree on a solution to a problem than to entertain other options that contradict their assumptions. Because they are homogeneous and self-reinforcing, such groups also tend to be shut off from dissenting views and input from the outside world, making them even more dysfunctional.

Groups that are prone to groupthink minimize internal conflict by encouraging all members to be team players. Group members may conform to steer clear of conflict or avoid appearing foolish, or simply because conforming is easier than challenging the group's assumptions. The result of this conformity, however, can be hasty or irrational decisions.

Leadership, Oligarchy, and Power

As we saw in Chapter 5, power shapes how we allocate resources, make rules and decisions, and define reality. In most organizations, especially workplaces, people struggle constantly over power (Edwards 1982; Edwards and Belanger 2009; Harrison, Lopez, and Martin 2015). One important characteristic of any organization, therefore, is its power structure.

In formal bureaucracies, people at each level of the organizational structure have power over those below and are subject to the authority of those above. As bureaucratic organizations expanded in the early twentieth century, sociologists raised questions about their potentially undemocratic impact. German sociologist Robert Michels (1876–1936), a student of Max Weber, coined the term **iron law of oligarchy** to describe what he saw as *the eventual and inevitable consolidation of power at the top of bureaucratic organizations.* (*Oligarchy* is rule by a powerful few.)

Michels argued that bureaucracies place too much power in the hands of those at the top. Inevitably, these select few misuse their power, which they consolidate through their unique access to information and resources. Once firmly entrenched in power, leaders are cut off from meaningful contact with others in the organization or the general public, rendering them unaccountable for their actions. Meanwhile, those lower down the bureaucratic hierarchy usually feel powerless to challenge the oligarchic leaders, though they may disapprove of them; as a result, they tend to be passive.

on social theory

Michels's analysis reflects the ideas of **conflict theory.** Have you encountered a situation in which power was concentrated at the top of an organization? If so, how did those below deal with this situation?

Despite Michels's fatalistic assessment, bureaucratic inequality can be contested through covert political conflict within organizations, including subtle forms of noncooperation and even sabotage (Courpasson 2016; Morrill, Zald, and Rao 2003). For example, employees sometimes "work to rule," completing only the minimum work required by company regulations, as a way of exercising power from below, a strategy that can dramatically undermine an organization. Sometimes subordinates react so slowly that they effectively prevent the implementation of policies they oppose. The inequality that is typical of hierarchical organizations can also lead workers to engage in overt efforts to change the balance of power—for example, by forming a labor union to protect their interests.

Although most traditional bureaucratic organizations do not operate on democratic principles, some bureaucratic organizations allocate positions in the hierarchy through democratic processes. Civic groups, for example, often elect officials. However, power is still likely to be distributed unequally, since election results place power in the hands of a few members—at least until the next election. More radical ways of distributing power within an organization involve consensus building and collective governance, which can dramatically reduce inequality (Schneiberg, King, and Smith 2008). Collective communities (sometimes referred to as communes), in which all members have an equal voice and all decisions are made through deliberative collective discussion, are a familiar example of such organizations. Worker-owned businesses are another example. Technology may also enable different forms of organization that distribute power more widely (Davis 2016).

Scientific Management and Workplace Control

As we have seen, industrialization led to the first large corporations with bureaucratic organizations in the late nineteenth and early twentieth centuries. There was no illusion of democracy in these bureaucratic workplaces. Owners wanted to control the workplace and limit workers' power to demand better wages or working conditions. A number of industries relied on skilled craft workers, however, many of whom were organized into trade unions. Their knowledge was central to successful production, and therefore they wielded considerable influence over the organization of the workplace and the conditions of their labor.

To consolidate power in the workplace, owners needed to transfer knowledge about the production process from these skilled workers to a small group of managers, while reducing complex jobs to simple tasks that could be done by easily replaceable unskilled and lower-paid workers. For employers, such top-down planning and control of production had the added benefit of being extremely efficient, increasing profits. For workers, it meant a loss of power in the workplace (Braverman 1974, 1998).

The process of de-skilling ordinary workers and increasing workplace efficiency through calculated study became known as **scientific management.** Frederick Taylor (1911) was the leading proponent of scientific management, and the approach is often referred to as Taylorism. Managers would carefully observe workers doing their jobs, noting all the individual steps and measuring the time each step took. Analysts would then examine the collected information to find ways of doing the work more quickly and efficiently. By breaking down complex and highly skilled work into simple components, managers could assign each element of the task to a different worker, who would need to know only one simple step.

The classic application of Taylorism was the assembly line. Although famous for its use in the auto industry, assembly-line work was first used in Chicago's meatpacking industry. Skilled employees once worked on an entire animal carcass, chopping

thinking about power

In bureaucratic organizations, **power** is concentrated in the upper ranks of an organization. In what ways can the "rank and file" members of an organization exert power? What hurdles do they face in doing so?

Source: Library of Congress [LC-USZ62-55730]

Butchers were once skilled workers who would cut up an entire carcass. Early assembly lines, like this one from a nineteenth-century meatpacking plant, broke down work into small tasks, such as splitting the backbone. An individual low-skill worker would complete his or her assigned task over and over. Each pig or cow, for example, would be worked on by as many as 300 different workers who each had a specific task to perform in transforming the animal carcass into steak or sausage.

and slicing the meat into the various cuts. With the application of Taylor's principles, the work was broken down into individual steps, each of which was performed by a separate worker, who could be hired at a lower wage and quickly trained for the monotonous and repetitious job.

Scientific management is not limited to the industrial context within which it was first applied. Standardized practices at fast-food restaurant chains and other establishments—so-called McDonaldization, discussed in Chapter 4—echo some features of Taylorism (Ritzer 2015). Today's high-tech workplaces often incorporate many of the Taylorist principles developed a century ago. Management control of the work process is almost universal in today's workplaces. Telemarketers at a call center, for example, typically use a prepared script and follow routine procedures when making phone calls. Managers monitor productivity by using software that records keystrokes on workers' computer keyboards and by occasionally listening in on calls—tactics that recall an earlier era of Taylorism.

Scientific management has its limits today, however. Professional jobs tend to be knowledge based, and workers need to use creativity, collaborate, and respond to rapidly changing markets. The result is a two-tier system of employment, reflecting the class system, in which knowledge workers enjoy considerable autonomy and flexibility, along with high pay, while most other workers are monitored closely, performing routine, repetitious tasks and receiving low pay. We examine the nature of work and the workplace more closely in Chapter 13.

A Changing World

"BACK-STAGE" PRIVACY AND SOCIAL MEDIA

In recent years, Facebook has been criticized for its lax privacy policies. However, getting users to share information is at the heart of its business model. As one business report put it, "Facebook Inc. is working to combat a decline in people sharing original, personal content, the fuel that helps power the money machine at the heart of its social network" (Frier 2016). Facebook's News Feed feature has long been the platform's most popular element. With it, users create and share content not available elsewhere on the internet. And this content attracts readers whose personal information Facebook then sells to advertisers, making the company's 30-something CEO, Mark Zuckerberg, a multibillionaire and one of the world's wealthiest people (Dolan and Kroll 2016).

News Feed content often includes personal details about friends, vacations, birthdays, family, and other actors and ordinary moments in daily life. As we saw earlier, this kind of personal information used to be the domain of the social "back stage" of Goffman's dramaturgical theory. In contrast to the "front stage," where social actors play a relatively formal public role for an intended audience, the "back stage" is where people can act informally among people close to them and shielded from the scrutiny of outsiders. Now, in the digital age, "back-stage" behavior—everything from goofy selfies to romantic drama—can be shared on a platform potentially viewable by millions.

Sharing information with an unbounded audience involves "context collapse" (Davis and Jurgenson 2014; Wesch 2009). That is, information—even when intended for a small group—potentially can be shared with many audiences simultaneously, stripping it of social context. The silly picture of you a little drunk that your friends find hilarious may strike your parents or a potential employer as not so funny. A risqué joke made among friends potentially takes on a different meaning when shared with the world.

Such concerns were fewer in the early days of social media, when participation was often skewed toward young early adopters. But with the use of social media now so widespread, "back-stage" information—meant to be personal and private—can circulate quickly, reaching unforeseen people with unimagined consequences. Revelations of how such information was used to target voters in 2016 is just one example.

That users should share such information about themselves, however, is precisely the foundation on which tech companies

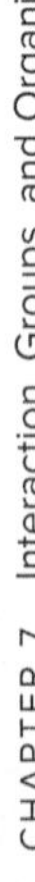

have built their business models, so it is important for them to convince users to keep sharing even as they reassure users about data privacy. Facebook CEO Zuckerberg famously argued that the protected privacy of the back stage is dead. "People have really gotten comfortable not only sharing more information and different kinds, but more openly and with more people," he has observed. "That social norm is just something that has evolved over time" (Johnson 2010).

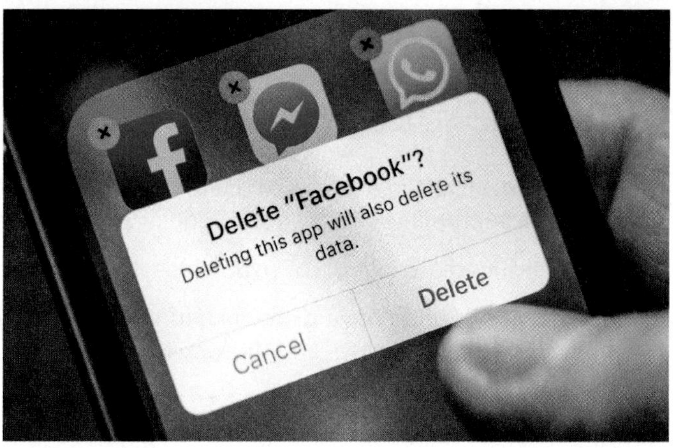

©True Images/Alamy Stock Photo

Zuckerberg is right that the norm around privacy has changed. Fewer people now feel the need to keep their personal and public person as rigidly separate, and more are comfortable sharing different parts of their lives with a broad audience. Nonetheless, social media users, and teen users in particular, are thoughtful about privacy issues. In one study, most teens said they kept their Facebook profiles private (60 percent), deleted unwanted people from their network or friends list (74 percent), removed their name from tagged photos (45 percent), used codes only their friends would understand to share inside information or jokes (58 percent), and even posted fake information, such as a fictitious name, age, or location, to help protect their privacy (26 percent) (Madden et al. 2013). Especially with the recent controversies involving Facebook, users have also learned about the negative consequences of indiscriminate sharing and have altered their behavior accordingly.

This reticence, however, was the source of Facebook's recent problem with a decline in sharing on the site. Personal stories on Facebook—as opposed to the reposting of widely available content—dropped by more than 20 percent between 2014 and 2015, posing a threat to the company's business model. In response, Facebook launched—with only limited effect—a series of initiatives to get users to share more. These included an "On This Day" feature that recycled old posts, aiming to inspire nostalgia-filled new posts; banners reminding users that it was their friend's birthday, in the hopes of encouraging new "happy birthday" posts; and live video broadcasting, a novelty intended to generate new responses (Ohlheiser 2016).

Facebook has another problem. In recent years, teens have wearied of the increased presence of adults on the site, of "excessive" sharing by some people, and of stress-inducing "drama" (Madden et al. 2013). Privacy concerns have even led some to encourage users to simply "delete Facebook." Some teens and young adults have enthusiastically adopted other social media platforms that promise greater privacy, such as Snapchat, which automatically deletes communications, and Telegram, which offers both encryption and self-destructing messages. At the same time, some tech companies have touted encryption and privacy as a key selling point for their products, most notably Apple with its iPhone (Cook 2016).

In fact, Americans continue to want—and to be concerned about—to maintain privacy broadly, not just on social media sites. One survey (Rainee 2016) found that

- 91 percent of adults agree or strongly agree that consumers have lost control of how companies collect and use personal information.
- 74 percent say it is "very important" for them to be in control of who can get information about them.
- 86 percent have taken steps online to remove or mask their digital footprints, and many say they would like to do more or are unaware of tools they could use.
- 18- to 29-year-olds are more likely than older adults to say they have paid attention to privacy issues and tried to protect their privacy.

This tug-of-war between sharing and privacy is likely to remain an issue of great contention in the future. But it seems likely that the distinction between public front-stage life and more restricted back-stage behaviors will survive in some form, despite the realities of social media and other technologies.

thinking sociologically about
Interaction, Groups, and Organizations

culture

- We are socialized in a particular culture, and we learn to see our world from that culture's perspective. That socially constructed viewpoint becomes reality for us.
- Cultures inform the nature of social roles and the expectations associated with them.
- Organizations often have distinct cultures that influence how they are structured, the values they espouse, and the way they operate.

structure

- Statuses and roles provide some of the glue that connects individuals to one another and to the behavioral patterns that constitute social structure.
- People create groups and organizations, which in turn become more formal social structures.
- After creating these social structures, people treat those socially constructed entities as objectively real, and structures in turn are influenced by the society they create.

power

- People with different statuses often receive differing levels of honor, prestige, power, and income, resulting in inequality.
- Even in small, informal groups, individuals tend to conform to the views of the majority and to obey authority figures.
- In bureaucracies, power is organized hierarchically. People at each level in a hierarchy have power over those below and are subject to the authority of those above. Positions in bureaucracies are starkly unequal.

REVIEW, REFLECT, AND APPLY

Looking Back

1. Face-to-face encounters, influenced by cultural norms, are the building blocks of social life. Through our social interactions we come to mutual understandings about reality. How we define reality can have real consequences.
2. People are involved collectively in the social construction of reality. Humans create society, treat it as an objective reality, and then are influenced by the social forces they have created.
3. A particularly important element in social life is social status, the position an individual occupies in the social system; social roles are the cultural expectations associated with a status. Statuses and roles link individuals to larger groups and institutions, helping create social structure.
4. In sociology, dramaturgy uses the metaphor of a theatrical performance to analyze roles and social interaction.
5. Society consists of links, groupings, and organizations. These include social networks that are formed out of our social ties as well as small-scale primary groups and large formal organizations.
6. The dynamics of groups, large and small, can be analyzed sociologically. For example, in small groups, conformity is an important social dynamic. People who engage in groupthink ignore evidence or ideas that contradict group beliefs.

7. Large organizations rely on bureaucratic structure to operate efficiently, but as the layers of bureaucracy multiply, they make organizations unwieldy and inefficient. The iron law of oligarchy holds that bureaucracies concentrate power in the hands of those at the top.
8. Contemporary developments, especially in technology, have affected how we interact with one another and have led to new types of social networks and to innovative forms of organizational structure.

Critical Thinking: Questions and Activities

1. Write a brief, realistic telephone exchange between two college-age friends. Now rewrite that same exchange, making explicit all the taken-for-granted information that the two speakers share. What type of information was left out of the original version?
2. List all the statuses you currently occupy. Write a brief description of the role expectations associated with three of your statuses. How did you learn about these role expectations? What consequences, if any, are there for deviating from these expectations?
3. Using elements of dramaturgical theory, describe an example of role playing from your own life. Were you successful in your performance? Why or why not?
4. Draw a diagram of the structure of a bureaucratic organization with which you are familiar—for example, a school, workplace, or community group—mapping the lines of authority. Can you explain the logic of the specific organizational structure? Does the organization operate effectively and efficiently? Can you imagine an alternative organizational structure?
5. How has the internet influenced your social networks? Do you think communication via the internet is replacing other forms of communication? Why or why not?

Key Terms

achieved status (p. 154) a social position that we voluntarily attain, to a considerable degree, as the result of our own efforts.

ascribed status (p. 154) a social position that is assigned to us from birth or that we assume later in life, regardless of our wishes or abilities.

bureaucracy (p. 163) a hierarchical administrative system with formal rules and procedures used to manage organizations.

dramaturgy (p. 155) an approach to the study of social interaction that uses the metaphor of social life as a theater.

groupthink (p. 168) a form of uncritical thinking in which people reinforce a consensus rather than ask serious questions or thoroughly analyze the issue at hand.

homophily (p. 158) the tendency for social contact to occur at a higher rate among people who are similar than it does among those who are different.

in-group (p. 166) a social group with which a person identifies and toward which he or she has positive feelings; members have a collective sense of "us."

intersubjectivity (p. 149) a common understanding between people about knowledge, reality, or an experience.

iron law of oligarchy (p. 169) the eventual and inevitable consolidation of power at the top of bureaucratic organizations.

master status (p. 154) a social position that is overwhelmingly significant, powerfully influences a person's social experience, and typically overshadows all the other social positions that person may occupy.

organizational environment (p. 165) factors that exist outside the organization but that potentially affect its operation.

organizations (p. 162) secondary groups that have a degree of formal structure and are formed to accomplish particular tasks.

out-group (p. 166) a social group toward which a person has negative feelings, considering its members to be inferiors, or "them."

primary groups (p. 159) people who have regular contact, enduring relationships, and a significant emotional attachment to each other.

reference groups (p. 160) the groups against which we choose to measure ourselves.

role conflict (p. 155) the problem that occurs when the expectations associated with different roles clash.

role strain (p. 155) the problem that occurs when the expectations associated with a single role compete with each other.

roles (p. 154) the sets of expected behaviors that are associated with particular statuses.

scientific management (p. 169) the process of de-skilling ordinary workers and increasing workplace efficiency through calculated study.

secondary groups (p. 160) people who interact in a relatively impersonal way, usually to carry out some specific task.

social groups (p. 159) collections of people who interact regularly with one another and who are aware of their status as a group.

social networks (p. 156) the collections of social ties that connect actors such as individuals and organizations to each other.

status (p. 154) a position in a social system that can be occupied by an individual.

status category (p. 154) a status that people can hold in common.

status hierarchy (p. 154) a ranking of social positions according to their perceived prestige or honor.

status set (p. 154) the collection of statuses that an individual holds.

stereotypes (p. 152) exaggerated, distorted, or untrue generalizations about categories of people that do not acknowledge individual variation.

Thomas theorem (p. 151) the idea that if people define situations as real, they are real in their consequences.

©Jenner Images/Moment/Getty Images

8 Deviance and Social Control

looking AHEAD

How does deviance reinforce the **structure** of your community or college?

How can we use our bodies to express deviance, in defiance of **cultural** norms?

How do your family, your teachers, and other agents of social control use **power** to promote conformity?

©J.B. Nicholas/Splash News/Newscom

Katendi Heald, a college student in London, acquires her food and furnishes her student house from other people's discards. She is part of a movement of Freegans, who are trying to minimize what they consume in an effort to create a more sustainable society. Freegan students like Heald also recognize that their anticonsumerist lifestyle can save them a great deal of money.

Instead of buying things, Freegans seek to "reclaim" other people's waste in a process they call "urban foraging": finding clothing, household goods, books and games, artwork—just about anything you can imagine—in the trash. That also means dumpster diving outside restaurants, supermarkets, and other food stores that routinely discard fresh fruits and vegetables that may be bruised or a bit overripe, day-old bread, canned goods that have expired recently, and prepared food, including sandwiches, salads, and even sushi (Barnard 2016; Perkin 2015).

Whereas millions of poor people around the world scavenge to survive, urban foraging is not common in affluent societies like that of England and the United States, and Freegans do it as a matter of choice, not necessity. Most people probably react negatively to the idea of eating trash, and in many places, dumpster diving is illegal. Most Freegans, like Heald, however, are not desperate, and they pay careful attention to food safety. They are also aware that the way they live is nonconformist. They believe, however, that by living as much as possible a life based on reusing, recycling, and reclaiming, they can drastically reduce their impact on the environment and oppose what they see as the wasteful "throwaway" mentality of a deeply entrenched consumer society.

By refusing to conform to the cultural norms that distinguish between trash and "acceptable" items, Freegans have crossed a line from normal to deviant behavior, and they risk becoming the target of criticism, even moral condemnation. Some will want to reform them, others will question their motives—are they sick, crazy, foolish, immoral, or just plain lazy?—and still others will have the power to punish them. By foraging for their food in this way, however, Freegans hope to call attention to the environmental challenge they believe consumer society poses and to encourage social change.

What is normal behavior, and how do we recognize it? Is normal what's most common? What's most desirable? What's healthiest? Who or what has the power to enforce normal behavior? We rarely think about these questions as we go about our daily lives. When you buy food in a supermarket or order a pizza in a restaurant, you're unlikely to think, "I'm behaving normally now." We have been socialized so effectively to accept our culture's norms that we rarely recognize them.

We begin to think about these questions, however, when we confront behaviors or beliefs that challenge, or deviate from, our expectations–when we react with disgust, for example, to the idea of eating a pizza pulled out of a garbage bin. In other words, nonconformity helps us clarify the boundary between normal and abnormal.

As we've seen in previous chapters, people develop their sense of self and identity through social interaction. Interactions in small groups form the basis for social structure, and social structure provides people with norms and expectations about appropriate behavior. But how do norms get established in the first place? Why do some people violate those norms? And how is this kind of norm-violating behavior related to the nonconformist's sense of self?

This chapter focuses on **deviance,** *behavior that does not conform to basic cultural norms and expectations,* and its relationship

Source: Library Of Congress [LC-F8- 8591]

©Andres Rodriguez/Alamy Stock Photo

FAST-FORWARD

Change and Beach Attire

Norms about what to wear to the beach have changed dramatically over the past 100 years. Women's bathing suits introduced in the late nineteenth century (*top*) were an innovation—and some would have considered them deviant—since they revealed more of a woman's body than had been shown previously. Men's swimsuits from the same period covered most of the body. The swimwear that we now define as normal (*bottom*) would have been viewed as shockingly deviant in an earlier era. How would you explain this change in the definition of deviant behavior?

to these questions of self and identity. As we will see, the lines between normal and abnormal, moral and immoral, appropriate and inappropriate, healthy and sick, and sane and crazy are flexible, even if most people within a society share an understanding of the distinction between normal and deviant. We also explore the consequences of violating norms, from subtle forms of social isolation to imprisonment or even execution. And we examine the various agents that encourage conformity.

Defining Deviance

Boundaries between normal and deviant are rarely clear-cut because people often disagree about where the line should be drawn. Ultimately what is defined as deviant depends on the particular social context in which the behavior occurs or a person lives and on the power of those who label it. For those defined as deviant, the negative effects can be long lasting, even devastating.

Deviance and Social Context

As Emile Durkheim established more than 100 years ago, a sociological perspective on deviance requires looking beyond particular behaviors to the connections between those behaviors and social norms. Durkheim argued that crime (and deviant behavior, more generally) could be defined only in relation to the social norms a criminal act violates. As Durkheim explained, we often misunderstand the relationship between crime and social norms. We are not offended by an action because it is a crime; rather, we define an act as criminal because it offends basic social norms. These basic norms contribute to what Durkheim called the **collective conscience,** *the shared norms, beliefs, and values in a community* (Durkheim [1893] 1997).

What is considered normal or deviant varies over time and across cultures, and definitions of normal often shift in response to social change. When we talk about deviance, then, we must bear in mind the social context in which it occurs, and we should remember that different communities may have different responses to the same behavior. For example, when women in the United States demanded the right to vote in the late nineteenth and early twentieth centuries, they were widely considered deviant, but these suffragists mobilized to gain power and change that label. Some people at the time no doubt continued to consider politics an inappropriate activity for women, but they no longer had the power to enforce such a judgment. Over time, our society's view of women as political actors changed. In some cultures today, however, women are still forbidden or highly discouraged from participating in politics—their participation is still considered deviant.

Midday naps are another example of varying definitions of deviance. An employee in the United States who went home for a rest at lunchtime would likely be branded as lazy or a slacker. However, in some places outside the United States, taking an extended midday break is standard procedure. In Spain, for example, shops and offices typically close for an hour or two after lunch to allow employees to go home for *siesta*—a short rest or cat nap—before returning to work in the midafternoon. In contrast to the U.S. standard of 9:00 a.m. to 5:00 p.m., the traditional workday in Spain includes a midday siesta and lasts until 8:00 p.m.

Siesta has become less common in recent years, but many businesses still take a midday break, albeit a shorter one than in previous generations. While global economic pressures and advocates for working mothers have successfully pushed to shorten siesta and end the workday earlier, support for siesta remains strong in some areas. For example, the mayor of the small town of Ador announced an official 2:00 p.m. to 5:00 p.m. siesta in 2015 (The Local 2015).

Labeling Theory: Defining Deviant Behavior

Some acts of deviance generate widespread, perhaps even universal, condemnation. Almost every society considers child molestation and unprovoked murder as deviant behavior. With other acts, however, the boundary between normal and deviant often depends on the specific social context (Downes, Rock, and McLaughlin 2016). Is it deviant for men to pierce their ears or for women to shave their heads? What about wearing a baseball cap in a restaurant or taking a break from work for afternoon prayers? How about killing animals for sport? Or torturing suspected terrorists for information?

You may have a strong opinion about each of these examples, but your individual response is not what marks an action as deviant. A behavior is defined as deviant when it is marked publicly as deviant by those with enough power to enforce that designation. This is the core insight of **labeling theory,** which *argues that deviance is the result of how others interpret a behavior and that individuals who are labeled deviant often internalize this judgment as part of their self-identity.* Sociologist Kai Erickson (1966) explains: "Deviance is not a property *inherent* in any particular kind of behavior; it is a property *conferred* upon that behavior by the people who come into direct or indirect contact with it," because they consider the behavior so dangerous or embarrassing that it requires special sanctions (6). Labeling theory highlights the interactive aspects of deviance—the interplay between behavior and the response to that behavior (Becker 1973). From this perspective, behavior is deviant only when it is labeled as such.

SPOTLIGHT

on social theory

Labeling theory, associated with the **symbolic interactionist approach,** emphasizes the power of groups within society to designate a given behavior as deviant. Can you think of an example of behavior that is labeled deviant in U.S. society and normal in another society?

The Effects of Deviant Labels

People who are labeled deviant are likely to face negative consequences and limited options in life. Indeed, those labeled criminal or otherwise dangerous may be locked up. But labeling may have other, less dramatic consequences. For example, people who are labeled mentally ill often have a difficult time finding employment because their deviant identity becomes a kind of *master status* that overshadows all other components of their identity. In this case, education, skills, and diligence all give way to a person's status as mentally ill so that potential employers or neighbors may perceive *only* the mental illness.

More generally, those who are labeled deviant must deal with the stigma or shame associated with their deviant label. **Stigma** refers to *the shame attached to a behavior or status that is considered socially unacceptable or discrediting.* Stigma can be a source of inequality because those who are stigmatized often experience isolation or discrimination that can reduce their social, economic, or political standing (see Figure 8.1).

The threat of stigmatization can be a powerful form of social control (Goffman 1963). For example, people who live on the street, regardless of the reasons, face tremendous uncertainty about food, health, and safety. But it is the stigma of their status as homeless that has perhaps the most profound social consequences. It may prevent them from making the kinds of social connections—getting a job interview, securing a loan, finding a friend to lend a hand—that can help homeless individuals cross back into a "normal" life.

Labeling people as deviant may lead them into **secondary deviance,** *deviant behavior that is a response to the negative consequences of labeling* (Lemert 1951). In other words, labeling creates a kind of self-fulfilling prophecy. A child who is labeled as a troublemaker and treated as such by adults may adopt the role of troublemaker, become hostile to authorities, and join with other so-called misfits in new forms of deviance. When parents label their children as rule violators, that label affects the

FIGURE 8.1 | COMPONENTS OF STIGMA

Human differences are distinguished and labeled.

Labeled persons are connected to undesirable characteristics via dominant cultural beliefs.

Labeled persons are categorized, accomplishing a separation between "us" and "them."

Labeled persons experience discrimination and suffer status loss.

Stigma occurs when labeling, separation, and discrimination are linked to inequality in social, economic, or political power.

Source: Link and Phelan 2001.

children's own self-appraisals and identity, leading to increased deviance (Matsueda 1992).

Using the National Longitudinal Survey of Youth, Davies and Tanner (2003) found that young people who had been labeled disciplinary problems at school or who had come into contact with the criminal justice system as teenagers and young adults had significantly reduced employment prospects and income potential later in life. The effect was especially significant among women. Even girls who had returned to school or completed high school after being suspended or expelled had problems finding jobs later in life. The stigma of their deviant status, it seems, stuck with them, leading employers to steer clear of them. In a more recent study, Wiley and Esbensen (2016) examined the experiences of middle school students with police at 31 schools in seven U.S. cities, tracking students' behavior and attitudes over a nearly two-year period. While most students (80 percent) had no contact with the police, about 14 percent of students had been stopped by police and another 6 percent had been arrested. The authors found negative consequences for students who experienced police contact, and this was not only the case for students who were arrested. The negative consequences extended to students who were stopped and questioned, but not arrested. One year later, in comparison with students who had no police contact, students who had been stopped were less likely to express a sense of guilt about the idea of participating in various delinquent activities; had a stronger commitment to peers who had been in trouble at school, home, or with the police; and were involved more frequently in delinquent acts ranging from skipping class and minor theft to selling drugs or physically attacking someone. Wiley and Esbensen conclude: "If simply being stopped and questioned has deleterious consequences, policing practices may inadvertently contribute to higher levels of delinquency" (299).

Labeling marks social boundaries between the normal and the deviant, between a socially defined "us" and "them." For those labeled deviant, the consequences may be diminished life chances, economic inequality, further deviance, and long-lasting stigma.

The Role of Deviance within Social Structures

In his treatise titled *The Rules of Sociological Method,* Emile Durkheim ([1895] 1982) pointed out that deviant behavior is a feature of all human societies. But Durkheim went further, arguing that deviance can be functional, playing a positive social role and reinforcing social structures. It does this in three specific ways:

- Deviance helps define group boundaries.
- Deviance helps create social solidarity.
- Deviance is a source of innovation.

Let's look in more detail at these three functions of deviance.

©Peter Dazeley/Photographer's Choice/Getty Images

How do you respond when people ignore no-smoking signs? Your response is likely to depend on the situation. How we respond to rule violations—whether we define them as minor transgressions or serious offenses—is a result, in part, of the specific social context.

Defining Group Boundaries

Deviant behavior helps clarify the boundaries of acceptable behavior within a given society. Especially because the line dividing deviant from nondeviant behavior is often subtle and hard to define, deviant behavior constantly reminds us of how to live within the boundaries of "normal"–and shows us the consequences of stepping outside those boundaries. In formal organizations, written rules and policies clearly define what behavior is and isn't tolerated. These rules reflect the identity and values of the organization. For example, cheating and plagiarism strike at the heart of academic integrity. As a result, colleges and universities have a formal system for punishing violators; suspension or even expulsion are common penalties. But not all rule violations are defined as serious enough to warrant suspension or expulsion. Although smoking indoors, for example, may violate a college's official rules, it is sometimes tolerated grudgingly.

Much of social life, however, is not governed by formal rules and policies. We don't get a handbook that tells us all the rules of our neighborhood, but that doesn't mean the rules don't exist. The boundaries between normal and deviant, acceptable and unacceptable, often remain implicit.

How do you decide who is inside or outside your closest group of friends? Presumably you don't have written rules about who can and cannot belong to this group. However, your network of friends almost certainly has basic values and norms that are enforced implicitly–and perhaps explicitly. Deciding whether someone fits in or does not belong, is accepted or rejected–these are the informal means groups use to maintain internal cohesion and label certain behaviors and attitudes as deviant.

More generally, think about how individuals in the various groups to which you belong respond to specific kinds of people—for example, atheists, gun enthusiasts, LGBT people, vegetarians, evangelicals, or teenage parents—and you'll begin to see the ways that community definitions of normal and deviant help establish, and sometimes change, social boundaries.

Creating Social Solidarity

In addition to defining boundaries, deviance helps build group solidarity by uniting people in opposition to, or disapproval of, a shared enemy. Deviant behavior reinforces conformity within a social structure; it also strengthens the bonds among those who feel outrage at displays of deviance. The threat of nonconformity, especially when people mobilize actively to stamp out nonconformist behavior, provides a powerful source of social connection among conformists.

A classic sociological illustration of this point is Kai Erickson's (1966) study of deviance within the seventeenth-century Massachusetts Bay Colony. Erickson explains how the hysteria about witchcraft in Salem resulted from change within the Puritan community. In 1672 in Salem, accusations of witchcraft were not taken seriously, and those who confessed to dealing with the devil were dismissed as liars. But just 20 years later the Puritans sensed that religious zeal was waning and members were turning against one another, an unsettling change for this deeply religious and insular community. In response to this threat, the community turned on presumed witches as a common enemy to all. For a brief period, lasting less than a year, the Salem Puritans united to root out the "witches," and 19 women and men were hanged. This case shows how a focus on deviance can bring together a community—and how collective hysteria about deviance can direct public vengeance at those labeled as deviant.

Even in complex, modern societies, deviance can help unite people. In the wake of the terrorist attacks of September 11, 2001, the mourning and fear helped, at least temporarily, to strengthen a sense of national unity in the United States. The shared sense of victimization, along with fear of additional attacks, produced a heightened sense that people in the United States, despite their differences, stood together. "United We Stand" bumper stickers and other public displays of patriotism were common sights at the time.

The way people respond to deviance can produce group solidarity. By highlighting group boundaries and giving sometimes diverse citizens an opportunity to express their shared distaste for behavior defined as immoral, criminal, or pathological, deviance brings people together.

Providing a Source of Innovation

Durkheim also argued that deviance provides a source of creativity and innovation in social life. In fact, Durkheim believed that healthy societies *need* deviance, since societies that are totally conformist are repressive and limit human possibility. Deviant people push boundaries and, as a result, can facilitate growth and change in social structures.

©Mark Scheuern/Alamy Stock Photo

After the September 11, 2001, terrorist attacks, Americans expressed their sense of national solidarity through patriotic displays. Sales of American flags skyrocketed, and "United We Stand" bumper stickers appeared on cars and trucks throughout the United States. Violent acts that caused enormous pain and suffering—in this case, acts that violated the norms of the international community and, in the perpetrators' targeting of civilians, even the norms of war—can produce a sense of social solidarity and national pride.

Many ideas and behaviors that we take for granted today were once considered deviant. Democracy is an example. Historically, democracy is a relatively new idea, having been implemented widely only within the past 200 years. Early advocates of democracy were generally considered to be radicals and irresponsible idealists (Dahl and Shapiro 2015).

Other "deviant" ideas have also proven to be powerful innovations. Until the early 1970s, women in the United States who put their children in full-time day care risked being labeled as neglectful mothers (Schur 1984). Now, however, this practice is common and widely accepted and, further, it is thought to provide children with an important educational and social experience. Many once-deviant notions have injected vibrant innovations into our culture and society. Public education, religious freedom, racial equality, and even rock and roll and hip-hop were all considered deviant at one time (Rose 1994).

on social theory

The **functionalist approach** emphasizes consensus in social life and looks at the ways in which deviant behavior may benefit society. How might adherents of this approach view people or behaviors that many people currently consider deviant, such as the Freegans described at the beginning of this chapter?

Explaining Deviance

Deviance is a product of the social relationship between those who affirm the boundaries of "normal" and those who cross such boundaries. What makes some people cross those lines?

How can we explain deviant behavior, and what do these explanations suggest about the best way to respond to deviance? Not surprisingly, given the wide range of deviant behaviors, sociologists and others have proposed a variety of answers to these questions (Levine and Marques 2016; Pfohl 2009).

Some explanations focus on *individual* sources of deviance, emphasizing the flaws or weaknesses of people who are considered deviant. Such explanations, which circulate in popular discourse but are generally rejected by sociologists, describe deviance in terms of immorality or as a symptom of an illness. A more sociological set of explanations emphasizes the *social* dynamics surrounding deviance, explaining it as a rational choice, the result of inadequate or improper socialization, or the product of mismatch between social norms and economic opportunities.

Deviance as Immorality

One way to explain deviance is as the consequence of *individual immorality.* The boundary between normal and deviant, from this perspective, is roughly the same as the line between good and evil. Some fundamentalist religions tend to see the world in these terms. More broadly, when people cannot understand or explain particularly horrendous deviant behavior—for example, the Holocaust during World War II, the genocide in Rwanda in the 1990s, or the actions of a ruthless serial killer—they sometimes simply label it as evil.

Although this approach may resonate emotionally, it does not help us uncover the actual nature of deviance. From a sociological standpoint, then, to explain deviance as the consequence of immorality does little to help us identify the social conditions that produce it or understand the ways people respond to it.

Deviance as Illness: Medicalization

A second approach based on individual behavior finds the sources of deviance in *pathology,* or *illness.* From this perspective, individuals who engage in deviant behavior are sick, suffering from a psychological or biological disorder. Here the boundary between normal and deviant coincides with the line between healthy and sick, sane and crazy. The roots of deviance as individual sickness are clearest in cases of mental illness, such as schizophrenia. But doctors now recognize an expanding list of deviant behaviors that result at least partially from underlying biological disorders and that they think will benefit from appropriate medical intervention. This process—*the designation of a deviant behavior as an illness that can be treated by medical professionals*—is what sociologists refer to as the **medicalization of deviance** (Conrad 2007; Conrad and Barker 2010; Conrad and Schneider 1980).

In some cases, specific deviant behaviors formerly identified as immoral have become reclassified as medical problems. A classic example is alcoholism (Gusfield 1996; Schneider 1978). In the early twentieth century, excessive drinking was considered a moral failure. In the 1960s and 1970s, the public understanding of alcoholism shifted, and people began to focus on disease as its underlying cause. Recent research suggests that alcoholism has a genetic component. As alcoholism was medicalized, the solution to alcoholism also shifted from moral rehabilitation to medical treatments and psychological therapies that might control the symptoms of the disease.

Treating a deviant behavior as a disorder can alter the stigma associated with it. People who drink too much, are addicted to gambling, or suffer from extreme anxiety may be considered deviant, but designating their behavior as a medical condition insulates them from some of the hostility that deviant groups have traditionally experienced. People with a medicalized deviance are more likely to be pitied than scorned. On the other hand, if the deviance is identified as the result of an inherited disease, it may still attract a lifelong stigma.

Sociologists have identified the growing power of the medical profession as a primary reason for the medicalization of deviance. As the authority of doctors, especially psychiatrists and pediatricians, expands, an ever-greater realm of social life is defined in medical terms. Just think about the range of issues for which we now seek medical advice and treatment: how to deal with hyperactive children, how to handle profound stress, and how to deal with trauma, to name just a few examples. The power of doctors to define issues in medical terms is only part of the picture. The pharmaceutical industry has also become a powerful engine of medicalization. Since 1997, when the U.S. Food and Drug Administration began permitting direct-to-consumer broadcast advertising of pharmaceutical products, drug companies have aggressively sought to medically define problems for which they have already developed new drug therapies. Viagra is a classic case. By actively promoting a sexual problem as a medical issue—erectile dysfunction—and identifying Viagra as the solution, pharmaceutical companies built remarkable public demand for Viagra and other similar drugs (Conrad 2005b).

There are five key stages in the medicalization of deviance (Conrad and Schneider 1980):

- ***Stage one.*** A behavior or condition is defined as deviant.
- ***Stage two.*** A medical explanation of this deviant behavior or condition is "discovered."
- ***Stage three.*** Organized interests—medical researchers, physicians, health care organizations, pharmaceutical companies—advance claims for applying a medical label to the deviant behavior or condition.
- ***Stage four.*** Those same interests appeal to government officials to legitimize the medical label.
- ***Stage five.*** The medical label is institutionalized, becoming an accepted part of the medical and legal classification system.

Medicalization can sometimes be successfully blocked or reversed, a process sociologists refer to as *demedicalization.* The most prominent example is homosexuality. In the late 1960s, gay and lesbian activists, newly visible with the emergence of the gay rights movement, pressured the American Psychiatric Association to change its classification of homosexuality as a "sexual deviation" in the 1968 edition of the *Diagnostic and Statistical Manual of Mental Disorders* (DSM-II). They argued that the classification was demeaning to gay men and women and had no scientific basis. In 1974 the American Psychiatric Association

©Studio 101/Alamy Stock Photo

In 2009 the FDA approved a new drug for the treatment of hypotrichosis, the medical term for a condition marked by inadequate eyelashes.

removed the "illness" label from homosexuality, classifying it as a disorder only for those who are unhappy about their sexuality.

Deviance as Rational Choice

Other explanations for deviance move beyond the individual level to include social factors. According to one such approach, deviance results from rational decision making; people are inclined to behave in deviant ways when deviance has significant rewards and limited costs. In many parts of the country, for example, you can drive well above the speed limit with little risk of being stopped by the police. Although individuals make strategic calculations about how to behave, the structure of incentives and penalties for deviance underlies their calculations. (Seeing more police officers stationed along your route would reduce the likelihood of your speeding.) When deviance does little harm, it may not be worth controlling. But when deviance is destructive, one way to control it is by increasing the penalties. This basic analysis underlies much of the "get tough on crime" rhetoric common in American politics.

Deviance and Socialization: Differential Association Theory

Two other social approaches explain deviance by focusing on socialization. One of these focuses on *inadequate* socialization. From this perspective, people engaged in deviant behavior have failed to internalize social norms and so are not regulated adequately by the moral framework of society. The root cause of this deviance is the inability of basic socializing agents, including family and schools, to transmit core values. When politicians or police argue that teenagers are getting in trouble because they haven't learned to respect authority, they are drawing from this perspective.

An alternative approach focusing on socialization views deviance as a result of social connections. Perhaps the most well-known articulation of this approach is Edwin Sutherland's (1893–1950) **differential association theory,** which suggests that *deviance is learned through interaction with other people involved in deviant behavior* (Sutherland 1947; Sutherland, Cressey, and Luckenbill 1992). Your parents' warning to be careful about whom you hang out with is a simple, commonsense version of this explanation. This perspective views people as socialized into a deviant subculture. By associating with other nonconformists, they learn how to be deviant and critical of social conventions, and they may be pressured into behaving in a deviant way or joining in deviant activities.

When deviant behavior becomes part of a group's collective identity, it creates strong social bonds among its members. From this perspective, the most effective way to control deviant social groups is to limit interaction among group members, thus breaking the social connections that lead people to violate social norms. As we will see, however, some subcultures are strong enough to withstand attempts to control them or break them up.

on social theory

Differential association theory explains deviance as a learned behavior. Can you think of a time when you or someone you knew felt pressured to engage in deviant behavior?

Deviant Subcultures

We all face social pressures to conform. In most cases—at home, school, or work—parents, teachers, and supervisors reward us for conformity and punish us for nonconformity. Over time, we internalize many of these prescriptions. Long-term deviance is likely to require the social support of a **deviant subculture,** *a group in which membership is based on a shared commitment to specific nonconformist beliefs or behaviors.*

Sometimes deviant subcultures promote behaviors and attitudes that challenge mainstream social norms. For example, members of white supremacist organizations often belong to a subculture that actively opposes racial equality. Before the civil rights movement, white supremacist attitudes were consistent with social norms within many white communities and were reflected in widespread racial segregation backed in many places by the force of law. The civil rights movement eliminated legal segregation and stigmatized overt racism, but white supremacists continue to promote white power and advocate the separation of people by race.

thinking about **culture**

How can the concept of **culture** help you analyze the meaning and significance of deviant subcultures, including any to which you belong?

The persistence of white power political activism in the Ku Klux Klan and Aryan Nations and various skinhead groups is rooted in a subculture that transmits white supremacist attitudes from one generation to the next, building a sense of shared identity (Simi and Futrell 2015). Through family gatherings, Bible study groups, informal parties, and other spaces hidden from public view, such groups "encourage members to safely and openly express their radical racist ideologies" (23). These local spaces are supported by conferences such as the World Aryan Congress and white power music festivals. In all these settings, members of the subculture share stories, listen to speeches, or wear clothing that reaffirms their commitment to white power, thus emphasizing the boundaries between their group and outsiders.

©Blickwinkel/Alamy Stock Photo

Music-based youth subcultures are familiar examples of deviant subcultures. They can provide valuable social support for alienated young people (Hancock and Lorr 2013; Howe and Friedman 2014). Members participate in a community that gives them an opportunity to express themselves and connect with others who feel as they do. In her exploration of suburban heavy metal culture, sociologist Donna Gaines (1991) found that deviant subcultures could help teenagers survive in difficult circumstances. The suburban teenagers that Gaines studied performed poorly in school, regularly smoked pot and drank alcohol, and had their share of encounters with local police. These teens knew they'd been labeled as losers, and the bonds they formed within their music subculture gave them a sense of self-worth, providing them with an identity that was more than that of troubled kid or loser.

Loner Deviance Deviance is not always connected to a subculture. In some cases, deviant behavior is intensely private, with little or no connection among those who engage in similar behaviors. Sociologists describe this behavior as **loner deviance,** *the activities of individuals who commit deviant acts without the social support of other participants* (Best and Luckenbill 1982). One study of self-injurers, or cutters—people who intentionally cut, burn, or otherwise mutilate their bodies—found that they have little contact with one another (Adler and Adler 2005). Cutters rarely share information about their activities and generally try to hide their self-induced injuries.

Without the support system of a subculture, most self-injurers ultimately stop injuring themselves on their own. The instability of loner deviance highlights an important sociological point: deviant behavior occurs within a specific social context. The growth of the internet and the proliferation of online communities, however, may provide new opportunities for loner deviants to interconnect. A virtual community can provide the kind of social support that is generally associated with deviant subcultures (Adler and Adler 2011, 2012).

Deviance and Structure: Merton's Strain Theory

Yet another social explanation of deviance emphasizes how underlying contradictions in the social or economic environment can drive people to deviance. From this perspective, nonconformity is caused primarily by inequality, which is embedded in social structure. Unequal access to money, power, education, or leisure leads some people to deviant behavior in pursuit of these socially valued goods. The most effective form of social control, then, is to decrease inequality and thereby weaken the structural foundations of deviance.

In his classic essay "Social Structure and Anomie," Robert K. Merton (1938) suggested that deviance results from the conflict between the dominant norms and goals of American society—the "normative structure"—and legitimate means of achieving these goals. Merton's approach was the basis of **strain theory,** *which emphasizes that strain or pressure on those who lack the means to achieve culturally defined goals leads them to pursue deviant routes to success.*

For example, most people in American society share the goal of financial success. Parents, schools, and the media all promote the importance of having a good job, as well as the satisfaction, status, comfort, and security that accompany financial success. But although many people share this goal, legitimate opportunities to achieve financial success are limited and unevenly distributed.

What happens when the goal of financial success is widely accepted but only some members of a society have the resources to achieve it? Most people will conform: they play by the rules and use socially acceptable means to try to achieve that goal. They will seek additional education, attempt to start businesses, or try to work their way up the company ladder. Others will find conventional avenues to success blocked off to them because of limited access to higher education, racial or gender discrimination in hiring, or a scarcity of good jobs in a particular area.

thinking about structure

What are some contemporary examples of the connection between deviance and a lack of legitimate access to resources? How might the **structural** inequality that causes this behavior be addressed?

FIGURE 8.2 | MERTON'S STRAIN THEORY OF DEVIANCE

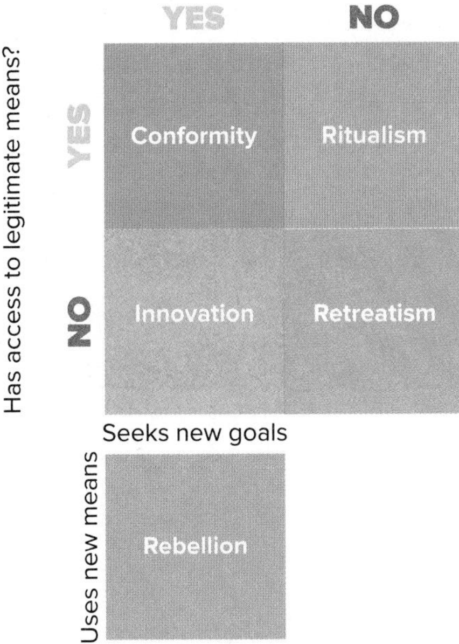

When conventional opportunities are blocked, people will find various ways to adapt to the disparity between goals and the legitimate means to achieve them, and some ways may lead them to nonconformist behavior (see Figure 8.2). One common deviant response is what Merton termed *innovation*—socially unacceptable (deviant) routes to success such as embezzling, drug dealing, or black market schemes. Thus strain theory understands deviance as a response to contradictions in the social structure.

Merton's theory explains other forms of behavior besides conformity and innovation. Those who have access to legitimate means to achieve success but reject culturally valued goals—say, burnt-out teachers no longer excited by their jobs—engage in *ritualism,* going through the motions but no longer believing in their work. Another response, *retreatism,* occurs when a person has no access to the means and rejects the goals, often leading to social isolation and withdrawal. Finally, those who *rebel* often create new goals and adopt new means of attaining them, thereby acting as agents of social change.

on social theory

The **functionalist approach** emphasizes consensus in social life and sees deviance as a means of reinforcing social structure. According to strain theory, which is associated with this approach, some people for whom conventional opportunities are blocked will use illegitimate means to achieve success. What examples of this behavior—other than street crime—can you think of?

Sociologist Elijah Anderson (1999) explored the development of deviant social norms in an extremely poor neighborhood in Philadelphia. He found that many young people felt alienated from mainstream American society, experienced racial discrimination, had few job prospects, and did not believe that the police would make their neighborhoods safe. Consistent with Merton's analysis, poverty, racism, and alienation led many young people to reject mainstream norms, adhering instead to what Anderson calls the "code of the street." These street norms are the foundation of an alternative social structure, one that emphasizes respect, the ability to defend oneself, and—often—the use of violence to gain or maintain respect.

As Anderson's study shows, in poor inner-city neighborhoods two social worlds collide: the mainstream social world of what he calls "decent families" and the oppositional world of "street families." These represent distinct norms and patterns of behavior—social structures—that coexist in the same physical space. Those who follow the code of the street are likely to be involved in the underground economy, including the sale of illegal drugs, and may have enough money to show off their fancy cars, clothes, and jewelry and to host a steady stream of visitors and parties in their homes. At the same time, the code of the street represents a rejection of traditional family life, low-wage jobs, and civility. Even those who do not live by street values are still likely to know the street code, since knowing this code is often necessary to ensure one's physical safety within inner-city communities.

Much of the classic research on juvenile delinquency and youth gangs has found that youth crime emerges in response to blocked opportunities and in the context of long-term inequality, as entrepreneurial young people look for alternative ways to get ahead (Cloward and Ohlin 1960; Thrasher 1927). The organized drug trade is also rooted in blocked opportunities, especially for young men of color in urban areas. In his study of "stickup kids" in the South Bronx, Randol Contreras (2013) describes how young men took to crack dealing as a route to economic success, only to have their lives turned upside down when the crack market declined. Similarly, Philippe Bourgois's (2003) study of crack dealers in New York's Puerto Rican community shows how young men and women deal with severely limited economic opportunities by working in the underground economy.

The point of these studies is not to demonize or glorify the young people who live by the code of the street or join gangs, but rather to explain the roots of such deviant behavior and the appeal of activities that are often dangerous and destructive. Such analysis tells us that any viable solution to the problems of inner-city alienation and violence must begin with an understanding of the structural roots of deviance.

Culture and Deviance: Deviant Bodies

So far we've looked primarily at questions about deviant behavior. However, we also know that powerful social norms define how our bodies should look and perform. Indeed, we most intimately experience society's definitions of normal and deviant in our own bodies. In this section, we look at how ideas about body weight, physical appearance, and disability are shifting and, in the process, sometimes literally changing us.

Body Weight

Although cultural norms about appropriate body size encourage us to look as slender as a Hollywood star and as fit as an Olympic athlete, the body size of average Americans does not match this culturally approved definition. The conflict between the widely accepted norm of thin-as-attractive and the actual size of most people is a source of substantial strain, especially for women (Bordo 1993). According to Gallup polling, more than half (52 percent) of adults in the United States say they want to lose weight (Norman 2017).

Widespread efforts to lose weight—and the growth of a diet industry that includes weight-loss programs and best-selling diet books—are a response to the increasing body weight of the U.S. population (see Figure 8.3). Because serious health problems are associated with obesity, losing weight is often part of a broader effort to live an active and healthy life.

At the same time, the desire to be thin is rooted in cultural norms that define fat bodies as deviant (Saguy 2013). Given the pervasiveness of the thin ideal, perhaps it is not surprising that people in the United States hold negative attitudes toward obese individuals (Puhl and Brownell 2001), and the stigma associated with obesity has real consequences (see the Through a Sociological Lens box).

Sociologist Katherine Mason (2012) analyzed a national survey of young adults in the United States and found that obese adults have lower incomes than their thinner counterparts. However, the income deficit for obese women is different than it is for obese men. Women defined as obese—those with BMI greater than 30—have lower incomes than women with BMI less than 30. For men, the income differential emerges only for very obese men (BMI > 35). Mason summarizes the results of her research, noting that "these findings provide evidence that weight-based income penalties begin at lower weights for women than for men . . . , but that very obese . . . men are heavily penalized relative to nonobese men" (424). These findings are consistent with substantial research documenting experiences of overweight stigma in workplace, educational, and health care settings, as well as in interpersonal relationships (Spahlholz et al. 2016).

©Wally McNamee/Corbis/Getty Images

People sometimes challenge their classification as deviant. In response to restrictive norms about appropriate body size, some overweight men and women have organized a size acceptance movement, demanding to be treated with respect and dignity.

CORE CONCEPTS CHALLENGE *What does this kind of demonstration suggest about the* **power** *of people who are considered deviant?*

If a powerful social stigma is attached to fat bodies, what about thin ones? Many young people, especially girls, desire a thinner body. Research indicates that 45 percent of teenage girls are dissatisfied with their body weight and see themselves as overweight (Boyd et al. 2011). More than half of adolescent girls (54.2 percent) and almost one-third of adolescent boys (32.1 percent) use "unhealthy weight-control behaviors," such as skipping meals, fasting, taking diet pills, smoking, and inducing vomiting (Vander Wal 2012).

At what point does weight-loss behavior itself become deviant, however? Is it socially acceptable to starve yourself or regularly force yourself to vomit after a meal? Those who struggle with eating disorders such as anorexia nervosa (an unwillingness to eat, accompanied by a distorted sense that one is overweight) or bulimia (binge eating, often accompanied by attempts to rid the body of its effects through purging) live at the intersection of

FIGURE 8.3 | OVERWEIGHT AND OBESITY TRENDS IN THE UNITED STATES

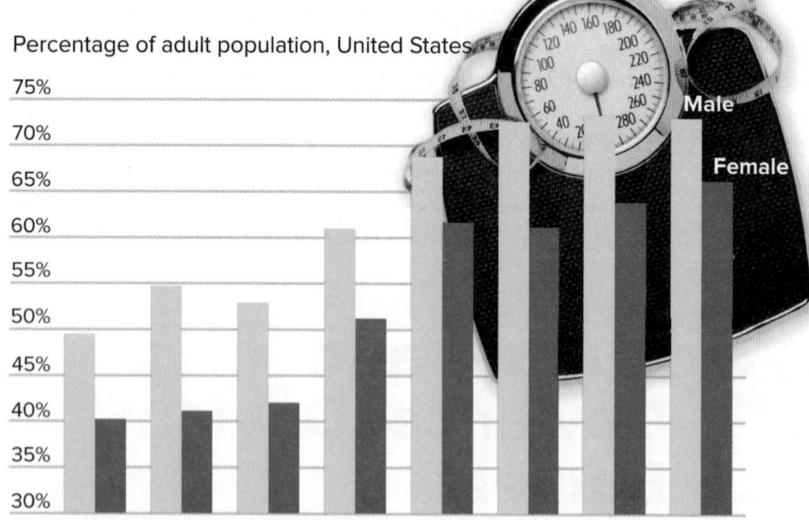

©Wally McNamee/Corbis/Getty Images

The percentage of adults in the United States who are overweight or obese has increased substantially since the early 1960s. According to data from 2011 to 2014, 73 percent of men and more than 66 percent of women were overweight or obese. Data shown here are for adults aged 20 to 74 and are age adjusted.

Source: National Center for Health Statistics. 2016. *Health, United States, 2015: With Special Feature on Racial and Ethnic Health Disparities.* Hyattsville, MD.

THROUGH A SOCIOLOGICAL LENS

Experiencing and Challenging the Stigma of Obesity

Eight years after being crowned "the biggest loser" in season 5 of NBC's weight-loss reality program, Ali Vincent had gained back most of the pounds she had dropped when she won the program's $250,000 cash prize in 2008. During the biggest loser competition, Vincent shed 112 pounds, about 48 percent of her body weight, reducing from 234 to 122 pounds. The first woman to win the competition, she had quickly earned celebrity status, becoming an author, a television personality, and a motivational speaker.

When she revealed that she had regained weight in a 2016 post on Facebook and during an appearance on *Oprah,* Vincent shared her embarrassment at her inability to keep the pounds off. In her April 19, 2016, Facebook post, Vincent explained: "I couldn't imagine a day again that I would weigh over 200 pounds. I feel ashamed. I feel embarrassed. I feel overwhelmed. I feel like a failure." Facing the stigma of her heavy body—after losing a formerly slender physique that had been celebrated on national television—Vincent announced plans to start a Weight Watchers regimen to lose weight again.

Heavy people—those defined as overweight or obese or sometimes simply called "fat"—face a pervasive stigma that is woven into the fabric of everyday life (Puhl and Heuer 2009). And since weight is widely perceived as something individuals can control through their choices about diet and exercise, the shame associated with a fat body is exacerbated by a broad cultural message that fat people have only themselves to blame for their stigmatized bodies.

In a recent study in the journal *Sociology of Health & Illness,* Marissa Dickens and her colleagues (2016) describe how online "fat acceptance" blogs offer powerful support in the face of obesity stigma. In-depth interviews with 44 bloggers reveal where obese people experience stigmatization: health care, media, and the weight-loss industry. For example, treating obesity as a medical problem—even when doctors are genuinely concerned about the health of their overweight patients—powerfully and negatively shapes the interactions fat people have with health providers. As one 42-year-old female blogger put it:

> You can't go to the doctor because they shame you, so do fat people have untreated medical conditions that get worse and worse over time? Yes. But that's because they can't go to the doctors because doctors treat them so badly because of their fat, and then don't treat them for medical conditions that have absolutely nothing to do with being fat. (802)

Media promote the ideal of a thin body, regularly emphasizing that being overweight is undesirable. And the weight-loss industry perpetuates the idea that fat people can and should do something to lose weight, showing fat bodies as the shameful "before" image to avoid at all costs.

In the context of such prevalent stigma, fat acceptance blogs—what bloggers refer to as the "fatosphere"—offer a social world where a heavy body is not a source of shame.

Ali Vincent, winner of the 2008 season of The Biggest Loser, *spoke out about the stigma of being overweight in 2016 after gaining back much of the weight she lost during the reality program.*

Instead of exclusion and blame, the fatosphere provides an experience of inclusion and support. Such support takes three distinct forms:

1. Intellectual support that gives community members new ways of thinking about their bodies
2. Social support, in which bloggers share their experiences in ways that help those facing discrimination or the cycle of weight loss–weight gain feel less isolated
3. Practical support, such as advice on traveling, buying clothes, and managing criticisms from friends or family

With a supportive online community, some people found themselves better prepared to stand up against weight discrimination. Ultimately, Dickens and her colleagues conclude that in the context of the online community's "efforts to remove the internalization of the negative and stigmatizing views of their bodies," the fatosphere "appears to assist individuals in further improving their physiological and psychological health" (807). Creating a positive online social space, one where moderators screen out hostile comments, offers community members new sources of protection and care in the face of the stigma they experience in daily life.

think about it

1. *How, specifically, do you think participation in an online community can help people cope with stigma?*
2. *Why do you think it is important for moderators to screen out hostile comments from fat acceptance blogs?*

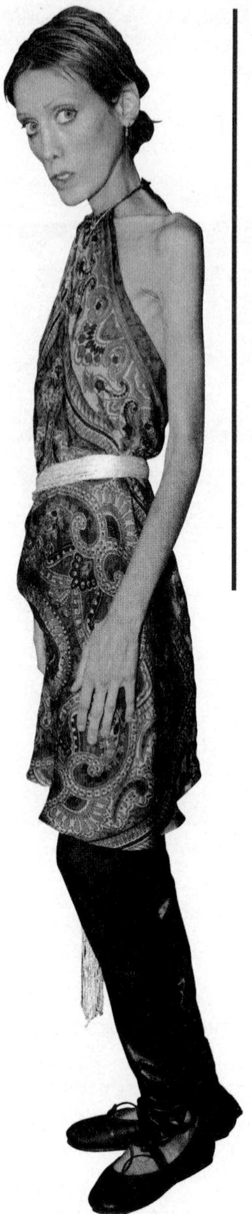

©Jules Motte/abacausa.com/Newscom

On websites supporting anorexic or bulimic lifestyles, images of extraordinarily thin women are intended to inspire people to maintain their commitment to losing weight and staying thin. Some of these "thinspiration" images depict women who are not merely trim but who appear to be dangerously malnourished as well.

CORE CONCEPTS CHALLENGE *What* **cultural** *norms might contribute to someone's perception that such a dangerous condition is desirable? Do people suffering from anorexia or bulimia constitute a deviant subculture? If so, would they have constituted a subculture before the emergence of web-based communities?*

conformity and deviance; they are conforming to cultural norms that encourage thinness, but following extreme—and dangerous—methods in their effort to achieve an exaggeration of the culturally preferred body type.

Eating disorders result from **overconformity,** or *following cultural expectations to an excessive degree.* People often respond negatively to overconformity; for example, gifted students are frequently shunned by their classmates as "rate-busters" (Shoenberger, Heckert, and Heckert 2015), and college students who do not consume alcohol often use elaborate strategies to avoid being labeled "losers" (Herman-Kinney and Kinney 2013). But *overconformity that gets a favorable response*—**positive deviance**—sometimes occurs. For example, we all appreciate unusually helpful neighbors, and we reward soldiers and police officers who take dramatic risks on our behalf.

Most of us perceive the overly thin, or anorexic, body as deviant, perhaps even frightening. In some communities, however, this painfully thin body is a symbol of positive deviance. A number of so-called pro-ana or pro-mia websites support an anorexic or bulimic lifestyle and display "thinspiration" images showing dangerously thin women. In the pro-ana community, anorexic bodies are held up as models to inspire those who reject the definition of their eating habits as deviant, disordered, or in need of treatment (Boero and Pascoe 2012).

Altering Bodies

Most of us think about much more than body weight when we judge who is, and is not, attractive. We often consider the size and shape of specific body parts, including breasts, eyes, nose, stomach, and lips. And people in our youth-oriented society feel pressure to keep their aging bodies looking young. Elective cosmetic surgery has become increasingly common as people try to make their bodies conform to prevailing cultural norms. More than 13 million cosmetic procedures were carried out in the United States in 2016, an increase of more than 750 percent since record-keeping began in 1997 (American Society for Aesthetic Plastic Surgery 2017).

Procedures such as facelifts or tummy tucks are highly invasive surgeries. They carry all the risks of hospital stays and the administration of anesthesia, and they require lengthy recovery periods. According to the website of the American Society of Plastic Surgeons (2018), during a tummy tuck (abdominoplasty) the surgeon will make "a horizontally-oriented incision in the area between the pubic hairline and belly button. . . . A second incision around the navel may be necessary to remove excess skin in the upper abdomen. The upper abdominal skin is pulled down like a window shade. The excess skin is trimmed and the remaining skin is sutured together. A new opening for the belly button is created. The belly button is popped through to the surface and sutured into position." Although the tone of this description is calm and clinical, it is clear that a tummy tuck is a major surgical procedure.

In previous generations, cosmetic surgery was far less common than it is today, and it had a stigma associated with it. It was widely considered to be a form of deviance stemming from vanity or anxiety about physical appearance. In fact, those who chose to undergo it for aesthetic reasons went to great lengths to keep their surgery secret. But attitudes change, and today that stigma has weakened considerably. Two-thirds of adults in the United States "would not be embarrassed" if family and friends learned they had undergone cosmetic surgery (American Society for Aesthetic Plastic Surgery 2011).

Today's favorable attitudes toward cosmetic surgery, and the declining stigma associated with it, reflect a shift in cultural norms known as **normalization,** in which *previously deviant behaviors become accepted as conventional.* As attitudes continue to shift, however, new pressures to conform emerge. We may be entering a period when those who do not have cosmetic surgery are increasingly defined as deviant because they are unwilling to conform to what may come to be viewed as easily achievable standards of beauty.

Rethinking the Disabled Body

Some people are automatically labeled as deviant because they are born with, or develop, a disability. Activists in the disability rights movement, however, have fought to establish equal rights and opportunities for people with disabilities, helping produce significant changes in how we think about disabled bodies. The Americans with Disabilities Act of 1990 (ADA), a landmark piece of legislation that established "a clear and comprehensive prohibition of discrimination on the basis of disability," was enacted in part because of a growing awareness that defining disabled bodies as deviant has real consequences. When potential employers, educators, community planners, and others see

©Alliance Images/Alamy Stock Photo

©Danita Delimont/Alamy Stock Photo

Advertisements for cosmetic surgery draw on the anxiety that many people feel about their appearance in a youth-oriented culture and suggest that we can choose how we want our bodies to look (*left*). Such notions are not unique to U.S. culture, as illustrated by this Ethiopian woman's lip plate, which conforms to her culture's standards of beauty (*right*).

disabled bodies as abnormal and less-than-capable, they have little incentive to open up opportunities and create accessible spaces. As a result, universal accessibility has become the norm for social spaces, a norm that a university, for example, would violate if it were not wheelchair accessible or did not provide sign language interpreters.

Legislation to outlaw discrimination, however, could only go part of the way in opening opportunities. Disability rights activists have long known that discrimination is connected to cultural definitions of what is normal. What is needed to prevent discrimination is a change in how we define normal bodies—a change that remains very much a work in progress. Many people with disabilities continue to experience hostility and stigma as a result of their status as deviant "others" (Corrigan 2014; Grue 2016). But the definition of a normal body is broadening.

Popular culture reflects these changes. For example, Michael J. Fox, an actor who has Parkinson's disease in real life, returned to television for several guest appearances and, in 2013, for his own television series. R. J. Mitte, who has mild cerebral palsy, costarred on the hit drama *Breaking Bad.*

The debate over Deaf Culture—spelled with a capital D—illustrates the stakes involved in changing definitions of normal and deviant bodies. Advocates of Deaf Culture do not consider deaf people to be disabled. Instead, they define the deaf community as a linguistic minority, rooted in a nonoral mode of communication: American Sign Language. Deaf Culture advocates insist that being deaf is not an impairment that should be corrected by medical procedures, and they celebrate the shared experience of being deaf in a hearing society. Their advocacy demonstrates how definitions of *normal*—as well as *disabled, deviant, nonconformist,* and other similar terms—are subject to a kind of power struggle between those defined as deviant and those who so define them.

Within Deaf Culture, there is nothing wrong with a deaf person's ears. Instead, the problem results from the distribution of power in a hearing-dominated society. From this perspective, members of the deaf community are a minority group that must deal with inequalities that reward the hearing and make life difficult for deaf people (Berbrier 1998).

Power and Deviance

The issue of power is a factor not only for those whom society has traditionally considered disabled, but for everyone who is labeled deviant as well. To understand the impact of deviance on society, we need to consider the concept of power and the inequality it fosters. Power is significant for four reasons:

1. ***Power is connected to our basic assumptions about what's normal and what's deviant.*** Some groups in society have the power to define norms, make rules, and decide that certain behaviors or attributes are deviant. Others do not have such power, and

consequently their interpretations have little consequence. As groups work to change the boundaries of socially acceptable behavior and to define certain types of behavior as deviant, tension and political conflict erupt frequently. In the end, the definition of what is normal and what is deviant often depends on the relative power of those who promote one particular view.

This social conflict is not always obvious. Consider the case of childrearing and housework, for example. Is it normal for women to do a majority of child care and housework? Is it deviant for men to stay at home as full-time caretakers of their children? Norms about men's and women's roles result in part from historical inequalities between men and women and the traditional power men have enjoyed to define appropriate family and gender roles. Men have historically reaped benefits from women's household labor, and women have struggled for the right to enter the paid workforce on an equal basis with their male colleagues.

©Frank Tozier/Alamy Stock Photo

In 1921 at age 39, Franklin Roosevelt was struck with polio, leaving him paralyzed from the waist down and unable to walk or even stand without braces. When he became president in 1933 and led the country for 12 years out of the Great Depression and through nearly all of World War II, he managed to largely conceal his disability, which would have been seen as a sign of weakness at the time. In 1997, when the Roosevelt Memorial was dedicated in Washington, D.C., Roosevelt's condition was still controversial and a statue of him in a wheelchair was not included. Disability advocates organized, lobbied, and raised private funds to add such a statue in 2001, pictured here. This example illustrates changing norms surrounding the acknowledgment and portrayal of disabilities, often as a result of activist efforts.

2. ***Power determines whether and how authorities enforce norms and punish deviance.*** The primary agents of social control—parents, teachers, religious leaders, police, judges—have the authority to enforce conformity. Because of their power, they can penalize rule breakers. For example, teachers have the power to enforce norms of appropriate classroom behavior; they can punish students who text in class or refuse to work quietly during an exam. The power of teachers and other school authorities to enforce norms and discipline students for deviance is often specified in official school policies.
3. ***Access to power enables some privileged groups to engage in distinct forms of deviant behavior.*** Political corruption, corporate accounting scandals, and other elite deviance require access to power. These types of deviant behavior can harm vast numbers of people or undermine confidence in society's basic institutions. In a classic work, Edwin Sutherland (1949) defined **white-collar crime** as *crime committed by people of high social status in the course of their occupation.* For example, Bernard Madoff, who ran a fraudulent investment fund that bilked people out of billions of dollars, was at one time chair of the NASDAQ stock exchange.
4. ***Power allows some people to escape being branded or punished as deviant.*** People with power can evade responsibility for deviant behavior at both an individual and an organizational level. Wealthy white college students who experiment with drugs are likely to be tolerated, perhaps even protected, by their parents and other adults. Unless they engage in large-scale drug distribution or develop a drug habit that seriously undermines their academic performance, these wealthy drug users will most likely be spared the consequences of being labeled deviant. In contrast, African American youth and teenagers in poor communities are more likely to be arrested and imprisoned for drug offenses (NAACP 2018; Reiman and Leighton 2017). They and their parents lack the power to protect themselves from the criminal label and the corresponding punishment.

Similarly, when organizations with political or economic power violate norms, they may not be defined as deviant or criminal. When construction companies cut corners in a way that results in shoddy housing, or when politicians accept campaign contributions in exchange for political favors, they are likely to define such acts as standard procedure in the real world of business or politics. Although ordinary citizens may see such behavior as irresponsible and corrupt—clearly deviant—they have little power to enforce such a label. Of course, powerful people caught breaking the law can be subject to public shame and criminal prosecution. But since rules and violations of them are defined, at least in part, by powerful people and organizations, a double standard partially insulates the powerful from being defined as deviant. Perhaps the role of power is most conspicuous in its connection to social control, the topic to which we now turn.

thinking about **power**

Powerful people can sometimes escape being defined as deviant even when they violate social norms, because they have the **power** to prevent potentially negative labels from sticking. Can you think of any nonconformist groups or individuals who avoid a deviant label as a result of their wealth, power, or status?

©Win McNamee/Getty Images

The 2010 explosion of BP's *Deepwater Horizon* oil rig in the Gulf of Mexico killed 11 workers and produced a four-million-barrel oil leak over a five-month period. BP eventually pleaded guilty to 11 counts of felony manslaughter, 1 count of felony obstruction of Congress, and violations of the Clean Water Act and the Migratory Bird Treaty Act.

Social Control and Deviance

We are all subject to subtle and not-so-subtle pressures to obey the rules, and we all face the possibility of negative consequences when we do not or cannot conform. In other words, we are all subject to **social control,** *the incentives and punishments that promote conformity in social life.* The relationship between deviance and social control has been described as a "battle to control the ways people think, feel, and behave" (Pfohl 2009). This battle may not always be obvious, especially because we all internalize, at least to some degree, social norms and expectations—a fundamental source of social control. This section examines both informal and formal means of social control.

Internal Influences: Socialization

When you were a child, you learned the norms of your culture, developed a moral framework for assessing right and wrong, and acquired an understanding of the range of attitudes, aspirations, and behaviors people expected from you. That's one way of describing the process of socialization, which we explored in Chapter 6. One important part of this process is learning to avoid what society defines as undesirable ways of thinking and acting.

As we internalize basic social norms through socialization, society becomes a part of us, shaping how we see the world, make decisions, and evaluate others. Because we have this internal regulator, we can often be our own most powerful agent of social control. For Durkheim, the internalization of social norms is one of the keys to understanding society. That's because Durkheim believed that the only force capable of limiting human desires and controlling human passions—giving us a sense of satisfaction and peace—is society. Without the forces of society operating within us, we would always want more and always feel miserably unstable. In Durkheim's ([1897] 1951) famous words, "inextinguishable thirst is constantly renewed torture." Policing ourselves, then, provides a kind of stability in social life and is necessary both for the smooth functioning of society and for individual satisfaction.

In contrast to Durkheim's view, French social theorist Michel Foucault (1926–1984) painted a bleak picture of our role as agents of self-control. Foucault described contemporary society as one in which "the judges of normality are present everywhere. We are in the society of the teacher-judge, doctor-judge, the educator-judge, the social-worker judge" (1979, 304). In this context, we are constantly under **surveillance,** *monitoring by authorities who police the boundaries of what is normal.*

We even watch ourselves. We "watch" our weight, what we say about politics, even how we dress and what we feel. For Foucault, this self-surveillance helps explain the complexity of social control. We are all incarcerated in the prison of social norms, judging ourselves and others according to standards of normality. And we are always both the subject and the object of normative judgments, so we are simultaneously both inmate and prison guard—and potential future offender.

Foucault's work challenges us to think carefully about our own relationship to processes of social control. After all, when we push ourselves to be more disciplined—to stick to that diet, exercise more intensely, or study harder—we are often our own most severe taskmasters. Foucault asks us to consider how deeply we've internalized prevailing definitions of what's normal, and he challenges us to understand how our own bodies and identities are where that social control happens.

External Influences: Control Theory

Interior belief systems are only one part of the story of social control. We need to consider how conformity is enforced. As we saw in Chapter 6, a variety of agents participate in socialization. These are also **agents of social control,** *the authorities and social institutions that enforce norms and rules, attempt to prevent rule violations, and identify and punish rule violators.*

As we saw in the discussion of power, the family, schools, and religion serve as primary agents of social control. In each of these settings, authority figures articulate and enforce cultural norms and impose consequences for breaking the rules. **Control theory** *suggests that our behavior is regulated by the strength of our connection to major social institutions, including family, school, and religion.* Instead of asking why people break

on social theory

Control theory suggests that our attachment to people who are important in our lives prevents us from breaking norms. Think of an example of a time when your social bonds prevented you from breaking a rule.

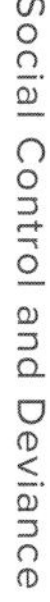

©Stefano Carnevali/Shutterstock

Video cameras are used for routine surveillance by both private security firms and government agencies in many urban areas. This photo shows security cameras above a road in a major city. Similar cameras are widespread in major urban areas, collecting large amounts of video data on both routine and extraordinary activities. For example, surveillance cameras in Boston's Back Bay neighborhood were used to help identify the two men who bombed the Boston Marathon in 2013.

CORE CONCEPTS CHALLENGE *Which institutions do surveillance cameras cover? What is the relationship between the location of surveillance cameras and the* **power** *of the institutions that installed them?*

rules, control theorists ask why we follow them. For these theorists, the key is the strength of our connection to the social control mechanisms that prevent us from violating rules. In his classic statement of control theory, *Causes of Delinquency,* Travis Hirschi (1969) suggested that social control operates through our attachment to parents, schools, and peers and our involvement in conventional family, school, and community activities. Our strong attachments to, and involvement with, these primary social networks prevent us from violating rules by increasing the cost of rule breaking. For example, people who are part of a close, loving family will not risk breaking those bonds by harming other family members. When social bonds are weak, however, people are far more likely to break the rules.

When people become involved in major or ongoing rule breaking, the costs of their actions are high and are likely to involve the criminal justice system—police, courts, prison.

Surveillance and Social Control in the Digital Age

Authorities have long used surveillance as a means of social control. In so doing, they have sought to develop new and ever more effective ways to monitor people's behavior.

One example is the idea of the *panopticon*, developed by eighteenth-century British social theorist Jeremy Bentham. A type of prison, the panopticon would permit guards to look out at all inmates all the time from one central observation post. This central watchtower would be opaque so that inmates would never know precisely when they were being watched. The power of the panopticon is that those subject to its control must live with the expectation of constant surveillance.

Few such buildings were ever constructed. However, in Foucault's powerful analysis of prisons, *Discipline and Punish* ([1975] 1995), he uses the panopticon as a metaphor for the various forms of everyday surveillance that encourage conformity, such as those in school and work settings. Reminding people that they are being watched can be a potent tool of social control, encouraging them to follow behavioral norms and act appropriately. The growing presence of security cameras—on public streets and in public parks, in shopping malls, in office buildings—is an example of this pervasive surveillance.

Today, as so many of our activities leave a digital trail that can be monitored, the possibilities for surveillance anytime and anyplace have expanded dramatically. Our daily routines—where we travel, whom we text or e-mail, where we shop, what we search for online, which ads we click on—are all subject to surveillance, though few of us think much about it.

Back in 2010, when *The Wall Street Journal* published a multipart investigative report, describing the many forms of electronic surveillance, digital tracking was still a relatively new phenomenon. The *Journal* reporters explained that "the tracking of consumers has grown both far more pervasive and far more intrusive than is realized by all but a handful of people in the vanguard of the industry" (Angwin 2010). The report, which characterized electronic surveillance as a form of online spying, found that the nation's top 50 websites each installed, on average, 64 different pieces of tracking technology on a visitor's computer, almost always without warning.

The basic outline of what the *Journal* reported in the early 2010s remains standard practice today; however, digital tracking has become even more sophisticated. For example, the *Journal's* report described how tracking firms plant third-party cookies on our computers, often through clickable ads or in free downloads, without our knowledge. Because the tracking companies that install these cookies may work with thousands of different websites, they accumulate a vast storehouse of information about our online activities, from where we shop and what we watch to what we "like" and where we go for news. The data are then sold to advertisers, who exploit this information to personalize product messages, targeting specific types of consumers and attempting to communicate more effectively with potential customers.

As users learned to identify and delete unwanted cookies from their computers, trackers created new "flash cookies" that can regenerate themselves after they have been deleted. Trackers also developed "beacons" that provide real-time data on a user's online activity, including what the person is typing and where his or her mouse pointer is moving. This information is compiled and auctioned off at lightning speed—often within seconds—through data exchanges to potential advertisers.

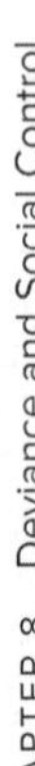

Today, digital tracking is both more widespread and even less transparent. For example, Facebook can still track what users "like" or "share," but it turns out that users don't even have to click the "like" or "share" buttons for Facebook to track the web pages they visit, even when they are not logged on to Facebook or don't have a Facebook account. One widely used tool for tracking users across the web is Facebook Pixel, an "invisible code that's dropped onto the other websites that allows that site and Facebook to track users' activity" (Singer 2018).

Digital tracking extends beyond collecting data on where users point their browsers. The proliferation of mobile phones, almost all of which have GPS embedded, has permitted the development of robust location tracking practices (Ghosh and Scott 2018). Most people who carry a smartphone are transmitting a steady stream of location data that are being collected and analyzed by marketers. The next time you visit the mall, for example, you may find that you receive e-mail, text messages, or social media posts alerting you to sale items just around the corner. Similarly, facial recognition software in cameras embedded covertly in commercial venues scans people's faces and compares them to a vast database of faces to differentiate valued customers, worthy of special deals and attentive service, from those who are unlikely to make a purchase or are even potential shoplifters (Angwin 2014b; Turow 2017).

In addition, the *Journal*'s report described what was then a new technique for linking data about our online and offline activities through "scraping," a practice that involves copying online conversations and personal information from social networking sites, resume and job-search sites, and online forums where people discuss their personal lives and political concerns (Angwin and Stecklow 2010). Scrapers mine these data to assemble profiles of individuals that are sold to employers, advertisers, and other websites; their activities can include linking people's real names to their various "screen names" and linking the identity of individual users of multiple digital devices, including laptop, tablet, and mobile phone.

Scraping strategies have intensified in recent years. For example, as Facebook sought to manage the 2018 fallout from revelations that the conservative political consulting firm Cambridge Analytica used personal data from Facebook to target up to 87 million U.S. voters during the 2016 presidential campaign, Facebook disclosed that the company had long been collecting call and text histories from users of its Messenger app on Android phones (Mello 2018). Similarly, Google Attribution aims to match online user activity with offline credit card purchases to track consumer behavior and measure the impact of Google's advertising platform (Kosoff 2017). Further, Princeton University researchers describe a sophisticated process of e-mail tracking, whereby third-party trackers collect personal data every time we view a commercial e-mail; "trackers can connect e-mail addresses to browsing histories and profiles, which leads to further privacy breaches such as cross-device tracking and linking of online and offline activities" (Englehardt, Han, and Narayanan 2018, 14).

In a 2018 story for *The Guardian,* reporter Dylan Curran (2018) describes the full range of data Google and Facebook have stored about users. The list in Figure 8.4 might surprise you.

FIGURE 8.4 | PERSONAL DATA LIKELY COLLECTED AND STORED ABOUT YOU (A PARTIAL LIST)

Google	Facebook
• Everywhere you have been since first launching Google on your phones (if you keep location tracking turned on to optimize various apps) • Everything you have ever searched (even if you have deleted your search history) • Every app you use • Your complete YouTube history • A detailed ad profile of you • Your email history • Your contacts • All your files from Google Drive • Every video you've uploaded to YouTube • All the photos you've taken on your phone • Your calendar history	• Every Facebook message you've ever sent or received • Every file you've sent or received • Every contact in your phone • All of the audio messages you've ever sent or received • All of your Facebook friends, including people you have "unfriended" • A log of every time you've logged on to Facebook, including the date, location, and device you used • All of the apps you've ever connected to your Facebook account • Your mobile call history • All of the files you've download • All the games you play • Your music

Sources: Chen 2018, Curran 2018.

Although most people likely lack a full understanding of the depth of everyday surveillance, research indicates that people in the United States are divided in the degree to which they trust authorities to protect their privacy. For example, a 2017 Pew Research Center survey found that half of adults do not trust either the federal government or social media companies to keep their personal data secure. In contrast, two-thirds of adults *do* trust their e-mail service, cell phone provider, and credit card companies to protect their data (Olmstead and Smith 2017). The same report found that people are far more likely to think their data has become less secure (49 percent) than more secure (18 percent) over the past five years, with people age 50 and older far more likely to be concerned about declining data security. Experience with data theft is widespread; more than 60 percent of adults have experienced some kind of data theft, ranging from fraudulent credit card charges to having a social media account hacked. Despite such experiences, the vast majority of U.S. adults (69 percent) say they are not concerned about the security of their online passwords.

Since the 2016 presidential election, amidst concerns about Russian efforts to influence the election, questions about just how much personal data Facebook and Google collect have been in the spotlight. Media scholars have coined the term "dataveillance" to describe the various ways personal digital data are used in surveillance activities (Lupton and Michael 2017). Still, the depth of commercial dataveillance pales in comparison to what government intelligence agencies are doing. Shrouded behind the veil of "national security," the extent and range of government data-gathering capacities in the United States and other countries are still largely unknown. What *is* known is that the degree of data gathering on citizens by governments around the world is vast and growing exponentially.

Following the September 11, 2001, terrorist attacks, Congress passed the USA PATRIOT Act, among whose provisions is the enhancement of law enforcement agencies' ability to search e-mail and telephone communications and to obtain information on internet users' personal data, including session times and durations and IP addresses. Subsequent legislation, the Protect America Act of 2007 and the Foreign Intelligence Surveillance Act (FISA) Amendments Act of 2008, permitted continued surveillance and immunized from legal action private telecommunications companies that cooperated with government intelligence gathering. Despite efforts by critics concerned that FISA permitted large-scale violations of privacy of U.S. citizens, including more than 30,000 warrantless searches of Americans' data every year (Guliani 2018), Congress voted in 2018 to extend the FISA surveillance program for another six years (Savage 2018).

Many people first learned the depth of the U.S. government's electronic surveillance activities in 2013, when whistle-blower Edward Snowden revealed that the National Security Agency (NSA) was collecting the phone records of millions of Americans; monitoring internet usage through direct access to the servers of nine leading technology companies; extracting e-mails, audio, video, and other content; and even had the capability to monitor what a person is typing in real time (Greenwald 2014; Lyon 2015). Reporting revealed that a secret court order had instructed the three major phone networks–Verizon, AT&T, and Sprint Nextel–to provide the NSA with daily information on the phone calls of its tens of millions of U.S. customers (Gorman, Perez, and Hook 2013). In addition, many of the leading internet companies, including Facebook and Google, had cooperated with the NSA by providing the agency with user content, including e-mails, chat logs, videos, and other data (Black 2013).

Digital surveillance is not just something others do to us. Many of us regularly use digital tools to monitor our own behavior, often inadvertently making our data available for others to see. You may post many of the details of your life on Facebook, regularly post photos to Instagram, or tweet about your daily activities. Some apps allow you to track and analyze specific aspects of your life, such as monitoring your health by tracking your daily step count, calorie intake, and sleep patterns. And "life-logging" apps, such as Foursquare's Swarm, track and map everyplace you go. Although many users find such tracking applications helpful, fun, or just plain cool, privacy advocates, such as the Electronic Frontier Foundation, are asking how we might protect our privacy so that corporations and governments cannot use this information in ways we never intended.

New practices of electronic surveillance are developing all the time. In 2018, for example, the city of Chicago pushed forward a plan to deploy surveillance drones, equipped with facial recognition software, to collect data on participants in public protests (Spielman 2018). Local police have been at the forefront of the adoption of new surveillance technologies, and some communities face more aggressive surveillance than others. A recent study, "The Eyes of Law Enforcement in the New Panopticon," concludes that while "surveillance is increasingly infiltrating modern-day society, its implementation differentially targets communities of color" (Hendrix et al. 2018).

Crime and Punishment

Perhaps the most obvious form of deviance is **crime,** *deviant behavior that violates a law.* Laws are specific rules, recognized in a community and adopted officially by a governing body, that are enforceable by established processes. Unlike those who merely violate a social norm, people who break the law may be subject to punishment by authorities.

Crime exists in all societies. As a result, communities have specialized agencies to handle potential and actual lawbreaking. The *criminal justice system,* which is designed to prevent crime and apprehend and punish those who commit crimes, is a powerful agent of social control. It includes the police, who maintain social order by upholding the law, investigating crimes, and arresting alleged criminals; the courts, which charge and try those who have been arrested; and prisons, which punish those who are found guilty.

The sociological study of crime focuses on the types of crime people commit, the social forces associated with the growth in or decline of crime, and the forms, goals, and consequences of punishment.

Types of Crime

When you think of crime, you probably picture the kinds of activities that are the subject of *Law and Order* or *CSI*–murder, robbery, assault, arson, or theft. These kinds of crimes, commonly referred to as *street crime,* can be classified as either violent crime or property crime. *Violent crime* includes murder, forcible rape, robbery, and aggravated assault. *Property crime* includes burglary, larceny, motor vehicle theft, and arson. Most discussions of crime and crime rates–including official statistics collected by the Federal Bureau of Investigation as part of the Uniform Crime Reporting program–focus on violent crime and property crime.

However, the most common crimes are those referred to as *public order crimes.* These crimes, such as prostitution, liquor law violations, drug offenses, and disorderly conduct, are sometimes called victimless crimes, although the offender's family and friends are often victims. For example, the children of a parent addicted to drugs or alcohol can be subject to neglect or even injury or death if that parent drives while impaired. In 2016, more people were arrested for violations of the drug laws than for any other offense; the second most common reason for arrest was

thinking about culture

Social theorist Michel Foucault argued that socialization makes us our own most effective social control agents, as we police our own behavior and attitudes to make sure they conform to social expectations and culture norms. Can you think of any examples when you have policed yourself in this way?

FIGURE 8.5 | MOST COMMON ARREST OFFENSES IN THE UNITED STATES, 2016

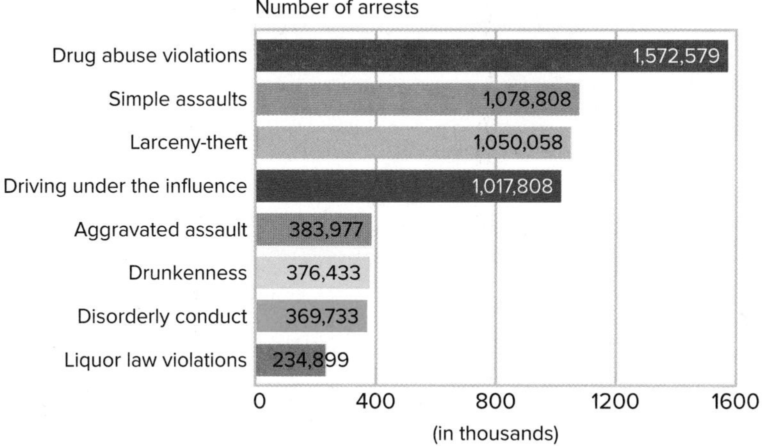

Nonviolent offenses, led by violations associated with drug abuse, are the most common causes of arrest in the United States.

Source: U.S. Department of Justice—Federal Bureau of Investigation 2017a.

larceny-theft (see Figure 8.5). One enduring question about public order crime focuses on **decriminalization,** *the process of making an illegal action legal.* Whether or not to decriminalize activities such as marijuana use and prostitution has been the subject of longstanding debate. In recent years, nine states, including Alaska, California, Colorado, Maine, Massachusetts, Nevada, Oregon, Vermont, and Washington, have legalized recreational marijuana use.

A fourth category of crimes is *hate crimes,* those motivated by bias against a victim's race, ethnicity, religion, sexual orientation, or disability. More than 6,100 hate crime incidents were reported in 2016; more than half were classified as racially motivated, while 21 percent were motivated by religious bias and another 18 percent by sexual orientation bias. Much debate centers on how best to assess the motivations of offenders and whether perpetrators of hate crimes should be classified (and punished) differently from others. Most states provide stiffer penalties for acts defined as hate crimes. The causes of and responses to bias-motivated crime are complex. If we take a sociological perspective on them, we need to consider how intergroup conflict is a source of hate crime and, just as important, how hate crimes (or the threat of such crimes) help reproduce and strengthen inequalities.

SPOTLIGHT

on social theory

According to the **conflict approach,** groups with more power in society are able to define norms and make rules. They also find it easier to hide criminal behavior or to escape its consequences if they are caught. What are the consequences of white-collar crime that could affect you, either directly or indirectly?

A final type of crime is *white-collar crime* (introduced earlier under the heading "Power and Deviance"). We know much less from officials and the media about the incidence of white-collar crime than about other categories. Many people are not even aware of the variety of white-collar crimes—including fraud, labor violations, insider trading, bribery, forgery, embezzlement, and tax evasion—perhaps in part because few white-collar criminals are ever prosecuted. The participants are commonly from the middle or upper classes, are likely to have authority in the workplace, and generally commit crimes that are difficult to identify, investigate, and prosecute. The exceptions are high-profile white-collar crime cases that saturate the media. For example, in the Enron case, which was the subject of the 2005 Academy Award–nominated documentary film *The Smartest Guys in the Room,* executives at that energy company used questionable accounting practices and other illegal methods in the late 1990s to hide billions of dollars in debt, which eventually led to the company's bankruptcy and the loss of many employees' pensions. Some Enron executives were eventually convicted of fraud and other charges. More typically, perpetrators of white-collar crime are neither prosecuted nor forced to admit wrongdoing. In 2016, Goldman Sachs agreed to pay up to $5 billion in fines in a settlement with federal prosecutors to resolve claims that it sold flawed mortgage-backed securities that helped produce the Great Recession (Goldstein 2016). Goldman joined several other major banks, including Bank of America and JPMorgan, that agreed to pay similar fines. Despite such penalties, none of the bank executives involved in these financial schemes were charged with crimes or prosecuted, as is typical with much white-collar crime.

White-collar crime is in fact quite common, and the financial costs are very high. In its 2018 Global Fraud Study, the Association of Certified Fraud Examiners estimates that $4 trillion was lost to occupational fraud in 2017. White-collar crime is also evolving in response to new opportunities, with various forms of online crime from identity theft and virtual currency scams to ransomware and tech support fraud, growing each year (Internet Crime Complaint Center 2017). White-collar crime has more than just financial consequences; by defrauding people and organizations, white-collar criminals undermine the trust that helps hold society together. In addition, white-collar crime has serious physical costs, including death and injury that result from unsafe workplaces, pollution, and the distribution of unsafe products (Croall 2016; Friedrichs 2009).

Crime Rates

Criminologists and sociologists study crime patterns most commonly by examining **crime rates,** which *measure the incidence of crime in relation to population size.* The most prominent measure tracks the number of crime incidents reported to law enforcement officials. Although incident-based measures include only crimes that are reported to the police, the measure has been used for many years and is considered reliable by law enforcement agencies and researchers. Figure 8.6 plots the rates of violent crime and property crime in the United States over a 30-year period. As the two graphs show, the rates for both violent crime and property crime increased substantially in the mid- and late 1980s but began a steady decline in the early 1990s.

FIGURE 8.6 | RATES OF VIOLENT CRIME AND PROPERTY CRIME, 1986–2016

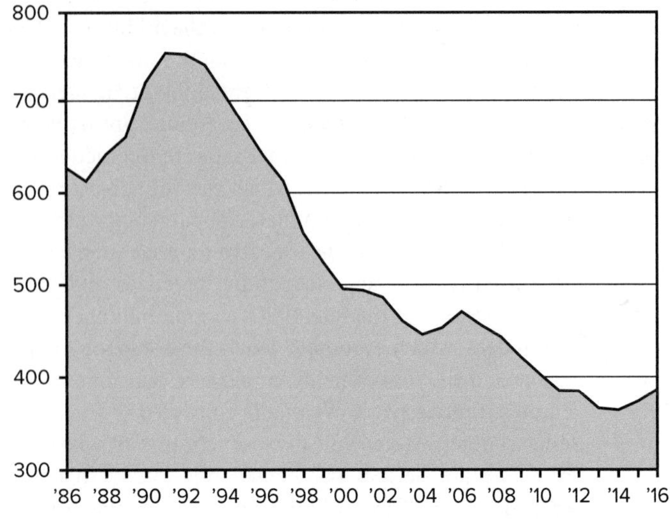

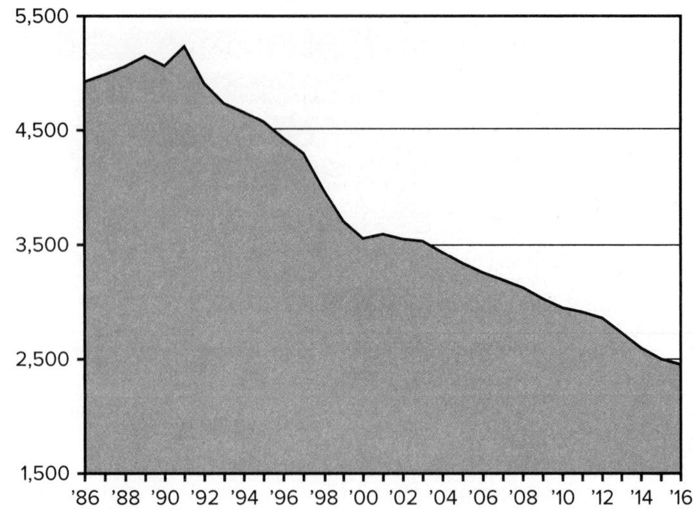

Violent crime and property crime rates peaked in the early 1990s, but declined sharply throughout the mid- to late 1990s. After remaining relatively stable in the early 2000s, crime rates began another multiyear decrease in the mid-2000s.
Source: FBI, Uniform Crime Reports, *Crime in the United States,* annual.

Sociologists have offered various explanations for the declining crime rates in the 1990s. The following are the most common (LaFree 1999):

- An improved economy that produced a decline in poverty and unemployment
- A more stable family structure, a primary form of social control, and the institutionalization of various nontraditional family forms, including dual-career, blended, gay or lesbian, and single-parent families
- A relative decline in the number of young people, who are the most common perpetrators and victims of crime
- A decrease in the number of crack cocaine users and, with it, a decline in the drug trade, which is closely associated with violent crime
- New, more effective policing strategies—including the development of *community policing* approaches that emphasize partnerships between police and neighborhood organizations
- A dramatic increase in the number of men and women in prison and jail

However, a precise explanation for the rise and fall of crime rates remains elusive, due largely to the absence of reliable crime data prior to the 1970s.

Debates about Punishment

Punishment is an unambiguous and universal social response to crime. But why do societies punish? In sociological terms, laws institutionalize social norms, and a crime, therefore, offends all law-abiding citizens by challenging the underlying moral framework of society (Durkheim [1895] 1982). Punishment strengthens social bonds among law-abiding citizens since it represents their collective disapproval of criminal conduct. At the same time, punishment reinforces people's commitment to basic social norms, since punishments represent a collective celebration of a shared moral framework. If crime threatens a community, punishment is a mechanism for defending, even strengthening, social solidarity in response.

Criminologists generally offer five competing rationales for punishment (Conklin 2010; Garland 1993; Sullivan and Tifft 2006):

1. ***Retribution.*** Perhaps the oldest rationale for punishment is retribution, or vengeance. To those who hold this view, the more severe the crime, the harsher the penalty. Governments act on behalf of individual victims and the broader community to deliver retribution to offenders. As we will see, some of those who advocate the death penalty for murder are applying the punishment-as-retribution approach.
2. ***Rehabilitation.*** Since the nineteenth century, one goal of punishment has been to rehabilitate offenders—to resocialize criminals into the basic values and norms of society. To adherents of this view, prisons are places where people not only serve their time for violating the law but also have the opportunity to become contributing members of society. People who hold this view generally advocate educational and job-training programs in prisons.
3. ***Deterrence.*** Those who agree with this rationale believe that when potential criminals see the consequences of committing a crime, they will be less likely to pursue criminal activity. The form and duration of punishment, therefore, need to be widely known. Those who believe that the crime rate declines

FIGURE 8.7 | U.S. INCARCERATION RATE TRENDS

Inmates in state and federal prisons per 100,000 population

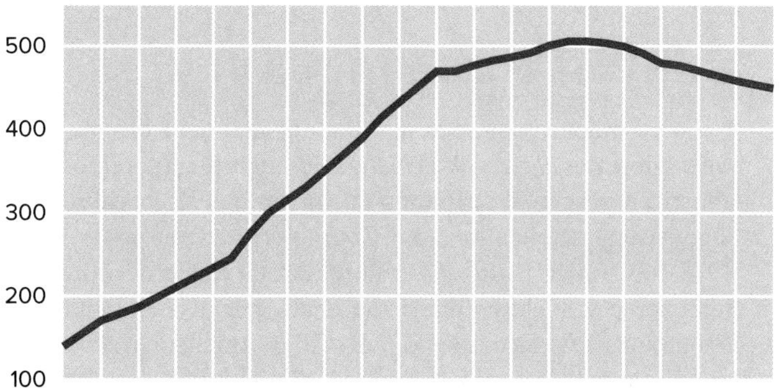

The incarceration rate in the United States increased dramatically in the 1980s and 1990s but leveled off in the early 2000s and began declining in 2009.

Source: Bureau of Justice Statistics 2012c, 2015b, 2018b.

in response to tougher punishment–longer prison sentences, under harsh conditions–generally advocate this approach.

4. ***Protection.*** Some people are imprisoned because they are defined as too dangerous to live among law-abiding citizens. This type of punishment is preventive; the criminal justice system removes people who may be a continuing threat to the community. Many of those who advocate life sentences for habitual criminals believe in punishment as protection.
5. ***Restoration.*** People advocating restoration as a rationale for punishment seek to repair the individual and social damage caused by a crime. The offender may be required to return or replace a victim's property. Offenders also help restore their victims' sense of security and dignity, giving victims a sense that justice has been served. Punishment as restoration also builds social support for perpetrators and helps restore their community bonds, with the goal of preventing future criminal behavior. Those who advocate mediation to reconcile victims and offenders are following a punishment-as-restoration approach.

In the United States the prison population increased substantially at the end of the twentieth century (see Figure 8.7). This expansion occurred while rates of violent crime and property crime were decreasing. The rate of increase slowed in the 2000s, and the prison population declined modestly between 2009 and 2016, reaching its lowest level since the late 1990s. In 2016, 1 in every 38 U.S. adults was under the supervision of the corrections systems–in federal or state prisons, in local jails, or on parole or probation (Bureau of Justice Statistics 2018a). The primary cause of the expansion of the prison population was policies that sent more nonviolent offenders to prison, sentencing guidelines that kept prisoners in custody for longer periods, and laws that imprisoned people for violating the rules associated with their parole or probation (Pew Center on the States 2008).

Punishment doesn't always build social solidarity, however. Inequalities associated with the administration of punishment can be a source of social conflict. The criminal justice system treats the poor far more severely than the rich: "*For the same criminal behavior,* the poor are more likely to be arrested; if arrested, they are more likely to be charged; if charged, more likely to be convicted; if convicted, more likely to be sentenced to prison; and if sentenced, more likely to be given longer prison terms than members of the middle and upper classes" (Reiman and Leighton 2017, 114).

Significant racial and ethnic disparities exist throughout the criminal justice system. For example, African Americans accounted for 39 percent of the male prison population in the United States in 2016, triple their proportion in the U.S. population. African American men have an imprisonment rate six times the white imprisonment rate, and Hispanics are imprisoned at more than twice the white rate. Whereas men are incarcerated far more frequently than women, significant racial and ethnic disparities are evident for both men and women (Bureau of Justice Statistics 2018b) (see Figure 8.8).

FIGURE 8.8 | INEQUALITY AND INCARCERATION

Estimated number of sentenced prisoners under state and federal jurisdiction per 100,000 of each group

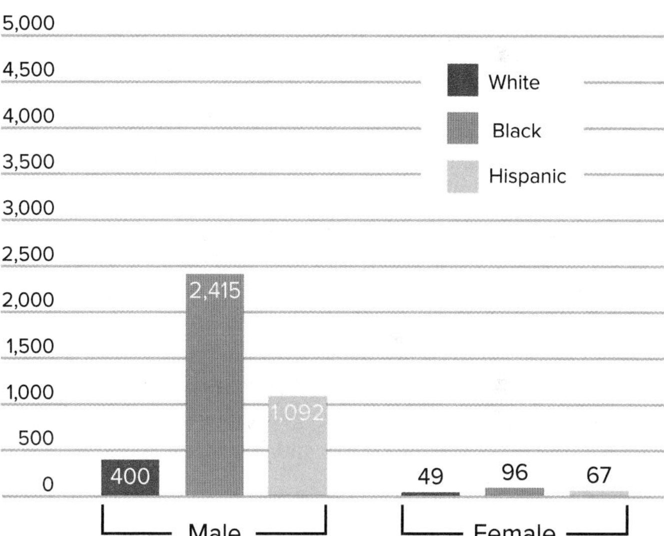

The bars represent the estimated number of prisoners with sentences of one year or longer in federal and state correctional facilities on December 31, 2016. Vast racial and gender disparities exist in incarceration rates in the United States. Black men are imprisoned at a rate six times higher than that for white men; for Hispanic men, the rate is more than double that for white men. The pattern among women is similar but less extreme. Black women are twice as likely as white women to be imprisoned, whereas the incarceration rate among Hispanic women is about 35 percent higher than the rate among white women.

Source: Bureau of Justice Statistics 2018b.

CORE CONCEPTS CHALLENGE *How do these inequalities in incarceration rates relate to social* ***structure****?*

TABLE 8.1 RECIDIVISM RATES AMONG PRISONERS RELEASED IN 2005

Time after Release	Rearrested All	Rearrested Male	Rearrested Female
1 year	43.9	44.9	35.1
5 year	77.0	78.0	69.0
9 years	83.4	84.2	76.8

More than 40 percent of released prisoners are arrested again during the first year after release, and more than four out of five are arrested within nine years of release.
Source: Bureau of Justice Statistics. 2018. *2018 Update on Prisoner Recidivism: A 9-Year Follow-up Period (2005-2014).* May, NCJ 250975.

Sociologists largely agree that these persistent patterns of racial disparity result from long-term social and economic inequalities in the United States (Wakefield and Uggen 2010; Western 2007). At the same time, these disparities help reinforce existing inequalities.

For those who complete their assigned punishment, serve their prison sentence, and return to community life, the social consequences of incarceration can be devastating. The stigma associated with serving time in prison can make it difficult for released prisoners to find jobs and housing and to rejoin the community. In addition, social networks among ex-convicts may provide discouraged ex-cons with incentives to return to criminal activities. (The Sociology in Action box describes the Women's Prison Association's ongoing efforts to provide effective support to women and their families.)

The rate of **recidivism,** or *return to criminal behavior,* is very high. Among those at risk for reincarceration in 2016—all adults exiting parole during that year—27 percent were returned to incarceration that year (Bureau of Justice Statistics 2018c). The most comprehensive study of recidivism in the United States, which examined the experiences of inmates released from prison in 30 states in 2005, found that more than three-quarters were rearrested within five years. Recidivism rates among men are higher than among women, but more than two-thirds of women were rearrested within five years of release from prison (see Table 8.1). Critics of the U.S. criminal justice system point to these high recidivism rates as evidence of the inability of our penal policies to prevent chronic crime. Public reintegration ceremonies can be an effective means of helping former prisoners rejoin a community and can reduce recidivism (Braithwaite 1989). In these ceremonies, offenders publicly acknowledge responsibility for their crimes and apologize for them, and community members forgive them and pledge to support their struggle to repair the damage they have caused. (See the Sociology Works box.)

Capital Punishment

No punishment is more severe than **capital punishment,** otherwise known as *the death penalty.* Although the Supreme Court effectively suspended capital punishment in 1972 because of its inconsistent application, the Court revisited the issue in the 1976 case *Gregg v. Georgia,* ruling that clearer procedures and sentencing guidelines made the death penalty constitutional. Executions resumed in 1977. By 2016, thirty-one states had provisions for sentencing convicted criminals to death, generally in murder cases (see Map 8.1). Between 1977 and mid-2018, 1,474 people were executed in the United States. More than 80 percent of these executions occurred in southern states, led by Texas, where 550 prisoners were executed during this time period (Death Penalty Information Center 2018). Explaining the concentration of executions in the southern states, sociologists Marquart, Ekland-Olson, and Sorensen (1994) point to "the cultural tradition of exclusion" in the southern states. "Before it is possible to justify the termination of life . . . it is morally necessary to define that life as lying outside the protective boundaries of the community. Such exclusion was a basic element of the legacy of slavery" (x–xi).

MAP 8.1 | CAPITAL PUNISHMENT BY STATE

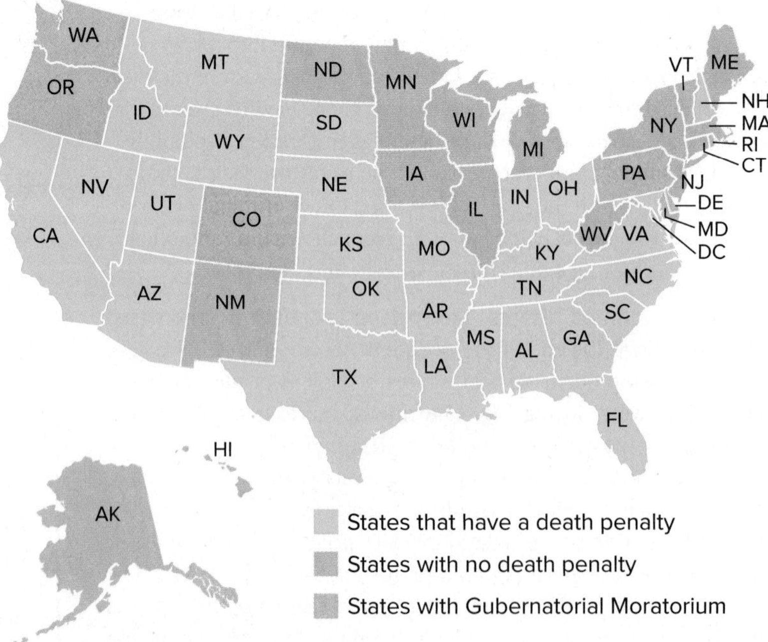

In 2018, 31 states had capital punishment statutes. Between 1977 and mid-2018, there were 1,474 executions in the United States, including 23 executions in 2017. Public support for capital punishment surged in the 1980s, reached a peak in the 1990s, and has remained above 60 percent throughout the 2000s. *Source:* Death Penalty Information Center 2016.

SOCIOLOGY in ACTION

Women's Prison Association

When Rochelle was 23, living with her drug-addicted mother and feeling hopeless about the future, she made a terrible mistake. In hopes of earning quick money, she got involved in transporting illegal drugs and ended up in jail. She was fortunate to connect with the Women's Prison Association (WPA). Rather than serving a prison sentence, Rochelle spent time in the WPA's alternative-to-incarceration program, where she got valuable support that helped her turn her life around. Working with the WPA, Rochelle received "counseling, parenting lessons, and anger management assistance" that helped prepare her to reconnect with her children and return to school. Eventually earning her bachelor's degree, she now manages a funeral home and operates her own funeral services business. She is a community leader, deeply involved in her local school district and her church, and she points to the WPA as a life-changing community. "WPA was the light at the end of my tunnel. They helped me become an outstanding citizen and someone who my kids, family, and friends could be proud of" (WPA n.d.).

While there are many more men than women in prison, the number of incarcerated women has grown at a much faster rate than the number of incarcerated men in the past 35 years. Between 1980 and 2014, the number of women in prison and jail leapt by more than 700 percent, growing from 26,378 to 215,332 (The Sentencing Project 2015). The experiences of women in prison (and their families outside of prison) are likely to be very different from the experiences of incarcerated men. Almost two-thirds of incarcerated women are mothers, most of whom were the primary caretakers of their children prior to their arrest. As a result, many incarcerated women must negotiate the complex process of finding care for their children while also maintaining their connections to them.

The majority of female prisoners are incarcerated for nonviolent offenses, including property (28 percent), drug (24 percent), and public order (9 percent) crimes (The Sentencing Project 2015). In 2016, more than half of all women in federal prison—56 percent—were serving time on drug-related charges (Bureau of Justice Statistics 2018b). In general, women prisoners are likely to be nonwhite, and many incarcerated women experienced childhood physical or sexual abuse (Moloney, van den Bergh, and Moller 2009). Female prisoners are more vulnerable to prison staff misconduct, including sexual harassment and assault.

The WPA draws upon sociological research to build a public conversation about women in the criminal justice system, no small task since most public discussion about the criminal justice system neglects questions of gender. The organization focuses on prison life, the experiences of recently released women as they reenter family and work life, and the impact on families and communities of incarcerating women. Former sociology student Sarah From helped develop the WPA's research and advocacy efforts. For From, sociology helped connect the dots, mapping the links between gender and crime, punishment, and policy.

©Rich Pedroncelli/AP Images

A woman prisoner plays with her 3-year-old son during a visit at California's Folsom Women's Facility.

The WPA seeks to build bridges between policymakers, police, prison officials, service providers, and researchers to reform the criminal justice system so that it will better serve women and their families. In 2014, the WPA reopened New York City's Hopper Home, a transitional shelter for single homeless women with criminal justice histories. According to the WPA: "Accounting for the intersection of mental illness, substance abuse, histories of abuse and trauma, and economic marginality that underlie a woman's criminal behavior and housing instability, Hopper Home provides services that are gender-responsive and based on research." The WPA also launched a new home-based alternative-to-incarceration program, JusticeHome, in 2013, and the program's first class of clients found support to maintain employment, pursue education, and stay connected to mental health services, reducing the likelihood of recidivism (Women's Prison Association 2015).

The WPA also created the Women's Advocacy Project to draw the voices of incarcerated women into the discussion. The project brings together women such as Rochelle who have been incarcerated or participated in drug treatment or other alternatives to prison sentences. The goal of the project is to build these women's skills in leadership, policy analysis, and public speaking. Since 2003 the Women's Advocacy Project has presented New York state officials with recommendations for improving the prison discharge process, proposed policies for better representing parents in New York City's family court, and presented proposals aimed at more effectively reuniting women in the criminal justice system with their families.

think about it

1. *What do you think policymakers could learn from listening to the perspectives of incarcerated women?*
2. *What kinds of support services do you think would be most helpful to women when they are released from prison?*

SOCIOLOGY WORKS

Nate Mandel and Parolee Outreach to Reduce Recidivism

For Nate Mandel, the recipient of a BA in sociology in 2010 and currently an outreach specialist with the Center for Employment Opportunities (CEO) in New York City, sociology is “a way of thinking and a way of life.” His background in sociology has given him a valuable perspective that informs his everyday work life, as well as specific skills with which to pursue fresh work opportunities.

As an outreach specialist, Mandel assists people coming home from prison to find paying jobs. He might help to place people in short-term transitional work or to connect formerly incarcerated men and women with employers who are seeking to hire full-time employees. Most of the time, Mandel is out in the field visiting parole bureaus throughout New York, where he talks with parole officers to identify recently released men and women who are in the job market and then follows up with potential clients to recruit them into the CEO’s program. His assignments can be challenging, and Mandel recognizes that his own life experience stands in sharp contrast to that of most of the former prisoners his work supports.

Mandel draws upon his sociology training on a daily basis. “Having a detailed understanding of systematic structures of power and inequality is a great resource to have in your back pocket. As a privileged white male, I can’t fully empathize with a person of color who has been incarcerated, but I can situate myself as someone who understands that there have been systemic factors working against that person since birth. Sometimes just showing someone that you understand the greater structures at play can go a long way.” In the field, a sociological outlook is an especially invaluable asset.

“A detailed understanding of systematic structures of power and inequality is a great resource to have in your back pocket. . . . Sometimes just showing someone that you understand the greater structures at play can go a long way.”

Back at the CEO office, Mandel manages the organization’s “Talk to Us” project that collects feedback from clients through surveys and focus groups to help the CEO evaluate and strengthen its life skills education, job placement, and postplacement support programs. Here again, a sociology background has been a real benefit for Mandel. His undergraduate training in sociological research methods helped prepare him to collect and analyze data and to understand the potential value of research that gives voice to former inmates. In describing the Talk to Us research, Mandel notes: “I’m especially interested in the project because people who have been incarcerated have been systematically prevented from speaking out and having their voices heard. This project is about empowering them and reminding them that their opinions and viewpoints matter.”

The Talk to Us project has opened new opportunities for Mandel. He now works as the CEO’s program innovator “to test and implement select program innovations across the enterprise to ensure that the CEO continues to improve its core model by designing effective programming and ensuring integrated implementation of model enhancements throughout the organization.” Ultimately, he will assist in launching versions of the Talk to Us project at all of the CEO’s offices around the United States “to help create a national solution to recidivism.”

Courtesy of Nathan Mandel
Nate Mandel

Developing and implementing programs that successfully reduce recidivism is no small task. Mandel recognizes what he has signed on for, however, and sociology is one reason why. In reflecting on his years studying sociology, he notes: “Intro sociology is just the beginning. Absorb the theoretical underpinnings of the field because they’ll be invaluable as you begin to apply them toward your passions; to eventually create meaningful change you’ll need to know how to identify a problem, theorize some solutions, and then present the information in approachable and actionable ways.”

Mandel is clear-eyed about his work. He remarks, “I carry a sociological lens in all aspects of life, to the point that it can be overwhelming. The benefit is knowing that when you do choose your battle, you’ll be well equipped to fight it.”

think about it

1. *Thinking sociologically, explain how you understand the relationship between recidivism and employment opportunities.*
2. *What kinds of questions would you include in a Talk to Us research project with formerly incarcerated men and women? Why?*

Although the death penalty has substantial public support, the underlying rationale for it is a source of continuing debate (Garland 2012). In the 1970s and 1980s, it was justified primarily as a deterrent and a form of protection. Advocates also argued that the death penalty would cost less than housing a prisoner for life. Researchers have found little empirical support for the deterrence, protection, or cost-savings arguments for capital punishment, however (Radelet and Borg 2000). A widely cited survey of leading criminologists in the United States found a broad consensus that the death penalty does not have a deterrent effect; 88 percent of these experts responded that the death penalty does not lower the murder rate (Radelet and Lacock 2009). In recent years, supporters have offered retribution as the most compelling rationale for the death penalty, asserting that people who commit the most hideous crimes simply deserve to die.

Critics of capital punishment argue that the death penalty should be abolished on humanitarian grounds. In addition, they note that sometimes innocent people are sentenced to death and executed. Many death sentences are not based on evidence obtained through DNA testing, which can establish whether a defendant was present at a specific crime scene. Since 1973, 162 death-row inmates were released after new evidence (often DNA evidence) proved their innocence (Death Penalty Information Center 2018).

Critics also point to significant racial disparities in the application of the death penalty. African Americans account for 35 percent of those executed since 1976 and for 42 percent of those on death row in 2016, even though they constitute only about 13 percent of the U.S. population (NAACP Criminal Justice Department 2017). One study in California found that those found guilty of murdering whites are far more likely to be sentenced to death than are those convicted of killing African Americans or nonwhite Hispanics (Pierce and Radelet 2005).

Public opinion about capital punishment also divides by race; whites are far more likely than people of color to favor the death penalty, a consistent pattern for 30 years (Cochran and Chamlin 2006; Unnever and Cullen 2007). A Pew Research Center survey (Oliphant 2016), for example, found that 57 percent of whites, in contrast to 29 percent of African Americans and 36 percent of Hispanics, support the death penalty. The dynamics underlying such longstanding attitudinal differences are complex, but research suggests that white racial animus–the belief that African Americans are "irresponsible" or "culturally deficient," the foundation of "white racism" (Feagin and O'Brien 2003)–is the most powerful "predictor of the degree to which Americans support the death penalty" (Unnever and Cullen 2007, 1291). Research outside the United States similarly found that Europeans who harbor negative attitudes toward immigrants–expressing racial and ethnic intolerance–are the most likely to support the death penalty (Unnever and Cullen 2010).

Since 1976, at least 70 countries have abolished the death penalty for all crimes. According to Amnesty International, more than two-thirds of countries no longer practice capital punishment. Only the United States in North America and only Belarus in Europe retained the death penalty as of 2017.

A Changing World

THE COMMERCIALIZATION OF DEVIANCE

As society changes, definitions of deviance change as well, bringing about new mechanisms of social control. One recent area of interest to sociologists is the *commercialization of deviance,* the process by which nonconformist activities or styles turn into commercial products. These products often create dilemmas for agents of social control.

Many cultures designate specific periods when otherwise deviant behavior is accepted and even encouraged. Brazil's Carnival and New Orleans's Mardi Gras celebrations, for example, can involve excessive public drinking, dancing in the streets, and public nudity. Recently these occasions have taken on a commercial tone. Mardi Gras and Carnival are tourist attractions more than religious festivals. Another example is spring break, which can offer the promise of unbridled partying while bringing much-needed dollars into local economies. Practicing deviance for fun in special times and places has become a form of short vacation from norms and rules and is

©Richard Bord/Getty Images

The X Games feature sports that once had a deviant image but now are embraced fully by mainstream corporate sponsors. How else do companies adopt "deviant" activities in their quest to reach consumers?

captured in the advertising slogan "What happens in Vegas, stays in Vegas."

One sociologist refers to these activities as "playful deviance": people "travel to symbolic spaces of leisure to participate in temporary forms of transgressions that they will not perform in places where they live" (Redmon 2003, 27). Playful deviance takes place apart from everyday life and is generally a short-term activity. People experience playful deviance as both exciting and liberating, an opportunity to act like someone else for a short time (Ravenscroft and Gilchrist 2009).

The marketing of vacations as opportunities for "playful deviance" is just one form of the marketing of deviance. Businesses also increasingly look to deviant subcultures for new opportunities, as in the cases of tattoos and body piercing. Skateboarding also used to be part of a deviant subculture involving young people who didn't play traditional sports, didn't wear traditional clothes or hairstyles, and often had a defiant attitude toward authorities. Skateboarding and other extreme sports were outsider activities in the 1970s and 1980s, but today they are popular and mainstream: top skateboarders have corporate sponsors, skateboard styles are available in suburban malls, and X Games broadcasts are highly popular on ESPN.

The world of indie music provides many similar examples, as alternative bands become popular on radio stations, on MTV, and in the major-label music business. Punk, rap, and grunge music began in deviant subcultures, and all three became commercial genres of music and fashion. The irony is that alternative music—and youth subcultures, more generally—become commercially successful *because* they have their roots in nonconformity. Deviance sells because it represents authenticity in a society full of mass-produced images (Moore 2009). Commercial success is a double-edged sword, however. As deviant activities and styles are marketed widely, they gain visibility and popularity that may undermine their initial authentic image. Once youth subcultures are absorbed into the mainstream corporate culture, these expressions of nonconformity often lose credibility.

Businesses have learned that deviance can be packaged and sold. The advertising campaigns and new product lines directed at the global youth market are saturated with images associated with individuality, authenticity, and rebellion. Advertisers and market researchers actively seek out deviant youth subcultures, trying to anticipate upcoming trends, making deviance a potentially valuable commodity.

Some scholars have examined the damage associated with "deviant leisure," including physical injuries to participants, environmental damage, and an emphasis on forms of extreme individualism that weaken social bonds (Raymen and Smith 2016; Smith and Raymen 2018). However, many types of nonconformist behavior are not obviously harmful, even though some people consider them offensive. In some cases—such as sporting a dramatically unconventional hairstyle at school or work—the potential stigma associated with deviance may become a kind of badge of honor, one that people wear proudly to proclaim their independence from stifling forms of convention. It would be a mistake, however, to conclude that the growth of deviance as a leisure activity or commercial product is a sign that social control has weakened substantially. Instead, embracing deviance and transforming nonconformity into a leisure activity are becoming new mechanisms of social control. Considered in this way, deviance-as-leisure is a kind of safety valve, allowing us to blow off steam from the pressure of social conformity without threatening basic social norms. In the age of tell-all reality television, YouTube videos, and near-constant social media sharing, we are fast becoming a society in which both performing and consuming deviance are popular forms of entertainment that may largely reinforce existing norms and social structures.

thinking sociologically about
Deviance

culture

- Cultural norms and beliefs define what society views as normal or deviant. These norms are taught through socialization and vary over time and across cultures.
- In some cases, deviance can result from inadequate or unsuccessful socialization. In such cases, people engaged in deviant behavior have not thoroughly internalized social norms and are not fully regulated by the moral framework of society.
- Because it runs counter to the dominant culture, long-term deviance is likely to require the social support of a deviant subculture, which helps nurture deviant behavior.

structure

- We learn norms and expectations about appropriate behavior through interactions in the small groups that form the basis for social structure. Through their actions, people can either reinforce or challenge norms about deviance.
- Merton's strain theory suggests that barriers posed by social structure can result in deviance when a conflict exists between the dominant goals of a society and legitimate means of achieving these goals. Strain on those who lack the means to achieve culturally defined goals leads them to pursue deviant routes to success.

power

- Often, powerful segments of society can promote and enforce their definition of deviance and effectively label less-powerful people as deviants. Access to power enables some privileged groups to engage in distinct forms of deviant behavior without being branded or punished as deviant.
- Those in society with few resources—money, power, education, or leisure—sometimes engage in deviant behavior in pursuit of these socially valued goods. Those who are stigmatized as deviant often experience isolation or discrimination that can contribute further to social, economic, or political inequalities.
- The criminal justice system, which is designed to prevent crime and apprehend and punish those who commit crimes, serves as a powerful agent of social control. It also reflects imbalances of power in society, since authorities can choose which norms to enforce and which forms of deviance to punish.

REVIEW, REFLECT, AND APPLY

Looking Back

1. Studying deviance, or nonconformist behavior, helps us understand how definitions of "normal" are the product of social processes. Definitions of normal and deviant are context specific. Different communities may respond differently to the same behavior.
2. Labeling theory focuses on the social reaction to nonconformist behavior and suggests that behavior is deviant only when it is so labeled by those in power.

3. Deviance is a feature of all human societies. Sometimes deviance that has been attributed to moral shortcomings is reclassified as a medical problem. Sociologists refer to this change as the *medicalization of deviance.*
4. Deviant subcultures provide an alternative community for people who do not fit in with, or choose not to be a part of, mainstream social groups.
5. One structural source of deviance is conflict between the dominant goals of a society and access to the means of achieving those goals. When legitimate opportunities are blocked, some people will use deviant behaviors to try to achieve these goals.
6. By focusing on body weight, cosmetic surgery, and disability, we can see how the body is a site where definitions of normal are experienced and sometimes contested.
7. Sociological approaches to deviance emphasize the relationship between deviance and social control. Socialization is a form of social control, since we often police ourselves to make sure we are conforming to social expectations. Other agents of social control, including family, school, and religion, articulate and enforce cultural norms and impose consequences for rule breaking.
8. The criminal justice system, designed to prevent crime and punish criminal offenders, is a powerful agent of social control. Sociological perspectives on punishment lead us to examine questions about the goals, forms, and consequences of punishment.
9. New cultural dynamics have made deviance a potentially marketable product. People sometimes practice deviance as a short-term leisure activity. In other cases, advertisers actively seek out deviant subcultures, trying to anticipate upcoming youth-culture trends.

Critical Thinking: Questions and Activities

1. Identify some unspoken rules or norms in your own family or friendship network. How are these rules communicated and enforced? What happens, if anything, when these rules are violated? Try to answer these questions by focusing on one specific rule or norm.
2. What is the relationship between deviance and inequality? How can persistent inequality be a source of nonconformist behavior? Would efforts to alleviate inequality lead to a decline in the frequency of deviant behavior? Why or why not?
3. Think of a specific example of how you police yourself. Make this a mini-research project, and keep a running list of moments when you encourage yourself to conform to social expectations, or when you deviate from these expectations. Looking back at your list, what does it tell you about socialization and social control?
4. Think about the five different rationales for punishment. Now apply these five rationales to the question of capital punishment. Do you believe capital punishment is justifiable? If not, why not? If you believe it is justifiable, which of the five rationales provides the strongest justification?
5. What is your "normal" body weight? Where would you look for a definition of normal body weight? How do we know the difference between normal and abnormal weight? What, if anything, happens to those who violate guidelines for normal weight?

Key Terms

agents of social control (p. 189) the authorities and social institutions that enforce norms and rules, attempt to prevent rule violations, and identify and punish rule violators.
capital punishment (p. 196) the death penalty.
collective conscience (p. 176) the shared norms, beliefs, and values in a community.
control theory (p. 189) a theory that suggests that our behavior is regulated by the strength of our connection to major social institutions, including family, school, and religion.
crime (p. 192) deviant behavior that violates a law.
crime rates (p. 193) statistics that measure the incidence of crime in relation to population size.
decriminalization (p. 193) the process of making an illegal action legal.
deviance (p. 175) behavior that does not conform to basic cultural norms and expectations.
deviant subculture (p. 181) a group in which membership is based on a shared commitment to specific nonconformist beliefs or behaviors.
differential association theory (p. 181) the theory that deviance is learned through interaction with other people involved in deviant behavior.
labeling theory (p. 177) the theory that deviance is the result of how others interpret a behavior and that individuals who are labeled deviant often internalize this judgment as part of their self-identity.
loner deviance (p. 182) the activities of individuals who commit deviant acts without the social support of other participants.
medicalization of deviance (p. 180) the designation of a deviant behavior as an illness that can be treated by medical professionals.
normalization (p. 186) a shift in cultural norms in which previously deviant behaviors become accepted as conventional.
overconformity (p. 186) following cultural expectations to an excessive degree.
positive deviance (p. 186) overconformity that gets a favorable response.
recidivism (p. 196) a return to criminal behavior.
secondary deviance (p. 177) deviant behavior that is a response to the negative consequences of labeling.
social control (p. 189) the incentives and punishments that promote conformity in social life.
stigma (p. 177) the shame attached to a behavior or status that is considered socially unacceptable or discrediting.
strain theory (p. 182) a theory that emphasizes that the strain or pressure on those who lack the means to achieve culturally defined goals leads them to pursue deviant routes to success.
surveillance (p. 189) monitoring by authorities who police the boundaries of what is normal.
white-collar crime (p. 188) crime committed by people of high social status in the course of their occupation.

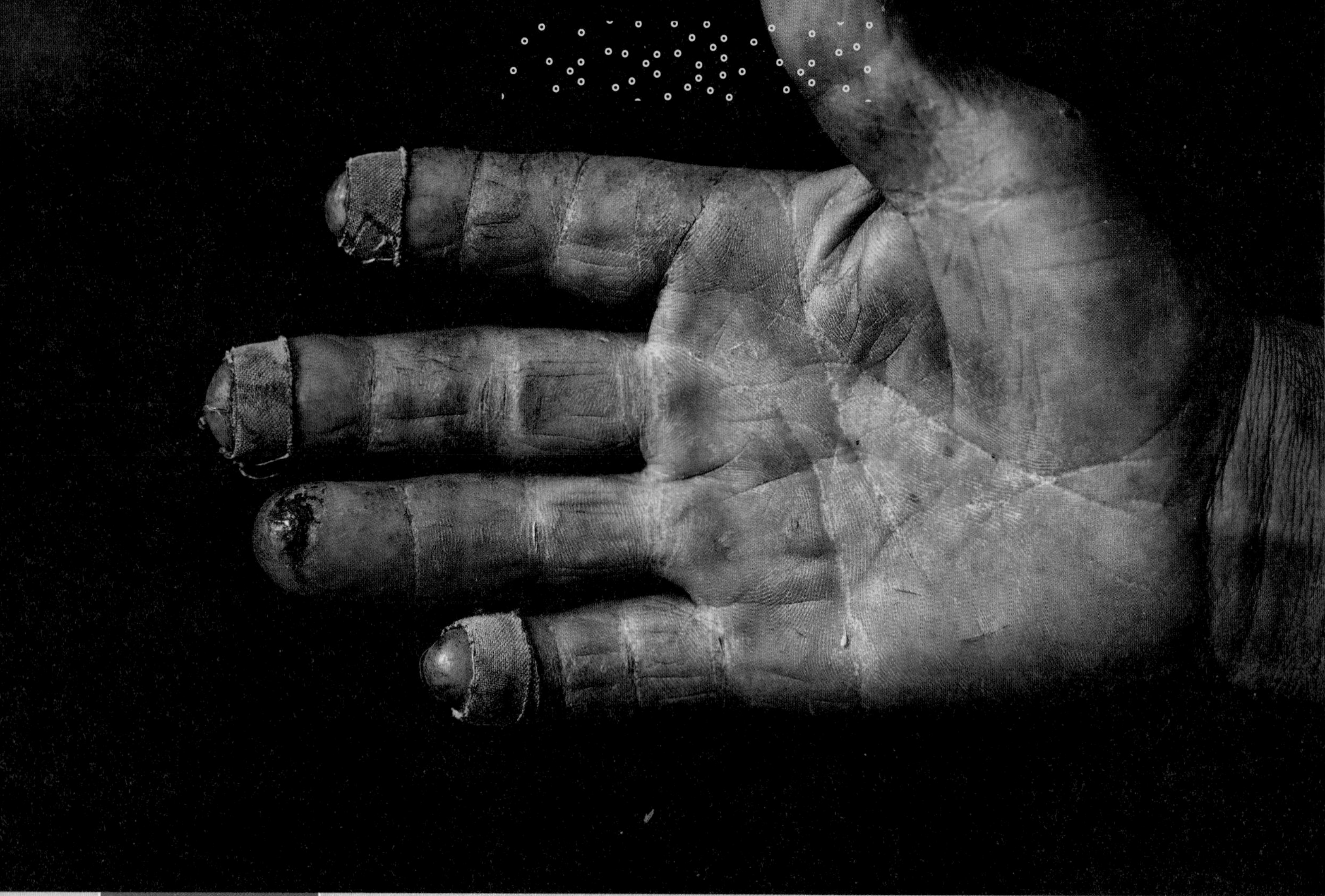

©Reza/Getty Images

9 Class and Global Inequality

looking AHEAD

How has class **structure** shaped your family's experiences?

How does **culture** influence how you experience class?

How does economic inequality affect and reflect the **power** of different players in the global economy?

©David Leahy/Getty Images

Alfred Lubrano grew up in a working-class family in New York. His father, a bricklayer, helped construct some of the buildings at prestigious Columbia University, which, ironically, Lubrano himself attended. As he notes wryly, "My dad has built lots of places in New York City he can't get into" (Lubrano 2004, 7). Lubrano went on to become a successful reporter, thus entering the middle class. In the process, however, he experienced what he calls "the pain of transition."

Lubrano loved the strong work ethic, lack of pretense, hearty humor, strong family ties, sense of loyalty, and forthright manner that characterized his working-class upbringing, but in countless ways, he didn't fit in. Like his male friends, he lifted weights and played in a neighborhood band, but he didn't share their enthusiasm for customizing cars. Unlike his resourceful father, who knew how to stretch every scarce dollar, he had neither the inclination nor the aptitude to fix household appliances. He cared about college, not Camaros; he didn't fix things, he read books.

But he didn't feel at home at Columbia, either. The mostly upper-middle-class students he met were confident, with a sense of entitlement and belonging that comes from shared experience and expectation. Courtesy of affluent parents, they lived on campus, didn't have to work long hours to pay expenses, graduated without debt, and often had family connections that led to career opportunities. Working-class students like Lubrano lived at home to limit expenses, spent hours working as well as studying, racked up heavy debts, and were on their own finding a job.

Fitting into his new middle-class life after school wasn't easy, either. There were little cultural things: eating Brie instead of Kraft slices; playing squash and racquetball instead of bowling; questioning authorities like doctors rather than being awed by their credentials. And there were big things: he learned to pursue a career rather than just get a job. His working-class culture was rooted in solidarity with family, neighborhood, church, and union. It was blunt and direct; you spoke your mind and said what you meant. Middle-class culture, in contrast, values individual achievement and success, which can require a self-promotion that many working-class folks find distasteful. And it involves diplomacy and office politics often pursued on the sly; you bite your tongue and tone down your language.

As a result, Lubrano (2004) writes, "I am two people. . . . With one foot in the working class, the other in the middle class, people like me are Straddlers, at home in neither world, living a limbo life" (1, 8).

Alfred Lubrano's story illustrates the importance of class in shaping who we are and how our society operates. As Lubrano (2004) himself puts it,

> Class is script, map, and guide. It tells us how to talk, how to dress, how to hold ourselves, how to eat, and how to socialize. It affects whom we marry; where we live; the friends we choose, the jobs we have; the vacations we take; the books we read; the movies we see; the restaurants we pick; how we decide to buy houses, carpets, furniture, and cars; where our kids are educated. . . . In short, class is nearly everything about you. And it dictates what to expect out of life and what the future should be. (5)

The way we experience class in our everyday lives (at the micro level) is linked to the social structure that helps perpetuate class inequality (at the macro level). Class, then, is about both personal experience and the broad structures of social inequality. In a global economy, the influence of class and economic inequality encompasses systems that are international in scope. What happens on this world stage can have a dramatic impact on you and your community. For example, new technologies and the export of good-paying manufacturing jobs over the past few decades have meant many more young Americans decided to attend college to improve their chances of getting a good job.

In Chapter 5, we examined the concept of power and its connection to inequality in society. We considered various forms of stratification and how race, class, and gender intersect to shape people's experience of inequality. In this chapter, we take a closer look at one form of inequality—class—in the United States and consider the broader context of global inequality.

Large steel-making equipment dwarfs the workers tending it. With the rise of industrialism, capital—needed to finance large manufacturing facilities like this one—became the key economic resource, giving industrial capitalism its name.

Understanding Class

In Chapter 5, we defined a **class** as *a group of people who share a roughly similar economic position and lifestyle.* Most of us have at least an intuitive understanding of class inequality. We know that being rich or poor shapes a person's life experiences in important ways. The streets of any major U.S. city include both the luxury automobiles of the wealthy and the shopping carts of the homeless. Your community likely has clubs, institutions, and businesses that are stratified by the class of the people who frequent them—everything from exclusive country clubs, fashionable shops, expensive gourmet restaurants, and private schools to bowling alleys, discount superstores, fast-food restaurants, and pawn shops.

Class permeates our popular language. Terms such as "middle class," "blue collar," and "professional" pepper our speech. Many of these terms have their roots in the sociological analysis of class and inequality. That analysis began with the efforts of Karl Marx and Max Weber in the late 1800s and early 1900s to understand the growing inequality and wrenching social changes that accompanied the rise of industrial capitalism. Their ideas, along with those of later sociologists, have given us insight into how class operates.

Marx's Analysis of Class

Karl Marx ([1867] 1976) based his analysis of class on the idea that if people are to survive, they must meet their basic material needs for food, clothing, and shelter. A society's *economy* is the system by which it meets these and other needs. How an economy is organized affects all other aspects of social life, Marx argued. For example, as we saw in Chapter 1, industrialization drove urbanization, changing where people lived as well as how they earned a living and organized their families.

Marx noted that through most of their history, humans lived in nomadic egalitarian societies and fed themselves by foraging for edible wild plants and by hunting. Because these societies produced few surplus goods, they had little economic inequality. However, the emergence of farming about 10,000 years ago enabled societies to live in permanent settlements, develop food surpluses, and accumulate material goods. As wealth increased, inequality also increased. Ever since then, the fundamental economic pattern has been the same: a division between those who own the means of production—the key resources in a particular economy—and those who do not. Marx argued that these groups constitute a society's two major classes, and the dynamics between them account for economic inequality.

In agricultural economies, for example, where land is the key resource, the central class division is between landowners and commoners such as peasants, serfs, and sharecroppers, who work the land but do not own it. In industrial economies, the key resource is **capital**—*the money to invest in factories, real estate, and other businesses.* In capitalism the basic division is between the **capitalist class** (or *bourgeoisie*), *those who control major capital and own the means of production,* and the **working class** (or *proletariat*), *those who survive on the wages they earn.*

Marx argued that because of their differing interests, the major classes are inevitably in conflict and that this class conflict has been the engine that has driven much of human history. Under capitalism, workers try to maximize their pay and benefits (often by forming labor unions), while owners try to maximize their profits by minimizing the costs of doing business, including labor costs. Thus the working class and the capitalists are locked in an eternal conflict that is part of the very structure of the capitalist system.

Furthermore, capitalists exploit workers, paying them less than the real value of their labor. The gap between what workers are paid and the value they bring is one of the sources of profits for owners. Eventually, according to Marx, this exploitation would result in an economic crisis, an unsustainable gap between rich and poor, and workers would unite to overthrow the capitalist system. The result, according to Marx, would be *socialism,* an economic arrangement in which the state owns the major means of production on behalf of the workers, thereby abolishing class distinctions based on the ownership of major property. So, for example, in a socialist country major enterprises such as education, health care, energy production, mass transportation, and telecommunications might be owned and operated by the government as public goods rather than being privately owned and operated for profit.

Marx was aware of other classes, but he did not see them playing a central role in capitalist systems. Small-business owners, for example, whom Marx called the *petite bourgeoisie,* neither generate profit primarily from other people's labor nor earn wages in somebody else's enterprise. Marx argued that over time the large capitalists would swallow up small-business owners. An example today would be local merchants who go bankrupt in the face of competition from big-box chains like Walmart and Home Depot.

As capitalism evolved, scholars adjusted Marx's theories to account for new developments, especially the rising importance of the middle class (Dahrendorf 1959; Walker 1979; Wright 1985). The major companies in Marx's day were not big by today's standards and were owned by families or small groups of capitalists who often played a direct role in running them. In contrast, today's corporations are massive, often global, and owned by tens of thousands of different people and institutions, none of which has direct control over a given company. Instead, authority in the workplace is in the hands of highly paid executives and managers who are part of the upper middle class but who usually do not own a significant part of the company. As a result, when analyzing class, some scholars focus on the role of authority rather than ownership in the workplace.

Weber's "Life Chances"

Max Weber ([1922] 1978), working a generation after Marx, differed from Marx in the way he conceptualized class. Whereas Marx saw class in terms of the organization of work and the struggle between owners and laborers, Weber looked at class from the perspective of **life chances,** *the likelihood a person has of obtaining valued economic and cultural resources.* Essentially, for Weber, a class is a group of people who share a common market situation—that is, they have a similar capacity to earn money and they pursue a similar lifestyle.

Weber's approach to class solves a problem with Marx's analysis. For Marx, a member of the working class is essentially anyone who earns a wage in a workplace that he or she does not own. By that definition, a corporate lawyer who earns $200,000 per year and a minimum-wage fast-food worker earning just over $15,000 per year are both members of the working class. Yet the life of a high-paid professional and that of a low-paid service worker are fundamentally different.

Weber's focus on life chances allowed him to highlight the importance of a middle class. The members of this class are primarily wage earners but are not capitalists (owners). Their formal education and training, however, provide them with a scarce resource that improves their life chances and thereby enables them to attain a higher standard of living than most members of the working class. In addition, people in the middle class and those in the working class often differ in everything from the leisure activities they enjoy to their preferences in music and food. In effect, different classes have different cultures.

More broadly, unlike Marx, Weber did not focus exclusively on class inequality and the economy. Instead, as discussed in Chapter 5, Weber emphasized the interaction of three dimensions of inequality: class, social status, and political power. The members of a group may have power because of their economic resources (class), but their power may also derive from their

©Photo12/UIG/Getty Images

©Kim Jae-Hwan/AFP/Getty Images

Through the late nineteenth and early twentieth centuries, labor struggles in the United States were more violent than in any other industrialized country, with hundreds killed and thousands injured in labor disputes. (The photo on the left is from a 1934 truck drivers' strike in Minneapolis, Minnesota, that expanded into a general strike. Truckers armed with pipes fought police in the streets.) Today, such violent clashes with police and military troops are more likely to occur in developing countries, where workers struggle for better wages and working conditions. (The photo on the right shows a 2003 clash between union members and the police in South Korea.)

CORE CONCEPTS CHALLENGE *What does the often-violent history of labor relations reveal about* **power** *in society?*

©Dan Dalton/Getty Images

To order a bottle of fine wine from a sommelier in a gourmet restaurant, a diner not only needs to be able to afford the wine, which can easily cost over $100 a bottle, but also must have some knowledge of grape vintages, the varieties of international cuisine that the wine might accompany, and perhaps even the foreign languages in which the names of wines and their labels are written. All of these reflect cultural aspects of class distinctions.

CORE CONCEPTS CHALLENGE *What other common social interactions reflect aspects of class* ***culture****?*

social status—as was the case in the power of whites over blacks in the segregated U.S. South—or from organized political efforts—as with the rise of the civil rights movement for racial equality. Thus, Weber's analysis of class is part of a wider multidimensional analysis of social inequality.

Is Class Stratification Functional?

For Marx and Weber, class inequality was intertwined with struggles for power in society. In contrast, American functionalists in the mid-twentieth century analyzed economic inequality in terms of the positive good it contributes to society as a whole (Alexander 1985; Merton 1968c). In this view, as expressed in a classic article by Kingsley Davis and Wilbert Moore (1945), economic stratification helps ensure "that the most important positions are conscientiously filled by the most qualified persons."

To Weber and Marx, class competition produces winners and losers, in part based on how much power each competitor has. In contrast, to functionalists, free competition among individuals for lucrative positions produces a win-win benefit for society. Functionalists argue that for society to survive, well-qualified people must fill important positions. These positions tend to require higher levels of training and often scarce talent. The higher rewards associated with these positions motivate people to train and compete to fill them. Who would undergo the expense and years of education and training required to become a doctor, for example, if a career in medicine provided no greater rewards than a job that required only a high school education? Instead of conflicting classes, then, functionalists see a continuum of occupations offering a variety of rewards and contributing to the survival and smooth functioning of society.

Critics of the functionalist perspective, however, point out that the real world doesn't operate this way (Tumin 1953). Instead, preexisting inequality affects how competitive a person can be, and barriers to mobility often prevent deserving individuals from advancing. In any society that produces more material goods than are necessary for basic survival, conflict inevitably emerges over how to distribute that surplus (Lenski 1966). Those who win the conflict can consolidate their power, alter a society's rules and laws, and pass on their advantages to their children. Critics argue that the functionalist analysis fails to account for this kind of enduring inequality and instead rationalizes and legitimizes existing inequality. Indeed, in the mid-twentieth century, when functionalists were formulating their approach to stratification, many social groups, including women and African Americans, were effectively barred from competing for society's best-rewarded positions.

Another problem with the functionalist approach to stratification is that it fails to define what is meant by "the most important positions." Who decides what they are? A top movie star can command tens of millions of dollars for a single film, while a teacher may earn a modest salary. Which job is more "important" to society?

Although functionalism proved to be an inadequate explanation of class inequality, it did describe some of the important dynamics of the labor market. Some of its ideas are still popular and, as we will see, are used in promoting education as a means of improving individual life chances.

Class Inequality in the United States

In the United States, the fortunes of the super-rich and everyone else often seem to be diverging. When a selfie just will not do, executives in San Francisco's high-tech Silicon Valley turn to photographer Kevin Abosch to take a portrait photo that costs them between $150,000 and $500,000 (Shontell 2016). Meanwhile, just outside the executive suites, one of seven children in the San Francisco Bay Area lives in poverty, a situation the mayor of nearby San Jose called "the moral shame of our community" (Silicon Valley Institute for Regional Studies 2015; Sutter 2015). Or consider the fate of Jamie Dimon, CEO of the nation's largest bank, JPMorgan Chase. When he helped boost profits at his company by eliminating more than 6,700 jobs in one year, he was rewarded with a 35 percent raise that lifted his compensation package to a comfortable $27 million a year—or about $74,000 a day (Whitehouse 2016). You do not need to follow the Rich Kids of Instagram or watch *Secret Lives of the Super Rich* to know that the United States is characterized by this sort of class inequality.

As we explored in Chapter 5, all stratification systems are characterized by three key elements:

1. The unequal distribution of valuable resources
2. Distinctive groups that make up the various strata in society
3. An ideology, or system of beliefs, that explains and justifies the existence of inequality

Class systems comprise all three of these key elements.

Mapping the Major Classes

The class structure of the United States can be described in various ways (Beeghley 2016; Gilbert 2015; Kerbo 2011; Marger 2014; Zweig 2011), and the data issues involved in making income and wealth estimates are complex (Piketty, Saez, and Zucman 2018). The four-class model used here (see Table 9.1) combines Weber's recognition of people's market situation with Marx's emphasis on the importance of ownership and control. In this model, each class is identified by the primary asset that it controls and contributes to the economy. Of course, the lines between classes are not hard and fast; people move up and down between them, and the characteristics of individual members in each class can vary considerably. Nonetheless, the broadly defined class distinctions illustrated in Figure 9.1 and summarized in Table 9.1 can give us insight into the dynamics of inequality in American society.

The Capitalist Class: Investments and Inherited Wealth **Wealth** refers to *the value of financial assets such as savings, real estate, stocks, and bonds, minus any outstanding debts.* **Income** is *money received from sources such as wages and salaries as well as from the interest, dividends, and rent generated by wealth.* Most people derive their income primarily from wages and salaries. In contrast, the defining characteristic of the *capitalist class* (or "upper" class) is that its members often generate income primarily through their wealth rather than through employment.

Some wealthy people have jobs that pay high salaries and bonuses, but generally speaking, the richer people are, the smaller the percentage of their income that comes from employment. Instead, businesses they own generate income for them, stocks produce dividends (profits distributed to shareholders), and real estate yields rental income. For some, management of these investments is their only "job," whereas others hire advisors to

TABLE 9.1 MAJOR U.S. SOCIAL CLASSES

	Major Economic Asset	Occupations	Education	Annual Income Level	Wealth
Capitalist (or Upper) Class	Investment capital	The wealthiest often do not work at a job. Some oversee the management of their investments. Some are top corporate executives.	Often college educated, but not necessarily, especially when wealth is inherited.	Top 1 percent of household income (about $443,000 or more). Higher end makes many times more.	Wealth is central. Major holdings in stocks, bonds, real estate, and other investments.
Middle Class Upper ("professional") middle class Lower middle class	Knowledge, expertise	Professionals: engineers, scientists, lawyers, doctors, etc. Other occupations requiring a college degree, such as schoolteacher.	College education is essential to success in this class.	55th–99th percentile (about $66,000–$443,000).	Ranges from limited assets such as a small home and savings to an expensive home, significant savings, and stock and other investments.
Working Class (including the working poor)	Skilled and unskilled labor, including service work	Wide variety, including office workers, factory workers, salesclerks, home health aides, customer service reps, etc.	High school diploma is the norm; technical school common; some college possible—especially when vocationally oriented.	10th–55th percentile (about $13,500–$66,000).	Usually little or no wealth; home is key investment; often in debt.
Underclass (or Lower Class)	None—chronically unemployed	Typically none; sometimes informal economy; public assistance.	Less than a high school diploma is common.	Bottom 9 percent or less (less than $13,500).	No assets; often in debt.

Sources: Estimate for income of top 1 percent is based on Saez 2016. Other income ranges are authors' estimates based on 2017 Current Population Survey household income data, retrieved from https://www.census.gov/data/tables/time-series/demo/income-poverty/cps-hinc.html.

FIGURE 9.1 | A MODEL OF THE U.S. CLASS SYSTEM

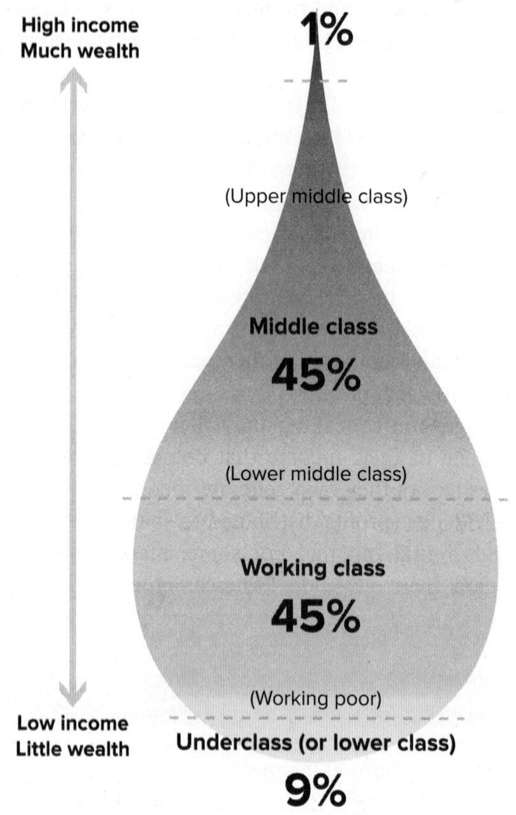

The bulk of the U.S. population is about evenly divided between the middle and the working classes. However, a broader range of incomes is found among the middle class, contributing to the elongated shape of this model. The highest incomes in the capitalist class extend far beyond what can be represented here.

manage their wealth and live a life of leisure. The number of families in the United States that are true capitalists is small, perhaps as little as 1 percent of all households. These families have average incomes of about $1.3 million a year—a few make hundreds of millions—and possess enormous wealth (Alvaredo et al. 2018).

Unlike income, wealth accumulates over time and can be passed on from generation to generation. As a result, the concentration of wealth in the United States is much greater than the concentration of income (as we will see), and much of the wealth of the upper class is inherited. In the 2018 *Forbes* magazine list of the nation's wealthiest people, three of the richest Americans (who are also among the 20 wealthiest people on the planet) were siblings who inherited their money from their father—Walmart founder Sam Walton. Each was worth over $46 billion. Your best chance of being part of this class is to be born into it.

The Middle Class: Pursuing the Benefits of Education

The **middle class** is *a group that contributes specialized knowledge and expertise to the economy.* To members of the middle class, education and training—usually obtained at college and professional schools—are essential resources. Encompassing roughly 45 percent of the population, the middle class is often subdivided informally into the upper middle class and the lower middle class. Those at the higher end have powerful jobs—often with considerable autonomy—that generate large salaries. Unlike capitalists, members of the upper middle class rely primarily on their salaries for their income, though they may also accumulate stocks and other investments and own expensive homes. Most lawyers, doctors, scientists, engineers, and other professionals fall into this category, as do most business executives.

Lower-middle-class occupations, such as schoolteacher, low-level manager, and social worker, generally offer lower income, fewer benefits, and less autonomy than upper-middle-class jobs. Members of the lower middle class may own their homes and have modest personal savings or retirement accounts but little else. Some lower-middle-class workers—such as teachers and government employees—are heavily unionized, which can help them improve their pay, benefits, and working conditions.

Although upper-class families can ensure their children's financial success by handing down wealth, education cannot be inherited; each generation must learn anew. As a result, middle-class parents are often especially concerned about obtaining the best education for their children so that they can maintain or improve upon their middle-class status.

The Working Class: Labor and Service

Like the middle class, the working class is broad and diverse, encompassing roughly 45 percent of the population. Whereas members of the middle class are generally engaged in knowledge work and earn a weekly or annual salary, members of the *working class* usually make a product or provide a service and earn hourly wages. The income range for the working class is considerably narrower than the range for the middle class.

All working-class jobs require some skill and knowledge (Rose 2004). However, these jobs can be placed on a continuum, with well-paid skilled trade workers such as mechanics, electricians, and technicians at one end and low-paid, relatively unskilled workers such as home health aides, garment workers, and food service employees at the other end. Skilled trade workers generally need specialized knowledge, but they also work with their hands. Some belong to trade unions that help them get better wages and benefits than their nonunion counterparts. Unskilled workers may be able to find only part-time or seasonal employment and—even if they work full time—earn low wages that may not keep a family above the poverty line. These working poor include farmworkers, hotel housekeeping staff, home health aides, garment workers, and food service employees. Union members in these occupations tend to enjoy modestly better wages and benefits than their nonunion counterparts, but they still struggle financially.

Historically the term "working class" has evoked images of blue-collar workers in factories and building construction. Although manufacturing jobs are still important, today working-class jobs in the United States—such as day care provider, food service worker, customer service representative, and retail salesclerk—are increasingly service oriented. Because members of the working class generally earn relatively modest paychecks, working-class families typically have only some savings, and they may own a modest home. Many families have no assets at all, living paycheck to paycheck or struggling with persistent debt.

The Underclass: Chronic Unemployment

Sociologists often use the term **underclass** (or *lower class*) to refer to *chronically unemployed people who have no ongoing relationship to the mainstream economy*. Members of the underclass include those only sporadically and briefly employed, those dependent on long-term public assistance, and those who earn money from the informal economy (off-the-books transactions that are not taxed or monitored by the government and can include everything from child care services and auto repair to begging and drug dealing). A variety of factors can prevent members of the underclass from finding or retaining regular employment. Their employer may have closed, they may have family responsibilities that prevent them from working, they may lack the skills and education for jobs that are available, or they may have physical disabilities or suffer from mental illnesses or substance abuse. Because they are either unable or unwilling to participate regularly in the mainstream economy, the members of this group typically live in poverty.

Income and Wealth Inequality

The differences among classes reflect substantial inequality in the distribution of income and wealth in the United States.

Income and wealth levels are usually measured by household rather than individual, because counting the income of multiple wage earners and the collective wealth of a household more accurately reflects people's standard of living. In Figure 9.2, the first pie chart divides U.S. households into five groups (known as *quintiles*), each of which makes up 20 percent of the population. The income pie chart shows the disproportionate distribution of income among these groups, with the highest-earning 20 percent of American households in 2016 receiving 51.5 percent of all household income. In contrast, households in the bottom 20 percent received only 3.1 percent of all income—barely visible on the chart. Income inequality is actually greater than suggested here, because the Census Bureau figures on which this graph is based do not include *capital gains* (money earned from stock and other investments), most of which flow to the richest households.

The wealth pie chart illustrates *net worth* (the value of assets minus debt) and shows that wealth is even more unequally distributed than income. The wealthiest 20 percent of households, with an average net worth of just under $3 million in 2016, owns 89.8 percent of the nation's total wealth. The bottom 20 percent has a negative net worth—these households are in debt and therefore are not shown on the wealth bar.

Both income and wealth in the top quintile are skewed toward the very top. The top 5 percent of households has 22.5 percent of income and 66.7 percent of wealth. In fact, 39.6 percent of all wealth is owned by just the top 1 percent of households (Wolff 2017). So many people have little or no wealth, and existing wealth is so heavily concentrated that the three wealthiest *individuals* in the United States—Bill Gates, Jeff Bezos, and Warren Buffett—have more wealth than the bottom half of the U.S. population—some 160 million people in 63 million households (Collins and Hoxie 2017).

Both income and wealth inequality in the United States have grown significantly. (The Through a Sociological Lens box examines growing income inequality among African Americans.) Using 2016 dollars (adjusted for inflation), Figure 9.3 shows that the average household income for most quintiles has remained stagnant, while the top quintile—especially the top 5 percent—has seen major increases, resulting in a much larger gap between those at the top and the rest of society. In 2016, the average household income for the top 5 percent of households was $375,088, the middle quintile was $59,149, and the bottom quintile was $12,943.

Class Mobility and Class Barriers

Because hierarchical class systems have fewer positions at the top, relatively few people can move up to the highest positions, regardless of talent, dedication, and hard work. As sociologist Jay MacLeod (2009) puts it, "Our society is *structured* to create

FIGURE 9.2 | THE DISTRIBUTION OF U.S. HOUSEHOLD INCOME AND WEALTH (BY QUINTILES)

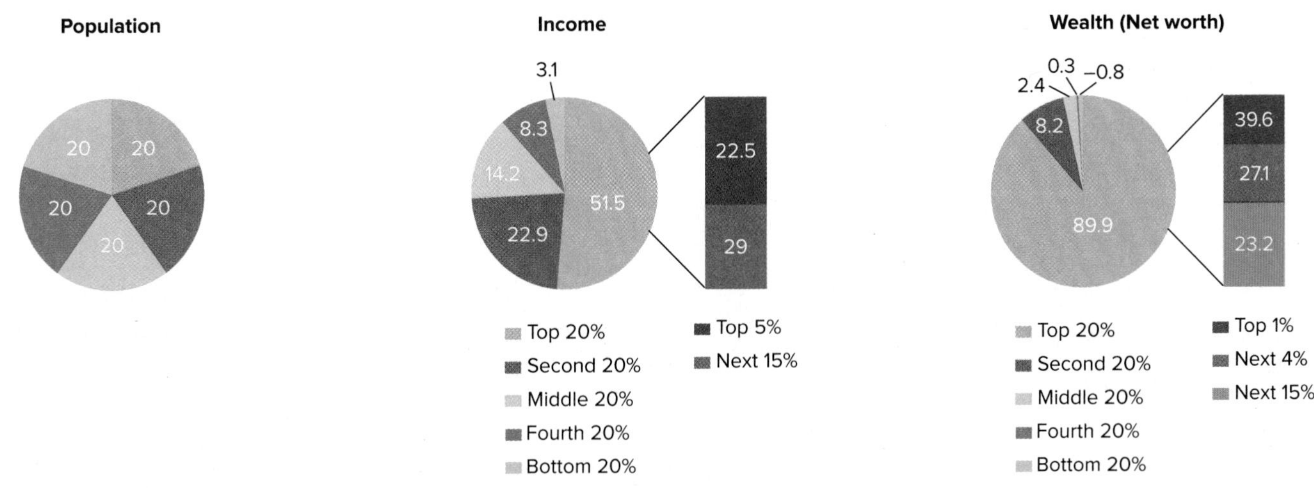

Both income and wealth are distributed unevenly in the United States. The top 20 percent of households receive over half of all income. Wealth is distributed far more unequally; nearly 40 percent of all wealth is owned by just the top 1 percent of households.
Sources: U.S. Census Bureau 2017b; Wolff 2017.

FIGURE 9.3 | AVERAGE U.S. HOUSEHOLD INCOME, 1967–2016 (BY QUINTILES AND TOP 5%)

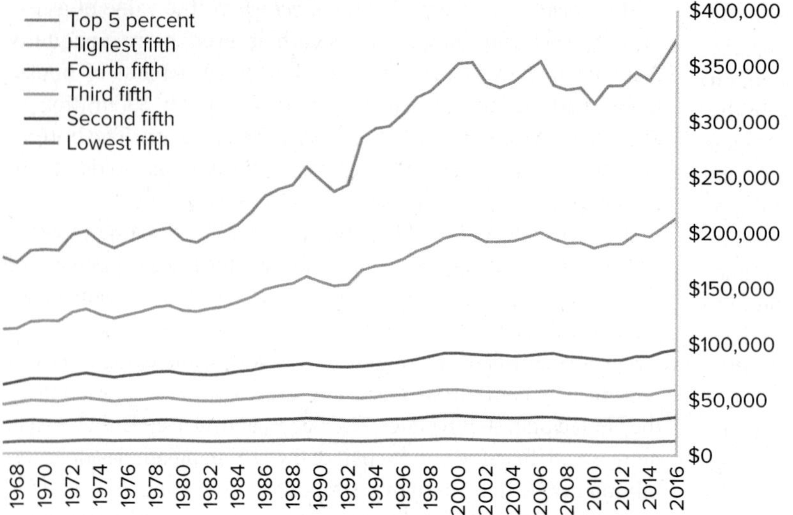

U.S. income inequality has been growing significantly in the last half century. Numbers are in constant 2016 dollars. *Source:* U.S. Census Bureau 2017c.

poverty and extreme economic inequality. . . . This roughly pyramidal structure ensures that even if everyone excels in school and strives ceaselessly for the top, the great majority are automatically bound to be disappointed" (241). Class structure, then, ultimately limits upward mobility and ensures inequality.

Still, class systems are less rigid than caste or feudal systems (see Chapter 5). In a caste system, the caste into which people are born almost completely determines their life chances. In contrast, class systems permit some **class mobility,** *the ability to move from one social class to another.* There are two general types of class mobility: structural and individual. **Structural mobility** occurs because *a shift in available occupations changes the class system as a whole.* For example, in the past several decades the number of relatively high-paying manufacturing jobs has declined, forcing people to find other types of work (Scott 2015). Since the fastest-growing occupations have been those with low wages (see Table 9.2), many people experienced downward mobility. Workers laid off from an automobile factory that provided good wages and benefits, for example, might have found themselves facing long-term unemployment or working instead at big-box stores or fast-food restaurants for much less (Chen 2015).

Individual mobility occurs *when a person's class position changes without any change in the larger class structure.* Alfred Lubrano's entry into the middle class, discussed in the chapter opener, is an example of this sort of mobility. Despite the popularity of rags-to-riches stories, however, most children end up with income levels similar to those of their parents (see Table 9.3).

TABLE 9.2 TEN OCCUPATIONS WITH THE LARGEST PROJECTED JOB GROWTH, 2016–2026

	Change, 2016–2026		Median Annual Wage, 2016
	Number	**Percent**	
Total, all occupations	*11,518,600*	*7.4*	*$37,040*
Personal care aides	777,600	38.6	$21,920
Combined food preparation and serving workers, including fast food	579,900	16.8	$19,440
Registered nurses	438,100	14.8	$68,450
Home health aides	431,200	47.3	$22,600
Software developers, applications	255,400	30.7	$100,080
Janitors and cleaners, except maids and housekeeping cleaners	236,500	9.9	$24,190
General and operations managers	205,200	9.1	$99,310
Laborers and freight, stock, and material movers, hand	199,700	7.6	$25,980
Medical assistants	183,900	29.0	$31,540
Waiters and waitresses	182,500	7.0	$19,990

Seven of the 10 occupations that the U.S. Labor Department projects to grow the most between 2016 and 2026 have median annual wages below the overall average of $37,040. What might these data suggest for the future of economic inequality in the United States?

Source: U.S. Bureau of Labor Statistics 2018a.

THROUGH A SOCIOLOGICAL LENS

Examining the Intersection of Race and Class: Growing Income Inequality among African Americans

In 1903, sociologist W. E. B. Du Bois ([1903] 2005) famously wrote, "The problem of the twentieth century is the problem of the color-line" (vii). In the ensuing years, activists targeted segregation and the legal barriers that prevented African Americans from participating fully in social, economic, and political life. By the latter half of the twentieth century, the strict color line that Du Bois had written about was crumbling, but deeply entrenched class divisions remained.

This shift is embodied in the career of Martin Luther King Jr. During the often-overlooked last five years of his life, King focused less on racial injustice and more on what he saw as the new social divide in the United States that cut across all races: class. As sociologist Michael Eric Dyson (2000) puts it, "King sensed the raging of a more powerful force than he had confronted in all the years of his civil rights struggles: structural economic inequality. . . . King saw that in the struggle to free Northern blacks, race mattered, but class mattered more" (82–83).

By 1980, sociologist William Julius Wilson confirmed that the life chances of individual blacks now were influenced more by their class position than by their interaction with whites. Race was still significant, Wilson (1980) argued, but "in the economic sphere, class has become more important than race in determining black access to privilege and power" (2). Because of class divisions within the black community, he argued, black people no longer share a uniform experience. A more complex social reality has replaced Du Bois's idea of a single "color line," requiring sociologists to examine the interaction of race and class.

Race continues to contribute to social inequality. For example, median family income for whites in the United States is nearly 40 percent higher than it is for blacks—$65,041 for whites; $39,490 for blacks (U.S. Census Bureau 2017b). However, income disparities among black households have grown significantly. As racial barriers fall and new opportunities arise, growing black middle and upper middle classes have emerged. In adjusted 2016 dollars the number of black households making at least $75,000 has more than tripled since 1967 (7.6 to 24.4 percent), while the percentage making $100,000 or more has nearly quintupled (3 to 14.9 percent). Meanwhile, the percentage living on $15,000 or less has declined much less (28.7 to 20.6 percent) (U.S. Census Bureau 2017b). The result is a growing class gap among African Americans.

Historian Henry Louis Gates Jr. argues that the "class divide" in the black community is "one of the most important and overlooked factors in the rise of Black Lives Matter" (Gates 2016). He observes that "today's black activists are the children of middle- and upper-middle-class parents" and their activism is, in part, motivated by the vast gulf they see between the college campuses they inhabit and the poor black communities where police violence, chronic unemployment, and poverty are so firmly entrenched. Gates suggests that these activists may turn out to be the grandchildren of what Du Bois once termed the "talented tenth"—the percentage of African Americans who would provide "college-trained" and "intelligent leadership" to understand and address the problems of the black community.

think about it

1. *How does increasing income disparity among African Americans illustrate why it is useful to consider the intersection of different types of inequality when examining a person's life chances?*
2. *Growing class differences among African Americans have been accompanied by growing cultural differences. How would you explain this relationship between social structure and culture?*

The best way to ensure economic success is to choose your parents wisely. Individual decisions, actions, effort, and ability are not irrelevant, but they always exist within a structural context that shapes the options available. This interplay between individual action and social structure, of course, is precisely the focus of sociological study.

The Impact of Class Inequality on Social Life

Class has a concrete impact on daily life. People who share a common class position often share conditions and experiences, such as their state of health, the quality of their education, the type of work they do, their level of political participation, and their lifestyle.

Health The impact of class on health lasts a lifetime (Chandola, Brunner, and Marmot 2006; Council on Community Pediatrics 2016; National Center for Health Statistics 2016). Compared to the poor, wealthier people in the United States eat better, enjoy better health care, experience less stress, and reside in safer neighborhoods. As a result, American men with the top 1 percent in income live 15 years longer than the poorest 1 percent of men; for women, the gap is 10 years. This gap has been growing in

thinking about structure

How have the structural conditions into which you were born helped shape your life options? How have your own choices and actions been influenced by these options?

TABLE 9.3 MOBILITY AND FAMILY INCOME

Parents' Family Income	Child's Family Income				
	Top 20%	Second 20%	Middle 20%	Fourth 20%	Bottom 20%
Top 20%	33.10	27.70	18.70	12.70	7.80
Second 20%	24.10	24.00	21.60	17.70	12.60
Middle 20%	17.70	19.60	21.90	21.80	18.90
Fourth 20%	13.50	16.10	20.70	24.10	25.60
Bottom 20%	11.70	12.60	17.00	23.70	35.10

Class systems allow for some mobility. However, parents' income level is strongly correlated with the eventual income level of their children—especially at the top and bottom of the income hierarchy. For example, children whose parents' income was in the top 20 percent of families are more than four times as likely to end up in the top 20 percent themselves as they are to be in the bottom 20 percent (33.1 percent versus 7.8 percent). *Source:* Saez et al. 2014.

CORE CONCEPTS CHALLENGE *Most of us would like to think that where we end up in life is the result of our own effort and ability. But the table suggests that social* **structure** *is a major influence as well. What factors might be contributing to the patterns shown in this table? What does the table suggest about the extent of intergenerational mobility?*

recent decades (Chetty et al. 2016). The more education and income you have, the less likely you are to develop–or die from–heart disease, diabetes, strokes, and many forms of cancer.

Your health is partly a result of your individual behavior, but your behavior is also influenced by the structural aspects of class. For example, people with lower incomes are less likely to learn about and adopt healthy eating habits, in part because they are less likely to live near grocery stores that offer fresh fruits and vegetables. Poor and working-class people are also more likely to have highly stressful and insecure jobs over which they have little or no control. Work stress is a major contributing factor to physical illness, including heart disease and diabetes, and also to mental illness, such as depression. People in higher-paying jobs with a great deal of responsibility may also experience considerable stress, but they generally have more personal control over their work and are more likely to have access to high-quality health care.

Education Education is part of what determines your class, but the class into which you are born affects the type of education you are likely to receive. Nobel Prize–winning economist Joseph Stiglitz put it succinctly: "Access to good education depends increasingly on the income, education and wealth of one's parents" (in Marginson 2016).

The class gap in education begins with the way public schools in the United States are funded (Baker, Sciarra, and Farrie 2015; Kozol 2005). Because school funding is based largely on local property taxes, schools in affluent communities are likely to be better funded than those in poorer communities and better able to provide children with early educational advantages. Increased income segregation in housing has been driven almost entirely by families with children seeking to live in high-income areas with strong school districts (Owens 2016). Affluent families are also better able to afford advantages outside the public school system, including private schools, tutors, and test-preparation courses. Affluent parents can provide expensive tutoring to help their children prepare for SAT and other standardized tests as well as to ensure their children get A's in regular high school courses. The class bias in such a system has been one reason more colleges have been dropping the SAT as a requirement (Schworm 2015).

The class into which you are born also influences whether you pursue higher education and, if you do, what type of college you are likely to attend. The more affluent your family, the more likely it is that you will go to college (Figure 9.4). Obviously, a major barrier to attendance is cost. In recent years, college has become less affordable for many middle- and low-income families. State cuts in higher-education funding have contributed to steeper tuition costs at public universities that have not been offset by increased financial aid; consequently, some students are priced out, and those who do attend face greater debt when they graduate (Goldrick-Rab 2016; Institute for Research on Higher Education 2016).

The fact that the cost of selective private universities can exceed $50,000 a year puts them far out of reach for most students and discourages those with modest means from applying. Even when such schools offer substantial financial assistance, their admissions processes favor better-prepared students who have had the early educational advantages that a higher-class position offers. Furthermore, in what is sometimes called "affirmative action for the rich" (Kahlenberg 2010), elite schools often give preference to legacy admissions–children of alumni–that increase the chance of admission for children of alumni over others by more than 20 percent, thereby helping perpetuate class inequality across generations (Espenshade, Chung, and Walling 2004; Hurwitz 2011). Chetty et al. (2017) found that "children whose parents are in the top 1% of the income distribution are 77 times more likely to attend an Ivy League college than those whose parents are in the bottom income quintile" (1).

Less selective schools are more accessible to those of more modest means, often because of both a lower price tag and looser admissions standards, although students from more affluent families are still overrepresented at these schools. The most diverse schools are two-year community colleges, which come the closest to drawing evenly from across class categories. These schools typically have open enrollment and lower costs. They serve students looking for a two-year degree, students planning on transferring to four-year institutions, and working adults looking to improve their job skills. Many community college students are adults who live at home and work full or part time while they commute to campus. Their college experience differs from that of students at a four-year residential college, an essential life experience for most people in the upper middle class (Leondar-Wright

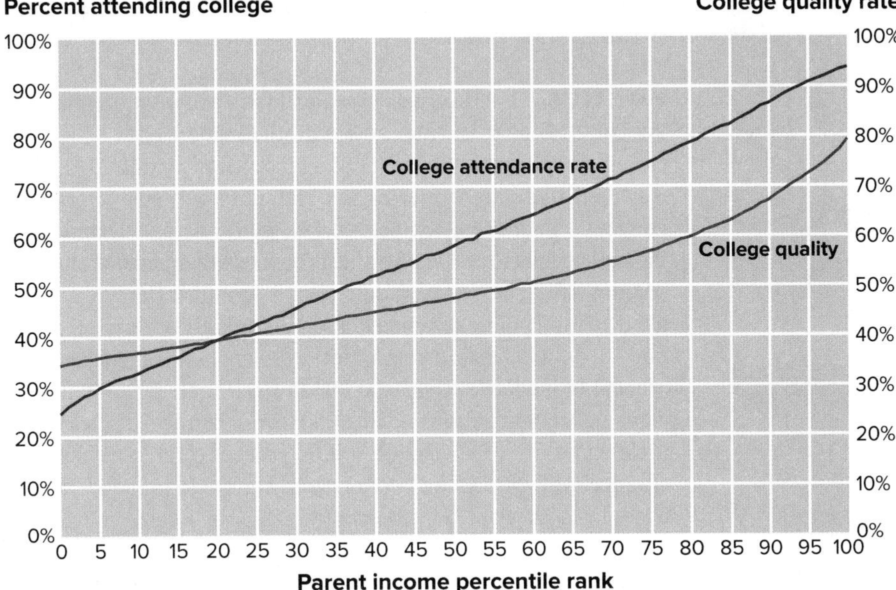

FIGURE 9.4 | COLLEGE ATTENDANCE RATE AND COLLEGE QUALITY BY PARENTS' INCOME

The higher parents' income, the more likely their children will go to college and the more likely they are to attend high-quality colleges. As the figure shows, about 24 percent of children of parents in the lowest income percentile ever attended college between ages 18 and 21, while 94 percent of children of parents in the highest income percentile did so. Parents' income was also strongly correlated with higher college quality (ranked based on the later earnings of those who attended).

Source: Adapted from data tables "Share of kids in parent bin ever attending college during age 18–21" and "College quality rank based on mean earnings at age 31 of children that attended the same college and were born in 1979–80," found at The Equality of Opportunity Project, www.equality-of-opportunity.org/index.php/data.

2005). In recent years, a growing number of for-profit private education companies such as the University of Phoenix have tailored college degrees to the needs of working adults by emphasizing flexible online classes that focus on job skills. Some of these schools have generated controversy, however, for being exceptionally expensive, failing to deliver marketable skills, and engaging in unethical recruitment practices. Too often, students never finish such schools, and they are left with considerable debt but with no degree or employable skills (Angulo 2016; McMillan Cottom 2016; Mettler 2014).

Beyond cost, differences in cultural capital can influence higher education choices. Families without a history of college attendance often do not have knowledgeable role models who can encourage and mentor younger family members to strive for college. Lower-income students are also more likely to attend high schools with limited resources for college preparation and so have less knowledge relevant to the college experience (St. John, Hu, and Fisher 2011).

Even when students do attend college, they enter an education system that is highly stratified along class lines (Karabel 2005; Lee 2013; Stevens 2007), with students from more affluent families more likely to attend higher-quality schools. One study found that even high school valedictorians from working-class backgrounds were less likely than those from more affluent families to attend high-quality schools. A key factor was that working-class valedictorians had fewer resources to guide them in their selection of a college, such as detailed information about the reputation of schools, the availability of financial aid, and the college-application process (Radford 2013).

Finally, before, during, and after college, a variety of other class-based differences provide students from more affluent families with advantages while creating hurdles for first-generation students (those whose parents did not attend college) (Banks-Santilli 2014; Lawrence 2016; Martin 2013). For example:

- Lower-income students often cannot afford multiple college applications and so settle for schools that are easier to get into rather than applying to a variety of competitive "stretch" schools.
- Lower-income students cannot afford to work for free as summer interns, thus missing out on a valuable experience that can benefit a future career.
- Parents without a college education usually lack the professional networks that can help children get their first jobs after college.

So, while higher education can provide opportunities for individuals to advance in society, the system of higher education also helps to perpetuate class-based inequality.

Work Your class also affects the experiences you will likely have at work. Working-class jobs tend to be regimented and closely supervised. Working-class employees often must punch a time clock, take breaks and lunch at specific times, and even ask for permission to use the bathroom. Their work is likely to be closely monitored electronically and by supervisors. Overall, they tend to have little or no control over their work, and the work tends to be relatively low paying with limited or no benefits.

By contrast, middle-class workers often enjoy a high degree of autonomy, looser work rules, less supervision, more-flexible work hours, and their own office space, and they are sometimes allowed to work from home. Often, middle-class workers supervise working-class employees.

Middle-class employees tend to work at desk jobs in quiet offices with climate-controlled environments on a regular weekday schedule. In contrast, many working-class employees toil in extremes of heat or cold and in exceptionally loud, stressful, and sometimes dirty and dangerous environments. Working-class occupations, such as truck driving, construction, logging, fishing, farming, and ranching, have the highest rates of death and injury on the job (U.S. Bureau of Labor Statistics 2018b). Working-class jobs often involve night shifts or rotating between shifts—all of which can disrupt family life.

©Danita Delimont/Gallo Images/Getty Images

©Image Source/Getty Images

FAST-FORWARD

Change and Conspicuous Consumption

In the last half of the nineteenth century, industrialization produced a "Gilded Age" dominated by so-called robber barons who controlled key industries. These newly wealthy industrialists often engaged in conspicuous consumption, as in the case of the castle-like Biltmore Estate in Asheville, North Carolina (*top*), which was completed in 1895 for one of the sons of Cornelius Vanderbilt, a shipping and railroad tycoon. Today, some members of the upper middle class have embraced a more modest version of conspicuous consumption, expressed through the "McMansions" (*bottom*) that helped fuel the housing boom—and bust—of the 2000s.

Many middle-class jobs—especially upper-middle-class positions—come with much better benefits than most working-class jobs, including private pension plans, medical insurance, generous sick leave, paid vacation, and paid educational leave. Top-level benefits can include expense accounts, company cars, membership in private clubs, company stock options, and tickets to sporting events. Access to these top-tier positions is heavily skewed to favor people from already-affluent backgrounds (Rivera 2015).

Politics Political participation varies according to class in the United States, leaving those with the highest rates of participation with the most power (Schlozman, Verba, and Brady 2012). However, there are bigger class differences between voters and nonvoters than there are between Republicans and Democrats; the higher a person's income, the more likely that person is to vote (Figure 9.5). The upper middle class and affluent are also most likely to fund political campaigns, either directly or through donations to political action committees (PACs), political parties, and other intermediaries. For example, over 40 percent of itemized campaign contributions ($200 and over) in the 2012 election cycle came from the wealthiest 0.01 percent of U.S. households (Bonica et al. 2013). Early donors get a chance to influence which candidates are viable long before a single vote is cast.

Lifestyle When you were growing up, did your family have *dinner* or *supper*? Was flying fairly routine for you or did you rarely, if ever, travel by air? Was it taken for granted that you would attend college, or was going to college an unusual accomplishment? Did your parents have an accountant, or did they make use of storefront check-cashing establishments? Such questions have to do with lifestyles, and lifestyles vary by class.

In an early work on class and lifestyles, sociologist Thorstein Veblen ([1899] 1973) coined the term **conspicuous consumption** to refer to *lavish spending, done to compete for status with others.* Veblen associated conspicuous consumption with the *nouveau riche* (French for "new rich"); in his day, these were mostly industrialists who had recently acquired their fortunes and often spent lavishly on mansions and other luxury items. Their lifestyle contrasted starkly with that of people who had so-called old money, wealth that had existed for generations. The old-money wealthy generally frowned upon ostentatious displays.

Many class-based status groups recognize members not merely by the amount of money they have but by social factors such as family heritage, race and ethnicity, educational background, and personal behavior. Such groups often develop formal or informal rules that identify who belongs and who does not. Joining an exclusive country club not only may cost thousands of dollars just to apply and thousands more for membership fees, but it also typically requires sponsorship from an existing member, ensuring that only the "right" people are allowed in. More informally, class-based status groups often share a lifestyle because they socialize together, send their children to the same schools, join the same organizations, and marry within exclusive social networks. These behaviors erect barriers of inclusion and exclusion that sometimes involve **classism,** *prejudice or discrimination based on social class.* Membership in a high-status group or low-status group can significantly affect an

thinking about culture

How did the culture you experienced growing up reflect your family's class status?

FIGURE 9.5 | REPORTED VOTING BY FAMILY INCOME, 2016

Percentage of citizens voting by family income

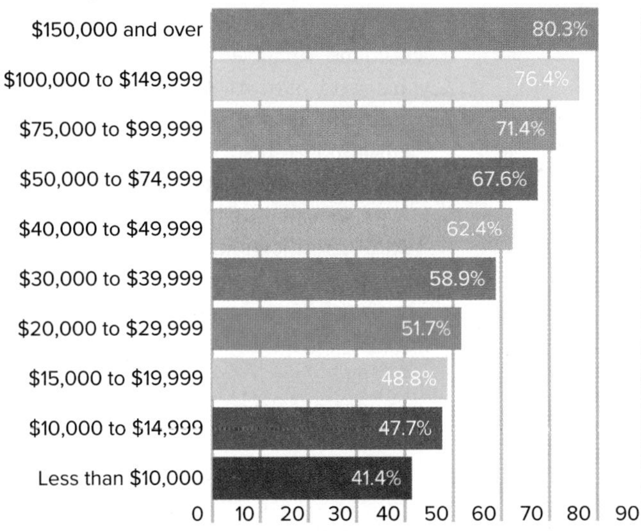

Those with higher incomes are more likely to vote (as shown here), volunteer for a campaign, and make a campaign contribution, skewing political participation by class.

Source: U.S. Census Bureau 2017d.

individual's life chances, including access to education, friendship networks, marriage opportunities, job opportunities, and business and professional contacts.

Poverty

"There's just no way, making $9 an hour as a single parent with two children, that I can live without assistance," says Erika McCurdy. A 40-year-old nurse's aide, McCurdy is in line outside Metropolitan Ministries in Chattanooga, Tennessee, where she's hoping to get help with paying some bills. Money has been tight, affecting all aspects of her life, big and small. Paying the electric bill is tough, and to see her son play on the school football team, she and her daughter sneak in at half-time for free; they can't afford the $6 entry fee (Greenhouse 2014).

McCurdy is not alone. The line she's standing in includes poultry workers, fast-food employees, housekeepers, and others who are also seeking help with paying their heating bills or feeding their families. Like poor people across the country, they are struggling to make ends meet. Perhaps no group in U.S. society feels the impact of class inequality more acutely than those who live in poverty.

Absolute poverty refers to *a scarcity of resources so severe that it is life-threatening.* Over 10 percent of the world's population lives on less than $1.90 a day, one indicator of absolute (or "extreme") poverty (United Nations 2018). **Relative poverty** refers to *a lack of the basic resources needed to maintain a standard of living considered acceptable in a particular society.* This form of poverty varies in different societies. Being forced to live without indoor plumbing or running water would certainly be seen as a sign of poverty in U.S. society today, but in some developing nations such conditions are common and do not by themselves necessarily distinguish people as poor.

Poverty is not "natural" or "inevitable." Poverty levels result, at least in part, from government decisions about the allocation of resources. For example, one reason the United States launched the Social Security system in the 1930s was to reduce the high level of poverty among those over age 65. Today this age group has the nation's lowest poverty rate. Similarly, new social programs introduced during the 1960s helped cut the poverty rate in half between 1960 and 1970 (U.S. Census Bureau 2017b).

Nations with similar degrees of wealth have significantly different relative poverty rates. The poverty rate in the United States is one of the highest among industrialized nations. In recent years the United States ranked 33rd among the 35 member nations of the Organization for Economic Cooperation and Development (OECD); only Israel and Mexico had higher rates. The U.S. poverty rate is more than three times that of the OECD countries with the lowest rates, Denmark and the Czech Republic (OECD 2016). Also, many of the other nations provide more noncash benefits (such as housing, health care, and food) than the United States does, making the impact of poverty less onerous than it is in the United States.

U.S. Poverty Rates

In the United States, the **poverty line** is *a measure of scarcity determined by figuring the cost of a minimal food budget and multiplying it by three.* Each year, the government adjusts poverty thresholds by recalculating the cost of food.

This formula (food cost × 3) dates back to the 1960s, when groceries took up one-third of a typical family budget. Considering that the cost of housing and other essentials has since increased faster than the cost of groceries, people today typically spend only one-fifth of their budget on food. Because the government still uses the outdated formula (food cost × 3), the official poverty line significantly undercounts the poor.

The U.S. **poverty rate** is *the percentage of the population that falls below the poverty line.* In 2016 this rate was 12.7 percent, meaning that nearly one of seven Americans–40.6 million people–lived in poverty (Figure 9.6).

Poverty threshold figures take into account family size, the age of family members, and the number of children in the household. The government counts as income not only wages but also child support and certain public assistance payments, but it excludes noncash benefits such as food stamps and housing subsidies. In 2016 a single parent with one child had to earn $16,543 to stay above the poverty line. However, if that parent worked full time at a job paying the federal minimum wage ($7.25 an hour in 2018), he or she would earn $14,500 and thus remain under the official poverty line. That's why some states and localities have higher minimum wage standards.

Misconceptions about Poverty

The characteristics of the poor are often misunderstood. One myth is that most people in poverty are black. Actually, two-thirds of poor people in 2016 were white (66.8 percent) and fewer than a quarter were black (22.7 percent). Children are more likely to be poor than people in any other age group, and more poor people live in rural or suburban areas than in urban areas. In the last half of the twentieth century, class and gender intersected in a

FIGURE 9.6 | NUMBER IN POVERTY AND POVERTY RATE, 1959–2016

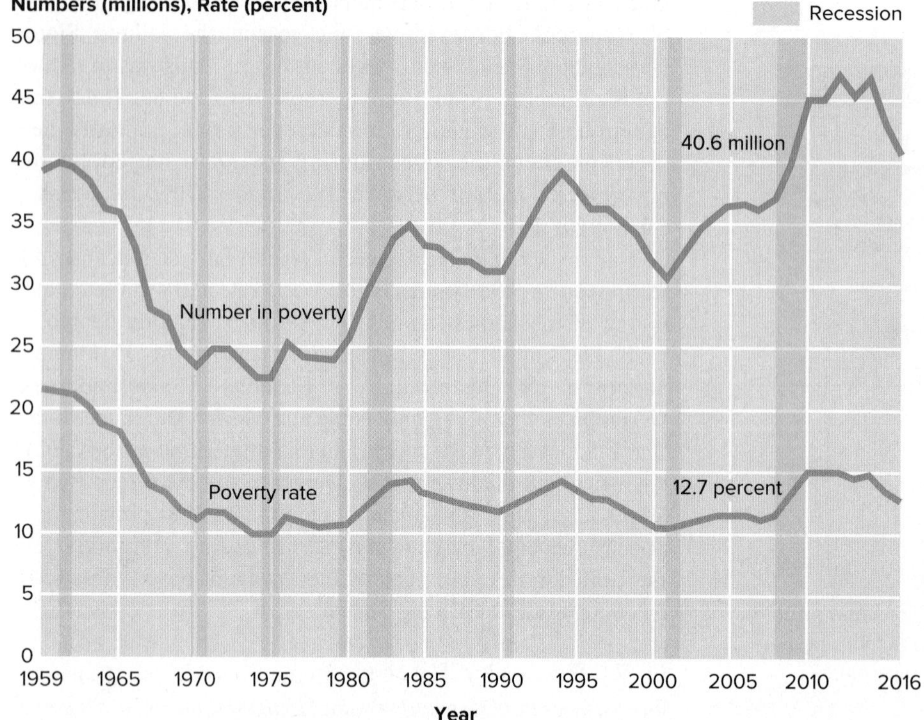

After dropping by nearly one-half in the 1960s, the poverty rate in the United States has hovered between 11 percent and 15 percent since the early 1980s.

Source: U.S. Census Bureau 2017b. "Income and Poverty in the United States: 2016."

CORE CONCEPTS CHALLENGE *The poverty rate increases during periods of recession (shaded), as it did in 2008–2009. How are such data an illustration of the role of social* ***structure****?*

feminization of poverty, *a trend in which women made up an increasingly large share of the poor.* Subsequently, by 2016, just over half of all poor families were headed by a single woman, about double the rate in 1960 (U.S. Census Bureau 2017b). Other characteristics of the poor are outlined in Table 9.4.

Another myth is that most of the poor remain in poverty for a long time. In fact, however, families and individuals move in or out of poverty from year to year, sometimes repeatedly. From 2009 through 2012, approximately 34.5 percent of the population fell below the poverty line for at least 2 months, but only 2.7 percent of the population lived in poverty for all 48 months (U.S. Census Bureau 2017b).

Perhaps the biggest misconception about poverty is that people are poor because they are unwilling to work. In fact, 43.8 percent of the poor are either too old (over 65) or too young (under 18) to work (U.S. Census Bureau 2017b). In addition, the poverty rate increases during periods of recession (when economic activity slows down) and declines when the economy improves, indicating that structural factors beyond individuals' control are a major cause of poverty. In reality, people live in poverty for many reasons. Some are born into it; others become poor as a result of job loss, divorce, the cost of a debilitating illness, or the addition of a child. People of sound mind rarely choose voluntarily to live in poverty. One reason for misconceptions about the causes and prevalence of poverty is ideology.

Ideology: Justifying Inequality

Growing up, were you told that you could be whatever you wanted to be? That with hard work and perseverance you could accomplish whatever you set your mind to? If so, you were learning an early lesson about ideology.

As we saw in Chapter 5, in the context of stratification, an *ideology* is a system of beliefs that explains and justifies the existence of inequality. An effective ideology helps legitimize inequality by making it appear natural, inevitable, and acceptable. In the past, belief in "God's will" justified strict systems of inequality. However, in modern societies other ideologies have emerged. If you were raised in the United States, you are probably familiar with these common ideas:

- Everyone has an equal opportunity to succeed (but is not guaranteed success).
- Success is based on merit (not on wealth, family ties, or other special statuses).
- People can achieve success through individual ability and hard work.

Together, these beliefs suggest that class stratification is the outcome of individual characteristics, unimpeded by structural constraints and unaided by group privilege. In other words, success comes from talent and effort; failure results from individual shortcomings. The message of such an ideology is clear: because everyone has an equal chance to succeed, society is basically fair.

To state these ideas more precisely, the dominant ideology in the United States generally includes the intertwined notions of equal opportunity, meritocracy, and individualism. **Equal opportunity** is *the idea that all people should have the same chance to achieve success.* **Meritocracy** is *a system in which people are rewarded and are able to advance because of their abilities.* These ideas suggest that our stratification system is open and fair. Finally, **individualism** is *a system of beliefs that highlights the importance of the single person over any social group.* Individualism is associated with personal rights and freedoms as well as personal responsibility and self-reliance. The idea of pulling yourself up by your bootstraps and the notion of the self-made man are popular expressions of individualism.

Ideologies help justify the advantages of those in power, and they are also crucial for maintaining social control; otherwise, subordinate groups would more readily challenge structural inequality. People who suffer the consequences of economic inequality sometimes believe the dominant ideology and blame themselves for their predicament. Many, however, see through these ideological myths but do not have the power to challenge or change the system of inequality. Although few people actually believe that class inequality results from merit and individual effort alone (Hunt and Bullock 2016; McCall 2013; Smith and Kluegel 1986), holding on to the promises offered by the dominant ideology can be a source of hope that things will one day improve.

Instead of relying on ideological myths, sociologists have studied how economic inequality really works and found that factors other than merit and individual effort heavily influence the likelihood of our success or failure.

TABLE 9.4 THE POOR IN THE UNITED STATES, 2016

RACE AND ETHNICITY

Most poor people are white. Of the 40.6 million poor:

- 66.8% are white (including white Hispanics)
- 42.5% are white non-Hispanics
- 22.7% are black
- 4.7% are Asian
- 27.4% are Hispanic (of any race)

The poverty rate is highest among blacks and Hispanics:

- Black, 22%
- Hispanic (of any race), 19.4%
- Asian, 10.1%
- White, 11%
- White (non-Hispanic), 8.8%

AGE

The poor are disproportionately children. Of the 40.6 million poor:

- Nearly one-third (32.6%) are children under the age of 18 (13.3 million)
- 11.2% are at least 65 years old (4.6 million)

More than one of six children live in poverty (18%)—making them the age group with the highest poverty rate; the lowest poverty rate is found among the elderly (9.3%); for adults aged 18 to 64, the rate is 11.6%.

FAMILY AND GENDER

Half of poor families are headed by single mothers. Of the 8.1 million poor families:

- 51.2% (4.1 million) have a single female householder
- 38.3% (3.1 million) have a married couple
- 10.5% (0.85 million) have a single male householder

WORK

Many poor adults work. Of the 22.8 million poor people aged 18–64 years:

- 10.6% work full time, year-round
- 27.8% work less than full time, year-round
- 61.6% did not work at least one week during the year

LOCATION

The number of poor people in urban and suburban areas is similar. Of the 40.6 million poor people:

- 16.6 million (40.8%) are in urban areas
- 17.2 million (42.3%) are in suburban areas
- 6.9 million (16.9%) are in rural areas

The poverty rate in rural and urban areas is similar:

- 15.9% in urban areas
- 10% in suburban areas
- 15.8% in rural areas

Source: U.S. Census Bureau 2017b.

Culture, Structure, and Class Reproduction

Why does class inequality persist? To begin with, families and schools socialize people to adopt beliefs, behaviors, and outlooks consistent with their class, thus reproducing the culture of that class. Public policy also helps reinforce class inequality. We look at these processes in more detail in the sections that follow.

Cultural Capital

To explain the reproduction of classes, French sociologist Pierre Bourdieu (1930–2002) built upon Weber's attention to culture and lifestyles. For Bourdieu, people reproduce classes across generations by passing on to young people not only money but also cultural assets. To describe these assets, Bourdieu coined the term **cultural capital,** which *consists of various types of knowledge, skills, and other cultural resources.*

Recall that earlier we noted that students from more affluent families were more likely than others to know how to navigate the process of choosing and applying to colleges. That knowledge is a form of cultural capital. Different forms of cultural capital are valuable within different social contexts. Bourdieu contended that young people are socialized differently depending on their family's class and that they learn class-based tastes, behaviors, and attitudes that distinguish them from people in other classes. As in other examples of socialization, people internalize these lessons, and the associated tastes, behaviors, and attitudes come to seem natural to them. These internalized lessons can help steer young people toward class positions similar to those of their parents. Bourdieu was especially interested in how everyday consumption—our choice of food, music, fashion, and leisure—marked class-based differences.

on social theory

Symbolic interactionism stresses the role of interpersonal interactions in reproducing culture and social structure. Have you ever been in a situation in which you felt at a disadvantage because you lacked the cultural capital to know what behavior was expected of you?

Bourdieu (1986) notes that cultural capital interacts with economic capital and with **social capital,** *relationships that are potentially economically valuable resulting from membership in a group.* For example, it is not enough to want to sail as a pastime; you need to have the economic capital to pursue such an expensive leisure activity. Similarly, knowing powerful, wealthy, or influential people—having social capital—can assist you in getting into high-status schools, companies, and professions.

Families: Training Children

Applying Bourdieu's framework to the contemporary United States, Annette Lareau (2011) studied the socialization of children in black and white middle-class and working-class families. She found that children of the same social class—regardless of race—have much more in common than children of the same race who belong to different social classes. Lareau speculates that as the children she studied grow up, race is likely to become a more significant factor.

In her study, Lareau distinguished between two types of childrearing. Parents who practice *concerted cultivation* actively assess their children's skills, interests, and behaviors. They arrange play dates; organize sports; provide music lessons, tutoring, and museum visits; engage children somewhat like "little adults"; and ask their children about their opinions, feelings, and thoughts. This approach to childrearing is especially prominent in middle-class families, regardless of race.

In contrast, working-class families tend to rely on what Lareau calls the *accomplishment of natural growth.* They focus on providing basic necessities and on creating opportunities for children to spend time at home, playing informally with peers, siblings, and other relatives. These parents also maintain a clear distinction between adults and children and are more inclined to tell their children what to do than to reason with them.

Each approach to childrearing offers advantages and disadvantages that in the end help reproduce class inequality. The constant challenges middle-class children face, and the frequent social interactions they encounter with a variety of people, socialize them to interact effectively with people in many different middle-class settings. However, their hectic schedules leave them little time to simply enjoy being with their families. By contrast, working-class children develop more independence and self-reliance, but they participate in a more limited range of activities. Consequently, they grow up to be less familiar and less comfortable with different social settings than are middle-class kids.

Schools: Individual Mobility and Class Reproduction

One purpose of schools, and higher education in particular, is preparing people for employment. In doing so, schools can provide individuals with a chance at social mobility while, paradoxically, helping reproduce class inequality for society as a whole.

Education Pays The role of education in helping individuals compete for good-paying jobs is well known and well documented. Figure 9.7 shows that higher educational attainment is associated with lower unemployment and higher wages. More variation exists within each category of educational attainment than these average numbers suggest, however. For example, income levels for people with a bachelor's degree vary significantly depending on their major and the type of school from which they graduated. Still, on the whole, the more education you have, the more likely you are to be employed and well paid.

SPOTLIGHT on social theory

How would **functionalist theory** explain the relationship between education and earnings? Do you think this theory adequately explains the levels of income of different people you know?

Education can help individuals compete, but it does not change the class structure. As we saw earlier in the chapter, structural factors—including the way public schools are funded and the high cost of higher education—create barriers to quality education that contribute to unequal educational outcomes. In addition, schools sort students by class. In high school, middle-class students are steered into college-prep courses emphasizing independent thinking and self-direction, which prepare them to move on to higher education and middle-class life. Working-class students are more likely to be channeled into classes that emphasize the importance of following rules and obeying authorities, thereby preparing them for working-class jobs that have similar expectations. In this way, although schools serve employers and the capitalist system by providing appropriately trained workers, they help reproduce class distinctions in society (Bowles and Gintis 1976, 2002).

Rewarding Cultural Capital Culture also plays a role in how schools reproduce inequality. Schools are generally organized to value the cultural capital of the higher classes and reward students accordingly. Since more-affluent students already possess that sort of cultural capital, the academic playing

FIGURE 9.7 | EARNINGS AND UNEMPLOYMENT BY EDUCATIONAL ATTAINMENT, 2017

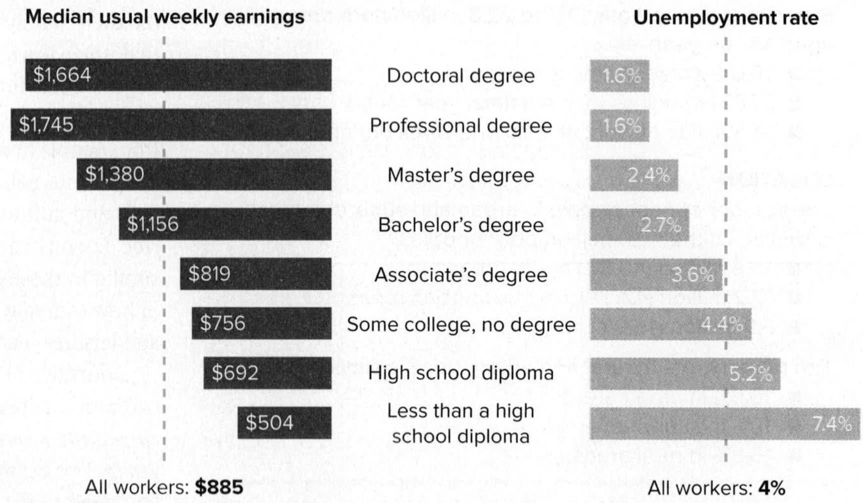

Source: U.S. Bureau of Labor Statistics 2017b.

field is tilted in their favor, increasing the odds they will achieve academic success. Working-class students are at a disadvantage when trying to meet the middle-class expectations of the school environment and often feel alienated. As a result, they can rebel, refuse to conform to academic expectations, and inadvertently help re-create their status in the working class (Willis 1977).

Jay MacLeod (2009) studied young, low-income black and white men in Boston, focusing specifically on the role of aspiration in their lives. The youth MacLeod studied related to their schoolwork quite differently based on their differing aspirations. MacLeod found that the young white men he studied had a fairly pessimistic outlook on their future. They saw their schooling as irrelevant and their prospects as lower than those of their parents because of the loss of good-paying working-class jobs. On the other hand, the young black men he studied were more optimistic, because they measured their prospects against the more repressive history of discrimination faced by African Americans in the past. They hoped their efforts in school would pay off, and they expected diligence in the workplace to be rewarded with increased responsibilities, promotions, and pay raises. However, aspiration by itself cannot overcome structural barriers. When MacLeod followed up with these black men seven years later, he found most ended up in dead-end jobs, like their white peers. Most now tempered their belief in the openness of American society but often blamed themselves for their failure.

Schools and Ideology When the students MacLeod studied blamed themselves for their failure, they were reflecting another influential role that schools play in reproducing class: ideology. Schools can strengthen class inequality by helping justify it and by reinforcing the idea that failure results from individual shortcomings, not structural biases.

We are so accustomed to accepting the connection between education and unequal rewards that we rarely see data such as those in Figure 9.7 as unfair. Instead, we usually understand them as a reflection of a generally fair system of meritocracy that rewards those who have ability, work hard, and make smart choices about their chosen field of study. In such an analysis, we tend to ignore the structural and cultural forces that work in favor of students from affluent backgrounds and against students from more modest backgrounds.

Public Policy and Inequality

Beyond the role of culture, economic inequality is caused in part by—and can be reduced through—government social policies. These policies tend to follow two different approaches.

One approach aims to create more *equal outcomes* by reducing the gap between the rich and the poor. One way of accomplishing this is to provide everyone with some basic public goods, such as health care and free education, which reduces the impact of income differences. Another way is to raise the floor (raise wages for those in low-income positions) and lower the ceiling (increase taxes on the highest income-earners). This ensures a living wage for those doing necessary but lower-paying work while limiting inequality that results from extremely high incomes. Government intervention of this sort produces less inequality.

The second approach focuses on encouraging *equal opportunity* by creating a more level playing field on which people compete for scarce good jobs. This is usually done by supporting more education as the means to individual mobility, thereby promoting fairer competition. This limits government intervention but results in more inequality.

U.S. society and government policy have mostly favored the equal opportunity approach over the equal outcomes approach, encouraging more education while accepting higher levels of inequality. As a result, the percentage of Americans over age 25 with at least a four-year college degree tripled between 1970 and 2017, from about 11 percent to 34 percent (U.S. Census Bureau 2017e), but during the same period economic inequality *increased* significantly. More education for more people did not reduce inequality because it did not change the overall class structure nor did it change the rewards associated with different types of employment. Instead, the United States has more economic inequality than is found in other industrialized nations. Those countries, in contrast, have placed higher value on reducing economic inequality and enacted different economic policies.

To give one example, the United States is the only advanced economy in the world that does not guarantee workers any paid vacation, whereas some countries mandate over 30 days of paid vacation annually (see Figure 9.8). Without the protection of federal mandates, U.S. workers in the private sector must rely on individual employers to provide paid vacations and holidays. As a result, nearly one of four workers gets no paid vacation time at all. Private-sector employees get an average of 10 paid vacation days a year—half the number mandated in most other wealthy countries—and six paid holidays, also less than in most other wealthy countries (Ray, Sanes, and Schmitt 2013).

Wages and Labor Laws Raising the wage floor helps reduce inequality, and the most direct way to raise low-income wages is to legislate a minimum wage. Because the federal minimum wage is not adjusted for inflation, its real value has fluctuated since it was first implemented in 1938. It peaked at about $11.56 in 1968 (in 2018 dollars), was allowed to reach a nearly 60-year low by 2007, and was increased to $7.25 an hour in 2009 (Elwell 2014). Given the relatively low federal minimum wage, some states implement their own, higher, minimum.

Labor unions have long worked to improve wages, benefits, and safety for workers by bargaining collectively with employers and establishing a work contract. In the middle of the twentieth century, about one of three workers in the United States belonged to a union. Such widespread union membership helped limit economic inequality by acting as a counterweight to the power of business owners, both in the workplace and at the ballot box (Figure 9.9). In the last few decades, however, union membership has declined significantly—to fewer than one in nine workers (10.7 percent)—contributing to the rise in economic inequality (unionstats.com 2018).

Technological change and global competition have been important elements in labor union decline. Another major factor has been the state of labor laws. These laws make it difficult for workers to join a union while making it relatively safe for private employers to try to get rid of existing unions ("union busting") or

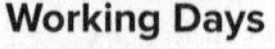

FIGURE 9.8 | PAID VACATION DAYS AND HOLIDAYS IN SELECT DEVELOPED COUNTRIES

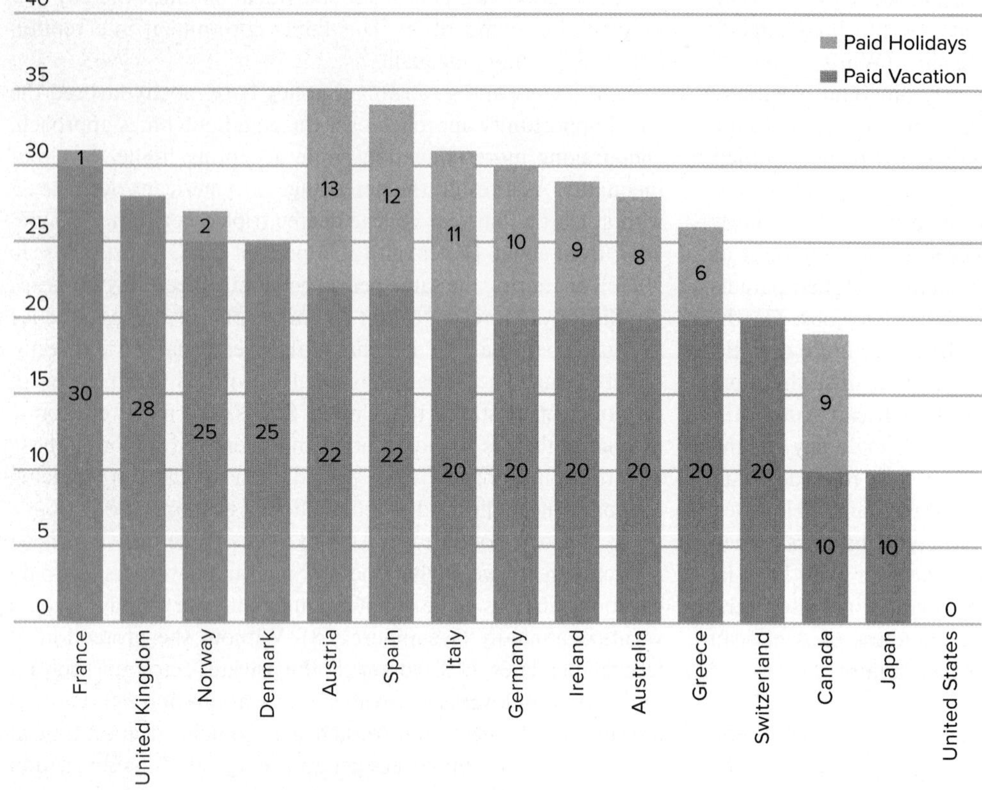

The United States is the only developed country that does not mandate a minimum number of paid vacation days and holidays for its workers. *Source:* Ray, Sanes, and Schmitt 2013.

to prevent workers from forming them, sometimes by firing workers who try to organize (Compa 2004; Logan 2006; Schmitt and Zipperer 2009; Warner 2013). Public-sector (government) employees have been less likely to face union-busting tactics and are five times as likely (34.4 percent) as private-sector workers (6.5 percent) to belong to a union (unionstats.com 2018). However, in recent years, some state legislatures have stepped up efforts to curtail or eliminate the rights of public-sector unions to bargain collectively, creating so-called "right to work" states (McCartin 2016).

Partly as a consequence of the low rate of unionization in the United States, many U.S. workers have relatively low wages and benefits compared to workers in other industrialized countries. (The Sociology in Action box examines how sociologists have studied the challenges facing workers' organizing efforts.)

Taxes If the minimum wage raises the floor to reduce inequality, then imposing higher taxes on the wealthy lowers the ceiling. But compared to a half century ago, the wealthy today enjoy substantially lower taxes whereas taxes on middle-income families are higher than they were (Piketty, Saez, and Zucman 2018). In a system of **progressive taxation,** *those with higher incomes pay a higher tax rate.* Throughout the 1950s the U.S. federal tax rate on personal income beyond the first $400,000 for married couples filing jointly was more than 90 percent—a highly progressive rate aimed at limiting the extremes of income inequality. However, that rate has been cut repeatedly since the 1980s and is 37 percent in 2018. The tax rate on capital gains—income earned from investments mainly by those in the highest income brackets—has similarly been cut by more than half since the mid-1970s and ranges from 15 to 20 percent in 2018. In contrast, the top tax rate for median family incomes rose substantially in the late 1960s and 1970s, and although it dropped again in the 1980s, it remains higher today than it was in 1955 (Tax Policy Center 2017a).

American workers pay more in taxes than they used to in part because corporations pay less. A congressional study found that more than two-thirds of all corporations paid no federal income tax, including nearly 20 percent of profitable large corporations with more than $10 million in assets (U.S. Government Accountability Office 2016). For example, some of the nation's best-known companies paid no federal income tax from 2006 to 2012, including CBS, General Electric, JetBlue, Mattel, Prudential, Time Warner, and Xerox (Citizens for Tax Justice 2015). The government has

FIGURE 9.9 | U.S. UNION MEMBERSHIP VS. INCOME INEQUALITY

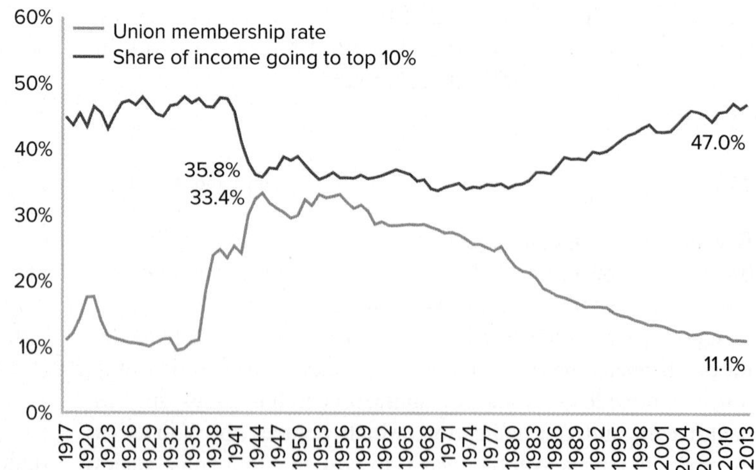

Workers in unions are better able to bargain for higher wages. A decline in union membership was one factor contributing to growing income inequality, with a greater share of income going to the top 10 percent.

Source: Mishel and Schieder 2016.

SOCIOLOGY in ACTION

Why David Sometimes Wins: Organizing Workers

Workers in the United States face an uphill battle in organizing. On paper, they have the right to join a labor union to pursue good wages, benefits, and working conditions. In reality, though, labor laws are stacked against them while giving employers an unfair advantage, according to the international human rights group Human Rights Watch (Compa 2004). For example, employers can legally launch aggressive pressure campaigns against employees attempting to organize, including holding mandatory meetings at which workers are often threatened with dire consequences if they join a union. Employers are even allowed to permanently replace workers who strike over wages and working conditions. Employers also often illegally fire workers who try to organize a union, exploiting a slow and ineffectual legal process that can tie up worker complaints about labor law violations for months or years and bring resolutions long after a union election is held (Compa 2004; Schmitt and Zipperer 2009).

Such laws and procedures contribute to a relatively weak labor union movement in the United States compared to many other industrialized countries. Union weakness contributes to higher poverty rates and greater economic inequality and is one of the key reasons why many U.S. workers do not have the sorts of wages and benefits that workers in other nations enjoy.

Sociologists have been studying the organizing efforts of workers and identifying their most effective organizing strategies. Because organizing traditional unions is so difficult, many of these strategies involve new tactics that are sometimes referred to as "social movement unionism" or "alt-labor" (Dixon 2014; Fiorito and Jarley 2012). For example, community-based worker centers have succeeded in providing basic services (such as language classes for recent immigrants) while helping to educate them about their rights and supporting them in their quest to improve working conditions and form a union (Milkman and Ott 2014). Other initiatives include the "Fight for $15" campaign targeting higher wages for food workers (fightfor15.org); the "Faculty Forward Network" effort (seiufacultyforward.org/) organizing low-paid—especially adjunct—faculty at public universities; and various local campaigns to raise the minimum wage (see raisetheminimumwage.com).

Sociologist Marshall Ganz draws on his own experience as a labor organizer in his work in labor studies. In the 1960s, Ganz dropped out of college to work with the United Farm Workers, best known for its charismatic leader César Chávez. Ganz eventually became the union's head of organizing, helping direct one of the most famous labor struggles in U.S. history. He later returned to school, got a PhD in sociology, and began teaching at Harvard University about organizing and leadership strategies. In 2008, Barack Obama's presidential campaign made him a key advisor for the training of the campaign's field organizers.

In 2009, Ganz wrote *Why David Sometimes Wins,* a sociological analysis of his experiences with the United Farm Workers whose title invokes the biblical struggle of an underdog against a giant—David versus Goliath. Ganz (2009) argues that the success of the farmworkers developed from diverse leadership teams—in terms of factors such as ethnicity and gender—with ties to different social networks. They built the union's strategic capacity—doing the most with what resources they had—through an ongoing process of experimentation, learning, and adaptation that involved taking risks, evaluating results, and implementing changes in strategy. In this way, ordinary workers built an organizational structure that had the power to influence employers with much greater resources. When such strategies were later abandoned, Ganz argues, the union's effectiveness declined.

Such nuanced sociological studies have provided organizers with a range of insights to improve the effectiveness of their work.

think about it

1. *What role do culture, structure, and power play in these sociological analyses of union organizing?*
2. *How might a stronger labor movement in the United States affect political decision making, as well as the conditions of workers?*

made up the difference by increasing the payroll taxes on workers (also known as FICA–Federal Insurance Contributions Act), which pay for Medicare and Social Security. Payroll taxes are a form of **regressive taxation** since they *disproportionately affect those with lower incomes.* For example, as of 2018, federal law exempted income above $128,400 per year from the Social Security payroll tax.

Taxing the inheritance of large estates has traditionally been another way to help reduce the concentration of wealth. When the first-ever U.S. billionaire, oil tycoon John D. Rockefeller, died in 1937, his children paid a 70 percent estate tax on most of his fortune they inherited, leaving them and their offspring with enough money to remain among the nation's wealthiest people to this day. The estate tax has since been slashed. As of 2018, the first $11.2 million an individual (or $22.4 million a couple) receives is tax-exempt. The amount in excess of this is taxed at 40 percent–a 43 percent tax cut since the days of John D. Rockefeller.

Public Assistance Public policy also affects economic inequality through the administration of public assistance programs. **Public assistance** *includes either tax credits or actual payments and benefits provided to citizens by the government.* Welfare for the poor is the best-known form of public assistance. It includes cash payments, food stamps, child care, and housing subsidies.

Since major welfare reform took effect in the mid-1990s, the focus of welfare benefits has shifted from direct cash payments to programs that promote work, such as job training and child care.

Contrary to popular perception, however, most public assistance goes to people in the middle and working classes—not the poor. If you are attending a state college or university, for example, you are benefiting from public assistance because the cost of your education is subsidized by taxpayers. Perhaps the most important form of middle-class public assistance is the home mortgage interest tax deduction, which allows homeowners to deduct the interest on a loan of up to $750,000 used to purchase or improve a home; the larger the price tag on the home, the larger the government tax break. Consequently, in recent years, about 75 percent of home mortgage interest tax benefits went to the top 20 percent of households in terms of income. The mortgage interest tax deduction program costs the federal government more than $70 billion a year. That amount was almost enough to cover the combined $79 billion cost in 2015 of all federal housing assistance for the poor (including public housing and low-income housing subsidies, aid for the homeless, and assisted housing for elderly and special-needs populations), food and nutrition programs (including WIC—the Special Supplemental Nutrition Program for Women, Infants, and Children), and other forms of assistance to low- and moderate-income people, such as heating fuel assistance and child care (Center on Budget and Policy Priorities 2016).

The public assistance provided to corporations, sometimes referred to as "corporate welfare," is also many times more generous than the assistance given to the poor. Corporations—and indirectly the shareholders who own them—receive billions in this kind of assistance in the form of direct subsidies and tax breaks and the free or low-cost use of public resources such as forests. For example, in 2015 the federal government paid over $20 billion in direct subsidies to agricultural concerns—many of which are large, profitable agribusiness corporations. Of that money, 85 percent went to the richest 10 to 15 percent of recipients (V. Smith 2015). The aerospace giant Boeing alone received over $13 billion in federal subsidies between 2000 and 2015 (Mattera and Tarczynska 2015). States and localities, too, often compete to attract businesses by slashing taxes, paying for infrastructure, subsidizing utilities, and providing other incentives, all at taxpayer expense.

The use of public resources to aid the middle and upper classes is the outcome of a political process. Those with the most political power write the rules, and they tend to write them for their own benefit. As we will see, political power also plays a role in global inequality.

Power and Global Inequality

In 2010, as its stock price surged, Apple surpassed Microsoft for the first time as the world's most valuable high-tech company, likely bringing smiles to the faces of its investors (Helft and Vance 2010). But in China, workers who assemble many Apple products, including the popular iPhone and iPad, were not celebrating the good news. Instead, 10 of them committed suicide in the first five months of the year, most by jumping off the balconies of company-built dormitories next to their massive factory complex in Shenzhen (BBC 2010a, 2010b). The workers were employed by Taiwan-based Foxconn Technology, the world's largest assembler of computers and handheld electronic devices, which contracts with Apple and other high-tech companies. Foxconn employees work six days a week for entry-level pay of $132 a month. They typically put in 10- to 12-hour workdays and are routinely expected to work overtime. They are forbidden to talk during their shifts and are subjected to what workers refer to as military-style discipline, leading one worker to tell reporters, "It's like a prison." Yet Foxconn is considered to be one of the better places to work. Conditions in many other Chinese factories are much worse.

The rash of suicides attracted embarrassing media coverage until government authorities ordered the Chinese press to tone down its coverage. After the Western media picked up the story and companies that contract with Foxconn expressed concern, the company instituted a 20 percent pay raise to improve morale and installed nets around its dormitories to foil suicide attempts.

Similar tales of bleak working conditions lurk behind many of the consumer electronics and other brand-name goods that dominate today's global economy (Bales 2016). The economic inequality that we have explored in the United States has parallels in other countries, and inequality *within* individual countries exists side-by-side with **global inequality,** *the differences in wealth and power among the countries of the world.* The economic systems of individual countries are increasingly interconnected, and to understand economic inequality in any one country, including the United States, we must consider that country's place in the global economic structure.

Categorizing National Economies

Researchers and others commonly use the terms *developed, developing,* and *underdeveloped* to summarize a country's level of industrial and technological development. A country at a higher level of development generally produces more goods. As a result, its people have a higher material standard of living than those in less-developed countries.

Analysts sometimes use more nuanced categorizations of national economies. For example, Map 9.1 sorts the world's countries into four income levels, according to an analysis by the World Bank. Widespread poverty in much of Africa and southern Asia makes these among the poorest places on earth, whereas the United States, Canada, the nations of Europe, Japan, and Australia are among the world's wealthiest countries.

We can get a more concrete idea of what high and low incomes mean on a global scale by considering *purchasing power,*

thinking about power

How do the social policies that the government enacts, such as tax policy, reflect the relative **power** of different segments of society?

MAP 9.1 | A GLOBAL VIEW OF PER-CAPITA INCOME LEVELS, 2017–2018

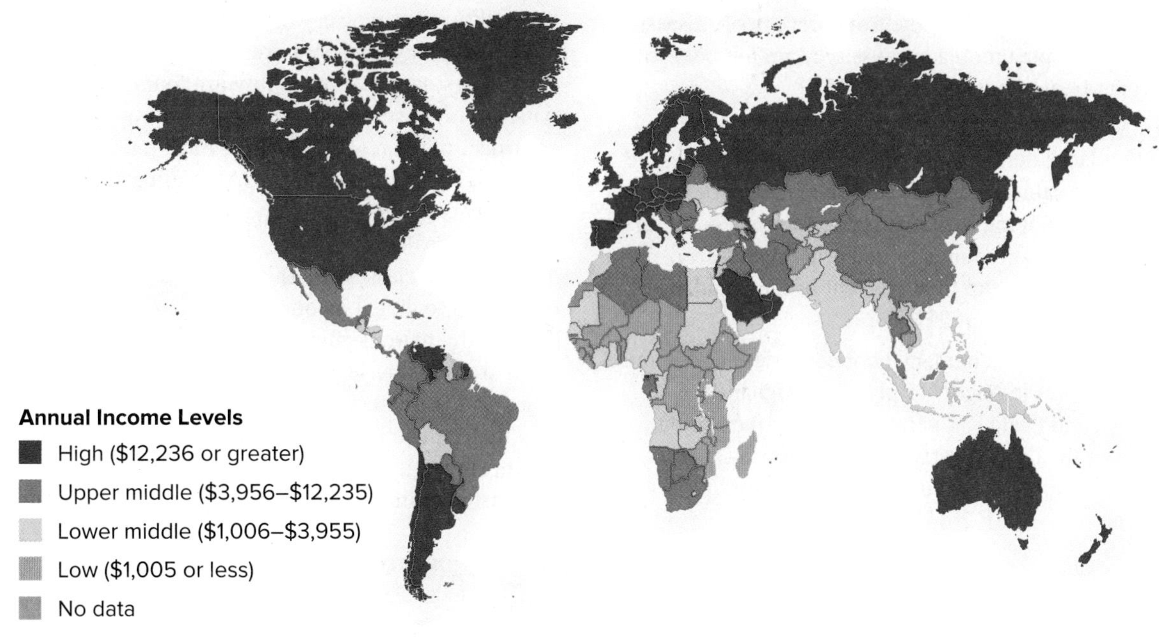

Source: World Bank 2018.

CORE CONCEPTS CHALLENGE *What does this map suggest about the relationship between a nation's wealth and its global political* **power**? *How might a nation's wealth influence its power? How might its political and military power influence its wealth?*

the average value of the goods and services people in a country can purchase in a year. As Figure 9.10 shows, purchasing power varies widely.

FIGURE 9.10 | PER-CAPITA PURCHASING POWER IN U.S. DOLLARS FOR SELECTED COUNTRIES, 2016

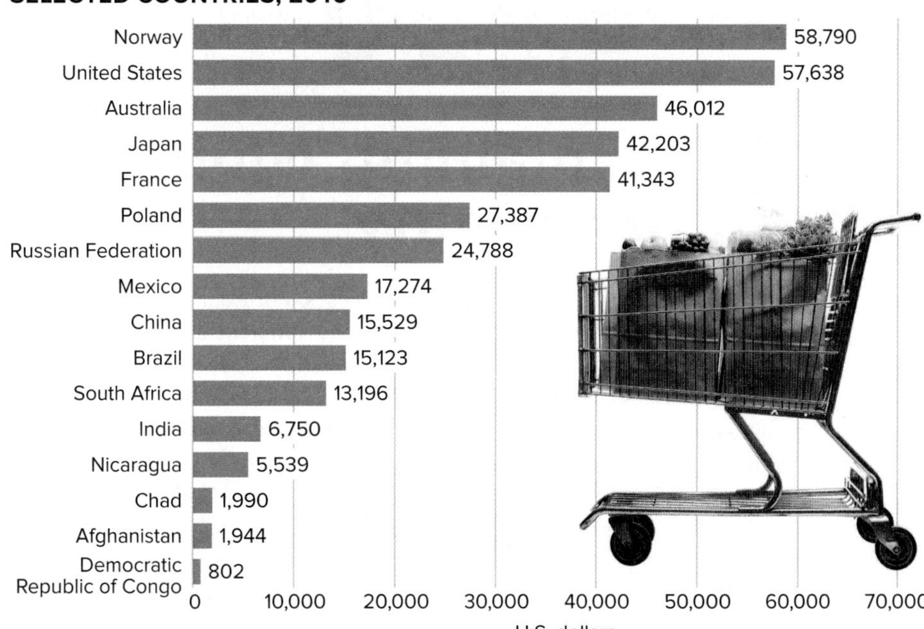

This graph illustrates, on average, how much a person from each country could purchase in a year in 2016. The data in U.S. dollars take into account the relative cost of goods and services in different countries.

Source: The World Bank, World Development Indicators. *Photo:* ©Mike Kemp/Rubberball/Getty Images RF

In addition, the global distribution of income is extremely unequal. Wealth distribution is even more unequal. The richest 1 percent of the world's population has about 50 percent of the world's wealth, while the bottom 80 percent has only 6 percent of the world's wealth (UN Development Programme 2015).

The Impact of Global Inequality

As we saw earlier in this chapter, your class status within the United States has implications for your health, education, and lifestyle. Similarly, a country's income level typically corresponds to a variety of social indicators, resulting in starkly unequal social conditions around the world:

- ***Life expectancy and health.*** Poverty kills. On average, life expectancy for people in the world's low-income countries is 17 years less than it is for people in high-income countries—62 versus 79 years (World Bank 2016). Poor countries have high rates of infant mortality, and people die at an early age from malnourishment, pneumonia, malaria, diarrhea, and HIV/AIDS. About 16,000 children under the age of five die every day due to poverty, nearly 6 million children a year. Often, these are children who die from preventable diseases like diarrhea and pneumonia because they are too poor to afford proper treatment (UNICEF 2015).

- ***Housing.*** More than 825 million people live in slums—housing that lacks durability, sufficient living area, access to clean water and sanitation, and secure occupancy rights. The rural poor in developing nations migrate to urban areas for jobs and schooling, often only to find grinding poverty and disease. In some cities, up to 80 percent of the population lives in slums (UN-Habitat 2016).
- ***Education.*** Most people in many poor countries are illiterate. Adult literacy rates in Niger (15 percent), Afghanistan (32 percent), and Chad (38 percent)—among the world's lowest—reflect the deep poverty of such countries, where schooling is often not free and children must work from a very early age (UNICEF 2015).

Over the past quarter century the number of people living in extreme poverty has decreased significantly. The World Bank estimated that 702 million people, or 9.6 percent of the global population, lived in extreme poverty in 2015, defined as earning less than $1.90 a day—a major drop from 25 years earlier, when 1.92 *billion* people (then 37.1 percent of the population) were in extreme poverty. This is the first time that the extreme poverty estimate has dipped below 10 percent and further reductions are forecast. The change has been largely due to dramatic economic growth in China and India, which together account for more than 35 percent of the world's population. However, in other parts of the world, particularly sub-Saharan Africa, poverty persists, and the number of people living in poverty there is higher than it was 25 years ago (Cruz et al. 2015).

©Pavel Gospodinov/Alamy Stock Photo

These global changes have had a direct impact on the United States. For example, as China and other countries with fast-growing economies used more resources, oil and food prices increased worldwide. The rise in fuel prices in turn contributed to increased energy production in the United States, including through the rapid growth of hydraulic fracturing, or "fracking." As growth in those countries has slowed, however, prices have declined. In addition, the shift of manufacturing to developing nations has reduced employment in U.S. factories, leading to an increase in the import of foreign goods and contributing to the U.S. trade deficit. In addition, poverty, despair, and inequality contribute to instability and conflict in various parts of the world, situations that have in some cases led to the involvement of U.S. military troops.

Inequality within Countries

Inequality exists in every country, produced in part by the kinds of public policy decisions we discussed earlier in this chapter. The highest levels of inequality are found in Central and South America and southern Africa. In these areas, a small elite controls limited resources, while most people live in poverty. In many highly unequal countries, the ruling and business elites use agreements with foreign corporations and governments to maintain their wealth and power at the expense of the nation's poor and working classes. In this way, inequality within nations is connected to global inequality.

Wealthy nations such as France and Sweden generally have comparatively low levels of economic inequality because of high taxes on the wealthy, generous minimum wages, and other policies that reduce inequality. The exception is the United States, the most unequal wealthy country in the world. In societies with the least amount of inequality, moderate and low-income groups tend to have much more power than they do in the United States. Compared to U.S. citizens, people in countries such as Norway and Canada are more likely to be organized into labor unions, to vote, and to have the option of voting for a political party that represents labor or the working class. In many respects, therefore, the nature and extent of inequality depends on the balance of power in a society.

Explaining Global Inequality

Global inequality has many causes. For example, different countries have different climates and different amounts of natural resources, both of which undoubtedly contribute to their degree of affluence or poverty. In addition, most sociologists acknowledge two major *social* causes of global inequality: culture and power.

Culture and Global Inequality: Modernization Theory

Through most of human history, people possessed relatively few material goods, so economic inequality was limited. However, as we saw in Chapter 1, industrialization transformed northern European societies by destroying traditional ways of life and creating unprecedented material abundance. But not all countries experienced this change.

Modernization theory *attributes global inequality to cultural differences among countries.* According to this theory, some societies resisted industrialization, preferring to retain traditional ways of life rather than adopt disruptive new technologies. Maintaining family and community relationships, the agricultural economy, and traditional religious beliefs were more important than adopting new means to produce greater material abundance. These differing cultural traditions helped open up an economic gap between industrialized nations and the developing world.

Power and Global Inequality: Dependency Theory

Many sociologists argue that today's global inequality is rooted in a much less benign process than cultural differences. Their alternative, **dependency theory,** *attributes global inequality to the exploitation of weaker, poor nations by wealthy, more powerful ones.* This theory locates the origin of growing global inequality in the increased exploration, travel, and trade that began roughly 500 years ago—long before industrialization. As European explorers ventured to Africa, the Western Hemisphere, and East Asia, they clashed with indigenous peoples, subjugated them, established colonies, and gained control of their natural resources and labor. Rather than voluntarily opting out of development, poor countries were prevented from developing by powerful colonizers who became wealthy by exploiting their natural resources and cheap labor. Typically, colonial powers would import raw materials from colonies and turn them into valuable manufactured goods. With slavery, colonial powers took West Africans to labor in American plantations, enriching the colonial nations while impoverishing the colonies.

©Kuni Takahashi/Getty Images

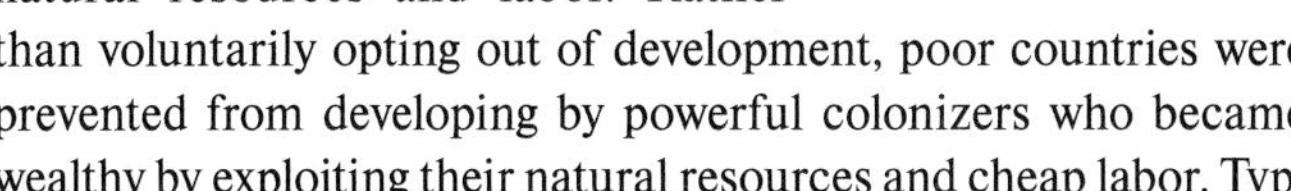

SPOTLIGHT on social theory

What makes **dependency theory** a type of **conflict theory**? How would dependency theory apply to countries you may have visited or to the countries in which you or your ancestors were born? How does it apply to the United States?

Colonialism and Neocolonialism

In the modern era, roughly since 1500, nations have struggled fiercely over resources. The most obvious type of global struggle was **colonialism,** *the use of military, political, and economic power by one society to dominate the people of another society, usually for economic benefit.* From the 1500s through the 1900s, European powers used their military might to subjugate other peoples across the globe. According to a famous saying, the sun never set on the British Empire because its colonial holdings were spread out across the world. The use of the English language in many regions of the world today is in part a legacy of this colonial subjugation. Africa, India, North America, much of South America, and other areas of the world were all conquered by colonial powers.

Colonial powers typically exerted direct political control over their colonies or established puppet governments (controlled by the outside colonial power) while engaging in military occupation and establishing cultural dominance. Most important, colonial powers usually sought to extract the natural resources from their colonies and exploit the labor available there.

Most colonies resisted their colonial occupiers. By the latter half of the twentieth century, independence movements had successfully brought an end to colonial rule. However, these new nations often struggled to overcome their colonial past, which had stripped them of vast resources, left them ill prepared to develop modern economic systems, and often institutionalized a culture of political corruption. Some observers argue that colonialism has been replaced by **neocolonialism,** *a system of economic domination of poorer nations by wealthier ones without formal political control or military occupation.*

In a neocolonial situation, former colonies continue to depend on wealthier nations for capital investment and technical expertise, giving these wealthier countries enormous influence over their development. In addition, former colonies often experience civil wars and political infighting as different factions struggle for control of resources, adding yet another hurdle to economic development (UN Development Programme 2015).

World Systems Analysis

Another approach to global inequality, **world systems analysis** *focuses on the interdependence among the countries in a single global economic system.* Sociologist Immanuel Wallerstein (1974, 1979) sees the poverty of some countries as connected directly to the wealth of others. He sorts countries into one of three primary groups, depending on their relationship to the global economy:

- ***Core nations*** include the United States, Canada, Japan, and the European countries. These, the world's wealthiest countries, are at the center of the global economy. Most core nations benefited from colonialism and continue to dominate the global economy through multinational corporations and global financial institutions.
- ***Periphery nations*** include many countries in Africa, Latin America, and parts of Asia. These are the world's poorest and least powerful countries, at the fringe of the global economy. They participate in the global economy by providing natural resources and cheap labor for the transnational corporations while also serving as markets for some goods.
- ***Semi-periphery nations*** include China, India, Mexico, and Pakistan. These middle-income nations are better integrated with the economies of core countries than are the periphery nations and often have a stronger domestic industrial base.

With modern communications and transportation, capital from core nations can move easily around the globe. Poorer countries are often dependent on this foreign investment to fund their economic development. They frequently compete against one another to attract foreign investment by offering low or no taxes, minimal environmental regulations, and a low-cost, nonunion labor force.

Typically based in core nations, multinational corporations look to cut costs and boost profits by shifting production to semi-periphery nations. This allows them to take advantage of low-wage labor and lax environmental regulation and to avoid paying some taxes in core nations. In doing so, they create jobs and stimulate the local economies in these poor countries.

This local economic development is often temporary, however. For example, in the 1990s—especially after the passage of the North American Free Trade Agreement (NAFTA)—some U.S. corporations moved manufacturing jobs to Mexico, which devastated some "rust belt" communities in the United States but helped Mexican workers, whose average manufacturing wage rose to $2.08 an hour. But these gains were short lived: many companies soon began the process over again by moving production to China, where manufacturing workers were earning an average of just 61 cents an hour (Faux 2013; Ferriss 2003).

This is an example of the *race to the bottom,* the process of poorer nations competing for foreign investment by sacrificing wages, tax revenue, worker safety, and environmental standards. The race to the bottom can keep periphery and semi-periphery nations poor while channeling profits back to investors in core countries. If workers in these poor countries organize into unions to improve their conditions—as workers once did in wealthier nations—or if national governments insist on high-quality environmental standards, corporate investors can simply move to a new country that offers more-favorable incentives. The existing rules for the global economy—rules that favor the free flow of capital—are coordinated through the world's global financial institutions (Scott 2015).

Global Financial Institutions

In recent decades, global financial organizations have had an enormous influence on the economic and social policies of poor countries (Kaplinsky 2007). The three major players in global finance are the World Bank, which provides poor countries with investments and loans for development; the International Monetary Fund (IMF), which provides financial and technical assistance to promote economic growth; and the World Trade Organization (WTO), which administers trade practices between countries. Although all three organizations ostensibly aim to promote development in and provide aid to poorer nations, many critics contend that they are key vehicles through which core nations and multinational corporations dominate poorer countries.

For example, critics contend that the conditions the World Bank sets for loans—known as *structural adjustment programs*—actually benefit foreign investors rather than the poor countries and in fact lead to increased poverty. In some cases, to receive assistance from the World Bank and the IMF, countries have been required to shift from producing essential food crops for domestic use, such as corn and beans, to cash crops intended for export, such as coffee and cotton, thereby worsening hunger locally. These organizations have also insisted that governments slash vital social service spending in order to repay foreign loans, sometimes with disastrous results for the health and education of the local population.

In recent years, activists from around the world have organized to promote basic labor and environmental standards and to advocate debt forgiveness. Activists have used education, the promotion of "fair trade" goods whose production meets basic labor and environmental standards, and street protests at the meetings of global financial institutions to advance their cause. Their advocacy has led to more public scrutiny of these institutions as well as some reforms (Stiglitz and Charlton 2007).

A Changing World

U.S. INEQUALITY IN GLOBAL CONTEXT

Economic inequality in the United States has long been closely connected to the global economy, and this close relationship has produced starkly different results in two recent periods. From 1945 to the 1970s, the U.S. economy experienced enormous growth. The economic infrastructure of most industrialized countries had been damaged or destroyed by World War II. With virtually no competition, U.S. manufacturers dominated much of the global marketplace. Plenty of well-paid working-class jobs were available in automobile plants, the steel industry, and other types of manufacturing. Strong labor unions fought for better working conditions and wages, and the benefits of this economic growth were spread across all income levels (see Figure 9.11).

By the 1970s, global economic conditions had changed. U.S. companies failed to invest adequately in newer technologies such as smaller, more-fuel-efficient automobiles and were caught off-guard by newly emerging global competition. To stay competitive, corporations based in the United States began exporting many of the high-paying manufacturing jobs that had provided economic security for working- and middle-class Americans to poor nations that offered lower wages, fewer labor and environmental regulations, and, often, repressive governments that maintained political stability and made labor organizing difficult or impossible. The result was **deindustrialization,** *the process by which investment in the nation's manufacturing capacity decreased,* devastating the economies of many communities, especially in the Midwest and Northeast. The export of good-paying working-class jobs often left middle-income workers scrambling for jobs with lower wages, while increased corporate profits translated into higher incomes for affluent stockholders. The result was increased inequality.

The economy continued to grow, but now, as Figure 9.11 shows, the benefits went disproportionately to those already making higher incomes. From 1979 to 2012, the income growth of the richest people remained high, while people at lower income levels had much lower growth or none at all. Working-class and lower-middle-class workers have actually fared worse

FIGURE 9.11 | CHANGE IN REAL FAMILY INCOME, 1947–1979 AND 1979–2016

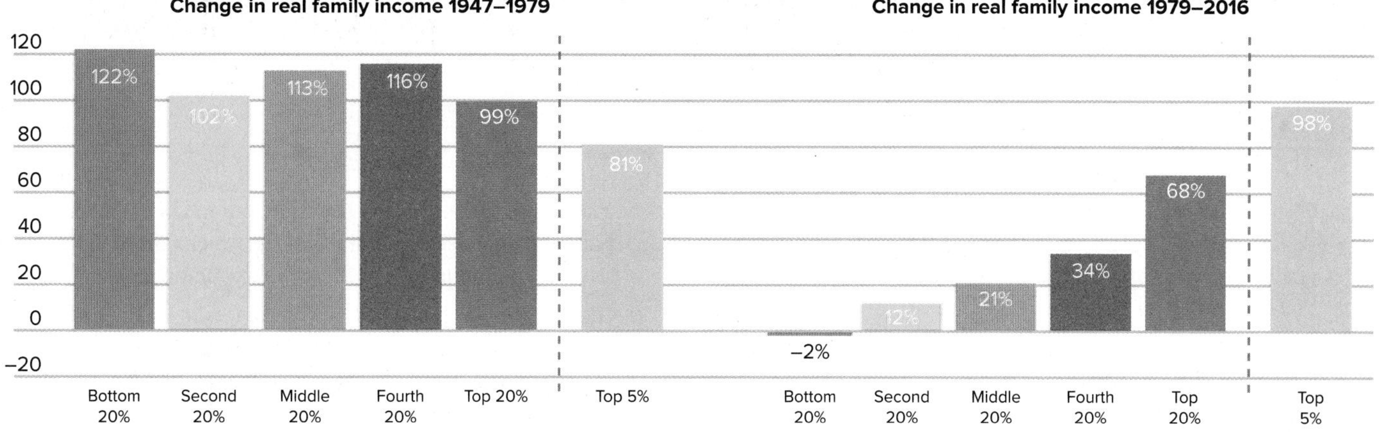

In the decades after World War II, the benefits of economic growth were spread evenly, and families at all income levels enjoyed significant increases in their income. In recent decades, however, those with already high incomes have seen the biggest gains; most people have experienced more modest gains or no gains at all.

Source: Calculated from U.S. Census Bureau, Current Population Survey, Annual Social and Economic Supplements, Table F03, using 2016 constant dollars.

than Figure 9.11 suggests, because in the past few decades more families have become two-income households. In a historic shift in family structure, both husband and wife in most families today work outside the home to improve or just maintain their standard of living (Levy 1998).

What all this means is that the gap between rich and poor has expanded significantly, and income inequality in the United States today is greater than at any time since the Great Depression of the 1930s. This growing inequality has profoundly affected both family structure and social structure as a whole. For example, because of stagnant wages, parents in many families work longer hours or take on a second job; as a result, they have less time to care for their children, volunteer, or become politically active. Many families have also taken on a growing amount of personal debt. The "Great Recession" of 2007-2009 further contributed to income inequality by lowering working- and middle-class wages for a decade. It took until 2017 for the real value of wages for most workers to return to 2007 levels (Gould 2018).

thinking sociologically about
Class and Global Inequality

culture

- Class is not just about money: it includes a major cultural component that is passed on through socialization, especially through the family and schools.
- Different societies have different cultural values that place more or less emphasis on limiting economic inequality.

structure

- Individual action is important in determining your class position, but it always takes place within a structural context that shapes the options available to you.
- The structure of the global economy helps shape the opportunities and living conditions of people around the globe.

power

- Because of their different levels of material and cultural resources, people from different classes have different levels of power in society.
- Wealthy, industrialized nations have considerably more power than poor or developing countries. Multinational corporations based in wealthy countries, along with global financial institutions, have considerable power to influence the global economy.

REVIEW, REFLECT, AND APPLY

Looking Back

1. Class is a system of stratification involving both economic and cultural resources. Marx explored class based on the relationship workers had to the means of production, whereas Weber emphasized people's life chances. Functionalists argued that economic stratification makes a useful contribution to the social order.
2. The U.S. class system includes the capitalist (upper) class, middle class, working class, and underclass. Considerable income inequality exists in the United States, and wealth is even more heavily concentrated at the top.
3. Class systems accommodate mobility; however, the class a person's family belongs to heavily influences the class to which he or she will belong as an adult. The impact of class on daily life can be seen in health, education, work, politics, and lifestyle.
4. Poverty can be defined in either absolute or relative terms. After declining sharply in the 1960s, U.S. poverty rates have remained relatively stable.
5. In the United States, class inequality is supported by an accompanying ideology that emphasizes equal opportunity, merit, and individual effort.
6. Class must be reproduced from generation to generation. Each class possesses cultural capital, which families and schools play an important role in reproducing.
7. Global inequality refers to the differences in wealth and power among countries. These differences affect health and life expectancy, housing, education, and many other conditions of daily life. Public policy influences the degree of within-country inequality found in different nations.
8. Modernization theory suggests that the vast gap between rich and poor nations is the result of cultural differences. Dependency theory explains global inequality by focusing on colonialism and neocolonialism. World systems analysis highlights the interdependence among countries, showing how domination of poorer countries by wealthy ones continues today. Some critics argue that this domination is achieved, in part, through global financial institutions.
9. The United States enjoyed economic domination in the post-World War II years, the benefits of which were spread evenly across people at all income levels. Since the 1970s, however, economic inequality has grown in the United States as the benefits of a more competitive global economy have gone disproportionately to those with higher incomes.

Critical Thinking: Questions and Activities

1. What is your family's class? In what ways has class helped shape your life? What privileges, if any, did you enjoy because of your family's class position? What barriers, if any, did you face? Were you taught some version of the ideas of equal opportunity, meritocracy, and individualism? What is the relationship between your family's class position and the ideology you learned?
2. Are you a first-generation college student? If so, has the experience exposed any class issues for you and your family? (Do you recognize some of the issues Alfred Lubrano raises in the opening of this chapter?) If not, what aspect of your family's cultural capital were you able to draw on in planning for and attending college?
3. Given what you now know, how would you explain why people are rich or poor? How do human action and structural forces figure in your explanations?
4. Do you think economic globalization has, on balance, been a positive development or a negative one? Explain.
5. The Walton family, of Walmart fame, has inherited a vast fortune generated from selling low-priced consumer goods to low-wage workers. Most of these products are manufactured abroad. Apply your understanding of deindustrialization and the global economy to explain the dramatic success of Walmart and stores like it.
6. Donald Trump's election as president in 2016 depended on a large number of votes from people without a college degree in "Rust Belt" states, such as Ohio, Michigan, Wisconsin, and Pennsylvania. How might such an outcome be connected to the process of deindustrialization, discussed in this chapter?

Key Terms

absolute poverty (p. 217) a scarcity of resources so severe that it is life-threatening.

capital (p. 206) the money to invest in factories, real estate, and other businesses.

capitalist class (p. 206) (or *bourgeoisie*) those who control major capital and own the means of production.

class (p. 206) a group of people who share a roughly similar economic position and lifestyle.

class mobility (p. 212) the ability to move from one social class to another.

classism (p. 216) prejudice or discrimination based on social class.

colonialism (p. 227) the use of military, political, and economic power by one society to dominate the people of another society, usually for economic benefit.

conspicuous consumption (p. 216) lavish spending, done to compete for status with others.

cultural capital (p. 219) various types of knowledge, skills, and other cultural resources.

deindustrialization (p. 228) the process by which investment in the nation's manufacturing capacity decreased.

dependency theory (p. 227) a theory that attributes global inequality to the exploitation of weaker, poor nations by wealthy, more powerful ones.

equal opportunity (p. 218) the idea that all people should have the same chance to achieve success.

feminization of poverty (p. 218) a trend in which women made up an increasingly large share of the poor.

global inequality (p. 224) the differences in wealth and power among the countries of the world.

income (p. 209) money received from sources such as wages and salaries as well as from the interest, dividends, and rent generated by wealth.

individual mobility (p. 212) a change in a person's class position that occurs without any change in the larger class structure.

individualism (p. 218) a system of beliefs that highlights the importance of the single person over any social group.

life chances (p. 207) the likelihood a person has of obtaining valued economic and cultural resources.

meritocracy (p. 218) a system in which people are rewarded and are able to advance because of their abilities.

middle class (p. 210) a group that contributes specialized knowledge and expertise to the economy.

modernization theory (p. 227) a theory that attributes global inequality to cultural differences among countries.

neocolonialism (p. 227) a system of economic domination of poorer nations by wealthier ones without the use of formal political control or military occupation.

poverty line (U.S.) (p. 217)a measure of scarcity determined by figuring the cost of a minimal food budget and multiplying it by three.

poverty rate (p. 217) the percentage of the population that falls below the poverty line.

progressive taxation (p. 222) a system of taxation in which those with higher incomes pay a higher rate.

public assistance (p. 223) either tax credits or actual payments and benefits provided to citizens by the government.

regressive taxation (p. 223) a system of taxation that disproportionately affects those with lower incomes.

relative poverty (p. 217) a lack of the basic resources needed to maintain a standard of living considered acceptable in a particular society.

social capital (p. 219) relationships that are potentially economically valuable resulting from membership in a group.

structural mobility (p. 212) a change in class position that occurs when a shift in available occupations changes the class system as a whole.

underclass (or lower class) (p. 211) chronically unemployed people who have no ongoing relationship to the mainstream economy.

wealth (p. 209) the value of financial assets, such as savings, real estate, stocks, and bonds, minus any outstanding debts.

working class (or *proletariat*) (p. 206) those who survive on the wages they earn.

world systems analysis (p. 227) an approach that focuses on the interdependence among the countries that make up a single global economic system.

©Jim West/Alamy Stock Photo

10 Race and Ethnicity

looking AHEAD

How does **culture** define your race?

How do individuals and institutional **structures** perpetuate racial and ethnic inequality?

How do majority and minority groups reflect inequalities in **power**?

©Charles Ommanney/The Washington Post/Getty Images

In 2010, early in Barack Obama's presidency, a Gallup poll found that the percentage of Americans who expressed a "great deal" of worry about race relations had hit an all-time low of 13 percent. To many, the election of the nation's first black president signaled progress in the long struggle for racial equality, perhaps even marking the beginning of a postracial America.

By 2017, early in Donald Trump's presidency, the percentage of Americans who expressed a "great deal" of worry about race relations had reached an all-time high of 42 percent (Gallup 2017a). Any thoughts of a postracial America now seemed hopelessly naïve.

While Trump has repeatedly claimed he is the "least racist" person around, he has a long history of words and deeds that critics view as bigoted and racist. He falsely claimed that Arab Americans in New Jersey were cheering when the World Trade Center towers collapsed on September 11, 2001, and later called for a "total and complete shutdown of Muslims entering the United States." Trump was a prominent proponent of the "birther" conspiracy theory that claimed Obama was not an American because he had been born in Kenya, even after his Hawaiian birth certificate made clear this was a lie. Trump launched his presidential campaign with a broadside attack on Mexican immigrants saying that, while some were good people, "They're bringing drugs. They're bringing crime. They're rapists," and called for the construction of a massive wall to seal the border. He re-tweeted material from white supremacist groups, including made-up statistics falsely claiming that blacks do most killings of whites. When Trump said that U.S.-born federal judge Gonzalo Curiel, who was overseeing a fraud case filed against "Trump University," had an "inherent bias" because of his Mexican heritage, even his own party's leader in the House of Representatives, Paul Ryan, responded, "Claiming a person can't do their job because of their race is sort of like the textbook definition of a racist comment" (Kreig 2016; Leonhardt and Philbrick 2018; McCammon 2016; Milbank 2015).

Trump's campaign drew support from and energized white supremacists after his election, including Nazi and Ku Klux Klan supporters, who took part in a "Unite the Right" rally in Charlottesville, Virginia, in August 2017. However, the appeal of Trump's nostalgic promise to "Make American Great Again" also reached far into mainstream America, often for reasons other than race. Still, having won 58 percent of the vote among whites, 29 percent among Latinos, and only 8 percent among African Americans (Roper Center 2016), the election of Donald Trump provides a stark reminder that race and ethnicity continue to be front-and-center issues for U.S. society, as they have been since before the nation's founding.

Debates involving race and ethnicity are as old as the country itself. Even before the United States existed, the arrival of Europeans in a land already populated by many native societies sparked conflict between people of different races and ethnicities. As we will see, neither race nor ethnicity is rooted in biological fact; both are cultural creations. But these cultural ideas have real-world consequences; they affect patterns of action–social structure–and they contribute to persistent inequalities in power and resources among racial and ethnic groups. In many ways, the social history of the United States is intertwined with the history of ideas about race and ethnicity, including debates about who is entitled to citizenship and equal rights.

Today, whether or not we realize it, whether or not we want them to be, race and ethnicity are parts of our identity, influencing our lives and the way people interact with us. To better understand ourselves and our increasingly diverse society, we need to grapple with the impact that race and ethnicity have had on our history and the role they continue to play today.

The Role of Culture: Inventing Ethnicity and Race

Many societies, including the United States, classify people in terms of *race* and *ethnicity*. **Ethnicity** refers to *a shared cultural heritage, often deriving from a common ancestry and homeland.* That cultural heritage can include, among other things, common language, traditions, customs, symbols, and distinctive foods and music.

In contrast, a **race** is *a category of people widely perceived as sharing socially significant physical characteristics such as skin color.* Ethnicity can be confused with race. For example, in the United States, many people mistakenly think of Hispanic as a "race" equivalent to "white," "black," or "Asian." In fact, the homelands from which Hispanics come are inhabited by people of Native American, African, European, and Asian origin. As a result, Hispanics may be of any race, though most identify as white.

While ethnic categories are based on culture and racial categories on perceived physical characteristics, both are socially constructed. That is, they are created by people, vary across cultures, and change over time.

Ethnicity as a Social Construction

Ethnicities are social constructions that exist only to the extent that people embrace them or have them imposed by others. People are constantly reinventing and redefining ethnic identities, which can make them fluid and murky. For example, in the United States, the ethnic label *Hispanic* applies to people who come from Spanish-speaking countries or whose ancestors did. The label was popularized in the 1970s by grassroots activists, newly emerging Spanish-language television broadcasters, and the federal government (Molina 2014). Activists believed a single label could help unite what were otherwise very different and geographically dispersed groups. With the single term "Hispanics" they sought to merge Puerto Ricans in the Northeast, Cuban Americans in the Southeast, and Mexican Americans in the Southwest, among others, into a single minority group. This single, larger group would then have greater political clout and be better positioned to compete for attention and resources from government agencies and philanthropies. Spanish-language television broadcasters, particularly Univision, helped to establish the term by creating content intended to appeal to a single, broad audience rather than specific nationalities. Finally, in 1980 the U.S. Census Bureau began including "Hispanic origin" as a category people could use to identify themselves, making the term a staple of U.S. culture.

However, many people categorized as Hispanic reject the label precisely because it lumps many cultures together. Instead, some prefer the term *Latino* (male), *Latina* (female), or *Latinx* (gender neutral) to specify a heritage from Latin America. Others prefer to identify with their specific ancestry as, for example, Mexican Americans (or Chicanos), Puerto Ricans, Cuban Americans, or Colombians. In addition, Hispanic is increasingly treated as if it were a racial category. In the 2010 Census, over 30 percent of Hispanic respondents chose "some other race" instead of one of the standard choices of white, black, Asian, American Indian, or Pacific Islander; about half wrote in "Mexican," "Hispanic," "Latin American," or "Puerto Rican" (Ríos, Romero, and Ramírez, 2014).

Race as a Social Construction

If you walk into a room full of people, you can usually tell just by looking who is white, Asian, or black. Isn't race, then, a biological reality? Although it is based on physical characteristics and thus reflects biological variation, race, like ethnicity, is a social construction (Mukhopadhyay, Henze, and Moses 2014). Races exist only to the extent that people use physical characteristics to assign one another to social categories, but those categories do not represent biologically meaningful divisions in the human species.

For example, most important biological differences among people—differences that affect health, longevity, susceptibility to disease, and so on—are invisible and do not play any role in the definition of racial categories. These differences include things like blood types or the presence of genetic markers that predispose people to certain diseases. In addition, people are arbitrarily selective in the visible physical characteristics they do use to define racial categories. In the United States, for example, they largely ignore eye color and hair color when making racial distinctions, focusing instead on skin color. Finally, no clear dividing line distinguishes one racial group from another. Physical variation occurs along a continuum, making it impossible to categorize humans neatly into a few distinct racial categories. For example, much more physical variation exists among whites than exists between whites and any other racial category; some people classified as white even have darker skin than some people classified as black.

In short, when it comes to race, we don't see many physical differences that matter, we ignore many differences we can see, and we classify people into supposedly sharply bounded categories when in fact the members of those categories have continuously overlapping physical characteristics.

In reality, there is only a single human race with no subcategories or subspecies. All humans share a common ancestral lineage that evolved in Africa about 100,000–200,000 years ago (Mukhopadhyay et al. 2014). As a result, no biological feature or cluster of features clearly distinguishes one category of humans racially from any other. To understand what this common origin means in terms of the socially constructed nature of race, consider the physical feature most closely identified with racial differences in the United States: skin color.

Skin color is determined mostly by varying amounts of a pigment called melanin. Humans are vulnerable to the harmful effects of intense sunlight, which include an increased probability of having a child with birth defects for women and reduced fertility for men. Melanin—and the dark skin associated with

©Commanding Artists/Botanica/Getty Images

©Dmitrii Rusev/EyeEm/Getty Images

©Image Source/Getty Images

People make racial distinctions in part by paying attention selectively to some physical variations while largely ignoring others. Why are the different skin tones in these men more socially significant than their different hair color? What does this selective attention suggest about the arbitrary nature of race?

it—protects against these adverse effects, but it also reduces the skin's ability to produce the essential nutrient vitamin D from sunlight. As a result, dark skin provides an evolutionary advantage in sunlight-intense tropical environments, whereas lighter skin provides an evolutionary advantage in regions of less intense sunlight (Jablonski and Chaplin 2002, 2010). As humans across many generations migrated and adapted to different geographic regions, they developed a range of skin tones that vary more or less continuously from dark to light between regions of intense sunlight and those of less intense sunlight (Map 10.1) (Jablonski and Chaplin 2002, 2010).

In addition, skin tone is not consistently connected to other physical features such as hair type or nose shape. Dark- or light-skinned people can have all types of hair, noses, and other physical attributes. Skin tone, in other words, is not a fixed biological attribute of any one race. To understand how it became linked with race in the popular imagination, we have to look to social factors—cultural beliefs, social structures, and power relationships—not to biology.

Pseudoscience and Race

The term *race* took on its popular contemporary connotations in the eighteenth century, when European scientists began systematically to name and classify the plants and animals of the natural world. When they turned their attention to humanity, however, ethnocentric assumptions of European superiority reduced their efforts to pseudoscience (Fish 2013; Smedley and Smedley 2012; Sussman 2014).

For example, the Swedish naturalist Carolus Linnaeus (1707–1778), who laid the foundation for the biological classification system still in use today, invented four subspecies of *Homo sapiens,* attributing to each not only physical traits but also judgmental character traits. White-skinned *Europeanus,* described as creative and governed by laws, was at the top. The other three were copper-skinned *Americanus,* described as stubborn, easily angered, and governed by customs; sallow-skinned (yellowish) *Asiaticus,* described as greedy and governed by opinions; and dark-skinned *Africanus,* described as lazy, negligent, and governed only by impulse (Smedley and Smedley 2012). This classification laid the groundwork for "scientific" justifications of **racism,** *the belief that one race is inherently superior to another.*

Later writers developed variations on this sort of racist classification system. These schemes often contradicted each other, proposing a widely varying number of "races," each based on different physical types and accompanying social characteristics. Whites, for example, were often divided into subgroups that purported to reflect the superiority of northern Europeans—labeled in various schemes as "Teutonic" or "Nordic"—over such other whites as "Celtics," "Semitics," and "Mediterraneans" (Smedley and Smedley 2012).

From today's perspective, the rationale used to justify these racial classification systems seems arbitrary and even bizarre. For example, in the nineteenth century, German anatomist and anthropologist Johann Blumenbach (1752–1840), apparently after admiring the symmetry of a particularly well-preserved skull from the Caucasus Mountains (located between Russia and Turkey), concluded that it must have been Caucasians whom God had created in his own image. Other races, he decided, had degenerated physically and morally from God's vision because they had moved and adapted to new environments. Thus, religion and folk belief, couched in pseudoscientific language, combined to give us the term *Caucasian,* still in common use as a synonym for "white" (Mukhopadhyay et al. 2014).

These arbitrary and conflicting classification systems went hand in hand with a belief in **racial essentialism**—*the idea that supposedly natural and immutable differences separate the races.* Whites who created the classification systems lived in societies

©PeopleImages/iStock/Getty Images

Human physical variation is too subtle and diverse to be captured accurately by a handful of racial or ethnic classifications.

with the power to enforce these ideas. Cultural notions of racial essentialism were used to justify white supremacy, slavery, and the European colonial domination of other peoples.

Race and Ethnicity over Time and across Cultures

Because races and ethnicities are cultural creations rather than biological facts, the definition and significance of racial and ethnic groups varies from culture to culture and changes over time. In nineteenth-century China, people drew distinctions based on body hair rather than skin tone. To them, extensive facial hair marked European missionaries as uncivilized barbarians (Mukhopadhyay et al. 2014). In many parts of the world, ethnicity is more important than race; people are much more concerned about one another's tribe, clan, or ethnic affiliation than about skin color or other physical characteristics (Cornell and Hartmann 2007).

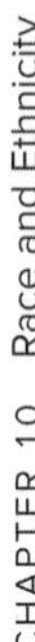

MAP 10.1 | GLOBAL DISTRIBUTION OF SKIN TONE

NORTH AMERICA
EUROPE
ASIA
AFRICA
SOUTH AMERICA
AUSTRALIA
From lightest skin to darkest skin
No data

Skin tone is roughly distributed along the earth's latitudes so that, for example, people in parts of Mexico, northern Africa, and portions of China all share similar skin tones, even though they are commonly classified as belonging to different racial groups. *Source:* Adapted from Jablonski and Chaplin (2002).

In countries where race does matter, definitions of race—and the standards for assigning people to one race or another—vary enormously. In the United States, sexual encounters between white owners and black slaves were common, and in the nineteenth century people of mixed race were often called "Mulattos." In the early twentieth century, however, whites began changing state laws so that racial categories became mutually exclusive, and in the case of mixed ancestry, the black status prevailed. For example, Virginia passed the "Racial Integrity Act" in 1924 mandating that all newborns be classified as either white or colored, with colored including those with *any* black or Native American ancestry. During the first half of the twentieth century, versions of this so-called one-drop rule—one drop of black blood makes a person black—were adopted by state legislatures throughout much of the South and Midwest (Murray 1997).

In recent years, however, the United States has returned to acknowledging mixed-race status. Since 2000, the U.S. Census Bureau (2011b, 2011c) has allowed people the option of indicating a mixed racial heritage, and by 2010 more than 9 million people—about 3 percent of the population—reported being of two or more races (see Figure 10.1).

The countries of Latin America and the Caribbean have long had a variety of categories for people of mixed descent—including

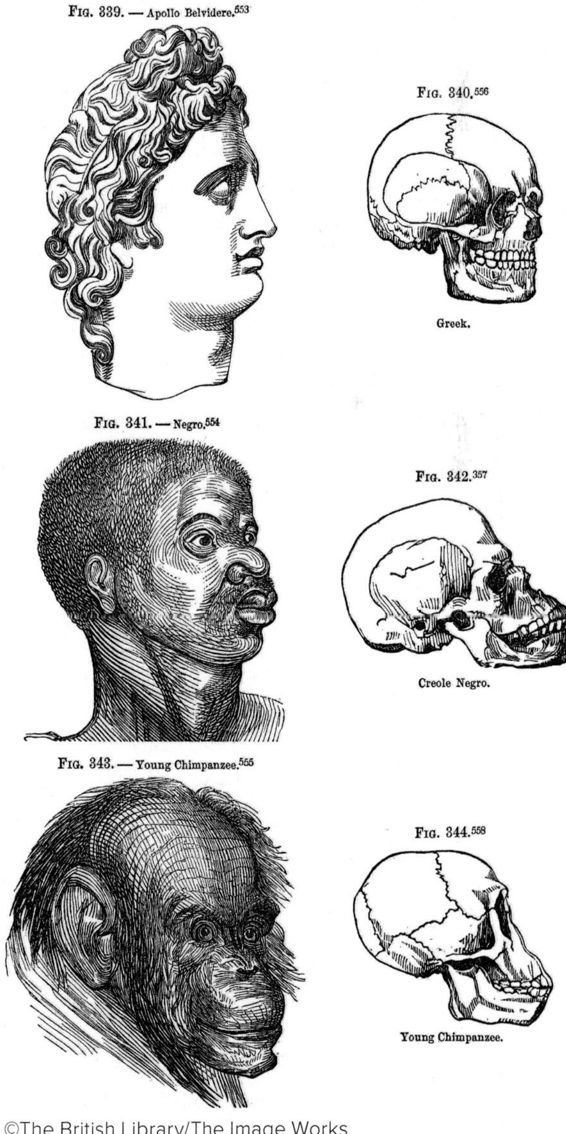

Early pseudoscientific classification schemes perpetuated racist beliefs. This image is from an 1857 book titled *Indigenous Races of the Earth* by physician Josiah Nott and Egyptologist George Gliddon. It suggests white biological superiority, with blacks somewhere in between whites and chimpanzees.

©The British Library/The Image Works

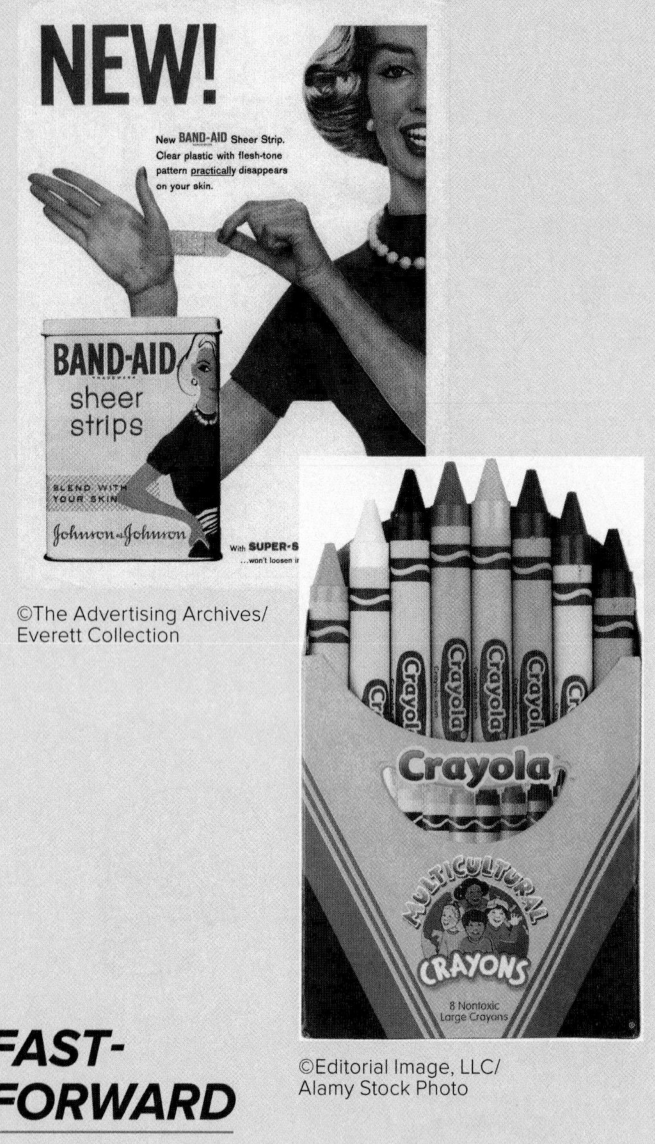

©The Advertising Archives/ Everett Collection

©Editorial Image, LLC/ Alamy Stock Photo

FAST-FORWARD

Social Change and Race

For many years, white people were the assumed norm when manufacturers created "flesh"-colored products such as adhesive bandages. Today, reflecting changes in the culture, manufacturers are more likely to recognize a diversity of skin tones, as with these "multicultural" crayons.

FIGURE 10.1 | RACE, ETHNICITY, AND THE U.S. CENSUS

Is this person of Hispanic, Latino, or Spanish origin?

- ☐ **No**, not of Hispanic, Latino, or Spanish origin
- ☐ Yes, Mexican, Mexican Am., Chicano
- ☐ Yes, Puerto Rican
- ☐ Yes, Cuban
- ☐ Yes, another Hispanic, Latino, or Spanish origin — *Print, for example, Salvadoran, Dominican, Colombian, Guatemalan, Spaniard, Ecuadorian, etc.*

What is this person's race?
Mark **X** *one or more boxes* ***AND*** *print origins.*

- ☐ White – *Print, for example, German, Irish, English, Italian, Lebanese, Egyptian, etc.*
- ☐ Black or African Am. – *Print, for example, African American, Jamaican, Haitian, Nigerian, Ethiopian, Somali, etc.*
- ☐ American Indian or Alaska Native - *Print name of enrolled or principal tribe(s), for example, Navajo Nation, Blackfeet Tribe, Mayan, Aztec, Native Village of Barrow Inupiat Traditional Government, Nome Eskimo Community, etc.*

☐ Chinese	☐ Vietnamese	☐ Native Hawaiian
☐ Filipino	☐ Korean	☐ Samoan
☐ Asian Indian	☐ Japanese	☐ Chamorro
☐ Other Asian – *Print, for example, Pakistani, Cambodian, Hmong, etc.*		☐ Other Pacific Islander – *Print, for example, Tongan, Fijian, Marshallese, etc.*

- ☐ Some other race – *Print race or origin.*

As usual, U.S. census includes questions about race and Hispanic origin. The categories included in these questions reflect the unique social history of the United States.
Source: U.S. Census Bureau.

mixtures of European, African, and Indian—and physical appearance carries much less social significance in the region than it does in the United States. For example, the legacy of slavery in Brazil endured in the ranking of people by racial category. However, in Brazil these categories were never codified legally. In addition, intermarriage and sexual relations among indigenous peoples, Africans, and Europeans were much more commonly accepted than in the United States. Brazilians now have dozens of racial categories based on differences in a variety of physical features, including hair, lips, eyes, and noses, as well as skin color. As a result, siblings from the same family can fall into different racial categories. Also, in Brazil the presence of any white ancestor helps determine a person's classification, and over half of Brazilians fall into the broad category of "white" (which is broken down into many smaller subcategories). However, many white Brazilians would be perceived as black if they traveled to the United States (Kephart 2003; Telles 2014). For a look at various systems of racial and ethnic classification, see Figure 10.2.

FIGURE 10.2 | RACE AND ETHNICITY ACROSS CULTURES

Australia 2016 Census

Is the person of Aboriginal or Torres Strait Islander origin?
For persons of both Aboriginal and Torres Strait Islander origin, mark both "Yes" boxes.

☐ No
☐ Yes, Aboriginal
☐ Yes, Torres Strait Islander

Brazil 2010 Census

Color or race:

☐ Branca [White]
☐ Peta [Black]
☐ Amaréta [Yellow]
☐ Parda [Mixed]
☐ Indigena [indigenous]

Bulgaria 2010 Census

What is your ethnic group?

☐ Bulgarian
☐ Turkish
☐ Roma
☐ Other

England 2011 Census

What is your ethnic group?

A) White
☐ English / Welsh / Scottish / Northern Irish / British
☐ Irish
☐ Gypsy or Irish Traveller
☐ Any other White background

B) Mixed / multiple ethnic groups
☐ White and Black Caribbean
☐ White and Black African
☐ White and Asian
☐ Any other Mixed / multiple ethnic background

C) Asian / Asian British
☐ Indian
☐ Pakistani
☐ Bangladeshi
☐ Chinese
☐ Any other Asian background

D) Black / African / Caribbean / Black British
☐ African
☐ Caribbean
☐ Any other Black / African / Caribbean background

E) Other ethnic group
☐ Arab
☐ Any other ethnic group

Canada 2016 Census

Is this person an Aboriginal person, that is, First Nations (North American Indian), Métis or Inuk (Inuit)?
If "Yes," mark the circle(s) that best describe(s) this person now.

☐ No, not an Aboriginal person
☐ Yes, First Nations (North American Indian)
☐ Yes, Métis
☐ Yes, Inuk (Inuit)

Is this person: (Mark more than one circle or specify, if applicable.)

☐ White
☐ South Asian (e.g., East Indian, Pakistani, Sri Lankan, etc.)
☐ Chinese
☐ Black
☐ Filipino
☐ Latin American
☐ Arab
☐ Southeast Asian (e.g., Vietnamese, Cambodian, Laotian, Thai, etc.)
☐ West Asian (e.g., Iranian, Afghan, etc.)
☐ Korean
☐ Japanese
☐ Other—specify

Mexico 2015 Census

Based on your culture, history, and traditions, do you consider yourself black, meaning Afro-Mexican or of African descent?

☐ Yes ☐ Yes, in part ☐ No

Based on your culture, are you indigenous?

☐ Yes ☐ Yes, in part ☐ No

South Africa 2011 Census

How would (name) describe him/herself in terms of population group?

☐ Black African
☐ Coloured
☐ Indian or Asian
☐ White
☐ Other

Because race and ethnicity are social constructions, they vary by culture. Different countries use different classification systems in their census collection. If you moved to another country, your race or ethnicity might change.

Source: Compiled by author from census forms online.

Structure and Power among Racial and Ethnic Groups

By identifying certain cultural or physical traits as socially significant, people create a social reality that influences how they behave with one another. In other words, "seeing" others in terms of race, ethnicity, and other social categories (such as religion, age, and sexual orientation) can affect how we act toward them and help legitimize social inequality based on those categories. Let's look at some of these dynamics.

Minority and Majority Groups

People often categorize different races and ethnicities within a society into minority and majority groups. A **minority group** is *a collection of people who suffer disadvantages and have less power because of identifiable physical or cultural characteristics.* In contrast, a **majority group** is *a collection of people who enjoy privileges and have more access to power because of identifiable physical or cultural characteristics.* Sociologists do not use these terms in a literal sense. A minority group need not be an actual minority of the population, and a majority group need not be an actual majority. In South Africa under the white supremacist apartheid regime, for example, the black population held the minority status even though they far outnumbered whites.

Although the status of individual members of a minority can vary widely, *as a group,* compared to the majority group, minorities tend to have lower incomes, less education, less political influence, and poorer health. Conversely, individual members of a majority group may not wield great power or have access to great resources, but, *as a group,* majorities dominate society. In addition to greater resources, the majority group also has the power to create and enforce the labels used to designate minority groups.

Members of minority groups tend to be conscious of their status and aware of the hurdles and barriers they face in society. To navigate a majority-dominated society successfully, they must learn how the majority group operates. In contrast, majority-group members often take their status for granted and are unaware of their relative privilege. They typically do not need to learn about minority cultures to be successful within a society their group dominates. Often, they argue that race and ethnicity should not matter.

Patterns of Majority-Minority Interaction

The relationship between majority and minority groups in a society can range from benign to destructive. In some cases, members of a minority group might find acceptance and equal standing with the majority group, whereas in other situations a minority group may be subjected to widespread prejudice and discrimination. To have **prejudice** means *to "pre-judge" someone or some group negatively based on inadequate information.* These judgments are often based on **stereotypes,** *exaggerated, distorted, or untrue generalizations about categories of people that do not acknowledge individual variation.* Stereotypes can be either negative or positive; examples of positive stereotypes are the Asian math whiz and the African American sports star. Prejudice is limited to beliefs and attitudes that individuals hold but may not act on. When prejudice is joined to action, however, it leads to **discrimination,** *unequal treatment that gives advantages to one group of people over another without justifiable cause.*

The patterns of interaction among majority and minority groups can take a variety of forms, sometimes straddling more than one category. In a society that embraces **pluralism,** *distinct ethnic and racial groups coexist on equal terms and have equal social standing.* Members of these groups recognize and maintain their differences, but the differences have no significant impact on anyone's political, social, or economic standing. Switzerland is a successful pluralistic society. The Swiss Confederation—Switzerland's official name—unites four cultures, each with its own regions and its own official language: German, French, Italian, or Romansch (based on Latin).

©McGraw-Hill Education/Christopher Kerrigan, photographer

Amalgamation is *the process by which a majority and a minority group blend or mix to form a new group.* This is typically accomplished through intermarriage over the course of several generations. For example, Mexican society today is primarily an amalgamation of Indian and Spanish cultures that have blended to create what is now a distinctly Mexican identity.

Assimilation is *the process by which members of a minority group come to adopt the culture of the majority group.* As we will see, the experience of many white European ethnic groups in the United States has been one of assimilation; ethnic groups largely abandoned their distinct cultures and were absorbed into the nation's dominant culture. The assimilation experience is often partially voluntary, as minority group members emulate the dominant culture, and partially coerced as majority-group members require others to conform to their cultural expectations.

Segregation involves *keeping distinct social groups physically and socially separate and unequal.* In the United States, segregation is most associated with the oppression of African Americans, especially in the South after the Civil War and before the civil rights movement.

Genocide is *the systematic killing of a group of people, based on their race, ethnicity, nationality, or religion.* Typically, genocide involves a majority group seeking to exterminate a minority group. The deliberate killing of Jews and others by the Nazi regime in Germany and other European countries during World War II is the most infamous example of genocide, but not the first and, unfortunately, not the last (Kiernan 2007).

Minority-Group Responses to Discrimination

Minority groups can respond to majority-group domination in a variety of ways:

- ***Withdrawal*** involves physically escaping the worst oppression. One example is the formation of racial and ethnic enclaves in urban areas: places with names like Germantown, Little Italy, and Chinatown.
- ***Passing*** involves blending in with the dominant group. White ethnics in the United States often changed their names on arrival to better blend into the dominant Anglo-Saxon culture. Germans with the name "Schmidt" would change it to "Smith," for example. Today many recent immigrants from Vietnam, China, India, and elsewhere similarly adopt names that are more familiar to native-born Americans and easier for them to spell and pronounce.

Passing can also occur when people in a minority group take advantage of physical similarities to the members of the majority group, as when light-skinned blacks conceal their race or even change their hair to appear more "white."

- *Code-switching*—a term coined by sociologist Elijah Anderson (1999)—refers to the strategy of complying with the social expectations of the majority by creating a front-stage self-presentation while maintaining a different more comfortable and authentic backstage identity. Code-switching may involve dressing "white" or using "white" English at work or school, while retaining a more comfortable mother tongue, ethnic slang, and ethnic dress at home.
- *Resistance* involves actively asserting oneself—either individually or collectively—in defiance of majority discrimination. The many civil rights struggles that have characterized U.S. history are examples of this strategy.

The Origins of Racial and Ethnic Diversity in the United States

In the United States, ideas about race and ethnicity are rooted in the country's early history—the European conquest of native peoples, the immigration of Europeans, the enslavement of Africans, and the recruitment of Asian laborers.

Native Peoples

In 1492, before Europeans established their first permanent settlements in the Western Hemisphere, an estimated 50 million people lived in North and South America, about 5 million of them in what is today the United States and Canada (Taylor 2001). When Europeans arrived, the Aztec capital of Tenochtitlán had a quarter of a million inhabitants—five times the size of London at the time (Gonzalez 2011). Native peoples formed hundreds of different societies with unique languages, religions, forms of government, and cultural traditions. These ranged from the Inuit, who lived in nomadic bands in what is today the Canadian Arctic, to the powerful urban civilizations of the Aztec and Maya in what is today Mexico and the Inca in what is today Peru.

The European invasion that began with Christopher Columbus's first voyage in 1492 had a devastating effect on native peoples. At any given place, within a decade after contact with Europeans, the native population typically fell to about half its precontact numbers, and within 50 years to just one-tenth (Taylor 2001). Most of this devastation was caused by disease. The native peoples had no immunity to the many infections the Europeans brought with them, including smallpox, measles, tuberculosis, and the bubonic plague, and they succumbed to them in huge numbers. Many European settlers interpreted the widespread deaths as a sign that God was "making room" for the colonists (Takaki 2008).

Of those who survived disease, many were killed as European powers, vying for control of the Americas, steadily dispossessed native peoples of their land and autonomy. By just before the American Revolution in 1776, the British and French controlled much of what became the United States and Canada. The Spanish were the dominant power in what is now the southwestern United States, Mexico, and much of Latin and South America, whereas the Portuguese controlled what is now Brazil.

After it achieved independence from Britain, the United States continued to subjugate and uproot the native populations of North America as it expanded westward. Its tactics included political deception, blatant treaty violations, forcible removal, and military conquest. By 1890, the country's Native American population had been reduced to less than 250,000 (Gibson and Jung 2002) who were confined largely to reservations that represented only a tiny fraction of the lands their ancestors had once occupied (Map 10.2). The U.S. government, which managed these reservations, sometimes seized Native American children and sent them to boarding schools where they were taught English and encouraged to adopt Christianity and abandon their own language and culture.

Native peoples struggled to maintain their cultural identity despite this invasion, and they have had an enduring and continuing impact on postconquest societies, especially in places with the densest precontact populations, such as Mexico, Guatemala, Ecuador, Peru, and Bolivia (Dunbar-Ortiz 2014).

Hispanics or Latinos

In the first half of the 1500s, various Spanish explorers traveled through what is today the southern half of the United States, claiming the region for Spain as they went. These expeditions—which took place decades before the 1607 founding of the first British colony at Jamestown, Virginia—gave names to many geographic features in the United States and established some of its earliest European settlements, including St. Augustine in Florida and Santa Fe in New Mexico (Gonzalez 2011).

Spanish control of areas that became Mexico, Puerto Rico, Cuba, and other nations of Central and South America laid the foundation for ethnic combinations that we now define as Hispanic or Latino.

Mexican Americans Mexican Americans are the largest Latino group in the United States, partly because when Mexico gained its independence from Spain in 1821, it included what are today the states of Texas, New Mexico, Arizona, California, Nevada, Utah, and part of Colorado. In the 1820s, thousands of white U.S. citizens illegally crossed the U.S.-Mexican border into the sparsely populated region of Téjas—present-day Texas. By 1835, U.S. citizens in the region outnumbered Mexicans by five to one. A year later they launched an insurrection that ended with the creation of the Republic of Texas. Its president, Sam Houston, declared in his inaugural address that the newly created republic reflected "glory on the Anglo-Saxon race" (Montejano 1987; Takaki 2008, 158).

In 1845 the United States annexed Texas, and an ensuing border dispute provided the justification for the Mexican-American War (1846–1848). By the end of the war, the United States seized nearly half of Mexico, including what is now California and the

MAP 10.2 | NATIVE AMERICAN LOSS OF TERRITORY FROM BEFORE 1850 TO 1890

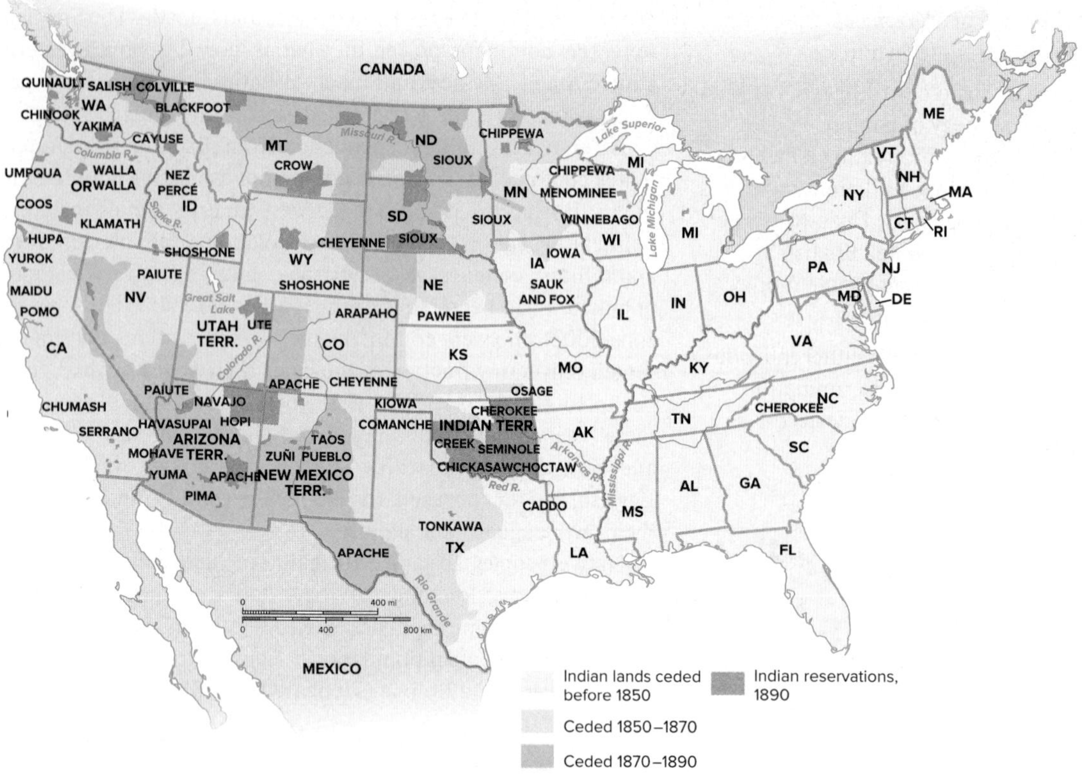

By 1890, conquest and expansion had confined most of the Native American population to a series of reservations, transforming North America from a land controlled by dozens of different native societies to one dominated by white European Americans. *Source:* Adapted from Davidson et al. (2014).

U.S. Southwest, fulfilling the common belief among whites in Manifest Destiny, which asserted that white Americans had a divinely ordained right and duty to occupy the continent from coast to coast (Horsman 1981).

The Treaty of Guadalupe Hidalgo that concluded the war in 1848 granted U.S. citizenship to about 80,000 formerly Mexican citizens who now found themselves living within the United States. Overnight, they had become, as Mexican American leader Pablo de la Guerra, later put it, "foreigners in their own land" (Takaki 2008, 165). In California, the discovery of gold that same year triggered a massive influx of Anglos—white English speakers—making Mexican Americans a minority there. Ironically, the newly arrived whites often saw the native Mexicans as "foreign" competitors for their land claims.

As they gained political power, Anglos began changing the laws already biased in favor of whites to give themselves further advantages at the expense of the native Mexican population, creating a de facto racial caste system. Throughout the Southwest, Mexican Americans faced the same segregation as African Americans. They were excluded from many restaurants and other public facilities, and their children attended segregated schools intended to prepare them to be farmworkers, not to help them get ahead. White-controlled courts also rejected the titles many Mexican Americans held to land, thus helping Anglos gain control of most of the Southwest. Deprived of land, many Mexican Americans worked for Anglos in mining, railroad construction, and ranching and farming, earning lower wages than their white counterparts (Montejano 1987). Both stoking and exploiting this racial and ethnic conflict, employers were able to blunt efforts by Mexican Americans and other workers to organize unions and strike for better conditions (Roediger 2007).

Some Mexican citizens, meanwhile, fled the political turmoil of the 1910 Mexican Revolution and headed north across the U.S.-Mexican border in search of security and work. But then, when work dried up during the Great Depression of the 1930s, 400,000 Mexicans—including many U.S.-born citizens—were sent back to Mexico, sometimes forcibly. Just a few years later, though, labor shortages that followed the outbreak of World War II prompted the U.S. government to recruit 200,000 Mexican laborers to work temporarily in the United States through the *bracero* program (from *brazos* for "arms"). Since then, agriculture in the Southwest has remained dependent on the labor of migrant Mexican and Mexican American farmworkers. The low pay and difficult conditions of this work sparked many labor disputes, which increased in the 1960s and 1970s with the rise of the United Farm Workers union led by César Chávez and Dolores Huerta (Pawel 2009, 2014).

Puerto Ricans Puerto Ricans, the second-largest Latino group in the United States, are also linked to U.S. expansion. The United States invaded and occupied Puerto Rico during the Spanish-American War of 1898, transforming the island from a Spanish colony to a U.S. colony. In the ensuing decades, U.S.

©Corbis/Getty Images

One way to dominate a population is to eradicate its culture. Native American boarding schools, typically run by Christian missionaries, taught native children to adopt European ways of life and abandon their own language, religion, traditions, and styles of dress.

sugar companies acquired vast tracts of land on the island, displacing small growers and prompting sometimes violent labor clashes. Many agricultural workers fled to the U.S. mainland in search of better opportunities. In 1917, Puerto Ricans became U.S. citizens and, in 1947, Puerto Rico became a commonwealth with the right to elect its own governor. Although it otherwise remains subject to U.S. law, it has only a nonvoting delegate to Congress and its residents cannot vote for president. Puerto Ricans are divided about the island's future political status. Some support the current arrangement, some favor gaining U.S. statehood, and some advocate independence (Takaki 2008; Wagenheim and Wagenheim 2013).

Cuban Americans The Spanish colony of Cuba, unlike Puerto Rico, gained formal independence after the Spanish-American War. However, it remained subject to U.S. military and economic intervention and suffered from political instability. In 1959, Fidel Castro led a revolution to overthrow the Cuban dictator Fulgencio Batista and instituted radical economic reform, eventually aligning his nation with the Soviet Union and communist bloc nations. Castro's reforms were popular among many of the country's poor, but not among the more affluent middle and upper classes, many of whom fled to the United States, forming the core of today's Cuban American community (Pérez 2015).

WASPs and White Ethnic Groups

The colonies founded by Great Britain on the east coast of North America were what became the early United States, and for many years the descendants of colonial-era immigrants from Great Britain—white Anglo-Saxon Protestants, or WASPS—were the country's most powerful ethnic group. Other white ethnic groups arrived in large numbers during the nineteenth and twentieth centuries.

White Anglo-Saxon Protestants The WASP label combines race, ethnicity, and religion. It refers mostly to people of English ancestry but also includes those of Scottish and Welsh ancestry. It excludes whites from other parts of Europe as well as Catholics and Jews. (The Through a Sociological Lens box explores the study of whiteness.)

WASPs were not a single unified group. Religious rivalries and class divisions made life better for some than for others. However, as the first immigrants to what was to become the United States, WASPs were able to develop and control the country's emerging government, business, and religious institutions. They thus amassed enormous power and avoided the sorts of discrimination that later immigrants would have to overcome. In the early years of the United States, WASPs typically believed in white racial superiority—often calling themselves the Anglo-Saxon race—and created laws to exclude nonwhites from the new nation (Horsman 1981).

The monopoly on power that WASPs maintained through much of U.S. history loosened considerably by the middle of the twentieth century (Kaufman 2004). The influence of this group endures, however, on much of U.S. culture, most noticeably in the use of English as the country's dominant language and the standing of Protestant Christianity as the country's largest religious affiliation.

White Ethnic Groups The first major wave of European immigrants who were not WASPs arrived in the early and mid-nineteenth century. After their English landlords evicted them to make way for more grazing lands for cattle and sheep, many impoverished Irish tenant farmers were left

thinking about culture

In what ways has the WASP influence on **culture** affected you? Consider common words you use, values you have, and the history you were taught in school.

THROUGH A SOCIOLOGICAL LENS

Understanding Whiteness

In a classic essay, feminist scholar Peggy McIntosh (1988) notes that whites are often taught to recognize the disadvantages that minorities face but not the advantages they enjoy as whites. She describes some of the dozens of ways that she benefits from white privilege in her daily life. When she shops, for example, she doesn't experience the suspicion and harassment to which minorities are often subjected. Minorities are often judged individually as if they represented their entire community: if they excel, they are a credit to the community; if they behave questionably, it's because of the deficiencies of their community. As a white person, McIntosh does not bear this burden. Cumulatively, these and similar advantages constitute an "invisible package of unearned assets," as McIntosh calls it, that reflects the dominant position of the white majority in the United States.

McIntosh's essay is one example of the study of whiteness. People often think of race in terms of minorities. But white majorities in the European colonies created the modern idea of "race" during the eighteenth century, and to understand "race" we must understand whiteness and its connection to power and inequality.

Although he is best known for writing about the condition of black Americans, African American sociologist and activist W. E. B. Du Bois ([1935] 1998) recognized the importance of whiteness a century ago. Although American society as a whole was divided by class, he noted, the working class was divided further along racial lines. White workers might be poorly paid, but they were "compensated in part by a sort of public and psychological wage. They were given public deference and titles of courtesy because they were white" (700). They, like white people of all classes, could attend public functions and enjoy public parks. They were served by a white police force, by a court system staffed by white jurists, and by white elected officials, and they had access to the best schools, which were reserved for them. Ironically, however, by embracing these race-based privileges, white workers lost the opportunity to organize with black workers to improve conditions for all of them.

Sociologists today are using Du Bois's sociological insights to inform their current analysis of race, particularly on the nature of whiteness (Rothenberg 2015). Sociologists engaged in whiteness studies examine both the historical roots and the contemporary processes associated with whiteness and white privilege. The questions they explore (some of which are discussed in this chapter) include: How did diverse ethnic groups once considered fundamentally different become lumped together as whites? How have the U.S. political, legal, and economic systems been structured to give advantages to whites? Does white privilege endure, and, if so, what forms does it take? As population changes make whites the "new minority" in the United States, how will they respond to the corresponding loss of privilege? How can whites help combat racism and its legacy?

The point is not to blame today's whites for the history of racial injustice. Instead, whiteness studies help us better understand that history of injustice, to recognize its continuing legacy today, and to use those insights to work toward a more just society.

think about it

1. *Has your education about race included consideration of what it means to be white? Explain.*
2. *How does the study of whiteness illustrate the sociological insight that power is a social relationship?*

dependent on potatoes for survival. When blight devastated the potato crop in Ireland in 1845, hundreds of thousands of Irish tenant farmers fled to the United States. At around the same time, large numbers of Germans arrived as well.

Many WASPs at first denied these and other European newcomers equal racial standing with themselves, referring to them instead as "Celtic" (Irish, Welsh, Scots), "Alpine" (German, Norwegian, Swedish, and other central European), and "Mediterranean" (Italian, Spanish, Greek, and other southern European). But as the new groups gained some power, they rejected these separate designations and claimed the mantle of racial superiority together with WASPs as part of a broadened white race (Mukhopadhyay et al. 2014).

The history of the Irish in America illustrates this process (Ignatiev 1996). The Irish had white skin, but they were Catholic, not Protestant, and many spoke Gaelic (Irish) rather than English. As a result, many WASPs considered the Irish a different race and discriminated against them as they did against black people, though never subjecting the Irish to the systematic legal discrimination blacks faced. Often poor and unskilled, the Irish commonly lived in the same neighborhoods as free blacks in northern cities and were often referred to as "white Negroes." Common stereotypes portrayed them as happy, lazy, and stupid with a penchant for drink, dance, and music—stereotypes that were also associated with blacks.

In time, the Irish learned English and took steps to differentiate themselves from black people, establishing their own churches and schools and forming their own social organizations. Although they had earlier supported the abolition of slavery, they gained political power by associating themselves with the Democratic Party, which at that time supported slavery. As a result, the Irish eventually came to be perceived as whites in American society—an option not available to darker-skinned people of African or Asian descent.

The second—and largest—wave of white ethnic immigrants arrived between 1890 and 1924. During that span, 20 million

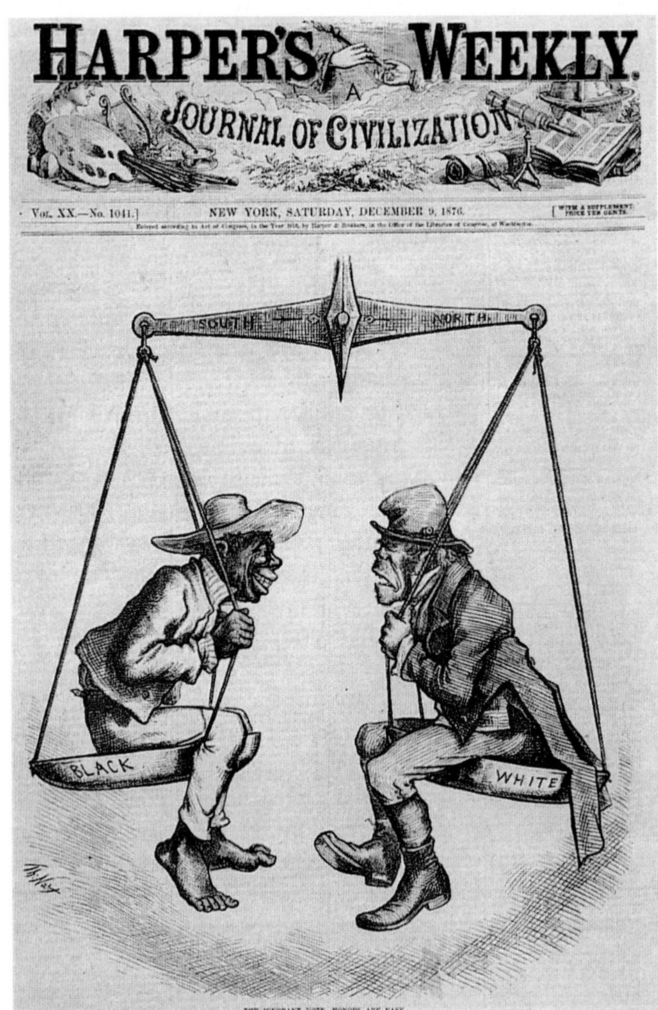

Source: Library of Congress Prints and Photographs Division [LC-USZ62-57340]

Racist imagery often compared Irish immigrants to African Americans, as in this 1876 political cartoon from *Harper's Weekly* magazine. Along with Italians, Jews, Greeks, and others, Irish immigrants were among those not considered white in the nineteenth century and subject to discrimination. Common complaints were that new immigrants did not speak English, held unfamiliar religious beliefs, had strange cultural practices, had too many children, engaged in crime and excessive drinking, and took away jobs from established Americans. How do such criticisms compare to today's discussions about immigration?

people came to the United States, most of them from southern and eastern Europe, including Italians, Poles, and Jews. Driven by poverty or political repression and drawn by the demand for labor in a rapidly industrializing United States, they were often met with resentment, prejudice, discrimination in housing and employment, and, sometimes, outright violence (Daniels 1997, 2004).

Anti-immigrant sentiment increased after World War I (1914–1918), resulting in the Immigration Act of 1924. This law slashed total immigration to 150,000 a year (excepting immigration from the Western Hemisphere) and dramatically reduced the percentage of foreign-born people in the United States for the next 40 years. The legislation effectively ended Asian immigration because it prohibited immigration by "aliens ineligible to citizenship" and naturalization was limited to whites only. It also slashed immigration from southern and eastern Europe through a severely restrictive quota system (Daniels 1997, 2004).

African Americans

Unique among the diverse racial and ethnic groups that make up the U.S. population, most African Americans are descended from people forcibly removed from their homeland, sent here against their will, and subjected to a lifetime of coerced labor. This experience is reflected in the distinctively North American idea of race that European colonists created to justify an economic system based on the slave labor of Africans. Before the American experience, slavery existed mostly independent of race. Greeks and Romans kept slaves with pale skin just like themselves, while some dark-skinned Africans captured and enslaved dark-skinned members of other African tribes. In what became the United States, however, a new notion of race was invented piecemeal, over a series of decades, and eventually used to justify a race-based slave system that was the foundation of the agricultural economy of the day, especially in the American South (Allen 2012; Smedley and Smedley 2012). This process so influenced the uniquely American notions of race—and the interaction between race and class in the United States—that it warrants close attention.

Indentured Servitude Race-based slavery emerged only after a labor system based on white indentured servitude failed. When English colonists settled the region that later became the United States, they needed workers to build settlements and raise crops. Especially during the early and mid-1600s, colonists relied primarily on the labor of indentured servants. These poor whites, mostly Britons and Germans, contracted to work for a period of four to seven years in exchange for transatlantic passage and sometimes "freedom dues"—which might include food, clothes, a gun, and, most important, land—upon completion of their contract. Some came voluntarily; others—including homeless children, convicts, beggars, and others considered by British officials to be social undesirables—were shipped forcibly. The work was brutal and the conditions harsh, and many indentured servants died before gaining their freedom. In many ways, they were essentially slaves: they were bought and sold as property, served at the whim of their employers, and were often chained and beaten. Unlike slaves, however, they suffered only temporary servitude; slavery was lifelong (Jordan and Walsh 2008).

Indentured servitude declined for multiple reasons. First, as word of the harsh conditions spread, fewer people volunteered to indenture themselves. Second, some indentured servants became defiant, most notably when white and black servants in Virginia joined black slaves in Bacon's Rebellion of 1676. Such multiracial agitation frightened wealthy white colonial officials, who responded by relying increasingly on race to divide poor whites from poor blacks and slaves.

Slavery as an Economic Institution In the early 1600s, Africans were only a small part of the colonial workforce. At first, many were treated similarly to white indentured

MAP 10.3 | THE TRIANGULAR TRANSATLANTIC SLAVE TRADE

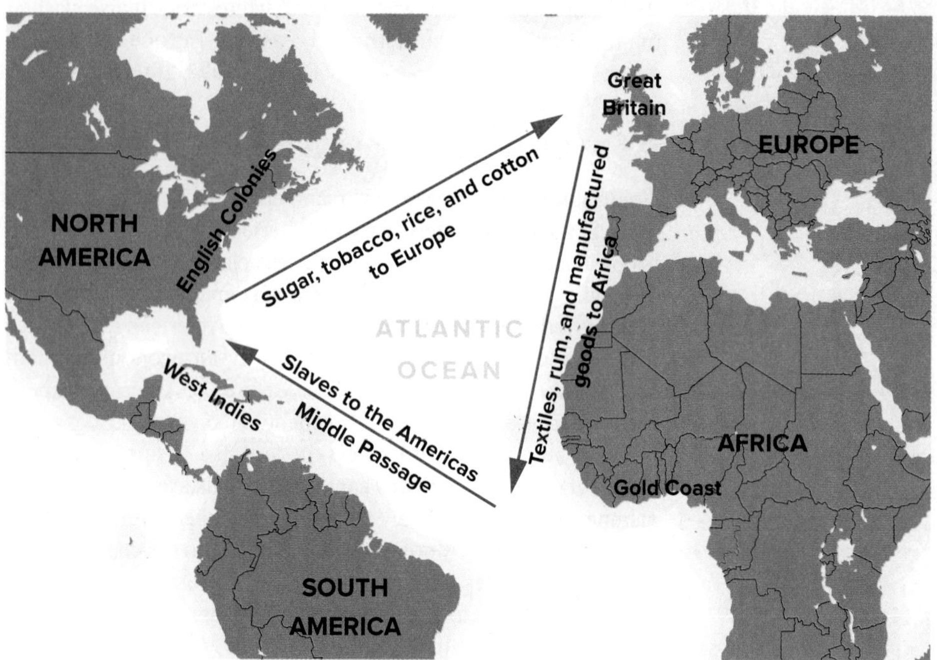

The triangular trade linked Europe, Africa, and the Americas economically.

servants. They lived with white servants; had similar legal rights, including the right to sign contracts; and could travel to some extent. As the supply of indentured servants dwindled, however, white planters began to rely increasingly on the labor of black African slaves. The enslaved Africans were the victims of an economic system that linked England, West Africa, and England's American colonies in a three-stage pattern of trade (see Map 10.3). In the first stage, English goods were shipped to West Africa and traded for Africans who had been kidnapped by fellow Africans and sold to European slavers. Packed into ships under horrific conditions, up to 20 million captives suffered the second stage, the infamous "middle passage" from Africa to the Americas that only half would survive. In the Americas, they were exchanged for raw materials such as tobacco, rice, and cotton. Finally, the raw materials were shipped to England and exchanged for finished goods, beginning the cycle again (Baptist 2014; Beckhert 2015; Rediker 2007).

The Racialization of Slavery As the importance of slave labor grew, the ideology justifying it changed. At first, colonists claimed that as non-Christians, Africans were unworthy of freedom. In a few cases, African slaves successfully sued for their freedom after converting to Christianity. By the end of the 1600s, however, with slaves increasingly converting to Christianity, religious differences no

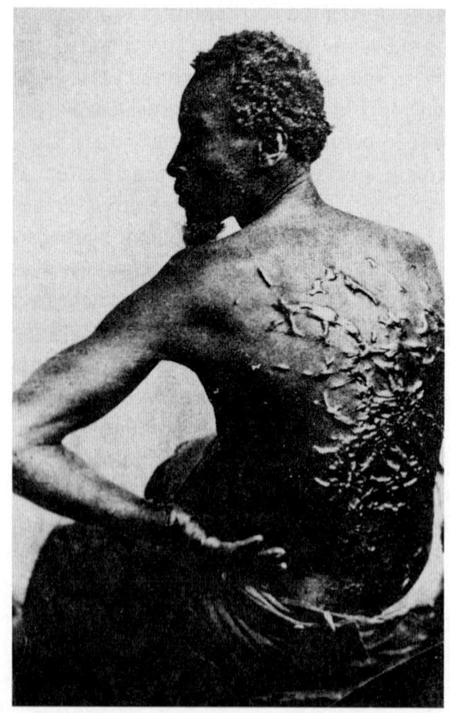

©Time Life Pictures/National Archives/Time Life Pictures/Getty Images

This man's back shows the scars left from brutal whippings he received as a slave in the American South.

©MPI/Getty Images

This idealized image of George Washington, painted in 1853, shows the nation's first president on his Mount Vernon plantation among his slaves. Like other large landowners of the time, Washington depended on slave labor to run his home and to generate his wealth by working his plantation.

CORE CONCEPTS CHALLENGE *What* **cultural** *beliefs about the nature of slavery does this painting promote? Who do you think is the intended audience for a picture like this?*

longer provided a convincing rationale for enslaving Africans and their descendants. Instead, whites now drew on pseudoscience and, ironically, biblical scripture to claim that black Africans were a different and inferior human subspecies fit only to serve the superior white race (Allen 2012; Smedley and Smedley 2012).

At the same time, wealthy southern landowners used their political clout to strip slaves of any legal rights and to define slave status legally in racial terms. In 1705 the Virginia Assembly for the first time passed laws designating slaves as property. Slave rebellions in the following years provoked increasingly restrictive laws, including laws making it illegal for slaves to learn to read (Horton and Horton 2005; Johnson and Smith 1999).

Slavery and Affluence Race-based slavery, justified by an ideology that viewed Africans as less than human, underlay the growing wealth of the new colonial elites and not just in the South. Members of a white planter aristocracy owned large estates and benefited directly from the labor of their many slaves. George Washington, among the wealthiest colonists of his day, owned more than 300 slaves. But even the northern colonies—not directly dependent on plantation agriculture—benefited from slavery. Merchants, shipbuilders, metal smiths, rum distillers, sawmill operators, and many others all profited directly or indirectly from the slave trade (Warren 2016).

Slaves lived under varied conditions, but their labor was always coerced, and the coercion was backed by force, often applied barbarically. White masters also often took it as their prerogative to rape their female slaves, and the offspring of these encounters were legally slaves at birth (Sublette and Sublette 2016). Slaves resisted their oppression in various ways, from avoiding work, to escaping, to joining rebellions (Breen 2015; Camp 2004).

Slavery's Legacy While Thomas Jefferson was writing "All men are created equal" in the Declaration of Independence, a slave in the next room was on call to attend to his every need. In 1776, some whites recognized that slavery was unjust and spoke out against it, but they were few. Slavery persisted for nearly 100 years in the newly independent United States until it was outlawed by the Thirteenth Amendment to the U.S. Constitution in the wake of the Civil War (1861-1865). The legacy of slavery endured, however, with the imposition of legalized (*de jure*) racial segregation in the South and segregation in fact (*de facto*), if not by law, in much of the rest of the country. Under the South's so-called Jim Crow laws, all aspects of life, including housing, employment, education, and political participation, were structured along racial lines, ensuring that blacks and whites would remain separate and unequal.

Racial segregation was enforced through violence and terror. Between 1882 and 1968, for example, white mobs lynched and killed an estimated 4,742 blacks (and many members of other ethnic minorities) (Allen et al. 2000). During the Great Migration of the early and middle twentieth century, many African Americans—some 2 million by 1930—fled the repressive South in search of economic opportunity in the urban North (Wilkerson 2010).

African Americans had long challenged their subordinate status under Jim Crow, and in the 1950s these efforts coalesced and intensified in the civil rights movement. By the mid-1960s, this landmark movement had succeeded in dismantling legal segregation and begun to significantly change the country's entrenched culture of racism.

Asian Americans

The experiences of African slaves in the plantation economy were unique. However, throughout U.S. history, race and ethnicity have been used repeatedly to divide workers for the benefit of the powerful. Asian Americans experienced this phenomenon as well.

Chinese Americans Early Chinese immigrants to the United States fled the violence of Britain's "Opium Wars," political turmoil resulting from peasant rebellions, and harsh economic conditions. The hope of finding possible riches in the California Gold Rush of 1849 motivated the earliest Chinese to

A group of white people in Indiana pose proudly for a photo after a lynching in 1930. Lynchings of this sort, often of alleged criminals, were conducted in broad daylight with the consent of local authorities. Some were treated as community events with a carnival atmosphere. Photos like this one—sometimes including children—were regularly taken to commemorate the occasion, and copies of these gruesome pictures were then sold as postcards.

©Dorothea Lange/Wra/The LIFE Picture Collection/Getty Images

U.S. soldiers stand guard as people of Japanese ancestry arrive at an internment camp in Santa Anita, California. Camps like this kept Japanese Americans confined for the duration of World War II.

emigrate. More came between 1863 and 1869—recruited to displace higher-paid Irish workers—to build the transcontinental railroad, a massive, sometimes brutally dangerous, labor-intensive project. After the railroad was completed, some Chinese workers moved to cities, most notably San Francisco, while others played a prominent role in California's emerging agricultural economy.

The Chinese were particularly vulnerable to discrimination because, as nonwhites, they were ineligible for U.S. citizenship. California, for example, targeted them with a special tax on foreign miners who were not going to become citizens. Over the years, white workers grew increasingly resentful of Chinese workers, often blaming them for taking their jobs and driving down wages. In the 1870s, Irish American politician Denis Kearney rose to prominence in California with the slogan "The Chinese must go!" and led violent attacks on Chinese workers. In the early 1890s, unemployed white workers rioted throughout California, beating and sometimes shooting Chinese immigrants and shipping them out of town in freight cars in what the Chinese would come to call the "driving out." Anti-Chinese feeling culminated in the Chinese Exclusion Act of 1882—the first U.S. law to prohibit immigration on the basis of a specific nationality—effectively ending Chinese immigration for a decade.

In the face of this hostility, Chinese immigrants already in the country often had to develop their own businesses and rely on their own community for support. Chinese laundries—which were inexpensive to start up—became a staple of many western cities, and urban "Chinatowns" emerged as the center of Chinese social and economic life (Lee 2015; Takaki 2008).

Japanese, Korean, and Filipino Americans Japanese, Koreans, and Filipinos have distinct cultures and sometimes conflicting histories, but they share some common experiences in the United States. In the late nineteenth and early twentieth centuries, some 200,000 Japanese, along with others from countries including China, Korea, and the Philippines, were recruited to work on sugarcane plantations in Hawaii, which was annexed as a U.S. territory in 1898. Plantation owners expected that this ethnic diversity would keep their workforce divided and vulnerable to exploitation. In 1919, however, the workers united in a successful strike and formed the Hawaii Laborers' Association, Hawaii's first interethnic union (Jung 2006; Lee 2015; Takaki 2008). From Hawaii, some Japanese, Korean, and Filipino immigrants went on to the mainland, most of them to work on farms in California. The Asian Exclusion Act, part of the Immigration Act of 1924, however, brought Asian immigration to a virtual stop.

In what was perhaps the most dramatically racist act against an Asian group in the country's history, the U.S. government interned nearly 120,000 Japanese Americans—two-thirds of them U.S. born—for the duration of World War II. In the wake of Japan's attack on Pearl Harbor in December 1941, the government uprooted entire families and sent them to camps in often remote and desolate areas of the country. Although the United States was at war with Germany and Italy as well as Japan, such widespread measures were not taken against white Americans with German or Italian ancestry. In 1988 the U.S. government paid survivors of the camps $20,000 each in reparations and apologized for what it called a "grave injustice," admitting that the internments were done "without adequate security reasons" and "were motivated largely by racial prejudice, wartime hysteria, and a failure of political leadership" [Public Law 100-383 (1988)].

Diversity Today

U.S. society is one of the most racially and ethnically diverse in the world. That is due to the country's past as well as more recent changes in immigration and demographic trends.

Racial and Ethnic Groups Today

Diversity in the United States varies significantly from region to region. For example, African Americans make up about 19.3 percent of the population in the South but only 4.6 percent in the West. People with German ancestry make up 25.3 percent of the population in the Midwest but only 9.6 percent in the

South (U.S. Census Bureau 2017f). However, all regions of the country are projected to become more racially and ethnically diverse in the coming years.

White Americans At 72.6 percent of the population (235 million), white people of many different ancestries continue to be by far the largest racial group in U.S. society. However, a growing proportion of whites are now Hispanic; non-Hispanic whites account for 61.1 percent of the population (see Table 10.1). Whites are found in substantial numbers throughout the country, with especially heavy concentrations in parts of the Midwest and northern New England. In 2016, only Hawaii, California, Nevada, New Mexico, and Texas (as well as the District of Columbia) were "majority minority" states with a non-Hispanic white population of less than 50 percent. In contrast, 22 states were at least 75 percent white and non-Hispanic (U.S. Census Bureau 2017f).

Hispanics or Latinos Latinos are the largest minority group in the United States. In 2016, they made up 17.8 percent of the U.S. population. About 65 percent identify themselves as white only, while another 20 percent report being of "some other race," likely treating Hispanic as a racial rather than ethnic category. Latinos are concentrated in the Southwest and West (reflecting the annexation of these areas from Mexico), in Florida (where Cuban Americans are concentrated), and in the New York metropolitan area.

TABLE 10.1 MAJOR RACIAL AND ETHNIC GROUPS IN THE UNITED STATES, 2016

Race		% of U.S. Population
White (any ethnicity)		72.6%
White, non-Hispanic	61.1	
White, Hispanic	11.5	
Black or African American		12.7
Asian		5.4
American Indian or Alaska Native		0.8
Native Hawaiian and Pacific Islander		0.2
Other		5.1
Two or more		3.2
Total		100%
Ethnicity/Ancestry		
Hispanic or Latino (collectively)		17.8%
German		13.9
Mexican		11.2
Irish		10.0
English		7.4
"American"		6.2
Italian		5.2

Source: U.S. Census Bureau 2017f.

African Americans African Americans make up about 12.7 percent of the U.S. population and are the nation's largest racial minority. Most African Americans live in the South, but they are also a major presence in cities of the Northeast and northern Midwest. In addition, recent immigrants are diversifying the African American community, especially in major metropolitan areas. In 2016, 9.6 percent of those who reported their race as only black were foreign born, compared with just 1 percent in 1960 (U.S. Census Bureau 2017f).

Asian Americans Asian Americans today account for 5.4 percent of the population in the United States. Chinese Americans are today's largest Asian subgroup. Those in the second-largest subgroup—from India—are relatively recent arrivals. Filipinos are the third-largest subgroup. In addition, many Koreans and Vietnamese emigrated to the United States in the wake of the Korean War and the Vietnam War. Asian Americans are mostly located on the West Coast, in major Hawaiian urban centers, and in the New York City region (U.S. Census Bureau 2017f).

Asian Americans are found at every class level, but on average they have both higher incomes and more education than members of other racial and ethnic groups, including whites. As a result, they are often perceived to be a "model minority," a label that overlooks the diversity within the Asian community and disregards the discrimination Asians have endured during much of American history. It can also place unfair pressure on Asian youth to live up to a stereotypical ideal.

Native Americans In 2016, an estimated 0.8 percent of the U.S. population was American Indian or Alaska Native. Another 0.7 percent included this category in combination with one or more other races (U.S. Census Bureau 2017f). As with other groups, most native peoples identify with a particular tribal heritage—such as Cherokee, Iroquois, or Navajo—more than with such generic, outsider-imposed terms as "Indian," "Native Peoples," or "Native American."

Not until the passage of the Indian Citizenship Act of 1924 were Native Americans granted the unlimited right to American citizenship. Before then, they had only limited access to citizenship that usually required them to give up tribal membership. Citizens or not, poverty and bleak prospects drove many to move away from reservations and into the white-dominated society. In the 1960s and 1970s, though, Native Americans organized to revive their traditional cultures and gain wider recognition of the injustices committed against them. In 1976 the Supreme Court ruled that states do not have the right to regulate activities on Indian reservations, opening the way for the establishment of the casinos and other gambling operations that have provided economic opportunity for some tribes.

Arab Americans About 0.6 percent of Americans identify as having Arab ancestry. The Arab world consists of more than 20 culturally varied Arabic-speaking countries. As a result, Arab Americans are a diverse ethnic group whose members, like those of other ethnic groups, often identify more with their specific ancestral homelands than with a broader ethnic label. The three largest Arab American subgroups are those who report ancestry from Lebanon (24.1 percent), Egypt (12.6 percent), and Syria (9.2 percent) (U.S. Census Bureau 2017f).

In the United States, many people confuse the ethnic label "Arab" (people from Arabic-speaking countries) with the religious label "Muslim" (adherents of Islam). In fact, about 80 percent of the world's Muslims live *outside* the Arab world, mostly in Southeast Asia and sub-Saharan Africa. Furthermore, 1 of 10 people in the Arab world is not Muslim. Among Arab Americans, between 50 percent and 63 percent are Christian, whereas between 24 percent and 50 percent are Muslim (Desilver and Masci 2017; Kayyali 2006).

The earliest Arab immigrants, mostly Lebanese Christians, began arriving in the 1880s. Among more recent immigrants, Muslims predominate. In a striking example of the social construction of race, in 1915, George Dow, a Syrian immigrant living in segregated South Carolina, successfully argued in court that Syrians were white and therefore eligible for citizenship under the existing immigration laws, which limited citizenship to "free white persons" (Naff 1985).

However, Arab American groups recently urged the Census Bureau to add a new category, "Middle Eastern/Northern Africa," as an alternative to "white" on the 2020 U.S. Census. The Census Bureau declined but advocacy for such a label is likely to continue. A MENA label could help unify a diverse group of people, as did "Hispanics." For example, many Christians with Arab ancestry do not self-identify as Arabs. A MENA category would allow them to join with a group of Americans who, by some estimates, could be as large as 3.6 million (Arab American Institute 2014).

A shift to MENA might also help avoid the stigma that some Americans attach to the term "Arab." As a result of the September 11, 2001, attacks and ongoing terrorist actions by ISIS and other Muslim extremists, many Arab Americans, particularly Muslims, have been unfairly profiled, demonized, and subjected to discrimination and even violence. One survey found that 55 percent of Muslim students in kindergarten through twelfth grade in California had been bullied based on their religious affiliation, and 20 percent said they had been discriminated against by a staff member (CAIR-CA 2015). Hate crimes against Muslims continue to occur at five times the rate they did before 9/11 (Ingraham 2015).

Immigration in the Post–Civil Rights Era

One major source of diversity in the United States today is the changing nature of immigration. The sheer volume of global migration has increased dramatically in recent decades, usually as people from poorer countries seek economic opportunity in the world's wealthier countries or flee wartime violence. In the United States, immigration has come from an increasingly diverse array of countries, because the civil rights movement of the 1950s and 1960s succeeded in dismantling legal discrimination for the first time in U.S. history, including getting Congress to change immigration laws.

Through most of the twentieth century, the United States had a discriminatory quota system for immigration that based admissions on the number of people who were already here from each country. As a result, the policy allotted the bulk of new admissions to immigrants from northern and western European countries that were already well represented in the U.S. population, while severely limiting the number of people from other parts of the world who were allowed to immigrate. This longstanding policy discriminated on behalf of whites.

That changed with the Immigration and Nationality Act of 1965, passed in the midst of the civil rights revolution. The act put in place a system that favored family members of U.S. citizens, skilled workers, and political refugees. New immigrants started arriving from more regions than before, and as a result, the percentage of foreign-born people in the United States from Latin America and Asia, especially, increased significantly, whereas the percentage of foreign-born people from Europe declined (see Figure 10.3).

Significantly, the 1965 legislation allowed naturalized immigrants to sponsor an unlimited number of family members as new immigrants. Once naturalized, these family members could in turn sponsor more family members, a process sometimes called "chain immigration." An unintended consequence

FIGURE 10.3 | FOREIGN-BORN POPULATION SINCE 1960

Percentage of foreign-born population by region of origin

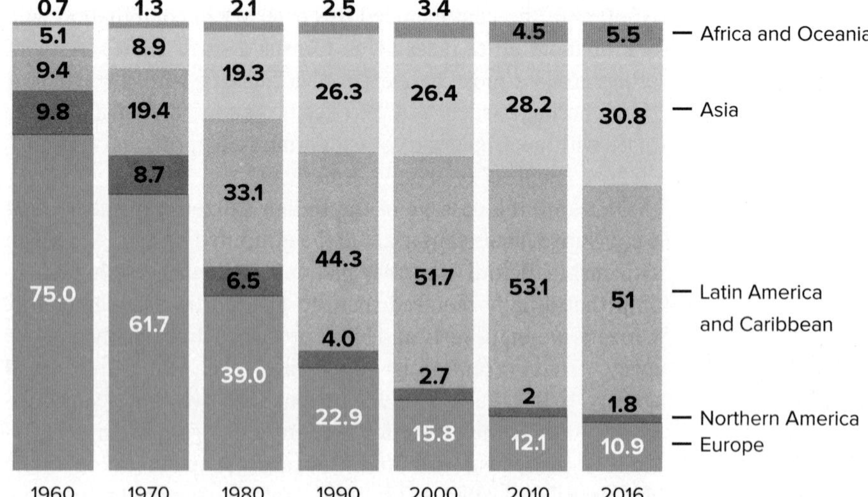

Changes in immigration law enacted in the 1960s eliminated preferences for European immigrants, contributing to a shift toward greater immigration from Latin American and Asian countries. *Sources:* U.S. Census Bureau 2010c, 2017f.

FIGURE 10.4 | FOREIGN-BORN POPULATION WITHIN THE UNITED STATES, 1850 TO 2016

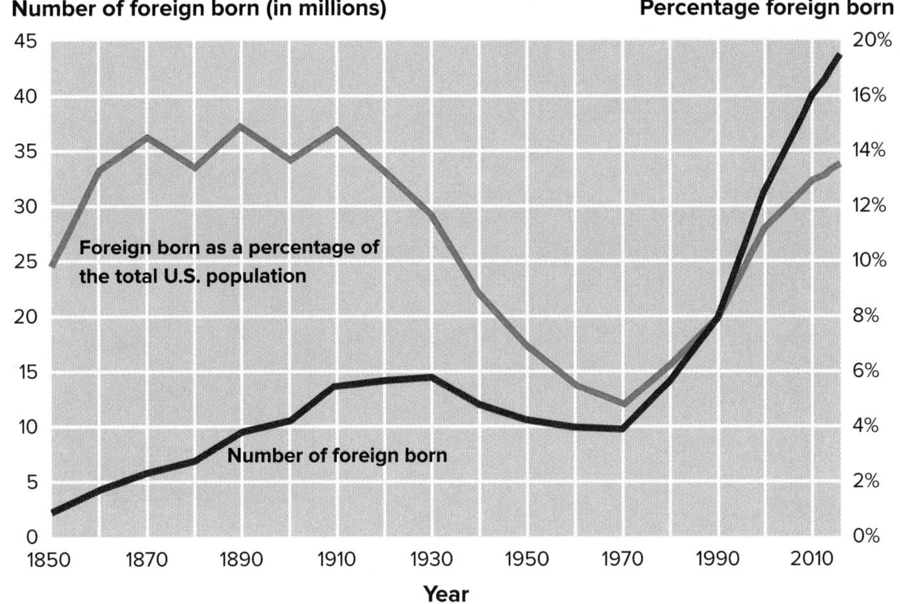

The *number* of people in the United States born elsewhere has reached unprecedented levels (purple line, left axis), but the *percentage* of the U.S. population that is foreign born is still less today than it was in the late 1800s and early 1900s (orange line, right axis). *Sources:* Gibson and Jung 2006; U.S. Census Bureau 2017f.

of this provision was to increase overall immigration to unprecedented levels, raising the foreign born as a percentage of the country's population to levels approaching those of the 1920s (see Figure 10.4). By 2016, more than one of eight people in the United States were born elsewhere. Because recent immigrants tend to have a higher birthrate than native-born Americans, the result will significantly affect the racial and ethnic composition of the United States in the coming decades. The Census Bureau projects that the percentage of foreign-born Americans will reach an all-time high (14.9 percent) in 2028 and increase to 17.2 percent by 2060 (U.S. Census Bureau 2018a). (The Sociology Works box explores a sociology major's work with immigrant tenants.)

Transnational Migrants

Unlike earlier immigrants, who often sought to assimilate into the dominant society and typically had limited contact with their homelands, many of today's immigrants are **transnational migrants** who *retain strong personal, cultural, and economic ties to both their country of birth and their newly adopted home.* Many recent immigrants have access to inexpensive telephone and internet services that can provide instantaneous communication with family at home. They can travel to their homeland more easily and can stay abreast of home country news and entertainment on satellite television and the internet. Transnational migrants often make *remittances*—money transfers to relatives back home—which make up a significant share of the national economies of most Central American countries, the Philippines, Pakistan, Egypt, and other nations. Recognizing these trends, some countries—such as the Philippines—make it easy for migrants to retain their citizenship even as they become

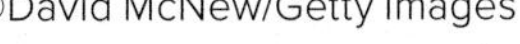
©David McNew/Getty Images

©Mohammed Elshamy/Anadolu Agency/Getty Images

The increase in unauthorized immigration has generated considerable controversy.

CORE CONCEPTS CHALLENGE *Some people advocate limiting immigration, stricter enforcement of immigration laws, and a clampdown on the borders. Others argue for continuing high levels of legal immigration and contend that unauthorized immigrants should have more access to citizenship. What role do* ***culture*** *and* ***power*** *play in these conflicts?*

SOCIOLOGY WORKS

Mikey Velarde and Community Organizing

When Mikey Velarde began college, he intended to study cognitive science. He had no idea that a few years later he would be helping organize a tenants' meeting in New York City's East Harlem as part of his new job as a community organizer. Motivated by a growing desire to understand—and challenge—racial and ethnic inequalities, Velarde switched from cognitive science to a major in sociology. He graduated with a bachelor's degree and now works primarily with immigrant tenants to help them secure dignified housing in the face of plans for urban development that threaten to displace low-income residents. Velarde has learned a broad array of skills as he works to support local community activists in myriad ways. He knocks on doors to build support networks and to staff meetings of the local tenant association; he organizes community protests; he corresponds with journalists; and he conducts research on housing code violations.

Velarde helps organize local tenants' associations and support the development of local leaders within these organizations. He sees the formation of these community-based organizations as serving a dual purpose: they contribute to a broader social justice movement and help deliver specific, immediate benefits to local tenants.

As an undergraduate, Velarde took a range of sociology courses that emphasized questions about the relationship between power and inequality with a specific focus on the experiences and perspectives of oppressed groups. These classes deepened and broadened his knowledge of the dynamic intersection of race, class, gender, sexuality, and nationality in contemporary U.S. society.

Just about every day Velarde is reminded of the relevance of sociology to his work and the lives of the people he serves. He recalls, for example, how, during a discussion at a community meeting, tenants began to grasp the connections among racial inequality, poor housing conditions, and city policies. The fragile housing situation in their neighborhood, they concluded, was more than an isolated phenomenon; it was an expression of structural relationships that kept them disadvantaged.

Courtesy of Michael Velarde
Mikey Velarde

Overall, Velarde concludes, "The best and most basic tool sociology has given me is, as Mills put it, a 'sociological imagination.'" Ultimately, he says, sociology "has given me a language to critique and contest unjust social arrangements. I am reminded even in the most difficult times that these very arrangements are within the reach of social actors." For community organizer Mikey Velarde, sociology encourages hope in the capacity of human beings to recognize—and challenge—injustice.

> Ultimately, he says, sociology "has given me a language to critique and contest unjust social arrangements."

Velarde has combined his personal experience as a Chicano from El Paso, Texas, with the insights he gained from sociology to cultivate a sociological imagination that he brings to bear on his efforts to help the residents of East Harlem improve their lives. He urges others to similarly bring the sociological imagination to bear on their own goals and circumstances. His advice? "Connect to the material from your own social location and life experience."

think about it

1. *What relationship does Mikey Velarde see between sociology and his work in East Harlem?*
2. *How does the sociological perspective encourage Velarde's optimism about our capacity to challenge injustice?*

citizens in their new homeland. These emerging models of citizenship are likely to become more common, promoting economic advancement and social integration without full cultural accommodation (Faist, Fauser and Reisenauer 2013; Vertovec 2009).

However, the scale and impact of widespread immigration has also generated some backlash, as it did during earlier waves of immigration (Schrag 2010; Tirman 2016). Critics argue that more immigration will "disunite" the country, undermine the economic well-being of workers by flooding the low-skill labor market, and contribute to more pollution and environmental strain since immigrants tend to have higher birthrates (Cafaro 2015; Schlesinger 1998).

Unauthorized Immigration

The Trump campaign's call to "Build the Wall" on the US-Mexico border reflects the fact that the focus of immigration debates in the United States is often on unauthorized immigrants. Because these immigrants are by definition "unauthorized" (they are also called "illegal" or "undocumented"), determining their exact number is impossible. Approximately 11 million unauthorized immigrants were estimated to be in the United States in 2015, a 10 percent decline from its peak in 2007 (Passal and Cohn 2017a). A third of these immigrants live in just five metropolitan areas: New York City, Los Angeles, Houston, Dallas, and Miami

(Passal and Cohn 2017b). They are employed mostly in agriculture, construction, and service occupations.

Several factors have contributed to the increase in undocumented immigrants. First, many Mexicans were recruited as legal temporary workers under the *bracero* program that began in the 1940s. When the program ended in 1964, many stayed in the United States without documentation (Durand, Massey, and Zenteno 2001). Second, the North American Free Trade Agreement (NAFTA) took effect in 1994, eliminating barriers to cross-border trade and investment and undermining broad sectors of the Mexican economy. In particular, many small-scale Mexican farms failed in the face of competition from government-subsidized U.S. agricultural products. As a result, displaced Mexican workers sought opportunities in the United States (Portes 2002). Finally, U.S. employers play a significant role in recruiting immigrant laborers, including undocumented workers, especially in agricultural and meat processing facilities (Rodriguez 2004).

Changing Population Trends

The saying "Children are our future" is certainly true when it comes to U.S. racial and ethnic diversity. Since 2011, less than half of all infants under 1 year of age have been non-Hispanic whites (U.S. Census Bureau 2012d). The factors that underlie this shift are straightforward. Recent immigrants tend to be young compared to white residents and are more likely to be of childbearing age. Also, white women tend to have fewer children than black, Hispanic, or Asian women (National Center for Health Statistics 2015a). Finally, the non-Hispanic white population in the United States is considerably older than other racial and ethnic groups, and these disproportionately white "baby boomers" born in the 1940s and 1950s are beginning to die in large numbers (Morello and Melnick 2013). As a result, the Census Bureau projects that by about 2045, non-Hispanic whites will make up less than half of the U.S. population, ushering in a new era where no single racial or ethnic group will be the "majority" (U.S. Census Bureau 2017a). However, there are countertrends that may slow this change: Hispanic Americans marry non-Hispanics at a high rate, immigration from Latin America is declining, and nearly a quarter of third-generation Hispanics (who identify as white) do not identify as Hispanic (López, Gonzalez-Barrera, and López 2017).

Culture, Structure, and Power: The Nature of Racial and Ethnic Inequality Today

Clearly, blatant racism fueled the nation's past (Kendi 2016). But you might be thinking, "Things are different now. Despite the increased visibility of white supremacists emboldened by the Trump election, the United States has moved on, outlawing racial discrimination, electing a black president, and broadly embracing racial and ethnic diversity."

All of that is true to a degree. But sociological research suggests that to understand racial and ethnic conditions today, we need to recognize more complex dynamics, including four seemingly contradictory developments that we sketch out in the remainder of the chapter:

1. ***"Old Racism" is largely dead.*** As is widely understood, the racist beliefs and practices of the past have largely been eliminated in mainstream society, though they continue to thrive in some subcultures. The civil rights struggle made a difference, paving the way for changes in the U.S. legal and political systems and helping drive a major cultural shift in racial attitudes toward more tolerance and an embrace of diversity.
2. ***Inequality persists.*** Despite the undeniable changes that occurred to restrict old-style racism, deep and profound racial and ethnic inequalities persist in all aspects of social life—sometimes virtually unchanged in the last half century.
3. ***"Old racism" left an influential legacy.*** Part of the explanation for persistent inequality is the powerful legacy of old-style racism, the effects of which continue to be felt today.
4. ***"New racism" has emerged.*** As old forms of racism have been overcome, new beliefs and practices have emerged that explicitly reject blatant racism but actually help perpetuate racial and ethnic inequality.

These four developments reflect aspects of changing culture, structure, and power in society. Before we explore them, we review the nature of discrimination at both the individual and institutional levels and consider some theories of prejudice and discrimination to inform our later discussion.

Prejudice and Discrimination: Individual and Institutional

Sociologists make an important distinction between the behaviors of individuals and the dynamics associated with social institutions. For most sociologists, racism is not just individual prejudice; it reflects the structure of our larger social system (Bonilla-Silva 1997, 2014).

Individual Attitudes and Behaviors: Prejudice and Discrimination While the legacy of the past continues to affect racial disparities today, many types of prejudice and discrimination are fresh creations of contemporary social life. Social-psychological theories that focus on individual attitudes and behaviors can help us understand how people come to adopt their views about inequality. As we noted in Chapter 7, people often define themselves as a member of an *in-group* and feel negatively toward members of an *out-group.* Racism creates an in-out group distinction based on a usually negative stereotype. According to the Thomas theorem (also discussed in Chapter 7), social characteristics that are defined as real have real consequences. Thus a widely accepted stereotype can become the basis for prejudicial attitudes toward the members of an out-group.

Stereotypes and prejudice are limited to beliefs and attitudes, but discrimination, as we have seen, involves actions and behaviors. Racial discrimination, for example, involves actions that help maintain the domination of one race over others based on the dominant group's belief in the subordinate group's inferiority. As such, discrimination is generally limited to those who have the power to act in ways that hinder others. Those who are relatively powerless may have prejudices of their own, but they generally lack the resources or ability to turn those prejudices into effective discriminatory action. In this sense, discrimination can be thought of as prejudice plus power (Clair and Denis 2015; Pager and Shepherd 2008).

Institutional Discrimination: Structural Barriers to Equality Individuals can discriminate—for example, a small-business owner might refuse to hire members of a different racial or ethnic group. However, racial and ethnic inequality is typically produced and reinforced through institutional discrimination, not just individual action. **Institutional discrimination** is *the unequal treatment that results from the structural organization, policies, and procedures of social institutions such as the government, businesses, and schools.* Institutional discrimination is especially powerful, since it affects large numbers of people. It is especially difficult to change, since it is not associated with any one individual but rather is a generalized feature of an institutional bureaucracy.

In some cases, institutional discrimination is intentional, as with Jim Crow laws in the pre–civil rights era South. In many cases, though, policies and practices that are not themselves overtly or intentionally discriminatory can have a discriminatory impact. For example, the hiring practices of many workplaces rely heavily on informal word-of-mouth communication. When those workplaces are nearly all white, the result can be institutional discrimination toward racial and ethnic minorities who do not have access to these informal channels of communication. Longstanding "redlining" practices by banks and real estate agencies that make it more difficult for minorities to finance or acquire a house in certain areas are also examples of institutional racism that have been particularly significant.

Theories of Prejudice and Discrimination: Culture and Group Interests

Sociological explanations for prejudice and discrimination tend to fall into one of two theoretical traditions, those emphasizing culture and those emphasizing group interests. Much sociological work on the subject, however, combines elements of each approach.

Learning Prejudice through Culture Cultural explanations focus on the way familiarity breeds comfort whereas unfamiliarity often produces anxiety or fear. Our socialization has made it easy for us to interact with people who look and behave like us because they are familiar and predictable. By contrast, interacting with people who look different or whose behavior is unfamiliar and therefore unpredictable, can make us uncomfortable.

As children grow up, their socialization often encourages them to form attachments with those in their own group, people like themselves, while often learning negative stereotypes about out-group members, people less like themselves (Teichman 2016). Some research suggests that youngsters learn stereotypes and develop prejudices as early as age three, often before fully comprehending their meaning or significance. Later in life, the mass media can perpetuate negative stereotypes with entertainment that presents such stock characters as the Asian martial-arts expert, the black criminal, the Arab terrorist, or the exotic Asian sex symbol (Wilson, Gutiérrez, and Chao 2013).

According to Gordon Allport's (1954) *contact hypothesis,* contact between members of different groups will reduce prejudice *if* the contact is sustained, involves groups with equal status who share common goals, and is sanctioned by authorities. Those are difficult conditions to meet, but college campuses often qualify. For example, one study found that white students randomly assigned a minority roommate had more contact and were more comfortable with members of other races than white students who were assigned a white roommate (Boisjoly et al. 2006). Another study found that the more white men were exposed to black students in their randomly assigned peer groups during their first year in college, the more likely they were to become roommates with black students in subsequent years (Carrell, Hoekstra, and West 2016). However, without a structure to encourage interaction, diversity on campus does not necessarily translate into increased interracial or interethnic contact.

Discriminating to Gain Advantage Group-interest explanations of prejudice and discrimination focus on the way groups compete with one another for scarce and valuable resources such as jobs or desirable housing. Such competition can lead to conflict and to discrimination by one group against another as a means of gaining an advantage over them. As we saw, discrimination often seems to increase in difficult economic periods as competition for scarce resources increases.

Split labor market theory *argues that ethnic and racial conflicts often emerge when two racial or ethnic groups compete for the same jobs.* According to this theory, employers, higher-paid workers, and lower-paid workers form three groups with separate and competing interests (Bonacich 1972, 1976; Gordon, Edwards, and Reich 1982). Employers recruit lower-paid workers to maximize

on social theory

Split labor market theory is in the tradition of ***conflict theory.*** Have you worked in or seen a workplace in which higher-paid workers and lower-paid workers were divided along ethnic or racial lines?

thinking about structure

The **structure** of an organization can contribute to institutional discrimination. How can an institution's structure help prevent discrimination?

their profits, thereby creating conflict between higher-paid workers and the lower-paid workers who are replacing them. As we have seen, employers often encouraged immigration as a source of inexpensive labor, sometimes stoking racial and ethnic divisions among workers to prevent them from organizing for better wages and working conditions. In the short term, discrimination against minorities also served the interest of higher-paid workers—often whites, in the context of American history—because it prevented minorities from competing with them for desirable jobs. In the long term, however, these divisions weakened the negotiating power of all workers.

More generally, members of one group can see those of another as a threat, especially when facing difficult circumstances. A **scapegoat** is *an individual or a group of people falsely blamed for a negative situation.* When people are frustrated by their inability to overcome difficulties, they sometimes seek simplistic explanations for their troubles in the form of a scapegoat. In the wake of World War I, for example, Germany faced enormously complex economic and political difficulties, but the Nazis scapegoated Jews and other minorities, blaming them for all the nation's problems. In the United States, blacks, Irish, Jews, communists, immigrants, and Muslims, among many others, have all been targeted as scapegoats at different times (Hardisty 1999; Iftikhar 2016). Today, politicians still can stir up votes by invoking Mexican immigrants, Muslims, or the Chinese as the source of U.S. problems.

The Death of "Old Racism": Changing Practices and Attitudes

Barack Obama's election as the nation's first black—or, more accurately, multiracial—president undoubtedly symbolized the changing nature of racial and ethnic conditions in the United States. In the past, blatant voter discrimination suppressed the black vote and made voting rights a central demand of the civil rights era. In a striking reversal, when Obama was elected president in 2008 and 2012, the rate of black voter turnout surpassed that of whites (Weiner 2013). More broadly, racial discrimination of the sort that marked Jim Crow has long been prohibited. Civil rights legislation bans racial segregation and makes discrimination in employment, housing, and other arenas illegal. While concerns about voter suppression and other discriminatory practices remain important (Wang 2012), the overall trend toward more fairness marks a stark contrast to the nation's long history of legal and overt discrimination based on race and ethnicity.

At the same time, individual attitudes about race have dramatically changed as well. For example, whereas only 4 percent of Americans approved of interracial marriage in 1958, 87 percent approved in 2013 (Newport 2013b). A majority of Americans embrace growing racial and ethnic diversity, with 70 percent agreeing that we will learn more and be enriched by exposure to many different cultures and 65 percent agreeing that as diversity increases, people will become more accepting and willing to find common ground (Teixeira and Halpin 2013).

These and other changes are real and significant. They confirm that old-style racial discrimination, while never eliminated entirely, is greatly marginalized However, perhaps because of such change, Americans significantly underestimate the enduring racial inequalities that continue to exist (Kraus, Rucker, and Richeson 2017).

Enduring Inequality

Even as practices and attitudes have changed, a huge volume of research has found that racial and ethnic inequality persists in virtually all aspects of social life, including the following:

- ***Economics.*** Blacks and Hispanics are about two-and-a-half times more likely to be poor than are non-Hispanic whites. The median income for non-Hispanic white households is nearly 40 percent greater than it is for black households and nearly 27 percent greater than for Hispanic households. Blacks have only about one-tenth the wealth of whites (Oliver and Shapiro 2006; U.S. Census Bureau 2017b).
- ***Housing.*** Numerous studies show that racial discrimination is a significant factor in the continuing stark racial and ethnic segregation of the nation's neighborhoods (Logan 2011; U.S. Department of Housing and Urban Development 2013). In addition, racial segregation between urban and suburban areas has actually been increasing in recent years (Lichter, Parisi, and Taquino 2015).
- ***Education.*** High school graduation rates are stratified by race. In 2016, the percentage of students receiving a high school diploma within four years of starting ninth grade differed between Asian (90 percent), white (88 percent), Hispanic (78 percent), black (75 percent), and American Indian/Alaska Native (72 percent) students (National Center for Education Statistics 2017a). The U.S. Department of Education's Office for Civil Rights has found deep racial and ethnic disparities across many facets of public education. For example, compared to white students, black students are more than four times as likely, and Latino students twice as likely, to attend schools where 20 percent or more of their teachers have not met state certification and licensing requirements (2014a). Black students are three times as likely to be suspended and expelled as white students (2014b). Enormous disparities in the rate of college completion make higher education a source of continuing racial inequality as well (Carnevale and Strohl 2013).
- ***Health.*** Racial and ethnic disparities across a host of health measures remain significant, often because of the association between race and economic inequalities (Phelan and Link 2015). For example, blacks in the

thinking about power

People in authority have often used scapegoats as a means of gaining or maintaining their **power** over others. Can you think of an example of the use of this tactic, from your own life or from recent history?

United States can expect to live 3.4 years less than whites, and they have the highest infant mortality rates and the highest rate of hypertension. Hispanic children and adolescents have the highest rate of obesity, and Hispanic adults are the group most likely to have gone without dental care in the previous year. On measures such as these, whites and Asians fare considerably better (U.S. Department of Health and Human Services 2016).

- ***Justice.*** The United States imprisons a larger share of its population than any country in the world, and that prison population is made up disproportionately of racial and ethnic minorities. More than a third of the prison population is black, and more than a third is Hispanic, numbers that are far higher than these groups' proportion in the population as a whole (Alexander 2012). Black men make up about 6 percent of the U.S. population, but they were 32 percent of the unarmed men shot to death by police in 2016–2017 (Sullivan et al. 2017). One response to this disparity has been the emergence of the Black Lives Matter movement (see the Sociology in Action box).
- ***Media.*** Stereotypical portrayals of racial and ethnic minorities have a long history in the media and are not entirely a relic of the past (Wilson, Gutiérrez, and Chao 2013).
- ***Hate Crimes.*** Race-based assault, vandalism, and even murder continue to be a reality in the United States. Of the 6,063 single-bias hate crimes the FBI documented in 2016, 58 percent were based on race, ethnicity, or ancestry. Of these, half (49.8 percent) were anti-black, one of five (20.6 percent) was anti-white, and one of ten (9.9 percent) was anti-Hispanic (Federal Bureau of Investigation 2017).

FIGURE 10.5 | RACIAL AND ETHNIC INEQUALITY, 2016

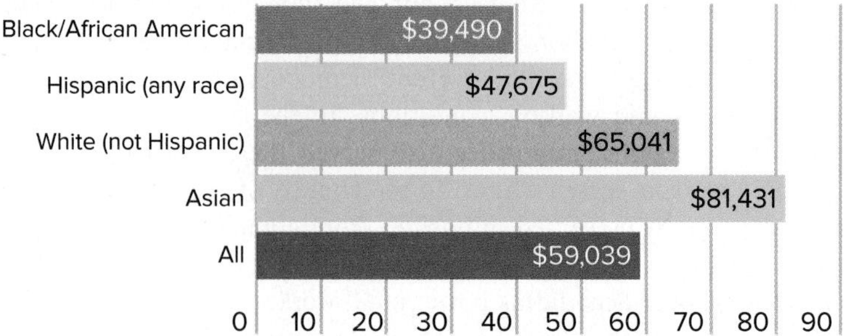

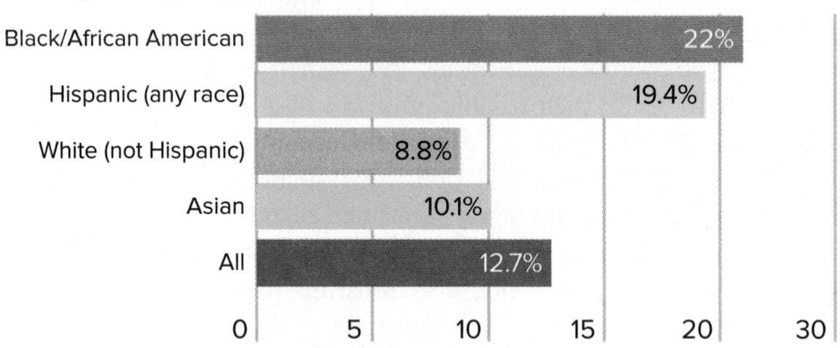

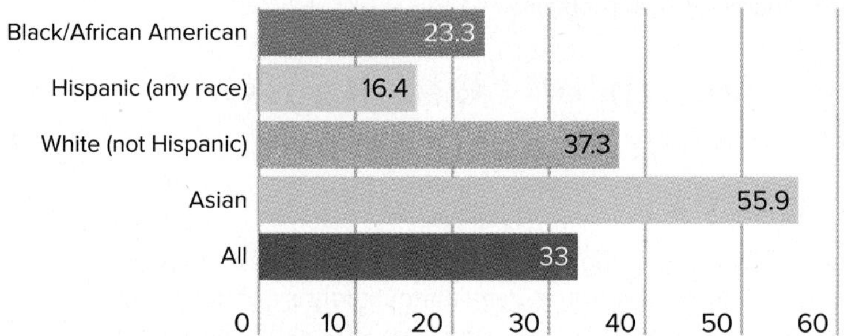

A half century after the civil rights movement, a number of measures indicate the persistence of racial and ethnic inequality in the United States today. *Sources:* U.S. Census Bureau 2017b.

CORE CONCEPTS CHALLENGE *How do the group disparities illustrated here reflect the relationship of race and ethnicity to American social* ***structure****?*

In these and other ways, racial and ethnic inequality continues to beset U.S. society. Such disparities are not a thing of the past, as shown in Figure 10.5.

Perhaps most disturbingly, some measures of racial and ethnic inequality have remained almost unchanged for 50 years, since the March on Washington for Jobs and Freedom where Martin Luther King Jr. delivered his famous "I Have a Dream" speech. For example, in 1963, the unemployment rate for blacks was 2.2 times the rate for whites; in 2017, the ratio was almost unchanged at 2.1 to 1 (U.S. Bureau of Labor Statistics 2018). Such lack of progress belies claims that the inequalities of the past no longer exist.

However, polls suggest that most people do not blame discrimination alone for enduring inequality. Though blacks (and Hispanics) have worse jobs, income, and housing than whites, 83 percent of whites and 60 percent of blacks say this situation is "mostly due" to factors *other than* racial discrimination. The last 20 years have seen a slow decline in the percentages of people who see this inequality as mostly the result of discrimination, from 21 to 15 percent for whites and from 44 to 37 percent among blacks. But discrimination is more likely to be seen in the area of criminal justice, where, for at least the past 20 years, about two-thirds of African Americans have consistently said they see the U.S. justice system as biased against blacks, while the percentage of whites who agree has declined from 33 percent in 1993 to 25 percent in 2013 (Newport 2013c).

The Legacy of Past Discrimination: The Black-White Wealth Gap

We have devoted considerable attention to the history of race and ethnicity in the United States because rather than being separate and unconnected to today's issues, the long history of "old racism" has set the stage for conditions today.

SOCIOLOGY in ACTION

Black Lives Matter

When George Zimmerman was acquitted in 2013 of the shooting death of unarmed 17-year-old Trayvon Martin in Sanford, Florida, Alicia Garza—a labor and community activist who self-identifies as queer—posted an impassioned response on Facebook that ended with "Black people. I love you. I love us. Our lives matter." Her friend, Patrisse Cullors—a gay artist and activist—adapted the phrase to create a Twitter hashtag: #BlackLivesMatter. Along with immigrant rights activist Opal Tometi, the daughter of undocumented Nigerians, the three black women set up Twitter and Tumblr accounts and began helping to build a diverse movement that eventually expanded to address a broad range of racial justice issues. The effort was gay-friendly, led by women of color, and decentralized across local chapters (Day 2015; blacklivesmatter.org).

Some sociologists took note, both personally, as they supported Black Lives Matter efforts, and professionally, as they began to study the fledgling movement (Fried 2014). When the 2014 police killing of Michael Brown in Ferguson, Missouri, led to demonstrations and a militarized response by police, a group of sociologists attending the American Sociological Association's (ASA) annual national meetings in San Francisco organized under the name "Sociologists for Justice" (McMillan Cottom 2014). They wrote a statement, eventually signed by more than 1,800 sociologists, that placed the unfolding events in a broader sociological context, citing "ingrained racial, political, social and economic inequities." It called for a variety of concrete measures—from adoption of police body cameras to a civil rights investigation into the events in Ferguson—and encouraged colleagues and fellow citizens to support the Black Lives Matter movement. The members of the group also produced a "Ferguson syllabus" that listed relevant readings on implicit bias, structural and institutional racism, police practices, economic inequality, and civil rights. They noted, "As scholars and advocates who study the various ways that race shapes our society and institutions, we are committed to sharing research, facilitating conversations and advancing solutions that promote racial equity and justice" (sociologistsforjustice.org). Not long afterward, a small group of sociologists also formed the Ferguson Research-Action Collaborative to study the Ferguson protests and the Black Lives Matter movement in the hope of contributing to the struggle for racial justice (Rios and Martino-Taylor 2016).

By the time sociologists held their 2016 ASA annual meeting in Seattle, the Black Lives Matter movement was a key item on the agenda. Charlene Carruthers and Mariame Kaba, leaders from the movement, spoke at key sessions, a variety of sociologists presented research on related topics, and even the theme of the meetings—Rethinking Social Movements: Can Changing the Conversation Change the World?—reflected the influence of Black Lives Matter.

think about it

1. *What do you know about the efforts related to the Black Lives Matter movement? How did you learn about them? What does that say about the way information about social issues is communicated today?*
2. *The most prominent leaders of the civil rights movement of the 1950s and 60s were mostly straight black men, often clergy, whereas Black Lives Matter has featured leadership from a much more diverse range of people. How might this affect the direction and success of the movement?*

Consider the following analogy. Imagine a long-distance foot race in which some competitors are shackled with leg irons at the start, while others can run freely. Partway through the race, a judge instructs the runners to stop where they are and orders the leg irons removed. The race then continues, but even though all competitors are now allowed to run freely, the gap between frontrunners and those who had been shackled continues to affect the outcome. This analogy reflects the dilemma facing U.S. society in dealing with the legacy of racism.

The conditions that originally created the inequalities no longer exist and the individuals who were responsible may not be around any longer, but the effects of those unequal conditions reverberate through subsequent generations. Sociological research shows that people's life chances are shaped dramatically by the families into which they are born. So, even those who have not directly experienced discriminatory practices can still indirectly inherit either the privileges or disadvantages that those practices create. One of the clearest examples of this legacy is the black-white wealth gap.

As we saw in Chapter 9, *income* refers to money a person receives over a set period of time. *Wealth* refers to what people own, including savings, real estate, stocks and bonds, and other investments. Recall that wealth is distributed much more unequally than income, because wealth can be accumulated and passed on to subsequent generations. The median income of blacks is less than 60 percent that of whites, but the median wealth of blacks has been less than 10 percent that of whites.

The racial wealth gap reflects the multigenerational nature of wealth accumulation. That is, advantages or disadvantages from the past continue to affect later generations. The race-specific barriers of old-style racism constitute what sociologists Melvin Oliver and Thomas Shapiro (2006) call the **racialization of the state,** *the implementation of government and private-sector policies that discriminated against minorities and provided whites with numerous advantages.* These policies included:

- The legalization and enforcement of slavery.
- Laws that barred blacks and other minorities from owning property.
- Local ordinances that barred blacks from entering certain occupations.
- Regulations that prevented blacks from selling to whites, making it nearly impossible for blacks to compete with white-owned businesses.
- Segregated and unequal schooling that ensured unequal opportunities in the job market based on race.
- Biased federal home loan programs that steered money to the rapidly growing white suburbs after World War II.
- Biased bank loan practices that required black applicants to meet more stringent mortgage criteria than white applicants and continued long after legal segregation ended.

These sorts of discriminatory practices made it far more difficult for blacks than whites to accumulate wealth and pass it on to their children. The impact of this legacy continues to be felt today.

Take the example of housing discrimination, one of the most important factors contributing to the racial wealth gap today. As we examine in more detail in Chapter 15, explicit residential racial segregation, blatant discriminatory lending practices, and discriminatory government policies once limited the demand for homes in nonwhite neighborhoods, artificially depressing their value. As a result, minorities who owned homes were not able to benefit from their increased value as much as white homeowners did. Today, because of existing wealth disparities passed on through inheritance and family financial assistance, white families are able to buy homes an average of eight years earlier than black families, make larger up-front down payments, and qualify for lower interest rates, all of which widen the racial wealth gap over time. And in recent years, African Americans are more likely than whites to have been the victim of predatory high-risk mortgages, and borrowers of color are twice as likely as whites to have lost their homes to foreclosure after the 2007 housing bust. Because owning a home makes up a larger part of the wealth black and Hispanic families have, compared to whites, the housing bust affected them disproportionately. By some estimates, the housing bust and ensuing Great Recession of 2007–2009 led to black families' collective loss of fully *one-half* of their wealth and to Hispanic families' loss of *two-thirds* of their wealth; these losses further contributed to a major increase in the racial wealth gap (McKernan et al. 2013; Shapiro, Meschede, and Osoro 2013).

So, even if we optimistically note that old-style racism has largely passed, the legacy of this historical discrimination combines with more recent developments to cast its shadow on today's world. One lesson of contemporary research, then, is that racial and ethnic inequality continues today because the discrimination of the past still matters. One attempt to overcome this legacy involves **affirmative action,** *policies and programs that aim to avoid discrimination and redress past discrimination through the active recruitment of qualified minorities for jobs, promotions, and educational opportunities.* Created by a presidential executive order in 1961, the U.S. policy of affirmative action forbid government agencies from discriminating in hiring based on race, religion, or national origin (sex was added as a protected category in 1967) and directed them to take "affirmative action" to promote equal hiring practices (Kennedy 2013). The term has since been applied to a variety of efforts to combat the effects of discriminatory practices in employment, college admissions, and other arenas.

Affirmative action based on race has long been controversial (Alon 2015; Cahn 2002; Wright and Garces 2018). Some critics contend that race-based affirmative action ignores the impact of class and that the greatest beneficiaries have been minorities from middle- and upper-class backgrounds. Others note that the programs can benefit the growing number of recent minority immigrants, even though they have not suffered the effects of American racism's historical legacy. Other critics contend that affirmative action policies have unintended detrimental effects, such as stigmatizing beneficiaries who face questions about preferential treatment and their qualifications. The most forceful critics even argue that some policies amount to reverse discrimination against whites.

The future of affirmative action remains unclear. Some states have prohibited the use of race-based affirmative action in public institutions. Federal court challenges have also resulted in limits being placed on how race-based affirmative action can be used but its basic constitutionality has been upheld.

The Emergence of "New Racism": Hidden, Implicit, and Color-Blind

While "old racism" has left a legacy that sheds light on today's enduring racial inequality, sociological research also suggests that new beliefs and practices help explain how racism operates in a society in which racial discrimination is often illegal and covert (Feagin 2014; Quillian 2006).

Hidden Prejudice Robert Merton (1949) recognized long ago that people who were not prejudiced could engage in discriminatory behaviors to conform to biased social norms. Some whites in the segregated South, for example, acquiesced to the dominant culture even though they personally rejected its racist assumptions. Similarly, prejudiced people may keep silent about their attitudes when the dominant norms condemn them but still engage in discriminatory behavior. Indeed, recent research suggests that, in some cases, norms promoting racial and ethnic equality in the post–civil rights era have not eliminated racism but rather have driven it underground, transforming overt prejudices into covert ones.

For example, some people refrain from racist talk or action in public but give vent to racial or ethnic stereotypes when among friends and family. In one study, over 1,000 students from a variety of colleges and universities kept journals recording their social interactions for several weeks during the 2002–2003 academic year (Picca and Feagin 2007). The journals of the more than 600 white students in the study showed them to be nearly always polite to their black peers, avoiding racially offensive language in public "frontstage" situations. However, in "backstage," white-only settings, students reported the frequent use of the word "nigger" and other racial epithets to refer to blacks. Some students reported feeling uncomfortable about the racist language but lacked the courage to object. In their journals, the white students also commonly referred to blacks in terms of racial stereotypes, describing them as lazy, criminally inclined, and oversexed. The results suggest that, even 50 years after the civil rights movement, these stereotypes and prejudices remain deeply entrenched and widely prevalent.

SPOTLIGHT
on social theory

As part of the ***symbolic interactionist*** tradition, **dramaturgical theory** draws attention to the differences between frontstage and backstage behaviors. Are research findings that racist backstage behavior is relatively common among college students, whereas frontstage behavior is noticeably free of such actions, consistent with your own experiences?

Although marginalized racist beliefs are usually kept "backstage," the internet offers a public stage on which racist ideas can be shared. In 2016, Microsoft introduced a chatbot named Tay that used artificial intelligence to learn from Twitter users how to simulate tweets and then send new tweets aimed at teens and young adults. Within a day, the chatbot was spewing racist tweets it had learned from internet trolls. Outrage quickly followed, and Microsoft deleted the offensive tweets and shut down the chatbot. The incident showed how racism is both rampant on the internet and not tolerated by mainstream actors (Perez 2016).

Hidden prejudices can also lead people who deny they are motivated by any personal prejudice to engage in discriminatory practices. White employers, for example, may justify their acknowledged reluctance to hire blacks by citing the prevalence of crime in black communities. Ironically, some managers admit to steering clear of hiring blacks precisely because of the public sanctions against racial discrimination: they fear a discrimination lawsuit if an African American employee needs to be fired (Wilson 1996).

Implicit Bias In 1926, sociologist Emory Bogardus published a study of the *social distance* between groups, based on a nationwide survey of college students. To measure social distance, he asked students how closely they were willing to interact with the members of certain other groups. Being willing to marry someone from a group, for example, indicated very little social distance, whereas wanting to bar members of a group from the country indicated great social distance. Bogardus—and later other researchers—repeated the survey over the years, refining the measures and expanding the sample to include the general population, not just college students (Bogardus 1967). The results show decreasing social distance over time, indicating a reduction in racial and ethnic prejudice. There are exceptions, though. In the wake of the September 11, 2001, terrorist attacks, for example, the acceptance of Muslims and Arabs declined (Parrillo and Donoghue 2005), and Muslims continue to be the major religious group Americans view most negatively (Pew Research Center 2017c).

As researchers learn more about how the brain works, however, they are finding that some biases may be more implicit—existing at the subconscious level—than overt and at a conscious level where they can be measured in surveys. Recent research suggests that we learn prejudices at a deep, unconscious level and respond to people with lightning-fast assessments that are beyond rational evaluation (Staats et al. 2015; Vedantam 2005). In our conscious activities, we can control our behaviors and overcome implicit biases, but this restraint is cognitively challenging and requires additional effort (Ito et al. 2015; Richeson et al. 2003). At the unconscious level, we may be acting on well-known stereotypes and deeply held prejudices.

Social psychologist Mahzarin Banaji and her colleagues have devised a series of implicit association tests (IAT) that measure unconscious biases by tapping into fast, unexamined responses. (You can take some of these tests yourself online at https://implicit.harvard.edu.) These researchers have found that most respondents show an unconscious preference for people like themselves, regardless of their stated beliefs. Even when people who feel and say they are not biased are tested, in most cases the results indicate they actually have unconscious biases based on race, ethnicity, sexual orientation, and class as well as other categories. These tests have their critics (Blanton and Jaccard 2015), but they appear to demonstrate that implicit bias is one source of enduring prejudice and discrimination in contemporary society. For example, one study using eye-tracking technology asked teachers to look for challenging behavior in videos of classrooms. Though there was no such misbehavior, teachers looked at and lingered on black boys more than other students (Gilliam et al. 2016). Another study found that from prekindergarten through high school, black students are disciplined with suspensions and expulsion at more than twice the rate of their white peers (U.S. Government Accountability Office 2018). Both studies concluded that implicit racial bias is likely a major contributing factor to such unequal treatment.

Racial discrimination persists in many areas of social life, whether because of prejudice, hidden racism, or implicit bias. One method sociologists use to measure discrimination is the *field audit* (Quillian 2006). In typical field audits, researchers pair people from different races or ethnic groups who are otherwise similar on all characteristics that might affect the study's outcome. They then send each member of the pair into social situations in which they may encounter discrimination, such as renting an apartment or applying for a job. Using this method repeatedly, researchers have documented persistent racial discrimination in housing, hiring, and other fields (Bertrand and Duflo 2016). One study even found discrimination based on no more than the name on otherwise comparable resumes mailed in response to ads for jobs. Resumes for people with white-sounding names, such as Emily and Greg, were 50 percent more likely to get a callback than were those for people with black-sounding names, such as Lakisha and Jamal (Bertrand and Mullainathan 2004). Another study found that employers were much more likely to hire a white person with a criminal record than a black person with a criminal record (Pager 2003). A meta-analysis of such field studies concluded racial discrimination in hiring has not diminished in 30 years (Quillian et al. 2017).

Color-Blind Racism Sociologists often refer to today's persistent racism as *the new racism,* and they describe its dynamics with a variety of approaches that have a variety of labels, including "symbolic racism" (Kinder and Sanders 1996), "laissez-faire racism" (Bobo, Kluegel, and Smith 1997), "color-blind racism" (Bonilla-Silva 2001, 2014), and "modern racism" (McConahay 1986). Although their analyses vary somewhat, these approaches agree on two points:

- Prejudice and discrimination persist in contemporary social life.
- The ways in which prejudice and discrimination manifest themselves have changed in the post–civil rights era.

For example, in a significant shift from earlier attitudes, many Americans today advocate race neutrality and a "color-blind" society. But ideas that once might have been progressive and antiracist can reinforce existing racial inequality in a different historical era. **Color-blind racism** is *a form of bias in which the promotion of race neutrality actually helps maintain existing racial and ethnic inequality.* It reveals itself in the rejection of efforts to reduce racial and ethnic inequality on the grounds that those efforts violate a color-blind approach to society and may even constitute reverse racism. Research suggests that many Americans are deeply ambivalent about how to embrace an ideology of color blindness while simultaneously embracing racial diversity as a positive development (Burke 2012). How can race matter but not matter at the same time?

Some who advocate color-blind policies are likely using race neutrality as a cover for prejudiced views, understanding that overt racism is no longer acceptable in our society. However, color-blind approaches are not inherently prejudicial, and some advocates of this view genuinely believe that race neutrality is the best route to racial justice. The result is a complex mix of racial and nonracial beliefs that in combination—intentionally or not—can help perpetuate racial inequality.

How do those who believe that racism is no longer a significant hurdle in our supposedly postracial society explain the continuing inequality among racial and ethnic groups in U.S. society? Some simply deny that inequality and discrimination exist, despite the vast body of social science research showing that they do. Some point to cultural differences to account for this variation and, in particular, to the success of Asian Americans as evidence that racial and ethnic discrimination no longer holds back social advancement. Some have argued that enduring racial inequality simply reflects the natural outcome of competition between groups with inherently different abilities. Richard Herrnstein and Charles Murray (1996), for instance, claimed that differences in scores on intelligence tests (IQ scores) reflect innate and unchangeable differences between the races. Critics have pointed out the inadequacies of such studies, which ignore the impact of environment on IQ scores and treat "intelligence" and "race" as clearly defined variables (Fischer et al. 1996). They argue that efforts to measure differences in intelligence are repackaged racist ideas that hark back to the ugly history of racist pseudoscience.

Critics of color-blind policies argue that to pretend that race no longer matters is to overlook the legacy of racism and the persistence of prejudice and discrimination. As U.S. Supreme Court Justice Harry Blackmun famously said in defending the use of affirmative action, "In order to get beyond racism, we must first take account of race." As the number of racially charged incidents and protests in the news has increased in the last few years, so has the percentage of Americans who feel change is needed. In one survey, 59 percent of whites and 83 percent of blacks responded that the country needed to make more changes in order to give blacks equal rights with whites (Pew Research Center 2015d).

In the nineteenth century, a civil war led to the end of slavery in the United States. In the twentieth century, the civil rights movement led to the end of racial segregation and legal discrimination. In both cases, social change came only after intense controversy and prolonged conflict. Just as those struggles were contentious in their day, so too are the efforts to understand inequality and advance racial and ethnic justice in a post-civil rights society. In particular, historians may look back at the dramatic shift from an Obama to a Trump presidency—and the backlash it generated—as another defining period in the nation's racial history.

A Changing World

MULTIRACIAL AND MULTIETHNIC IDENTITIES

When E. Dolores Johnson's white mother wanted to marry her black father in the 1940s, she had to leave her home state of Indiana, which outlawed interracial marriage. Although born multiracial in New York, Johnson's birth certificate said "Negro," and she grew up in a society where people always wanted to pigeonhole her into a single racial category and often insulted her because of her multiracial origins. In 2000, though, the U.S. Census Bureau finally began allowing respondents to say they had more than one race and, as Johnson put it, "I felt as if my country could finally see me" (Johnson 2017).

The country will be seeing many more multiracial and multiethnic people in the coming years—both because more people are willing to acknowledge their ancestry and because of the growth of intermarriage. This growth in multiracial and multiethnic identities will be another development in our ever-evolving social construction of race and ethnicity.

When Barack Obama filled out his 2010 census form while president, he indicated his race as African American, even though his mother was white. The move disappointed many multiracial Americans (Chang 2010), but Obama was conforming to the cultural norm of his generation that still encouraged people to identify with only one race. For example, in the 2010 census, only 7.4 percent of blacks indicated they had a multiracial background, even though the U.S. Census Bureau estimates that at least 75 percent of black Americans have a multiracial ancestry (Daniel 2002). Even Martin Luther King Jr. had white Irish ancestors (The Grio 2011).

Multiracial identities are becoming more socially accepted, however, and young people are the most likely to say they are multiracial. The number of people in the United States who identify as multiracial varies depending on how researchers ask the question. One estimate of the multiracial population is 6.9 percent and growing; more than 1 of 10 babies is now multiracial (Pew Research Center 2015k). Much of this growth is due to the rise in intermarriage.

As we saw earlier in the chapter, the 1965 Immigration and Nationality Act set the stage for people from many different backgrounds to come to the United States. Just two years later, in 1967, the Supreme Court struck down laws in 15 states that prohibited interracial marriage. Since then, immigration and intermarriage have resulted in more children who are multiracial and multiethnic. (Intermarriage in this context typically means between a Hispanic and a non-Hispanic or as between non-Hispanics from any two of the major U.S. racial categories.) In 1967, just 3 percent of new marriages were intermarriages; in 2016 that figure was 18 percent and growing (Livingston and Brown 2017).

Rising intermarriage is one sign that the boundaries between racial and ethnic groups have become less rigid. Intermarriage between members of different white ethnic groups was rare 100 years ago but is now so common that researchers no longer categorize such unions as interethnic. In recent decades, intermarriage has increased for all groups. Since 1980, for example, the share of African Americans who married someone of a different race or ethnicity has more than tripled from 5 percent to 18 percent. Asians and Hispanics are the most likely to intermarry; whites are the least likely to do so. Intermarriage rates also vary by sex, especially for blacks and Asians. (See Figure 10.6.)

Younger people and native-born adults are more likely to marry outside their racial or ethnic group than are older people and immigrants, suggesting intermarriage will likely increase in the coming years as any remaining taboo against it fades and recent immigrants become more established. As the trend toward intermarriage continues, it promises to alter the nature of racial and ethnic relations in the United States. Perhaps it will even diminish the social significance of racial and ethnic categories altogether.

©SWNS.com

Some people perceive these fraternal multiracial twins as being "black" and "white." But the 21st-century understanding of human genetics tells us that the whole idea of race is a human invention" (Edmonds 2018). If two children of the same parents can appear to be of different races, what does "race" really mean? And who is most likely to perceive these differences as meaningful? The growing numbers of multiracial children in the United States will likely change some of the discussion about such issues.

FIGURE 10.6 | INTERMARRIAGE RATES OF NEWLYWEDS, 2015

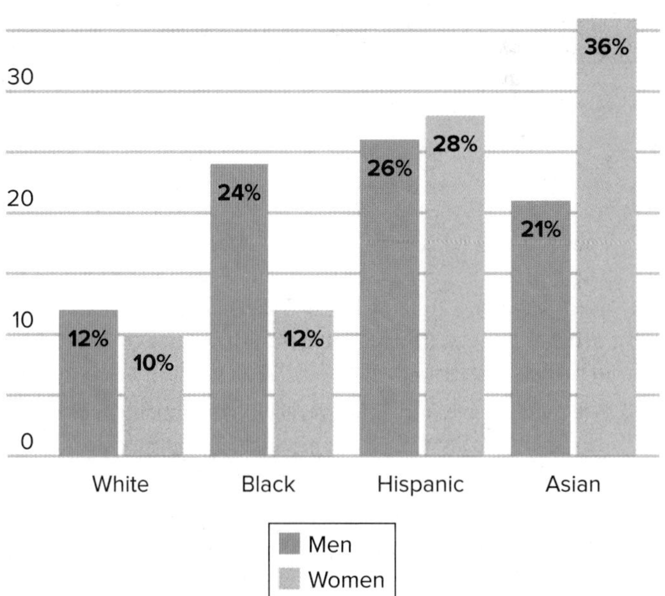

Intermarriage rates vary by race, ethnicity, and sex but they have been rising for all groups in recent decades.

Note: "Newlyweds" refers to people who got married in the 12 months before the survey. All groups (other than Hispanic) are non-Hispanic single races.

Source: Livingston and Brown 2017.

thinking sociologically about
Race and Ethnicity

culture

- Race and ethnicity are social constructs whose definitions change over time and vary across cultures.
- Social norms about race and ethnicity—both racist and antiracist—are learned through the process of socialization.

structure

- Interpretations of race and ethnicity influence patterns of social interaction.
- The policies and practices of social institutions can both reflect racist beliefs and perpetuate racial and ethnic inequality.
- Groups, from slaves to the activists of the civil rights movement and later, have resisted racial discrimination, sometimes producing long-lasting changes in the social structure.

power

- Racial and ethnic inequality reflects differences in power within society.
- Powerful groups have historically justified their privileges on the basis of their supposed racial or ethnic superiority.
- The post–civil rights era has seen both enduring racial and ethnic inequality as well as new relations of power, reflecting the increasing diversity of society.

REVIEW, REFLECT, AND APPLY

Looking Back

1. Race is not a biological reality, but rather a social construct whose origin lies in eighteenth- and nineteenth-century pseudoscience. Ethnicity is also a social construct that, like race, has been interpreted differently in different cultures and in various historical periods.
2. Grouping people into different races and ethnicities sets up majority-minority group dynamics that become a part of the social structure and reflect inequalities in power.
3. The social history of the United States resulted in unique ideas and practices concerning race and ethnicity. In particular, whites used ideas about race and racial superiority to justify slavery and adopt laws that enshrined racial inequality.
4. Native societies were decimated by the arrival of European colonizers. Spanish colonists, the ancestors of today's Hispanics, took control of what is now the southwestern United States. White Anglo-Saxon Protestants settled primarily on the east coast and rapidly expanded their landholdings westward. African slaves were imported in growing numbers as labor for an agrarian economy. In the nineteenth century, Asian laborers—especially Chinese—were recruited to work on railroads and in other industries.
5. Rising immigration from throughout Europe in the nineteenth and early twentieth centuries increased ethnic diversity. Some groups—including Jews, the Irish, and Italians—were not considered white until they gradually assimilated.
6. The civil rights movement helped transform society, making racial and ethnic discrimination illegal and promoting tolerance. One consequence was a change in immigration laws that opened the way to new diversity. Recent immigrants, who come mostly from Asia and Latin America rather than Europe, are substantially changing the racial and ethnic makeup of the country.

7. Despite the gains of the civil rights movement, racial and ethnic inequalities endure, reflecting racism's historical legacy as well as contemporary practices. Racial prejudice and discrimination operate at different levels of social life, involving individual attitudes and behaviors and the structural barriers created by institutions. Prejudice and discrimination can be fueled by cultural differences or by the pursuit of group interests. In a post–civil rights society, prejudice and discrimination can be hidden, implicit, or produced by support for color-blind policies.
8. One consequence of our increasing diversity is the growth of multiethnic and multiracial identities, in part the result of an increase in interracial marriage.

Critical Thinking: Questions and Activities

1. A friend asks, "Are you blind? Of course race exists!" Explain to your friend why race is, in fact, a social construction, rather than a biological fact.
2. How did you first learn about race and ethnicity? Did this early socialization include the perpetuation of stereotypes? Explain. What socializing forces later influenced your understanding of these issues?
3. Is the social history of race and ethnicity in the United States summarized here consistent with what you learned in high school? If not, how is it different?
4. How do you think changing demographics in the United States will influence other aspects of life 50 years from now?
5. Do you think racial attitudes today among people under age 30 differ significantly from those held by older people? Why or why not? (How could you find out for sure?) What factors do you think contributed to this situation?
6. Do you think the election of Donald Trump has made a difference in how Americans view and discuss issues of race and ethnicity? Explain.

Key Terms

affirmative action (p. 258) policies and programs that aim to avoid discrimination and redress past discrimination through the active recruitment of qualified minorities for jobs, promotions, and educational opportunities.

amalgamation (p. 240) the process by which a majority and a minority group blend or mix to form a new group.

assimilation (p. 240) the process by which members of a minority group come to adopt the culture of the majority group.

color-blind racism (p. 260) a form of bias in which the promotion of race neutrality actually helps maintain existing racial and ethnic inequality.

discrimination (p. 240) unequal treatment that gives advantages to one group of people over another without justifiable cause.

ethnicity (p. 234) a shared cultural heritage often deriving from a common ancestry and homeland.

genocide (p. 240) the systematic killing of a group of people, based on their race, ethnicity, nationality, or religion.

institutional discrimination (p. 254) unequal treatment that results from the structural organization, policies, and procedures of social institutions such as the government, businesses, and schools.

majority group (p. 240) a collection of people who enjoy privileges and have more access to power because of identifiable physical or cultural characteristics.

minority group (p. 239) a collection of people who suffer disadvantages and have less power because of identifiable physical or cultural characteristics.

pluralism (p. 240) a situation in which distinct ethnic and racial groups coexist on equal terms and have equal social standing.

prejudice (p. 240) the "pre-judgment" of someone or some group negatively based on inadequate information.

race (p. 234) a category of people widely perceived as sharing socially significant physical characteristics such as skin color.

racial essentialism (p. 235) the idea that supposedly natural and immutable differences separate the races.

racialization of the state (p. 257) the implementation of government and private-sector policies that discriminated against minorities and provided whites with numerous advantages.

racism (p. 235) the belief that one race is inherently superior to another.

scapegoat (p. 255) an individual or a group of people falsely blamed for a negative situation.

segregation (p. 240) keeping distinct social groups physically and socially separate and unequal.

split labor market theory (p. 254) the theory that ethnic and racial conflicts often emerge when two racial or ethnic groups compete for the same jobs.

stereotypes (p. 240) exaggerated, distorted, or untrue generalizations about categories of people that do not acknowledge individual variation.

transnational migrants (p. 251) immigrants who retain strong personal, cultural, and economic ties to both their country of birth and their newly adopted home.

©MoMo Productions/DigitalVision/Getty Images

11 Gender and Sexuality

looking AHEAD

How has **culture** influenced your understanding of gender roles and sexuality?

How are your ideas about gender and sexuality reinforced through social **structures** such as your family and your school?

Are differences in **power** in your family or friendships the result of inequalities based on gender and sexual orientation?

©Bettmann/Getty Images

On April 19, 1967, 20-year-old Kathrine Switzer was running the Boston Marathon when a truck carrying photographers and race officials drove by slowly. One of the officials, Jock Semple, was stunned when he noticed Switzer. Jumping off the vehicle and yelling, "Get the hell out of my race!" Semple lunged at the young runner and tried to rip off her official race number. He missed the number but grabbed the back of Switzer's sweatshirt, momentarily preventing her from advancing. Switzer's boyfriend, who was also running, shoved the race official, allowing Switzer to escape and finish the race.

What had Switzer done to evoke such an angry outburst? She had dared to run a marathon at a time when women were banned from competing. A year earlier, Roberta Gibb had become the first woman to finish the Boston Marathon, but she had run unofficially, and she even had to hide in the bushes near the start so that race officials would not spot her. Switzer managed to obtain an official number by registering under a gender-neutral name, K. V. Switzer (Switzer 2007).

At the time, the men who organized long-distance road races in the United States used their power to ban women from competing in marathons for what they argued were biologically obvious reasons: women were simply too frail to complete the grueling 26.2-mile event safely. Conventional wisdom held that even if some women could finish the race, doing so would likely cause physiological damage, perhaps even preventing them from having children. Women could not compete officially in U.S. marathons until 1971 or in an Olympic marathon until 1984.

Today, hundreds of thousands of women run in marathons each year. Their safe participation shows that what was widely considered biological reality just a few decades ago was, in fact, a social construction—a part of the structure of sports produced by the power of men that created needless social barriers for women.

In this chapter, we examine the idea of gender and consider how people mistake socially constructed differences as natural. We look at how cultural norms are reinforced or modified in daily life and within social structures, and how artificial distinctions between women and men contribute to gender inequality. In addition, we consider similar issues of social construction as they apply to human sexuality. We also look at how people have organized to challenge inequality based on gender and sexuality.

Biology and Culture: Sex and Gender

In everyday life, you often see the terms *sex* and *gender* treated as if they meant the same thing. For example, a questionnaire might ask for your "gender," expecting you to indicate either "male" or "female." Sociologists distinguish between sex and gender, however, to highlight the difference between biology and culture (Stoller 1968).

Sex is *the biological distinction between females and males.* In contrast, **gender** refers to *the socially constructed cultural expectations associated with women and men.* Biology makes us male or female; culture teaches us to be men or women. To take two simple examples, most females have the physical capacity to give birth to children, but males do not. This ability is a sex difference. In our culture, women are free to wear dresses in daily life, but men are generally discouraged from doing so. This restriction is a gender difference. It is based on culture and has nothing to do with biology.

The distinctions between sex and gender are not always so clear-cut. Scholars debate the influence of biologically based sex differences on social behavior. However, much of what our culture associates with *sex* differences is, in fact, socially

produced *gender* differences. For example, when Kathrine Switzer ran in the 1967 Boston Marathon, the women's world record in the marathon—from competitions outside the United States—was 3:19:33, while the men's record was 2:12:00. Some men pointed to this 67-minute gap as evidence that women were biologically unfit for the difficult race. As of early 2018, however, women runners had narrowed the gap to less than 13 minutes: 2:15:25 for women and 2:02:57 for men. Clearly, social factors, not biological ones, were responsible for most of the gap between women's and men's performance in the past. In sports, as in many other areas of life, we can mistakenly attach biological explanations to what are primarily social factors. To help unravel the relationship between sex and gender, let's examine each more closely.

The Biology of Sex

A person's sex is determined at conception when the mother's ovum (or egg cell) contributes an X chromosome to the embryo and the father's sperm contributes either an X or a Y chromosome. An XX combination produces a female; an XY combination a male. Chromosomes help determine physical development, including distinctions between the sexes. *Primary sex characteristics,* including the genitals and reproductive organs, are sex differences that are directly involved in reproduction. *Secondary sex characteristics,* including wider hips and breast development in females and more extensive body hair and increased muscle mass in the upper body in males, are not directly involved in reproduction.

Sex differences can be grouped loosely into two categories: absolute differences and differences of degree. Absolute sex differences include those related to reproduction. Only females menstruate, ovulate, become pregnant, and breastfeed their babies; only males can impregnate females. Other differences, though, are of degree. Both men and women possess the same hormones, for example, but in different amounts.

Most individuals are clearly biologically female or male. But some people are **intersexual**—*individuals born with ambiguous reproductive or sexual anatomy.* Intersexual people have some ambiguity in their genitals, chromosomes, gonads (female ovaries or males testes), or hormones. Being intersexual can include conditions such as having external female genitals but internal testes, an additional sex chromosome (XXY), or hormonal irregularities that at puberty produce secondary sex characteristics associated with the other sex. Because of the range of conditions involved, experts disagree about who and how many people qualify as intersexual, with one study estimating between 0.2 and 1.7 percent of the population (Blackless et al. 2000).

The Limits of Biology

Imagine that researchers devise a project to investigate whether the ability to walk in high-heeled shoes is biologically based. They choose a random sample of women and men, have them strap on some heels, and record the results. Lo and behold, it turns out that, on average, women perform significantly better than men. The researchers might suggest that these results are likely due to biological differences between the sexes in body mass, balance, and coordination.

Actually, the ability they are measuring has been learned with practice—as anyone proficient in walking in heels can tell you. With some effort, it's entirely possible for men to develop this skill, but in our culture they are not encouraged to acquire it. Socialization, not biology, produced the difference.

In fact, studies show an overwhelming number of similarities in the psychology and abilities of women and men, with more variation occurring within each sex than between the two (Hyde 2005, 2014). Yet the popular media often highlight misinterpretations and pseudoscience regarding supposedly innate differences between the sexes. For example, a once-popular book touting that "men are from Mars and women from Venus" (J. Gray 2004) simply treats cultural stereotypes—such as women are passive while men are active—as innate differences, without adequately considering the role of gender socialization in producing them. We can recognize the falseness of such claims in an outrageous example such as our hypothetical study of walking in high heels, but more subtle real-world studies can be misleading.

For example, men often outperform women in tasks that require subjects to use visualization and mentally manipulate objects. Researchers sometimes attribute such superior performance to innate differences that developed during evolution and cite these results as a reason why men dominate some scientific fields such as engineering. An understanding of how gender influences human development, however, provides us with a different perspective on this research.

Numerous studies have shown that playing action video games affects the ability to process visual information (Bediou et al. 2018). In one study, researchers briefly showed subjects a grid that contained two dozen identical objects and one object that was different (Feng, Spence, and Pratt 2007). The subjects had to determine the location of the odd object quickly. Consistent with the idea that they have evolved better spatial abilities, men succeeded in the task 68 percent of the time, whereas women succeeded only 55 percent of the time, a statistically significant difference. However, after some of the subjects spent 10 hours playing a video game that involved shooting at a target (a game popular with boys, less so with girls), the difference between the sexes disappeared upon retesting both at once and five months later. A difference in skill that researchers and others could have misinterpreted as the result of innate physiological differences instead turned out to be easily influenced—and erased—by environmental conditions, in this case, access to and practice with video games.

There *are* actual differences in the architecture of male and female brains. In the coming years we will likely learn more about these differences and how men and women use their brains in different ways to get the same job done. As we saw in Chapter 6, though, the human brain has a remarkable ability—known as brain plasticity—to restructure and reorganize itself in response to social experiences and learning. As we will see, expectations about gender create different social experiences for women and men from the moment of birth. Just as the gender gap in marathon performance was due largely to culture, not biology, so are many of the differences measured by today's research. If we want to understand the social life of women and men, then, we need to look beyond biology to gender and its social construction.

Gender as a Social Construction

Almost all the differences we associate with men and women are culturally produced, not biologically based. From infancy, we are taught our culture's expectations regarding gender, we develop identities that are based on those expectations, and we view the world through the lens of gender expectations that we usually take for granted. For example, if you got into a taxi cab with a female driver, you would probably take note; without even thinking about it, you most likely expect a man to drive a taxi. Similarly, you might be surprised to encounter a male dental hygienist or day care provider.

If we look at how notions of gender differ over time and across cultures, we can see the powerful influence of culture.

Gender in a Different Time Throughout the history of the United States, activists have challenged—and, over time, changed—widely accepted ideas about gender. In 1848, participants at a groundbreaking women's rights convention in Seneca Falls, New York, pointed out some of the oppressive political, legal, educational, and economic conditions that women faced. In a document modeled after the Declaration of Independence, these activists produced an inventory of grievances that included the fact that women could not vote, had no legal or property rights, could be abused by their husbands at will, were excluded from most occupations and professions, and were prevented from obtaining a college education. "The history of mankind," they concluded, "is a history of repeated injuries and usurpations on the part of man toward woman, having in direct object the establishment of an absolute tyranny over her" (Stanton 1889, 70–71). The Seneca Falls activists were part of the movement that eventually helped secure women's right to vote with the passage of the Nineteenth Amendment to the Constitution in 1920.

In hindsight, we can see the biases behind the gender claims that dominated nineteenth-century America, even as we recognize their persistence in some parts of contemporary society.

Gender in a Different Culture Blatant and comprehensive discrimination against women continues in many parts of the world, illustrating how ideas about gender vary not only across time but also across cultures. In Saudi Arabia, for example, a close ally of the United States, women have few social rights and are not treated as equal members of society (U.S. Department of State 2016). Although women compose more than half of university students, the types of work they can perform are restricted, and they make up only 21 percent of the workforce. They are expected to remain at home caring for husband and family. By law and custom, schools, workplaces, and transportation are segregated by sex, and women cannot attend most public events unless a close male relative accompanies them. Before 2018, Saudi women could not drive. They generally still cannot appear in public with their heads uncovered, or travel abroad without permission from a male relative or guardian. A woman cannot conduct financial transactions (even if she owns a business) without deputizing a male relative as her representative. In the court system in Saudi Arabia, which is

©The Advertising Archives

©The Advertising Archives

FAST-FORWARD

Change and Gender

Cultures promote gender norms through images in mass media. Over time, these images can reveal the socially constructed and changing nature of gender. In the mid-twentieth century, ads such as this one for a kitchen mixer painted a picture of a stark gender division of labor, with men as breadwinners and women as cooks and homemakers. In more recent years, images of women have been more diverse, including ad campaigns such as this one that challenge traditional norms of beauty. If a historian from the future looked back at today's ads, what would she or he learn about gender in our society?

based on Islamic law, the testimony of a woman is given half the weight of the testimony of a man.

Many of these gender practices contrast sharply with contemporary Western values, but they are similar to those in the United States a century and a half ago, when the activists at Seneca Falls produced their inventory of grievances. Despite strong restrictions on political protest, some Saudi women have dared to challenge their treatment publicly.

Gender Identities and Transgender People

As these examples of difference over time and across cultures show, gender is a social construction that originates in culture but that becomes a part of a person's sense of self. **Gender identity** is *a person's identification as a woman, a man, or some combination of the two.* Most males learn to identify as men; most females learn to identify as women. (Some cultures recognize three or four genders; see the Through a Sociological Lens box.) We explore this process in more detail later in this chapter.

Gender identity is largely learned; however, it remains unclear whether, and to what degree, biology—especially prenatal hormones—might influence its development. This is another example of the current recognition that both biology and culture play a role in human development, although much work remains to be done to specify this relationship (Fausto-Sterling 2000, 2012). Researchers broadly agree, however, that biology does not *determine* gender identity.

Gender expression is *the communication of a person's gender identity to others, through behavior, clothing, hairstyle, and other means.* Since gender (based on culture) is different from sex (based on biology), gender identity and gender expression are not necessarily consistent with biology. The differentiation between sex and gender is central to the idea of transgender identity. **Transgender people** are *individuals who identify with a gender different from the one associated with their sex.* Some transgender people report that they feel trapped in a body of the opposite sex. Some wear the clothes and hairstyles of the gender with which they identify and adopt the vocal pitch, speech patterns, posture, and body language associated with that gender. Being transgender is not necessarily connected to sexual orientation, nor is it the same as being a *transvestite,* a person of one sex who dresses in clothing associated with the other sex.

Increasingly, governments are recognizing the legal rights of individuals who are transgender or who do not identify with either gender. Oregon was the first U.S. state to offer a "non-binary" option (in addition to "male" and "female") on government documents (Mele 2016). This follows the lead of countries, among them Australia, that offer an "other" or "unspecified" option. Also, India and several other Southeast Asian countries recognize a third gender that is neither male nor female (Knight and Ghoshal 2016).

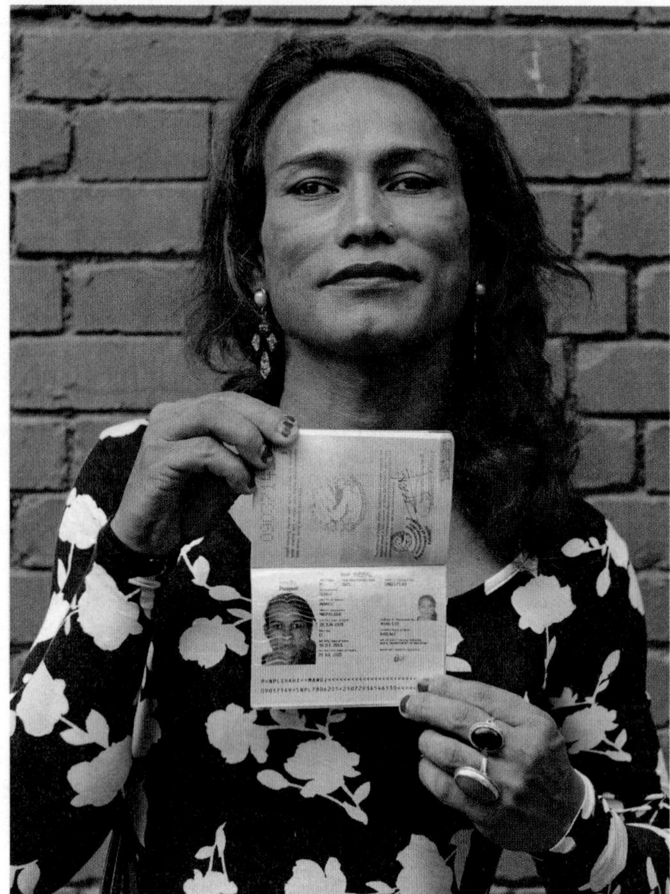

The first recipient of a Nepalese transgender passport, Monica Shahi, displays her new passport with "O" for "other" in the document's gender section, in 2015. Nepal no longer restricts the country's third gender population to describe themselves as male or female in their travel documents. Do you think U.S. passports should offer an option for people who are transgender? Why or why not?

Some transgender people become **transsexuals,** *people who have sex reassignment surgery to change their physical appearance.* Such surgery alters their genitalia and is usually accompanied by hormone treatments that promote secondary sex characteristics, such as breasts for women and facial hair for men. Though it is not biologically possible to change a person's sex—for example, males who undergo sex change operations cannot bear children, and they still have XY chromosomes—surgery and hormone treatments can make a person's body more consistent with the gender with which he or she identifies.

Masculinities

As we have seen, ideas about gender vary over time and across cultures. Even within U.S. society today, people often have

thinking about culture

Ideas about gender vary by **culture**. Have you experienced a culture or subculture in which some gender norms differed from those commonly found in the dominant U.S. culture?

THROUGH A SOCIOLOGICAL LENS

Examining the Case of Two-Spirits

In 1886, anthropologist Matilda Coxe Stevenson, one of the country's first female social scientists, toured Washington, D.C., with We'wha, a representative of the New Mexican Zuni tribe. The newspapers covered We'wha's visit. She was photographed, demonstrated Zuni weaving techniques on the National Mall, and even met with then-president Grover Cleveland. Although We'wha was six feet tall and had distinctly male physical features, Americans understood her to be a woman. What her audiences didn't realize was that We'wha was a biological male but her culture considered her to belong to a third gender, neither male nor female (Roscoe 1992).

Our society is used to dividing men and women into two distinct genders. However, many cultures see more than two genders, allowing for a blending of characteristics. For example, well over 100 Native American cultures have recognized a gender that is now commonly known as "two-spirit" (Gilley 2006; Jacobs, Thomas, and Lang 1997). Although they may be physiologically male or female, two-spirits such as We'wha take on some of the social roles generally associated with the other sex.

Historically, most two-spirits were males who dressed in women's clothes and did work associated with women, such as handcrafts, cooking, and childrearing. They adopted, in effect, a third gender. A smaller number of tribes recognized two-spirit females who took on roles associated with men, including hunting, warfare, and tribal leadership. Some tribes considered female two-spirits to be a fourth gender distinct from male two-spirits.

Social roles, not sexuality, defined two-spirits. However, homosexuality and bisexuality were common among both male and female two-spirits, with two-spirits sometimes marrying someone of the same sex who was not a two-spirit.

The treatment two-spirits received within their cultures varied widely, ranging from reverence to scorn. Sometimes they held a high social status. Mystical or healing powers were attributed to them, or they played important pragmatic roles, such as mediating disputes between women and men. In some cultures, two-spirits were not particularly distinct from others except for their adoption of cross-gender roles. In other cultures, however, two-spirits were marginalized and might be excluded from many tribal activities.

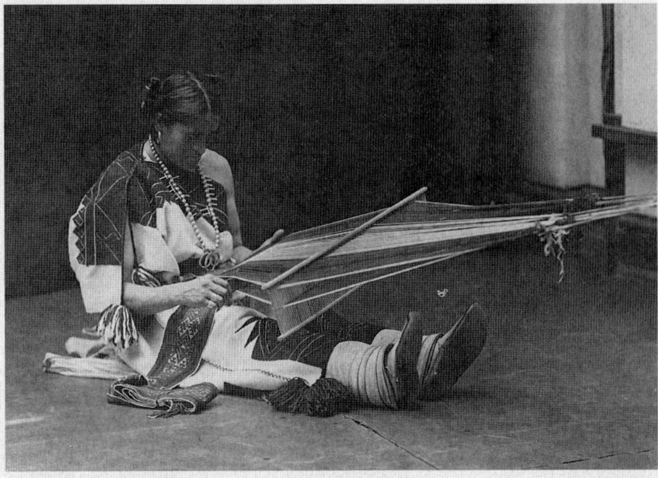

Source: U.S. National Archives [523797]
A common tradition of two-spirits goes back many generations and includes We'wha of the Zuni tribe, pictured in an 1886 photo.

European Americans failed to understand—and were perhaps threatened by—the role of two-spirits, since this category contradicted their strict two-gender culture. They labeled such people pejoratively as *berdache,* a word whose origin is connected with male prostitution, which is inaccurate and offensive to most native people. The word for people who had both female and male gender characteristics was different in various tribal languages, but since the early 1990s the Ojibwa term *two-spirits* has been widely adopted. Today, some two-spirits people meet in annual gatherings to affirm their unique identities (Lang 2016; Moore 2015).

think about it

1. *How do two-spirits illustrate the socially constructed nature of gender?*
2. *What are the advantages and disadvantages of recognizing more than two genders in a culture?*

different ideas about what it means to be a woman or a man, depending on their class, race, and other social characteristics.

The women's movement has long promoted the idea that there is no single way to be a woman; many femininities exist. Similarly, although a broad dominant definition of *masculinity*—the properties and characteristics associated with men—pervades society, various subcultures have differing social norms and expectations for "masculine" behavior and attitudes. Researchers talk about Latino masculinity, gay masculinity, working-class masculinity, and so on. Furthermore, even within these subgroups, ideas about masculinity can vary.

Instead of a single interpretation of masculinity, the intersection of gender with race and class creates a variety of masculinities (Kimmel 2012; Pascoe and Bridges 2016). Working-class men, especially those involved in manual labor, often have a sense of masculinity that values group solidarity, physical strength and toughness, and resistance to those in authority. By contrast, middle-class men often value self-reliance, individual ability, and

©Roger Hutchings/Alamy Stock Photo

©Eric Lafforgue/Alamy Stock Photo

©Imagemore Co., Ltd./Getty Images

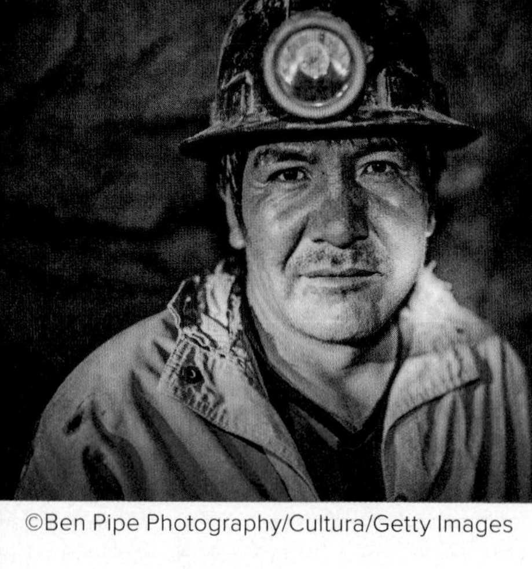

©Ben Pipe Photography/Cultura/Getty Images

These people are all biologically male and culturally men. However, differences in culture, age, race, and class—among other characteristics—help produce a variety of masculinities. Being a man means different things in different contexts.

mental proficiency (Slutskaya et al. 2016; Tolson 1977). A male college student from a working-class or poor background may be acutely aware of these differences since his college education is preparing him for a middle-class social world that is different from that experienced by his father and other male relatives and friends.

A person's race and ethnicity also influence his or her experience of gender. African Americans of both sexes, for example, are more likely than whites to be critical of gender inequality, to recognize that it is socially produced, and to support social action to reduce it (Harnois 2015; Kane 2000). Those who experience racial or ethnic inequality and discrimination (or both) tend to become more aware of the degree and social origins of gender inequality. However, this is not always true. Hispanics typically favor more traditional gender roles, with a greater degree of separation between genders, than do either white or African American men. However, evidence indicates that differences among racial and ethnic groups regarding gender have been declining over time, which suggests that ideas about gender are converging (Harnois 2015, 2017; Kane 2000).

Gender Distinctions and Power

Traditionally, men have set up so-called masculine characteristics in opposition to feminine characteristics, often claiming masculine qualities as superior to and more desirable than feminine characteristics, thereby promoting **sexism,** *the ideology that one sex is superior to the other.* Boys learn to be boys, in large part, by learning *not* to behave like girls. Boys are often warned that "big boys don't cry" (presumably unlike girls) and criticized for throwing or running "like a girl." A culture that encourages boys to be different from girls limits the options available to boys and teaches them that characteristics associated with girls are undesirable. This attitude is probably part of the reason gay men are so often subject to abuse from straight men; according to traditional gender norms they are seen as not adequately masculine and are associated with inferior feminine qualities (Kimmel 2012; Pascoe and Bridges 2016).

EVERY GIRL EVERY BOY

FOR EVERY GIRL WHO IS TIRED OF ACTING WEAK WHEN SHE IS STRONG, THERE IS A BOY TIRED OF APPEARING STRONG WHEN HE FEELS VULNERABLE. FOR EVERY BOY WHO IS BURDENED WITH THE CONSTANT EXPECTATION OF KNOWING EVERYTHING, THERE IS A GIRL TIRED OF PEOPLE NOT TRUSTING HER INTELLIGENCE. FOR EVERY GIRL WHO IS TIRED OF BEING CALLED OVER-SENSITIVE, THERE IS A BOY WHO FEARS TO BE GENTLE, TO WEEP. FOR EVERY BOY FOR WHOM COMPETITION IS THE ONLY WAY TO PROVE HIS MASCULINITY, THERE IS A GIRL WHO IS CALLED UNFEMININE WHEN SHE COMPETES. FOR EVERY GIRL WHO THROWS OUT HER E-Z-BAKE OVEN, THERE IS A BOY WHO WISHES TO FIND ONE. FOR EVERY BOY STRUGGLING NOT TO LET ADVERTISING DICTATE HIS DESIRES, THERE IS A GIRL FACING THE AD INDUSTRY'S ATTACKS ON HER SELF-ESTEEM. FOR EVERY GIRL WHO TAKES A STEP TOWARD HER LIBERATION, THERE IS A BOY WHO FINDS THE WAY TO FREEDOM A LITTLE EASIER.

Based on a poem by Nancy R. Smith, this poster, available in English and Spanish, highlights the parallel impact that gender expectations have on girls and boys. Gender distinctions limit the options available to both sexes.

Like race and class, gender involves social relationships and power dynamics between groups of people, in this case women and men. In a society in which gender signals both difference and male superiority, men will have considerably more power than women. Men perpetuate this domination by treating culturally produced gender differences as if they were unchangeable sex differences. We examine such gender inequality in more detail later in this chapter.

Socialization in Structural Context

Since it is not biologically based, gender must be taught through socialization. To a considerable degree, men and women behave the way they do because they are conforming to the cultural expectations about gender they have learned. Like other social constructions, gender is not fixed; our ideas about gender are reproduced or modified as we interact with other people every day. However, we are not free to reinvent gender without consequences because our interactions take place within social structures such as the family, school, and work that enforce certain gender expectations. These structures can impose negative sanctions, or punishments, on those who violate gender expectations, while rewarding those who conform. In this section, we consider how these interactions work.

Learning Gender: Socialization and Gender Roles

As we discussed in Chapter 7, sociologists define roles as the sets of expectations that are associated with different social positions. The roles you occupy do not exist in isolation; instead, a role gives you a part to play in social life, complete with expectations governing proper behavior, appearance, language, and attitudes. A **gender role** is *a set of social expectations regarding behavior and attitudes based on a person's sex.* Men and women are equally capable of folding laundry or changing the oil in a car. But in heterosexual couples, women usually do the laundry whereas men do auto maintenance—or at least bring the car to the garage. The fact that some couples share or reverse these assignments highlights their arbitrary nature.

Traditional advice to "man up" or "act like a lady" is loaded with social expectations that reflect our culture's beliefs about gender. In fact, gender roles help shape our identity by influencing a wide range of characteristics, including the following:

- ***Appearance.*** What clothing, hairstyles, jewelry, and makeup are appropriate?
- ***Activities.*** Who loves shopping? Who uses power tools? Who initiates a date?
- ***Behaviors and emotions.*** Who is expected to be nurturing and expressive? Who is expected to be tough and stoic?
- ***Aspirations.*** What kind of future should a man or woman want or expect? What job? What role in the family?

When socialization is effective, people want to be female or male as defined by their culture, and they perceive this learned desire to be both normal and natural. A child who violates these expectations is often chastised, sometimes by being labeled a tomboy or sissy.

"Doing Gender": Social Interaction and Power

How are gender roles created? How are they perpetuated or changed? In a classic article, Candace West and Don Zimmerman (1987) argued that gender is constantly being created—and potentially altered—through the process of **"doing gender,"** *creating gender through interactions in particular social settings.* Gender is an "accomplishment" that is achieved through our interactions with others. Thus ideas about gender may be contested and changed, both in our individual interactions and in institutional settings.

©McGraw-Hill Education/Mark Dierker, photographer

Because gender must be reproduced, it can also be modified. Parents who use children's books that challenge traditional gender roles are exposing children to alternative ideas about gender. Growing up, were you exposed to traditional gender socialization? Or did you receive nontraditional messages as well?

Individual Interactions Two students who don't know each other walk toward a campus building. When they get to the entrance, the male student darts forward and opens the door for the female student, who smiles, says "Thanks," and walks in. He nods and says, "No problem." What just occurred? Perhaps the male student was flirting or was raised to be a polite "gentleman" and hold doors open for women (though not for men). The student is behaving according to the expectations he has learned through socialization.

However, in terms of "doing gender" what just happened is one of the countless tiny–often trivial–ways that gender is re-created in daily life. The students were reinforcing a notion of gender through their actions in a particular social setting (school). Whether the gesture was a sign of courteous respect or was based on a largely unconscious assumption that women are the weaker sex and need help from men, it marks a traditional gender difference. (It's unlikely that the woman would have darted ahead to open the door for the male student.) Over time, such actions reinforce the notion that gender differences are natural. In this sense, gender is not who we are but rather what we do.

SPOTLIGHT on social theory

In the tradition of **symbolic interactionism,** "doing gender" is a part of **feminist theory** that highlights the ability of actors to create social reality in daily life. How have you acted in ways that reinforced traditional gender roles recently? How have you acted in ways that redefine their meaning?

People "do gender" in a variety of situations. How does a married or cohabitating heterosexual couple decide how to divide their household chores? Who does the cooking or the dishes? Who takes out the garbage or unclogs the drain? The answers to such questions often reflect different levels of power in personal relationships–and sometimes women are the ones with more power at home. One study asked straight couples whether the man or woman is most responsible for making four decisions: what couples do together on weekends, who manages household finances, who decides about big purchases for the home, and who most often decides what to watch on television. In 26 percent of cases, men made the decision in more areas than women; 31 percent of couples split decision-making responsibilities equally; and in 43 percent of couples, women made more decisions than men (Morin and Cohn 2008).

In making daily decisions, couples constantly negotiate and create gender, sometimes redefining its meaning. For example, sociologists have long known that when men take on equal or primary responsibility for child care, they can develop the close emotional and nurturing behaviors popularly associated with mothers, thus redefining the meaning of gender to incorporate the father's caregiving role (Coltrane 1989; Rehel 2014).

Interactions within Institutions Within their families, schools, and workplaces, people use their power to enforce social expectations, making it easier for all of us to conform to gender roles than to defy them. Family members, teachers and classmates, and colleagues tend to praise and encourage conformity, thus reinforcing it. Men and women who challenge or reject established gender roles, though, are likely to encounter criticism and sanctions. Thus gender is not only taught through socialization and re-created daily in individual interactions; it is also enforced within the context of social structures and institutions.

For example, sociologist Karen Davies (2003) shadowed nurses and doctors in Sweden as they did their daily work and later conducted in-depth interviews with them about their experiences. Despite a recent influx of women doctors, she found an assumption of male dominance throughout the institutional culture of hospitals and the broader professional culture of medicine that shapes the way people experience gender on the job and influences how doctors and nurses interact.

Davies found that male doctors were more accustomed than female doctors to being in a dominant position in relation to nurses. One female nurse, noting that she was more willing to follow a male doctor's orders, commented, "The male doctor is usually more authoritarian. . . . [I]f he says to me, 'Go and take that patient's blood pressure,' then I go and do it. I don't stop and think about it, whereas with a woman I might have thought that she could go and do it herself" (Davies 2003, 731). Female doctors, too, recognized this gender difference. One said, "I find it difficult to ask for help with things I could do myself–yesterday I hesitated in asking an assistant nurse to clean the floor when an incontinent woman wet herself–I mean it's preposterous to imagine that I should clean the floor and be late for my outpatients–and yet all the same . . . it's hard asking another woman for help with the dirty work" (731).

©Christina Kennedy/Alamy Stock Photo

The deeply contradictory messages about the role of mothers within U.S. culture illustrate how class and gender intersect for women. Middle- and working-class women who work outside the home are often criticized for not staying at home with their children. On the other hand, public assistance policies, such as Temporary Assistance for Needy Families (TANF), explicitly require poor women to leave their children for work, school, or job training.

CORE CONCEPTS CHALLENGE *How do these contrasting standards for people of different classes reflect differences in* **power** *between the classes?*

Gender contributed to differences in power relations, too. After working together for a time, female nurses were more likely to seek to establish a collaborative relationship with female doctors than with male doctors. In turn, female doctors were more likely to see nurses as part of a team that worked together to decide on the best care for patients. In contrast, male doctors often overlooked or ignored the insights of experienced nurses, arguing that since the doctor is responsible for the final decision, he should make it on his own. A study of American nurses similarly found gendered power interactions (Apker, Propp, and Ford 2005). Nurses—who were mostly female—were expected to show deference when working with physicians—who were mostly male. Nurses who challenged this deferential arrangement could become the target of arrogant, condescending, and even abusive behavior by physicians. As the health professions evolve, gender continues to have an impact on all aspects of this work (Watts 2015). Hospitals are just one example of places where "doing gender" happens in daily life and social structure influences power relations between men and women.

Gender and the Family

Of all the social environments we encounter, the family probably has the most influence on our understanding of gender—an impact that starts from the moment we are born.

Gender Socialization from Birth Upon learning of a woman's pregnancy or the birth of a child, many people immediately ask, "Is it a boy or a girl?" From the earliest moments of life, then, adults view infants through the lens of gender and treat newborns differently depending on their sex, thus beginning the gender socialization process.

As more than 40 years' worth of research has documented, gender socialization occurs almost from the moment a baby is born. Since the early research studies, however, gender norms have evolved, and so have parents' expectations and behaviors. For example, a classic study from the mid-1970s found that parents, especially fathers, engaged in significant gender stereotyping (Rubin, Provenzano, and Luria 1974). When asked, fathers were more likely than mothers to rate their newborn girls as softer, weaker, and more delicate than boys. Both parents described their daughters as little, beautiful, pretty, and cute and their sons as big. A similar study, done over 20 years later, found that although these gender stereotypes still existed, they had become less intense. In addition, the gap between the gender stereotyping of fathers and mothers was gone (Karraker, Vogel, and Lake 1995).

Parents and others reinforce gender in infants in a variety of routine ways, such as with greeting cards and gifts containing messages and images that fit with gender stereotypes (for example, blue for boys, pink for girls) (Bridges 1993). The toys parents choose for their children in their first year also influence the preferences infants develop (Boe and Woods 2017).

©Baris Simsek/Getty Images

Parents often construct a gendered environment for their babies well before infants even know what the toys, images, and colors in their nursery represent. Here hearts, flowers, and the "feminine" color pink dominate this designer nursery, which is clearly intended for a girl.

CORE CONCEPTS CHALLENGE *How do nursery designs reflect our* **culture's** *gender expectations? What might a stereotypical boy's nursery look like? What lessons are infants taught through the creation of such environments? In what other ways do we affirm gender at a young age?*

Gender Socialization throughout Childhood Early lessons about gender continue as a child grows up. While there is no difference between the behavior of female and male babies in early months, studies show that parents interact differently with them based on a child's sex. For example, mothers respond to and speak more to their daughters than their sons, thereby encouraging earlier verbal development with girls. Mothers also interact more with their daughters during lab observations, often comforting and hugging them, while leaving their sons to explore independently. Fathers and mothers each respond more readily to vocalizations of children of their own sex (Clearfield and Nelson 2006; Johnson et al. 2014; Sung et al. 2013).

©Ariel Skelley/Blend Images/Getty Images

As youngsters, girls and boys play easily together at games such as soccer. However, even at such a young age they are being taught about the differences between the genders, and soon most will resist playing with members of the other sex. Did this happen to you?

By the time their children are 18 months old, parents routinely encourage them to play with gender-stereotyped toys. Parents give their children more praise and other forms of feedback and encouragement when they engage in gender-traditional activities, such as boys playing with trucks, than when they engage in cross-gendered activities, such as boys playing with dolls (Caldera and Sciaraffa 1998; Erden 2014; Freeman 2007). Throughout childhood girls and boys are treated differently. Their clothes, chores, play, and sports all carry gendered messages. In the earliest years of their lives, children have already been subjected to intense and near-constant affirmation of the expectations society has for their gender, and they begin to respond accordingly. Parental beliefs and attitudes can affect this process, however. For example, adopted children with same-sex parents are less likely to engage in stereotyped play than adopted children of heterosexual parents (Goldberg, Kashy, and Smith 2012).

Teaching Gender in School

The first regular experience most children have outside of their families is with school. Gender socialization here begins at a very early age and continues throughout a child's education.

In a classic work, sociologist Karin Martin (1998) found that preschools help children develop a gendered identity by altering how they relate to their own bodies. Their generally relaxed movement and free activity on the playground contrasts with the more formal discipline and proper behavior they are taught once they are inside the school building: waiting in line, raising their hands, sitting still in neatly organized rows of desks, and following many other rules and procedures. These lessons are different for boys and girls, however. Martin found that teachers reprimanded girls more often for not behaving formally but allowed boys to be more disruptive and to behave more informally by sitting in relaxed positions and engaging in freer play than girls. Girls were told to be quiet three times as often as boys were, even though boys were frequently much noisier. Even the clothes parents chose for their children signaled differences in self-discipline. Many girls wore dresses, which limited their ability to move freely and left them vulnerable to potentially embarrassing exposure. Thus the bodies of young children are conditioned to conform to gendered expectations.

As children grow older, school continues to foster and reinforce gender differences, often through choice of curriculum. In high school, girls not planning on going to college often train for traditionally female professions such as cosmetology and secretarial work, whereas boys are more likely to take courses in traditionally male trades such as auto mechanics and welding. As we see later in this chapter, gendered curriculum distinctions continue in college.

As awareness of gender issues increases, families and schools are adopting more flexible attitudes about gender. Some schools make it a policy to support whatever choice children make regarding their gender. When a specific dress code for boys and girls exists, transgender students are allowed to wear the clothing that corresponds to their gender identity. Some schools permit students to choose the pronoun by which they are referred, the bathroom they use, and the athletic team—either boys' or girls'—they will play on. LGBT advocates want to mandate such policies to help ensure the civil rights of transgender students, though the courts have not yet decided this issue (Dean 2016; Orr and Baum 2016).

thinking about structure

In many ways, the **structure** of school reinforces what children have learned about gender in their families. What did your school's structure teach you about gender? In what ways did your school reinforce or challenge gender stereotypes?

©Mads Perch/Getty Images

Gender socialization can be a positive influence. Same-sex friends can bond and provide mutual support, even while reinforcing some traditional gender norms. What positive experiences resulted from your same-sex peers? How did they reinforce gender norms?

Gender Lessons from Peers

As young people become sexually active, develop an adult persona, and become independent of the family, regular interaction with peers—friends and classmates who are usually of the same general age and, often, of the same sex—reinforces and expands on the lessons about gender they have learned from their family and schools. Peer groups can have a positive impact on a person's self-esteem and result in long-lasting friendships. They also tend to reproduce dominant gender norms.

As boys become men, for example, they often bond with other young men, forming relationships that promote the dominant masculine identity of their culture (Kimmel 2008, 2012). Our society often encourages young men to belong to sports teams, fraternities, the military, and other primarily male groups. Though this peer socialization can offer mutual support, it also can pass on to new members the sexist ideas and behaviors the group's culture accepts and promotes, such as sexual jokes that degrade women and attitudes that are dismissive of women's intelligence and disrespectful of their abilities.

Peer socialization can exaggerate and reinforce gender distinctions by encouraging a person to develop a sense of self that is connected to a group of people of the same gender—and disconnected from the other gender. Young men can adopt an air of detachment or an exaggerated posture of toughness while denigrating signs of weakness or emotionality they supposedly detect in others. Young women often concentrate on their own physical appearance—including norms regulating clothing, weight, hairstyles, and makeup—while policing that of their peers. Both women and men often adopt the norms for appearance promoted in the media.

Media and Gender

Media portrayals of gender in television shows, movies, music videos, as well as the news can signal appropriate or acceptable behavior and attitudes, especially to young men and women. Sometimes media images and portrayals can challenge traditional gender roles, but often they repackage cultural stereotypes (Ward and Aubrey 2017).

Women are underrepresented across media platforms and formats, both as subjects of coverage and as producers of content. For example, one report (Women's Media Center 2017) found that:

- Female journalists wrote 40 percent of newspaper news stories; and female TV journalists were responsible for 32 percent of broadcast news reports.
- Women make up about one-third of the radio and TV news directors.
- Women hosted 13 of the top 100-rated radio talk shows.
- Women comprised roughly one-third of the speaking characters in film, TV, and digital shows.
- Men outnumbered women two to one as film leads in 2014–2015.
- On the 250 top-grossing domestic films of 2015–2016, women were only 17 percent of the directors, writers, producers, executive producers, editors, and cinematographers, combined.

Women are more likely than men to use social media—80 percent to 73 percent in 2015 (Anderson 2015)—but some women have been the target of sometimes-vicious harassment and bullying in comments and on forums frequented more often by men (Buni and Chemaly 2014; Duggan 2014).

Perhaps as a consequence of women's underrepresentation, media of all sorts reinforce gender stereotypes. Traditional gendered stereotypes are still found in children's play. For

©Stacy Walsh Rosenstock/Alamy Stock Photo

Idealized images of women have long been a staple of media content. But idealized—and airbrushed—images of male bodies create unrealistic standards for men, too.

CORE CONCEPTS CHALLENGE *Do you think such advertising helps reproduce gender stereotypes in our* **culture,** *or are they harmless? Whatever their effect, do you think the impact of idealized images in advertising and other media is different for men and women? Why or why not?*

example, the Disney Store website, featuring many products from Disney movies, sharply divides girls' and boys' toys. Toys labeled for boys are sold in bold colors and include action figures, building toys, weapons, and vehicles. Items labeled for girls are predominantly pink or purple and are likely to be dolls, cosmetics, jewelry, and beauty- and domestic-oriented toys. Most toys labeled for both boys and girls resembled the boys' toys in terms of color palette (Auster and Mansbach 2012). These days, gendered stereotypes are often wrapped in a layer of women-friendly packaging that appropriates feminist images and slogans to sell traditional gendered products, as with Cover Girl's #GirlsCan campaign to boost makeup sales (Douglas 2010; Zeisler 2016).

The gender images provided by the media are more than just meaningless entertainment. Photographs of rail-thin, airbrushed models present unrealistic standards of beauty for women to aspire to. Nevertheless, after viewing images of models in magazine advertisements for just three minutes, women reported being more dissatisfied with their own bodies—regardless of their own weight, height, or age (Hamilton, Mintz, and Kashubeck-West 2007). Idealized images of men in the media highlight muscular bodies and youthfulness. One study showed that although men are cynical about such photographs, they believe the images show the "ideal" male body that women appreciate. Younger men, especially, acknowledge that such images constantly remind them that their own bodies may not match up to the ideal. Perhaps that is why few men of any age report being satisfied with their own bodies (Pompper, Soto, and Piel 2007).

Culture, Power, and Gender Inequality

As we all learn about gender through socialization and then help reproduce gender roles by "doing gender" in our daily lives, we become part of the way gender is structured in society. This structure reflects differences in power between men and women. As a result, every social institution is marked by substantial gender inequality. **Gender stratification** refers to *the systematic and unequal distribution of power and resources in society between women and men.* Though the United States has made significant progress in overcoming gender inequality over the past century, men continue to dominate positions of power. In this section, we consider the origins of inequality between women and men and then review some examples of gender inequality in the United States.

Sex and the Origins of Patriarchy

Patriarchy refers to *a social system dominated by men.* In a patriarchal society, men hold most of the powerful political and economic positions and benefit from cultural expectations that limit the role and influence of women. Patriarchal societies have existed around the globe and throughout history. There have been various *matrilineal* societies in which kinship and sometimes property pass through the female line. However, most scholars agree that no clear example of a **matriarchy**—*a social system dominated by women*—is known to have ever existed (Eller 2001; Motz 1997).

Although matriarchies may never have existed, anthropological evidence suggests that early hunting and gathering cultures had little stratification, gender-based or otherwise. Private property did not exist, family structure was fluid, and women's labor and men's labor were comparably valued because both were essential for survival.

So, why did patriarchy become so pervasive? Sociologist Joan Huber (2007) argues that male dominance stemmed largely from sex differences—especially women's role in carrying, bearing, and breastfeeding children—coupled with economic changes. Throughout human evolution, the vast majority of women were either pregnant or lactating through most of their adult lives. Although pregnancy had a significant impact on women, lactation may have had an even greater effect. Until the modern era, infants and toddlers depended entirely on their mothers for sustenance because the food consumed by older humans was too difficult for them to chew and digest. Mothers needed to breastfeed their infants frequently during the day (and less frequently at night) for the first two years, then with less frequency for an additional two years. Such frequent breastfeeding over an extended period limited the activities in which mothers could engage.

This limitation had minimal impact in early hunting and gathering cultures, because they had relatively little inequality overall. However, when human groups began practicing agriculture and raising animals for food about 10,000 years ago, men were in a better position to control the newly created food and material surpluses that emerged with this new economic system, resulting in more inequality. Men's exemption from pregnancy and lactation—coupled with their generally larger physical size and greater strength—enabled them to dominate social, political, and economic life, thus increasing their power relative to women (Collins et al. 1993). Friedrich Engels ([1884] 1972), a close collaborator of Karl Marx, also argued that with the creation of material surplus and the rise of private property, male property owners now needed to control the sexuality of women to know who their rightful heirs were. The result was a new emphasis on premarital virginity, monogamous marriage, and the rigid modern family. Thus, physical domination, coupled with economic changes, likely contributed to the emergence of patriarchal societies across the planet.

Culture Trumps Biology

Biology may go a long way in explaining the *origins* of patriarchy. But the ability of humans to alter the social environment has accelerated exponentially in just a couple of centuries, undermining the significance of sex differences. Today, machinery often replaces the need for physical strength. Medication can moderate the impact of menstruation. Couples can prevent pregnancy by using effective birth control. Women can terminate a pregnancy through safe abortion. Women can become pregnant through artificial insemination, and emerging biotechnologies will likely create more options for reproduction. Once a baby is born, mothers can manage breastfeeding with the use of a breast pump, or supplement or replace it with other foods and nutrients.

Such cultural interventions are quite recent. Women did not begin to abandon old-style, near-continuous lactation until the late nineteenth or early twentieth century. The emergence of the germ theory of disease led to safer public drinking water and ways to prepare food for infants, which enabled women to breastfeed less frequently and to use bottle-feeding as an alternative (Huber 2007). As a result of such cultural innovations, the sex differences between women and men became less significant. Once men had accumulated power in society, however, they tended to resist sharing it with women, producing gender-based inequality that continues today.

FIGURE 11.1 | PERCENTAGE OF 25- TO 29-YEAR-OLDS WITH FOUR YEARS OF COLLEGE OR MORE, BY SEX, 1947–2015

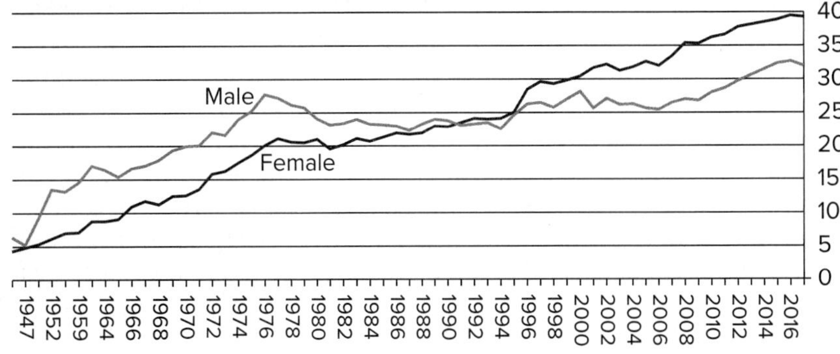

Source: U.S. Census Bureau 2017g.

Work and Education: The Pay Gap and Its Sources

Since the passage of the Equal Pay Act in 1963, it has been illegal for U.S. employers to pay women less than men for the same job just because of their sex. Yet in the United States, women still are paid only about 82 percent of what men are paid. While this wage gap has narrowed since the 1950s, when women were paid only 64 percent of what men were paid, its persistence makes the workplace one of the best-known examples of gender discrimination (U.S. Bureau of Labor Statistics 2017c). If we could wipe out workplace discrimination, the wage gap between women and men would be reduced but it wouldn't be eliminated. By some estimates, factors other than direct workplace discrimination explain roughly 60 to 75 percent of the wage gap (Council of Economic Advisers 2015a; Dey and Hill 2007). Taking a comprehensive sociological approach to this issue can help us see the many different factors that contribute to this inequality (Tharenou 2013).

Education, Majors, and Occupations On average, workers with college degrees earn more than those without. Traditionally, men have surpassed women in educational achievement, and this educational attainment gap contributed to the gender wage gap. In recent decades, however, women have caught up with and surpassed men in terms of education (see Figure 11.1). This is one factor contributing to the decline in the wage gap. Overall, men still hold more college degrees than women do, but this discrepancy is a legacy of the past. In 2017, among young adults aged 25 to 29 years, 39.3 percent of women but only 32 percent of men possessed a bachelor's degree or higher—and the gap is growing (U.S. Census Bureau 2017g). As women continue to outpace men in educational achievement, the wage gap between the sexes—especially among young workers—should continue to decline.

The salaries of college graduates vary greatly by major. Although women and men currently have similar access to education, the fields of study they choose to major in and the professions they pursue are still often segregated along gender lines, likely reflecting early gender socialization. Women earn the majority of bachelor's degrees in relatively low-paying fields such as education, psychology, and the health professions—three traditionally female fields—whereas men earn more degrees in relatively high-paying—and traditionally male—fields such as engineering, mathematics, and the physical sciences (National Center for Education Statistics 2017b). (The Sociology in Action box shows how sociology has helped inform efforts to encourage women to become engineers.) These differences between women's and men's choices of college major contribute to the wage gap. Even in fields that do not require a college degree, women tend to cluster in low-paying service and retail jobs (see Table 11.1).

©Alexander Koerner/Getty Images

Without the labor of women at home—both the unpaid labor of wives and the low-paid labor of service workers—most highly paid male corporate executives would be unable to work long hours to achieve personal success in their fields. How else do women who work in the home contribute to the success of men?

SOCIOLOGY in ACTION

Using Sociological Insight to Encourage Women Engineers

When Naomi Chesler, now a distinguished professor of biomedical engineering at the University of Wisconsin–Madison, took an aptitude test in high school, she learned that her talents in math and science would suit her well for engineering. This profession—one of the highest-paid occupations—is dominated by men. Confident in her abilities, however, Chesler majored in engineering as an undergraduate, earned her PhD in medical engineering, and obtained a university position. As a young faculty member, she was mentored in a program that encouraged individual competition and placed obstacles in her path on the assumption that overcoming such challenges would help produce success. Despite her love for the field and her ability to excel at it, she found this traditional, hierarchical, and masculine approach less than satisfying (Maurer 2009).

She began talking with her father, Mark Chesler, a sociologist who has researched race and gender discrimination in higher education, about how she might take gender differences into account to create a different kind of mentoring program for female junior engineering faculty. Drawing upon sociological research, the Cheslers realized that because of different socialization, women and men often have different learning styles, and these differences were not being accommodated in traditional mentoring programs. For example, many women prefer collaborative and interactive ways of learning rather than the isolated and individualistic style that dominates engineering departments. This mismatch was one factor causing female students to drop out of engineering.

The Cheslers collaborated to develop a model for mentoring young women engineers that used a supportive and collaborative approach rather than emphasizing aggressive individual competition. The medical engineer and the sociologist teamed up to write an article that encouraged "multiple mentoring" from numerous sources instead of reliance on one mentor, mutually supportive "peer mentoring" to deemphasize hierarchical relationships, and "collective mentoring" that puts responsibility for effective mentoring on an entire department or organization rather than on the individual mentee (Chesler and Chesler 2002). They also emphasized the need for organizational change, not just individual efforts, to help ensure success. This sociologically informed model has helped Chesler establish award-winning mentoring programs. Naomi Chesler and her colleagues have since shown that women's motivation to persist in engineering can be increased if women experience "authentic" engineering simulations early in their studies (Arastoopour, Chesler, and Shaffer 2014).

©Jonathan Fickies/Boys & Girls Clubs of America/AP Images

A CA Technologies employee coaches girls as they reassemble the components of a desktop computer at the Children's Aid Society East Harlem Boys & Girls Club in New York. The girls are participating in the new Tech Girls Rock initiative, launched by Boys & Girls Clubs of America and CA Technologies.

Whereas the Cheslers' program helps retain women in engineering, the Society for Women Engineers (SWE) promotes mentoring as a way to encourage girls to enter the field in the first place. SWE targets girls in elementary and high school with programs that encourage collaborative hands-on engineering activities, celebrate the accomplishments of women engineers, and introduce girls to engineers and engineering college students who can serve as role models. By intervening in girls' early socialization, SWE hopes to encourage more girls to become the engineers of the future.

Mentoring is just one way to help overcome the gender gap in high-paid professions. But when built upon a sociological understanding of gender, such programs can make a difference.

think about it

1. *What sociological insights about gender informed the creation of the mentoring programs mentioned here?*
2. *Have you ever been involved in a mentoring program? If so, what impact did it have on you? If not, in what aspect of your life might such a program have helped you?*

TABLE 11.1 TEN LEADING OCCUPATIONS OF EMPLOYED WOMEN, 2017

Occupation	Women Employed (thousands)	Percentage of Women in Occupation	Women's Median Weekly Earnings	Women's Earnings as Percentage of Men's
Total, 16 years and older, full-time	**50,291**	**44.4%**	**$770**	**81.8%**
Registered nurses	2,253	88.8%	1,143	90.7%
Elementary and middle school teachers	2,224	78.4%	987	86.7%
Secretaries and administrative assistants	2,046	94.5%	735	86.3%
Customer service representatives	1,234	65.6%	637	89.5%
Nursing, psychiatric, and home health aides	1,223	88.2%	493	84.6%
Managers, all other	1,163	38.7%	1,251	76.8%
First-line supervisors of retail sales workers	1,013	42.4%	639	71.7%
Cashiers	982	72.2%	422	85.6%
Accountants and auditors	890	58.9%	1,065	76.7%
First-line supervisors of office and administrative support workers	854	67.7%	819	83.0%

Source: U.S. Bureau of Labor Statistics, Current Population Survey. 2018a. Retrieved from www.bls.gov/cps/cpsaat39.htm.

Workforce Participation Women's participation in the paid workforce nearly doubled from about 33 percent in 1950 to 60 percent in 2000. Since then, it has declined slightly to about 57 percent in 2017 (compared to about 69.1 percent for men) (U.S. Bureau of Labor Statistics 2018b). This change happened for a variety of reasons. Effective and convenient birth control in the form of "the Pill"–introduced in the early 1960s–enabled women to control the timing and number of pregnancies; as a result, they needed to spend less time raising children and could devote more time to paid employment. At roughly the same time, the women's movement helped change cultural norms and the legal environment in ways that made working outside the home more feasible for women. Because wages for male workers have remained stagnant over the last 40 years, many families have needed the additional income that employed women could offer to maintain or improve their lifestyle.

Women and men have different work patterns, however, which contributes to the wage gap. These different patterns are largely due to gender norms about family. Among full-time workers with few family responsibilities–unmarried workers (never married, divorced, separated, and widowed) with no children under 18 at home–women make nearly as much (95 percent) as men do (U.S. Bureau of Labor Statistics 2017c). But women are much more likely than men to reduce work hours, take significant time off, quit a job, or turn down a promotion because of family responsibilities (Parker 2015). By interrupting their careers, women with families are at a disadvantage when they later return to the workforce, a phenomenon sometimes referred to as the "motherhood penalty" (Correll and Benard 2007; Manchester, Leslie, and Dahm 2018). These differences reflect choices people make in the context of a highly gendered culture that encourages such behavior. In addition, these work patterns are facilitated by the absence of supporting social programs in the United States, such as paid family leave and subsidized child care, that would make women's uninterrupted workforce participation more feasible and likely reduce the wage gap (Budig, Misra, and Boeckmann 2016). Other choices people make can contribute to the wage gap. For example, couples are more likely to relocate because of a man's career, a change that usually advances the man's career and interrupts the woman's. In part because of these differences in labor force participation, the pay gap between women and men–even within the same field–widens as workers get older.

Discrimination and the Glass Ceiling Research shows that women face discrimination in male-dominated environments, and since occupations with the highest salary and prestige tend to be male dominated, women may face the most discrimination in jobs that have the highest pay and status (Koch, D'Mello, and Sackett 2015). The relative absence of women in high-level, high-paying positions is popularly explained by the **glass ceiling,** *the often-invisible barrier created by individual and institutional sexism that prevents qualified women from advancing to high levels of leadership and management.* For example, at the upper levels of corporate management, the relative absence of women is startling (see Figure 11.2).

FIGURE 11.2 | WOMEN IN S&P 500 COMPANIES

Women comprise over 44 percent of employees in the large corporations that make up the S&P 500. However, the percentage of women holding powerful management positions decreases dramatically at higher levels of the companies.

Source: Adapted from Catalyst. Pyramid: Women in S&P 500 Companies. New York: Catalyst, 2018.

Similar patterns prevail in other institutional sectors such as education and government (see Figure 11.3).

In their various forms, workplace bias and discrimination continue to be a reality for many women (Dovidio et al. 2010; Ezzedeen, Budworth, and Baker 2015; Livingstone, Pollock, and Raykov 2016). Although intentional and overt workplace sexism was once the central source of workplace discrimination and the glass ceiling, recent research has focused on so-called "second generation" gender bias, which is subtler but often just as harmful (Ibarra, Ely, and Kolb 2013). Such bias includes both individual- and institutional-level sources.

Individuals discriminate, sometimes unintentionally. Gender discrimination can be especially difficult to combat when it results from subconscious prejudice that colors how people view and evaluate one another's work (Barres 2006). In professional environments, coworkers and supervisors are more likely to see men as competent and logical and women as unreliable and emotional, and over time these skewed perceptions can influence the way they evaluate coworkers and employees (Koch, D'Mello, and Sackett 2015). At the institutional level, cultural norms can promote workplace discrimination by discouraging married heterosexual women from focusing on career advancement rather than on raising a family or from having greater success than their husbands. Lack of encouragement, the absence of role models, and negative perceptions of others can undermine women's self-confidence and blunt their ambitions. Women themselves often end up ambivalent about whether they want to advance to the highest levels of leadership, especially if doing so involves sacrificing family and household responsibilities (Ibarra, Ely, and Kolb 2013). These differences in ambition or competitiveness are then misread as innate rather than culturally created (Fels 2005).

As women have slowly gained more power in organizations, research has begun to probe into the consequences of these changes. Some studies suggest that women in top leadership positions feel pressured to adopt the attitudes and behaviors of the men who preceded them, including limiting advancement opportunities for other women (Mavin, Grandy, and Williams 2014). Other research, though, suggests that women in top leadership can pave the way for women in lower-level positions (Kurtulus and Tomaskovic-Devey 2012), as well as help to change an institution's culture of bias (Stainback, Kleiner, and Skaggs 2016).

The wage gap is just one example of the multifaceted impact of gender. Gender inequality is pervasive throughout society–in the family, politics, the media, and religion–and power disparities are also reflected in sexual harassment and violence against women.

Home and Family

In the last half century, the lives of women and men have changed significantly. More women today spend more hours doing paid labor outside the home than in the past. But in one classic study, Arlie Hochschild and Anne Machung ([1989] 2012) found that

FIGURE 11.3 | GENDER STRATIFICATION IN LEADERSHIP POSITIONS

	Men	Women
S&P 500 CEOs	94.8%	5.2%
S&P 500 board of directors	78.8%	21.2%
S&P 500 executive officers	73.5%	26.5%
U.S. Senate	77%	23%
U.S. House of Representatives	80.9%	19.1%
State governors	88%	12%
Mayors of 100 largest cities	81%	19%
State legislatures	74.6%	25.4%
U.S. college presidents	70%	30%

Men continue to dominate the leadership positions in business (in 2018), government (in early 2018), and higher education (in 2016).

Sources: American Council on Education 2017; Catalyst 2018; Center for American Women and Politics 2018.

CORE CONCEPTS CHALLENGE *How do the data presented here challenge the idea that women and men now have equal* **power** *in society? Do you expect such numbers to change significantly during your lifetime? Why or why not?*

as growing numbers of women worked at full-time jobs, they still came home to a **second shift**—*the phenomenon of employed women still having primary responsibility for housework and child care.* In households with two wage earners, heterosexual couples still viewed the man's position as the primary career, while the woman's job was often seen as supplemental. Whereas men might "help" with the housework, women worked outside the home to "help" pay the bills.

The specific findings of recent research vary depending on the methodology used, but the general trends are clear (Bianchi et al. 2012; Gerson 2009; Pew Research Center 2015e; U.S. Bureau of Labor Statistics 2016g). The overall number of hours women and men spend working is about the same, but women spend a larger share of their time in unpaid housework while men spend more time working outside the home for pay. This gap has shrunk significantly as women have cut the number of hours they spend on housework by nearly half while men have more than doubled the number of hours they spend doing housework (Chesters 2011). However, this convergence has stalled in recent years, and the housework gap persists. In about half of two-parent families, both partners work full time outside the home, but men tend to work more hours for pay. In the other half of families, women are seven times as likely as men to be the one parent who works outside the home only part time or not at all (Pew Research Center 2015e).

Increasingly, both women and men say they would like to share household responsibilities equally, and young couples without children often do just that. However, a gender gap in household duties appears after a couple has children, because women take on a larger share of the new child care responsibilities than men do (Yavorsky, Dush, and Schoppe-Sullivan 2015). Making the problem worse is that, reflecting cultural expectations for more intensive parenting, today's parents spend more time caring for children than parents of earlier generations (Craig, Powell, and Smyth 2014).

At first glance, how a couple divides household chores would seem to be purely a matter of individual choice. However, larger workplace and social policies matter, illustrating the influence of social structure on personal decisions. For example, in societies with relatively *less* gender equality, women tend to earn a lower percentage of what their husbands earn and are more likely to give up a job to care for children. In countries with *more* gender equality, women earn higher wages that are closer to those of men; this advantage makes their time in the workforce more valuable to the household and increases their power in negotiating the division of housework (Fuwa 2004). In the United States, gendered work expectations and a lack of flexible policies regarding leave and work hours create barriers for couples seeking to manage household responsibilities more equally. But when flexible policies do exist, women are still more likely to take advantage of them, while men are more likely to remain in the full-time workforce (Pedulla and Thebaud 2015). Research shows that same-sex couples tend to divide housework more equally than heterosexual couples, but when they do adopt a division of labor, it is usually justified on pragmatic grounds that have to do with workplace status: the partner who earns less money and has more-flexible work hours usually ends up doing more housework (Bauer 2016; Goldberg 2013). Such findings suggest that to eliminate the gender gap in housework, both cultural norms and social policies must continue to change.

Political Power

The degree to which women have been marginalized in the halls of political power is symbolized by the bathrooms in the U.S. Capitol. A restroom for female senators was not installed until 1992 (Taley 2006). Female members of the House of Representatives did not get their own restroom until 2011. More important, as of early 2018, women held just 23 of the 100 Senate seats (23 percent) and just 83 of the 435 seats in the House of Representatives (19.1 percent) (Center for American Women and Politics 2018).

Around the world, women accounted for just 23.6 percent of the members of all national legislative bodies in 2018 (see Table 11.2). In 1995 the UN Economic and Social Council

TABLE 11.2 COUNTRIES WITH THE HIGHEST AND LOWEST PERCENTAGES OF WOMEN IN NATIONAL LEGISLATIVE BODIES, 2018

Highest Percentage of Women		Lowest Percentage of Women	
1 Rwanda	61.3%	1 Micronesia	0%
2 Bolivia	53.1%	2 Oman	1.2%
3 Cuba	48.9%	3 Solomon Islands	2.0%
4 Namibia	46.2%	4 Haiti	2.5%
5 Nicaragua	45.7%	5 Kuwait	3.1%
6 Costa Rica	45.6%	6 Lebanon	3.1%
7 Sweden	43.6%	7 Thailand	4.8%
8 Mexico	42.6%	8 Nigeria	5.6%
9 South Africa	42.4%	9 Sri Lanka	5.8%
10 Finland	42.0%	10 Iran	5.9%
		Maldives	5.9%

Note: Rankings are based on the lower or single house. The United States was 102nd out of the 193 countries ranked.
Source: Inter-Parliamentary Union 2018.

thinking about culture

Culture norms regarding gender have a powerful effect on the behavior of men and women in the workforce and on their careers. What kinds of norms influence men? What effect do these norms have—both positive and negative—on their careers?

TIME magazine chose "The Silence Breakers" as the 2017 "Person of the Year." These women, who spoke out about sexual harassment and assault, sparked the #MeToo movement. The accompanying profile noted, "Women have had it with bosses and co-workers who not only cross boundaries but don't even seem to know that boundaries exist. They've had it with the fear of retaliation, of being blackballed, of being fired from a job they can't afford to lose. They've had it with the code of going along to get along. They've had it with men who use their power to take what they want from women" (Zacharek, Dockterman, and Edwards 2017). These efforts led to the firing or resignations of dozens of high-profile business, entertainment, news, and political figures (below). In some cases, legal proceedings are ongoing.

Harvey Weinstein
Producer and co-founder of the Weinstein Company

Accusation: Rape of three women; sexual assault and harrassment of dozens of others

Fallout: Fired from his company and expelled from the Academy of Motion Pictures Arts and Sciences

Matt Lauer
Co-host of *Today*

Accusation: Sexually inappropriate behavior with multiple women

Fallout: Fired by NBC

John Conyers Jr.
U.S. representative for Michigan

Accusation: Sexual harrassment of employees

Fallout: Resigned

Mario Batali
Chef, restaurant owner and co-host of ABC show *The Chew*

Accusation: Sexual misconduct with four women

Fallout: Fired by ABC, stepped away from his businesses

Russell Simmons
Co-founder of Def Jam Records and other businesses

Accusation: Rape of three women; sexual assault of two others

Fallout: Stepped down from his businesses

CORE CONCEPTS CHALLENGE *How does the concept of* **power** *help us to analyze and better understand both sexual harassment and sexual assault against women as well as the rise of the #MeToo movement?*

Sources: Almukhtar, Gold, and Buchanan, 2018; Zacharek et al. 2017.

adopted a goal of 30 percent representation for women in each country's legislative body (Elson and Keklik 2003). By 2018, however, only 50 (of 193) countries had met the goal, many of them through legislated or voluntary quotas. The percentage of women in the U.S. Congress is well below the UN goal, and as of early 2018, the United States ranked 102nd (of 193). The absence of women in positions of political power means women are underrepresented in the groups that are responsible for creating public policy, passing laws, directing resources, and setting political priorities.

Religion and Gender

Because the world's religions are numerous and varied, it is difficult to generalize about gender roles. However, the world's major religions—including forms of Judaism, Islam, Buddhism, Hinduism, and Christianity—severely restrict the role of women in rituals and in institutional governance. In most cases, sacred texts in these religions personify God and the major prophets and disciples as male. Religious writings and teachings are often used to justify male domination in social life. For example, the Christian Bible

thinking about structure

How do cross-national comparisons of gender inequality illustrate that macro-level social **structure** can influence micro-level decisions, such as the division of housework?

notes that "wives should submit to their husbands in everything" (Ephesians 5:24), while the Qur'an (4.34) instructs that if wives are not obedient, men may "admonish them, and leave them alone in the sleeping-places and beat them." However, as with other religious beliefs, religious leaders reinterpret doctrines of faith regarding gender relations to reflect changing cultural values in the society at large. Thus, as gender equality has become a mainstream value, many religions are beginning to affirm the role of women in their sacred traditions. For example, there are women rabbis, and some Protestant denominations have women pastors or priests.

Sexual Harassment

Another form of gender discrimination is **sexual harassment,** *unwelcome sexual advances, requests for sexual favors, and other verbal or physical harassment of a sexual nature* (U.S. Equal Employment Opportunity Commission 2016). Harassment can take place anywhere: at work, on campus, or in the community. Most cases of sexual harassment are committed by men against women, but the perpetrator and victim can be of either gender.

Some harassment involves the abuse of power. The clearest cases are *quid pro quo* ("this for that") harassment, which involves a proposed exchange of some benefit, or withholding of some sanction, for sexual favors: sleep with me and I'll raise your salary; refuse and you're fired. Such cases are clearly abuses of authority and blatantly illegal. Other cases involve severe or pervasive sexual harassment that creates a hostile work environment, including inappropriate sexual jokes, sexually explicit e-mails or screen-savers, pornography, sexual cartoons, or unwanted verbal comments or physical contact. Typically, for such cases to be prosecuted, the offensive behavior must continue after a victim has lodged a complaint.

The legal standard for the creation of a hostile work environment—that a "reasonable person" in the same or similar circumstances would find the situation offensive—is not easy to meet, since there are many gray areas where reasonable people can disagree. In fact, some sexual harassment is unintentional. One person may think he or she is saying something funny or complimentary, but a colleague is offended—a good example of the failure to achieve intersubjectivity, as discussed in Chapter 7. The 2017 #MeToo movement, though, illustrates that much sexual harassment is blatant and goes unpunished until victims are able to speak out. Still, concern about the issue is uneven. In one poll, nearly twice as many Democrats (62 percent) as Republicans (33 percent) said men getting away with sexual harassment or assault was a major problem (Graf 2018).

Gendered Violence

Abuse of power, which is sometimes involved in sexual harassment, takes another, extreme form in gendered violence. The victims of violence are usually women and the perpetrators are usually men, but this is not always the case, as we will see. Still, violence against women by men carries with it a unique gendered dynamic on which we focus here. As in other relations that involve power, violence against women is both a consequence and a cause of inequality. Usually it is men who carry out this violence on an individual level as well as in more organized and systematic ways.

Domestic Violence and Sexual Assault

For much of history, violence against women in the home was widely accepted. In the United States, men had the legal right to assault their wives physically as recently as the late 1800s. Even today, other societies tolerate domestic violence. In many countries, though, feminist activists have been successful in changing cultural norms, legal standards, and law enforcement practices regarding domestic violence. In the United States, domestic violence is now widely recognized as a major social problem and is treated as a crime (Horth 2015).

The U.S. Department of Justice (2016) defines **domestic violence** as "*a pattern of abusive behavior in any relationship that is used by one partner to gain or maintain power and control over another intimate partner.*" (The term *intimate partner violence* is also commonly used.) Such abuse may include physical, sexual, psychological, emotional, and economic components. According to the Department of Justice, it includes "any behaviors that intimidate, manipulate, humiliate, isolate, frighten, terrorize, coerce, threaten, blame, hurt, injure, or wound someone."

In 2016, over 10 percent of all violent crime involved intimate partner violence. About 55 percent of the reported incidents consisted of relatively less severe behaviors such as being slapped, pushed, or shoved, leaving about 45 percent designated as "serious," a category that includes aggravated assault, sexual assault, and rape (Morgan and Kena 2017). Men and women engage in intimate partner violence at about the same rate. However, women tend to commit less serious forms of violence that often develop from escalating arguments (referred to by researchers as "situational couple violence"), while men's actions tend to be more serious, carry more severe consequences, and are more often aimed at controlling women's behavior (referred to as "intimate terrorism") (Johnson 2008). Female murder victims, for example, are much more likely (39.3 percent) than their male counterparts (2.8 percent) to have been killed by an intimate partner (Catalano 2013). In their lifetime, about one of four women and one of seven men have been the victim of at least one act of severe physical violence by an intimate partner, ranging from being slammed against something, punched, or hit with something hard to being sexually assaulted or raped (Breiding et al. 2014).

Rape overlaps with domestic violence since some domestic violence involves sexual assault. About a quarter of rapes are committed by a current or former spouse or intimate partner, another half by other acquaintances, and less than a quarter by strangers. While rape on campus has received much-needed attention recently, among 18- to 24-year-old women the rate of rape and sexual assault is actually 1.2 times higher for *non*-students than students (Sinozich and Langton 2014).

Male sexual victimization has been notoriously underreported in part because of stigma and in part because most surveys do not include prison and detention populations, in which male victimization is especially likely to occur (Stemple and Meyer 2014). More generally, there is growing awareness of the problem of violence in same-sex relationships. Lesbian, gay, and bisexual individuals are more likely to be the victim of severe physical violence by an intimate partner than are heterosexuals (Walters, Chen, and Breiding 2013). In the United States, increased awareness of the problem of domestic violence, changing cultural values that reject violence against women, and better prosecution of perpetrators contributed to a dramatic 72 percent decline in the rate of serious intimate partner violence against women from 1994 to 2011 (Catalano 2013).

Internationally, the situation is even more troubling. The World Health Organization (2013) estimates that the rates of intimate partner violence in Southeast Asia, the Middle East, and Africa are more than 50 percent higher than those in Europe and North America. A United Nations (2015) report found that intimate partner violence accounts for the majority of women's experience of violence worldwide. However, cultural acceptance of violence against women has been declining in almost all countries. At least 119 countries now have laws against domestic violence, 125 against sexual harassment, and 52 against marital rape. (The Sociology Works box examines one sociology major's work with recent immigrants for gender justice.)

State Violence against Women

We usually think of violence against women in terms of crimes committed by individuals, but governments are also implicated in this type of crime. Some governments willfully ignore sexual assault by failing to pass or enforce laws against it. In times of war, governments and military groups have organized and carried out systematic violence against women, including sexual slavery, in which women are forced to serve as prostitutes for soldiers (Kurtz and Kurtz 2015).

Military groups have used mass rape to terrorize civilian populations. Soldiers often murder the rape victims afterward. In 1994, for example, men raped as many as 500,000 women in Rwanda as part of that central African country's genocidal civil war. During the violence in Croatia and Bosnia-Herzegovina in southeastern Europe in the early 1990s, the number of rape victims was as high as 60,000 (United Nations 2016).

Sometimes, women are participants in wartime sexual violence and men are the victims. For example, during the 1994 genocide in Rwanda, women encouraged, ordered, and participated in the rape and killing of victims. In 2003, female U.S. soldiers participated in the sexual abuse and humiliation of Iraqi prisoners in the Abu Ghraib prison. Researchers have rarely asked whether men were victims in wartime, but when one study in the Congo did so, 23 percent of men reported experiencing some form of sexual violence (Cohen, Green, and Wood 2013).

In 2008, the United Nations Security Council passed a resolution (1820) condemning the use of sexual violence as a tool of war, making rape and other forms of sexual violence grounds for prosecution as war crimes or "crimes against humanity."

Human Trafficking and Globalization

Another form of organized violence against women involves human trafficking, in which criminal networks recruit, entrap, and transport individuals, holding them against their will for either sexual exploitation or forced labor. Such activities have increased significantly as globalization has made travel and immigration easier. In recent years, an increasing percentage of human trafficking has been for labor rather than sexual exploitation; more men have been victims than in the past, and more in-country—rather than international—trafficking has been detected.

Estimates about the number of people involved in human trafficking are unreliable. What is known is that of the victims detected, about half were trafficked for sexual exploitation and about 40 percent were for labor. Of every 10 detected victims, about 5 are adult women, 2 are girls, 2 are adult men, and 1 is a boy. About two-thirds of convicted traffickers are men; one-third are women (UN Office on Drugs and Crime 2016). Although the crime is widely recognized, little has been done so far to effectively combat it.

Genital Cutting

Female genital cutting is an umbrella term covering a variety of procedures that involve the partial or total removal of the external female genitalia. The most common form involves the removal of the clitoris and the labia minora, a procedure that traditional circumcisers or medical personnel often perform without anesthetic anytime from infancy through adolescence. Some cultures use the practice to encourage virginity until marriage and fidelity afterward. Others use it as an initiation rite to a community of adult women. Still others perform the procedure in the mistaken belief that it has hygienic benefits or enhances fertility. Whatever the reason, an estimated 125 million women have undergone some form of genital cutting in the 29 countries in Africa and the Middle East where the practice is concentrated (United Nations 2015).

Although it has long been an accepted part of some cultures and religious practices, especially in Africa, many human rights advocates consider genital cutting to be a form of organized violence against women, and some women from the cultures that condone it have organized to stop the practice. Some female genital cutting interferes with sexual pleasure, and some procedures can interfere with urination and contribute to complications during childbirth (World Health Organization 2016a). Whereas male circumcision—the removal of the foreskin from the penis—is also prominent in some cultures, its purpose and significance differ starkly from female genital cutting. In particular, male circumcision has no significant effect on sexual functioning, is not performed to inhibit sexual activity, and may help the man reduce his chance of HIV infection (World Health Organization 2016b).

As genital cutting illustrates, sexuality is another area related to gender in which cultural differences result in many variations.

Sexuality

Sexuality refers to *a person's sexual desires, behaviors, and identity.* Like gender, sexuality is related to biologically based sex characteristics but is also a social construction. Sexuality is about much more than biological reproduction. As a social behavior, sexuality is heavily influenced by norms and expectations that vary by culture and change over time. In discussing sexuality, then, we need to consider both biology and culture.

Biology, Culture, and Sexuality

There are two basic ways to approach human sexuality. On the one hand, we can look at humans as highly evolved animals for whom sex is simply a "natural" biological activity necessary for reproduction, as it is for other animals. Hormones help fuel a sex

SOCIOLOGY WORKS

Mona Moayad and Gender Justice

After earning her undergraduate degree in sociology, Mona Moayad received job offers in Washington, D.C., from the Federal Trade Commission, which oversees consumer protection and competition issues, and the little-known Tahirih Justice Center (2011), which describes itself as a "nonprofit organization that works to protect immigrant women and girls from gender-based violence through legal services, advocacy, and public education programs." Choosing the small nonprofit over the big federal agency, Moayad took an important step toward a career promoting social justice.

As a paralegal in immigration and family law at the center, Moayad worked with women and girls who had been victims of gender-based persecution. Her day-to-day work included conducting intake meetings for those seeking services, drafting and presenting case summaries, preparing complaints for family law cases, and interviewing clients to help them complete immigration forms. The center's programs include providing *pro bono* (free) legal services to immigrant women who have fled their home countries to escape torture, rape, human trafficking, forced marriage, domestic abuse, female genital cutting, and crimes committed against them in the name of family honor or because they had become widows.

"Sociology gave me the framework to understand why direct legal services are so important and necessary to empower disadvantaged communities," Moayad notes. "Studying social stratification gave me a clearer understanding of what challenges my clients were facing: characteristics of the 'working poor,' the wage gap between women and men, institutionalized racism that is deeply woven into every aspect of society which limited my clients' abilities to move up the 'social ladder' and have access to more opportunities for themselves and for their children. This knowledge gave me the context to understand where my clients were coming from and gave me the stats to defend and advocate for my clients." Moayad used her sociology degree and experience at the Tahirih Justice Center as stepping-stones to law school, earning a law degree from the City University of New York (CUNY) School of Law in pursuit of a career as an activist lawyer.

Courtesy of Mona Moayad

Mona Moayad

Although her mother also has a degree in sociology, and is, as Moayad puts it, "very passionate about the subject," Moayad says, "[I] had no idea I would major in sociology" and she did not decide to do so until after she took introductory sociology in her second year of college. "I was fascinated by sociology; it helped me understand what was going on in the world around me in every aspect."

"Sociology gave me the framework to understand why direct legal services are so important and necessary to empower disadvantaged communities."

"Sociology has given me a heightened awareness about the inequalities that exist within society. It has given me the framework to understand the deficiencies of the legal system and why—although insufficient—reform legal work is necessary in order to bring about change in society."

think about it

1. *How are power and inequality central to Moayad's work?*
2. *Have you ever thought of using a degree in sociology as a stepping-stone to law school or other professional training? If so, what type of training might you be interested in, and how could sociology help prepare you for it?*

drive that enables human beings to reproduce successfully—perhaps *too* successfully, since population growth strains the planet's resources. In this vein, some people invoke "nature" to make judgments about what is "normal" sexual activity, and some observers condemn homosexuality as "unnatural" because it cannot result in conception. However, contrary to common belief, other nonhuman primates—our closest animal cousins who are social beings and have relatively large brains and facial features similar to humans—engage in a variety of sexual activities, some of which have nothing to do with reproduction. Bonobo chimpanzees (also known as pygmy chimps), for example, use sex as play, to mark an end to an argument, to help form a friendship, to trade for food, and more. Since bonobos often engage in homosexual sex, oral sex, or sex with juveniles, their sexual behavior is not only for procreation. Therefore, even in nature, sex includes a broad range of practices with a variety of purposes.

On the other hand, human behavior is the product of culture as well as biology, and in this sense, human sexuality isn't so much "natural" as it is a set of socially regulated practices that vary across cultures and over time. Religious belief—which often includes ideas about right and wrong expressions of sexuality—has been one way of communicating cultural norms about sexuality. For example, the use of birth control was forbidden by all Protestant denominations until 1930 and is still considered sinful by the Catholic Church today. The Catholic Church also condemns masturbation and homosexuality (Jutte 2008).

Cultures typically have a variety of norms and expectations regarding sexuality. At what age is sexual activity appropriate? Is sex with a first cousin acceptable? Is sex outside of marriage acceptable? Is monogamy—commitment to a single sexual partner—necessary? Different cultures answer these questions differently. However, all cultures have some form of **incest taboo,** *a norm restricting sexual relations between certain relatives.* Since reproduction between close relatives increases the risk that offspring will be born with harmful physical or mental effects, incest taboos reduce this risk. Incest taboos also promote social integration by encouraging people to reach beyond their immediate family for a sexual partner and reduce conflict within the family by marking boundaries that restrict competition for sexual partners. Other taboos, such as age restrictions, protect vulnerable children not yet mature enough to consent to sexual activity.

©StockPhotosArt/Alamy Stock Photo

As with other aspects of human social life, sociologists understand that sexuality is the result of both nature and nurture; it has a biological basis but varies culturally. As such, it is another aspect of our lives that is socially constructed.

Sexuality as a Social Construction

The bedroom may seem like the last place that would be submitted to a sociological analysis. But sociology applies not only to our public actions but also to the most personal and private aspects of our lives. Sex reflects a culture's collective norms (Fitzgerald and Grossman 2018; Seidman 2015).

Culture heavily influences when, how often, where, with whom, and how humans have sex (Kimmel 2012). Researchers have documented a variety of sexual customs around the world. A passionate kiss on the lips frequently initiates a sexual encounter in U.S. culture. But the Thonga of Mozambique and Siriono of Bolivia, among others, find such kissing to be repulsive because of the possibility of exchanging saliva; mouths are intended to be used for food. The Zande people of central Africa typically have sex several times a night but, in contrast, the Yapese people of the Pacific Islands typically have sex only about once a month. In some cultures, sexual intercourse always occurs outside so as not to "contaminate" the living quarters; in others it always happens indoors. Oral sex is a staple of sexual encounters in some cultures but is absent from others. Men typically initiate sex in many cultures, whereas women typically do so in others.

Because all these sexual behaviors and more are considered "normal" in their cultural context, there clearly is no single understanding of human sexuality. Amid all these variations in sexual behavior, humans manage to reproduce, express love, form strong social bonds, experience pleasure, and simply have fun.

Changing Norms: The Sexual Revolution in the United States

To get a sense of the social construction of sexuality, consider how sexual attitudes, behaviors, and norms have evolved in the United States. In a major cultural shift, the past century has seen an increasing willingness to discuss sexuality openly and a greater emphasis on individual freedom and personal choice in matters of sexuality.

Through much of the twentieth century, sexuality was closely controlled by restrictive social norms. Morality and religion preached that the only appropriate use of sex was to have children. Reflecting the inequality of the day, women were subjected to a double standard: premarital sex by men was commonly tolerated, whereas women were expected to remain virgins until marriage. Because women didn't have easy access to effective birth control or safe legal abortions, and unmarried mothers were subjected to severe social stigma, female abstinence before marriage was a practical necessity.

By the mid-twentieth century, however, a number of factors helped change sexual attitudes and behaviors in the United States, creating what came to be called the sexual revolution:

- In 1948, Alfred Kinsey and his colleagues helped spark serious public discussion of sexuality when they published the first of two books on male and female sexuality (Kinsey, Pomeroy, and Martin [1948] 1998; Kinsey et al. [1953] 1998). Though crude by today's standards, the work used a social scientific approach to explore what had largely been taboo subjects, including homosexuality. Their findings suggested that many people were more open to a variety of sexual experiences than was often acknowledged. Such work was significant, since sexuality was typically considered a private matter not to be discussed in public, and most people lacked even basic sexual information to a degree that is difficult to imagine today.
- The vibrant youth culture of the post–World War II baby boom generation during the latter 1950s and 1960s rebelled against many social conventions, including restrictive sexual norms. Students living away from home in rapidly growing residential college campuses encountered a social environment that enabled sexual experimentation. By the late 1960s, some members of this youth subculture were advocating the wholesale rejection of sexual conventions and promoting sexuality for pleasure, not just procreation.
- The introduction of the Pill in 1960 helped make such sexual freedom possible. Oral contraceptives made it easier for women to control if and when they had children.
- A broader women's movement decried the sexual double standard and affirmed the right of women to control their own bodies and enjoy their sexuality.

FIGURE 11.4 | SEXUAL IDENTITIES

		Degree of Different-Sex Attraction	
		High	*Low*
Degree of Same-Sex Attraction	*High*	Bisexual	Homosexual
	Low	Heterosexual	Asexual

This new freedom was not without consequences. As people engaged in more frequent sex with a greater number of partners, the frequency of sexually transmitted diseases (STDs) and teen pregnancies rose in the 1970s, which helped spark a backlash against the sexual revolution. Social conservatives advocated a return to "family values," including a revival of earlier norms regarding sexuality and gender roles. Debates over these cultural values continue to this day, but most aspects of the sexual revolution have long since moved into the cultural mainstream, influencing the expression of our sexual identities.

Sexual Identities

Queer theory argues that sexual identities are socially constructed, evolve, and can change during a person's life (Hall and Jagose 2013; Seidman 1996). **Sexual identity** (or sexual orientation) refers to *our sense of self as it relates to the type of sexual attraction we have for others.* Sexual identities exist along a continuum, but in our society, there are four basic sexual identity groups (summarized in Figure 11.4):

- **Heterosexuals** *are attracted to people of a different sex.*
- **Homosexuals** *are attracted to people of the same sex.*
- **Bisexuals** *are attracted to people of both sexes.*
- **Asexual people** *experience no sexual attraction for anyone.*

Although it remains an area of debate, growing evidence suggests that sexual identity is rooted in biology but influenced by culture. For example, the American Academy of Pediatrics has long offered its clinicians advice that is typical of this growing consensus: "Sexual orientation probably is not determined by any one factor but by a combination of genetic, hormonal, and environmental influences" (Frankowski 2004, 1828). Research shows that acceptance of various sexual identities and behaviors has grown significantly in the United States during the last few decades. For example, the percentage of Americans who said same-sex activity is "not wrong at all" has nearly quadrupled from just 13 percent in 1990 to 49 percent in 2014 (Twenge, Sherman, and Wells 2016).

Sexuality is a sensitive and private topic, and many people are guarded about discussing it. Also, given the continuum of attitudes and behaviors that marks sexuality, classifying people into distinct categories can be difficult and misleading. For example, one U.S. study found that of people aged 18 to 44, 17.4 percent of women and 6.2 percent of men had ever had any same-sex contact, but much smaller percentages identified as lesbian or gay (1.3 percent of women, 1.9 percent of men) or as bisexual (5.5 percent of women, 2 percent of men) (Copen, Chandra, and Febo-Vazquez 2016). Thus the percentage of the population that falls within each type of sexual identity is a matter of debate.

A variety of research puts the gay and lesbian population at about 1.6 percent of U.S. adults, but there is more variation in results regarding the percentage who identify as bisexual. The National Health Interview Survey, the government's annual look at health and behaviors, found 96.6 percent of U.S. adults identify as straight, 1.6 percent as gay or lesbian, and 0.7 percent as bisexual, with 1.1 percent declining to respond or choosing "I don't know" or "something else" (Ward et al. 2014). Some surveys, though, report that the percentage of people who are bisexual is as high as 1.8 percent (Gates 2011).

Inventing Heterosexuals and Homosexuals

Just as culture influences how people understand sexual behavior, it also influences how we understand sexual identity. In fact, the very idea of linking identity to sexuality—of identifying as "straight," "gay," or "bi"—is a relatively recent social invention.

All forms of sexual behaviors have existed throughout human history. Some forms of homosexual activity were a routine part of social life in some societies, as we saw from the example of the two-spirits earlier in this chapter. Perhaps most famously, homoexuality was prevalent in ancient Greek culture, and the word *lesbian* is derived from the island of Lesbos, home of the ancient Greek poet Sappho, who wrote her love poems for women and girls.

However, through most of human history, sexual behavior and what we now call sexual identity have been separated. That is, engaging in a particular sexual *behavior* did not necessarily result in the attachment of a label—gay, straight, and so on—to a person. In earlier times, engaging in heterosexual or homosexual activity did not necessarily mean a person was regarded as a heterosexual or a homosexual. Not until early scientific efforts to categorize human sexual behavior in the mid-nineteenth century was the notion of "homosexuals" as a distinct category of people created to contrast with "heterosexuals."

In *The History of Sexuality,* Michel Foucault (1980) argued that in the mid-nineteenth century, in part because of the increasingly diverse and rapidly growing populations concentrated in recently industrialized cities, scientists undertook new efforts to study sexual behaviors. For the first time, sexuality—which had always been a part of daily life—was scrutinized and analyzed. In the process of studying sexual behaviors, researchers began classifying them into distinct categories—including "normal" and "deviant." Increased knowledge about sexual practices led to efforts by those in power to restrict them. Governments began trying to regulate and control these newly labeled deviant practices. For example, they enacted sodomy laws banning practices associated with homosexuality (though performed by many heterosexuals as well), such as anal intercourse and oral sex. By the end of the nineteenth century, Western societies treated someone who engaged in homosexual activity as a member of a new and distinct social category: homosexuals.

In the latter half of the twentieth century, however, skepticism about the strict separation of sexualities and efforts to enforce it increased. As early as 1948, Kinsey suggested that rather than belonging to one of two distinct categories, men's sexuality fell along a continuum, with many men experiencing both heterosexual and homosexual feelings and behaviors to varying degrees. Many researchers have confirmed Kinsey's findings, though popular culture often still views "gay" and "straight" as sharply divided and mutually exclusive identities.

Bisexuality and Asexuality

Are you gay or straight? As noted, our culture generally insists on dichotomous—either-or—sexual identities. But what if your answer to that question is "both" or "neither"? Being *bisexual* means having a sexual identity based on attraction to both women and men. People in various cultures have long engaged in sexual activity with people of both sexes, but the notion of bisexuality as a distinct identity emerged in the nineteenth century. The term *bisexual* was not commonly used until the mid-twentieth century.

Being *asexual* means lacking sexual attraction to either gender. This identity, too, violates our culture's expected norms about sexuality. Asexual people don't choose to refrain from sex, resist sexual urges, fail to find a sexual partner, or have moral or religious objections to sex. Instead, asexuals are simply not sexually attracted to anyone. They may or may not engage in sexual activity and may be in long-term romantic relationships without sex; they simply are not sexually attracted to others. Because precise definitions of asexuality vary, research findings about the number of people who are asexual also vary considerably. After reviewing the range of findings, one leading researcher suggests that 1 percent is a reasonable estimate for the percentage of people who are asexual (Bogaert 2015).

Sexual Identities and Inequality

Cultures have widely divergent views about lesbian, gay, bisexual, and transgender (LGBT) people. **Heterosexism,** *a set of attitudes and behavior that indicates an assumption that everyone is heterosexual,* is common. Assuming a female friend is referring to a man when she mentions a date is an example of heterosexism. People with heterosexist attitudes don't necessarily have negative feelings toward LGBT people; they simply overlook their existence. In contrast, **homophobia** is *the disapproval and fear of LGBT people.* Homophobia is often the source of hostility and discrimination.

Lesbian, gay, bisexual, and transgender people have long faced discriminatory homophobic laws and customs that often forced them to stay "in the closet." However, the LGBT community organized effectively, became more public, and eventually catalyzed powerful changes in public attitudes, social policies, and the law (Bronski 2011; Faderman 2015). For example:

- The American Psychiatric Association (APA) once included homosexuality in its influential manual of "mental disorders," providing "scientific" justification for those who saw it as a sickness. As research evidence to the contrary accumulated and as gay activists became more vocal, the APA dropped the listing in 1973.
- Sodomy laws (named after a biblical tale in Genesis) typically outlawed anal and oral sex but were used almost exclusively to target gay men until the U.S. Supreme Court ruled them unconstitutional in 2003.
- Homosexuals were banned from military service until 1993, when a compromise "don't ask, don't tell" policy (designed by sociologist Charles Moskos) permitted gays and lesbians to serve as long as they did not openly disclose their sexual identity. In 2010, a federal court found this policy unconstitutional, prompting congressional action that overturned the ban. In 2016, the Pentagon announced it would also allow transgender people to serve openly in the military. In 2018, though, the Trump administration reversed this position, approving a new policy stating "transgender persons who require or have undergone gender transition are disqualified from military service" (Cooper and Gibbons-Neff 2018).
- Same-sex relationships were not legally recognized, with widespread implications for medical, tax, property, parenting, and other legal arenas. Beginning with Massachusetts in 2003, activists succeeded in getting a growing number of individual states to recognize domestic partnerships, civil unions, and same-sex marriage through court orders, legislative action, and referenda. In 2015, when the U.S. Supreme Court legalized same-sex marriage nationwide, the United States joined more than 20 countries that had already done so.

Despite progress, barriers remain. LGBT people often lack basic civil rights protections and consequently can encounter discrimination in the workplace, housing, and other areas. Employers, for example, can fire or refuse to hire people simply because they are gay, bisexual, or transgender. Transgender individuals can be barred from using the bathroom of their choice. In a strategy similar to the one that led to nationwide same-sex marriage, activists have been organizing to get individual states to enact civil rights protections barring discrimination based on sexual orientation, gender identity, and gender expression, with the goal of eventually achieving such protections on the federal level. As of 2018, though, about half of LGBT people in the United States live in states where they can be legally discriminated against because of a lack of civil rights protections (freedomforallamericans.org).

Homophobic beliefs are often rooted in religious doctrine, but there is no consensus among the world's religions regarding the status of LGBT people. Indeed, debates about homosexuality, the role of gays in each faith, same-sex marriage, and LGBT civil rights have deeply divided some denominations. Some faiths have embraced LGBT members. For example, the Reverend V. Gene Robinson, once a bishop in the Episcopal Church, has been an articulate advocate for the rights of LGBT people, often challenging myths about the Bible's stance on homosexuality (Robinson 2010a). Other religious groups have actively resisted advances in

thinking about **power**

Once scientists categorized people as homosexual or heterosexual, governments sought to use their **power** to control individuals with sexual identities they considered deviant. In what ways do governments still use power to control people's sexual identity?

MAP 11.1 | SEXUAL ORIENTATION LAWS AROUND THE WORLD

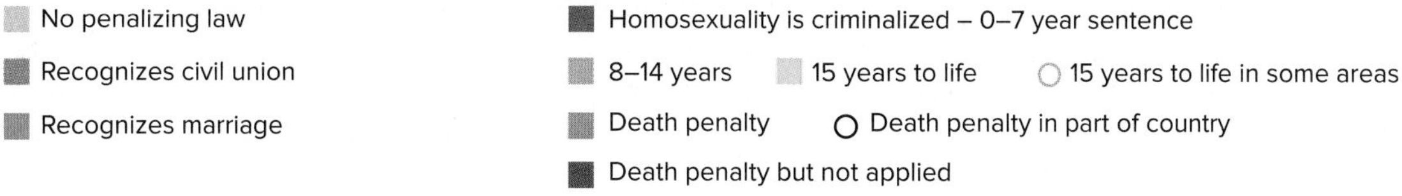

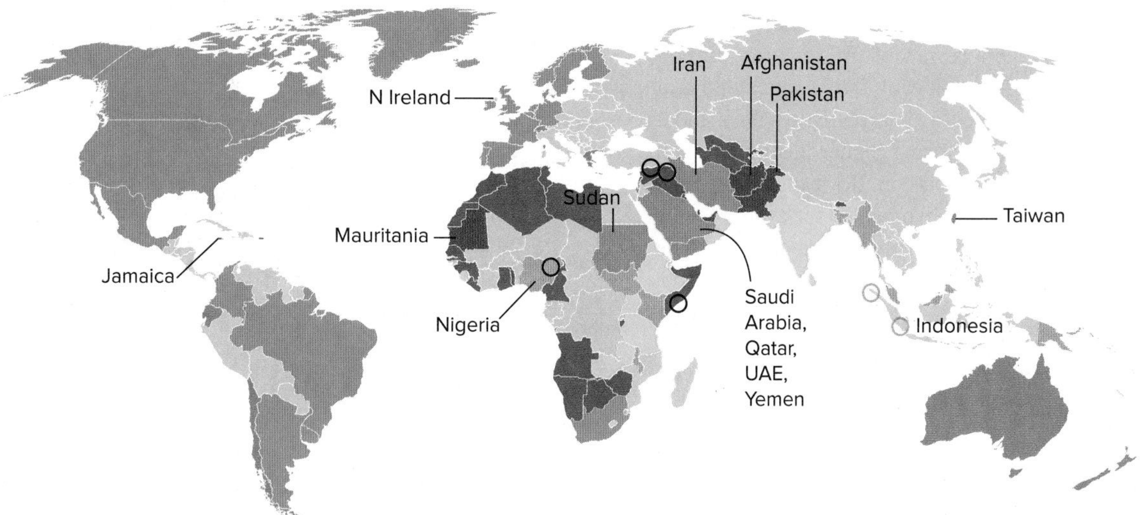

Laws addressing same-sex couples vary significantly around the world and include everything from legal marriage for same-sex couples to the death penalty for homosexuality. *Source:* Duncan, Pamela. "Gay relationships are still criminalised in 72 countries, report finds." The Guardian. July 27,2017; ilga.org/maps-sexual-orientation-laws.

CORE CONCEPTS CHALLENGE *How do the core concepts of* **culture** *and* **power** *help to explain this wide spectrum of laws.*

LGBT rights, sometimes by promoting "religious freedom bills" that would enable individuals and businesses to use religious belief to justify their refusal to serve LGBT individuals. Abroad, intolerance can be extreme. As of 2017, 72 countries and territories still criminalize same-sex relationships. (See Map 11.1.) In eight Muslim countries, including Saudi Arabia, Iran, and Iraq, homosexuality is still punishable by death (ILGA 2018).

More informally, homophobia still pervades our culture. For many young people, *gay* is a synonym for *lame* or *stupid.* "Gay bashing" ranges from well-known insulting slang terms—such as *fag* and *dyke*—to hate crimes such as harassment, assault, and even murder. Such harassment sometimes leads to suicides, especially by beleaguered gay teens. In 2016, a homophobic individual even targeted the patrons of a gay nightclub in Orlando, Florida, killing 49 people.

In one particularly horrendous period of persecution, German Nazis arrested and beat tens of thousands of gay men—sometimes castrating them—and used them as forced laborers in concentration camps. Once imprisoned, they were forced to wear pink triangles, which activists have since recast as a powerful symbol of the LGBT movement.

Sexuality and the Internet

The internet has made a vast range of material about sexuality easily available. Some sites provide information about sex and sexuality, others serve as support communities for sexual minorities, and many offer pornography. The term *pornography* refers to material that explicitly portrays sexual acts or naked people and is primarily intended to stimulate sexual excitement. With the rise of the internet, pornography is more easily available than ever before. Consequently, porn has increasingly drawn the attention of sociologists and others for its portrayal of human sexuality.

The porn industry is vast. Though accurate data are difficult to obtain, some estimates are that porn generates over $13 billion each year in the United States alone and that the internet features well over 4 million websites devoted to pornography (Dines 2010). Pornography is a major part of the bottom line not only for its producers but also for mainstream corporations. For example, sexually explicit television channels are highly profitable for cable providers, and most hotels offer lucrative pay-per-view porn movies.

Pornography helped fuel many of the internet's early innovations, including online payment systems, video streaming, and video chat, as well as many of its nuisances, among them spam, malware, and pop-up ads (Tynan 2008). Owing to the internet, porn has also become increasingly do-it-yourself, with "amateur" photos and videos commonly uploaded to porn websites. Some of these postings are malicious, as in the case of "revenge porn," which involves uploading sexually explicit photos or videos—sometimes obtained surreptitiously—without the knowledge or consent of the person in them.

One concern about the growth of pornography is that child and teen internet users now have access to a sea of sexually explicit material. This development has toppled a traditional social barrier that once separated adults and children. Loaded with clichés that are far removed from real-world sexual practice, including portrayals of women whose only role is to fulfill male fantasies, and sometimes laced with misogynistic images of women being mistreated, pornography badly distorts young people's understanding of healthy sexuality, many observers argue (Dines 2010; Gallup 2011). One review of the research on pornography and young people (Horvath et al. 2013) concluded that early exposure to porn is associated with unrealistic beliefs about sex and the adoption of attitudes favoring gender inequality, such as male dominance and female submission. Boys and young men are more likely than girls and young women to seek out pornography, and they tend to have more-positive views about it. The review also found that while not necessarily a causal relationship, access and exposure to pornography are associated with higher rates of risky sexual behaviors, including practicing unprotected sex, combining sex with alcohol and drug use, having sex with multiple partners, and engaging in "sexting"—the sending of sexually explicit photos or messages by smartphone.

Observers have noted that, in part due to the easy availability of sexually explicit material over the internet, pornography has moved into mainstream culture (Sarracino 2009). Music videos adopt poses and conventions from pornographic films, often featuring submissive women. Television programs and stand-up comics routinely celebrate porn use. The 2011 erotic novel *50 Shades of Grey,* sold mostly as an e-book, mixed a traditional romance formula with explicit sex scenes of bondage and sadomasochism to reach the *New York Times* best-seller list and sell over 70 million copies. Other self-published "erotic novels" have gained considerable popularity among e-book readers, especially women (Berlatsky 2013). Oprah Winfrey's magazine, *O,* has featured an adult film guide for women suggesting that using such material can lead to a more satisfying sex life.

As porn has gone mainstream, its content has diversified. Illegal pornography involving children or deadly violence is still rampant. Traditional "hardcore" adult pornography includes depictions that degrade women, portray humiliating sexual acts, and involve coercion, abuse, and violence. But a growing segment of pornography can be labeled *erotica*, a subjective term referring to sexually explicit material that is not violent, degrading, or exploitative and that features compassionate sexual encounters. Such material appears to be reaching new and wider audiences including many women (Hambleton 2016).

Feminist scholars and activists have long debated the nature of and appropriate response to pornography (Cornell 2000). Some critiques of pornography note the negative impact of stereotypical and violent porn on consumers and the broader society, as well as the disturbing exploitative and dangerous practices that characterize the porn industry and affect porn workers. Critics sometimes call for the censoring of pornography, considering it to be "sexual slavery" that inevitably constitutes violence against women. Groups such as Stop Porn Culture are "dedicated to challenging the pornography industry and an increasingly pornographic pop culture" (stoppornculture.org).

Other feminists condemn traditional pornography but endorse sexually explicit material produced in a noncoercive way, which treats women and men as equals and portrays healthy, caring sexual encounters in the context of larger relationships (O'Connor 2013). Further, feminist porn highlights diversity and aims to "contest and complicate dominant representations of gender, sexuality, race, ethnicity, class, ability, age, body type, and other identity markers" (Taormino 2013, 9). That is, it challenges dominant images of sexuality, many of which are the result of traditional porn.

Debates among these critics continue even as the study of pornography itself has become more mainstream. In 2014, *Porn Studies* was launched, the first academic journal devoted to the study of pornography.

Challenging Inequality Based on Gender and Sexual Identity

A half century ago, a chapter such as this one simply would not have appeared in a sociology textbook; gender and sexuality were on the margins of sociology. In an example of how human action can change cultures and social structures, however, feminists and LGBT activists have helped modify political, legal, and cultural reality as well as the scholarly agenda. This section briefly explores some of these efforts.

Gender in Sociology

As we saw in Chapter 1, most early mainstream sociologists ignored issues of gender and sexuality, reflecting the sexist views of the societies in which they were working (Kandal 1988). The "founding fathers" of sociology in the nineteenth and early twentieth centuries often based their generalizations about society on the experiences of heterosexual men. Women writing sociological works at the time were mostly excluded from formal academic positions. As a result, gender played a marginal role in early conventional sociology.

One exception was a critical theory of gender stratification developed by Friedrich Engels, a close collaborator of Karl Marx. As noted earlier in this chapter, Engels ([1884] 1972) tied gender stratification to the rise of private property and class. Later, capitalism elevated the importance of wage labor outside the home but depended upon women's devalued and unpaid labor in the home to feed and care for current and future workers. Thus, for Engels, gender stratification emerged from changes in the economy. Although he made gender secondary in importance to class, Engels at least recognized gender inequality as unjust and saw the intersection of class and gender stratification. Consistent with his work, the emancipation of women was a goal of many socialist political movements.

Gender Stratification as Functional By the middle of the twentieth century, Talcott Parsons was one of a number of sociologists who wrote about "sex roles." Parsons recognized the role strain involved in being a woman in middle-class America, especially the tension between being a mother and working in paid employment. However, reflecting his functionalist theoretical orientation, Parsons accepted uncritically the idea that the specialization of sex roles served a useful function in society.

SPOTLIGHT
on social theory

Parsons's **functionalist** approach to gender rationalized inequality between the sexes. Do you agree that specialized roles for each sex can serve a positive function? How might such specialization be dysfunctional for society?

According to Parsons, paid labor serves an *instrumental* function because it is task oriented, with short-term, impersonal interactions, while the family serves the *expressive* functions involved in stable, long-term, personal relationships. With work separated from home life, men specialized in instrumental functions, whereas women focused on the expressive tasks of nurturing children and caring for husbands. Parsons seemed to assume that women and men voluntarily accepted this state of affairs and embraced the values associated with it. For Parsons, this clear separation of sex roles reduced competition between husband and wife for status in the family. "If both were equally in competition for occupational status, there might indeed be a very serious strain on the solidarity of the family unit," Parsons wrote (1954, 79). He argued that the useful functions provided by sex role segregation helped explain why "the feminist movement has had such difficulty in breaking it down" (80). In the 1960s and 1970s, the women's movement challenged these assumptions.

Feminist Scholarship Objecting to the functionalists' assumptions, feminist scholars pointed out that there was no reason why individuals could not perform *both* instrumental and expressive tasks, or if these tasks were to be separated, why men had to be limited to instrumental and women to expressive. They also pointed out that functionalist arguments ignored reality: first, a significant portion of women—overwhelmingly members of the working class—were already in the labor force, and second, Parsons's model of family life was limited to a particular middle-class version that was dominant in the United States in the middle of the twentieth century. Since that time, feminist scholarship has influenced every subfield in the discipline (Risman, Froyum, and Scarborough 2018). This chapter reflects many insights from feminist scholars.

Women's Activism

Feminism is *a philosophy that advocates social, political, and economic equality for women and men.* Activism on behalf of women's equality has been a constant force in the modern world, but various periods of especially intense activism are commonly identified as "waves." *First-wave feminism* took place mainly in the United States and the United Kingdom during the late nineteenth and early twentieth centuries, when activists working on behalf of women's political and social rights won the right to vote for women. The Seneca Falls convention mentioned earlier in this chapter is from this era, as are such noted feminist leaders as Susan B. Anthony and Elizabeth Cady Stanton. The activists of this period had broad goals beyond winning the right to vote, including eliminating discriminatory laws, increasing access to higher education, and working to make birth control more readily available.

Second-wave feminism refers to the period of intense activism during the 1960s and 1970s, when activists tackled issues related to gender inequality, including discrimination in the workplace and in education, gender stereotypes in popular culture, restrictive gender roles, reproductive rights, and sexual freedom. During this era well-known activists such as Betty Friedan, the author of *The Feminine Mystique* (a book that helped inspire a revival of interest in women's rights), helped form the National Organization for Women (NOW), and Gloria Steinem, another important activist, founded *Ms.* magazine as a platform for feminist ideas.

©The Advertising Archives/Everett Collection

©Mladen Antonov/AFP/Getty Images

In 1969, gays and lesbians were forced to live almost entirely "in the closet," and public gay rights activism was so rare that the clash (*left*) between police and gay men outside New York's Stonewall Inn became iconic. Today, activism has led to more support for LGBT rights, even among mainstream political institutions. When the Supreme Court ruled in 2015 that marriage was a constitutionally guaranteed right for same-sex couples, the Obama administration celebrated the occasion by lighting the White House in the rainbow colors of the LGBT movement.

Third-wave feminism refers to activism beginning in the 1990s, though some feminist scholars and activists view this period as a continuation of second-wave feminism. Activism today promotes female self-empowerment and sexual self-esteem, gives special attention to race and class diversity within women's experiences, and often includes a playful subversion of popular culture. For example, third-wave feminists combated the patronizing use of the word *girl* to refer to women by reclaiming it as "grrl power," a confident affirmation of women's strength.

LGBT Activism

Sexual identity and gender identity are not just private issues; they are also public and political concerns. As discussed earlier in this chapter, social activism has made the public increasingly aware of issues affecting LGBT people (Bronski 2011; Faderman 2015; Miller 2006). On June 28, 1969, the New York City police raided a gay bar called the Stonewall Inn, as they had done many times before. This time, however, patrons refused to go quietly to jail, and while the police waited for patrol wagons, a crowd gathered outside the bar and began heckling and then attacking the officers. The spontaneous demonstration that followed was repeated on subsequent nights in what has become known as the Stonewall Riots, a defining moment for the LGBT community and a symbolic turning point in the history of social movements. After years of being forced to hide from police harassment, gay people took to the streets to demand their rights. Today, these actions are commemorated in the Stonewall National Monument, the first such monument devoted to LGBT rights (National Park Service 2016).

Stonewall primarily involved white, gay men. Since then, a diverse LGBT rights movement has emerged, taking on a broad range of issues, including supporting LGBT people of color; combating hate crimes; supporting LGBT teens who face bullying, harassment, and estrangement from their families; mobilizing people of faith to support LGBT rights; combating discriminatory laws and practices; working for equality in the workplace; and helping same-sex parents. College campuses have been especially active in cultivating LGBT activism and developing movement leaders. Over the years, activists have shifted the nation's culture and laws toward considerably more equality for the LGBT community, though much remains to be done.

A Changing World

CONVERGENCE IN GENDER AND SEXUALITY

As we have seen, ideas about gender and sexuality are changing constantly. In recent years, one ongoing change has been that women and men have become more similar in both gender and sexuality.

Gender Convergence

Gender convergence is *a trend toward increasing similarity in how women and men live.* This convergence varies depending on social context, much like gender itself. Some women in booming developing countries, for example, are experiencing increased economic opportunities and independence for the first time, newfound freedom that is allowing them to carve out new gender roles in otherwise traditional societies. Those most affected are middle-class, educated women who have the chance to defer marriage and motherhood while pursuing careers in fields such as business and technology. In India, for example, a growing population of young, single women has chosen to live independently rather than staying at their parents' house or getting married. Although Indian women marry young compared to their Western counterparts, the average age at which they marry has risen slightly, with college-educated women putting off marriage the longest. Although arranged marriages are still common and traditional gender roles still deeply entrenched, new economic realities are enabling some women to pursue careers and lifestyles once limited to men (Clark 2016).

In wealthy developed countries, traditional ways of dividing responsibility between work and family are becoming less common and gender roles less rigid (Altintas and Sullivan 2016; Galinsky, Aumann, and Bond 2013). As we have seen, women and men participate in the labor force at rates that are converging. Consequently, they now have increasingly similar attitudes toward the best way to allocate their time: both women and men report they want to strike a balance between work and family life.

In particular, younger men and women in wealthy societies are increasingly taking on similar roles. Younger fathers spend more time doing child care than their own fathers did (Gerson 2010b; McGill 2014). College students of both sexes have similar aspirations to pursue advanced degrees and careers, have similar attitudes about the appropriate role of women in society, provide similar answers to a variety of questions about personal values (including about the desire to raise a family), and hold comparable opinions about some social and political issues (Astin 1998; Eagan et al. 2016).

Sexual Convergence

Over the past few decades, gender convergence has gradually changed the sexual double standard between men and women, especially among younger people. Though differences remain, the age at which women and men become sexually active, their number of sexual partners, and their attitudes toward sexuality have become more similar. One phase of this convergence occurred in the wake of the sexual revolution of the 1960s and 1970s, when girls became more sexually active at an earlier age, thereby behaving more like boys. A second phase got under way in the 1990s, when boys began delaying the age of their first sexual activity, thereby behaving more like girls.

Risman and Schwartz (2002) suggest that the traditionally large gap between the rate of girls' and boys' sexual activity before the sexual revolution meant that a few sexually active girls were having relations with a larger number of boys. Gender norms of the time discouraged sexual activity on the part of "good girls," leaving boys to pursue sex with "bad girls," who were ostracized as "sluts." As gender norms changed, girls' sexual activity has become more accepted and widespread. Consequently, boys' early sexual activities are now more likely to be in the context of an ongoing relationship with a girlfriend rather than a fleeting encounter with a "bad girl." Sex in such ongoing relationships is more likely to be safe and responsible, contributing to some positive trends. In recent years, the rates of sexually transmitted diseases, teen pregnancies, and abortions have all declined, suggesting that teens are being more sexually responsible.

thinking sociologically about

Gender and Sexuality

culture

- *Gender* refers to the socially constructed cultural expectations associated with men and women. Different cultures produce different gender norms.
- From infancy, we are socialized into our culture's gender expectations, develop gendered identities, and view the world through the lens of gender expectations that we usually take for granted.
- Sexuality also varies by culture, and different cultures have different norms regarding sexual identities that must be taught through socialization.

structure

- Gender is built into social structure, as when social institutions enforce gender expectations.
- Gender must constantly be maintained and re-created—actions that sociologists call "doing gender." Gender roles and identities are fragile and may be contested and changed.
- Social structures often reflect expectations regarding sexuality, as when the legal system is tailored to heterosexual couples.

power

- In every society, differences in power between men and women have resulted in social institutions with considerable gender inequality.
- Inequality based on sexuality also reflects differences in power in society.
- Feminists and LGBT activists have organized, using their collective power to promote change.

REVIEW, REFLECT, AND APPLY

Looking Back

1. *Sex* refers to the biological characteristics that distinguish females and males. *Gender* refers to the socially constructed expectations associated with women and men. Transgender people, who identify with a gender not typically associated with their sex, illustrate the difference between sex and gender.
2. Much of what our society attributes to sex is, in fact, gender. Notions of gender vary over time and across cultures. Gender is taught through socialization, and "doing gender" refers to daily interactions in a variety of social settings that involve the reinforcement or modification of gender.

3. Gender inequality and stratification are part of the structure of society. Sex differences likely played an important role in the establishment of patriarchy, whereas cultural developments have radically reduced the importance of sex in relation to gender.
4. Gender inequality can be found in all the major social institutions, including the workplace, family, media, politics, and religion. Individual or organized violence against women is one way male power is used to dominate women.
5. Norms about sexuality and sexual identity are culturally produced, resulting in wide variations. In Western society, the invention of distinct sexual orientations is a relatively recent phenomenon. Sexual minorities are often subject to discrimination.
6. Feminist efforts have helped create more equality between women and men. Activism has also helped reduce discrimination against LGBT people. Gender and sexual convergence have occurred in many areas of social life, as standards become more similar for men and women.

Critical Thinking: Questions and Activities

1. Both gender and race have socially constructed characteristics that are mistakenly attributed to biology. Using a sociological perspective, describe how else race and gender are similar. How are they different?
2. Take note of how the words *sex* and *gender* are used to refer to women and men in popular media and other places. Can you find examples in which the word *gender* is being used to mean biological differences?
3. What do you think are the major differences, if any, between how gender affects your life and how it affected the lives of your parents?
4. Where do you see the most entrenched forms of gender inequality? Why has this particular area been so resistant to change?
5. How were you socialized to understand different sexual identities? Did this socialization include homophobic biases?

Key Terms

asexual people (p. 287) people who experience no sexual attraction for anyone.

bisexuals (p. 287) people who are attracted to people of both sexes.

doing gender (p. 271) creating gender through interactions in particular social settings.

domestic violence (p. 283) (or intimate partner violence) a pattern of abusive behavior in any relationship that is used by one partner to gain or maintain power and control over another intimate partner.

feminism (p. 291) a philosophy that advocates social, political, and economic equality for women and men.

gender (p. 265) the socially constructed cultural expectations associated with women and men.

gender convergence (p. 292) a trend toward increasing similarity in how women and men live.

gender expression (p. 268) the communication of a person's gender identity to others, through behavior, clothing, hairstyle, and other means.

gender identity (p. 268) a person's identification as a woman, a man, or some combination of the two.

gender role (p. 271) a set of social expectations regarding behavior and attitudes based on a person's sex.

gender stratification (p. 276) the systematic and unequal distribution of power and resources in society between women and men.

glass ceiling (p. 279) the often-invisible barrier created by individual and institutional sexism that prevents qualified women from advancing to high levels of leadership and management.

heterosexism (p. 288) a set of attitudes and behavior that indicates an assumption that everyone is heterosexual.

heterosexuals (p. 287) people who are attracted to people of a different sex.

homophobia (p. 288) the disapproval and fear of LGBT people.

homosexuals (p. 287) people who are attracted to people of the same sex.

incest taboo (p. 286) a norm restricting sexual relations between certain relatives.

intersexual people (p. 266) individuals born with ambiguous reproductive or sexual anatomy.

matriarchy (p. 276) a social system dominated by women.

patriarchy (p. 276) a social system dominated by men.

second shift (p. 281) the phenomenon of employed women still having primary responsibility for housework and child care.

sex (p. 265) the biological distinction between females and males.

sexism (p. 270) the ideology that one sex is superior to the other.

sexual harassment (p. 283) unwelcome sexual advances, requests for sexual favors, and other verbal or physical harassment of a sexual nature.

sexual identity (p. 287) (or sexual orientation) our sense of self as it relates to the type of sexual attraction we have for others.

sexuality (p. 284) a person's sexual desires, behaviors, and identity.

transgender people (p. 268) individuals who identify with a gender different from the one associated with their sex.

transsexuals (p. 268) people who have sex reassignment surgery to change their physical appearance.

©P. Deliss/Corbis Documentary/Getty Images

12

Family and Religion

looking AHEAD

How does **culture** influence your understanding of family and religion?

How are the **structures** of family and religion that you experience today different from those of previous generations?

How does **power** operate in your family? How much **power** does religion have in your life?

©Honeymonster/Shutterstock

Joe Morrow was a middle-aged ordained Southern Baptist minister. Raised in the tradition of American Evangelicalism, he became a leader in his church, serving as a teacher, preacher, and pastoral counselor. He even went on international trips as a missionary. His family life revolved around his faith. His wife, Lisa, was a fellow Christian and they were raising their two young children in their faith's traditions. Religion helped structure their family life, through everything from prayer before meals and daily Bible study to church-based rituals and fellowship activities. As he puts it, "I lived a life devoted to bringing the 'Good News of Jesus Christ' to a world that I sincerely believed needed it" (Morrow 2017).

That is why it was so difficult for him to—as he puts it—"come out" as an atheist. In retrospect, he realizes his transformation was a long, slow process decades in the making. His growing understanding of scientific evidence for things such as human evolution contradicted his faith's teachings about the literal truths of the Bible. The more he studied science, the more it made sense to him. Not willing to see the Bible as merely allegorical, he came to reject religion entirely. Ironically, he writes, "The Bible states in the book of John, chapter eight, verse 32, 'Then you will know the truth, and the truth will set you free.' The truth is there is no God, and this truth has truly set me free."

Joe's realizations were difficult. "It's a scary place to be when you find yourself doubting everything you've based your life on for so long, when you find yourself at odds with so many people you have loved." Living in the South made it more difficult. "To a lot of religious people here in the Bible Belt, atheists are on the same level as rapists, devil worshipers, and pedophiles." That is why many non-believers in the region shy away from the atheist label, preferring terms like "humanist" or "freethinker" that carry less social stigma.

Joe, however, told his family directly: He was an atheist. Fortunately, he and his wife had a strong relationship that remained solid. (Years later, she also became an atheist.) Joe read accounts of other ministers who had left their faith (Barker 2006; DeWitt 2013) and learned about organizations such as "Recovering from Religion" that offer support for people who doubt their religious beliefs and are thinking of leaving their faith. Eventually, he went public with his story. Sounding a bit like the preacher he had once been, he encouraged others to do the same. "[B]rothers and sisters, you are not alone. Our numbers are growing. Come out with us!"

Joe Morrow's story is not an isolated one. Growing numbers of Americans–young people, especially–are leaving organized religion, sometimes declaring themselves atheists or agnostics, other times embracing personalized spiritual beliefs unattached to any organized religion (Voas and Chaves 2016). At the same time, though, the majority of Americans embrace religion from a wide variety of traditions and many make their faith a central part of their family life. Perhaps more than ever, these diverse views reflect religion in transition, both in the United States and around the world. In this chapter, we explore family and religion in a changing world, considering their variations within and across cultures, and their evolution over time.

Understanding the Family

We begin by examining the sociological definition of the family and the functions families perform in society.

The Family as a Social Institution

Sociologists define a **family** as *two or more people, related either by birth or through social commitment, who share resources, care*

for any dependents, and often maintain close emotional relationships. This broad definition helps identify "Who is family?" as well as "What do families do?" With its enduring patterns of relationships and behaviors, the family is a key *social institution.* Biologically based relationships—so-called blood relations—play a role in establishing family links, but social commitment such as adoption, marriage, civil union, or a steadfast enduring relationship can also establish **kinship,** or *family bonds.*

Ultimately, the meaning of family is culturally defined. A culture's notions about family establish, for example, whose relationships are significant, what obligations individuals have to each other, and what actions are expected from each. Families vary enormously because they are social constructions that reflect the norms and beliefs of different cultures at different points in history. However, as in all social institutions, it is the actions of individuals that maintain or change family structures. Finally, the family is influenced by broader social forces, some of which help create differences in power that perpetuate inequality.

Families take many forms. Some families include caregivers with children or elders as dependents; others consist solely of an adult couple. Some families live together, but some extend well beyond a single household. Love is often central to marriage and family life, but relationships in some marriages and families are quite formal, without loving, intimate interaction. Despite these variations, all families perform at least some core social functions, as we see next.

Social Functions of the Family

Sociologically speaking, what is important about families is less the form they take than the roles they play in society. Sociologists working in the functionalist tradition have highlighted several positive social functions of families (Parsons and Bales 1955).

- ***Social stability.*** Families create kinship ties. On a micro level, these relationships create a social bond between individuals and their relatives. On a macro level, kinship ties can create intricate social networks that include extended family and multiple generations. In preindustrial societies, these networks were an especially important source of social stability because they promoted solidarity. The marriage of two individuals could serve as a political alliance between separate kinship networks for common defense and shared prosperity. In industrialized societies, formal governmental and economic institutions have displaced many of the functions of these extended kinship networks, but smaller kinship units—families—continue to play a significant role.
- ***Material aid.*** Family members typically help one another by pooling their material resources and labor. In some cases, they work together to produce their necessities of life, including food, clothing, and shelter. In wage-based economies, earnings are used for the material benefit of family members, whereas unpaid labor in the home contributes to the family's maintenance and well-being. Regardless of the model, pooling resources is a common feature of families. Power within the family often resides with those in control of these resources.
- ***Descent and inheritance.*** *Descent* refers to the way people trace kinship over multiple generations. *Inheritance* refers to the rules regarding the reallocation of property within a family after someone dies. In modern industrial societies, descent is commonly *bilateral,* traced through both mother and father. In many traditional, preindustrial societies, descent is *unilineal,* traced through either the father (*patrilineal descent*) or the mother (*matrilineal descent*). Because the family serves as the primary agent for inheritance of property and other wealth, it is central to the reproduction of class in society. When inheritance favors male heirs, these practices can also help perpetuate gender inequality.
- ***Care and socialization of dependents.*** Families often care for a variety of dependents, especially children, family members with disabilities, and elders. In addition to teaching children practical skills, family members socialize them in particular values and beliefs, as we saw in Chapter 6, including gender roles, morality, and religion. Caring for elders is increasingly important as more people live longer and some of them begin to experience debilitating physical and mental conditions.
- ***Sexual regulation.*** Cultural norms typically indicate which sexual relations are socially acceptable. As we saw in Chapter 11, incest taboos prohibit sex with certain family members. Some societies have strict prohibitions against sex between unmarried couples. Marriage simultaneously legitimates a sexual partnership while typically defining sex outside the partnership as illegitimate.
- ***Emotional support.*** In addition to its practical functions, the modern family is often expected to be a source of emotional comfort and intense emotional bonds. Love is expected to figure centrally in marriage, and family members are expected to assist one another out of a sense of mutual responsibility, commitment, and concern.

The family is a social institution that retains its central role throughout the life course, from infancy to old age. However, in industrialized societies today, other social institutions have emerged to take on functions previously performed by the family. The education system instructs children and socializes them to be adults. The health care system cares for those who are sick and elderly.

on social theory

Functionalist theories emphasize a variety of tasks that are carried out by families. How did the family you grew up in accomplish these tasks?

thinking about structure

The patterns of behavior found in families are a part of social **structure**. What are some of the ways that your family structures social life by enabling specific patterns of behavior?

©PeopleImages/E+/Getty Images

©Inmagineasia/Getty Images

This Christian family saying grace before a meal (*left*) is the distinct product of U.S. culture. It contrasts starkly with this Muslim family from Malaysia (*right*), who are also about to share a meal. Their geography, culture, race, nationality, and religion may differ, yet both families perform remarkably similar social functions.

The government provides for our defense; citizenship, rather than membership in a clan, tribe, or other kin group, entitles us to protection.

Family Diversity in Global Context

Whatever type of family you belong to, it's probably very different from that of the Na, an ethnic minority at the foot of the Himalayan Mountains in southwestern China (Hua 2001). The Na are a matrilineal society, tracing descent from mothers to daughters. Until the 1990s, when the Chinese government began to pressure the Na to change their way of life, social concepts of marriage and fatherhood were irrelevant to them. Instead of getting married when they reached adulthood, Na men and women continued to live in their mothers' homes but were free to have consenting heterosexual relations with others in the village. A woman and her family raised any children she bore. Because monogamy was not expected of anyone, paternity was usually uncertain and unimportant. As this example suggests, families can vary radically in form and still perform essential social functions.

Global Variations in Family and Marriage

Families vary in a variety of ways, including the following:

- ***Family networks.*** Families vary by size and composition. A **nuclear family** (sometimes referred to as a conjugal family) *consists of a parent or parents and any children.* An **extended family** *consists of the nuclear family plus other relatives such as grandparents who commonly live together.* For example, in some cases newly married adults move in with one set of parents permanently. Such arrangements provide assistance for young couples, who are expected to care for their parents as they age.
- ***Marriage and cohabitation.*** The nature of the social bond between couples in a nuclear family varies. **Marriage** is *a social relationship that creates family ties, typically involves sexual intimacy, and is formalized by legal contract, religious ceremony, or both.* **Cohabitation** is *a social relationship that can create family ties and typically involves sexual intimacy, in which people live together as unmarried partners.* In some cultures cohabitation carries a negative stigma, whereas other cultures accept cohabitation as either a prelude to marriage or, increasingly, a legitimate alternative to it.
- ***Marriage eligibility.*** Cultures vary according to how they limit eligible marriage partners. Sometimes cultures enforce **endogamy,** *the restriction of marriage by either law or custom to people within the same social category.* People might be forbidden or discouraged from marrying across caste, class, or racial lines, for example. As we saw in Chapter 5, marriage across caste lines in India was once strictly forbidden. In other cases, cultures allow or require **exogamy,** *marriage between people from different social categories.* Because of the incest taboo, many societies require marriage outside of one's immediate family. A culture might at the same time require endogamy within certain categories but exogamy between others.
- ***Marriage arrangements.*** In some cultures, romantic love figures prominently in marriage and people are typically responsible for choosing their own mates. But marriages are arranged in some cultures based on economics and status rather than romantic love. In such arrangements, parents often play a significant and sometimes determining role in

©Patrick Aventurier/Gamma-Rapho/Getty Images

A Na woman in China poses with her daughters. The Na's matrilineal society, using a family form quite different from our own, successfully meets the basic functions of family as a social institution.

CORE CONCEPTS CHALLENGE *What effect do you think a family* **structure** *like that of the Na might have on gender relations and the relative status of women in Na society?*

choosing spouses for their children. In practice, most marriages for young people have some degree of parental involvement and include practical concerns such as financial stability as well as consideration of personal compatibility, if not outright love.

- ***Marriage forms.*** **Monogamy** is *the practice of restricting sexual relations to one partner.* In most marriages and committed long-term relationships, expectations of monogamy are strong, and violation of this norm can break up the union. However, some cultures permit **polygamy,** *a marriage system in which an individual is allowed multiple spouses.* The most common form of polygamy is *polygyny,* the marriage of one man to multiple wives. *Polyandry,* the marriage of one woman to multiple husbands, is less common but is still practiced in parts of Tibet.
- ***Gender roles.*** Families also vary in the degree to which they are organized along gender lines. In some cultures, the roles of women and men overlap. Women often work outside the home and men often play a significant—though usually secondary—role in childrearing and housework. In other cultures, however, gender distinctions within the family are relatively rigid. Stricter gender roles often preclude women from working outside the home and assign them sole responsibility for child care and maintenance of home life. Men take on the dominant role in life outside the home and are expected to provide financially for the family. In some societies, gender stratification overtly perpetuates male domination of women—physically, legally, and culturally.

Global Trends in Family Life

Despite the diversity of family types around the world, several large-scale trends can be identified in many parts of the world in recent years, though they are by no means universal or uniform in their progress (Abela and Walker 2014; Berardo and Shehan 2004):

- ***Families are getting smaller.*** In preindustrial societies, large families can be beneficial since they provide labor to work the land and otherwise contribute to the family's sustenance. As societies industrialize, however, a large family can become an economic burden, representing more mouths to feed with little economic return. Such economic incentives, coupled with greater access to contraception, have contributed to smaller families.
- ***Extended families are less common.*** As more of the world industrializes and as some regions become more affluent, more people can afford smaller households and the privacy they offer. As a result, the nuclear family household has been replacing extended family households.
- ***Open-mate selection is growing.*** Increasingly, the world's societies are moving away from arranged marriages, and some of the ethnic, racial, religious, and other boundaries that once limited mate selection are eroding. Instead, individual freedom in choosing a mate is growing.
- ***Women are waiting longer to get married.*** Often women postpone marriage in order to continue their education or to work outside the home. This delay contributes to smaller family size.
- ***People spend fewer years of their lives being married.*** Cohabitation and divorce rates are rising; as a result, people today are spending a smaller portion of their lives married than in the past.
- ***More women are joining the paid labor force.*** This increased economic independence for women has likely been a factor fueling some of the other changes in marriage and family life, including smaller families.
- ***Families increasingly include more elderly members.*** Advances in health information and medical treatment have prolonged human life, resulting in an increasingly large number of elderly people, some of whom require special care from family members.

The Social History of Family Life in the United States

Some of the broad global trends in family life are reflected in the United States, where families have been evolving and becoming more diverse than ever. These changes have been the subject of sometimes deeply divisive political debates. Often framed in

©ABC/Photofest

©20TH CENTURY FOX TV/Album/Newscom

FAST-FORWARD

Media Images of Families

Idealized images of the white, middle-class family, with its prominent patriarch, distinguished numerous television programs of the 1950s. Among them was *Beulah*, whose title character was a black servant—one of the first major television roles for an African American. Programs today are more diverse in the family types they portray. While still upper-middle class, the long-running hit *Modern Family* includes an interethnic family and a white same-sex couple who adopt an Asian child.

terms of "family values," many of these debates have centered on the decline of the "traditional" two-parent, one-wage-earner nuclear family and the perceived negative social consequences of this shift.

But social histories of the family and marriage (Coontz 2006, 2016; D'Emilio and Freedman 2012), along with the work of a variety of feminist scholars (Few-Demo 2014; Fox 2015), suggest that what is decried today as the "decline" of the family may simply be the most recent phase in ongoing change.

The Mythical "Traditional" Family

The popular story often told about family goes something like this: Once upon a time, U.S. society was anchored by strong, traditional, nuclear families headed by married heterosexual couples. The husband assumed the role of breadwinner, the wife that of homemaker. Such families were stable, with low divorce rates and healthy, well-mannered children who were taken care of by nurturing mothers and strong fathers. Compared to those idyllic days, the story continues, today's families have fallen apart, contributing to numerous social ills. Divorce is rampant, unwed mothers are common, fathers are absent. Further, even in two-parent families, the hectic schedules of two wage earners means families rarely spend time together, undermining social bonds and proper socialization. A picture emerges of families under threat, marriages in crisis, and children left neglected, unsupervised, and out of control (Popenoe 2009; Wilson 2002).

As we will see, families in America today have changed, and some of these changes have created new challenges for family life. But sociological research shows that the often-told story of the traditional family is an inaccurate and idealized one that leaves out important aspects of a more complicated truth.

Families Reconsidered: History, Class, and Race

The myth of the "traditional" family is built on a number of misconceptions (Coontz 2006, 2016; D'Emilio and Freedman 2012). First, rather than representing longstanding tradition, the two-parent, one-wage-earner family was dominant only during a brief window in U.S. history: the unique post–World War II period that combined relative economic affluence with limited aspirations for consumer goods. As a result of this historical anomaly, many people could live comfortably on a single income. But these conditions were not traditional; they did not exist prior to World War II and began to disappear by the 1970s.

Second, the notion of doting parents caring for their children and enforcing conservative social norms was also not traditional. In colonial America, parents routinely sent their children and adolescents to live in other households as servants and apprentices or simply let them be raised by other relatives. Sexual activity sometimes started at a young age—the "age of consent" in most states was twelve or younger, as late as 1896. In the early 1900s, thousands of children worked in factories, mines, and mills, often living away from their parents. In middle-class and affluent families, servants often handled childrearing tasks. Practices considered "traditional"—from the daily family sit-down dinner to much of what we take for granted as proper childrearing—are in reality mid-twentieth-century creations that represent just one of the many ways families have been structured at various times (Coontz 2006, 2016; Fischer and Hout 2006). Indeed, in recent years parents have been spending *more* time caring for children than they did in years past (Bianchi, Robinson, and Milkie 2006; Parker and Wang 2013). (The Through a Sociological

THROUGH A SOCIOLOGICAL LENS

Delaying Adulthood

©Studio 101/Alamy Stock Photo

"Children grow up so fast today." We've all heard this popular refrain. But as we saw in Chapter 6, the social trend has long been to *delay* entry into full adulthood, as with the creation of "adolescence." Today, for the first time since the 1800s, adults aged 18 to 34 are more likely to be residing in their parents' home than they are to be living with a spouse or partner in their own household (Fry 2016). This trend has provided rich fodder for popular media commentaries about "boomerang kids" and this generation's "failure to launch." Social scientists, though, see what they call *emerging adulthood* as simply another example of how life stages are based on social definitions that vary over time and are influenced by broader social developments (Arnett 2015; Henig 2010).

The transition to adulthood does not follow consistent age-specific rules. In the United States, you can join the military at 18 but can't drink alcohol legally until you are 21. You can drive at 16, but if you are a full-time student living at home, the Internal Revenue Service considers you a legal dependent until you are 24 years old, and children can be covered by their parents' health insurance plans through age 26. Emerging adulthood can be a period of creative exploration when young adults fully develop their identity, but it can also be a time of anxious instability and transitional preparation for an uncertain future.

Adulthood in the latter half of the twentieth century was often marked by the milestones of completing school, leaving home, becoming financially independent, marrying, and having a child. These milestones now commonly occur later in life. Many people are postponing or forgoing marriage and parenthood and pursuing more education than in the past, delaying the completion of their schooling. An uneven economy and high levels of student debt have created hurdles to financial security for many young adults. As a result, more young people are still living at home with a parent or parents. Compared to 1960, young people today are also about half as likely to be living with a spouse or romantic partner in their own household, once a key marker of full adulthood (Fry 2016).

Studies find variation in who is more likely to live in their parents' home: men more than women; blacks, Hispanics, and Asians more than whites; those with just a high school diploma more than those with a bachelor's degree. In turn, parents housing adult children are more likely than others to have higher incomes, live in a single family home, and own their home (Fry 2016; Kreider 2007).

During the twentieth century, the idea of adolescence as a distinct life phase was identified and eventually widely accepted. It remains to be seen if the same will happen to emerging adulthood in the twenty-first century.

think about it

1. *When do you think adulthood begins? Why?*
2. *How, if at all, has your life followed the trend of emerging adulthood?*

Lens box addresses other ways in which our understanding of family and life stages has changed.)

A third reason that the story of the "traditional" two-parent one-breadwinner (male) family is incomplete is that even at its height during the 1950s, it was never universal; it coexisted with other family forms. The idealized model was most prevalent among middle-class whites.

Better-paying unionized jobs also enabled some in the working class to adopt this family model, but many working-class and poor people did not have access to the good-paying jobs that enabled a single wage earner to support a family. As a result, in working-class and poor families, mothers were often part of the paid workforce long before the women's movement of the 1960s and 1970s. More than one-third (37.7 percent) of all women were already in the paid labor force in 1960 (Toossi 2002). That year, one of three children was in a household that was *not* a two-parent, one-wage-earner home; half of those were in two-wage-earner families (Cohen 2014).

As a result of discrimination, African Americans and other racial and ethnic minorities were especially likely to be shut out of better-paying employment and thus more likely to be in two-wage-earner families. In much of the South, especially, many black women had to leave their own children at home while they worked in white middle-class homes as servants, often caring for the children of their employers. In fact, just as today, the lifestyles of many middle-class and affluent families in the mid-twentieth century were made possible in part by the availability of low-wage minority workers to do household chores, cook, and care for children (Jones 2010).

Gender, Power, and the Family

The idealized traditional family of the mid-twentieth century was also highly stratified by gender, reflecting a deep imbalance of power (Coontz 2006, 2016). Fathers supported the family financially but were largely absent from the lives of their children and often spent leisure time away from the family. Childrearing was left almost entirely to the mother.

The barriers produced by this imbalance of power left many women deeply frustrated, but divorce was not an easy option due to its deep social stigma, strict divorce laws, and the lack of economic opportunities for women. Low divorce rates could mask profoundly unhappy relationships and dysfunctional family life. During this period, deep social ills, including child and spousal abuse, went largely unacknowledged and unaddressed publicly. Finally, families of the idealized traditional type were based strictly on heterosexual couples; gay and lesbian families would have been impossible to maintain publicly in the homophobic environment of the time.

Even today, when gender relations are far more equitable, family life continues to be shaped by the same inequalities that influence the broader society. Many contemporary heterosexual wedding ceremonies still carry the symbolic vestiges of patriarchy, with the father "giving away" his daughter to a new male who, in turn, bestows his name upon his bride. Growing up in a family, we learn, and often internalize, the gendered social expectations of a previous generation, as well as today's more subtle but enduring gender stratification. For example, one recent survey found that 70 percent of adults in the United States believe it is ideal for fathers of young children to work full time; in contrast, only 12 percent of adults think it is best for mothers with young children to hold full-time jobs (Pew Research Center 2013d). As we saw in Chapter 11, however, gendered social relations are complex interactions that people actively create in everyday life. Just as families can serve to perpetuate gender inequalities, they can also help create new expectations about gender equality.

Trends in U.S. Family Life

Although the families of the mid-twentieth century were never as homogeneous as is sometimes believed, today's families are more diverse than ever. Significant changes have occurred in family structure and other family characteristics. Some changes may be cause for concern; others merely represent new ways of meeting social needs. (See the Sociology Works box.)

FIGURE 12.1 | LIVING ARRANGEMENTS OF ADULTS 18 AND OLDER, SELECT YEARS

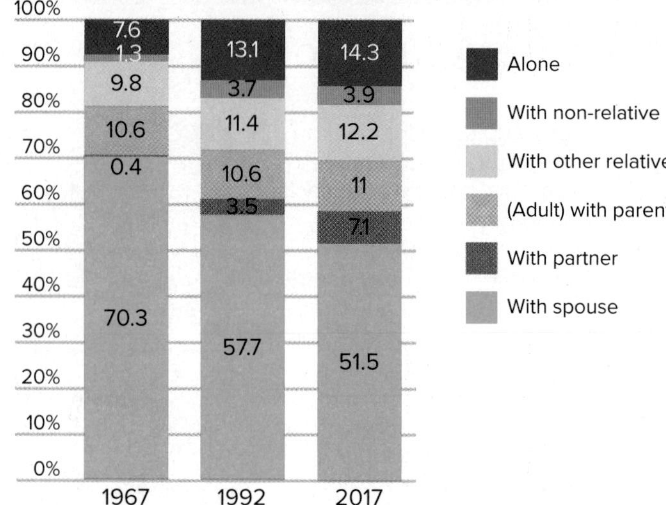

Source: U.S. Census Bureau, Current Population Survey, Annual Social and Economic Supplement, 1967 to 2017.

Marriage and Cohabitation

The growing diversity in family life over the last half century can be seen in how adults' living arrangements have changed (Figure 12.1). Fifty years ago, more than two-thirds of adults lived with a spouse. Now that proportion is closer to half. As married couples have become less common, other types of living arrangements have grown, especially people living with unmarried partners (7.1 percent) and people living alone (14.3 percent).

People in the United States today are less likely to marry than at any time in the nation's history. In recent years, about one in five adults 25 or older has never been married, double the percentage in 1960 (Parker and Stepler 2017; Wang and Parker 2014). Even if couples do marry, they are waiting longer to do so. As Figure 12.2 shows, in the 1950s the median age at marriage in the United States reached a modern-day historic low (another way in which this period was an anomaly), at about age 20 for women and 23 for men. In the 1960s, median age at first marriage began to rise, reaching 27.4 for women and 29.5 for men in 2017.

Marriage patterns are changing as well, with important implications for class inequality. In contrast to earlier years, marriage is now significantly more common among college-educated people than among others. Since people tend to marry a partner from roughly the same class background, college graduates are likely to marry other college graduates, often resulting in relatively affluent two-income households. Meanwhile, poor and working-class individuals likewise look for financial stability in a partner but are less likely to find it in people from their own class, a trend contributing to lower marriage rates among these economic strata (Cherlin 2014; Kuo and Raley 2016; Pew Research Center 2010a). When affluent people marry each other, and poorer people stay single, economic inequality between

SOCIOLOGY WORKS

April Bombai Pongtratic and Family Assistance

Many families face economic challenges in meeting basic needs and preparing for the future. Sociology major April Bombai Pongtratic helps make a difference in the lives of some low-income families in her work as an executive assistant at the Long Beach Community Action Partnership (CAP) in Long Beach, California. The agency is part of a national network of approximately 1,100 Community Action Partnerships whose mission is to empower low-income individuals and families with educational, social, or economic barriers and foster their personal development and self-sufficiency through education, training, and cultural awareness. For those who qualify, the Long Beach CAP offers a variety of free services, including youth programs, job training, energy assistance, and job development opportunities.

Pongtratic's role includes administrative duties, serving as a liaison between the agency and the community, and maintaining the agency's social networking platforms. Such work relates directly to her early interests. She notes, "I was always interested in how society works and how things like race, religion, economic status, and geographic location are factors in its operation. I felt that it was important to understand why there were certain inequalities and how some issues can be remedied. . . . I wanted to be an advocate for those who may not have an outlet to speak up for themselves."

Pongtratic cites hands-on experience as her best asset, but she's also benefited from her sociology training. "My studies in sociology have assisted me in my current job when writing grants or when dealing with clients and understanding the socioeconomic background they come from and the barriers they face," she says. And "knowing how to read statistics and apply them to reports has also been helpful."

She advises students, "If you feel passionate about what is going on in your community, stay with sociology. If you want a major that will keep your mind engaged, major in sociology because it allows you to explore a wide range of topics including health care, the justice system, economic issues, and race."

Pongtratic's work experience and preparation in sociology have put her on the front lines of efforts to help today's diverse families.

"If you feel passionate about what is going on in your community, stay with sociology. If you want a major that will keep your mind engaged, major in sociology."

Courtesy of April Bombai Pongtratic

April Bombai Pongtratic

think about it

1. *Did your family or someone you know ever benefit from social services of the sort provided by the Long Beach CAP? Explain.*
2. *In what specific ways might the skills that April Pongtratic learned from her sociology training help you in your planned (or current) career?*

households increases (Greenwood et al. 2014). In one exception to this trend, those who belong to a labor union are more likely to have higher income, better benefits, and more stable employment and thus are more likely to be married, even without a college degree (Sawhill 2013; Schneider and Reich 2014).

The decline in marriage rates has been accompanied by the growth of cohabitation—people living with an unmarried partner. The legal protections provided by marriage were always less relevant for poor and working-class people with few economic assets, so they were more likely to cohabit. Because of the social stigma attached to cohabitation, relatively few affluent heterosexual couples lived together before marriage. However, cohabitation increased substantially across class lines beginning in the 1960s, a period of cultural change during which people began to question the value and necessity of marriage. Also, the introduction of the birth control pill reduced the threat that sexual relationships would result in unwanted pregnancy (Coontz 2006; Lundberg, Pollak, and Stearns 2016).

In recent years, just over half of young adults live with their partner before they get married. However, living together does not mean that young people reject marriage. After the third year, nearly 6 in 10 couples who lived together are married, 19 percent have split up, and 23 percent continue to cohabitate. Some couples are choosing cohabitation as an alternative to marriage entirely, but about half of those who cohabit have been married in the past (Copen, Daniels, and Mosher 2013; Pew Research Center 2014d). Forty percent of cohabitating couples have children (about the same rate as married couples) (Vespa, Lewis, and Kreider 2013). Cohabitation, though, is still more common in many other countries than it is in the United States.

FIGURE 12.2 | MEDIAN AGE AT FIRST MARRIAGE, 1890–2017

Median age

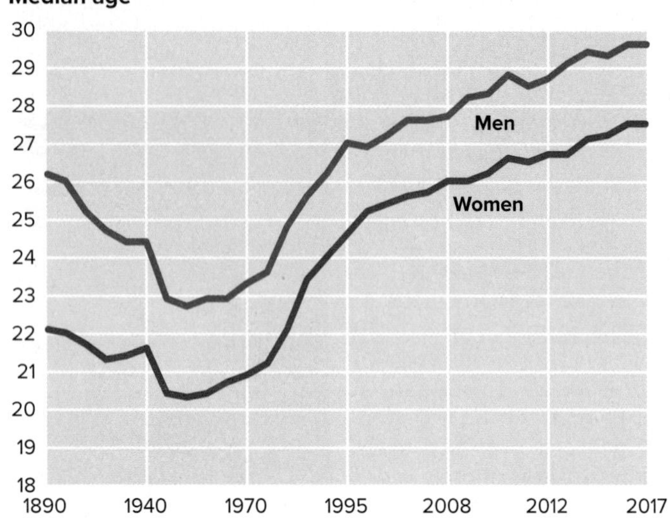

The age at first marriage has risen from historic lows in the 1950s to historic highs today. *Source:* U.S. Census Bureau, Current Population Survey, March and Annual Social and Economic Supplements, 2017 and earlier.

Divorce and Blended Families

The increasingly fluid nature of families can be seen in the rise of divorce. Once taboo, divorce has become common and accepted in mainstream society. There is even a *Divorce Magazine* that touts itself as providing help for "Generation Ex."

A variety of legal and cultural changes contributed to the sharp increase in divorce rates in the 1960s and 1970s. Legal restrictions severely limited divorces for much of U.S. history. To qualify, an individual typically had to prove wrongdoing such as infidelity or cruelty by his or her partner. That requirement changed in the 1970s with the introduction of "no-fault" divorces in which family courts could grant a divorce based solely on the request of one of the partners. Earlier generations often regarded marriage as a practical necessity and an irrevocable commitment. People who marry today are more likely to see it as a means to achieve personal happiness and self-fulfillment. If it fails to meet these expectations, couples are more willing to dissolve the partnership and, often, try again with a new partner. Ironically, as love increasingly has become the basis for marriage, it has raised the expectations for personal satisfaction and made the institution of marriage more fragile (Coontz 2006).

Nearly 50 percent of all first marriages eventually end in divorce. The annual rate of divorce more than doubled between the mid-1960s and early 1980s and then declined significantly (Figure 12.3).

Divorce varies by class and race. People with four-year college degrees tend to get married later than those with less education, but their marriages are less likely to end in divorce. This is probably due to the fact that more education contributes to financial stability, while financial troubles are a leading cause of divorce. Among women with bachelor's degrees, about 8 in 10 first marriages are still intact after 20 years, a rate that is double that of women who have not completed high school. Relatedly, nearly 7 in 10 first marriages for Asian women survive 20 years—the highest rate for any racial/ethnic group—but less than 4 in 10 marriages for African American women do—the lowest rate (Copen et al. 2012; Wang 2015).

FIGURE 12.3 | U.S. DIVORCE RATE, 1950–2016

Divorces per 1,000 population

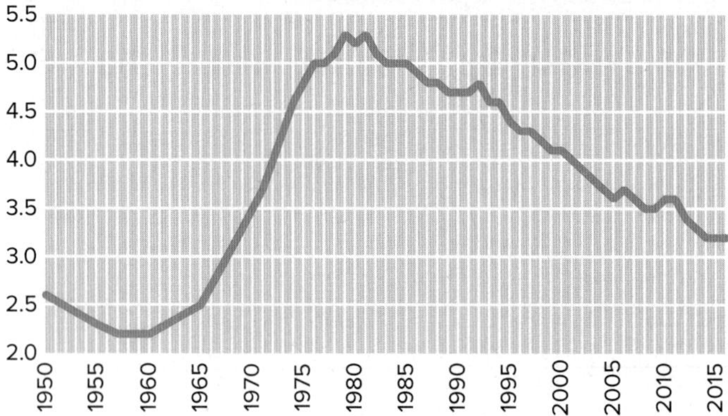

Divorce rates rose dramatically from 1960 to about 1980 but have since been falling. *Source:* National Center for Health Statistics.

Divorce can end an unhappy and damaging marriage and free children from feuding parents and a tension-filled home. However, it is stressful for everyone involved. As Cherlin (2013) summarizes, research shows the following:

- Almost all children experience an initial period of intense emotional upset after their parents separate.
- Most resume normal development without serious problems within about two years after the separation.
- A minority of children experience some long-term problems that may persist into adulthood.

After a divorce, the parent who has custody of the children—usually the mother—typically sees a decline in income, often leading to stressful changes such as relocation to less expensive housing and a change of schools. The stress of divorce can make parents less available to supervise their children or to provide them with emotional support.

Long-term issues affecting children can include higher risks of dropping out of school or having a child as a teenager and greater likelihood of being divorced as an adult (Cherlin 2013; McLanahan, Tach, and Schneider 2013). However, studies suggest that some of these effects are due to the lingering negative impact of conflict in their parents' bad marriage rather than to the divorce. Children whose parents are in marriages with high levels of conflict seem to do better if their parents divorce than if they stay together, whereas children of parents with low-conflict marriages do worse after divorce than those whose parents stay together (Amato and Booth 2000; Gagera, Yabikub, and Linvera 2016).

Increased divorce and subsequent remarriage have led to the creation of more "blended" stepfamilies that include two adults and at least one child from a previous marriage or relationship. However, such families are diverse and are not necessarily the result of divorce and remarriage. For example, some are created after the death of one parent and more than a third of blended families feature parents

FIGURE 12.4 | LIVING ARRANGEMENTS OF CHILDREN UNDER 18 YEARS OLD, SELECT YEARS

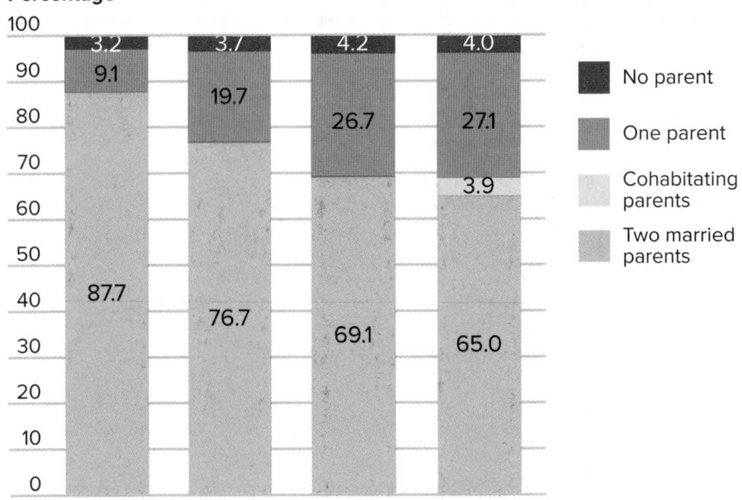

Note: Data regarding cohabitation are not available for earlier years; in those years, children with cohabitating parents are included in "one parent."
Source: Census Bureau, Current Population Survey (Table CH-1. Living Arrangements of Children under 18 Years Old: 1960 to Present; Table C3. Living Arrangements of Children under 18 Years and Marital Status of Parents: 2017).

who are not married. Transitioning to the new status of a blended family can be challenging as people negotiate new identities and family roles. However, children in such families show considerable resilience and even do better on some measures of well-being than do children in first-marriage families (Papernow 2013; Pryor 2014).

Unmarried and Single Parents

One of the most significant changes in family life has been the increased diversity of the families in which children are being raised. In 1960, more than 87 percent of children lived with two parents; by 2017 that figure was less than 70 percent (Figure 12.4). As "traditional" families have become less common, children are increasingly being raised in households with single parents or unmarried cohabitating parents.

In 1950, only 1 of every 25 births was to an unmarried woman. That figure rose consistently in subsequent decades, and in recent years about 2 of every 5 births have been to unmarried women (National Center for Health Statistics 2015a). But "unmarried" does not necessarily mean "single." Because researchers have started to collect such data, we now know that most births to unmarried women—nearly 6 in 10—occur in the context of cohabitating parents (Child Trends Databank 2015).

The percentage of single-parent families with children under age 18 has tripled, from about 9 percent in 1960 to 27 percent in 2017. While the percentage of single-parent fathers has been inching upward, more than 8 of 10 single-parent families are headed by women. The rate of single parenthood varies considerably by race and ethnicity. Asian Americans are least likely to raise children in a one-parent household, and African Americans most likely to do so (Figure 12.5).

The continuing increase in the prevalence of single-parent families is a cause for concern. Considerable evidence indicates that, all other things being equal, children fare better in households with two parents than they do in single-parent families. It does not appear to matter whether those parents are married or cohabitating or are a same-sex couple. Compared to their peers growing up in two-parent households, children from a single-parent household are twice as likely to drop out of high school, are more likely to become single parents themselves, and are one-and-a-half times more likely to have unsteady employment as young adults (Brown 2010; McLanahan, Tach, and Schneider 2013).

A major reason for this difference is that single-parent households are much more likely to be poor. In some cases, women are poor before they have children. In others, divorce leads to a drop in income. Either way, single-parent families generally do not have access to as many economic resources as do two-parent families. In addition, a single parent typically cannot provide the same level of supervision and social support that two parents can. Finally, divorce and limited financial resources tend to create unstable living situations for children. Divorce and poverty make it more likely that a child's family will move into a lower-income neighborhood with fewer resources, causing a loss of friends and connections to other sources of social support.

The United States and the nations of Western Europe have approached family issues in starkly different ways that have a disproportionate impact on single-parent families. The United States relies heavily on promoting marriage (and thus two incomes) to combat child poverty, whereas European nations limit income inequality (through progressive taxes) and provide more income

FIGURE 12.5 | U.S. CHILDREN AND FAMILY TYPE, 2017

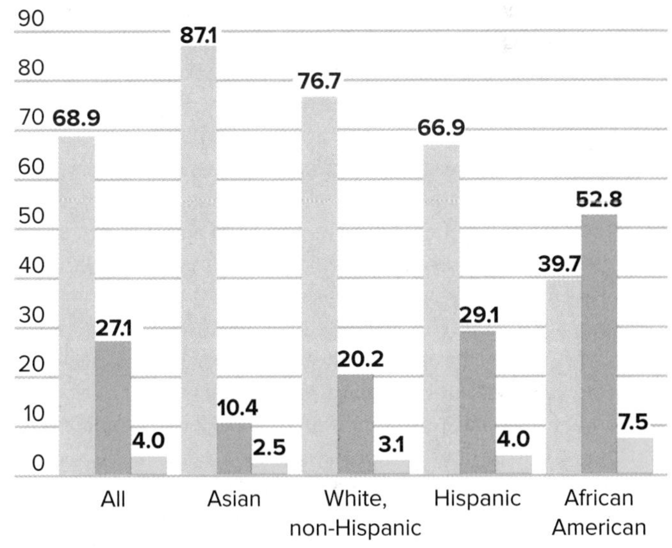

The family structure within which children are raised varies considerably by race and ethnicity. Children with "neither parent" often live with other relatives. *Source:* U.S. Census Bureau, Current Population Survey, 2017 Annual Social and Economic Supplement.

support to single parents. The result is that the children of single mothers in the United States are more than twice as likely to be poor than their counterparts in France and four to six times as likely to be poor than single mothers in Sweden, Belgium, and Finland (Heuveline and Weinshenker 2008; OECD 2018a).

Similarly, although many people struggle to balance the need to work in order to provide for their families with the responsibility to care for dependents, the United States generally does not offer government-supported child care or paid parental leave. In contrast, many European countries do. For example, France offers free, full-day child care for children up to two years old and provides preschool programs for children over age two on a sliding-scale fee. In Norway, a new mother must take six weeks of paid leave and fathers must take at least four weeks of paid paternity leave. In addition, either the mother or father is entitled to a full year of leave at 80 percent pay or 10 months at full pay (OECD 2018b; Ray, Gornick, and Schmitt 2009). The effect of such policies is greater support for healthy childrearing in all families.

Fertility Rates and Childfree Couples

Women are choosing to delay having children and are having fewer children over their lifetime, resulting in lower fertility rates. The U.S. **fertility rate**—*the average number of births per female*—has fluctuated throughout the country's history. At the beginning of the twentieth century, it was far higher than it is today, with women averaging between four and five children (though many of the children died at birth or soon thereafter). The fertility rate dropped to just over 2 births per woman during the Great Depression of the 1930s (likely due to women deciding to defer childbearing and to the effects of poverty on women's health), before rising during the "baby boom" of the 1950s to more than 3.5 births per woman. By the mid-1970s the average fertility rate had declined by nearly half to 1.8 births per woman (see Figure 12.6). It then rose to 2.1 by 2007 and has declined since then to about 1.8, below the rate needed to replace the current population (Fischer and Hout 2006; National Center for Health Statistics 2018).

Some women choose not to have children at all. In the 1970s, about one in ten women in her 40s (the end of childbearing years) was childless. That figure increased to about one in six in the 1990s and has stayed relatively stable since then (National Center for Health Statistics 2018).

National data on childlessness do not differentiate between those who cannot have children and those who choose to be childfree. The latter often face unique challenges in a society where wanting to have children is often considered a social norm and choosing to be childfree can be considered deviant. Researchers find that the reasons to be childless by choice are varied and include changing cultural norms and economic realities, such as women's increased reproductive choice and labor force participation. Also, those who remain childfree often cite the benefits that result from being childless by choice, including increased autonomy, opportunity for self-fulfillment, and freedom, as well as the ability to avoid negative lifestyle changes that typically come with parenthood (Blackstone and Stewart 2012, 2016).

FIGURE 12.6 | U.S. FERTILITY RATE

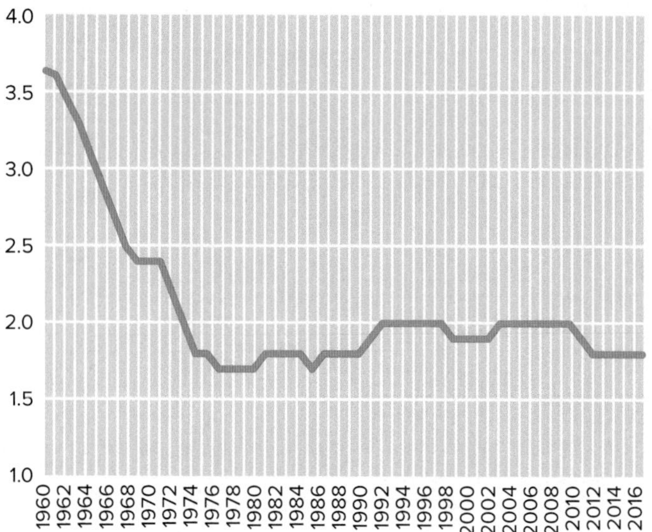

The U.S. fertility rate declined sharply after the "baby boom" years of the 1950s. Since the mid-1970s the rate has remained relatively stable. *Source:* National Center for Health Statistics. 2018.

Research has found that U.S. parents are 12 percent *less* happy than people who are childfree. The primary reason is the absence of family-friendly social policies that might relieve parental stress and strain. In countries where such policies exist, parents often are *more* happy than their childfree counterparts (Glass, Simon, and Andersson 2016).

Same-Sex Families

In addition to the structural changes in families already discussed in this chapter, the growing diversity of family life involves other features, including the rise of LGBT families. However, research on families has historically focused on heterosexual relationships, so there is less work on same-sex family life and even less on transgender parents. Even basic estimates about the number of same-sex couples is still being clarified as researchers find the best ways to collect accurate data (Lewis, Bates, and Streeter 2015). The 2020 census, for the first time, will have separate categories for "opposite-sex" and "same-sex" spouses and unmarried partners, which should produce better data. (The Census Bureau is also exploring if and how to add questions about sexual orientation and gender identity to future surveys [Holzberg et al. 2018].)

Currently, the U.S. Census Bureau estimates that there are about 887,000 same-sex couple households, split almost evenly between male-male (49 percent) and female-female (51 percent) households. These make up about 1.4 percent of all U.S. family households (U.S. Census Bureau 2017h). Over 60 percent of same-sex cohabitating couples are now married, a significant increase since the legalization of same-sex marriage nationwide in 2015 (Gallup 2017b). (See the Sociology in Action box for a discussion of sociological research and this case.)

Research on LGBT families is growing, revealing considerable diversity (Moore and Stambolis-Ruhstorfer 2013; van Eeden-Moorefield et al. 2018). We know, for example, that 35 percent of

SOCIOLOGY in ACTION

Research, Public Policy, and the Law

Sociological research often provides information that is relevant in policymaking and judicial processes. One way sociologists participate in public life is by communicating social science research findings to public officials, including legislators and the courts. When the U.S. Supreme Court considered whether same-sex couples had the right to marry in the 2015 case *Obergefell v. Hodges,* the American Sociological Association (ASA) offered the Court a compelling assessment of the conclusions of scholarly research on the key questions.

One of the foundations of laws limiting marriage to heterosexuals has long been the claim that it is harmful to children to live in a household with gay parents. In its "friend of the court" brief to the Supreme Court, the ASA tackled this claim head-on, explaining that its comprehensive review of research shows no evidence of such harmful effects on children. "The clear and consistent social science consensus is that children raised by same-sex parents fare just as well as children raised by different-sex parents" (ASA 2015, 2).

The ASA's brief provided the justices with a comprehensive review of research findings on the experiences of children whose parents are same-sex couples. This review details the range of ways that children of same-sex couples and different-sex parents are similar: academic performance, cognitive development, social development, psychological health, teenage sexual activity, substance abuse, and delinquent behavior. Measures of each of these dimensions consistently show no significant differences in the outcomes for children raised by gay couples in comparison to those raised by straight couples. Summarizing the ASA's assessment, the brief concludes that "the overwhelming body of social science research confirms that a child's well-being is not dependent on whether the child's parents are of the same or different sex. Instead, the consensus is that the key factors affecting child well-being are stable family environments and greater parental socioeconomic resources, neither of which is related to the sex or sexual orientation of a child's parents" (13).

Given these findings, the ASA's brief articulated a clear position in support of marriage rights for same-sex couples. As its authors explicitly argued, research indicates that permitting same-sex couples to marry "has the potential to improve child well-being insofar as the institution of marriage may provide social and legal support to families and enhances family stability, which are key drivers of positive child outcomes" (27).

©Bao Dandan/chine nouvelle/SIPA/Newscom

The American Sociological Association (ASA) weighed in on the case in which the Supreme Court ruled that the U.S. Constitution guarantees the right of same-sex couples to marry. The ASA pointed out that research overwhelmingly shows that children fare as well when raised by same-sex parents as they do with different-sex parents.

When the Supreme Court announced its landmark decision recognizing the right of same-sex couples to marry, sociologists generally praised the decision. But many also cautioned that a single court ruling had not solved all problems. As one noted, "There's a whole lot more work to be done, both in terms of completing the equalization of rights and the broader work of social justice and institutional change" (Gamson 2015).

think about it

1. *Do you think it is appropriate for social scientists to weigh in on research findings to inform current debates? Why or why not?*
2. *On what other issues do you think a summary of sociological research findings could be useful to policymakers or judges?*

LGBT people live in the South and that same-sex couples are more likely to be interracial than are different-sex couples. Same-sex couples without children typically have attained relatively high levels of education and enjoy a middle-class income. In contrast, same-sex couples with children are more likely to be working class or poor.

Same-sex couples most commonly become parents as a result of a previous heterosexual relationship on the part of one partner. But as social acceptance of same-sex families grows, more same-sex couples are initiating families through adoption, donor insemination, or surrogacy (Biblarz and Savci 2010). In fact, compared to their heterosexual counterparts, same-sex couples raising children are four times as likely to be raising an adopted child (Mallon 2017). As the American Sociological Association (2015) summarizes, the "clear and consistent social science

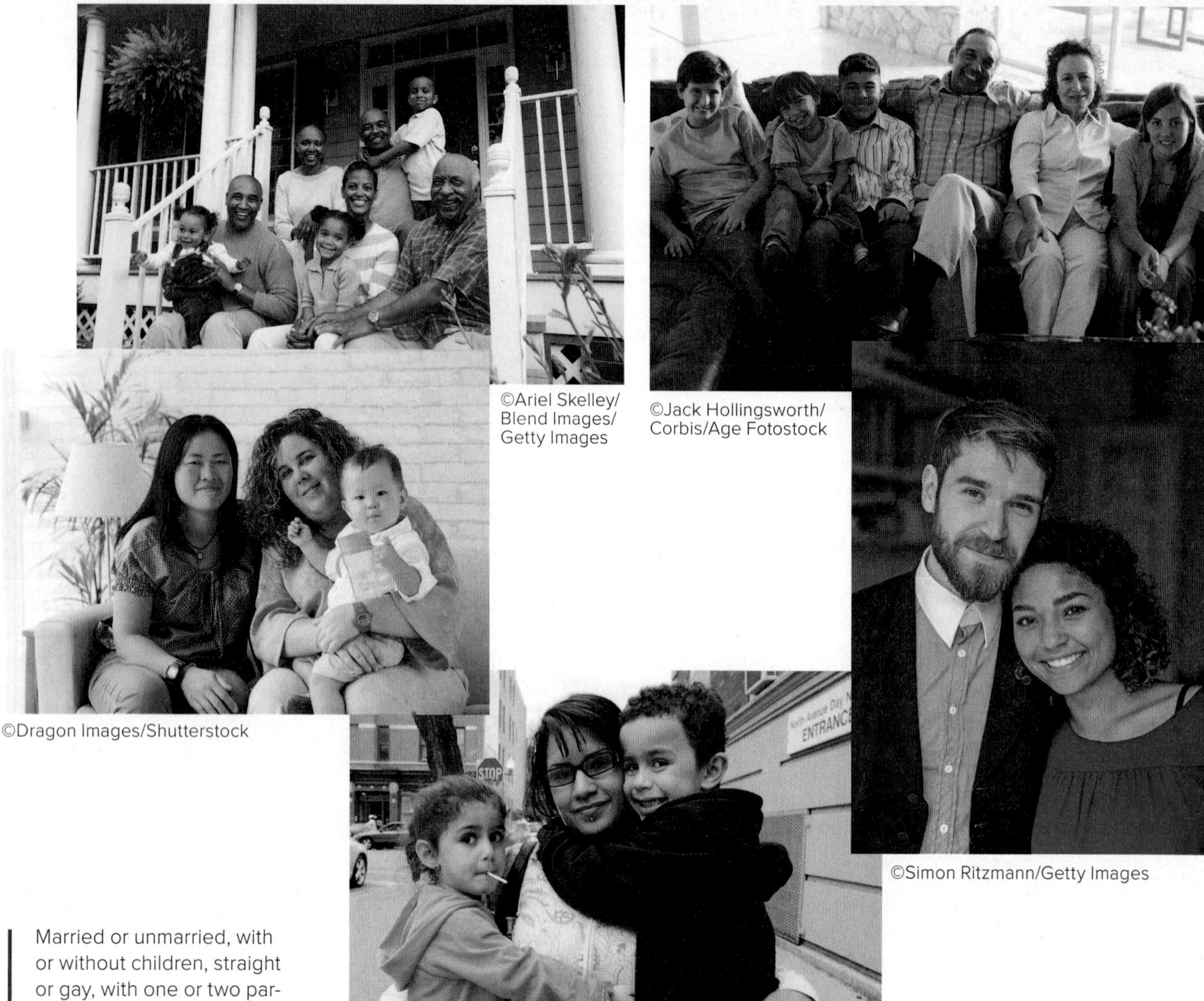

©Ariel Skelley/Blend Images/Getty Images

©Jack Hollingsworth/Corbis/Age Fotostock

©Dragon Images/Shutterstock

©Simon Ritzmann/Getty Images

©Charles Rex Arbogast/AP Images

Married or unmarried, with or without children, straight or gay, with one or two parents, nuclear or extended, blended, interracial—all of these and more are now part of the diverse fabric of American families.

consensus is that children raised by same-sex parents fare just as well as children raised by different-sex parents . . . across a wide spectrum of factors [including] academic performance and cognitive development, social development, psychological health, early sexual activity, and substance abuse and behavioral problems" (p. 5).

Yet research also suggests that same-sex couples may differ in some ways from different-sex couples. For example, same-sex parents appear to be less concerned about gender nonconformity, are less likely to use corporal punishment, and are more likely to share child care duties equally (Biblarz and Stacey 2010). Same-sex couples also have more conversations about end-of-life planning than heterosexual couples, primarily because of the absence of legal protections and concerns about discriminatory actions by family members (Thomeer et al. 2017).

Interracial and Interethnic Families

As we saw in Chapter 10, interracial and interethnic marriages have increased significantly in recent decades, contributing to another form of family diversity. In 1967, just 3 percent of new marriages were intermarriages; by 2016 that figure had grown sixfold to 18 percent. That means one in six new marriages is now interracial or interethnic, while one in ten marriages overall is an intermarriage. Intermarriage is about a third more common among college-educated newlyweds (19 percent) compared to those with a high-school diploma or less (14 percent). In order of commonality, intermarriages include Hispanics and non-Hispanic whites (42 percent), Asians and whites (15 percent), multiracial people and whites (12 percent), blacks and whites

(11 percent), Hispanics and blacks (5 percent) (Livingston and Brown 2017). Indications are that such intermarriages will continue to become a more common feature of family life.

Understanding Religion

Like the family, religion is an enduring social institution that varies across cultures and is undergoing significant change. Many people are socialized into a religion at an early age in the context of the family. In this section we explore how sociologists have approached religion as a topic of sociological study, examine how it varies across cultures, and consider how it is changing in contemporary society.

The Sociology of Religion

As a social science, sociology is committed to understanding the social world—including religion—based on empirical evidence. But people experience religion typically through **faith**—*belief grounded in personal conviction or divine revelation rather than scientific evidence.* How can social science study a faith-based phenomenon? That is, how can there be a sociology of religion? Sociologists don't try to assess the conflicting truth claims of the world's many religions; they study religion to understand the role it plays in social life. As we saw in Chapter 7, the *Thomas theorem* notes that if people define situations as real, they are real in their consequences. For sociologists, the impact of religion in social life comes from some people's *believing* in the truth of their faiths and adjusting their behavior accordingly.

Religion has figured prominently throughout human history and consequently attracted the attention of some of the earliest sociologists. Here we take a look at Emile Durkheim's, Karl Marx's, and Max Weber's still influential analyses of religion and then turn to Peter Berger's more recent contribution.

Durkheim on Religion: The Sacred and the Profane

In his last major work, *The Elementary Forms of the Religious Life,* Emile Durkheim ([1915] 2001) focused on the most rudimentary forms of religion and their social functions. The descendant of a long line of rabbis in predominantly Christian France, who himself became agnostic, Durkheim was familiar with a variety of religious traditions. He used the religion of Australian aborigines as a key case study because he believed it embodied the simplified essential elements of religion.

Durkheim concluded that all religions share three basic elements:

- A set of core beliefs
- A set of ritual practices
- A community of adherents

In Durkheim's view, the most important belief of any religion is that the world can be divided into the "sacred" and the "profane." The **sacred** is *something extraordinary, to be treated respectfully, with reverence and awe.* Almost anything can be sacred, including objects, actions, and words. Sacred texts, idols, gods, symbols, gestures, and even animals populate various religions. In various versions of Christianity, for example, the Bible, holy water, consecrated bread and wine, and the crucifix can all be considered sacred. What makes the sacred special is that it is set apart from the **profane,** or *the ordinary world of everyday life.*

Rituals are *symbolic actions, typically performed at specified times, that help evoke an emotional bond among participants.* The sacred is embodied in ritual practices such as attending worship services, taking communion, offering sacrifices, reciting prayers or incantations (verbal charms or spells), singing, dancing, and giving blessings. These actions help create a sense of a shared community that has common norms and values. With rituals, whether a believer's prayers are "answered" is less significant

©Jahi Chikwendiu/The Washington Post/Getty Images

©Eric Lafforgue/Alamy Stock Photo

A Christian evangelical gathering and a Haitian voodoo ceremony are examples of rituals. Each is directed at something considered to be sacred, and each helps affirm a shared moral community of believers. How would you analyze a religious ritual using Durkheim's concepts?

than the fact that praying can bring comfort and strength to the faithful, as well as a sense of social solidarity to a group that shares this practice.

Beliefs and practices are developed and passed on through communities of *adherents*–those who share a faith and join in its rituals. A community of adherents becomes a **church** when it has developed into a more *formal religious organization with broad mainstream acceptance.* Churches often have well-organized subgroups with varying interpretations of their faith, known as *denominations,* such as Baptists and Methodists among Christians and Sunni and Shiite among Muslims. A **sect** is *a small dissenting faction of a church that promotes new beliefs or practices.* Newer religious communities typically must struggle to gain acceptance as a legitimate church from mainstream society. Those with power in society–including established churches–sometimes label *small religious communities whose beliefs and practices are at odds with the dominant culture* as **cults,** often to discredit them.

SPOTLIGHT

on social theory

Symbolic interactionist theories focus on how people use shared symbols and construct society as a result of their everyday interactions. How do the religious rituals you may have observed illustrate this idea?

The Social Functions of Religion

Durkheim's classic analysis is the basis for a sociological definition of **religion:** *a unified system of beliefs and ritual practices relating to the sacred that bond people into a moral community.* Significantly, this definition does not include a reference to **theism**–*a belief in the existence of a god or gods.* Religion needs to include an idea of the sacred but not necessarily a supernatural power or a god. Buddhism, for example, teaches followers to seek enlightenment through right conduct but does not necessarily include belief in any supernatural forces. Similarly, some new religious movements focus on the common bonds that link humanity rather than the divine or supernatural.

SPOTLIGHT

on social theory

Functionalist approaches to religion focus on its positive contributions to social life. Does religion serve some of the purposes in your life that functionalist theory suggests? Why or why not?

Regardless of its particular teachings, religion serves a variety of functions:

- ***Religion promotes social solidarity.*** When people of similar beliefs participate in religious activities, they develop social bonds (or "fellowship"). Because of these shared beliefs and practices, followers often consider themselves to be part of a special group (for example, "saved," "the chosen people," or "enlightened") that differentiates them from outsiders and promotes internal solidarity.
- ***Religion operates as a form of social control.*** By promoting values and norms, religious organizations can play an important role in socialization. Believers in a particular religion are typically expected to adhere to a code of ethics and to avoid behaviors labeled as immoral, sinful, evil, and worthy of punishment. These regulations are taught and promoted through religious activities as well as in sacred texts. The social control produced by religion is especially powerful because adherents often believe the religion's mandates emanate from the sacred. The Bible's commandments–and most other religions' teachings–would carry less moral authority if they were understood as having been drafted by a committee of humans rather than as being part of the "word of God."
- ***Religion can provide believers with deep social-psychological benefits.*** For example, it can relieve people's fears and anxieties about difficult topics, such as death, human suffering, and powerlessness, and can serve as a source of strength for those struggling through life's challenges. The belief in divine intervention can be a source of hope and comfort, especially in times of crisis. Religion can provide answers to challenging questions such as the origin of life and the purpose of human existence. The moral code of a religion also provides a guide for living, reducing the burden of making individual judgments and decisions.
- ***Religion can motivate social action.*** The morals and values taught through religion can move people to take action in society. Sometimes that action focuses on *proselytizing*–spreading an adherent's religious beliefs–through everything from door-to-door testimonials and religious broadcasting to international missionary work and military conquest. Action can also involve everything from charity work and service to the poor to terrorist actions and the oppression of nonbelievers. Drawing on their moral beliefs, religious adherents also engage in action for what they see as social justice, such as antiwar protests or antiabortion organizing.

Religion can also be dysfunctional. For example, the social solidarity promoted by religion can lead to intolerance toward people of differing beliefs and can fuel conflict between different faiths. Similarly, the norms and values promoted by religion may create a rigid orthodoxy (traditional beliefs that are judged to be true and correct) that prevents needed changes in new circumstances. The Catholic Church sometimes resisted the insights of emerging science that contradicted religious doctrine, as when it convicted Galileo of heresy for arguing that the earth revolved around the sun (Lindberg and Numbers 2008). Even today, conservative religious belief is associated with skepticism about science (Sherkat 2017). More broadly, some religious traditions–but not others–have long been used to oppose women's equality, abortion rights, same-sex marriage, LGBT rights, and other social changes (Fowler et al. 2014; Wald and Calhoun-Brown 2014). In addition, the emotional consolation and support that religion provides can sometimes discourage action for necessary social change–an idea that Karl Marx ([1844] 1978) emphasized, as we see later.

Society and Religion

For Durkheim, humans create gods and religions to embody the shared values of a society, which he termed the *collective conscience* (see Chapter 1).

Because these values vary across cultures and change over time, notions of gods and religion also vary. Nevertheless, many religions share a comparable core message. For example, some variation of the **ethic of reciprocity**—*the "golden rule" that encourages people to treat others as they would like to be treated*—is a part of all major religions including Christianity ("love your neighbor as yourself"), Islam ("Hurt no one so that no one may hurt you"), and Hinduism (the concept of *karma*—the idea that a person's actions toward others determine his or her fate in the next incarnation).

The sacred represents the shared values of a society. As Durkheim ([1915] 2001) put it, "The idea of society is the soul of religion" (314). That is, the sacred—in whatever forms it was or is imagined—is a symbol for society. Thus it is common for religions to teach some variation of the following:

- God is far more powerful than any individual.
- God exists everywhere; God is both within all of us and outside us.
- God makes us what we are (I am the product of God; without God, I am nothing).
- In return for God's gifts, we are obligated to adhere to God's rules.
- God has laid out the way we should live.
- If we violate God's wishes, we risk being punished or cast out.
- Those who do not adhere to ways of God cannot be trusted.

If we replace the word *God* in these statements with *society,* each one still makes sense. As we have seen throughout this text, society is indeed something bigger and more powerful than any individual; we are dependent on the creations of society—its social structures—for our existence and for our identity; and society's continued functioning requires that we adhere to basic social norms. In a sense, for Durkheim, religion is society worshipping itself.

Yet adherents of any particular religion do not understand their beliefs in this way. Instead, they often ascribe mystical, magical, supernatural, or spiritual powers to their faith. Sociologically speaking, though, the result is the same: a moral community.

Marx on Religion: The Opium of the People

Karl Marx warned against the dark side of religion. He never focused significantly on religion in his work but famously described it as "the opium of the people." His words are best understood if read with more context:

> *Man makes religion,* religion does not make man. . . . Religion is the sigh of the oppressed creature, the sentiment of a heartless world, and the soul of soulless conditions. It is the *opium* of the people. The abolition of religion as the *illusory* happiness of men is a demand for their *real* happiness. The call to abandon their illusions about their condition is a *call to abandon a condition which requires illusions.* (Marx [1844] 1978, 53–54)

In its broader context, the famous phrase takes on new nuances. As Durkheim would over 70 years later, Marx saw gods and religion as human creations. By contrast, however, Marx focused on two dimensions of religion that differed from Durkheim's later emphases:

- ***Religion offers false comfort to believers.*** Marx argued that religion's power over people derived from the temporary solace it provided from the real and relentless oppression and emptiness of daily life. For Marx this was a tragedy because, for example, although religions might encourage charity toward the poor, they accepted poverty as inevitable. Many believers interpreted quotes, such as Jesus's saying, "Blessed are you who are poor, for yours is the kingdom of God" (Luke 6:20–21), as meaning that followers should take comfort in a blissful afterlife rather than seek justice here on earth. Like a narcotic, claimed Marx, religion provides temporary relief from a painful, heartless life of oppression but does nothing to address the conditions that produce such pain in the first place.
- ***People in power manipulate religion.*** Carrying Marx's opium analogy further, we might say that members of the ruling class—the very people who benefit from economic oppression—play the role of drug dealers by encouraging this addiction. In Marx's view, religion serves the interests of the ruling class by keeping the oppressed compliant and docile. Rather than working here and now for real social change, religion encourages the downtrodden instead to anticipate an imaginary world where they will find relief in the future.

For Marx, then, religion is merely a reflection of the underlying economic structure. He saw religion as a problem only insofar as it is a form of "false consciousness" that prevents people from seeing the true source of their unhappiness.

SPOTLIGHT on social theory

Marxist **conflict theory** argues that those in power use religion to promote "false consciousness" among ordinary people. Can you think of examples in which people who are following their religious beliefs might be working against their material self-interests?

Revolutionary movements inspired by Marx often invoked these ideas to advocate atheism. However, others, including Marx's collaborator Friedrich Engels, recognized that religious belief could support radical political action (Marx and Engels 2008). In the United States, for example, religious activists have long used their faith to advocate for the poor (Day 1952), fight for civil rights (Marsh 2006), oppose war (Macgregor 1954), and support labor unions (Interfaith Worker Justice 2018). Beginning in the 1960s, some Latin American Catholic leaders combined their religious belief with Marxist economic critiques to create **liberation theology,** *a form of Christian belief dedicated to combating poverty and other forms of social injustice.* Today, many variations of liberation theology exist around the world, addressing issues such as the inequalities created by global capitalism and environmental degradation (Barger 2018; Floyd-Thomas and Pinn 2010).

Weber on Religion: Disenchantment of the World

Max Weber paid special attention to the relationship between religion and economic life. As we saw in Chapter 1, in *The Protestant Ethic and the Spirit of Capitalism,* Weber ([1905] 1958) described how some Protestant values unintentionally contributed to the rise of capitalism and industrialization. Calvinist Protestants believed in extreme self-denial, frugality, and hard work and saw the resulting economic success as a sign of divine favor. According to Weber, this belief system, which he called *the Protestant ethic,* and the drive to earn and save, which he called the *spirit of capitalism,* allowed adherents to accumulate the considerable capital necessary to invest in the machinery of industrialization. In later works, he showed how religions in China and India, by not promoting such values, contributed to the delayed emergence of capitalism in those countries.

One of Weber's other major contributions, however, was to detail the long-term process by which rationality replaced tradition as the basis for organizing social and economic life (see Chapter 1). This *rationalization of society* was accompanied by a decline in the influence of religion. As Weber ([1919] 1946b) famously put it—quoting a phrase from German playwright Friedrich Schiller—"The fate of our times is characterized by rationalization and intellectualization and, above all, the 'disenchantment of the world'" (155). The ability of science and rational thought to explain more and more of the world—sometimes in ways that clashed with religious beliefs—helped displace the power of religion in daily life. But as we saw in Chapter 5, Weber knew that charismatic leaders, including religious leaders, could sometimes inspire groups of people to act.

Weber ([1915] 1946a) foresaw the negative consequences of rationalization, including the rise of the impersonal "iron cage" of bureaucracy and the influence of money:

> Money is the most abstract and "impersonal" element that exists in human life. The more the world of the modern capitalist economy follows its own immanent [or inherent] laws, the less accessible it is to any imaginable relationship with a religious ethic of brotherliness. (331)

Thus Weber was writing not just about rationalization and the secularization of *society* but also about *personal* disenchantment; without religion's "ethic of brotherliness," individual life might have no clear meaning or direction. Weber noted that every religion begins precisely with the assumption that life *has* meaning and that religion's promise is to make this meaning accessible and understandable.

By contrast, science is silent on the issue of meaning. Perhaps, as existentialist philosophy contends, life is without meaning until individuals create it (Hayim 1995). The absence of God presents the possibility of a radically free individual. But this freedom brings with it heavy responsibilities and challenges. Some people, as Weber ([1919] 1946b) put it, "cannot bear the fate of the times" and instead return to seek solace in religion, where "[t]he arms of old churches are opened widely and compassionately" for them (155).

Berger on Religion: The Sacred Canopy

Because rationalization of society often has seemed to drain life of its meaning, people continue to long for the comfort of the sacred. A half century after Weber, sociologist Peter Berger (1967) emphasized that religion is primarily an effort to create a meaningful reality in which to live. Religion helps us make sense of our existence and provides order to an otherwise chaotic world. It serves as a "shield against terror," protecting humans from the "danger of meaninglessness" in which "the individual is submerged in a world of disorder, senselessness, and madness" (22). Thus religion provides a "sacred canopy" under which, together, a society's members can find shelter.

However, as the metaphor suggests, religion works best when all members of a society share a single interpretation of reality—when a single canopy provides shelter. As we will see, in the contemporary world, competing and incompatible interpretations have emerged, changing the nature of religion and perhaps even helping undermine it.

Religion in Global Context

In this section we sketch briefly the distribution of religious traditions and nonbelief around the world and in the United States. We also examine the rise of secularism in Western society and the fundamentalist resistance to it.

Religion throughout the World

About 84 percent of humanity identifies with one of the world's hundreds of religions, though not all those people are active participants in communities of worship. As shown in Figure 12.7, Christianity is the most widespread religion, with a significant presence in all areas except Asia/Pacific and the Middle East/North Africa. In contrast, Islam is relatively narrowly concentrated, with the highest percentage of Muslims in the Middle East and North Africa. About 16 percent of the world's population is nonreligious—including agnostics and atheists—who are found most commonly in Asia, Europe, and North America (Pew-Templeton Global Religious Futures Project 2018).

People in the world's wealthier, modernized nations are least likely to be religiously active, as measured, for example,

thinking about culture

How can religion help promote the values cherished in a **culture**?

FIGURE 12.7 | MAJOR RELIGIOUS TRADITIONS BY REGION, 2020 ESTIMATE

Percentage

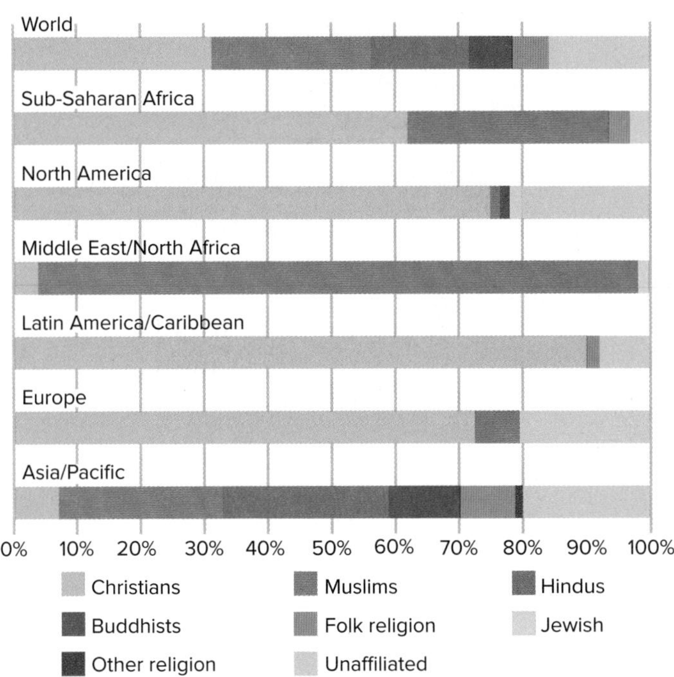

What you believe is influenced by where you live. Two-thirds of the world's population adheres to one of the world's three largest religious traditions: Christianity (31.1 percent), Islam (24.9 percent), or Hinduism (15.2 percent). *Source:* Pew-Templeton Global Religious Futures Project 2018.

FIGURE 12.8 | GLOBAL ATTENDANCE AT WEEKLY RELIGIOUS SERVICES

Percentage who attend religious services at least weekly

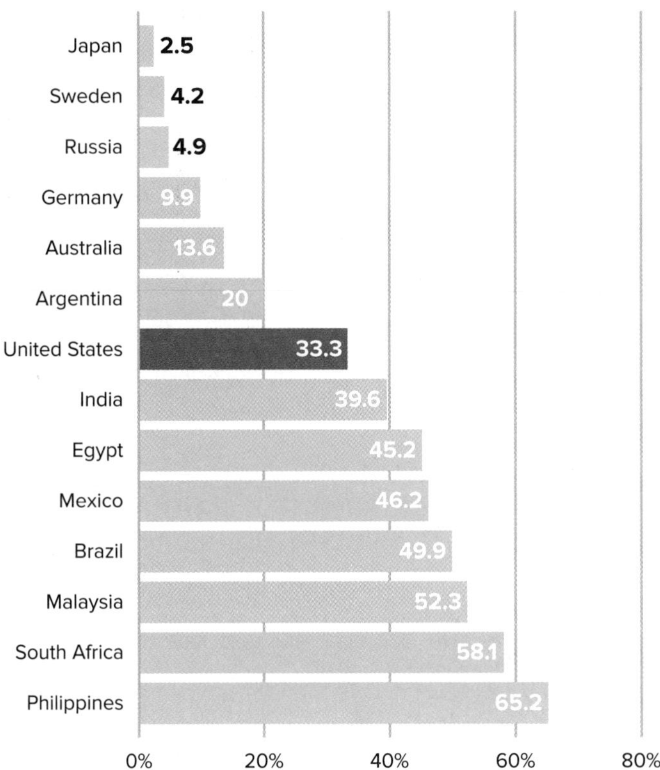

People in the United States (purple) are typically less religious than those in poorer, more traditional societies such as Egypt and Malaysia. However, Americans report the highest level of religious participation among wealthy industrialized societies, surpassing countries such as Japan and Germany. *Source:* World Values Survey 2010–2014.

by the percentage of the population who attend weekly services (Figure 12.8). Following this pattern, religious participation in the United States is lower than in most of the world's countries. However, among wealthy modernized nations, the United States has the highest rate of religious participation.

Religious Adherence in the United States

Data on religious affiliation varies somewhat based on how questions are asked and how response categories are structured. About 7 in 10 adult Americans (70.6 percent) identify as Christian. Of these, Protestants (46.6 percent) and Catholics (20.8 percent) are the largest subgroups. Protestantism, though, is fragmented into hundreds of denominations. Although only 1.9 percent of the adult population, Jews make up the largest non-Christian religion in the United States; Muslims are second with 0.9 percent. Over one-fifth (22.8 percent) of the population consists of people unaffiliated with any religion (Pew Research Center 2015f).

Religious affiliations are subject to significant shifts (Figure 12.9), and more than a quarter (28 percent) of all adults—44 percent if we include people shifting between Protestant denominations—have left the religion of their childhood (Pew Forum on Religion and Public Life 2008a). Sometimes they move to another faith; sometimes they leave religion altogether. Nearly a third of people raised Catholic have left the Church, the biggest loss of any faith, but Catholic numbers have been supplemented by recent immigrants, among whom Catholics outnumber Protestants by nearly two-to-one. Compared to the population as a whole, recent immigrants are also more likely to be Muslim, Hindu, or Buddhist, but these adherents still make up only a tiny fraction of the U.S. population. Still, as a result of declining membership and a growing unaffiliated population, Protestants now make up less than half of the U.S. population (Pew Research Center 2015f).

The fastest-growing religious category in recent years has been the "unaffiliated" (22.8 percent in 2015), whose percentage of the overall population has doubled since the early 1990s. This category includes atheists (3.1 percent), agnostics (4 percent), and those who simply describe their religion as "nothing in particular" (15.8 percent). The unaffiliated do not identify with a specific religious group, but they are not uniformly secular. One-third (33 percent) of the unaffiliated say that religion is very or

FIGURE 12.9 | RELIGIOUS COMPOSITION OF THE UNITED STATES, 1972–2016

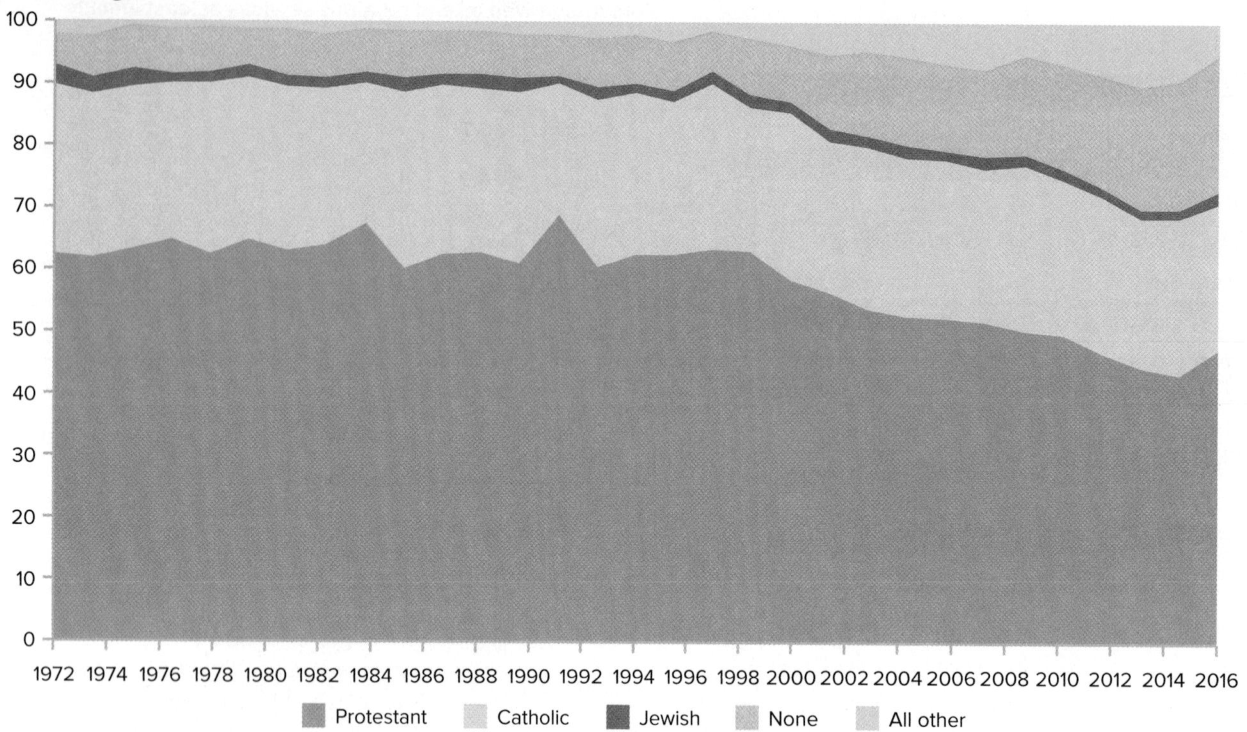

After remaining relatively stable during the last decades of the twentieth century, the religious composition in the United States has changed in the twenty-first century. While still a minority, those who say their religious preference is "none" have been the fastest-growing segment of the population. These include people who are unaffiliated with any formal religion, as well as atheists and agnostics.

Note: Excludes those who responded "don't know" and "no answer."

Source: National Opinion Research Center 2018.

somewhat important in their lives, and 6 in 10 (61 percent) believe in God, although more than half are not certain about the existence of God (Pew Research Center 2015g).

The religious composition of the U.S. population has shifted over time, with mainline Protestant churches losing the greatest share and greatest growth occurring in the unaffiliated category. Muslims are projected to overtake Jews as the second-largest religion (after Christians) around 2035 (Mohamed 2016).

Shopping for God in the Religious Marketplace

The relatively high level of religiosity in the United States is accompanied by a great deal of religious diversity and widespread religious tolerance (Putnam and Campbell 2010). This can likely be attributed to the country's longstanding separation of church and state. By protecting religious freedom but never having an official state religion, the United States created a vibrant climate for competition among faiths. Religion came to resemble a commodity in a marketplace—a product "sold" by competing religious organizations eager to attract adherents and "bought" (or not) by consumers who often comparison shop before making a decision (Stark and Bainbridge 1996). A diverse array of religious beliefs undermines the power of any single church and results in greater tolerance and religious freedom for everyone (Heclo et al. 2007; Hutchison 2003; Norenzayan 2016).

Sociologists using this type of analysis assume that the "demand" for religion is more or less constant. However, the relative health of religion depends on how well religious organizations provide the "supply." Because traditional religious institutions often have not adapted to changing social conditions and "consumer" tastes, mainline religions in the United States—as well as European state-sponsored religions—have seen a dramatic loss of membership. In the United States, this loss is offset by innovative religions and practices that provide an almost infinite variety of choices in the religious marketplace. For individuals, having more religions to choose from makes it more likely that they can find a faith that suits their personal needs. Thus, this analysis contends, religious choice and competition is good for adherents, for religious organizations, and for religion itself.

Does all this choice make U.S. society as a whole more religious? Yes, say some researchers (Stark 1999; Stark and Bainbridge 1985). But others contend that the very idea that religion is treated as a commodity is strong evidence of religion's decline (Bruce 2011). If a multitude of religious institutions merely provides consumers in various market segments with a product they want,

SPOTLIGHT
on social theory

Rational choice theories draw upon economic analyses and view people as actors rationally weighing the costs and benefits of their actions, as when they choose between competing religions. Is the idea of a religious marketplace relevant to your choice (or rejection) of religion? Why or why not?

and "the customer is always right," then religion has lost its authority to promote a widely shared set of values or enforce a common set of social norms.

Further, Bruce (2011) argues that religion today survives in large part because it engages in activities other than connecting individuals to the supernatural—often its traditional sacred role. Contemporary religious organizations are instead involved in promoting basic moral values (often in interfaith efforts), fellowship, charitable work, and political causes.

Indeed, most Americans equate religion with personal ethics and behavior and think that more religion would help counter crime, greed, uncaring parents, and materialism. But, overwhelmingly, Americans of faith have also accepted the need to coexist with adherents of other religions and with nonbelievers, and they understand the need for pragmatic compromise (Farkas et al. 2001). For example, of those people who claim a religious affiliation in the United States, only 27 percent say their religion represents the one true faith leading to eternal life; 67 percent say that many religions—or none at all—can lead to eternal life (Pew Research Center 2015g).

Secularization

As we've seen, the fastest-growing religious category in the United States is made up of those who say they have no religious affiliation—now nearly 23 percent of the population. An even higher portion (36 percent) of young Americans (born between 1990 and 1996) say they have no religious affiliation, a figure that has more than doubled in 20 years (Pew Forum on Religion and Public Life 2010a; Pew Research Center 2015f). Do such trends suggest that the influence of religion is decreasing in the United States? That question is part of a broader debate regarding **secularization,** *the decline in the social significance of religious beliefs, practices, and institutions.* There is little doubt that secularization has occurred in parts of the world during the past two centuries, but major questions and debates remain about the nature and degree of secularization.

The founders of sociology saw that the influence of religion was diminishing due to the emergence of modernity. According to Weber, the rise of science and rationality marked a new way of thinking that emphasized the need for skepticism, questioning, and empirical evidence as the basis for knowledge and action. This was a stark alternative to the heavy reliance on faith and divine revelation found within religion. The very creation of sociology was a by-product of this shift in thinking.

Religion's influence declined in more-affluent societies where science and industrialization first took root. According to the **secularization thesis,** *the social significance of religion has declined in the face of modernity.* Some sociologists criticize this thesis, pointing to the relatively high levels of religious activity in the United States and to the rise of fundamentalist forms of religious belief around the world (Stark 1999)—a topic we examine later in this chapter. Other scholars suggest that religion has not declined so much as secularism has arisen as a competing ideology (Fox 2016). However, the secularization thesis does not predict the *disappearance* of religion, only its declining influence on social life in modern societies. Just as when Weber first observed the decline of religion's influence, today's secularization tends to be in the wealthier societies that are more modernized, while remaining more limited in parts of the world that are less affluent and less modernized (Norris and Inglehart 2012; Warner, VanAntwerpen, and Calhoun 2010).

Secularization is a multidimensional social process that operates at various levels of society.

- ***Secularization at the macro level*** is the general decline of religion's influence in society that occurs when religion is separated from other aspects of social life. In nonsecular societies,

©Paul Harris, BWP Media/atticusimages/Newscom

Mega-churches like the 9,000-seat Southeast Christian Church in Louisville, Kentucky, adapt modern technology and marketing to compete in the religious marketplace. Modeled on the venues used for sports competition and rock concerts, these churches feature dramatic lighting, a central stage, giant video screens, and powerful sound systems in their services, which are often broadcast via radio and television and streamed on websites.

CORE CONCEPTS CHALLENGE *How would the analyses of Durkheim, Marx, Weber, and Berger apply to this type of contemporary religious* ***culture****?*

religion permeates all of society and the practices promoted by religious institutions shape family life, work, education, the law, and government. But when modernization divides social life into separate spheres, the influence of religion in society is diminished. With industrialization, work becomes separated from home, and religion is primarily a matter for private life. Modern governments and other bureaucracies rationalize and begin operating based on policies, procedures, and rules rather than on religious tradition. Religious doctrine no longer is the basis for legal rulings. Science advances learning through evidence-based analyses of the world rather than religious teaching. In modern secular societies, the Bible or Qur'an is not the basis for court decisions; retail businesses remain open on religious holidays; public schools do not promote a particular religious doctrine; and science, not faith, informs health care decisions. In short, once religion and its institutions are separated from government, the economy, schools, and the law, their influence in society declines.

- ***Secularization at the meso level*** is the loss of authority for the truth claims of any particular religion. Modernity's urbanization and industrialization bring together people of different cultures, with different ideas about religion from which people can choose. Rather than all-encompassing divinely inspired bearers of truth, religious groups became more like other social movements or advocacy groups competing for members and sometimes trying to influence political and cultural debates. This sort of secularization has been supported by some theologians and people of faith because it accommodates the peaceful coexistence of competing belief systems (Smith 2003).
- ***Secularization at the micro level*** is a decline in the significance of religion for people's daily lives. Researchers often measure micro-level secularization by indicators such as whether people claim a religious affiliation and how often they attend religious services. With some variation, church membership, religious activities, and religious belief all decline in modern societies. For example, weekly religious attendance has fallen worldwide and is below 10 percent in France and Germany and even lower in Scandinavian countries (Bruce 2011; Pew Research Center 2016a). Immigrants to the West are often highly religious people from rural areas in developing countries. However, the children of these immigrants, who now live in a more secular, modern, urban environment, tend to be much less religious (Crockett and Voas 2006; Voas and Fleischmann 2012).

Today the continued growth of individual freedoms, egalitarian democratic ideals, and respect for diversity has further challenged traditional religious authority (Bruce 2002, 2011). A rigid church hierarchy can seem out of date in an era that celebrates equality and adaptability; reliance on specially trained clergy to interpret religious doctrine can contradict a democratic spirit that emphasizes an individual's right to think freely; and a unique claim to divinely inspired truth can seem outdated when respect for the insights of differing cultural traditions increases. Further, the patriarchal nature of many religious doctrines and organizations has put them at odds with the trend toward greater gender equality.

For all these reasons, to varying degrees in different countries, religion has become a limited component of social life. The result has been a rise of **secular humanism,** *a belief system that emphasizes morality and decision making based on reason, ethics, and social justice rather than religious doctrine or the supernatural.* Instead of divinity, other values—especially democracy—have more commonly united modern societies. In effect, such societies have developed **civil religion,** *a set of common beliefs and ritual practices that bind people in a predominantly secular society.* The "sacred" symbols and rituals of democratic freedom—such as flags, the Pledge of Allegiance, national anthems, and military medals—serve as a secular equivalent of religious icons and rituals. Durkheim ([1922] 1956, [1925] 1961, [1938] 1977) recognized this trend and advocated using modern schools for secular moral education, another displacement of religion.

However, if modernity is supposed to secularize societies, why has religious fundamentalism experienced a resurgence in recent decades? We turn now to an analysis of this development.

Fundamentalist Resistance to Change

Relying on a literal interpretation of the Bible, Kentucky's Creation Museum teaches visitors that humans and dinosaurs coexisted in the Garden of Eden, Earth is barely 6,000 years old, and evolution is a myth—but overwhelming scientific evidence contradicts all these notions. The museum's rejection of aspects of modern thought is an example of **fundamentalism,** *a religious movement that advocates strict adherence to traditional principles in all aspects of social life, usually based on literal interpretation of a religion's infallible sacred texts.*

At first glance, the resurgence in fundamentalist religions in recent decades might seem to contradict the secularization thesis. But, ironically, religious fundamentalists are perhaps the greatest advocates of the secularization thesis because they see their efforts to reinsert religious belief into all aspects of social life as a defense against secularism's rising tide.

As noted, signs of secularization in the United States abound. The percentage of people identifying as unaffiliated has grown, and each generation is becoming less religious in terms of affiliation, religious practice, and belief (Voas and Chaves 2016). However, this secularization has come primarily from those who were religious moderates; conservative fundamentalists have retained high levels of religiosity (Schnabel and Bock 2017). The result is a growing gap between conservative fundamentalists and the rest of U.S. society. Similar dynamics are playing out worldwide.

Fundamentalism Then and Now The term *fundamentalist* comes from a series of religious manifestos first published by conservative Protestants beginning in 1910 under the title *The Fundamentals.* This original fundamentalism was more a response to other religious sects than to the secular world. After the 1925 Scopes "monkey" trial—in which a Tennessee high school teacher was prosecuted for teaching the scientific theory of human evolution instead of relying on biblical teaching—fundamentalists were marginalized from much of

©Sarah Sachs/Arizona Diamondbacks/Getty Images

With a huge American flag on the field, players and fans stand for the national anthem before a baseball game. Such ritualistic practices are evidence of a civil religion that promotes common values and creates emotional bonds of solidarity within a predominantly secular context. Where else have you seen evidence of civil religion in the United States?

mainstream American society. They reemerged in the 1970s, though, resisting the social and cultural changes of the 1960s. This time they became politically active, helping drive a resurgent conservative political movement within the Republican Party that peaked in the 1980s but is still influential (Emerson and Hartman 2006; Fox 2018; Putnam and Campbell 2010). Today's Christian fundamentalists tend to oppose secular humanism as the framework for political life; to reject the scientific theory of evolution; to condemn practices such as abortion, homosexuality, and gender equality that they claim violate biblical injunctions; and to reject what they see as a violent, decadent, and sexualized popular culture that contradicts their interpretation of Christian values.

In 1979, at about the same time as the resurgence of Christian fundamentalism, Islamic fundamentalism hit the world stage when Iranian revolutionaries deposed the American-backed Shah of Iran and replaced a secular government with a fundamentalist Islamic state. Since then, Islamic fundamentalists in many countries have resisted Western cultural influences, especially mass media, and opposed the imposition of Western power in Muslim countries. In their place, they seek to enforce Islamic law (*sharia*) in daily life and in government (Roy 2004, 2007).

Fundamentalism today applies to many religious sects, including forms of Christianity, Islam, Judaism, and Hinduism, though some of these groups do not always accept this label. Despite important differences, the many forms of fundamentalism share a resistance to the changes in modern life, especially secularization, and seek to restore their sacred texts as absolute authority in all matters (Bruce 2008; Emerson and Hartman 2006; Goodine 2014).

The significance of fundamentalism depends on your perspective. As Emerson and Hartman (2006) summarize,

> From a modern, secular viewpoint, fundamentalists are reactionaries, radicals attempting to grab power and throw societies back into the dark ages of oppression, patriarchy, and intolerance. . . . Conversely, for fundamentalists and their sympathizers, Western versions of modernization rush over them in a tidal wave of change, ripping apart communities, values, social ties, and meaning. . . . [They] see their stand against the tidal wave of change as honorable, right, life preserving, and a life calling. (131)

This clash of perspectives presents some major challenges.

Fundamentalism and Democracy Can a fundamentalist worldview based on absolutist beliefs be compatible with a democratic system based on individual freedoms and tolerance of different beliefs? This question lurks behind many contemporary debates (Benhabib 2002; Göle 2011; Scott 2010). In the United States, some religious groups reject secularism and assert that the country was founded as a Christian nation whose laws and institutions should embody those Christian beliefs. This has been part of what Casanova (1994) calls the "deprivatization" of religion—moving previously private beliefs into the public sphere. For example, religious opponents of equal rights for gays and lesbians or abortion rights—including many fundamentalists—want to use their interpretation of religious teachings as the basis for laws that affect everyone. Some of this activism has spilled over into violence, as in the cases of abortion clinic bombings and the shooting of abortion providers. The vast bulk of domestic Christian fundamentalism, however, has been nonviolent; its advocates organize politically to work within the electoral system.

Similarly, conflicts have erupted in Europe regarding Muslim immigrants, some of whom are fundamentalists, who advocate veiling (*hijab*), female genital cutting, arranged marriages, polygamy, and sex segregation. Especially worrisome has been the propensity for some extremist sects—claiming to be doing God's will in a cosmic war between good and evil—to endorse violence and terrorist acts as a means to advance their cause (Juergensmeyer 2003; Rausch 2015). For these reasons, some critics contend that Islam is incompatible with modern Western secular values (Huntington 1998; Lewis 2004)—a claim once made against Catholicism in parts of Europe (Gross 2004).

The increase in terrorist violence today carried out in the name of Islam is disturbing and disheartening. Some right-wing movements have sought political gain from such terrorism by cultivating *Islamophobia*—an unfounded dread or hostility toward Muslims—by portraying Islam as monolithic, unchanging,

©Tref/Alamy Stock Photo

Unlike fundamentalists, some people blend traditional religious practices with contemporary beliefs. Here a Muslim transgender woman takes part in a Gay Pride March in London wearing a traditional hijab veil or headscarf. Where else have you seen traditional religious practice adapted to contemporary conditions?

inferior, and an inevitable threat (Cesari 2013; Green 2015; Lean and Esposito 2012). However, scholars point out that Islam and Islamic movements are diverse and vary by region and context; most are not fundamentalist, nor are they violent (Rippen 2012; Roy 2007). In the same way that Christian fundamentalist violence is carried out by extremists who are disavowed by the vast majority of Christians, Islamic extremism also is a tiny portion of the spectrum of Islamic belief that is unrepresentative of the vast majority of Muslims (Lipka 2016). Evidence suggests that terrorist violence carried out in the name of Islam is in fact often political conflict that is being justified by a religious veneer. This violence is frequently in response to Western military and economic domination or is part of nationalist power struggles. It is more likely to originate in settings where religion is repressed or a single religion is imposed by the state (Brubaker 2015; Cesari 2014; Gunning and Jackson 2011).

In societies with separation of religion and government, and free competition among varying religious groups, tolerance is more common and religiously based violence is relatively rare. In addition, when Islamic fundamentalism is incorporated into democratic societies, evidence suggests that it becomes more moderate by becoming globalized (separated from the national cultures) and individualized (allowing for variation in observance and belief), much in the same way that Protestantism and Catholicism were. Even when militant religious movements take part in the political process, they tend to become more secularized and to moderate their views (Cesari 2004, 2014; Roy 2007, 2013; Schwedler 2006).

The future of fundamentalism is not clear. Some sociologists see the resurgence in fundamentalism as a relatively short-term phenomenon, the last gasp of resistance to the wave of modernization and secularism that has swept over the developed world over the past two centuries. Others see modernization and secularism as continuously creating alienating conditions that will fuel fundamentalism indefinitely (Riesebrodt 2000). This leaves still others to suggest a postsecular age, in which religious worldviews—of all sorts—will coexist and interact with secular worldviews (Habermas 2002).

A Changing World

THE FUTURE OF RELIGION

Religious identity is quite fluid in the United States, and a number of changes give clues about where religion might be going in the future (Sherkat 2014).

First, evidence indicates that religion in the United States is increasingly a source of individual emotional comfort rather than the basis of a comprehensive, collective worldview. For example, Wolfe (2005) finds that Protestants, Catholics, and Jews in the United States increasingly focus on emotional involvement with worship instead of on an intellectual engagement with a religion's history or doctrine. The result is a more personalized and individualistic approach to religion. People participate in the rituals of worship but pick and choose which doctrines to believe and, as we have seen, are more tolerant of the choices and lifestyles of others.

In stark contrast to fundamentalists' emphasis on doctrine and sacred texts, this shift to more emotional, individualized varieties of faith means less emphasis on doctrinal knowledge. Some surveys show that those most knowledgeable about the core teachings and history of major world religions are atheists and agnostics (Pew Forum on Religion and Public Life 2010b). In a society with overwhelmingly Christian adherents, surveys find that Bible-reading has declined for at least a quarter century and basic knowledge of the Bible's contents is at an all-time low (Prothero 2007). But such knowledge may not be necessary for the type of personal spiritual experience many people seek today.

In fact, a second change in recent decades has been a rise in the growing popularity of many forms of "spirituality." **Spirituality** can be thought of as *an inner sense of meaning or purpose, especially as it involves a person's relationship to something greater than the self.* As we saw in Chapter 1, some postmodern thought reacts to the central tenets of modernity, including rationalization and secularization. It rejects the idea that reality can be known only through science or any other method for achieving impartial understanding. Instead, these postmodern thinkers contend that, at best, all knowledge is partial and fragmented and that we live in a world with multiple realities from which to choose. In this context, some people embrace mystical or supernatural ways of knowing.

People can be both "spiritual" and "religious" (Ammerman 2013), but some forms of spirituality emphasize a personal relationship to a higher power without the need for a religious institution (Masci and Lipka 2016). Such practices can amount to God without religion or what one study dubbed "believing without belonging" (Davie 1994). In this situation, people continue to express belief in God but are no longer active in any religion. Some analysts see spirituality, broadly defined (including astrology, witchcraft, and paganism, for example), as likely to persist (Heelas and Woodhead 2005; Pearson 2003; Spencer 2003).

But spirituality doesn't require the supernatural or gods. Durkheim's definition of the sacred did not necessarily involve the supernatural, just the identification of something as extraordinary, to be treated respectfully, with reverence and awe. Acknowledging "a greater power" can mean simply an appreciation of the common fate of humanity, our interconnection through our natural environment, or even the sense of empowerment that comes from self-help efforts; it is a "spirituality without religion" (Harris 2014). Faiths and practices that profess such ethical and moral principles offer their adherents the chance to experience shared spiritual activity without necessarily invoking a divine being; they are religions without God. Such beliefs are often associated with "new age" religions, though they can also be found in established denominations such as the Unitarian Universalists, who note that "diverse beliefs about the existence of a higher power are welcome in Unitarian Universalism" (Unitarian Universalist Association of Congregations 2013).

©John Warburton-Lee Photography/Alamy Stock Photo

The growth of spirituality often does not include supernatural beliefs. Meditative practices, for example, can promote mental and physical health while encouraging practitioners to be mindful of the connections between people and their natural environments.

The rejection of modernist rationality in favor of postmodernist spirituality can be seen throughout popular culture. Television programs, books, and movies are filled with images and stories that involve spirits, supernatural events, and mysterious beings with superpowers. Whether they are angels, vampires, alien lifeforms, superheroes, or some other entity, the characters in these stories often remind humans of core values and their common destiny, as powerful religious texts have always done.

Embracing the certainty of traditional faith can offer believers comfort and reassurance in a time of change and uncertainty. But globalization has brought people, information, and competing beliefs into contact with one another as never before. The result is likely to be an increasing emphasis on the need for religious tolerance, the growth of individualized spirituality, and the declining influence—though not necessarily declining visibility—of fundamentalist religions. It is also likely to involve the continued expansion of secular humanism.

While not choosing sides in religious debates, sociologists know that if societies are to survive, they will need to identify and affirm shared values and social norms that enable them to operate peacefully in the midst of a multitude of conflicting beliefs. Perhaps this search for common ground—among nonbelievers and believers of all stripes—will be what characterizes the future the most.

©AF archive/Alamy Stock Photo

The broad interest in supernatural phenomena can be seen in popular culture's portrayals of vampires, ghosts, and characters like *Game of Thrones*'s "White Walkers," an ancient race of humanoid creatures who possess ice-related magical powers and the ability to reanimate the dead.

thinking sociologically about
Family and Religion

culture

- Family and religion are both institutions through which culture is passed on to the next generation. Both institutions vary considerably by culture and over time, reflecting different norms and beliefs.

structure

- Families help structure daily life by performing a variety of social functions, but people can also act to change the structure of families, adapting to different circumstances and adopting new values.
- Religion has long served to provide some structure to social life by focusing on values and moral behavior and thereby serving as a mechanism of social control. The structure of religion itself has changed considerably as a large number of belief systems compete for adherents.

power

- How families are organized and operate reflects the relative levels of power held by members, sometimes contributing to gender inequality.
- Changes in religion, including the rise of various aspects of secularization, have diminished the power that religious institutions have in modern societies.

REVIEW, REFLECT, AND APPLY

Looking Back

1. The family as a social institution can perform a variety of social functions, including encouraging social stability, caring for dependents, and providing emotional comfort. But the gender roles established in families can help perpetuate inequality.
2. Families vary around the world by structure and size, marriage types, and gender roles. However, some common global trends in family life include smaller families, the growth of open-mate selection, and a delay in marriage.
3. The idealized image of the "traditional" family in the United States obscures a complicated reality that included distinct imbalances in power as well as gender, class, and racial inequalities.
4. Families in the United States today are undergoing significant changes, including fewer and later marriages, a rise in divorce rates, an increase in blended families and other family forms, an increase in single-parent families, and a reduction in the number of children born to couples.
5. Since its inception, sociology has examined religion as a social phenomenon, considering its role in social life and its functions in society. Durkheim viewed religions as a mechanism to promote the norms of society. Marx saw religion as a way for those in power to keep oppressed people submissive. Weber emphasized the displacement of religion by the rationalization of modernity.
6. Religion can promote social solidarity, exert social control, provide personal comfort, and motivate social action. But it can also be dysfunctional, contributing to social conflict and perpetuating orthodox myths.

7. Although religion has declining influence within modern industrialized societies, religiosity in the United States is relatively high. U.S. religious life in the postmodern period is characterized by a diverse spiritual marketplace, featuring many varied forms of religious and spiritual life.
8. The debate over secularization focuses on the degree to which the social significance of religion is in decline. Ironically, increasing secularism may be fueling a resurgence of fundamentalism among some religious groups that want their religious prescriptions to prevail in society.

Critical Thinking: Questions and Activities

1. How has the American family changed in the past half century? Does your family reflect some of these changes?
2. Overall, do you think the changes in marriage and the family found in the United States have been positive for society? Why or why not?
3. Growing up, were you encouraged to believe in a particular religious tradition? If not, were you encouraged to disbelieve, or was your family simply indifferent to religion? How did you learn about the different beliefs held by other people?
4. Do you think competing and contradictory claims of absolute truth, often contained within religious doctrine, pose a threat to society? Why or why not? How can such potential conflicts be avoided in a diverse society?
5. Do you think society is becoming more secularized? Less so? What is the evidence for your position?

Key Terms

church (p. 310) a formal religious organization with broad mainstream acceptance.

civil religion (p. 316) a set of common beliefs and ritual practices that bind people in a predominantly secular society.

cohabitation (p. 298) a social relationship that can create family ties and typically involves sexual intimacy, in which people live together as unmarried partners.

cult (p. 310) a small religious community whose beliefs and practices are at odds with the dominant culture.

endogamy (p. 298) the restriction of marriage by either law or custom to people within the same social category.

ethic of reciprocity (p. 311) the "golden rule" that encourages people to treat others as they would like to be treated.

exogamy (p. 298) marriage between people from different social categories.

extended family (p. 298) consists of the nuclear family plus other relatives such as grandparents who commonly live together.

faith (p. 309) belief grounded in personal conviction or divine revelation rather than scientific evidence.

family (p. 296) two or more people, related either by birth or through social commitment, who share resources, care for any dependents, and often maintain a close emotional relationship.

fertility rate (p. 306) the average number of births per female.

fundamentalism (p. 316) a religious movement that advocates strict adherence to traditional principles in all aspects of social life, usually based on literal interpretation of a religion's infallible sacred texts.

kinship (p. 297) the bonds of family relationships.

liberation theology (p. 311) a form of Christian belief dedicated to combating poverty and other forms of social injustice.

marriage (p. 298) a social relationship that creates family ties, typically involves sexual intimacy, and is formalized by legal contract, religious ceremony, or both.

monogamy (p. 299) the practice of restricting sexual relations to one partner.

nuclear (conjugal) family (p. 298) parent(s) and any children.

polygamy (p. 299) a marriage system in which an individual is allowed multiple spouses.

profane (p. 309) the ordinary world of everyday life.

religion (p. 310) a unified system of beliefs and ritual practices relating to the sacred that bond people into a moral community.

rituals (p. 309) symbolic actions, typically performed at specified times, that help evoke an emotional bond among participants.

sacred (p. 309) something extraordinary, to be treated respectfully, with reverence and awe.

sect (p. 310) a small dissenting faction of a church that promotes new beliefs or practices.

secular humanism (p. 316) a belief system that emphasizes morality and decision making based on reason, ethics, and social justice rather than religious doctrine or the supernatural.

secularization (p. 315) the decline in the social significance of religious beliefs, practices, and institutions.

secularization thesis (p. 315) the argument that, in the face of modernity, the social significance of religion has declined.

spirituality (p. 318) an inner sense of meaning or purpose, especially as it involves a person's relationship to something greater than the self.

theism (p. 310) a belief in the existence of a god or gods.

©Sturti/E+/Getty Images

13 Education and Work

looking AHEAD

How—and what—have schools taught you about the social norms and values of your **culture**?

Do schools provide a **structure** that promotes social equality—or do they reinforce social inequality?

How does **power** operate in workplaces such as those where you have had experience?

©Ariel Skelley/DigitalVision/Getty Images

Nique Williams, 27, worked as a cashier at a Target store in Emeryville, California, where she made almost $15 an hour. The job paid well, but over time, coordinating her work hours with her five-year-old daughter's school schedule had become increasingly difficult. When she was hired, Williams had been clear about her availability. She had to drop Nyla off at kindergarten and pick her up afterward from Monday through Friday, so her weekday hours were limited. On weekends, though, she could work as long as necessary. Eventually, Williams was asked to work longer hours that conflicted with Nyla's school schedule. When she pushed back, refusing to accommodate Target's demands, she lost her job.

Although prioritizing Nyla's education cost Williams her job, she understands the cost her daughter would have paid if she had agreed to the new schedule. Nyla struggles with a learning disability, even in kindergarten. Williams knows that in the years to come, the school's demands on Nyla will only intensify, and she is committed to being there to help her daughter manage those demands. Today, with more and more employers expecting workers to live with flexible or on-call work hours, parents like Williams, struggling to balance work with their children's needs, face tough choices. Williams opted for less pay to work at a local credit union, where managers respect her commitment to a school-friendly schedule (Quart 2016).

Among working parents in the United States, Nique Williams's experience is a familiar one. Many parents work evening or overnight shifts, which often prevent them from taking part in afterschool activities or from helping their children with homework. For the children, the parents' absence during these hours can be a real disadvantage, for education is a crucial factor in childhood development. Recent research indicates that for parents as well, irregular work schedules can take a toll, making childrearing especially difficult (Morsy and Rothstein 2015).

From a sociological point of view, education and work are closely interconnected. One of the aims of education is to teach individuals the knowledge and skills they will need to get jobs and lead happy, productive lives. In this chapter we look closely at these two intertwined social institutions. We consider their roles and functions in society, their structure, and their relationship to social equality and inequality. We also emphasize the various social and cultural factors that shape people's school and workplace experiences.

Education and Schooling

Education is a word you know well. If you are reading this book, you are probably pursuing a college education. The news is full of stories about education, politicians often talk about the importance of education, and potential employers ask job candidates about their education. Sociologists define **education** as *the social institution through which individuals acquire knowledge and skills and learn cultural norms and values.* Education is vital to the transmission of basic cultural knowledge from one generation to the next, including traditions and an understanding of history. Education also imparts knowledge and skills related to specific jobs and household management.

The learning associated with education occurs in different settings beyond schools. For example, learning takes place at home, on the playground, and at work and involves parents, friends and neighbors, and employers. However, the sociological study of education focuses foremost on schools, which are the primary arena of formal education, and on **schooling,** *organized instruction by trained teachers.*

Schooling is an important part of social life throughout the world. Most countries emphasize the value of schooling and invest in organized instruction for their citizens. Three key indicators highlight the widespread belief in the importance of schooling (Brint 2017). First, young people throughout the developed world, and in much of the developing world, spend a great deal of their childhood in school. In the United States, children typically attend school six hours a day for about 180 days each year. Children in some countries have an even longer school year. In Australia, Japan, and Mexico, for example, the school year for primary students is 200 or more days each year.

TABLE 13.1 AVERAGE NUMBER OF INSTRUCTION DAYS PER YEAR, PRIMARY SCHOOL, PUBLIC INSTITUTIONS, SELECT COUNTRIES, 2017

Country	Days per Year
Australia	200
Brazil	200
Canada	183
Denmark	200
England	190
France	162
Germany	188
Israel	219
Italy	200
Japan	201
Mexico	200
Russia	169
Spain	175
United States	180

Source: Organization for Economic Cooperation and Development 2017.

In Israel, primary school students attend school for 219 days each year. (See Table 13.1.)

Second, most wealthy nations make a substantial investment in schooling by financing a system of formal education. A key reason is that political participation and economic growth depend, in part, on schooling to teach citizenship and job skills. Perhaps the most fundamental of these skills is **literacy,** *the ability to read and write.* In 2016, the global adult literacy rate was 86 percent. However, as Map 13.1 illustrates, literacy rates vary throughout the world. Adult literacy is nearly universal (99 percent) in developed countries, and literacy has increased substantially in developing countries in recent decades. In Latin America and the Caribbean, adult literacy stands at 94 percent; in East and Southeast Asia, 96 percent; in Northern Africa and West Asia, 81 percent; in Southern Asia, 72 percent; and in sub-Saharan Africa, 65 percent (UNESCO Institute for Statistics 2017). The overall global adult literacy rate of 86 percent is an increase from 76 percent in 1990. In the United States and throughout most of the developed world, government funds help finance schools from elementary schools through colleges and universities. Developing countries typically have fewer resources to invest in schools, but spending on formal education is still often a very high priority. UNESCO's Global Education Monitoring Report (2017) cites instruction in a language different from students' home language as a key source of low rates of primary school completion, particularly in sub-Saharan Africa, where most students go to schools where they do not learn to read their first language.

Third, a large number of adults have jobs in education, working as teachers, support staff, and administrators in schools and school offices. Schools are a major employer in the United States. In 2017, there were more than 3.2 million elementary and middle school teachers, more than 1 million high school teachers, and more than 900,000 school administrators (U.S. Bureau of Labor Statistics 2018c), with hundreds of thousands of others employed in schools as teaching assistants, librarians, custodians, and food service workers, among many different occupations. Similarly, from preschools to universities, schools are a major employer throughout the world.

Education in the United States: A Brief Social History

Until the nineteenth century, most children in the United States did not attend school. Instead, children typically worked in the household, on the farm, or as wage laborers. Some children received an education in a specific trade by serving an apprenticeship. Formal education, though available, was offered almost exclusively to upper-class children, who attended private schools and private universities.

Leaders of the American Revolution, notably Thomas Jefferson, advocated the development of a public elementary school system as a way to unify the new nation and promote active citizenship and democratic self-government. Yet in the late 1700s and early 1800s, education in the United States remained a patchwork of schools with minimal government funding and limited enrollment. Women, African Americans, and Native Americans were largely excluded (Urban and Wagoner 2009).

Public schools—"common schools" at the time—did not emerge until the early 1830s, when educational reformers in the Northeast argued for the development of free taxpayer-supported schools that would be accessible to all children. With the United States amid a transformation from a rural and agrarian society to one shaped by industrialization, urbanization, and an influx of new immigrants, advocates of common schools emphasized the civic value of education. During this period of social change, according to historian William J. Reese (2011), "schools were expected to strengthen the moral character of children, reinvigorate the work ethic, spread civic and republican values, and along the way teach a common curriculum to ensure a literate and unified public" (p. 3).

After the Civil War, school enrollment increased and common schools expanded dramatically. In 1870, 57 percent of 5- to 18-year-olds were enrolled in school. By the turn of the century, there were more than 250,000 public schools in the United States, and 72 percent of children were attending school (Reese 2011). Starting with Massachusetts in 1852, states began enacting compulsory attendance laws in the middle of the nineteenth century. By 1918, all 48 states had laws requiring children to attend school, usually through eighth grade—and the foundation of our contemporary system of universal compulsory education was established.

MAP 13.1 | LITERACY RATES AROUND THE WORLD

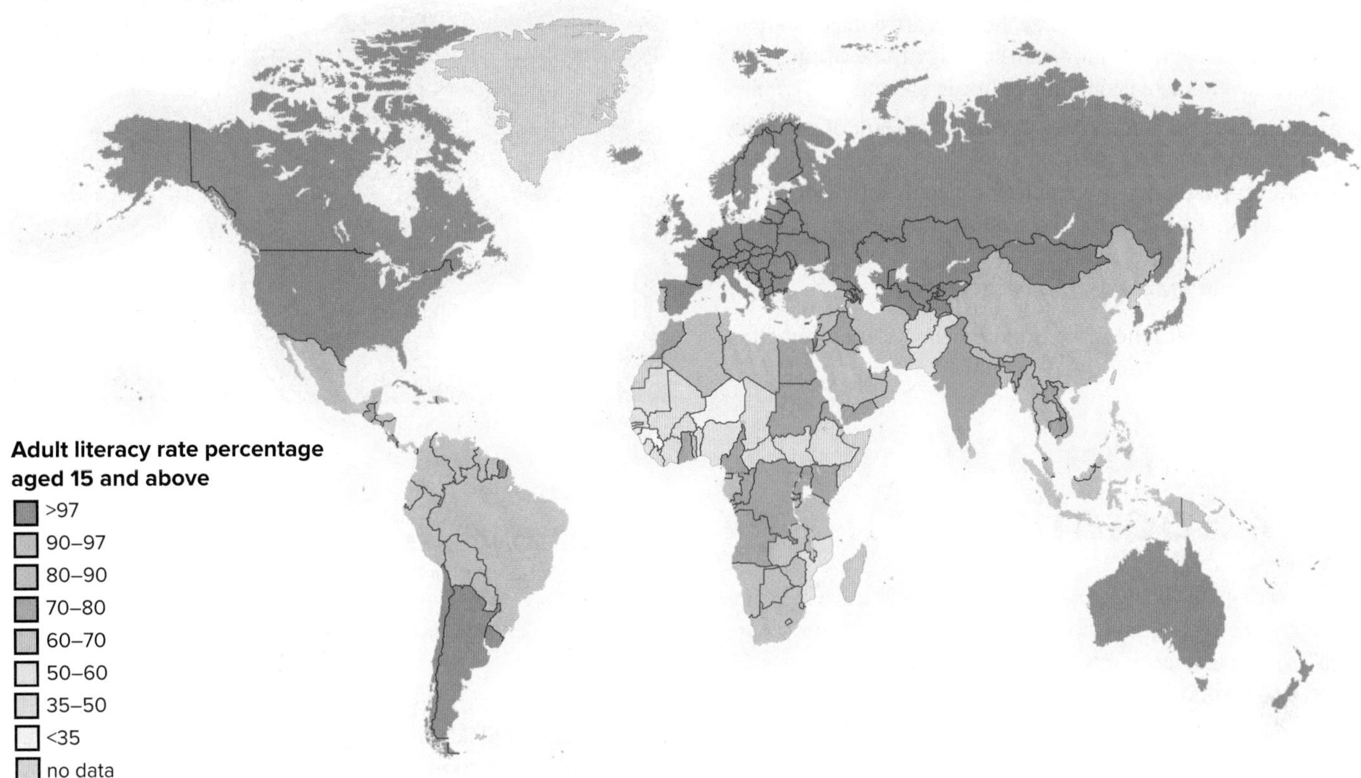

National literacy rates vary considerably. Literacy exceeds 97 percent in North America, Australia, and most of Europe, but literacy rates are significantly lower in most of Africa, Asia, and South America.

Source: United Nations Development Programme. 2016. *Human Development Report 2016: Human Development for Everyone*. New York: UNDP.

Public education continued to expand in the first half of the twentieth century as a high school education became increasingly common. Between 1900 and 1950, the school year lengthened from an average of 144 days to 178 days, and total public school enrollment climbed from 15.5 to 25.7 million students (Reese 2011). Local governments increasingly invested in schools, which were becoming the largest public expenditure in many communities. Then, as now, schools were the focus of public scrutiny and became an arena for debate and controversy over the substance of the curriculum, teaching methods, academic standards, the goals of education, and, more generally, the place of education in society.

The Functions of Schooling

What are schools for? This question is deceptively complex and cannot be answered adequately with the obvious response, "Schools are a place to learn." A sociological perspective directs us to consider seven fundamental functions of contemporary schools:

1. ***Transfer of knowledge.*** Schools are a vital site where children and teenagers acquire knowledge defined as important by previous generations, including subjects from history and literature to math and science.
2. ***Job preparation.*** Schools play an important role in teaching job skills. Most schools help prepare future workers. Many high schools, colleges, and adult education programs emphasize specific job-related skills.
3. ***Occupational sorting.*** In preparing young people for future jobs, schooling helps sort people into different kinds of jobs. Not all schools are the same. Some schools emphasize specific trades, giving students skills in, say, plumbing or auto repair, whereas other schools focus on college preparation and send many graduates off to college and, subsequently, graduate school.
4. ***Child care.*** Schools are responsible for children for the bulk of the workday and thus serve as a major source of child care for working parents. Some of the demand for a longer school day and an extended school year comes from those in need of the kind of full-time child care that schools provide.
5. ***Social integration.*** Schools teach common cultural traditions that help build social solidarity. Schools build community by connecting children and adults in the shared activity of teaching and learning. Schools often emphasize local and national history, helping reinforce a sense of community and national identity.

on social theory

A **functionalist** perspective emphasizes the role of education in society. Do you think the functions of schooling are changing in the twenty-first century?

6. ***Change and innovation.*** In bringing students and faculty together to study and learn, schools are a site from which new ideas and practices emerge. Schools are a major source of technological innovation, and schools can be a source of ideas that stimulate economic, political, and cultural change.
7. ***Socialization.*** Schools serve as a powerful agent of socialization, teaching lessons that extend well beyond the subject-specific curriculum. Contemporary schools often adopt an explicit socialization role, integrating into the school day educational activities about issues such as diversity, health, sexuality, and drug and violence prevention.

In the sections that follow, we explore many of these functions of education.

©Ariel Skelley/DigitalVision/Getty Images

Schoolchildren say the Pledge of Allegiance at the start of the day.

CORE CONCEPTS CHALLENGE *What are public schools teaching when the Pledge of Allegiance is a part of the school's daily routine? How are the values of U.S.* **culture** *reflected in the messages conveyed in the Pledge?*

Education, Culture, and Socialization

There is widespread consensus that schools should teach the "three Rs"—reading, writing, and arithmetic—but what else do schools teach? As you will see in this section, schools provide lessons that extend well beyond specific academic knowledge and skills.

The Hidden Curriculum

Much of the socialization that happens in schools takes place outside the formal subject-matter curriculum. In the early twentieth century, Emile Durkheim ([1925] 1961) coined the term **moral education** to describe *the role of schools in teaching children the central values and beliefs of their society.* For Durkheim and many later sociologists, schools play a vital part in instructing children about their culture's core values.

Schools, for example, teach children lessons about the value of hard work, discipline, obedience to authorities, being on time, following the rules, and the consequences of misbehaving. In addition, typical evaluation systems teach kids about inequality (some students receive higher grades than others), and the school's structure teaches about hierarchy (the chain of command in schools, leading up to the principal). Sociologists refer to these implicit teachings as the **hidden curriculum,** or *the lessons students learn simply by attending school, in contrast to the lessons from the formal subject-specific curriculum.*

In recent years, politicians and parents have increasingly demanded that schools instruct children about core values and appropriate behavior. In many communities, schools are expected to help solve social problems by educating children about violence, sex, drugs, intolerance, health, nutrition, and basic civility. As a result, a new cast of school employees—among them, student assistance counselors, violence prevention coordinators, health educators, and diversity trainers—is becoming increasingly important on the public school stage.

Students also learn a great deal about national identity during the school day. Public schools in the United States adhere to a relatively standard set of patriotic rituals that identify both the school and its population as American. For example, many public school students recite the Pledge of Allegiance each day and participate in school assemblies to recognize national holidays such as Veterans Day and Memorial Day. One study suggests that the rapid spread of American public schools since the nineteenth century was part of a broader process of nation building in which the school became the central arena for forging national solidarity and preparing future generations to be engaged citizens (Meyer et al. 1979).

Schools also transmit fundamental social values connected to religious definitions of national identity. Consider how the Pledge of Allegiance, in referring to "one nation under God" (a phrase inserted in 1954 in the midst of the Cold War), emphasizes a religious basis for American identity. In contrast, public schools in France present a far more secular version of national identity, and religious displays are banned in French public schools. Consequently—and controversially—Muslim girls are not permitted to wear headscarves in France's public schools (Vaisse 2004). In 2008 the European Commission on Human Rights found that the headscarf ban in public schools does not violate the European Convention on Human Rights (ECHR 2017).

Socialization Messages in Schools

Schools teach about behavior and values in both formal instruction and informal interactions between students and school

thinking about culture

The ethnic diversity of the U.S. school population has increased in recent years. Did your high school stick to teaching traditional lessons about U.S. **culture**—or did it take into account the cultural values of recent immigrants?

©Francois Lo Presti/AFP/Getty Images

A Muslim girl in France arrives at school, where she must remove her headscarf before classes. Have you seen religious displays at schools in your community? If so, do you think they should be permitted? Why or why not?

©St. Petersburg Times/ZUMAPRESS/Newscom

This elementary school student is learning math with the help of M&M's. Some teachers see this practice as a way to engage students in school, making math fun—and perhaps rewarding, too. When teachers use popular products like brand-name candy and pizza as rewards, what are students learning beyond addition and fractions?

officials. Brint, Contreras, and Matthews (2001) identified five ways in which socialization messages are disseminated in U.S. primary schools:

1. Teacher-initiated interactions with students
2. Everyday classroom routines
3. Student participation in schoolwide activities and programs
4. Visual displays and oral rituals in public spaces
5. Subject matter in the formal curriculum

The authors found that the content of socialization messages outside the formal curriculum consists largely of traditional lessons about appropriate behavior. For example, most teacher-initiated interactions with students stress the importance of orderliness and effort, as when a teacher reminds students to "listen quietly when someone else is speaking" and to "finish on time." Broader, schoolwide activities are likely to emphasize the values of participation and respect and include conflict resolution programs and public recognition of students for positive contributions. Public spaces typically transmit messages that highlight the importance of obeying school rules and respecting authority—say, by means of a poster that reminds students to act responsibly or by requiring students' silence during the principal's morning announcements.

Brint (2006) identifies three dimensions by which schools evaluate students, producing specific language for describing students who conform to their socialization messages:

1. ***Behavior conformity.*** Daily life in schools is full of informal instruction on proper behavior. For example, you must raise your hand and wait to be called on before speaking, and you must request permission to use the bathroom. School authorities call students who follow these rules "well disciplined."
2. ***Moral conformity.*** Schools train students to internalize values about what is moral, right, or proper (see the Through a Sociological Lens box). Teachers and school officials commonly emphasize the importance of "honesty, tolerance, courage, hard work, or fairness . . . [and] may also assign reading materials that illustrate the consequences of not being guided by these moral virtues" (Brint 2006, 134). Students who appear to conform to these moral standards are generally regarded as "good" students.
3. ***Cultural conformity.*** Schools also instruct students on what Brint calls "approved styles and outlooks"—culturally desirable behaviors and perspectives. These are likely to vary significantly by school setting. For example, large urban public schools may teach students how to get along in complex, rule-based organizations by completing assignments precisely as instructed by the teacher. In contrast, elite private schools are far more likely to encourage students to demonstrate their creative thinking by producing quirky projects that may even question the assumptions of a given assignment. Brint notes that those who conform to cultural styles are perceived to be "well adjusted" to the cultural expectations of their specific school environment.

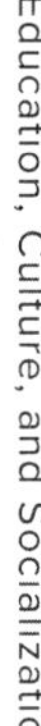

THROUGH A SOCIOLOGICAL LENS

Tracing the Links between Moral Authority and School Discipline

A high school teacher before returning to graduate school to study sociology, sociologist Richard Arum was keenly aware of the complex problems facing public schools. As Arum (2003) reports in the preface to his book *Judging School Discipline,* he taught in an urban public school system where disorder and violence were common.

Arum recognized that most of the research literature and media coverage of public schools focused on measures of educational achievement—test scores, dropout rates, college admissions statistics. For his part, Arum was concerned about the ability of a school "to foster moral development and successfully socialize youth in its charge" (viii). His interests were influenced by social theorist Emile Durkheim's writings on moral education, by the longstanding public concern about ineffective school discipline, and by the increasing burdens schools must bear in an age when adults spend more time at work—and less time with their children. Arum set out to explore the relationship between school discipline and what he saw as a crisis in moral authority in U.S. schools.

To focus his investigation, Arum turned his attention to the courts, specifically probing how court decisions might have contributed to a "decline in moral authority and the erosion of effective disciplinary practices in American public schools" (4). Arum examined court data, along with data on thousands of schools from four national surveys that had studied school disciplinary practices, student and teacher perceptions of school discipline, and educational achievement. He identified more than 6,000 relevant state and federal court cases that involved questions of school discipline, and employed a series of statistical techniques to analyze the patterns in these cases.

Arum's analysis showed that some states had pro-school judicial climates (in which courts were more likely to rule in favor of schools) whereas other states had pro-student court climates (in which courts were more likely to rule in favor of students). He sought to identify whether these differing court climates affected how teachers and students act in school. He found that in pro-school judicial climates, teachers felt they had more classroom control and greater support for rule enforcement from their principals. In contrast, in pro-student climates, court rulings helped undermine the legitimacy of school disciplinary practices because of the ever-present threat of lawsuits from parents and students. More recently, Arum and Velez (2012) reported that about half of all U.S. teachers and administrators say fear of a legal challenge affects their ability to manage their classrooms and schools.

Applying his sociological training, Arum relied on Durkheim's view of schools' role in moral education to interpret these results. He noted that although pro-student court rulings were important in educating students about the core democratic rights of free expression and due process, these rulings also had significant unintended consequences. In particular, Arum argues that pro-student court decisions have been part of a broader weakening of the school as a respected institution and of the teacher as a legitimate authority—two shifts that make it much more difficult for schools and teachers to do their jobs of educating and socializing young people. Arum argues that his research suggests that courts and state legislatures need to expand the discretion and legal protections granted to teachers and school administrators so that they can develop effective disciplinary practices that will maintain order in schools—and be perceived by students and parents as legitimate.

©Myrleen Pearson/Alamy Stock Photo

think about it

1. *Do you think schools should focus on moral development rather than just academic achievement? Explain.*
2. *Arum argues that schools have lost their "moral authority" and have experienced a decline in "effective disciplinary practices." Do you agree or disagree? Was this your experience in high school or not?*

Mixed Messages about Socialization

The values that schools teach are a dynamic mix of old and new. They reflect both the schools' traditional interest in an orderly, achievement-oriented environment and wider, more recent social trends that encourage tolerance and respect for diversity. For example, formal instruction—including that in textbooks, assignments, and in-class lessons—now often emphasizes respect for cultural diversity and the importance of inclusiveness.

Sometimes conflicts arise within the community—or, more broadly, in the nation—about the mix of old and new messages. Educational historian Jonathan Zimmerman's *Whose America?* (2002) examines a series of longstanding conflicts over what public schools should teach about history, religion, and sexuality. Zimmerman shows that these conflicts are rooted in such deeply held beliefs that there seems to be little room for compromise or even discussion. For example, debates about prayer in school, demands to include creationist theories in science classes as an alternative to Darwin's theory of evolution, and disagreements over whether and what to teach about sex and sexuality pit different worldviews, values, and understandings of morality against one another.

The point is that socialization in schools reflects specific historical and social circumstances. Disagreements about the values children should learn have therefore made American public schools a site of ongoing political conflict (Zimmerman and Robertson 2017).

Beyond their role as agents of socialization, schools are commonly seen as engines of social mobility and economic opportunity. In the next section, we look at how sociologists describe and interpret the relationship between education and opportunity.

Educational Structure and Inequality

Education is the great equalizer. If you want to get ahead in the world, the best route to success is through education, right? This is the official story, and it reflects the important relationship between achievement in school and career opportunities for adults. But education is not a simple equalizer. Not all people have the same educational opportunities, and research suggests that although schools sometimes reduce inequality, they also sometimes reinforce it. In this section, we examine the ways schools sort people into different kinds of jobs, often perpetuating existing inequalities, and we probe the issue of why school structure matters for students and teachers.

Education and Income

As Figure 13.1 shows, one thing is clear: those with more education, on average, make more money. At each educational level, average income rises substantially for both men and women. In 2016, the most recent year for which data are available, the median income for individuals with a bachelor's degree was double that of people who had not completed high school. People with a master's degree had a median income that was almost double those who had completed high school but not attended college.

There are exceptions to this link between education and income. You may have a neighbor who never went to college but has a very high income as a building contractor. Or you may know someone who completed graduate school but struggles on the salary of a part-time teacher. Research suggests that some types of expensive for-profit colleges also do not pay off for students (McMillan Cottom 2016). Despite such examples, the

FIGURE 13.1 | EDUCATIONAL ATTAINMENT AND MEDIAN INCOME, MEN AND WOMEN AGED 25 TO 34, 2016

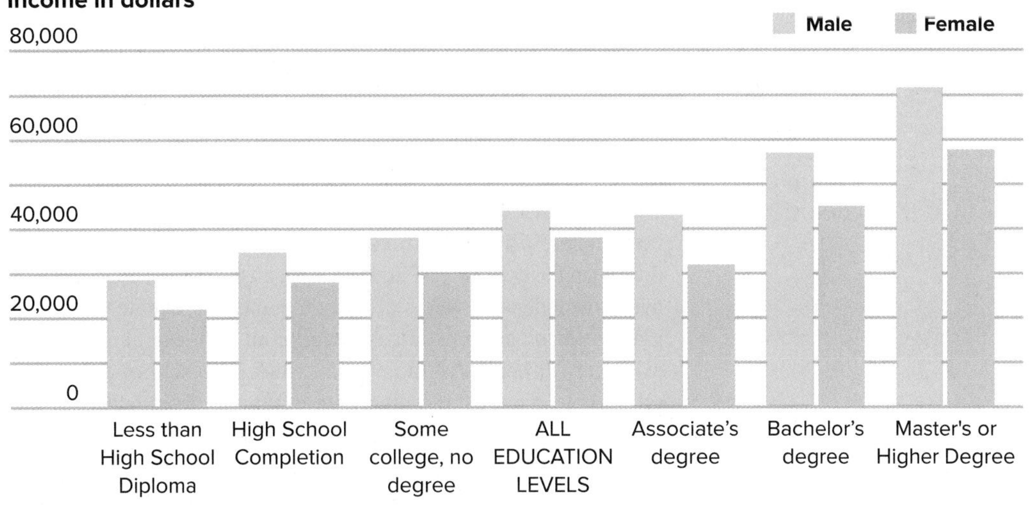

Source: National Center for Education Statistics 2018.

education-income link is well established and quite strong. As a general rule, the more education you have, the higher your income will be as an adult.

Education and Social Mobility

Education helps an individual get a better job with greater rewards. It also substantially increases an individual's chance of upward social mobility. The benefits of schooling may affect subsequent generations as well. One highly regarded study tracked the educational achievement of three generations over a 30-year period and found that when women from disadvantaged backgrounds have the opportunity to attend college, their future children are more likely than the children of their peers who did not attend college to be successful in school and ultimately to complete college themselves (Attewell et al. 2007). However, only about one-third of adults in the United States have completed college; by 2017, 34.1 percent of U.S. adults aged 25 and over had a bachelor's or graduate degree (see Figure 13.2).

Although school achievement is a route to occupational success, the relationship among education, social mobility, and economic advancement is complex. As we saw earlier in this book, systems of stratification are made up of structural positions, the rewards associated with each position, and the people who occupy these positions. Education can help an individual advance within a stratified, unequal system, but it does little or nothing to reduce structural inequality itself.

Suppose, for example, that we could give every working adult in the United States a college education. Would everyone then advance to a better job? The answer is no for a couple of reasons.

First, the value of a college education would plummet, because a college degree would no longer be scarce. Indeed, consider that a college degree is valuable precisely *because* some people do not have one. As college degrees become increasingly common, graduate or specialized professional degrees become more necessary for career advancement. Second, even if everyone had a college degree, some people would still have to collect garbage, serve coffee, clean streets, and work as cashiers. There will always be a need for low-skill jobs that do not require higher education. Changing the workforce's level of education will not change this structural reality.

What *would* reduce economic inequality, though, would be to change the rewards associated with different positions, perhaps by increasing wages at the bottom and raising taxes on top income earners. In other words, to reduce economic inequality, we need to pay attention to issues such as wages and taxes, not just education. Proving the point, in the United States today, a larger percentage of the population than ever has a college degree, yet economic inequality hovers at an all-time high.

FIGURE 13.2 | EDUCATIONAL ATTAINMENT, U.S. ADULTS AGED 25 AND OVER, 2017

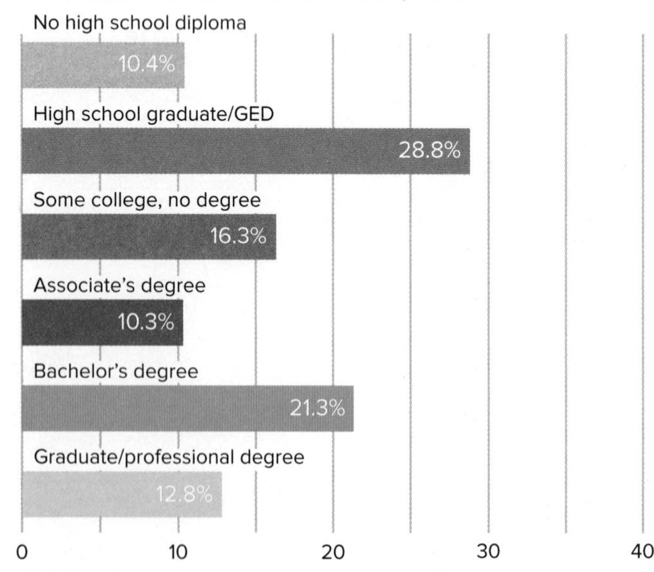

Source: U.S. Census Bureau, Current Population Survey, 2017 Annual Social and Economic Supplement.

How Schools Reinforce Social and Economic Inequality

Ironically, the schools themselves—the very institutions that society counts on to pave the way to opportunity and equality—reinforce social and economic inequality (Brathwaite 2017). They do so through various means, some of which are unintended. **Social reproduction theory** *explores the ways that schools help reproduce systems of inequality.* Social reproduction theorists argue that social and economic inequalities are built into the experience of schooling and the curriculum and inevitably result in unequal educational opportunities.

Access to Resources In August 2010, the new Newton North High School in Newton, Massachusetts, opened its doors to student and teacher raves. This state-of-the-art complex houses two theaters, a student cafe, an Olympic-size swimming pool, tennis courts, indoor and outdoor tracks, and a climbing wall, in addition to 119 gleaming instructional areas. The price tag? $197.5 million (Thomas 2010). Meanwhile, a few miles away in budget-strapped Boston, most of the public school buildings in the city need to be renovated or significantly repaired. A 2017 city report described significant educational consequences of the old buildings, such as inadequate space for art and music rooms, cafeterias and gymnasiums, and classrooms large enough for hands-on project-based learning activities (Vaznis 2017).

Perhaps the clearest reason that schools reproduce inequality is their dramatically unequal access to financial resources. Jonathan Kozol's (2012) account of daily life in public schools in poor neighborhoods features heartbreaking stories of young children trying to do their best in crumbling, unsafe school buildings with overcrowded, windowless classrooms and inadequate textbooks. Under such circumstances, academic achievement can be extremely difficult. As Table 13.2 shows, high school graduation rates also vary substantially by state, ranging from a 2016 graduating class low of 69 percent in Washington, D.C., to a high of 91 percent in Iowa (U.S. Department of Education 2017a).

The money that could improve such deplorable conditions is scarce because public schools are funded primarily from local

©Hill Street Studios/Blend Images/Getty Images

©J Pat Carter/AFP/Getty Images

Learning environments can vary widely from one school district to another. Some schools in well-off communities have state-of-the-art facilities (*left*). In some poor districts, however, schooling takes place in dilapidated—and often unsafe—buildings (*right*). How might differences in school facilities have an impact on educational opportunities for students?

property taxes. Therefore, poor communities have far fewer resources for their schools than wealthier communities. Given these realities, children in well-off neighborhoods (like Newton) are far more likely to attend schools that spend more money on teachers, counselors, computers, laboratories, educational materials, buildings, and playgrounds than schools in poorer districts (like many in Boston). From the starting gate, then, we have public schools that—because they reflect existing variations in the wealth of school districts—provide unequal opportunities (see the Sociology in Action box).

The inequality of public schools' financial resources is only the tip of the iceberg. Beyond this factor, some well-off families have the resources to send their children to elite private day schools or boarding schools. Here students not only receive educational advantages but also prepare for future power—making beneficial social connections, building up their self-esteem, and getting encouragement to see themselves as the leaders of tomorrow (Khan 2011). Untold numbers of other children, including those whose families lack the financial means for such privileged learning, do not have access to such educational opportunities.

In addition, even as access to higher education continues to expand, the high cost of college and the enormous debt incurred by many families who struggle to afford college (see Table 13.3) mean that educational inequality persists from kindergarten through college. And the quality of a college education can vary

TABLE 13.2 U.S. STATES WITH THE LOWEST AND HIGHEST HIGH SCHOOL GRADUATION RATES, 2016

Lowest graduation rates		Highest graduation rates	
Washington, DC	69	Iowa	91
New Mexico	71	New Jersey	90
Nevada	74	West Virginia	90
Oregon	75	Kentucky	89
Alaska	76	Missouri	89
Colorado	79	Nebraska	89
Georgia	79	Tennessee	89
Louisiana	79	Texas	89

Overall U.S. graduation rate = 84%

Source: U.S. Department of Education 2017a.

SOCIOLOGY in ACTION

Challenging the Structure of School Financing

The public school system in Syosset, New York, a wealthy community in Long Island, offers students an incredibly rich curriculum: courses in seven foreign languages as well as American Sign Language, almost 30 advanced placement (AP) classes, and a nationally recognized arts education program. Public school students in Ilion, New York, an economically depressed community in upstate New York, by contrast, have far fewer curricular opportunities: courses in only one foreign language (Spanish), just four AP classes, and a financial situation that makes it difficult to purchase necessary equipment for science classes (*New York Times* 2011b).

For Cassie Schwerner, Senior Vice President of National Partnerships at the Schott Foundation for Public Education, sociology provided a framework for thinking about how to challenge these educational inequities. In the 1980s and 1990s, Schwerner assisted school reform advocate Jonathan Kozol on his award-winning book *Savage Inequalities*. Kozol's book contrasts the conditions between schools in poor neighborhoods and those in affluent areas.

Working with Kozol gave Schwerner a close-up view of what's wrong with our public education system and showed her that the structure of school financing is a primary problem. Schwerner turned to her sociology background to map a route for equalizing school financing. In graduate school she had studied a variety of organized social change efforts, looking at how advocates work with media to define social issues and how activists build coalitions. Schwerner's doctoral dissertation, "Sing a Song of Justice," examined initiatives to build multicultural organizations for social change. Schwerner paid particular attention to the complex relationships among race and class differences.

©Scott Olson/Getty Images

Since she joined the Schott Foundation in 1997, Schwerner has worked to organize and fund the Fair Funding Initiative, which seeks to bring racial and fiscal equity to public schools in New York State. She was a prominent participant in the Campaign for Fiscal Equity (CFE), a grassroots New York City organization dedicated to ensuring that adequate resources and opportunities are available for all schoolchildren, regardless of their place of residence or their parents' income.

The CFE went to court to challenge New York State's school financing, arguing that the current system was unfair and inadequate and led to schools that could not properly serve students in poorer communities. The problems were especially acute in New York City, where more than 85 percent of the students are African Americans, Latinos, or other racial or ethnic minorities. Schwerner guided the CFE in forging alliances among community, school, and parent organizations and helped organize the funding community to support the reform campaign.

In 2006, after a protracted court battle, New York State agreed to a settlement of $11 billion for new school construction. Then in 2007, the state legislature voted to enact a major increase in state aid to public schools, along with other reforms, such as smaller class sizes and initiatives to improve teacher quality. Throughout this campaign, Schwerner and Schott supported the CFE financially and strategically.

The Schott Foundation continues to support efforts to promote educational opportunity for all students. The foundation currently supports the *Campaign for Fair Education Funding* in Pennsylvania, which advocates for equitable public education funding among school districts across the state; the *Schools Our Girls Deserve Campaign* in New York City, which works to create school environments that support girls, LGBTQ, and gender nonconforming students of color; and the *Fair Share Constitutional Amendment Campaign* in Massachusetts, which supports a constitutional amendment ballot initiative that would raise tax revenue specifically to promote educational equity. A 2017 report in honor of the foundation's 25 years of grant making emphasized Schott's continuing commitment to education equity:

"Through our efforts to expand access to early childhood education in Massachusetts, or increase fiscal equity in New York, or the myriad campaign activities in between, the Schott Foundation is committed to building and sustaining platforms that elevate grassroots voices demanding that all students have the access and opportunity to learn" (Schott Foundation for Public Education 2017).

think about it

1. *In what tangible ways might the New York City public schools improve as a result of additional state funding?*
2. *What challenges and obstacles do you think are likely to remain after an increase in state funding for New York City's public schools?*

significantly as well, with more-affluent and better-prepared students benefiting disproportionately from the nation's best colleges and universities (see Figure 13.3).

Sorting by Class School districts differ in far more subtle ways than just in their monetary resources. In their classic work *Schooling in Capitalist America,* Samuel Bowles and Herbert Gintis (1976) argued that a key function of schools is to mold future workers. Thus, they said, part of schools' job is to sort students by class, preparing them for different kinds of jobs.

A primary way that schools sort by class, according to Bowles and Gintis, is by teaching students class-specific lessons about authority. For instance, students in working-class communities are more likely to be taught about the importance of obedience and following directions. This emphasis prepares them for working at the lower levels of an organization, in jobs that encourage compliance and often permit little autonomy. In contrast, children from more privileged communities generally attend high schools (and, later, colleges) that encourage creativity, innovation, and independent-mindedness. This educational focus trains students to deal with authority in ways that are more suited to future managers and executives.

Teaching styles and subject-matter curricula are also likely to vary according to students' class status. Rigidly structured, discipline-oriented instructional methods—such as those featuring military-style boot-camp principles and a curriculum focused exclusively on preparation for end-of-year state tests—are increasingly common in schools that serve students from poor communities. In contrast, teaching methods that emphasize collaborative exploration and self-discovery are found far more often in wealthy public school districts and selective private schools. Furthermore, public schools in working-class and poor communities are far more likely to feature vocational and technical classes, whereas public schools in higher-income communities are more likely to include arts education, a wider range of academic subject areas beyond the state-mandated core classes, and opportunities to pursue college-level courses.

TABLE 13.3 COLLEGE COST AND STUDENT DEBT, 2006 AND 2016

	Average Price (Four-Year Institution, Tuition, Fees, Room and Board, in 2016 dollars)		
Year	**2005–06**	**2015–16**	**% Increase, 2005–06 to 2015–16**
Public	14,765	19,558	+32.5
Private	34,988	43,997	+25.7
	Percentage of Students Who Graduated with Debt		
Year	**2005–06**	**2015–16**	
Bachelor's Degree Recipients at Public and Private Nonprofit Four-Year Institutions	58	60	
	Average Debt per Borrower among Graduating Seniors (2016 dollars)		
Year	**2005–06**	**2015–16**	**% Increase, 2005–06 to 2015–16**
Public	22,000	27,000	+22.7
Private Nonprofit	28,800	32,000	+11.1

Sources: National Center for Education Statistics 2017c; Baum, Ma, Pender, and Welch 2017.

FIGURE 13.3 | HOW EDUCATION REPRODUCES SOCIAL AND ECONOMIC INEQUALITY

Photos: (*top*): ©Bananastock/age fotostock; (*bottom*): National Archives and Records Administration (NWDNS-412-DA-13449) *Source:* National Archives and Records Administration (NWDNS-412-DA-13449)

Chapter 9, **cultural capital** refers to *various types of knowledge, skills, and other cultural resources.* Sociologists recognize that high-status groups use knowledge, taste, preferences, and styles to signal their status and to exclude others from their social circles (Bourdieu and Passeron 1977). For example, knowledge of classical music or fine art, opportunities for study abroad, and experience with diverse cuisines are forms of cultural capital. Such knowledge, experiences, and tastes provide people with advantages in high-status social networks, whether on the job, in school, or in more-informal settings. Cultural capital can serve as both a ticket to enter high-status groups and a sign of one's membership.

Cultural capital gives students advantages in school. It prepares them to fit in with others, to understand what schools expect from successful students, and to use their cultural knowledge for higher grades. Furthermore, sociologists have shown that *parents'* cultural capital can have a significant impact on their children's educational opportunities and experiences. Kaufman and Gabler's (2004) study of the college admissions process in the United States found that the cultural activities of parents help explain which students ultimately attend elite colleges. Specifically, students with parents who visit art museums regularly are far more likely to attend an elite college than students whose parents do not, even when the students themselves are not regular museumgoers. Parents not only transmit their cultural capital to their daughters and sons, but also use it to help their children secure future membership in advantaged groups. A recent Danish study found that children with a high degree of cultural capital—defined as participation in "highbrow cultural activities," the frequency and volume of reading books, participation in extracurricular activities, and "how often parents discuss cultural and social issues with children"—are far more likely to complete the college prep track in Danish high schools than those students with lower levels of cultural capital. However, this relationship holds only for students whose parents have a college education, suggesting that some college-educated parents have resources that allow them to help their children convert cultural capital into educational benefits. This study suggests that the key difference is likely schooling context: the inequality "in returns to cultural capital arises from differences

Credentialing Universities, colleges, and professional schools play a vital role in what sociologists call **credentialing,** *the process whereby individuals with advanced educational degrees and formal certificates monopolize access to the most rewarding jobs.* According to sociologist Randall Collins (1979), educational certification is so important for future career opportunities that the United States is in effect a "credential society." This state of affairs helps explain the often-intense competition for limited slots in select colleges and universities and why degree holders are quick to highlight their recognized credentials. Inequality is built into the credentialing system because the value of educational credentials stems to some degree from limited access to these credentials.

Cultural Capital Schools respond to—and help reproduce—people's unequal access to cultural resources. As we saw in across schooling contexts in their ability to enable children to convert their cultural capital (for example, intellectual creativity and academic competence) into educational success" (Jaeger and Møllegaard 2017, 140). This helps to explain why highly educated parents invest so much time, attention, and anxiety in placing their children into their preferred kindergarten programs (Lareau, Evans, and Yee 2016).

Parental cultural capital—or lack of it—can also significantly shape younger children's early educational experiences. Education scholar Adrian Blackledge (2001) found that Bengali-speaking immigrant mothers in England did not have the cultural capital to meet teachers' expectations for appropriate parental involvement, so school officials concluded they were not committed to their children's education. In Blackledge's view, these mothers had the "wrong" kind of cultural capital—knowledge of Bengali but not English—to the disadvantage of their children's current educational experiences and future job opportunities. Similarly, a recent study of Iraqi immigrant families in Australia found that mothers unfamiliar with Australian schools and with limited knowledge of English found it difficult to support their children's education, even when they had earned college degrees in their home country. Al-deen and Windle (2017) argue that having the wrong kind of cultural capital can produce emotional distress for mothers, who see themselves as bad parents, and end up limiting their children's educational opportunities.

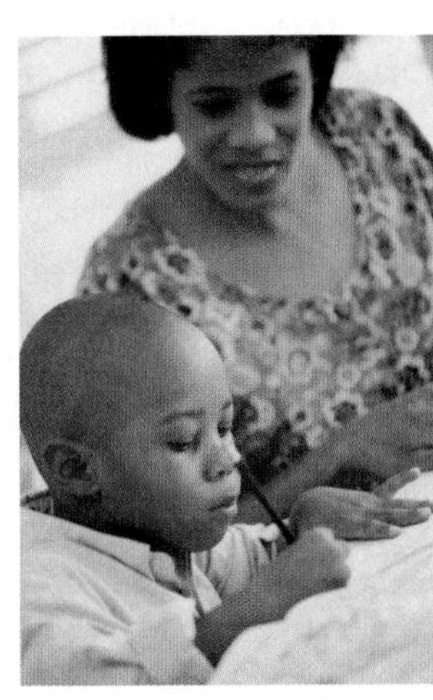
©Photodisc Collection/ Getty Images

Education experts stress the importance of parents' involvement with teachers and officials at their children's schools (Herman and Reinke 2017). Lareau and Weininger (2003), in their now-classic paper, argue that middle-class parents have real advantages over working-class parents in fulfilling educators' expectations in this regard. Specifically, middle-class parents have forms of cultural capital that make it much easier for them to engage actively with educators and are far more likely to be comfortable with educational jargon. Further, these parents display a sense of entitlement and a confidence that they can advocate strongly for their children. Such attitudes are far less common among working-class parents.

Racial Segregation In 1954 the U.S. Supreme Court ruled in *Brown v. Board of Education* that **racial school segregation,** *the separation of students into exclusively white and exclusively black public schools,* was unconstitutional. The Court declared, "In the field of public education, the doctrine of 'separate but equal' has no place. Separate educational facilities are inherently unequal."

More than a half century later, however, U.S. public schools are still remarkably segregated. After desegregation efforts during the 1960s and 1970s, a process of *resegregation* began in the late 1980s that has continued into the 2000s. A 2016 report by the Civil Rights Project at UCLA highlights the deepening segregation in U.S. schools, finding that the number of intensely segregated schools, those with less than 10 percent white enrollment, has increased dramatically since the late 1980s, more than tripling from 5.7 percent to 18.6 percent of public schools. In some areas, a majority of students of color go to intensely segregated schools. For example, in New York State, more than 65 percent of black students and more than 56 percent of Latino students attend schools that have enrollment that is more than 90 percent nonwhite (Orfield, Ee, Frankenberg, and Siegel-Hawley 2016). As a result of resegregation, racial segregation in U.S. schools is nearly as extreme as it was in the 1960s.

Why did resegregation happen? Research shows that racial segregation in schools results in large part from residential segregation and is associated closely with concentrations of poverty. Since neighborhoods are typically segregated by race, local schools often reflect these patterns as well. In addition, the rise of charter schools, magnet schools, and other "school choice" programs (discussed later in this chapter) appears to have magnified racial segregation because white families are far more likely to take their children out of multiracial neighborhood schools when they find other options (Mordechay and Ayscue 2017; Orfield 2014).

The quality of education at segregated schools—and its impact on achievement—is also an issue. According to the U.S. Department of Education's Office for Civil Rights (2015), "Racially isolated schools often have fewer effective teachers, higher teacher turnover rates, less rigorous curricular resources (e.g., college preparatory courses), and inferior facilities and other educational resources."

The effects of segregated schools are likely to extend beyond issues of academic achievement. For example, one study found that minority students in racially segregated schools are far more likely, as adults, to spend time in prison or jail than are their counterparts at integrated schools and that the incarceration rate for black students in segregated schools has increased over time (LaFree and Arum 2006). More recently, Nance (2017) found that segregated schools with a school population consisting primarily of students of color rely on more extensive surveillance practices than do schools with primarily white students. Nance argues that such "disproportionate exposure to intense surveillance methods may contribute to the vast racial inequalities in school discipline, academic achievement, and involvement in the justice system" (798).

Even so, some research suggests that under certain circumstances, there may be some benefits to racially segregated schools. One study found that in schools with predominantly minority students *and predominantly minority teachers,* students were more optimistic about their post–high school educational opportunities and future job prospects and had more positive attitudes about teachers and schools than did minority students in predominantly white schools (P. Goldsmith 2004). Subsequent research has found that exposure to same-race teachers leads to lower levels of serious disciplinary action, such as suspension and expulsion, among black students, both male and female, in elementary, middle, and high school grades (Lindsay and Hart 2017), and that both black and white elementary school students show stronger academic performance in reading and math when they have same-race teachers (Egalite, Kisida, and Winters 2015).

Similarly, historically black colleges and universities—including Howard University, Morehouse College, Spelman College, and Tuskegee University, among more than 100 such schools—have served for generations as sources of educational opportunity for African Americans when they were excluded from many private and public colleges and universities. Even today, when many colleges and universities actively pursue a diverse student body, historically black colleges and universities offer African American students a learning environment that supports confidence building and academic achievement and that establishes social networks for subsequent job and educational opportunities (Espinosa, Turk, and Taylor 2017; Palmer, Davis, and Maramba 2010; Upton and Tanenbaum 2014).

Schools as Complex Organizations

Schools are complex organizations that are shaped by policies and rules, their own organizational histories, and powerful social forces. To understand what happens in schools, why, and with what consequences, we need to consider how the size and organizational structure of schools influence the educational process.

School Size In one widely cited study, education scholars Valerie Lee and Julia Smith (1995) distinguished between schools organized as a bureaucracy and those organized as a community, and they show that these two structural forms are related to school size. Large schools are typically bureaucratic organizations structured along traditional, hierarchical lines, with teachers reporting to administrators. They usually have a uniform curriculum, and information is sent home to parents about how best to help their children. In contrast, small schools are more likely to have a communal organization that gives teachers time to plan lessons together, emphasizes curricular flexibility and cooperative learning, and actively involves parents.

Does school size affect students' level of achievement and engagement? School size *does* matter. In an analysis of 57 studies of the impact of school size from 1990 to 2007, Leithwood and Jantzi (2009) found that small schools are associated with higher academic achievement than large schools, particularly at the elementary level. Disadvantaged students benefit most from the support they receive in a small school environment. The study found strong evidence that students are more engaged at small schools than at large schools and are more involved with extracurricular activities. A more recent review of international research on school size found that the positive impact of small schools to be more significant in the United States than in other countries (Scheerens, Hendriks, and Luyten 2014). The lesson for school reformers might be for large schools to adopt some of the mechanisms through which small schools support academic success and facilitate student engagement.

Tracking Many schools adopt formal or informal structures of **tracking**, *placing students into different curricular paths intended to accommodate varying levels of academic work.* Tracking systems allow schools to manage students with widely varying skills and interests. Sometimes these tracks are rigid, with some students on a college-prep track and others on a vocational or jobs-skills track. In other situations, the tracks are informal and involve various courses labeled as remedial, general, advanced, AP, or honors.

Tracking was a common feature of U.S. high schools through the mid-1960s. But concerns arose that tracking was an obstacle to social mobility—that tracks locked students into a particular path from an early grade and limited future educational and work opportunities for those not on a college-prep track. Given these concerns, most U.S. high schools eliminated or substantially modified their tracking procedures between 1965 and 1975, according to Sam Lucas (1999). Lucas found, however, that even when the tracking barriers were removed and students were permitted to take a wider range of classes in high school, course placement was not based on prior achievement in a subject area. Instead, parents from economically advantaged families, who had more information about curricular choices, acted to have their children placed in more advanced courses. Thus, although in some schools formal tracking systems may be a thing of the past, informal curricular tracks, reinforced by class and educational differences among parents, remain an organizational reality.

Researchers have examined how the informal tracking structure that persists in U.S. high schools might affect academic achievement. In general, they have found that students in "higher" tracks learn more than students with similar abilities in "lower" tracks. Carbonaro (2005) examined the relationship between school structure (the learning opportunities in each curricular track) and student action (the degree of student effort) with an eye to understanding how both structure and action shape academic achievement. He found that action—in this case, student effort—matters. Those who work harder learn more and are more successful, as measured by grades and test scores.

However, the tracking structure itself remains a significant factor in shaping both effort and learning. Students in higher tracks generally put more effort into their schoolwork than do students in lower tracks. Even when students in lower-track classes apply a great deal of effort, they still learn less than comparable students in higher-track classes. In other words, effort matters, but the tracking structure exerts a powerful constraint, limiting the potential of hard work for students in lower academic tracks and rewarding those who work hard in higher tracks. Subsequent research showed that teachers have lower expectations for student achievement for those tracked into "lower" level classes, and students internalize these low expectations (Kelly and Carbonaro 2012; Van Houtte, Demanet, and Stevens 2013). The lesson from these findings: we need to pay attention to students' effort while recognizing that the action students take is shaped by a tracking structure that influences their effort, expectations, and opportunities to learn.

thinking about structure

Why might students engage more, and learn more, if they attend a school with a communal **structure**? What structure did your grade school and high school have, and how did that structure affect your learning?

MAP 13.2 | COMMON CORE IN THE STATES

Kept Its Common-Core Adoption

Never Adopted the Common Core

Announced a Major Common-Core Rewrite or Replacement

Adopted the Common Core Only in English/Language Arts

Broad parent and teacher criticism of the Common Core State Standards Initiative has led to substantial change. By late 2017, 11 of the 46 states that had initially adopted the Common Core had announced plans to significantly rewrite or replace the Common Core approach. Debate continues about the relationship between educational accountability and standardized tests.
Source: "Map: Tracking the Common Core State Standards," *Education Week*, September 18, 2017.

Contemporary Educational Issues and Trends

Shifts in the economy, advances in digital technologies, an influx of immigrants, and political change have had an impact on the U.S. educational landscape. In this section, we look briefly at some educational challenges confronting citizens and policymakers.

Accountability for Basic Skills

The No Child Left Behind Act (NCLB), passed by the U.S. Congress in 2001, aimed to make schools more accountable for student performance. NCLB's best-known provision required schools to test all children in reading and math each year from grades three to eight. Researchers referred to these examinations as high-stakes tests because student performance on them is tied to federal school funding (Dworkin 2005). This rigid national testing regime, which punished teachers, students, and underperforming schools, engendered substantial criticism (Meier and Wood 2004). In 2015, Congress replaced NCLB with the Every Student Succeeds Act (ESSA). Although the new act gives states more flexibility than NCLB in how to conduct and respond to tests, it leaves in place NCLB's focus on test scores as the centerpiece of school accountability.

©Blend Images/John Lund/Marc Romanelli/Getty Images

The Common Core State Standards Initiative has sparked broad public discussion about the meaning of accountability. Coordinated by the National Governors Association and the Council of Chief State School Officers, the Common Core program emphasizes the development of new math and English language arts standards and assessments for K-12 students. While 46 states initially adopted the Common Core standards in the 2010s, and began implementing new curriculum and assessment tools, the Common Core faced substantial opposition from parents and teachers who are concerned about the impact of new tests on the curriculum content (see Map 13.2). Many worry that the early elementary curricular guidelines are not developmentally appropriate and that the tests associated with them will be used to evaluate teachers (Rethinking Schools 2013). The push-back against Common Core intensified in 2015 with the emergence of a national movement encouraging parents to have their children "opt out" of Common Core tests. In New York State, for example, about 20 percent of students opt out of standardized tests each year (Schutzman 2018). By late 2017, 11 states had announced plans to significantly rewrite or replace the Common Core (Education Week 2017).

Supporters of reforms like Common Core argue that this kind of testing regimen will push schools with low test scores to perform better and will help address inequalities in academic achievement. Sociologists of education emphasize, however, that a successful approach to school reform must pay careful attention to outside social forces. Understanding differences in academic performance requires an examination of broader patterns of inequality affecting access to health care, housing, job opportunities, adequate income, and supportive communities (Karen 2005; Payne and Ortiz 2017).

Bilingual Education

U.S. schools are home to students from diverse backgrounds, including a growing number of children for whom English is not their first language. For children in the early years of elementary school, school policies often emphasize English language acquisition with the expectation that younger students will quickly become fluent in English. However, English language instruction for new immigrant students in middle school or high school is often far more complex.

Source: Library of Congress [LC-USF346-033071-D]

©Maskot/Getty Images

FAST-FORWARD

Education and Change

U.S. schoolchildren in the mid- and late twentieth century experienced their formal education in traditional classrooms. Students sat tall at desks arranged in neat rows and focused on the teacher at the front of the room. Today, with ongoing advances in computer and media technology, as well as in online teaching and learning resources, learners from grade-schoolers to graduate students have a world of information at their fingertips.

Since the 1970s, Americans have passionately debated the value of **bilingual education,** in which *students receive instruction in both their first language and English.* Although some organized immigrant groups have pressed for robust bilingual programs, opposition to bilingual education grew in the early 2000s. Voters in several states, including California, Arizona, and Massachusetts, supported ballot initiatives that largely eliminated bilingual education programs (Gandara and Hopkins 2010; Menken 2017). At the same time, the number of English language learners, as students who are not proficient in English are called, was growing rapidly. The U.S. Department of Education (2017b) reports that 16.7 percent of kindergarten students and, overall, 9.4 percent of public school students (4.6 million students) are English language learners.

Research points to the complexity of the questions raised by bilingual education advocates and critics. For example, in his study of children of immigrants in Florida and California, sociologist Alejandro Portes (2011) observed a "positive association between bilingualism and better academic performance" (569). Portes also identified benefits of bilingualism beyond academic performance; bilingual high school students had higher self-esteem and higher educational aspirations than similarly situated monolingual children of immigrants. Despite these positive findings, however, other research indicates that immigrants who do not achieve English language proficiency are more likely to drop out of high school and to have lower incomes than their counterparts who learn English (Bleakley and Chin 2004; Claster and Blair 2013).

Much of the debate ultimately centers on whether bilingual programs help or hinder students' capacity to learn English and other subjects in school. One study of elementary school students in New York City (Conger 2010) found that students in bilingual programs may learn English less quickly than students in English as a second language (ESL) classes. At the same time, however, evidence indicates that non-English-speaking students learn science, math, and history more effectively in bilingual programs than in English-only classrooms. One five-year study of Spanish-speaking elementary school students in the United States found that bilingual and English-immersion classrooms were equally effective at teaching children to read English proficiently, concluding that the quality (rather than language) of instruction is what matters most (Slavin et al. 2010).

School Choice and the Debate over Charter Schools

The vast majority of U.S. elementary and secondary school students (90 percent) go to public schools. In most such cases, place of residence limits families' options about which school their children can attend.

One longstanding school reform approach revolves around the concept of **school choice,** *various policies that give families options for deciding which school their children will attend.* School choice advocates argue that granting parents the power to choose where their children are schooled will produce competition among public schools that creates incentives for positive reform. Critics of these policies argue that market-oriented school choice programs undermine the integrity of the public education system and further benefit already advantaged families who have access to better information about educational options for their children (Fabricant and Fine 2012; Ravitch 2016).

Perhaps the most talked-about school reform initiative in the 2010s has been the development of **charter schools,** *public schools* *run by an organization independent from local school districts.* As part of their charter from state government, these schools are exempt from some rules and regulations that govern typical public schools. Charter schools have expanded dramatically since they first appeared in the 1990s. By 2017, charter schools were operating in 44 states and Washington, D.C., and there were more than 7,000 charter schools in the United States, with a total of 3.2 million students (National Alliance for Public Charter Schools 2018). In light of these schools' autonomy from state regulations and school district authorities, some reformers believe that charter schools can develop innovative approaches to teaching and learning—and thus can genuinely offer families a local and public choice, especially in communities with low-performing public schools.

Betsy DeVos, U.S. Secretary of Education in the Trump administration, has been a vocal supporter of charter schools, arguing that they improve student learning. However, large-scale research on learning outcomes of students enrolled in charter schools presents a mixed picture. Some studies have found no difference in the academic performance of charter school and public school students, whereas other studies have reported that students admitted to charter schools performed better than public school students who applied to but did not attend charter schools (Renzulli and Roscigno 2011).

The most comprehensive examination of charter schools, published by Stanford University's Center for Research on Education Outcomes, found that the charter school student body has become increasingly diverse. Specifically, students from poor households and African American students now represent a higher percentage of charter school students than they do overall public school students. In addition, academic performance among charter school students has improved in recent years, although reading and math scores for charter school students are similar to the corresponding scores of local public school students. Independent charter school reading scores, for example, are no different from local public schools' scores in 51 percent of cases. Charter schools outperform their local counterparts in 29 percent of cases, but local public schools score higher than charter schools in 20 percent of cases (Center for Research on Education Outcomes 2017).

The Online Classroom

Today's digital technologies mean that education no longer has to take place in the physical space of a school building. In recent years, higher education has moved online at a rapid pace. By the Fall of 2016, more than 6 million U.S. college students—about one of three—were taking at least one online course; about half of these were studying online exclusively (Seaman, Allen, and Seaman 2018). More than 80 million people from around the globe who are not enrolled in degree programs sign up for massive open online courses (MOOCs) offered by organizations such as Udacity, edX, and Coursera.

Online education has made it easier for working adults to earn a college credential by making travel to the school site unnecessary and providing scheduling flexibility. But proponents of online courses point to more than just the flexibility they offer working adult students—who are often juggling family obligations in addition to a job and school. These supporters say that online learning makes college more accessible to students from a wider range of backgrounds, saves students and universities money, allows students to earn a degree faster, and helps universities manage demand for limited classroom space (Parry 2010). Questions abound regarding the quality and rigor of online education, the degree of student effort required for online classes, and the training of faculty to use innovative online teaching tools effectively. An early leader in online education, the for-profit University of Phoenix has seen a dramatic decline in enrollment, falling from 470,000 in 2010 to 130,00 in 2016. Nonprofit institutions, led by Western Governors University and Southern New Hampshire University, are now the leading growth engines of online higher education (McKenzie 2018).

Even as online learning opportunities make a college education more widely accessible, the growth in online college programs may be producing a two-tier system of higher education. To date, little comparative research has examined the learning outcomes of online versus face-to-face education. Nonetheless, one highly regarded survey of academic leaders from more than 2,800 colleges and universities found that the academic reputation of online learning is improving. By 2016, 71.4 percent of the academic leaders rated online education as "at least as good" as a traditional classroom, up from 57 percent in 2003. Still, more than one-quarter of academic leaders judge distance learning to be inferior to face-to-face instruction. Concern about the quality of online education is far greater at schools that offer exclusively traditional classroom instruction—and these schools disproportionately are highly selective private colleges (Allen and Seaman 2016). Elite private colleges are likely to retain their focus on traditional classroom instruction, providing one-on-one mentoring and academic guidance that is largely absent from online programs.

Cyberbullying

Bullying and harassment in schools are problems with a long history and no simple solutions. Most school districts in the United States have adopted antibullying policies as part of broader efforts to maintain a safe school climate. In recent years, several high-profile cases of repeated harassment through text messages and on social networking sites, including incidents in Missouri and Massachusetts that involved teenage suicides, have helped make electronic forms of bullying, known as *cyberbullying,* an issue of national concern. What constitutes cyberbullying is still evolving, as are the legal issues associated with electronic and sometimes anonymous harassment.

Cyberbullying usually follows a pattern of repetitive actions, such as sending hostile or insulting text messages, posting inappropriate photos to embarrass someone, and rumor-mongering on social media. One recent study defined cyberbullying as "aggression that is intentionally and repeatedly carried out in an electronic context where a power imbalance exists between the perpetrator and victim" (Kim et al. 2018, 661).

The typical victims and the primary perpetrators are teenagers. Research indicates that cyberbullying "is a prevalent problem, similar to school bullying," experienced by up to one-quarter of students (Wade and Beran 2011, 45). Teachers, parents, and others who work with teenagers point to cyberbullying as a significant social problem, and news media accounts have helped

©Photodisc Collection/Getty Images

Elder care is a rapidly growing field. Some elder care providers work in residential settings such as nursing homes and assisted living facilities, whereas others are home health care aides who tend to senior citizens in their own residences. What kind of pay and benefits do you think are typical of jobs in the health care sector?

focus public attention on its dangers. Research indicates that cyberbullying can lead to an array of negative consequences, including fear and embarrassment, interpersonal violence, school difficulties, substance use, low self-esteem, and suicidal thoughts (Sabella, Patchin, and Hinduja 2013).

Schools are a primary site for responding to and preventing cyberbullying. School counselors, many of whom are already well versed in the problem of bullying, can educate students and parents about the forms and impacts of cyberbullying, help build programs to offer peer support to victims, work to implement effective school policies regarding electronic bullying and harassment, and develop clear guidelines for reporting cyberbullying (Sabella 2012). One recent study found that student concern about punishment from schools and parents is far more effective in deterring cyberbullying than concern about police involvement (Patchin and Hinduja 2018).

Workplace Structure and Power

Work experiences are incredibly diverse. Some people work at home; others go to an office, a factory, or a retail store; and still others report to a different job site every day. Some people work for large companies with staff all around the globe, others work for small businesses with only a handful of employees in one location, and still other people are self-employed.

Sociologists who study work examine both the specificity of individual work experiences and the shared features of diverse workplaces. As we will see, broad social and structural forces shape people's work lives, and work is a source of inequality in the distribution of both status and income. In addition, workplaces teach people profound lessons about how power works (see the Sociology Works box).

Occupational Structure and Status Attainment

Work and socioeconomic status are closely connected. Differences in pay help produce, and reinforce, inequalities of income and wealth. Table 13.4 shows some wide variations in average hourly earnings in the United States. These financial disparities have far-reaching effects, since high earners are much more likely than low earners to live in upscale neighborhoods and to pass on the rewards of their pay to their children. As we saw earlier in this chapter, these rewards include the wider educational opportunities

TABLE 13.4 AVERAGE HOURLY EARNINGS, U.S. PRIVATE NONFARM EMPLOYEES, SELECT INDUSTRIES, MARCH 2018

Industry	Average Hourly Earnings (U.S. $)
Professional and technical services	41.12
Management of companies and enterprises	40.25
Utilities	40.24
Information	39.15
Financial activities	34.40
Mining and logging	32.52
Wholesale trade	30.30
Construction	29.43
Manufacturing	26.87
Education and health services	26.81
Real estate	26.54
Transportation and warehousing	24.31
Administrative and waste services	20.44
Retail trade	18.47
Leisure and hospitality	15.79

Source: U.S. Bureau of Labor Statistics 2018d.

SOCIOLOGY WORKS

Kimberly Jones and Educational Publishing

Kimberly Jones has found her sociological training and imagination to be a valuable resource in her job. The recipient of a bachelor's degree in sociology from Cornell University in 2006, Jones works in McGraw-Hill's Reading Department, where she collaborates with the editorial team that develops K–12 reading textbooks and creates online learning tools for teachers and students. Jones was unfamiliar with the sociological perspective until she took Sociology 101, through which she became intrigued by sociology's emphasis on the relationship between the individual and society.

Jones's sociology courses trained her to be a careful and critical reader, learning how to extract important information from articles and books, an essential skill in her work. However, becoming a thoughtful reader was only the first step. As Jones gained confidence in talking with classmates and instructors in the sociology classroom about their readings, she developed vital communication skills, including the ability to present her own ideas about a text and to listen attentively to and absorb different perspectives on that same text. As for the discipline itself, Jones notes that sociology helped her open her eyes and ears to different ways of thinking about issues, a vital skill in all realms of public life. These various communication and critical-thinking skills are essential components of a sociological imagination.

Sociology also gave Jones strong writing and analytical skills—key assets in *any* workplace. Jones stresses the value of writing assignments that required her to examine sociological theory critically. As a sociology major, Jones explains, "you'll learn how to compose well-written essays in which you build and defend your arguments with an engaging style. Learning all of these skills will take you far as a student"—and in a future career.

Courtesy of Kimberly Jones
Kimberly Jones

Jones focused her study of sociology on business and organizations. Her courses taught her a great deal about what happens beneath the surface in the workplace. For example, Jones learned that there are often complex power dynamics in an office setting and that a person's official job title doesn't always align with his or her power on the job. The ability to recognize these dynamics and to respect the knowledge that low-ranking administrative staff often have in the day-to-day activities of the workplace has helped Jones successfully navigate a fast-paced and competitive work world. Ultimately, Jones observes, there are "endless possibilities as a sociology major."

> "With some creativity and courage, your sociology degree can take you wherever you want to go."

think about it

1. *How are strong communication skills—the ability to listen, speak, and write effectively—helpful in one's work life?*
2. *How do you think the ability to recognize the complex workplace power dynamics that Jones describes can be helpful in navigating the work world?*

SPOTLIGHT on social theory

According to the **conflict approach,** groups with more power in a society have an advantage in acquiring good jobs. Think of the job you eventually hope to obtain. What factors determine that job's prestige and earnings?

that are disproportionately more available to high-income families.

One of the oldest traditions in the sociology of work focuses on **status attainment,** *the process by which people come to occupy a certain level in a social hierarchy.* Status attainment research examines the economic and educational factors that shape an individual's life chances, particularly one's adult occupation. The classic work in this approach is Blau and Duncan's *The American Occupational Structure* (1967), which mapped the patterns in U.S. work life. Blau and Duncan found that the circumstances that lead some people into high-status or high-paying jobs, and others into lower-status or low-paying jobs, are not based primarily on merit. Instead, the two researchers found that factors such as parents' education, race, and community of residence were major determinants of a person's adult job and earnings.

Blau and Duncan's research was part of a broader trend within American sociology to understand the roots of socioeconomic inequality and to evaluate the degree of social mobility in contemporary societies. Much of this research focuses on people's work lives because work plays such a significant role in shaping how—and often where—we live.

Occupational Prestige and Job Satisfaction

Work-related inequalities extend beyond income disparity. An individual's job is also a source of his or her social status, and some jobs are widely perceived to have higher status than others. Income and status levels of jobs do not always go together. Some jobs are high paying yet not high status; others are high status but not particularly high paying.

We are usually aware of these work-based status differences, and we may respond to people in ways that reflect their (or our) occupational status. For example, you probably are willing to wait patiently for a doctor who is running late to see you, even when you have an appointment for a specific time. But you are probably not going to be as patient if you must wait for help from a store clerk or an insurance agent. Because the profession of doctor is among the most prestigious jobs in the United States, you are more willing to wait for the doctor's attention than you are for that of people—such as store clerks and insurance agents—whose jobs do not carry the same high status.

Various surveys measure what researchers call **occupational prestige,** *collective attitudes about the status of various jobs.* The measure is based on surveys that ask people to rate their view of the prestige of different jobs. A 2016 public opinion survey (McCarthy 2016) indicates that doctor, scientist, and firefighter are the most prestigious professions in the United States (see Table 13.5).

Sociologists also study what makes people happy with their work. A key assumption of their research is that **job satisfaction**—*the degree to which a person is content in his or her job*—is an integral part of one's overall happiness or well-being. Research shows a connection between occupational prestige and job satisfaction, but the link is not as strong as you might expect. The most comprehensive study of job satisfaction found that about one-third of people with low-prestige jobs are "very satisfied" with their work and that more than half of those with high-status jobs are "very satisfied" (Smith 2007). However, the jobs with the highest levels of satisfaction are not the same as the ones with the highest status. So, holding a high-status job is no guarantee of job satisfaction. Research on job satisfaction is more focused on *levels* of satisfaction than on the reasons why people are satisfied—or not—with their work. Still, survey research indicates that "the most satisfying jobs are mostly professions, especially those involving caring for, teaching, and protecting others and creative pursuits" (Smith 2007, 1).

TABLE 13.5 OCCUPATIONAL PRESTIGE IN THE UNITED STATES

Most Prestigious Occupations
1. Doctor
2. Scientist
3. Firefighter
4. Military Officer
5. Engineer
6. Nurse
7. Architect
8. Emergency Medical Technician
9. Veterinarian
10. Police Officer

Source: McCarthy 2016.

The Gender Gap at Work

A central concern for sociologists who study work is the **gender division of labor,** *differences between men and women in access to jobs.* One result of the gender division of labor is that, historically, men have monopolized higher-paying jobs and have therefore earned more money than women. Although the pay gap between men and women in the United States has closed considerably since 1980, the difference between their earnings remains significant. In 2017 the median income for women who worked full time for a full year was 81.8 percent of men's median income (see Figure 13.4).

As we saw in Chapter 11, sociologists seek to understand the diverse sources and the dynamics of the gender wage gap. One underlying factor is gender socialization, which likely steers girls and young women toward often lower-paying jobs such as preschool teacher and receptionist while encouraging boys and young men to enter higher-paying occupations such as engineer and architect. After marriage, moreover, women are much more likely than men to leave the workforce to care for children, a pattern again reflecting a cultural value.

Another part of the explanation for the gender division of labor is discrimination. Peterson and Saporta (2004) identify three different types of discrimination that might explain the persistent inequality in earnings between men and women:

1. ***Allocative discrimination:*** Patterns in processes of hiring and promotion that place women in lower-paying jobs than men.
2. ***Within-job wage discrimination:*** The practice of giving women lower pay than men for doing the same job at the same firm.
3. ***Valuative discrimination:*** The devaluation and lower compensation of occupations dominated by women in comparison to those dominated by men, even though similar skills may be required.

Peterson and Saporta report that within-job wage discrimination is not a significant contributor to the gender wage gap but that valuative discrimination is. For this reason, advocacy groups working on behalf of equal pay for women emphasize the concept of **comparable worth,** *a commitment to setting salaries for different job titles based on their value to an employer, regardless of the typical gender of those working in such jobs.* Allocative discrimination is also a factor; lower wages start at the point of initial hiring, when women are typically offered jobs that are lower in pay and status than men.

The gender wage gap is not just a problem in low-wage or low-skill jobs. Even among the most highly trained workers, earning differences persist between men and women. One study of University of Michigan Law School graduates showed that male and

FIGURE 13.4 | THE FEMALE EARNINGS GAP

Women's earnings as a percentage of men's

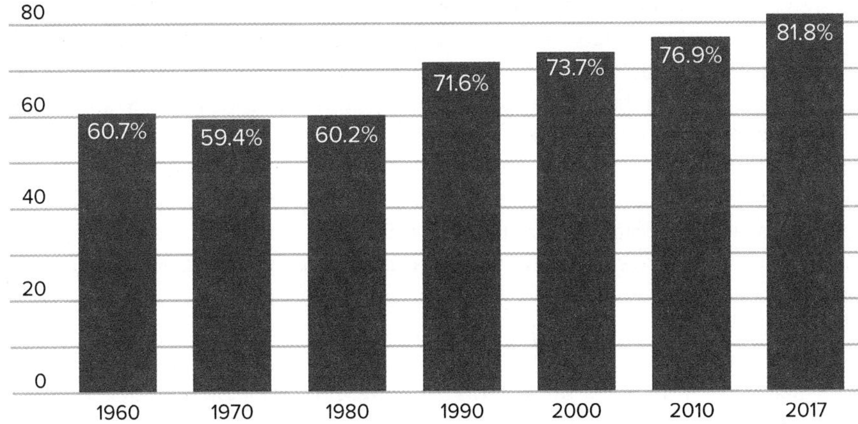

Women's median annual earnings as a percentage of men's median annual earnings, full-time workers, United States, 1960–2017.

Source: Institute for Women's Policy Research 2018.

CORE CONCEPTS CHALLENGE *What traditions in U.S.* **culture** *have been factors in these income differences? As more and more women attain professional jobs in which they exercise* **power,** *do you anticipate that the pay gap will close more?*

female lawyers earn about the same in the first year out of law school (Noonan, Corcoran, and Courant 2005). But 15 years later, the female lawyers earned far less than male lawyers with the same training—less than 65 percent of their male counterparts' earnings. The researchers noted that female lawyers work fewer hours than male lawyers and are far more likely to work part time or take time off for child care. However, the authors find little support for these as the reasons that women earn less. In fact, women *without* children earn about the same as women *with* children, and single women earn about the same as married women. Noonan and her colleagues concluded that the persistent earnings gap is a result, at least in part, of unequal treatment in the legal profession.

A subsequent study of early career lawyers working full time in private practice (Dinovitzer, Reichman, and Sterling 2009) found evidence of a persistent gender wage gap. Even when controlling for law school credentials, size and type of law firm, areas of law practiced, and city—factors that might explain different pay levels—male lawyers still earned salaries more than 5 percent higher than female lawyers. The authors concluded that their findings "make clear that in professional settings such as law firms, where work is defined by a complex assemblage and hierarchy of tasks, the mechanisms underlying gender inequity combine to generate a consistent devaluation of women" (847). A recent study of medical doctors in Sweden found similar inequity. Even when accounting for differences in specialization, male doctors earned about 7 percent more than female doctors, and the gender wage gap among doctors in Sweden has increased over time (Magnusson 2016).

Power on the Job

For just about all of us, work is a place where we can see and experience power in action. Let's start with a simple premise: most people who work are not their own boss. They report to, are supervised by, or are accountable to someone else. But some workers operate in the middle of a workplace hierarchy, reporting to their boss while also supervising other employees. With this kind of complexity, how can we understand power in the workplace?

One useful approach, summarized in Table 13.6, is to analyze three key assets—ownership, control, and credentials—that are distinct sources of workplace power (Wright 1985). This approach provides a valuable framework for thinking about power at work and the individual and institutional forces that wield it—owners, managers, professionals, and labor unions.

Owners

One form of occupational power is the ability to influence broad decisions about the operation of a particular organization or company, including how the firm will operate, who will run the day-to-day operations, and what resources are invested in the company. This is the power of ownership. Owners may not be on the scene every day, but they have a distinctive form of power that is a result of their ownership status. For example, billionaire Robert Kraft, who owns the New England Patriots football team, does not make decisions about game strategy or even hire all of the team's personnel. But he establishes the budget, hires senior management, and has final say on major decisions, including those concerning large investments in players and stadium improvements.

In many instances, ownership lies in the hands of a large group of *shareholders*—individuals who own shares of stock in a company. Shareholders may not exercise power in the same way as an owner, but they can still significantly shape workplace dynamics, especially in the case of those with a large ownership stake. In the early 2000s, major newspapers throughout the United States were forced to terminate newsroom staff when shareholders demanded increased profits through cost cutting.

Managers

A second form of occupational power is the ability to make decisions about the day-to-day activities at a workplace. This is the domain of a company's managers.

TABLE 13.6 SOURCES OF WORKPLACE POWER

Key Assets	Who Has Them
Ownership of capital	Owners of companies
Control of organizations (employees, budgets, decision making)	Managers of companies
Possession of credentials	Highly skilled professionals

Managers have the power to direct other workers—to tell them what to do and how to do it. A given organization may have multiple layers of management, and some managers have more power and authority than others.

The source of managerial power is the organizational hierarchy. A given business or government agency will have formal guidelines that specify managers' roles within the organization and the degree of authority they have. Patriots owner Kraft has a general manager who is responsible for acquiring players for the team, as well as a coaching staff that makes daily decisions about the line-up and game strategy.

The source of management's power can be very unstable. Managers, including general managers of football teams, are fired all the time; organizations are frequently restructured, and job titles change. That's why managers have sought a potentially more durable basis for power: credentials. Graduate schools of business—which confer the degree of MBA (master's in business administration)—provide managers with a specific credential that certifies their managerial training and differentiates those who hold a degree from those who do not.

The emergence of graduate degrees in business in the early twentieth century reflected a broader trend in U.S. business, as managers sought to develop new strategies for securing power, as we discussed in Chapter 7. Many companies adopted engineer Frederick Taylor's philosophy of **scientific management** (also known as Taylorism), *the effort by trained managers to study workflow and develop precise procedures that govern the completion of work tasks.* Taylor's approach rested on time and motion studies that used a stopwatch to measure and examine the specific body motions involved in a given job. Taylor would then reconstruct the job—identifying the precise way employees should stand and move their arms and legs, and the exact number of seconds they should take in each of these motions—in an effort to improve efficiency. Often, more complex tasks performed by skilled workers were redesigned into separate steps requiring little skill or training.

In Taylor's method, only managers, not workers, understood the overall production process. Moreover, lower-skill workers could be hired, paid a lower wage, and easily replaced. The advent of scientific management marked a substantial change from earlier periods when skilled crafts and trades workers not only performed the labor but also held the knowledge about how to do a job.

Although scientific management claimed to focus on efficiency, it was also a strategy for asserting a particular form of managerial power over workers (Braverman [1974] 1998). Today's managers may use different strategies to wield power in the workplace, often relying on the credentials of a graduate degree to legitimize their authority.

Professionals For some employees, workplace power derives almost entirely from having valued skills that are typically the result of a credentialing process that includes specialized training and an advanced degree. For example, physicians typically have an MD, lawyers have a JD, and most college professors hold a PhD. These are all examples of **professionals,** *a class of workers who are highly educated, hold degrees to certify their education, and have jobs that require a particular form of expertise.* Professionals make up about 16 percent of the U.S. workforce (Gilbert 2015).

Professionals typically have a great deal of control over the conditions of their own work. They are rarely subject to the kind of supervision that nonprofessional workers experience; instead, typical professionals are largely self-directed. Having control over one's own work is a significant form of workplace power.

The power of professionals is rooted in our collective belief in their expertise, which we trust because they have credentials. Perhaps that is why so many professionals—doctors, lawyers, engineers, architects, professors—display their framed diplomas on their office walls. Derber, Schwartz, and Magrass (1990) argue that professionals have learned how to "spin knowledge into gold" by turning their advanced degrees into jobs that generally pay substantial salaries and give them significant control over their own work lives.

An official-sounding credential suggests expertise, usually expertise backed by a professional association that certifies the credential-holder's training. But not all credentials are equal. For example, a financial advisor might have any of the following credentials, and it can be difficult to know what kinds of training or experience are associated with any of the specific titles:

- Certified senior advisor
- Certified retirement financial advisor
- Registered financial gerontologist
- Certified retirement counselor
- Certified financial planner
- Chartered financial analyst

The first four credentials require very little training—less than one week of classroom instruction. In contrast, the final two credentials typically require years to complete and include significant work experience as part of the certification process (Duhigg 2007).

Some professionals are certified experts in management with a graduate degree in, for example, business administration, public administration, or arts administration. Sociologists sometimes refer to these experts as the *professional managerial class.* They typically have the power to supervise and direct other workers, but their power is legitimized further by their education and certification. For *management consultants,* the high-priced experts that companies hire to help them reorganize or solve problems, power comes largely from their credentials as specialists in how to manage an organization. The recommendations of management consultants have the mark of expert objectivity because they are outsiders who have no loyalties to any specific

thinking about power

Reflect on a job you have held. Did you have **power** in this workplace? If so, how did you know? What were some of the consequences of your status?

group within an organization. These outside experts have the power and autonomy in their work that comes from their education and claims to expertise.

FIGURE 13.5 | UNION MEMBERS AS A PERCENTAGE OF ALL U.S. WAGE AND SALARY WORKERS, 1984–2017

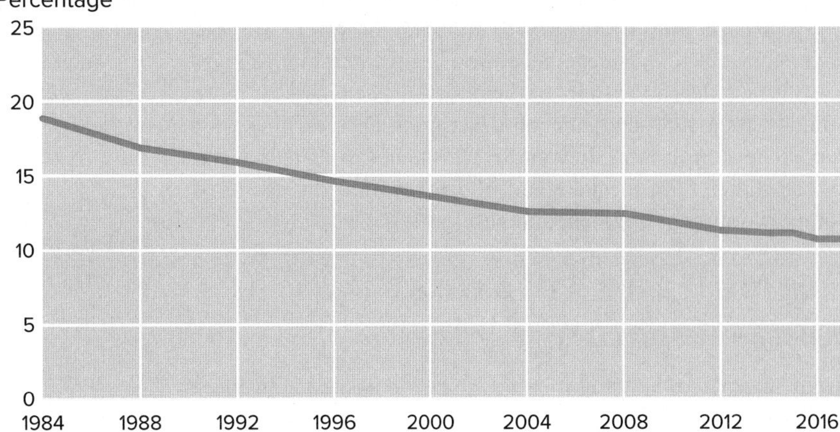

Source: Hirsch and Macpherson 2018.

Labor Unions Most employees do not wield a great deal of individual power in their workplaces. In contrast to professionals, the majority of employees are subject to control by superiors or by organizational rules that specify when, where, and how to work. However, far from being passive actors, employees use various strategies to cope with, oppose, evade, or otherwise act in response to workplace power.

In a widely cited study, James Scott (1992) described the diverse ways that individual employees seek to assert their power. Some arrive late to work, steal supplies or food from an employer, share information about a supervisor's whereabouts with other employees, and engage in nonwork activities during the workday. Greta Foff Paules (1992) studied how waitresses in a highway diner exercised power. Paules found that these waitresses were active agents who defined themselves as independent businesswomen trying to control the flow of people, food, and money or as soldiers fighting against both management and customers for control of the diner floor.

Individual acts of resistance often have little, if any, larger effect, however. When employees organize themselves and work together, they often have more power in the workplace than when they act alone. **Labor unions,** *associations of employees who join together for the purpose of improving their working conditions,* give workers the power to speak to their employers with a collective voice. By joining forces to address management, unions give employees power based on the group's solidarity.

The foundation for unions' power is the possibility that workers will act collectively and demand recognition for their grievances. If employers refuse to work toward a solution, unionized workers may strike to protest working conditions. A strike was the strategy adopted by teachers in Arizona, Kentucky, Oklahoma, and West Virginia in 2018. They went on strike demanding higher pay for teachers, who are among the lowest paid in the nation, and increased funding for public schools. The teachers had broad public support, including among many parents of school-aged children. Teachers in Arizona, Oklahoma, and West Virginia won pay raises, while Kentucky teachers went back to work after a statewide school funding budget bill passed.

The basic power of union workers is that their employers need workers—perhaps not any individual worker but the group of employees as a whole. More highly skilled workers, or those in whom a company has invested by training them for specific jobs, often have more power when they organize because they may be more difficult to replace than less skilled workers.

Strikes or work slowdowns are relatively uncommon in the United States. The primary way contemporary labor unions try to exercise power is through collective bargaining. In **collective bargaining,** *unionized workers typically authorize union representatives to negotiate with their employer on questions of pay, benefits, and working conditions.* When union representatives reach an agreement with management, and union members approve the agreement, an employer and a union sign a contract that specifies the terms of the negotiated agreement. These contracts typically specify wage and benefit agreements over a multiyear period, as well as issues associated with work schedules and other working conditions.

The presence of a union generally means that workers receive higher wages and better working conditions, but employers can also benefit. Unionized workers tend to be a more stable workforce. This stability means a higher quality of work and lower employer costs for recruitment and training.

In recent years, though, employers have been exerting their own power in resisting unionization efforts, and the proportion of workers who are union members has declined (see Figure 13.5). Taking advantage of labor laws that generally favor employers, bosses at many companies have actively fought union efforts. Tactics commonly used include firing workers who lead organizing drives, intimidating workers sympathetic to unions in "one-on-one" meetings, hiring consultants from "union-busting" firms, and threatening to relocate a company abroad to avoid unionization. In the past, these anti-union tactics have been used mostly against private-sector unions, but in recent years, efforts to limit or eliminate unions in the public sector–including those of teachers, police, and government workers–have increased.

Workplace Culture

In the cartoon strip *Dilbert,* frustrated, powerless employees struggle for job survival in an environment in which clueless managers create pointless rules and preside over nasty office politics. Just as workers vary in the kind of power they hold (or, as in the case of the Dilbert workers, do not hold), each workplace has what sociologist Gary Alan Fine (2006) calls a **shopfloor culture**–*a distinctive set of norms and rules that shape* *daily behavior and interaction on the job.* Likewise, specific occupations have their own norms and rules that help define how to be a baker, a teacher, an electrician, or an accountant.

Workplace and occupational cultures, however, are not always obvious to outsiders. When you begin a new job, you typically have to learn the ropes of the position. The task is far more complex than studying your job description and learning your specific responsibilities. In your first few weeks, you are likely to be socialized, both formally and informally, into the norms of your new work environment and new job.

Formal and Informal Socialization

Many workplaces have an orientation session for new employees to discuss the company's formal expectations. Some workplaces establish formal peer-mentoring programs that pair new employees with experienced workers who can give newcomers tips on how to navigate an unfamiliar shopfloor culture.

More informally, in some work settings, new employees go through an initiation process that is usually organized by fellow employees and often not officially recognized by management. The seasoned employees' intent is to teach newcomers the work group's informal rules. For example, when Major League Baseball teams travel to away games, first-year players are typically expected to carry veteran ballplayers' luggage. Experienced coal miners, according to a classic study by Charles Vaught and David Smith (2003), subject new miners to beatings and humiliation in their first days in the underground mine, as a way of "making a miner" out of the new hires. In both examples, newcomers learn that they are expected to respect old-timers and that each individual employee is subject to the work group's demands.

©George Marks/Retrofile/Getty Images

Clothing styles reflect trends in the larger culture. In the first half of the twentieth century—an era when formality and tradition prevailed—professional men and women dressed in a tailored, buttoned-down manner. In today's more relaxed business culture, a looser, more individualized corporate look is in vogue. With what broader social shifts—or changes in workplace culture—might these changing norms about appropriate business clothing be connected?

Much workplace socialization occurs through informal interaction with other employees, supervisors, and clients during the workday. Think for a moment about all the questions you might have on the first day of a new job. For example,

- What should I wear?
- Do I refer to my bosses by their first names or as Mr. and Ms.?
- What tools, if any, should I bring with me to work?
- Is it okay to check my personal e-mail while I'm at work? If I do, will anyone know?
- Do I really have to work overtime if my boss asks me to stay late?

You are not likely to ask these kinds of questions in a formal orientation session. Instead, you will learn the informal rules of your workplace by interacting with others. At first, you'll probably be keenly aware that you do not know the answers to these questions. However, once you are socialized into the norms of the work group, you will know when to show up, what to wear, how to address your bosses, and when it is okay to leave at the end of the day—without having to think about these issues. If you move on to a different job within the same company, you might have to learn the norms and expectations of your new job.

Emotional Labor: Managing Feelings on the Job

When you sit down in a restaurant, you probably expect a friendly smile from your server. If you've ever worked as a babysitter, you may have recognized that your employer expected you to be warm and nurturing. These examples illustrate an aspect of workplace culture that has become increasingly important as service jobs have proliferated in the U.S. economy—specifically, the norms of jobs that involve what sociologist Arlie Hochschild (1983) has called emotional labor. **Emotional labor** describes *jobs that require employees to manage their feelings and to display specific feelings to their customers or clients.* Flight attendants, for example, are expected to smile throughout the flight and to project an attitude of calm reassurance. Those who are successful do not appear to be putting on an act. For service workers, bosses and customers typically expect their "performance of friendliness" (Simpson 2008) to seem genuine.

One recent study (Singh and Glavin 2017), drawing on a nationally representative sample of U.S. workers, identified the jobs requiring the highest levels of emotional labor to be primarily in the areas of policing, emergency response, health, education, and service work (see Table 13.7). This study found that employees who work in emotionally demanding jobs often find satisfaction in the relationships they build at work. However, workers with limited autonomy and those who work for employers that do not provide support for dealing with difficult customers or clients are likely to experience negative consequences, such as job dissatisfaction or stress-related health problems.

TABLE 13.7 15 OCCUPATIONS WITH THE HIGHEST EMOTIONAL LABOR REQUIREMENTS

1. Police patrol officers and sheriffs
2. Emergency service dispatchers
3. Flight attendants
4. Health-care social workers
5. Correctional officers and jailers
6. Emergency medical technicians and paramedics
7. Bailiffs
8. Child, family, and school social workers
9. Criminal investigators and special agents
10. Education administrators, elementary and secondary school
11. Reservation and transportation ticket agents and travel clerks
12. Licensed practical and licensed vocational nurses
13. Radiologic technologists
14. Educational, guidance, school, and vocational counselors
15. Fish and game wardens

Source: Singh and Glavin 2017.

Workers doing similar jobs can face unequal emotional demands from their clients or customers. For example, female and male coworkers may experience different expectations for how they display emotion in client interactions. A recent study of college teachers found that students make more emotional demands, including requests for special favors, on their female professors than they do on their male professors (El-Alayli, Hansen-Brown, and Ceynar 2018). Some workers experience emotional labor as a source of empowerment, the foundation of agency in workplaces that offer little opportunity for workers to control the conditions of their own work. In their study of how restaurant servers manage the tipping system, Brewster and Wills (2013) found that "while servers report feeling powerless over the structural features of their labor (e.g., policies and procedures), they perceive themselves to have considerable influence over their interactions with customers.... Servers also report exercising agency in the service encounter by purposively employing techniques to avoid problems from arising or by using humor and excessive expressions of kindness strategically to cultivate the desired positive affect among their customers" (205).

A Changing World

UNCERTAINTY IN THE TWENTY-FIRST-CENTURY WORKPLACE

Workplace trends are tightly connected to the sweeping social, technological, and economic changes of recent years. **Globalization**—*the worldwide interaction or integration of social life, including economies, cultures, political systems, and populations*—is one noteworthy factor. The development and application of new technologies, and the emergence of new industries, are also contributing to dramatic shifts in people's work experiences in the United States and around the world.

To begin, the nature of the U.S. workforce has been changing. Today only a small segment of the population works in agriculture, and the proportion of people in industrial jobs also has declined significantly. New kinds of work have emerged and grown. For example, an increasing number of Americans work in jobs that provide services to other people and to businesses, such as health care, child care, and financial and other support services. And many new jobs are in the information sector, where workers collect, analyze, and store data about individuals and organizations.

The way work is done within the workplace has also been changing. Many workplaces now stress teamwork and flexibility—in contrast to more rigid and hierarchical management traditions. The work-team approach emphasizes employee participation and worker "empowerment." However, researchers have long debated the merits of team-oriented workplaces, with some arguing that teamwork is liberating for workers and others insisting that it is simply a new strategy for controlling workers (Hodson 2001; Tweedie 2013). Your understanding of structure and action should remind you, however, that as management imposes new work rules, employees will find ways to make sense of—and respond to—shifting management strategies (Vallas 2007).

In a significant shift, more and more U.S. corporations have been relying on **outsourcing,** *moving jobs out of the country to take advantage of cheaper labor costs elsewhere.* A wide range of jobs—in manufacturing, information technology, telemarketing, tax preparation, market research, and pharmaceutical research, to name only a few—has migrated from U.S. to overseas factories and offices, where wages are typically far lower. During the

thinking about culture

What initiation processes into a workplace culture have you experienced? Was there a difference between what you learned through formal and informal socialization? Why?

2016 presidential campaign, candidate Donald Trump promised to stop outsourcing and bring jobs back to the United States. In the first year of the Trump presidency, however, outsourcing of jobs continued at a steady pace (Greenwood 2017). Sociologists who study work are paying careful attention to the impact of outsourcing on education, family life, and other arenas beyond the workplace.

When corporations outsource jobs, workers must look for other sources of employment. In recent years, a growing number of people have begun to earn an income in the so-called sharing economy. Typically, these people are self-employed service providers who rely on the internet to connect with clients. The best-known examples of sharing-economy services are home-sharing platforms, such as Airbnb and HomeAway, and ride-hailing apps, such as Uber and Lyft. These innovative arrangements serve as alternatives to hotels and taxis, allowing people to rent their rooms, apartments, or entire homes to others, and car owners to earn money driving strangers from one place to another. The basic idea, in both cases, is for people to put their existing resources—home or car—to work to earn an income.

The range of services available continues to grow. TaskRabbit helps busy customers connect with cleaners, handymen, and delivery people. Online moving sites allow people to book local furniture movers by the hour. Other providers will board your dog, play cards with an elderly parent, or lend you money. Such arrangements are typical of a "gig economy," where temporary and short-term jobs are carried out by independent workers who contract with an employer.

In all these examples, strangers come together in transactions that require substantial trust. For many people, renting out your apartment to someone you've never met, hopping in a stranger's car, or dropping your dog off with someone you don't know is unthinkable. The internet solves the trust problem through what sociologist Juliet Schor (2015) calls "crowdsourcing of reputational information"—that is, the online ratings that build confidence in customers and providers. Still, most adults in the United States do not use these services. In 2017, about one-quarter of adults in the United States used sharing economy services, such as a ride-hailing app or online home-sharing service (Enberg 2017).

Can this kind of activity really be considered sharing? Some sociologists think not. In the high-profile examples mentioned here, the primary activity is selling or renting rather than sharing. Home-sharing clients are purchasing access to a room or home for a specific period. The owner may offer them a friendly welcome and a hearty breakfast, but the relationship is still more like staying at a hotel than with family or friends. Sites like Freecycle and Couchsurfing, which connect people who want to share goods or sleeping space for free, represent a more genuine form of sharing.

Most important, however, as sociologist Edward Walker (2015) points out, is the impermanence of this kind of employment. Workers in the sharing economy are essentially freelance workers, temporary contractors who do not receive the benefits of traditional full-time employees. Although these workers may enjoy flexible schedules, they do not receive health insurance, retirement benefits, or paid vacations, and they have little job security.

For all workers, the rapidly changing nature of work is a source of uncertainty. Sociologist Arne Kalleberg (2009; Kalleberg and Vallas 2018) argues that the contemporary employment climate in the United States is characterized increasingly by "precarious work," which he defines as "employment that is uncertain, unpredictable, and risky from the point of view of the worker" (Kalleberg 2009, 2). Kalleberg has identified five components of the rise in precarious work in the United States:

1. Workers' attachment to their employers has weakened; on average, individual employees in the private sector spend fewer years with a specific employer than in years past.
2. Long-term unemployment—remaining jobless for six months or longer—has increased in the 2000s.
3. U.S. workers are more and more concerned about the security of their own jobs, according to surveys; indeed, the perception of job insecurity has risen since the 1970s.
4. A growing sector of the job market consists of jobs that diverge from the standard, full-time, full-year schedule; more jobs are now temporary or represent "contract" work.
5. Employers continue to transfer risk to workers; employee benefit plans continue to shift the burden for retirement and health insurance from employer to worker.

©Paul Warner/AP Images

In today's uncertain employment climate, many jobs, such as that of a pizza delivery driver, require irregular hours, offer limited benefits, and are typically short-term positions.

Pointing to the significance of the growth in precarious work, Kalleberg and Vallas (2018) remind us that the consequences "are not restricted to work and the workplace but also affect many non-work domains, including individual health and well-being (e.g., owing to mental stress, poor physical health, and uncertainty about educational choices), family formation (delayed entry into marriage and having children), and the nature of social life more generally (community disintegration and declining social cohesion)" (2).

What are the implications of the changing nature of work for your own career? You will most likely change jobs several times during your adult life and work for different organizations. You probably will even change your career at least once. This employment path will stand in sharp contrast to the experiences of people in your grandparents'—and perhaps even your parents'—generation, who were much more likely to work for one organization for many years, maybe even their entire adult lives. Today, because large employers are far less loyal to their employees than they once were, many young workers assume that they will not be able to retain the same job over the long haul. Sociologist Allison Pugh (2015), in her book *The Tumbleweed Society*, notes that "low expectations for employers and high ones for workers shape the emotions that people are allowed to feel about the new ways of working, about workplace insecurity and the ascendance of flexibility in an era in which workers are responsible for their own careers, their own employability, and their own risks" (32).

thinking sociologically about

Education and Work

culture

- Education plays a vital part in instructing children about the core values of their culture.
- Each workplace has its own distinctive culture, which shapes people's everyday experiences at work. When people begin a new job, they typically undergo a process of socialization, learning the norms and rules of a new workplace culture.

structure

- Schools reinforce social and economic inequality through various, often unintended, means. Since existing inequalities are built in to the structure of the educational system, schools reflect and reaffirm these inequalities.
- Mapping the patterns in work life reveals the contours of the occupational structure in the United States. Research shows that the circumstances that lead some people into high-status or high-paying jobs, and others into low-status or low-paying jobs, are not based primarily on merit but on factors such as parents' education, race, and community of residence.

power

- Education helps reproduce social and economic inequality. Schooling can be a source of power for privileged students—those who have educational advantages, make beneficial social connections, build their self-esteem, and are encouraged to see themselves as future leaders.
- Workplace power is typically based on the possession of key organizational assets, which include ownership of capital (company owners), control of budgets and decision making (managers), and possession of valued credentials (professionals).

REVIEW, REFLECT, AND APPLY

Looking Back

1. Education is vital to the transmission of basic cultural knowledge from one generation to the next. The sociological study of education focuses foremost on schools—the primary arena of formal education—and on the process of schooling.
2. A sociological perspective highlights the various functions of schooling: transfer of knowledge, job preparation, occupational sorting, child care, social integration, change and innovation, and socialization.
3. Schools are among the primary agents of socialization in contemporary societies, teaching broad lessons that extend well beyond specific academic skills.
4. Schools reinforce social and economic inequality through various, often unintended, means. Because existing social and economic inequalities are built in to the educational system, schools reflect and reaffirm these inequalities.
5. Schools are complex organizations that are shaped by policies and rules, their own organizational histories, and wider social forces.
6. With today's digital technologies, education no longer has to take place in the physical space of a school building. More and more high school and higher education classes are being held in virtual classrooms over the internet.
7. Work and socioeconomic inequality are very closely connected because differences in work-related income help produce, and reinforce, inequalities of income and wealth.
8. To understand workplace power, we can analyze three key assets—which serve as sources of power—that people bring to their jobs. Company owners have capital assets, managers have control of organizational assets, and professionals possess credential assets. In addition, unions exercise a collective form of power that derives from their members' numbers and significance to a particular company's functioning.
9. Each workplace has its own culture—a distinctive set of norms and rules that shape daily behavior and interaction on the job. When an individual begins a new job, he or she typically has to learn the ropes of the job.
10. Globalization, the development of new technologies, and the emergence of new industries are contributing to change in and producing uncertainty about the work experiences of people in the United States and around the world.

Critical Thinking: Questions and Activities

1. Identify some socialization messages from your school experience. How have traditional and new messages coexisted in your own educational experience? Are the implicit socialization messages you are receiving in college consistent with those from high school? Explain.
2. Would making a college education available to all high school students reduce economic inequality? Why or why not? Consider what your response suggests about the relationship between education and inequality.
3. What do you think are the most important differences between online and face-to-face education? How would you evaluate the relative effectiveness of these two learning environments?
4. Consider the occupations that are ranked highest in job satisfaction. What, if anything, do these jobs have in common? What do you think are the qualities of a satisfying work experience?
5. How does an employee learn the shopfloor culture at a new job? What are some differences between formal and informal workplace socialization?

Key Terms

bilingual education (p. 338) instruction in both a student's first language and English.

charter schools (p. 338) public schools run by an organization that is independent from local school districts.

collective bargaining (p. 345) negotiations between union representatives and an employer on questions of pay, benefits, and working conditions.

comparable worth (p. 342) a commitment to setting salaries for different job titles based on their value to an employer, regardless of the typical gender of those working in such jobs.

credentialing (p. 334) the process whereby individuals with advanced educational degrees and formal certificates monopolize access to the most rewarding jobs.

cultural capital (p. 334) various types of knowledge, skills, and other cultural resources.

education (p. 323) the social institution through which individuals acquire knowledge and skills and learn cultural norms and values.

emotional labor (p. 346) jobs that require employees to manage their feelings and to display specific feelings to their customers or clients.

gender division of labor (p. 342) differences between men and women in access to jobs.

globalization (p. 347) worldwide interaction or integration among various aspects of social life, including economies, cultures, political systems, and populations.

hidden curriculum (p. 326) the lessons students learn simply by attending school, in contrast to the lessons from the formal subject-specific curriculum.

job satisfaction (p. 342) the degree to which a person is content in his or her job.

labor unions (p. 345) associations of employees who join together for the purpose of improving their working conditions.

literacy (p. 324) the ability to read and write.

moral education (p. 326) the role of schools in teaching children the central values and beliefs of their society.

occupational prestige (p. 342) collective attitudes about the status of various jobs.

outsourcing (p. 347) moving jobs out of the country to take advantage of cheaper labor costs elsewhere.

professionals (p. 344) a class of workers who are highly educated, hold degrees to certify their education, and have jobs that require a particular form of expertise.

racial school segregation (p. 335) the separation of students into exclusively white and exclusively black public schools.

school choice (p. 338) various policies that give families options for deciding which school their children will attend.

schooling (p. 323) organized instruction by trained teachers.

scientific management (p. 344) (also known as Taylorism) the effort by trained managers to study workflow and develop precise procedures that govern the completion of work tasks.

shopfloor culture (p. 345) a distinctive set of norms and rules that shape daily behavior and interaction on the job.

social reproduction theory (p. 330) theory that explores the ways that schools help reproduce systems of inequality.

status attainment (p. 341) the process by which people come to occupy a certain level in a social hierarchy.

tracking (p. 336) placing students into different curricular paths intended to accommodate varying levels of academic work.

©Damien Meyer/AFP/Getty Images

14

Media and Consumption

looking AHEAD

How do you experience the **power** of media in your daily life?

How might the role of media in your life be changing as the **structures** of media evolve?

How has the growth of consumer **culture** affected your social life and your community?

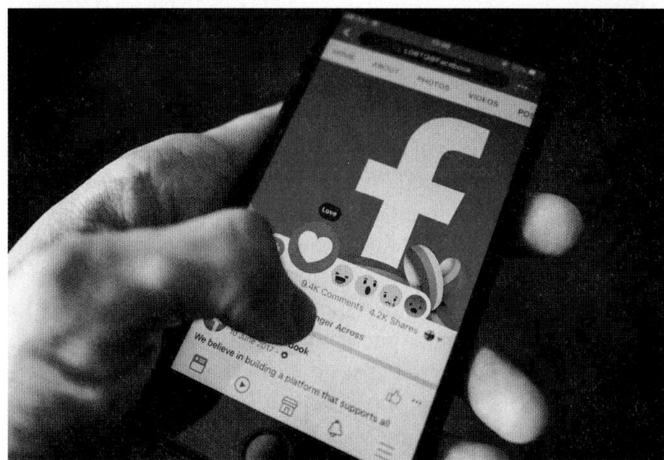

©Wachirawit Iemlerkchai/Alamy Stock Photo

If you have a Facebook account, have you ever seen the data the company has gathered about you? (Some of it is available from the site's "Accessing your Facebook Data" page; other data requires third-party apps to find, and some is inaccessible to users.) Much of your data may not be surprising but it is substantial (Gallagher 2018; Haselton 2018; Nield 2017). Your files include any "About Me" profile information you provided, such as your birthday, hometown, gender, relationship status, and employer. Everything you ever posted in your timeline is there, including all messages, photos, and videos, along with any file you included and any sticker you added. Facebook tracks every ad you have ever clicked on and every video you have ever watched on its site. It has every "friend" invitation you have ever made, accepted, declined, or deleted. It also has all of your friends' contact information, and it retains every Facebook event invitation you have ever received. Facebook archives all of your Messenger conversations (and Facebook owns Instagram and WhatsApp, which collect your data, too).

Some data Facebook collects is less obvious and extends beyond the platform itself. Even if you have not activated the facial recognition feature, Facebook has used your photos to compile the data needed to identify your face. Facebook tracks every date, time, IP address, make and model of device, and browser you have ever used to log on. When you use a smartphone, Facebook knows your location and the other apps you use. If you have an Android phone, Facebook has gathered all of the metadata from your phone calls and texts, including your contacts' names, their phone numbers, and the length of calls—whether or not they have Facebook accounts.

There's more. Facebook remembers every item you have ever "liked" on any website. By having other sites load code called Facebook Pixel, Facebook tracks what you do on those sites too, even when you are not using Facebook. As a result, Facebook has data on your movement across the internet, logging what sites you visit and how long you stay, what articles you read, what videos you watch, and what items you look at when shopping. Facebook's proprietary algorithms also create new data by making guesses about you (sometimes incorrectly). If you do not provide the information, Facebook will guess your age, race, sex, home location, and much more. If you buy textbooks online, it may categorize you as a student; buy diapers and you'll likely be tagged as a parent.

All of this is legal. With some variation based on your settings, you gave Facebook permission to gather this data when you accepted a user agreement that you didn't read. (No one does.) Facebook is free for you to use because you are not the customer; conveniently sorted and categorized for advertisers based on your detailed information, you are the product.

Media saturate our daily lives. We learn about our world, our society, and ourselves through the media's delivery of news and entertainment. We use social media platforms to communicate with people in our networks as well as to access and share media content, both serious and silly. Media profoundly influence our understanding of reality, play a crucial role in socialization, and are a central part of contemporary culture. The structure of the media industry shapes the content of popular media and the experiences we have with social media. As a pervasive presence, media have a powerful influence on contemporary society.

Commercial companies create much of the media content that surrounds us as well as the social media platforms that we use. These companies make money by selling media products to audiences, selling audiences to advertisers, or both. Consequently, most media are inextricably linked to promoting consumption. In this chapter, we consider both media and consumption in contemporary society. We apply a sociological framework to understand media as a social institution, looking at the interactions among the media industry, content, users, and technology within the broader social context. We then consider the role of consumption in society, examining how it is promoted and the consequences of a consumer culture.

A Sociological Approach to Media

Karl Marx, Max Weber, Emile Durkheim, and other early sociologists never saw television, imagined the internet, or conceived of a tweet. When they were writing more than a century ago, media played a very different and much more limited role. As the variety and significance of media have grown, media's role in society has become a central topic of sociological study (Croteau and Hoynes 2019).

Media Use and Types

Media is the plural of the word *medium,* derived from the Latin word *medius,* meaning "middle." **Media** are *the various technological processes that enable communication between (and are in the "middle" of) the sender of a message and the receiver of that message.* Print, telephony, radio, broadcast and cable television, film, and the internet are among the many types of media that exist.

While specific numbers vary based on the methodology used, it is clear that Americans spend an enormous amount of time watching, listening to, reading, or otherwise using various forms of media. For example, Figure 14.1 shows estimates by Nielsen (a firm that measures media audiences) of the average time members of different generations spend each day with select media. Often, people use media while engaging in other activities, such as listening to the radio while driving or cooking dinner with the television on. With people receiving vast exposure to media at all ages, media are arguably the dominant social institution in contemporary society, supplanting the influence of older institutions, such as schools, religion, and the family.

All mediated communication involves a sender, message, medium, and receiver. The different technologies that underlie various media are what result in different types of communication. We can categorize media based upon these various characteristics, summarized in Table 14.1.

Interpersonal media *enable primarily private interactive communication between known individuals.* With the traditional telephone, for example, you typically know whom you are trying to reach. You don't dial a number randomly; you don't try to reach a large number of people at once; and you don't expect an audience for your conversation. However, you do anticipate two-way interactive communication.

Mass media *enable primarily public one-way communication that reaches a potentially large and mostly anonymous audience.* Mass media producers who publish magazines, record music, broadcast radio content, create television programs, and make films generally hope to reach large numbers of people, most of whom they do not know. Such media typically have very limited or no mechanism for interaction. These one-way communication channels create a clear distinction between producers and receivers of media content. Producers of most mass media content are professionals in commercial companies, nonprofit media organizations, and governments, whereas ordinary users generally are limited to being in the audience consuming media content.

In just the last few decades, new technologies have enabled a third category of media to emerge and supplant other media forms. Originally—and sometimes still—referred to as "new" media, we can more usefully call these "hybrid" media. **Hybrid media** *have features of both interpersonal and mass media, enabling private communication with known individuals, public communication with a potentially large unknown audience, or both.* Such media were able to develop because of digital convergence and the rise of the internet. **Digital convergence** is *the merging of different forms of media through their transformation into digital information.* Historically, different media had clear material differences that kept them separate: print was on paper; movies were on film;

FIGURE 14.1 | DAILY TIME SPENT WITH SELECT MEDIA BY GENERATION, U.S., 2017

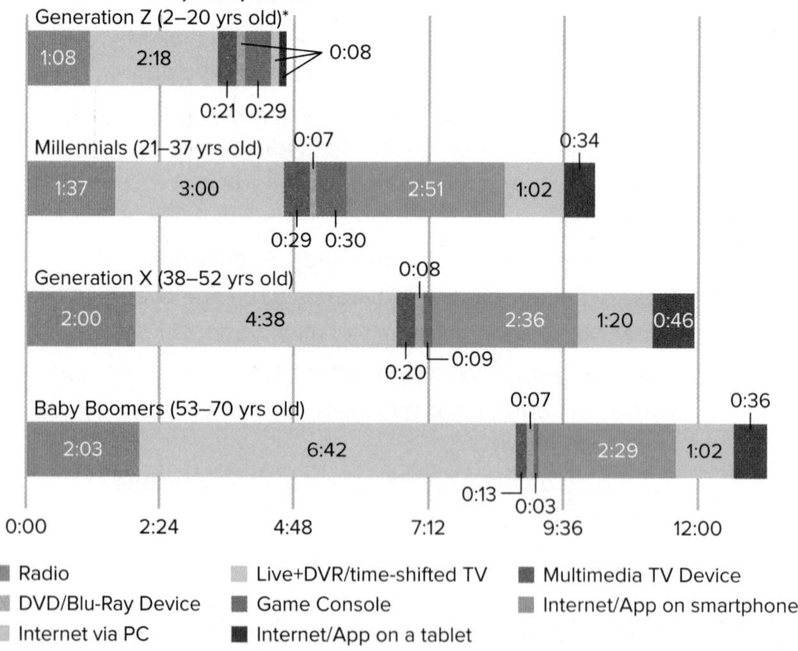

*Generation Z does not include smartphone data due to privacy; radio data are for 12–20 years old only.

Media use changes during the life cycle but is a significant factor at any age. These figures do not take into account the fact that more than one type of media can be used at the same time (e.g., using the internet while listening to music on the radio for an hour appears as two hours of media exposure: one hour for radio, one hour for internet use). *Source:* Nielson, 2017

TABLE 14.1 TYPES OF MEDIA AND THEIR USUAL CHARACTERISTICS

Interpersonal Media	Mass Media	Hybrid (or "New") Media
Examples: written letters, traditional telephone	Examples: print, movies, television, recorded music	Examples: internet and related devices
One-to-one private communication	One-to-many public communication	Private one-to-one and/or public one-to-many communication
Known receiver	Anonymous receivers	Known and/or anonymous receivers (and senders)
Individuals can be both senders (producers) and receivers of messages	Senders (producers) are distinct from receivers (audiences)	Users can be either/both senders (producers) and/or receivers
Two-way communication (interactive)	One-way communication (producer to audience)	Either/both one- and two-way communication

music was recorded on vinyl records or magnetic tape; television and radio content were broadcast with analog signals. However, new technologies enabled producers to convert all of these media into the 1's and 0's of digital code. For example, a compact disc can hold digital files with text, sound, images, or video, erasing the practical distinctions between these forms of media.

Furthermore, the internet and related devices (especially smartphones) enabled the quick and easy communication of digital content to anyone with internet access. Internet users can share media of any type—text, image, audio, video—either privately with individuals in their social network (e.g., e-mail, text, or direct message on social media apps) or by posting it publicly on a platform available to any user (e.g., Facebook, Instagram, Twitter, YouTube). Ordinary users, not just professional media organizations, can create some of this content in the form of photos, tweets, videos, posts, and entire websites. Online, this user-generated content can be shared widely and potentially go viral, reaching a mass audience.

We tend to take contemporary media capabilities for granted, but they represent a revolutionary change in how communication takes place. The variable boundaries between private interpersonal communication and public mass communication have created changes—and a new way of living—with which we are still grappling.

The Functions of Media

Reading this book gives you access to information. Watching a movie or listening to the radio can entertain you. Using social media can enable you to stay in touch with friends. Clearly, the many hours we spend with media serve different functions for us personally. The media serve similarly varied functions for society as a whole.

Sources of Information Media serve as the storehouse and conduit for a society's accumulated knowledge and information, from the mundane to the profound. By examining media content, we can learn everything from the latest sports scores and celebrity sightings to vital medical information and the policy positions of political candidates. In recent years, media have made information more accessible more quickly than ever before, transforming human society. Whereas information once was scant and difficult to obtain, a central challenge now is to make sense of the glut of information at our fingertips.

Agents of Socialization Whether serious or just for entertainment, media can socialize us by telling stories and informing us about our culture and its norms. Media provide models of appropriate behavior for the various social roles that are part of our lived experience, such as friend, parent, and citizen. Over time, our steady diet of media content influences how we come to understand ourselves, our society, and our world. Indeed, most of what we know about the world has reached us through media. Media socialization can be especially influential for children. They have limited life experience and have not yet fully developed their own identity, and yet they are increasingly barraged with media messages on TV and the internet. Children, in fact, spend more time with media than they do in the classroom or interacting with their parents (Rideout, Foehr, and Roberts 2010; Valkenburg, Peter, and Walther 2016). This constant media exposure shapes their understanding of the world.

Promoters of Ideology In discussing stratification in previous chapters, we defined ideology as a system of beliefs that justifies the existence of social inequality. But ideology also helps us define, explain, and make value judgments about the world more broadly. The dominant ideology promotes the interests and reflects the worldview of the powerful. The media's ideological function is not carried out by a single depiction in a movie or news story, but through the cumulative effect of exposure to many such depictions—and to the persistent absence of other depictions.

For example, U.S. news media typically take for granted the desirability of free markets, downplaying their negative features. They raise few questions about the growing economic inequality discussed in Chapter 9 or about the exploitation of workers in a global economy. Instead, the vast bulk of economic news coverage is actually "business" news, presented from the perspective of investors and managers, not workers (Kollmeyer 2004;

Verhoeven 2016). Much media content is linked to the promotion of consumption, with little regard for the social or environmental consequences of consumer culture. Even the recent uptick in environmental news coverage is often accompanied by the call for more consumption—this time of "green" products. The end result is coverage that explains the economic world from a particular perspective and treats this perspective as if it were the only reality.

As media carry out their various functions, they are enmeshed in a variety of social relationships that make the media a key social institution.

Media as a Social Institution

We summarize many of the key dynamics that make up media as a social institution in Figure 14.2 (Croteau and Hoynes 2019). The figure features four central elements: the media industry, media content, ordinary users (who both consume and create media), and the technology that enables mediated communication. Double-headed arrows throughout the figure indicate that influence is always bidirectional, reflecting the push and pull of structure and action. Each element of the model exerts influence on and is affected by other elements. For example, technology can influence how people use media, but users ultimately choose whether to adopt or reject these technologies. Technology also influences what the media industry can do but industry personnel ultimately decide if and how to apply new technologies.

FIGURE 14.2 | SIMPLIFIED MODEL OF MEDIA AND SOCIETY

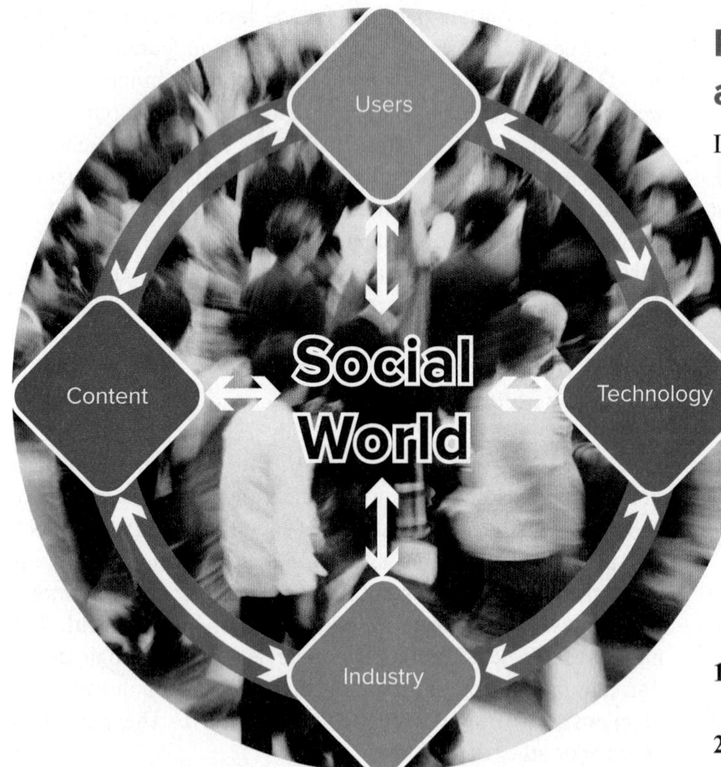

©Ken Usami/Getty Images

A sociological approach to media highlights the bidirectional influence shown in this graphic. For example, the messages within media content can influence ordinary users by shaping how people think; at the same time, user preferences can have a powerful influence on what type of media content is created.

Our figure also reminds us that the media process occurs within a broader social world that both influences the media and is influenced by it. Social forces—including cultural norms, legal standards, and regulatory practices of different societies—influence how the media operate. In turn, the presence of media in society influences how that society operates.

We will look briefly at each element of this media model, beginning with the media industry.

The Structure of the Media Industry

As we have seen, the rise of hybrid media changed the structure of communication, enabling ordinary users to produce and share content with their social networks and beyond. However, even with this growth in user-generated content, the importance of the media industry has not diminished. Instead, the industry has evolved, both producing traditional content and providing the platforms that shape user experiences (Croteau and Hoynes 2006, 2019).

Products, Platforms, and Pipes

In recent decades, the overall media industry has grown larger and individual media corporations have grown bigger because of mergers and acquisitions. In 1980, the American Broadcasting Company (ABC) was the nation's largest media company, with about $6.8 billion in revenues (in 2018 dollars) (Advertising Age 1984). By 2018, ABC had long been part of the Walt Disney Company, which had $55 billion in revenues—about eight times as big as ABC had been in 1980 (Forbes 2018).

However, Disney is far from being the largest player on the contemporary media landscape (Table 14.2). Today, the definition of a "media" company has evolved to include both traditional producers of media content, like Disney, and companies that were, until recently, more likely to be considered technology or telecommunications companies. These companies perform three key media-related tasks, providing the following:

1. **Products**—the media content that we watch, read, and listen to, such as movies, original journalism, or music recordings.
2. **Platforms**—the sites and services that find, host, and display media content, such as Google, YouTube, and Facebook. This includes streaming services—such as Netflix, Hulu, and Amazon for video content and Spotify, Apple Music, and Pandora for music. It also includes live programming via streaming services such as Sling, YouTube Live, and DirecTV Now.
3. **Pipes**—the conduits by which we access media content and platforms, such as wireless, cable, DSL, and fiber optics that

TABLE 14.2 SELECT MEDIA-RELATED COMPANIES BY REVENUE, 2017

Company	Revenue (in billions)	Key Activities
Apple	$217.5	Hardware (iPhone, iPod, Mac computers), streaming services
AT&T	$163.8	Telecommunications, cable, satellite and streaming (DirectTV)
Amazon	$136	Online retail, cloud services, hardware (Kindle, Echo) streaming services, original media content
Verizon	$126	Telecommunications and cable operations, internet (Yahoo!, AOL)
Alphabet (Google)	$89.9	Internet services (search, ads, maps), platforms (YouTube), hardware (Home)
Microsoft	$85.3	Software, hardware, cloud services
Comcast	$80.4	Telecommunications, broadcast TV and cable (NBC), movies (Universal), internet services
Sony	$69.2	Hardware, movies, television, music, gaming
Walt Disney	$54.9	Theme parks, broadcast and cable TV (ABC, ESPN), movies, publishing
Time Warner	$29.3	Cable services, movies (Warner Bros.), publishing, cable television (HBO, Turner)
Charter Communications	$29	Cable and broadband services (Spectrum)
Twenty-First Century Fox	$28.1	Broadcast and cable TV (FOX, FOX Sports, FX), movies
Facebook	$27.6	Social media platform
Altice Group	$20.6	Telecommunications, cable/pay-TV, television and movies
CBS	$13.2	Broadcast TV and cable (CBS, Showtime), radio, publishing, internet sites

Source: Forbes 2018.

Some well-known, others not, the largest media-related companies are involved in providing some combination of hardware, telecommunications services, internet platforms, and/or media content.

are the arena of telephone (Verizon and AT&T), cable (Comcast and Charter Communications), and satellite companies (DirecTV, owned by AT&T, and Dish Network).

Although it is useful to disentangle these functions to better understand how the media industry works, in reality it is increasingly difficult to separate companies into neat categories such as "media," "telecommunications," and "technology." Instead, integrated companies populate the media landscape.

Integrated Companies Media companies are often integrated. In **vertical integration,** *a media company owns the different stages of production and distribution of a single media form.* For instance, Netflix produces original content and distributes it exclusively through its own streaming service, thus controlling both production and distribution. **Horizontal integration** occurs *when a media company owns different forms of media.* An example would be a corporation that owns television stations, radio outlets, and newspapers. Figure 14.3 illustrates these two forms of integration; many large media conglomerates are both vertically and horizontally integrated.

Large integrated media corporations have distinct advantages. Horizontally integrated companies can create and promote products that are sold in different media forms: a comic book can be transformed into a television cartoon series and then made into a movie with an accompanying video game. Each form of media helps promote the other. Consider the blockbuster film trilogy *The Hunger Games.* This story about extreme class inequality and exploitative violence for entertainment generated millions of dollars at the box office, but that was just the tip of the iceberg. DVD sales, action figures, a game app, and advertising agreements with Cover Girl makeup, Subway restaurants, and others provided a wide range of additional revenue. There was even talk of a possible Hunger Games theme park (Maloney 2013). Whether it's the long-running *Star Wars* franchise, the

thinking about power

Commercial media are typically produced by hierarchical organizations, where **power** is concentrated in high-level executive positions. Decisions about what to make and how to produce media most efficiently are largely top-down processes. How do you think this top-down process influences media content?

©Michael Hurcomb/Corbis/Getty Images

As media companies grew in size and became more diverse, their products expanded into more areas of popular culture. For example, *The Hunger Games*, originally a trilogy of novels for teens and young adults, was transformed into a popular movie franchise and marketed aggressively through licensing agreements for hundreds of consumer products spin-offs including games, toys, clothes, school supplies, coloring books, posters, cell phone cases, jewelry, mugs, mouse pads, doormats, and umbrellas.

magic of Harry Potter, or the universe of Marvel superheroes, the mix of media and merchandise is a staple of the industry.

Concentrated Ownership As the media became more integrated, ownership of media became more concentrated. As the nature of the media industry evolved, ownership concentration changed as well.

Media ownership concentration occurs when more media outlets come to be owned by a diminishing number of media corporations. Journalist and media scholar Ben Bagdikian (2004) tracked ownership patterns over 20 years in various editions of his classic book *The Media Monopoly*. When the first edition of his book was published in 1983, Bagdikian determined that 50 media firms controlled the majority of all media products used by U.S. audiences. By the final 2004 edition of his book, he found that just five global conglomerates–Time Warner, Disney, News Corporation, Viacom, and Bertelsmann–"own most of the newspapers, magazines, book publishers, motion picture studios, and radio and television stations in the United States" (3).

Since then, the media landscape has changed considerably. First, several of the traditional media giants Bagdikian identified may have overreached in their efforts to acquire competitors.

FIGURE 14.3 | VERTICAL AND HORIZONTAL INTEGRATION OF MEDIA COMPANIES

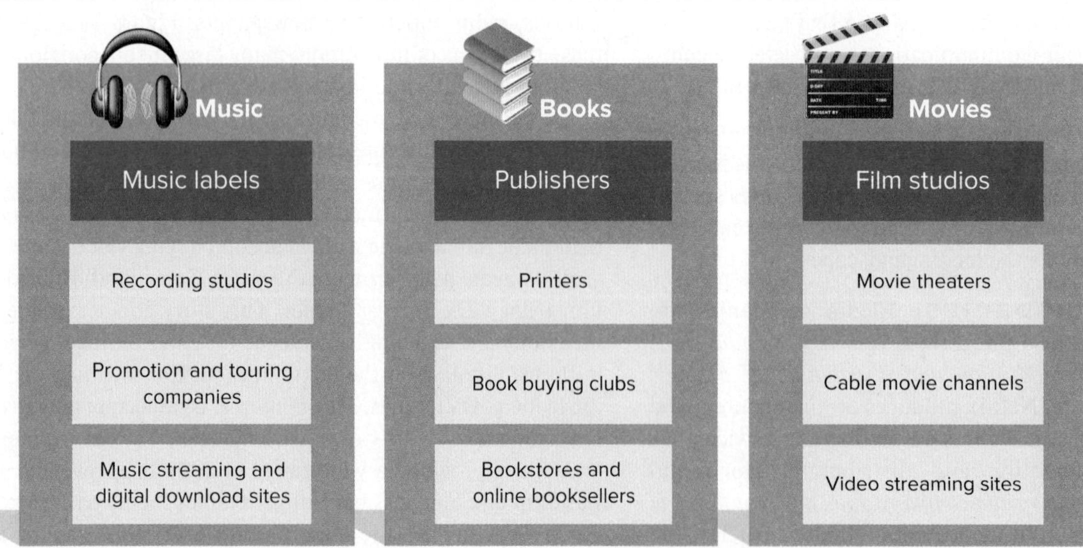

With vertical integration, illustrated in each column, a media company owns different stages of production and distribution of a single media form. Horizontal integration, illustrated by the blue boxes, occurs when one media company owns different forms of media.

CORE CONCEPTS CHALLENGE *How do media conglomerates gain forms of* **power** *from having each type of integration?*

Viacom, News Corporation, and Time Warner, for example, each split up into smaller units, selling parts of their multimedia conglomerates to focus their businesses more narrowly. Second, although not traditional media companies, technology giants like Facebook and Google emerged as new media giants in their own right by dominating online advertising revenue and fundamentally changing how users experience media. However, as the older media giants scrambled to compete in the new media landscape, they turned again to consolidation as a business strategy. Verizon's 2017 purchase of Yahoo! signaled the beginning of a new wave of consolidation. In 2018, a federal judge approved the merger of AT&T and Time Warner, combining Time Warner's media products with AT&T's vast network of pipes. The ruling set the stage for a bidding war between Disney and Comcast to buy 21st Century Fox's television and movie business (Kang 2018). Even in the face of change in the media industry, media ownership will continue to be highly concentrated.

Global Media Conglomerates

About one of nine of Facebook's 2.1 billion active monthly users are in the United States; the vast majority are scattered elsewhere around the world (We Are Social 2018). Google (2018) has offices in over 50 countries; Twitter (2018) is available in 34 languages. All major media corporations have an international presence, distributing their content worldwide, too. (See Figure 14.4.)

FIGURE 14.4 | WALT DISNEY COMPANY, SELECT HOLDINGS, 2018

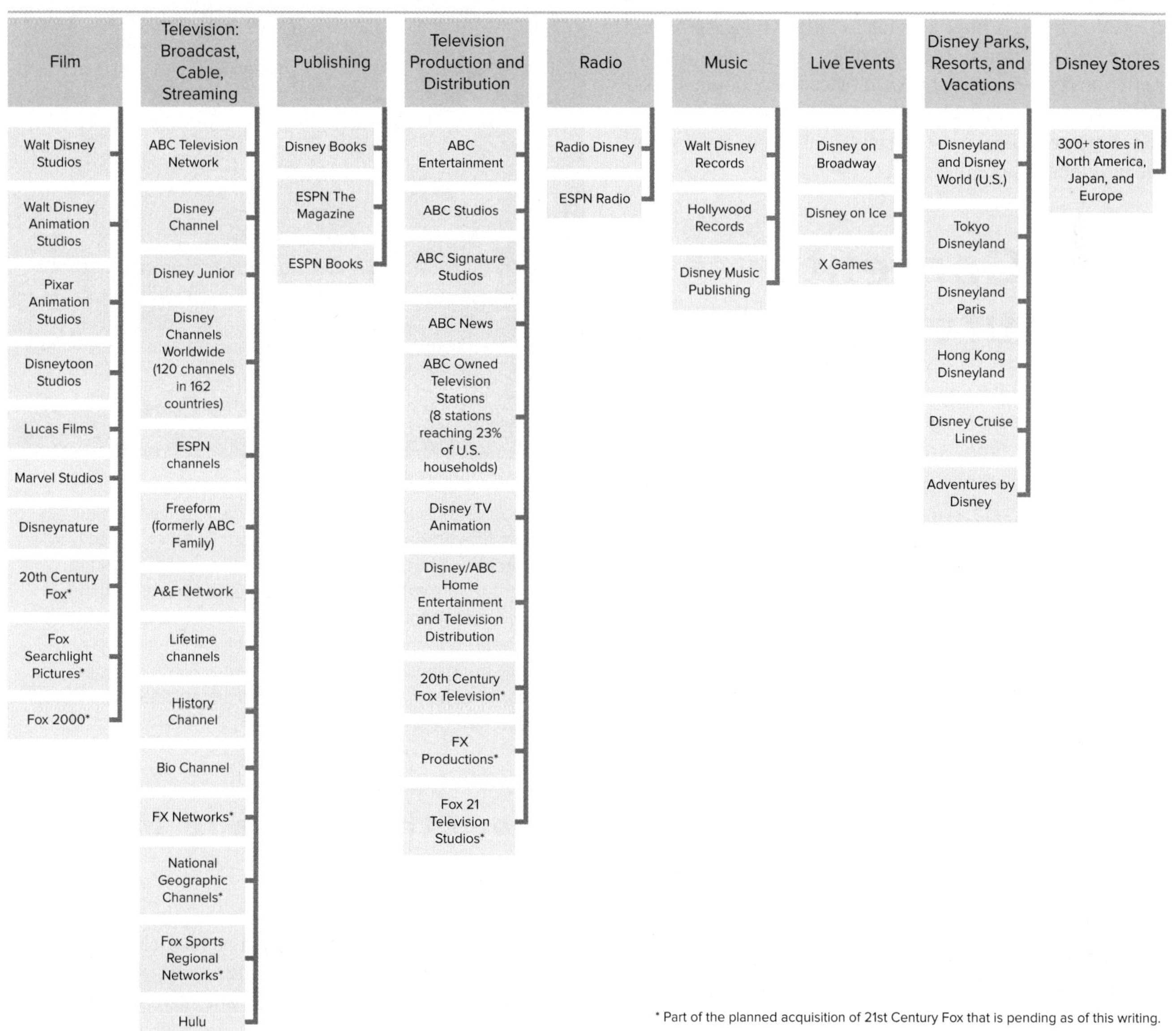

The Walt Disney Company is one example of an integrated media conglomerate with global reach.
Sources: Disney and Fox Company websites.

CORE CONCEPTS CHALLENGE *How might control of a vast range of media holdings be a form of* **power** *in contemporary society?*

Twenty-First Century Fox (2017) touts that its "global video brands–FOX, National Geographic, FOX News, FOX Sports, FX, Star India, Hulu, and Sky . . . connect over 1 billion subscribers in approximately 50 languages in more than 170 countries" (9).

Integrated media companies are global players and this often influences how they operate. For example, U.S. box office receipts alone once determined the success of Hollywood movies. Now, about three-quarters of box office revenue for all films produced worldwide is generated outside the United States (Motion Picture Association of America 2018). To capture a share of that revenue, U.S. studios try to appeal to global viewers by creating films that will export easily to other cultures. Dialogue-heavy films and subtle humor often do not cross-cultural boundaries readily. Instead, expensive Hollywood blockbusters geared to a global audience are often characterized by cartoonish adventure stories in which visual action and special effects dominate. A huge hit such as 2018's *Avengers: Infinity Wars* made $630 million in U.S. box office revenue the first few weeks after it was released, but earned twice that amount abroad during the same period (Box Office Mojo 2018). Such a film followed the proven blockbuster formula, shaped in part by concern for the global marketplace.

©BFA/Alamy Stock Photo

First appearing in 1966 during the civil rights and Black Power movements, the original Black Panther comic book character was the first African American protagonist in either the Marvel or DC universes. Superhero, political leader, and religious figure rolled into one, Black Panther reappeared in the 2018 Hollywood film of the same name. Part of the growing Afrofuturism genre, Black Panther is an example of how even fantasy and science-fiction content can comment on the "real" world.

Media Content as Culture

Media content is a central part of our popular culture. There is so much content that sociologists and other media scholars are usually interested in broad trends, rather than specific items, using several approaches to study it (McQuail 2011):

1. ***Compare media depictions to social reality.*** How does the depiction of women in movies compare with their real-world roles in society?
2. ***Compare content between two or more types of media.*** How does news reported on television compare with that found in online news sites?
3. ***Examine media content as an expression of broader cultural values and beliefs.*** How do music videos reflect contemporary values in the United States?
4. ***Evaluate the quality and performance of media based on certain criteria.*** How well did the news media perform in its coverage of the most recent election?
5. ***Examine the potential effects of media content on audiences.*** Do violent video games encourage real-world violence?
6. ***Study media content as a text, with its own structure, grammar, and syntax.*** To what purposes are musical soundtracks used in films and how have they evolved?

Because media play an important role in socialization, sociologists have been especially interested in the first of these approaches, considering how media content compares to social reality. We illustrate this briefly by using the example of race and ethnicity.

Race, Ethnicity, and Media Content

Media content reflects–and reproduces–the broader social inequalities that exist in society based on race, class, gender, and sexual orientation. Studies exploring media depictions have found plenty of underrepresentation and stereotypes, but they have also shown that the images of various groups improve as those groups gain more power in society.

For example, there has been much interest in content analysis that examines how media messages address race and ethnicity (Dávila and Rivero 2014; Dines, Humez, Yousman, and Yousman 2018; Lind 2017; Luther, Lepre, Clark 2018; Rodman 2014;

Squires 2009). Affluent, white men have historically controlled the mainstream mass media, often perpetuating racist stereotypes in the content they produced. In their overview of U.S. press history, Gonzalez and Torres (2011) contend that white-controlled "newspapers, radio, and television played a pivotal role in perpetuating racists' views among the general population. They did so by routinely portraying nonwhite minorities as threats to a white society and by reinforcing racial ignorance, group hatred, and discriminatory government policies" (2).

Throughout much of U.S. media history, blacks, Native Americans, Asians, Latinos, and other racial and ethnic minorities have been either ignored or stereotyped in roles such as the Black Mammy, the Indian Maiden, the Latin Lover, or the sinister Asian Warlord (Wilson, Gutiérrez, and Chao 2013). (The Sociology in Action box explores the efforts of one advocacy group to combat media stereotypes.) Kenya Barris, creator of ABC's sitcom *black-ish*, recalled that, when growing up, "I saw *Friends* and *Seinfeld* and thought, 'What part of New York is this?'" (Bauder, Elber, and Moore 2015). Both long-standing hits from the 1990s were almost exclusively white.

In recent years, though, racial and ethnic diversity has become a staple of many prime-time television programs, with barriers being regularly broken. In the 2010s, Fox's sitcom *The Mindy Project* starred a South Asian American actress—a first for network TV; ABC's political drama *Scandal* starred an African American woman—the first black female lead in a network series in nearly 40 years. Barris's *black-ish*, along with *Empire, Fresh Off the Boat, Atlanta,* and a host of other recent hits, have continued the trend.

More broadly, since the 2016-2017 season, African American and Asian American representation on prime-time broadcast television has been at or above their representation in the general population. Latino representation, though, lags far behind (GLAAD 2018). (See Figure 14.5.) Although varied in methodology and precise results, other studies have also documented the growing racial and ethnic diversity on television (Chin et al. 2017; Smith, Choueiti, and Pieper 2016). As one watchdog group summarized in its annual diversity study, "It seems that the broadcast networks are finally making serious strides towards more racially diverse representations" (GLAAD 2018, 14).

Trends can change, but for the moment we seem poised for continued growing inclusiveness in media content. But why? We can better understand what is likely to be going on with these changes by using our sociological approach to media and considering the interaction of industry, users, technology, and the broader social context.

First, most mainstream media are commercial ventures that pay close attention to user trends. Racial and ethnic diversity has increased in the population as a whole, and inclusive content is more likely to attract these diverse audiences to sell to advertisers. In this way, increased diversity is a money-making proposition. However, this may not extend to portrayals of poor and working-class life, which are not popular with advertisers and still relatively rare in the media.

Second, changes in media technology have resulted in more media outlets and content, making it easier to accommodate a wider variety of representations. For example, mostly due to the expansion of cable and internet streaming, the number of

FIGURE 14.5 | RACIAL AND ETHNIC REPRESENTATION ON PRIME-TIME BROADCAST TV NETWORKS BY SEASON, 2005–2018

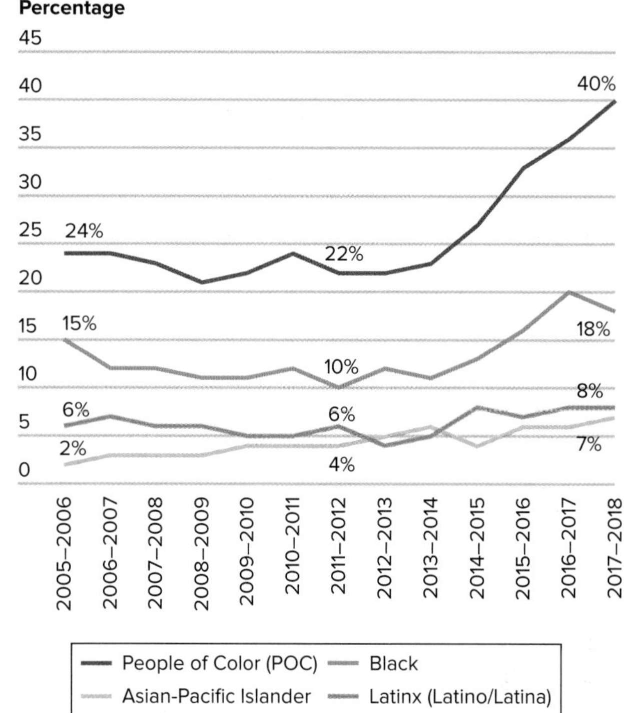

The percentage of regularly recurring characters who are racial and ethnic minorities on prime-time scripted broadcast series has increased significantly in the last couple of years. Since the 2016–2017 season, African Americans and Asians have been represented at or above their rate in the U.S. population, but Latinx characters remain significantly under-represented. In the 2017–2018 season, a full 40 percent of broadcast characters were people of color. (In 2016, the U.S. population was 61.3% white [non-Hispanic], 13.3% black, 5.7% Asian, 17.8% Hispanic [of any race] [U.S. Census Bureau 2018b].)

scripted television series more than doubled from 182 in 2002, to 487 by 2017 (Schneider 2018). Although the growth in abundance likely facilitates growing diversity, ironically it may undermine the impact of that diversity. With more choices, audiences are fragmenting and many Americans are not seeing the growing diversity in media content. Instead, television viewing is often segregated. During the 2017 season, none of the top five most-popular scripted series among African American viewers were among the top five of white viewers (Levin 2017). This segmentation of media audiences raises the possibility that the media are losing their role as a common socializing agent.

Finally, activists from both inside and outside of the industry have worked tirelessly to change media practices. Watchdog groups have long advocated for change. Various annual diversity reports on media content and personnel are common. Individual and collective efforts to promote more diverse hiring in key positions have been undertaken within different media sectors. Symbolic protests targeting major awards programs, such as #OscarsSoWhite and #GrammysSoMale, call attention to

SOCIOLOGY in ACTION

Combating Media Stereotypes

For decades, sociologists have been documenting how the media often stereotype groups of people, helping perpetuate racism, sexism, classism, and homophobia. Influenced by the evidence compiled by such research, numerous advocacy groups now track and combat media stereotypes, sometimes using the latest sociological studies. One such group is the Media Action Network for Asian Americans (MANAA). Among other activities, MANAA works "to advocate and provide reinforcement for fair, accurate, sensitive, and balanced depictions of persons of Asian Pacific descent in all facets of the media." As part of that effort, the group has compiled a list of common media stereotypes of Asians and the "stereotype-busters" that the media could employ to combat inaccuracies. Some of these are listed below:

Media Stereotype	Stereotype-Buster
Asian Americans as foreigners who cannot be assimilated	Portraying Asians as an integral part of the United States; more portrayals of acculturated Asian Americans speaking *without* foreign accents
Asian Americans restricted to clichéd occupations (for example, grocers, martial artists, laundry workers)	Asian Americans in diverse, mainstream occupations: doctors, lawyers, therapists, educators, U.S. soldiers, etc.
Asian racial features, names, accents, or mannerisms as inherently comic or sinister	Asian names or racial features as no more unusual than those of whites
Asians relegated to supporting roles in projects with Asian or Asian American content	More Asian and Asian American lead roles
Asian male sexuality as negative or nonexistent	More Asian men as positive romantic leads
Asian women as "China dolls"	Asian women as self-confident and self-respecting, pleasing themselves as well as their loved ones
Asian women as "dragon ladies"	Whenever villains are Asian, not attributing their villainy to their ethnicity
Asian Americans as the "model minority"	Asian characters with flaws and foibles, with whom audiences can empathize
"Asian-ness" as an explanation for the magical or supernatural	Asian cultures as no more or less magical than other cultures

Source: Media Action Network for Asian Americans.

The efforts of researchers who document media stereotyping and activists who advocate for more accurate and diverse portrayal can help make a difference. Media scholar Jack Shaheen has studied film and television images of Arabs for more than three decades. He explains the formula for successfully challenging media stereotypes: "People worked together, until finally they managed to become filmmakers themselves, producing, directing, and appearing in courageous movies that elevated their humanity" (Shaheen 2009, 6).

think about it

1. *What would you include in a list of media stereotypes about college students? What "stereotype-buster" would you suggest for each?*
2. *What TV programs have perpetuated stereotypes? What shows have "busted" them?*

continuing underrepresentation of women and people of color and invite users to express their support for more diverse representation. All of these efforts reflect the growing power of people who have been underrepresented in mainstream media.

Of course, increased inclusion says nothing about the quality of the roles available for racial and ethnic minorities. It is still possible, without much effort, to find examples of stereotypical racial images in film, television, novels, and other media. However, with some variation—research suggests the portrayal of Arab Americans has gotten worse, for example (Shaheen 2014)—the trend has been away from such unabashed stereotyping.

We have used the case of race and ethnicity to discuss content but, with some variation, we could tell a similar story about women and the LGBT community. Decades of simple, blatantly stereotypical images—or almost no images at all—dominated the earlier years of mass media. As media audiences and the media industry felt the influence of movements struggling for equal rights, these stereotypical images gave way to a wider diversity of images and roles for women and LGBT actors.

The Economics of Content

As we have seen, the economics of media influences the content. Most media firms operate in what is called a **dual product market**, in which *a company sells two completely different types of "products" to two completely different sets of buyers.* One set of buyers are media users, who purchase media products such as books and movie DVDs or who buy access to media products as with cable and streaming services. However, for most media, the primary buyer is advertisers who pay for online and print ads, television and radio commercials, and in-program product placement. In this case, it is important to attract the audience that advertisers want.

For example, if a television program with modest ratings reaches a demographic group that advertisers want, it may be renewed, whereas a program with higher ratings but demographics less appealing to advertisers might be dropped. Higher-income viewers are typically more appealing than low-income viewers. Similarly, younger audiences (who tend to spend more disposable income and are still solidifying what may become lifelong brand loyalties) tend to be more attractive to advertisers than older audiences are.

Dual product markets, therefore, are important because the way they are structured determines who has the power to influence media content. For decades, advertiser-supported "free" broadcast television had little competition. Advertisers wanted network TV to reach a broad audience. Networks accommodated by creating often-bland content that would be inoffensive to advertisers and mainstream audiences—and that often ignored minority audiences. Cable television and later streaming services introduced competition and operated on a different economic model. Premium channels like HBO and streaming services like Netflix asked users to pay for ad-free content. Such channels could appeal to a smaller slice of the audience and thus risk creating more diversity, more specialized programming, and edgier content that some might find offensive.

The economics of broadcast television resulted in content shared by broad mainstream audiences. The economics of cable television and streaming, as well as the internet more generally, resulted in content aimed at relatively narrow demographic and interest groups. Whether television programs, pop music, movies, or political discussion, specialized media content addressing smaller and more fragmented audiences results in a society with less cultural common ground.

Global Media and Cultural Imperialism

We typically think of culture as reflecting the values and beliefs of a society. But what happens when cultural products are imported from other societies on a massive scale? The result is what some critics call **cultural imperialism**, *the tendency of media corporations from wealthier nations—especially the United States—to export so many of their media products that they come to dominate the local cultures of other, especially poorer, nations.*

For many years, most nations simply did not have the resources to develop the infrastructure necessary to produce expensive media products. In contrast, well-financed Western media companies could add to their profits without incurring additional production costs by exporting content already created for the domestic market to foreign markets at a relatively cheap price. This helped to undermine the development of local media industries. In addition, U.S. media content tended to be secular and promote individualism and consumerism, which often conflicted with the traditional values of other nations. The impact on local cultures, critics contended, could be devastating (Hamm and Smandych 2005; Holton 2016; Schiller 1992).

While the cultural imperialism approach usefully put a spotlight on the power of Western media conglomerates, it has limitations (Elasmar and Bennett 2003; Tomlinson 2008). In particular, it does not distinguish between capital-intensive media sectors and less-expensive fare, thereby underestimating the role played by local media. A single feature film costs well over $100 million to make, let alone promote (Verrier 2009), and some episodes of *Game of Thrones* cost $15 million each to make (Ryan and Littleton 2017). This is far more than most non-U.S. production studios can afford. However, such high-ticket items are the exception. It is relatively cheap to produce high-quality music recordings, and Western and American music faces much more competition from local recording artists. Print and radio

In Singapore, a country with a large Muslim minority, a woman in a traditional headscarf walks past a Western-style advertisement featuring women in revealing bathing suits. The clash between Western media content and the different cultural values found in many societies is part of the debate regarding cultural imperialism.

have always been local because they are affordable to create, rely on local languages, and are based on local issues. Locally produced media content, finely attuned to local cultures, tends to be enormously popular. Thus, local producers have often successfully competed with the global media conglomerates by providing localized alternatives that differentiate themselves from homogenized international media fare, even if they don't have the big budgets of Western media products.

In addition, digital technologies have lowered the cost of producing media content in recent years even in the most expensive types of media, film and television. Local indigenous content has grown, and regional export centers have developed. For example, India, China, and Nigeria all have flourishing regional film industries. Indeed, some signs suggest that the tide of U.S. imports may have reached its peak as local and regional media industries compete more effectively for markets.

Still, as television, movies, film, and music become globally mass-produced, cultures may begin to lose their distinctive elements. In response, some governments provide financial support to nurture a local alternative to imported foreign media.

Media Power and Influence

Do images of rail-thin models contribute to eating disorders? Does spending lots of time on social media help create friendships or leave users dissatisfied? Have the media changed how politics works? Since the advent of mass media, researchers have examined the potential power and influence media may have on individuals, institutions, and society as a whole. There is no doubt that media have changed how people live and social institutions operate. However, those effects are often more subtle and complex than is generally acknowledged.

Active Audiences and Users

Early studies in the first half of the twentieth century emphasized media's power to influence audiences, as with propaganda campaigns during the two world wars. Later critics called these the *hypodermic model* of media influence, since they seemed to suggest that media could inject ideas into the public mind, much like a hypodermic needle. Another approach, *mass society theory,* argued that modern society had experienced a decline in traditional social bonds, such as the family and the neighborhood, leaving audiences susceptible to the influence of mass media. These approaches treated people as passive recipients of media messages.

In response, a variety of researchers began paying more attention to how **active audiences** *make choices about how they use the media and actively interpret media content.* First, "uses and gratifications" researchers examined *what* people do with media and *why* they are using media. This research found that users played an active role in choosing what media they were exposed to (known as "selective exposure") and that they often did so to meet particular needs, such as finding information, spending time relaxing with family, or escaping from the mundane demands of daily life.

A second approach, critical cultural studies, focused on how people interpret and make meaning out of the media content they use. Researchers found that media content does not usually have a single meaning and that people actively interpret such content in variable ways, based on their social identities, including their race, class, gender, age, and nationality (Storey 2015). In a classic study, media scholars Jhally and Lewis (1992) found that white and black audiences liked the popular 1980s sitcom *The Cosby Show* for dramatically different reasons. Blacks appreciated the references to African American culture and the positive portrayal of a black family. Whites, though, tended to see the show as evidence that successful blacks could be just like whites; they liked the portrayal because it was nonracial. In a dynamic observed in many audience studies, *Cosby* audiences were active interpreters of media content, but their social positions influenced those interpretations.

The internet enables active use and interpretation within the context of online communities. Some people are involved in fan communities, sharing opinions, analysis, and criticism about media personalities and media content in fan forums or their own blogs. They may create "fan fiction," writing alternative storylines for characters, or even attend in-person events with other fans. Users watching television can employ a "second screen" (e.g., mobile phone, tablet) to access Twitter and other internet platforms to discuss what they are seeing on television in real time. In doing so, audience members create and contribute to a real-time, user-generated media landscape that exists alongside, and in response to, traditional mass circulation television (Highland, Harrington, and Bruns 2013; McClelland 2012).

Influencing Individuals: Setting Agendas and Cultivating Beliefs

The existence of active users does not mean that the media have no influence. It does mean that such influence is more nuanced than early research recognized. Media effects are difficult to prove definitively because people experience many influences at once in their complex social environment. Nevertheless, numerous studies using various methodologies have given us significant insight into the media's social influence.

For example, **agenda-setting theory** *holds that media may not be able to tell people what to think, but they can significantly influence what people think about.* They do so through their emphasis (or silence) on various issues. This effect is especially true for the news media, but entertainment media, too, can raise or stifle awareness of specific social and political issues.

Also, **cultivation theory** *argues that by repeated and long-term exposure to the media's portrayal of the world (especially on television), people come to accept many of these depictions as reality.* For example, local broadcast news programs are notorious for emphasizing crime, fires, and accidents, and entertainment television often focuses on crime. In what is called the "mean world syndrome," researchers found that long-term heavy viewers of such broadcasts are more likely than light or moderate viewers to believe that the world is dangerous, people cannot be trusted, and most people are selfishly looking out for themselves (Gerbner et al. 2008; Morgan and Shanahan 2014). In effect, exposure to constant images of danger and violence lead heavy viewers to believe that this depiction accurately represents their community.

Affecting Society: Mediatization

Rather than focus on how media might influence individuals, **mediatization** *examines how the omnipresence of media has changed various aspects of society.* The examples are endless (Esser and Strömbäck 2014; Hepp, Hjarvard, and Lundby 2015). Smartphones, texting, and video chatting have changed how families communicate and stay in touch. Medicine is different because patients can now Google health information before consulting a doctor. Online shopping and product reviews have changed consumption, business, and the economy more broadly. Online information resources have altered education. Everything from campaign commercials to presidential tweeting has transformed political life. Perhaps most obviously, an endless supply of media content has transformed leisure time across the globe.

Mediatization incorporates theories of individual influence but emphasizes macro-level processes, similar to the ideas of individualization or globalization (Hjarvard 2008). While mediatization has been occurring since the rise of media itself, most observers argue that it has accelerated since the latter part of the twentieth century. Winfried Schulz (2004) groups the changes brought about by mediatization into four key categories:

1. Media extend the ability of humans to communicate across both time and space.
2. Media replace some forms of face-to-face interactions, as with online banking.
3. Media infiltrate and coexist with everyday communication, as with checking your cell phone while talking with a friend, or "talking around" a television program while watching with others.
4. "Media logic" encourages people to adjust their attitudes and behaviors to accommodate the needs of a medium, as when politicians speak in pithy sound bites that are easy for journalists to insert in a news story, or social media users present an "ideal self" online to appeal to others in their network.

There is no single mediatization process; it manifests itself differently in different social and cultural contexts. However, these changes are profound. Indeed, sociologists Couldry and Hepp (2017) argue for the need to rethink the character of the entire social world "starting out from the principle that the social is constructed from, and through, technologically mediated processes and infrastructures of communication, that is, through what we have come to call 'media'" (1).

Inequality: Digital Divides

The potential influence of media, as well as their potential benefits, is tempered by social inequality. The **digital divide** refers to *the gap between those who have the knowledge and resources needed to use digital information technology, especially computers and the internet, and those who do not.*

Within the United States, the digital divide has closed substantially since the early days of the internet. By 2018, about 9 of 10 adults used the internet, three-quarters were online daily, and about one-quarter said they were online almost constantly (Perrin and Jiang 2018). There was almost no gap in usage based on race or gender, but there were gaps based on age, class (income, educational attainment), and community type. (See Figure 14.6). Gaps based on age and class have decreased substantially over the last two decades, but the gap based on community type has remained essentially unchanged. While 9 of 10 adults use the internet, only about two-thirds have home broadband access (Pew Research Center 2018b). The largest gap in broadband access is based on class (income and education), likely due to high costs.

One survey found that, of those who do not use the internet, about one-third said it was not relevant (e.g., no interest, waste of time, too busy), another third found it difficult to use (e.g., frustrating, physically unable, concerns about spam, viruses,

FIGURE 14.6 | DIGITAL DIVIDE: U.S. ADULTS WHO DO NOT USE THE INTERNET, 2018

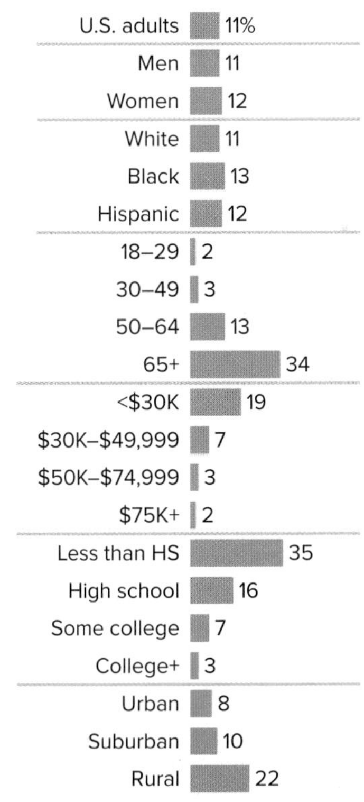

Early digital divides based on race and gender have all but disappeared; only those associated with age, class (income and education), and community type remain.
Source: Anderson, Perrin, and Jiang 2018.

FIGURE 14.7 | GLOBAL INTERNET USE, 2018

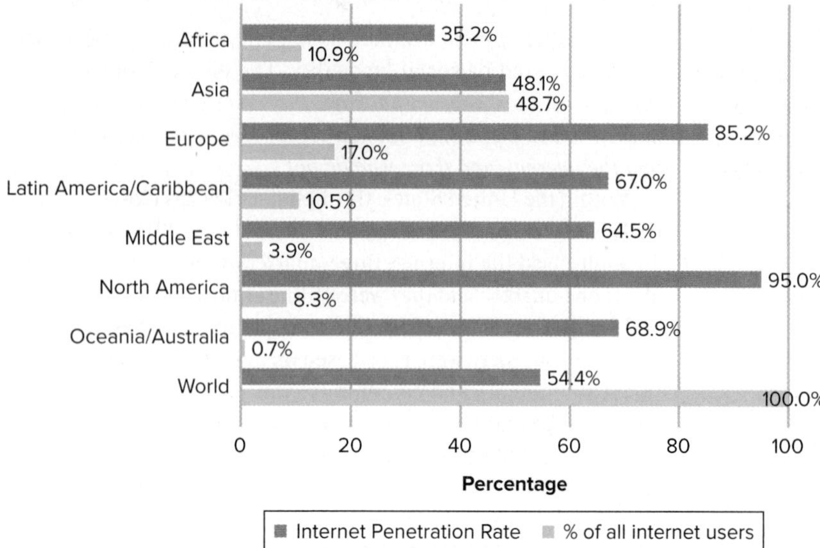

Much of the world still lacks access to the internet. Whereas 95 percent of North Americans can go online, only 35 percent of Africans are able to do so. Such dramatic discrepancies in internet access can have economic and political consequences. *Source:* World Internet Stats 2018.

CORE CONCEPTS CHALLENGE *In what ways can access to the internet be a source of power? How might the "digital divide" help perpetuate global inequalities?*

spyware, and hackers); one of five said it was too expensive; and about 7 percent did not have available internet access where they lived (Zickuhr 2013).

Another digital divide exists between wealthy and poor regions of the world. Comparable figures can be difficult to obtain, but as of early 2018, estimates of the percentage of the population with internet access (known as the "penetration rate") ranged from a high of 95 percent in North America to a low of 35 percent in Africa. (See Figure 14.7.) Just as the infrastructure for traditional mass media developed unevenly following preexisting lines of economic inequality, so too has access to the internet. Rather than being a forum for a shared "global village," the internet remains the preserve of the world's privileged. Even in 2018, a full 45 percent of the world's population was not online. In addition, largely because of language barriers, even those who are online remain almost invisible to most American users. It is easy to forget that nearly half (48.7 percent) of all internet users are in Asia, while only one of twelve (8.3 percent) are in North America.

The Social Impacts of Technology

For most people, the "Triple Revolution" (Rainie and Wellman 2012) of expanding internet, mobile communications, and social networks has been a positive occurrence. One survey of Americans found that 70 percent of users saw the internet's impact as a good thing for society, and 88 percent said it had been a good thing for them personally, especially in providing access to more information and strengthening their relationships with family and friends (Smith and Olmstead 2018). However, those numbers were a small decline from just a few years earlier. As the internet matures, many scholars and ordinary citizens are raising concerns about the consequences these technologies might be having for society.

Social Media: Connection, Distraction, and Compulsion

A "network effect" is said to exist when the value of a product or service increases the more people use it. Social media are certainly an example of this. For users, the benefits of a particular platform increase when other people they know also use it. For companies that own the platforms—and for advertisers using them to target potential customers—their economic value increases with more people joining and staying active. From a social media company's perspective, making more money always involves attracting more users and keeping existing users engaged as long as possible.

To do this, social media encourage self-disclosure, erasing the line between public and private identity, and self-promotion, sharing your thoughts, what you are doing, where you are going, what you are consuming (Curran, Fenton, and Freedman 2016). The content users create on a social media platform like Snapchat, Instagram, YouTube, Facebook, Twitter, and Reddit attracts and retains more eyeballs to sell to advertisers thereby adding value to these companies. Social media sites quantify engagement by tracking the number of "followers" or "friends" each user has, or how many "shares," "likes," and "retweets" a post receives. These numbers serve as a measure of popularity and, for some people, can be a compelling reason to keep returning to the site. Carefully grooming a public image of oneself to maximize that popularity becomes a common feature of social media. The reciprocal nature of this process—such as following those who follow you, retweeting others in the hope they will retweet you—also helps to promote engagement.

All of this can make social media use compulsive. For example, about 45 percent of U.S. teens 13 to 17 years old say they are on social media "almost constantly," while another 44 percent say they use social media several times a day. The result of such use is a mixed bag, though. Nearly a third (31 percent) of teens say social media is a mostly positive experience for people their age, primarily because it helps them connect with friends. However, a quarter of teens (24 percent) say social media's effect is mostly negative because it facilitates bullying and rumor-spreading, a loss of in-person contact, unrealistic views of others' lives, distraction or addiction, and peer pressure. Nearly half of teens (45 percent) see social media as neither good nor bad (Anderson and Jiang 2018).

Research suggests that the effects of social media and internet use are dependent on social factors users bring to the experience (Nadkarni and Hofmann 2012; Oh et al. 2014). Most users enjoy and benefit from social media use. However, for some users, comparing themselves against idealized online persona can leave them envious, dissatisfied, and focused on the negative shortcomings of their own lives, even to the point of depression (Appel, Gerlach, and Crusius 2016; Feinstein et al. 2013; Shakya and Christakis 2017). Some analysts even argue that people with certain preexisting psychological conditions can become "addicted" to internet use just as they can to gambling. Components of such addiction include preoccupation with internet use; repeated unsuccessful attempts to reduce use; disturbances in mood when attempting to reduce use; greater use than anticipated or desired; lying about the extent of use; and overuse to the point of jeopardizing employment, education, or relationships (Christakis 2010).

Source: U.S House of Representatives Permanent Select Committee on Intelligence Democrats.

Source: U.S House of Representatives Permanent Select Committee on Intelligence Democrats.

In the run-up to the 2016 presidential election, Russian agents created fake Twitter and Facebook accounts and placed ads targeting potential voters. Many of the ads aimed to inflame divisions around race, religion, guns, and immigration. Others attacked Democratic candidates or supported Donald Trump's campaign.

Some of the very people who have designed social media's best-known and most compulsive features have since denounced their negative influence. Jason Rosenstein, the Facebook engineer who designed the "like" button says, "It is very common for humans to develop things with the best of intentions and for them to have unintended, negative consequences." He now goes to great extremes to avoid addictive aspects of the internet and says, "One reason I think it is particularly important for us to talk about this now is that we may be the last generation that can remember life before." Tristan Harris, a former Google employee turned public critic agrees, warning, "All of our minds can be hijacked. Our choices are not as free as we think they are" (Lewis 2017).

Some observers contend that compulsive social media use is part of a broader culture of distraction. Technology writer Maggie Jackson (2008) argues that our embrace of social media and the internet has produced a sort of attention-deficit culture. Characterized by constant stimulation, interruption, and multitasking, this culture provides little intellectual nutritional value and undermines our ability to focus, concentrate, and attend to deeper and substantive issues. Others suggest that the immediacy and personalized nature of social networking promotes a focus on novelty, the self, and friends. Information or news that is not about this narrow world is often ignored. The result is a worldview that promotes entitlement and self-centeredness, what social psychologist Jean Twenge (2014) dubbed "Generation Me."

As with many things, moderation may be the happy middle ground. The ability of the internet and social media to connect people is one of its greatest features. Media writer and scholar William Powers (2010) agrees, but argues that wisdom, insight, and perspective are gained from being *disconnected*—by creating time and space for solitude and contemplative thought. A healthy and vibrant life in the digital age, he argues, needs to involve a balance between the advantages of connectivity and the benefits of solitude.

Algorithms and Bots: Filter Bubbles and Propaganda

Media scholar Siva Vaidhyanathan (2018) argues, "If you wanted to build a machine that would distribute propaganda to millions of people, distract them from important issues, energize hatred and bigotry, erode social trust, undermine journalism, foster doubts about science, and engage in massive surveillance all at once, you would make something a lot like Facebook" (19). One factor leading to this assessment is Facebook's use of algorithms.

As we saw in Chapter 5, the algorithms that programmers create can be influential and produce unintended results. Algorithms—the software code created to accomplish various tasks without human intervention—are usually designed to promote continued online engagement so they tend to steer users toward things they already like. This may not be much of an issue when it comes to suggesting music or fashion, but it does create major problems with social and political content. Being fed only the things an algorithm knows you already like can result in "echo chambers" (Sunstein 2017) or "filter bubbles" (Pariser 2011), where users are never exposed to alternative views while having their existing views constantly reinforced. Over time, Facebook newsfeeds, Twitter streams, YouTube recommendations, and other sources can all amplify a single point of view. If users "like" or simply view stories or videos taking one side or another on a social or political issue, the algorithms will highlight similar stories and downplay opposing views. Further, there is evidence that over time these recommendations tend to suggest content with more extreme views, contributing to political polarization (Tufecki 2018).

Autocratic leaders have found ways to use social media's algorithms to promote misinformation and discourage dissent—an effort sometimes called "computational propaganda" (Woolley and Howard 2017). The best-known example is the Russian meddling with the 2016 U.S. presidential election. While the impact it had on voter turnout or voter preference is unclear, various U.S. intelligence agencies concluded that the inference was intended to help Donald Trump win the presidency (Intelligence Community Assessment 2017). From this assessment and media accounts (Dewey 2016; Parkinson 2016; Reed 2016), we know that Russian operatives bought online ads to spread false information (targeting audiences identified through Facebook's algorithms), created fake Facebook groups and Twitter accounts to rile up the electorate and spread disinformation, and even organized both sides of competing protests to stir up discord, often around hot-button anti-immigration, religious, or race-related issues. Many of the messages were generated by Twitter "bots," software that controls a fake Twitter account, making it look like a real person by tweeting, retweeting, "liking," "following," and even sending direct messages to other users. Researchers who study cases like this note, "The most powerful forms of computational propaganda involve both algorithmic distribution and human curation—bots and trolls working together" (Woolley and Howard 2017, 5).

Misinformation, Hatred, and Online Censorship

Forty-seven minutes after news appeared about a high school mass shooting in Parkland, Florida, in 2018, right-wing posters on an anonymous chat board known for racist and anti-Semitic content were already plotting a response. They decided to try to influence public perception of the event by spreading the lie that the students interviewed afterward were "crisis actors"—performers pretending to be students—and that the event was a "false flag"—staged to generate support for gun restrictions. Before the end of the day,

Source: Vox Media Inc.

Right-wing memes like this one falsely suggest that tragic mass shootings were actually staged by liberals and populated by "crisis actors" playing the role of victims. Such messages try to sow seeds of doubt about the authenticity of news, encourage divisiveness, and undermine any calls for gun legislation.

right-wing conspiracy radio host Alex Jones was raising the possibility of a "false flag" on his *Infowars* program. Within the week, the number-one "Trending" video on YouTube labeled a student who was the son of an FBI agent a fake "actor." As one regular poster in another right-wing forum put it the day after the Parkland attack, "There's a war going on outside . . . and it is only partially being fought with guns. The real weapon is information and the attack is on the mind" (Timberg and Harwell 2018; Yglesias 2018).

The ability of a small number of anonymous users to influence the national discussion of major issues speaks to the power of social media. By bypassing traditional news media gatekeepers, information—and misinformation—can travel quickly and unimpeded across social networks because of how social media platforms work (Cacciatore, Dietram, and Iyengar 2016). Algorithms that identify content with which users are engaged may well end up promoting content that is inaccurate, hateful, and shocking, or controversial. Inflaming passions promotes engagement; discussing calmly usually does not. When misinformation and lies attacking other people routinely enter the information network, the consequences can be serious. At least some of the partisan gridlock of recent years is very likely attributable to this "juiced up" information environment that delivers a constant stream of highly provocative, highly selective, and often misleading or false messages.

Sometimes new technology is being used to promote old hatreds. At home, a broad variety of hate groups use the internet to recruit, organize, and spread lies. Racist hatred flourishes online (Jakubowicz et al. 2017) through tweets (Cisneros and Nakayama 2015), viral videos (Gray 2015), memes (Yoon 2016), and even biased search engine results (Noble 2018). Globally, terrorist groups communicate through social media sites like YouTube as well as their own websites, which include discussion groups, videos, political articles, instruction manuals, and leaders' speeches (Seib and Janbek 2011).

©Stuwdamdorp/Alamy Stock Photo

Because the internet is unfiltered, it can serve as a platform for user-generated content—like this white supremacist website—produced by groups that promote hate and violence.

CORE CONCEPTS CHALLENGE *How might hate groups take advantage of the internet to build and sustain a racist* ***subculture****? How might the internet be used to combat such efforts?*

In the wake of Russian interference in the 2016 U.S. presidential election, public concern grew and elected officials began considering possible regulation if media companies did not address the most egregious issues. Now on alert, the corporations that owned the platforms began trying to identify and prevent "fake news" and hate sites. Google announced new steps to combat terrorism content on its YouTube platform, including hiring more humans to staff their "Trusted Flagger" program and tweaking their algorithms to more quickly find and remove extremist and terrorism-related content (Walker 2017). Twitter (2017), too, announced that it had shut down nearly 300,000 accounts for "promoting terrorism." In 2017, when racist alt-right demonstrators in Charlottesville, Virginia, sparked violence, including the killing of a counter-demonstrator, Facebook moved to shut down a variety of accounts associated with the movement. The day before, it had already shut down "Unite the Right," the page used to organize the rally (Herrman 2017). Efforts such as these are ongoing.

These developments expose the contradiction of having public discourse on privately owned social media sites. Who decides what views warrant attention or banishment? In civic life—in the public sphere—the First Amendment guarantees freedom of speech against attempts at government control. However, in the private world of YouTube and Facebook, the First Amendment does not apply. Private corporations that created the spaces to promote profits judge the limits of speech to protect those profits. Whether and how governments should regulate such sites—either to compel them to do more to eliminate extremist hate content or to insist they abide by free speech standards—will be a continuing concern in the coming years.

As media have come to permeate society, they have been accompanied by relentless messages promoting consumption. These messages have contributed to the rise of consumer culture, a defining characteristic of contemporary society.

Consumer Culture

Twenty-five-year-old Reema Patel thinks that "the first class in college should be about credit cards." That's because by the time she was 21 she had accumulated $28,000 in credit card debt and has been working hard to pay it off ever since. Like many college students, Reema was sucked into the trap of easy credit and the allure of consumer culture, spending much more than she should have on travel, shopping, and partying. Reema's experiences occurred at the peak of easy credit on college campuses. Since then, the Great Recession has prompted belt-tightening, and passage of the Credit CARD Act of 2009 reformed industry practices and led to tighter lending standards. In 2016, more than half (56 percent) of college students had a credit card, up from only 30 percent of students in 2013, when post-recession credit was much tighter. Most college students (63 percent) now pay their credit card balance in full each month, and fewer than 10 percent of student credit card holders make only the minimum monthly payment (which can accumulate debt quickly). Still, one quarter of students worry that their credit card debt is out of control (SallieMae 2016).

Easy credit is just one feature of a broader consumer culture that incessantly promotes **consumption,** *the process of choosing, purchasing, and using goods.* A sociological approach to consumer culture emphasizes its economic, political, cultural, and social dimensions (Sadian 2018; Warde 2015; Zukin and Maguire 2004). To sociologists, consumption

- Is structured by the economic institutions, political regulations, and social norms that help organize the production and sale of consumer goods
- Is promoted through advertising and the media
- Involves the values, beliefs, and behaviors of consumers who, beyond meeting basic needs, use consumption to form and express their identities

Humans have consumed basic goods—such as clothing, tools, and simple household goods—for centuries. But modern technological advances—especially the rise of industrialization and capitalism—fundamentally changed the nature and significance of consumption as a social process. (The Sociology Works box explores an applied sociologist's efforts to better understand consumers.)

The Rise of Consumer Culture

Consumer culture in the United States and Europe emerged in the late nineteenth and early twentieth centuries, enabled by several key developments:

- *Industrialization made it possible to produce an unprecedented quantity of goods.* Factories could mass-produce a surplus of common personal and household items.
- *Mass production greatly reduced the cost of many items, making them affordable to a much larger number of people.* More

SOCIOLOGY WORKS

Hy Mariampolski and Consumer Research

Hy Mariampolski has been hired by the likes of Nissan, Clorox, Citibank, Microsoft, McDonald's, and dozens of other well-known corporations as well as numerous not-for-profits. With a PhD in sociology, Mariampolski moved into consumer behavior studies after trying out work in an academic setting. Mariampolski and his spouse and business partner, Sharon Wolf, run a firm that specializes in qualitative data on how consumers use everyday products. Although the company, QualiData, conducts focus groups and interviews to learn about some consumer needs, it is best known for pioneering the use of ethnographic research in marketing.

Ethnographic research involves taking account of evolving cultural habits and observing consumers as they buy various brands and use products in their homes and workplaces. Mariampolski (2001, 2005) has written two books teaching these research methods and shares his tools and techniques in workshops he conducts worldwide. Firsthand observations in natural settings can shed new light on how customers use products, on their frustrations with product design, and on how they may use products in ways that manufacturers never intended. Such insights help manufacturers design better products and market more effectively to consumers.

Mariampolski likes to think of himself as representing the "voice of the consumer," providing manufacturers with feedback on what people like and don't like. For example, one of his projects highlighted how working-class men avoid many pain relievers because they cause drowsiness, which can interfere with their ability to perform their jobs. His firm was also involved in a variety of ad campaigns involving sexual health. He helped condom manufacturers find more "life-affirming" ways to advertise that encouraged consumers to integrate condoms into their "natural eroticism." "People are not necessarily motivated by ads threatening them with death," Mariampolski observed.

Mariampolski endorses the trend among consumers that demands more socially responsible business practices, such as caring about nutrition and the environment. Nevertheless, he sometimes gets criticized for "his enthusiastic endorsement of free-market capitalism" that runs counter to sociologists whose research documents the negative effects of consumer culture and corporate advertising. Mariampolski, though, is comfortable in his alliance with corporate America. "We help corporations implement their good intentions," he says. "We're not outside throwing bricks" (Rice 2007).

> "I use my [sociology] background and knowledge every day of the week when I explain to my clients how their products may have to be adapted for new or growing demographic categories."

Courtesy of Hy Mariampolski
Hy Mariampolski

think about it

1. *Should sociologists use their knowledge and research techniques to help companies market their products effectively? What ethical issues, if any, might this form of research raise?*
2. *What insights might you gain from observational research that you might not learn from an interview or a focus group?*

people became consumers of manufactured goods rather than producers of their own items. Fewer clothes, for example, were made in the home as more were purchased in stores.

- *The immense capital investments needed to create mass manufacturing facilities gave rise to larger, more centralized business firms.* Eventually, the production and sale of most consumer goods shifted from craftsmen and small merchants to large corporations and retail chain stores.
- *Over time, competition to produce and sell goods more cheaply came to dominate much of the consumer market.* As part of this process, manufacturers introduced **planned obsolescence,** *the intentional design and manufacture of consumer goods so as to ensure a loss of utility in a relatively short period of time.* Products made cheaply could sell for less but would also break or become outdated more quickly, fueling another round of profitable consumption.
- *Excessive manufacturing capacity contributed to the rise of advertising as a way to promote more consumption.* Advertising also generated new kinds of consumer "needs" (Ewen 2001; Powers 2016). As social historian Stephanie Coontz (2016) notes, with the rise of consumer society, "The word consumption increasingly lost its earlier connotations of destroying, wasting, or using up, and came instead to refer in a positive way to the satisfying of human needs and desires" (225).

Even when consumer culture was still in its infancy, it did not escape the notice of early sociologists. In the late nineteenth century, Karl Marx in particular considered the links between the changing methods of production and the new culture of consumption.

Alienated Labor and Commodity Fetishism

Have you ever experienced the satisfaction of doing it yourself—say, repairing a car, completing a craft project, or creating a website? For Marx, work that we engage in to meet our human needs is, ideally, creative and satisfying. Growing food, building a home, or knitting a sweater are all inherently meaningful tasks that help develop human potential. The rise of industrial capitalism, however, distorted our relationship to work so that it became separated from meeting basic needs. Rather than working for themselves to create useful things, wage laborers work at the discretion of employers for money to buy goods that will meet their needs. This system creates a distance between what we *do* (for money) and what we *use* (as consumers). One consequence of this distance, according to Marx, is **alienation,** *the separation and isolation of workers as a result of the structure of capitalist society.* Alienation under capitalism has several dimensions:

©Florescu Productions/age fotostock

- *Workers are separated from their natural state as creative, autonomous beings.* They become largely interchangeable cogs in a productive machine.
- *Workers are separated from one another.* Instead of working toward a common good, workers are often pitted against one another competitively.
- *Workers are separated from what they produce.* Little or no connection exists between workers and the products of their labor, which are owned by their employers.
- *Workers are separated from the process of production.* For many, work is a meaningless, tedious activity with few, if any, intrinsic rewards.

Ironically, later researchers have found that the impersonal, isolating nature of work creates dissatisfaction and unhappiness that advertisers then exploit by encouraging consumption as a solution for this alienation. The beneficiaries of this system of production and consumption are capitalists, who gain, first, by exploiting workers—paying them less than the value of the goods they generate—and, second, by profiting from the sales of such goods back to workers.

When we no longer create or grow the goods we consume, the source of consumer products can seem obscure. Marx used the term **commodity fetishism** to describe *the failure of people to recognize the labor that created the value in the commodities they use.* In the study of primitive religions, *fetish* refers to objects that have magical powers. When we buy jeans or a T-shirt, they seem to appear magically at the local mall with a price tag, entirely separate from the workers who made them. We generally do not think about the labor process involved in an item's creation: the likely low-paid workers—perhaps even child laborers—who made the item, the extensive mark-up added to the price to create profit, or the natural resources consumed in its production and transportation. This disconnect between production of goods and their consumption has become a feature of our consumer culture.

Consumption and Identity

Your great-grandparents probably had identities that reflected where they were born and lived and worked, their religious beliefs, and their strong ties to a particular community. Your identity is no doubt still forming as a result perhaps of various moves, changing schools and peer groups, and living on your own and considering future career choices while you attend college. The nature of our identities reflects, in large part, the nature of our society.

As sociologist Peter Berger (1963) once put it, "[T]raditional societies assign definite and permanent identities to their members" (48). In such societies, identity is often rooted firmly in the family and community, with rigid and permanent roles that are recognized widely. With the rise of modernity, radical economic, social, and political changes contributed to the creation of modern identities, partially freed from the influences of family and place. "In modern society," Berger notes, "identity itself is uncertain and in flux." Since our family of origin and place of birth do not necessarily determine our future, our sense of self does not develop automatically.

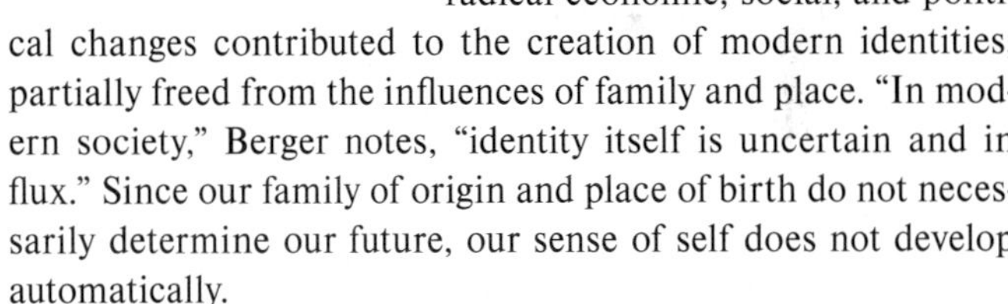

Today's postmodern era requires us to choose who we will become. We have more freedom to choose or construct our own social roles, decide where to live and what to do, and much more. A paramount question—one nearly unthinkable in traditional societies—becomes "Who do we want to be?"

In a highly commercial society, where nearly everything is a product for sale, what you buy and where you buy it can take on great importance as an affirmation of your identity. **Consumerism** is *an emphasis on shopping and the possession of material goods as the route to personal happiness.* Advertisers sell an identity through products, and individuals express their identity through the choices they make as consumers (or by their rejection of consumerism).

In a classic book, *The Conquest of Cool,* cultural historian Thomas Frank (1997) showed how advertisers in the 1960s tapped into the popular culture of the day by promoting consumption as a type of creative self-expression. A variety of

Source: Under Armour®, Inc.

Source: GUESS?, Inc.

©Splash News/Newscom

Regardless of the product being sold or the audience being targeted, many advertisers sell their products by associating them with a particular image and lifestyle. Are these ads really about athletic wear, clothing, watches, or perfume?

©Francis Dean/Dean Pictures/ The Image Works

consumer products were touted as the choice of nonconformists, rebels, and the "hip," such as Volkswagen vans, Old Gold cigarettes, Polaroid cameras, and Suzuki motorcycles. Ads encouraged consumers to reject conformity—by following the ads' advice to buy a product. The result, of course, is conformity among all those who buy the product. The spectacle of major corporations selling mass consumption as a means of self-expression and individual rebellion—ironic though it may be—surfaces frequently in advertising campaigns. The Gap's "Do You" campaign celebrated individual creativity. American Eagle Outfitters' #WeAllCan campaign featured young people's personal stories of empowerment. Patagonia even ran a "Don't Buy This Jacket" ad campaign, which led many people to . . . buy a Patagonia Jacket (MacKinnon 2015).

Advertisers often promote their products to particular demographic groups, sometimes reinforcing differences based on gender, race, age, and class. Products not only do something, they also *say* something about who we want to be and the group to which we belong. Far removed from Marx's notion that products meet human needs, today's consumer products are often about image and identity. This phenomenon is not entirely new. As we saw in Chapter 9, Thorstein Veblen explored the "conspicuous consumption" of the leisure class a century ago. However, this kind of consumption has expanded to include most of society. The brands we choose become infused with social meaning that go well beyond the practical use of the product. Prestigious commodities (such as cars, electronics, and clothes) are taken to be a reflection of our own social value (Baudrillard 1988a).

Promoting Consumption

Advertising is ubiquitous in contemporary society. Just think of the various places you've observed ads in the past week: on large highway billboards, on taxis and buses, at the airport, throughout your local mall, in the stalls in public restrooms, on a sticker on a piece of fruit—and in most of the media you consume. Advertising provides the primary source of revenue for most media. You don't have to pay for broadcast television and radio because advertisers foot the bill. The fees for cable television and print subscriptions are affordable because the majority of operating revenue typically comes from advertising. Online media platforms, such as Google and Facebook, have adopted the broadcast model—advertising-supported and free to users—for online sites. Most successful high-traffic websites, from news and entertainment sites to medical advice and "how to" sites, are supported by advertisers willing to pay a premium for a carefully targeted audience. Similarly, social media are supported by ads and by collecting data on user activity that is sold to advertisers seeking to target specific audiences.

At its most basic level, advertising provides consumers with information about specific products and services. On the whole, however, advertising promotes more than just a particular product; it encourages us to embrace buying as a way of life.

A great deal of thought, money, and effort goes into encouraging people to be consumers. Advertisers must make people unhappy with what they have and lead them to believe that a purchase will improve their condition. They cultivate dissatisfaction by encouraging consumers to feel insecure, bored, anxious, envious, or frustrated about the life they lead and then evoke an image or a lifestyle that consumers supposedly want to emulate, a process called "emotional obsolescence." The cycles of fashion, the new car models, the constant upgrades of media devices are all techniques designed to promote dissatisfaction with the older version of a product and plant the seed of desire for the new product. This endless cycle of consumption, dissatisfaction, and consumption is an inherent part of consumer culture. Increasingly, advertisers are also exploiting the emotional vulnerabilities of children, as the Through a Sociological Lens box describes.

One problem for the advertising industry is that people generally do not like advertisements. As a result, the ad industry is constantly developing new ways to overcome audience resistance and promote consumption, including through advertising in public spaces, product integration, and stealth advertising.

Public Spaces and Captive Audiences

One way to overcome resistance to ads is simply to place them in public spaces that are difficult to avoid. In recent years, for example, ads have appeared on the exterior of airplanes, inside school classrooms, all around sports arenas, and just about everywhere on the internet. Another strategy is to show ads in places where people are temporarily a captive audience: in elevators, taxicabs, airports, waiting rooms in doctors' offices, and restrooms.

Product Integration Today's television viewers have various ways to avoid commercials: fast forwarding, muting the sound, cord-cutting by subscribing to ad-free streaming services instead of cable or satellite television. In response to such audience resistance, *advertisers make ads unavoidable by integrating the product being promoted into media content*, a technique known as **product placement.** For example, viewers of Netflix's hit science-fiction series *Stranger Things* surely noticed that Eggo waffles were incorporated into the story line as the favorite food of one of the principal characters. Similarly, the 2017 blockbuster film *The Fate of the Furious*, part of the *Fast and Furious* franchise, features Dwayne (The Rock) Johnson wearing Under Armour apparel throughout the film. These and many more subtle efforts are product placements.

Product placement is most effective when viewers do not recognize they are the target of advertising (Eagle and Dahl 2018). For example, in one experimental study, after a few seconds'

©Bruce Bennett Studios/Getty Images

©Cal Sport Media/Alamy Stock Photo

FAST-FORWARD

Change and Sports Advertising

Until the mid-1980s, players in the National Hockey League skated on rinks with plain white ice and boards. When today's players take to the rink, they skate past countless commercial advertisements plastered on the boards and painted right into the ice on which they play. It is impossible to watch professional sports today without being forced to view the logos and other advertisements that cover and surround the playing surfaces and sometimes the players themselves. Even sports arenas and ballparks carry the names of corporate sponsors and are designed to promote consumption.

Examining the Commercialization of Childhood

More than ever before, advertisers are using media to target children. Today's ad campaigns are much more sophisticated than those of the past. For example, children fill out marketing surveys in schools, and sponsored classroom materials sometimes include brand-name acknowledgments that serve as advertisements for youth-oriented products. Marketers also employ psychologists who help craft messages to exploit the emotional vulnerabilities of children, especially their feelings that they are "uncool," a "loser," or simply "left out" if they don't have the latest product. Children are even being hired for "stealth advertising" efforts (described later), for example, by participating in slumber parties sponsored by the research and marketing firm Girls Intelligence Agency, at which the children try to learn about and influence their friends' tastes and habits.

Once a tiny portion of the advertising industry, children's advertising has grown dramatically in recent years as corporations have found new ways to tap parents' wallets through their kids. This barrage of ad messages, says sociologist Juliet Schor, is literally making children sick, causing an array of health and psychological problems. Schor has used sociological inquiry to study the inside operations of advertising agencies that target children, and she has explored the effects of advertising on children. Her findings are alarming.

Today's children are being inundated with many more ads than any other generation has ever experienced. In the 1970s, children watched an estimated 55 television commercials a day. By the 1990s this figure had doubled to 110 (or 40,000 a year), and it continues to increase. By the late 2010s, the flood of advertising targeting children across the full range of media—television, video games, music and video streaming, social media, within e-mail, at all kinds of websites—was so omnipresent that it became impossible to count reliably. Still, the nonprofit research institute Children and Screens notes that kids see tens of thousands of ads each year. One recent review of research on children and advertising indicates that "marketers reaching children in online settings are acting with little oversight and are often more aggressive with their marketing strategies" (Lapierre et al. 2017, S154).

Children have a keen awareness of themselves as consumers and are often the first to try new technology. As Schor points out, "Children have become conduits from the consumer marketplace into the household, the link between advertisers and the family purse." As such, children drive many forms of household consumption, often by nagging parents until they give in or using their own allowance to purchase products. Advertisers understand this process and target children accordingly.

All this exposure to advertising, says Schor, has led to a public health crisis. An epidemic in childhood obesity can be traced in part to a sedentary lifestyle (often spent watching television and playing video games) coupled with a spike in the consumption of high-fat and high-sugar junk food (advertised on children's programs). Research shows that television commercials for fast-food restaurants routinely target children by highlighting toy giveaways and movie tie-ins (Bernhardt et al. 2013) and that ads for foods with minimal nutritional value are common in schools (Molner et al. 2013). More broadly, Schor's research suggests that the more children are caught up in the consumer culture, the more likely they are to suffer from depression, anxiety, low self-esteem, and a variety of physical complaints brought on by emotional distress. The ability of advertising to promote dissatisfaction and envy can take a toll on young psyches.

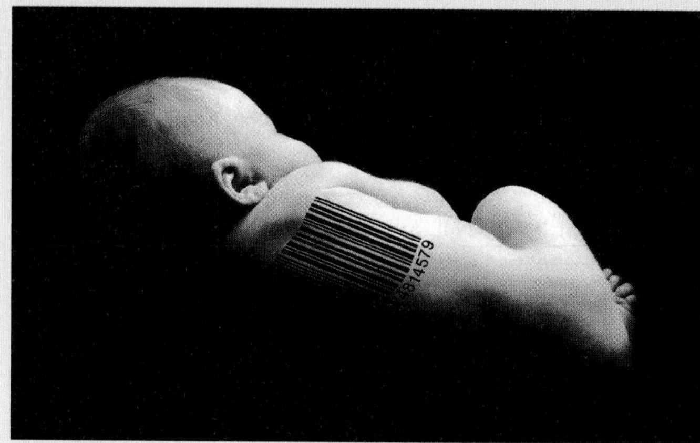

Courtesy of Media Education Foundation

Surveys show that 4 in 5 Americans think there should be more restrictions on children's advertising, and nearly 9 in 10 think that our consumer culture makes it more difficult to instill positive values in children. Even many of the marketers that Schor interviewed for her study knew something was wrong; they spontaneously expressed ambivalence and guilt about what their work was doing to children.

Sources: American Academy of Pediatrics 2006; Babb 2004; Center for the New American Dream, http://newdream.org; Schor 2004; Strasburger and Wilson 2002; Strasburger, Wilson, and Jordan 2009.

think about it

1. *What sorts of regulations, if any, do you think should be placed on advertising to children?*
2. *List all the consequences for children who are overly commercialized. Think about the psychic as well as the economic consequences. What might these children be missing in their lives?*

observation of a breakfast cereal that was covertly placed in a TV sitcom, viewers were three times as likely to recall the cereal and to have a positive attitude toward the brand afterward. That influence is significantly reduced, however, if the paid product placement is disclosed to viewers (Campbell, Mohr, and Verlegh 2013). While such disclosure mitigates the effectiveness of sponsorship among adults, disclosure does not seem to undermine the persuasiveness of product placement among adolescents (van Reijmersdal et al. 2017).

Other media use product placement as well. In movies, the car the hero drives, the computer the police detective uses, and the wristwatch the spy consults are all likely to be products provided to the movie producers and inserted into the film, sometimes for a fee. Movie producers keep costs down by using such free (or paid-for) props, advertisers get to associate their products with popular movie stars, and audiences experience a form of advertising that is woven seamlessly into the film.

Product placement has become increasingly sophisticated. Advertisers think strategically about how best to build their products into the story line of a movie, television series, or video game, creating apparently natural product placements that may be hard to recognize. Chefs on cooking shows use and talk about brand-name cooking products, the judges on *American Idol* drink prominently displayed cans of Coca-Cola, and Papa John's pizza appeared prominently in the 2016 *Ghostbusters* remake.

Similarly, video game developers continue to develop innovative forms of in-game advertising to more fully integrate products into the game environment. While in-game billboards advertising real-world products have long been a staple of video games—on the walls of race tracks, inside sports arenas, in city scenes—video games now feature more brand-name products for game players to drive, wear, and consume. As product placement opportunities continue to grow, advertisers now speak of "branded entertainment," such as *The Lego Movie* and its spinoffs, in which the brand is the center of the media product.

One trend linking products with media content involves complex partnerships that advertisers call "brand integration." In some of these partnerships, companies contribute products or props that keep film production costs down, while other cases involve joint marketing campaigns to promote both a film or television program and the brand-name products. For example, AMC's hit television series *The Walking Dead* partnered with PepsiCo, maker of soft drink Mountain Dew, to create an augmented-reality app that allows fans into a game environment to interact with some of the show's popular zombie "walkers" by unlocking the characters in Mountain Dew advertisement and product packaging. As one PepsiCo executive described the strategy: "We are really rewarding people for engaging in our commercials. This gets them to use their smartphones, which we know they are likely already using, to actively seek out our commercial and rewards them for doing so" (Steinberg 2017). These forms of brand integration may be effective precisely because they are difficult for consumers to avoid and the sales pitch appears less intrusive, perhaps even appealing.

©Stephen Lioy/Alamy Stock Photo

American fast-food restaurants line a street in Shenzhen, China. Consumer cultures of this sort, once limited to affluent Western countries, have now expanded to some developing nations. But U.S.-style levels of consumption cannot be sustained globally; the planet simply does not contain sufficient resources.

Stealth Advertising Another increasingly common practice is stealth advertising. Sometimes called "guerrilla marketing," **stealth advertising** is *the creation of covert advertising in everyday real-life situations.* For example, many advertisers take advantage of social media sites and consumer review features of online retail sites to plant surreptitious advertising for their products. Advertisers hire employees to pose as ordinary users of these sites and praise the attributes of their employer's products by posting enthusiastic reviews. In a 2016 high-profile case, the Federal Trade Commission found that Warner Bros. paid online "influencers" for posting favorable game-play videos of *Middle Earth: Shadow of Mordor* without adequately disclosing that the reviewers had been paid by Warner Bros. These promotional videos were viewed more than 5 million times on YouTube and other social media (Federal Trade Commission 2016).

Advertisers also hire people to promote their products subtly by, for example, going to bars and ordering a particular brand of beer, in effect becoming a walking advertisement. Camera companies have hired people to pose as tourists and ask passersby to take their picture in front of a popular landmark. As this innocuous exchange takes place, the "tourists" praise the virtues of their new camera, creating another stealth ad. Such advertising techniques, which rely on people's trust and goodwill, are deceptive and insert commercial motivations into everyday social interactions.

The Social Impact of Consumer Culture

What happens to a culture in which consumption becomes the center of social life and citizens are subject to an endless stream of advertising? We note some of the social implications in the sections that follow.

Inequality and Consumption Social and economic inequality is important to keep in mind when considering the impact of consumer culture. The affluence necessary for consumer spending is not distributed evenly. As we saw in

FIGURE 14.8 | NUMBER OF MIDDLE-CLASS ADULTS (IN MILLIONS) BY REGION AND SELECT COUNTRIES, 2015

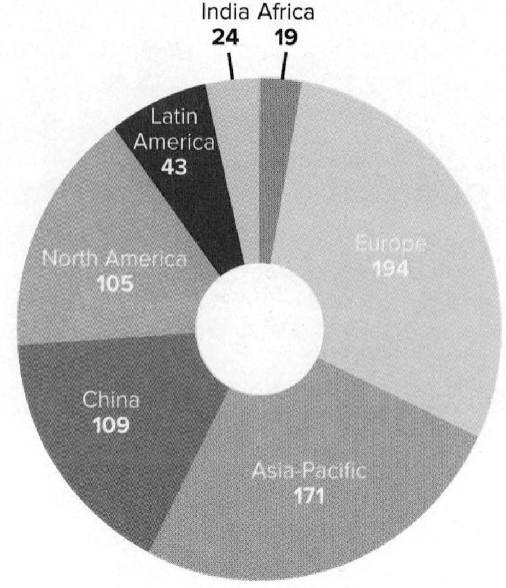

If the middle class is measured as those people who have the equivalent of $50,000 to $500,000 in wealth, then China has the largest middle class in the world. The middle class emerged in the last century, in the industrialized countries of the West. In the twenty-first century, the growing populations and increased affluence of China and other Asian-Pacific nations have made them the center of the global consumer culture.

Source: Credit Suisse Research Institute 2015.

CORE CONCEPTS CHALLENGE *Worldwide, what might the geographic location of members of the middle class suggest about who will have the most* ***power*** *to shape consumer culture in the twenty-first century?*

Chapter 9, inequality within our own society produces very different living standards, and globally, large segments of the world's population still endure poverty and subsistence living. The transformation to consumer culture came first to the more affluent Western societies in the nineteenth and early twentieth centuries, and only later to parts of the developing world that are now integrated into the global economy. After the fall of communism in 1989, Eastern Europe saw a dramatic expansion in consumer culture. In the early twenty-first century, consumer culture in Asian nations—especially China—grew rapidly, by some measures overtaking the West. As Figure 14.8 shows, the number of people in the middle class in China alone now exceeds that in the United States. Still, the vast majority of the world's population is unable to participate in consumer culture because of starkly limited resources.

Debt and Dissatisfaction As we saw in Chapter 12, Marx regarded religion as an "opiate" that gave temporary, but ultimately false, comfort to people suffering from society's injustices. Since the middle of the twentieth century, critical theorists have suggested that consumerism fills a similar role in modern society (Adorno and Horkheimer [1944] 2000). Shopping is often touted as an escape from the drudgeries of daily life. "Treating yourself," "living for the weekend," and "splurging" because "you are worth it" are all popular notions that encourage guilt-free consumption. However, the fleeting comfort of consumption is often coupled with the accumulation of burdensome debt, producing more stress and anxiety in a person's life. Consumption and working to pay for it become a cyclical way of life (Gabriel and Lang 2015; Schor 1999, 2010).

on social theory

Marx and contemporary **conflict theorists** emphasize the inability of consumption ultimately to offer satisfaction. Has consumption helped give you a sense of satisfaction? Who has benefited from your participation in consumer culture?

As far back as Durkheim, sociologists have understood that satisfaction in life comes from understanding and staying within limits and boundaries. Insofar as advertising and consumer culture encourage boundless desires that can never be satisfied, they can be a source of social instability and can undermine human happiness.

Excessive consumption cannot substitute for addressing the underlying social conditions that create unhappiness. Since the cycle of consumption is at bottom based on perpetual dissatisfaction (Ewen 2001; Koles, Wells, and Tadajewski 2018), any comforting effects are likely to be temporary, leaving deep-seated troublesome issues unchanged. What is more likely to produce happiness and satisfaction? Scholars point to rewarding interpersonal relationships, meaningful employment, outlets for creative self-expression, and gratifying civic and community participation (Kasser 2003; Lane 1994; Schor 2010).

Commodification **Commodification** is *the process of transforming all things into a product to be bought and sold.* Social relationships that used to be based on, and promoted by, mutual aid and trust are often just commercial transactions today. For example, a variety of goods and services that were once produced and shared among family and friends—such as yard work, pet sitting, home repairs, and child care—are now more likely to be paid services. Today we even shop for mates on the internet.

Religious holidays and communal festivals that once promoted social solidarity are now celebrations of consumption. Thanksgiving now marks the early Christmas sales. Birthdays, Mother's Day and Father's Day, Valentine's Day, and other events are marked by the obligatory mass-produced greeting card and the purchase of a consumer item. Big sales are associated with Presidents' Day, Labor Day, and Memorial Day. The newest civic holiday, the Super Bowl, is as notable for the unveiling of new advertisements as for the game played on the field. Shopping has been transformed from a necessary chore to America's favorite pastime.

With commodification, monetary terms increasingly measure social life. If carried to an extreme, such a development can undermine the social trust necessary for a healthy society. A society in which everything—and everyone—has a price is one in which emptiness and alienation are likely to thrive (Gabriel and Lang 2015; Sandel 2013; Slater 1999; Warde 2017).

Environmental Degradation Finally, the spread of the culture of consumption around the globe has taken a toll on the environment (Klein 2015; Wilk 2016). For decades, affluent nations, especially the United States, have consumed the earth's resources at a vastly disproportionate level. With about 5 percent of the earth's population, Americans consume about 25 percent of the world's resources. Now, billions of residents of developing nations are seeing improvements in their standards of living and are themselves becoming consumers. For some, consumer culture is a step up from the grinding pain of poverty. The more widespread availability of basic, affordable consumer goods has been a major positive development.

The overall expansion of consumer culture, however, has resulted in environmental destruction on a massive, unprecedented, and unsustainable scale—including slashed and burned forests, polluted air and water, toxic landfills, crippling carbon dioxide emission, holes in the atmosphere's protective ozone layer, and wholesale climate change. We explore some of these effects in Chapter 15.

A Changing World

TARGETING CONSUMERS IN THE DIGITAL AGE

As we saw with the example of social media in this chapter's opening vignette, the internet has taken advertising to a whole new level because it is the only medium that allows advertisers to track the activity of potential consumers and to harvest information about users' interests and habits (Schneier 2015; Turow 2017).

Advertisers use sophisticated software to collect a treasure trove of personal data—what we search, click, post, share, read, and buy—often without our clear understanding of just how thoroughly our online activity is gathered and analyzed (Ghosh and Scott 2018). These new tracking tools are the foundation for a promotional approach known as **behavioral targeting,** *advertising sent to online users based on their earlier internet activities.*

The best-known form of online tracking involves the installation of cookies. Cookies help websites store information such as your name, address, and payment preferences. This information can help users learn about new products that might match their interests and can make online shopping fast and easy.

In recent years, however, cookies have been installed primarily by companies that specialize in tracking and recording users' online activity and selling this information to advertisers. These companies pay websites to permit them to install tracking tools on the computers of visitors to the site. In addition, tracking tools are often hidden in commercial e-mails, allowing advertisers to track who opens, deletes, or forwards e-mail and connect these data to information on our web browsing and buying habits.

By piecing together bits of information you leave behind as you browse the internet, advertisers can anticipate your likely interests and pitch products to you based on your past online activity. Records of your searches on Google or other sites, the products you have viewed, the articles you have read, the zip code you entered to get local weather, your Facebook likes and Instagram photos—all these pieces of information can be assembled to construct a sophisticated consumer profile that allows marketers to create a targeted online consumer experience, steering you to advertisements tailor-made to your specific interests. Your cell phone, too, is a treasure trove of information for marketers. Since cell phones rely on relay towers, they communicate your location, transmitting GPS coordinates to those with access. By default, photos taken with your phone have your GPS coordinates embedded in the metadata; you must deactivate that feature to hide the information. Marketers can use your location data to track and better understand your likely consumer behavior.

The forms of behavioral targeting are likely to increase with the growth of the "internet of things," the growing network of connected devices in our homes, schools, and offices. One recent study argues that the internet of things is opening a new frontier for advertising that "takes advantage of a huge collection of smart devices, such as wearables, home appliances, vehicles, and many other connected digital instruments which end users constantly interact with in their daily lives" (Aksu et al. 2018).

Research suggests there is substantial public concern about online tracking. Public opposition to behavioral targeting is connected to broader concerns about online privacy. A recent review of research on behavioral targeting found that consumers have become increasingly uneasy about online privacy issues over the past decade; most consumers find personalized online advertising to be invasive, even "creepy" (Boerman, Kruikemeier, and Borgesius 2017). People who are most concerned about privacy are also the most careful online, typically sharing less personal information online and taking more privacy protective actions online. However, this connection between concern and caution does not seem to apply to social media, where the **privacy paradox,** *when people's concerns about privacy are not consistent with their privacy management activities,* helps to explain the widespread use of media that vacuum up huge stores of personal data about individual consumer interests, activities, and preferences (Baruh, Secinti, and Cemalcilar 2017).

In the face of the growing sophistication of behavioral targeting and other data-gathering techniques, consumer advocates have called for government regulations. However, efforts to enact meaningful regulations in the United States have made little headway. Several attempts to develop "do not track" rules failed in the 2010s amidst disagreements about what such policies would mean for digital advertisers and whether companies whose business model is built on collecting data would follow voluntary guidelines (Volz 2015). In 2016, the Federal Communications Commission announced new regulations requiring internet service providers to get advance permission from customers before

thinking about culture

As consumer culture spreads throughout the globe, environmental pollution is spreading as well. What aspects of U.S. consumer culture might create these problems?

©Ann Little/Alamy Stock Photo

At this 2013 "Stop Watching Us" protest outside the U.S. Capitol in Washington, DC, demonstrators rallied to demand an end to mass surveillance.

sharing sensitive personal data, such as a person's web browsing history, health information, or precise location. Before the new regulations even took effect, President Trump signed legislation that repealed these new online privacy rules (Reilly 2017). The situation is much different in Europe, where the General Data Protection Regulation (GDPR) went into effect in May 2018. One of the key principles of the GDPR is that people own their personal data, so they can withdraw their consent for companies to use their data. Among its key provisions is the right to be forgotten: "also known as Data Erasure, the right to be forgotten entitles the data subject to have the data controller erase his/her personal data, cease further dissemination of the data, and potentially have third parties halt processing of the data" (EUGDPR 2018).

The debate about online advertising techniques is sure to continue as citizens and policymakers sort through the various arguments about consumer privacy and efficient marketing. In this new era of customized consumption, sociologists are likely to pay careful attention to the power associated with information tracking and the cultural consequences of the proliferation of personalized advertising (and political) messages.

thinking sociologically about
Media and Consumption

culture

- Media reflect and promote cultural norms.
- Consumption has become central to our culture and is used to help form social identities.

structure

- The structure of the media industry shapes the content of popular media.
- Media organizations must operate within the structural constraints imposed by their legal, political, economic, and cultural environments.
- The widespread presence of advertising helps structure consumer society.

power

- Major media ownership is highly concentrated; those who control the media wield considerable power in society.
- Consumerism is linked to inequality and reflects disparities in economic power in society.

REVIEW, REFLECT, AND APPLY

Looking Back

1. There are three major types of media, each with unique features: (a) interpersonal media, (b) mass media, and (c) hybrid (or "new") media.
2. Media act as sources of information, agents of socialization, and as a means for those in power to promote ideology.
3. As a social institution, media involve the interaction of several key elements: the media industry, media content, users, technology, and the broader social context.
4. Media companies are involved in providing (a) *products* (or content), (b) *platforms* that host and display content, and (c) *pipes* that deliver content to users. The media industry has been expanding, integrating (vertically and horizontally), and globalizing, while its ownership has become more concentrated.
5. As illustrated with the case of race, media content often reflects the broader social inequalities in society, sometimes perpetuating them through the socialization process. Economic interests often drive this content, and the export of media content sometimes raises concerns about "cultural imperialism."
6. Users make choices about their media use and interpret media content, often based on their social position. But extensive and long-term exposure to media does have an impact on audiences, influencing what they think about and how they view the world. More broadly, the omnipresence of media has changed various aspects of society, a process known as mediatization.
7. The explosive growth of media technology in everyday life has raised questions about its social impact. Concerns include the distracting and compulsive features of the internet; the role of algorithms in helping create "filter bubbles" and inflaming political divisions; and the use of social media for misinformation, propaganda, and hate-mongering.
8. The rise of consumer culture was accompanied by an increase in advertising delivered through various media. Advertising has become a ubiquitous force, and advertisers use a variety of techniques to influence our identities and promote consumption.
9. Consumer culture has had a significant social impact on how we live, work, and value our lives. It has also been a key factor in the escalation of environmental degradation.

Critical Thinking: Questions and Activities

1. In what ways and for how long do you use media in a typical day? Keep a log for one or two days, noting every use of media. How would you summarize the role that media play in your life? How do you think your lifelong exposure to media has influenced how you understand the world? How does the influence of media extend beyond *what* you know to include *how* you relate to the social world?
2. If someone relied exclusively on popular media portrayals to understand the life of a college student today, would he or she get a reasonably accurate picture of your real-world experiences in college? What does this say about the role of media in teaching about aspects of the world we don't experience firsthand?
3. Do you share any of the concerns mentioned in this chapter about the potential impact of media technology? If not, why not? If you do, which do you think are the biggest problems and why?
4. Note your exposure to advertising for one day. What techniques did advertisers use to get your attention? Is there any part of your life that is free from brand names, logos, and ads?
5. Would you agree to have a corporate advertiser pay for your wedding ceremony in exchange for incorporating the corporation's logo into the event (for example, printed on invitations and napkins, displayed on a banner at the reception, announced as part of the ceremony)? Why or why not? What issues does this "product placement" raise about the appropriate limits for advertising?
6. In what ways do you participate in consumer culture? Do you have any concerns about the role of consumption in your life?

Key Terms

active audiences (p. 364) audiences that make choices about how they use the media and actively interpret media content.

agenda-setting theory (p. 364) a theory that holds that media may not be able to tell people what to think but can significantly influence what people think about.

alienation (p. 371) the separation and isolation of workers as a result of the structure of capitalist society.

behavioral targeting (p. 377) advertising sent to online users based on their earlier internet activities.

commodification (p. 376) the process of transforming all things into a product to be bought and sold.

commodity fetishism (p. 371) consumers' failure to recognize the labor that created the value in the commodities they use.

consumerism (p. 371) an emphasis on shopping and the possession of material goods as the route to personal happiness.

consumption (p. 369) the process of choosing, purchasing, and using goods.

cultivation theory (p. 364) a theory that argues that, by repeated and long-term exposure to the media's portrayal of the world (especially on television), people come to accept many of these depictions as reality.

cultural imperialism (p. 363) the tendency of media corporations from wealthier nations—especially the United States—to export so many of their media products that they come to dominate the local cultures of other, especially poorer, nations.

digital convergence (p. 354) the merging of different forms of media through their transformation into digital information.

digital divide (p. 365) the gap between those who have the knowledge and resources needed to use digital information technology, especially computers and the internet, and those who do not.

dual product market (p. 362) the situation that occurs when a company sells two completely different types of "products" to two completely different sets of buyers.

horizontal integration (p. 357) what occurs when a media company owns different forms of media.

hybrid (or "new") media (p. 354) have features of both interpersonal and mass media, enabling private communication with known individuals, public communication with a potentially large unknown audience, or both.

interpersonal media (p. 354) enable primarily private interactive communication between known individuals.

mass media (p. 354) enable primarily public one-way communication that reaches a potentially large and mostly anonymous audience.

media (p. 354) the various technological processes that enable communication between (and are in the "middle" of) the sender of a message and the receiver of that message.

mediatization (p. 365) examines how the omnipresence of media has changed various aspects of society.

planned obsolescence (p. 370) the intentional design and manufacture of consumer goods so as to ensure a loss of utility in a relatively short period of time.

privacy paradox (p. 377) when people's concerns about privacy are not consistent with their privacy management activities.

product placement (p. 373) the integration into media content of a product that is being advertised.

stealth advertising (p. 375) the creation of covert advertising in everyday real-life situations.

vertical integration (p. 357) what occurs when a media company owns the different stages of production and distribution of a single media form.

©John Seaton Callahan/Getty Images

15 Communities, the Environment, and Health

looking AHEAD

How does the **structure** of *where* you live—whether it's an urban, suburban, or rural community—influence *how* you live?

How does your **culture** influence your understanding of your community and the environment?

How does the amount of **power** you have affect the likelihood that you will face environmental hazards and develop health problems?

©Lzf/iStock/Getty Images

When Fan Qun moved from a rural community to the city of Beijing looking for economic opportunity, every aspect of his and his family's life changed. Unlike many others who struggled, Qun became affluent working for a consulting firm that advises Western pharmaceutical companies doing business in China.

Yet "everyone is unhappy," says Fan Hanlin, Qun's 70-year-old father. Because Qun and his wife view their marriage as their main priority, rather than their relationship with Qun's father, Hanlin has lost his traditional role as respected elder. Qun's father and mother are also upset by behaviors that contrast starkly with their lifelong frugality: Qun and his wife employ two housekeepers, frequently eat in expensive restaurants, and each own a car.

Millions have moved into China's growing cities, abandoning a centuries-old way of life and adopting the new norms of an urban, market-oriented society. Affluence has enabled many city dwellers to afford their own apartments, and some even put their elderly parents into nursing homes, a practice unheard of just a few years ago (Babones 2018; Chen 2005).

Perhaps the most dramatic impact of change has been on China's environment, with significant health consequences. To fuel massive growth, China's land has been overcultivated, overgrazed, and sometimes deforested, with 90 percent of trees cut in some provinces. Over a quarter of China's landmass is a desert today, contributing to massive sandstorms that sometimes halt air traffic in major cities. To attract investment, the government allowed foreign corporations to locate toxic-waste-producing factories in China, where environmental protection laws are almost nonexistent. China is the world's biggest producer of carbon dioxide emissions, opening a new coal-fired power plant every week. Researchers estimate that in recent years air pollution contributed to the premature deaths of more than a million Chinese people annually (Chen 2005; Health Effects Institute 2018; Wong 2013). In an effort to reduce the negative environmental and health effects of its rapid growth, China launched a national program that includes massive investments in nonpolluting, renewable energy sources, including tripling its solar power capacity between 2015 and 2020 (The Lancet Commission 2018). Whether such an approach can succeed remains to be seen.

Whether we look at the way it is changing individual families, transforming the nation, or influencing the planet, China's experience with urbanization illustrates three themes we explore in this chapter. First, *where* we live influences *how* we live. The move from traditional rural communities to the new physical and social environment of cities changes cultural norms, creates new social structures, and alters power relationships. Second, although growth creates affluence for some, it also creates environmental challenges that result in major social problems. Sociology can help us better understand the dynamics behind our environmental crises and suggest options for addressing them. Third, health is more than a medical issue; it is a social issue connected to broad social patterns. The sociological perspective can help us understand the social dynamics that influence health-related issues and the way our environment contributes to those issues.

The Structure and Evolution of Communities

Films and television have often told the tale: a small-town innocent finds his or her way to the big city and is overwhelmed. City life is so different from home! Buildings shoot up to the sky, crowds of people bustle frantically, the noise is deafening, and

con artists prey on the naïvely trusting innocent. In a similar story line, a bewildered "city slicker" struggles with the foreign ways of a rural community.

Though now clichés, these tales reflect basic sociological insights. Social life *can* be vastly different in the dissimilar structures of different locations. In short, place matters (Gieryn 2000). Sociologists are well aware of online communities and social media networks that enable virtual relationships (Rainie and Wellman 2012). But these often have less influence on us than place-based communities, and virtual communities can exist only because their members occupy a physical space and use material infrastructure to access internet experiences and cell phone communication. Even with the growth of virtual communities, place and physical environment still matter.

Community: Place, People, and Relationships

The term *community* has different meanings depending on its context (Cere 2017; Goe and Noonan 2007). It can refer to a *place,* as in, "I just moved to this community earlier this year." It can also refer to a *group of people* who share some common characteristic or identity, such as "the Latino community." Finally, it can refer to the *social relationships* that unite people in groups, as in "College sports can promote community spirit on campus."

Here, we look at where these ideas overlap, the connection between the place where people live and work and the type of social bonds that unite them as a group. In this context, **community** is *a set of social relationships, typically arising from living in a particular place, that give people a sense of identity and belonging.* It refers simultaneously to a place, the people who share that place, and the social relationships that result.

Sociologists have long examined the relationships between *where* people live and *how* they live. To do so, they use the lenses provided by sociology's subfields, including urban sociology, rural sociology, human ecology, environmental sociology, and the sociology of community. Drawing on these perspectives, we can sketch the evolution of human communities and sample the social changes that humans created and that in turn changed their physical and social environments (Johnson and Earle 2000; Mumford 1968; Scott 2017).

We distinguish among three kinds of environments. First, the **social environment** refers broadly to *the cultural context and patterns of relationships within which humans live,* including groups, institutions, social networks, and social positions. We have been discussing social environment throughout this book. In addition, there is a physical environment with two components. The **built environment** is *the physical surroundings that humans create.* These include the buildings, roads, dams, homes, and consumer products we use every day. The **natural environment** is *the land, water, air, vegetation, and organisms that make up the physical world.* (See Figure 15.1.)

As humans shifted from being primarily hunter-gatherers, to farmers, and then to industrial manufacturers, their relationship to the natural and built environments changed. As a result, the communities in which they lived changed as well.

FIGURE 15.1 | SOCIAL, BUILT, AND NATURAL ENVIRONMENTS

(natural): ©ImageMore Co., Ltd./Getty Images; (built): ©TongRo Image Stock/Alamy Stock Photo; (social): ©Megapress/Alamy Stock Photo

Our social environment is nested within the human-built environment, which is located within the broader natural environment.

Nomadic Life: Hunting and Gathering

Modern humans (*Homo sapiens*) have been around for roughly 200,000 years. For about 95 percent of that time, they were hunters and gatherers living in small groups and foraging their natural environment for subsistence. Rather than forming a permanent settlement, they were nomadic, following the migration of animals and the seasonal availability of plant foods around a relatively large but circumscribed territory. This way of life had its advantages: extracting food from different environments resulted in a diversified and nutritious diet that could withstand the loss of any single food source; daily activity meant healthier lifestyles; small communities limited any spread of disease.

Since there was so little of it, the built environment was much less significant to such communities than the natural environment was. Besides clothing and basic tools, there was little substantial material culture, no ownership of land, limited private ownership of property, and little economic inequality. Men and women typically did different kinds of work, but they were generally social equals.

Rural Life: Settlements, Surpluses, and Inequality

Some 10,000–12,000 years ago, humans in some areas of the world gradually began to cultivate crops, such as wheat, rice, and corn, and to raise animals for food, raw materials, and transport. For several thousand years, limited cultivation coexisted with continued hunting and gathering. Eventually, though, around 5,000 years ago, the balance shifted toward more settled, rooted lifestyles. These developments brought several changes to their communities.

First, it became more difficult to follow a nomadic life. Crops in the fields needed to be tended over long periods of time, tying people to specific plots of land and contributing to a more sedentary lifestyle. A community became a group of people connected to a particular place.

Second, the establishment of rural communities produced an increasingly significant built environment. By staying in one place, people were able to invest more time, effort, and resources in constructing substantial homes, plowing farmland, and digging irrigation canals, thus forming permanent settlements.

Third, the cultivation of crops and raising of food animals enabled people to produce and store food surpluses, protecting themselves from droughts and other natural disasters but restricting the diversity of their diet. Surpluses were also useful for trade with other communities, diversifying the goods available.

Fourth, the ability to produce material surpluses led to the specialization of labor. In hunting-gathering societies, nearly everyone's work was focused on collecting, producing, or processing food. But the production of food surplus allowed some people to develop other skills and knowledge. Craftspeople, for example, began to focus on making clothing, constructing buildings, and creating useful implements. The result was new divisions of labor and more complex variation in social roles.

Finally, with more material goods available and more distinct social roles emerging, social inequality increased. Coordinated by the early state, which could tax land and grains, ownership of land, animals, and the surplus goods they helped produce became the basis for growing social stratification. People with more resources gained more power, often enabling them to acquire even more resources.

Various forms of rural life centered on villages, and small towns remained the dominant type of human community as

©Edward S. Curtis/Library of Congress/Corbis/Getty Images

As recently as the nineteenth century, some Native American nations of the Great Plains had cultures based on a nomadic lifestyle. They could readily dismantle their tipis to follow the seasonal movement of bison, a central source of food, clothing, and shelter.

©Florian Kopp/Alamy Stock Photo

©South Idaho Press/Ashley Smith/AP Images

Even today, rural agricultural communities—like these in Thailand (*top*) and the United States (*bottom*)—are home to billions of people around the globe.

CORE CONCEPTS CHALLENGE *Both of these farmers live in rural communities. How might their* **cultures** *have more in common with each other than they do with the culture of a major Thai or U.S. city? What does your answer suggest about the role of place in social life?*

©Jaysi/123RF

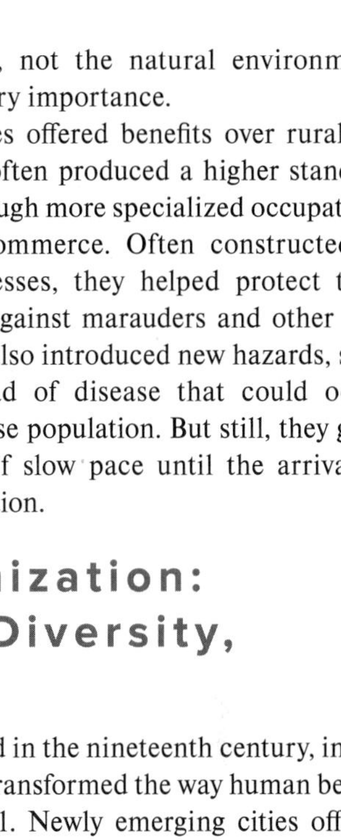

Security was a central purpose of some early cities. The walls that once protected the medieval city of Carcassonne, France, are still clearly visible.

recently as the early twentieth century; today they persist in many less-industrialized nations. But the creation of human settlements began a process that eventually led to the rise of cities.

Preindustrial Cities: Protection and Prosperity

The change from rural to city life took thousands of years. The earliest "cities," found in the Middle East, were towns by today's standards, sometimes containing fewer than 1,000 inhabitants. But as farmers increased their capacity to produce surplus food, they could support larger populations who were able to live in larger, more densely populated communities. These early settlements were the initial steps toward urban life in which the built environment, not the natural environment, was of primary importance.

Early cities offered benefits over rural villages. They often produced a higher standard of living through more specialized occupations and more commerce. Often constructed as walled fortresses, they helped protect their inhabitants against marauders and other enemies. Cities also introduced new hazards, such as the spread of disease that could occur among a dense population. But still, they grew at a steady if slow pace until the arrival of industrialization.

Modern Urbanization: Opportunity, Diversity, and Problems

Over a remarkably short period in the nineteenth century, industrialization and urbanization transformed the way human beings lived, as we saw in Chapter 1. Newly emerging cities offered unprecedented economic opportunities and created a vital and diverse intellectual environment, though they also became the site of deep social problems (see Table 15.1).

The foundation of the Industrial Revolution was a massive new capacity to manufacture consumer goods. Industrialization brought large numbers of wage laborers from the surrounding

TABLE 15.1 COMMUNITY TYPES AND FEATURES

	Nomadic/ Hunter-Gatherer	Rural/Agricultural	Preindustrial Cities	Industrial and Postindustrial Cities
Key period of development	Until about 10,000 B.C.E.	10,000–3000 B.C.E.	3000 B.C.E.–1700 C.E.	1700s–today
Experience of natural/ built environment	Dependence on natural environment; minimum built environment	Significant dependence on natural environment; some built environment	Limited experience with natural environment; significant built environment	Pervasive built environment; little experience with natural environment
Key economic feature	Hunting and gathering	Farming (crops) and herding (animals)	Manual crafts and trades	Mass manufacturing and, later, growing information-based employment
Surplus and extent of inequality	No significant material surplus; therefore, little economic inequality	Increased material surplus and increased inequality	Significant surpluses with extensive inequality	Massive surpluses with extremes of wealth and poverty
Specialization of labor	Very limited, by gender	Limited specialization	Significant specialization	Extensive specialization

countryside together in centralized factories, producing an explosion in urban populations. For example, in 1790, the four largest U.S. cities had a *combined* population of fewer than 100,000 people; by 1900 *each* of the four largest U.S. cities (New York, Boston, Chicago, and Philadelphia) had populations of at least 1 million (Gibson 1998). Urbanization eventually required sophisticated built environments. Electrical power plants powered factory machinery and lit homes at night. The icon of city life—the skyscraper—became possible once architects and developers introduced steel-framed buildings and electric elevators in the late nineteenth century. In this way, changes in the built environment enabled the creation of new urban communities.

The gathering of people of diverse ideas, skills, and talents provided a vibrant and stimulating intellectual and cultural environment in large cities. For those interested in new scientific ideas, the creative arts, and business opportunities, cities were the place to be. But while modern cities created enormous wealth for some, they could be places of horror for the poor. Abject squalor marked some neighborhoods. Oppressive factories or sweatshops often featured brutal 12-hour days, a hazardous environment, and dangerous machinery that could maim or kill. Overcrowded slums arose side-by-side with commercial districts and pollution-spewing workplaces, resulting in health and sanitation problems such as lung disease from air pollution and dysentery from open sewers.

TABLE 15.2 TEN LARGEST METROPOLITAN AREAS, PROJECTED, 2030

City, Country	Population, in millions
1. Tokyo, Japan	37.2
2. Delhi, India	36.1
3. Shanghai, China	30.8
4. Mumbai (Bombay), India	27.8
5. Beijing, China	27.7
6. Dhaka, Bangladesh	27.4
7. Karachi, Pakistan	24.8
8. Al-Qahirah (Cairo), Egypt	24.5
9. Lagos, Nigeria	24.2
10. Ciudad de Mexico (Mexico City), Mexico	23.9

Source: UN Department of Economic and Social Affairs 2017a.

Sunbelt Cities and Global Growth

In the latter half of the twentieth century, urbanization in the United States was most intense in cities such as Atlanta, Houston, and Phoenix in the South and Southwest, the area known as the Sunbelt. Most of these cities expanded rapidly by annexing adjacent lands. As a result, unlike older cities, Sunbelt cities are often decentralized environments heavily dependent on the automobile.

Today, industrialization and urbanization are increasingly global phenomena. In 2008, the world reached what the United Nations called "an invisible but momentous milestone" (UN Population Fund 2008, 1). For the first time in human history, a majority of people live in urban areas. By 2016, 54.5 percent of the world's population—4 billion people—called a city home, and that figure is expected to grow to 60 percent (to 5.1 billion) by 2030. In 2016, nearly a quarter of the world's population (23 percent, 1.7 billion people) lived in a city with at least 1 million inhabitants (UN Department of Economic and Social Affairs 2017a).

Urbanization occurs in developing nations today for largely the same reasons it occurred in Europe and the United States in earlier periods. Cities hold out the promise of economic opportunity for people from rural areas who often suffer from grinding poverty. In 2030, 9 of the 10 largest metropolitan areas will be in developing nations (see Table 15.2).

Just as in earlier periods, however, cities in poorer developing nations cannot live up to the expectations of the masses of people flocking to them. Like Fan Qun, the man described in the chapter-opening vignette, some people find upward mobility in cities. But many others struggle for a modest existence, and some are left destitute and without the support of the families they left in their communities of origin. In the miserable shantytowns that surround the more affluent cities in India, Mexico, China, Brazil, and elsewhere, a stunning inequality between rich and poor echoes what occurred in Europe in the nineteenth century.

Understanding the Culture of Urban Life

The urbanization that began in the West and continues in developing countries radically transformed rural ways of life that had existed for centuries. Early sociologists analyzed how social cohesion developed in this new urban environment.

Tönnies: Cities as a New Form of Social Organization

The most systematic early comparison of traditional rural and modern urban life came from German sociologist Ferdinand Tönnies (1855–1936). In 1887, he published a book that used the German words *Gemeinschaft* and *Gesellschaft*—usually translated as community and society—to label two distinct ways of life, summarized in Table 15.3.

Gemeinschaft refers to *social organization in which most relationships are based on the long-term personal ties of collective kinship, common tradition, and shared values.* Such forms of social organization are quite stable and are typically found in small

TABLE 15.3	ELEMENTS OF TÖNNIES'S *GEMEINSCHAFT* AND *GESELLSCHAFT*
Gemeinschaft	***Gesellschaft***
Typified by traditional rural communities	Typified by large cities
Culture is rooted in stable tradition	Culture is newly emerging and changing
People share common life experiences	People have diverse backgrounds and experiences
Social interactions often involve multilayered personal relationships	Social interactions are often impersonal and task specific, based on a single narrowly defined role
Little privacy and no anonymity	Considerable privacy and anonymity amid dense population
Culture tends to conformity, intolerance of difference, punishment of even mild deviance	Culture tends to tolerance of difference and some deviance
Social control is largely maintained through informal cultural norms and personal relationships	Social control is maintained through formal means (for example, police force)
Collective goals and community cooperation are common	Individual goals and pursuit of self-interest dominate

rural communities where residents are very similar, often related by blood and marriage, and typically employed in similar work, often agricultural. The people usually share common religious beliefs and other cultural traditions, too. Virtually all interactions—in school, on the street, in commerce, at work—include personal relationships as well as the task at hand. For example, the merchant who sells supplies may also be a neighbor, relative, fellow church member, and former schoolmate. "In Gemeinschaft we are united from the moment of our birth with our own folk for better or for worse," Tönnies wrote ([1887] 2001, 18). As sociologist Zygmunt Bauman (2001) further noted, the distinctiveness of a *Gemeinschaft* community provides a boundary between members of the community and outsiders, and its relative self-sufficiency makes extensive contact with outsiders unnecessary. Common life experiences produce strong, often emotionally based group norms that reinforce common identity and values, encourage conformity, and discourage deviance. The result is strong social cohesion based on commonality.

In contrast, ***Gesellschaft*** is Tönnies's term for *social organization in which most social relationships are impersonal, temporary, and based primarily on the pursuit of individual rational self-interest.* Such social organization characterizes modern city life. Urban centers attract people from various locales who often have little in common, who work in specialized occupations, and who remain relatively anonymous in the city's vast population. Identifying and enforcing common social norms can be difficult because people come from different places and cultures. Most social interactions in the city, therefore, are impersonal and do not extend beyond the task at hand. Tönnies argued that urban life undermines social solidarity and loosens social control mechanisms. These changes lead to more individualism and social isolation, weaker ties between people, and more deviance than in *Gemeinschaft* communities.

Tönnies insightfully argued that if people change *where* they live, they will likely change *how* they live. He suggested that something important—including a comforting sense of stable and secure community—may have been lost in the transition from rural to urban life. But sociologists caution against romanticizing traditional communities. Bauman (2001) noted that the restrictive homogeneity of *Gemeinschaft* can foster deep prejudice toward outsiders and anyone who dares to be different. Family duty and community responsibility override individual aspirations. So while modern urban life did represent a loss of safe and secure tradition, it also introduced new individual freedoms. This tension

©Viviane Moos/Corbis/Getty Images

The rapid growth of cities around the world has been accompanied by stark differences between newly emerging wealth and grinding poverty. Here, a poor slum area sits across the river from high-rise apartments for the wealthy in Mumbai, India.

between security (resulting from sameness) and freedom (resulting from diversity) has been a central one in modern social life (Bauman 2001).

Durkheim: Organic Solidarity in the City

Tönnies suggested that the individualism of urban life could undermine social solidarity. Durkheim, however, argued that a new form of collective cohesiveness emerges from the new social organization of cities (Durkheim [1893] 1997).

As we saw in Chapter 1, for Durkheim homogeneous rural communities exhibited *mechanical solidarity*—social cohesion based on shared experience, personal ties, and a limited sense of individuality. With the growth of cities, social solidarity was gradually replaced by *organic solidarity,* a new form of social cohesion based on interdependence. In modern industrial society, people depend on one another precisely *because* their work and social roles are so specialized. The baker, merchant, factory worker, doctor, and teacher all need and rely upon one another. For Durkheim, the rise of specialization created interdependence, providing urban populations with a different, but effective, form of social cohesion.

Jane Addams and the "Chicago School": Community in City Life

Tönnies and Durkheim both believed the personal ties of rural life were not a common feature of urban life. However, close studies of late-nineteenth-century Chicago neighborhoods revealed a more complex reality in which immigrants and other marginalized groups maintained personal connections in urban situations.

Between 1850 and 1900, Chicago's population exploded from 30,000 people to 1.7 million, making the city the fifth largest in the world. By 1930 the population had almost doubled again to 3.3 million (Gibson 1998). This rapid growth created severe social problems including poor sanitation, crowded housing, increasing crime, and exploitation of workers. To help address some of these issues, as we saw in Chapter 1, pioneering sociologist Jane Addams cofounded Hull House in 1889, a settlement house that provided community services for ethnically diverse poor and working-class residents. (See the Sociology in Action box.) In researching Chicago's neighborhoods and their needs, Addams and her collaborators at Hull House invented a new form of urban sociology that relied on gathering detailed data and mapping the demographic characteristics of different neighborhoods (Deegan 1988).

In the 1920s and 1930s, sociologists at the University of Chicago built upon the Hull House work and began formal "community studies" of urban life that employed small-scale direct observation. **Community studies** *typically look at groups of people who share some common tie and engage in social interaction within a particular geographic area.* According to these "Chicago School" studies, even in the heart of urban centers, ethnic enclaves—neighborhoods whose residents were often working-class immigrants of the same ethnic group—retained a distinct cultural identity, indicated by a distinct common language, religious practices, food, music, family relations, and other cultural traditions. Thus some of the social cohesion that marked traditional rural life survived in the new urban ethnic enclaves. Over time, though, immigrants became more fully assimilated into the dominant U.S. culture.

Some of the sociological insights gained by studying early European immigrants apply to today's city neighborhoods and communities. Like their earlier counterparts, today's immigrants often speak a language other than English, have different religious traditions, and observe distinctive norms and customs. Seeking the economic opportunities that cities offer, they form new ethnic enclaves as a means of providing mutual aid and maintaining social cohesion in a new environment (Buccitelli 2016; Foner et al. 2014).

The Impact of Place on Social Life: Human Ecology

Early work on urbanization showed that the physical environment influences the social life that takes place within it. This fundamental insight is the foundation of **human ecology,** *the study of the links between the physical environment—natural and built—and social life.*

The human ecology approach reveals that the physical environment is important at all levels of social life (Appold 2007; Steiner 2016). At the macro level, we can explain the location and development of cities by looking at their physical context. Major cities are usually located next to oceans, rivers, and large lakes, since these are natural resources that have facilitated travel, provided hydropower, and supplied necessary water for drinking, sanitation, and other applications. On the other hand, humans can alter the natural environment by building dams, reservoirs, and levees, actions that allow the construction of cities in the unlikeliest of places, such as the desert of Las Vegas.

Also at the macro level, the built environment of cities can reflect and reinforce broader cultural values. In Europe, as power shifted from religion to government and finally to corporations, the built environment followed suit. The tallest buildings of medieval cities were cathedrals near the city center. Towering city halls marked the rise of civil government, whereas in modern cities corporate skyscrapers dominate the skyline.

At the meso level, human ecologists note that cities are organized into distinct subsections—residential, commercial, industrial, and the like—that evolve in relationship to one another. Growth or decline of any one area can disrupt and disorganize a community, resulting in crime and neglect, but typically stability eventually returns as people establish new social norms and structures. These processes in cities resemble

on social theory

Human ecologists draw upon **functionalist theories** that view society as made up of distinct but interrelated parts. What are some of the distinct parts of the community in which you live? What functions do they serve?

SOCIOLOGY in ACTION

Jane Addams and Hull House

Sociology and social work have common roots that go back to the nation's first graduate department of sociology at the University of Chicago, which combined study and practice. Reflecting the gender inequality of the day, men dominated the main sociology department, but a strong contingent of women sociologists, most famously Jane Addams, was affiliated with it (Deegan 1988; Feagin, Vera, and Ducey 2015).

Beginning in the 1890s and continuing for a quarter century, many of these women worked with Hull House, a settlement house that provided community services for poor and working-class people and served as an intellectual center for residents and scholars alike. Cofounded by Jane Addams, a scholar and activist who worked for women's rights and labor reforms and was awarded the Nobel Peace Prize in 1931, Hull House grew to encompass an entire city block in one of Chicago's poorest and most ethnically diverse neighborhoods. Several thousand visitors a week came for its dormitory and bathing facilities, day care, health clinic, employment assistance, gymnasium, coffeehouse, reading room, adult evening classes, and more.

Source: Library of Congress Prints and Photographs Division [LC-USZ61-144]

Addams and her Hull House collaborators campaigned to end child labor and improve health and working conditions, goals that helped define the liberal reform period known as the Progressive Era. To improve conditions in nearby neighborhoods, they had to understand the issues residents faced. Hull House thus served, in effect, as a center of applied sociology, where research teams gathered data, applied their findings to shape the work of the settlement house, and provided evidence used in legislative reform efforts. In doing so, Hull House workers pioneered forms of urban sociology and heavily influenced the development of community studies at the University of Chicago.

Some male sociology faculty joined Addams and her colleagues in their social reform efforts, but most focused on developing theoretical models of urbanization and its effects. They viewed the city as a "laboratory" within which to conduct their work, regarding residents more as subjects for study than as partners for change.

Over time the university institutionalized the distinction between studying urban issues and working to bring about social reform. In 1920, it transferred all the women affiliated with the sociology department to the social work department. On most U.S. campuses, sociology and social work continue to exist as separate departments, the former emphasizing the study of society, the latter focusing on providing social services.

However, Jane Addams, often referred to as a founder of social work, thought of herself as a sociologist, not a social worker. In her Hull House work she integrated study and practice, and her advocacy for social change continues today as "public sociology" and related work.

think about it

1. *How does Addams's work compare to your understanding of social work today?*
2. *Do you think sociologists should act upon the knowledge they have to help address social problems, or should they remain detached observers, studying but not advocating for any particular change? What are the advantages and pitfalls of each approach?*

growth and decline in natural ecological systems. But human action can intervene, such as with modern zoning practices that define how different areas can be used (residential, commercial, industrial, and so on).

Human ecologists also point out that function, not political boundary, defines urban areas and shapes our experience of them. So, to understand urban dynamics—the way a city functions—we must look at the entire area, including the region beyond its formal boundaries. To help in this analysis, researchers distinguish between the various physical spaces that make up urban communities (see Figure 15.2), including

- The ***inner city,*** typically the most densely developed portion
- The ***city proper,*** a city's legal boundary
- The ***suburbs,*** less densely developed and populated areas that surround a city's official boundaries
- ***Edge cities,*** mini-cities that develop outside the city proper and that include major business, commercial, and even industrial districts to which people travel for work, shopping, and recreation
- ***Exurbs,*** residential areas beyond the suburbs that have a quasi-rural atmosphere
- ***Metropolitan area,*** the region that encompasses a city plus the surrounding suburbs, exurbs, and edge cities
- ***Megalopolis,*** a continuous urban region that incorporates multiple cities

FIGURE 15.2 | THE ZONES OF COMMUNITY LIFE

Metropolitan Area
(city plus surrounding areas)

Inner city
City proper (legal boundary)
Suburbs
Edge cities
Exurbs

Megalopolis
(continuous developed region with more than one city)

A metropolitan area is made up of different zones, including the inner city, the city proper, the suburbs, edge cities, and the exurbs. When two or more developing cities blend together, they form a megalopolis.

Finally, at the micro level, the physical environment within a city can also influence social life. If you look around your campus to see where students like to hang out, you will probably find physical features that make these locations appealing. Benches, a wall, a green and shady lawn can all make a difference in whether and how people use a physical space. Urban planners and architects apply these social-psychological insights in designing buildings, public spaces, and neighborhoods.

Power and Inequality in City Life

What fuels urban growth? Who has the power to help determine the investment and development that will occur? How are valuable resources, including housing, transportation, and city services, distributed in a city? In studying urban life, sociologists have asked such questions and documented how the powerful disproportionately influence urban development, often to the disadvantage of those with less power. An example of this research is **new urban sociology,** *an approach to studying cities that focuses on the interactions of politics and economics and locates them in the larger context of the global economy* (Hutchison and Ryan 2015). Here we consider examples of the insights that have emerged from this approach.

Class Inequality and the Urban "Growth Machine"

Class inequality is pervasive in urban spaces. The gap between the rich in luxurious settings and the homeless on the street is just one indicator of economic inequality. In addition to comfortable homes, people in affluent areas typically enjoy low rates of street crime and better community services.

We also see class inequality in the attention paid to the needs of commuters. For decades, governments have built and expanded roads to accommodate mostly middle-class drivers commuting from the suburbs while often neglecting public transportation–the buses, trains, light rail, and subways relied upon by poor and working-class city residents. Stratification is emerging even among drivers, however, as some localities introduce private toll roads that allow paying drivers to bypass congestion others must endure (Vanoutrive 2016).

Class inequality is also reflected in the way cities grow. Developers, realtors, bankers, builders, and other business owners all have a stake in promoting the growth of cities because more people means more potential profits for their businesses. For politicians, growth results in grateful business owners to fund their campaigns and an expanding commercial tax base to fund government budgets. Consequently, some sociologists have referred to cities as **"growth machines,"** *a label that highlights how powerful businesses and politicians work together to promote urban development, often while ignoring the interests of ordinary citizens* (Molotch 1976).

©Michael Matthews/Alamy Stock Photo

A poster in Seattle, Washington, protests the high cost of housing. The clashing interests of residents and developers are reflected in the conflicts that emerge over the gentrification of neighborhoods.

CORE CONCEPTS CHALLENGE *How do such clashes reflect economic inequality and differences in* ***power****?*

thinking about power

How is **power**, and its distribution, reflected in the way your community is arranged? What are the desirable neighborhoods, and who lives in them? What neighborhoods are considered to have problems? Who lives in those neighborhoods?

Developers pursuing profits move from project to project and do not have to live with the consequences of what they create. But for ordinary citizens, cities are not merely growth machines but the places where they live and work, communities to which they have a long-term commitment. Sometimes the growth interests of business and politicians harm the interests of ordinary citizens. Poorly maintained housing for low-income residents with high eviction rates can be a profitable business for some landlords but a nightmare for residents (Desmond 2016). On the other hand, **gentrification** is *the process of rehabilitating older housing stock and investing in neighborhood development in a way that typically attracts new higher-income residents and displaces current middle- and low-income residents.* Because they transform relatively inexpensive properties into more desirable—and more expensive—housing, such projects can be highly profitable for investors. But gentrification often displaces middle- and low-income residents who cannot afford to buy and are unable to pay the newly increased rents (Brown-Saracino 2017). Meanwhile, investors and politicians often neglect low-income housing—a key to tackling the homelessness that exists in all urban areas—because of its relatively low profit margins.

SPOTLIGHT

on social theory

Conflict theorists highlight the power struggles that often occur to control scarce resources. How do such struggles apply to urban development? Have you seen evidence of such conflict in your community?

Conflicts therefore arise between investors who pursue short-term growth and profits and residents who want to protect their quality of life. Community-based social movements often emerge to advocate for residents' interests. They typically face an interlocking concentration of power consisting of developers, realtors, and both appointed and elected officials.

In addition, because local governments play a key role in the regulation and distribution of valuable resources, such as housing, education, transportation, and social welfare benefits, they are often involved in conflict. Local disputes between government and citizen grassroots organizations represent new forms of community-based class conflict in capitalist societies that Karl Marx did not anticipate when he focused on workplace class conflict (Castells 1983).

FIGURE 15.3 | CONTINUING RACIAL AND ETHNIC SEGREGATION

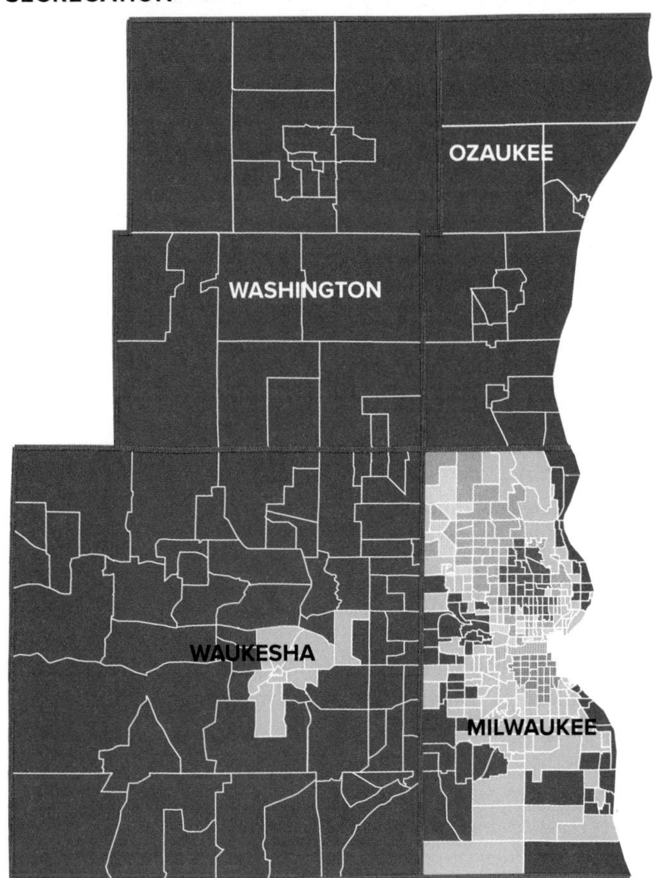

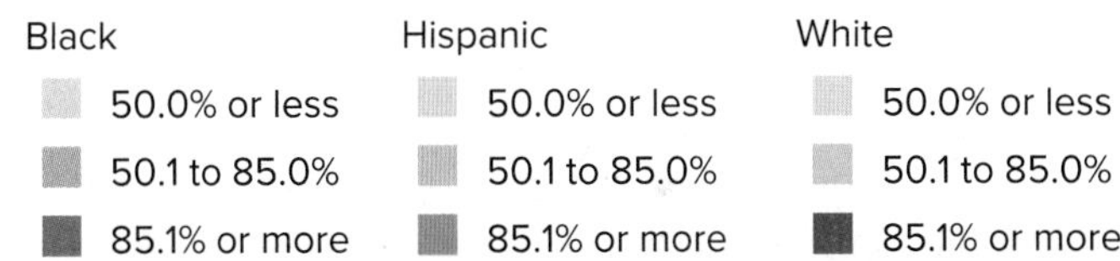

Although overall segregation levels have been declining, racial and ethnic segregation remains stark in many cities. In Milwaukee, Wisconsin, and surrounding counties—the nation's most segregated urban area according to the 2010 Census—black, Hispanic, and white residents live in largely separate areas. *Source:* Denvir 2011.

Race and Urban Inequality

At the end of the nineteenth century, W. E. B. Du Bois, working in Philadelphia, carried out the first sociological study of African Americans. In *The Philadelphia Negro* ([1899] 1996), Du Bois used innovative methods—from mapping to personal interviews and statistics—to document employment, family composition, religion, street activity, community institutions, crime, interracial contacts, and other aspects of black urban life. His nuanced assessment of the black community included an indictment of the role white racism played in creating deplorable conditions that contrasted with affluent white neighborhoods.

Over a century later, urban communities are still divided by race, due to the legacy of segregation (which created single-race neighborhoods), continuing economic inequality, and ongoing institutional racism (see Figure 15.3). Even long after the end of legal segregation, institutional discrimination in the housing industry played a role in the form of **redlining,** *the use of discriminatory practices in the sale or rental of housing to minorities.* (The term comes from real estate agents' practice of marking maps with a red line indicating neighborhoods they deemed off limits to minorities.) Banks sometimes informally wrote off minority neighborhoods, denying mortgages to potential buyers and home improvement loans to owners, regardless of their financial status. Real estate agents sometimes also refused to show prospective buyers homes in these neighborhoods. These tactics contributed to the downward spiral of some minority neighborhoods. Studies show that minorities in rental and housing markets today continue to be treated differently from whites (Rosen 2014; Squires, Friedman, and Saidat 2002; Turner and Ross 2005).

In a twist on this sort of discrimination, the housing mortgage crisis that began at the end of 2007 featured "reverse redlining," or predatory lending. Unscrupulous brokers and financial institutions targeted poor and working-class minorities, encouraging them to shoulder complex mortgages with high interest rates that they often did not understand and could not afford. One study found that blacks and Hispanics were twice as likely to get these high-cost "subprime" loans as whites with comparable income (Bajaj and Fessenden 2007). Then minority borrowers were disproportionately more likely to be evicted from their homes (Sharp and Hall 2014).

The segregation picture today is mixed (Iceland et al. 2010; Lichter, Parisi, and Taquino 2017; Logan and Stults 2011). Although significant racial segregation persists, fair housing legislation, the growth of the black middle class, and declining racial prejudice among individuals have enabled some desegregation to occur. However, this has largely been due to working- and middle-class minorities moving into formerly all-white areas, leaving behind neighborhoods made up predominately of poor minorities. It is far less common for whites to move into these poor minority neighborhoods, which now often feature lower-quality schools, higher crime rates, and less valuable homes (Logan and Stults 2011).

Segregation between blacks and whites peaked in the 1960s and has been declining slowly but steadily, reaching new lows in the 2010s. Hispanics and Asians are considerably less segregated than African Americans, and there has been little change in segregation levels for these groups in the past decade. However, the rapidly growing Hispanic population is resulting in larger homogeneous Hispanic communities.

©Ken Wolter/Shutterstock

The consolidation of economic power into the hands of large, often global, chain stores has meant that strip malls and other commercial development across the country look remarkably similar, featuring the same handful of national chains, big-box retailers, and indistinctive architecture. How are local communities affected by this sort of development?

Urbanization in a Global Economy

Just a few decades ago, local businesses and political leaders made the decisions affecting the future of a city, so decisions about where to invest and locate new businesses were controlled locally. For example, as late as the 1960s, most hardware stores, clothing stores, restaurants, and so on were independent and owned locally or regionally. In recent decades, however, globalization has centralized much of business. Instead of hundreds of independent hardware stores scattered across the country, most communities have only a Home Depot or a Lowe's outlet. Instead of countless local restaurants, a small handful of national and international fast-food chains dominate the market. The same is true for many other industries.

SPOTLIGHT on social theory

According to Wallerstein's **world systems theory,** a global economy links the countries of the world. How do the actions of transnational corporations within this global system affect your community?

This massive growth of chains has brought lower prices for consumers but has concentrated economic power in the hands of a few corporate players, against which small local businesses often cannot effectively compete. Control over a local community's fate—its ability to attract business, promote commercial development, and so on—has often shifted to the boardrooms of major national and transnational corporations (Gottdeiner and Hutchison 2015).

An influx of investment dollars can bring jobs and prosperity, while a withdrawal of investment can lead to economic decline and urban blight. Over decades, many U.S. cities in the North and Midwest experienced difficulties as transnational corporations pursuing higher profits moved the manufacturing jobs that provided steady employment for local residents to foreign countries with fewer regulations and lower wages (Bluestone and Harrison 1982; Harvey 1990; Koistinen 2014). Critics argue that "free trade" agreements have only made it easier for companies to move jobs abroad. At the same time, the movement of capital abroad has helped fuel the development of cities in China, Mexico, India, and other nations. Understanding urbanization today requires understanding such global dynamics.

The Structure and Culture of the Suburbs

Since 2010, big cities—especially Sunbelt cities—have been growing faster than the suburbs, signaling an urban revival in some places (Frey 2016). That development could be temporary, though. The longer trend in the United States has not been urbanization but rather suburbanization. In this section we examine this development and sample some of the issues it raises.

Suburban Growth and Urban Decline

The rise of the suburbs dates to the post-World War II period. As the United States emerged from the war with a strong manufacturing infrastructure and few foreign competitors, it began a period of unprecedented prosperity. With the help of their unions, many U.S. workers acquired well-paid manufacturing jobs.

Newfound affluence among the working class allowed many to pursue a dream unthinkable before the war: home ownership. In the postwar years, the federal government made vast amounts of money available to help citizens achieve this goal, offering home mortgages with low interest rates to veterans and tax breaks to homeowners. However, as discussed in Chapter 10, these programs were often racially biased, favoring white home buyers. The government guaranteed mortgages in "low risk" areas—often interpreted as newly built (white) suburbs—while neglecting existing housing stock in central cities (Oliver and Shapiro 2006; Wilson 1996). For whites, such financing, combined with mass-produced modest tract homes, made housing in the suburbs more affordable than ever. New road and highway programs facilitated transportation from central cities to the suburbs. All these structural conditions encouraged a migration, mostly white, from cities to suburbs in the 1950s and 1960s.

While public policy was making the suburbs attractive, a number of developments made cities increasingly unattractive. In the 1960s, media images of urban rioters protesting racial and economic inequality, police brutality, and other grievances left many viewers with the impression that the inner city was dangerous and crime-ridden. The export of urban manufacturing jobs overseas that began in the 1970s and 1980s undermined the economic health of many cities, forcing unemployment rates up and deepening poverty. As a result, the need for social services increased just as cities were beginning to lose tax revenue, provoking urban financial crises. The perception of these urban problems further enhanced the appeal of the suburbs for those who could afford them, and their departure for the suburbs left the people behind with few options. Since 1950, more than 90 percent of U.S. population growth in metropolitan areas has occurred in the suburbs. Some cities saw an "urban renaissance" in recent years in large part due to young adults—often referred to as millennials (Ehrenhalt 2012). Millennials found employment in cities, remained single, and delayed purchasing a home in the face of a difficult economy, high student loan debt, and the housing crisis (Pinsker 2015). However, as more millennials achieve financial stability and get married, many are moving to the suburbs where homes are more affordable. The result has been slowed urban growth and a new resurgence of suburbs, where about two-thirds of Americans live (Kolko 2015, 2017; Morris 2016).

Suburban Problems

The automobile made the growth of suburbs possible. Henry Ford, the father of automobile mass-manufacturing, was sure the future lay in the suburbs. "The modern city is the most artificial and unlovely sight this planet affords," Ford once said. "The ultimate solution is to abandon it. We shall solve the city problem only by leaving the city" (in Flint 2006, 29). The suburbs did indeed become an attractive option for many people. But rather than solving city problems, the growth of the suburbs brought unanticipated new challenges for our health, environment, and social lives.

Sprawl The growth of the suburbs has resulted in **sprawl,** *low-density development that disperses people over a wide area, separates homes from workplaces and stores, and depends heavily on cars for transportation.* Suburban sprawl quickly consumes land that had been wildlife habitat or devoted to agriculture. As the distance between home, work, and shopping grew, sprawl also created enormous traffic congestion and long commutes to work (see Figure 15.4) (Ross 2014). On average, U.S. workers spend 51 minutes a day traveling to and from work. About 8.1 percent of commuters—some 10.8 million people—have "long commutes" of two hours round-trip, and about 600,000 have "mega-commutes" in which they spend three hours or more a day going to and from work (McKenzie 2013).

Only 5 percent of people take public transportation to work. Instead, with three cars for every four people, 86 percent get to work by car and 76 percent drive alone (see Figure 15.5). With all that driving, Americans around major cities are estimated to spend an average of 38 hours a year stuck in traffic, wasting 2.9 billion gallons of fuel (Schrank, Eisele, and Lomax 2012). Driving takes a toll on health, too. As commuting times increase, physical activity and cardiovascular health decline, while weight, blood pressure, and heart attack risk increase (Hoehner et al.

thinking about structure

How does the physical **structure** of suburban communities shape social life in the suburbs and distinguish it from urban life?

FIGURE 15.4 | SUBURBAN SPRAWL

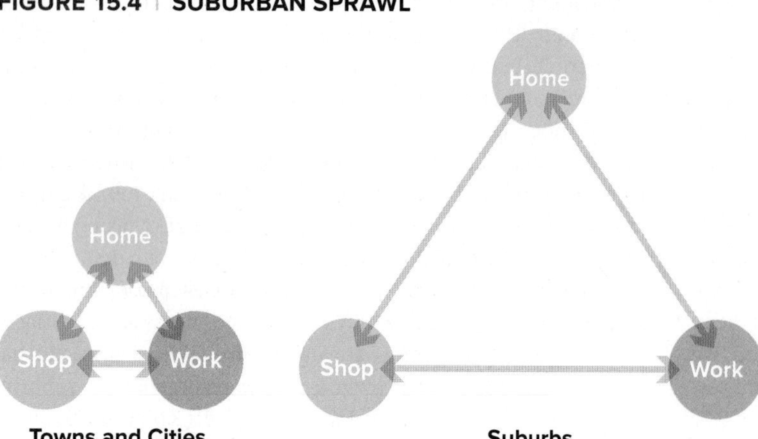

Imagine a triangle between your home, the place you work, and the key places you shop. In smaller communities or dense urban environments, the sides of the triangle typically represent relatively short distances. In suburban sprawl, though, these distances become much greater, separating various social activities so that longer car travel is required and a unifying sense of community is less likely. What are some of the other consequences of making the legs of this triangle longer?

2012). Driving and congestion also contribute to the degradation of our natural environment, through both air pollution and inefficient use of land. Although the price fluctuates periodically, expensive gasoline also burdens commuters with a higher cost of living.

The most common response to congestion—building more roads—usually makes the situation worse because it attracts more suburban development, which produces more traffic. In metropolitan areas with the most added road capacity in the 1990s, the hours commuters were stuck in traffic jumped by 70 percent (Flint 2006). More broadly, traffic increases proportionately to the new roads added; more roads simply results in more traffic and no reduction in congestion (Duranton and Turner 2011).

Higher Taxes Local governments lose money on suburban residential growth, making growth expensive for taxpayers (Flint 2006; Thompson 2013). In most cases, the tax revenue new residents bring in is not enough to offset the costs of infrastructure such as roads and schools and the ongoing salaries of additional teachers, firefighters, and other workers needed to serve the increased population. To pay these costs, suburban governments usually increase residential property taxes, making taxpayers subsidize the residential real estate development industry.

Social Isolation Unlike that of cities, the built environment of suburbs often makes social life more isolated and private. Some of this privacy is desirable and one of the reasons the suburbs are attractive to many. But it also has social consequences. The suburbanite's need to drive almost everywhere reduces face-to-face social interaction by reducing casual encounters on neighborhood streets (which often even lack sidewalks) or on public transportation (which often doesn't exist). The design of suburban homes frequently features back decks rather than front porches, discouraging socializing with any passersby. Private suburban backyards partially replace the urban experience of public parks; private media rooms supplant public movie theaters.

The orientation to privacy can carry over to a broader decline in civic engagement. For example, in many suburban developments, homeowner associations arrange for services such as private trash pick-up, snow removal, and road maintenance—tasks that used to be the responsibility of local governments. As a result, participation in these associations sometimes displaces broader public civic engagement.

More broadly, in his classic work, *Bowling Alone,* Robert Putnam (2000) found that "*each additional ten minutes in daily commuting time cuts involvement in community affairs by 10 percent*—fewer public meetings attended, fewer committees chaired, fewer petitions signed, fewer church services, less volunteering, and so on" (p. 213). Of all the factors affecting how much civic activity people undertake, time spent commuting is second only to educational level in importance.

FIGURE 15.5 | HOW U.S. WORKERS GET TO WORK

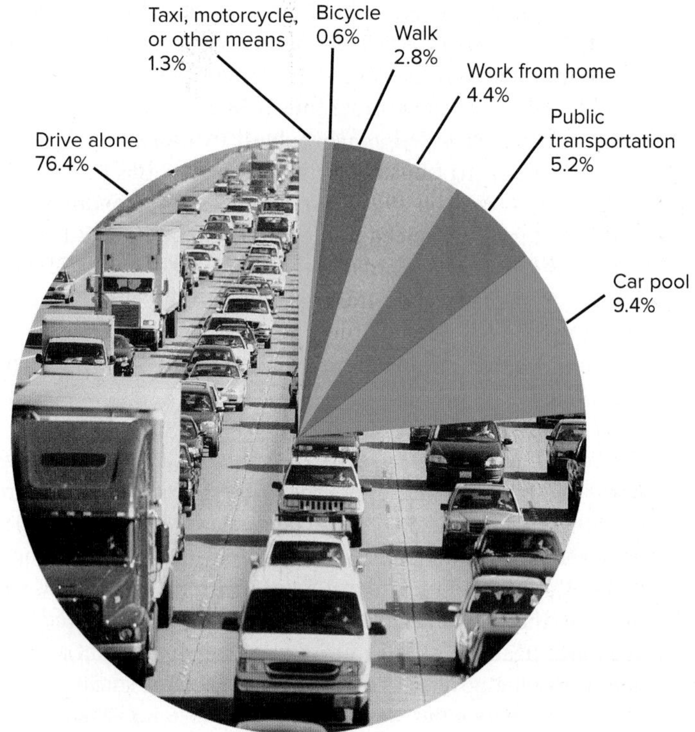

©Comstock/Getty Images

The vast majority of U.S. workers commute by car, usually driving alone. *Source:* McKenzie 2015.

CORE CONCEPTS CHALLENGE *How do you get to school? How does the* **structure** *of your community influence your decision to travel this way?*

©John Carnemolla/Corbis/Getty Images

An expanding suburban development (*foreground*) crowds a neighboring farm. As the suburbs grow, they take up land once used for agriculture and wildlife habitat, strain local water supplies, and transform the local ecosystems.

Putnam argues that commuting cuts into civic participation for three reasons. First, as noted, navigating sprawl takes time. Second, sprawl is associated with increased social segregation, reducing opportunities to make connections that cross class and racial lines. Finally, sprawl disrupts community "boundedness"—the sense of living in a distinct community. People in the suburbs, whose attention is divided between where they live and where they work, have less sense of belonging to a distinct community (and thus of participating in community life) than do urban dwellers, who are more likely to live near work.

Today's Changing Suburbs

The popular image of the suburbs in the 1950s was of quiet neighborhoods, with white residents living in modest homes surrounded by picket fences. But the suburbs have changed dramatically, and today they also vary significantly from one another. Older inner suburbs have developed many social problems formerly associated with cities, such as significant crime, gang violence, poverty, pollution, and neighborhood blight. In stark contrast, other suburbs feature a relatively secure life in high-end luxury homes behind the protective walls of gated communities. Spatial development also differs greatly across suburban areas. The exurbs, for example, sometimes have no real neighborhoods at all, since homes are spread out on large multiacre lots. Some new suburbs have followed "smart-growth" principles, however, emphasizing dense development that allows residents to live, work, and shop in walkable neighborhoods—features that used to distinguish city life.

Suburbs, overall, have also become more racially and ethnically diverse. In the twenty-first century, most emigrants to the United States have moved to small towns and suburbs rather than large urban areas (Farrell 2016). As more racial and ethnic minorities achieve middle-class status and governments and lenders eliminate overtly racist housing policies, many minorities have done exactly what an earlier generation of whites did: they have left the city and moved to the suburbs, leaving behind poorer residents in urban minority neighborhoods.

In some cases, modern technology has helped overcome the social isolation of the suburbs. Many housing developments have their own websites, forums, Facebook groups, and e-mail lists that allow news to be shared and help organize face-to-face social and community events. Multifamily housing units are more common today in the suburbs, and wealthier suburban developments even hire professional activities directors to coordinate social events and community gatherings (McCrummen 2005a; Sisson 2017).

These technological and professional fixes can help people of similar incomes (who can afford to live in the subdivision) and interests make connections, but they do not promote broad civic engagement with the larger community. In fact, affluent suburban housing developments can be very homogeneous and inward looking, epitomized by gated communities that physically exclude neighbors of more modest means who often lived in the area long before the new developments were constructed (McCrummen 2005b). Such a built environment speaks volumes about the types of social connections being cultivated—and discouraged.

The Enduring Significance of Rural Life

Different government agencies use different definitions to distinguish between urban and rural. Although cities and suburbs often receive the most attention, about 72 percent of the land in the United States is classified as "nonmetropolitan" and thus rural. These rural areas are home to about 46.1 million people—14 percent of the population in 2017 (Cromartie 2018).

The overall rural population in the United States has remained relatively stable for more than 50 years but, because the urban population has increased during the same period and some rural counties with major population growth have been reclassified as nonrural, the rural population has declined as a percentage of the overall population. Some rural communities have shrunk in recent decades, while others have grown in population since the 1990s. So far, "rural rebound" has occurred mostly in areas that cater to tourists looking for outdoor activities such as skiing, boating, and hiking. But as more people are able to work from home over the internet, they may begin to migrate back to smaller communities.

Regardless of their population, rural areas continue to play crucial roles in social life (Flora and Flora 2013; Lobao 2007). For one thing, cities themselves depend on rural areas for a variety of resources. The rural farmlands and ranches that are home to crops and animals feed urban populations. Rural mines generate the coal and uranium, oil and gas fields the oil and natural gas, and wind turbines and solar farms the wind and solar energy that fuel urban life. Wood, steel, and other construction materials that form the infrastructure of cities are harvested from rural forests and mines. Most of the garbage generated in urban areas ends up in rural landfills. Many tourist destinations–getaways for restoring the mental health of urban dwellers–are also located in rural areas.

Rural communities are no longer as isolated or as homogeneous as they once were. Modern highways and road systems make traveling to them easier, while telecommuting and "extreme commuting" open up many more jobs to rural residents than just agriculture or ranching. Satellite communications bring television and the internet to sparsely populated rural areas, connecting them to all facets of the broader culture. Local agricultural and meat processing jobs often attract new immigrants, especially from Mexico and Central America. In short, today's rural communities can increasingly include the diversity found in the broader society.

Regardless of these changes, the fields, forests, and green spaces of rural communities continue to link their residents to the natural environment. In contrast, many urban dwellers do not think about where their food is grown, where their water comes from, or where their wastes end up. For most city residents, attention to nature is largely limited to deciding whether they will need an umbrella today. But increasingly the natural environment demands everyone's attention because the impact of human activity has created an environmental crisis.

Source: NASA

NASA's "blue marble" photo, the first clear picture of a fully lit face of Earth, helped symbolize the fragile nature of Earth's environment.

Environmental Sociology

On December 7, 1972, while on their way to the moon, astronauts in NASA's Apollo 17 took the first crystal-clear picture of a fully lit Earth, the "blue marble" photo, as it became known. Huge distances, vast terrains, and seemingly endless oceans confront people who travel the surface of the planet. But this single photo, taken from 18,000 miles away, shows that our tiny planet in the vast darkness of space has very real limits. Released just as concerns about environmental issues were growing–the first-ever Earth Day had taken place in 1970–the "blue marble" photo became a symbol of our planet's limited resources and the common challenge of protecting them that we face.

Like the rest of society, sociologists have paid increasing attention to environmental issues since the days of the "blue marble" photo (Bell and Ashwood 2016; Burns and Caniglia 2016). As Dunlap and Marshall (2007) note, "[E]nvironmental problems are fundamentally social problems: They result from human social behavior, they are viewed as problematic because of their impact on humans (as well as other species), and their solution requires societal effort" (329). **Environmental sociology** *focuses on the interaction between social life, the built environment, and the natural environment.* Pellow and Brehm (2013) note that environmental sociology is unique in highlighting "the inseparability of human society from nonhuman natures and the centrality of inequality and power that shape both" (232). In examining our natural world, environmental sociologists focus on three key issues: (1) why societies are producing such daunting environmental problems, (2) how people come to recognize and understand them, and (3) how changes in social structure and behavior can help address them. We consider each of these issues, but we start with a quick reminder of the range of problems in our current environmental crisis (Blunden and Arndt 2016; United Nations Environment Programme 2016).

Environmental Threats

In brief, the following are among the environmental challenges we face:

- ***Climate change.*** The use of fossil fuels generates carbon dioxide pollution, forming a shield that prevents heat from escaping the earth's atmosphere. This process helps to produce global warming, an increase in the average temperature of the earth's oceans and atmosphere. Climate change contributes to the melting of glaciers and likely increases the severity of extreme weather, such as droughts, flooding, hurricanes, and tornadoes. For example, heat fuels hurricanes and studies suggest that warming oceans are making hurricanes more destructive. Warmer oceans contributed to disastrous amounts of rainfall in 2017's Hurricane Harvey that dumped 60 inches of rain on parts of Texas, the most ever recorded from a single storm in the United States (Trenberth et al. 2018). Hurricanes are becoming more extreme and ramping up to peak wind speeds more quickly than in the past, resulting in more damage (Balaguru, Foltz, and Leung 2018). (The Through a Sociological Lens box explores sociology's take on climate change.)

- ***Air pollution.*** Gases emitted by cars, trucks, and industrial processes enter the air we breathe. They can combine with water molecules in the atmosphere and be reintroduced into the soil and water as acid rain (precipitation high in acid content). Or these toxic gases can rise into the air and reduce the effectiveness of the ozone layer—the layer of atmosphere that protects the earth against ultraviolet radiation from the sun, a source of skin cancer and other health problems.
- ***Water pollution.*** Numerous pollutants threaten water quality: industrial pollutants (including industrial waste dumped into rivers, waste oil dumped into the ocean, and chemicals used in fracking, which may contaminate ground and surface waters); household waste (sewage treated with chemicals and dumped in rivers, drugs flushed down the toilet); erosion from development (mud in creeks and streams); and agricultural runoff (including pesticides and fertilizers). These pollutants can create health problems and destroy habitats for microorganisms and larger water animals.
- ***Solid waste.*** The quantity of garbage has been exploding, and the space we have for it is limited. Nonbiodegradable trash (waste that cannot be broken down by living organisms) fills our landfills, where most garbage is buried and will remain intact essentially forever. Leaks and seepage of toxic wastes into the groundwater and the release of polluting gases into the air pollute areas near landfills. A fast-growing form of garbage is "e-waste," the electronic devices that make up to 70 percent of all toxic waste in landfills (Holgate 2017).
- ***Resource depletion.*** Human activity destroys, depletes, and pollutes a variety of natural resources. Logging and burning destroy rain forests, often to make room for cattle ranching or farming. But rain forests are like the earth's lungs in reverse; they absorb carbon dioxide from the atmosphere and produce oxygen. They are also home to an estimated three-quarters of the earth's plant species. Clean water is becoming a scarce commodity, and a water shortage could be one of the biggest threats in this century.
- ***Energy consumption.*** Energy consumption depletes natural resources (such as oil), produces toxic pollutants (such as radioactive waste from nuclear power plants), and contributes to climate change (via waste from coal-fired electrical plants, for example). Because energy use affects the environment in so many ways, developing the ability to produce clean renewable energy is a huge challenge for the future of our environment.

Many of these problems have been emerging for decades. What is new is the *scale* of consumption, pollution, and resource depletion as industrialization and urbanization spread around the world.

©Tony Waltham/Robert Harding/Newscom

©Tony Waltham/Robert Harding/Newscom

FAST-FORWARD

Change and the Environment

One of the ways we can see the effects of climate change is in the extensive melting of many of the world's massive glaciers. These pictures contrast a glacier in Norway photographed in 2002 (*top*) with the same glacier photographed in 2011 (*bottom*). Glacial melting has clearly accelerated in just the past few years.

Analyzing Environmental Problems

How can we analyze and better understand environmental problems that threaten us? One way is to draw upon the sociological perspective on environments and community life we have used throughout this chapter. The natural environment is the context within which social life occurs. The actions humans take, especially in constructing a built environment, alter that environment. The altered natural environment, in turn, influences human action.

THROUGH A SOCIOLOGICAL LENS

Climate Change

Why would sociologists want to study climate change? That's easy: by disrupting the environment on which we depend for life, climate change "threatens the future of society" (Dunlap and Brulle 2015, 1).

This grave assessment opens a collected volume of sociological research called *Climate Change and Society: Sociological Perspectives,* which was assembled by the American Sociological Association. Typically, we think of *natural* scientists as the ones who study climate change: climatologists, biologists, oceanographers, glaciologists, and the like. However, sociologists bring their own unique perspective to the topic, asking questions and highlighting the human dimensions of climate change, which are often neglected.

For example, sociologists study the social forces that have contributed to the rise of climate change. At a macro level, those forces include the role of capitalism in fueling unbridled growth, along with the question of how capitalist theory might be modified to address environmental concerns. At a meso level, sociologists study the part corporations play in producing greenhouse gases and often in resisting efforts to regulate or reduce such emissions. At a micro level, sociologists take a critical look at how consumers drive climate change by participating in a culture that encourages them to acquire status and express their identity by buying things.

Sociologists also examine the social impact of climate change, paying close attention to the role of inequality. The poor are disproportionately affected by the negative consequences of climate change, while affluent consumers disproportionately contribute to the problem. Understanding how climate change both reflects and helps to reinforce social inequalities is another sociological lens through which to see this topic.

Finally, sociologists examine how people respond to the challenge of climate change, individually, institutionally, and as a society. How do people think about and understand climate change, and how does their thinking affect the way they respond to the crisis? This topic includes social movements that aim to change public opinion, corporate behavior, and government regulations. It also includes countermovements, such as the climate change denial movement, which is dedicated to sabotaging the environmental movement and potential government regulation. And it includes political institutions and their role in regulating emissions and promoting environmentally friendly policies.

As the editors of *Climate Change and Society* note, "Human-caused climate change is clearly one of the most important issues of the twenty-first century, and understanding climate change—its sources, impacts, and potential amelioration—is an inherently sociological concern" (Brulle and Dunlap 2015, 15). Rather than accept the inevitability of a climate change disaster, sociologists remind us that as a society, we still have the power to choose a healthier future.

think about it

1. *What ideas from your sociology course do you think are especially relevant to thinking about climate change?*
2. *What sociological questions related to climate change do you think are important to answer?*

The spectacular growth of Brazil's Rio de Janeiro has meant the destruction of the adjacent Atlantic rain forest. Urban growth around the world has put unprecedented strains on natural resources, contributing to the expanding environmental crisis.

The issue that underlies most environmental crises is a lack of sustainability. **Sustainability** refers to *a balance between resource protection and consumption that can be maintained indefinitely.* Unfortunately, humans are engaged in a number of *unsustainable* practices with enormous consequences (Blewitt 2015).

Our natural environment provides essential assets that serve key functions for our survival, but their overuse results in critical environmental problems, as summarized in Figure 15.6. The three basic functions of our environmental assets are to provide a place in which to live, to provide resources needed for survival (including air, water, food, and energy), and to provide a place to dispose of wastes. Our global ecosystem has only a limited ability to serve these three functions (Dunlap and Marshall 2007).

Unsustainable practices put excess demands on the environment, creating three corresponding problems. First, dramatic growth in human population is leading to overcrowding. Second, we are consuming resources at a pace that outstrips long-term supply, resulting in resource depletion. Third, pollution is overwhelming the ecosystem's ability to absorb waste products. For example, water pollution is creating dramatic "dead zones" in the world's

FIGURE 15.6 | FUNCTIONS OF THE ENVIRONMENT AND THE CONSEQUENCES OF OVERUSING THEM

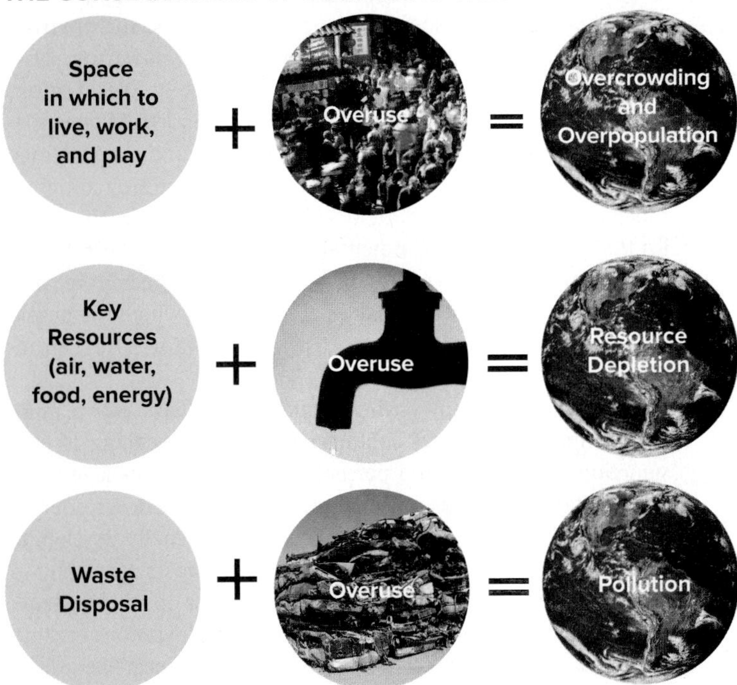

(overuse top): ©JLImages/Alamy Stock Photo; (overuse middle): ©Comstock Images/Alamy Stock Photo; (overuse bottom): ©Image Source/Getty Images; (earth): ©Brand X Images/PunchStock

Our natural environment provides essential assets that serve a key function for our survival, but our overuse of them results in critical environmental problems.

oceans—areas so toxic that virtually nothing survives in them—whereas excess carbon dioxide is contributing to climate change.

Overuse in one area can create problems in the others. Pollution, for example, can make an area uninhabitable, while overpopulation can contribute to resource depletion. Thus the environmental problems we face are closely interrelated.

Power, Inequality, and Environmental Justice

Who is most likely to be a source of environmental pollution and degradation, and who is most likely to be exposed to and harmed by them? In analyzing these questions, sociologists consider issues of power and inequality, both on a global scale and locally.

When you buy a new laptop or cell phone, you probably don't think about the labor—often in slave-like conditions—that went into extracting the minerals needed to make it. That labor comes from developing countries such as the Democratic Republic of the Congo, where children as young as 11 years old toil as miners to extract the rare minerals (Bales 2016). And when that electronic device is outdated, you probably don't think about where the toxic waste it will produce ends up. Again, it's likely to be in a developing country, where so-called e-waste is exported and discarded, often illegally (Basel Action Network 2016).

For decades, wealthier nations have been extracting resources from—and then shipping their toxic wastes and other environmentally hazardous goods to—poorer nations. This is one way in which power and inequality determine the impact of environmental problems. Those with more power and privilege generally reap the benefits of environmental degradation through affluent lifestyles and the ability to protect themselves from pollution. Those with less power and privilege, like slave miners and those who handle toxic wastes, often bear the brunt of environmental crises (Ammons and Roy 2015; McMichael 2017).

Even in the United States, class and race play a part in disproportionately burdening poor and minority communities with environmentally hazardous materials (Bullard 2000; Schlosberg 2013; Taylor 2014; Walker 2012). Governments and corporations are more likely to place toxic waste dumps, chemical plants, incinerators, landfills, sewage treatment facilities, and other pollution hazards near the homes of racial minorities and people with lower incomes, and rarely in affluent communities, whose residents have the power to resist such threats. Even noise pollution is higher in neighborhoods populated by low-income residents and racial and ethnic minorities (Casey et al. 2017).

Since the mid-1980s, in response to this form of inequality, activists have organized campaigns for **environmental justice,** *the prevention of harmful practices that unfairly burden low-income people and racial minorities with disproportionate exposure to environmental hazards.* In the workplace as well, class distinctions shape exposure to environmental hazards. Working-class employees are most likely to be exposed to dangerous environmental conditions that can cause disease or injury. For decades, labor unions have promoted the adoption of occupational health and safety regulations that protect workers from environmental hazards such as exposure to harmful chemicals on the job.

©Johannes Eisele/AFP/Getty Images

Affluent nations export much of the electronic waste ("e-waste") they produce from computers, cell phones, and other electronic devices. Poor people in developing countries, such as these Chinese workers in Shantou City, Guangdong Province, are often employed to extract usable metals from the waste, a process that sometimes exposes them to high levels of toxins. Have you disposed of any electronic devices in recent years? If so, do you know where they ended up?

Structure: The "Treadmill of Production"

Environmental problems have no single source, but sociologists, rather than focusing solely on the actions of individuals, focus also on the effect of structural forces in creating those problems. According to one structural analysis, *capital-intensive industries and the modern state, in pursuit of continual growth as a central good, have created* a **treadmill of production** *that results in increasing resource depletion and worsening pollution* (Gould, Pellow, and Schnaiberg 2008; Schnaiberg 1980).

In a capitalist market economy, corporations increase their profits by growing bigger. For workers, economic growth provides jobs, the income from which enables them to consume more. For the state, growth represents low unemployment and an expanding tax base, as we saw with urban "growth machines." But the promotion of growth by corporations, governments, and workers produces two negative environmental consequences. First, growth contributes to resource depletion by increasing exploitation of natural resources and energy. In a world with finite resources, continuous growth that increases resource consumption is unsustainable. Second, growth creates pollution and waste, which we have seen contribute to environmental problems (Klein 2015). As long as humanity continues to pursue an unsustainable growth strategy, we will be on this destructive treadmill.

Culture and the Social Construction of Environmental Problems

The common belief that growth is a good thing instead of a strain on our natural environment illustrates how our cultural beliefs and traditions shape our perception of the environment and the threats to it. Environmental problems have a physical reality–rising pollution levels, loss of animal habitat, and declining resources, for example. But sociologists have long understood that for these objective conditions to be recognized as social problems, people must frame them accordingly. This framing is the task of *sponsors*–people who work to bring these problems to the attention of the media, public officials, and the public, seeking support in addressing them (Hannigan 2014). Their work is a type of social construction of reality.

SPOTLIGHT

on social theory

Symbolic interactionists highlight how humans interpret and make meaningful the world around them. Do you think the meaning of the natural environment is different for young people today than it was for past generations? Why or why not?

In the 1960s and 1970s, environmental activists played a pioneering role in raising the public's consciousness about environmental issues, resulting in some important legislative initiatives. Between 1970 and 1973, Congress passed the Clean Air Act, the Clean Water Act, and the Endangered Species Act. Environmental protection seemed an overwhelmingly important priority. But enforcement has been lax, and counterefforts have chipped away at these and other environmental legislative initiatives.

In fact, as recent sociological research shows, the environmental movement has stalled, evolving from a powerful grassroots social movement into a fragmented set of Washington, D.C.-based lobbying groups and isolated local efforts. Meanwhile, conservative countermovements, think tanks, and corporations with a financial stake in growth have been promoting antienvironmental messages and attempting to discredit scientific studies that document environmental destruction. Since the 1970s, the passage of proenvironment legislation has been rare, and some indicators show a *decline* in the degree to which the public sees environmental protection as a priority (Dalton 2015; Ogrodnik and Staggenborg 2016).

Meanwhile, as many environmental threats have grown more serious, the United States continues to embrace a culture of consumption. With less than 5 percent of the world's population, the United States consumes about 25 percent of the world's resources and produces about 30 percent of its waste. Rapidly developing nations are emulating the U.S. record and ramping up consumption at an unprecedented pace. China, as noted in our opening vignette, has rapidly transformed many urban areas into high-consumption centers, complete with cars, consumer products, meat-filled diets, and energy-guzzling homes. But the U.S. level of consumption is impossible to reproduce on a global scale; the earth simply does not have enough resources. According to one estimate, for just India and China to consume resources and pollute at a per-capita level comparable to that of the United States, we would need two more planet Earths (Worldwatch Institute 2006). Each year, a group of researchers and activists mark "Earth Overshoot Day," the estimated point at which humans have used more resources than the earth can renew and generated more pollution than the earth can absorb in a year. During the 1980s, that day was in November; by 2017 it had moved up to August 2 (Global Footprint Network 2018). Organizers argue that the change signals the increased pace at which we are using up the earth's resources in an unsustainable manner.

Seriously addressing environmental threats requires a change in attitudes, values, and understanding–a change of culture. Environmental activists work to bring about a culture that recognizes the hazards of overconsumption, resource depletion, and pollution while prioritizing limited consumption and the reuse of goods and materials.

The U.S. culture of individualism also can handicap us. The trend seems to be away from protecting the environment toward protecting the individual (Szasz 2007, 2011). For example, many people are concerned about the contamination of their tap water with chemicals, a concern highlighted by the water crisis in Flint, Michigan, in 2014 (Carmody 2016). A social response would include political action to ensure stricter water pollution measures and more funding for water treatment facilities. Instead, most people protect only themselves by purchasing bottled water and water filters. This individualized approach shields those who can afford it, while society's most vulnerable bear the brunt of environmental damage.

The use of bottled water has also increased plastic consumption, adding nonbiodegradable trash to our landfills. Individualized responses like this are expensive and often ineffective (the production of bottled water is unregulated, and some products are just tap water), and they may only hinder more effective political action to achieve real change.

Still, there are occasional signs of growing environmental awareness in the culture and its subcultures. For example, more than 200 prominent Christian evangelicals have signed "Climate Change: An Evangelical Call to Action." The document used scientific research findings and relevant biblical passages to call upon Christians to make protecting the environment a major priority, noting that "the consequences of climate change will be significant and will hit the poor the hardest" (Evangelical Climate Initiative 2016). The call is part of a larger, ongoing "Green Evangelical" movement (Kearns 2014).

The Search for Solutions

Environmental sociologists have also studied how best to address environmental challenges. Buttel (2003) identifies four basic mechanisms of "environmental reform":

1. ***Environmental activism and social movements,*** which raise awareness of issues, promote changes in individual and institutional behavior, and advocate for legislative regulation and reforms
2. ***Environmental regulation by governments,*** which can promote energy efficiency, put curbs on inefficient development, and limit polluting
3. ***International environmental governance,*** including global treaties and intergovernmental organizations
4. ***Ecological modernization,*** or the use of environmentally friendly new technologies and greater technological efficiencies

Social movements outside the halls of power can be especially important in environmental reform because they are effective catalysts for other forms of action (Giugni and Grasso 2015). As we saw, a vibrant grassroots movement in the 1960s and 1970s helped jump-start important environmental legislation. More recently, leaders from 175 countries signed the nonbinding Paris Accord, aiming to slow the production rate of carbon dioxide and other greenhouse gases that contribute to climate change. (In 2017, the Trump administration announced it would withdraw the United States from the Accord, effective in late 2020.) Such a treaty could only have come after years of social movement campaigns to pressure governments to act. The 2014 People's Climate Change March in New York City, which featured over 300,000 people and over 2,500 simultaneous solidarity events in more than 160 countries, was one such campaign (Foderaro 2014; 2014.peoplesclimate.org). Some advocates argue that such action by noninstitutional players is essential to environmental reform.

Some sociologists, though, say that the capitalist quest for profit can actually help the environment, an approach referred to as ecological modernization theory (Mol, Spaargaren, and Sonnenfeld 2014). These theorists maintain that the destructive aspects of modernization can be dealt with by new, environmentally sound technologies and policies. In fact, they suggest that technological advances are humankind's best hope for an ecologically sustainable future. For example, as companies recognize that energy inefficiency represents lost profits, the theory goes, they will adopt energy-efficient technologies.

Such ideas are controversial (Arsel and Büscher 2012). The cases used to illustrate success are often atypical plants, corporations, and industries that use methods others cannot adopt on a scale large enough to make a difference (Dunlap and Marshall 2007). History suggests that pursuit of profit may just as likely encourage destructive practices (Jenks 2011). The examples of environmental disasters that involved cost cutting, negligence, or a disregard for safety are many: the toxic waste dump of New York's Love Canal, which caused cancers and birth defects well into the 1970s; Union Carbide's 1984 toxic gas leak in Bhopal, India, which killed over 2,000 people; Russia's 1986 nuclear power plant explosion at Chernobyl, which spread radiation, immediately killing over 30 people and resulting in countless cancer deaths; and the 2010 BP Deep Horizon oil spill, which killed 11 workers and spewed oil into the Gulf of Mexico for several months. Only enforcement of government regulations can protect people and the natural environment from such abuses.

Perhaps the most visible recent effort to protect the environment is the marketing of "eco-friendly" products. However, Buttel (2004) and others argue that "green" consumerism is not a viable approach. First, as we have seen, pressure toward growth originates not with individuals who are the target of green consumerism but with institutional players—corporations and governments of the "growth machine" and "treadmill of production." Second, corporate and government decisions heavily influence the choice of products available to consumers. Corporate failure to invest in more-efficient cars and government failure to require higher fuel efficiency have long limited consumers' options, regardless of their preferences. Third, many products and practices promoted as environmentally friendly are of marginal benefit and may be merely "greenwashing" efforts aimed at improving the corporation's public image (Lyon and Montgomery 2015). Finally, evidence suggests that many who *say* they are concerned about the environment simply do not change their consumer behavior voluntarily.

Many sociologists therefore argue that focusing on individuals rather than larger social systems is unlikely to produce change on the necessary scale. This is not to say that individual choices do not matter but that, as sociologists have long observed, human action takes place within existing social structure. Real social change requires changing those structures.

thinking about **culture**

How does a **culture** that values high levels of consumption and individualism help contribute to our environmental crisis? How might that culture change to encourage a more sustainable future?

The Sociology of Health

Just as sociologists see community and environmental issues in a broader social context, they also emphasize how culture, social structure, and power influence health and illness. For example, culture influences our understanding of health and illness. Which conditions are recognized as illnesses? Which are stigmatized? How do we define a healthy lifestyle? Answers to such questions vary across cultures and over time, and are part of the social construction of health and illness (Cooper and Thorogood 2013).

Similarly, the structure of health care varies across societies. How are health care services organized? Who pays? Is health care a universal right or a privilege? Social structure affects the answer to such questions (Toth 2016). Finally, inequalities in power influence the disparities that exist both in access to health care resources and in the outcomes of health care (Barr 2014). In short, rather than focus on clinical or biological issues, sociologists emphasize the social causes and consequences of health and illness (Cockerham 2016; Weiss and Lonnquist 2015; Weitz 2017).

©Corbis/Getty Images

Before doctors gained the exclusive right to prescribe prescription drugs, some powerful drugs were unregulated and included in over-the-counter medicines intended for children.

CORE CONCEPTS CHALLENGE *How does this ad reflect the* **culture** *of the era in which it was produced?*

Culture, Structure, Power, and the Medical Profession

One example of the sociological approach to health issues concerns the rise of the medical profession. Today, the occupation of doctor is among the most prestigious and highly paid in the United States. But that is a relatively recent cultural development that resulted from doctors effectively organizing to institutionalize their profession and gain power over health care. Sociologist Paul Starr's classic book *The Social Transformation of American Medicine* traces doctors' shifting status in nineteenth- and twentieth-century U.S. society. Starr (1983) cites an 1869 medical journal that complains "medicine has ever been and is now, the most despised of all the professions" (7).

Few doctors enjoyed any financial success before 1900. They lacked uniform training and universal standards of practice and were not particularly successful at diagnosis and treatment. Many people distrusted them and preferred traditional home remedies. Doctors also faced challenges from other practitioners with very different approaches to illness, including midwives, herbalists, and peddlers of "patent medicines," typically made from exotic ingredients and sold as "miraculous" cures for virtually all illnesses.

Doctors Organize In the early twentieth century, doctors organized into a unified group emphasizing their specialized knowledge and skills and forming what would become a powerful voice on their behalf: the American Medical Association (AMA). Its members built alliances with the growing number of hospitals in the United States and devised standards for medical training and practice. Especially important, rather than competing among themselves, doctors united around an approach to health care based on science and research, which increased their success at diagnosing and treating illness. This scientific emphasis bound the medical profession with universities, where training and ongoing research now took place.

By the early twentieth century, U.S. doctors had established a powerful **professional authority,** *legitimate power to define the terms of discussion within a specific field.* Citizens looked to doctors for medical advice on staying healthy and for treatment when they became ill. Mindful of the complexity of the human body and aware of doctors' distinctive knowledge, patients learned to doubt their own ability to diagnose and treat illness. A growing public trust in science, and dramatic success in reducing the incidence of dreaded diseases such as tetanus and diphtheria, elevated doctors as unparalleled authorities on health and illness. Their influence soon extended beyond medicine, as people turned to them for advice on matters from childrearing to sexual conduct.

Monopolizing Medical Practice Building on the high status of their powerful professional authority, doctors established an institutional monopoly on medical practice that drove out rival practitioners. They secured legislation that permitted only officially licensed doctors to practice medicine. The AMA certified medical schools, and each medical school limited enrollment, thereby controlling the supply of doctors. In this new medical system, professional authority became a means of increasing doctors' incomes to unprecedented heights.

Just as important, doctors came to act as gatekeepers, controlling access to prescription drugs and influencing policies that required people to consult them before participating in specific activities. Public schools and summer camps often won't admit children without evidence of a physical examination by a doctor. Some employers depend on company-paid doctors to screen new hires, and insurance companies require medical examinations when people make health- or injury-related insurance claims.

The Weakening of Doctors' Authority

Changes in health care in the United States have undermined the power, status, and authority of doctors. McKinlay and Marceau (2002) identify eight key factors in this shift:

1. The decline in government support for doctors in private practice
2. The bureaucratization of medical practice, as an increasing number of doctors have left private practice and gone to work for large health care corporations
3. The emerging competitive threat from other lower-cost health care workers, including nurse-practitioners and physicians' assistants, who have some of the same medical privileges as doctors
4. Globalization and the information revolution, which gives patients access to international health care options and vast amounts of medical information
5. Changes in the public conception of the body, which threaten to reduce the physician from a professional who cures illness to a technician who repairs the body
6. Changes in the doctor-patient relationship and the erosion of patient trust, as doctors increasingly work in for-profit contexts and heed the demands of health insurance providers
7. Growth in the number of doctors, leading to a general oversupply
8. The weakening and fragmentation of the AMA, which has historically represented doctors' shared interests

In addition, the internet has given people easier access to medical information without the need for doctors (Clarke et al. 2015). Although some of these trends may be plusses for patients, they all threaten the authority and autonomy of doctors (Draper 2003; Reich 2014). More physicians are becoming employees of large organizations, including health maintenance organizations (HMOs), since it has grown increasingly difficult and expensive to enter private practice. Many work for major corporations, supervising health care and wellness programs for employees and working with policy makers on health-related workplace issues. Increasingly, employers demand that doctors satisfy organizational—often profit-driven—goals that clash with the professional norms of independent physicians.

The Social Determinants of Health

In 2011, the Association of American Medical Colleges (AAMC) added sociology and other social science content to the Medical College Admissions Test (MCAT). The move was a response to accumulating research that shows that doctors need to understand the social context in which patients live in order to serve them best. An AAMC report on the change noted that doctors should be able to draw on sociology to "accurately describe how social determinants of health influence health outcomes and how physicians can incorporate this knowledge in the care of patients" (AAMC 2011, 24).

Although an understanding of the social determinants of health is a relatively new requirement for health practitioners, it is not new to sociology. Our understanding of how to improve health outcomes has varied over time (Booske et al. 2010). In the United States, the last century can be divided into four periods, each of which emphasized a different way to improve health outcomes:

- ***1930–1950: Sanitation and environmental health.*** In this period, the leading causes of disease and death were infectious diseases like pneumonia, influenza, tuberculosis, and diarrhea, all of which were related to the environment in which people lived and worked. Thus the biggest improvements in health during this period came from better sanitation and safety, through cleaner food production, water fluoridation, control of infectious diseases, and occupational safety laws. Many of these measures were related to community life and the environment, discussed earlier in this chapter.
- ***1950–1970: Health care.*** In this period, heart disease and cancer became the leading causes of death. The focus shifted from sanitation and safety to the detection and treatment of diseases through clinical interventions. Health officials emphasized vaccination for childhood illnesses, improved maternal and prenatal care, and the detection and treatment of high blood pressure.
- ***1970–1990: Health behaviors.*** In this period, stroke and lung disease joined heart disease and cancer as the leading causes of death. The focus shifted to how individuals could improve their health by changing their behavior. Based on accumulating evidence, doctors advised patients to stop smoking, drink less alcohol, maintain a healthier diet, and exercise regularly.
- ***1990–present: Social and economic factors.*** In recent decades, the focus of health care has shifted from individual health behaviors to the social determinants of health. The sociological factors that can affect health include social class inequality, racial inequality, the strength of social networks and support systems, working conditions, and social capital (see Figure 15.7).

This overview is a stark reminder that health is not limited to—or even primarily affected by—clinical interventions. Instead, a much broader range of factors plays a crucial role in maintaining or damaging health. It is these "big picture" issues that sociologists address in attempting to improve health outcomes. As the cost of clinical interventions has skyrocketed, researchers have concentrated on finding more cost-effective interventions based on the social determinants of health and illness. (The Sociology Works box examines one sociology major's work in promoting community health.)

Inequality and Health Disparities

Like other patterns in social life, disease and death are not distributed equally or randomly throughout a population. Instead,

FIGURE 15.7 | WHAT IMPROVES HEALTH OUTCOMES TODAY?

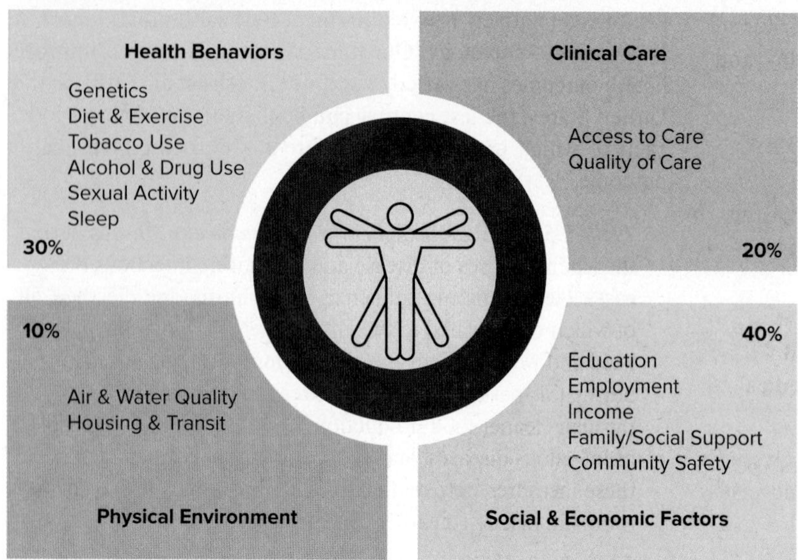

When researchers studied the factors that affect health outcomes today, they concluded that social and economic factors were the largest single influence. Clinical care accounted for only 20 percent of outcomes, even though the cost of that care accounted for 88 percent of health care spending. As a result, future health care policy is likely to place greater emphasis on cost-effective preventive measures that address the social environment and social inequality.

Sources: Booske et al. 2010; Remington, Catlin, and Gennuso 2015.

social inequalities shape the likelihood that someone will be healthy or sick, die young or live a long life. In short, social inequalities are related to inequalities in health (Barr 2014). Sociologists refer to these *persistent patterns of inequality in health* as **health disparities.**

In general, social inequality works in predictable ways: people with less income and education are likely to experience more illness and to die younger. Childhood asthma is far more prevalent in low-income households than in middle- or upper-income households. The death rate associated with diabetes is also correlated with family income and is highest in the poorest households. The lowest-income adults are far more likely to experience "fair" or "poor" health whether they are male, female, white, black, or Hispanic (National Center for Health Statistics 2016). Health disparities exist on a global scale, too: wealthier nations' populations live longer, healthier lives than do those in poorer nations (Marmot 2015).

Evidence of health disparities is clear and long-standing. Syme and Berkman (1976) note that high death rates and shorter life expectancy for the lower classes have been observed since the twelfth century. Multifaceted "pathways" have been identified that connect inequality in socioeconomic status (SES) and in race/ethnicity with health disparities, suggesting that each component of SES—education, income, and occupation—as well as race, contributes directly to health disparities (Adler and Newman 2002; Braveman et al. 2010; Phelan and Link 2015).

- ***Education*** shapes future job opportunities and helps determine adult income. Just as important, education gives people social capital—the knowledge, confidence, and skills that increase access to information and resources, promoting health and healthy lifestyles.
- ***Income*** is necessary to purchase health care services or health insurance. Those who can afford high-quality health services—including preventive and specialist care—are likely to be healthier, in the long run, than those who cannot. Income is also associated with improvements in nutrition, recreation, and housing—all of which contribute to health.
- ***Occupation*** relates to health disparities in that people with jobs and job security have fewer health problems. However, specific jobs can contribute to health disparities. Lower-status jobs are often more dangerous than higher-status ones, exposing workers to toxic substances and increasing the risk of on-the-job injuries. In addition, the unemployed, part-timers, flexible workers in the "gig economy," and those in lower-status jobs are far less likely than full-time professionals to have a high-quality employer-sponsored health insurance plan, further increasing the health disparities associated with occupation. The implementation of the Affordable Care Act ("Obamacare") reduced the number of people without health insurance. However, the Trump administration has opposed and chipped away at the policy, leaving the future of the program uncertain (Starr 2013, 2018).
- ***Race and ethnicity*** intersects with class to create distinct disparities. As we saw in Chapter 10, institutional racism resulted in policies and procedures that reduced access to good housing, schools, and employment for minorities. Cultural racism can result in negative stereotypes and discrimination, which can trigger health-damaging responses. Finally, the experience of racial discrimination creates stress, which can increase health risks and produce adverse health outcomes.

In addition, lower socioeconomic groups are also more likely to smoke and less likely to eat a healthy diet and get sufficient exercise—all of which contribute to health problems. They are also more likely to be socially isolated. Their isolation leaves them at far greater risk of physical illness and death, as well as of mental health problems such as depression, which can lower energy levels and reduce motivation to seek proper medical care when needed. A tragic example of the effect of social isolation is documented in Eric Klinenberg's (2003) study of the 1995 heat wave in Chicago, which resulted in more than 700 deaths. Klinenberg found that the underlying cause of these very preventable deaths was social isolation. The victims were largely poor elderly residents who lived alone and had little access to support, resources, government assistance, or even information about how to deal with the intense heat and the power shortages that made air conditioning unavailable.

SOCIOLOGY WORKS

Tristan Sanders and Healthy Communities

When students think about working in health care, they often think of medical or nursing school. But Tristan Sanders took a different route, using the BA in sociology he earned. "I always knew I wanted to work in a health-related field," he says, "and majoring in sociology allowed me to do that at a population level, which has allowed me to have far greater influence than if I were to have gone to medical school and become a doctor." Rather than treating individual sick patients, Sanders helps promote healthy living in entire communities.

He works for Kaiser Permanente in the Institute for Health Research in Denver, Colorado, where he helps evaluate a nonprofit organization that Kaiser supports financially called LiveWell Colorado (livewellcolorado.org). LiveWell is a statewide organization that provides multiyear grants to local communities to implement healthy eating and active living strategies to fight obesity. These strategies include the creation of safe routes to schools (to encourage walking), farmers markets and community gardens (to improve access to healthy foods), comprehensive bicycle and pedestrian plans (to encourage healthier commuting and recreation), and school- and work-based wellness programs (to educate about and encourage healthy lifestyles).

On any given day, Sanders may be working with technical assistance providers and local community coordinators, implementing an interactive voice response (IVR) survey to monitor behavioral and health patterns, conducting focus groups during site visits, helping write grant applications, or developing evaluation plans. To advance his career, he has completed a master's degree in public health with a focus in health systems, management, and policy.

Sanders couldn't be happier with his choice of major: "Sociology has provided me nothing but opportunities. Opportunities to thrive academically because I was studying something I was interested in. Opportunities to thrive professionally because I was able to understand and apply the many things I have learned. Even opportunities to thrive socially because of the diverse base of knowledge I gained while studying sociology." Among his most memorable sociology courses, he cites methods classes that taught him about evaluation techniques and one course called "What It Means to Be Sick," a historical look at the evolution of health and wellness and of changes in the treatment of persons who are ill over time.

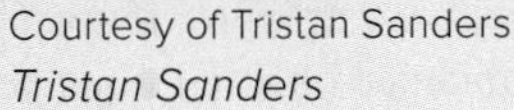
Courtesy of Tristan Sanders
Tristan Sanders

> "Sociology opened my mind to a world of possibilities."

Says Sanders, "Sociology opened my mind to a world of possibilities, most specifically being able to work in the field I ultimately wanted to work in [health care and population health] without going to medical school." And he confesses, "My experience with sociology has been a bit of a love affair. The more I engage myself in the material, the more I get out of it."

think about it

1. *How does Sanders's work reflect a sociological perspective on health issues?*
2. *How might a sociology degree be a stepping-stone to a health-related career?*

A Changing World

COMMUNITY AND ENVIRONMENTAL INFLUENCES ON HEALTH

Is new research redefining our idea of health? Although it has long been known that personal behavioral choices influence well-being, health researchers today are increasingly recognizing the many ways that place—both the built environment and the natural environment—affects our health (Duncan and Kawachi 2018). A large body of new research connects "neighborhood disadvantage"—high community poverty rates and accompanying unemployment, racial segregation, crime, reduced physical activity, and even traffic problems—with "a wide range of detrimental health outcomes, including low birth weight, infant mortality, asthma, tuberculosis, depression, and poor self-rated health" (Do et al. 2008, 1259).

Housing also influences health. Deteriorating lead paint poses a major health hazard to children exposed to elevated levels of lead in the air and water inside their homes. Poor ventilation, leaky pipes, and pest infestations can fill a home with allergens, a primary source of childhood asthma. Poor insulation in winter and lack of ventilation in summer create health problems, too, especially for older people. Overcrowding contributes to a variety of illnesses, including infectious diseases and psychological stress.

Even the high cost of housing can add indirectly to health problems by forcing difficult trade-offs. Hefty rent or mortgage payments may be met at the expense of heat, prescription medications, or health insurance, with potentially serious health consequences (Robert Wood Johnson Foundation 2008). Foreclosures or evictions can make matters worse (Arcaya 2018).

The relationship between community and health is not limited to disadvantaged neighborhoods. People who live in compact cities where walking is common have lower rates of diabetes, hypertension, heart disease, and stroke than do those in suburbs where driving is the norm. Suburban dwellers are on average six pounds heavier than their counterparts in cities. In response, however, some communities are designing built environments that promote good health by encouraging physical activity, especially walking and cycling along new networks of bike and pedestrian trails (Flint 2006; Stock and Ellaway 2013).

Society is growing more aware that environmental factors also influence health. Public health officials in the United States and around the world have identified **environmental health**—*the aspects of health, illness, and disease that result from environmental factors*—as one of the keys to a healthy population. Environmental factors such as air, water, and soil pollution; household lead; unsanitary drinking water; and climate change can produce major health consequences. Diseases most commonly associated with environmental causes are diarrhea, respiratory infections, malaria, birth-related conditions, and certain heart diseases. The World Health Organization (2016c) estimates that 23 percent of all deaths globally—12.6 million people a year—are attributable to the environment.

Improving and expanding access to safe water and sanitation systems can make a major contribution to global health. Deaths from diseases associated with water, sanitation, and hygiene problems are particularly high in Africa and parts of South Asia. These rates contribute to the significant disparity in global life expectancy (see Map 15.1). The U.S. government's report *Healthy People 2020* identifies improvements in air and water quality and the proper use and disposal of toxic substances and hazardous waste as among the primary environmental health objectives in the twenty-first century (U.S. Department of Health and Human Services 2010).

What are the key characteristics of healthy places? A growing body of evidence shows that places that bring people into contact with the natural environment, that facilitate interaction

MAP 15.1 | GLOBAL DISPARITIES IN LIFE EXPECTANCY

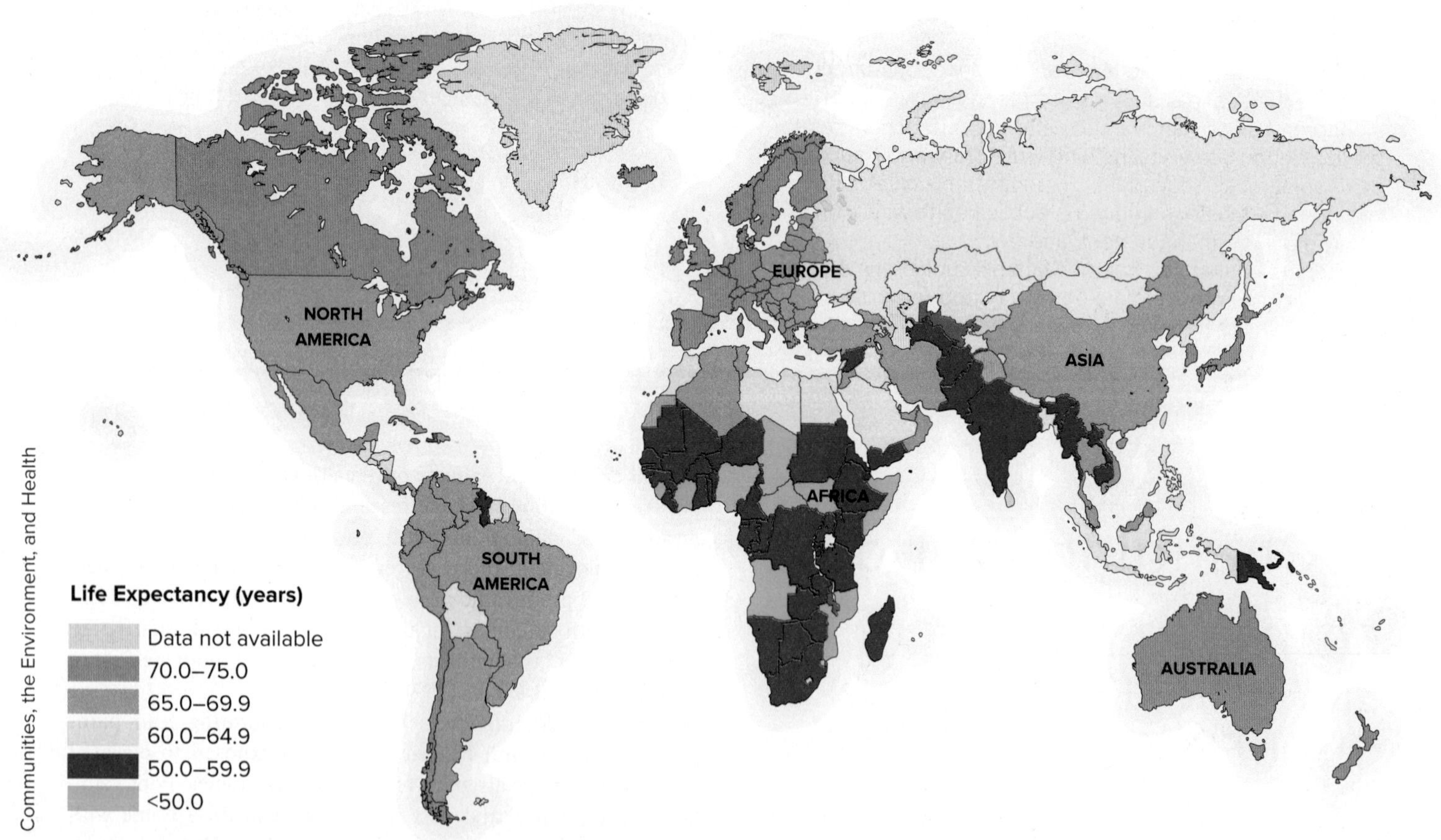

The poorer nations in Africa and South Asia have the shortest life expectancy, while the wealthy nations in Europe, Canada, Japan, and Australia are among those with the longest life expectancy. *Source:* World Health Organization 2016c.

among people, that encourage regular physical activity, and that build structures along environmentally sound principles (using nontoxic building materials and cleansers, effective ventilation, and natural lighting) promote good health among the people who live, work, and play in them (Eriksson and Emmelin 2013; Hensley, Mateo-Babiano, and Minnery 2014; Korpela, De Bloom, and Kinnunen 2015).

The sociology of health asks us to pay attention to the many ways in which health and illness are social issues. Understanding the community and environmental factors that influence people's physical health—both the factors that contribute to illness and disease and those that promote good health and healthy lifestyles—has emerged as a central component of the contemporary sociological analysis of health and illness.

thinking sociologically about
Communities, the Environment, and Health

culture

- The places where we live—our communities—both reflect our culture and help promote certain types of cultural practices.
- Our perception of and relationship to the natural environment are influenced by our culture.
- Evolving cultural norms have influenced our understanding of health and the role of health care professionals.

structure

- The social environment that people create exists within the broader built and natural environments that help structure daily life.
- The action of doctors in the early twentieth century helped structure the medical profession in such a way as to greatly influence the health care field as we know it.

power

- Communities are shaped by the struggles between those with more and less power, reflecting broader class and race inequalities.
- Natural resource consumption and environmental hazards are distributed unevenly, reflecting inequalities in power.
- Social inequalities play a major role in shaping the likelihood that someone will have the power to remain healthy and avoid sickness.

REVIEW, REFLECT, AND APPLY

Looking Back

1. Human communities evolved from nomadic hunter-gatherer societies, to rural agriculturally based communities, to modern industrial cities and megalopolises. Each type of community featured different sorts of social relationships, levels of inequality, degrees of specialization, and relationships to the natural environment.
2. Humans have created an extensive built environment that provides the physical context within which social life occurs. This built environment influences social life and reflects the culture of the people who live there.
3. The rise of modern cities prompted early sociologists to analyze the social differences between urban and rural life, to research city life, and to help address urban social problems. Today, human ecology focuses on how the physical environment of cities influences social life.
4. Analyses that examine cities as "growth machines" explore how government policy and powerful economic interests heavily influence urban development, reflecting inequalities in power.
5. The suburbs offer an alternative to city life but create their own set of social problems, including sprawl, higher taxes, and social isolation.
6. Environmental sociologists examine the sources of the crises that currently threaten our natural environment, study how people understand those crises, and examine what changes can help address them.
7. Unsustainable growth is a major contributor to climate change and the pollution and massive resource depletion that plague the planet. The benefits and consequences of environmental destruction are distributed unequally, with the poor and relatively powerless facing the worst conditions while the affluent benefit from a lifestyle of consumption. Environmental action will require changes not only in individual behavior but also in the basic "treadmill of production" that fuels unsustainable growth.
8. In the early twentieth century, the status, income, and power of doctors rose dramatically. Doctors organized themselves into a unified group, emphasizing their specialized knowledge and skills; built alliances with hospitals; established widely shared standards for both medical training and medical practice; and united around an approach to health care that was based on science and research. Now, in the early twenty-first century, the health care industry is undermining the power, status, and authority of doctors.
9. To study health sociologically, we need to consider what it means to have a healthy community and what contributes to the overall well-being of the members of a given society. Social inequalities related to education, income, occupation, and race and ethnicity shape the likelihood that someone will be healthy or sick, die young or live a long life.

Critical Thinking: Questions and Activities

1. Have you ever moved from one type of community (rural community, small town, suburb, city) to another? If so, what struck you as being different in your new physical environment? Did these differences influence your social life?
2. How did institutional and structural changes, such as government policy and economic conditions, help fuel suburbanization in the United States? How did such policies also promote inequality?
3. The earth's resources are not adequate to enable today's developing countries to consume at the level of the United States. So now what? What do you see as the most important steps needed to help avoid a crisis of resource depletion and pollution?
4. What, if anything, does your community do to promote healthy lifestyles? What *should* it be doing?
5. Given that inequalities in education, income, work, and race and ethnicity contribute to health disparities, do you think it is possible to make changes that would reduce these health disparities? If so, what would you recommend?

Key Terms

built environment (p. 383) the physical surroundings that humans create, including the buildings, roads, dams, homes, and consumer products we use every day.

community (p. 383) a set of social relationships, typically arising from living in a particular place, that give people a sense of identity and belonging.

community studies (p. 388) a field that typically looks at groups of people who share some common tie and engage in social interaction within a particular geographic area.

environmental health (p. 406) the aspects of health, illness, and disease that result from environmental factors.

environmental justice (p. 399) the prevention of harmful practices that unfairly burden low-income people and racial minorities with disproportionate exposure to environmental hazards.

environmental sociology (p. 396) the study of the interaction between social life, the built environment, and the natural environment.

Gemeinschaft (p. 386) social organization in which most relationships are based on the long-term personal ties of collective kinship, common tradition, and shared values.

gentrification (p. 391) the process of rehabilitating older housing stock and investing in neighborhood development in a way that typically attracts new higher-income residents and displaces current middle- and low-income residents.

Gesellschaft (p. 387) social organization in which most social relationships are impersonal, temporary, and based primarily on the pursuit of individual rational self-interest.

growth machines (p. 390) a label for cities that highlights how powerful businesses and politicians work together to promote urban development, often while ignoring the interests of ordinary citizens.

health disparities (p. 404) persistent patterns of inequality in health.

human ecology (p. 388) the study of the links between the physical environment—natural and built—and social life.

natural environment (p. 383) the land, water, air, vegetation, and organisms that make up the physical world.

new urban sociology (p. 390) an approach to studying cities that focuses on the interactions of politics and economics and locates them in the larger context of the global economy.

professional authority (p. 402) legitimate power to define the terms of discussion within a specific field.

redlining (p. 391) the use of discriminatory practices in the sale or rental of housing to minorities.

social environment (p. 383) the cultural context and patterns of relationships within which humans live.

sprawl (p. 393) low-density development that disperses people over a wide area, separates homes from workplaces and stores, and depends heavily on cars for transportation.

sustainability (p. 398) a balance between resource protection and consumption that can be maintained indefinitely.

treadmill of production (p. 400) a term that refers to the way capital-intensive industries and the modern state, in pursuit of continual growth as a central good, have led to increasing resource depletion and worsening pollution.

©Drew Angerer/Getty Images

16 Politics and the Economy

looking AHEAD

Capitalism? Socialism? How do different types of economies reflect the values in the culture of different societies?

How do politics structure the way our society operates?

How is power organized in different types of governments?

©ZUMA Press, Inc./Alamy Stock Photo

Donato Soberano came from the Philippines for his new job in Arizona (Goldstein 2018). His employer had been unable to find enough American workers to fill jobs with long hours, high stress, and modest wages. It turned to the federal government's J-1 visa program to recruit people to work temporarily in the United States. As the head of the human resources department put it, "In these times, you have to be innovative and creative in recruiting." In 2017, more than 2,800 foreign workers came to the United States to do the same job as Donato: teach in a public school.

Importing public school teachers from abroad is one of the peculiar side effects of the complex interaction between government policy and economic reality. Many Arizona teachers argued that, after repeatedly cutting taxes, the state had badly underfunded education. With salaries well below the national average, some teachers moved in with their parents or applied for food stamps to make ends meet. Others complained of having to pay out of pocket for basic classroom supplies that schools could no longer afford.

Teachers are just one category of workers who have seen their pay stagnate and their working conditions decline in recent decades, even as the incomes of wealthy Americans have skyrocketed. Long a feature of working-class life, poor pay and working conditions are moving up well into the middle class. Weak labor laws are part of the problem. Arizona is a so-called "right-to-work" state, which forbids unions from requiring membership for employment. You can receive the pay and benefits of a job without joining the union that negotiated them. Typically, the results of such laws are weak unions and poorer working conditions. In Arizona, workers simply refused to take the teaching jobs and the school district turned to another government law—the J-1 visa program—to fill the gap.

This did not help Arizona teachers who eventually went on strike in a distinctive #RedforEd campaign. (Teachers in West Virginia, Oklahoma, Kentucky, and other states have also gone on strike in recent years for similar reasons.) Arizona's strike led to a compromise that included a teacher pay raise. As the leader of the coalition that led the labor action put it, "The war is not over, but we've won an important battle here to move the Legislature this far" (Flaherty 2018).

What rights will workers have? How will taxes be structured to raise revenue? What will be the government's spending priorities? How will immigration work? Such questions involve both politics and the economy–the two social institutions on which we focus in this chapter. We begin by examining the role of politics and the government in society. Then we look at the structure of the economy and the government's role in relation to it. We conclude by considering concerns about populism and its impact on democracy.

The Structure of Politics

Politics is *the struggle over power.* (As we have seen, **power** is *the ability to bring about an intended outcome, even when opposed by others.*) One of the distinctive features of political sociology (in contrast to political science) is that it analyzes power and politics in all arenas of social life. That is why power has been a key theme throughout this book. When we popularly refer to "family politics" or "office politics," we are taking a sociological approach to politics by recognizing power struggles in these contexts.

In this chapter, though, we focus primarily on power struggles involving the **government,** *the system by which authority is exercised over a specific territory,* and all the actors who seek to influence government decision making, including ordinary citizens, social movement organizations, businesses, and lobbyists. Governmental politics are especially important because the outcome of these power struggles helps answer key questions about what type of society we will have. How much freedom will we as citizens have? How will our resources be used? Will we go to war? How will we address crime and respond to our health care, energy, education, and transportation needs?

You've probably heard people use the term *politics* in a negative way, as in, "It's all just politics." Because so much is at stake in politics, it is an arena often full of conflict, deception, hypocrisy, and self-interest. At its worst, politics can produce murderous regimes that oppress and terrorize their own people. But at its best, politics can produce many benefits for a society, such as a well-run, responsive government that protects the quality of people's lives through regulations that minimize environmental threats, promote food safety, ensure fair treatment of workers, and guard against fire and other hazards. Government agencies can provide roads and public transportation; supply clean water; and offer social services, education, and health care. And through the military, police, and courts, government can help defend our physical safety and civil liberties. In short, the government that results from politics enables citizens to collectively achieve what individuals cannot (Dobratz, Walder, and Buzzell 2012; Drake 2010; Nash 2010).

Systems of Government

German sociologist Max Weber ([1919] 1946a) recognized that politics is about power—how it is maintained, distributed, challenged, and transferred. Authority is power that is recognized as legitimate by those who are governed. Weber argued that the defining characteristic of governments (or "the state") is their successful claim of a monopoly on the legitimate use of physical force within a given territory. This distinguishes them from all other social organizations. A government can authorize military personnel to kill on its behalf in wars; its police can arrest and even shoot people in the line of duty; and its prison guards can keep people incarcerated, depriving them of their freedom.

Because political processes are socially constructed, governments around the world differ in the way they choose leaders and how politically engaged their citizens are. We can classify government structures into three basic types: monarchies, authoritarian governments, and democracies.

A **monarchy** is *a system of government headed by a single person, the monarch, who typically inherits the position as a member of a ruling family.* Monarchs' titles signify their royal status (king, queen, sultan, emir, or emperor) and are passed from one generation to the next. There are two broad types of monarchies. In *traditional* (or *absolute*) *monarchies,* a single royal leader enjoys essentially unconditional power. This form of government is very rare today, existing only in a few countries, such as Saudi Arabia (king), Qatar (emir), Oman (sultan), and Swaziland (king). Instead, most contemporary monarchies are *constitutional monarchies,* democracies that recognize a limited and often only symbolic role for the royal family. Queen Elizabeth II—the monarch of the United Kingdom of Britain and Northern Ireland—is the best-known constitutional monarch today. She plays a ceremonial role as head of state, while an elected parliament and a prime minister run the government. Upon her death, she will be succeeded by her son Charles, the Prince of Wales.

Instead of monarchies, two broad types of government now predominate: authoritarian and democratic. An **authoritarian government** *typically features self-appointed leaders who exert great control over the lives of citizens that includes severely limiting their civil liberties.* Central ruling parties or the military usually run authoritarian governments, as with China's Communist Party. They do not rely on popular support from citizens or tolerate meaningful political opposition, though authoritarian leaders may rig elections to try to legitimize their power, as is the case in Russia. Disdainful of civil liberties, authoritarian governments often intrude in the lives of citizens, directing, for example, what people may read or publish, what religion they practice, or where they may travel. They often go to considerable expense to monitor the private lives of citizens through various forms of surveillance.

A democratic government, or **democracy**, is *a political system in which government leaders are selected through multiparty elections and the right to vote is widespread.* In its literal definition, democracy is "rule by the people." However, the specific mechanisms by which "the people" rule can vary. In a *direct democracy,* citizens themselves participate in political decision making in such venues as town hall meetings or in referendums (direct citizen votes on a possible law) to decide the fate of a proposed policy. More common is *representative democracy,* in which citizens elect delegates who carry out the policymaking processes of government on their behalf. Democratic systems often include elements of both direct and representative democracy, as does the United States. Free and fair elections are a fundamental component of all representative democracies.

The widespread embrace of democracy is relatively recent in human history. Many nations have not yet adopted democracy, though some leaders use its rhetoric to help legitimize their rule. The Democracy Index, published by *The Economist*'s Economist Intelligence Unit (2018), identifies five key components of a democratic government:

- Free and fair competitive elections
- Civil liberties, including freedom of speech, expression, and the press; freedom of religion; freedom of assembly and association; and the right to due judicial process

thinking about **power**

According to Weber and other sociologists, the legitimate use of force distinguishes governments from other **powerful** organizations. When might a government's use of force cease to be legitimate?

- A functioning government that can implement democratically based decisions
- Active political participation by citizens in public life
- A democratic political culture in which supporters of losing candidates accept the judgment of voters and permit the peaceful transition of power

For 2017, Economist Intelligence Unit researchers, awarding points in each of these categories, labeled only 11.4 percent of the world's countries as "full democracies"; 34.1 percent as "flawed democracies"; 31.3 percent as authoritarian; and the remaining 23.4 percent as hybrids (see Map 16.1). About half the world's population (49.3 percent) lives in a democracy of some sort; the remainder does not. The Democracy Index has been recording an average decline in democracy for several years running. U.S. democracy—once categorized as "full"—has been categorized as "flawed" since 2016, in part because of a significant decline of public trust in U.S. political institutions.

Political Structure and Political Action

The political structure of a society shapes the possibilities for political action by its members, and political action can sometimes have a significant impact on the political structure.

An authoritarian society allows little opportunity for dissent, limiting the possibilities for political action. To oppose the ruling party by speaking out or joining an underground movement is to risk harsh consequences, including harassment, jail, or execution. But even in an authoritarian society, actions matter. Compliance or cooperation may help reinforce the existing political structure. But with broad enough participation, as history has repeatedly shown, even small challenges can over time turn into public protests, demands for reform, or a revolution that changes the political structure.

Citizens in democracies, in contrast, have a wide range of options for political participation with little fear of reprisal. In turn, the way citizens use—or don't use—their rights helps determine a democracy's future.

Democracies vary. For example, voters elect the head of government in *presidential* systems, whereas voters elect members of the legislature who, in turn, elect (and dismiss) the prime minister in a *parliamentary* system. Another major distinction between democratic systems is that some offer plurality voting whereas others feature proportional representation. **Plurality voting** is *a "winner-take-all" system in which the candidate with the most votes wins the office being contested.* For example, in U.S. federal elections each House and Senate seat is awarded to the candidate receiving the most votes in that seat's district. Even if a candidate loses by a single vote, his or her party goes unrepresented in that district. In **proportional representation** systems, *parties are awarded seats in government based on the percentage of votes they receive in an election.* A party that wins 20 percent of the vote might be awarded 20 percent of the seats in the legislature. Many countries, including Japan, Ireland, Brazil, Hungary, Canada, and South Africa, have some form of proportional representation.

MAP 16.1 | DEMOCRACY INDEX, 2017

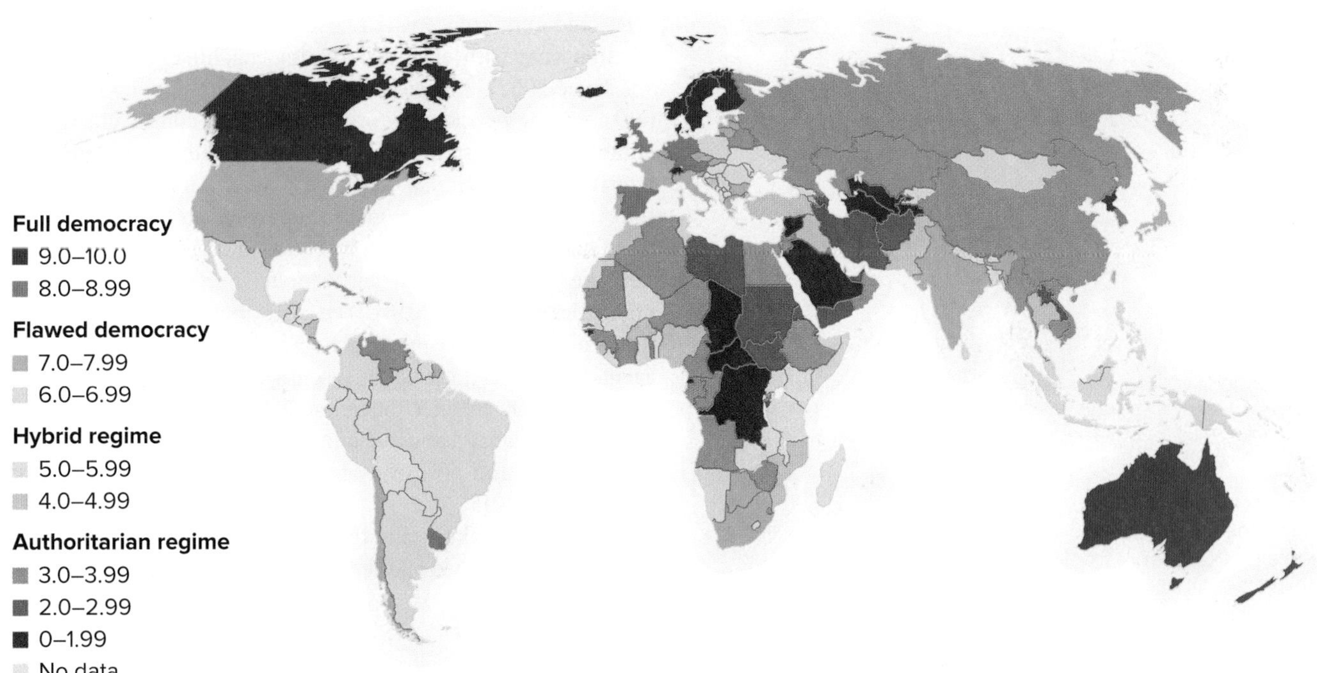

The degree of democratic rule varies considerably from country to country. On the 1 to 10 scale used here, darkest green color indicates the most democratic countries, while the darkest orange/brown color indicates the most authoritarian regimes. *Source:* Economist Intelligence Unit 2018.

In the United States, plurality voting has been a major factor in the emergence of a system dominated by two parties, the Republicans and the Democrats. Although small political parties such as the Libertarian Party and the Green Party do exist, few voters know much about them. Debate organizers typically exclude third-party candidates, and news organizations rarely cover their campaigns, helping ensure that small parties remain on the margins of political life. Because of the structural limitations of the two-party system, major change to the system must often originate from outside the two major parties, often through social movements (see Chapter 17).

Many countries have a more diverse multiparty system, often due to their system of proportional representation. (See Figure 16.1.)

FIGURE 16.1 | MULTIPARTY LEGISLATURES: POLITICAL PARTIES IN CANADA AND GERMANY

Canada 2018

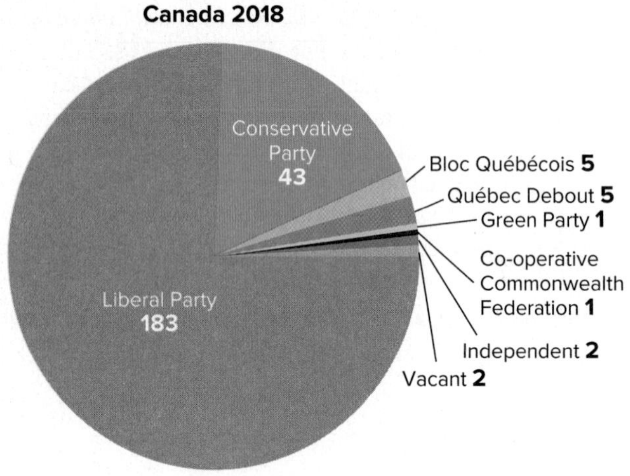

Germany 2018

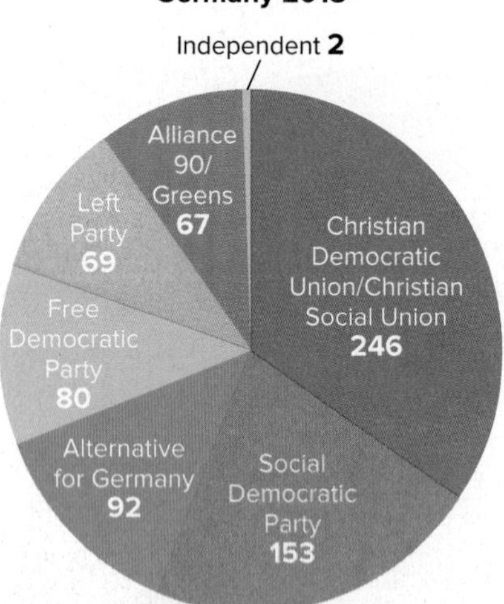

Unlike the United States, other democracies have legislatures with significant representation from more than two parties.
Sources: German Bundestag 2018; Parliament of Canada 2018.

Citizens in multiparty systems are more likely to find a party that represents their views, thereby contributing to higher voter turnout than is typical in the United States. Such systems, though, can produce fragmented and unstable governments.

Political Culture

Like any social institution, politics features culturally specific norms and practices. The cultural norms we learn influence what issues we consider political and whether we speak out about them.

Political Socialization

Political socialization *teaches us basic norms and expectations about political life and attitudes toward involvement in politics.* Democratic political systems, like that of the United States, encourage citizens to participate in politics, at least to a degree. Schools typically teach students basic lessons about civics, including the significance of voting rights. During election season, news coverage regularly stresses the importance of voting as a basic act of citizenship. Freedom and democracy are celebrated through patriotic cultural events, from schoolchildren's recitation of the Pledge of Allegiance to the playing of the national anthem at the start of sporting events.

But the U.S. political process and citizens' relationship to politics are in fact more complicated than our celebrations suggest. For most of U.S. history, the majority of citizens were denied even the basic right to vote. Though not nearly as pervasive as some suggest, scholars have documented election fraud past and present, including voting by dead people, uncounted votes, and interference with registration as well as the possibility of tampering with electronic voting machines (Alvarez, Hall, and Hyde 2008). Allegations of voter manipulation and inaccurate counting periodically produce election controversies, most notably the contested 2000 presidential election settled by the intervention of the U.S. Supreme Court. And in recent years, state voter ID laws that supposedly were enacted to combat voter fraud have been struck down by court findings that they actually were created to suppress voter turnout, specifically among racial minorities (Newkirk 2016). The 2016 presidential election featured new efforts to manipulate voters, this time by Russian agents using social media (as discussed in Chapter 15). Further, some observers criticize the news media for failing to adequately serve their crucial democratic functions of being a watchdog on the powerful and effectively informing citizens about politics (McChesney 2015).

Such shortcomings take their toll. Research suggests, as one survey summary noted, "Americans generally agree on democratic

thinking about **structure**

The **structure** of the two-party system in the United States limits the range of candidates who can realistically be elected to Congress or the presidency. Have you been satisfied with the choice of candidates available to you in the two major parties? Do you think a major third party will ever emerge in U.S. politics? Why or why not?

©Karen Bleier/AFP/Getty Images

A girl watches her mother voting at a polling station. Were political discussions and activities a part of your upbringing? Where do your political views come from?

TABLE 16.1 VOTER TURNOUT IN TOP 20 DEMOCRATIC COUNTRIES

Rank	Country	Voter Turnout[1] (as percentage of voting age population)
1	Singapore	93.6%
2	Malta	92.1%
3	Luxembourg	91.2%
4	Australia	91.0%
5	Belgium	89.4%
6	Uruguay	88.6%
7	Denmark	85.9%
8	Sweden	85.8%
9	Botswana	84.8%
10	Malaysia	82.3%
11	Philippines	82.0%
12	Netherlands	81.9%
13	Peru	81.9%
14	Ecuador	81.7%
15	Sri Lanka	81.5%
16	Brazil	80.6%
17	Austria	80.0%
18	New Zealand	79.8%
19	Iceland	79.2%
20	Norway	78.2%
49	United States	65.4%

Among the countries considered "full" or "flawed" democracies (see Map 16.1), U.S. voter turnout ranked 49th. What factors do you think contribute to the relatively low voter turnout in the United States?

[1]Voter turnout is for the most recent presidential or parliamentary election as of 2017.

Source: International Institute for Democracy and Electoral Assistance 2018.

ideals and values that are important for the United States. But for the most part, they see the country falling well short in living up to these ideals" (Pew Research Center 2018c, 1). For example, 84 percent of respondents said it is very important that "the rights and freedoms of all people are respected," but only 47 percent thought this describes the United States "very" or "somewhat" well. Also, 83 percent thought elected officials should "face serious consequences for misconduct," but only 30 percent thought this describes the United States "very" or "somewhat" well.

As a result, many Americans are at best highly skeptical of the political process and political figures. Millions simply avoid politics and decline to vote. Ironically, the United States–which often prides itself on being a global symbol of freedom and democracy–typically has one of the lowest voter turnouts of any Western industrialized democracy (see Table 16.1). Such widespread mistrust of political institutions and alienation from the political process are signs of the significant challenges U.S. democracy faces. (We consider threats to democracy in the United States and elsewhere in the "A Changing World" section at the end of the chapter.)

Political Norms and the "Spiral of Silence"

In democratic political systems, the legitimacy of governments is dependent on public support. But since long periods often separate one election from the next, how do the people "govern"

thinking about culture

Who benefits from a **culture** of political cynicism and mistrust?
What needs to happen to help rebuild faith in U.S. political institutions?

between elections? One way is by expressing their opinions about the issues of the day. However, talking about politics is not always easy, especially for those with unpopular views.

As we saw in Chapter 7, experimental studies have long suggested that people tend to conform to group expectations (Asch 1952, 1955). Political researchers have long known of the "bandwagon effect," whereby people adopt positions or support candidates because they are perceived to be popular (Dizney and Roskens 1962). The **spiral of silence** is *a theory that explains how people keep quiet about controversial issues when they think their opinions are not widely shared, in order to avoid social isolation.*

The theory came from Elisabeth Noelle-Neumann (1916–2010), a conservative German public opinion researcher. Once affiliated with Nazi organizations during World War II, she later denied ever personally being a Nazi (Bogart 1991; *New York Times* 1991; Noelle-Neumann 1991). Upon the defeat of Nazi Germany, once-dominant racist views became marginalized in the postwar era. It is from this environment that Noelle-Neumann (1974, 1993) developed the idea that those who held minority views were likely to remain silent when they believed that others disagreed.

One comprehensive review of spiral of silence theory and research summarizes the five key dynamics of this process (Scheufele and Moy 2000):

1. Societies require some degree of agreement about basic values and goals and exert social pressure on individuals to agree, including an implicit threat of isolation for those who do not.
2. As individuals develop their own opinions, they fear social isolation and seek to conform to what they see as the prevailing views in their community.
3. People monitor their environment, paying careful attention to the opinions of others as they try to decipher the most common opinions and future opinion trends.
4. People are likely to express their opinions when they believe their views are popular or rising in popularity. However, when they believe their views are unpopular or declining in popularity, they are likely to be guarded and remain silent.
5. "The tendency of the one to speak up and the other to be silent starts off a spiraling process which increasingly establishes one opinion as the prevailing one" (Noelle-Neuman 1974).

The spiral of silence narrows public discussion by squeezing out minority views and overstating the degree of political consensus. The media play an important role in this process because people often look to media for indications of which views are currently popular. If they do not see their perspectives reflected there, they are likely to believe that their views are marginal, making it more likely they will be quiet. This is not necessarily a bad thing since dominant political and social norms can effectively keep in check views that are widely considered dangerous or abhorrent, such as racist or misogynistic attitudes.

The unexpected 2016 election of Donald Trump triggered renewed interest in the spiral of silence. Popular commentators suggested it might help explain why polls often underestimated support for Trump and why, in the wake of his election, far right supporters felt emboldened to express racist and anti-Semitic views that had previously been marginalized (Mecking 2017; Whiteley 2016). As spiral of silence theory suggests, Trump's election may have animated some who had previously been silent because they had not seen their views included in the mainstream media. When the mainstream media began covering far-right support for Trump, it inadvertently helped to encourage it (Phillips 2018).

The spiral of silence received renewed attention, as well, because of the rise of social media. As we saw in Chapter 15, autocratic leaders have found ways to use social media to discourage dissent by flooding the medium with misinformation, an effort sometimes called "computational propaganda" (Spaiser et al. 2017; Woolley and Howard 2017). In addition, the internet offers many venues for discussion with like-minded individuals. It may be that people who had previously felt isolated—trapped in the spiral of silence—are now more likely to be emboldened by seeing others who share their views. For those unjustly marginalized in the past, this can be a blessing, but insofar as it may also inspire others who hold hateful or violent views, it poses a challenge for society.

Cultural Values and Political Ideologies

Political ideologies embody the values of political culture. (An *ideology*, as we discussed in Chapter 3, is *a system of meaning that helps define and explain the world and that makes value judgments about that world.*) Political ideologies vary by society and advocates debate their meaning, so universal agreement on simple definitions surely does not exist. However, some of the most common political ideologies in the United States include the following:

- *Conservativism* argues that traditional beliefs and institutions should be retained, supporting only change that is limited and gradual. Conservatives often emphasize limited and fiscally responsible government.
- *Liberalism* endorses change by using government to protect individual rights and freedoms, as well as to provide citizens with an economic safety net.
- *Libertarianism* endorses unrestricted individual freedom achieved by minimizing the role of government.
- *Progressivism* highlights the use of government to check the influence of powerful institutions—especially corporations—and to create programs promoting social and economic justice.

Political parties draw upon but do not line up neatly with these basic ideologies. In fact, advocates endorse a wide range of specific policies, depending on how they interpret these sometimes-overlapping ideologies.

Political Issues and Private Matters

If politics is the social institution whereby societies make collective decisions about priorities and policies, it matters a great deal

SPOTLIGHT
on social theory

Feminist theory and activism have been important in advancing the notion that "the personal is political." How might actions in your personal life have political implications?

what issues count as politics. A mixture of culture and power determines the way a society defines politics. Feminist activists in the 1970s challenged traditional definitions of politics, arguing that "the personal is political" because power pervades all aspects of social life (Evans 1980). In other words, politics is not just about what happens in government but also includes many aspects of our daily and personal lives, such as the food we choose to buy and eat, the choices we make about the work we do, and the way we structure our personal relationships.

Social theorist Nancy Fraser (1992) points out that one consequential question that reflects our political culture is what gets defined as "private" and therefore inappropriate for public discussion. A variety of issues–including child abuse, domestic violence, sexual orientation, and mental illness–were, until quite recently, considered private matters and excluded from politics. Political and cultural changes have transformed these into political issues to which public policy is attuned and about which public discussion is permissible. On the other hand, asserting the right to have a private life–free of surveillance or intrusion–is itself a political position. Ongoing debates about the government's right to use surveillance on citizens, conduct searches at airports, and legislate personal behavior illustrate that the relationship between public and private is always being contested and creates power struggles, to which we now turn (Rotenberg, Scott, and Horwitz 2015).

©Cris Bouroncle/AFP/Getty Images

In Lima, Peru, a woman holds a sign during a rally that was part of the International Day for the Elimination of Violence Against Women. Feminist activists helped to make legislation against domestic abuse—once considered a private matter—a public policy issue.

Power and Politics

By definition, politics is the struggle over power. Whoever makes the rules for a society gets to influence the direction of that society. In the United States today, do "the people" rule? Do "special interests"? Does someone else? Sociologists have long examined such issues of power, considering who takes part in politics and how government policies reflect this participation.

Theories of Political Power: Pluralism, Elites, and Class Domination

Three broad classic approaches help us understand the distribution of political power in U.S. society (Table 16.2). **Pluralist theory** *argues that political power is fragmented among many different competing groups.* Business owners, labor unions, teachers, retired people, gun owners, environmentalists, antiabortion advocates, and a host of other interests are represented by organizations that try to influence public policy by educating the public, lobbying elected officials, and supporting sympathetic candidates. Developed mostly by political scientists and adopted by some functionalist sociologists, pluralism suggests that politics is a constant negotiation among these various interests and that policies change as one or another group gains more influence (Dahl 1961).

In contrast, **power elite theory** *suggests that political power is concentrated in the hands of a small dominant group of business, government, and military leaders.* Developed by sociologist C. Wright Mills (1956), power elite theory is a form of conflict theory that argues power is heavily concentrated in the hands of those who head society's major bureaucratic institutions: the very wealthy who own or control big business, politicians and bureaucrats who run government, and the military brass who head the United States' military structure. Elites move back and forth among these three fields, as when a general leaves the military to become an executive for a defense contractor or when a banking executive becomes secretary of the U.S. Treasury. The flow of people among the three sectors helps solidify the power these elites have over the policies and budgets of their interlocking bureaucracies. According to power elite theory, ordinary citizens' influence is minimal in the face of such concentrated power, except when elites disagree among themselves and thereby open the door to possible citizen influence.

TABLE 16.2 THEORIES OF POLITICAL POWER

Theory	Key Idea	Sociological Tradition
Pluralist theory	Power is fragmented among many competing groups that are constantly shifting.	Functionalist
Power elite theory	Power is concentrated in the hands of a small number of elites within business, government, and the military.	Conflict
Class domination theory	Power is concentrated in the hands of a small number of wealthy people who own or control key economic resources.	Conflict (especially Marx)

Class domination theory *suggests that political power is concentrated in the hands of the rich, who own or control a large share of the nation's economic resources.* Based on the work of Karl Marx and adapted by modern interpreters (Domhoff 2013), class domination theory is a form of conflict theory that views the economic system as the ultimate source of power. Those who control this system—especially super-wealthy owners and executives of major corporate conglomerates—use their financial clout to influence government by funding lobbyists, financially supporting political campaigns, and bankrolling "astroturf" campaigns that advance corporate goals through what appear to be grassroots citizen efforts (Walker 2014). Corporations also influence the cultural and ideological landscape by bankrolling research at tax-exempt think tanks, thereby helping to shape discussions of public policy from behind the scenes (Lipton and Williams 2016). Corporate-owned media outlets also help limit the range of political debate on news and other programs. These uses of economic resources undermine the ability of ordinary citizens to significantly influence the political system. Although efforts to rein in the power of the rich—through higher taxes and limits on campaign contributions, for example—are sometimes criticized as promoting "class warfare," proponents of class domination theory say that it's the other way around—ordinary citizens are the real targets of class warfare. As investor Warren Buffett, one of the richest men in the United States, once put it, disapprovingly, "There's class warfare, all right, but it's my class—the rich class—that's making war, and we're winning" (quoted in Stein 2006).

SPOTLIGHT on social theory

Both **power elite** and **class domination theory**—forms of **conflict theory**—argue that political power is not really in the hands of ordinary citizens, as **pluralist theory** suggests. Can you think of an example that seems to support such claims? Can you think of a situation in which ordinary citizens seem to have prevailed over powerful interests?

Many sociologists would likely agree that the United States follows some aspects of the pluralist model, especially on issues that are not fundamentally economic, such as abortion, immigration, and gun control, where lively debates are pursued by various groups. But there is little doubt that elites—especially corporations—wield disproportionate influence on political life, particularly economic affairs, though the precise nature and degree of this influence is a topic of ongoing study and debate (Bartels 2016; Mizruchi 2013).

Class Differences in Political Participation

Societies with a healthy democratic political system have broad public participation in politics, even if only in elections. But more than in many other democracies, political participation in the United States is stratified by class. Working-class and poor people are less likely to vote in the United States than are middle-class people (Schlozman, Brady, and Verba 2018). As we saw in Chapter 9, one likely reason is the absence of a strong labor or socialist party that can speak on behalf of working-class voters. All other Western democracies have such a party, and the class gap in voter turnout is considerably less in those countries. In contrast, both major parties in the United States are closely aligned with major corporate interests and depend heavily on their financial contributions.

The political socialization of young people is another important influence on political participation. Informed political discussion benefits from self-confidence, education, knowledge, and a time commitment, and these resources are not distributed equally. Although a healthy democracy requires the inclusion of diverse

©Patrick McMullan/Getty Images

To celebrate the one year anniversary of President Trump's time in office, over 800 guests attended a reelection fund raiser at his Mar-a-Lago Club in Palm Beach, Florida on January 18, 2018. Couples were charged $100,000 to attend the event; those who paid $250,000 got to talk with the president at a rountable (Jacobs and Allison 2018). Here, donors at that event pose with a cardboard cut-out of the first couple.

perspectives from all sectors of society, research suggests that higher levels of education and income contribute significantly to a sense of political competence (Jacobs and Skocpol 2007; Leighley and Nagler 2013). Children from highly educated, wealthier, and higher-status families enjoy numerous advantages that encourage and enable them to become active in politics: their parents are more likely than working-class parents to participate in politics and to talk to their children about political activity; their teachers and school officials are more likely to encourage students to become active in school and community activities; and their peer networks are more likely to support interest and involvement in politics. People from poor or working-class backgrounds are less likely to perceive themselves as adequately prepared for political discussions and are less likely to be active in an arena that seems to reward the affluent.

Campaign Contributions, Lobbying, and Policy Outcomes

Class differences in political participation are even more pronounced in activities beyond voting. Not surprisingly, financial contributions—the lifeblood of political campaigns—come disproportionately from affluent voters. The rich have more money to contribute. For example, in the 2016 election, Hillary Clinton and Donald Trump received 81 percent and 72 percent of their funds, respectively, from large donors who gave more than $200 each (Center for Responsive Politics 2016). While also receiving tens of millions of dollars in support from large donors, Donald Trump spent an additional $66 million of his own money on his campaign (Levinthal 2018).

Campaign money also flows through political action committees (PACs), organizations that raise and contribute money to candidates' campaigns or to party organizations. Although the amount of money PACs can raise and spend is restricted, the Supreme Court's highly controversial 2010 *Citizens United* decision eliminated restrictions on spending by so-called super PACs. Unlike PACs, which contribute to a candidate or party, super PACs spend the money independently, usually on advertising or mailings for or against a particular candidate. The result can be massive "outside money" contributions. In the 2016 election cycle, hedge fund manager Tom Steyer donated $91 million to support liberal campaigns; casino owner Sheldon Adelson contributed $82 million to support conservative candidates (Center for Responsive Politics 2018b).

Moreover, the *Citizens United* decision, as well as other legal developments, have increased the influence of tax-exempt "dark money" groups, which don't need to disclose the source of the money they spend so there are millions more of untraceable money entering election campaigns. The result of these changes has been a massive increase in the amount of money spent on elections, along with a decrease in accountability for the expenditures (Albert 2017; Beckel and Bennett 2015).

Once candidates have been elected, they must immediately begin raising funds for their reelection. Today's politicians run a "permanent campaign," one that has intensified with the increasing influx of money into politics. Officials must raise funds for reelection while lobbyists encourage lawmakers to vote in their clients' interests—often the same clients who make major campaign contributions (Figure 16.2).

FIGURE 16.2 | LOBBYING EXPENDITURES BY SECTOR, 1998 TO MID-2018

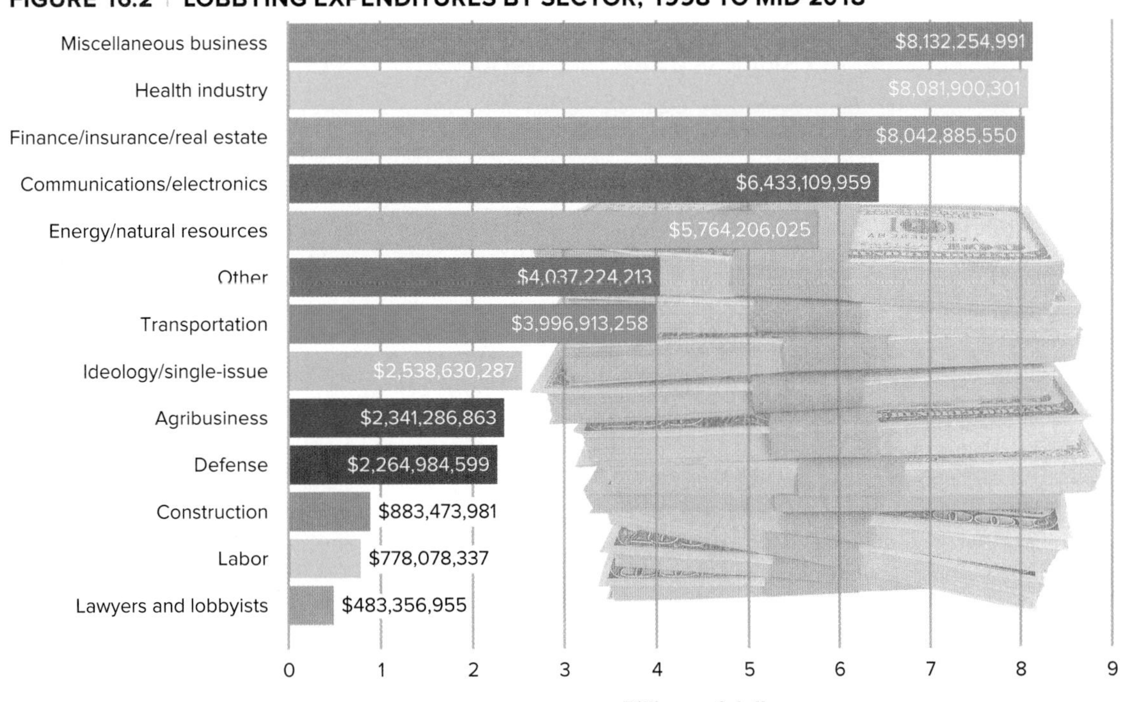

©Comstock Images/Alamy Stock Photo

Business-sector spending on lobbyists far surpasses that of labor groups or single-issue organizations such as environmental, gay rights, and gun rights groups. *Source:* Center for Responsive Politics 2018c.

Campaign donations give donors and lobbyists unique access to elected officials, which they often parlay into special assistance that benefit them directly (Drutman 2015; Walker and Rea 2014). These benefits tend to fall into two categories. First, companies are interested in eliminating regulations that limit how they can operate. Set up to do things such as protect public health, prevent corrupt practices, shield worker rights, defend consumers, and safeguard the environment, regulations add to the cost of doing business and are a main target of lobbying efforts. Second, rather than lobby to be left alone by the government, corporate lobbyists often compete for lucrative government contracts providing military hardware, infrastructure construction, logistical services, and other projects. One study found a direct correlation between the amount of a firm's corporate political activity and the size of the government contracts they were later awarded (Hadani, Munshi, and Clark 2017).

In addition, wealthy corporations and individuals lobby for lower tax rates and tax loopholes (Johnston 2005, 2007, 2018). One government analysis found that with loopholes and tax deductions, large companies (with assets of $10 million or more) paid an average of 14 percent in taxes on their profits—well below the 35 percent corporate tax on the books. One in five of these large, profitable companies paid no income taxes (U.S. Government Accountability Office 2016). In 2015, for example, some of the country's largest and most profitable companies paid no income taxes, including automaker General Motors, United Continental Airlines, media giant News Corporation, drugmaker Pfizer, and Xerox Business Services (Krantz 2016). Higher-income earners—who pay more income taxes—get the biggest piece of common tax breaks, such as deductions for mortgage payments, tax-free pension contributions, employee premiums for employer-sponsored health insurance, and lower tax rates on capital gains income (Congressional Budget Office 2013). It was business as usual with the first Trump-era tax cut in 2017 that, despite rhetoric to the contrary, massively favored the richest households. (See Figure 16.3.)

Considerable research suggests that the government is most responsive to the affluent classes. In a series of works, political scientist Martin Gilens (2005, 2012) focused on issues for which the policy preferences of high-income people differed from those of middle- and low-income citizens. The inheritance tax, government-funded health care, and affirmative action are supported substantially more by those with modest incomes than by those with higher incomes. Gilens (2012) concluded that "government policy appears to be fairly responsive to the well-off and virtually unrelated to the desires of the low- and middle-income citizens" (81).

Inequality, Power, and Politics

Connecting the dots between economic inequality, campaign finances, lobbying, and legislation, some critics argue that concentrated wealth is undermining democratic institutions (Collins and Yeskel 2005; Johnston 2014). (See Figure 16.4.) Those with money use their resources to influence the political system, while those struggling to earn a living have little time to take part in the political process and no money to contribute. Because political parties and politicians speak to and respond mostly to the more affluent, the less affluent often do not see

FIGURE 16.3 | **AVERAGE ANNUAL FEDERAL TAX SAVINGS BY INCOME GROUP, 2017 TAX CUTS AND JOB ACT**

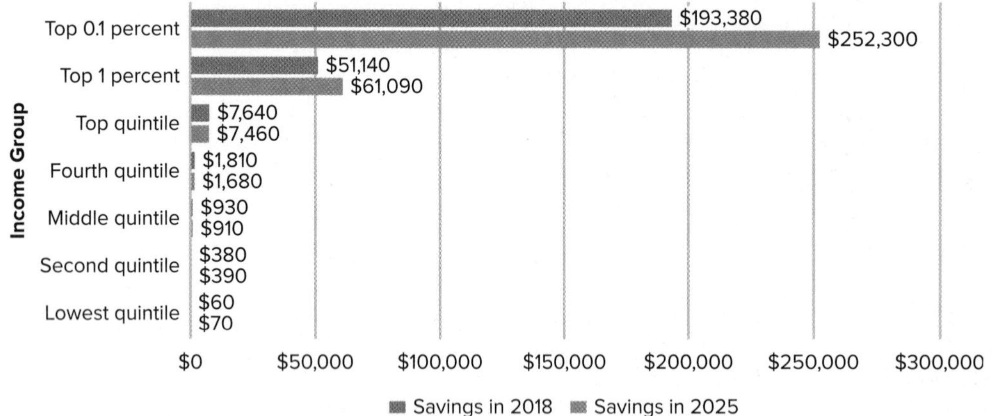

Taxes are one of the direct ways that government policy affects personal economics. Higher income groups pay more in taxes but enjoy the biggest tax breaks. With 2017 legislation, the nation's richest families received another massive tax break, while middle- and low-income families saw modest or minimal savings. Provisions in the bill are scheduled to increase the benefits for the wealthy even more by 2025.

Note: Average federal tax includes individual and corporate income tax, payroll taxes for Social Security and Medicare, the estate tax, and excise taxes. *Source:* Tax Policy Center 2017b.

CORE CONCEPTS CHALLENGE *Do you think this distribution pattern is related to the amount of* ***power*** *various income groups have in society? Why or why not?*

FIGURE 16.4 | INEQUALITY, POWER, AND POLITICS: A MODEL

Economic inequality can endanger the health of a democracy—and unhealthy democracy can lead to greater inequality. *Source:* Adapted from Collins and Yeskel (2005).

CORE CONCEPTS CHALLENGE *Do you think this model summarizes accurately the way political* ***power*** *works in contemporary U.S. politics? Why or why not?*

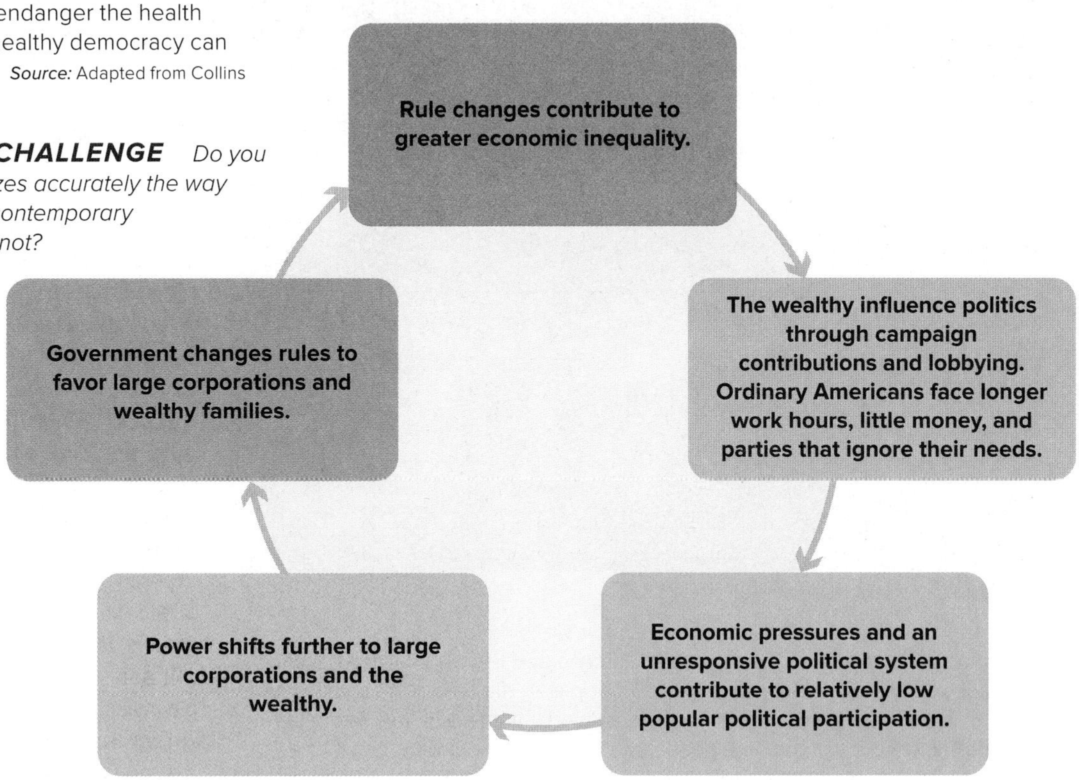

political participation as a wise investment of time and energy. However, by opting out of the political process, the less affluent virtually guarantee that politicians and the government will continue to neglect their interests. The vacuum they leave makes it easier for powerful players to shape laws, rules, and regulations to benefit their own interests, some of which increase inequality. Powerful elites do not need to convince most people to support their efforts; they merely need to convince them that government is inefficient, ineffective, and not worth fighting for. Cynicism and alienation among citizens benefit those who are already powerful.

Democracies, however, always contain within them the possibility for reform. As long as basic civil rights remain in place, such as freedom of speech and assembly and the right to vote, citizens can promote change through the electoral process. If that process is not working properly, then social change can occur through the efforts of social movements that challenge authority outside the electoral system (discussed in Chapter 17). It remains to be seen whether and in what ways citizens will act to reform our democracy in the coming years.

War and the Military

Mao Zedong ([1936] 2010), the leader of the Communist Revolution in China, famously justified armed insurrection with the slogan "Political power grows out of the barrel of a gun" (24). As Mao knew, **war**—*organized armed conflict among two or more specially trained military groups*—is often used to overcome opposition. Or as nineteenth-century German military theorist Carl von Clausewitz ([1832] 1976) put it, war is "the continuation of policy [or politics] by other means" (87).

Some sociologists argue that war is a permanent feature of modern societies, since preparing for war is now a routine and perpetual government activity that absorbs an enormous amount of resources. A sociological approach to war and the military includes a consideration of the military's role in society and the socialization processes that create citizens who accept war and soldiers who fight it (Centeno and Enriquez 2016; Kestnbaum 2009; Malešević 2010).

The Rise of the National Security State

During its first 125 years or so of existence—with the exception of the Civil War—the U.S. government kept a relatively small military force, even as it fought its way across the continent, acquiring new territories and subjugating indigenous peoples. At the end of the nineteenth century, U.S. territory stretched from the Atlantic to the Pacific. The country faced no real military threat but some political leaders—most famously Theodore Roosevelt—wanted to continue expanding U.S. influence abroad. This goal required a much larger military, especially a modern navy that could move beyond defense to project U.S. power overseas. The United States began building such a navy, and after its 1898 war with Spain, it quickly acquired colonies in the

©Digital Vision/Photodisc/Getty Images

The distinctive Pentagon building, just outside Washington, D.C., is the headquarters of the U.S. Department of Defense and the world's largest office building, with a daily workforce of 24,000 people. At the time of its construction at the start of World War II, it was widely assumed that the building would be converted after the war to some peacetime use, perhaps as an archive or a hospital. Instead, the military never left (Vogel 2007). Does the military have a visible presence in your community?

Philippines, Cuba, Guam, and Puerto Rico. Its time as a traditional colonial power was short, however; armed insurrections and resistance movements forced the United States to give up most of its newly acquired colonies. But the growing U.S. military continued to play an ever-larger role in society, expanding dramatically during the two world wars.

After World War II ended, the United States maintained a military of unprecedented size as it engaged in the Cold War (1945–1989), an ongoing state of military tension between the United States and the Soviet Union. Although these superpowers never directly engaged in war, the United States developed a **national security state,** *a government dominated by powerful military, foreign policy, and intelligence agencies.* The key moment in the development of the national security state was the passage of the National Security Act of 1947. The act created the National Security Council to advise the president on foreign policy and the Central Intelligence Agency, which collects and analyzes security information and engages in covert operations abroad. It also consolidated the military under the newly formed Department of Defense, headquartered at the recently built Pentagon (Hogan 1998).

The national security state is not monolithic. Debates often exist within its circles about the proper priorities and allocation of resources. But as a whole it wields enough power to influence major economic and political policy decisions and priorities. In the eyes of critics, the national security state has an unhealthy preoccupation with foreign and domestic enemies that distorts economic and political policy decisions and priorities (Bacevich 2010, 2013).

For example, military spending receives priority well beyond the amount needed to ensure territorial security (Greider 2010; Thorpe 2014). Intelligence-gathering capacities have been used in ways that critics contend violate basic democratic values, since they include secrecy, surveillance, and limits on civil liberties at home and often occur without public knowledge or review (Cole and Dempsey 2006; Greenwald 2014). As a *Washington Post* investigation concluded, "The top-secret world the government created in response to the terrorist attacks of Sept. 11, 2001, has become so large, so unwieldy and so secretive that no one knows how much money it costs, how many people it employs, how many programs exist within it or exactly how many agencies do the same work" (Priest and Arkin 2010). The information revealed by whistleblower Edward Snowden in 2013 especially exposed some of the massive surveillance efforts of the National Security Agency (NSA), which gathers data on the e-mails, internet activity, and cell phone communications of millions of people inside and outside the United States.

The rise of the national security state was part of a broader change in which the U.S. military grew much more powerful, enjoying unprecedented peacetime funding, and the federal government increasingly defined international affairs in military terms. In his farewell speech to the nation in 1961, outgoing Republican president (and supreme commander of the Allied Forces during World War II) Dwight D. Eisenhower warned of the growth of a military establishment and arms industry, cautioning that "in the councils of government, we must guard against the acquisition of unwarranted influence, whether sought or unsought, by the military-industrial complex. The potential for the disastrous rise of misplaced power exists and will persist."

Eisenhower's warnings were extraordinary given that they came from an army general, but they were not new. C. Wright Mills (1956), in his analysis *The Power Elite,* had already documented the rise of military influence in political life, the declining influence of civilian diplomats, the growing impact of military spending on the economy, and the influential role of military money and priorities on research on university campuses. Mills observed that "the professional military believe firmly in the military definition of world reality and . . . are genuinely frightened for their country" (202). With their growing influence, military leaders were able to promote these fears and definitions of reality, thereby helping transform the United States into a more militarized society.

In recent years, the fear of terrorism served as a new catalyst for massive investments in military and a widespread "war on terror." Since just 2015, the United States has conducted bombings in Iraq, Afghanistan, Yemen, Somalia, Libya, Pakistan, and Syria. The assault on ISIS in Syria by the United States and its allies in 2017–2018 produced what Amnesty International (2018) called a "War of Annihilation" because, they say, the vast scale and recklessness of the attack killed thousands of civilians.

The Pentagon rejects that characterization but admits that it killed nearly 500 civilians in 2017 alone (Cooper 2018), while acknowledging that "no one will ever know" the exact number of civilian deaths resulting from U.S. bombings (Sonne 2018). Meanwhile, at home, polls indicated that most Americans came to believe that the wars in Iraq and Afghanistan were "not worth fighting" (ABC/Washington Post 2013).

Military Funding

The United States is bounded by oceans on both the east and west coasts and shares its northern and southern borders with close allies, making it among the most geographically safe countries in the world. Yet, since the middle of the twentieth century, it has maintained the most powerful military in the world, on which it spends far more than any other country (see Figure 16.5.) The United States in 2017 accounted for about 36 percent of the world's $1.69 trillion in military spending (Stockholm International Peace Research Institute 2018) and in recent years has devoted more than half of its federal discretionary budget to military spending (Figure 16.6).

Much of the United States' military spending is devoted to projecting power worldwide. In addition to military sites in all 50 states, the United States has about 800 military sites—big and small—in over 70 countries. Ever since World War II, the United States has as one analyst put it (Vine 2015), "an unparalleled global military presence, unmatched by any prior people, nation, or empire in history" (18).

FIGURE 16.5 | GLOBAL MILITARY SPENDING, 2017

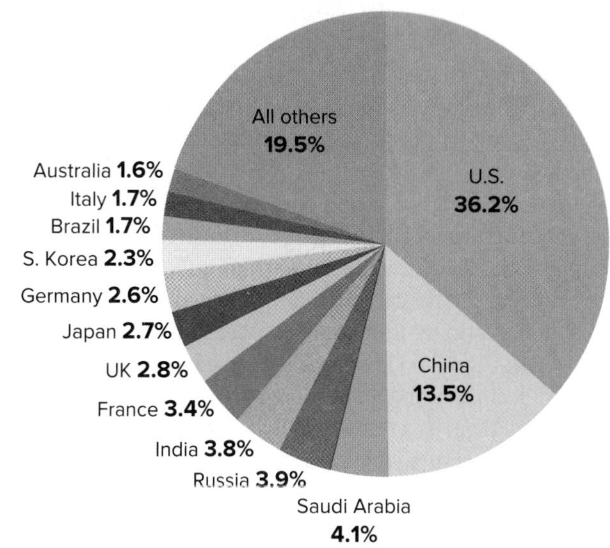

In 2017, the United States spent over $609 billion on direct military expenditures, about the same amount as the next eight countries combined. *Source:* Stockholm International Peace Research Institute [SIPRI] 2018.

The Politics of Fear and Civil Liberties

Ironically, massive U.S. military spending intended to promote security has long been accompanied by a deep sense of fear and insecurity among many citizens. The postwar arms race between the United States and the former Soviet Union raised concern that nuclear annihilation could occur at any moment and that communism threatened U.S. democratic freedoms. With the collapse of the Soviet Union in 1991 and the 2001 attacks on 9/11, terrorists replaced communists as the perceived threat to security.

Fear can lead people to take actions that they otherwise would not consider, including accepting policies that threaten civil liberties and jeopardize basic democratic principles in the name of security. As we saw in Chapter 10, thousands of Asian Americans were sent to internment camps during World War II. During the Cold War, the FBI monitored the peaceful political

FIGURE 16.6 | U.S. DISCRETIONARY SPENDING, FY 2018

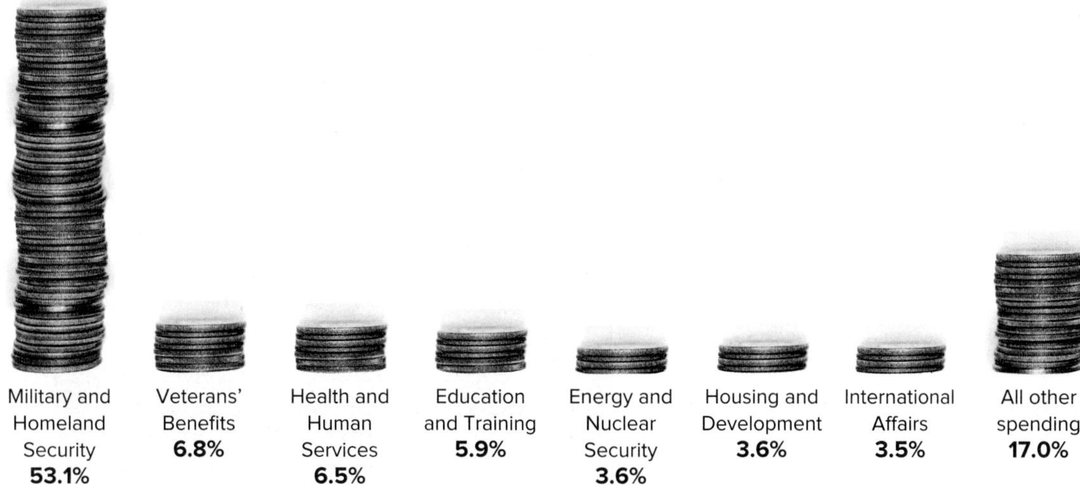

©Stockbyte/PunchStock

Most U.S. discretionary spending is used on the military, far surpassing the amount spent on health, human services, education, housing, and other programs. Discretionary spending is the portion of the federal budget that must be allocated each year. It does not include dedicated trust funds, such as Social Security and Medicare, which are paid largely from payroll taxes, not income taxes. *Source:* Committee for a Responsible Federal Budget 2018.

activities of citizens; as a condition of employment, schools and other institutions demanded "loyalty oaths" (some of which are still required today); and a congressional committee—the House Un-American Activities Committee—questioned public figures about their political views and loyalty. Many of these activities are now recognized as misguided efforts that undermined basic civil liberties.

The 2001 USA Patriot Act, adopted after 9/11, included a range of new government policies meant to fight terrorism, including wiretapping phone lines without a warrant; collecting information about citizens' phone calls, e-mail, financial data, and health records; and detaining immigrants without criminal charges. In just a few years, these policies have been used against tens of thousands of U.S. citizens and many more foreign visitors. So far, most have accepted them as a trade-off between security and liberty.

To many observers, the politics of fear were embodied in Donald Trump's 2016 presidential "campaign of fear" (New York Times Editorial Board 2016). Trump's acceptance speech at the Republican National Convention, for example, was widely seen as "one of the darkest, most foreboding, and aggressively fear-mongering speeches in modern political memory." His campaign repeatedly stoked voters' fear of illegal immigrants, Muslims, foreigners, terrorism, crime, and more (Matthews 2016). Once in office, Trump repeatedly returned to the theme of fear-inducing threats, including immigrants (Long 2018), gangs (Guariglia 2018), Muslims (Beinart 2017), and asylum seekers (Human Rights First 2018). He even justified new tariffs by citing longtime ally Canada as a threat to "national security" (Da Silva 2018). (The Through a Sociological Lens Box considers how threats motivated Trump voters in 2016.)

Terrorism

In recent years, the most widely discussed threat to society has been terrorism. Sociologists, along with scholars in the broader social sciences, have contributed to our understanding of how to combat terrorism (Brym 2007; Cronin 2009; Hoffman 2006; Sageman 2008; Vertigans 2013). Some of their insights include the following:

- ***Terrorism is socially constructed.*** Much of what we now call terrorism used to be referred to simply as political violence; its perpetrators were referred to as guerrillas, revolutionaries, or insurgents. Over time, often for political reasons, various actors have defined some political violence as "terrorism" and its perpetrators as "terrorists" (Richards 2015; Stampnitzky 2013). Consequently, there is no universally accepted definition of terrorism. Rather, the term encompasses a wide range of activities, organizations, circumstances, and beliefs. Typically, we reserve the label **terrorism** for *politically motivated violence that intentionally targets noncombatants.* When we identify an act of violence as terrorism in this way, we are affixing a powerful label to it, one that is often controversial. We tend to apply the label *terrorist* only to groups that we oppose, often failing to see that our allies and even our own government have acted in similar ways.
- ***Governments can engage in terrorism.*** **State terrorism** is *political violence directed at civilians by governments.* Although terrorists are often assumed to be non-state actors, throughout history, many governments—from the Soviet Union under Joseph Stalin to Syria under Bashar al-Assad—have unleashed political violence against civilians at home and abroad. Even the United States has targeted civilian populations. For example, in World War II, to undermine enemy morale, the United States targeted German civilians (by firebombing cultural centers like Dresden) and Japanese civilians (by dropping atomic bombs on Hiroshima and Nagasaki). Indeed, political violence was first described as terror during the French Revolution (1789–1799), when the revolutionary government executed thousands of French civilians, often by guillotine, in what became known as the Reign of Terror.
- ***Terrorists are not crazy.*** Studies of failed suicide bombers have found that nearly all of them engage in such actions for rational, strategic reasons. Indeed, terrorist organizations typically root out anyone who appears to have psychological problems, out of concern that unstable individuals could jeopardize the successful completion of their missions or the safety of their members (Hafez 2006; Pape 2005).
- ***There is no single face of terrorism.*** Stereotypes about cultures, religions, and practices that are different from our own can cloud our understanding of terrorism. Over the years, terrorist acts have been carried out by a wide variety of groups that hold diverse beliefs and worldviews and espouse a range of political causes, including white supremacy, radical leftism, and Islamic extremism.

Maximilien de Robespierre (1758–1794), leading figure of the French Revolution, is guillotined in the Place de la Révolution on July 28. The revolution's "Reign of Terror" marked the first time the word *terror* was applied to political violence.

Understanding Trump Voters

In the aftermath of the unexpected 2016 election of Donald Trump, polls identified the basic characteristics of those who voted for each candidate. However, understanding what voter characteristics were most important—and why—involved some more-nuanced analysis from researchers, including sociologists.

Election-day exit polls found that Hillary Clinton received the majority of votes of women, younger voters (under 40), racial and ethnic minorities, those with a college education, those from low-income and lower-middle income households ($50,000 or less), those for whom the economy and foreign policy were their top concerns, and those who wanted a candidate with experience. Conversely, Donald Trump won with men, older voters, whites (including those 18–29 years old), those without a college education, those with upper-middle household incomes from $50,000 to $100,000 (the candidates evenly split voters with incomes above $100,000), those for whom immigration and terrorism were their top concerns, and those who wanted a candidate of change (CNN 2016; Tyson and Maniam 2016).

Small changes in the electorate compared to earlier elections proved important. Black voter turnout declined from the historic high of the Obama years, harming Clinton's chances. However, analysts identified white working-class voters as the real key to the Trump victory, especially in crucial midwestern battleground states (McQuarrie 2017; Morgan and Lee 2017, 2018). By some estimates, nearly one of four white working-class Obama voters switched to Trump (Cohn 2017).

Some analysts found that Trump received support among white working-class voters because of their economic predicament. Voters without a college degree face an uphill climb in a profoundly unequal economy that offers them few opportunities. Even though Trump was a child of privilege, he spoke of rebuilding manufacturing and returning to an earlier era of American economic dominance. He tied unfair free trade, the threat of China, and resentment toward immigrants directly to working-class economic security (Lamont, Park, and Ayala-Hurtado 2017; McCall and Orloff 2017; Swedberg 2018).

Analysts also found that the bigotry and racism that tinged Trump's anti-immigration and Muslim ban rhetoric had significant appeal (Smith and Hanley 2018). Research has long shown that whites, threatened by growing diversity in a country where they will be the minority by 2045, are more likely to endorse conservative policy positions on immigrants and racial minorities, making them a prime target for Republican candidates (Craig and Richeson 2014; Vespa, Armstrong, and Medina 2018).

Finally, another key factor was the cultural divide that Trump highlighted by praising traditional patriotic values, flaunting a politically incorrect persona, and attacking elites in society—the politicians in Washington and the cultural snobs in Hollywood and the media that seemed to look down on the unsophisticated working class. Studies found this tapped into fears among white working-class voters—especially religious voters—that America's best days had passed and that outside influences were eroding the country's cultural values and distinct identity. Exposing the depth of this alienation, half of white working-class voters surveyed agreed that "things have changed so much that I often feel like a stranger in my own country" (Cox, Lienesch, and Jones 2017). (Long before the election, sociologist Arlie Hochschild [2016] studied conservative Tea Party supporters, many of whom later supported Trump, similarly concluding—as the title of her book emphasized—that such voters felt like *Strangers in Their Own Land*.)

Rather than see these factors as competing explanations, though, we can understand them all as part of a broader "status threat" (Mutz 2018), where people who previously had power feel threatened by change. White working-class voters—who were once more comfortable economically, who enjoyed the privileges of being in a white-majority country, and whose culture dominated the mainstream—now felt threatened by changes on all fronts and responded favorably to Trump's nostalgic message to "Make America Great Again."

think about it

1. *How do insights from sociology help explain voter preferences in this election? What factors do you think were most important? Why?*
2. *Do you think the Trump election more likely represents a new direction for the country's future or a last stand for those defending a fading past? Why?*

- ***Terrorism is rooted in perceived injustice.*** Terrorism is fueled by moral outrage over a perceived injustice that is interpreted in a way consistent with people's lived experience. The injustice is usually political in nature, involving the social organization of power. Consequently, sociologists emphasize the importance of understanding the political and social context that gives rise to terrorist acts. Responding effectively to terrorism often means addressing the long-simmering inequalities and conflicts that fuel it.
- ***Terrorism is an act of relative powerlessness.*** Terrorism by non-state actors is committed by those who are powerless and who believe they must resort to extreme measures to advance their cause. Because the vast majority of terrorist efforts fail to accomplish their goals, terrorism is rarely an attractive option if other avenues exist for pursuing justice. Thus, one way of combating terrorism is to open the legitimate political process to groups wishing to advocate for change.

©Everett Collection, Inc./Alamy Stock Photo

©J. G. Domke/Alamy Stock Photo

FAST-FORWARD

Change and Politics

Despite a safe homeland and unrivaled spending on the military, U.S. citizens have long been plagued by a sense of fear and insecurity. In the 1950s and 1960s, fear of communism led to military action abroad and a clampdown on political freedom at home. In recent years, terrorism and Islamic extremism have become the justification for wars abroad and surveillance at home.

- ***Terrorists are socialized.*** The willingness to participate in terrorist acts is acquired during a socialization process, through which individuals learn the knowledge, values, and worldview of the terrorist organization. Thus, another way to combat terrorism is to intervene and disrupt the radicalization process at an early stage before recruits join secret networks or cells.
- ***The internet has changed terrorism.*** The internet has proven an effective platform for terrorist organizations to articulate their messages, recruit adherents, and inspire action through social media and video (Jarvis, MacDonald, and Chen 2015). One of the most vexing problems facing counterterrorist efforts is dealing with "lone wolf" terrorists, isolated individuals (some of whom may be mentally unstable) who are inspired by social media to engage in unsophisticated yet deadly terrorist acts. Thus, another response to terrorism is to understand the appeal of online messages and counter them with effective communications.
- ***Violent counterterrorism can be counterproductive.*** Combating terrorism through violence can inspire retaliatory violence, creating a seemingly endless cycle (Brym and Araj 2006). More broadly, aggressive acts aimed at combating terrorism—from bombings, drone strikes, and surveillance measures to immigration restrictions and religious prohibitions—can actually be useful to terrorists' recruitment efforts, especially when they produce civilian casualties. From the terrorists' point of view, such countermeasures are consistent with and confirm the group's perception of an injustice.

Socialization for War

The United States has engaged in wars and major military actions for much of the past 80 years, including World War II (1941–1945), the Korean War (1951–1953), the Vietnam War (1960–1975), Panama (1989), the Persian Gulf War (1991), Bosnia-Herzegovina (1999), the Iraq War (2003–2011), and Afghanistan (2001–current). This partial list does not include countless covert CIA operations, Special Operations actions, smaller bombing runs, drone strikes, missile attacks, and other displays of military strength in Yemen, Somalia, Libya, Syria, Pakistan, and many other countries. U.S. citizens have grown accustomed to living in a nation that is usually at war.

Preparing Citizens to Accept War Responding to this near-continuous engagement, U.S. culture encourages citizens to affirm their support for military actions and to revere the soldiers who fight them. Soldiers are honored in the media and with monuments, memorials, museums, national holidays, and countless "Support our troops" car magnets. School textbooks often mark the progress of history in relation to the start or end of a war. Socialization for war encourages citizens to

thinking about culture

Have you or someone you know experienced military basic training? If so, what did the experience suggest about the differences between civilian and military culture?

SOCIOLOGY in ACTION

Peace Studies

If peace is widely valued, then why do we so rarely study how to achieve and maintain it? That question animates peace studies, a multidisciplinary field that was founded with the significant input and insight of sociologists (Galtung and Fischer 2013). Peace studies seeks alternatives to violence and promotes conflict resolution and social justice. These efforts include many campus-based programs, collaborations between activists and academics through professional associations such as the Peace and Justice Studies Association in the United States and the International Peace Research Association, and real-world implementation of the ideas developed in peace studies through the United Nations and nongovernmental organizations.

Perhaps the best-known founder of peace studies is Norwegian sociologist Johan Galtung, who has spent 60 years studying, teaching about, and promoting peace. Galtung is an internationally recognized advocate of innovative methods of nonviolent conflict resolution. He helped create the International Peace Research Institute in Oslo in 1959 and later started the *Journal of Peace Research,* an arena for an ongoing global conversation about the causes of war and violence, strategies of peace-building and nonviolence, and approaches to peace education.

Galtung's (1996, 2000, 2015) work reflects a sociological orientation to peace and conflict. It incorporates a structural analysis of violence, considering the forms of inequality that often underlie war and highlighting the human capacity to create a more just society. His work has included an emphasis on the importance of building a culture of peace, in which primary agents of socialization—parents, schools, media—promote values, attitudes, and behaviors that emphasize nonviolence, human rights, and social justice. Instructors in peace studies courses often teach military personnel and tackle these cultural issues, recognizing and respecting military experience but questioning the idea of "defense" and assumptions that violence is the inevitable focus of defense policies (Page 2007).

For Galtung, violence is more than just acts of physical brutality. It includes what he calls "structural violence," the underlying social conditions of inequality and injustice that prevent people from achieving their full potential and that often lead to direct physical violence. Likewise, peace is more than just the absence of overt conflict (what he dubs "negative peace"); it is the existence of social justice ("positive peace").

Galtung has participated in over 120 mediations in dozens of countries, including Afghanistan, Colombia, Israel and the Palestinian Territories, Kashmir, Korea, Northern Ireland, Rwanda, and Sri Lanka, often with positive results. For example, his mediation was central to the resolution of a border conflict between Peru and Ecuador that had led to war three times in the past. He has worked as a consultant to the United Nations on a wide range of peace-building and peacekeeping projects and since 1993 has been director of TRANSCEND, a network of like-minded colleagues from more than 80 countries who work with him to mediate conflict and provide training in conflict resolution, nonviolence, and reconciliation (transcend.org).

In a book dedicated "to a country I love, the United States of America," Galtung (2009) argued that the United States as a global power (what he calls the U.S. Empire) is unraveling, like other empires before it, as its reliance on the military to achieve economic and political ends proves increasingly economically burdensome and politically ineffective. But Galtung sees this as an opportunity for the United States as a nation (what he calls the U.S. Republic) to blossom, relieved of the burdens of empire.

think about it

1. *How might U.S. culture give greater priority to promoting peace?*
2. *Do you agree with Galtung that the United States has an opportunity to blossom by refocusing from projecting power abroad toward caring for domestic needs? Why or why not?*

---

accept, even actively support, military action. In many European nations, in contrast, after the devastations of two world wars fought partially on European soil, military values have much less appeal (Sheehan 2008). (For efforts to promote a culture of peace, see the Sociology in Action box.)

Training Soldiers to Fight Citizens may be socialized to support wars, but soldiers must learn how to fight them, typically beginning with "basic training" or "boot camp." Military training camps are a classic example of a "total institution" (discussed in Chapter 6). In addition to developing physical fitness, intensive basic training resocializes young people to behave in ways that contradict much of what they have already learned (Dyer 2004; Kooistra and Mahoney 2016). Raised in a culture that emphasizes freedom and individuality, recruits must learn to obey their commanding officers, follow orders unquestioningly, work as part of a unit, suppress their emotions, and kill as a normal job requirement.

To achieve this transformation, recruits, usually young, are taken away from mainstream society and kept in relative isolation for a number of weeks. Their individual identity is stripped away through the use of standardized close-cropped haircuts, identical clothing and gear, and collective barracks with no privacy. The recruits are then subjected to just enough physical and mental stress to wear them down, while—in the U.S. services—enabling about 90 percent to successfully complete basic training.

Adopting military culture can come at a cost, though. The traumatic events soldiers sometimes experience in combat, combined with the ongoing stress caused by lengthy deployments and separation from family, create enormous strains for many, resulting in mental health issues and suicides. The military lifestyle also tends to create distinct new identities for soldiers, some of whom find it difficult to reintegrate into civilian life after their service is over; substance abuse, posttraumatic stress disorders, and other psychological difficulties are persistent problems for some (Breitbach, Rabinowitz, and Warner 2018; Hoge 2010).

Social Inequality and the Military

The military is a social institution with its own traditions, values, norms, and organizational structure (Kestnbaum 2009; Siebold 2001). But it is also influenced by issues found in broader society, including social inequality.

Race, Gender, and Sexual Orientation in the Military The clash between the ideal of fighting for freedom and the reality of inequality in the United States has always been especially stark in the military. African American soldiers, for example, fought overseas in World War II against the ideology of racial supremacy in Nazi Germany, only to return home to racial segregation in the United States. Like other social institutions at the time, the military was a bastion of racist behaviors and policies. But the military is also a unique institution in that authority within it is intensely enforced from the top down, and, as a consequence, it is able to introduce and enforce new ideas and behaviors.

In 1948—long before the peak of the civil rights movement—President Truman issued an executive order to begin a swift process of racial integration in the military. Since then, the military has often taken the lead in promoting progressive racial policies, making it a particularly attractive career choice for African Americans, Latinos, and other minorities who face continuing discrimination in civilian employment.

Women and gays and lesbians have had a more mixed experience. The military first excluded women and then grudgingly allowed them entry to an often hostile "macho" environment in which sexism and sexual violence remain major concerns to this day. The pressure to avoid being either too feminine (defined as soft and unprepared for military life) or too masculine (therefore not womanly) makes the military a site of ongoing negotiation for women (Herbert 2000; MacKenzie 2015).

The military has lagged behind the broader society in its treatment of lesbian and gay soldiers. It banned gays and lesbians until 1993, when it adopted a "don't ask, don't tell" policy that allowed them to serve as long as they kept their sexual orientation a secret. The policy was repealed in 2010, and gays and lesbians may now serve openly. Beginning in 2017, transgender personnel, too, were officially allowed in the military. An attempt by the Trump administration to once again ban transgender personnel was overturned in a court ruling. Subsequent restrictive policies are being contested in the courts (Cooper and Gibbons-Neff 2018).

Class and Military Service Class distinctions have long marked military service in the United States. The nation's first national mandatory service (known as *conscription* or *the draft*) was instituted—and fiercely resisted—during the Civil War when both North and South allowed wealthy citizens to avoid service by hiring substitutes. In World War I substitutes were not allowed, but biased local draft boards sent a disproportionate number of poor and working-class people to war (Hodges 2016; Keith 2003). In World War II a more equitable lottery system was used, but during the Vietnam War class bias returned in the form of exemptions for college students, and medical deferments for well-connected individuals who were disproportionately middle and upper class. In 1973 the U.S. government ended required military service and instituted an all-volunteer force (Janowitz and Moskos 1979; Talbot and Oplinger 2014).

The military does not keep data on the family income of its recruits, but some studies suggest that the all-volunteer military draws disproportionately from working-class and lower-middle-class families. The poor (who often cannot meet the entry requirements), the upper middle class, and especially the wealthy are underrepresented (National Priorities Project 2011). To attract recruits who have limited job prospects and cannot afford a college education, the military highlights its education and training programs. Recruitment is considerably easier in periods of economic recession. Thus class inequality continues to mark the all-volunteer force.

Some sociologists have argued that the shift to an all-volunteer military has gradually changed military service from a widely shared experience to a specialized occupation isolated from society. Indeed, in recent years, the rate of military service among members of the U.S. Congress has been the lowest in history. Of the last four commanders-in-chief, none served on active duty. As of 2016, veterans made up only 7 percent of the

©Alexandre Fagundes/Alamy Stock Photo

An all-volunteer military provides employment opportunities, especially for working-class and lower-middle-class people with few options for good jobs. Given this economic bias, do you think an all-volunteer system is fair? Why or why not?

population, a decline from 18 percent in 1980 (Bialik 2017). Meanwhile, over 80 percent of new military recruits—disproportionately working class, people of color, from the South—have a family member who also served in the military, raising concerns about an emerging "soldier class" or "warrior caste" that, surveys show, is increasingly alienated from the civilian population (Schafer 2017).

The reliance on a small "soldier class" to carry out military duties has also had political consequences. It makes troops less likely to actively oppose a war (as draftees during the Vietnam War commonly did) and, by eliminating the risk of being drafted, may reduce civilian opposition to wars. The vast majority of Americans can remain disengaged from debates about war and the military because they and their loved ones are not directly affected (Schafer 2017). As Schafer (2017) notes, while appreciated, for many military personnel, the popular "Thank you for your service" greeting "carries with it the notion of a disengaged public for whom the wars and those who fight them are largely an abstraction" (10). Perhaps most important, if children of the more affluent and powerful are not a major component of the military, government officials may be less hesitant to put troops in harm's way (*Los Angeles Times* 2015).

While governments are clearly concerned about their citizens' physical security, they must help ensure their **economic security** as well, *the condition of having a stable means of financial support adequate to maintain a given standard of living.* We turn now to a consideration of the economy as a social institution and to the government's influence on economic life.

The Economy

We have already considered topics related to the economy, such as class inequality (Chapter 9), the world of work (Chapter 13), consumerism (Chapter 14), and the connection between types of communities and the economy (Chapter 15). Here we focus on the social nature of the economy and the role of government in relation to economic affairs.

The Economy as an Evolving Social Institution

The **economy** is *a social institution that includes a society's production, distribution, and consumption of goods and services.* Like other aspects of social life, economies are neither "natural" nor inevitable; they are created through human action and vary considerably over time and across cultures.

Because they are socially constructed, economies exist in many forms. In Chapter 15, we traced the evolution of economies from those based on hunting and gathering to today's information-based economies. As the name suggests, *hunter-gatherer* societies obtained food and other materials by hunting animals and gathering seeds, roots, fruits, and other foodstuffs. Often these were collective efforts in which nearly the entire community took part, sharing resources and serving as a single economic unit. This arrangement was an economy, though it lacked many of the elements we associate with today's wage-based economies, such as markets, buyers, sellers, and wages. When a hunter's kill was divided among community members, or when coastal dwellers exchanged some of their fish catch for the skins of animals taken by hunters living inland, these transactions had as much to do with establishing and affirming social bonds as they did with gaining access to goods (Polyani 1977).

Later, when plants and livestock became domesticated, paving the way for agricultural and pastoral economies, the family became the primary economic unit. Family members, including children, typically worked together on land they owned, shared, or sharecropped for landowners to produce food and other goods for use, trade, or sale. The family was the center of both work and consumption, in a model that still dominates in many parts of the world today.

When industrialization expanded in the nineteenth century, economic life became increasingly separated—culturally and physically—from other aspects of social life. People left their homes and families to earn wages in workplaces where social relationships were not tied to family or personal links. Home was now associated with consumption, and work with production.

Modern economies came increasingly to rely on the **corporation,** *a business that is treated legally as an entity separate from its owners.* Corporations have many of the rights of individuals—including the right to make contracts, incur debt, and engage in political speech—but their owners are not responsible for the corporation's obligations and liabilities and so corporations are able to take more risks. This has enabled corporations to grow substantially. Today, many are huge *multinational* (or *transnational) corporations* with facilities spread across the globe.

The Social Economy

Regardless of the type of economy, politics and culture affect economic life just as economic conditions influence politics and culture (Carruthers and Babb 2013; Granovetter 2017). Economic activities are inherently *social* activities requiring interaction, cooperation, coordination, and exchanges among individuals, organizations, and even governments. Max Weber ([1949] 2011) coined the term *social economics* to emphasize this connection between social and economic life, a connection we can view in relation to social cohesion, to culture, and to other social institutions.

Economies and Social Cohesion

First, economic life is social because economic relationships can take place only with a level of trust. As we saw in Chapter 1, Durkheim argued that social cohesion is necessary for the maintenance of a well-functioning society, and the same is true for economic life. Economic agreements—to purchase something, to provide a service, to pay for labor—will succeed only if the parties can trust each other to follow through. That is, a

on social theory

As Durkheim—whose ideas helped form the **structural-functionalist tradition**—saw, the trust that results from social cohesion is needed for an economy to function effectively. How is trust a part of your economic life?

social relationship must exist prior to the economic relationship. Generalized trust—sometimes called *precontractual solidarity*—assures us that obligations will be honored and disputes resolved to allow economic life to proceed smoothly. Faith in the rule of law and the legal system to resolve disputes is essential. Thus, when social relationships collapse, as in war and civil unrest, economies often collapse as well.

Economies and Culture A second reason economic life is social is that economies are embedded within and reflect the cultural values of a society (Granovetter 1985). For example, our society discourages the marketing of crack cocaine and of child pornography, even though they are often profitable ventures, because cultural values outweigh the opportunity for economic gain. Different cultures also value different features of economic life. In recent years, the United States usually has emphasized "free trade" and "free-market" principles that encourage the relative autonomy of the economic sphere and a highly individualistic competitive economy that holds out the possibility of some people getting rich. Other societies focus more on achieving freedom from want, directing the economy toward meeting collective human needs such as equal access to good schools, housing, and health care. In either case, economic priorities and policies are being filtered through broader cultural values.

Economies and Other Social Institutions

A third reason economic life is social is that the economy is intertwined with other social institutions. We saw in Chapter 13 how education and work are often closely connected. Another especially important relationship exists between the government and the economy.

Here is a simple example. Imagine you and some friends start a small business making accessories for cell phones. Being independent-minded entrepreneurs, you want to run your business your own way, without government interference. However, ironically, the very existence of your business and its success depend on government intervention and assistance at every step of the way:

- The government produces deeds and titles certifying the ownership of your building and the land it is on. (If you rent, your lease agreement complies with government regulations protecting both landlord and tenant.)
- A police force monitors and enforces your property rights, and firefighters help lower your risk of loss due to fire.
- A legal system provides a mechanism (courts) for settling disputes and enforcing your contracts.
- The government issues and enforces trademark protection for your company's name and logo. Copyright law protects some of the designs you use on your merchandise, and patents protect your innovative products.
- Public utilities commissions manage access to rights-of-way for power lines, water pipes, and fiber-optic cables through public spaces, making available the power you purchase from the electric company and other services.
- A government-financed system of roads and airports enables you to ship products anywhere.
- Government-issued currency enables you to carry out your business.

Because all contemporary economies depend on government intervention of one sort or another, the real question isn't *whether* the government will be involved in the economy but rather *how* and *to what extent.* Different societies answer these questions in ways that result in different economic systems.

Major Economic Systems

Capitalism and socialism have been the modern world's two dominant economic systems. Here we take a basic look at the idealized theory behind each system (see Table 16.3 for a summary); then, following this section, we consider the more complex economic conditions that exist in the real world.

Ideal Capitalism

Capitalism is *an economic system that emphasizes private ownership of the means of production, which are operated for profit.* Under capitalism, businesses that produce and sell goods and services are owned by private individuals, either directly or, through stock ownership, indirectly. These businesses seek to generate profit for their owners by selling goods and services at a price higher than the cost of producing them. Profits are the incentive for companies to be innovative and efficient. By providing a product or service many consumers want and keeping costs as low as possible, owners can maximize their profit. The profit incentive drives the capitalist system; profit is the yardstick by which success is measured.

Capitalism relies on competitive markets to operate successfully. Ideally, informed consumers get to choose between multiple providers who compete to offer the best product at the best price. Collectively, these purchasing choices decide the fate of various products and businesses. Meanwhile, workers look for

TABLE 16.3 IDEAL CHARACTERISTICS OF MAJOR ECONOMIC SYSTEMS

	Capitalism	Socialism
Major means of production	Owned privately	Owned publicly
Driving incentive	Personal profit	Public good
Economic structure	Markets	Government planning

jobs that offer the best wages, benefits, and conditions, and employers try to attract the talent they need at the lowest possible cost. The system as a whole emphasizes individual freedom: of owners to operate their business, consumers to make choices in purchasing, and workers to choose employment.

Ideal Socialism

Socialism is *an economic system that emphasizes public ownership of the major means of production, which are operated to meet human needs and promote social justice.* Major industries—energy production, communications, banking, health care, and the like—are publicly owned through the government. (Smaller businesses providing retail consumer goods and services may be privately owned.) Ideally, instead of focusing on generating profits for owners, these state-owned industries meet basic human needs by making essential goods and services available to all citizens. Free or subsidized public goods and services can include health care, education, housing, day care, public transportation, and other essentials. These are paid for, in part, through a system of progressive taxation (which taxes higher incomes at a higher rate), thereby limiting economic inequality.

A socialist system relies on government to coordinate key economic functions. Since they are nonprofit and able to eliminate the wasteful costs of marketplace competition (advertising, duplication of services and administrative bureaucracy, excessive executive salaries, and so on), well-functioning socialist governments can help meet basic needs efficiently. Because they make major economic decisions in the name of the public good to promote social justice, they can take into account the collective benefits of labor rights and environmental protection, for example, rather than just their costs for individual private firms. The system as a whole emphasizes the collective good by directing resources to meet basic human needs.

Often confused with socialism, *communism* can refer to both an economic and a political system. Economically, communism is an egalitarian system in which property is owned collectively and class inequality is nonexistent. Some simple hunter-gatherer societies can be considered a form of primitive communism, but no modern economies have been truly communist. Politically, communism is a system associated with Russian revolutionary Vladimir Lenin, in which an elite political party supposedly leads the nation toward an egalitarian (thus communist) future. The Soviet Union and China were communist societies in the political sense—led by a communist party—but not in the economic sense of a classless society with collective ownership of the means of production.

The realities of capitalism and socialism are more complicated than the simple ideal theories we have just outlined. Neither system has worked in the way economic theory suggests, in part because economies are affected by broad social forces, especially inequalities in power.

Capitalism in Reality

Adam Smith, capitalism's best-known theorist and advocate, argued in his classic book *The Wealth of Nations* (1776) that society was best served by self-interested competition, carried out within a set of basic rules in the form of laws and contracts. Capitalism has indeed proved very successful at unleashing productivity and innovation. A competitive marketplace motivates producers to search constantly for new goods and services to offer consumers, promoting innovation and reacting quickly to new market conditions and needs. Pursuing higher profits by lowering costs motivates producers to look constantly for ways to be more efficient and productive.

"Free-market" capitalist theory argues that governments should ensure the conditions necessary for businesses to operate and then leave them free to function as they see fit (which is why it is also called *laissez-faire* capitalism—*laissez faire* is French for "leave alone"). Free-market adherents often oppose labor, environmental, and consumer protections, all of which add to the cost of doing business.

Nineteenth-century industrial capitalism is probably the closest we have come to a fully free-market system, and in many ways it was a disaster. One problem is that without government intervention and regulation, unfettered capitalism tends to produce a concentration of enormous wealth and power in the hands of a small elite who can then use that power to prevent others from competing fairly, undermining the very premise of a capitalist system. Shrewd late-nineteenth-century U.S. industrialists—"captains of industry" to their admirers—became more commonly known as "robber barons" for their unscrupulous business behavior. They used their early success to build "trusts," powerful companies that unfairly forced out competitors and monopolized key industries, including railroads (Cornelius Vanderbilt), steelmaking (Andrew Carnegie), and oil (John D. Rockefeller). These industrialists then used their resources to help undermine democracy by financing political campaigns and improperly influencing government decision making. As a result, government provided them with special favors and enormous giveaways of public resources such as vast tracts of land for building commercial railroads.

©Ross D. Franklin/AP Images

In recent decades, U.S. capitalism has produced enormous rewards for the affluent while millions of workers struggle just to survive. The result has been a dramatic growth in economic inequality and worker campaigns to increase the minimum wage.

While producing great wealth for a few in the period during the late nineteenth century known as the Gilded Age, this system also produced enormous hardship and poverty for many. Powerful industrialists often subjected their workers to grueling working conditions, including 12-hour workdays, six days a week, for poverty wages. Exhaustion coupled with inadequate safety equipment often made work deadly. Steel mill workers sometimes roasted alive in spills of molten metal. Workers—sometimes children—were decapitated or had limbs torn from their bodies by rapidly moving machinery. Early reformers documented thousands of such cases (MacLaury 2011). Meanwhile, the advantages some families reaped from early industrial activity were passed from generation to generation, fueling a cycle of inequality. To this day, the names Vanderbilt, Carnegie, and Rockefeller are icons of inherited wealth and power.

A variety of social movements of the late 1800s and early 1900s pressed for more government intervention in the economy. In the United States, these included the early labor movement, the Populist Movement (which included farmers and small-business owners oppressed by the large business trusts), and the Progressive Movement (which advocated various economic, political, and social reforms, including workplace safety). These movements pressured federal and state governments to introduce reforms, including outlawing anticompetitive monopolies and cartels, setting wage and safety standards, and protecting the right of workers to form unions. Eventually, government intervention limited the power of industrialists, protected the basic rights of workers, and, many historians argue, helped save capitalism from itself (Schlesinger 2003).

Reforming Capitalism

Governments around the world have repeatedly intervened since then to address the excesses of capitalism and to shore up unstable capitalist economies subject to cycles of "boom and bust," or rapid growth followed by collapse. The second period of major government intervention in the United States took place in the wake of the Great Depression of the 1930s. A variety of causes contributed to this worst economic depression, or deep economic slump, of the twentieth century. One source was the 1929 stock market crash, which followed a boom in speculation (high-risk investment in stocks or other ventures in the pursuit of high profits). Other factors were the collapse of thousands of U.S. banks that cost millions of workers their savings and high levels of economic inequality that helped undermine the economy.

Elected in 1932 following this calamity, President Franklin Roosevelt did not respond by implementing socialism in the form of a government takeover of banks and major industry. Instead, the New Deal policies he introduced in 1933 were intended to revive the economy and help stabilize capitalism. Though business leaders opposed many of his reforms, the New Deal was extremely popular and included the following:

- New spending for public works programs that created jobs by building roads, dams, and national parks. (Later, massive military spending for World War II created even more jobs and an endless demand for military supplies.)
- New social programs, notably Social Security, that helped create a social safety net to protect modest- and low-income workers from economic setbacks.
- New government regulation and intervention in the financial system, such as the creation of the Federal Deposit Insurance Corporation (FDIC), which insures bank deposits.
- New worker protections through the Wagner Act, which recognized the right to form unions in the workplace and to strike for better wages and working conditions.

These reforms became a central feature of the U.S. economic system during the period of post–World War II prosperity.

By the 1980s, though, the global economy had enabled large businesses to move production to foreign countries and flee government regulation, giving them greater leverage in negotiations with government. Employers aggressively opposed labor unions, undermining their political power. In this new climate, conservatives called for the deregulation of business, financial institutions, and the economy. In the 1980s, deregulation of savings and loan institutions (S&Ls), which had been limited to providing savings accounts and mortgage loans, allowed them to operate more like banks, but without any of the regulations that governed banks. This deregulation contributed to a new financial crisis in which more than 700 S&Ls failed, requiring government action to clean up and stabilize the industry through new regulations. The S&L scandal cost taxpayers at least $125 billion and led to some bank executives serving time in prison (Black 2013; Pizzo, Fricker, and Muolo 1989).

The Housing Bubble and Global Economic Crisis

The S&L crisis of the 1980s was small compared to the global financial meltdown, rooted in the housing industry, that occurred in 2007–2009 with effects that continued for more than a decade (Financial Crisis Inquiry Commission 2011; Foster and Magdoff 2009; Friedman and Posner 2009; Sorkin 2010; U.S. Senate Permanent Subcommittee on Investigations 2011). A closer look at this most recent crisis reveals the economy as an integrated social system—from micro-level consumers to macro-level global investors—that can sometimes be dysfunctional.

Sources of the Crisis The 2007–2009 global economic crisis—sometimes referred to as the Great Recession—stemmed from several factors:

- Facing stagnant wages, many ordinary U.S. households relied increasingly on credit. Meanwhile the world's richest investors searched for investments that would yield steady profits, eventually buying much of this consumer debt.
- Deregulation in the financial services industry enabled commercial banks to engage in high-risk speculation, which had been prohibited before.

- The financial services industry developed new forms of complex and unregulated investment devices (known as *derivatives*) that led to massive high-risk speculation.
- Corporations engaged in misleading and fraudulent behavior. Some of the world's largest financial firms—including JPMorgan Chase, Citibank, and Merrill Lynch—had often been caught laundering money, defrauding customers, and committing accounting fraud. In most such cases, the firms agreed to pay large fines—sometimes well over $100 million—but did not have to admit to any wrongdoing. But when fraudulent tactics were used in the housing market, the impact was much more widespread.

When these factors combined, the result was disastrous.

The Housing Bubble and Burst A "bubble" occurs when the price of a good or service is overinflated. The housing crisis of 2007-2009 was made possible by social relationships between various parties in a chain that connected individual homeowners to global investors, linking micro-level economic decisions with macro-level economic forces:

- Homebuyers acquired cheap mortgages featuring low rates in the early months that increased dramatically over the life of the loan. Some borrowers used poor judgment in entering these contracts; others were greedy and bought more expensive houses than they should have. Many, though, either did not understand the conditions of their mortgage or were defrauded by unscrupulous lenders who misled applicants and approved high-risk mortgages to clearly unqualified borrowers.
- Some lenders used deceptive or fraudulent sales tactics to entice borrowers into mortgages they could not afford. Lenders had an incentive to make as many loans as possible, regardless of people's ability to pay, because they sold the individual loans to investment banks. The banks preferred these risky, so-called subprime loans because they carried higher interest rates and, thus, the potential for higher profits.
- Investment banks bought a large number of mortgages from lenders, combined these with other debt, such as student loans and credit card debt, and then sold pieces of this debt as a type of derivative called *collateralized debt obligations* (CDOs). Major investment firms such as Goldman Sachs were selling CDOs to investors as a safe investment, while simultaneously betting that CDOs they didn't own would fail.
- Ratings agencies (Standard & Poor's, Moody's, Fitch)—which are paid by the investment banks—evaluated CDOs and often gave them the highest possible grade, AAA, obscuring their actual high-risk nature.
- Investors from around the world in search of steady profits purchased CDOs, believing them to be safe investments, thereby generating massive profits for the investment banks that sold them.

In the short term, everyone in the chain benefited. Homebuyers had a chance to experience the American Dream of homeownership. Lenders, rating agencies, investment banks, and investors made money. Wall Street executives and traders, especially, became enormously rich on bonuses they generated from these often-tainted deals. For example, between 2000 and 2007, the CEO of the Lehman Brothers investment firm, Richard Fuld, took home about $529 million (Sterngold 2010).

Since almost anyone could get a mortgage in this system, the housing market boomed, creating an artificial bubble in which housing prices nearly doubled in less than 10 years. The FBI and some leading economists warned of massive and widespread mortgage fraud, but those warnings went unheeded and the government failed to step in to regulate the industry. In fact, many major government regulators and economic advisors were former finance industry executives. Henry Paulson, for example, was paid $35 million in 2005 as CEO of investment firm Goldman Sachs while it was issuing billions of dollars in high-risk CDOs, and in 2006 he was appointed secretary of the U.S. Treasury (Sloan 2007).

By 2007 the housing bubble had burst. When homebuyers could not keep up with mortgage payments, families lost their homes and were evicted (Desmond 2016). Investment banks found themselves still holding tens of thousands of mortgages whose values were plummeting and that could not be sold. Investors began losing their money. The impact of these failures rippled through the economy as banks and the insurance companies that insured them teetered on the brink of bankruptcy. The stock market plunged, and everyone from major institutional investors to individuals with retirement accounts invested in stocks suffered

The housing crisis of 2007–2009 disrupted life for many families. Here, Cynthia and Michael French of Redding, California, react after being served an eviction notice. The couple developed financial problems when Cynthia's state disability compensation ended and Michael later lost his job.

major losses. Unemployment increased as firms facing financial trouble began laying off workers.

At the height of the crisis, the federal government responded with massive spending to bail out major commercial firms and stimulate the economy. After years of criticism that the U.S. Department of Justice had not pursued Wall Street criminals aggressively enough, the government reached an agreement with JPMorgan Chase in 2013 directing the firm to pay the largest civil fine ever: $13 billion for its role in knowingly bundling "toxic" loans and selling them to unsuspecting investors (Barrett and Fitzpatrick 2013). The government did not prosecute any of the corporate executives who helped destroy their companies, wrecked the economy, and walked away with the fortunes they accumulated carrying out these actions. After the crisis, U.S. banks became bigger, more concentrated, and more powerful than ever before. They have been able to use their political clout to successfully resist any significant reform of Wall Street.

Periodic crises lead many observers to conclude that capitalist markets seem to operate best when they are well regulated to prevent fraud and abuse by powerful economic players. Canada, for example, had much stronger regulation of its banking industry and largely avoided the economic crisis that affected the U.S. banking industry. In addition, capitalism seems to require a robust social safety net to assist those left behind in the competitive marketplace. Critics of these measures, however, see such developments as an abandonment of capitalist ideals and the encroachment of socialism.

Socialism in Reality

By prioritizing social needs over personal profit, a socialist economy can effectively reduce inequality and drastically reduce or even eliminate some social problems commonly found in capitalist economies, such as homelessness, lack of health care, and lack of affordable access to higher education (Lebowitz 2010). But as the most prominent experiment with socialism—the former Soviet Union—has illustrated, this system can also lead to disaster.

Soviet-Style Socialism Russia was an agricultural society, lagging far behind Western industrialized nations in economic development, when the Russian Revolution of 1917 ended its monarchy and eventually brought an authoritarian communist government into power. This government began a massive transformation of the economy that introduced gigantic industrialization campaigns, dramatically raised living standards, and catapulted the newly formed Soviet Union into a global superpower in a single generation. But, especially under the leadership of Joseph Stalin, the authoritarian government also used its power to ruthlessly suppress political dissent, condemning those accused of anti-Soviet or anticommunist activity to remote penal labor camps (*gulags*), where prisoners often died or disappeared. These camps played a key economic function for the then-industrializing Soviet Union, which exploited the labor of millions of imprisoned criminals and political dissidents to work in mines, on infrastructure projects like roads and bridges, and on other development efforts.

By the 1960s, the economic role of the gulags had declined dramatically. However, the government's significant expenditures on a large military to compete with its Cold War adversary, the United States, worsened the bureaucratic inefficiencies of centralized economic planning right up to the country's formal dissolution in 1991. Economic inequality in the Soviet Union and the Soviet-dominated countries of Eastern Europe was very low by Western standards, but so too was the standard of living.

Under the leadership of Mikhail Gorbachev in the late 1980s, the Soviet Union sought to simultaneously reform its economic structure (*perestroika*) while introducing more democratic freedoms (*glasnost*). The changes proved too radical, and the Soviet Union disintegrated into separate nation-states. Since the collapse of Soviet-style socialism, Russia and other Eastern European nations formerly under Soviet control have experienced widely divergent fates. With the privatization of public resources, capitalism has created enormous wealth and even some billionaires (sometimes due to rampant fraud and corruption). However, rising unemployment has pushed millions of other people into poverty and created a vast new set of social problems, including skyrocketing alcoholism and a resurgence of tuberculosis, a disease typically associated with poverty.

A basic problem with Soviet-style socialism was that it was administered by an authoritarian government with no accountability. Socialism coupled with democracy, however, has achieved greater success.

Democratic Socialism Whereas capitalism needs government intervention to curb the excesses of concentrated economic power, socialism needs a democratic political system to curb the excesses of concentrated government power. Scandinavian countries that feature both democratic political systems and socialist economies are among the most affluent and democratic countries in the world.

One example is Norway, a constitutional monarchy in which real power rests in a parliamentary system where a half-dozen major political parties regularly compete for power. In the three decades following World War II, the country developed a system that features state ownership of major industrial, financial, and communications firms and a major role for labor unions in deciding workplace issues. It also includes free universal health care, nearly free higher education, and a generous lifelong social welfare system that includes 12 months of paid leave for new parents. Combined, these programs make up about half the country's goods and services. Since the 1970s, Norway has maintained its programs in part because the government, rather than private corporations, controls its major oil and natural gas resources. But during this period it has decentralized control of its government assets, allowing local and regional authorities to adapt social and economic programs to their own particular needs. It has also introduced more market-based competition as it has become a significant participant in the global economy. While the global economic crisis caused much of the industrialized world to stagger, close regulation of its financial sector, large public-sector employment, astute management of natural resources, and a culture of financial thrift largely insulated Norway from the worst effects.

The Rise of Mixed Economies

Our brief survey of economies shows that four ideal types of political-economic systems exist. They differ based on the degree of government intervention in the economy and the presence or absence of a democratic political system (see Table 16.4). We have already considered capitalist democracies, state socialism, and democratic socialism. The final form of political-economic system is authoritarian capitalism.

China is an authoritarian capitalist system. Over the past several decades, China has allowed many aspects of market capitalism and encouraged foreign investment, though state-run enterprises still play a major role in the economy. However, China's leaders maintain strict political control by suppressing dissent, most famously during the 1989 uprisings in Beijing's Tiananmen Square, which unsuccessfully called for democratic reforms. Russia is also an authoritarian capitalist system, combining private ownership with authoritarian leadership.

Today, the world's largest and most vibrant economies are all mixed economies to varying degrees, and the line between socialism and capitalism is becoming murkier every year. **Mixed economies** *contain elements of both market-based capitalism and the significant government intervention associated with socialism.* Successful socialist nations have learned to harness the power of markets to spur innovation and respond to consumer needs, while still directing key industries to meet social needs, guarding public resources for the common good, and providing a broad social safety net for citizens. Successful capitalist nations have learned that reasonable government regulation of business and markets can help protect against abuses of concentrated economic power, that a social safety net blunts the excesses of capitalist inequality, and that government intervention can help limit capitalism's characteristic boom-and-bust cycles.

Countries use a variety of approaches in setting up their social-welfare safety nets. One classic categorization sorts welfare states around the world into three broad types (Esping-Andersen 1990, 2002):

- ***Liberal welfare states,*** like those in the United States, Canada, and Australia, generally provide only minimal benefits, such as K–12 public schooling, to everyone (these are called "universal" benefits). Instead, these countries target public assistance at people whose incomes are low enough to qualify (these are called "means-tested" benefits). In such contexts, welfare often comes with a social stigma.
- ***Conservative/corporatist welfare states,*** like those in France, Germany, and Italy, provide universal social insurance that is an entitlement, not a form of means-tested assistance. Benefits are typically based on contributions already made through taxes. Often, both the contributions and benefits vary based on a person's income. Because such programs are universal, welfare does not carry a significant social stigma. The goal of social insurance is often to support traditional families–for example, by providing subsidies that enable a parent to stay home and care for children.
- ***Social-democratic welfare states,*** like those in Scandinavian countries, offer high levels of universal benefits, including free health care and free college education, in exchange for higher taxes. Such welfare programs are universal and broadly embraced. Benefits are aimed at making people independent–for example, state-run child care helps parents to remain in the labor force.

©Comstock/PunchStock

TABLE 16.4 BASIC POLITICAL AND ECONOMIC SYSTEMS

Economic System		Political System: Democratic	Political System: Authoritarian
	Capitalist	**Capitalist democracies** have democratic political systems and private ownership of industry with modest state intervention in the economy. Example: United States	**Authoritarian capitalism** is found in countries that have considerable private ownership of industry and market-based economies but few civil rights or political freedoms. Example: China
	Socialist	**Democratic socialism** is found in countries that have democratic political systems, public ownership of some key industries, and significant state intervention in the economy. Example: Norway	**State socialism** features an authoritarian government that dominates a largely centralized economy. Example: North Korea

All three types of mixed economy represent an attempt to promote citizens' health and well-being while harnessing the benefits of markets.

Convergence theory *suggests that capitalist and socialist economies are becoming increasingly similar.* Globalization appears to have accelerated the process, introducing competitive markets to economies around the world and making them more capitalistic. Globalization has also made many capitalist economies more volatile and vulnerable to the pressures of competition from other nations. This is in large part the reason for the decline of manufacturing industries in the United States and the global financial crisis. Governments in capitalist economies have responded to such economic difficulties by intervening more actively in economic affairs, a tendency typically associated with socialist economies. The result has been the global rise of mixed economies.

A Changing World

POPULISM AND THE THREAT TO DEMOCRACY

Populist leaders and movements have surged in recent years, often invoking the rhetoric of democracy, while simultaneously engaging in behaviors that chip away and undermine democratic norms and institutions. These movements have sometimes emerged from the political left, but they are usually from the right. Some are extreme, producing tyranny; others are mostly moderate in their methods and aims. Populists of recent years include Venezuela's Hugo Chávez, Russia's Vladimir Putin, the Philippines' Rodrigo Duterte, Hungary's Viktor Orbán, Turkey's Recep Tayyip Erdoğan, India's Narendra Modi, a variety of nationalist parties across Europe, and, of course, Donald Trump. Far from being unprecedented, such movements have popped up repeatedly during times of historical discontent and they tend to have some common features (Friedman 2017; Judis 2016; Mudde and Kaltwasser 2017; Müller 2016; Oliver and Rahn 2016).

Most political ideologies articulate a vision for how people should organize their government, economy, and society, but populism is defined more by what it is against, rather than what it is for. Populists advocate throwing out elites while rarely specifying who or what should replace them. In fact, populism thrives on intensifying divisions rather than finding solutions. It typically divides the world into "us" versus "them," contrasting supposedly authentic, moral, "real" citizens against some "other" used as a scapegoat for society's ills, often foreigners, immigrants, racial minorities, and economic elites. Not just a partisan divide in the political arena, populists oppose establishment forces in all aspects of social life, including the media and popular culture, education, and the economy. Stylistically, appealing to "real" common people often involves simplistic, crude, and coarse language and the calculated embrace of appearing uneducated. This helps distinguish populists from the sophisticated, refined "elites" against which they battle.

Even in power, populists paint themselves as victims of attacks, thriving in the underdog role. This victim mentality helps to justify their unconventional behavior, violating social and political norms, sometimes lying and breaking the law, all in the name of advancing a greater cause. Populist movements usually have charismatic, authoritarian leaders who often attack the free press and the courts (both pillars of democratic societies), along with any others forces that are seen as a threat to their power.

When populists demonize their opponents, there can be no compromise or cooperation. Consequently, populists are often short-lived. Their simple incendiary rhetoric is good fuel for a fight, but actually governing and getting things done requires compromise and negotiation. However, moderation risks losing populist support based on moral absolutes, while continued provocations risk gridlock with opponents that prevents any real change from occurring. That recipe often leads to a loss of support.

Because they depend on the support of "the people" for their legitimacy, populists must find ways to explain away the absence of that support, claiming polls are rigged, voter fraud is rampant, news is "fake," the media are the "enemy of the people," protesters are actually paid professionals, and secret conspiracies aimed at thwarting their efforts are everywhere. Their promotion of propaganda based on misinformation and lies helps to undermine the essential role of an informed citizenry in democratic life. The most recent round of populism has been fueled by underlying social forces such as globalization and growing inequality, as well as by the rise of social media that populists have used effectively to promote their cause. By covering the rise of right-wing populism and extremism, the mainstream media inadvertently amplified their messages (Phillips 2018).

Surveys find that most Americans believe that politicians engaged in misconduct will not be held accountable, that Donald Trump lacks respect for democratic institutions, and that people who disagree politically can't agree on basic facts. Ironically, a majority does not even have "trust and confidence in the wisdom of American people in making political decisions." Falling far short of democratic ideals, there is widespread public support for "significant change" in the fundamental "design and structure" of American government but there is no consensus on what those changes should be (Pew Research Center 2018c).

Populism exacerbates the loss of faith in democratic institutions (Mounk 2018). Believing that the media are not telling the truth; that the economic system is "rigged" against ordinary people; that elections are tainted by widespread voter fraud; that judges constantly distort the law; that universities promote political correctness rather than pursue honest truth; that complicated conspiracies explain political developments, are all signs of problems for a democratic society because they suggest a loss of faith in basic democratic norms, processes, and institutions. Some contend they indicate, as one book is titled, *How Democracies Die* (Levitsky and Ziblatt, 2018).

In the face of such challenges, some observers call for political and economic reform, such as eliminating laws that make it difficult to vote, abolishing the Electoral College and electing the president by popular vote, and investing in infrastructure, education, and health to address the underlying inequalities that generate discontent (Dionne, Ornstein, and Mann 2017). Others call for a more fundamental "reckoning with twenty-first-century questions: whether we have ever been democratic, and whether the versions of capitalism that have emerged in the last forty years are compatible with democracy" (Purdy 2018). They contend that deep-seated problems require more-radical solutions of the sort that the labor and civil rights movements advocated in their day and the New Deal legislation of the Roosevelt administration enacted amidst the Great Depression.

Populism taps into—and intensifies—widespread discontent about the state of our politics and economy. The actions of citizens in the coming years will determine whether or not such anger can be channeled into productive efforts that reinvigorate democratic life and bring about meaningful change.

thinking sociologically about
Politics and the Economy

culture

- Cultural values help shape both political and economic systems.
- A broad sense of insecurity and a culture of fear help support a large investment in the military.
- Differing cultural approaches to individual freedom and social justice inform capitalist and socialist economies.

structure

- The political structure of a society shapes the possibilities for political action, creating specific constraints and opportunities for individuals and groups to engage in political action.
- Similarly, economic structures help shape the opportunities people have.

power

- Politics in the struggle over power decides priorities and policies for society.
- The type of government helps determine who has power in society.
- The decisions governments make can have a profound impact on levels of inequality, especially since the way in which economies are organized can either increase or decrease economic inequality.
- Socialist economies make reducing inequality a priority, whereas capitalist economies accept greater levels of inequality and prioritize the free pursuit of profit.

REVIEW, REFLECT, AND APPLY

Looking Back

1. Politics is the arena in which societies make collective decisions about priorities and policies, and government is the focus of political activity. Governments claim a monopoly on the legitimate use of force in a given territory. Contemporary forms of government include democracies, authoritarian governments, and monarchies. Political culture influences whether and how we become involved in politics.
2. Pluralism, power elite theory, and class domination theory each explain power and politics in a different way. Political involvement in the United States reflects class inequality: people in the middle class are more active than those in the working class, and the political system responds most readily to concerns of the affluent.
3. As part of the national security state, the size, reach, and financial resources of the U.S. military are unrivaled. But a politics of fear continues to shape how we think about the world, leading to policies that would otherwise be unlikely to be adopted. People are socialized to accept war, and recruits are resocialized to become soldiers. The military reflects some of the social inequality that exists in society. Sociology and the social sciences have made significant contributions to better understanding and combating terrorism.
4. The economy is a social institution that includes a society's production, distribution, and consumption of goods and services. Economies reflect the cultural values and political priorities of the societies in which they exist.
5. Capitalism and socialism have been the modern world's two dominant economic systems. The ideals of both these systems contrast with complicated realities that expose each of their shortcomings, including the periodic crisis of capitalism and the repressive nature of state socialism. Capitalist and socialist economies have become more similar to each other, producing mixed economies that incorporate elements of each system.
6. The rise of populist movements worldwide has tapped into—and intensified—anger about how governments operate, posing new challenges to democratic institutions.

Critical Thinking: Questions and Activities

1. Do you feel prepared to participate in politics? Do you vote? How can you explain your specific engagement with—or disengagement from—the world of politics?
2. Why do you think the United States spends so much more on the military than any other country? Do you think this is a wise investment of resources for the country? Why or why not?
3. What are the basic differences between capitalist and socialist economies? Do you think the U.S. economic system is best described as capitalist, socialist, or mixed? Why?
4. The 2016 election of Donald Trump put a capitalist billionaire in the office of president for the first time in U.S. history. What do you know about his administration's approach to economic policy so far? Do you approve of these policies? Explain. Where would these policies fall in the typologies of economies presented in this chapter?
5. Are you optimistic about the future of democracy in the United States? Why or why not? What changes, if any, do you think need to happen to repair widespread discontent with our system of government?

Key Terms

authoritarian government (p. 412) a government that typically features self-appointed leaders who exert great control over the lives of citizens, which includes severely limiting their civil liberties.

capitalism (p. 430) an economic system that emphasizes private ownership of the means of production, which are operated for profit.

class domination theory (p. 418) a theory that suggests that political power is concentrated in the hands of the rich, who own or control a large share of the nation's economic resources.

convergence theory (p. 435) a theory that suggests capitalist and socialist economies are becoming increasingly similar.

corporation (p. 429) a business that is treated legally as an entity separate from its owners.

democracy (p. 412) a political system in which the right to vote is widespread and government leaders are selected through multiparty elections.

economic security (p. 429) the condition of having a stable means of financial support adequate to maintain a given standard of living.

economy (p. 429) a social institution that includes a society's production, distribution, and consumption of goods and services.

government (p. 412) the system by which authority is exercised over a specific territory.

mixed economies (p. 435) economies that contain elements of both market-based capitalism and the significant government intervention associated with socialism.

monarchy (p. 412) a system of government headed by a single person, the monarch, who typically inherits the position as a member of a ruling family.

national security state (p. 422) a government dominated by powerful military, foreign policy, and intelligence agencies.

pluralist theory (p. 417) a theory that argues that political power is fragmented among many different competing groups.

plurality voting (p. 413) a "winner-take-all" electoral system in which the candidate with the most votes wins the office being contested.

political socialization (p. 414) the inculcation of basic norms and expectations about political life and attitudes toward involvement in politics.

politics (p. 411) the struggle over power.

power (p. 411) the ability to bring about an intended outcome, even when opposed by others.

power elite theory (p. 417) a theory that suggests that political power is concentrated in the hands of a small dominant group of business, government, and military leaders.

proportional representation (p. 413) an electoral system in which parties are awarded seats in government based on the percentage of votes they receive in an election.

socialism (p. 431) an economic system that emphasizes public ownership of the major means of production, which are operated to meet human needs and promote social justice.

spiral of silence (p. 416) a theory that explains how people keep quiet about controversial issues when they think their opinions are not widely shared, in order to avoid social isolation.

state terrorism (p. 424) political violence directed at civilians by governments.

terrorism (p. 424) politically motivated violence that intentionally targets noncombatants.

war (p. 421) organized armed conflict among two or more specially trained military groups.

©Matt McClain/The Washington Post/Getty Images

17 Social Change: Globalization, Population, and Social Movements

looking AHEAD

How has globalization affected your experience of **culture**?

How will the coming changes in the population **structure** affect social life in your lifetime?

What are the sources of **power** in the social movements that are important to you?

©Johnrochaphoto/China/Alamy Stock Photo

Twenty-three-year-old Feng Jianme had no idea that a picture of her would help end China's one-child policy. In 2012, while she was seven months pregnant with her second child, government family planning agents forcibly injected Feng with a chemical that killed the fetus and then induced her to give birth. This procedure violated Chinese law, which prohibited abortion after six months. Outraged by this abuse of power, Feng's sister posted photos on the internet of Feng lying in her hospital bed next to her dead baby. The graphic pictures went viral on Sina Weibo, China's version of Twitter, and then circulated around the globe. Some of the officials responsible for the death were fired, and the government formally apologized. But the damage to the controversial policy's public image had been done. The incident helped galvanize a long-simmering protest movement against the policy, which ultimately was replaced with a two-child policy in 2016.

Implemented in 1979, the one-child policy had been one of China's responses to an internal population explosion. Officials had feared that drastic population growth would outstrip China's resources, creating economic and environmental catastrophes and derailing the government's attempts to improve people's standard of living. The family planning policy limited many women to having one child, especially in urban areas, although there were numerous exceptions. Also, families could pay a hefty fine to have a second child, an option Feng Jianme could not afford. The policy had long been opposed by people who resented the government's intrusion into the personal lives of citizens, and Feng's case—elevated by the global exposure it received via social media—was another factor that contributed to the policy's eventual repeal (Fong 2016). Once the policy was removed, more families did have a second child. However, the country's overall birth rate declined a bit as more urban, educated women chose to not have children at all (Fincher 2018).

The case of China's one-child policy highlights three areas of contemporary social change that we examine in this chapter: globalization, population change, and social movements. These forces represent types of change, as well as being catalysts for further social change.

The theme of social change is highlighted throughout this book because change is an important aspect of social life and an essential topic of sociological inquiry. Our world is in transition, and sociology helps us understand these ongoing developments. At its best, sociology can inform our efforts to promote positive social change. In this chapter, we explore examples of contemporary change. First, however, we consider some broad features of social change itself.

Social Change: Structure and Culture

Social change is *the modification of structure or cultural patterns over time.* Structural change includes shifting patterns of behavior and interaction. Cultural change involves the transformation of values, beliefs, knowledge, and norms, as well as the introduction and adoption of new cultural objects, such as new technologies.

Characteristics of Change

Although social change covers a broad range of behaviors and cultural objects, we can nevertheless make some generalizations about it. First, change is continuous—society is always changing, never static. Despite this continuous change, however, certain aspects of society persist. Second, change occurs at different levels, from micro to meso to macro. Third, change usually is not planned; often it is unintended. And fourth, in most cases, change is resisted by certain segments of society.

Change Is Continuous but Partial "Nothing endures but change," observed Greek philosopher Heraclitus 2,500 years ago. Indeed, because society is not static, change is a *continuous* feature of social life and a major focus of sociology

(Harper and Leicht 2016; Weinstein 2010). People must constantly reproduce social structures and cultural norms, and their actions can alter society. This is part of the interplay between structure and action that is so central to a sociological perspective.

Although change is continuous, the *pace* of change varies considerably. Sometimes change is slow and difficult to perceive as it is happening. Long periods of human history were characterized by stability and slow incremental change. Individuals could expect to live as generations of ancestors had, experiencing a similar lifestyle, employed in similar sorts of labor, and holding similar cultural values, beliefs, and norms. But other historical eras have featured a frantic pace of change. As we saw in Chapter 1, sociology first emerged in the nineteenth century as an effort to understand a period of particularly rapid and widespread change. At the time, industrialization, urbanization, and democratic movements were among other forces dramatically altering the Western social landscape. Today, we are once again living in a period when the pace of social change is swift and highly visible. (The Sociology Works box examines how sociology majors are doing in a changing job market.)

Though continuous, social change is always *partial,* and certain aspects of social life are persistent. One central reason for the existence of cultural traditions, organizations, and social institutions is to help ensure that they outlive any particular individuals and provide society with some stability and permanence. As a result, some structural patterns and cultural perspectives linger even as others change. For example, the U.S. government today is vastly different from the government in power at the nation's founding, yet key structural features such as the three separate branches of government have provided relative stability and continuity for more than two centuries. Also, the central cultural values that informed the creation of the U.S. government, such as democracy and personal freedom, continue to be important, even though citizens' interpretation of those values has changed significantly since the eighteenth century. In short, continuity coexists with social change.

Change Occurs at Different Levels One helpful way to think about various types of structural change is to consider the *level* at which a given change occurs (Harper and Leicht 2016). Changes that originate at various macro, meso, or micro levels can affect other levels. For example, free trade agreements among multiple nations occur at a transnational, or world, level. However, the impact of such changes can trickle down to individual societies and their economies, as well as to specific companies and in turn to those firms' employees. Conversely, some changes start at the micro level and eventually have worldwide implications. Whatever the direction of change, humans often initiate change unwittingly, and the change they create is frequently unintended.

Change Is Often Unintended A **social trend** happens *when many individuals act independently but similarly.* Often the cumulative—and unintentional—effect of such behavior is to produce social change.

An interplay between individual action and larger social forces usually propels any social trend. For example, as we saw in Chapter 15, in the post-World War II era many U.S. couples decided to move from cities to suburbs. Individual couples did not start out wanting to change society; rather, they acted for personal reasons. Collectively, though, their behavior led to social change. Importantly, people's choices during this period were significantly influenced by outside social forces, such as the prosperous postwar economy and the government's decision to use tax credits to encourage homeownership. Structural and cultural forces influenced individual actions; in turn, the cumulative effect of those actions helped create social change.

In addition to the inadvertent change caused by social trends, many human actions have **unintended consequences,** *results that are unplanned and unforeseen.* For example, because people increasingly get their news and information on the internet for free, newspapers have lost paid subscriptions and much of their advertising as sources of revenue, leading to drastic personnel cuts in many newsrooms (McChesney and Pickard 2011).

Change Is Often Resisted Change is often resisted by one segment of society or another. Sometimes, for example, cultural change poses a challenge to deeply held values, as when growing secularization within a society threatens religious communities. Sometimes social change brings an end to meaningful ways of life, as when residential development destroys the longstanding routines and rhythms of a rural community. In other cases, people simply are comfortable with the status quo and uneasy about new ways of doing things, such as using new technologies for

Cell phones are used virtually everywhere in U.S. society, creating a new driving hazard as an unintended consequence.

CORE CONCEPTS CHALLENGE *How has the advent of cell phones affected U.S.* ***culture****? What other unintended consequences for society have resulted from the widespread use of cell phones?*

thinking about structure

What are some **structure**-related changes that have begun at the micro or meso level and spread over time to the macro level—thus having global significance? What impact have these changes had on you?

SOCIOLOGY WORKS

Sociology Majors after Graduation

The Sociology Works box in Chapter 1 explored the ways in which a degree in sociology can prepare you for a variety of jobs. But what do sociology majors do once they graduate? Here are some answers from students:

- "I am an ongoing caseworker for abused and neglected children."
- "I work in the business development of technology hardware and professional services."
- "I am a paralegal."
- "I research climate change policies in several western states."
- "I am a seventh- and eighth-grade social studies teacher in a middle school in a large urban city."
- "I am a police officer in a large urban city."
- "I am a marketing consultant for a broadcasting company."
- "I am a statistician in the Fertility and Family Statistics Branch of the U.S. Census Bureau."

"I am a caseworker." "I research climate change policies." "I am a teacher." "I am a police officer." "I am a marketing consultant." "I am a statistician."

These responses are from an American Sociological Association (ASA) study surveying sociology majors from a variety of schools, part of the ASA's work analyzing the experiences of sociology majors both before and after graduation. These ongoing efforts have included surveys and in-depth interviews with students from the classes of 2005 and 2012 (Senter, Van Vooren, and Spalter-Roth 2013; Spalter-Roth and Van Vooren 2008; Spalter-Roth, Van Vooren, and Senter 2014).

Two years after graduation, 83 percent of the class of 2012 were working in jobs or paid internships, and some of them were also attending graduate school. Another 10 percent were attending graduate school but not working for pay. For the class of 2005, the most frequent job category was social services. Over 90 percent of students reported being "very" or "somewhat" satisfied with their jobs. Four years after graduation, many students reported having moved from entry-level positions, such as those with clerical or administration support duties, to service or management positions in their chosen fields.

Reflecting the versatility of an undergraduate sociology degree, more than half (57 percent) of sociology majors who were seniors in 2012 planned to attend graduate or professional school in a wide range of fields. The most popular fields of graduate study were sociology, social work, psychology, education, criminal justice, public policy, public health, business management, and law.

One challenge, the ASA study noted, is that few jobs are listed as "sociologist." Students therefore must identify the skills and knowledge they have developed as sociology majors (such as learning about racial and ethnic groups and understanding data in tables and charts), include them on their resume, and discuss them during job interviews. Many students in master's programs focus on honing their research skills and using statistical software packages, as competencies in these areas can increase an applicant's opportunities in many fields.

think about it

1. *What is your desired career path? How might a sociology major be an asset in helping you land a good job?*
2. *List the main knowledge and skills you are developing in your sociology course. How would you describe these on your resume? What other skills do you hope to develop before you graduate?*

interpersonal communication. Often individuals resist change because it represents a shift in the balance of power between social actors—and therefore threatens them directly or indirectly. The rise of right-wing populist movements in the United States, Europe, and elsewhere are a recent example of this sort of resistance to change (Cas 2016; Judis 2016).

Theories of Social Change

Traditionally, historical accounts have highlighted the actions and accomplishments of powerful individuals—presidents, judges, generals, business tycoons, and others who have made key and far-reaching decisions. Such actors can play an important role in social change. However, many contemporary historians examine the larger social factors that contribute to change, writing what is known as *social history*.

Similarly, various sociological theories emphasize two broad sources of change instead of focusing on the actions of particular individuals. Some theories look at change that originates because of *material factors* in the physical world, such as economic conditions, structural complexity, and technology. Other theories are concerned with change that is driven by *ideas* from within the human mind, such as thoughts, values, and beliefs. Recall from Chapter 1 that these "objective" (material) and "subjective" (idea-based) approaches make up an important dimension of all sociological theory.

Material Theories of Change: Historical Materialism, Complexity, and Technology

The best-known materialist theory of social change comes from Karl Marx ([1859] 1978). The part of Marx's work now referred to as **historical materialism** *suggests that the economic base of a society is the primary force driving change in other aspects of social life.*

To survive, Marx argued, humans must work with the resources found in nature to produce the material necessities of life, among them food, shelter, and clothing. A society's economy—its *mode of production,* in Marxist terms—defines how these basic necessities are created. Humans work collectively to produce these material necessities and in so doing enter into social relationships, or what Marx called *relations of production.* These social relations involve the roles people play in the production process, as well as other factors, such as the laws and regulations that affect how businesses operate.

According to Marx, *forces of production*—primarily the type of technology that is available to produce material necessities—determine the specific relations of production in a society. For example, the advent of the plow helped make large agriculturally based societies possible; the invention of various machines, such as the mechanical loom and the steam engine, enabled the growth of industrial manufacturing; and the microchip and related developments in computers have facilitated our information-based economy. Each of these changes in the forces of production contributed to change in communities and transformed many social institutions. In other words, a change in the economic base of the society had a powerful impact on other aspects of social life. Marx's theory reminds us that understanding social change often involves attending closely to the economy.

Another largely materialist approach, evolutionary theory, does not adopt a Marxist analysis, but highlights instead the cumulative changes brought about as societies evolve from relatively simple hunter-gatherer structures to players in today's postindustrial world (Lenski 2005). As societies grow, evolutionary theorists contend, their development paths may diverge based on their interactions with the environment, their use of available technologies, and other variables. Yet eventually, they all create increasingly complex social structures with increasingly elaborated and diversified cultures. This process of meeting social needs through growing complexity drives social change.

Other materialist approaches developed more specific arguments about technology's role in social change without adopting a broader Marxist framework. Writing mostly in the 1930s, American sociologist William Ogburn identified three routes by which technology and other forces could change society: invention, discovery, and diffusion. *Invention* involves the creation of new materials, ideas, or patterns of behavior; consider, for example, how the microchip, used in computers and countless other devices, has revolutionized social life. *Discovery* entails finding something new that already exists, such as DNA or the neutron. *Diffusion* occurs when new technology or ideas spread from one society to another, as when the machinery that enabled industrialization spread around the world. Ogburn argued that material things like technological innovations generally change more rapidly than a culture's ideas, values, and beliefs. The result is *cultural lag,* a delay in a culture's adaptation to technological innovation, often resulting in social problems.

A dramatic example of cultural lag was noted by scientist Albert Einstein at the end of World War II when he warned, "The unleashed power of the atom has changed everything save our modes of thinking and we thus drift toward unparalleled catastrophe" (Einstein [1946] 1999). Though Einstein himself had played a prominent role in encouraging the development of the first atomic weapons, he concluded that people of the time did not fully grasp their destructive power—and therefore did not change their behavior accordingly. As Ogburn might have observed, society's ideas and beliefs about warfare had not yet caught up with the new technological reality that made the annihilation of humanity a real possibility. Today, our generation may be experiencing a similar cultural lag as many people struggle to accept the reality of humankind's negative impact on the global environment.

In the end, technology has important implications for three reasons (Harper and Leicht 2016):

1. It creates new alternatives for a society.
2. It alters patterns of social interaction.
3. It gives rise to new social problems that must be addressed.

One of Ogburn's examples—the introduction of the automobile into American life—illustrates all three points. With cars, individuals could travel farther in less time than ever before and could do so more comfortably. It became possible for people to live at some distance from where they worked, and this new option in turn spurred suburban growth. Cars also changed how people interacted: for example, the automobile made visits to distant relatives easier and provided young dating couples with a newfound privacy. Finally, cars contributed a host of new social problems, including road accidents, air and noise pollution, and traffic congestion.

Cultural Theories of Change: Weber's Protestant Ethic and Ideology The ideas, values, and beliefs that are part of a culture can also fuel social change. Whereas Marx analyzed the rise of industrial capitalism in materialist terms, Max Weber argued that religious belief also played a key role.

Weber's study, *The Protestant Ethic and the Spirit of Capitalism* ([1905] 1958), suggested that capitalism emerged first in certain areas because it was compatible with the Calvinist version of Protestantism. Calvinists saw economic success as a sign of God's blessing. Therefore, their religious values and beliefs encouraged hard work and frugality, which facilitated the accumulation of money. This money became available for investment in the new technologies and infrastructure that enabled industrial capitalism to grow. In this way, the Protestant ethic's emphasis on hard work and frugality contributed to the rise of capitalism.

thinking about culture

Has your college's **culture** (in the form of norms and rules) lagged behind the introduction of cell phones and laptops in the classroom? If so, has this lag created any problems? Explain.

Weber argued that societies with different religious beliefs did not encourage the same accumulation of capital and therefore did not smooth the way for the rise of capitalism. Thus, according to Weber, a particular set of religious ideas advanced economic development.

A wide range of cultural values and beliefs can drive social change efforts. For example, the ideal of democracy in U.S. culture and elsewhere has provided a powerful spark for many social movements. In this way, ideas can encourage action that leads to social change.

Change in Context Most sociologists today adopt **contextual analyses** that *take into account the particular historical and social context within which change is occurring and do not assume that a single factor is the most important in all situations.* This orientation is less a consistent theory about change in particular than a general approach to studying any aspect of social life. A contextual analysis might find that in a particular situation, the adoption of new technology may be the leading factor driving change, but in another case economic conflict may play a role that is equally—or more—important. Government action, new ideas, changing population trends, and other factors can be crucial sources of change in particular situations. In short, the question "What causes change?" can best be answered by saying, "It depends."

Globalization as Change

Apple iPhones are a global product. Minerals used in the battery are mined in the Congo; the display screens are manufactured in Japan and South Korea; the gyroscopes come from France and Italy; and the sensors from the Netherlands. These components are assembled into phones in China. The global ad agency that markets the finished phones is based in the United States, and the product is sold worldwide: see Map 17.1 (Minasians 2016).

You may not think of globalization when you see an iPhone, but like many other products sold today, it is an example of how globalization enters your daily life. The coffee you sip, the semester you might spend abroad, the foreign film you stream via Netflix, the price you pay for gasoline, the clothes you wear, the news report live from Afghanistan, the Chilean grapes you eat, the internet, the Afro-pop tracks you stream on Spotify, the new immigrants in your community (and perhaps you)—all are the result of globalization trends.

Throughout this book we have traced the impact of globalization—on culture, the economy, the media, and other areas of society. In this section, we link these many different dimensions by considering globalization as a social process and by examining how it is both a type of change and a catalyst for change.

MAP 17.1 | LOCATION AND NUMBER OF APPLE SUPPLIERS PER COUNTRY

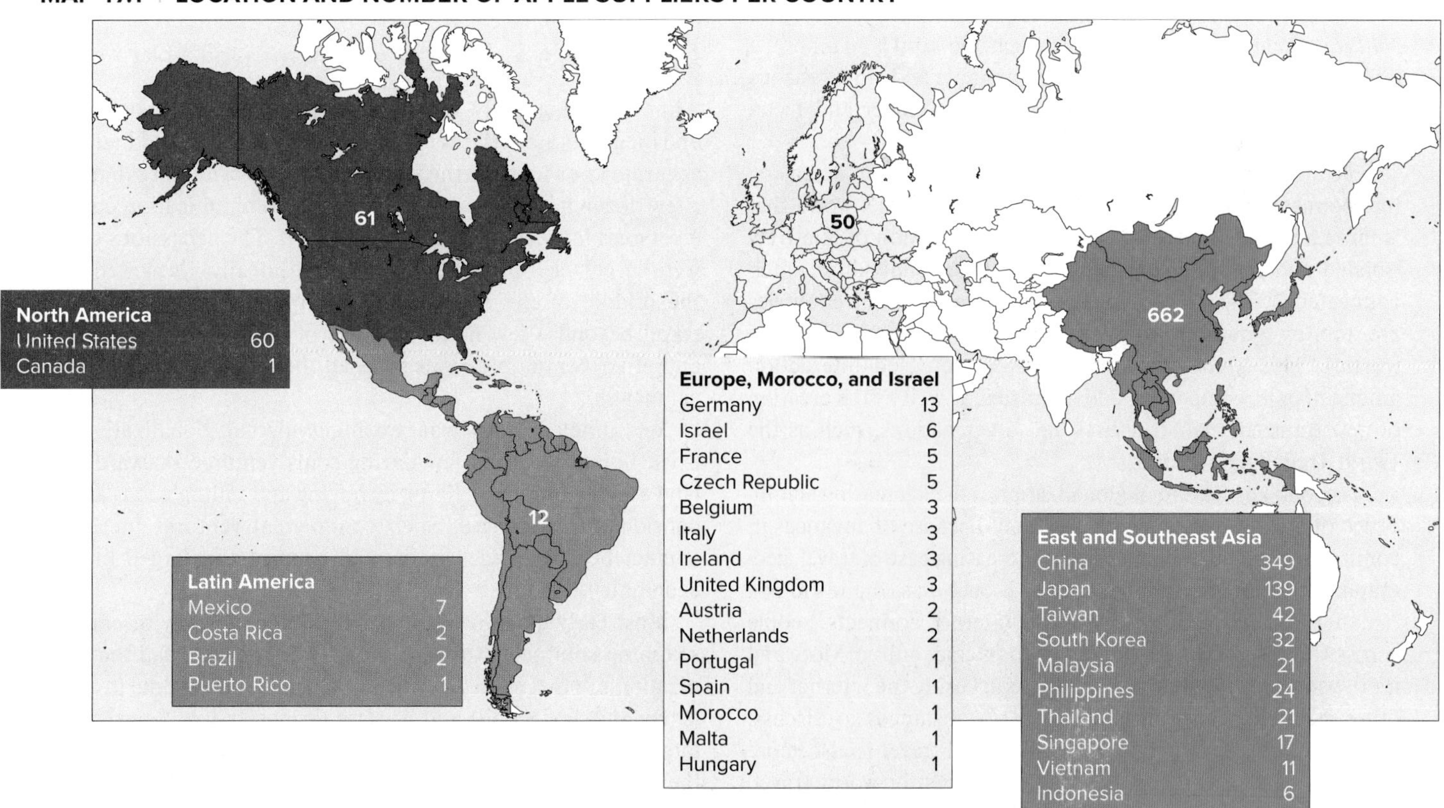

Like many other electronic devices, Apple's iPhone is a global product, with parts produced by hundreds of manufacturers scattered across dozens of countries. *Source:* CompareCamp 2014.

©Allen Creative/Steve Allen/Alamy Stock Photo

Communicable diseases, such as tuberculosis, sometimes can be spread between travelers through just coughing or sneezing. People can be exposed to other diseases by traveling to areas where outbreaks are occurring. Here, travelers in Georgia's Atlanta International Airport—the world's busiest airport—are cautioned about visiting countries experiencing Zika outbreaks in 2016, a disease spread primarily by mosquito bites. What other problems are created or made worse by globalization?

©US Air Force Photo/Alamy Stock Photo

Through advances in communication technology, soldiers can operate drones for either reconnaissance or attack from command centers thousands of miles from the battlefield. This capability has decreased the significance of both distance and physical location. Pilots at Creech Air Force Base in Indian Springs, Nevada, control aircraft from a remote console in 2015.

Globalization: Integrating Societies

Globalization refers to *the worldwide interaction or integration among various aspects of social life, including economies, cultures, political systems, and populations.* As such, the word is an umbrella term that highlights the links among multiple and simultaneous developments that are continually evolving (Ritzer and Dean 2015; Smith 2013).

The most significant feature of globalization is the increasing interconnection of societies. Globalization reflects a world that is more a single, integrated place than a collection of relatively isolated and separate societies. Not only are individuals interconnected by means of instant communication, but countries are, too, by global networks of trade agreements and political treaties. This global dynamic involves increased interaction among people, companies, and countries, as well as the creation of new transnational structures and organizations, such as the World Trade Organization.

A second key feature of globalization is the decreasing significance of distance and physical location. Because of advances in communication technology and the increasing ease of travel, geographic space is less significant than it once was; the world is a "smaller" place. Think of how the internet connects people across vast distances, allowing them to interact online. More and more people throughout the world interact using the internet and other technological bridges across major distances to discuss, buy, learn, organize, and have fun. Physical travel is also more accessible and commonplace, and consequently world travel, tourism, and international business have grown dramatically. People from far-flung locations now routinely come into social contact within the same physical space.

As stunning and rapid as these developments have been, you probably already take them for granted. To appreciate the significance of globalization, we must consider what came before it.

Early Globalization's Colonial Roots

Almost unimaginably, for much of human history, people lived and died in or near the communities of their birth and had little accurate knowledge of the wider world. Travel of more than just a few dozen miles was uncommon, and communication outside a person's immediate region was limited. The necessities of life were largely self-produced or acquired locally. Even well into the middle of the nineteenth century, most people did not travel beyond a few hundred miles of their home, and letters and other communications reached their destination by physical means.

Yet limited forms of what we might now call globalization did exist. For centuries, a few daring souls ventured outward over land and sea to make a living by buying and selling goods across considerable distances. Such commercial ventures increased contact between widely separated peoples and forged limited economic ties.

Most early globalization, however, came by way of empires spanning continents through military domination and the colonization of other societies. Technological developments in travel (ships and navigation) and warfare (armor and weapons) facilitated the colonization of less developed societies. From roughly the 1500s through the early 1900s, European colonialism in particular expanded the reach of a few powerful countries, making events in foreign countries relevant to people in a new way (Map 17.2). Colonial populations were subjugated by governments

MAP 17.2 | THE BRITISH EMPIRE IN THE 1920s

Early globalization derived primarily from the establishment of colonial empires such as Britain's. The effects of colonialism's past continue to be felt worldwide today. *Source:* Based on archival maps at www.probertencyclopaedia.com and www.britishempire.co.uk.

CORE CONCEPTS CHALLENGE *What forms of* **power** *did colonizing nations use to build large empires and spread their influence?*

that sometimes ruled from halfway around the globe. At the same time, individuals in the home countries of the colonial powers became linked to events that occurred in distant colonies, and in this way they began to learn about the other societies that were now a part of their empire.

In the postcolonial era, the formal ties of colonialism have been severed as former colonies have gained their independence. However, new means of influencing national and regional politics have arisen. As we saw in Chapter 9, critics contend that *neocolonialism* (economic domination without formal political control or military occupation) is often carried out through transnational economic organizations such as the World Bank and the International Monetary Fund (Blanton, Blanton, and Peksen 2015). Transnational corporations, which have no allegiance to any particular country, have also taken center stage in the global economy and have had a major impact on the economies of smaller, poorer nations, in particular. The continuing legacy of colonialism, with power imbalances and inequality among nations and regions of the world, has contributed to persistent international tensions and conflict.

Contemporary Globalization's Multiple Dimensions

Since the mid-twentieth century and especially in the past few decades, globalization has become more pervasive, far reaching, swiftly developing, and technology dependent than ever before. The very term *globalization* came into wide use only in the 1980s as these trends became more readily apparent and began to have an impact on growing numbers of people. Globalization is now one of the most important social forces affecting societies around the world.

Many issues can no longer be understood merely by looking at a single society; the dynamics involved are now global or transnational. Moreover, globalization affects a diverse array of overlapping areas of social life, including the following:

- ***Economy.*** Globalization has meant an increased flow of goods (trade), capital (investment), and people (migration) across national boundaries.
- ***Culture.*** Globalization has powered a surge of ideas, beliefs, and lifestyles across national boundaries–everything from democratic movements, media products, religious

©Nicolas Asfouri - Pool/Getty Images

Typically carried out behind closed doors, global economic meetings such as the 2016 G20 Summit in Hangzhou, China, bring together leaders of the world's major industrialized countries to make economic decisions that can affect billions of people worldwide. How do such meetings reflect aspects of power and inequality on a global scale?

proselytizing, and travel and tourism to sporting events such as World Cup soccer and the Olympic Games.

- ***Communications technology.*** More than 1,100 communication satellites orbit Earth, an ever-growing number that facilitates the flow of communications on a vast scale. Instantaneous global communication has been crucial to the staggering reduction in the significance of distance and time.
- ***Transnational entities.*** Globalization has led to the creation of new social structures to deal with the increase in social relations across national boundaries. Transnational corporations; economic organizations such as the International Monetary Fund, the World Trade Organization, and the World Bank; and political institutions such as the United Nations and the European Union are prominent transnational structures. International relief agencies such as the Red Cross/Red Crescent and Doctors Without Borders, and even international professional associations such as the International Sociological Association are part of this trend.
- ***Transnational identities.*** Globalization has contributed to the emergence of new social identities. Ever more eclectic consumers mix cultural products from across the globe, including music, food, film, and clothing styles. It is not unusual to find, say, Jordanian teen girls in traditional hijab dress listening to American pop music or to find U.S. teens who are fans of Japanese anime and Indian food. Immigrants moving from one country to another often live a life of cultural hybrids, speaking one language at home and another at school or work; watching both native-language television programs via satellite and programs in the language of their adopted country; listening to both traditional music from their homelands and Western pop music; adopting values, behaviors, and dress that combine the cultures of their original and newly adopted homes. Websites often serve internationally diverse users. For example, the Google search engine, truly a global phenomenon, supports more than 140 languages, and the company's popular Translate service accommodates over 100 languages.
- ***Global cities.*** As globalization disperses economic activity worldwide, these scattered economic processes are coordinated from a few key locations where managers, lawyers, financiers, and engineers navigate the legal and technical complexities of multinational transactions (Sassen 2019). *Global cities* are home to many companies that provide key financial, legal, technical, and other high-level services and are thus strategic nodes in the networks that constitute the global economy. Among the most important global cities are New York, London, Tokyo, Paris, Frankfurt, Zurich, Amsterdam, Sydney, Hong Kong, Mexico City, and São Paulo. Global cities are also cosmopolitan, catering to sophisticated international workers through diverse restaurants, entertainment, religious and other cultural offerings. Global cities, then, are urban centers that transcend the nations in which they are located.

©K M Asad/ZUMA Press, Inc/Alamy Stock Photo

Fans in Bangladesh watch a 2018 FIFA World Cup soccer match in Russia between Brazil and Belgium projected on a big screen.

CORE CONCEPTS CHALLENGE *How does the broadcast of such games worldwide exemplify the globalization of* ***culture****? What are other examples of global cultural events?*

SOCIOLOGY in ACTION

Sociological Research in the International Arena

It was a small victory that could change lives. Through its housing program for low-income families, Argentina's third-largest city, Rosario, began setting aside 10 percent of the city's new public housing for victims of domestic abuse. Women who once could not leave their abusers because they had no other place to go would now have a potentially lifesaving alternative.

Sociological research can make a real difference in people's lives, but the route to change is often complex and indirect. In this case, the new housing effort was advanced by local advocates in the wake of extensive media reports about the link between inadequate housing and the perpetuation of domestic violence. That coverage involved both mainstream media, like the BBC and major regional news outlets, and advocacy networks, like Amnesty International, Habitat for Humanity, and the Women's UN Report Network. All that media attention was triggered by a report from the Swiss-based Center on Housing Rights and Evictions, an international human rights organization. The report was prepared by staff sociologist Mayra Gómez, who cites its impact as one example of how sociological research can make the world a better place (Gómez 2014).

Social change results from the accumulated efforts of many people engaged in many types of action, and this particular change was no different. Gómez is just one of many sociologists who inform and support international nongovernmental organizations and social change groups that promote human rights, fair trade, labor rights, women's rights, environmental protection, and other social justice issues. Their work is often unglamorous and unnoticed, but it can make an important contribution toward the slow progress of social justice.

Doing such work can have its rewards, too. Gómez is now with the Global Initiative for Economic, Social, and Cultural Rights, a human rights organization based in Minnesota. She notes, "I have been fortunate enough to travel to about 40 countries covering every region of the world. Many have been poor, many war-torn and disaster-struck. It's hard to articulate the impact this really has on you. Each place deepens my commitment to creating a better, more just, world and each place reminds me of our fundamental connectedness to one another and to the beautiful planet we share" (*Duluth News Tribune* 2013).

think about it

1. *What elements of a sociological perspective might be especially useful in doing social justice work on an international scale?*
2. *What global issues do you think sociologists might be well prepared to address? Why?*

- ***Global social movements.*** As social problems have gone global, so too have the responses of social movement activists (Moghadam 2013). Environmental groups reach across national boundaries to tackle global climate change and the loss of wildlife habitat. Labor groups, including unions, work across national boundaries to protect employees of transnational corporations. Human rights groups try to mobilize worldwide support to pressure repressive governments to cease human rights abuses.

These developments represent some of the most significant changes that the world has undergone in the past century. The impact of these changes is raising a number of pressing sociological questions.

The Impact of Globalization on Culture, Structure, and Power

We conclude this section with a look at some of the issues resulting from the expansion of globalization, grouping them by sociology's core concepts.

Culture Has globalization improved understanding among people of different cultures? Or has it resulted in the homogenization of cultures as wealthier nations come to dominate in global relationships? These questions have driven the debate over globalization and its impact on culture.

Global culture has many dimensions (Berger 1997; Buhari-Gulmez and Robertson 2016). Beyond *popular culture* in the form of music, movies, and clothing, the global economy has contributed to a common *business culture* of economic elites. In addition, *religious* organizations from wealthier nations—especially evangelical Protestants—have exported their beliefs and practices to other nations, another sort of cultural globalization. In the realm of *ideas,* Western intellectuals, through academic networks and nongovernmental organizations, have advanced a culture rooted mostly in democratic egalitarian values. Combined, these processes have had a massive impact on how people around the globe are socialized.

When different cultures have contact, they exchange influences, such as when languages adopt foreign words and when music or literature integrates foreign traditions. Cross-cultural contact in turn can promote greater understanding, tolerance, and mutual appreciation, all of which can diffuse tensions,

©Mark Schiefelbein/AP Images

In Beijing, China, people walk past a poster for the movie *Star Wars: The Force Awakens* in 2016. Well-known Chinese actors were cast in the film to attract Chinese audiences and the film was a huge box-office hit there. Unlike most governments, Chinese officials allow only a handful of foreign films to be officially released each year, thereby limiting the impact of such cultural products on the local culture. How many foreign-made films have you seen in the past year? What does this suggest about the flow of global media into and out of the United States?

reduce conflict, and facilitate a more stable, peaceful world. It also paves the way to advances in knowledge that can potentially improve people's quality of life, as often happens when scholars share scientific advances.

But most cross-cultural contact also leads to challenges. First, some ideas and values from different cultures are incompatible. For example, a belief in complete gender equality—a hallmark of most secular democratic societies—clashes with some patriarchal religious traditions that limit women's role in religion and sometimes even social and civic life. When one country promotes egalitarian and democratic principles, is it imposing its cultural values on the political culture of other peoples? Or is it asserting universal rights that unite humanity, irrespective of culture? The fact that different cultures offer different answers to such questions is one of the challenges societies face in a globalized world.

Patriarchy versus gender equality, and theocratic states versus secular democracies, are among the volatile issues that will continue to characterize the debate over global culture and that will be an ongoing source of conflict. Because of greater economic and political integration, the risk of a large-scale global conflict such as the two world wars of the twentieth century is probably reduced. However, insofar as globalization results in increased contact among cultures with irreconcilable differences, it will likely result in *more* conflicts than in the past.

Second, because the world's societies are not equally wealthy and powerful, their ability to be heard in a global exchange of culture is unequal. For a long time, wealthy, predominantly Western societies exported most of the cultural goods traveling in the global economy. Recently, however, major changes have occurred in the nature of cultural exports. First, the volume of such exports has increased dramatically, doubling between 2003 and 2013. Because of digitization, however, some of the most popular and influential goods—especially music and movies—are now more likely to be streamed online than to be exported as physical goods. As such they are not counted in some measures of exports. Today, art objects (jewelry, sculptures, paintings, and crafts) represent an increasing percentage of the physical cultural goods being exported. These objects come from emerging economies, such as China, which is now the largest exporter of cultural goods (UNESCO 2016b). Even so, Western domination of movies and music continues. In 2013, for example, the world's three major film producers were India (1,724 films), the United States (738 films), and China (638 films), but because most Chinese and Indian films are viewed only domestically, U.S. movies still dominate international film distribution (UNESCO 2016c).

At a time when most of the world can be exposed to the same media content, sometimes simultaneously, that content is still most likely to come from wealthy Western societies. This situation raises the issue of cultural domination. Recall from Chapter 3 the concerns that sociologists have about the potential homogenizing effects of mass media and cultural products. Although many people around the world have embraced Western cultural products and values, others have resisted their influence. In some cases, such as in India, they have simply embraced locally produced films and music. In others, such as in China, governments have limited the import of Western films and censored the internet.

Structure Has globalization reduced hierarchy and bureaucracy by promoting decentralized social networks and direct communication? Or have the large transnational entities that have emerged concentrated control more centrally and made hierarchy and bureaucracy increasingly resistant to change? These are among the questions sociologists and other observers debate in relation to the impact of globalization on structure and action.

Globalization has stimulated contradictory trends involving social structures and social action. On the one hand, new social structures have been created to facilitate and manage the increase in transnational relations. For example, on the economic front, the large transnational corporations that have emerged are massive global organizations employing thousands of people in many different countries and often organized into fairly traditional bureaucratic, pyramidal structures. On the other hand, the increased accessibility of new technologies has enabled communication and interaction that involve far fewer layers of bureaucratic hierarchies—that is, a flattened structure—because people interact more directly through networks (Castells 1996; Rainie and Wellman 2012). Even small businesses can use the internet, telephone, and overnight package delivery services to conduct business directly with consumers around the globe, cutting out the need for large corporate intermediaries. On the downside, such developments have contributed to an increase in less stable "contingent" work, performed by freelancers and temporary contract workers who are less likely to receive benefits than traditional permanent workers.

Do such trends empower people and organizations to act more freely? Or does the unprecedented size of global companies restrict the practical options that are available to people? We do not yet have complete answers to these questions because these structures are still in transition.

Power Does globalization help improve living standards throughout the world, or is it a new form of colonialism, reinforcing and even intensifying economic divisions? How has power shifted since globalization has become so pervasive? These two related questions are central to the ongoing debates over the effect of globalization on power and inequality.

It is difficult to answer questions about globalization and inequality definitively, in part because individual countries vary significantly in how much they have participated in globalization (see Table 17.1). Wealthier nations tend to be the most globalized, and poorer countries are the least integrated globally. Even within individual countries, generally only the relatively affluent can afford computers, broadband access, and other communications technologies that enable them to participate in aspects of globalization, such as information gathering, online music and video streaming, long-distance education, and e-commerce.

Deep inequalities and power imbalances among different countries and regions clearly have been intrinsic to globalization. Extreme poverty worldwide has been cut in half since 1990 (United Nations 2018). However, not all nations have benefited equally. For example, some developing countries have struggled with international debt and have had to impose domestic austerity programs, which cut social services to the poor, in order to meet repayment obligations. Even workers in wealthier nations have experienced mixed results. Although they have benefited from the availability of cheaper goods, many have seen their jobs shift to low-wage countries where workers enjoy few if any labor rights or democratic freedoms. Such shifts have devastated communities and entire regions that had previously benefited from stable, well-paid manufacturing jobs. As transnational corporations continuously seek lower wages and lower production costs in what some critics call a "race to the bottom," workers lose their ability to maintain a living wage.

Sociologists arguing from the perspective of world systems theory maintain that wealthy "core" countries exert considerable influence over less affluent countries that are part of the poor "periphery" or middle-income "semi-periphery" of the world's economy. In this way, the dynamics inherent in the global economy maintain a significant imbalance of power and ensure continued inequality among wealthy and poor nations. Wealthy, powerful nations have created, and continue to enforce, the ground rules according to which global capitalism operates. A

TABLE 17.1 MOST AND LEAST GLOBALIZED COUNTRIES, 2017

Most Globalized		Least Globalized	
Country	Globalization Index	Country	Globalization Index
1. Belgium	90.5	1. Eritrea	28.7
2. Netherlands	90.2	2. Central African Republic	34.7
3. Switzerland	89.7	3. Afghanistan	38.7
4. Sweden	88.1	4. Burundi	39.0
5. Austria	87.9	5. Myanmar	39.8
6. Denmark	87.8	6. Chad	40.1
7. France	87.3	7. Comoros	40.2
8. United Kingdom	87.2	8. Guinea-Bissau	40.4
9. Germany	86.9	9. Bhutan	40.8
10. Finland	86.0	10. Solomon Islands	41.0
24. United States	80.0		

One globalization index combines measures of economic, political, and social globalization to score 192 countries on a scale of 0 (low) to 100 (high). This table shows the results for the 10 most globalized and the 10 least globalized countries, as well as for the United States. The U.S. ranking is high but not among the top few in large part because, like Australia (27th), Japan (35th), and China (87th), it has a large domestic economy and is more inward-looking economically than many other countries. What similarities do you see among the 10 most globalized countries? How about among the 10 least globalized countries?

Source: Gygli, Haelg, and Sturm 2018.

©Nicolas Liponne/NurPhoto/Getty Images

Globalization has produced clashes over immigration. Increased immigration—often of Muslims—generated right-wing, anti-immigrant, and anti-Islam protests in many parts of Europe. These were sometimes led by fascist parties reviving the symbols and language of Nazism. That right-wing backlash, though, has been met by antiracism advocates like these in Lyon, France. During a 2018 rally, their banner reads "Nazis off of our streets."

SPOTLIGHT

on social theory

World systems theory—a form of **conflict theory**—highlights the interconnections among the economies of different countries. How are your activities as a consumer or a worker linked to this global economic activity?

variety of international economic and political organizations implement these rules, including the World Bank, the International Monetary Fund, the World Trade Organization, and the United Nations (Peet 2009; Steger 2017; Wallerstein, Rojas, and Lemert 2012).

As a result of the actions of wealthier, more powerful nations, national governments in weaker countries now have less authority to regulate their own economies than they once did. To participate in the global economy, these countries must follow the ground rules established by the international economic organizations and must court investment from large multinational firms. To some observers, this situation represents a shift of power from national governments to transnational organizations. Since these transnational organizations in turn are dominated by wealthier countries, this shift has reinforced the power of wealthy countries over poorer ones.

This approach to economic globalization is known as *neoliberalism* (not to be confused with the liberal/conservative political spectrum) (Eagleton-Pierce 2016; Springer, Birch, and MacLeavy 2016). **Neoliberalism** refers to *an economic philosophy that promotes markets, deregulation, privatization, and reduced government social expenditures.* Typical neoliberal policies include the deregulation of economic sectors, the reduction of taxes, the elimination of tariffs and trade barriers, opposition to labor unions, and the privatization of government-owned industries. Neoliberals favor a shift in power away from government and toward private enterprise.

In reality, critics point out, neoliberal policies are often applied selectively as the government intervenes to promote certain business interests. With respect to agriculture, for example, the United States and Europe provide farmers with subsidies that enable growers to sell their crops at a lower price than they otherwise could. Subsidization forces prices downward, sometimes harming nations whose major exports are agricultural products. Critics contend that neoliberalism ultimately favors policies that, first and foremost, protect the interests of investors. They note that neoliberal policies can be used to shift power from governments that are democratically elected and accountable to the people to corporations that are privately owned and accountable only to investors.

Supporters of neoliberal policies promote their version of economic globalization as the only legitimate form (Griswold 2009; Irwin 2015). They blast critiques of neoliberalism as "antiglobalization"—a label some activists use as well. But in reality, most of the critics oppose the neoliberal version of globalization, not globalization itself. For example, rather than endorse unqualified "free trade," opponents of neoliberalism advocate "fair trade" policies that protect workers' rights and are environmentally sustainable. In effect, they argue for a globalization that would help reduce inequality and empower workers in the global economy.

The Limits of Globalization

The forces of globalization are neither inevitable nor invincible, as recent developments have shown. For example, the global economic crisis of the late 2000s produced a significant short-term decline in global trade, capital flows, and foreign investments, as countries tried to protect their domestic industries. Although these activities gradually returned to pre-crisis levels, the frightening economic turmoil highlighted some of the shortcomings of an interconnected global economy. In many countries, efforts were made to restrict immigration in the wake of perceived job losses to new immigrants. Ongoing fears about terrorism, too, have sometimes fueled bigotry and suspicion toward immigrants, especially Muslims (Dickinson 2017; Robinson 2014). Nevertheless, the trend toward globalization is strong and will withstand the setbacks caused by changing political tides and temporary economic downturns.

It's important, though, to keep globalization in perspective. Billions of people live in poverty and are left out of globalization processes. In addition, local, regional, and national factors still heavily influence a nation's economic, political, cultural, and social life. In the future, social life will be neither exclusively local nor primarily global; instead, local and global issues and concerns will become increasingly intermeshed.

The particular neoliberal policies associated with globalization have been undergoing some reform, however. Emerging economies, especially China and India, have challenged the dominance of Western countries in international organizations, prompting some change (Hopewell 2016). A diverse global justice movement has pursued increased transparency (openness) in the operations of the organizations that oversee the global economy, as well as a greater focus on combating poverty and protecting the environment (Klein 2014). At the other end of the political spectrum, right-wing nationalist and populist movements have criticized many aspects of globalization as well. In the United States, Donald Trump's "America First" emphasis included withdrawals from international treaties and attempts to increase tariffs and other trade barriers (McCarthy 2018). These reform efforts are among a host of social movements promoting social change, a topic we examine later in the chapter. First, we consider another significant form of social change: the population shifts that are reshaping societies.

Population Change

World War II created enormous uncertainly for young Americans. Because many had been drafted or had volunteered to serve in the military, their fate was in doubt for the war's duration. Millions of young people put off plans to get married and delayed having children until the future was clearer.

At the end of the war in 1945, the survivors of the conflict were able to carry out their marriage plans. Many couples were soon enjoying the economic good times that followed the war. They could now afford to have children, and the popular culture of the day encouraged attention to family life. Consequently, the number of marriages increased, and the percentage of childless marriages decreased. Individually, these people were simply starting the family life that they had put on hold during the war. Collectively, they were unintentionally creating one of the best-known social trends of the twentieth century: the post–World War II "baby boom."

The term *baby boomers* applies to people born in the postwar period roughly spanning 1946 to 1964, when the U.S. birth rate soared. Because the boomers' numbers are so much greater than usual, this cohort of Americans has had a powerful impact on the country throughout their lives. When they reached college age, they were part of an explosion in the size of higher education. When they had children, they created a *baby boomlet*—a smaller echo of the previous generation's baby boom. As they have aged and begun to retire, they are contributing to the "graying of America" and putting strains on the nation's health care and Social Security systems.

The baby boomers exemplify how social factors—war, economic good times, and cultural norms—can influence personal decisions. In turn, the changes in population that result from these individual actions can ripple throughout society for decades to come.

Demography is *the study of human population trends* such as the baby boom. It considers a wide array of population characteristics, including rates of birth, marriage, household occupancy, income, and education. In the United States, the Census Bureau is the agency responsible for collecting such data. Internationally, the United Nations is a key clearinghouse for demographic data.

In studying human population trends, sociologists not only document patterns but also look for explanations as to *why* various developments occur. In this section, we examine population change, some social explanations for it, and the effects of this change on society.

The Population Explosion and Its Sources

The world is currently in the midst of a population explosion. The effects of this population surge are being felt globally and in many different ways, including increased urbanization and the environmental crisis we examined in Chapter 15.

It took all of human history—tens of thousands of years—for the world's population to reach an estimated 1 billion in about 1804. After that, each subsequent billion took less time than the preceding one. We reached

2 billion people in just 123 years (1927),
3 billion in 33 years (1960),
4 billion in 14 years (1974),
5 billion in 13 years (1987),
6 billion in 12 years (1999),
7 billion in 12 years (2011).

Although this pace of growth is expected to slow somewhat, our global population will continue to increase to a massive 11 billion by about 2088 (Figure 17.1).

Why is the human population increasing so rapidly? You might think the obvious answer is that people are having more children than in the past. In fact, the rate at which women are bearing children has *declined* in many societies during the precise period in which the overall population has increased. Instead, the population explosion is due to two global developments.

First, more infants are surviving into childhood and then into adulthood than in the past. As a result of scientific advances and growing affluence, many infants now receive better nutrition and health care, factors that help them survive their critical early years. Thus the population boom is, in part, one of the unintended consequences of scientific progress. This trend is

FIGURE 17.1 | WORLD POPULATION IN BILLIONS, 1 C.E. TO 2088 (PROJECTED)

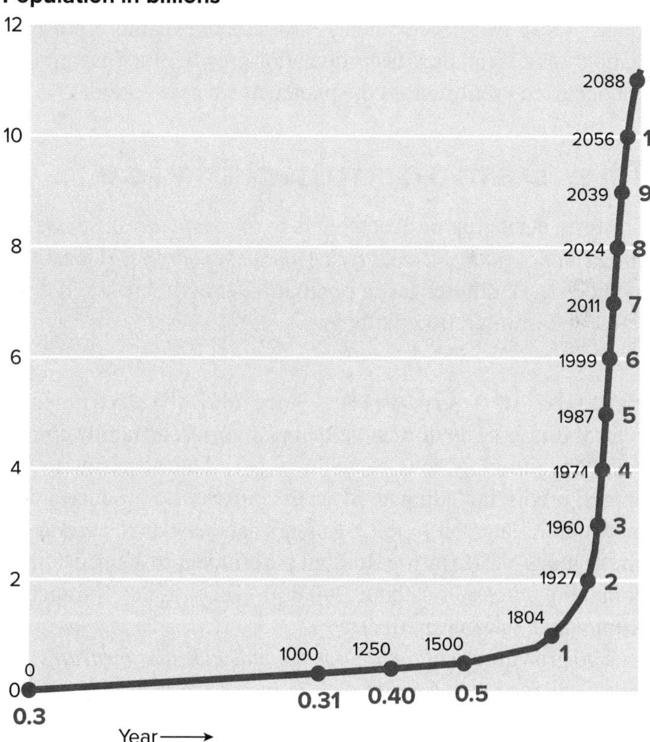

It took all of human history for the world's population to reach an estimated 1 billion people in about 1804, as the graph shows. What happened after that milestone was reached?

Source: UN Department of Economic and Social Affairs, Population Division 2017a.

©Irene Abdou/Alamy Stock Photo

A Society for Family Health volunteer speaks to women in Kano, Nigeria about family planning and child spacing.

measured by looking at the **infant mortality rate,** *the number of infants less than a year old who die per 1,000 live births.* In recent decades, the infant mortality rate across the world has been declining significantly, though unevenly.

Second, around the world, people are living longer. The human life span has increased because of improved nutrition, medical care, and knowledge about the causes of disease and illness. **Life expectancy** refers to *the median number of years a person is likely to live given the current conditions.* This figure can be measured by nation, by sex, or by other subpopulations and can vary considerably by subpopulation even within a single country. When the life expectancy in a nation is low, it is a sign that many of its citizens are dying prematurely. Common reasons for early death include disease (AIDS is a major killer in some countries), lack of clean water, malnourishment, and famine.

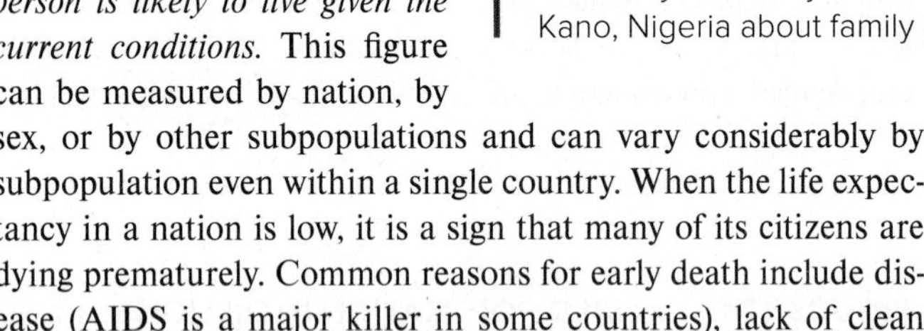

As more infants survive into adulthood and more adults live longer, these two developments have combined into a powerful demographic trend that fuels population growth. But this trend has not occurred evenly across the planet, as we next consider.

The Demographic Divide

The term **demographic divide** refers to *the inequality in population and health conditions between rich and poor countries.* This divide includes stark differences in population growth, birth and death rates, and immigration patterns.

Population Growth

Since 2007, the government of central Russia's Ulyanovsk region has sponsored "family contact day," encouraging couples to have sex. The government has offered prizes, including an SUV, to couples who produce a baby nine months later, on June 12, Russia's national day. The contest is one of many efforts by the Russian government to stem an annual population *decline* of about 700,000 (Haas 2008; Karabchuk, Kumo, and Selezneva 2017).

The **growth rate** *of a nation is the indicator that measures how quickly that country's population is increasing.* The growth rate combines two figures: the difference between births and deaths plus the difference between immigrants (those moving into a country permanently) and emigrants (those leaving a country permanently). In Russia, declining birth rates, high death rates, and significant emigration have combined to create a negative growth rate; despite the Russian government's best efforts, the country's population is on course to decline by more than 10 percent by 2050. All of Europe and several dozen other relatively wealthy countries are also experiencing unprecedented negative population growth. Declining birth rates in these countries are associated with both economic and cultural characteristics. Broadly speaking, women tend to have fewer children when they live in wealthy nations with high-quality health care and readily available contraception. Women also tend to have fewer children where they have greater social equality, are more educated, and are more likely to work outside the home (May 2012; UNFPA 2016).

Russia's declining population contrasts starkly with trends in Nigeria, an African nation whose population growth is among the world's highest. Nigeria's population of about 182 million in 2015 is projected to rise to an astounding 548 million by 2060—more than tripling in size. It is these vast differences in population growth that underlie the demographic divide. Despite high infant mortality, the world's less developed countries continue to experience relatively high birth rates, resulting in high growth rates. The contrast in population trends between wealthier and poorer countries means that a greater percentage of the world's people live in less developed regions than in the past, and this trend is projected to continue. By 2050 nearly 9 out of 10 people will inhabit less developed—and therefore poorer—regions (Figure 17.2).

FIGURE 17.2 | POPULATION GROWTH IN MORE, LESS DEVELOPED REGIONS, 1950–2100 (PROJECTED)

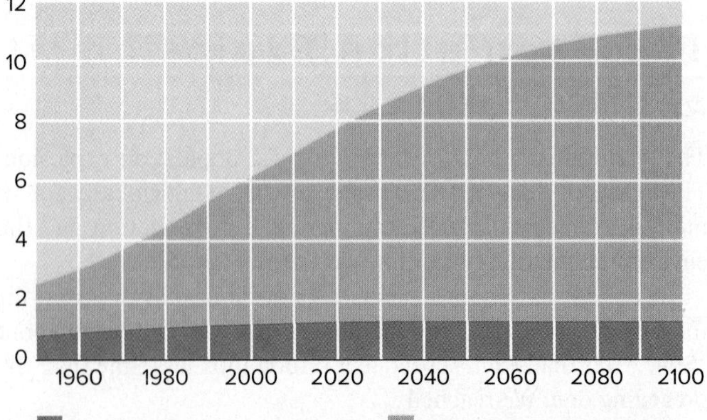

Note: "More developed" regions are Europe, North America, Australia/New Zealand, and Japan. "Less developed" regions include Africa, Asia (except Japan), Latin America, and the Caribbean. *Source:* UN Department of Economic and Social Affairs, Population Division 2017a.

FIGURE 17.3 | WORLD POPULATION STRUCTURES BY REGIONAL LEVEL OF DEVELOPMENT, 2020

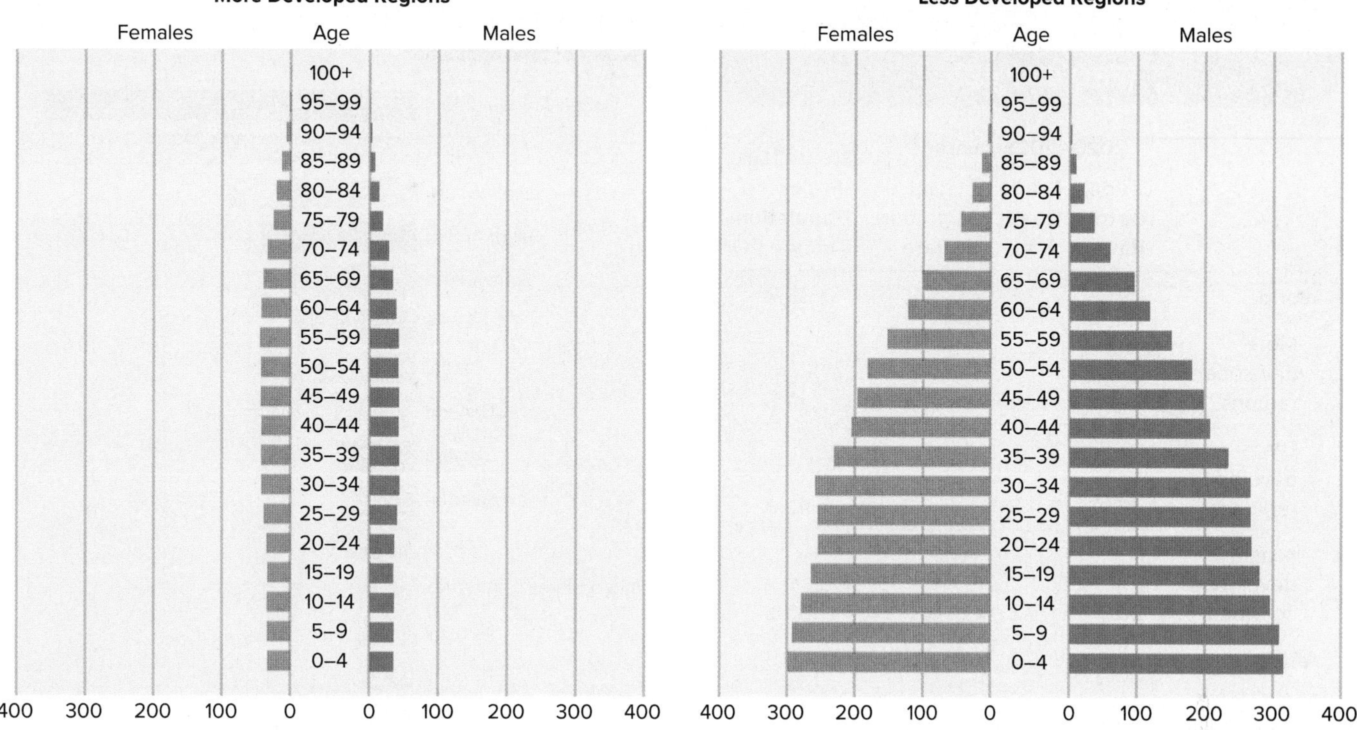

These two bar graphs show the distribution of a population by age and sex for more developed regions (*left*) and less developed regions (*right*).

Note: "More developed" regions are Europe, North America, Australia/New Zealand, and Japan. "Less developed" regions include Africa, Asia (except Japan), and the Caribbean. *Source:* UN Department of Economic and Social Affairs, Population Division 2017a.

CORE CONCEPTS CHALLENGE *What is the significance of these different population* **structures**? *How will the future of these regions differ in the coming years?*

Differences in growth rates can be seen in a country's **population pyramid,** *a bar chart that shows the distribution of a population by age and sex.* The population structure of a country with a high birth rate will be a pyramid shape, showing the large number of young people who account for the high population growth. By contrast, the population structure of a country with a more modest birth rate will be the shape of a pillar, showing a balanced replacement of the population. As Figure 17.3 illustrates, the population structures in less versus more developed regions of the world are conspicuously different.

Birth and Death Rates

The most significant element of a country's growth rate is the difference between its birth and death rates. The **crude birth rate** is *the number of live births per 1,000 people in a population.* Similarly, the **crude death rate** is *the number of deaths per 1,000 people in a population.* These are rough (or "crude") figures because they are based on the population as a whole rather than taking into account the number of women of childbearing age (for birth rate) or the overall age distribution (for death rate).

As shown in Table 17.2, crude birth and death rates vary substantially around the globe. Most strikingly, Africa's crude birth rate is more than triple that of Europe, part of a broader trend in which less developed nations have higher birth rates than wealthier nations.

Death rates also vary worldwide. Europe has the highest death rate (owing to its aging population) and a low birth rate; consequently, the continent's native-born population has fallen. Africa's death rate has declined in recent years but it is still relatively high, largely due to its high infant mortality and poor health conditions.

Immigration and Emigration

A country's population growth is also affected by **migration,** *the movement of people from one place to another.* Table 17.2 shows significant variation in the migration rates of different regions around the world, with people moving from less developed to more developed countries. Migration is an example of a social trend in which people respond individually to social forces and, by doing so, collectively create social change.

The primary reason people move to another country is economic opportunity. The search for economic betterment is also the most important "pull" factor that attracts people to certain countries. However, the world's poorest countries tend to have few emigrants, because they do not have the resources to travel.

TABLE 17.2 BIRTH, DEATH, MIGRATION, AND POPULATION CHANGE (PROJECTED)

	2020–2025 Average			2020–2070
	Crude Birth Rate	Crude Death Rate	Net Migration Rate	Projected Population Change (%)
World	17.6	7.8	0	35.7
More developed regions	10.6	10.4	1.8	1.5
Less developed regions	18.9	7.3	−0.3	42.3
Least developed countries	30.0	7.3	−0.7	133.2
Africa	31.6	7.7	−0.3	150.9
Asia	15.2	7.4	−0.3	12.2
Europe	10.0	11.4	1.2	−8.4
Latin America/ Caribbean	15.2	6.3	−0.4	17.5
North America	12.4	8.4	3.1	26.6
Oceania*	15.7	6.8	3.4	52.7

Crude birth rate = births per 1,000 population
Crude death rate = deaths per 1,000 population
Net migration rate = migrations per 1,000 population
Population change = percent of population
*Oceania refers to a region in the Pacific Ocean that includes Australia, Papua New Guinea, New Zealand, and numerous other Pacific islands.
Source: UN Department of Economic and Social Affairs, Population Division 2017a.

FIGURE 17.4 | INTERNATIONAL MIGRANTS AS PERCENTAGE OF TOTAL POPULATION, SELECT COUNTRIES, 2017

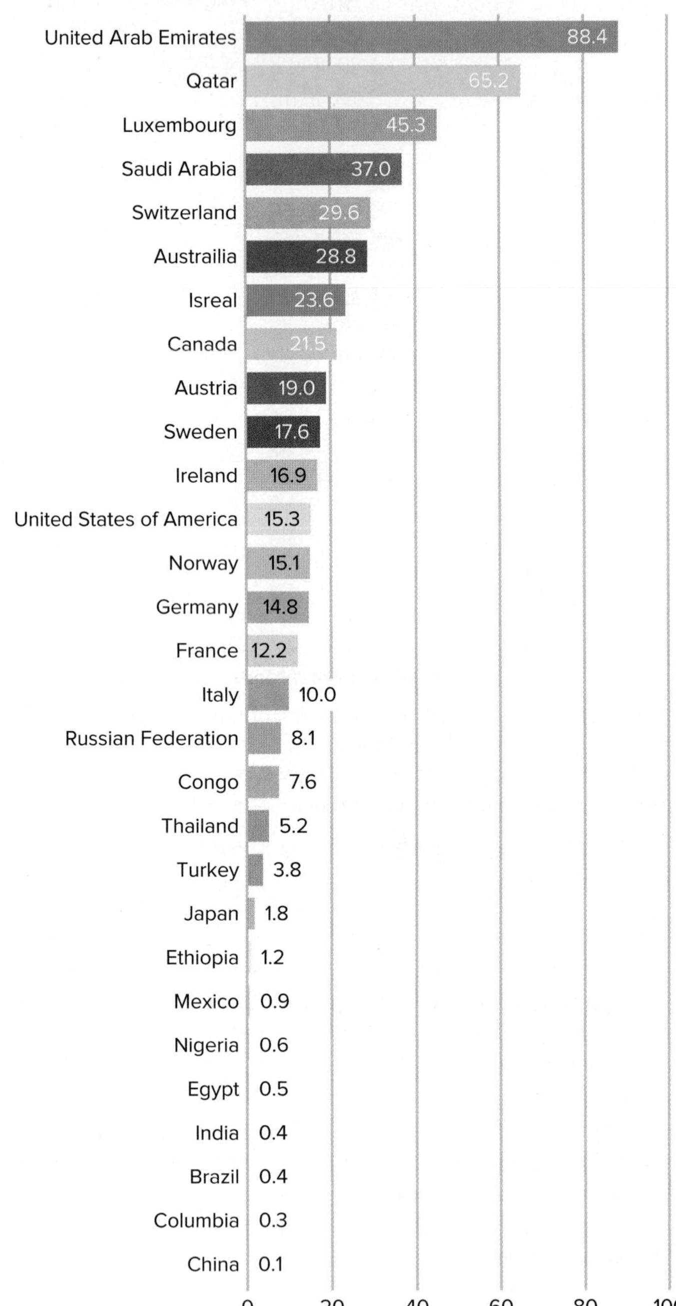

The percentage of foreign-born individuals in the populations of different countries varies widely. How does the United States compare with other countries in this regard?
Source: UN Department of Economic and Social Affairs, Population Division 2017c.

Another significant "pull" is the presence of relatives in another country. But certain "push" factors also drive people away from their homelands, including war, violence, oppression, instability, and disasters such as droughts, famines, and typhoons. For example, in 2017, 16.2 million people worldwide were displaced due to persecution, conflict, violence, or human rights violations (UNHCR 2018a).

About 3.4 percent of the world's people live in a country other than the one in which they were born. In the United States today, resistance to immigration is a major issue. The United States has the largest number of international migrants of any country in the world. The 49.8 million immigrants in the United States represent about one of five migrants worldwide. (Saudi Arabia and Germany, with 12.2 million immigrants each, have the next largest migrant populations.) However, migrants are a smaller percentage of the U.S. population than in many other countries (see Figure 17.4). In 2017, 3 of every 20 people living in the United States (15.3 percent) were born in another country. Indeed, a significant portion of the population growth in the United States and other wealthy nations today comes from immigrants' movement to these countries. Because of its mounting immigration rate, and because its birth rate is higher than Europe's, the United States has avoided the sorts of population losses that have affected many European nations. If current trends continue, 88 percent of the population increase in the United States between 2015 and 2065 will be due to immigrants and their U.S.-born descendants (Pew Research Center 2015j). This trend will have a major impact on education, politics, media, and other aspects of social life.

Aging Nations One side effect of increased life spans and declining birth rates is that many of the world's wealthier nations are aging rapidly. By 2070, one of four residents of the United States is expected to be over 65 years of age; that figure will be closer to one of three in more than a dozen countries, including Germany, China, and Japan. (Meanwhile, only about 1 of 12 people in Africa will be 65 or older.) Worldwide, the percentage of people over 65 years of age is expected to double between 2020 (9.4 percent) and 2070 (18.8 percent) (UN Department of Economic and Social Affairs, Population Division 2017a).

An aging population is associated with a variety of social phenomena. A "bulge" in the number of young people within a population is associated with increases in crime and political violence, so an aging population may serve as a counterbalance to these problems. At the same time, however, an aging population means a rising percentage of workers who are retired and need expensive health care and other social services, a situation that puts enormous economic strain on governments.

In the United States, the "graying of America" will present the nation with notable challenges. For example, as baby boomers retire, the nation faces the problem of fewer younger workers supporting the benefits of a larger number of retirees. In 1965, when the baby boom ended, there were 4 workers for every Social Security beneficiary. By 2010, when the oldest boomers were beginning to retire, the ratio was 2.9 to 1, and it is projected to drop to 2.2 to 1 by 2035 (Social Security Board of Trustees 2016). With fewer workers paying into Social Security, the system has had to adjust benefits to stay solvent. It has reduced benefits and delayed the retirement age at which workers receive full benefits. This means fewer jobs for younger workers.

In addition, increased life expectancy has meant that many older Americans are living longer and suffering from the chronic illnesses typical of old age. The growing number of older Americans is driving up demand for health services and senior housing and causing a significant redeployment of medical facilities and resources to care for this aging population.

Other challenges facing a graying United States are more cultural. In the past, aging Americans often were isolated from mainstream life. But as their life expectancy increases and their health prospects improve, seniors' social role is in transition. Older Americans are healthier and more vigorous than previous generations, and many are enjoying active retirements. Some are even pursuing "encore careers" doing community service work.

The Threat of Overpopulation: The Neo-Malthusian View

The historian and political economist Thomas Robert Malthus published a book in 1798 arguing that the human population was growing faster than the available food supply. Although the details of his arguments are out of date, the insight that the earth's population growth is unsustainable remains relevant. A more contemporary analysis, known as the **neo-Malthusian perspective,** *warns that human overpopulation is threatening the planet.* As evidence, supporters of this perspective point to environmental degradation, the rampant consumption pursued by wealthier nations, and high birth rates in poorer nations (Ehrlich 1986; Ehrlich and Ehrlich 2013). Such trends are unsustainable over time. The massive food shortages that Malthus and his later followers predicted were delayed by advances in agriculture, sometimes referred to as the "green revolution," but such technological advances cannot be maintained indefinitely. The dynamic of growth outpacing the supply of natural resources remains in effect.

To help correct ecological imbalances between the planet's population and its resources, neo-Malthusians support the empowerment of women. They maintain that women should have the right to make their own reproductive decisions, and they advocate the widespread availability and voluntary use of contraceptives. In addition, neo-Malthusians argue for a curb on rampant consumption and waste in wealthier societies.

What happens when the population grows at an unsustainable pace? Simply put, people die prematurely. Enormous progress has been made in recent years to reduce the child mortality rate, but in the world's poorer nations, infants and children are still dying at a frightening rate because they lack access to basic nutrition and medical care. Inequality and poverty are at the heart of this situation, but high birth rates make it worse. In Angola, Somalia, and Chad, some of the poorest countries, nearly one in eight children dies before age five, usually because of poverty-related conditions such as malnutrition and illnesses that could have been easily prevented (World Health Organization 2016d).

Demographic Transition

The threat of overpopulation should lessen as wealthier nations achieve negative growth and as more resources are put into stemming population growth in poorer countries. In fact, the rate of overall population growth globally has eased in recent years. This development is consistent with **demographic transition theory,** which suggests that *a society's population patterns are influenced decisively by its level of affluence and its adoption of new technology.* The theory originally focused on technological development but has evolved to reflect the fact that other factors associated with affluence—especially education and changing social norms—influence population patterns.

Although nations vary considerably and there are exceptions to this model, human societies have tended to move through four demographic stages (see Table 17.3). First, societies experienced high birth and death rates, a pattern yielding little overall change in population. In preindustrial societies throughout history, high death rates were the result of poor nutrition and hygiene, lack of knowledge about illness and disease, and the general difficulty of human survival. Because death rates were so

TABLE 17.3	DEMOGRAPHIC TRANSITION MODEL OF TYPICAL SOCIETAL EVOLUTION		
	Birth Rates	**Death Rates**	**Population**
First phase	High	High	Steady
Second phase	High	Lower	Enormous growth
Third phase	Lower	Lower	Slowed growth
Fourth phase	Low	Low	Steady

high, people had no incentive to reduce birth rates. In fact, most cultures placed a high value on fertility, and families had large numbers of children as a source of needed labor in agricultural societies—and as insurance of survival.

Second, those societies that industrialized reduced their death rates at all age levels. Industrialization contributed to greater affluence, which in turn allowed for better nutrition and more-sanitary living conditions. The scientific advances that led to industrialization also contributed to expanded knowledge about nutrition, sanitation, and disease. With the spread of such understanding and the adoption of healthier practices, infant mortality declined and adult illnesses became less deadly. But limited birth control options, along with cultural norms that discouraged contraception, kept birth rates high. Because the death rate declined while birth rates remained high, populations ballooned.

on social theory

Demographic transition theory suggests that population patterns are affected by affluence and the adoption of new technology. What features of **functionalist theory** are reflected in this analysis?

Third, as cultural norms changed and people developed more knowledge about and options for family planning—and as societies amassed the resources needed to make contraception widely available—the birth rate gradually declined and the rate of population increase slowed. Fourth, societies achieved **zero population growth**—*a balance between birth rates and death rates, which maintains stable population numbers.*

About a third of the world's societies—the affluent nations—have moved through these stages and are in or approaching the fourth stage. They are growing at relatively modest rates or reducing their population in some cases. The remaining nations are mostly in the second stage and are contributing to the continuing increase in the global population. However, change is occurring rapidly. As one report from the United Nations put it, "the end of high fertility is near" because developing countries around the world have had "declining levels of lifetime fertility" (UN Department of Economic and Social Affairs, Population Bureau 2017b).

Explaining the Demographic Divide

The social structure of a society influences birth rates. In agricultural societies, large families are highly valued since they provide labor for work on farms and in fields. Influenced by these structural conditions, agricultural societies have developed cultural norms that place great value—and confer high status—on large families.

As less developed nations industrialize, however, the cultural preference for large families begins to outlive its structural usefulness. Today, young people in such countries often work in factories, bringing needed income to the family from that source (as they did when Western nations first industrialized), but big families are not the economic asset they once were. In wealthier industrialized societies, in fact, having a large number of children is considered an expensive liability rather than an economic asset, and families feel pressure to reduce their reproduction rate (though norms still favor having children, instead of choosing to be child-free). In this way, social structure and cultural norms interact to influence individual action.

The interaction of socioeconomic and cultural factors also influences growth rates. For example, the relative affluence of wealthy societies is associated with improved education, which in turn results in a more informed population and expanded access to effective birth control. In contrast, people in poorer societies are less likely to have access to reproductive health services and accurate information about family planning. In 2017, the Trump administration cut international funding for family planning aid to programs that also provided abortions. Without access to contraceptives, both unwanted pregnancies and dangerous backstreet abortions increased (Elbagir, Leposo, and Mackintosh 2018). Because more-affluent societies also tend to have greater gender equality, women in such societies have more power to make their own decisions about reproduction. As women gain such rights, they tend to decide to have smaller families—or no children at all. Thus, increased affluence, higher levels of education, women's rights, and access to and cultural acceptance of birth control all contribute to lower birth rates. Securing equal rights for women is an example of the sorts of issues that spawn social movements, our next topic.

The Power of Social Movements

As we have seen, many social changes are unintentional and unanticipated. In this section, though, we examine efforts by people to promote change *deliberately* by participating in social movements.

Understanding Social Movements

On December 1, 1955, seamstress Rosa Parks was riding home on a bus in Montgomery, Alabama, when the driver told her to give up her seat for a white passenger and to move to the back in accordance with local segregation laws (Loeb 2010; Morris 1984). Tired from a long day at work, Parks refused—and was arrested. Her spontaneous act of individual defiance sparked the ensuing Montgomery bus boycott, a pivotal event in and catalyst for the U.S. civil rights movement.

At least, that is the usual story told about this famous incident. However, the real Rosa Parks and the actual bus boycott were more complicated, and they illustrate some common elements of social movement campaigns.

Parks's resistance did not happen without preparation. Parks was a civil rights activist long before her arrest. For over a decade, she had been active in a local chapter of the National Association for the Advancement of Colored People (NAACP), the leading civil rights group of the time, and had been mentored by E. D. Nixon, a labor union leader. A few months before her arrest, she had attended a 10-day training program at a labor and civil rights organizing school, where she had met like-minded activists and discusssed recent civil rights cases with them, including previous bus boycotts.

Shortly before Parks's arrest, the local NAACP had planned to challenge bus segregation in Montgomery using the case of Claudette Colvin, who had also been arrested for refusing to move to the back of the bus. Colvin's name is now largely lost to history; since she was unmarried and pregnant, the NAACP decided she would not be the right person to represent the message of their campaign. Rosa Parks, on the other hand, was perfect. Hardworking, dedicated, and churchgoing, she became the campaign's symbol—and an icon in the civil rights movement.

Parks could not have achieved change on her own. The power of the movement came from collective action by thousands of people. The local Women's Political Council took the lead in printing and distributing flyers encouraging a boycott. The newly formed Montgomery Improvement Association pooled money, automobiles, and all the resources necessary to sustain a year-long bus boycott. A young, relatively unknown preacher who was new in town and had not made any enemies was chosen to lead this group: Martin Luther King Jr. The NAACP took on the legal challenge and eventually won the Supreme Court case that settled the dispute and ended segregation on Montgomery's buses.

The real story of the Montgomery bus boycott features many aspects of social movement activism that are familiar to sociologists (Jasper 2014; Meyer 2015; Staggenborg 2016; Tarrow 2011; Tilly and Tarrow 2015). Successful movements need to develop a clear message; have effective organizations that can recruit members, mobilize resources, nurture new leaders, and draw upon experienced activists; and be persistent, because most of their efforts fail until the right opportunities come along. Despite difficult odds, successful movements by ordinary citizens can help make history—a topic explored in the Through a Sociological Lens box.

©Don Cravens/The LIFE Images Collection/Getty Images

Source: Black Lives Matter

FAST-FORWARD

Social Movement Communications

During the civil rights movement, organizers called mass meetings at local churches to enlist and communicate with members and build solidarity among African Americans. The meeting shown here was held during the 1956 Montgomery bus boycott. Such gatherings drew on many aspects of black church culture, including Gospel hymns, Bible readings, and powerful speeches by local pastors.

Today's movements are still grounded in face-to-face protest, but they draw on social media to reach a broader audience and share information more widely. The Black Lives Matter movement, for example, made extensive use of social media, posting information and videos from the movement's official accounts on Twitter, Facebook, and other platforms. Supporters used #blacklivesmatter to tag their Twitter communications and YouTube to share videos of their actions.

Defining Social Movements

Why don't corporate executives ever march in the streets holding picket signs? The answer is simple: they don't need to. Powerful executives have more conventional avenues by which to pursue their goals, such as hiring lobbyists, making campaign contributions, and networking with political officials. In the wake of the 2007–2009 financial crisis, for example, U.S. corporations received hundreds of billions of dollars in taxpayer-funded assistance without needing to take to the streets to ask for it.

THROUGH A SOCIOLOGICAL LENS

Democracy Isn't Easy: "Making Life" versus "Making History"

The understanding that people create society is a basic principle of sociology. The idea that ordinary citizens should have both the right and the power to change society is the essence of democracy. An interesting thread connects sociology, democracy, and social change—a thread examined by sociologist Richard Flacks.

Flacks, a leader in the student and antiwar movements of the 1960s, became a sociologist and later wrote *Making History* (1988), a now-classic book about social change. In the tradition of C. Wright Mills's analysis of the relationship between biography and history, Flacks highlights the difference between what he calls "making life" and "making history."

Most of us, most of the time, spend our time and energy "making life." We do household chores, shop, go to school or work, study, care for our families, enjoy leisure, pursue our hobbies—all the things we need to do to survive and to maintain and develop ourselves and our dependents.

"Making history" is different in that it involves the survival, maintenance, and development of *society,* not just individuals. In other words, making history influences the rules that govern everyday life for groups of people. If Congress votes to provide publicly funded day care, if corporate executives close down a factory in your hometown, if students come together to successfully resist a tuition increase, each of these acts changes the terms and conditions under which people live—and each is thus making history.

History making is usually associated with those who have considerable power. In fact, Flacks argues that we can think of power as "the capacity to make history" (5). People in powerful positions—such as political leaders and major corporate executives—make history as a routine part of their daily work lives. For them, "making life" and "making history" overlap substantially. The more that power is concentrated in the hands of such elites, the more that ordinary people feel like the objects of historical forces acting upon them, and the more *powerless* they feel to make history.

In fact, for most of us, history making is usually beyond our reach; we focus instead on making life. Democracy, though, is the idea that power should *not* be highly centralized in the hands of elites. Instead, democratic ideals suggest that ordinary citizens should have the power to choose priorities and create the rules for society. A healthy democratic system is routinely responsive to people's wishes, generally carrying out the will of the people through elections, referenda, and other mechanisms. This democratic ideal is in fact a radical notion that challenges the concentrated power of elites wherever it exists—in local communities, universities, workplaces, corporate boardrooms, or the halls of political power.

Much of U.S. history has been driven by the tension between the ideal of democracy and a reality that has fallen far short. Democratic rhetoric, however, was and is inspirational, and it has motivated generations of social movement activists who have worked to change U.S. society so that it more closely resembles the democratic ideal.

But participation in social movements can be stressful, because social movement activists often carry out the task of "making history" at the expense of "making life." Participation in a social movement can require major commitments of time and energy, and sometimes dedicated activists neglect friends, family, jobs, and other relationships. Since this level of commitment is difficult to sustain in the long term, social movement activism often occurs in bursts. For a relatively short period of time, people will give priority to "making history," and an upturn of activism will result. But because the mundane responsibilities of "making life" eventually must be attended to, the higher level of commitment that activism requires becomes unsustainable over the long haul for many people. Nonetheless, these bursts of heightened social movement activity—lasting from days to a few years—can leave a permanent mark on social life. They "make history."

think about it

1. *How do "making life" and "making history" differ in sociological terms?*
2. *Have you ever been involved in "history making"? If so, did it take a toll on your ability to "make life"? Explain.*
3. *In what specific ways can you, as an ordinary citizen, get involved in "making history"?*

Most people do not command such significant resources. The halls of power are not routinely open to them, so when normal political channels fail, they must find other ways to be heard. One such mechanism is social movements.

Social movements are *organized, ongoing collective efforts by relatively powerless people engaging in extrainstitutional action to promote or resist change.* That formal definition highlights several characteristics that distinguish social movements from other forms of social and political action. For example, movements are organized and ongoing; they are not just spontaneous onetime actions (as might be the case, say, with a riot). Movements are collective; they are not just courageous acts by individuals or the cumulative effect of individual actions (as with a social trend).

The single biggest distinction between social movements and other kinds of politics is that social movement activists use *extrainstitutional* tactics–measures that are outside the regular, routine political processes of voting, lobbying, or making campaign contributions, for example. Extrainstitutional tactics include everything from boycotts and nonviolent street demonstrations to armed insurrection. The participants use such tactics because they typically lack access to routine channels of power and thus are relatively powerless compared to their opponents.

At the turn of the twentieth century, for example, women agitating for the right to vote were shut out of mainstream politics and relied on unconventional tactics to advance their cause.

There are various types of social movement. For example, movements can mobilize either to promote or to resist change. In fact, often a social movement will face off against a countermovement, as in the longstanding clash between the "pro-life" and "pro-choice" movements over abortion.

Although social movements seldom fall neatly into one single category, and can change over time, they can be loosely classified by some of their characteristics. In particular:

- Social movements vary by the *degree of change* they seek. Does a movement seek modest changes or a radical transformation?
- Social movements also vary by the *level of change* they seek. Does a movement ask *individuals* to change their behavior (micro change), *institutions* to change the way they operate (meso change), or entire *societies* to change their structure or cultural values (macro change)?

Specific social movements can be analyzed in terms of both these characteristics, as summarized in Table 17.4. Movements seeking change at the individual level can advocate partial change ("alterative" movements, such as one aiming to stop substance abuse through a 12-step support group) or total change ("redemptive" movements, such as a cloistered religious order requiring total withdrawal from society). Movements seeking change at the institutional or societal level may also seek partial change ("reformative" movements, such as one pursuing mandatory recycling legislation) or total change ("transformative" movements, such as a revolutionary effort to overthrow a national government).

In many cases, participants in social movements engage in conventional political action, such as voting and lobbying, in addition to their other activities on the movement's behalf. The line between social movement activism and conventional political participation can therefore be blurry. As well, many social movements have advocates within the political system. For example, Tea Party and other right-wing activists, in addition to holding demonstrations and other events, work with supporters in the Republican Party's conservative wing. These two elements are often mutually beneficial, as social movement agitation pressures elected officials and makes it possible for allies within the system to move an agenda forward. Support from insiders gives legitimacy to activists' efforts and helps ensure that their cause gets serious consideration.

TABLE 17.4 TYPES OF SOCIAL MOVEMENT CHANGE

		Degree of Change	
		Partial	Total
Level of Change	Individual (micro)	Alterative	Redemptive
	Institutional (meso) or societal (macro)	Reformative	Transformative

Source: Adapted from Aberle ([1966] 1991).

Another major distinguishing feature of social movements is that they involve advocacy for social change—such as the passage of specific legislation or the enactment of institutional policies—rather than the provision of charity or social services (see Table 17.5). For example, a homeless shelter might provide vital services that meet the immediate needs of those without a home. However, such short-term relief does not change the underlying conditions that created homelessness in the first place, such as the scarcity of low-income housing and the lack of adequate jobs that pay a living wage. Although social services are essential, making long-term improvements requires tackling the *underlying cause* of a given social problem, not just treating the symptoms.

This distinction is important because it helps explain the often different dynamics involved in social movements as opposed to social services or charities. Because social movements seek to change structural, institutional, or cultural conditions, they inevitably come into conflict with those resisting this change. This struggle is ultimately about power.

TABLE 17.5 SOCIAL SERVICE AND SOCIAL CHANGE

	Social Services/Charitable Efforts	Social Change
Primary goal is to . . .	Meet immediate needs	Change structural conditions, underlying causes of a problem, or the balance of power
Focus of activities is on . . .	Providing a direct service (often aimed at individuals)	Structural, institutional, or cultural change
Parties involved include . . .	A service provider (for example, social worker, expert, volunteer) Client (recipient of goods and/or services)	Change advocates and supporters "Target" group or institution (suggests conflict is likely)

Power, Conflict, and Social Movements

Social movements typically face the dilemma that those who support (or resist) change through a social movement have little power, whereas those who have power and benefit from the current social structure generally resist movement efforts. As a result, when ordinary people advance their cause through social movements, they come into conflict with people in power. The conflict might be minimal and brief, or it might be violent and long-lasting. However, if conflict does not occur—if everyone already agrees on the issue at hand—then there is no social change.

A letter written in 1849 by Frederick Douglass (2003), the former slave and abolitionist leader, famously expresses this point. In his poetic prose, Douglass presents a sociological analysis of the role of power in enforcing order, and of ordinary people's potential to challenge that power:

> If there is no struggle there is no progress. Those who profess to favor freedom, and yet depreciate agitation, are men who want crops without plowing up the ground. They want rain without thunder and lightning. . . . Power concedes nothing without a demand. It never did and it never will. Find out just what people will submit to, and you have found the exact amount of injustice and wrong which will be imposed upon them; and these will continue until they are resisted with either words or blows, or with both. (42)

As was the case with Douglass's fight against slavery, social movement organizers face daunting odds. By their nature, these movements are efforts by underdogs with little obvious power to challenge entrenched and powerful interests. Given this situation, it is not surprising that the vast majority of these efforts fail to achieve their stated aims. Yet sometimes social movements succeed and spark significant social change, often overcoming enormous odds. How is this possible?

As we saw in Chapter 5, power is the ability to bring about an intended outcome, even when it is opposed by others. Power is thus a social dynamic rather than a "thing" to be possessed. For a person or group to be given power over others, people must be convinced, rewarded, or threatened into obeying. But obedience is not inevitable; it is voluntary and can be withdrawn. So ordinary people have more power then they realize, because the orderly functioning of society requires their tacit cooperation to continue. This threat that noncompliance will disrupt a part of society is a major element of social movements' power. By **organizing**—*coordinating and directing the efforts of many individuals to work for a cause*—activists pool the power of individuals into a substantial collective force for change (Bobo, Kendall, and Max 2010; Jobin-Leeds and AgitArte 2016).

Those in positions of power who are being targeted by a specific social movement can resist in various ways. First, they can often prevail simply by relying on cultural norms and routines. For example, they might take advantage of the fact that most people have been socialized to "follow the rules" and "not rock the boat" and know that individuals generally do not want to take risks, be seen as deviant, or look foolish. To encourage compliant behavior, people in power often give activists labels with a negative social stigma, such as "outside agitators," "extremists," "romantic idealists," "troublemakers," "politically correct," "radicals," and "terrorists." Similarly, those in power can encourage common attitudes of cynicism, fatalism, or apathy, all of which discourage activism and are thus useful in preventing change. Activists often counter this tactic by linking their efforts to mainstream cultural values (democracy, freedom, justice, God) or by affirming a positive counterculture that promotes solidarity. Sometimes they even appropriate a "deviant" label once used against them, as in the case of the gay rights chant, "We're queer, we're here; get used to it."

Second, those in power can use material or political sanctions to either reward or punish individual activists. They can try to co-opt opponents—lure the activists to their side—by using rewards such as job offers or promotions, grants, and concessions on smaller issues. Or they can threaten to punish activists by, for example, firing them, expelling them from school, or fining them. Often merely the *threat* of such action is enough to secure compliance. In response, activists typically stress the importance of solidarity for success, try to protect individuals, and discourage the co-opting of members.

Third, as a last resort, those in power can use physical control, including arrests, beatings, and even the execution of individuals who participate in social movements. In opposing a movement's efforts, those in power must often be careful not to overreact and respond in an overly aggressive manner that might generate additional support for the movement. For their part, activists must reduce fears of participating in the movement—for example, by using social media to publicize successful demonstrations by activists.

Movement Actors

Community organizers—activists who organize people to address local problems—have long noted that there are two basic sources of power: money and people. Powerful elites have few people among their ranks, but they do have lots of money and other resources with which to carry out their agendas. Social movements, on the other hand, may not have piles of money, but they have the potential to organize many people into a powerful force—and in this way to change the balance of power. To succeed, they need to develop viable organizations to coordinate their members' action.

Movements are usually made up of a number of different social movement organizations. For example, two of the most prominent social movement organizations within the human rights movement are Amnesty International and Human Rights

thinking about power

Name two or three present-day social movements that are seeking change. What are the activists' goals? Where would these movements fall in Table 17.4? What gives the movements their **power**? How successful do you think they have been?

Watch. The organizations that compose a movement usually have different goals, audiences, and tactics. But all such organizations must operate on a field that includes three groups of actors: supporters, opponents, and bystanders.

Supporters assist a movement and can be either *activists,* the core staff and volunteers who are directly involved in planning and carrying out the organization's goals, or *adherents,* those who agree with and occasionally assist the movement's efforts but with less intensity than the core activist supporters. A movement's *opponents* include the *target group,* the individuals and organizations that are being pressured, as well as any *countermovements,* social movements that have organized to oppose the movement's efforts. Finally, in any given conflict, the vast majority of people are uninvolved *bystanders,* individuals with little or no stake in the outcome and who often know little or nothing about the issues. Nevertheless, bystanders play a potentially pivotal role, because the resolution of any conflict depends on whether they get involved and, if they do, which side they support. It is especially important for social movements to enlist the support of bystanders since movements typically have less power in the conflict; with little money, they can win only by expanding their numbers. Those in power usually want to contain the conflict, not to expand it to include bystanders.

Movement Success: Message, Resources, and Opportunity

Sociologists highlight three important ingredients for social movement success: an effective message, adequate resources, and opportunity in the form of a favorable political environment. The significance of these factors will vary depending on the movement, but to some degree, they all affect the possibility of a movement's success.

Framing: Articulating the Message and Forging a Collective Identity

Are proposed cuts to the education budget a sensible step toward fiscal responsibility or an assault on students' future? In answering such a question, social movement activists engage in **framing,** *interpreting and assigning meaning to events and conditions in order to shape a movement's message and the collective identity that develops among members.* In framing issues and events, social movement activists try to mobilize support for their cause by communicating with the public (Snow and Benford 1988).

A movement must communicate by framing the issue it is addressing in a way that is consistent with its goals (Snow et al. 1986). In particular, to be successful, a movement must

- Persuade people to see the condition they are concerned about as an injustice
- Advance a viable alternative
- Convince people that they are responsible for and capable of effecting change

Social movements attempt to spread these messages to the general public through one-on-one organizing, public events, their websites, and social media, as well as by mainstream media coverage.

Further, movements encourage the development of a collective identity through an organizational culture that involves shared values, music, logos, T-shirts, literature, and knowledge of movement history. A strong collective identity can be a crucial means of promoting solidarity and the willingness to sacrifice on behalf of a cause, both of which are essential if a movement is to be effective.

SPOTLIGHT on social theory

Framing originates in the work of **symbolic interactionist** Erving Goffman (1974). How does a movement's need to frame issues reflect the basic insights of this theoretical perspective?

Resource Mobilization

Resource mobilization is *the process by which social movements generate the assets necessary to build and sustain the movement.* This process, which is vital to the movement's success, includes raising money, recruiting members, developing tactics and strategies, finding people with necessary skills, and training leaders (McCarthy and Zald 1977).

The likelihood of a person's being successfully mobilized by a social movement is influenced by his or her structural location. Individuals are more likely to join a social movement effort if they

- Have prior contact with a movement activist, which provides a personal connection and a social incentive for participation
- Belong to other—even nonmovement—organizations, because such affiliations make them more likely to learn about movement issues and events and come into contact with activists
- Have few personal constraints, such as childrearing responsibilities, marriage, and full-time employment (parents acting specifically to protect the future of their children are an exception)

Middle-class college students typically have relatively high rates of participation in social movements. Why? Many often have few personal constraints, are involved in other organizations and activities, and live on campus—a common setting for social movement organization and mobilization.

Political Opportunity

The environment in which a social movement operates can be critical to the success—or failure—of a movement (Jasper and Goodwin 2011; Tilly 2004a). **Political opportunities** are *the factors outside a social movement that can influence whether it emerges and is successful.*

Sometimes a dramatic event can create political opportunities. High-profile mass shootings helped gun control activists spark widespread public debate about possible legislation.

External actors can also affect a movement's success or failure. A government, for example, can repress a movement, ignore it, or accommodate some of its demands, each of which will affect the movement differently. If a government is divided internally, movement activists are more likely to find political opportunities in aligning with allies within the halls of power.

The mainstream media are also external players with the potential to exercise considerable influence over the outcome of a movement's efforts. Media coverage, along with social media messages, can help mobilize support and protect activists from violent government repression.

©Bill Clark/CQ Roll Call/Getty Images

Advocates for the decriminalization of marijuana attract attention from the media (and police) by carrying a giant 50-foot replica of a joint during a demonstration in front of the White House in 2016. What other tactics do demonstrators use to attract media attention? How might such tactics help or harm the demonstrators' cause?

Finally, other social movement organizations can have an impact on the results of a movement's efforts. Countermovements can effectively undermine support for a movement. On the other hand, other organizations within a movement can often be allies in a broader struggle.

Movement Stages

Although each social movement is unique, successful movements tend to follow a cyclical pattern of birth, growth, success, and decline (Tarrow 2011; Taylor 1989). Movements often begin at the margins of society when a few activists—who are often influenced by earlier movement efforts—start raising an issue. These efforts attract the attention of a few others who are sympathetic to the cause. Over time, these contacts among individuals become routine, and the early activists create a social movement organization to coordinate and fund a movement campaign (see Figure 17.5).

Most movements end at this stage, with an ineffectual organization that eventually disbands. But in successful cases, social movement organizations grow, drawing more supporters, creating a more coherent collective identity, and clarifying positions on the issues. As the movement builds, it can make substantial—though typically partial—progress toward achieving its goals.

Eventually, though, the movement declines. Sometimes historical events overtake the movement and make the issue it is addressing a lower priority. Sometimes opponents can effectively respond to movement challenges by diverting their energies toward unproductive efforts such as forming a new committee to study the issue being contested (*co-optation*) and agreeing to a token settlement that does not address the movement's fundamental demands (*accommodation*), or by using force to defeat the movement (*repression*). Sometimes, ironically, decline comes about because of success. When a movement succeeds at least partially in achieving a primary goal, that success can eliminate a unifying focus for its members and make it vulnerable to fragmentation and infighting over new goals and priorities. Also, a sudden surge in growth of the movement can change its composition, culture, and internal dynamics, planting the seeds for its disintegration (Gitlin 2003). Finally, the movement disbands entirely or enters a period of retrenchment sustained by a handful of committed activists, with minimal support and activity. These remnants of past movements can often be a resource for the emergence of new movements.

The Impact of Social Movements on Culture, Structure, and Power

Movement activism is a central mechanism for social change. It takes ideas that often originate at the margins of society and incorporates them into mainstream society, sometimes changing culture, social structures, and power relations. Many of the basic rights and privileges we enjoy are the result of the struggles of activists who came before us.

At first, new ideas about how social life should be organized can seem so foreign to common experience that the people who support them are not taken seriously. Overthrowing British rule in the North American colonies, abolishing slavery, establishing the 40-hour workweek, ensuring equal rights for women, providing free public education, ensuring access to safe and legal contraceptives, legalizing same-sex marriage—all seemed absurd at one time, and advocates for these causes were ignored or ridiculed. As movements advancing such ideas gain momentum, those resisting change often see these advocates as a threat, and criticize, vilify, and even attack them as dangerous. Often, these movements achieved partial success but remained controversial during a period of transition. Gradually, though, some movements achieve a critical mass of support, tipping the scales in their favor (see Figure 17.6). When social change resulting from such movements is finally implemented and fully incorporated into society, it appears to those who come after to have been inevitable and to be just common sense—the way things ought to be. Thus, controversial change that seems radical or even revolutionary in one historical period can become the norm—until, perhaps, new efforts challenge prevailing assumptions, either advancing change further or rolling back earlier gains.

FIGURE 17.5 | A SUCCESSFUL MOVEMENT CYCLE

A few people are concerned → Activists form a social movement organization → Movement grows to include many supporters → Change occurs—usually partial → Movement declines → A few activists remain committed to the cause

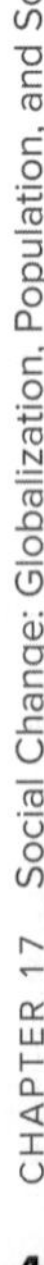

FIGURE 17.6 | CHANGING VALUES: U.S. SUPPORT FOR SAME-SEX MARRIAGE, 2001–2017

Percentage who favor same-sex marriage

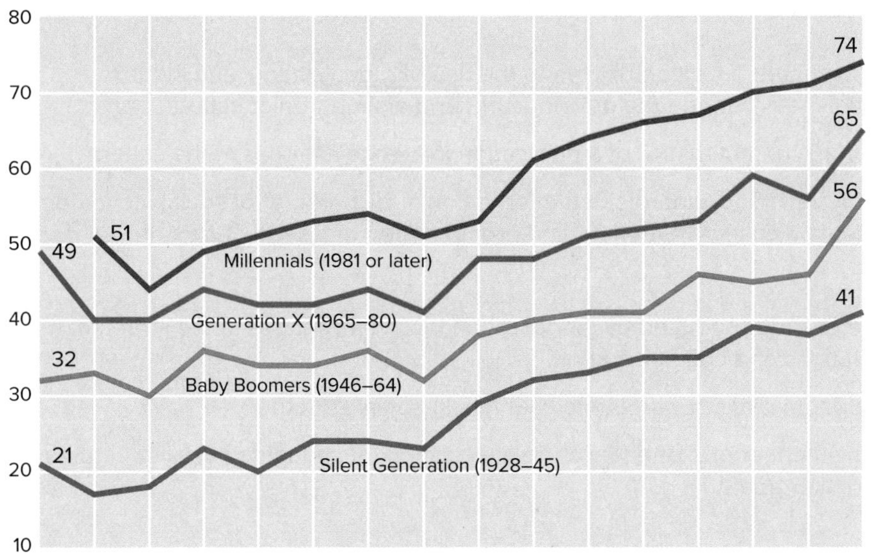

A successful social movement can help change a society's cultural values. Advocates of marriage equality, for example, have gradually succeeded in making their ideas more acceptable to each successive generation. Eventually, social institutions responded and in 2015 same-sex marriage was recognized nationally.

Source: Pew Research Center 2017d.

A Changing World

MOVEMENTS AND THE STRUGGLE OVER THE INTERNET

The ability to communicate effectively with the public is a crucial component of social movement success. It is also a dimension of social organizing that has undergone breathtaking change. Earlier movements relied on face-to-face communication, public speeches, and the printed word. All those techniques are still important today, but contemporary social movements have increasingly relied on the internet and mobile devices to distribute information, contact people, and raise money (Carty 2015). Organizational websites, Facebook pages, Twitter accounts, and other social media are standard communication channels for social movement initiatives. Perhaps most dramatically, pro-democracy movements in repressive nations such as Egypt, Iran, Russia, and China have used these media to help organize and communicate around the world.

However, the opponents of pro-democracy and other social movement efforts have responded with tactics of their own to *limit* communication. Freedom House, a watchdog group advocating political rights and civil liberties, monitors internet freedom around the world and releases its annual "Freedom on the Net" analysis. By the 2017 edition of the report, the group had documented the seventh consecutive year of overall *decline* in internet freedom. It subtitled this edition of the report "Manipulating Social Media to Undermine Democracy" when it found that online manipulation and disinformation tactics were a significant factor in the elections of at least 18 countries the previous year, including the United States. Led by Russia and China, but used in at least 30 countries including Turkey, the Philippines, and Venezuela, governments around the world have employed armies of people—and created countless automated bots—to go online to promote government propaganda, shape public opinion, and attack critics in social movements. These tactics are more subtle and difficult to combat than those governments used in earlier years. Those more blunt efforts are still employed, though, and include these common practices:

- ***Censorship of social media.*** In response to the popularity of social networking sites among movement organizers, countries implement consistent or temporary bans on social media services.
- ***Repression of internet users.*** Countries detain, arrest, or imprison bloggers, online journalists, and human rights activists for their internet communications.
- ***Cyberattacks against critics.*** Increasingly, governments and their supporters are launching cyberattacks to disrupt online social networks, cripple movement websites, and spy on electronic communications.
- ***Censorship and manipulation of internet content.*** Some countries consistently block politically relevant internet content, including the sites of news organizations and human rights groups.
- ***Limits on internet access.*** In some countries, the government targets centralized internet infrastructure to limit its citizens' access to international internet traffic, even cutting off the internet entirely in some cases during political turmoil.

Of the 65 countries analyzed by the Freedom House monitors, 16 (including the United States) were categorized as "free" when it comes to internet access; 28 (including India and Mexico) were "partly free," and 21 (including China, Russia, Saudi Arabia, and Turkey) were "not free."

The clash over internet freedom is one example of the broader social change struggles around the world. People striving for justice and freedom face intimidating obstacles in the form of powerful adversaries and entrenched social structures. Yet the study of sociology reveals that just as human beings created the prevailing social conditions, they can take action to change them. Understanding that people can make a difference—both in changing their own lives and in helping transform society—is an exciting, liberating, and hopeful insight.

In the end, nothing is more persistent than change. The only questions are, What direction will change take, and what role will you play in it?

thinking sociologically about Social Change

culture

- Changes in culture have contributed to the rise of globalization, and in turn globalization has changed the development and distribution of culture.
- The changing characteristics of a population influence changes in the culture.
- Culture plays an important role in the formation and character of social movements as they create a collective identity and promote their message of change.

structure

- Part of the change produced by globalization involves changes in the structure of organizations and communication.
- Changing populations contribute to changes in social structure.
- Social movement efforts often face the difficult task of changing social structures to achieve their goals.

power

- Globalization has shifted the amount of power held by various players, including national governments and transnational corporations.
- As populations change in a society, some communities become more powerful, while others become less so.
- Social movements involve struggles over power.

REVIEW, REFLECT, AND APPLY

Looking Back

1. Social change involves modification of social structure or cultural patterns. Change is a continuous process, is often unintended, occurs at different levels, and often produces conflict.
2. Sociological theories, such as Marx's theory emphasizing material factors and Weber's case for the influence of ideas, highlight differing causes of social change. However, change must be understood in the specific context within which it occurs, taking into account multiple sources.
3. *Globalization* is an umbrella term referring to the interaction or integration among various aspects of social life, including economies, cultures, political systems, and populations. This integration helps overcome the barriers of physical space and time.
4. Globalization is rooted in colonialism and is still characterized by deep global inequalities and controversies over the distribution of power, including concern about the homogenization of culture and about neoliberal policies that favor wealthy nations.
5. The world's population is growing rapidly, often due to improvements in health and life expectancy, and most of the growth is occurring in poorer nations. Meanwhile, many wealthier nations are experiencing stable or declining populations, producing a demographic divide. Explanations for this divide include socioeconomic and cultural factors.
6. Demographic trends include an increase in the share of the world's population in developing nations and in immigration to wealthier nations, as well as an overall aging population.

7. Social movements are efforts by relatively powerless people engaging in extrainstitutional action to promote or resist change. Unlike social services, social movement activism targets the causes of social problems, not just the symptoms, and involves conflict between opposing parties.
8. Successful social movements must frame their efforts effectively, mobilize resources, and navigate the political environment. An important goal is often to convince bystanders to support the movement.
9. Movements tend to operate in cycles, and even successful movements decline eventually. Social movements tend to start at the margins of society. When successful, their ideas become part of mainstream social life.

Critical Thinking: Questions and Activities

1. What do you think is more important as a cause of most social change: economic factors or ideas? Why?
2. What is globalization? Give examples of ways in which globalization has affected your life. Overall, do you think globalization has had a positive or negative impact on your life? Explain.
3. Social movements on both the left and right have criticized some features of globalization. What do these critiques have in common? How are they different?
4. Do the earth's rapidly growing population and the demographic divide concern you? Why or why not? What challenge do they pose in the coming years? What, if anything, do you think should be done to address the issue?
5. Visit the website of a social movement organization of your choice. What cultural values and symbols is the movement invoking in communicating with readers?
6. Do you think the spread of disinformation and propaganda by governments and their supporters is a significant threat to the future of the internet? Why or why not? What, if anything, can be done about it?

Key Terms

contextual analyses (p. 445) analyses that take into account the particular historical and social context within which change is occurring and do not assume that a single factor is the most important in all situations.

crude birth rate (p. 455) the number of live births per 1,000 people in a population.

crude death rate (p. 455) the number of deaths per 1,000 people in a population.

demographic divide (p. 454) the inequality in population and health conditions between rich and poor countries.

demographic transition theory (p. 457) the view that a society's population patterns are influenced decisively by its level of affluence and its adoption of new technology.

demography (p. 453) the study of human population trends.

framing (p. 463) interpreting and assigning meaning to events and conditions in order to shape a movement's message and the collective identity that develops among members.

globalization (p. 446) the worldwide interaction or integration among various aspects of social life, including economies, cultures, political systems, and populations.

growth rate (p. 454) the indicator that measures how quickly a country's population is increasing.

historical materialism (p. 444) the part of Marx's work suggesting that the economic base of a society is the primary force driving change in other aspects of social life.

infant mortality rate (p. 454) the number of infants less than a year old who die per 1,000 live births.

life expectancy (p. 454) the median number of years a person is likely to live given the current conditions.

migration (p. 455) the movement of people from one place to another.

neoliberalism (p. 452) an economic philosophy that promotes markets, deregulation, privatization, and reduced government social expenditures.

neo-Malthusian perspective (p. 457) the view, derived from Malthus's thought, warning that human overpopulation is threatening the planet.

organizing (p. 462) coordinating and directing the efforts of many individuals to work for a cause.

political opportunities (p. 463) factors outside a social movement that can influence whether it emerges and is successful.

population pyramid (p. 455) a bar chart showing the distribution of a population by age and sex.

resource mobilization (p. 463) the process by which social movements generate the assets necessary to build and sustain a movement.

social change (p. 441) the modification of structural or cultural patterns over time.

social movements (p. 460) organized, ongoing collective efforts by relatively powerless people engaging in extrainstitutional action to promote or resist change.

social trend (p. 442) the direction a society takes when many individuals act independently but similarly.

unintended consequences (p. 442) results that are unplanned and unforeseen.

zero population growth (p. 458) a balance between birth rates and death rates, which maintains stable population numbers.

Glossary

A

absolute poverty a scarcity of resources so severe that it is life-threatening.

achieved status a position in a social system that a person attains voluntarily, to a considerable degree, as the result of his or her own efforts.

action the ability to behave independent of social constraints.

active audiences audiences that make choices about how they use the media and actively interpret media content.

affective action behavior guided by emotions and feelings.

affirmative action policies and programs that aim to avoid discrimination and redress past discrimination through the active recruitment of qualified minorities for jobs, promotions, and educational opportunities.

agenda-setting theory a theory that holds that media may not be able to tell people what to think, but they can significantly influence what people think about.

agents of social control the authorities and social institutions that enforce norms and rules, attempt to prevent rule violations, and identify and punish rule violators.

agents of socialization people and groups who teach us about our culture.

alienation the separation and isolation of workers as a result of the structure of capitalist society.

amalgamation the process by which a majority and a minority group blend or mix to form a new group.

anomie social normlessness, without moral guidance or standards.

anticipatory socialization the process by which individuals practice for a future social role by adopting the norms or behaviors associated with a position they have not yet achieved.

applied research research that has the primary goal of directly addressing some social problem or need.

ascribed status a social position that is assigned to us from birth or that we assume later in life, regardless of our wishes or abilities.

asexual people people who experience no sexual attraction for anyone.

assimilation the process by which members of a minority group come to adopt the culture of the majority group.

authoritarian government a government that typically features self-appointed leaders who exert great control over the lives of citizens, which includes severely limiting their civil liberties.

B

basic research research that has the primary goal of describing some aspect of society and advancing our understanding of it.

behavioral targeting advertising sent to online users based on their earlier internet activities.

behaviors the actions associated with a group that help reproduce a distinct way of life.

beliefs the specific convictions or opinions that a people generally accept as being true.

bilingual education instruction in both a student's first language and English.

biological determinism a theory that contends that biology, specifically our genetic makeup, almost completely shapes human behavior.

bisexuals people who are attracted to people of both sexes.

breaching experiments social situations in which the individuals involved intentionally break social rules, violating basic norms and patterns of behavior.

built environment the physical surroundings that humans create, including the buildings, roads, dams, homes, and consumer products we use every day.

bureaucracy a hierarchical administrative system with formal rules and procedures used to manage organizations.

C

capital the money to invest in factories, real estate, and other businesses.

capital punishment the death penalty.

capitalism an economic system that emphasizes private ownership of the means of production, which are operated for profit.

capitalist class (or bourgeoisie) those who control major capital and own the means of production.

caste system stratification based on various ascribed characteristics determined at birth.

charismatic authority power whose legitimacy is derived from the extraordinary personal characteristics of an individual leader, which inspire loyalty and devotion.

charter schools public schools run by an organization that is independent from local school districts.

church a formal religious organization with broad mainstream acceptance.

civil religion a set of common beliefs and ritual practices that bind people in a predominantly secular society.

class a group of people who share a roughly similar economic position and lifestyle.

class domination theory a theory that suggests that political power is concentrated in the hands of the rich, who own or control a large share of the nation's economic resources.

class mobility the ability to move from one social class to another.

class system stratification determined by economic position, which results from a combination of individual achievement and family of birth.

classism prejudice or discrimination based on social class.

coerce to force people's compliance by threatening, intimidating, pressuring, or harming them.

cohabitation a social relationship that can create family ties and typically involves sexual intimacy, in which people live together as unmarried partners.

collective bargaining negotiations between union representatives and an employer on questions of pay, benefits, and working conditions.

collective conscience the shared norms, beliefs, and values in a community.

colonialism the use of military, political, and economic power by one society to dominate the people of another society, usually for economic benefit.

color-blind racism a form of bias in which the promotion of race neutrality helps maintain existing racial and ethnic inequality.

commodification the process of transforming all things into a product to be bought and sold.

commodity fetishism consumers' failure to recognize the labor that created the value in the commodities they use.

community a set of social relationships, typically arising from living in a particular place, that give people a sense of identity and belonging.

community studies a field that typically looks at groups of people who share some common tie and engage in social interaction within a particular geographic area.

comparable worth a commitment to setting salaries for different job titles based on their value to an employer, regardless of the typical gender of those working in such jobs.

conflict theories social theories that focus on issues of contention, power, and inequality, highlighting the competition for scarce resources.

conspicuous consumption lavish spending, done to compete for status with others.

consumerism an emphasis on shopping and the possession of material goods as the route to personal happiness.

consumption the process of choosing, purchasing, and using goods.

content analysis a variety of techniques that enable researchers to systematically summarize and analyze the content of various forms of communication—written, spoken, or pictorial.

contextual analyses analyses that take into account the particular historical and social context within which change is occurring and do not assume that a single factor is the most important in all situations.

control theory a theory that suggests that our behavior is regulated by the strength of our connection to major social institutions, including family, school, and religion.

convention a practice or technique that is widely used in a particular social setting.

convergence theory a theory that suggests capitalist and socialist economies are becoming increasingly similar.

conversation analysis a method of analyzing the patterns in face-to-face conversation that produce the smooth, back-and-forth turn-taking of such exchanges.

corporation a business that is treated legally as an entity separate from its owners.

correlation a relationship in which change in one variable is connected to change in another variable.

counterculture a subculture that champions values and lifestyles distinctly opposed to those of the dominant culture.

credentialing the process whereby those with advanced educational degrees and formal certificates monopolize access to the most rewarding jobs.

crime deviant behavior that violates a law.

crime rates statistics that measure the incidence of crime in relation to population size.

critical social science research carried out explicitly to create knowledge that can be used to bring about social change.

crude birth rate the number of live births per 1,000 people in a population.

crude death rate the number of deaths per 1,000 people in a population.

cult a small religious community whose beliefs and practices are at odds with the dominant culture.

cultivation theory a theory that argues that, by repeated and long-term exposure to the media's portrayal of the world (especially on television), people come to accept many of these depictions as reality.

cultural capital various types of knowledge, skills, and other cultural resources.

cultural imperialism the tendency of media corporations from wealthier nations—especially the United States—to export so many of their media products that they come to dominate the local cultures of other, especially poorer, nations.

cultural lag the ways that new technological developments often outpace the norms that govern our collective experiences with these new technologies.

cultural object a physical item that is created by and associated with people who share a culture.

cultural relativism the practice of understanding a culture by its own standards.

culture the collection of values, beliefs, knowledge, norms, language, behaviors, and material objects shared by a people and socially transmitted from generation to generation.

culture shock the experience of being disoriented because of a lack of knowledge about an unfamiliar social situation.

culture war an intense disagreement about core values and moral positions.

D

decriminalization the process of making an illegal action legal.

deindustrialization the process by which investment in the nation's manufacturing capacity decreased.

democracy a political system in which the right to vote is widespread and government leaders are selected through multiparty elections.

demographic divide the inequality in population and health conditions between rich and poor countries.

demographic transition theory the view that a society's population patterns are influenced decisively by its level of affluence and its adoption of new technology.

demography the study of human population trends.

dependency theory a theory that attributes global inequality to the exploitation of weaker, poor nations by wealthy, more powerful ones.

dependent variable the entity that changes in response to the independent variable.

deviance behavior that does not conform to basic cultural norms and expectations.

deviant subculture a group in which membership is based on a shared commitment to specific nonconformist beliefs or behaviors.

dialect a variant of a language with its own distinctive accent, vocabulary, and in some cases grammatical characteristics.

differential association theory a theory that deviance is learned through interaction with other people involved in deviant behavior.

digital convergence the merging of different forms of media through their transformation into digital information.

digital divide the gap between those who have the knowledge and resources needed to use digital information technology, especially computers and the internet, and those who do not.

discrimination treating others unequally based on their background or other personal characteristics.

division of labor the way people specialize in different tasks, each requiring specific skills.

doing gender creating gender through interactions in particular social settings.

domestic violence (or **intimate partner violence**) a pattern of abusive behavior in any relationship that is used by one partner to gain or maintain power and control over another intimate partner.

dominant culture a culture that permeates a society and that represents the ideas and practices of those in positions of power.

dominant ideology a widely held and regularly reinforced set of assumptions that generally support the current social system and serve the interests of authorities.

dramaturgy an approach to the study of social interaction that uses the metaphor of social life as a theater.

dual product market the situation that occurs when a company sells two completely different types of "products" to two completely different sets of buyers.

dysfunctional inhibiting or disrupting the working of a system as a whole.

E

economic security the condition of having a stable means of financial support adequate to maintain a given standard of living.

economy a social institution that includes a society's production, distribution, and consumption of goods and services.

education the social institution through which individuals acquire knowledge and skills and learn cultural norms and values.
emotional labor jobs that require employees to manage their feelings and to display specific feelings to their customers or clients.
empirical evidence evidence that can be observed or documented using the human senses.
empowerment an increase in the capacity of people to bring about an intended outcome.
endogamy the restriction of marriage by either law or custom to people within the same social category.
environmental health the aspects of health, illness, and disease that result from environmental factors.
environmental justice the prevention of harmful practices that unfairly burden low-income people and racial minorities with disproportionate exposure to environmental hazards.
environmental security the safe management of natural resources to protect social stability.
environmental sociology the study of the interaction between social life, the built environment, and the natural environment.
epigenetics the study of changes in gene expression (some of which can be passed on to children) that are produced without changing the underlying genetic code.
equal opportunity the idea that all people should have the same chance to achieve success.
ethic of reciprocity the "golden rule" that encourages people to treat others as they would like to be treated.
ethnicity a shared cultural heritage often deriving from a common ancestry and homeland.
ethnocentrism the judging of other cultures by the standards of one's own on the assumption that one's own is superior.
ethnomethodology an approach that examines the methods people use to make sense of their daily activities, emphasizing the ways in which they collectively create social structure in their everyday activities.
exogamy marriage between people from different social categories.
experiment a data-gathering technique in which the researcher manipulates an independent variable under controlled conditions to determine if change in an independent variable produces change in a dependent variable, thereby establishing a cause-and-effect relationship.
extended family consists of the nuclear family plus other relatives such as grandparents who commonly live together.

F

faith belief grounded in personal conviction or divine revelation rather than scientific evidence.
family two or more people, related either by birth or through social commitment, who share resources, care for any dependents, and often maintain a close emotional relationship.
feminism a philosophy that advocates social, political, and economic equality for women and men.
feminization of poverty a trend in which women made up an increasingly large share of the poor.
fertility rate the average number of births per female.
field research a data collection technique in which the researcher systematically observes some aspect of social life in its natural setting.
folkways group habits or customs that are common in a given culture.
framing interpreting and assigning meaning to events and conditions in order to shape a movement's message and the collective identity that develops among members.
functionalist theories see "structural-functionalist theories."
fundamentalism a religious movement that advocates strict adherence to traditional principles in all aspects of social life, usually based on literal interpretation of a religion's infallible sacred texts.

G

Gemeinschaft social organization in which most relationships are based on the long-term personal ties of collective kinship, common tradition, and shared values.
gender the socially constructed cultural expectations associated with women and men.
gender convergence a trend toward increasing similarity in how women and men live.
gender division of labor differences between men and women in access to jobs.
gender expression the communication of a person's gender identity to others, through behavior, clothing, hairstyle, and other means.
gender identity a person's identification as a woman, a man, or some combination of the two.
gender role a set of social expectations regarding behavior and attitudes based on a person's sex.
gender stratification the systematic and unequal distribution of power and resources in society between women and men.
generalize the ability to describe patterns of behavior of a larger population based on findings from a sample.
generalized other the values and orientations of one's overall community rather than those of specific individuals.
genocide the systematic killing of a group of people, based on their race, ethnicity, nationality, or religion.
gentrification the process of rehabilitating older housing stock and investing in neighborhood development in a way that typically attracts new higher-income residents and displaces current middle- and low-income residents.
Gesellschaft social organization in which most social relationships are impersonal, temporary, and based primarily on the pursuit of individual rational self-interest.
glass ceiling the often-invisible barrier created by individual and institutional sexism that prevents qualified women from advancing to high levels of leadership and management.
global inequality the differences in wealth and power among the countries of the world.
globalization worldwide interaction or integration among various aspects of social life, including economies, cultures, political systems, and populations.
government the system by which authority is exercised over a specific territory.
groupthink a form of uncritical thinking in which people reinforce a consensus rather than ask serious questions or thoroughly analyze the issue at hand.
growth machines a label for cities that highlights how powerful businesses and politicians work together to promote urban development, often while ignoring the interests of ordinary citizens.
growth rate the indicator that measures how quickly a country's population is increasing.

H

Hawthorne effect the tendency of humans to react differently than they otherwise would when they know they are in a study.
health disparities persistent patterns of inequality in health.
hegemony a condition that exists when those in power have successfully spread their ideas—and marginalized alternative viewpoints—so that their perspectives and interests are accepted widely as being universal and true.
heterosexism a set of attitudes and behavior that indicates an assumption that everyone is heterosexual.
heterosexuals people who are attracted to people of a different sex.
hidden curriculum the lessons students learn simply by attending school, in contrast to the lessons from the formal subject-specific curriculum.
high culture cultural forms associated with—and especially valued by—elites.

historical materialism the part of Marx's work suggesting that the economic base of a society is the primary force driving change in other aspects of social life.
homophily the tendency for social contact to occur at a higher rate among people who are similar than among those who are different.
homophobia the disapproval and fear of LGBT people.
homosexuals people who are attracted to people of the same sex.
horizontal integration what occurs when a media company owns different forms of media.
human ecology the study of the links between the physical environment—natural and built—and social life.
hybrid media media that have features of both interpersonal and mass media, enabling private communication with known individuals, public communication with a potentially large audience, or both.
hypothesis a statement about the relationship between variables that is to be investigated.

I

ideal culture what the members of a culture report to be their values, beliefs, and norms.
ideology a system of meaning that helps define and explain the world and that makes value judgments about that world.
illegitimate power a form of authority that relies on force or coercion to generate obedience.
incest taboo a norm restricting sexual relations between certain relatives.
income money received from sources such as wages and salaries as well as from the interest, dividends, and rent generated by wealth.
independent variable the entity that is associated with and/or causes change in the value of the dependent variable.
individual mobility a change in a person's class position that occurs without any change in the larger class structure.
individualism a system of beliefs that highlights the importance of the single person over any social group.
industrialization the use of large-scale machinery for the mass manufacture of consumer goods.
inequality the unequal distribution of resources among groups of people.
infant mortality rate the number of infants less than a year old who die per 1,000 live births.
informed consent the principle that subjects in any study must know about the nature of the research project, any potential benefits or risks that they may face, and that they have the right to stop participating at any time, for any reason.
in-group a social group with which a person identifies and toward which he or she has positive feelings; members have a collective sense of "us."
institutional discrimination unequal treatment that results from the structural organization, policies, and procedures of social institutions such as the government, businesses, and schools.
intensive interview a data-gathering technique that uses open-ended questions during somewhat lengthy face-to-face sessions.
interpersonal media media that enable primarily private interactive communication between known individuals.
interpretive social science an approach that focuses on understanding the meaning that people ascribe to their social world.
intersectionality theory a perspective that highlights the connections and interactions between various forms of inequality, especially race, class, and gender.
intersexual people individuals born with ambiguous reproductive or sexual anatomy.
intersubjectivity a common understanding between people about knowledge, reality, or an experience.
iron law of oligarchy the eventual and inevitable consolidation of power at the top of bureaucratic organizations.

J

job satisfaction the degree to which a person is content in his or her job.

K

kinship the bonds of family relationships.
knowledge (cultural) the range of information, awareness, and understanding that helps us navigate our world.

L

labeling theory the theory that deviance is the result of how others interpret a behavior and that individuals who are labeled deviant often internalize this judgment as part of their self-identity.
labor unions associations of employees who join together for the purpose of improving their working conditions.
language an elaborate system of symbols that allows people to communicate with one another in complex ways.
latent functions the largely unrecognized and unintended consequences of social phenomena.
legitimate power or **authority** power that is voluntarily accepted by those who are subject to it.
liberation theology a form of Christian belief dedicated to combating poverty and other forms of social injustice.
life chances the opportunities offered by a person's economic position.
life-course perspective an approach that looks at how age, time, and place shape social identities and experiences over a lifetime.
life expectancy the median number of years a person is likely to live given the current conditions.
literacy the ability to read and write.
loner deviance the activities of individuals who commit deviant acts without the social support of other participants.
looking glass self the idea that our sense of self develops as a reflection of the way we think others see us.

M

macro level of analysis a focus on large-scale social systems and processes such as the economy, politics, and population trends.
majority group a collection of people who enjoy privileges and have more access to power because of identifiable physical or cultural characteristics.
manifest functions the recognized and intended consequences of social phenomena.
marriage a social relationship that creates family ties, typically involves sexual intimacy, and is formalized by legal contract, religious ceremony, or both.
mass media communications that reach a relatively large and mostly anonymous audience.
master status a social position that is overwhelmingly significant, powerfully influences a person's social experience, and typically overshadows all the other social positions that person may occupy.
material culture the physical objects produced by people in a particular culture, including tools, clothing, toys, works of art, and housing.
matriarchy a social system dominated by women.
matrix of domination the interlocking systems of oppression associated with race, class, and gender.
Mead's "I" the part of the self that is spontaneous, impulsive, creative, and unpredictable.
Mead's "me" the sense of self that has been learned from interaction with others.
media the various technological processes that enable communication between (and are in the "middle" of) the sender of a message and the receiver of that message.
mediatization the process that examines how the omnipresence of media has changed various aspects of society.

medicalization of deviance the designation of a deviant behavior as an illness that can be treated by medical professionals.
meritocracy a system in which people are rewarded and are able to advance because of their abilities.
meso level of analysis a focus somewhere between very large and very small social phenomena—on organizations or institutions, for example.
micro level of analysis a focus on small-scale, usually face-to-face social interaction.
middle class a group that contributes specialized knowledge and expertise to the economy.
migration the movement of people from one place to another.
minority group a collection of people who suffer disadvantages and have less power because of identifiable physical or cultural characteristics.
mixed economies economies that contain elements of both market-based capitalism and the significant government intervention associated with socialism.
modernity a historical era in the eighteenth and nineteenth centuries characterized by the growth of democracy and personal freedom, increased reliance on reason and science to explain the natural and social worlds, and a shift toward an urban industrial economy.
modernization theory a theory that attributes global inequality to cultural differences among countries.
monarchy a system of government headed by a single person, the monarch, who typically inherits the position as a member of a ruling family.
monogamy the practice of restricting sexual relations to one partner.
moral education the role of schools in teaching children the central values and beliefs of their society.
mores norms that are strictly enforced, with potentially severe penalties for violating them.
multiculturalism the recognition, valuing, and protection of the distinct cultures that make up a society.

N

national security state a government dominated by powerful military, foreign policy, and intelligence agencies.
natural environment the land, water, air, vegetation, and organisms that make up the physical world.
nature versus nurture debate a disagreement about the relative importance of biology ("nature") and the social environment ("nurture") in influencing human behavior.
neocolonialism a system of economic domination of poorer nations by wealthier ones without the use of formal political control or military occupation.
neoliberalism an economic philosophy that promotes markets, deregulation, privatization, and reduced government social expenditures.
neo-Malthusian perspective the view, derived from Malthus's thought, warning that human overpopulation is threatening the planet.
new urban sociology an approach to studying cities that focuses on the interactions of politics and economics and locates them in the larger context of the global economy.
nonmaterial culture the ideas of a culture, including values and beliefs, accumulated knowledge about how to understand and navigate the world, and standards or "norms" about appropriate behavior.
normalization a shift in cultural norms in which previously deviant behaviors become accepted as conventional.
norms a culture's rules and expectations for "appropriate" behavior.
nuclear (conjugal) family parent(s) and any children.

O

occupational prestige collective attitudes about the status of various jobs.
occupational socialization the process of learning the informal norms associated with a type of employment.
operationalize to define clearly the variables to be studied so that they can be measured.
organizational environment factors that exist outside the organization but that potentially affect its operation.
organizational structure the rules and routines, both formal and informal, that shape daily activity within organizations.
organizations secondary groups that have a degree of formal structure and are formed to accomplish particular tasks.
organizing coordinating and directing the efforts of many individuals to work for a cause.
out-group a social group toward which a person has negative feelings, considering its members to be inferiors, or "them."
outsourcing moving jobs out of the country to take advantage of cheaper labor costs elsewhere.
overconformity following cultural expectations to an excessive degree.
ownership concentration what occurs when more media outlets come to be owned by a diminishing number of media corporations.

P

patriarchy male domination through social institutions and cultural practices.
peer group a group of people, usually of comparable age, who share similar interests and social status.
peer-review process the process in which scholars evaluate research manuscripts before they are published in order to ensure their quality.
persuade to get people's compliance by convincing them of the correctness of your position and goals.
planned obsolescence the intentional design and manufacture of consumer goods so as to ensure a loss of utility in a relatively short period of time.
pluralism a situation in which distinct ethnic and racial groups coexist on equal terms and have equal social standing.
pluralist theory a theory that argues that political power is fragmented among many different competing groups.
plurality voting a "winner-take-all" electoral system in which the candidate with the most votes wins the office being contested.
political opportunities factors outside a social movement that can influence whether it emerges and is successful.
political socialization the inculcation of basic norms and expectations about political life and attitudes toward involvement in politics.
politics the struggle over power.
polygamy a marriage system in which an individual is allowed multiple spouses.
popular culture cultural forms that are widespread and commonly embraced within a society.
population pyramid a bar chart showing the distribution of a population by age and sex.
positive deviance overconformity that gets a favorable response.
positivism a belief that accurate knowledge must be based on the scientific method.
positivist social science an approach that assumes that the social world, like the natural world, is characterized by laws that can be identified through research and used to predict and control human affairs.
postmodernity a historical period beginning in the mid-twentieth century characterized by the rise of information-based economies and the fragmentation of political beliefs and ways of knowing.
poverty line (U.S.) a measure of scarcity determined by figuring the cost of a minimal food budget and multiplying it by three.
poverty rate the percentage of the population that falls below the poverty line.
power the ability to bring about an intended outcome, even when opposed by others.

power elite theory a theory that suggests that political power is concentrated in the hands of a small dominant group of business, government, and military leaders.
power tactics the specific strategies people use to influence others in everyday life.
prejudice the "pre-judgment" of someone or some group negatively based on inadequate information.
primary groups people who have regular contact, enduring relationships, and a significant emotional attachment to each other.
privacy paradox occurs when people's concerns about privacy are not consistent with their privacy management activities.
privilege a special advantage or benefit that not everyone enjoys.
product placement the integration into media content of a product that is being advertised.
profane the ordinary world of everyday life.
professional authority legitimate power to define the terms of discussion within a specific field.
professionals a class of workers who are highly educated, hold degrees to certify their education, and have jobs that require a particular form of expertise.
progressive taxation a system of taxation in which those with higher incomes pay a higher rate.
proportional representation an electoral system in which parties are awarded seats in government based on the percentage of votes they receive in an election.
provisional knowledge the idea that truth claims are tentative and open to revision in the face of new evidence.
public assistance either tax credits or actual payments and benefits provided to citizens by the government.
public sociology efforts to reach beyond an academic audience to make the results of sociological research, both basic and applied, known to the broader public.

Q

qualitative data any kind of evidence that is not numerical in nature, including evidence gathered from interviews, direct observation, and written or visual documents.
quantitative data evidence that can be summarized numerically.

R

race a category of people widely perceived as sharing socially significant physical characteristics such as skin color.
racial essentialism the idea that supposedly natural and immutable differences separate the races.
racial school segregation the separation of students into exclusively white and exclusively black public schools.
racialization of the state the implementation of government and private-sector policies that discriminated against minorities and provided whites with numerous advantages.
racism the belief that one race is inherently superior to another.
random sample a sample in which every element of the population has an equal chance of being chosen.
rational action behavior motivated by calculations of efficiency.
rationalization of society the long-term historical process by which rationality replaced tradition as the basis for organizing social and economic life.
rational-legal authority power that has legitimacy because it is based on established laws, rules, and procedures.
real culture what members of a culture actually do, which may or may not reflect the ideal.
recidivism a return to criminal behavior.
redlining the use of discriminatory practices in the sale or rental of housing to minorities.
reference groups the groups against which we choose to measure ourselves.
regressive taxation a system of taxation that disproportionately affects those with lower incomes.
relative poverty situation that exists when people do not have the basic resources needed to maintain a standard of living considered acceptable in their society.
religion a unified system of beliefs and ritual practices relating to the sacred that bond people into a moral community.
research methods the procedures used by sociologists to collect and analyze data.
resocialization the process by which individuals replace old norms and behaviors with new ones as they move from one role or life stage to another.
resource mobilization the process by which social movements generate the assets necessary to build and sustain a movement.
reward to encourage people's compliance by offering some compensation as a positive incentive.
rites of passage activities that mark and celebrate a change in a person's social status.
rituals symbolic actions, typically performed at specified times, that help evoke an emotional bond among participants.
role conflict the problem that occurs when the expectations associated with different roles clash.
role strain the problem that occurs when the expectations associated with a single role compete with each other.
roles the sets of expected behaviors that are associated with particular statuses.

S

sacred something extraordinary, to be treated respectfully, with reverence and awe.
sample part of the population a researcher is studying that represents the whole.
Sapir-Whorf hypothesis the idea that because of their different cultural content and structure, languages affect how their speakers think and behave.
scapegoat an individual or a group of people falsely blamed for a negative situation.
school choice various policies that give families options for deciding which school their children will attend.
schooling organized instruction by trained teachers.
science a method of inquiry that uses logic and the systematic collection of evidence to support claims about the world.
scientific management the process of de-skilling ordinary workers and increasing workplace efficiency through calculated study (also known as Taylorism); the effort by trained managers to study workflow and develop precise procedures that govern the completion of work tasks.
second shift the phenomenon of employed women still having primary responsibility for housework and child care.
secondary data analysis a type of research using data previously collected by other researchers.
secondary deviance deviant behavior that is a response to the negative consequences of labeling.
secondary groups people who interact in a relatively impersonal way, usually to carry out some specific task.
sect a small dissenting faction of a church that promotes new beliefs or practices.
secular humanism a belief system that emphasizes morality and decision making based on reason, ethics, and social justice rather than religious doctrine or the supernatural.
secularization the decline in the social significance of religious beliefs, practices, and institutions.
secularization thesis the argument that, in the face of modernity, the social significance of religion has declined.
segregation keeping distinct social groups physically and socially separate and unequal.

sense of self the collection of thoughts and feelings you have when considering yourself as an object.
sex the biological distinction between females and males.
sexism the ideology that one sex is superior to the other.
sexual harassment unwelcome sexual advances, requests for sexual favors, and other verbal or physical harassment of a sexual nature.
sexual identity (or **sexual orientation**) our sense of self as it relates to the type of sexual attraction we have for others.
sexuality a person's sexual desires, behaviors, and identity.
shopfloor culture a distinctive set of norms and rules that shape daily behavior and interaction on the job.
social capital relationships that are potentially economically valuable resulting from membership in a group.
social change the modification of structural or cultural patterns over time.
social closure the process whereby a status group maximizes its own advantages by restricting access to rewards only to members of the group.
social control the incentives and punishments that promote conformity in social life.
social determinism a theory that contends that culture and the social environment almost completely shape human behavior.
social environment the cultural context and patterns of relationships within which humans live.
social groups collections of people who interact regularly with one another and who are aware of their status as a group.
social institutions the major arenas of social life in which durable routines and patterns of behavior take place.
social integration the process by which values and social structures bind people together within a society.
social mobility movement from one stratum of a stratification system to another.
social movements organized, ongoing collective efforts by relatively powerless people engaging in extrainstitutional action to promote or resist change.
social networks the collections of social ties that connect actors such as individuals and organizations to each other.
social reproduction theory theory that explores the ways that schools help reproduce systems of inequality.
social solidarity the collective bonds that connect individuals.
social structure recurring patterns of behavior.
social theory a set of principles and propositions that explains the relationships among social phenomena.
social trend the direction a society takes when many individuals act independently but similarly.
socialism an economic system that emphasizes public ownership of the major means of production, which are operated to meet human needs and promote social justice.
socialization the process through which people learn their culture's basic norms, values, beliefs, and appropriate behaviors.
society a group of people who live together in a specific territory and share a culture.
sociological perspective a view of the social world that focuses on discovering and understanding the connections between individuals and the broader social contexts in which they live; what C. Wright Mills called the *sociological imagination.*
sociology the systematic study of the relationship between individuals and society.
spiral of silence a theory that explains how people keep quiet about controversial issues when they think their opinions are not widely shared, in order to avoid social isolation.
spirituality an inner sense of meaning or purpose, especially as it involves a person's relationship to something greater than the self.
split labor market theory the theory that ethnic and racial conflicts often emerge when two racial or ethnic groups compete for the same jobs.
sprawl low-density development that disperses people over a wide area, separates homes from workplaces and stores, and depends heavily on cars for transportation.
standpoint theory a theory that questions taken-for-granted assumptions about society by looking at it from multiple viewpoints, especially from the perspective of people in subordinate positions.
state terrorism political violence directed at civilians by governments.
status a position in a social system that can be occupied by an individual.
status attainment the process by which people come to occupy a certain level in a social hierarchy.
status category a status that people can hold in common.
status hierarchy a ranking of social positions according to their perceived prestige or honor.
status set the collection of statuses that an individual holds.
stealth advertising the creation of covert advertising in everyday real-life situations.
stereotypes exaggerated, distorted, or untrue generalizations about categories of people that do not acknowledge individual variation.
stigma the shame attached to a behavior or status that is considered socially unacceptable or discrediting.
strain theory a theory that emphasizes that the strain or pressure on those who lack the means to achieve culturally defined goals leads them to pursue deviant routes to success.
stratification systems social structures and cultural norms that create and maintain inequality by ranking people into a hierarchy of groups that receive unequal resources.
structural mobility a change in class position that occurs when a shift in available occupations changes the class system as a whole.
structural-functionalist theories theories that focus on consensus and cooperative interaction in social life, emphasizing how different parts of a society contribute to its overall operation. Often referred to simply as "functionalist theories" or "functionalism."
structure the recurring patterns of behavior in social life.
subculture a culture associated with smaller groups in society that has distinct norms, values, and lifestyles setting it apart from the dominant culture.
surveillance monitoring by authorities who police the boundaries of what is normal.
survey a data collection technique that involves asking someone a series of questions.
sustainability a balance between resource protection and consumption that can be maintained indefinitely.
symbol anything–a sound, a gesture, an image, an object–that represents something else.
symbolic interactionist theories social theories that focus on how society emerges from people's use of shared symbols in the course of their everyday interactions.

T

taboo a norm whose violation carries severe stigma.
terrorism politically motivated violence that intentionally targets noncombatants.
theism a belief in the existence of a god or gods.
Thomas theorem the idea that if people define situations as real, they are real in their consequences.
total institution a confining social setting in which an authority regulates all aspects of a person's life.
tracking placing students into different curricular paths intended to accommodate varying levels of academic work.
traditional action behavior motivated by custom.
traditional authority power that has legitimacy because of compliance with well-established cultural practices.
transgender people individuals who identify with a gender different from the one associated with their sex.

transnational migrants immigrants who retain strong personal, cultural, and economic ties to both their country of birth and their newly adopted home.

transparency the requirement that researchers explain how they collected and analyzed their evidence and how they reached their conclusions.

transsexuals people who have sex reassignment surgery to change their physical appearance.

treadmill of production a term that refers to the way capital-intensive industries and the modern state, in pursuit of continual growth as a central good, have led to increasing resource depletion and worsening pollution.

U

underclass (or **lower class**) chronically unemployed people who have no ongoing relationship to the mainstream economy.

unintended consequences results that are unplanned and unforeseen.

urbanization the growth of cities.

user-generated content content that is created by ordinary media users, rather than by media organizations, and that is available to a potentially large audience.

V

value a deeply held principle or standard that people use to make judgments about the world, especially in deciding what is desirable or worthwhile.

value-neutrality the goal of removing any personal views from the research process; part of positivist social science.

variables measures that can change (or vary) and thus have different values.

vertical integration what occurs when a media company owns the different stages of production and distribution of a single media form.

W

war organized armed conflict among two or more specially trained military groups.

wealth the value of financial assets such as savings, real estate, stocks, and bonds minus any outstanding debts.

white-collar crime crime committed by people of high social status in the course of their occupation.

working class (or **proletariat**) those who survive on the wages they earn.

world systems analysis an approach that focuses on the interdependence among the countries that make up a single global economic system.

X

xenophobia an unreasonable fear or hatred of foreigners or people from other cultures.

Z

zero population growth a balance between birth rates and death rates, which maintains stable population numbers.

References

AAMC (American Association of Medical Colleges). 2011. Behavioral and social science foundations for future physicians. Washington, DC. Retrieved from www.aamc.org/download/271020/data/behavioralandsocialsciencefoundationsforfuturephysicians.pdf.

ABC News/Washington Post. 2013. A decade on, most are critical of the U.S.-led war in Iraq. Retrieved from www.langerresearch.com/wp-content/uploads/1147a6IraqandAfghanistan.pdf.

Abela, Angela, and Janet Walker. 2014. *Contemporary issues in family studies: Global perspectives on partnerships, parenting and support in a changing world.* Malden, MA: Wiley.

Aberle, David F. (1966) 1991. *The peyote religion among the Navaho.* Norman: University of Oklahoma Press.

Ackerman, Peter, and Jack Duvall. 2000. *A force more powerful.* New York: Palgrave.

Addams, Jane. (1895) 2007. *Hull House maps and papers.* Chicago: University of Illinois Press.

Addams, Jane. (1902) 2002. *Democracy and social ethics.* Urbana and Chicago: University of Illinois Press.

Adler, Nancy E., and Katherine Newman. 2002. Socioeconomic disparities in health. *Health Affairs* 21 (2): 60–76.

Adler, Patricia A., and Peter Adler. 2005. Self-injurers as loners: The social organization of solitary deviance. *Deviant Behavior* 26 (4): 345–78.

Adler, Patricia A., and Peter Adler. 2011. *The tender cut: Inside the hidden world of self-injury.* New York: NYU Press.

Adler, Patricia A. and Peter Adler. 2012. Self-injury in cyberspace. *Contexts* 11 (1): 59–61.

Adorno, Theodor W., and Max Horkheimer. (1944) 2000. The culture industry: Enlightenment as mass deception. In *The consumer society reader,* ed. Juliet B. Schor and Douglas B. Holt, pp. 3–19. New York: New Press.

Advertising Age. 1984. 100 Leading Media Companies. June 28.

Akpabio, Eno, and Kayode Mustapha-Lambe. 2008. *Nollywood* films and the cultural imperialism hypothesis. *Perspectives on Global Development and Technology* 7 (3): 259–70.

Aksu, Hidayet, Leonardo Babun, Mauro Conti, Gabriele Tolomei, and A. Selcuk Uluagac. 2018. Advertising in the IoT era: Visions and challenges. *IEEE Communications Magazine.* doi:10.1109/MCOM.2017.1700871.

Albert, Zachery. 2017. Trends in campaign financing, 1980–2016. Washington, DC: Bipartisan Policy Center. Retrieved from https://bipartisanpolicy.org/wp-content/uploads/2018/02/Trends-in-Campaign-Financing-1980-2016.-Zachary-Albert.pdf.

Al-deen, Taghreed Jamal, and Joel Windle. 2017. "I feel sometimes I am a bad mother": The affective dimension of immigrant mothers' involvement in their children's schooling. *Journal of Sociology* 53 (1): 110–26.

Aldrich, Daniel P., and Michelle A. Meyer. 2015. Social capital and community resilience. *American Behavioral Scientist* 59 (2): 254–69.

Alexander, Jeffrey, ed. 1985. *Neofunctionalism.* Beverly Hills, CA: Sage.

Alexander, Michelle. 2012. *The new Jim Crow: Mass incarceration in the age of colorblindness.* New York: New Press.

Allen, Amy. 1999. *The power of feminist theory.* Boulder, CO: Westview Press.

Allen, Amy. 2008. *The politics of our selves: Politics, autonomy, and gender in contemporary political theory.* New York: Columbia University Press.

Allen, I. Elaine, and Jeff Seaman. 2016. Online report card: Tracking online education in the United States. Babson Survey Research Group. Retrieved from: http://onlinelearningsurvey.com/reports/onlinereportcard.pdf.

Allen, James, Jon Lewis, Leon F. Litwack, and Hilton Als. 2000. *Without sanctuary: Lynching photography in America.* Santa Fe, NM: Twin Palms.

Allen, Theodore W. 2012. *The invention of the white race,* vol. 2, *The origin of racial oppression in Anglo-America.* New York: Verso.

Allport, Gordon. 1954. *The nature of prejudice.* Cambridge, MA: Addison-Wesley.

Almukhtar, Sarah, Michael Gold, and Larry Buchanan. 2018. After Weinstein: 71 men accused of sexual misconduct and their fall from power. Retrieved from http://time.com/time-person-of-the-year-2017-silence-breakers/.

Alon, Sigal. 2015. *Race, class, and affirmative action.* New York: Russell Sage Foundation.

Altintas, Evrim, and Oriel Sullivan. 2016. Fifty years of change updated: Cross-national gender convergence in housework. *Demographic Research* 35: 455–69.

Alvaredo, Facundo, Lucas Chancel, Thomas Piketty, Emmanuel Saez, and Gabriel Zucman. 2018. World Inequality Report. Retrieved from http://wir2018.wid.world/.

Alvarez, R. Michael, Thad E. Hall, and Susan D. Hyde, eds. 2008. *Election fraud.* Washington, DC: Brookings Institution Press.

Amato, Paul R., and Alan Booth. 2000. *A generation at risk.* Cambridge, MA: Harvard University Press.

American Academy of Pediatrics. 2006. Children, adolescents, and advertising. Policy statement. *Pediatrics* 118 (6): 2563–69. Reaffirmed March 2010. Retrieved from http://pediatrics.aappublications.org/cgi/content/full/118/6/2563#R2.

American Council on Education. 2017. American College President Study, 2017. Retrieved from www.acenet.edu/news-room/Pages/American-College-President-Study.aspx.

American Folklife Center. 2018. What is folklife? Retrieved from www.loc.gov/folklife/whatisfolklife.html.

American Social History Project. 2007. *Who built America?* New York: Bedford/St. Martin's.

American Society for Aesthetic Plastic Surgery. 2011. Survey shows that more than half of Americans approve of cosmetic plastic surgery. April 4. Retrieved from www.surgery.org/media/news-releases/survey-shows-that-more-than-half-of-americans-approve-of-cosmetic-plastic-surgery.

American Society for Aesthetic Plastic Surgery. 2017. *2016 Cosmetic Surgery National Data Bank Statistics.*

American Society of Plastic Surgeons. 2018. *Tummy tuck: Abdominoplasty.* Retrieved from www.plasticsurgery.org/cosmetic-procedures/tummy-tuck/procedure.

American Sociological Association. 1999. Code of ethics. Retrieved from www.asanet.org/page.ww?section=Ethics&name=Code+of+Ethics+Table+of+Contents.

American Sociological Association. 2015. Brief of amicus curiae. *Obergefell v. Hodges.* Retrieved from www.asanet.org/sites/default/files/savvy/documents/ASA/pdfs/ASA_March_2015_Supreme_Court_Marriage_Equality_Amicus_Brief.pdf.

American Sociological Association. 2018. ASA letter to commerce secretary regarding census citizenship question. Retrieved from www.asanet.org/asa-letter-commerce-department-regarding-census-citizenship-question.

Amichai-Hamburger, Yair, Mila Kingsbury, and Barry M. Schneider. 2013. Friendship: An old concept with a new meaning? *Computers in Human Behavior* 29: 33–39.

Ammerman, Nancy T. 2013. Spiritual but not religious? Beyond binary choices in the study of religion. *Journal for the Scientific Study of Religion* 52 (2): 258–78.

Ammons, Elizabeth, and Modhumita Roy, eds. 2015. *Sharing the earth: An international environmental justice reader.* Athens: University of Georgia Press.

Amnesty International. 2018. "War of annihilation": Devastating toll on civilians, Raqqa–Syria. Retrieved from www.amnesty.org/download/Documents/MDE2483672018ENGLISH.PDF.

Anderson, Elijah. 1999. *Code of the street.* New York: Norton.

Anderson, Margaret. 2015. *Thinking about women: Sociological perspectives on sex and gender.* Boston, MA: Pearson.

Anderson, Margaret, and Patricia Hill Collins, eds. 2013. *Race, class & gender: An anthology,* 8th ed. Belmont, CA: Cengage.

Anderson, Monica. 2015. Men catch up with women on overall social media use. Washington, DC: Pew Research Center. Retrieved from www.pewresearch.org/fact-tank/2015/08/28/men-catch-up-with-women-on-overall-social-media-use/.

Anderson, Monica, and Jingjing Jiang. 2018. Teens, social media and technology, 2018. Washington, DC: Pew Research Center. Retrieved from http://assets.pewresearch.org/wp-content/uploads/sites/14/2018/05/31102617/PI_2018.05.31_TeensTech_FINAL.pdf.

Anderson, Monica, Andrew Perrin, and Jinjing Jiang. 2018. 11% of Americans don't use the internet. Who are they? Washington, DC: Pew Research Center. Retrieved from www.pewresearch.org/fact-tank/2018/03/05/some-americans-dont-use-the-internet-who-are-they/.

Angulo, A. J. 2016. *Diploma mills: How for-profit colleges stiffed students, taxpayers, and the American dream.* Baltimore, MD: Johns Hopkins University Press.

Angwin, Julia. 2010. The web's new gold mine: Your secrets. *Wall Street Journal,* July 30. Retrieved from http://online.wsj.com/article/SB10001424052748703940904575395073512989404.html.

Angwin, Julia. 2014a. Meet the online tracking device that is virtually impossible to block. *ProPublica,* July 21.

Angwin, Julia. 2014b. *Dragnet nation.* New York: St. Martin's Griffin

Angwin, Julia. 2016. Verizon to pay $1.35 million to settle zombie cookie privacy charges. *ProPublica,* March 7.

Angwin, Julia, and Terry Parris Jr. 2016. Facebook lets advertisers exclude users by race. Retrieved from www.propublica.org/article/facebook-lets-advertisers-exclude-users-by-race.

Angwin, Julia, and Steve Stecklow. 2010. "Scrapers" dig deep for data on the web. *Wall Street Journal,* October 12. Retrieved from http://online.wsj.com/article/SB10001424052748703358504575544381288117888.html.

Angwin, Julia, Madeleine Varner, and Ariana Tobin. 2017. Facebook enabled advertisers to reach "Jew haters." Retrieved from www.propublica.org/article/facebook-enabled-advertisers-to-reach-jew-haters.

Apker, Julie, Kathleen M. Propp, and Wendy S. Zabava Ford. 2005. Negotiating status and identity tensions in healthcare team interactions: An exploration of nurse role dialectics. *Journal of Applied Communication Research* 33 (2): 93–115.

Appel, Helmut, Alexander L Gerlach, and Jan Crusius. 2016. The interplay between Facebook use, social comparison, envy, and depression. *Current Opinion in Psychology* 9: 44–49.

Appelbaum, Eileen, and Ruth Milkman. 2011. *Leaves that pay: Employer and worker experience with paid family leave in California.* Center for Economic and Policy Research, Center for Women and Work, Institute for Research on Labor and Employment, and the Murphy Institute.

Appelbaum, Eileen, Ruth Milkman, Luke Elliott, and Teresa Kroger. 2014. *Good for business: Connecticut's Paid Sick Leave Law.* Center for Economic and Policy Research and the Murphy Institute.

Appold, Stephen. 2007. Human ecology. In *21st century sociology: A reference handbook,* ed. Clifton D. Bryant and Dennis L. Peck, pp. 444–54. Thousand Oaks, CA: Sage.

Arab American Institute. 2014. Demographics. Washington, DC. Retrieved from https://d3n8a8pro7vhmx.cloudfront.net/aai/pages/9843/attachments/original/1460668240/National_Demographic_Profile_2014.pdf.

Arastoopour, Golnaz, Naomi C. Chesler, and David Williamson Shaffer. 2014. Epistemic persistence: A simulation-based approach to increasing participation of women in engineering. *Journal of Women and Minorities in Science and Engineering* 20 (3): 211–34.

Arcaya, Mariana C. 2018. Neighborhood foreclosures and health. In *Neighborhoods and health,* ed. Dustin T. Duncan and Ichiro Kawachi, pp. 293–320. New York: Oxford University Press.

Aries, Philippe. 1965. *Centuries of childhood: A social history of family life,* trans. Robert Baldick. New York: Vintage.

Arnason, Johann P. 2001. History of civilizational analysis. In *International encyclopedia of the social and behavioral sciences,* ed. Neil J. Smelser and Paul B. Baltes. Oxford and New York: Elsevier.

Arnett, Jeffrey Jensen. 2015. *Emerging adulthood: The winding road from the late teens through the twenties.* New York: Oxford University Press.

Arsel, Murat, and Bram Büscher. 2012. Nature™ Inc.: Changes and continuities in neoliberal conservation and market-based environmental policy. *Development and Change* 43 (1): 53–78.

Arum, Richard. 2003. *Judging school discipline.* Cambridge, MA: Harvard University Press.

Arum, Richard, and Melissa Velez. 2012. Class and racial differences in U.S. school disciplinary environments. In *Improving learning environments,* ed. Richard Arum and Melissa Velez, pp. 278–330. Stanford, CA: Stanford University Press.

Asch, Solomon E. 1952. *Social psychology.* Englewood Cliffs, NJ: Prentice Hall.

Asch, Solomon E. 1955. Opinions and social pressures. *Scientific American* 193 (5): 31–35.

Association of Certified Fraud Examiners. 2018. Report to the nations: 2018 global study on occupational fraud and abuse.

Astin, Alexander W. 1998. The changing American college student: Thirty-year trends, 1966–1996. *Review of Higher Education* 21 (2): 115–35.

Attewell, Paul, David Lavin, Thurston Domina, and Tania Levey. 2007. *Passing the torch: Does higher education for the disadvantaged pay off across the generations?* New York: Russell Sage Foundation.

Auster, Carol, and Claire Mansbach. 2012. The gender marketing of toys: An analysis of color and type of toy on the Disney Store website. *Sex Roles* 67 (7): 375–88.

Axelrad, Hila, and Jacquelyn B. James. 2017. Employers, attitudes toward older-worker job seekers: A comprehensive review with recommendations for action. Boston College Center on Aging & Work.

Babb, Sarah. 2004. Born to buy: Sarah Babb interviews Juliet Schor. In *Sociology speaks 2003–2004.* Chestnut Hill, MA: Boston College Department of Sociology.

Babbie, Earl. 2016. *The practice of social research,* 14th ed. Boston: Cengage.

Babones, Salvatore. 2018. China's middle class is pulling up the ladder behind itself. Retrieved from http://foreignpolicy.com/2018/02/01/chinas-middle-class-is-pulling-up-the-ladder-behind-itself/.

Bacevich, Andrew J. 2010. *Washington rules: America's path to permanent war.* New York: Macmillan.

Bacevich, Andrew J. 2013. *The New American militarism: How Americans are seduced by war.* New York: Oxford University Press.

Bagdikian, Ben. 2004. *The new media monopoly.* Boston: Beacon Press.

Bailey, Carol A. 2018. *A guide to qualitative field research,* 3rd ed. Thousand Oaks, CA: Sage.

Bajaj, Vikas, and Ford Fessenden. 2007. What's behind the race gap? *New York Times,* November 4, 2007. Retrieved from www.nytimes.com/2007/11/04/weekinreview/04bajaj.html?_r=2&ref=business &oref=slogin&oref=slogin.

Baker, Bruce D., David G. Sciarra, and Danielle Farrie. 2015. *Is school funding fair?: A national report card,* 4th ed. Education Law Center. Newark, NJ: Rutgers University. Retrieved from http://schoolfundingfairness.org/National_Report_Card_2015.pdf.

Baker, Peter, and Eileen Sullivannov. 2017. Trump shares inflammatory anti-Muslim videos, and Britain's leader condemns them. Retrieved from www.nytimes.com/2017/11/29/us/politics/trump-anti-muslim-videos-jayda-fransen.html.

Baker, Rachel. 2016. The effects of structured transfer pathways in community colleges. *Educational Evaluation and Policy Analysis* 38 (4): 626–46.

Baker, Rachel. 2018. Understanding college students' major choices using social network analysis. *Research in Higher Education* 59: 198–225.

Baker, Wayne E. 2005. *America's crisis of values: Reality and perception.* Princeton, NJ: Princeton University Press.

Balaguru, Karthik, Gregory R. Foltz, and L. Ruby Leung. 2018. Increasing magnitude of hurricane rapid intensification in the central and eastern tropical Atlantic. Geophysical Research Letters. https://doi.org/10.1029/2018GL077597.

Bales, Kevin. 2016. *Blood and earth: Modern slavery, ecocide, and the secret to saving the world.* New York: Spiegel & Grau.

Banks-Santilli, Linda. 2014. First-generation college students and their pursuit of the American dream. *Journal of Case Studies in Education* 5: 1–32.

Baptist, Edward E. 2014. *The half has never been told: Slavery and the making of American capitalism.* New York: Basic Books.

Barabási, Albert-László. 2002. *Linked.* New York: Plume.

Barger, Lilian Calles. 2018. *The world come of age: An intellectual history of liberation theology.* New York: Oxford University Press.

Barker, Dan. 2006. *Losing faith in faith: From preacher to atheist.* Madison, WI: Freedom from Religion Foundation.

Barnard, Alex V. 2016. *Freegan: Diving into the wealth of food waste in America.* Minneapolis: University of Minnesota Press.

Barr, Donald. 2014. *Health disparities in the United States: Social class, race, ethnicity, and health.* Baltimore, MD: Johns Hopkins University.

Barres, Ben A. 2006. Does gender matter? *Nature,* July 13, pp. 133–36.

Barrett, Devlin, and Dan Fitzpatrick. 2013. J.P. Morgan, U.S. settle for $13 billion. *Wall Street Journal,* November 19. Retrieved from http://online.wsj.com/news/articles/SB10001424052702304439804579207701974094982.

Bartels, Larry M. 2016. *Unequal democracy: The political economy of the new gilded age.* Princeton, NJ: Princeton University Press.

Bartky, Sandra Lee. 1990. *Femininity and domination.* New York: Routledge.

Baruh, Lemi, Ekin Secinti, and Zeynep Cemalcilar. 2017. Online privacy concerns and privacy management: A meta-analytical review. *Journal of Communication* 67: 26–53.

Basel Action Network. 2016. e-Trash transparency project. Seattle, WA. Retrieved from www.ban.org/trash-transparency.

Battani, Marshall, John R. Hall, and Mary Jo Neitz. 2003. *Sociology on culture.* New York: Routledge.

Bauder, David, Lynn Elber, and Frazier Moore. 2015. TV networks make unequal progress toward on-screen diversity. Retrieved from www.apnews.com/a86e495dbe714a1e849d3d72d5d8d0ff.

Baudrillard, Jean. 1988a. Consumer society. In *Selected writings,* ed. Mark Poster, pp. 29–56. Stanford, CA: Stanford University Press.

Baudrillard, Jean. 1988b. For a critique of the political economy of the sign. In *Selected writings,* ed. Mark Poster, pp. 57–97. Stanford, CA: Stanford University Press.

Bauer, Gerrit. 2016. Gender roles, comparative advantages and the life course: The division of domestic labor in same-sex and different-sex couples. *European Journal of Population* 32 (1): 99–128.

Baum, Sandy, Jennifer Ma, Matea Pender, and Meredith Welch. 2017. *Trends in student aid 2017.* New York: The College Board.

Bauman, Zygmunt. 2001. *Community: Seeking safety in an insecure world.* Cambridge, UK: Polity Press.

Baxter, Janeen, and Tsui-O. Tai. 2016. Inequalities in unpaid work: A cross-national comparison. In *Handbook on well-being of working women*, ed. Mary L. Connerley and JiyunWu, pp. 653–71. Dordrecht, Netherlands: Springer.

BBC. 2010a. Suicide-hit Foxconn factory to increase wages. Retrieved from http://news.bbc.co.uk/2/hi/business/10184186.stm.

BBC. 2010b. Taiwan iPhone-maker Foxconn suffers another death. Retrieved from http://news. bbc.co.uk/2/hi/world/asia_ pacific/10182824.stm.

BBC. 2014. The Islamic veil across Europe. July 1. Retrieved from www.bbc.com/news/world-europe-13038095.

Beckel, Michael, and Jared Bennett. 2015. 12 ways "Citizens United" has changed politics. Center for Public Integrity. Retrieved from www.publicintegrity.org/2015/01/21/16626/12-ways-citizens-united-has-changed-politics.

Becker, Howard. 1973. *Outsiders: Studies in the sociology of deviance.* New York: Free Press.

Beckhert, Sven. 2015. *Empire of cotton: A global history.* New York: Vintage Books.

Bediou, Benoit, Deanne M. Adams, Richard E. Mayer, Elizabeth Tipton, Shawn C. Green, and Daphne Bavelier. 2018. Meta-analysis of action video game impact on perceptual, attentional, and cognitive skills. *Psychological Bulletin* 144 (1): 77–110.

Beeghley, Leonard. 2016. *The structure of social stratification in the United States.* New York: Routledge.

Beer, David. 2009. Power through the algorithm? Participatory web cultures and the technological unconsciousness. *New Media & Society* 11 (6): 985–1002.

Beier, Jonathan S., and Elizabeth S. Spelke. 2012. Infants' developing understanding of social gaze. *Child Development* 83 (2): 486–96.

Beinart, Peter. 2017. Trump's anti-Muslim political strategy. Retrieved from www.theatlantic.com/politics/archive/2017/11/trumps-anti-muslim-retweets-shouldnt-surprise-you/547031/.

Bell, Michael Mayerfeld, and Loka L. Ashwood. 2016. *An invitation to environmental sociology.* Thousand Oaks, CA: Sage.

Bellah, Robert N., Richard Madsen, William M. Sullivan, Ann Swidler, and Steven M. Tipton. 2007. *Habits of the heart: Individualism and commitment in American life,* 3rd ed. Berkeley: University of California Press.

Benhabib, Seyla. 2002. *The claims of culture: Equality and diversity in a global era.* Princeton, NJ: Princeton University Press.

Benton, Ted. 1977. *Philosophical foundations of the three sociologies.* Boston: Routledge.

Berardo, Felix M., and Constance L. Shehan. 2004. Family problems in global perspective. In *Handbook of social problems: A comparative international perspective,* ed. George Ritzer, pp. 246–60. Thousand Oaks, CA: Sage.

Berbrier, Mitch. 1998. Being deaf has very little to do with one's ears: Boundary-work in the Deaf Culture movement. *Perspectives on Social Problems* 10: 79–100.

Berger, Peter. 1963. *Invitation to sociology.* New York: Doubleday.

Berger, Peter. 1967. *The sacred canopy.* Garden City, NY: Doubleday.

Berger, Peter. 1997. Four faces of global culture. *National Interest* 49 (Fall): 23–29.

Berger, Peter L., and Thomas Luckmann. 1966. *The social construction of reality.* New York: Doubleday.

Berlatsky, Noah. 2013. A self-published erotic novelist pioneers a new kind of porn. *Salon.* Retrieved from www.salon.com/2013/10/19/a_self_published_erotic_novelist_ pioneers_ a_new_kind_of_porn/.

Berners-Lee, Tim. 2018. The web is under threat. Join us and fight for it. Retrieved from https://webfoundation.org/2018/03/web-birthday-29/.

Bernhardt, Amy M., Cara Wilking, Anna M. Adachi-Mejia, Elaina Bergamini, Jill Marijnissen, and James D. Sargent. 2013. How television fast food marketing aimed at children compares with adult advertisements. Retrieved from www.rwjf.org/en/research-publications/find-rwjf-research/2013/08/how-television-fast-food-marketing-aimed-at-children-compares-wi.html.

Bernhardt, Annette, Diana Polson, and James DeFilippis. 2010. *Working without laws.* New York: National Employment Law Project.

Bernhardt, Annette, Ruth Milkman, Nik Theodore, Douglas Heckathorn, Mirabai Auer, James DeFilippis, Ana Luz González, Victor Narro, Jason Perelshteyn, Diana Polson, and Michael Spiller. 2009. *Broken laws, unprotected workers: Violations of employment and labor laws in America's cities.* Center for Urban Economic Development, the National Employment Law Project, and the UCLA Institute for Research on Labor and Employment.

Bertrand, Marianne, and Esther Duflo. 2016. Field experiments on discrimination. Working Paper No. 22014. National Bureau of Economic Research. Retrieved from www.nber.org/papers/w22014.

Bertrand, Marianne, and Sendhil Mullainathan. 2004. Are Emily and Greg more employable than Lakisha and Jamal? A field experiment on labor market discrimination. *American Economic Review* 94 (4): 991–1013.

Best, Joel, and David F. Luckenbill. 1982. *Organizing deviance.* Englewood Cliffs, NJ: Prentice Hall.

Bialik, Christen. 2017. The changing face of America's veteran population. Washington, DC: Pew Research Center. Retrieved from www.pewresearch.org/fact-tank/2017/11/10/the-changing-face-of-americas-veteran-population/.

Bianchi, Suzanne M., John P. Robinson, and Melissa A. Milkie. 2006. *Changing rhythms of American family life.* New York: Russell Sage Foundation.

Bianchi, Suzanne M., Liana C. Sayer, Melissa A. Milkie, and John P. Robinson. 2012. Housework: Who did, does or will do it, and how much does it matter? *Social Forces* 91 (1): 55–63.

Biblarz, Timothy J., and Evren Savci. 2010. Lesbian, gay, bisexual, and transgender families. *Journal of Marriage and Family* 72 (3): 480–97.

Biblarz, Timothy J., and J. Stacey. 2010. How does the gender of parents matter? *Journal of Marriage and Family* 72 (1): 3–22.

Bick, Johanna, and Charles A. Nelson. 2016. Early adverse experiences and the developing brain. *Neuropsychopharmacology Reviews* 41: 177–96.

Biggs, Simon. 2018. *Negotiating ageing: Cultural adaptation to the prospect of a long life.* New York: Routledge.

Black, Edwin. 2012. *War against the weak: Eugenics and America's campaign to create a master race.* Washington, DC: Dialog Press.

Black, Ian. 2013. NSA spying scandal: What we have learned. *The Guardian*, June 10. Retrieved from www.guardian.co.uk/world/2013/jun/10/nsa-spying-scandal-what-we-have-learned.

Black, Michele C., Kathleen C. Basile, Matthew J. Breiding, Sharon G. Smith, Mikel L. Walters, Melissa T. Merrick, Jieru Chen, and Mark R. Stevens. 2011. The National Intimate Partner and Sexual Violence Survey: 2010 Summary Report. Atlanta, GA: Centers for Disease Control and Prevention (CDC). Retrieved from www.cdc.gov/violenceprevention/pdf/nisvs_report2010-a.pdf.

Black, William K. 2013. *The best way to rob a bank is to own one: How corporate executives and politicians looted the S&L industry.* Austin: University of Texas Press.

Blackledge, Adrian. 2001. The wrong sort of capital? *International Journal of Bilingualism* 5 (3): 345–69.

Blackstone, Amy, and Mahala Dyer Stewart. 2012. Choosing to be childfree: Research on the decision not to parent. *Sociology Compass* 6 (9): 718–27.

Blackstone, Amy, and Mahala Dyer Stewart. 2016. "There's more thinking to decide": How the childfree decide not to parent. *The Family Journal* 24 (3): 296–303.

Blair, Johnny, Ronald F. Czaja, and Edward A. Blair. 2014. *Designing surveys,* 3rd ed. Thousand Oaks, CA: Sage.

Blake, Mariah. 2005. Stations of the cross. *Columbia Journalism Review* (May/June): 32–39.

Blanton, Hart, and James Jaccard. 2015. Not so fast: Ten challenges to importing implicit attitude measures to media psychology. *Media Psychology* 18 (3): 338–69.

Blanton, Robert G., Shannon Lindsey Blanton, and Dursun Peksen. 2015. The impact of IMF and World Bank programs on labor rights. *Political Research Quarterly* 68 (2): 324–36.

Blau, Peter, and Otis D. Duncan. 1967. *The American occupational structure.* New York: Wiley.

Bleakley, Hoyt, and Aimee Chin. 2004. Language skills and earnings: Evidence from childhood immigrants. *Review of Economics and Statistics* 86: 481–96.

Blewitt, John. 2015. *Understanding sustainable development.* New York: Routledge.

Bluestone, Barry, and Bennett Harrison. 1982. *The deindustrialization of America.* New York: Basic Books.

Blumer, Herbert. 1986. *Symbolic interactionism: Perspective and method.* Berkeley: University of California Press.

Blunden, Jessica, and Derek S. Arndt, eds. 2016. State of the climate in 2015. *Bulletin of the American Meteorological Society* 97 (8): S1–S275. Retrieved from www.ametsoc.org/ams/index.cfm/publications/bulletin-of-the-american-meteorological-society-bams/state-of-the-climate/.

Bobo, Kim, Jackie Kendall, and Steve Max. 2010. *Organizing for social change: Midwest Academy manual for activists.* Santa Ana, CA: Seven Locks Press.

Bobo, Lawrence, James R. Kluegel, and Ryan A. Smith. 1997. Laissez-faire racism: The crystallization of a kinder, gentler, antiblack ideology. In *Racial attitudes in the 1990s: Continuity and change,* ed. Jack K. Martin and Steven A. Tuch, pp. 15–42. Westport, CT: Praeger.

Boe, Josh L., and Rebecca J. Woods. 2017. Parents' influence on infants' gender-typed toy preferences. *Sex Roles* 1–16. Retrieved from https://doi.org/10.1007/s11199-017-0858-4

Boerman, Sophie C., Sanne Kruikemeier, and Frederik J. Zuiderveen Borgesius. 2017. Online behavioral advertising: A literature review and research agenda. *Journal of Advertising* 46 (3): 363–76.

Boero, Natalie, and C. J. Pascoe. 2012. Pro-anorexia communities and online interaction: Bringing the pro-ana body online. *Body & Society* 18 (2): 27–57.

Bogaert, Anthony F. 2015. Asexuality: What it is and why it matters. *Journal of Sex Research* 52 (4): 362–79.

Bogardus, Emory S. 1967. *A forty-year racial distance study.* Los Angeles: University of Southern California Press.

Bogart, Leo. 1991. The pollster & the Nazis. Retrieved from www.commentarymagazine.com/articles/the-pollster-the-nazis/.

Boisjoly, Johanne, Greg J. Duncan, Michael Kremer, Dan M. Levy, and Jacque Eccles. 2006. Empathy or antipathy? The impact of diversity. *American Economic Review* 96: 1890–905.

Bonacich, Edna. 1972. A theory of ethnic antagonism: The split labor market. *American Sociological Review* 37 (5): 547–59.

Bonacich, Edna. 1976. Advanced capitalism and black/white relations in the United States: A split labor market interpretation. *American Sociological Review* 41 (1): 34–51.

Bonanno, Rina A,. and Shelley Hymel. 2013. Cyber bullying and internalizing difficulties: Above and beyond the impact of traditional forms of bullying. *Journal of Youth and Adolescence* 42 (5): 685–97.

Bond, Rod, and Peter B. Smith. 1996. Culture and conformity: A meta-analysis of studies using Asch's line judgment task. *Psychological Bulletin* 119: 111–37.

Bonica, Adam, Nolan McCarty, Keith T. Poole, and Howard Rosenthal. 2013. Why hasn't democracy slowed rising inequality? *Journal of Economic Perspectives* 27 (3): 103–24.

Bonilla-Silva, Eduardo. 1997. Rethinking racism: Toward a structural interpretation. *American Sociological Review* 62 (3): 465–80.

Bonilla-Silva, Eduardo. 2001. *White supremacy and racism in the post-civil rights era.* Boulder, CO: Lynne Rienner.

Bonilla-Silva, Eduardo. 2014. *Racism without racists: Color-blind racism and the persistence of racial inequality in America.* Lanham, MD: Rowman & Littlefield.

Booske, Bridget C., Jessica K. Athens, David A. Kindig, Hyojun Park, and Patrick L. Remington. 2010. Different perspectives for assigning weights to determinants of health. University of Wisconsin, Population Health Institute. Retrieved from http://uwphi.pophealth.wisc.edu/publications/other/different-perspectives-for-assigning-weights-to-determinants-of-health.pdf.

Bordo, Susan. 1993. *Unbearable weight.* Berkeley: University of California Press.

Borg, Emma. 2017. Mirroring, mind-reading and smart behaviour-reading. *Journal of Consciousness Studies* 24 (5–6): 24–49.

Borgatti, Stephen P., Martin G. Everett, and Jeffrey C. Johnson. 2013. *Analyzing social networks.* Thousand Oaks, CA: Sage.

Boruchoff, Judith. 2013. Transnational engagement of Mexican migrant organizations in Chicago. *Latino Studies* 11 (1): 21–27.

Bourdieu, Pierre. 1986. The forms of capital. In *Handbook for theory and research for the sociology of education,* ed. J. G. Richardson, pp. 241–58. Westport, CT: Greenwood Press.

Bourdieu, Pierre, and Jean Claude Passeron. 1977. *Reproduction in education, society, and culture.* Thousand Oaks, CA: Sage.

Bourgois, Philippe. 2003. *In search of respect,* 2nd ed. New York: Cambridge University Press.

Bowen, Elizabeth A., Berg Miller, Anamika Barman-Adhikari, Kyla Fallin, and Dale Zuchlewski. 2017. Emerging adult homelessness in geographic perspective: A view from the rust belt. *Children and Youth Services Review* 73: 213–19.

Bowles, Samuel, and Herbert Gintis. 1976. *Schooling in capitalist America.* New York: Basic Books.

Bowles, Samuel, and Herbert Gintis. 2002. Schooling in capitalist America revisited. *Sociology of Education* 75: 1–18.

Box Office Mojo. 2018. 2018 domestic grosses. Retrieved from www.boxofficemojo.com/yearly/chart/?yr=2018&p=.htm.

Boyd-Barrett, Oliver. 2015. *Media imperialism.* Thousand Oaks, CA: Sage.

Boyd, Emily M., John R. Reynolds, Kathryn Harker Tillman, and Patricia Yancey Martin. 2011. Adolescent girls' race/ethnic status, identities, and drive for thinness. *Social Science Research* 40: 667–84.

Braithwaite, John. 1989. *Crime, shame, and reintegration.* New York: Cambridge University Press.

Brathwaite, Jessica. 2017. Neoliberal education reform and the perpetuation of inequality. *Critical Sociology* 43 (3): 429–48.

Braveman, Paula A., Catherine Cubbin, Susan Egerter, David R. Williams, and Elsie Pamuk. 2010. Socioeconomic disparities in health in the United States: What the patterns tell us. *American Journal of Public Health* 100 (S1): S186–S196.

Braverman, Harry. (1974) 1998. *Labor and monopoly capital.* New York: Monthly Review Press.

Breen, Patrick H. 2015. *The land shall be deluged in blood: A new history of the Nat Turner Revolt.* New York: Oxford University Press.

Breiding, Matthew J., Sharon G. Smith, Kathleen C. Basile, Mikel L. Walters, Jieru Chen, and Melissa T. Merrick. 2014. Prevalence and characteristics of sexual violence, stalking, and intimate partner violence victimization—National Intimate Partner and Sexual Violence Survey, United States, 2011. Centers for Disease Control and Prevention. *Morbidity and Mortality Weekly Report* 63 (SS-8): 1–18. Retrieved from www.cdc.gov/mmwr/preview/mmwrhtml/ss6308a1.htm.

Breitbach, Jill E., Yaron G. Rabinowitz, and Christopher H. Warner. 2018. Combat and operational stress. In *Military and veteran mental health,* ed. Laura Weiss Roberts and Christopher H. Warner, pp. 245–63. New York: Springer.

Brenan, Megan. 2017. Nurses keep healthy lead as most honest, ethical profession. Retrieved from http://news.gallup.com/poll/224639/nurses-keep-healthy-lead-honest-ethical profession.aspx?g_source=CATEGORY_SOCIAL_POLICY_ISSUES&g_medium=topic&g_campaign=tiles.

Brewster, Zachary W., and Jeremiah B. Wills. 2013. The institution of tipping as a source of employee agency: The case of restaurant servers. *Sociological Focus* 46: 193–210.

Bridges, J. S. 1993. Pink or blue: Gender-stereotypic perceptions of infants as conveyed by birth congratulations cards. *Psychology of Women Quarterly* 17: 193–205.

Brint, Steven. 2006. *Schools and societies,* 2nd ed. Palo Alto, CA: Stanford University Press.

Brint, Steven. 2017. *Schools and societies,* 3rd ed. Stanford, CA: Stanford University Press.

Brint, Steven, Mary F. Contreras, and Michael T. Matthews. 2001. Socialization messages in primary schools. *Sociology of Education* 74 (July): 157–80.

Bromley, Victoria L. 2012. *Feminisms matter.* Tonawanda, NY: University of Toronto Press.

Bronski, Michael. 2011. *A queer history of the United States.* Boston: Beacon Press.

Brothers, Leslie. 1997. *Friday's footprint: How society shapes the human mind.* New York: Oxford University Press.

Brown, Gregory Hippolyte, Lisa M. Brunelle, and Vikas Malhotra. 2017. Tagging: Deviant behavior or adolescent rites of passage. *Culture & Psychology* 23 (4): 487–501.

Brown, Susan. 2010. Marriage and child well-being: Research and policy perspectives. *Journal of Marriage and Family* 72 (5): 1059–77.

Brownmiller, Susan. 1975. *Against our will: Men, women, and rape.* New York: Ballantine.

Brown-Saracino, Japonica. 2017. Explicating divided approaches to gentrification and growing income inequality. *Annual Review of Sociology* 43: 515–39.

Brubaker, Rogers. 2015. Religious dimensions of political conflict and violence. *Sociological Theory* 33 (1): 1–19.

Bruce, Steve. 2002. *God is dead: Secularization in the West.* Malden, MA: Wiley-Blackwell.

Bruce, Steve. 2011. *Secularization: In defense of an unfashionable theory.* New York: Oxford University Press.

Bruce, Steven. 2008. *Fundamentalism.* Malden, MA: Polity Press.

Bruinius, Harry. 2006. *Better for all the world: The secret history of forced sterilization and America's quest for racial purity.* New York: Alfred A. Knopf.

Brulle, Robert J., and Riley E. Dunlap. 2015. *Climate change and society: Sociological perspectives.* New York: Oxford University Press.

Brym, Robert J. 2007. Six lessons of suicide bombers. *Contexts* 6 (4): 40–45.

Brym, Robert J., and Bader Araj. 2006. Suicide bombing as strategy and interaction: The case of the Second Intifada. *Social Forces* 84 (4): 1965–82.

Bryson, Valerie. 2016. *Feminist political theory.* New York: Palgrave.

Buccitelli, Anthony Bak. 2016. *City of neighborhoods: Memory, folklore, and ethnic place in Boston.* Madison: University of Wisconsin Press.

Buckingham, David. 2011. *The material child: Growing up in consumer culture.* Malden, MA: Polity Press.

Budig, Michelle J., Joya Misra, and Irene Boeckmann. 2016. Work-family policy trade-offs for mothers? Unpacking the cross-national variation in motherhood earnings penalties. *Work and Occupations* 43 (2): 119–77.

Bugental, D. B., & Jeffrey C. Lewis. 1999. The paradoxical misuse of power by those who see themselves as powerless: How does it happen? *Journal of Social Issues* 55 (1): 51–64.

Buhari-Gulmez, Didem, and Roland Robertson, eds. 2016. *Global culture: Consciousness and connectivity.* New York: Routledge.

Bullard, Robert. 2000. *Dumping in Dixie: Race, class and environmental quality.* Boulder, CO: Westview Press.

Buni, Catherine, and Soraya Chemaly. 2014. The unsafety net: How social media turned against women. *The Atlantic,* October 9. Retrieved from www.theatlantic.com/technology/archive/2014/10/the-unsafety-net-how-social-media-turned-against-women/381261/.

Burawoy, Michael, ed. 2014. Precarious engagements: Combat in the realm of public sociology. Special issue of *Current Sociology* 62 (2), March.

Bureau of Justice Statistics. 2012a. Arrests in the United States, 1990–2010. U.S. Department of Justice, October. Retrieved from www.bjs.gov/index.cfm?ty=pbdetail&iid=4515.

Bureau of Justice Statistics. 2012b. Correctional populations in the United States, 2011. U.S. Department of Justice, November. Retrieved from www.bjs.gov/index.cfm?ty=pbdetail&iid=4537.

Bureau of Justice Statistics. 2012c. Prisoners in 2011. U.S. Department of Justice, December. Retrieved from www.bjs.gov/index.cfm?ty=pbdetail&iid=4559.

Bureau of Justice Statistics. 2015a. Correctional population in the United States, 2014. U.S. Department of Justice, December.

Bureau of Justice Statistics. 2015b. Prisoners in 2014. U.S. Department of Justice, September.

Bureau of Justice Statistics. 2015c. Probation and parole in the United States, 2014. U.S. Department of Justice, November.

Bureau of Justice Statistics. 2018a, April. Correctional population in the United States, 2016. U.S. Department of Justice.

Bureau of Justice Statistics. 2018b, January. Prisoners in 2016. U.S. Department of Justice.

Bureau of Justice Statistics. 2018c, April. Probation and parole in the United States, 2016. U.S. Department of Justice.

Bureau of Labor Statistics. 2018d, January 19. Employed persons by detailed occupation, sex, race, and Hispanic or Latino ethnicity. Labor Force Statistics from the Current Population Survey.

Burke, Meaghan. 2012. *Racial ambivalence in diverse communities: Whiteness and the power of color-blind ideologies.* Lanham, MD: Lexington Books.

Burns, Thomas J., and Beth Schaefer Caniglia. 2016. *Environmental sociology: The ecology of late modernity.* Norman, OK: Mercury Academic.

Bush, George W. 2001. Address to a Joint Session of Congress and the American People. September 20. Office of the Press Secretary, White House. Retrieved from http://georgewbush-whitehouse.archives.gov/news/releases/2001/09/20010920-8.html.

Buttel, Frederick H. 2003. Environmental sociology and the explanation of environmental reform. *Organization & Environment* 16 (3): 306–44.

Buttel, Frederick H. 2004. The treadmill of production: An appreciation, assessment, and agenda for research. *Organization & Environment* 17 (3): 323–36.

Byrd, W. Carson, and Matthew W. Hughey. 2017. Biological determinism and racial essentialism: The ideological double helix of racial inequality. *The ANNALS of the American Academy of Political and Social Science* 661 (1): 8–22.

Cacciatore, Michael A., Dietram A. Scheufele, and Shanto Iyengar. 2016. The end of framing as we know it . . . and the future of media effects. *Mass Communication and Society* 19 (1): 7–23.

Cafaro, Philip. 2015. *How many is too many? The progressive argument for reducing immigration into the United States.* Chicago: University of Chicago Press.

Cahn, Stephen M., ed. 2002. *The affirmative action debate.* New York: Routledge.

CAIR-CA (Council on American Islamic Relations-California). 2015. MISLABELED: The impact of school bullying and discrimination on California Muslim students. Santa Clara, CA. Retrieved from https://ca.cair.com/sfba/wp-content/uploads/2015/10/CAIR-CA-2015-Bullying-Report-Web.pdf.

Caldera, Y. M., and M. A. Sciaraffa. 1998. Parent-toddler play with feminine toys: Are all dolls the same? *Sex Roles* 39: 657–62.

Calhoun, Craig, Joseph Gerteis, James Moody, Steven Pfaff, and Indermohan Virk, eds. 2012. *Classical sociological theory.* Malden, MA: Wiley-Blackwell.

Callero, Peter. 2003. The sociology of the self. *Annual Review of Sociology* 29: 115–33.

Camber, Warren, T. 2014. Not by the sword alone: Soft power, mass media, and the production of state sovereignty. *International Organization* 68 (1): 111–41.

Camp, Stephanie M. H. 2004. *Closer to freedom: Enslaved women and everyday resistance in the plantation South.* Chapel Hill: University of North Carolina Press.

Campbell, Donald, and Julian Stanley. 1963. *Experimental and quasi-experimental design for the social sciences.* Chicago: Rand McNally.

Campbell, Margaret, Gina S. Mohr, and Peeter W. J. Verlegh. 2013. Can disclosures lead consumers to resist covert persuasion? The important roles of disclosure timing and type of response. *Journal of Consumer Psychology* 23 (4): 483–95.

Carbonaro, William. 2005. Tracking, students' effort, and academic achievement. *Sociology of Education* 78 (1): 27–49.

Carey, Nessa. 2012. *The epigenetics revolution: How modern biology is rewriting our understanding of genetics, disease, and inheritance.* New York: Columbia University Press.

Carini, Frank. 2016. Rising Rhode Island rents drive homelessness. Retrieved from www.ecori.org/social-justice-archive/2016/10/24/some-simple-maths-adds-up-to-more-housing.

Carmody, Tim. 2016. How the Flint River got so toxic. *The Verge,* February 26. Retrieved from www.theverge.com/2016/2/26/11117022/flint-michigan-water-crisis-lead-pollution-history.

Carnevale, Anthony P., and Jeff Strohl. 2013. Separate and unequal: How higher education reinforces the intergenerational reproduction of white racial privilege. Washington, DC: Georgetown Public Policy Institute. Retrieved from www9.georgetown.edu/grad/gppi/hpi/cew/pdfs/Separate&Unequal.FR.pdf.

Carrell, Scott E., Mark Hoekstra, and James E. West. 2016. The impact of college diversity on behavior toward minorities. NBER Working Paper w20940.

Carruthers, Bruce G., and Sarah Louise Babb. 2013. *Economy/society: Markets, meanings, and social structure.* Thousand Oaks, CA: Sage.

Carty, Victoria. 2015. *Social movements and new technology.* Boulder, CO: Westview Press.

Casanova, Jose. 1994. *Public religions in the modern world.* Chicago: University of Chicago Press.

Casey, Joan A., Rachel Morello-Frosch, Daniel J. Mennitt, Kurt Fristrup, Elizabeth L. Ogburn, and Peter James. 2017. Race/ethnicity, socioeconomic status, residential segregation, and spatial variation in noise exposure in the contiguous United States. *Environmental Health Perspectives* 125 (7). doi:10.1289/EHP898

Caspi, Avshalom, Joseph McClay, Terrie E. Moffitt, Jonathan Mill, Judy Martin, Ian W. Craig, Alan Taylor, and Richie Poulton. 2002. Role of genotype in the cycle of violence in maltreated children. *Science* 297: 851–54.

Castaneda, Laura. 2017. "Spanish fluency in the U.S. decreases with each generation." *USA Today.* September 10. Retrieved from https://www.usatoday.com/story/life/2017/09/10/spanish-fluency-u-s-decreases-each-generation/636773001/.

Castells, Manuel. 1983. *The city and the grassroots.* Berkeley: University of California Press.

Castells, Manuel. 1996. *The rise of network society.* Oxford, UK: Blackwell.

Catalano, Shannan. 2013. Intimate partner violence: Attributes of victimization, 1993–2011. Washington, DC: U.S. Department of Justice, Bureau of Justice Statistics. Retrieved from www.bjs.gov/content/pub/pdf/ipvav9311.pdf.

Catalyst. 2018. Women in S&P 500 companies. Retrieved from www.catalyst.org/knowledge/women-sp-500-companies.

Centeno, Miguel A., and Elaine Enriquez. 2016. *War and society.* Malden, MA: Polity Press.

Center for American Women and Politics. 2016. Facts: Current numbers and historical data on women in politics. New Brunswick, NJ: University of Rutgers. Retrieved from www.cawp.rutgers.edu/facts.

Center for American Women and Politics. 2018. Current numbers. Rutgers University. Retrieved from www.cawp.rutgers.edu/current-numbers.

Center for Research on Education Outcomes. 2017. Charter management organizations 2017. CREDO, Stanford University.

Center for Responsive Politics. 2016. 2016 presidential race. Retrieved from www.opensecrets.org/pres16/.

Center for Responsive Politics. 2018a. National Rifle Association. Retrieved from www.opensecrets.org/orgs/summary.php?id=d000000082.

Center for Responsive Politics. 2018b. Top individual contributors: All federal contributions. Retrieved from www.opensecrets.org/overview/topindivs.php?cycle=2016&view=fc.

Center for Responsive Politics. 2018c. Lobbying: Ranked sector (all years 1998–2018). Retrieved from www.opensecrets.org/lobby/top.php?showYear=a&indexType=c.

Center on Budget and Policy Priorities. 2016. Policy basics: Non-defense discretionary programs. Retrieved from www.cbpp.org/research/policy-basics-non-defense-discretionary-programs.

Cere, Rinella. 2017. Constructing community: Notes on a slippery concept. In *Representing communities,* ed. Ruth Sanz Sabido, pp. 19–34. Cham, Switzerland: Palgrave MacMillan.

Cerulo, Karen. 2008. Social relations, core values, and the polyphony of the American experience. *Sociological Forum* 23 (2): 351–62.

Cesari, Jocelyne. 2004. *When Islam and democracy meet.* New York: Palgrave Macmillan.

Cesari, Jocelyne. 2013. *Why the West Fears Islam.* New York: Palgrave Macmillan.

Cesari, Jocelyne. 2014. *The awakening of Muslim democracy: Religion, modernity, and the state.* New York: Cambridge University Press.

Chandola, Tarani, Eric Brunner, and Michael Marmot. 2006. Chronic stress at work and the metabolic syndrome: Prospective study. *British Journal of Medicine* 332: 521.

Chang, Elizabeth. 2010. Why Obama should not have checked "black" on his census form. Retrieved from www.washingtonpost.com/wp-dyn/content/article/2010/04/28/AR2010042804156.html.

Charles, Maria. 2011. What gender is science? American Sociological Association. Retrieved from https://contexts.org/articles/what-gender-is-science/.

Charles, Maria. 2017. Venus, Mars, and math: Gender, societal affluence, and eighth graders' aspirations for STEM. *Socius: Sociological Research for a Dynamic World* 3: 1–16.

Chazan, David. 2010. Row over "torture" on French TV. BBC News, March 18. Retrieved from http://news.bbc.co.uk/2/hi/europe/8573755.stm.

Chen, Brian X. 2018. I downloaded the information that Facebook has on me: Yikes. Retrieved from www.nytimes.com/2018/04/11/technology/personaltech/i-downloaded-the-information-that-facebook-has-on-me-yikes.html.

Chen, Henglien Lisa. 2010. Welfare and long-term care in the East and West. *International Journal of Sociology and Social Policy* 30 (3/4): 167–81.

Chen, Kathy. 2005. China's growth places strains on a family's ties. *Wall Street Journal*, April 13, pp. A1, A15.

Chen, Victor. 2015. *Cut loose: Jobless and hopeless in an unfair economy.* Berkeley: University of California Press.

Chenoweth, Erica, and Maria J. Stephan. 2011. *Why civil resistance works: The strategic logic of nonviolent conflict.* New York: Columbia University Press.

Cherlin, Andrew J. 2013. *Public and private families.* New York: McGraw-Hill.

Cherlin, Andrew J. 2014. *Labor's love lost: The rise and fall of the working-class family in America.* New York: Russell Sage Foundation.

Cheshire, Tamara. 2006. American Indian families: Strength and answers from our past. In *Families in global and multicultural perspective,* 2nd ed., ed. Bron B. Ingoldsby and Suzanna D. Smith, pp. 315–27. Thousand Oaks, CA: Sage.

Chesler, Naomi C., and Mark A. Chesler. 2002. Gender-informed mentoring strategies for women engineering scholars: On establishing a caring community. *Journal of Engineering Education* 91 (9): 49–55.

Chesters, Jenny. 2011. Gender convergence in core housework hours. *Journal of Sociology* 49 (1): 78–96.

Chetty, Raj, John N. Friedman, Emmanuel Saez, Nicholas Turner, and Danny Yagan. 2017. Mobility report cards: The role of colleges in intergenerational mobility. Retrieved from www.equality-of-opportunity.org/papers/coll_mrc_paper.pdf.

Chetty, Raj, Michael Stepner, Sarah Abraham, Shelby Lin, Benjamin Scuderi, Nicholas Turner, Augustin Bergeron, and David Cutler. 2016. The association between income and life expectancy in the United States, 2001–2014. *Journal of the American Medical Association* 315 (16): 1750–66.

Child Trends Databank. 2015. Births to unmarried women. Bethesda, MD. Retrieved from www.childtrends.org/wp-content/ uploads/2015/03/75_Births_to_Unmarried_Women.pdf.

Chin, Christina B., Meera E. Deo, Faustina M. DuCros, Jenny Jong-Hwa Lee, Noriko Milman, and Nancy Wang Yuen. 2017. Tokens on the small screen: Asian Americans and Pacific Islanders in prime time and streaming television. Retrieved from www.aapisontv.com/uploads/3/8/1/3/38136681/aapisontv.2017.pdf.

Chinn, Sarah. 2009. *Inventing modern adolescence.* Rutgers, NJ: Rutgers University Press.

Chou, Hui-Tzu Grace, and Nicholas Edge. 2012. "They are happier and having better lives than I am": The impact of Facebook on perceptions of others' lives. *Cyberpsychology, Behavior, and Social Networking* 15: 117–21.

Christakis, Dimitri A. 2010. Internet addiction: A 21st century epidemic? *BMC Medicine* 8: 61.

Christakis, Nicholas A., and James H. Fowler. 2007. The spread of obesity in a large social network over 32 years. *New England Journal of Medicine* 357: 370–79.

Christakis, Nicholas A., and James H. Fowler. 2008. The collective dynamics of smoking in a large social network. *New England Journal of Medicine* 358: 2249–58.

Cisneros, J. David, and Thomas K. Nakayama. 2015. New media, old racisms: Twitter, Miss America, and cultural logics of race. *Journal of International and Intercultural Communication* 8 (2): 108–27.

Citizens for Tax Justice. 2015. Fifteen (of many) reasons why we need corporate tax reform. Retrieved from http://ctj.org/ctjreports/2015/04/fifteen_of_many_reasons_why_we_need_corporate_tax_reform.php#.Vzoz6IQrLRY.

Clair, Matthew, and J. Denis. 2015. Sociology of racism. In *International encyclopedia of the social & behavioral sciences,* 2nd ed., ed. James Wright, pp. 857–63. New York: Elsevier. Retrieved from http://dx.doi.org/10.1016/B978-0-08-097086-8.32122-5.

Clark, Alice. W. 2016. *Valued daughters: First-generation career women.* Thousand Oaks, CA: Sage.

Clarke, Martina A., Joi L. Moore, Linsey M. Steege, Richelle J. Koopman, Jeffery L. Belden, Shannon M. Canfield, Susan E. Meadows, Susan G. Elliott, and Min Soon Kim. 2015. Health information needs, sources, and barriers of primary care patients to achieve patient-centered care: A literature review. *Health Informatics Journal,* pp. 1–25. doi:10.1177/1460458215602939

Classen, Timothy J., and Owen Thompson. 2016. Genes and the intergenerational transmission of BMI and obesity. *Economics & Human Biology* 23: 121–33.

Claster, Patricia Neff, and Sampson Lee Blair. 2013. Latino and Latina educational attainment: An investigation of bi-lingual language abilities and the familial context. *Sociological Viewpoints* 29 (1): 59–86.

Clayman, Steven E. 2013. Conversation analysis in the news interview. In *The handbook of conversation analysis*, ed. Jack Sidnell and Tanya Stivers, pp. 630–656. Boston: Wiley-Blackwell.

Clayman, Steven, and John Heritage. 2002. *The News Interview.* New York: Cambridge University Press.

Clearfield, Melissa W., and Naree M. Nelson. 2006. Sex differences in mothers' speech and play behavior with 6-, 9-, and 14-month-old infants. *Sex Roles: A Journal of Research* 54 (1-2): 127–37.

Clegg, Stewart R., David Courpasson, and Nelson Phillips. 2006. *Power and organizations.* Thousand Oaks, CA: Sage.

Clift, Rebecca. 2016. *Conversation analysis.* Cambridge, MA: Cambridge University Press.

Cloward, Richard A., and Lloyd E. Ohlin. 1960. *Delinquency and opportunity.* New York: Free Press.

CNN. 2016. Exit polls. Retrieved from www.cnn.com/election/2016/results/exit-polls.

CNN. 2018. Florida student to NRA and Trump: "We call BS." Retrieved from www.youtube.com/watch?v=ZxD3o-9H1lY.

Cochran, John K., and Mitchell B. Chamlin. 2006. The enduring racial divide in death penalty support. *Journal of Criminal Justice* 34: 85–99.

Cockerham, William C. 2016. *Medical sociology.* New York: Routledge.

Cohen, Dara Kay, Amelia Hoover Green, and Elisabeth Jean Wood. 2013. Wartime sexual violence misconceptions, implications, and ways forward. Washington, DC: United States Institute of Peace. Retrieved from www.usip.org/sites/default/files/resources/SR323.pdf.

Cohen, Phillip. 2014. Family diversity is the new normal for America's children. Austin, TX: Council on Contemporary Families. Retrieved from https://contemporaryfamilies.org/the-new-normal/.

Cohn, Nate. 2017. A 2016 review: Turnout wasn't the driver of Clinton's defeat. Retrieved from www.nytimes.com/2017/03/28/upshot/a-2016-review-turnout-wasnt-the-driver-of-clintons-defeat.html.

Cole, David, and James X. Dempsey. 2006. *Terrorism and the Constitution: Sacrificing civil liberties in the name of national security.* New York: New Press.

Collins, Chuck and Josh Hoxie. 2017. Billionaire bonanza: The Forbes 400 and the rest of us. Washington, DC: Institute for Policy Studies. https://inequality.org/wp-content/uploads/2017/11/BILLIONAIRE-BONANZA-2017-Embargoed.pdf.

Collins, Chuck, and Felice Yeskel. 2005. *Economic apartheid in America.* New York: New Press.

Collins, Patricia Hill, and Sirma Bilge. 2016. *Intersectionality.* Malden, MA: Polity Press.

Collins, Patricia Hill. 2000, 2009. *Black feminist thought.* New York: Routledge.

Collins, Randall. 1979. *Credential society.* New York: Academic Press.

Collins, Randall, Janet Saltzman Chafetz, Rae Lesser Blumberg, Scott Coltrane, and Jonathan H. Turner. 1993. Toward an integrated theory of gender stratification. *Sociological Perspectives* 36 (3): 185–216

Coltrane, Scott. 1989. Household labor and the routine production of gender. *Social Problems* 36 (5): 473–90.

Committee for a Responsible Federal Budget. 2018. Appropriations watch: FY 2018. Retrieved from www.crfb.org/blogs/appropriations-watch-fy-2018.

Common Sense Media. 2015. *The common sense census: Media use by tweens and teens.* San Francisco, CA: Common Sense Media, Inc. Retrieved from www.commonsensemedia.org/research/the-common-sense-census-media-use-by-tweens-and-teens.

Compa, Lance. 2004. *Unfair advantage: Workers' freedom of association in the United States under international human rights standards.* Ithaca, NY: ILR Press/Cornell University Press.

CompareCamp. 2014. How and where iPhone is made: Comparison of Apple's manufacturing process. Retrieved from http://comparecamp.com/how-where-iphone-is-made-comparison-of-apples-manufacturing-process/.

Conger, Dylan. 2010. Does bilingual education interfere with English-language acquisition? *Social Science Quarterly* 91 (4): 1103–22.

Congressional Budget Office. 2013. The distribution of major tax expenditures in the individual income tax system. Retrieved from www.cbo.gov/sites/default/files/cbofiles/attachments/43768_DistributionTax Expenditures.pdf.

Conklin, John E. 2010. *Criminology,* 10th ed. Boston: Allyn & Bacon.

Conrad, Peter. 2005a. General introduction. In *The sociology of health and illness,* 7th ed., ed. Peter Conrad. New York: Worth.

Conrad, Peter. 2005b. The shifting engines of medicalization. *Journal of Health and Social Behavior* 46 (March): 3–14.

Conrad, Peter. 2007. *The medicalization of society.* Baltimore, MD: Johns Hopkins University Press.

Conrad, Peter, and Kristin K. Barker. 2010. The social construction of illness; key insights and policy implications. *Journal of Health and Social Behavior* 51: S67–79.

Conrad, Peter, and Joseph Schneider. 1980. *Deviance and medicalization.* St. Louis, MO: Mosby.

Contreras, Randol. 2013. *The stickup kids.* Berkeley: University of California Press.

Cook, Tim. 2016. Apple's commitment to your privacy. Retrieved from www.apple.com/privacy/.

Cooley, Charles Horton. (1902) 1964. *Human nature and the social order.* New York: Schocken Books.

Coontz, Stephanie. 2006. *Marriage, a history: How love conquered marriage.* New York: Penguin.

Coontz, Stephanie. 2016. *The way we never were: American families and the nostalgia trap.* New York: Basic Books.

Cooper, Helene. 2018. U.S. strikes killed nearly 500 civilians in 2017, Pentagon says. Retrieved from www.nytimes.com/2018/06/01/us/politics/pentagon-civilian-casualties.html.

Cooper, Helene, and Thomas Gibbons-Neff. 2018. Trump approves new limits on transgender troops in the military. Retrieved from www.nytimes.com/2018/03/24/us/politics/trump-transgender-military.html.

Cooper, Sara, and Nicki Thorogood. 2013. Social construction of health and health promotion. In *Health promotion theory,* ed. Liza Cragg, Maggie Davies, and Wendy Macdowell, pp. 20–34. New York: McGraw-Hill.

Copen, Casey E., Anjani Chandra, and Isaedmarie Febo-Vazquez. 2016. Sexual behavior, sexual attraction, and sexual orientation among adults aged 18–44 in the United States: Data from the 2011–2013 National Survey of Family Growth. *National Health Statistics Reports* 88 (January 7). Retrieved from www.cdc.gov/nchs/data/nhsr/nhsr088.pdf.

Copen, Casey E., Kimberly Daniels, and William D. Mosher. 2013. First premarital cohabitation in the United States: 2006–2010 National Survey of Family Growth. *National Health Statistics Report* 64 (April): 1–15. Retrieved from www.cdc.gov/nchs/data/nhsr/nhsr064.pdf.

Copen, Casey E., Kimberly Daniels, Jonathan Vespa, and William D. Mosher. 2012. *First marriages in the United States: Data from the 2006–2010 National Survey of Family Growth.* National Health Statistics Reports, No. 49. Hyattsville, MD: National Center for Health Statistics.

Cornell, Drucill, ed. 2000. *Feminism and pornography.* New York: Oxford University Press.

Cornell, Stephen, and Douglas Hartmann. 2007. *Ethnicity and race: Making identities in a changing world.* Thousand Oaks, CA: Pine Forge Press.

Cornwell, Benjamin, and Fedor Dokshin. 2014. The power of integration: Affiliation and cohesion in a diverse elite network. *Social Forces* 93 (2): 803–31.

Correll, Shelley J., and Stephen Benard. 2007. Getting a job: Is there a motherhood penalty? *American Journal of Sociology* 112 (5): 1297–1338.

Corrigan, Patrick W., ed. 2014. *The stigma of disease and disability.* Washington, DC: American Psychological Association.

Corriveau, Kathleen H., Grace Min, and Katelyn Kurkul. 2014. Cultural differences in children's learning from others. In *Trust and skepticism,* ed. Elizabeth J. Robinson and Shiri Einav, pp. 95–109. New York: Psychology Press.

Coser, Lewis. 1956. *The functions of social conflict.* New York: Free Press.

Costa-Font, Joan, David Elvira, and Oscar Mascarilla-Miro. 2009. "Ageing in place?" Exploring elderly people's housing preferences in Spain. *Urban Studies* 46 (2): 295–316.

Cottingham, Marci D., Austin H. Johnson, and Rebecca J. Erickson. 2018. "I can never be too comfortable": Race, gender, and emotion at the hospital bedside. *Qualitative Health Research* 28 (1): 145–58.

Couldry, Nick, and Andreas Hepp. 2017. *The social construction of mediated reality.* Malden, MA: Polity Press.

Council of Economic Advisers. 2015a. Gender pay gap: Recent trends and explanations. Washington, DC: Council of Economic Advisers. Retrieved from http://permanent. access.gpo.gov/gpo62962/equal_pay_issue_brief_final.pdf.

Council on Community Pediatrics. 2016. Poverty and child health in the United States. *Pediatrics* (April). doi:10.1542/peds.2016-0339. Retrieved from http://pediatrics.aappublications.org/content/early/2016/03/07/peds.2016-0339.

Courpasson, David. 2016. Impactful resistance: The persistence of recognition politics in the workplace. *Journal of Management Inquiry* 25 (1): 96–100.

Cox, Daniel, Rachel Lienesch, and Robert P. Jones. 2017. Beyond economics: Fears of cultural displacement pushed the white working class to Trump. Public Religion Research Institute/ *The Atlantic Report.* Retrieved from www.prri.org/research/white-working-class-attitudes-economy-trade-immigration-election-donald-trump/.

Craig, Lyn, Abigail Powell, and Ciara Smyth. 2014. Towards intensive parenting? Changes in the composition and determinants of mothers' and fathers' time with children 1992–2006. *The British Journal of Sociology* 65 (3): 555–79.

Craig, Maureen and Jennifer A. Richeson. 2014. On the precipice of a "majority-minority" America: Perceived status threat from the racial demographic shift affects white Americans' political ideology. *Psychological Science* 25 (6): 1189–97.

Credit Suisse Research Institute. 2015. *Global wealth report 2015.* Retrieved from https://publications.credit-suisse.com/tasks/render/file/?fileID=F2425415-DCA7-80B8-EAD989AF9341D47E.

Crenshaw, Kimberlé. 1989. Demarginalizing the intersection of race and sex: A black feminist critique of antidiscrimination doctrine, feminist theory, and antiracist politics. *University of Chicago Legal Forum* 1: 139–67.

Croall, Hazel. 2016. What is known and what should be known about white-collar crime victimization. In *The Oxford handbook of white-collar crime,* ed. Shanna R. Van Slyke, Michael L. Benson, and Francis T. Cullen, pp. 59–77. New York: Oxford University Press.

Crockett, Alasdair, and David Voas. 2006. Generations of decline: Religious change in 20th-century Britain. *Journal for the Scientific Study of Religion* 45 (4): 567–84.

Cromartie. John. 2018. Population & migration: Overview. Washington, DC: U.S. Department of Agriculture. Retrieved from www.ers.usda.gov/topics/rural-economy-population/population-migration/.

Cronin, Audrey Kurth. 2009. *How terrorism ends: Understanding the decline and demise of terrorist campaigns.* Princeton, NJ: Princeton University Press.

Croteau, David, and William Hoynes. 1994a. All the usual suspects: *MacNeil/Lehrer* and *Nightline.* In *By Invitation Only: How the Media Limit Political Debate,* pp. 105–37. Monroe, ME: Common Courage Press.

Croteau, David, and William Hoynes. 1994b. *By invitation only: How the media limit political debate.* Monroe, ME: Common Courage Press.

Croteau, David, and William Hoynes. 2006. *The business of media: Corporate media and the public interest.* Thousand Oaks, CA: Pine Forge Press.

Croteau, David, and William Hoynes. 2014. *Media/society: Industries, images, and audiences,* 5th ed. Thousand Oaks, CA: Sage.

Croteau, David, and William Hoynes. 2019. *Media/society: Technology, industries, content, and users.* Thousand Oaks, CA: Sage.

Croteau, David, William Hoynes, and Kevin Carragee. 1996. The political diversity of public television. *Journalism and Mass Communication Monographs* 157: 1–55.

Croteau, David, William Hoynes, and Stefania Milan. 2011. *Media/society: Industries, images, and audiences,* 4th ed. Thousand Oaks, CA: Pine Forge Press.

Crothers, Lane. 2009. *Globalization and American popular culture,* 2nd ed. Lanham, MD: Rowman & Littlefield.

Cruz, Marcio, James Foster, Bryce Quillin, and Philip Schellekens. 2015. Ending extreme poverty and sharing prosperity: Progress and policies. World Bank. Retrieved from http://pubdocs.worldbank.org/pubdocs/publicdoc/2015/10/109701443800596288/PRN03-Oct2015-TwinGoals.pdf.

Curran, Dylan. 2018. Are you ready? Here is all the data Facebook and Google have on you. Retrieved from www.theguardian.com/commentisfree/2018/mar/28/all-the-data-facebook-google-has-on-you-privacy.

Curran, James, Natalie Fenton, and Des Freedman. 2016. *Misunderstanding the internet.* New York: Routledge.

Czaja, Ronald, and Johnny Blair. 2004. *Designing surveys,* 2nd ed. Thousand Oaks, CA: Pine Forge Press.

D' Emilio, John, and Estelle B. Freedman. 2012. *Intimate matters: A history of sexuality in America.* Chicago: University of Chicago Press.

Da Silva, Chantal. 2018. DHS announces "strengthened northern border strategy" amid growing tensions between U.S. and Canada. Retrieved from www.newsweek.com/dhs-announces-strengthened-northern-border-strategy-amid-growing-tensions-973115.

Dahl, Robert, and Ian Shapiro. 2015. *On democracy*, 2nd ed. New Haven, CT: Yale University Press.
Dahl, Robert. 1957. The concept of power. *Behavioral Science* 2: 201–15.
Dahl, Robert. 1961. *Who governs? Democracy and power in an American city.* New Haven, CT: Yale University Press.
Dahrendorf, Ralf. 1959. *Class and class conflict in industrial society.* Stanford, CA: Stanford University Press.
Dalton, Russell J. 2015. Waxing or waning? The changing patterns of environmental activism. *Environmental Politics* 24 (4): 530–52.
Daniel, G. Reginald. 2002. *More than black: Multiracial identity and new racial order.* Philadelphia, PA: Temple University Press.
Daniels, Roger. 1997. *Not like us: Immigrants and minorities in America, 1890–1924.* Chicago: Ivan R. Dee.
Daniels, Roger. 2004. *Guarding the golden door: American immigration policy and immigrants since 1882.* New York: Hill and Wang.
Dasgupta, Samir, and Peter Kivisto, eds. 2014. *Postmodernism in a global perspective.* Thousand Oaks, CA: Sage.
Davenport, Christian. 2007. State repression and political order. *American Review of Political Science* 10: 1–23.
Davidov, Eldad, Bart Meuleman, Jaak Billiet, and Peter Schmidt. 2008. Values and support for immigration: A cross-country comparison. *European Sociological Review* 24 (5): 583–99.
Davidson, James West, et al. 2014. *Experience History: Interpreting America's Past.* New York: McGraw-Hill Education.
Davie, Grace. 1994. *Religion in Britain since 1945: Believing without belonging.* Oxford, UK: Blackwell.
Davies, Karen. 2003. The body and doing gender: The relations between doctors and nurses in hospital work. *Sociology of Health & Illness* 25 (7): 720–42.
Davies, Scott, and Julian Tanner. 2003. The long arm of the law: Effects of labeling on employment. *Sociological Quarterly* 44 (3): 385–404.
Dávila, Arlene, and Yeidy M. Rivero, eds. 2014. *Contemporary Latina/o media: Production, circulation, politics.* New York: New York University Press.
Davis, Betsy, Renda Dionne, and Michelle Fortin. 2014. Parenting in two cultural worlds in the presence of one dominant worldview: The American Indian experience. In *Parenting across cultures: Childrearing, motherhood and fatherhood in non-Western cultures*, ed. Helaine Selin, pp. 367–77. New York: Springer Dordrecht.
Davis, Donna Z. 2013. A study of relationships in online virtual environments. In *Advancing research methods with new technologies*, ed. Natalie Sappleton, pp. 187–205. Hershey, PA: Information Science Reference.
Davis, Gerald F. 2016. Can an economy survive without corporations? Technology and robust organizational alternatives. *The Academy of Management Perspectives* 30 (2): 129–40.
Davis, Jenny, and Nathan Jurgenson. 2014. Context collapse: Theorizing context collusions and collisions. *Information, Communication & Society* 17 (4): 476–85.
Davis, Kingsley, and Wilbert Moore. 1945. Some principles of stratification. *American Sociological Review* 10: 242–49.
Davis, Kingsley. 1947. Final note on a case of extreme isolation. *American Journal of Sociology* 52 (5): 432–37.
Day, Dorothy. 1952. *The long loneliness.* New York: Harper & Row.
Day, Elizabeth. 2015. #BlackLivesMatter: The birth of a new civil rights movement. *The Guardian,* July 19. Retrieved from www.theguardian.com/world/2015/jul/19/blacklivesmatter-birth-civil-rights-movement.
Dean, Mensah M. 2016. Philly schools pass sweeping policy protecting transgender students. *Philadelphia Inquirer,* June 18. Retrieved from http://articles.philly.com/2016-06-18/news/73844286_1_transgender-students-new-policy-district-spokesman-fernando-gallard.
Death Penalty Information Center. 2016. *Facts about the death penalty.* Washington, DC. April 28.
Death Penalty Information Center. 2018. Facts about the death penalty. Retrieved from https://deathpenaltyinfo.org/documents/FactSheet.pdf.
Deegan, Mary Jo. 1988. *Jane Addams and the men of the Chicago School, 1892–1918.* New Brunswick, NJ: Transaction.
DeLaure, Marilyn, Moritz Fink, and Mark Dery, eds. 2017. *Culture jamming: Activism and the art of cultural resistance.* New York: New York University Press.
Denvir, Daniel. 2011. The 10 most segregated urban areas in America. Retrieved from http://politics.salon.com/2011/03/29/most_segregated_cities/slide_show/10/.
Derber, Charles, William A. Schwartz, and Yale Magrass. 1990. *Power in the highest degree.* New York: Oxford University Press.
Desilver, Drew, and David Masci. 2017. World's Muslim population more widespread than you might think. Retrieved from www.pewresearch.org/fact-tank/2017/01/31/worlds-muslim-population-more-widespread-than-you-might-think/.
Desmond, Matthew. 2016. *Evicted: Poverty and profit in the American city.* New York: Penguin Random House.
Devlin, Bernie, Stephen E. Fienberg, Daniel P. Resnick, and Kathryn Roeder, eds. 1997. *Intelligence, genes, and success: Scientists respond to the bell curve.* New York: Springer-Verlag.
Dewey, Caitlin. 2016. Facebook fake-news writer: "I think Donald Trump is in the White House because of me." Retrieved from www.washingtonpost.com/news/theintersect/wp/2016/11/17/facebook-fake-news-writer-i-think-donald-trump-isin-the-white-house-because-of-me/.
DeWitt, Jerry. 2013. *Hope after faith: An ex pastor's journey from belief to atheism.* Boston: Da Capo Press-Perseus Books.
Dey, Judy Goldberg, and Catherine Hill. 2007. *Behind the pay gap.* Washington, DC: American Association of University Women Educational Foundation.
Dickens, Marissa, Colette Browning, Susan Feldman, and Samantha Thomas. 2016. Social inclusion and the fatosphere: The role of an online weblogging community in fostering social inclusion. *Sociology of Health and Illness* 38 (5): 797–811.
Dickinson, Eliot. 2017. *Globalization and migration: A world in motion.* Lanham, MD: Rowman & Littlefield.
Dimitrova, Radosveta, Michael Bender, and Fons van de Vijver, eds. 2014. *Global perspectives on well-being in immigrant families.* New York: Springer Science + Business Media.
Dinas, Elias. 2014. Why does the apple fall far from the tree? How early political socialization prompts parent-child dissimilarity. *British Journal of Political Science* 44 (4): 827–52.
Dines, Gail. 2010. *Pornland.* Boston: Beacon Press.
Dines, Gail, Jean M. Humez, Bill Yousman, and Lori Bindig Yousman, eds. 2018. *Gender, race, and class in media.* Thousand Oaks, CA: Sage.
Dinovitzer, Ronit, Nancy Reichman, and Joyce Sterling. 2009. The differential valuation of women's work: A new look at the gender gap in lawyers' incomes. *Social Forces* 88 (2): 819–64.
Dionne Jr, E. J., Norman J. Ornstein, and Thomas E. Mann. 2017. *One nation after Trump: A guide for the perplexed, the disillusioned, the desperate, and the not-yet deported.* New York: St. Martin's Press.
Dixon, Marc. 2014. Union organizing and labor outreach in the contemporary United States. *Sociology Compass* 8 (10): 1183–90.
Dizney, Henry F., and Ronald W. Roskens. 1962. An investigation of the "bandwagon effect" in a college straw election. *The Journal of Educational Sociology* 36 (3): 108–14.
Do, D. Phuong, Brian Karl Finch, Ricardo Basurto-Davila, Chloe Bird, Jose Escarce, and Nicole Lurie. 2008. Does place explain racial health disparities? *Social Science & Medicine* 67: 1258–68.
Dobratz, Betty, Lisa K. Waldner, and Timothy Buzzell. 2012. *Power, politics, and society: An introduction to political sociology.* New York: Routledge.
Dolan, Kerry, and Luisa Kroll. 2016. Forbes 2016 world's billionaires: Meet the richest people on the planet. *Forbes.* Retrieved from www.forbes.com/sites/luisakroll/2016/03/01/forbes-2016-worlds-billionaires-meet-the-richest-people-on-the-planet/#f34962641cbf.
Domhoff, G. William. 2013. *Who rules America?* New York: McGraw-Hill.
Donovan, Todd and Kenneth Hoover. 2014. *The elements of social scientific thinking,* 11th ed. Boston: Wadsworth.
Douglas, Susan. 2010. *The rise of enlightened sexism: How pop culture took us from girl power to girls gone wild.* New York: St. Martin's Press.
Douglass, Frederick. 2003. *Frederick Douglass on slavery and the Civil War: Selections from his writings,* ed. Joslyn T. Pine. Mineola, NY: Dover.
Dovidio, John F., Miles Hewstone, Peter Glick, and Victoria M. Esses, eds. 2010. *The SAGE handbook of prejudice, stereotyping and discrimination.* Thousand Oaks, CA: Sage.
Downes, David, Paul Rock, and Eugene McLaughlin. 2016. *Understanding deviance: A guide to the sociology of crime and rule-breaking,* 7th ed. New York, NY: Oxford University Press.
Drake, Michael. 2010. *Political sociology for a globalizing world.* Malden, MA: Polity Press.
Draper, Elaine. 2003. *The company doctor.* New York: Russell Sage Foundation.
Dreifus, Claudia. 2005. A sociologist confronts "the messy stuff" of race, genes and disease. *New York Times,* October 18, p. 2.
Drutman, Lee. 2015. *The business of America is lobbying: How corporations became politicized and politics became more corporate.* New York: Oxford University Press.
Du Bois, W. E. B. (1899) 1996. *The Philadelphia negro: A social study.* Philadelphia: University of Pennsylvania Press.
Du Bois, W. E. B. (1903) 2005. *The souls of black folk.* New York: Simon & Schuster.
Du Bois, W. E. B. (1935) 1998. *Black reconstruction in the United States, 1860–1880.* New York: Free Press.
Dudley, Kathryn Marie. 1997. *The end of the line: Lost jobs, new lives in postindustrial America.* Chicago: University of Chicago Press.

Dugan, Máire A. 2003. Empowerment. In *Beyond intractability,* ed. Guy Burgess and Heidi Burgess. Boulder, CO: Conflict Research Consortium, University of Colorado. Retrieved from www .beyondintractability.org/essay/empowerment.

Duggan, Maeve. 2014. Online harassment. Washington, DC: Pew Research Center. Retrieved from www.pewinternet.org/2014/10/22/online-harassment/.

Duhigg, Charles. 2007. For elderly investors, instant experts abound. *New York Times,* July 8, pp. 1, 14.

Duluth News Tribune. 2013. 20 under 40 Q&A: Mayra Gomez. September 19. Retrieved from www.duluthnewstribune.com/content/20-under-40-qa-mayra-gomez.

Dunbar-Ortiz, Roxanne. 2014. *An indigenous peoples' history of the United States.* Boston: Beacon.

Duncan, Dustin T. and Ichiro Kawachi, eds. 2018. *Neighborhoods and health.* New York: Oxford University Press.

Dunlap, Riley E. and Robert J. Brulle. 2015. *Climate change and society: Sociological perspectives.* New York: Oxford University Press.

Dunlap, Riley E., and Brent K. Marshall. 2007. Environmental sociology. In *21st century sociology: A reference handbook,* ed. Clifton D. Bryant and Dennis L. Peck, pp. 329–40. Thousand Oaks, CA: Sage.

Durand, Jorge, Douglas S. Massey, and Rene Zenteno. 2001. Mexican immigration to the United States: Continuities and changes. *Latin American Research Review* 36 (1): 107–11.

Duranton, Gilles, and Matthew A. Turner. 2011. The fundamental law of road congestion: Evidence from US cities. *American Economic Review* 101 (6): 2616–52.

Durkheim, Emile. (1893) 1997. *The division of labor in society.* New York: Free Press.

Durkheim, Emile. (1895) 1982. *The rules of sociological method,* trans. Sarah A. Solovay and John H. Mueller. New York: Free Press.

Durkheim, Emile. (1897) 1951. *Suicide,* trans. John A. Spaulding and George Simpson. New York: Free Press.

Durkheim, Emile. (1915) 2001. *The elementary forms of the religious life,* trans. Carol Cosman. New York: Oxford University Press.

Durkheim, Emile. (1922) 1956. *Education and sociology,* trans. D. F. Pocock. Glencoe, IL: Free Press.

Durkheim, Emile. (1925) 1961. *Moral education,* trans. Everett K. Wilson. Glencoe, IL: Free Press.

Durkheim, Emile. (1938) 1977. *The evolution of educational thought,* trans. Peter Collins. Boston: Routledge/Kegan Paul.

Duster, Troy. 2003. *Backdoor to eugenics.* New York: Routledge.

Dworkin, A. Gary. 2005. The No Child Left Behind Act: Accountability, high-stakes testing, and roles for sociologists. *Sociology of Education* 78 (2): 170–74.

Dyer, Gwynne. 2004. *War: The lethal custom,* rev. ed. New York: Carol & Graf.

Dyson, Michael Eric. 2000. *I may not get there with you: The true Martin Luther King Jr.* New York: Free Press.

Eagan, Kevin, Ellen Bara Stolzenberg, Joseph J. Ramirez, Melissa C. Aragon, Maria Ramirez Suchard, and Cecilia Rios-Aguilar. 2016. *The American freshman: Fifty-year trends 1966–2015,* expanded ed. Los Angeles: Higher Education Research Institute, UCLA. Retrieved from www.heri.ucla.edu/monographs/50YearTrendsMonograph2016.pdf.

Eagle, Lynne, and Stephan Dahl. 2018. Product placement in old and new media: Examining the evidence of concern. *Journal of Business Ethics* 147 (3): 605–18.

Eagleton-Pierce, Matthew. 2016. *Neoliberalism.* New York: Routledge.

Eagly, Alice H., and Steven J. Karau. 2002. Role congruity theory of prejudice toward female leaders. *Psychological Review* 109: 573–98.

Economist Intelligence Unit. 2018. Democracy index 2017: Free speech under attack. Retrieved from www.eiu.com/topic/democracy-index.

Edelman, Laren B., and Mark C. Suchman. 1997. The legal environments of organizations. *Annual Review of Sociology* 23: 479–515.

Edmonds, Patricia. 2018. These twins, one black and one white, will make you rethink race. Retrieved from www.nationalgeographic.com/magazine/2018/04/race-twins-black-white-biggs/.

Education Week. 2017. Map: Tracking the common core state standards. Retrieved from www .edweek.org/ew/section/multimedia/map-states-academic-standards-common-core-or.html.

Edwards, Paul, and Jacques Belanger. 2009. The multinational firm as contested terrain. In *Images of the multinational firm,* ed. Simon Collinson and Glen Morgan, pp. 193–216. San Francisco: Wiley.

Edwards, Richard. 1982. *Contested terrain: The transformation of the workplace in the twentieth century.* New York: Basic Books.

Egalite, Anna J., Brian Kisida, and Marcus A. Winters. 2015. Representation in the classroom: The effect of own-race teachers on student achievement. *Economics of Education Review* 45: 44–52.

Ehrenhalt, Alan. 2012. *The great inversion and the future of the American city.* New York: Vintage.

Ehrlich, Paul R. 1986. *The population bomb.* New York: Ballantine Books.

Ehrlich, Paul R., and Anne H. Ehrlich. 2013. Can a collapse of global civilization be avoided? *Proceedings of the Royal Society B* 280 (1754): 1–9. Retrieved from http://rspb.royalsocietypublishing.org/content/roysprsb/280/1754/20122845.full.pdf.

Einstein, Albert. (1946) 1999. Quoted in *The Oxford Dictionary of Quotations,* ed. Elizabeth Knowles, p. 290. New York: Oxford University Press.

Eisenstadter, Dave. 2015. Student debt: More college, university students across valley take on loan obligations that follow them for years. *Daily Hampshire Gazette,* September 4. Retrieved from www.gazettenet.com/home/18050337-95/student-debt-more-college-university-students-across-valley-take-on-loan-obligations-that-follow.

Eisenstein, Zillah. 1979. *Capitalist patriarchy and the case for socialist feminism.* New York: Monthly Review Press.

El-Alayli, Amani, Ashley A. Hansen-Brown, and Michelle Ceynar. 2018. Dancing backwards in high heels: Female professors experience more work demands and special favor requests, particularly from academically entitled students. *Sex Roles.* Retrieved from https://doi.org/10.1007/s11199-017-0872-6.

Elasmar, Michael G., and Kathryn Bennett. 2003. The cultural imperialism paradigm revisited: Origin and evolution. In *The impact of international television,* ed. Michael G. Elasmar, pp. 1–16. New York: Routledge.

Elbagir, Nima, Lillian Leposo, and Eliza Mackintosh. 2018. Trump's ban on global abortion funding has led to more abortions. Retrieved from www.cnn.com/2018/05/24/health/trump-mexico-city-policy-abortion-ban-kenya-asequals-intl/index.html.

Elder, Glen. 1999. *Children of the Great Depression.* Boulder, CO: Westview Press.

Elder, Glen H., Jr. 2006. Life course perspective. In *The Blackwell encyclopedia of sociology,* ed. George Ritzer, pp. 2634–39. Boston: Blackwell.

Eller, Cynthia. 2001. *The myth of patriarchal prehistory.* Boston: Beacon.

Ellison, G. T. H., and T. De Wet. 2017. Biological determinism. In *The International Encyclopedia of Biological Anthropology.*

Elson, Diane, and Hanke Keklik. 2003. *Progress of the world's women, 2002,* vol. 2. New York: UN Development Fund for Women.

Elwell, Craig K. 2014. Inflation and the real minimum wage: A fact sheet. Congressional Research Service. Retrieved from www.fas.org/sgp/crs/misc/R42973.pdf.

Emerson, Michael O., and David Hartman. 2006. The rise of religious fundamentalism. *Annual Review of Sociology* 32: 127–44.

Enberg, Jasmine. 2017. Uber, Airbnb lead the way as sharing economy expands. Retrieved from www.emarketer.com/Article/Uber-Airbnb-Lead-Way-Sharing-Economy-Expands/1016109.

Engels, Fredrerick. (1884) 1972. *The origin of the family, private property and the state.* New York: International.

Englehardt, Steven, Jeffrey Han, and Arvind Narayanan. 2018. I never signed up for this! Privacy implications of email tracking. *Proceedings on Privacy Enhancing Technologies 2018.*

Erden, Feyza Tantekin. 2014. Parents' toy preferences: Is gender still an issue? In *Contemporary perspectives and research on early childhood education,* ed. Mustafa Yasar, Ozkan Ozgun, and Jeanne Galbraith, pp. 322–32. Cambridge, MA: Cambridge Scholars Publishing.

Ericcson Mobility Report. 2017, November. Middle East and Africa Appendix.

Erickson, Kai. 1966. *Wayward puritans: A study in the sociology of deviance.* New York: Wiley.

Ericsson. 2015a. *On the pulse of the networked society: Ericsson Mobility Report.* November. Stockholm.

Ericsson. 2015b. *Sub-Saharan Africa: Ericsson Mobility Report.* November. Stockholm.

Ericsson. 2016. *Financial services for everyone: An Ericsson Consumer Insight Report.* February. Stockholm.

Eriksson, Malin, and Maria Emmelin. 2013. What constitutes a health-enabling neighborhood? *Social Science & Medicine* 97: 112–23.

Espenshade, Thomas J., Chang Y. Chung, and Joan L. Walling. 2004. Admission preferences for minority students, athletes, and legacies at elite universities. *Social Science Quarterly* 85 (5): 1422–46.

Esping-Andersen, Gøsta. 1990. *The three worlds of welfare capitalism.* Princeton, NJ: Princeton University Press.

Esping-Andersen, Gøsta. 2002. *Why we need a new welfare state.* New York: Oxford University Press.

Espinosa, Lorelle L., Jonathan M. Turk, and Morgan Taylor. 2017. Pulling back the curtain: Enrollment and outcomes at minority serving institutions. American Council on Education, Center for Policy Research and Strategy.

Esser, Frank, and Jesper Strömbäck, eds. 2014. *Mediatization of politics.* London, UK: Palgrave Macmillan.

Eubanks, Virginia. 2017. *Automating inequality: How high-tech tools profile, police, and punish the poor.* New York: St. Martin's Press.

EUGDPR.ORG. 2018. GDPR key changes. Retrieved from www.eugdpr.org/key-changes.

European Audiovisual Observatory. 2015. Focus 2014: World film market trends. Retrieved from www.obs.coe.int/en/shop/focus.

European Convention on Human Rights. 2017, December. Factsheet: Religious symbols and clothing. Press Unit.

Evangelical Climate Initiative. 2016. Climate change: An evangelical call to action. Retrieved from www.christiansandclimate.org/.

Evans, Louwanda. 2013. *Cabin pressure: African American pilots, flight attendants, and emotional labor.* Lanham, MD: Rowman & Littlefield.

Evans, Peter. 1997. Review of *The clash of civilizations and the remaking of the world order. Contemporary Sociology* 26 (6): 691–93.

Evans, Sarah. 1980. *Personal politics.* New York: Vintage.

Ewen, Stuart. 2001. *Captains of consciousness: Advertising and the social roots of consumer culture.* New York: McGraw-Hill.

Ezzedeen, Souha R., Marie-Helene Budworth, and Susan D. Baker. 2015. The glass ceiling and executive careers: Still an issue for pre-career women. *Journal of Career Development* 42 (5): 355–69.

Fabricant, Michael, and Michelle Fine. 2012. *Charter schools and the corporate makeover of public education.* New York: Teachers College Press.

Facebook. 2013. Facebook for business. Retrieved from www.facebook.com/business/overview.

Faderman, Lillian. 2015. *The gay revolution: The story of the struggle.* New York: Simon & Schuster.

Fadiman, Anne. 2012. *The spirit catches you and you fall down.* New York: Farrar, Straus & Giroux.

Faist, Thomas, Margit Fauser, and Eveline Reisenauer. 2013. *Transnational migration.* Malden, MA: Polity Press.

Falomir-Pichastor, Juan Manuel, Armand Chatard, Leila Selimbegovic, Paul N'Dri Konan, and Gabriel Mugny. 2013. Conformity and counter-conformity to anti-discrimination norms: The moderating effect of attitude toward foreigners and perceived in-group threat. *Journal of Applied Social Psychology* 43: E206–E215.

Farkas, Steve, Jean Johnson, and Tony Foleno with Ann Duffett and Patrick Foley. 2001. For goodness' sake: Why so many want religion to play a greater role in American life. New York: Public Agenda. Retrieved from www.publicagenda.org/files/pdf/for_goodness_sake.pdf.

Farrell, Chad R. 2016. Immigrant suburbanisation and the shifting geographic structure of metropolitan segregation in the United States. *Urban Studies* 53 (1): 57–76.

Fausto-Sterling, Anne. 2000. *Sexing the body.* New York: Basic Books.

Fausto-Sterling, Anne. 2012. *Sex/gender: Biology in a social world.* New York: Routledge.

Faux, Jeff. 2013. NAFTA's impact on US workers. Economic Policy Institute. Retrieved from www.epi.org/blog/naftas-impact-workers/.

Feagin, Joe. 2014. *Racist America: Roots, current realities, and future reparations.* New York: Routledge.

Feagin, Joe R., and Eileen O'Brien. 2003. *White men on race power, privilege, and the shaping of cultural consciousness.* Boston: Beacon Press.

Feagin, Joe R., Hernan Vera, and Kimberly Ducey. 2015. *Liberation sociology.* New York: Routledge.

Federal Trade Commission. 2010. FTC approves final order settling charges that public relations firm used misleading online endorsements to market gaming apps. November 26. Retrieved from www.ftc.gov/opa/2010/11/ reverb.shtm.

Federal Trade Commission. 2016. Warner Bros. settles FTC charges it failed to adequately disclose it paid online influencers to post gameplay videos. Retrieved from www.ftc.gov/news-events/press-releases/2016/07/warner-bros-settles-ftc-charges-it-failed-adequately-disclose-it.

Feinstein, Brian A., Rachel Hershenberg, Vickie Bhatia, Jessica A. Latack, Nathalie Meuwly, and Joanne Davila. 2013. Negative social comparison on Facebook and depressive symptoms: Rumination as a mechanism. *Psychology of Popular Media Culture* 2 (3): 161–70.

Feloni, Richard. 2016. Zappos' CEO says this is the biggest misconception people have about his company's self-management system. *Business Insider,* February 2. Retrieved from www.businessinsider.com/zappos-ceo-tony-hsieh-on-misconception-about-holacracy-2016-2.

Fels, Anna. 2005. *Necessary dreams: Ambition in women's changing lives.* New York: Anchor.

Feng, Jing, Ian Spence, and Jay Pratt. 2007. Playing an action video game reduces gender differences in spatial cognition. *Psychological Science* 18 (10): 850–55.

Ferriss, Susan. 2003. Free trade's broken promises. (Austin) *American-Statesman,* November 5. Retrieved from www.statesman.com/specialreports/content/specialreports/mexico_farms/1102 mexfactory.html.

Few-Demo, April L. 2014. Intersectionality as the "new" critical approach in feminist family studies: Evolving racial/ethnic feminisms and critical race theories. *Journal of Family Theory & Review* 6 (2): 169–83.

Fielding, Nigel G., Raymond M. Lee, and Grant Blank, eds. 2017. *The SAGE handbook of online research methods,* 2nd ed. London, UK: Sage.

Filson, Jennifer, Emilio Ulloa, Cristin Runfola, and Audrey Hokoda. 2010. Does powerlessness explain the relationship between partner violence and depression? *Journal of Interpersonal Violence* 25 (3): 400–15.

Financial Crisis Inquiry Commission. 2011. *The financial crisis inquiry report.* New York: Public Affairs.

Fincher, Leta Hong. 2018. China dropped its one-child policy. So why aren't Chinese women having more babies? Retrieved from www.nytimes.com/2018/02/20/opinion/china-women-birthrate-rights.html.

Fine, Gary Alan. 2006. Shopfloor cultures. *Sociological Quarterly* 47: 1–19.

Finnegan, Ruth. 2014. *Communicating: The multiple modes of human communication.* New York: Routledge.

Fiorina, Morris. 2011. *Culture war? The myth of a polarized America,* 3rd ed. Boston: Longman.

Fiorito, Jack, and Paul Jarley. 2012. Union organizing and membership growth: Why don't they organize? *Journal of Labor Research* 33: 461–86.

Fischer, Claude. 1992. *America calling: A social history of the telephone to 1940.* Berkeley: University of California Press.

Fischer, Claude S. 2011. *Still connected: Family and friends in America since 1970.* New York: Russell Sage Foundation.

Fischer, Claude, and Michael Hout. 2006. *Century of difference: How America changed in the last one hundred years.* New York: Russell Sage Foundation.

Fischer, Claude, Michael Hout, Martín Sánchez Jankowski, Samuel R. Lucas, Ann Swidler, and Kim Voss. 1996. *Inequality by design: Cracking the bell curve myth.* Princeton, NJ: Princeton University Press.

Fish, Jefferson M. 2013. *The myth of race.* Allen, TX: Argo-Navis.

Fishman, Mark. 1980. *Manufacturing the news.* Austin: University of Texas Press.

Fitzgerald, Kathleen J., and Kandice L. Grossman. 2018. *Sociology of sexualities.* Thousand Oaks, CA: Sage.

Flacks, Richard. 1988. *Making history.* New York: Columbia University Press.

Flaherty, Joseph. 2018. The teachers won. Retrieved from www.phoenixnewtimes.com/news/the-teachers-won-how-arizonas-strike-unfolded-10403354.

Fletcher, Colin. 1974. *Beneath the surface.* Boston: Routledge.

Flew, Terry. 2007. *Understanding global media.* New York: Palgrave Macmillan.

Flint, Anthony. 2006. *This land: The battle over sprawl and the future of America.* Baltimore, MD: Johns Hopkins University Press.

Flora, Cornelia Butler and Jan L. Flora. 2013. *Rural communities,* 4th ed. Boulder, CO: Westview Press.

Floyd-Thomas, Stacy M., and Anthony B. Pinn, eds. 2010. *Liberation theologies in the United States.* New York: New York University Press.

Foderaro, Lisa W. 2014. Taking a call for climate change to the streets. *New York Times,* September 21. Retrieved from www.nytimes.com/2014/09/22/nyregion/new-york-city-climate-change-march.html.

Foner, Nancy, Jan Rath, Jan Willem Duyvendak, and Rogier van Reekum, eds. 2014. *New York and Amsterdam: Immigration and the new urban landscape.* New York: New York University.

Fong, Mei. 2016. *One child: The story of China's most radical experiment.* New York: Houghton Mifflin Harcourt.

Forbes. 2018. The world's biggest public companies. Retrieved from www.forbes.com/sites/kristinstoller/2018/06/06/the-worlds-largest-public-companies-2018/#56ca31d1769f.

Forsyth, Donelson. 2019. *Group dynamics.* Boston, MA: Cengage.

Foster, John Bellamy, and Fred Magdoff. 2009. *The great financial crisis: Causes and consequences.* New York: Monthly Review Press.

Foucault, Michel. 1979. *Discipline and punish,* trans. Alan Sheridan. New York: Vintage.

Foucault, Michel. 1980. *The history of sexuality,* vol. 1. New York: Vintage.

Foucault, Michel. 1995. *Discipline and punish: The birth of the prison,* trans. Alan Sheridan. New York: Vintage.

Fowler, James H., and Nicholas A. Christakis. 2008. Dynamic spread of happiness in a large social network: Longitudinal analysis over 20 years in the Framingham Heart Study. *British Medical Journal* 337: a2338.

Fowler, Robert Booth, Allen D. Hertzke, Laura R. Olson, and Kevin R. Den Dulk. 2014. *Religion and politics in America: Faith, culture, and strategic choices.* Boulder, CO: Westview Press.

Fox, Bonnie. 2015. Feminism on family sociology: Interpreting trends in family life. *Canadian Review of Sociology* 52 (2): 204–11.

Fox, Jonathan. 2016. Secular-religious competition in Western democracies: 1990 to 2014. *Journal of Religious and Political Practice* 2 (2): 155–74.

Fox, Jonathan. 2018. *An introduction to religion and politics: Theory and practice*. New York: Routledge.

Francis, Richard C. 2011. *Epigenetics: How environment shapes our genes*. New York: Norton.

Frank, Thomas. 1997. *The conquest of cool*. Chicago: University of Chicago Press.

Frankowski, Barbara L. 2004. Sexual orientation and adolescents. *Pediatrics* 113 (6): 1827–32.

Franks, David D. 2010. *Neurosociology: The nexus between neuroscience and social psychology*. New York: Springer.

Franks, David D., and Jonathan H. Turner, eds. 2013. *Handbook of neurosociology*. New York: Springer.

Fraser, Nancy. 1992. Rethinking the public sphere: A contribution to the critique of actually existing democracy. In *Habermas and the Public Sphere*, ed. Craig Calhoun, pp. 109–42. Cambridge, MA: MIT Press.

Fraser, Steve, ed. 1995. *The bell curve wars*. New York: Basic Books.

Freedman, Des. 2014. *The contradictions of media power*. New York: Bloomsbury Academic.

Freedom House. 2017. Freedom on the net 2017: Manipulating social media to undermine democracy. Retrieved from https://freedomhouse.org/sites/default/files/FOTN_2017_Final.pdf.

Freeman, Kathlee, and Fridah Mubichi. 2017. ICT use by smallholder farmers in rural Mozambique: A case study of two villages in Central Mozambique. *Journal of Rural Social Sciences* 32 (2): 1–19.

Freeman, Nancy K. 2007. Preschoolers' perceptions of gender appropriate toys and their parents' beliefs about genderized behaviors: Miscommunication, mixed messages, or hidden truths? *Early Childhood Education Journal* 34 (5): 357–66.

Freese, Jeremy, and Sara Shostak. 2009. Genetics and social inquiry. *Annual Review of Sociology* 35: 107–28.

Friedland, Nehemia. 1976. Social influence via threats. *Journal of Experimental Social Psychology* 12: 552–63.

Freire, Paulo. 1970. *Pedagogy of the oppressed*, trans. Myra Bergman Ramos. New York: Seabury Press.

French, John R. P., Jr., and Bertram Raven. (1959) 2001. The bases of social power. In *The negotiation sourcebook*, ed. Ira G. Asherman and Sandra Vance Asherman, pp. 61–73. Amherst, MA: HRD Press.

Frey, William H. 2016. Mid-decade, big-city growth continues. Washington, DC: Brookings Institute. Retrieved from www.brookings. edu/2016/05/23/mid-decade-big-city-growth-continues/.

Fried, Mindy. 2008. The evaluator in the field as an outsider within. *Footnotes* 36 (3). Retrieved from www.asanet.org/footnotes/mar08_R/fn6.html.

Fried, Mindy. 2014. How sociologists can support Black Lives Matter. Feminist Reflections: The Society Pages. Retrieved from https://thesocietypages.org/feminist/2014/12/15/how-sociologists-can-support-black-lives-matter/.

Friedman, Jeffrey, and Richard A. Posner, eds. 2009. *What caused the financial crisis*. Philadelphia: University of Pennsylvania Press.

Friedman, Uri. 2017. What is a populist? Retrieved from www.theatlantic.com/international/archive/2017/02/what-is-populist-trump/516525/.

Friedrichs, David O. 2009. *Trusted criminals: White collar crime in contemporary society*, 4th ed. Belmont, CA: Wadsworth.

Frier, Sarah. 2016. Facebook wants you to post more about yourself. *Bloomberg*. Retrieved from www.bloomberg.com/news/articles/ 2016-04-07/facebook-said-to-face-decline-in-people-posting-personal-content.

Fry, Richard. 2016. For first time in modern era, living with parents edges out other living arrangements for 18–34-year-olds. Washington, DC: Pew Research Center. Retrieved from www.pewsocialtrends.org/files/2016/05/2016-05-24_living-arrangement-final.pdf.

Fry, Richard. 2017. It's becoming more common for young adults to live at home—and for longer stretches. Pew Research Center. Retrieved from www.pewresearch.org/fact-tank/2017/05/05/its-becoming-more-common-for-young-adults-to-live-at-home-and-for-longer-stretches/.

Fussell, Elizabeth. 2006. Leaving New Orleans: Social stratification, networks, and hurricane evacuation. In *Understanding Katrina: Perspectives from the social sciences*. Retrieved from http://understandingkatrina.ssrc.org/Fussell/.

Fussell, Elizabeth. 2018. Population displacements and migration patterns in response to Hurricane Katrina. In *Routledge handbook of environmental displacement and migration*, ed. Robert McLeman and François Gemenne, pp. 277–88. New York: Routledge.

Fuwa, Makiko. 2004. Macro-level gender inequality and the division of household labor in 22 countries. *American Sociological Review* 69 (6): 751–67.

Gabriel, Yiannis, and Tim Lang. 2015. *The unmanageable consumer*. Thousand Oaks, CA: Sage.

Gagera, Constance T., Scott T. Yabikub, and Miriam Linvera. 2016. Conflict or divorce? Does parental conflict and/or divorce increase the likelihood of adult children's cohabiting and marital dissolution? *Marriage & Family Review* 52 (3): 243–61.

Gaines, Donna. 1991. *Teenage wasteland*. New York: Pantheon.

Galinsky, Ellen, Kerstin Aumann, and James T. Bond. 2013. Times are changing: Gender and generation at work and at home in the USA. In *Expanding the boundaries of work-family research: A vision for the future*, ed. Steven Poelmans, Jeffrey Greenhaus, and Mireia Las Heras Maestro, pp. 276–96. New York: Palgrave Macmillan.

Gallagher, Sean. 2018. Facebook scraped call, text message data for years from Android phones. Retrieved from https://arstechnica.com/information-technology/2018/03/facebook-scraped-call-text-message-data-for-years-from-android-phones/.

Gallian, Joseph A. 2004. A conversation with Melanie Wood. *Math Horizons* (September): 13–14, 31.

Galliher, John F. 2016. *Troy Duster: Berkeley sociologist, teacher, and civil rights activist*. Lanham, MD: Hamiltwon Books.

Gallup, Cindy. 2011. *Make love, not porn: Technology's hard-core impact on human behavior*. TED Books.

Gallup. 2017a. Americans' worries about race relations at record high. Retrieved from http://news.gallup.com/poll/206057/americans-worry-race-relations-record-high.aspx?g_source=link_NEWSV9&g_medium=TOPIC&g_campaign=item_&g_content=Americans%27%2520Worries%2520About%2520Race%2520Relations%2520at%2520Record%2520High.

Gallup. 2017b. In U.S., 10.2% of LGBT adults now married to same-sex spouse. Retrieved from http://news.gallup.com/poll/212702/lgbt-adults-married-sex-spouse.aspx.

Galtung, Johan. 1996. *Peace by peaceful means*. London: Sage.

Galtung, Johan. 2000. *Conflict transformation by peaceful means*. New York: United Nations.

Galtung, Johan. 2009. *The fall of the US empire—and then what?* Grenzach-Whylen, Germany: TRANSCEND University Press.

Galtung, Johan. 2015. *World politics of peace and war*. New York: Hampton Press.

Galtung, Johan, and Dietrich Fischer. 2013. Peace studies and conflict resolution: The need for transdisciplinarity. In *Johan Galtung*, pp. 139–49. New York: Springer

Gamson, Joshua. 2015. The moment of maybe. *Contexts*. Washington, DC: American Sociological Association. Retrieved from https://contexts.org/blog/the-moment-of-maybe/.

Gamson, William A., Bruce Fireman, and Steven Rytina. 1982. *Encounters with unjust authority*. Homewood, IL: Dorsey Press.

Gandara, Patricia, and Megan Hopkins. 2010. *Forbidden language: English learners and restrictive language policies*. New York: Teachers College Press.

Gans, Herbert J. 1999. *Popular culture & high culture*, rev. ed. New York: Basic Books.

Ganz, Marshall. 2009. Why David sometimes wins: Leadership, organization, and strategy in the California farm worker movement. New York: Oxford University Press.

García-Manglano, Javier. 2015. Opting out and leaning in: The life course employment profiles of early baby boom women in the United States. *Demography* 52 (6): 1961–93.

Garey, Anita Ilta, and Karen V. Hansen, eds. 2011. *At the heart of work and family: Engaging the ideas of Arlie Hochschild*. New Brunswick, NJ: Rutgers University Press.

Garfinkel, Harold. 1967. *Studies in ethnomethodology*. New York: Prentice Hall.

Garland, David. 1993. *Punishment and modern society*. Chicago: University of Chicago Press.

Garland, David. 2012. *Peculiar institution: America's death penalty in an age of abolition*. Cambridge, MA: Belknap Press.

Gates, Gary J. 2011. How many people are lesbian, gay, bisexual and transgender? Los Angeles: Williams Institute, UCLA School of Law.

Gates, Henry Louis, Jr. 2016. Black America and the class divide. *New York Times*, February 1. Retrieved from www.nytimes.com/2016/02/07/education/edlife/black-america-and-the-class-divide.html.

Gaventa, John. 1982. *Power and powerlessness*. Urbana: University of Illinois Press.

Gazzaniga, Michael. 1998. *The mind's past*. Berkeley: University of California Press.

Gelder, Ken, ed. 2005. *The subcultures reader*, 2nd ed. New York: Routledge.

Gelles, David. 2016. The Zappos exodus continues after a radical management experiment. *New York Times*, January 13. Retrieved from http://bits.blogs.nytimes.com/2016/01/13/after-a-radical-management-experiment-the-zappos-exodus-continues.

Gerbner, George, Larry Gross, Michael Morgan, and Nancy Signorielli. 2008. Growing up with television: Cultivation processes. In *Media effects: Advances in theory and research*, ed. Jennings Bryant and Dolf Zillmann. Hillsdale, NJ: Erlbaum.

German Bundestag. 2018. Distribution of seats in the 19th German Bundestag. Retrieved from www.bundestag.de/en/parliament/plenary/distributionofseats.

Gerson, Kathleen. 2009. *The unfinished revolution: Coming of age in a new era of gender, work, and family.* New York: Oxford University Press.

Gerson, Kathleen. 2010. *Hard choices: How women decide about work, career, and motherhood.* Berkeley: University of California Press.

Gerson, Kathleen. 2010b. *The unfinished revolution: How a new generation is reshaping family, work and gender in America.* New York: Oxford University Press.

Ghosh, Dipayan, and Ben Scott. 2018. #Digital-Deceit: The technologies behind precision propaganda on the internet. New America Public Interest Technology Program.

Gibson, Campbell, and Kay Jung. 2002. Historical census statistics on population totals by race, 1790 to 1990, Table 1. Washington, DC: U.S. Census Bureau. Retrieved from www.census.gov/population/www/ documentation/twps0056/twps0056.html.

Gibson, Campbell, and Kay Jung. 2006. Historical Census Statistics on the Foreign-Born Population of the United States: 1850 to 2000. Working Paper No. 81. U.S. Census Bureau. Retrieved from https://www.census.gov/population/www/documentation/twps0081/twps0081.pdf.

Gibson, Campbell. 1998. Population of the 100 largest cities and other urban places in the United States: 1790 to 1990. Retrieved from www.census.gov/population/www/documentation/twps0027/twps0027.html.

Gieryn, Thomas F. 2000. A space for place in sociology. *Annual Review of Sociology* 26: 463–96.

Gilbert, Dennis. 2015. *The American class structure in an age of growing inequality,* 9th ed. Thousand Oaks, CA: Sage.

Gilens, Martin, and Benjamin I. Page. 2014. Testing theories of American politics: Elites, interest groups, and average citizens. *Perspectives on Politics* 12 (3): 564–81.

Gilens, Martin. 2005. Inequality and democratic responsiveness. *Public Opinion Quarterly* 69 (5): 778–96.

Gilens, Martin. 2012. *Affluence and influence: Economic inequality and political power in America.* Princeton, NJ: Princeton University Press.

Gilley, Brian Joseph. 2006. *Becoming two-spirit: Gay identity and social acceptance in Indian country.* Omaha: University of Nebraska Press.

Gilliam, Walter S., Angela N. Maupin, Chin R. Reyes, Maria Accavitti, and Frederick Shic. 2016. Do early educators' implicit biases regarding sex and race relate to behavior expectations and recommendations of preschool expulsions and suspensions? Yale University Child Study Center. Retrieved from www.addressingracialmicroaggressions.com/wp-content/uploads/2016/10/Preschool-Implicit-Bias-Policy-Brief_final_9_26_276766_5379.pdf.

Gimenez, Martha E. 2001. Marxism, and class, gender, and race: Rethinking the trilogy. *Race, Gender & Class* 1: 23–33.

Gitlin, Todd. 2003. *The whole world is watching: Mass media in the making and unmaking of the new left.* Berkeley, CA: University of California Press.

Giugni, Marco, and Maria T. Grasso. 2015. Environmental movements in advanced industrial democracies: Heterogeneity, transformation, and institutionalization. *Annual Review of Environment and Resources* 40: 337–61.

GLAAD. 2018. Where we are on TV: 17–18. Retrieved from https://glaad.org/files/WWAT/WWAT_GLAAD_2017-2018.pdf.

Glass, Jennifer, Robin W. Simon, and Matthew A. Andersson. 2016. Parenthood and happiness: Effects of work-family reconciliation policies in 22 OECD countries. *American Journal of Sociology, 122*(3): 886–929.

Glasser, Irene, Eric Hirsch, and Anna Chan. 2014. Reaching and enumerating homeless populations. In *Hard-to-survey populations*, ed. Roger Tourangeau, Brad Edwards, Timothy P. Johnson, Kirk M. Wolter, and Nancy Bates, pp. 180–200. Cambridge, UK: Cambridge University Press.

Global Footprint Network. 2018. Why past Earth overshoot day dates keep changing. Retrieved from www.overshootday.org/why-past-earth-overshoot-day-dates-keep-changing/.

Gloor, Storm. 2014. Songs as branding platforms? A historical analysis of people, places, and products in pop music lyrics. *Journal of the Music & Entertainment Industry Educators Association* 14 (1): 39–60.

Goe, W. Richard, and Sean Noonan. 2007. The sociology of community. In *21st century sociology: A reference handbook,* ed. Clifton D. Bryant and Dennis L. Peck, pp. 455–64. Thousand Oaks, CA: Sage.

Goffman, Erving. 1959. *The presentation of self in everyday life.* Garden City, NY: Doubleday Anchor Books.

Goffman, Erving. 1963. *Stigma: Notes on the management of spoiled identity.* New York: Simon & Schuster.

Goffman, Erving. 1974. *Frame analysis.* New York: Harper & Row.

Göhler, Gerhard. 2009. Power to and power over. In *The SAGE handbook of power,* ed. Stewart R. Clegg and Mark Haugaard, pp. 27–39. Thousand Oaks, CA: Sage.

Goldberg, Abbie E. 2013. "Doing" and "undoing" gender: The meaning and division of housework in same-sex couples. *Journal of Family Theory & Review* 5 (2): 85–104.

Goldberg, Abbie, Deborah Kashy, and JuliAnna Smith. 2012. Gender-typed play behavior in early childhood: Adopted children with lesbian, gay, and heterosexual parents. *Sex Roles* 67 (9/10): 503–15.

Goldrick-Rab, Sara. 2016. *Paying the price: College costs, financial aid, and the betrayal of the American dream.* Chicago: University of Chicago Press.

Goldsmith, Marshall. 2004. Why even thinking about retirement can be a bad idea. *Fast Company* 78 (January).

Goldstein, Dana. 2018. Teacher pay is so low in some U.S. school districts that they're recruiting overseas. *New York Times*, May 2.

Goldstein, Matthew. 2016. Goldman to pay up to $5 billion to settle claims of faculty mortgages. *New York Times*, January 15, p. B1.

Göle, Nilüfer. 2011. *Islam in Europe.* Princeton, NJ: Markus Weiner.

Gómez, Mayra. 2014. Human rights and the sociological imagination: How sociologists can help make the world a better place. In *Sociologists in action: Sociology, social change, and social justice,* ed. Kathleen Odell Korgen, Jonathan M. White, and Shelley K. White, pp. 6–10. Thousand Oaks, CA: Sage.

Gonzalez, Juan. 2011. *Harvest of empire: A history of Latinos in the United States.* New York: Penguin.

Gonzalez, Juan, and Joseph Torres. 2011. *News for all the people: The epic story of race and the American media.* Brooklyn, NY: Verso.

Goodine, Bradley. 2014. Religious fundamentalism. In *The encyclopedia of political thought*, ed. Michael T. Gibbons, Diana Coole, Elisabeth Ellis, and Kennan Ferguson. Malden, MA: Wiley-Blackwell.

Goodwin, Kerri A., Passion J. Hannah, Meg C. Nicholl, and Jenna M. Ferri. 2017. The confident co-witness: The effects of misinformation on memory after collaborative discussion. *Applied Cognitive Psychology* 31 (2): 225–35.

Google. 2018. Our offices. Retrieved from www.google.com/about/locations.

Gordon, David M., Richard Edwards, and Michael Reich. 1982. *Segmented work, divided workers.* New York: Cambridge University Press.

Gorman, Siobhan, Evan Perez, and Janet Hook. 2013. U.S. collects vast data trovc. *Wall Street Journal,* June 7.

Gottdiener, Mark, and Ray Hutchison. 2015. *The new urban sociology.* Boulder, CO: Westview Press.

Gould, Elise. 2018. The state of American wages, 2017. Washington, DC: Economic Policy Institute. Retrieved from www.epi.org/publication/the-state-of-american-wages-2017-wages-have-finally-recovered-from-the-blow-of-the-great-recession-but-are-still-growing-too-slowly-and-unequally/.

Gould, Kenneth A., David N. Pellow, and Allan Schnaiberg. 2008. *The treadmill of production: Injustice and unsustainability in the global economy.* Boulder, CO: Paradigm.

Gould, Stephen Jay. 1996. *The mismeasure of man.* New York: Norton.

Government Accounting Office. 2015. Contingent workforce. GAO-15-168R. Washington, DC. Retrieved from www.gao.gov/assets/670/669766.pdf.

Graf, Nikki. 2018. Sexual harassment at work in the era of #MeToo. Washington, DC: Pew Research Center. Retrieved from http://assets.pewresearch.org/wp-content/uploads/sites/3/2018/04/03161853/Pew-Research-Center-Sexual-Harassment-Report-April-2018-FINAL.pdf.

Gramsci, Antonio. 1971. *Selections from the prison notebooks,* ed. and trans. Quintin Hoare and Geoffrey Nowell Smith. New York: International.

Granfield, Robert. 1992. *Making elite lawyers.* New York: Routledge.

Granfield, Robert, and Thomas Koenig. 1990. From activism to pro bono. *Critical Sociology* 17 (1): 57–80.

Granovetter, Mark S. 1973. The strength of weak ties. *American Journal of Sociology* 78 (6): 1360–80.

Granovetter, Mark S. 1974. *Getting a job.* Cambridge, MA: Harvard University Press.

Granovetter, Mark. 1985. Economic action and social structure: The problem of embeddedness. *American Journal of Sociology* 91 (3): 481–510.

Granovetter, Mark. 2017. *Society and economy: Framework and principles.* Cambridge, MA: Harvard University Press.

Gray, Herman. 2015. The feel of life: Resonance, race, and representation. *International Journal of Communication* 9: 1108–19.

Gray, John. 2004. *Men are from Mars, women are from Venus.* New York: Harper.

Green, Todd H. 2015. *The fear of Islam: An introduction to Islamophobia in the West.* Minneapolis, MN: Fortress Press.

Greenhouse, Steven. 2014. Low-wage workers are finding poverty harder to escape. *New York Times,* March 16. Retrieved from www.nytimes.com/2014/03/17/business/ economy/low-wage-workers-finding-its-easier-to-fall-into-poverty-and-harder-to-get-out.html.

Greenwald, Glenn. 2014. *No place to hide: Edward Snowden, the NSA, and the U.S. surveillance state.* New York: Metropolitan Books.

Greenwood, Jeremy, Nezih Guner, Georgi Kocharkov, and Cezar Santos. 2014. Marry your like: Assortative mating and income inequality. National Bureau of Economic Research Working Paper No. 19829. Retrieved from http://pareto.uab.es/nguner/ggksPandP-December2013.pdf.

Greenwood, Max. 2017. Number of jobs lost to foreign competition up since Trump's election: Report. *The Hill.* November 30. Retrieved from https://thehill.com/policy/finance/362526-number-of-jobs-lost-to-foreignw-trade-since-trumps-election-on-par-with.

Greider, William. 2010. *Come home, America.* New York: Rodale Press.

Griffin, Larry J. 2004. "Generations and collective memory" revisited. *American Sociological Review* 69 (4): 544–57.

Griswold, Daniel T. 2009. *Mad about trade: Why main street America should embrace globalization.* Washington, DC: Cato Institute.

Gross, Michael B. 2004. *The war against Catholicism.* Ann Arbor: University of Michigan Press.

Groth, Aimee. 2015. Internal memo: Zappos is offering severance to employees who aren't all in with Holacracy. *Quartz.* Retrieved from http://qz.com/370616/internal-memo-zappos-is-offering-severance-to-employees-who-arent-all-in-with-holacracy/.

Grue, Jan. 2016. The social meaning of disability: A reflection on categorisation, stigma, and identity. *Sociology of Health & Illness* 38 (6): 957–64.

Grusky, David B., and Manwai C. Ku. 2008. Doom, gloom, and inequality. In *Social stratification,* ed. David B. Grusky, pp. 2–28. Boulder, CO: Westview Press.

Grusky, David B., Bruce Western, and Christopher Wimer, eds. 2011. *The great recession.* New York: Russell Sage Foundation.

GSMA. 2017. *The mobile economy: Sub-Saharan Africa 2017.*

Guariglia, Matthew. 2018. The real goal of Donald Trump's MS-13 fearmongering. Retrieved from www.washingtonpost.com/news/made-by-history/wp/2018/04/09/the-real-goal-of-donald-trumps-ms-13-fearmongering.

Guba, Egon, and Yvonna Lincoln. 1994. Competing paradigms in qualitative research. In *Handbook of qualitative research,* ed. N. Denzin and Yvonna Lincoln, pp. 105–17. Thousand Oaks, CA: Sage.

Guliani, Neema Singh. 2018. Congress just passed a terrible surveillance law. Now what? Retrieved from www.aclu.org/blog/national-security/privacy-and-surveillance/congress-just-passed-terrible-surveillance-law-now.

Gunning, Jeroen, and Richard Jackson. 2011. What's so "religious" about "religious terrorism"? *Critical Studies on Terrorism* 4 (3): 369–88.

Guo, Guang, Michael E. Roettger, and Tianji Cai. 2008. The integration of genetic propensities into social-control models of delinquency and violence among male youths. *American Sociological Review* 73 (4): 543–68.

Gusfield, Joseph. 1996. *Contested meanings: The construction of alcohol problems.* Madison: University of Wisconsin Press.

Gygli, Savina, Florian Haelg, and Jan-Egbert Sturm. 2018. The KOF globalisation index revisited. Working Paper 439. Retrieved from https://doi.org/10.3929/ethz-b-000238666.

Haas, Mark L. 2008. Pax Americana Geriatrica. *Miller-McCune,* August, pp. 31–39.

Habermas, Jurgen. 2002. *Religion and rationality,* trans. E. Mendieta. Cambridge, MA: MIT Press.

Hadani, Michael, Natasha Munshi, and Kim Clark. 2017. The more you give, the more you get? The impact of corporate political activity on the value of government contracts. *Business and Society Review* 122 (3): 421–48.

Haenfler, Ross. 2014. *Subcultures: The basics.* New York: Routledge.

Hafez, Mohammed M. 2006. Suicide terrorism in Iraq: A preliminary assessment of the quantitative data and documentary evidence. *Studies in Conflict and Terrorism* 29 (6): 591–619.

Hall, Donald E. and Annamarie Jagose, eds. 2013. *The Routledge queer studies reader.* New York: Routledge.

Hall, Richard, and Pamela Tolbert. 2009. *Organizations.* Englewood Cliffs, NJ: Prentice Hall.

Hambleton, Alexandra. 2016. When women watch: The subversive potential of female-friendly pornography in Japan. *Porn Studies* 3 (4): 427–42.

Hamilton, Emily A., Laurie Mintz, and Susan Kashubeck-West. 2007. Predictors of media effects on body dissatisfaction in European American women. *Sex Roles* 56 (5–6): 397–402.

Hamm, Bernd, and Russell Smandych, eds. 2005. *Cultural imperialism.* Toronto, Ontario, Canada: University of Toronto Press.

Hancock, Ange-Marie. 2016. *Intersectionality: An intellectual history.* New York: Oxford University Press.

Hancock, Black Hawk, and Michael J. Lorr. 2013. More than just a soundtrack. *Journal of Contemporary Ethnography* 42 (3): 320–46.

Handel, Gerald, Spencer Cahill, and Frederick Elkin. 2007. *Children and society: The sociology of children and childhood socialization.* Los Angeles: Roxbury Publishing Company.

Hanisch, Carol. 1970. The personal is political. In *Notes from the second year: Women's liberation.* Retrieved from www.carolhanisch.org/CHwritings/PIP.htm.

Hannan, Cheryl Kamei. 2006. Neuroscience and the impact of brain plasticity on Braille reading. *Journal of Visual Impairment & Blindness* 100 (7): 397–413.

Hannigan, John. 2014. *Environmental sociology.* New York: Routledge.

Harding, Sandra. 1991. *Whose science? Whose knowledge? Thinking from women's lives.* Ithaca, NY: Cornell University Press.

Harding, Sandra, ed. 2004. *The feminist standpoint theory reader.* New York: Routledge.

Hardisty, Jean. 1999. *Mobilizing resentment.* Boston: Beacon.

Harnois, Catherine E. 2015. Race, ethnicity, sexuality, and women's political consciousness of gender. *Social Psychology Quarterly* 78 (4): 365–86.

Harnois, Catherine E. 2017. Intersectional masculinities and gendered political consciousness: How do race, ethnicity and sexuality shape men's awareness of gender inequality and support for gender activism? *Sex Roles* 77 (3–4): 141–54.

Harper, Charles L., and Kevin T. Leicht. 2016. *Exploring social change: America and the world.* New York: Routledge.

Harris, Sam. 2014. *Waking up: A guide to spirituality without religion.* New York: Simon & Schuster.

Harrison, Jill Ann, Steven H. Lopez, and Andrew W. Martin. 2015. Rethinking organizational decoupling: Fields, power struggles, and work routines. *Social Currents* 2 (4): 341–60.

Hartman, Andrew. 2015. *A war for the soul of America: A history of the culture wars.* Chicago: University of Chicago Press.

Hartsock, Nancy. 1983. *Money, sex, and power: Toward a feminist historical materialism.* Boston: Northeastern University Press.

Harvey, David. 1990. *The condition of postmodernity.* Oxford, UK: Blackwell.

Haselton, Todd. 2018. I checked and it turns out Facebook knows a lot about me. Retrieved from www.cnbc.com/2018/03/27/facebook-knows-a-lot-about-me.html.

Hatch, Mary Jo. 2018. *Organization theory: Modern, symbolic, and postmodern perspectives.* New York: Oxford University Press.

Hawley, George. 2017. *Making sense of the alt-right.* New York: Columbia University Press.

Hayim, Gila. 1995. *Existentialism and sociology: The contribution of Jean-Paul Sartre.* New Brunswick, NJ: Transaction Publishers.

He, Wan, and Mark N. Muenchrath. 2011. ACS-17, 90+ in the United States: 2006–2008. U.S. Census Bureau, American Community Survey Reports. Washington, DC: U.S. Government Printing Office.

Health Effects Institute. 2018. State of global air 2018. Boston, MA: Health Effects Institute. www.stateofglobalair.org/sites/default/files/soga-2018-report.pdf.

Hearn, Jonathan. 2012. *Theorizing power.* New York: Palgrave Macmillan.

Heclo, Hugh, Theda Skocpol, Mary Jo Bane, and Alan Wolfe. 2007. *Christianity and American democracy.* Cambridge, MA: Harvard University Press.

Heelas, Paul, and Linda Woodhead. 2005. *The spiritual revolution.* Malden, MA: Blackwell.

Held, Virginia. 1993. *Feminist morality: Transforming culture, society, and politics.* Chicago: University of Chicago Press.

Helft, Miguel, and Ashless Vance. 2010. Apple passes Microsoft as No. 1 in tech. *New York Times,* May 26, p. B1. Retrieved from https://www.nytimes.com/2010/05/27/technology/27apple.html.

Hendrix, Josh A., Travis A. Taniguchi, Kevin J. Strom, Kelle Barrick, and Nicole J. Johnson. 2018. The eyes of law enforcement in the new panopticon: Police-community racial asymmetry and the use of surveillance technology. *Surveillance & Society* 16 (1): 53–68.

Henig, Robin Marantz. 2010. What is it about 20-somethings? *New York Times Magazine,* August 22. Retrieved from www.nytimes.com/2010/08/22/magazine/ 22Adulthood.

Hensley, Melissa, Derlie Mateo-Babiano, and John Minnery. 2014. Healthy places, active transport and path dependence: A review of the literature. *Health Promotion Journal of Australia* 25 (3): 196–201.

Hepp, Andreas, Stig Hjarvard, and Knut Lundby. 2015. Mediatization: Theorizing the interplay between media, culture and society. *Media, Culture & Society* 37 (2): 314–24.

Herbert, Melissa. 2000. *Camouflage isn't only for combat: Gender, sexuality, and women in the military.* New York: New York University Press.

Heritage, John, and Tanya Stivers. 2013. Conversation analysis and sociology. In *The handbook of conversation analysis*, ed. Jack Sidnell and Tanya Stivers, pp. 659–73. Boston: Wiley-Blackwell.

Herman, Edward S., and Noam Chomsky. 2002. *Manufacturing consent: The political economy of the mass media.* New York: Pantheon Books.

Herman, Keith C., and Wendy M. Reinke. 2017. Improving teacher perceptions of parent involvement patterns: Findings from a group randomized trial. *School Psychology Quarterly* 32 (1): 89–104.

Herman-Kinney, Nancy J., and David A. Kinney. 2013. Sober as deviant: The stigma of sobriety and how some college students "stay dry" on a "wet" campus. *Journal of Contemporary Ethnography* 42 (1): 64–103.

Herrman, John. 2017. How hate groups forced online platforms to reveal their true nature. Retrieved from www.nytimes.com/2017/08/21/magazine/how-hate-groups-forced-online-platforms-to-reveal-their-true-nature.html.

Herrnstein, Richard, and Charles Murray. 1996. *The bell curve: Intelligence and class structure in American life.* New York: Free Press.

Heuveline, Patrick, and Matthew Weinshenker. 2008. The international child poverty gap: Does demography matter? *Demography* 45 (1): 173–91.

Highland, Tim, Stephen Harrington, and Axel Bruns. 2013. Twitter as a technology or audiencing and fandom: The #Eurovision phenomenon. *Information, Communication & Society* 16 (3): 315–39.

Hirsch, Barry T., and David A. Macpherson. 2018. Union membership and coverage database from the CPS. Retrieved from www.unionstats.com.

Hirsch, Eric. 2016. Forcing homeless off street is wrong. Retrieved from www.providencejournal.com/opinion/20160408/eric-hirsch-forcing-homeless-off-street-is-wrong.

Hirschi, Travis. 1969. *Causes of delinquency.* Berkeley: University of California Press.

Hjarvard, Stig. 2008. The mediatization of society. *Nordicom Review* 29 (2): 105–32.

Hochschild, Arlie. 1979. Emotion work, feeling rules, and social structure. *American Journal of Sociology* 85: 551–75.

Hochschild, Arlie. 1983. *The managed heart.* Berkeley: University of California Press.

Hochschild, Arlie. 2012. *The managed heart: The commercialization of human feeling,* 3rd ed. Berkeley: University of California Press.

Hochschild, Arlie Russell. 2016. *Strangers in their own land.* New York: New Press.

Hochschild, Arlie, with Anne Machung. 1989/2012. *The second shift: Working families and the revolution at home,* paperback ed. New York: Penguin.

Hodges, Adam J. 2016. *World War I and urban order: The local class politics of national mobilization.* New York: Palgrave Macmillan.

Hodson, Randy. 2001. *Dignity at work.* New York: Cambridge University Press.

Hoehner, Christine M., Carolyn E. Barlow, Peg Allen, and Mario Schootman. 2012. Commuting distance, cardiorespiratory fitness, and metabolic risk. *American Journal of Preventive Medicine* 42 (6): 571–78.

Hoffman, Bruce. 2006. *Inside terrorism.* New York: Columbia University Press.

Hofstede, Geert, Gert Jan Hofstede, and Michael Minkov. 2010. *Cultures and organizations: Software of the mind.* New York: McGraw-Hill.

Hogan, Dennis P. 1978. The variable order of events in the life course. *American Sociological Review* 43 (August): 573–86.

Hogan, Dennis P., and Nan Marie Astone. 1986. The transition to adulthood. *Annual Review of Sociology* 12: 109–30.

Hogan, Michael H. 1998. *A cross of iron: Harry S Truman and the origins of the national security state, 1945–1954.* New York: Cambridge University Press.

Hoge, Charles W. 2010. *Once a warrior—Always a warrior: Navigating the transition from combat to home—Including combat stress, PTSD, and mTBI.* Guilford, CT: Globe Pequot.

Holgate, Peter. 2017. The model for recycling our old smartphones is actually causing massive pollution. Retrieved from www.recode.net/2017/11/8/16621512/where-does-my-smartphone-iphone-8-x-go-recycling-afterlife-toxic-waste-environment.

Holmes, Leslie. 2009. *Communism.* New York: Oxford University Press.

Holsti, Ole. 1968. *Content analysis for the social sciences and humanities.* Reading, MA: Addison-Wesley.

Holton, Robert. 2016. Globalization's cultural consequences revisited. In *Global culture: Consciousness and connectivity,* ed. Roland Robertson and Didem Buhari-Bulmez. New York: Routledge.

Holyfield, Lori, Matthew Ryan Moltz, and Mindy S. Bradley. 2009. Race discourse and the U.S. Confederate flag. *Race, Ethnicity, and Education* 12 (December): 517–37.

Holzberg, Jessica L., Renee Ellis, Matthew Virgile, Dawn V. Nelson, Jennifer Edgar, Polly Phipps, and Robin Kaplan. 2018. Assessing the feasibility of asking about gender identity in the current population survey: Results from focus groups with members of the transgender population. Working Paper RSM2018-05. U.S. Census Bureau. Retrieved from www.census.gov/library/working-papers/2018/adrm/rsm2018-05.html.

Hook, Jennifer L. 2010. Gender inequality in the welfare state: Sex segregation in housework, 1965–2003. *American Journal of Sociology* 115 (5): 1480–523.

hooks, bell. 1994. *Teaching to transgress: Education as the practice of freedom.* New York: Routledge.

hooks, bell. 2000. *Feminist theory: From margin to center.* Boston: South End Press.

hooks, bell. 2015a. *Feminist theory: From margin to center,* 3rd ed. New York: Routledge.

hooks, bell. 2015b. *Ain't I a woman: Black women and feminism.* New York: Routledge.

Hopewell, Kristen. 2016. *Breaking the WTO: How emerging powers disrupted the neoliberal project.* Stanford, CA: Stanford University Press.

Horo, Prabha Renuka. 2014. Impact of emotional labour on employee well-being: A conceptual framework. *Review of HRM* 3: 21–27.

Horsman, Reginald. 1981. *Race and manifest destiny: The origins of American Anglo-Saxonism.* Cambridge, MA: Harvard University Press.

Horth, Aaron. 2015. Toward a comprehensive gender-based violence court system. *Boston University Public Interest Law Journal* 24 (2): 221–45.

Horton, James Oliver, and Lois Horton. 2005. *Slavery and the making of America.* New York: Oxford University Press.

Horvath, Miranda A. H., Llian Alys, Kristina Massey, Afroditi Pina, Mia Scally, and Joanna R. Adler. 2013. "Basically . . . porn is everywhere": A rapid evidence assessment on the effects that access and exposure to pornography has on children and young people. London: Middlesex University. Retrieved from www.mdx.ac.uk/Assets/BasicallyporniseverywhereReport.pdf.

Hougham, Victoria. 2005. Sociological skills used in the capture of Saddam Hussein. *Footnotes* 33 (6): 3.

Howe, Tasha R., and Howard S. Friedman. 2014. Sex and gender in the 1980s heavy metal scene. *Sexuality & Culture* 18: 608–629.

Hsieh, Elaine. 2007. Interpreters as co-diagnosticians. *Social Science & Medicine* 64: 924–37.

Hua, C. 2001. *A society without fathers or husbands: The Na of China.* New York: Zone Books.

Huber, Joan. 2007. *On the origins of gender inequality.* Boulder, CO: Paradigm.

Hughes, Everett C. 1945. Dilemmas and contradictions of status. *American Journal of Sociology* 50: 353–59.

Human Rights First. 2018. Fear mongering and alternative facts: The Trump administration's attacks on asylum. Retrieved from www.humanrightsfirst.org/resource/fear-mongering-and-alternative-facts-trump-administrations-attacks-asylum.

Hunt, Matthew O., and Heather E. Bullock. 2016. Ideologies and beliefs about poverty. In *The Oxford handbook of social science of poverty,* ed. David Brady and Linda M. Burton, pp. 93–115. New York, NY: Oxford University Press.

Hunt, Stephen J. 2017. *The life course: A sociological introduction.* New York: Palgrave Macmillan.

Hunter, James Davisown. 1991. *Culture wars: The struggle to define America.* New York: Basic Books.

Hunter, James Davison. 1994. *Before the shooting begins: Searching for democracy in America's culture war.* New York: Free Press.

Huntington, Samuel. 1993. The clash of civilizations? *Foreign Affairs* 72 (3): 22–49.

Huntington, Samuel. 1998. *The clash of civilizations and the remaking of world order.* New York: Simon & Schuster.

Huntington, Samuel. 2005. *Who are we? The challenges to America's national identity.* New York: Simon & Schuster.

Hurwitz, Michael. 2011. The impact of legacy status on undergraduate admissions at elite colleges and universities. *Economics of Education Review* 30 (3): 480–92.

Hutchison, Ray, and Michael T. Ryan. 2015. *The new urban sociology.* Boulder, CO: Westview Press.

Hutchison, William R. 2003. *Religious pluralism in America.* New Haven, CT: Yale University Press.

Hyde, Janet S. 2014. Gender similarities and differences. *Annual Review of Psychology* 65: 373–98.

Hyde, Janet Shibley. 2005. Gender similarities hypothesis. *American Psychologist* 40 (6): 581–92.

Ibarra, Herminia, Robin J. Ely, and Deborah Kolb. 2013. Women rising: The unseen barriers. *Harvard Business Review* 91: 60–66.

Iceland, John, Matthew Hall, Kris Marsh, Luis Sanchez, and Gregory Sharp. 2010. Racial and ethnic residential segregation in the United States: Comparisons across racial and ethnic groups, 1970–2009. Retrieved from http://projects.pop.psu.edu/canc/segregation/Cross-group-report-12-19-2010.pdf.

Iftikhar, Arsalan. 2016. *Scapegoats: How Islamophobia helps our enemies and threatens our freedoms.* New York: Skyhorse Publishing.

Ignatiev, Noel. 1996. *How the Irish became white.* New York: Routledge.

ILGA (International Lesbian, Gay, Bisexual, Trans and Intersex Association). 2018.

Inglehart, Ronald. 2018. *Cultural evolution.* New York: Cambridge University Press.

Inglehart, Ronald, and Pippa Norris. 2003. The true clash of civilizations. *Foreign Policy* 135: 62–70.

Inglehart, Ronald, and Christian Welzel. 2005. *Modernization, cultural change, and democracy.* New York: Cambridge University Press.

Ingraham, Christopher. 2015. Anti-Muslim hate crimes are still five times more common today than before 9/11. *Washington Post,* February 11. Retrieved from www.washingtonpost.com/news/wonk/wp/2015/02/11/anti-muslim-hate-crimes-are-still-five-times-more-common-today-than-before-911/.

Institute for Research on Higher Education. 2016. College affordability diagnosis: National report. Philadelphia: Institute for Research on Higher Education, Graduate School of Education, University of Pennsylvania. Retrieved from www2.gse.upenn.edu/irhe/affordability-diagnosis.

Institute for Women's Policy Research. 2018, April. The gender wage gap by occupation 2017 and by race and ethnicity. IWPR Working Paper C467.

Intelligence Community Assessment. 2017. Assessing Russian activities and intentions in recent US elections. Retrieved from www.dni.gov/files/documents/ICA_2017_01.pdf.

Interfaith Worker Justice. 2018. Issues. Retrieved from www.iwj.org/issues.

International Institute for Democracy and Electoral Assistance. 2018. Voter turnout database. Retrieved from https://www.idea.int/data-tools/data/voter-turnout.

Internet Crime Complaint Center. 2017. 2016 Internet Crime Report.

Inter-Parliamentary Union. 2018. Compare data on parliaments. Retrieved from https://data.ipu.org/compare.

Irwin, Douglas A. 2015. *Free trade under fire.* Princeton, NJ: Princeton University Press.

Irwin, Rachel. 2007. Culture shock: Negotiating feelings in the field. *Anthropology Matters* 9 (1): 1–11.

Ito, Tiffany A., Naomi P. Friedman, Bruce D. Bartholow, Joshua Correll, Chris Loersch, Lee J. Altamirano, and Akira Miyake. 2015. Toward a comprehensive understanding of executive cognitive function in implicit racial bias. *Journal of Personality and Social Psychology* 108 (2): 187–218.

Jablonski, Nina G., and George Chaplin. 2002. Skin deep. *Scientific American* 287 (4): 74–82.

Jablonski, Nina G., and George Chaplin. 2010. Human skin pigmentation as an adaptation to UV radiation. *Proceedings of the National Academy of Sciences USA* 107: 8962–68.

Jackson, David. 2015. Republican candidates appeal to religious conservatives. *USA Today,* October 18. Retrieved from www.usatoday.com/story/news/politics/elections/2016/2015/10/18/prestonwood-baptist-trump-carson-fiorina-carson-bush-cruz-huckabee-santorum/74175226/.

Jackson, Pamela Braboy, and Alexandra Berkowitz. 2005. The structure of the life course: Gender and racioethnic variation in the occurrence and sequencing of role transitions. *Advances in Life Course Research* 9: 55–90.

Jackson, Philip. 1968. *Life in classrooms.* New York: Holt, Rinehart and Winston.

Jacobs, Jennifer, and Bill Allison. 2018. Trump to mark one-year anniversary with gala at Mar-a-Lago. Retrieved from www.bloomberg.com/news/articles/2018-06-12/u-s-s-navarro-apologizes-for-inappropriate-trudeau-comments.

Jacobs, Lawrence R., and Theda Skocpol. 2007. *Inequality and American democracy.* New York: Russell Sage Foundation.

Jacobs, Sue Ellen, Wesley Thomas, and Sabine Lang, eds. 1997. *Two-spirit people: Native American gender identity, sexuality, and spirituality.* Urbana: University of Illinois Press.

Jacoby, William G. 2014. Is there a culture war? Conflicting value structures in American public opinion. *American Political Science Review* 108 (4): 754–71.

Jæger, Mads Meier, and Stine Møllegaard. 2017. Cultural capital, teacher bias, and educational success: New evidence from monozygotic twins. *Social Science Research* 65: 130–44.

Jakubowicz, Andrew, Kevin Dunn, Gail Mason, Yin Paradies, Ana-Maria Bliuc, Nasya Bahfen, Andre Oboler, Rosalie Atie, and Karen Connelly. 2017. Racism and the affordances of the internet. In *Cyber racism and community resilience*, pp. 95–145. Cham, Switzerland: Palgrave Macmillan.

Janis, Irving L. 1972. *Victims of groupthink: A psychological study of foreign-policy decisions and fiascoes.* Boston: Houghton Mifflin.

Janis, Irving L. 1989. *Crucial decisions.* New York: Free Press.

Janowitz, Morris, and Charles C. Moskos Jr. 1979. Five years of the all-volunteer force: 1973–1978. *Armed Forces and Society* 5 (2): 171–218.

Jarvis, Lee, Stuart MacDonald, and Thomas M. Chen, eds. 2015. *Terrorism online: Politics, law and technology.* New York: Routledge.

Jasper, James M. 2014. *Protest: A cultural introduction to social movements.* Malden, MA: Polity Press.

Jasper, James M., and Jeff Goodwin. 2011. *Contention in context: Political opportunities and the emergence of protest.* Stanford, CA: Stanford University Press.

Jelen, Ted G. 2017. Religion and American public opinion: Social issues. In *The Oxford handbook of religion and American politics*, ed. Corwin E. Smidt, Lyman A. Kellstedt, and James L. Guth, pp. 217–41. New York: Oxford University Press.

Jenks, Andrew L. 2011. *Perils of progress: Environmental disasters in the 20th century.* Upper Saddle River, NJ: Pearson.

Jhally, Sut, and Justin Lewis. 1992. *Enlightened racism.* Boulder, CO: Westview Press.

Jobin-Leeds, Greg, and AgitArte. 2016. *When we fight, we win: Twenty-first-century social movements and the activists that are transforming our world.* New York: New Press.

Johnson, Allan G. 2005. *Privilege, power and difference.* New York: McGraw-Hill.

Johnson, Allen, and Timothy Earle. 2000. *The evolution of human societies: From foraging groups to agrarian state.* Stanford, CA: Stanford University Press.

Johnson, Bobbie. 2010. Privacy no longer a social norm, says Facebook founder. *The Guardian,* January 10. Retrieved from www.theguardian.com/technology/2010/jan/11/facebook-privacy.

Johnson, Carolyn Y. 2008. Study finds culture a factor in female math achievement. *Boston Globe,* October 10, p. A4.

Johnson, Charles, and Patricia Smith. 1999. *Africans in America: America's journey through slavery.* New York: Harvest Books.

Johnson, E. Dolores. 2017. When the census recognized mixed-race people, I felt as if my country could finally see me. Retrieved from www.vox.com/first-person/2017/11/16/16658738/census-mixed-race.

Johnson, Katharine, Melinda Caskey, Katherine Rand, Richard Tucker, and Betty Vohr. 2014. Gender differences in adult-infant communication in the first months of life. *Pediatrics* 134 (6): 1603–10.

Johnson, Stephen. 2004. *Mind wide open: Your brain and the neuroscience of everyday life.* New York: Scribner.

Johnston, David Cay. 2003. *Perfectly legal: The covert campaign to rig our tax system to benefit the super rich—and cheat everybody else.* New York: Portfolio/Penguin.

Johnston, David Cay. 2007. *Free lunch: How the wealthiest Americans enrich themselves at government expense.* New York: Penguin.

Johnston, David Cay. 2018. *It's even worse than you think: What the Trump administration is doing to America.* New York: Simon & Schuster.

Johnston, David Cay, ed. 2014. *Divided: The perils of our growing inequality.* New York: New Press.

Jones, Jacqueline. 2010. *Labor of love, labor of sorrow: Black women, work, and the family, from slavery to the present.* New York: Basic Books.

Jones, Lucy. 2016. If a Muslim says "homo," nothing gets done: Racist discourse and in-group identity construction in an LGBT youth group. *Language in Society* 45 (1): 113–33.

Jordan, Don, and Michael Walsh. 2008. *White cargo: The forgotten history of white slaves in America.* New York: New York University Press.

Judis, John B. 2016. *The populist explosion: How the great recession transformed American and European politics.* New York: Columbia Global Reports.

Juergensmeyer, Mark. 2003. *Terror in the mind of God: The global rise of religious violence.* Berkeley: University of California Press.

Jung, Moon-Kie. 2006. *Reworking race: The making of Hawaii's interracial labor movement.* New York: Columbia University Press.

Juszkiewicz, J. 2015. *Trends in community college enrollment and completion data, 2015.* March. Washington, DC: American Association of Community Colleges.

Jutte, Robert. 2008. *Contraception: A history.* Malden, MA: Polity Press.

Jylha, Marja, and Marja Saarenheimo. 2010. Loneliness and aging: Comparative perspectives. In *The SAGE handbook of social gerontology,* ed. Dale Danaher and Chris Phillipson, pp. 317–28. Los Angeles: Sage.

Kahlenberg, Richard D., ed. 2010. *Affirmative* Action for the Rich. New York: The Century Foundation.

Kalkhoff, Will, Shane R. Thye, and Joshua Pollock. 2016. Developments in neurosociology. *Sociology Compass* 10 (3): 242–58.

Kalleberg, Arne L. 2009. Precarious work, isecure workers: Employment relations in transition. *American Sociological Review* 74 (1): 1–22.

Kalleberg, Arne L. and Steven P. Vallas. 2018. Probing precarious work: Theory, research, and politics. *Research in the Sociology of Work* 31: 1–30.

Kandal, T. R. 1988. *The woman question in classical sociological theory.* Miami: Florida International University Press.

Kane, Emily W. 2000. Racial and ethnic variations in gender-related attitudes. *Annual Review of Sociology* 26: 419–39.

Kang, Cecilia. 2018. Why the AT&T-Time Warner case was so closely watched. Retrieved from www.nytimes.com/2018/06/12/business/dealbook/att-time-warner-trial-antitrust-ruling.html.

Kant, Immanuel. (1784) 1999. An answer to the question: What is enlightenment? In *Practical Philosophy,* ed. Mary J. Gregor, pp. 11–22. Cambridge, UK: Cambridge University Press.

Kantrowitz, Alex. 2017. Google allowed advertisers to target "Jewish parasite," "black people ruin everything." Retrieved from www.buzzfeed.com/alexkantrowitz/google-allowed-advertisers-to-target-jewish-parasite-black.

Kaplinsky, Raphael. 2007. *Globalization, poverty and inequality.* Malden, MA: Polity Press.

Karabchuk, Tatiana, Kazuhiro Kumo, and Ekaterina Selezneva. 2017. *Demography of Russia: From the past to the present.* London, UK: Palgrave Macmillan.

Karabel, Jerome. 2005. *The chosen: The hidden history of admissions and exclusion at Harvard, Yale, and Princeton.* New York: Houghton Mifflin.

Karen, David. 2005. No child left behind? Sociology ignored! *Sociology of Education* 78 (2): 165–69.

Karp, David. 1996. *Speaking of sadness.* New York: Oxford University Press.

Karp, David. 2017. *Speaking of sadness: Depression, disconnection, and the meanings of illness.* New York, NY: Oxford University Press.

Karraker, Katherine Hildebrandt, Dena Ann Vogel, and Margaret Ann Lake. 1995. Parents' gender-stereotyped perceptions of newborns: The eye of the beholder revisited. *Sex Roles* 33 (9–10): 687–702.

Kasser, Tim. 2003. *The high price of materialism.* Cambridge, MA: MIT Press.

Kastelle, Timothy. 2013. Hierarchy is overrated. *Harvard Business Review.* Retrieved from https://hbr.org/2013/11/hierarchy-is-overrated/.

Kaufman, Eric P. 2004. The decline of the WASP in the United States and Canada. In *Rethinking ethnicity: Majority groups and dominant minorities,* ed. Eric P. Kaufman, pp. 54–73. New York: Routledge.

Kaufman, Jason, and Jay Gabler. 2004. Cultural capital and the extracurricular activities of girls and boys in the college attainment process. *Poetics* 32: 145–68.

Kaufman, Joan, Bao-Zhi Yang, Heather Douglas-Palumberi, Shadi Houshyar, Deborah Lipschitz, John H. Krystal, and Joel Gelernter. 2004. Social supports and serotonin transporter gene moderate depression in maltreated children. *Proceedings of the National Academy of Sciences* 101 (5): 17316–21.

Kay, Paul, and Willett Kempton. 1984. What is the Sapir-Whorf hypothesis? *American Anthropologist* 86 (1): 65–79.

Kayyali, Randa A. 2006. *The Arab Americans.* Westport, CT: Greenwood Press.

Kearns, Laura. 2014. Green Evangelicals. In *The new evangelical social engagement,* ed. Brian Steensland and Philip Goff, pp. 157–78. New York: Oxford University Press.

Keaten, Jamey. 2010. French polemic over fake game show electrocutions. Associated Press, March 17.

Keith, Jannette. 2003. *Rich man's war, poor man's fight.* Durham: University of North Carolina Press.

Kelly, Sean, and William Carbonaro. 2012. Curriculum tracking and teacher expectations: Evidence from discrepant course taking models. *Social Psychology of Education* 15 (3): 271–94.

Kendi, Ibram X. 2016. *Stamped from the beginning: The definitive history of racist ideas in America.* New York: Nation Books.

Kennedy, Randall. 2013. *For discrimination: Race, affirmative action, and the law.* New York: Random House.

Kephart, Ronald. 2003. Latin America and the Caribbean. In *Race and ethnicity: An anthropological focus on the United States and the world,* ed. Raymond Scupin, pp. 288–308. Upper Saddle River, NJ: Prentice Hall.

Kerbo, Harold. 2011. *Social stratification and inequality.* New York: McGraw-Hill.

Kestnbaum, Meyer. 2009. The sociology of war and the military. *Annual Review of Sociology* 35: 235–54.

Khan, Shamus Rahman. 2011. *Privilege: The making of an adolescent elite at St. Paul's School.* Princeton, NJ: Princeton University Press.

Khan, Shamus Rahman. 2012. The sociology of elites. *Annual Review of Sociology* 38: 361–77.

Kheirandish, P., and F. Chinegwundoh. 2011. Ethnic differences in prostate cancer. *British Journal of Cancer* 105: 481–85.

Kiernan, Ben. 2007. *Blood and soil: A world history of genocide and extermination from Sparta to Darfur.* New Haven, CT: Yale University Press.

Kim, Heejung, and Hazel Rose Markus. 1999. Deviance or uniqueness, harmony or conformity? A cultural analysis. *Journal of Personality and Social Psychology* 77 (4): 785–800.

Kim, Soyeon, Scott R. Colwell, Anna Kata, Michael H. Boyle, and Katholiki Georgiades. 2018. Cyberbullying victimization and adolescent mental health: Evidence of differential effects by sex and mental health problem type. *Journal of Youth and Adolescence* 47: 661–72.

Kim, Young K., Julie J. Park, and Katie K. Koo. 2015. Testing self-segregation: Multiple-group structural modeling of college students' interracial friendship by race. *Research in Higher Education* 56 (1): 57.

Kimball, Will, and Lawrence Mishel. 2015. Unions' decline and the rise of the top 10 percent's share of income. Washington, DC: Economic Policy Institute. www.epi.org/publication/unions-decline-and-the-rise-of-the-top-10-percents-share-of-income/?utm_source=Economic+Policy+Institute&utm_campaign=cc4d4c40a2-EPI_News_08_21_158_21_2015&utm_medium=email&utm_term=0_e7c5826c50-cc4d4c40a2-55906029.

Kimmel, Michael. 2008. *Guyland: The perilous world where boys become men.* New York: HarperCollins.

Kimmel, Michael. 2012. *Manhood in America: A cultural history.* New York: Oxford University Press.

Kimmel, Michael S., and Michael A. Messner. 2013. *Men's lives,* 9th ed. Boston, MA: Pearson.

Kinder, Donald R., and Lynn M. Sanders. 1996. *Divided by color: Racial politics and democratic ideals.* Chicago: University of Chicago Press.

King, Barbara J. 2013. Diaperless Babies: "Lunatic" or "Positive" Parenting? *Cosmos & Culture.* NPR.org. May 2. Retrieved from www.npr.org/sections/13.7/2013/05/02/ 179880234/diaperless-babies-lunatic-or-positive-parenting.

Kinsey, Alfred C., Wardell B. Pomeroy, and Clyde E. Martin. (1948) 1998. *Sexual behavior in the human male.* Bloomington: Indiana University Press.

Kinsey, Alfred C., Wardell B. Pomeroy, Clyde E. Martin, and Paul H. Gebhard. (1953) 1998. *Sexual behavior in the human female.* Bloomington: Indiana University Press.

Klein, Alec. 2003. *Stealing Time: Steve Case, Jerry Levin, and the collapse of AOL Time Warner.* New York: Simon & Schuster.

Klein, Naomi. 2014. *This changes everything: Capitalism vs. the climate.* New York: Simon & Schuster.

Klinenberg, Eric. 2003. *Heat wave.* Chicago: University of Chicago Press.

Klinenberg, Eric. 2012. *Going solo: The extraordinary rise and surprising appeal of living alone.* New York: Penguin.

Kluckhohn, Clyde. 1968. *Mirror for man.* New York: Fawcett Crest.

Knight, Kyle, and Neela Ghoshal. 2016. Recognizing the rights of transgender people. Human Rights Watch. Retrieved from www.hrw.org/news/2016/02/13/recognizing-rights-transgender-people.

Koch, Amanda J., Susan D. D'Mello, and Paul R. Sackett. 2015. A meta-analysis of gender stereotypes and bias in experimental simulations of employment decision making. *Journal of Applied Psychology* 100 (1): 128–61.

Koch, Pamela Ray, and Lala Carr Steelman. 2009. From molehills mountains made: An examination of red and blue state cultural stereotypes. *Cultural Sociology* 3 (1): 165–89.

Kohn, Melvin L. 1977. *Class and conformity: A study in values,* 2nd ed. Chicago: University of Chicago Press.

Koistinen, David. 2014. *Confronting decline: The political economy of deindustrialization in twentieth-century New England.* Gainesville: University Press of Florida.

Kolb, Bryan, and Robbin Gibb. 2014. Searching for the principles of brain plasticity and behavior. *Cortex* 58: 251–60.

Koles, Bernadett, Victoria Wells, and Mark Tadajewski. 2017. Compensatory consumption and consumer compromises: A state-of-the-art review. *Journal of Marketing Management,* 34 (1–2): 96–133. doi:10.1080/0267257X.2017.1373693.

Kolko, Jed. 2015. How suburban are big American cities? *FiveThirtyEight,* May 21. Retrieved from http://fivethirtyeight.com/features/how-suburban-are-big-american-cities/.

Kolko, Jed. 2017. Americans' shift to the suburbs sped up last year. Retrieved from https://fivethirtyeight.com/features/americans-shift-to-the-suburbs-sped-up-last-year/.

Kollmeyer, Christopher. 2004. Corporate interests: How the news media portrays the economy. *Social Problems* 51 (3): 432–52.

Kooistra, Paul G., and John S. Mahoney. 2016. The road to hell: Neutralization of killing in war. *Deviant Behavior* 37 (7): 761–83.

Koonse, Tia, Miranda Dietz, and Annette Bernhardt. 2015. *Enforcing city minimum wage laws in California.* UCLA Center for Labor Research and Education and UC Berkeley Center for Labor Research and Education.

Korpela, Kalevi, Jessica De Bloom, and Ulla Kinnunen. 2015. From restorative environments to restoration in work. *Intelligent Buildings International* 7 (4): 215–23.

Kosfeld, Michael, Markus Henrichs, Paul J. Zak, Urs Fischbacher, and Ernst Fehr. 2005. Oxytocin increases trust in humans. *Nature* 435 (2): 673–76.

Kosoff, Maya. 2017. Google is secretly monitoring your real-world purchases, too. Retrieved from www.vanityfair.com/news/2017/05/google-tracking-credit-card-data-advertisers.

Kozol, Jonathan. 2012. *Savage inequalities.* New York: Broadway Books.

Krantz, Matt. 2016. 27 giant profitable companies paid no taxes. *USA Today,* March 7. Retrieved from www.usatoday.com/story/money/markets/2016/03/07/27-giant-profitable-companies-paid-no-taxes/81399094/.

Kraus, Michael W., Julian M. Rucker, and Jennifer A. Richeson. 2017. Americans misperceive racial economic equality. *Proceedings of the National Academy of Sciences* 114 (39): 10324–31.

Kreider, Marilyn. 2007. Young adults living in their parents' home. Paper presented at the American Sociological Meeting, New York, August 12. Retrieved from www.census.gov/population/www/socdemo/hh-fam/young-adults-in-parents-home.pdf.

Krieg, Gregory. 2016. 14 of Trump's most outrageous "birther" claims—half from after 2011. CNN. September 16. Retrieved from www.cnn.com/2016/09/09/politics/donald-trump-birther/index.html.

Kriesberg, Louis. 1982. *Social conflicts.* Englewood Cliffs, NJ: Prentice Hall.

Kuo, Janet Chen-Lan, and R. Kelly Raley. 2016. Diverging patterns of union transition among cohabitors by race/ethnicity and education: Trends and marital intentions in the United States. *Demography* (June): 1–15.

Kurtulus, Fidan Ana, and Donald Tomaskovic-Devey. 2012. Do female managers help women to advance? A panel study using EEO-1 records. *Annals of the American Academy of Political and Social Science* 639: 173–97.

Kurtz, Mariam, and Lester R. Kurtz, eds. 2015. *Women, war, and violence: Topography, resistance, and hope.* Santa Barbara, CA: Praeger.

Kwon, Jong Bum, and Carrie M. Lane, eds. 2016. *Anthropologies of unemployment: New perspectives on work and its absence.* Ithaca, NY: Cornell University Press.

LaFree, Gary, and Richard Arum. 2006. The impact of racially inclusive schooling on adult incarceration rates among U.S. cohorts of African Americans and whites since 1930. *Criminology* 44 (1): 73–103.

LaFree, Gary. 1999. Declining violent crime rates in the 1990s: Predicting crime booms and busts. *Annual Review of Sociology* 25: 145–68.

Lam, Bourree. 2016. Why are so many Zappos employees leaving? *The Atlantic,* January 15. Retrieved from www.theatlantic.com/business/archive/2016/01/zappos-holacracy-hierarchy/424173/.

Lammers, J., A. D. Galinsky, E. H. Gordijn, and S. Otten. 2008. Illegitimacy moderates the effects of power on approach. *Psychological Science* 19: 558–64.

Lamont, Michèle, Bo Yun Park, and Elena Ayala-Hurtado. 2017. Trump's electoral speeches and his appeal to the American white working class. *The British Journal of Sociology* 68: S153–80. doi:10.1111/1468-4446.12315.

Landecker, Hannah, and Aaron Panofsky. 2013. From social structure to gene regulation, and back: A critical introduction to environmental epigenetics for sociology. *Annual Review of Sociology* 39: 333–57.

Landsbaum, Claire, and Greta Weber. 2015. What happened at the University of Missouri? *Slate,* November 9. Retrieved from www.slate.com/blogs/the_slatest/2015/11/09/ timeline_of_u_of_missouri_protests_and_president_resignation.html.

Lane, Carrie M. 2011. *A company of one: Insecurity, independence, and the new world* of *white-collar unemployment.* Ithaca, NY: Cornell University Press.

Lane, Robert E. 1994. The road not taken: Friendship, consumerism, and happiness. *Critical Review* 8 (4): 521–54.

Lang, Sabine. 2016. Native American men-women, lesbians, two-spirits: Contemporary and historical perspectives. *Journal of Lesbian Studies* 20 (3–4): 299–323.

Lapierre, Matthew A., Frances Fleming-Milici, Esther Rozendaal, Anna R. McAlister, and Jessica Castonguay. 2017. The effect of advertising on children and adolescents. *Pediatrics* 140 (S2): 152–56.

Lareau, Annette. 2011. *Unequal childhoods: Class, race, and family life,* 2nd ed. Berkeley: University of California Press.

Lareau, Annette. 2015. Cultural knowledge and social inequality. *American Sociological Review* 80 (1): 1–27.

Lareau, Annette, Shani Adia Evans, and April Yee. 2016. The rules of the game and the uncertain transmission of advantage: Middle-class parents' search for an urban kindergarten. *Sociology of Education* 89 (4): 279–99.

Lareau, Annette, and Elliot B. Weininger. 2003. Cultural capital in educational research. *Theory and Society* 32 (5–6): 567–606.

Lawrence, Matthew. 2016. Unequal advantages: The intergenerational effects of parental educational mobility. *American Educational Research Journal* 53 (1): 71–99.

Lean, Nathan, and John L. Esposito. 2012. *The Islamophobia industry: How the right manufactures fear of Muslims.* New York: Palgrave Macmillan.

Lee, Elizabeth M. 2013. Elite colleges and socioeconomic status. *Sociology Compass* 7: 786–98.

Lee, Erika. 2015. *The making of Asian America: A history.* New York: Simon & Schuster.

Lee, Nam-Jin, Dhavan V. Shah, and Jack M. McLeod. 2012. Processes of political socialization: A communication mediation approach to youth civic engagement. *Communication Research* 40 (5): 669–97.

Lee, Valerie E., and Julia B. Smith. 1995. Effects of high school restructuring and size on early gains in achievement and engagement. *Sociology of Education* 68 (4): 241–70.

Leighley, Jan E., and Jonathan Nagler. 2013. *Who votes now? Demographics, issues, inequality, and turnout in the United States.* Princeton, NJ: Princeton University Press.

Leithwood, Kenneth, and Doris Jantzi. 2009. A review of empirical evidence about school size effects: A policy perspective. *Review of Educational Research* 79 (1): 464–90.

Lelkes, Yphtach. 2016. Mass polarization: Manifestations and measurements. *Public Opinion Quarterly* 80 (S1): 392–410.

Lemert, Edwin M. 1951. *Social pathology.* New York: McGraw-Hill.

Lende, Daniel H., and Greg Downey, eds. 2012. *The encultured brain: An introduction to neuroanthropology.* Cambridge, MA: MIT Press.

Lenhart, Amanda. 2015. Teens, social media & technology overview 2015. Pew Research Center. Retrieved from www.pewinternet.org/2015/04/09/teens-social-media-technology-2015.

Lenhart, Amanda, Aaron Smith, Monica Anderson, Maeve Duggan, and Andrew Perrin. 2015. Teens, technology and friendships. Pew Research Center. August. Retrieved from www.pewinternet.org/2015/08/06/teens-technology-and-friendships/.

Lenski, Gerhard. 1966. *Power and privilege: A theory of social stratification.* New York: McGraw-Hill.

Lenski, Gerhard. 2005. *Ecololgical-evolutionary theory.* Boulder, CO: Paradigm Publishers.

Leondar-Wright, Betsy. 2005. *Class matters.* Gabriola Island, BC: New Society.

Leondar-Wright, Betsy. 2014. *Missing class: Strengthening social movement groups by seeing class cultures.* Ithaca, NY: Cornell University Press.

Leonhardt, David, and Ian Prasad Philbrick. 2018. Donald Trump's racism: The definitive list. Retrieved from www.nytimes.com/interactive/2018/01/15/opinion/leonhardt-trump-racist.html.

Levin, Gary. 2017. Who's watching what: TV shows ranked by racial and ethnic groups. Retrieved from www.usatoday.com/story/life/tv/2017/06/27/whos-watching-what-tv-shows-ranked-racial-and-ethnic-groups/103199848/.

Levine, John M., and Jose M. Marques. 2016. Norm violators as threats and opportunities: The many faces of deviance in groups. *Group Processes & Intergroup Relations* 19 (5): 545–52.

Levinthal, Dave. 2018. Actions, not words, tell Trump's political money story. Washington, DC: Center for Public Integrity. Retrieved from www.publicintegrity.org/2018/01/19/21480/actions-not-words-tell-trumps-political-money-story.

Levitsky, Steven, and Daniel Ziblatt. 2018. *How democracies die.* New York: Penguin Random House.

Levitt, Peggy. 2004. Salsa and ketchup: Transnational migrants straddle two worlds. *Contexts* 3 (2): 20–26.

Levy, Frank. 1998. *The new dollars and dreams.* New York: Russell Sage Foundation.

Lewis, Bernard. 2004. *The crisis of Islam: Holy war and unholy terror.* New York: Random House.

Lewis, Jamie M., Nancy Bates, and Matthew Streeter. 2015. Measuring same-sex couples: The what and who of misreporting on relationship and sex. SEHSD [Social, Economic & Housing Statistics Division] Working Paper 2015-12. Washington, DC: U.S. Census Bureau. Retrieved from www.census.gov/content/dam/Census/library/working-papers/2015/demo/SEHSD-WP2015-12.pdf.

Lewis, Paul. 2017. "Our minds can be hijacked": The tech insiders who fear a smartphone dystopia. Retrieved from www.theguardian.com/technology/2017/oct/05/smartphone-addiction-silicon-valley-dystopia?CMP=share_btn_tw.

Lichter, Daniel T., Domenico Parisi, and Michael C. Taquino. 2015. Toward a new macro-segregation? Decomposing segregation within and between metropolitan cities and suburbs. *American Sociological Review* 80 (4): 843–73.

Lichter, Daniel T., Domenico Parisi, and Michael C. Taquino. 2017. Together but apart: Do US whites live in racially diverse cities and neighborhoods? *Population and Development Review* 43 (2): 229–55.

Lind, Rebecca Ann. 2017. *Race and gender in electronic media*. New York: Routledge.

Lindberg, David C., and Ronald L. Numbers. 2008. *When science and Christianity meet.* Chicago: University of Chicago Press.

Lindsay, Constance A., and Cassandra M. D. Hart. 2017. Exposure to same-race teachers and student disciplinary outcomes for black students in North Carolina. *Educational Evaluation and Policy Analysis* 39 (3): 485–510.

Ling, Rich, and Scott W. Campbell, eds. 2012. *Mobile communication: Bringing us together and tearing us apart.* New Brunswick, NJ: Transaction.

Ling, Rich. 2008. *New tech, new ties.* Cambridge, MA: MIT Press.

Ling, Rich. 2012. *Taken for grantedness: The embedding of mobile communication into society.* Cambridge: MIT Press.

Link, Bruce G., and Jo C. Phelan. 2001. Conceptualizing stigma. *Annual Review of Sociology* 27: 363–85.

Lipka, Michael. 2016. Muslims and Islam: Key findings in the U.S. and around the world. Washington, DC: Pew Research Center. Retrieved from www.pewresearch.org/fact-tank/2016/07/22/muslims-and-islam-key-findings-in-the-u-s-and-around-the-world/.

Lipton, Eric, and Brooke Williams. 2016. Researchers or corporate allies? *New York Times,* August 7. Retrieved from www.nytimes.com/2016/08/08/us/politics/think-tanks-research-and-corporate-lobbying.html.

Livingston, Gretchen, and Anna Brown. 2017. Intermarriage in the U.S. 50 years after *Loving v. Virginia*. Washington, DC: Pew Research Center. http://assets.pewresearch.org/wp-content/uploads/sites/3/2017/05/19102233/Intermarriage-May-2017-Full-Report.pdf.

Livingstone, D. W., Katina Pollock, and Milosh Raykov. 2016. Family binds and glass ceilings: Women managers' promotion limits in a "knowledge economy." *Critical Sociology* 42 (1): 145–66.

Livingstone, Sonia, and Julian Sefton-Green. 2016. *The class: Living and learning in the digital age.* New York: New York University Press.

Lobao, Linda. 2007. Rural sociology. In *21st Century sociology: A reference handbook,* ed. Clifton D. Bryant and Dennis L. Peck, pp. 465–75. Thousand Oaks, CA: Sage.

Loeb, Paul Rogat. 2010. *Soul of a citizen*. New York: St. Martin's Press.

Logan, John R., and Brian J. Stults. 2011. The persistence of segregation in the metropolis: New findings from the 2010 Census. Census brief prepared for Project US2010. Retrieved from www.s4.brown.edu/us2010/Data/ Report/report2.pdf.

Logan, John. 2006. The union avoidance industry in the United States. *British Journal of Industrial Relations* 44 (4): 651–75.

Logan, John. 2011. Separate and unequal: The neighborhood gap for blacks, Hispanics and Asians in metropolitan America. Providence, RI: Brown University. Retrieved from www.s4.brown.edu/us2010/Data/Report/report0727.pdf.

Long, Clara. 2018. Trump's fearmongering about migrant caravan. Human Rights Watch. www.hrw.org/news/2018/04/04/trumps-fearmongering-about-migrant-caravan.

Lopez, Edward S., and Nurcan Ensari. 2014. The effects of leadership style, organizational outcome, and gender on attributional bias toward leaders. *Journal of Leadership Studies* 8 (2): 19–37.

López, Mark, Ana Gonzalez-Barrera, and Gustavo López. 2017. Hispanic identity fades across generations as immigrant connections fall away. Washington, DC: Pew Research Center. www.pewhispanic.org/2017/12/20/hispanic-identity-fades-across-generations-as-immigrant-connections-fall-away/.

Lorber, Judith, and Lisa Jean Moore. 2010. *Gendered bodies: Feminist perspectives.* New York: Oxford University Press.

Los Angeles Times. 2015. Special report: America's all-volunteer army. *Los Angeles Times,* May 23. Retrieved from www.latimes.com/nation/la-na-volunteer-army-sg-storygallery.html.

Lubrano, Alfred. 2004. *Limbo: Blue-collar roots, white-collar dreams.* Hoboken, NJ: Wiley.

Lucas, Samuel. 1999. *Tracking inequality.* New York: Teachers College Press.

Lui, Wenlin, and John Gastil. 2014. Pathways of immigrant political socialization: Examining the role of news media, social connections, and community interaction. *Journal of Intercultural Communication Research* 43 (3): 238–63.

Lukes, Steven. 2005. *Power: A radical view,* 2nd ed. New York: Palgrave Macmillan.

Lundberg, Shelly, and Robert A. Pollak. 2015. The evolving role of marriage: 1950–2010. *Future of Children* 25 (2): 29–50.

Lundberg, Shelly, Robert A. Pollak, and Jenna Stearns. 2016. Family inequality: Diverging patters in marriage, cohabitating, and childbearing. *Journal of Economic Perspectives* 30 (2): 79–102.

Lupton, Deborah, and Mike Michael. 2017. Depends on who's got the data: Public understandings of personal digital dataveillance. *Surveillance & Society* 15 (2): 254–68.

Lutendo, Malisha, Pranitha Maharaj, and Michael Rogan. 2008. Rites of passage to adulthood: Traditional initiation schools in the context of HIV/AIDS in the Limpopo Province, South Africa. *Health, Risk and Society* 10 (6): 585–98.

Luther, Catherine A., Carolyn Ringer Lepre, and Naeemah Clark. 2018. *Diversity in U.S. mass media.* Malden, MA: John Wiley & Sons.

Lyon, David. 2015. *Surveillance after Snowden.* Malden, MA: Polity Press.

Lyon, Thomas P., and A. Wren Montgomery. 2015. The means and end of greenwash. *Organization & Environment* 28 (2): 223–49.

MAA (Mathematical Association of America). 2017. U.S. students bring home medals at international mathematics competition in Brazil. Retrieved from www.maa.org/news/us-students-bring-home-medals-at-international-mathematics-competition-in-brazil.

Macgregor, G. H. C. 1954. *The New Testament basis of pacifism.* Nyack, NY: Fellowship Publications.

MacKenzie, Megan. 2015. *Beyond the band of brothers: The US military and the myth that women can't fight.* New York: Cambridge University Press.

MacKinnon, J. B. 2015. Patagonia's anti-growth strategy. *The New Yorker,* May 21.

MacLaury, Judson. 2011. *Government regulation of workers' safety and health, 1877–1917.* Washington, DC: U.S. Department of Labor. Retrieved from www.dol.gov/oasam/programs/history/mono-regsafeintrotoc.htm.

MacLeod, Jay. 2009. *Ain't no makin' it: Aspirations and attainment in a low-income neighborhood.* Boulder, CO: Westview Press.

MacMillan, Ross. 2005. The structure of the life course: Classic issues and current controversies. *Advances in Life Course Research* 9: 3–24.

Madden, Mary, Amanda Lenhart, Maeve Duggan, Sandra Cortesi, and Urs Gasser. 2013. Teens and technology 2013. Washington, DC: Pew Internet and American Life Project. Retrieved from www.pewinternet.org/~/media//Files/Reports/2013/PIP_TeensandTechnology 2013.pdf.

Magnusson, Charlotta. 2016. The gender wage gap in highly prestigious occupations: A case study of Swedish medical doctors. *Work, Employment and Society* 30 (1): 40–58.

Malešević, Siniša. 2010. *The sociology of war and violence.* New York: Cambridge University Press.

Mallon, Gerald P. 2017. Practice with LGBT parents. In *Social work practice with lesbian, gay, bisexual, and transgender people,* pp. 165–97. New York: Routledge.

Maloney, Devon. 2013. The marketing tactics for *Hunger Games: Catching Fire* would make Panem's Capitol proud. *Wired,* November 22. Retrieved from www.wired.com/underwire/2013/11/catching-fire-marketing/.

Manchester, Colleen Flaherty, Lisa M. Leslie, and Patricia C. Dahm. 2018. Family responsibilities and career outcomes: Discriminatory and non-discriminatory explanations. In *The Oxford handbook of workplace discrimination*, ed. Adrienne J. Colella and Eden B. King. New York: Oxford University Press.

Manger, Christian. 2014. Endogenous age discrimination. *Journal of Population Economics* 27 (4): 1087–1106.

Mann, Michael. 2012. *The sources of social power.* New York: Cambridge University Press.

Mannheim, Karl. (1928) 1952. The problem of generations. In *Essays on the sociology of knowledge,* pp. 276–322. London: Routledge/Kegan Paul.

Manning, Nathan, and Kathy Edwards. 2014. Does civic education for young people increase political participation? A systemic review. *Educational Review* 66 (1): 22–45.

Mao Zedong. (1936) 2010. *Quotations from Chairman Mao Zedong during the Cultural Revolution.* Fairfax, CA: Intercultural.

Marger, Martin N. 2014. *Social inequality.* New York: McGraw-Hill.

Marginson, Simon. 2016. Higher education and growing inequality. *Academic Matters.* Retrieved from www.academicmatters.ca/2016/01/higher-education-and-growing-inequality/.

Mariampolski, Hy. 2001. *Qualitative market research: A comprehensive guide.* Thousand Oaks, CA: Sage.

Mariampolski, Hy. 2005. *Ethnography for marketers: A guide to consumer immersion.* Thousand Oaks, CA: Sage.

Marini, Margaret Mooney. 1984. The order of events in the transition to adulthood. *Sociology of Education* 57 (2): 63–84.

Marmot, Michael. 2015. *The health gap: The challenge of an unequal world.* New York: Bloomsbury.

Marquart, James W., Sheldon Ekland-Olson, and Jonathan R. Sorensen. 1994. *The rope, the chair, and the needle: Capital punishment in Texas, 1923–1990.* Austin: University of Texas Press.

Marsh, Charles. 2006. *The beloved community: How faith shapes social justice from the civil rights movement to today.* New York: Basic Books.

Martin, John E. 1986. *Feudalism to capitalism: Peasant and landlord in English agrarian development.* London: Palgrave Macmillan.

Martin, Karin A. 1998. Becoming a gendered body: Practices of preschools. *American Sociological Review* 63 (4): 494–511.

Martin, Molly A. 2008. The intergenerational correlation in weight: How genetic resemblance reveals the social role of families. *American Journal of Sociology* 114: S67–S105.

Martin, Nathan D. 2013. Forms of social capital: Family resources, campus networks, and dominant class advantage at an elite university. In *Networks, work and inequality,* Research in the Sociology of Work, vol. 24, ed. Steve McDonald, pp. 359–86. Bingley, UK: Emerald Group Publishing.

Martineau, Harriet. (1837) 2009. *Society in America.* New York: Cambridge University Press.

Martineau, Harriet. (1838) 2009. *How to observe morals and manners.* Charleston, SC: BiblioLife.

Marx, Karl. (1844) 1978. Contribution to the critique of Hegel's *Philosophy of Right*: Introduction. In *The Marx-Engels reader,* ed. Robert C. Tucker, pp. 53–65. New York: Norton.

Marx, Karl. (1845) 1978. Theses on Feuerbach. In *The Marx-Engels Reader,* 2nd ed., ed. Robert C. Tucker. New York: Norton.

Marx, Karl. (1852) 1978. The eighteenth Brumaire of Louis Bonaparte. In *The Marx-Engels Reader,* 2nd ed., ed. Robert C. Tucker. New York: Norton.

Marx, Karl. (1859) 1978. Preface to *A contribution to the critique of political economy.* In *The Marx-Engels reader,* 2nd ed., ed. Robert C. Tucker, pp. 3–6. New York: Norton.

Marx, Karl. (1867) 1976. *Capital,* trans. Ben Fowkes. New York: Vintage.

Marx, Karl, and Friedrich Engels. 2008. *On religion.* Mineola, NY: Dover.

Masci, David, and Michael Lipka. 2016. Americans may be getting less religious, but feelings of spirituality are on the rise. Washington, DC: Pew Research Center. Retrieved from www.pewresearch.org/ fact-tank/2016/01/21/americans-spirituality/.

Mason, Katherine. 2012. The unequal weight of discrimination: Gender, body size, and income inequality. *Social Problems* 59 (3): 411–35.

Massey, Douglas S., and Nancy Denton. 1993. *American apartheid: Segregation and the making of the underclass.* Cambridge, MA: Harvard University Press.

Matsueda, Ross. L. 1992. Reflected appraisals, parental labeling, and delinquency. *American Journal of Sociology* 97 (6): 1577–611.

Mattera, Philip, and Kasia Tarczynska. 2015. Uncle Sam's favorite corporations: Identifying the large companies that dominate federal subsidies. Washington, DC: Good Jobs First. Retrieved from www.goodjobsfirst.org/sites/default/files/docs/pdf/UncleSamsFavoriteCorporations.pdf.

Matthews, Dylan. 2016. Donald Trump's convention speech was an overwhelming victory for fear. *Vox,* July 22. Retrieved from www.vox.com/2016/7/22/12254826/donald-trump-convention-speech-rnc-fear.

Maurer, Lora. 2009. Naomi Chesler: Teacher, researcher, mentor, mom. *The Connector* 23 (1): 8–9. Harvard-MIT Division of Health Sciences and Technology. Retrieved from http://hst.mit.edu/images/upload/Connector_Winter09.pdf.

Mavin, Sharon, Gina Grandy, and Janine Williams. 2014. Experiences of women elite leaders doing gender: Intra-gender micro-violence between women. *British Journal of Management* 25: 439–55.

May, John F. 2012. *World population policies: Their origin, evolution, and impact.* New York: Springer Science + Business Media.

McAdam, Doug. 1989. The biographical consequences of activism. *American Sociological Review* 54 (5): 744–60.

McCall, Leslie. 2013. *The undeserving rich: American beliefs about inequality, opportunity, and redistribution.* New York: Cambridge University Press.

McCall, Leslie, and Ann Shola Orloff. 2017. The multidimensional politics of inequality: Taking stock of identity politics in the U.S. presidential election of 2016. *The British Journal of Sociology* 68: S34–56. doi:10.1111/1468-4446.12316.

McCammon, Sarah. 2016. Trump says comments about judge "have been misconstrued." National Public Radio, June 7. Retrieved from www.npr.org/2016/06/07/481013560/ryan-trumps-criticism-of-judge-textbook-definition-of-a-racist-comment.

McCarthy, Daniel. 2018. The case for Trump's tariffs and "America first" economics. Retrieved from www.nytimes.com/2018/03/08/opinion/trump-tariffs-economics.html.

McCarthy, John D., and Mayer N. Zald. 1977. Resource mobilization and social movements: A partial theory. *American Journal of Sociology* 82 (6): 1212–41.

McCarthy, Justin. 2015a. In U.S., socialist presidential candidates least appealing. June 22. Retrieved from www.gallup.com/poll/183713/socialist-presidential-candidates-least-appealing.aspx.

McCarthy, Niall. 2016. America's most prestigious professions in 2016. Retrieved from www.forbes.com/sites/niallmccarthy/2016/03/31/americas-most-prestigious-professions-in-2016-infographic/#56af52291926.

McCartin, Joseph. 2016. Public sector unionism under assault: How to combat the scapegoating of organized labor. *New Labor Forum.* Retrieved from http://newlaborforum.cuny.edu/2016/01/19/public-sector-unionism-under-assault-how-to-combat-the-scapegoating-of-organized-labor.

McChesney, Robert. 2015. *Rich media, poor democracy.* New York: New Press.

McChesney, Robert W., and Victor Pickard, eds. 2011. *Will the last reporter please turn out the lights: The collapse of journalism and what can be done to fix it.* New York: New Press.

McClelland, Stephen. 2012. Social networks and the second screen. *Intermedia* 40 (3): 16–21.

McConahay, John B. 1986. Modern racism, ambivalence, and the modern racism scale. In *Prejudice, discrimination and racism,* ed. John F. Dovidio and Samuel L. Gaertner, pp. 91–125. Orlando, FL: Academic Press.

McCrummen, Stephanie. 2005a. Building unity in subdivisions. *Washington Post,* February 27, pp. A1, A13.

McCrummen, Stephanie. 2005b. Subdivisions impose social divide. *Washington Post,* May 1, pp. A1, A16.

McFarland, Daniel A., and Reuben J. Thomas. 2006. Bowling young: How youth voluntary associations influence adult political participation. *American Sociological Review* 71 (3): 401–25.

McGill, Brittany S. 2014. Navigating new norms of involved fatherhood: Employment, fathering attitudes, and father involvement. *Journal of Family Issues* 35 (8): 1089–1106.

McGregor, Richard. 2010. *The party: The secret world of China's communist rulers.* New York: HarperCollins.

McIntosh, Peggy. 1988. *White privilege and male privilege: A personal account of coming to see correspondences through work in women's studies.* Wellesley, MA: Center for Research on Women.

McKenzie, Brian. 2013. Out of state and long commutes, 2011. Washington, DC: U.S. Census Bureau. Retrieved from www.census.gov/hhes/commuting/files/2012/ACS-20.pdf.

McKenzie, Brian. 2015. Who drives to work? Commuting by automobile in the United States: 2013. Washington, DC: U.S. Census Bureau. Retrieved from www.census.gov/hhes/commuting/files/2014/acs-32.pdf.

McKenzie, Lindsay. 2018. The 100K club. Retrieved from www.insidehighered.com/news/2018/04/23/nonprofits-poised-unseat-u-phoenix-largest-online-university.

McKernan, Signe-Mary, Caroline Ratcliffe, Eugene Steuerle, and Sisi Zhang. 2013. Less than equal: Racial disparities in wealth accumulation. Washington, DC: Urban Institute. Retrieved from www.urban.org/UploadedPDF/412802-Less-Than-Equal-Racial-Disparities-in-Wealth-Accumulation.pdf.

McKinlay, John B., and Lisa D. Marceau. 2002. The end of the golden age of doctoring. *International Journal of Health Services* 32 (2): 379–416.

McLanahan, Sara, Laura Tach, and Daniel Schneider. 2013. The causal effects of father absence. *Annual Review of Sociology* 39: 399–427.

McLaughlin, Kenneth. 2016. *Empowerment: A critique.* New York: Routledge.

McMichael, Philip. 2017. *Development and social change: A global perspective.* Thousand Oaks, CA: Sage.

McMillan Cottom, Tressie. 2014. Public sociology at ASA14. Retrieved from https://tressiemc.com/2014/08/20/public-sociology-at-asa14/.

McMillan Cottom, Tressie. 2016. *Lower ed: The troubling rise of for-profit college in the new economy.* New York: New Press.

McPherson, Miller, Lynn Smith-Lovin, and James M. Cook. 2001. Birds of a feather: Homophily in social networks. *Annual Review of Sociology* 27: 415–44.

McQuail, Denis. 2011. *Mass communication theory.* Thousand Oaks, CA: Sage.

McQuarrie, Michael. 2017. The revolt of the rust belt: Place and politics in the age of anger. *The British Journal of Sociology* 68: S120–52.

Mcveigh, Ryan. 2016. Basic-level categories, mirror neurons, and joint-attention schemes: Three points of intersection between G. H. Mead and cognitive science. *Symbolic Interaction* 39 (1): 45–65.

Mead, George Herbert. (1934) 1962. *Mind, self, and society,* ed. Charles W. Morris. Chicago: Chicago University Press.

Mecking, Olga. 2017. This scientific theory explains why people keep quiet on things that matter. Retrieved from http://theweek.com/articles/685976/scientific-theory-explains-why-people-keep-quiet-things-that-matter.

Meier, Deborah, and George Wood. 2004. *Many children left behind: How the No Child Left Behind Act is damaging our children and our schools.* Boston: Beacon Press.

Mele, Christopher. 2016. Oregon court allows a person to choose neither sex. *New York Times,* June 13. Retrieved from www.nytimes.com/2016/06/14/us/oregon-nonbinary-transgender-sex-gender.html.

Mello, John P., Jr. 2018. Facebook phone-scraping takes users by surprise. Retrieved from www.technewsworld.com/story/85227.html.

Meloni, Maurizio. 2015. Epigenetics for the social sciences: Justice, embodiment, and inheritance in the postgenomic age. *New Genetics and Society* 34 (2): 125–51.

Menken, Kate. 2017. Leadership in dual language bilingual education. Center for Applied Linguistics.

Merton, Robert K. 1938. Social structure and anomie. *American Sociological Review* 3: 672–82.

Merton, Robert K. 1949. Discrimination and the American creed. In *Discrimination and the national welfare,* ed. R. M. MacIver, pp. 99–126. New York: Harper & Row.

Merton, Robert K. 1968a. The bearing of empirical research on sociological theory. In *Social Theory and Social Structure,* pp. 156–71. New York: Free Press.

Merton, Robert K. 1968b. The Matthew effect in science. *Science* 159 (3810): 56–63.

Merton, Robert K. 1968c. *Social theory and social structure.* New York: Free Press.

Mettler, Suzanne. 2014. *Degrees of inequality: How the politics of higher education sabotaged the American dream.* New York: Basic Books.

Meyer, David S. 2015. *Politics of protest: Social movements in America.* New York: Oxford University Press.

Meyer, John W., David Tyack, Joane Nagel, and Audri Gordon. 1979. Public education as nation-building in America: Enrollments and bureaucratization in the American states, 1870–1930. *American Journal of Sociology* 85 (3): 591–613.

Meyrowitz, Joshua. 1985. *No sense of place: The impact of electronic media on social behavior.* New York: Oxford University Press.

Michener, H. A., and E. J. Lawler. 1975. The endorsement of formal leaders: An integrative model. *Journal of Personality and Social Psychology* 31: 216–33.

Milgram, Stanley. 1963. Behavioral study of obedience. *Journal of Abnormal and Social Psychology* 67 (4): 371–78.

Milgram, Stanley. 1965. Some conditions of obedience and disobedience to authority. *Human Relations* 18 (1): 57–76.

Milgram, Stanley. 1969. *Obedience to authority.* New York: HarperCollins.

Milkman, Ruth, and Stephanie Luce. 2017. *The state of the unions 2017: A profile of organized labor in New York City, New York State, and the United States.* New York: The Joseph S. Murphy Institute for Worker Education and Labor Studies. Retrieved from www.gc.cuny.edu/CUNY_GC/media/CUNY-Graduate-Center/PDF/Press%20Room/Union_Density_2017_C.pdf.

Milkman, Ruth, and Steve Ott, eds. 2014. *New labor in New York: Precarious workers and the future of the labor movement.* Ithaca, NY: Cornell University Press.

Milkman, Ruth. 1997. *Farewell to the factory: Auto workers in the late twentieth century.* Berkeley: University of California Press.

Miller, Alan S., and Tmoko Mitamura. 2003. Are surveys on trust trustworthy? *Social Psychology Quarterly* 66 (1): 62–70.

Miller, Kristen, and J. Michael Ryan. 2011. *Design, development and testing of the NHIS Sexual Identity Question.* Questionnaire Design Research Laboratory, Office of Research and Methodology, National Center for Health Statistics. October.

Miller, Neil. 2006. *Out of the past: Gay and lesbian history from 1869 to the present.* Los Angeles: Advocate Books.

Mills, C. Wright. 1948. *The new men of power.* New York: Harcourt.

Mills, C. Wright. 1952. *White collar.* New York: Oxford University Press.

Mills, C. Wright. 1956. *The power elite.* New York: Oxford University Press.

Mills, C. Wright. 1959. *The sociological imagination.* New York: Oxford University Press.

Minasians, Christopher. 2016. Where are the iPhone, iPad and Mac designed, made and assembled? *Macworld,* April 18. Retrieved from www.macworld.co.uk/feature/apple/are-apple-products-truly-designed-in-california-made-in-china-iphonese-3633832/.

Miranda, Candice. 2003. In Kenya, television opens window mainly in the west. *Washington Post,* April 28, p. A19.

Mishel, Lawrence and Jessica Schieder. 2016. "As union membership has fallen, the top 10 percent have been getting a larger share of income." Economic Policy Institute. Retrieved from https://www.epi.org/publication/as-union-membership-has-fallen-the-top-10-percent-have-been-getting-a-larger-share-of-income/.

Mizruchi, Mark S. 2013. *The fracturing of the American corporate elite.* Cambridge, MA: Harvard University Press.

Moghadam, Valentine M. 2013. *Globalization and social movements.* Lanham, MD: Rowman & Littlefield.

Mohamed, Besheer. 2016. A new estimate of the U.S. Muslim population. Washington, DC: Pew Research Center. Retrieved from www.pewresearch.org/fact-tank/2016/01/06/a-new-estimate-of-the-u-s-muslim-population/.

Mohanty, Chandra Talpade, ed. 2003. *Feminism without borders: Decolonizing theory, practicing solidarity.* Durham, NC: Duke University Press.

Mol, Arthur P. J., Gert Spaargaren, and David A. Sonnenfeld. 2014. Ecological modernization theory: Taking stock, moving forward. In *Handbook of social and environmental change,* ed. Stewart Lockie, David A. Sonnenfeld, and Dana R. Fisher, pp. 15–30. New York: Routledge.

Molina, Natalia. 2014. *How race is made in America: Immigration, citizenship, and the historical power of racial scripts.* Berkeley: University of California Press.

Molm, L. D. 1997. Risk and power use: Constraints on the use of coercion in exchange. *American Sociological Review* 62: 113–33.

Molner, Alex, Faith Boninger, Michael D. Harris, and Ken M. Libby. 2013. Promoting consumption at school: Health threats associated with schoolhouse commercialism. Boulder, CO: National Education Policy Center. Retrieved from http://nepc.colorado.edu/files/commercialism-2012_0.pdf.

Moloney, K. P., B. J. van den Bergh, and L. F. Moller. 2009. Women in prison: The central issues of gender characteristics and trauma history. *Public Health* 123: 426–30.

Molotch, Harvey L. 1976. The city as a growth machine. *American Journal of Sociology* 82 (2): 309–30.

Montejano, David. 1987. *Anglos and Mexicans in the making of Texas, 1836–1986.* Austin: University of Texas Press.

Moody, Harry R. 2010. *Aging: Concepts and controversies,* 6th ed. Thousand Oaks, CA: Pine Forge Press.

Moore, Chadwick. 2015. Joining the annual gathering of the Two Spirit Society in Montana. *Out,* September 22. Retrieved from www.out.com/news-opinion/2015/9/22/joining-annual-gathering-two-spirit-society-montana.

Moore, Christopher J. 2004. *In other words.* New York: Levenger Press/Walker & Company.

Moore, Mignon R., and Michael Stambolis-Ruhstorfer. 2013. LGBT sexuality and families at the start of the twenty-first century. *Annual Review of Sociology* 39: 491–507.

Moore, Ryan. 2009. *Sells like teen spirit.* New York: NYU Press.

Moraga, Cherríe, and Gloria Anzaldúa, eds. 2015. *This bridge called my back: Writings by radical women of color.* Albany, NY: SUNY Press.

Mordechay, Kfir, and Jennifer Ayscue. 2017. White growth, persistent segregation: Could gentrification become integration? The Civil Rights Project, UCLA.

Morello, Carol. 2012. Census chief Robert Groves: We've got to stop counting like this. *Washington Post,* August 5. Retrieved from http://articles.washingtonpost.com/2012-08-05/politics/35493263_1_census-bureau-census-records-census-questions.

Morello, Carol, and Ted Melnick. 2013. *Washington Post,* June 13. Retrieved from www.washingtonpost.com/local/white-deaths-outnumber-births-for-first-time/2013/06/13/3bb1017c-d388-11e2-a73e-826d299ff459_story.html.

Morgan, Michael, and James Shanahan. 2014. Effects and cultivation. In *The SAGE handbook of television studies,* ed. Manuel Alvarado, Milly Buonanno, Herman Gray, and Toby Miller, pp. 356–65. Thousand Oaks, CA: Sage.

Morgan, Rachel E., and Grace Kena. 2017. Criminal victimization, 2016. Washington, DC: Bureau of Justice Statistics. Retrieved from www.bjs.gov/content/pub/pdf/cv16.pdf.

Morgan, Stephen L. 2018, May 11. Fake news: Status threat does not explain the 2016 presidential vote. Retrieved from https://osf.io/preprints/socarxiv/7r9fj/. doi:10.17605/OSF.IO/7R9FJ.

Morgan, Stephen L. and Jiwon Lee. 2017. The white working class and voter turnout in U.S. presidential elections, 2004 to 2016. *Sociological Science* 4: 656–85. doi:10.15195/v4.a27.

Morgan, Stephen L., and Jiwon Lee. 2018. Trump voters and the white working class. *Sociological Science* 5: 234–45. doi:10.15195/v5.a10.

Morin, Rich, and D'Vera Cohn. 2008. Women call the shots at home; public mixed on gender roles in jobs. Pew Research Center. Retrieved from http://pewresearch.org/pubs/967/gender-power.

Morin, Richard. 1994. That misleading Holocaust survey; A flawed poll overstated the public's skepticism. *New York Times,* March 20, p. C3.

Morrill, Calvin, Mayer N. Zald, and Hayagreeva Rao. 2003. Covert political conflict in organizations: Challenges from below. *Annual Review of Sociology* 29: 391–415.

Morris, Aldon. 1984. *The origins of the civil rights movement.* New York: Free Press.

Morris, David. Z. 2016. Why millennials are about to leave cities in droves. Retrieved from http://fortune.com/2016/03/28/millennials-leaving-cities/.

Morrow, Joe. 2017. Honey, I'm an atheist: Losing my faith and telling my wife about it. Retrieved from www.patheos.com/blogs/excommunications/2017/05/honey-im-an-atheist-losing-my-faith/.

Morsy, Leila, and Richard Rothstein. 2015. Parents' non-standard work schedules make adequate childrearing difficult. Economic Policy Institute. Issue Brief #400. August 6.

Mosco, Vincent. 2009. *The political economy of communication,* 2nd ed. Thousand Oaks, CA: Sage.

Motion Picture Association of America. 2018. Theatrical and home entertainment market environment report 2017. Retrieved from https://pmcdeadline2.files.wordpress.com/2018/04/mpaa-theme-report-2017.pdf.

Motz, Lotte. 1997. *The faces of the goddess.* New York: Oxford University Press.

Mounk, Yascha. 2018. *The people versus democracy.* Cambridge, MA: Harvard University Press.

Mouw, Ted, and Barbara Entwisle. 2006. Residential segregation and interracial friendship in schools. *American Journal of Sociology* 112 (2): 394–441.

Mudde, Cas, ed. 2016. *The populist radical right: A reader.* New York, NY: Routledge.

Mudde, Cas, and Cristóbal Rovira Kaltwasser. 2017. *Populism: A very short introduction.* New York: Oxford University Press.

Mukhopadhyay, Carol C., Rosemary Henze, and Yolanda T. Moses. 2014. *How real is race? A sourcebook on race, culture, and biology,* 2nd ed. Lanham, MD: Rowman & Littlefield.

Müller, Jan-Werner. 2016. *What is populism?* Philadelphia, PA: University of Pennsylvania Press.

Muller-Hill, B. 1988. *Murderous science: Elimination by scientific selection of Jews, Gypsies, and others, Germany, 1933–1945.* Oxford, UK: Oxford University Press.

Mumford, Lewis. 1968. *The city in history.* New York: Harvest.

Murray, Damian R., and Mark Schaller. 2012. Threat(s) and conformity deconstructed: Perceived threat of infectious disease and its implications for conformist attitudes and behavior. *European Journal of Social Psychology* 42 (2):180–88.

Murray, Pauli, ed. 1997. *States' laws on race and color.* Athens: University of Georgia Press.

Mutz, Diana C. 2018. Status threat, not economic hardship, explains the 2016 presidential vote. *Proceedings of the National Academy of Sciences.* www.pnas.org/content/early/2018/04/18/1718155115.

NAACP. 2018. Criminal justice fact sheet. Retrieved from www.naacp.org/criminal-justice-fact-sheet/.

NAACP Criminal Justice Department. 2017. Death penalty fact sheet. Retrieved from www.naacp.org/wp-content/uploads/2017/01/Death-penalty-fact-sheet-1-17-1.pdf.

Nadkarni, Ashwini, and Stefan Hofmann. 2012. Why do people use Facebook? *Personality and Individual Differences* 52 (3): 243–49.

Naff, Alixa. 1985. *Becoming American: The early Arab immigrant experience.* Carbondale: Southern Illinois University Press.

Nance, Jason P. 2017. Student surveillance, racial inequalities, and implicit racial bias. *Emory Law Journal* 66: 765–837.

Napoli, Philip M. 2010. *Audience evolution.* New York: Columbia University Press.

Nash, Kate. 2010. *Contemporary political sociology: Globalization, politics and power.* Malden, MA: Wiley.

National Alliance for Public Charter Schools. 2013. Back to school tallies: Estimated number of public charter schools & students, 2012–2013. January. Retrieved from http://dashboard.publiccharters.org/dashboard/home.

National Alliance for Public Charter Schools. 2018. 2017 Annual Report.

National Cancer Institute. 2016. What factors might contribute to the disproportionate burden of prostate cancer among African American/Black men? In *Cancer Health Disparities.* Retrieved from www.cancer.gov/about-nci/organization/crchd/cancer-health-disparities-fact-sheet#q10.

National Center for Education Statistics. 2017a. The conditions of education. https://nces.ed.gov/pubs2017/2017144.pdf.

National Center for Education Statistics. 2017b. *Digest of education statistics.* https://nces.ed.gov/programs/digest/current_tables.asp.

National Center for Education Statistics. 2017c. *Digest of education statistics.* Table 330.10. Average undergraduate tuition and fees and room and board rates charged for full-time students in degree-granting postsecondary institutions, by level and control of institution: Selected years, 1963-64 through 2016-17.

National Center for Education Statistics. 2018. The condition of education: Annual earning of young adults.

National Center for Health Statistics. 2015a. Births: Final data for 2014. *National Vital Statistics Reports* 64 (12). Hyattsville, MD. Retrieved from www.cdc.gov/nchs/data/nvsr/nvsr64/nvsr64_12.pdf.

National Center for Health Statistics. 2015b. Life stages and populations. Retrieved from www.cdc.gov/nchs/fastats/life-stages-and-populations.htm#.

National Center for Health Statistics. 2016. *Health, United States, 2015.* Hyattsville, MD: U.S. Department of Health and Human Services. Retrieved from www.cdc.gov/nchs/data/hus/hus15.pdf.

National Center for Health Statistics. 2018. Births and natality. Retrieved from www.cdc.gov/nchs/fastats/births.htm.

National Opinion Research Center. 2016. General Social Survey. Data analysis retrieved from http://gssdataexplorer.norc.org.

National Opinion Research Center. 2018. General Social Survey. Data analysis retrieved from http://gssdataexplorer.norc.org.

National Park Service. 2016. Stonewall National Monument. Retrieved from www.nps.gov/ston/index.htm.

National Priorities Project. 2011. Military recruitment 2010. Retrieved from http://nationalpriorities.org/analysis/2011/military-recruitment-2010/.

Natrajan, Balmurli. 2012. *The culturalization of caste in India.* New York: Routledge.

Nature Editorial Group. 2012. Life stresses. *Nature* 490: 143.

Nave, Gideon, Colin Camerer, and Michael McCullough. 2015. Does oxytocin increase trust in humans? A critical review of research. *Perspectives on Psychological Science* 10 (6): 772–89.

Nelson, Charles A., Nathan A. Fox, and Charles H. Zeanah Jr. 2013. Anguish of the abandoned child. *Scientific American* 308 (4): 62–67.

Nelson, Margaret K. 2010. *Parenting out of control.* New York: New York University Press.

Nevarez, Leonard. 2018, February 3. Urban lift-off amid the rural amenity economy: Riverfront cities and the "Brooklynization" of the Hudson Valley. Paper presented at the Annual Meeting of the Eastern Sociological Society. Baltimore, MD.

New American Economy. 2017. Not lost in translation: The growing importance of foreign language skills in the U.S. job market. Retrieved from http://www.newamericaneconomy.org/wp-content/uploads/2017/03/NAE_Bilingual_V6.pdf.

New York Times. 1991. Professor is criticized for anti-Semitic past. Retrieved from www.nytimes.com/1991/11/28/us/professor-is-criticized-for-anti-semitic-past.html.

New York Times. 2009. Workers in America, cheated. September 2, p. A30.

New York Times. 2011a. Netizens gain some privacy. January 29. Retrieved from www.nytimes.com/2011/01/30/opinion/30sun3.html.

New York Times. 2011b. Rich district, poor district. March 26. Retrieved from www.nytimes.com/2011/03/27/opinion/27sun1.html?_r=2.

New York Times Editorial Board. 2016. Donald Trump's campaign of fear. *New York Times,* July 22. Retrieved from www.nytimes.com/2016/07/22/opinion/donald-trumps-campaign-of-fear.html.

Newkirk, Vann. 2016. Voter-fraud laws are all about race. *The Atlantic,* August 2. Retrieved from www.theatlantic.com/politics/archive/2016/08/voting-rights-court-decisions-racism/493937/.

Newkirk, Vann R., II. 2018. A year after Hurricane Maria, Puerto Rico finally knows how many people died. *The Atlantic.* August 2018. Retrieved from https://www.theatlantic.com/politics/archive/2018/08/puerto-rico-death-toll-hurricane-maria/568822/.

Newman, Jason. 2014. Old videos, new ads: Advertising's shocking next frontier. *Rolling Stone.* Retrieved from www.rollingstone.com/music/features/old-videos-new-ads-advertisings-shocking-next-frontier-20141104.

Newman, Katherine S. 2004. *Rampage: The social roots of school shootings.* New York: Basic Books.

Newman, Katherine S. 2012. *The accordion family: Boomerang kids, anxious parents, and the private toll of global competition.* Boston: Beacon Press.

Newman, Mark. 2016. Maps of the 2016 U.S. presidential election results. Retrieved from www-personal.umich.ed/~mejn/election/2016/.

Newport, Frank. 2013a. Gulf grows in black-white views of U.S. justice system bias. Gallup. Retrieved from www.gallup.com/poll/163610/gulf-grows-black-white-views-justice-system-bias.aspx.

Newport, Frank. 2013b. In U.S., 87% approve of black-white marriage, vs. 4% in 1958. Gallup. Retrieved from www.gallup.com/poll/163697/approve-marriage-blacks-whites.aspx.

Newport, Frank. 2013c. Fewer blacks in U.S. see bias in jobs, income, and housing. Gallup. Retrieved from www.gallup.com/poll/163580/fewer-blacks-bias-jobs-income-housing.aspx.

Nield, David. 2017. How to find out what Facebook knows about you. Retrieved from www.popsci.com/everything-facebook-knows-about-you.

Nielsen. 2017. The Nielsen total audience report, Q1 2017. Retrieved from www.nielsen.com/content/dam/corporate/us/en/reports-downloads/2017-reports/total-audience-report-q1-2017.pdf.

Noam, Eli M. 2016. *Who owns the world's media? Media concentration and ownership around the world.* New York: Oxford University Press.

Noble, Safiya Umoja. 2018. *Algorithms of oppression: How search engines reinforce racism.* New York: New York University Press.

Noelle-Neuman, Elisabeth. 1974. The spiral of silence: A theory of public opinion. *Journal of Communication* 24 (2): 43–51.

Noelle-Neumann, Elisabeth. 1991. Accused professor was not a Nazi. Retrieved from www.nytimes.com/1991/12/14/opinion/l-accused-professor-was-not-a-nazi-257591.html.

Noelle-Neuman, Elisabeth. 1993. *The spiral of silence.* Chicago: University of Chicago Press.

Noonan, Mary C., Mary E. Corcoran, and Paul N. Courant. 2005. Pay differences among the highly trained. *Social Forces* 84 (2): 853–72.

Norenzayan, Ara. 2016. Theodiversity. *Annual Review of Psychology* 67: 465–88.

Norman, Jim. 2017. Americans weigh more, but shun "overweight" label. Retrieved from http://news.gallup.com/poll/222578/americans-weigh-shun-overweight-label.aspx.

Norris, Pippa, and Ronald Inglehart. 2012. *Sacred and secular: Religion and politics world-wide,* 2nd ed. New York: Cambridge University Press.

NRATV. 2018. We will never waver. Retrieved from www.nratv.com/series/wayne-lapierre/episode/wayne-lapierre-season-3-episode-1-we-will-never-waver.

Nyberg, Renee Smith, and Trine C. Jensen. 2009. Honoring the Kun Lun way: Cross-cultural organization development consulting to a hospitality company in Datong, China. *Journal of Applied Behavioral Science* 45: 305–37.

O'Connor, Russell. 2013. What does feminist porn look like? *Role/Reboot.* Retrieved from www.rolereboot.org/sex-and-relationships/details/2013-02-what-does-egalitarian-porn-look-like.

OECD (Organisation for Economic Co-operation and Development). 2016. Poverty rate. Retrieved from https://data.oecd.org/inequality/poverty-rate.htm.

OECD (Organisation for Economic Co-operation and Development). 2018a. OECD Family Database: Child poverty. Retrieved from www.oecd.org/els/family/database.htm.

OECD (Organisation for Economic Co-operation and Development). 2018b. OECD Family Database: Child-related leave. Retrieved from www.oecd.org/els/family/database.htm.

Ogburn, William. 1922. *Social change.* New York: Huebsch.

Ogrodnik, Corinne, and Suzanne Staggenborg. 2016. The ebb and flow of environmentalism. *Sociology Compass* 10 (3): 218–29.

Oh, Hyun Jung, Elif Ozkaya, and Robert LaRose. 2014. How does online social networking enhance life satisfaction? The relationships among online supportive interaction, affect, perceived social support, sense of community, and life satisfaction. *Computers in Human Behavior* 30: 69–78.

Ohlheiser, Abby. 2016. Facebook is trying to get its users to share more about their personal lives. *Washington Post,* April 8. Retrieved from www.washingtonpost.com/news/the-intersect/wp/2016/04/08/facebook-is-trying-to-get-its-users-to-share-more-about-their-personal-lives/.

Okin, Susan Moller. 1999. *Is multiculturalism bad for women?* Princeton, NJ: Princeton University Press.

Olds, Kris. 2013. Mapping Coursera's global footprint. *Inside Higher Ed,* November 19. Retrieved from www.insidehighered.com/blogs/globalhighered/mapping-courseras-global-footprint.

Oliphant, Baxter. 2016, September 29. Support for death penalty lowest in more than four decades. Pew Research Center.

Oliver, J. Eric, and Wendy M. Rahn. 2016. Rise of the Trumpenvolk: Populism in the 2016 election. *The ANNALS of the American Academy of Political and Social Science* 667 (1): 189–206.

Oliver, Melvin L., and Thomas M. Shapiro. 2006. *Black wealth, white wealth: A new perspective on racial inequality.* New York: Routledge.

Olmstead, Kenneth, and Aaron Smith. 2017, January. *Americans and cybersecurity.* Pew Research Center.

Orfield, Gary. 2014. Tenth Annual Brown Lecture in Education Research: A new civil rights agenda for American education. *Educational Researcher* 43 (6): 273–92.

Orfield, Gary, Jongyeon Ee, Erica Frankenberg, and Genevieve Siegel-Hawley. 2016, May 16. Brown at 62: School segregation by race, poverty and state. Civil Rights Project, UCLA.

Organisation for Economic Cooperation and Development (OECD). 2017. *Education at a glance 2017: OECD indicators.* Paris: OECD Publishing.

Orme, Nicholas. 2003. *Medieval children.* New Haven, CT: Yale University Press.

Orr, Asaf, and Joel Baum. 2016. Schools in transition: A guide for supporting transgender students in K-12 schools. Washington, DC: Human Rights Campaign. Retrieved from http://hrc-assets.s3-website-us-east-1.amazonaws.com//files/assets/resources/Schools-In-Transition.pdf.

Owens, Ann. 2016. Inequality in children's contexts: Income segregation of households with and without children. *American Sociological Review,* April 27. doi:10.1177/0003122416642430.

Page, James S. 2007. Teaching peace to the military. *Peace Review* 19 (4): 571–77.

Pager, Devah. 2003. The mark of a criminal record. *American Journal of Sociology* 108 (5): 937–75.

Pager, Devah. 2007. *Marked: Race, crime, and finding work in an era of mass incarceration.* Chicago: University of Chicago Press.

Pager, Devah, and Hana Shepherd. 2008. The sociology of discrimination: Racial discrimination in employment, housing, credit, and consumer markets. *Annual Review of Sociology* 34: 181–209.

Painter, Christopher, and Jorge Tiago Martins. 2017. Organisational communication management during the Volkswagen diesel emissions scandal: A hermeneutic study in attribution, crisis management, and information orientation. *Knowledge and Process Management* 24 (3): 204–218.

Palmer, Robert T., Ryan J. Davis, and Dina C. Maramba. 2010. Role of an HBCU in supporting success for underprepared black males. *Negro Educational Review* 61 (1–4): 85–106.

Panofsky, A. 2014. *Misbehaving science: Controversy and the development of behavior genetics.* Chicago: University of Chicago Press.

Pape, Robert A. 2005. *Dying to win: The strategic logic of suicide terrorism.* New York: Random House.

Papernow, Patricia L. 2013. *Surviving and thriving in stepfamily relationships.* New York: Routledge.

Pariser, Eli. 2011. *The filter bubble: How the new personalized web is changing what we read and how we think.* New York: Penguin.

Park, Heejung, and Anna S. Lau. 2016. Socioeconomic status and parenting priorities: Child independence and obedience around the world. *Journal of Marriage and Family* 78 (1): 43–59.

Parker, Kim. 2015. Women more than men adjust their careers for family life. Washington, DC: Pew Research Center. Retrieved from www.pewresearch.org/fact-tank/2015/10/01/women-more-than-men-adjust-their-careers-for-family-life/.

Parker, Kim, and Renee Stepler. 2017. As U.S. marriage rate hovers at 50%, education gap in marital status widens. Washington, DC: Pew Research Center. www.pewresearch.org/fact-tank/2017/09/14/as-u-s-marriage-rate-hovers-at-50-education-gap-in-marital-status-widens/.

Parker, Kim, and Wendy Wang. 2013. *Modern parenthood: Roles of moms and dads converge as they balance work and family.* March 14. Washington, DC: Pew Research Center.

Parkinson, Hannah Jane. 2016. Click and elect: How fake news helped Donald Trump win a real election. Retrieved from www.theguardian.com/commentisfree/2016/nov/14/fake-news-donald-trump-election-alt-right-social-media-tech-companies.

Parliament of Canada. 2018. Party standings in the House of Commons. Retrieved from www.ourcommons.ca/Parliamentarians/en/partystandings.

Parrillo, Vincent N., and Christopher Donoghue. 2005. Updating the Bogardus social distance studies: A new national survey. *Social Science Journal* 42 (2): 257–72.

Parry, Marc. 2010. Tomorrow's college. *Chronicle of Higher Education,* October 31. Retrieved from http://chronicle.com/article/Tomorrows-College/125120/.

Parsons, Talcott. 1949. The social structure of the family. In *The family: Its function and destiny,* ed. R. N. Asher, pp. 173–201. New York: Harper.

Parsons, Talcott. 1951. *The social system.* Glencoe, IL: Free Press.

Parsons, Talcott. 1954. An analytical approach to the theory of social stratification. In *Essays in sociological theory,* pp. 69–88. New York: Free Press.

Parsons, Talcott. 1960. The distribution of power in American society. In *Structure and process in modern societies.* New York: Free Press.

Parsons, Talcott, and Robert F. Bales. 1955. *Family: Socialization and interaction process.* New York: Free Press.

Pascoe, C. J. 2011. *Dude, you're a fag: Masculinity and sexuality in high school.* Berkeley: University of California Press.

Pascoe, C. J., and Tristan Bridges. 2016. *Exploring masculinities: Identity, inequality, continuity and change.* New York: Oxford University Press.

Pasquale, Frank. 2015. *The black box society: The secret algorithms that control money and information.* Cambridge, MA: Harvard University Press.

Passal, Jeffrey S. and D'Vera Cohn. 2017a. As Mexican share declined, U.S. unauthorized immigrant population fell in 2015 below recession level. Washington, DC: Pew Research Center. www.pewresearch.org/fact-tank/2017/04/25/as-mexican-share-declined-u-s-unauthorized-immigrant-population-fell-in-2015-below-recession-level/.

Passal, Jeffrey S. and D'Vera Cohn. 2017b. 20 metro areas are home to six-in-ten unauthorized immigrants in U.S. Washington, DC: Pew Research Center. www.pewresearch.org/fact-tank/2017/02/09/us-metro-areas-unauthorized-immigrants/.

Patchin, Justin W., and Sameer Hinduja. 2018. Deterring teen bullying: Assessing the impact of perceived punishment from police, schools, and parents. *Youth Violence and Juvenile Justice* 16 (2): 190–207.

Patillo, Mary. 2013. *Black picket fences: Privilege and peril among the black middle class.* Chicago: University of Chicago Press.

Paules, Greta Foff. 1992. *Dishing it out.* Philadelphia: Temple University Press.

Pawel, Miriam. 2009. *The union of their dreams: Power, hope, and struggle in Cesar Chavez's farm worker movement.* New York: Bloomsbury Press.

Pawel, Miriam. 2014. *The crusades of Cesar Chavez: A biography.* New York: Bloomsbury Press.

Payne, Charles M., and Cristina M. Ortiz. 2017. Doing the impossible: The limits of schooling, the power of poverty. *The Annals of the American Academy of Political and Social Science* 673 (1): 32–59.

Pearson, Jo. 2003. "Witchcraft will not soon vanish from this Earth": Wicca in the 21st century. In *Predicting religion: Christian, secular and alternative futures,* ed. Grace Davie, Paul Heelas, and Linda Woodhead, pp. 170–92. Burlington, VT: Ashgate.

Pedulla, David S., and Sarah Thebaud. 2015. Can we finish the revolution? Gender, work-family ideals, and institutional constraint. *American Sociological Review* 80 (1): 116–39.

Peet, Richard. 2009. *Unholy trinity: The IMF, World Bank, and WTO.* New York: Zed Books.

Pellow, David N., and Hollie Nyseth Brehm. 2013. An environmental sociology for the twenty-first century. *Annual Review of Sociology* 39: 229–50.

Perc, Matjaž. 2014. The Matthew effect in empirical data. *Journal of the Royal Society Interface* 11 (98): 20140378.

Pérez, Louis A. 2015. *Cuba: Between reform and revolution.* New York: Oxford University Press.

Perez, Sarah. 2016. Microsoft silences its new A.I. bot Tay, after Twitter users teach it racism. *TechCrunch,* March 24. Retrieved from https://techcrunch.com/2016/03/24/microsoft-silences-its-new-a-i-bot-tay-after-twitter-users-teach-it-racism/.

Perkin, Bethany. 2015. Freegan freshers: The students making savings by living off waste. *The Guardian*, January 23. Retrieved from www.theguardian.com/education/2015/jan/23/freegan-freshers-the-students-making-savings-by-living-off-waste.

Perrin, Andrew, and Jingjing Jiang. 2018. About a quarter of U.S. adults say they are "almost constantly" online. Washington, DC: Pew Research Center. Retrieved from www.pewresearch.org/fact-tank/2018/03/14/about-a-quarter-of-americans-report-going-online-almost-constantly/.

Perry, Richard J. 2015. *Killer apes, naked apes, and just plain nasty people: The misuse and abuse of science in political discourse.* Baltimore, MD: Johns Hopkins University Press.

Peterson, Trond, and Ishak Saporta. 2004. The opportunity structure for discrimination. *American Journal of Sociology* 109 (4): 852–901.

Pew Center on the States. 2008. *One in 100: Behind bars in America 2008.* Washington, DC: Pew Charitable Trusts.

Pew Forum on Religion and Public Life. 2008a. Many Americans say other faiths can lead to eternal life. Washington, DC: Pew Research Center. Retrieved from http://pewforum.org/Many-Americans-Say-Other-Faiths-Can-Lead-to-Eternal-Life.aspx#1.

Pew Forum on Religion and Public Life. 2008b. *U.S. Religious Landscape Survey.* Washington, DC: Pew Research Center.

Pew Forum on Religion and Public Life. 2010a. *Religion among the millennials.* Washington, DC: Pew Research Center.

Pew Forum on Religion and Public Life. 2010b. *U.S. Religious Knowledge Survey.* Washington, DC: Pew Research Center.

Pew Global Attitudes Project. 2015. Washington, DC: Pew Research Center. Retrieved from Question Database, www.pewglobal.org/question-search/?qid=408 &cntIDs=&stdIDs=/.

Pew Research Center. 2007a. *Blacks see growing values gap between poor and middle class.* Washington, DC: Pew Research Center.

Pew Research Center. 2007b. *Muslim Americans: Middle class and mostly mainstream.* Washington, DC: Pew Research Center.

Pew Research Center. 2010a. The decline of marriage and the rise of new families. Washington, DC: Pew Research Center. Retrieved from http://pewresearch.org/pubs/1802/decline-marriage-rise-new-families.

Pew Research Center. 2010b. Support for same-sex marriage edges upward; majority continues to favor gays serving openly in military. Retrieved from http://people-press.org/ report/662/same-sex-marriage.

Pew Research Center. 2011. The American-Western European values gap. Washington, DC. Retrieved from www.pewglobal.org/files/2011/11/Pew-Global-Attitudes-Values-Report-FINAL-November-17-2011-10AM-EST1.pdf.

Pew Research Center. 2013a. Big racial divide over Zimmerman verdict. Retrieved from www.people-press.org/2013/07/22/big-racial-divide-over-zimmerman-verdict/.

Pew Research Center. 2013b. "Borders first" a dividing line in immigration debate. Washington, DC: Pew Research Center. Retrieved from www.people-press.org/2013/06/23/borders-first-a-dividing-line-in-immigration-debate/.

Pew Research Center. 2013c. Changing attitudes on gay marriage. Retrieved from http://features.pewforum.org/same-sex-marriage-attitudes/slide2.php.

Pew Research Center. 2013d. Modern parenthood: Roles of moms and dads converge as they balance work and family. Washington, DC: Pew Research Center.

Pew Research Center. 2013e. The world's Muslims: Religion, politics, and society. Washington, DC. Retrieved from www.pewforum.org/files/2013/04/worlds-muslims-religion-politics-society-full-report.pdf.

Pew Research Center. 2014a. Political polarization and media habits. October 2014. Retrieved from www.pewresearch.org/topics/political-polarization/.

Pew Research Center. 2014b. Emerging and developing economies much more optimistic than rich countries about the future. Washington, DC. Retrieved from www.pewglobal.org/files/2014/10/Pew-Research-Center-Inequality-Report-FINAL-October-17-2014.pdf.

Pew Research Center. 2014c. How Americans feel about religious groups. Washington, DC. Retrieved from www.pewforum.org/2014/07/16/how-americans-feel-about-religious-groups/.

Pew Research Center. 2014d. Record share of Americans have never been married. Washington, DC. Retrieved from www.pewsocialtrends.org/files/2014/09/2014-09-24_Never-Married-Americans.pdf.

Pew Research Center. 2015. Global Attitudes Project. 2015. Retrieved from www.pewglobal.org/files/2015/11/Pew-Research-Center-Democracy-Report-FINAL-November-18-2015.pdf.

Pew Research Center. 2015a. In debate over legalizing marijuana, disagreement over drug's dangers. April 14. Retrieved from www.people-press.org/2015/04/14/in-debate-over-legalizing-marijuana-disagreement-over-drugs-dangers/#survey-report.

Pew Research Center. 2015b. Cell phones in Africa: Communication lifeline. April 15. Retrieved from www.pewglobal.org/2015/04/15/cell-phones-in-africa-communication-lifeline/.

Pew Research Center. 2015c. Multiracial in America: Proud, diverse and growing in numbers. Washington, DC. Retrieved from www.pewsocialtrends.org/files/2015/06/2015-06-11_multiracial-in-america_final-updated.pdf.

Pew Research Center. 2015d. Across racial lines, more say nation needs to make changes to achieve racial equality. Washington, DC. Retrieved from www.people-press.org/files/2015/08/08-05-2015-Race-release.pdf.

Pew Research Center. 2015e. Raising kids and running a household: How working parents share the load. Washington, DC. Retrieved from www.pewsocialtrends.org/2015/11/04/raising-kids-and-running-a-household-how-working-parents-share-the-load/.

Pew Research Center. 2015f. America's changing religious landscape. Washington, DC. Retrieved from www.pewforum.org/files/2015/05/RLS-08-26-full-report.pdf.

Pew Research Center. 2015g. U.S. public becoming less religious. Washington, DC. Retrieved from www.pewforum.org/files/ 2015/11/201.11.03_RLS_II_full_report.pdf.

Pew Research Center. 2015h. Teens, social media, technology overview 2015. Washington, DC: Pew Research Center. Retrieved from www.pewinternet.org/files/2015/04/PI_TeensandTech_Update2015_0409151.pdf.

Pew Research Center. 2015i. The middle class is losing ground. Washington, DC. Retrieved from www.pewsocialtrends.org/files/2015/12/2015-12-09_middle-class_FINAL-report.pdf.

Pew Research Center. 2015j. Modern immigration wave brings 59 million to U.S., driving population growth and change through 2065. Washington, DC. Retrieved from www.pewhispanic.org/files/2015/09/2015-09-28_modern-immigration-wave_REPORT.pdf.

Pew Research Center. 2015k. Multiracial in America proud, diverse and growing in numbers. http://assets.pewresearch.org/wp-content/uploads/sites/3/2015/06/2015-06-11_multiracial-in-america_final-updated.pdf.

Pew Research Center. 2016a. The gender gap in religion around the world. Washington, DC. Retrieved from www.pewforum.org/files/2016/03/Religion-and-Gender-Full-Report.pdf.

Pew Research Center. 2016b. Shared, collaborative, and on demand: The new digital economy. May. www.pewinternet.org.

Pew Research Center. 2016c. Changing attitudes on gay marriage. Washington, DC. Retrieved from www.pewforum.org/2016/05/12/changing-attitudes-on-gay-marriage/.

Pew Research Center. 2017a, September. *News use across social media platforms.*

Pew Research Center. 2017b, July. *Online harassment 2017.*

Pew Research Center. 2017c. U.S. Muslims concerned about their place in society but continue to believe in the American dream. http://assets.pewresearch.org/wp-content/uploads/sites/11/2017/07/09105631/U.S.-MUSLIMS-FULL-REPORT-with-population-update-v2.pdf.

Pew Research Center. 2017d. Changing attitudes on gay marriage. Retrieved from www.pewforum.org/fact-sheet/changing-attitudes-on-gay-marriage/.

Pew Research Center. 2018a. Mobile fact sheet. February 5. www.pewinternet.org/fact-sheet/mobile/.

Pew Research Center. 2018b. Internet/broadband fact sheet. www.pewinternet.org/fact-sheet/internet-broadband/.

Pew Research Center. 2018c. The public, the political system and American democracy. Retrieved from http://assets.pewresearch.org/wp-content/uploads/sites/5/2018/04/26140617/4-26-2018-Democracy-release.pdf.

Pew-Templeton Global Religious Futures Project. 2018. Pew Research Center's Religion & Public Life Project. www.globalreligiousfutures.org/.

Pfohl, Stephen. 2009. *Images of deviance and social control.* Long Grove, IL: Waveland Press.

Phelan, Jo C., and Bruce G. Link. 2015. Is racism a fundamental cause of inequalities in health? *Annual Review of Sociology* 41: 311-30.

Phillips, Whitney. 2018. The oxygen of amplification: Better practices for reporting on extremists, antagonists, and manipulators online. New York: Data & Society Research Institute. https://datasociety.net/wp-content/uploads/2018/05/FULLREPORT_Oxygen_of_Amplification_DS.pdf.

Picca, Leslie Houts, and Joe Feagin. 2007. *Two-faced racism: Whites in the backstage and frontstage.* New York: Routledge.

Pierce, Glenn L., and Michael L. Radelet. 2005. The impact of legally inappropriate factors on death sentencing for California homicides, 1990-1999. *Santa Clara Law Review* 46: 1-41.

Piketty, Thomas, Emmanuel Saez, and Gabriel Zucman. 2018. Distributional national accounts: Methods and estimates for the United States. *The Quarterly Journal of Economics* 1-57. doi: 10.1093/qje/qjx043. http://gabriel-zucman.eu/files/PSZ2018QJE.pdf.

Pillet-Shore, Danielle. 2016. Criticizing another's child: How teachers evaluate students during parent-teacher conferences. *Language in Society* 45 (1): 33-58.

Pinker, Steven. 2007. *The language instinct: How the mind creates language.* New York: Harper Perennial Modern Classics.

Pinsker, Joe. 2015. Young Americans: Yearning for the suburbs, stuck in the city. Retrieved from www.theatlantic.com/business/archive/2015/01/young-americans-yearning-for-the-suburbs-stuck-in-the-city/384752/.

Pizzo, Stephen, Mary Fricker, and Paul Muolo. 1989. *Inside job: The looting of America's savings and loans.* New York: McGraw-Hill.

Plain, Bob. 2015. Eric Hirsch, Renaissance workers win Red Bandana Awards. May 5. www.rifuture.org/eric-hirsch-renaissance-workers-win-red-bandana-awards.html.

Poggi, Gianfranco. 2001. *Forms of power.* Malden, MA: Blackwell.

Pollin, Robert, and Stephanie Luce. 1998. *The living wage: Building a fair economy.* New York: New Press.

Polyani, Karl. 1977. *The livelihood of man.* New York: Academic Press.

Pompper, Donnalyn, Jorge Soto, and Laren Piel. 2007. Male body image and magazine standards: Considering dimensions of age and ethnicity. *Journalism and Mass Communication Quarterly* 83: 3 (Autumn): 525-45.

Popenoe, David. 2009. *Families without fathers.* Piscataway, NJ: Transaction.

Portes, Alejandro. 2002. NAFTA and Mexican immigration. Working Paper No. 351. Princeton University, Woodrow Wilson School of Public and International Affairs, Center for Migration and Development. Retrieved from http://cmd.princeton.edu/papers/NAFTA%20and%20Mexican%20Immigration.pdf.

Portes, Alejandro. 2011. English-only triumphs, but the costs are high. In *The structure of schooling: Readings in the sociology of education,* ed. Richard Arum, Irenee R. Beattie, and Karly Ford, pp. 567-71. Los Angeles: Sage.

Powers, Devon. 2016. Advertising and consumerism. In *A companion to popular culture,* ed. Gary Burns, pp. 243-60. Malden, MA: Wiley.

Powers, William. 2010. *Hamlet's BlackBerry.* New York: Harper.

Priest, Dana, and William M. Arkin. 2010. A hidden world, growing beyond control. *Washington Post,* July 19. Retrieved from http://projects.washingtonpost.com/top-secret-america/articles/a-hidden-world-growing-beyond-control/.

Prothero, Stephen. 2007. *Religious literacy.* New York: HarperCollins.

Prothero, Stephen. 2016. Why liberals win the culture wars (even when they lose elections). New York: HarperCollins.

Pryor, Jan. 2014. *Stepfamilies: A global perspective on research, policy, and practice.* New York: Routledge.

Pugh, Allison J. 2009. *Longing and belonging: Parents, children and consumer culture.* Berkeley: University of California Press.

Pugh, Allison J. 2015. *The tumbleweed society: Working and caring in an insecure age.* New York: Oxford University Press.

Puhl, Rebecca, and Kelly D. Brownell. 2001. Bias, discrimination, and obesity. *Obesity Research* 9 (12): 788-805.

Puhl, Rebecca M., and Chelsea A. Heuer. 2009. The stigma of obesity: A review and update. *Obesity* 17 (5): 941-64.

Pullen, John Patrick, Casey Quackenbush, Jennifer Calfas, and Abigail Abrams. 2018. What to know about alleged Florida shooter Nikolas Cruz. Retrieved from http://time.com/5159134/who-is-the-florida-shooter-parkland-nicolas-cruz/.

Purdy, Jedediah. 2018. Normcore. Retrieved from www.dissentmagazine.org/article/normcore-trump-resistance-books-crisis-of-democracy.

Putnam, Robert D. 2000. *Bowling alone: The collapse and revival of American community.* New York: Simon & Schuster.

Putnam, Robert, and David E. Campbell. 2010. *American grace: How religion divides and unites us.* New York: Simon & Schuster.

Quan-Haase, Anabel, and Alyson L. Young. 2010. Uses and gratifications of social media: A comparison of Facebook and instant messaging. *Bulletin of Science, Technology & Society* 30: 350-61.

Quart, Alissa. 2016. Homework inequality: The value of having a parent around after school. *The Atlantic,* June 5.

Quillian, Lincoln. 2006. New approaches to understanding racial prejudice and discrimination. *Annual Review of Sociology* 32: 299-328.

Quillian, Lincoln, and Mary E. Campbell. 2003. Beyond black and white: The present and future of multiracial friendship segregation. *American Sociological Review* 68: 540-66.

Quillian, Lincoln, Devah Pager, Ole Hexel, and Arnfinn H. Midtbøen. 2017. Meta-analysis of field experiments shows no change in racial discrimination in hiring over time. *Proceedings of the National Academy of Sciences* 114 (41): 10870-75.

Quraishi-Landes, Asifa. 2016. Five myths about Sharia law. Retrieved from www.washingtonpost.com/opinions/five-myths-about-sharia/2016/06/24/7e3efb7a-31ef-11e6-8758-d58e76e11b12_story.html.

Radelet, Michael L., and Marian J. Borg. 2000. The changing nature of death penalty debates. *Annual Review of Sociology* 26: 43-61.

Radelet Michael L., and Traci L. Lacock. 2009. Do executions lower homicide rates? The views of leading criminologists. *Journal of Criminal Law and Criminology* 99 (2): 489-508.

Radford, Alexandria Walton. 2013. *Top student, top school?: How social class shapes where valedictorians go to college.* Chicago: University of Chicago Press.

Rainey, James. 2006. Aiming for a more subtle fighting force. *Los Angeles Times,* May 9, p. A1.

Rainie, Lee. 2016. The state of privacy in America: What we learned. Pew Research Center. Retrieved from www.pewresearch.org/fact-tank/2016/01/20/the-state-of-privacy-in-america/.

Rainie, Lee, and Maeve Duggan. 2016. Privacy and information sharing. Pew Research Center. January. www.pewinternet. org/files.

Rainie, Lee, and Barry Wellman. 2012. *Networked: The new social operating system.* Cambridge, MA: MIT Press.

Rao, Anupama. 2009. *The caste question: Dalits and the politics of modern India.* Berkeley: University of California Press.

Rasinski, Kenneth. 1989. The effect of question wording on public support for government spending. *Public Opinion Quarterly* 53: 388-94.

Ratcliff, Amanda Jo, Josh McCarty, and Matt Ritter. 2017. Religion and new media: A uses and gratifications approach. *Journal of Media and Religion* 16 (1): 15-26.

Rausch, Cassandra Christina. 2015. Fundamentalism and terrorism. *Journal of Terrorism Research* 6 (2).

Ravenscroft, Neil, and Paul Gilchrist. 2009. Spaces of transgression: Governance, discipline, and reworking the carnivalesque. *Leisure Studies* 28 (1): 35-49.

Ravitch, Diane. 2016. *The death and life of the great American school system.* New York: Basic Books.

Ray, Rebecca, Janet C. Gornick, and John Schmitt. 2009. Parental leave policies in 21 countries: Assessing generosity and gender equality. Washington, DC: Center for Economic and Policy Research. Retrieved from www.cepr.net/documents/publications/parental_2008_09.pdf.

Ray, Rebecca, Milla Sanes, and John Schmitt. 2013. No-vacation nation revisited." Washington, DC: Center for Economic and Policy Research. Retrieved from http://cepr.net/documents/publications/no-vacation-update-2013-05.pdf.

Raymen, Thomas, and Oliver Smith. 2016. What's deviance got to do with it? Black Friday sales, violence and hyper-conformity. *British Journal of Criminology* 56: 389-405.

Rectanus, Mark. 2002. *Culture incorporated: Museums, artists, and corporate sponsorships.* Minneapolis: University of Minnesota Press.

Rediker, Marcus. 2007. *The slave ship: A human history.* New York: Viking.

Redmon, David. 2003. Playful deviance as an urban leisure activity. *Deviant Behavior* 24 (1): 27-51.

Reed, Brian J., and David R. Segal. 2006. Social network analysis and counter-insurgency operations: The capture of Saddam Hussein. *Sociological Focus* 39 (4): 251-64.

Reed, Max. 2016. Donald Trump won because of Facebook. Retrieved from http://nymag.com/selectall/2016/11/donaldtrump-won-because-of-facebook.html.

Rees, Courtney, and Sonia Ruiz. 2003. Compendium of cultural competent initiatives in health care. Menlo Park, CA: Henry J. Kaiser Family

Foundation. Retrieved from www.kff.org/uninsured/loader.cfm?url=/commonspot/security/getfile.cfm&PageID=14365.

Reese, William J. 2011. *America's public schools: From the common school to "No Child Left Behind,"* updated ed. Baltimore, MD: Johns Hopkins University Press.

Rehel, Erin M. 2014. When dad stays home too: Paternity leave, gender, and parenting. *Gender & Society* 28 (1): 110–32.

Reich, Adam Dalton. 2014. *Selling our souls: The commodification of hospital care in the United States.* Princeton, NJ: Princeton University Press.

Reid, Joan A., Rachael A. Haskell, Christina Dillahunt-Aspillaga, and Jennifer A. Thor. 2013. Contemporary review of empirical and clinical studies of trauma bonding in violent or exploitative relationships. *International Journal of Psychology Research.* 8 (1): 37–73

Reilly, Katie. 2017. President Trump signs bill overturning internet privacy protections. Retrieved from http://time.com/4724128/donald-trump-internet-history-isp-privacy-browser-history/.

Reiman, Jeffrey, and Paul Leighton. 2017. *The rich get richer and the poor get prison,* 11th ed. New York: Routledge.

Reinharz, Shulamit. 1992. *Feminist methods in social research.* New York: Oxford University Press.

Remington, Patrick L., Bridget B. Catlin, and Keith P. Gennuso. 2015. The county health rankings: Rationale and methods. *Population Health Metrics* 13: 11. Retrieved from http://pophealthmetrics.biomedcentral.com/articles/10.1186/s12963-015-0044-2.

Renkema, Lennart J., Diederik A. Stapel, and Nico W. Van Yperen. 2008. Go with the flow: Conforming to others in the face of existential threat. *European Journal of Social Psychology* 38: 747–56.

Renzulli, Linda A., and Vincent J. Roscigno. 2011. Charter schools and the public good. In *The structure of schooling: Readings in the sociology of education,* ed. Richard Arum, Irenee R. Beattie, and Karly Ford, pp. 572–57. Los Angeles: Sage.

Rethinking Schools. 2013. The trouble with Common Core. *Rethinking Schools* 27 (4, Summer).

Revers, Matthias. 2014. The Twitterization of news making: Transparency and journalistic professionalism. *Journal of Communication* 64 (5): 806–26.

Rice, LaVon. 2007. Shameless lackey or consumer advocate? *Footnotes* (January): 7.

Richards, Anthony. 2015. *Conceptualizing terrorism.* New York: Oxford University Press.

Richeson, Jennifer A., Abigail A. Baird, Heather L. Gordon, Todd F. Heatherton, Carrie L. Wyland, Sophie Trawalter, and J. Nicole Shelton, 2003. An fMRI investigation of the impact of interracial contact on executive function. *Nature Neuroscience* 6 (12): 1323–28.

Rideout, Victoria J., Ulla G. Foehr, and Donald F. Roberts. 2010. *Generation M2: Media in the lives of 8- to 18-year olds.* Menlo Park, CA: Kaiser Family Foundation.

Riesebrodt, Martin. 2000. Fundamentalism and the resurgence of religion. *Numen* 47: 266–87.

Ríos, Merarys, Fabián Romero, and Roberto Ramírez. 2014. Race reporting among Hispanics: 2010. Washington, DC: Population Division, U.S. Census Bureau. Retrieved from www.census.gov/content/dam/Census/library/working-papers/2014/demo/ POP-twps0102.pdf.

Rios, Victor M., and Lisa Martino-Taylor. 2016. Documenting and participating in history in the making. *Berkeley Journal of Sociology.* Retrieved from http://berkeleyjournal.org/2016/03/documenting-and-participating-in-history-in-the-making/.

Rippen, Andrew. 2012. *Muslims: Their religious beliefs and practices.* New York: Routledge.

Risman, Barbara J., Carissa M. Froyum, and William J. Scarborough, eds. 2018. *Handbook of the sociology of gender,* 2nd ed. Cham, Switzerland: Springer Publishers.

Risman, Barbara, and Pepper Schwartz. 2002. After the sexual revolution: Gender politics in teen dating. *Contexts* 1 (1): 16–24.

Ritschard, Gilbert, Reto Burgin, and Reto Schumacher. 2017. Changes in the order of family life events in 20th-century Europe: A cross-regional perspective. *Historical Life Course Studies* 4: 41–58.

Ritzer, George. 1975. *Sociology: A multiple paradigm science.* Boston: Allyn & Bacon.

Ritzer, George. 2015. *The McDonaldization of society.* Thousand Oaks, CA: Sage.

Ritzer, George. 2019. *The McDonaldization of society: Into the digital age,* 9th ed. Los Angeles, CA: Sage.

Ritzer, George, and Paul Dean. 2015. *Globalization: A basic text.* Malden MA: Wiley.

Ritzer, George, and Jeffrey Stepinsky. 2014. *Sociological theory.* New York: McGraw-Hill.

Rivera, Lauren A. 2015. *Pedigree: How elite students get elite jobs.* Princeton, NJ: Princeton University Press.

Robert Wood Johnson Foundation. 2008. *Where we live matters for our health: The links between housing and health.* Issue Brief 2, September.

Robinson, Gene. 2010a. What does the Bible really say about homosexuality? *On Faith.* Retrieved from https://www.onfaith.co/onfaith/2010/12/06/what-does-the-bible-really-say-about-homosexuality.

Robinson, William I. 2014. *Global capitalism and the crisis of humanity.* New York: Cambridge University Press.

Robles, Frances, Kenan Davis, Sheri Fink, and Sarah Almukhtar. 2017. Official toll in Puerto Rico: 64. Actual deaths may be 1,052. Retrieved from www.nytimes.com/interactive/2017/12/08/us/puerto-rico-hurricane-maria-death-toll.html.

Rodman, Gilbert B., ed. 2014. *The race and media reader.* New York: Routledge.

Rodriguez, Nestor. 2004. Workers wanted: Employer recruitment of immigrant labor. *Work and Occupations* 31 (4): 453–73.

Roediger, David. 2007. *The wages of whiteness: Race and the making of the working class.* New York: Verso.

Roethlisberger, Fritz Jules. 1939. *Management and the worker.* Cambridge, MA: Harvard University Press.

Roettger, Michael E., Jason D. Boardman, Kathleen Mullan Harris, and Guang Guo. 2016. The association between the MAOA 2R genotype and delinquency over time among men: The interactive role of parental closeness and parental incarceration. *Criminal Justice and Behavior* 43 (8): 1076–94.

Rohter, Larry. 2006. Billboard ban in São Paulo angers advertisers. *New York Times,* December 12. Retrieved from www.nytimes.com/2006/12/12/world/americas/12iht-brazil.html.

Roper Center for Public Opinion Research. 2016. How groups voted 2016. Cornell University. Retrieved from https://ropercenter.cornell.edu/polls/us-elections/how-groups-voted/groups-voted-2016.

Roscigno, Vincent J., Lisa M. Williams, and Reginald A. Byron. 2012. Workplace racial discrimination and middle class vulnerability. *American Behavioral Scientist* 56 (5): 696–710.

Roscigno, Vincent J., Sherry Mong, Reginald Byron, and Griff Tester. 2007. Age discrimination, social closure and employment. *Social Forces* 86 (1): 313–34.

Roscoe, Will. 1992. *The Zuni woman-man.* Albuquerque: University of New Mexico Press.

Rose, Mike. 2004. *The mind at work.* New York: Penguin.

Rose, Tricia. 1994. *Black noise.* Wesleyan University Press.

Rosen, Eva. 2014. Rigging the rules of the game: How landlords geographically sort low-income renters. *City & Community* 13 (4): 310–40.

Ross, Benjamin. 2014. *Dead end: Suburban sprawl and the rebirth of American urbanism.* New York: Oxford University Press.

Rotenberg, Marc, Jeramie Scott, and Julia Horwitz, eds. 2015. *Privacy in the modern age: The search for solutions.* New York: New Press.

Rothenberg, Paula S. 2014. *Race, class, and gender in the United States,* 9th ed. New York: Worth.

Rothenberg, Paula S., ed. 2015. *White privilege: Essential readings on the other side of racism.* Boston: Worth.

Routhier, Ray. 2018. Maine high school students to join national walkout for gun control. Retrieved from www.pressherald.com/2018/03/12/maine-students-join-national-gun-control-movement-with-school-walkouts/.

Roy, Olivier. 2004. *Globalized Islam.* New York: Columbia University Press.

Roy, Olivier. 2007. *Secularism confronts Islam.* New York: Columbia University Press.

Roy, Olivier. 2013. *Holy ignorance: When religion and culture part ways.* New York: Oxford University Press.

Rubin, Beth A. 1996. *Shifts in the social contract.* Thousand Oaks, CA: Pine Forge Press.

Rubin, Beth A. 2012. Shifting social contracts and the sociological imagination. *Social Forces* 91: 327–46.

Rubin, Herbert J. and Irene S. Rubin. 2012. *Qualitative interviewing: The art of hearing data,* 3rd ed. Thousand Oaks, CA: Sage.

Rubin, J. Z., F. J. Provenzano, and Z. Luria. 1974. The eye of the beholder: Parents' views on sex of newborns. *American Journal of Orthopsychiatry* 44: 512–19.

Russell, Bertrand. 2004. *Power: A new social analysis.* New York: Routledge.

Ryan, Maureen, and Cynthia Littleton. 2017. TV series budgets hit the breaking point as costs skyrocket in peak TV era. Retrieved from http://variety.com/2017/tv/news/tv-series-budgets-costs-rising-peak-tv-1202570158/.

Sabella, Russell. 2012. Cyberbullying: How school counselors can help. In *Cyberbullying prevention and response: Expert perspectives,* ed. Justin W. Patchin and Sameer Hinduja, pp. 72–92. New York: Routledge.

Sabella, Russell A., Justin W. Patchin, and Sameer Hinduja. 2013. Cyberbullying myths and realities. *Computers in Human Behavior* 29: 2703–11.

Sabia, Joseph J. 2008. There's no place like home: A hazard model analysis of aging in place among older homeowners in the PSID. *Research on Aging* 30 (1): 3–35.

Sadian, Samuel. 2018. Consumer studies as critical social theory. *Social Science Information* 57 (2): 273-303.

Saez, Emmanuel. 2016. Striking it richer: The evolution of top incomes in the United States (updated with 2015 preliminary estimates). Retrieved from https://eml.berkeley.edu/~saez/saez-UStopincomes-2015.pdf.

Saez, Emmanuel, Raj Chetty, Nathan Hendren, and Patrick Kline. 2014. Where is the land of opportunity? The geography of intergenerational mobility in the United States. *Quarterly Journal of Economics* 129 (3): 1553–1623.

Sageman, Marc. 2008. A strategy for fighting international Islamist terrorists. *The ANNALS of the American Academy of Political and Social Science* 618 (1): 223–31.

Saguy, Abigail. 2013. *What's wrong with fat?* New York: Oxford University Press.

Sallie Mae. 2013. How America pays for college 2013. Retrieved from www.salliemae.com/assets/Core/how-America-pays/howamericapays2013.pdf.

SallieMae. 2016. Majoring in money: How American college students manage their finances. Retrieved from http://news.salliemae.com/research-tools/majoring-in-money.

Sandel, Michael J. 2013. *What money can't buy: The moral limits of markets.* New York: Farrar, Straus, and Giroux.

Sanders, Bernie. 2015. Prepared remarks: Senator Bernie Sanders on democratic socialism in the United States. November 19. Retrieved from https://berniesanders.com/democratic-socialism-in-the-united-states/.

Sapiro, Virginia. 2004. Not your parents' political socialization: Introduction for a new generation. *Annual Review of Political Science* 7: 1–23.

Sappleton, Natalie, ed. 2013. *Advancing research methods with new technologies.* Hershey, PA: Information Science Reference.

Sarracino, Carmine. 2009. *The porning of America.* Boston: Beacon Press.

Sassen, Saskia. 2019. *Cities in a world economy.* Thousand Oaks, CA: Sage.

Savage, Charlie. 2018. Senate, rebuffing privacy concerns, clears path to extend surveillance law. Retrieved from www.nytimes.com/2018/01/16/us/politics/senate-vote-section-702-fisa-amendments-surveillance.html.

Sawhill, Isabel V. 2013. Family structure: The growing importance of class. Washington, DC: Brookings Institute. Retrieved from www.brookings.edu/research/articles/2013/01/family-structure-class-sawhill.

Schafer, Amy. 2017. Generations of war: The rise of the warrior caste & the all-volunteer force. Washington, DC: Center for a New American Security. www.socalgrantmakers.org/sites/default/files/resources/CNASReport_GenerationsofWar-Final.pdf.

Scharf, Deepti. 2003. *Melanie Wood: The making of a mathematician.* Durham, NC: Duke University Office of News and Communications. Retrieved from www.dukenews.duke.edu/2003/05/melaniewood0503.html.

Scheerens, Jaap, Maria Hendriks and Hans Luyten. 2014. School size effects: Review and conceptual analysis. In *School size effects revisited*, ed. H. Luyten, M. Hendricks, and J. Scheerens, pp. 7–40. Cham, Switzerland: Springer.

Scheufele, Dietram A., and Patricia Moy. 2000. Twenty-five years of the spiral of silence: A conceptual review and empirical outlook. *International Journal of Public Opinion Research* 12 (1): 3–28.

Schiller, Herbert I. 1992. *Mass communications and American empire,* 2nd ed. Boulder, CO: Westview Press.

Schlaug, Gottfried. 2015. Musicians and music making as a model for the study of brain plasticity. In *Progress and brain research, volume 217,* ed. Eckart Altenmüller.

Schlesinger, Arthur. 1998. *The disuniting of America.* New York: Norton.

Schlesinger Jr., Arthur M. 2003. *The coming of the new deal, 1933–1935.* Boston: Houghton Mifflin.

Schlosberg, David. 2013. Theorising environmental justice: The expanding sphere of a discourse. *Environmental Politics* 22 (1): 37–55.

Schlozman, Kay, Henry Brady, and Sidney Verba. 2018. *Unequal and unrepresented: Political inequality and the people's voice in the new gilded age.* Princeton, NJ: Princeton University Press.

Schlozman, Kay Lehman, Sidney Verba, and Henry E. Brady. 2012. *The unheavenly chorus: Unequal political voice and the broken promise of American democracy.* Princeton, NJ: Princeton University Press.

Schmidt, Alvin. 1997. *The menace of multiculturalism.* Westport, CT: Praeger.

Schmitt, John, and Ben Zipperer. 2009. Dropping the ax: Illegal firings during union election campaigns. Washington, DC: Center for Economic and Policy Research. Retrieved from http://cepr.net/documents/publications/unions_2007_01.pdf.

Schnabel, Landon, and Sean Bock. 2017. The persistent and exceptional intensity of American religion: A response to recent research. *Sociological Science* 4: 686–700.

Schnaiberg, Allan. 1980. *The environment.* New York: Oxford University Press.

Schneiberg, Marc, Marissa King, and Thomas Smith. 2008. Social movements and organizational form: Cooperative alternatives to corporations in the American insurance, dairy, and grain industries. *American Sociological Review* 73: 635–67.

Schneider, Daniel, and Adam Reich. 2014. Marrying ain't hard when you got a union card? Labor union membership and first marriage. *Social Problems* 61 (4): 625–43.

Schneider, Joseph. 1978. Deviant drinking as a disease: Alcoholism as a social accomplishment. *Social Problems* 25 (4): 361–72.

Schneider, Michael. 2018. Peak TV tally: There were more shows than ever in 2017, which is why it's impossible to keep up. Retrieved from www.indiewire.com/2018/01/how-many-shows-on-tv-2017-fx-john-landgraf-tca-1201913645/.

Schneier, Bruce. 2015. *Data and Goliath: The hidden battles to collect your data and control your world.* New York: Norton.

Schor, Juliet. 1999. *The overspent American.* New York: Basic Books.

Schor, Juliet. 2004. *Born to buy: The commercialized child and the new consumer culture.* New York: Scribner.

Schor, Juliet. 2010. *True wealth.* New York: Penguin.

Schor, Juliet B. 2015. Getting sharing right. *Contexts* 14 (1): 14–15.

Schott Foundation for Public Education. 2017. *Resourcing movements: Philanthropy and advocacy partnerships to secure the opportunity to learn.* Cambridge, MA: Schott Foundation.

Schrag, Peter. 2010. *Not Fit for Our Society: Immigration and Nativism in America.* Berkeley: University of California Press.

Schrank, David, Bill Eisele, and Tim Lomax. 2012. *2012 urban mobility report.* College Station, TX: Texas A&M Transportation Institute. Retrieved from http://d2dtl5nnlpfr0r.cloudfront.net/tti.tamu.edu/documents/mobility-report-2012.pdf.

Schulz, Winfried. 2004. Reconstructing mediatization as an analytical concept. *European Journal of Communication* 19 (1): 87–101.

Schur, Edwin M. 1984. *Labeling women deviant.* New York: Random House.

Schutz, Alfred. 1962. *Collected papers: The problem of social reality,* ed. Maurice Natanson. The Hague: Martinus Nijhoff.

Schutzman, Nina. 2018. State math test opt-outs drop in local school districts. Retrieved from www.poughkeepsiejournal.com/story/news/education/2018/05/04/new-york-state-math-test-opt-outs-drop-local-districts/569631002/.

Schwartz, Raz, and Germaine R. Halegoua. 2015. The spatial self: Location-based identity performance on social media. *New Media & Society* 17 (10): 1643–60.

Schwartz, Shalom. 2017. Refined theory of values. In *Values and behavior*, ed. Sonia Roccas and Lilach Sagiv, pp. 51–72. Dordrecht, Netherlands: Springer.

Schwartz, Shalom H., Gian Vittorio Caprara, Michele Vecchione, Paul Bain, Gabriel Bianchi, Maria Giovanni Caprara, Jan Cieciuch, et al. 2014. Basic personal values underlie and give coherence to political values: A cross national study in 15 countries. *Political Behavior* 36 (4): 899–930.

Schwartz, Shalom, Gian Vittorio Caprara, and Michele Vecchione. 2010. Basic personal values, core political values, and voting: A longitudinal study. *Political Psychology* 31: 421–452.

Schwartz, Shalom H., Gila Melech, Arielle Lehmann, Steven Burgess, Mari Harris, and Vicki Owens. 2001. Extending the cross-cultural validity of the theory of basic human values with a different method of measurement. *Journal of Cross-Cultural Psychology* 32: 519–42.

Schwedler, Jillian. 2006. *Faith in moderation.* New York: Cambridge University Press.

Schworm, Peter. 2015. SAT losing favor as more Mass. colleges end requirement. *Boston Globe,* November 6. Retrieved from www.bostonglobe.com/metro/2015/11/05/more-mass-colleges-foregoing-sat/7fBsxwseXxVetpEY0zzunO/story.html.

Scott, James. 1987. *Weapons of the weak.* New Haven, CT: Yale University Press.

Scott, James C. 1992. *Domination and the arts of resistance.* New Haven, CT: Yale University Press.

Scott, James C. 2017. *Against the grain: A deep history of the earliest states.* New Haven, CT: Yale University Press.

Scott, Joan Wallach. 2010. *The Politics of the Veil.* Princeton, NJ: Princeton University Press.

Scott, John. 2012. *Social network analysis.* Thousand Oaks, CA: SAGE Publications.

Scott, Robert E. 2015. Globalization lowers the wages of U.S. workers. Economic Policy Institute. Retrieved from www.epi.org/publication/unfair-trade-deals-lower-the-wages-of-u-s-workers/.

Scott, Robert E. 2015. Manufacturing job loss: Trade, not productivity, is the culprit. Economic Policy Institute. Retrieved from www.epi.org/publication/manufacturing-job-loss-trade-not-productivity-is-the-culprit/.

Scott-Clayton, Judith. 2011. The shapeless river: Does a lack of structure inhibit students' progress at community colleges? (CCRC Working Paper No. 25). Community College Research Center. New York: Columbia University Teachers College. Retrieved from http://ccrc.tc.columbia.edu/publications/lack-of-structure-students-progress.html.

Seaman, Julia E., I. Elaine Allen, and Jeff Seaman. 2018. Grade increase: Tracking distance education in the United States. Babson Survey Research Group.

Segel-Karpas, Dikla, Liat Ayalon, and Margie E. Lachman. 2018. Loneliness and depressive symptoms: The moderating role of the transition into retirement. *Aging & Mental Health* 22 (1): 135–40.

Seib, Philip, and Dana M. Janbek. 2011. *Global terrorism and new media*. New York: Routledge.

Seidman, Steven, ed. 1996. *Queer theory/sociology.* Malden, MA: Blackwell.

Seidman, Steven. 2015. *The social construction of sexuality.* New York: Norton.

Sennett, Richard. 2006. *The culture of the new capitalism.* New Haven, CT: Yale University Press.

Senter, Mary S., Nicole Van Vooren, and Roberta Spalter-Roth. 2013. Sociology majors: Before graduation in 2012. Washington, DC: American Sociological Association. Retrieved from www.asanet.org/documents/research/pdfs/BachBeyond_Sociology_Majors_Brief_2013.pdf.

Shaheen, Jack G. 2009. *Reel bad Arabs: How Hollywood vilifies a people.* Northhampton, MA: Olive Branch Press.

Shakya, Holly B. and Nicholas A. Christakis. 2017. Association of Facebook use with compromised well-being: A longitudinal study. *American Journal of Epidemiology* 185 (3): 203–11.

Shanahan, Michael J. 2000. Pathways to adulthood in changing societies: Variability and mechanisms in life course perspective. *Annual Review of Sociology* 26: 667–92.

Shanahan, Michael J., and Scott M. Hofer. 2005. Social context in gene-environment interactions: Retrospect and prospect. *Journals of Gerontology, Series B* 60 (March): 65 (12).

Shanahan, Michael J., Jeylan T. Mortimer, and Monica Kirkpatrick Johnson, eds. 2016. *Handbook of the life course, volume II.* New York: Springer International Publishing.

Shapiro, Thomas, Tatjana Meschede, and Sam Osoro. 2013. *The roots of the widening racial wealth gap: Explaining the black-white economic divide.* Waltham, MA: Brandeis University, Institute on Assets and Social Policy. Retrieved from http://iasp.brandeis.edu/pdfs/Author/shapiro-thomas-m/racialwealthgapbrief.pdf.

Sharp, Gene. 1973a. *Power and struggle.* Boston: Porter Sargent.

Sharp, Gene. 1973b. *The politics of nonviolent action, Parts 1-3.* Boston, MA: Porter Sargent.

Sharp, Gene. 2010. *From dictatorship to democracy.* Boston: Albert Einstein Institute. Retrieved from www.aeinstein.org/organizations/org/fdtd.pdf.

Sharp, Gregory, and Matthew Hall. 2014. Emerging forms of racial inequality in homeownership exit, 1968–2009. *Social Problems* 61 (3): 427–47.

Sheehan, James. 2008. *Where have all the soldiers gone?* New York: Houghton Mifflin.

Sherkat, Darren E. 2014. *Changing faith: The dynamics and consequences of Americans' shifting religious identities.* New York: New York University Press.

Sherkat, Darren E. 2017. Religion, politics, and Americans' confidence in science. *Politics and Religion* 10 (1): 137–60.

Sherwood, Jessica Holden. 2010. *Wealth, whiteness, and the matrix of privilege.* Lanham, MD: Rowman and Littlefield.

Shontell, Alyson. 2016. This photographer takes $150,000 portraits of Silicon Valley's most powerful people. *Business Insider,* January 20. Retrieved from www.businessinsider.com/kevin-abosch-career-art-and-famous-portraits-2016-1.

Siebold, Guy L. 2001. Core issues and theory in military sociology. *Journal of Political and Military Sociology* 29 (1): 140–59.

Silicon Valley Institute for Regional Studies. 2015. Poverty in the San Francisco Bay Area. Retrieved from www.jointventure.org/images/stories/pdf/poverty-brief-2015-03.pdf.

Simi, Pete, and Robert Futrell. 2015. *American swastika: Inside the white power movement's hidden spaces of hate,* 2nd ed. Lanham, MD: Rowman & Littlefield.

Simmel, Georg. (1903) 1950. The metropolis and mental life. In *The sociology of Georg Simmel,* trans. and ed., Kurt H. Wolff. New York: Free Press.

Simmel, Georg. (1922) 1955. *Conflict & the web of group affiliations,* trans. and ed. Kurt H. Wolff and Reinhard Bendix. New York: Free Press.

Simmel, Georg. (1908) 1964. *The sociology of Georg Simmel,* trans. Kurt H. Wolff. New York: Free Press.

Simpson, Miles. 1990. Political rights and income inequality: A cross-national test. *American Sociological Review* 55 (October): 682–93.

Simpson, Tim. 2008. The commercialization of Macau's cafes. *Ethnography* 9 (2): 197–234.

Singer, Natasha. 2018. What you don't know about how Facebook uses your data. Retrieved from www.nytimes.com/2018/04/11/technology/facebook-privacy-hearings.html.

Singh, Diana, and Paul Glavin. 2017. An occupational portrait of emotional labor requirements and their health consequences for workers. *Work and Occupations* 44 (4): 424–66.

Sinozich, Sofi, and Lynn Langton. 2014. Rape and sexual assault victimization among college-age females, 1995–2013. Washington, DC: U.S. Department of Justice, Bureau of Justice Statistics. Retrieved from www.bjs.gov/content/pub/pdf/rsavcaf9513.pdf.

Sisson, Patrick. 2017. New high-end developments bring the city to the suburbs. Retrieved from www.curbed.com/2017/1/31/14452382/real-estate-development-suburb-community-city-center.

Slater, Don. 1999. *Consumer culture and modernity.* Malden, MA: Polity/Blackwell.

Slavin, Robert E., Nancy Madden, Margarita Calderon, Anne Chamberlain, and Megan Hennessy. 2010. *Reading and language outcomes of a five-year randomized evaluation of transitional bilingual education.* Baltimore, MD: Johns Hopkins University.

Sloan, Allan. 2007. House of junk: Junk mortgages under the microscope. *Fortune,* July 29.

Slutskaya, Natasha, Ruth Simpson, Jason Hughes, Alexander Simpson, and Selçuk Uygur. 2016. Masculinity and class in the context of dirty work. *Gender, Work & Organization* 23 (2): 165–82.

Smedley, Audrey, and Brian D. Smedley. 2012. *Race in North America: Origin and evolution of a worldview.* Boulder, CO: Westview Press.

Smith, Aaron, and Monica Anderson. 2018, March 1. *Social media use in 2018.* Pew Research Center.

Smith, Aaron, and Kenneth Olmstead. 2018. Declining majority of online adults say the internet has been good for society. Washington, DC: Pew Research Center. http://assets.pewresearch.org/wp-content/uploads/sites/14/2018/04/27165144/PI_2018.04.30_Internet-Good-Bad_FINAL.pdf.

Smith, Adam. (1776) 1994. *The Wealth of Nations.* (Edited with an introduction and notes by Edwin Cannan.) New York: Random House.

Smith, Christian, ed. 2003. *The secular revolution.* Berkeley: University of California Press.

Smith, David Norman, and Eric Hanley. 2018. The anger games: Who voted for Donald Trump in the 2016 election, and why? *Critical Sociology* 44 (2): 195–212.

Smith, Dorothy. 1974. Women's perspective as a radical critique of sociology. *Sociological Inquiry* 44: 7–14.

Smith, Dorothy. 1989. *The everyday world as problematic: A feminist sociology.* Boston: Northeastern University Press.

Smith, Dorothy. 1990. *The conceptual practices of power.* Boston: Northeastern University Press.

Smith, Eliot R., and James R. Kluegel. 1986. *Beliefs about inequality.* Hawthorne, NY: Aldine Transaction.

Smith, Keri E. Iyall, ed. 2013. *Sociology of globalization: Cultures, economies, and politics.* Boulder, CO: Westview Press.

Smith, Oliver, and Thomas Raymen. 2018. Deviant leisure: A criminological perspective. *Theoretical Criminology* 22 (1): 63–82.

Smith, Sharon. 2015. *Women and socialism.* Chicago: Haymarket Books.

Smith, Stacy L., Marc Choueiti, and Katherine Pieper. 2016. Inclusion or invisibility? Comprehensive Annenberg Report on Diversity in Entertainment. Annenberg School for Communication, University of Southern California. http://annenberg.usc.edu/sites/default/files/2017/04/07/MDSCI_CARD_Report_FINAL_Exec_Summary.pdf.

Smith, Tom W. 2007. *Job satisfaction in the United States.* Chicago: NORC/University of Chicago.

Smith, Vincent. 2015. Should Washington end agriculture subsidies? *Wall Street Journal,* July 12. Retrieved from www.wsj.com/articles/should-washington-end-agriculture-subsidies-1436757020.

Smith-Lovin, Lynn, and Miller McPherson. 1993. You are who you know: A network perspective on gender. In *Theory on gender. Feminism on theory,* ed. Paula England, pp. 223–51. New York: Aldine.

Snelson, Chareen, Christopher I. Wertz, Kimberly Onstott, and Jason Bader. 2017. Using World of Warcraft to teach research methods in online doctoral education. *The Qualitative Report* 22 (5): 1439–56.

Snow, David A., and Robert D. Benford. 1988. Ideology, frame resonance, and participant mobilization. In *International social movement research,* pp. 197–217. Greenwich, CT: JAI Press.

Snow, David A., E. Burke Rochford Jr., Steven K. Worden, and Robert D. Benford. 1986. Frame alignment processes, micromobilization, and movement participation. *American Sociological Review* 51: 464–81.

Snyder, Timothy. 2017. *On tyranny: Twenty lessons from the twentieth century.* New York: Penguin Random House.

Social Security Board of Trustees. 2016. *The 2016 annual report of the Board of Trustees of the Federal Old-Age and Survivors Insurance and Federal Disability Insurance trust funds.* Washington, DC: U.S. Government Publishing Office. Retrieved from www.ssa.gov/oact/tr/2016/tr2016.pdf.

Sonne, Paul. 2018. Pentagon: "No one will ever know" how many civilians U.S. has killed in fight against ISIS. Retrieved from www .washingtonpost.com/world/national-security/pentagonno-one-will-ever-know-how-many-civilians-us-has-killed-in-fight-against-isis/2018/06/05/4b3fec30-6900-11e8-bbc5-dc9f3634fa0a_story.html.

Sorkin, Andrew. 2010. *Too big to fail: The inside story of how Wall Street and Washington fought to save the financial system—and themselves.* New York: Viking.

Spahlholz, S., N. Baer, H.-H. Konig, S.G. Riedel-Heller, and C. Luck-Sirorski. 2016. Obesity and discrimination—A systematic review and meta-analysis of observational studies. *Obesity Reviews* 17 (1): 43–55.

Spaiser, Viktoria, Thomas Chadefaux, Karsten Donnay, Fabian Russmann, and Dirk Helbing. 2017. Communication power struggles on social media: A case study of the 2011–12 Russian protests. *Journal of Information Technology & Politics* 14 (2): 132–53.

Spalter-Roth, Roberta, and Nicole Van Vooren. 2008. *What are they doing with a bachelor's degree in sociology?* Washington, DC: American Sociological Association.

Spalter-Roth, Roberta, Nicole Van Vooren, and Mary Senter. 2014. *Recent sociology alumni: Would they major again?* Washington, DC: American Sociological Association.

Spencer, Wayne. 2003. Are the stars coming out? Secularization and the future of astrology. In *Predicting religion: Christian, secular and alternative futures,* ed. Grace Davie, Paul Heelas, and Linda Woodhead, pp. 214–28. Burlington, VT: Ashgate.

Spielman, Fran. 2018. ACLU sounds the alarm about bill allowing use of drones to monitor protesters. Retrieved from https://chicago.suntimes.com/politics/aclu-sounds-the-alarm-about-bill-allowing-use-of-drones-to-monitor-protesters/.

Springer, Simon, Kean Birch, and Julie MacLeavy, eds. 2016. *The handbook of neoliberalism.* New York: Routledge.

Squires, Catherine. 2009. *African Americans and the media.* Malden, MA: Polity Press.

Squires, Gregory D., Samantha Friedman, and Catherine E. Saidat. 2002. Experiencing residential segregation: A contemporary study of Washington, DC. *Urban Affairs Review* 38 (2): 155–84.

St. John, Edward P., Shouping Hu, and Amy S. Fisher. 2011. *Breaking through the access barrier: How academic capital formation can improve policy in higher education.* New York: Routledge.

Staats, Cheryl, Kelly Capatosto, Robin A. Wright, and Danya Contractor. 2015. State of the science: Implicit bias review 2014. Columbus: Kirwan Institute, Ohio State University. Retrieved from http://kirwaninstitute.osu.edu/wp-content/uploads/2015/05/2015-kirwan-implicit-bias.pdf.

Staggenborg, Suzanne. 2016. *Social movements.* New York: Oxford University Press.

Stainback, Kevin, Sibyl Kleiner, and Sheryl Skaggs. 2016. Women in power: Undoing or redoing the gendered organization? *Gender & Society* 30 (1): 109–35.

Stampnitzky, Lisa. 2013. *Disciplining terror: How experts invented "terrorism."* New York: Cambridge University Press.

Stanton, Elizabeth Cady. 1889. *A history of woman suffrage,* vol. 1. Rochester, NY: Fowler and Wells. Retrieved from www. fordham.edu/halsall/mod/Senecafalls.html.

Stark, Rodney. 1999. Secularization RIP. *Sociology of Religion* 60: 249–73.

Stark, Rodney, and William Sims Bainbridge. 1996. *A theory of religion.* New Brunswick, NJ: Rutgers University Press.

Stark, Rodney, and William Sims Bainbridge. 1985. *The future of religion: Secularization, revival, and cult formation.* Berkeley: University of California Press.

Starr, Paul. 1983. *The social transformation of American medicine.* New York: Basic Books.

Starr, Paul. 2013. *Remedy and reaction: The peculiar American struggle over health care reform.* New Haven, CT: Yale University Press.

Starr, Paul. 2018, February 4. A new strategy for health care. American Prospect. http://prospect.org/article/new-strategy-health-care.

Steger, Manfred B. 2017. *Globalization: A very short introduction.* New York: Oxford University Press.

Stein, Ben. 2006. In class warfare, guess which class is winning. *New York Times,* November 26. Retrieved from www.nytimes.com/2006/11/26/business/yourmoney/26every.html.

Steinberg, Brian. 2017. Walking Dead zombies shamble forward for Mountain Dew. Retrieved from https://variety.com/2017/tv/news/walking-dead-mountain-dew-amc-advertising-1202548606/.

Steiner, Frederick R. 2016. *Human ecology: How nature and culture shape our world.* Washington, DC: Island Press.

Stelmach, Aleksandra, and Brigitte Nerlich. 2015. Metaphors in search of a target: The curious case of epigenetics. *New Genetics and Society* 34 (2): 196–218.

Stemple, Lara, and Ilan H. Meyer. 2014. The sexual victimization of men in America: New data challenge old assumptions. *American Journal of Public Health* 104 (6): 19–26.

Stepler, Renee. 2016. Smaller share of women ages 65 and older are living alone. Pew Research Center. Retrieved from www.pewsocialtrends.org/2016/02/18/smaller-share-of-women-ages-65-and-older-are-living-alone/.

Sterngold, James. 2010. How much did Lehman CEO Dick Fuld really make? *Bloomberg Businessweek,* April 29. Retrieved from www .businessweek.com/print/magazine/content/10_19/b4177056214833.htm.

Sternheimer, Karen. 2018. *The social scientist's soapbox: Adventures in writing public sociology.* New York: Routledge.

Stevens, Mitchell. 2007. *Creating a class: College admissions and the education of elites.* Cambridge, MA: Harvard University Press.

Stewart, David W., and Prem N. Shamdasani. 2015. *Focus groups: Theory and practice,* 3rd ed. Thousand Oaks, CA: Sage.

Stiglitz, Joseph, and Andrew Charlton. 2007. *Fair trade for all.* New York: Oxford University Press.

Stock, Christianne, and Anne Ellaway. 2013. *Neighbourhood structure and health promotion.* New York: Springer.

Stockholm International Peace Research Institute (SIPRI). 2018. SIPRI military expenditure database. www.sipri.org/databases/milex.

Stohlberg, Carol Gay. 2011. Shy U.S. intellectual created playbook used in a revolution. *New York Times,* February 16. Retrieved from www.nytimes.com/2011/02/17/world/middleeast/17sharp.html.

Stoller, Robert. 1968. *Sex and gender: On the development of masculinity and femininity.* New York: Science House.

Storey, John. 2015. *Cultural theory and popular culture: An introduction.* New York: Routledge.

Strangleman, Tim, and James Rhodes. 2014. The "new" sociology of deindustrialisation? Understanding industrial change. *Sociology Compass* 8 (4): 411–421.

Strasburger, Victor C., and Barbara J. Wilson. 2002. *Children, adolescents, and the media.* Thousand Oaks, CA: Sage.

Strasburger, Victor C., Barbara J. Wilson, and Amy B. Jordan. 2009. *Children, adolescents, and the media,* 2nd ed. Thousand Oaks, CA: Sage.

Sublette, Ned, and Constance Sublette. 2016. *The American slave coast: A history of the slave-breeding industry.* Chicago: Chicago Review Press.

Suchman, Mark C. 2015. Organizations and the law. In *International encyclopedia of the social & behavioral sciences,* 2nd ed., vol. 17, pp. 397–404. Elsevier. Retrieved from http://dx.doi.org/10.1016/B978-0-08-097086-8.86089-4.

Sullivan, Dennis, and Larry Tifft. 2006. *Handbook of restorative justice: A global perspective.* New York: Routledge.

Sullivan, John, Reis Thebault, Julie Tate, and Jennifer Jenkins. 2017. Number of fatal shootings by police is nearly identical to last year. Retrieved from www.washingtonpost.com/investigations/number-of-fatal-shootings-by-police-is-nearly-identical-to-last-year/2017/07/01/98726cc6-5b5f-11e7-9fc6-c7ef4bc58d13_story.html.

Summers, Alicia, and Monica K. Miller. 2014. From damsels in distress to sexy superheroes. *Feminist Media Studies* 14 (6): 1028–40.

Sumner, William Graham. 1906. *Folkways.* Boston: Ginn.

Sundar, S. Shyam, and Anthony M. Limperos. 2013. Uses and grats 2.0: New gratifications for new media. *Journal of Broadcasting & Electronic Media* 57 (4): 504–25.

Sung, Jihyun, Anne Fausto-Sterling, Cynthia Garcia Coll, and Ronald Seifer. 2013. The dynamics of age and sex in the development of mother–infant vocal communication between 3 and 11 months. *Infancy* 18 (6): 1135–58.

Sunstein, Cass. 2017. *#Republic: Divided democracy in the age of social media.* Princeton, NJ: Princeton University Press.

Sussman, Robert Wald. 2014. *The myth of race: The troubling persistence of an unscientific idea.* Cambridge, MA: Harvard University Press.

Sutherland, Edwin H. 1947. *Principles of criminology,* 4th ed. Philadelphia: Lippincott.

Sutherland, Edwin H. 1949. *White collar crime.* New York: Dryden Press.

Sutherland, Edwin H., Donald R. Cressey, and David F. Luckenbill. 1992. *Principles of Criminology,* 11th edition. Lanham, MD: Rowman & Littlefield.

Sutter, John D. 2015. The argument for a basic income. CNN. Retrieved from www.cnn.com/2015/03/01/opinion/sutter-basic-income/.

Swedberg, Richard. 2018. Folk economics and its role in Trump's presidential campaign: An exploratory study. *Theory and Society* 47: 1–36. doi:10.1007/s11186-018-9308-8.

Sweeney, Megan. 2016. Socioeconomic standing and variability in marriage timing in the twentieth century. *The Annals of the American Academy of Political and Social Science* 663 (1): 270–91.

Switzer, Kathrine. 2007. *Marathon woman.* New York: Carroll & Graf.

Syme, S. Leonard, and Lisa F. Berkman. 1976. Social class, susceptibility, and sickness. *American Journal of Epidemiology* 104: 1–8.

Szasz, Andrew. 2007. *Shopping our way to safety: How we changed from protecting the environment to protecting ourselves.* Minneapolis: University of Minnesota Press.

Szasz, Andrew. 2011. Is green consumption part of the solution? In *The Oxford Handbook of Climate Change and Society,* ed. John S. Dryzek, Richard B. Norgaard, and David Schlosberg, pp. 594–608. New York: Oxford University Press.

Tahirih Justice Center. 2011. About us. Retrieved from www.tahirih.org/about-us/.

Takaki, Ronald. 2008. *A different mirror: A history of multicultural America.* New York: Back Bay Books.

Talbot, Richard P., and Jon T. Oplinger. 2014. Social stratification and ethnic mobilization: U.S. military deaths in Southeast Asia. *Race, Gender & Class* 21 (1/2): 195–210.

Taley, Margaret. 2006. When nature calls, women in House hike. *Denver Post,* December 12. Retrieved from www.denverpost.com/rockies/ci_4911077.

Taormino, Tristan. 2013. Introduction: The politics of producing pleasure. In *The feminist porn book,* ed. Tristan Taormino, Constance Penley, Celine Parrenas Shimizu, and Mireille Miller-Young, pp. 9–20. New York: Feminist Press at the City University of New York.

Tarrow, Sidney. 2011. *Power in movement.* New York: Cambridge University Press.

Tax Policy Center. 2017a. Historical highest marginal income tax rates. Retrieved from www.taxpolicycenter.org/statistics/historical-highest-marginal-income-tax-rates.

Tax Policy Center. 2017b. Distributional analysis of the conference agreement for the Tax Cuts and Jobs Act. Retrieved from www.taxpolicycenter.org/publications/distributional-analysis-conference-agreement-tax-cuts-and-jobs-act/full.

Taylor, Alan. 2001. *American colonies: The settling of North America.* New York: Penguin.

Taylor, Dorceta. 2014. *Toxic communities: Environmental racism, industrial pollution, and residential mobility.* New York: New York University Press.

Taylor, Frederick Winslow. 1911. *The principles of scientific management.* New York: Harper Brothers.

Taylor, Verta. 1989. Social movement continuity: The women's movement in abeyance. *American Sociological Review* 54 (5): 761–75.

Taylor, Verta, Leila Rupp, and Nancy Whittier, eds. 2012. *Feminist frontiers.* New York: McGraw-Hill.

Teichman, Yona. 2016. Stereotypes and prejudice in conflict: A developmental perspective. In *A social psychology perspective on the Israeli-Palestinian conflict,* ed. Keren Sharvit and Eran Halperin, pp. 17–30. New York: Springer International.

Teixeira, Ruy, and John Halpin. 2013. Building an all-in nation. Washington, DC: Center for American Progress. Retrieved from www.americanprogress.org/wp-content/uploads/2013/10/AllInNationReport.pdf.

Telles, Edward, and the Project on Ethnicity and Race in Latin America. 2014. *Pigmentocracies: Ethnicity, race, and color in Latin America.* Chapel Hill: University of North Carolina Press.

TenHouten, Warren D. 1980. Social dominance and cerebral hemisphericity: Discriminating social groups by performance on two lateralized tests. *International Journal of Neuroscience* 10: 223–32.

TenHouten, Warren D. 1999. Text and temporality: Patterned-cyclical and ordinary-linear forms of time consciousness, inferred from a corpus of Australian Aboriginal and Euro-Australian life-historical interviews. *Symbolic Interaction* 22: 121–37.

Tharenou, Phyllis. 2013. The work of feminists is not yet done: The gender pay gap—a stubborn anachronism. *Sex Roles* 68 (3): 198–206.

The Economist. 2017. The world's most valuable resource is no longer oil, but data. Retrieved from www.economist.com/leaders/2017/05/06/the-worlds-most-valuable-resource-is-no-longer-oil-but-data.

The Grio. 2011. DNA used to reveal MLK and Garvey's European lineage. Retrieved from https://thegrio.com/2011/01/13/dna-used-to-reveal-mlk-and-garveys-african-lineage/.

The Lancet Commission. 2018. The Lancet Commission on pollution and health. *Lancet* 391: 462–512.

The Local. 2015. Spanish town brings in compulsory siesta law. July 16. Retrieved from www.thelocal.es/20150716/siesta-made-compulsory-by-law-in-spain.

The Sentencing Project. 2015. Fact sheet: Incarcerated women and girls. Washington, DC: Bureau of Justice Statistics. November. Retrieved from www.sentencingproject.org

Thomas, Sarah. 2010. Students, teachers agog at New Newton North High School. Retrieved from www.boston.com/yourtown/news/newton/2010/08/students_leaders_agog_at_new_n.html.

Thomas, William I., and Dorothy Swain Thomas. 1928. *The child in America: Behavior problems and programs.* New York: Knopf.

Thomeer, Mieke Beth, Rachel Donnelly, Corinne Reczek, and Debra Umberson. 2017. Planning for future care and the end of life: A qualitative analysis of gay, lesbian, and heterosexual couples. *Journal of Health and Social Behavior* 58 (4): 473–87.

Thompson, David. 2013. Suburban sprawl: Exposing hidden costs, identifying innovations. Ottawa, ON: Sustainable Prosperity. http://thecostofsprawl.com/report/SP_SuburbanSprawl_Oct2013_opt.pdf.

Thorpe, Rebecca U. 2014. *The American warfare state: The domestic politics of military spending.* Chicago: University of Chicago Press.

Thrasher, Frederick Milton. 1927. *The gang.* Chicago: University of Chicago Press.

Tilly, Charles. 2004a. *Social movements 1768–2004.* Boulder, CO: Paradigm.

Tilly, Charles. 2004b. Terror, terrorism, terrorists. *Sociological Theory* 22 (1): 5–13.

Tilly, Charles, and Sid Tarrow. 2015. *Contentious politics.* New York, NY: Oxford University Press.

Timberg, Craig, and Drew Harwell. 2018. We studied thousands of anonymous posts about the Parkland attack—and found a conspiracy in the making. Retrieved from www.washingtonpost.com/business/economy/we-studied-thousands-of-anonymous-posts-about-the-parkland-attack—and-found-a-conspiracy-in-the-making/2018/02/27/04a856be-1b20-11e8-b2d9-08e748f892c0_story.html.

Tirman, John. 2016. *Immigration and the American backlash.* Cambridge, MA: MIT Press.

Tolson, A. 1977. *The limits of masculinity.* London: Tavistock.

Tomlinson, John. 2008. *Cultural imperialism: A critical introduction.* London: Continuum.

Tönnies, Ferdinand. (1887) 2001. *Community and civil society,* trans. Margaret Hollis. Cambridge, UK: University of Cambridge Press.

Toossi, Mitra. 2002. A century of change: The U.S. labor force, 1950–2050. *Monthly Labor Review.* Washington, DC: Bureau of Labor Statistics. Retrieved from www.bls.gov/opub/mlr/2002/05/art2full.pdf.

Toth, Federico. 2016. Classification of healthcare systems: Can we go further? *Health Policy* 120 (5): 535–43.

Trenberth, Kevin E., Lijing Cheng, Peter Jacobs, Yongxin Zhang, and John Fasullo. 2018. Hurricane Harvey links to ocean heat content and climate change adaptation. Earth's Future. Retrieved from https://doi.org/10.1029/2018EF000825.

Truth and Reconciliation Commission of Canada. 2015. Honouring the truth, reconciling for the future: Summary of the final report of the Truth and Reconciliation Commission of Canada. Retrieved from www.trc.ca/websites/trcinstitution/File/2015/Findings/Exec_Summary_2015_05_31_web_o.pdf.

Tufecki, Zeynep. 2018. YouTube, the great radicalizer. Retrieved from www.nytimes.com/2018/03/10/opinion/sunday/youtube-politics-radical.html.

Tumin, Melvin. 1953. Some principles of stratification: A critical analysis. *American Sociological Review* 18: 387–94.

Turkle, Sherry. 1995. *Life on the screen.* New York: Simon & Schuster.

Turkle, Sherry. 2011. *Alone together: Why we expect more from technology and less from each other.* New York: Basic Books.

Turkle, Sherry. 2015. *Reclaiming conversation: The power of talk in a digital age.* New York: Penguin.

Turner, Jonathan. 2000. *On the origins of human emotions: A sociological inquiry into the evolution of human affect.* Stanford, CA: Stanford University Press.

Turner, Jonathan H., and Richard S. Machalek. 2018. *The new evolutionary sociology: Recent and revitalized theoretical and methodological approaches.* New York: Routledge.

Turner, Margery Austin, and Stephen L. Ross. 2005. How racial discrimination affects the search for housing. In *The geography of opportunity,* ed. Xaviar de Souza Briggs, pp. 81–100. Washington, DC: Brookings Institution Press.

Turow, Joseph. 2006. *Niche envy: Marketing discrimination in the digital age.* Cambridge, MA: MIT Press.

Turow, Joseph, Jennifer King, Chris Jay Hoofnagle, Amy Bleakley, and Michael Hennessy. 2009. Contrary to what marketers say, Americans reject tailored advertising and three activities that enable it. Retrieved from http://papers.ssrn.com/sol3/papers.cfm?abstract_id=1478214.

Turow, Joseph. 2017. *The aisles have eyes: How retailers track your shopping, strip your privacy, and define your power.* New Haven, CT: Yale University Press.

Tweedie, Dale. 2013. Making sense of insecurity. *Work, Employment, and Society* 27 (1): 94–104.

Twenge, Jean M. 2014. *Generation me.* New York: Atria/Simon & Schuster.

Twenge, Jean M., Ryne A. Sherman, and Brooke E. Wells. 2016. Changes in American adults' reported same-sex sexual experiences and attitudes, 1973–2014. *Archives of Sexual Behavior* doi:10.1007/s10508-016-0769-4

Twenty-First Century Fox. 2017. 2017 annual report. www.21cf.com/investor-relations/annual-reports.

Twitter. 2017. Twitter transparency report. www.transparency.twitter.com.

Twitter. 2018. Twitter for websites supported languages. https://dev.twitter.com/web/overview/languages.

Tyler, T. R. 2005. Introduction: Legitimating ideologies. *Social Justice Research* 18: 211–15.

Tyler, T. R., and S. L. Blader. 2003. The group engagement model: Procedural justice, social identity, and cooperative behavior. *Personality and Social Psychology Review* 7: 349–61.

Tynan, Dan. 2008. Thank you, porn! 12 ways the sex trade has changed the web. *PC World.* Retrieved from www.pcworld.com/article/155745/porn_on_the_web.html.

Tyson, Alec, and Shiva Maniam. 2016. Behind Trump's victory: Divisions by race, gender, education. Retrieved from www.pewresearch.org/fact-tank/2016/11/09/behind-trumps-victory-divisions-by-race-gender-education/.

U.N. Office on Drugs and Crime. 2016. Global report on trafficking in persons, 2106. Retrieved from www.unodc.org/documents/data-and-analysis/glotip/2016_Global_Report_on_Trafficking_in_Persons.pdf.

U.S. Bureau of Labor Statistics. 2015a. May 2014 national occupational employment and wage estimates, United States. Retrieved from www.bls.gov/oes/current/oes_nat.htm#00-0000.

U.S. Bureau of Labor Statistics. 2015b. Highlights of women's earnings in 2014. BLS Report 1058. Retrieved from www.bls.gov/opub/reports/womens-earnings/archive/highlights-of-womens-earnings-in-2014.pdf.

U.S. Bureau of Labor Statistics. 2016a. Injuries, illnesses, and fatalities. Retrieved from www.bls.gov/iif/.

U.S. Bureau of Labor Statistics. 2016b. Occupations with the most job growth. Retrieved from www.bls.gov/emp/ep_table_104.htm.

U.S. Bureau of Labor Statistics. 2016c. Employment projections. Retrieved from www.bls.gov/emp/ep_chart_001.htm.

U.S. Bureau of Labor Statistics. 2016d. Union members summary. Retrieved from www.bls.gov/news.release/union2.nr0.htm.

U.S. Bureau of Labor Statistics. 2016e. Occupations with the largest job growth. Retrieved from www.bls.gov/emp/ep_table_ 104.htm.

U.S. Bureau of Labor Statistics. 2016f. Labor force statistics from the Current Population Survey, "Women in the Labor Force." Retrieved from www.dol.gov/wb/stats/stats_data.htm.

U.S. Bureau of Labor Statistics. 2016g. American Time Use Survey, 2015. Retrieved from www.bls.gov/tus/.

U.S. Bureau of Labor Statistics. 2016h. Current Employment Statistics (CES) National. Table B-3a. Average hourly and weekly earnings of all employees on private nonfarm payrolls by industry sector, seasonally adjusted. June 3.

U.S. Bureau of Labor Statistics. 2017a, March 31. May 2016 national occupational employment and wage estimates, United States. Retrieved from www.bls.gov/oes/2016/may/oes_nat.htm#00-0000.

U.S. Bureau of Labor Statistics. 2017b. Employment projections. Retrieved from www.bls.gov/emp/ep_chart_001.htm.

U.S. Bureau of Labor Statistics. 2017c. Highlights of women's earnings in 2016. Retrieved from www.bls.gov/opub/reports/womens-earnings/2016/home.htm.

U.S. Bureau of Labor Statistics. 2018a. Median weekly earnings of full-time wage and salary workers by detailed occupation and sex. Retrieved from www.bls.gov/cps/cpsaat39.htm.

U.S. Bureau of Labor Statistics. 2018b. Employment status of the civilian noninstitutional population 16 years and over by sex, 1977 to date. Retrieved from www.bls.gov/cps/cpsaat02.htm.

U.S. Bureau of Labor Statistics. 2018b. Injuries, illnesses, and fatalities. Retrieved from www.bls.gov/iif/.

U.S. Bureau of Labor Statistics. 2018c. Labor force statistics from the current population survey. Retrieved from www.bls.gov/web/empsit/cpsee_e16.htm.

U.S. Bureau of Labor Statistics. 2018d, June 1. Current employment statistics. Table B-3a. Average hourly and weekly earnings of all employees on private nonfarm payrolls by industry sector, seasonally adjusted.

U.S. Census Bureau, Current Population Survey, Annual Social and Economic Supplement, 1967 to present. www.census.gov/.

U.S. Census Bureau. 2010a. America's families and living arrangements. Retrieved from www.census.gov/population/www/socdemo/hh-fam/cps2010.html.

U.S. Census Bureau. 2010b. Income, poverty, and health insurance coverage in the United States: 2009. Retrieved from www.census.gov/prod/2010pubs/p60-238.pdf.

U.S. Census Bureau. 2010c. Race and Hispanic origin of the foreign-born population in the United States: 2007. Retrieved from www.census.gov/prod/2010pubs/acs-11.pdf.

U.S. Census Bureau. 2011a. Current Population Survey, March and annual social and economic supplements, 2010 and earlier, Table AD-1. Retrieved from www.census.gov/population/www/socdemo/hh-fam.html#ht.

U.S. Census Bureau. 2011b. The Hispanic population: 2010. Retrieved from www.census.gov/prod/cen2010/briefs/c2010br-04.pdf.

U.S. Census Bureau. 2011c. Overview of race and Hispanic origin: 2010. Retrieved from www.census.gov/prod/cen2010/briefs/c2010br-02.pdf.

U.S. Census Bureau. 2012a. Current Population Survey, March and annual social and economic supplements, 2012 and earlier. Retrieved from www.census.gov/hhes/www/poverty/publications/pubs-cps.html.

U.S. Census Bureau. 2012b. Current Population Survey, November. Retrieved from www.census.gov/hhes/www/socdemo/voting/publications/p20/2012/tables.html.

U.S. Census Bureau. 2012c. Current Population Survey, 2012 annual social and economic supplement. Retrieved from www.census.gov/hhes/www/poverty/publications/pubs-cps.html.

U.S. Census Bureau. 2012d. Most children under 1 are minorities, Census Bureau Reports. Retrieved from www.census.gov/newsroom/releases/archives/population/cb12-90.html.

U.S. Census Bureau. 2012e. *Statistical abstract of the United States*: 2012. Table 1149: Cellular telecommunications industry: 1990–2010. Retrieved from www.census.gov/compendia/statab/cats/information_communications/telecommunications.html.

U.S. Census Bureau. 2016a, November. Current population survey.

U.S. Census Bureau. 2016b. Educational attainment in the United States: 2015. Retrieved from www.census.gov/content/dam/Census/library/publications/2016/demo/p20-578.pdf.

U.S. Census Bureau. 2016c. 2014 American Community Survey 1-year estimates. Data retrieved from census.gov/programs-surveys/acs/.

U.S. Census Bureau. 2016d. 2014 Population projections. Retrieved from www.census.gov/population/projections/data/national/2014.html.

U.S. Census Bureau. 2016e. Educational attainment. Retrieved from www.census.gov/hhes/socdemo/education.

U.S. Census Bureau. 2017a. Table HH-4: Households by size: 1960 to present. Current population survey, March and annual social and economic supplements.

U.S. Census Bureau. 2017b. Income and poverty in the United States: 2016. Retrieved from www.census.gov/content/dam/Census/library/publications/2017/demo/P60-259.pdf.

U.S. Census Bureau. 2017c. Table H-3. Mean household income received by each fifth and top 5 percent, all races: 1967 to 2016. Retrieved from www.census.gov/data/tables/time-series/demo/income-poverty/historical-income-households.html.

U.S. Census Bureau. 2017d. Voting and registration in the election of November 2016. Retrieved from www.census.gov/data/tables/time-series/demo/voting-and-registration/p20-580.html.

U.S. Census Bureau. 2017e. Educational attainment in the United States: 2017. Retrieved from www.census.gov/data/tables/2017/demo/education-attainment/cps-detailed-tables.html.

U.S. Census Bureau. 2017f. 2016 American Community Survey 1-year estimates. Retrieved from census.gov/programs-surveys/acs/.

U.S. Census Bureau. 2017g. Table A-4. Detailed years of school completed by people 25 years and over: 2000 to 2017. Retrieved from www.census.gov/data/tables/time-series/demo/educational-attainment/cps-historical-time-series.html.

U.S. Census Bureau. 2017h. Characteristics of same-sex couple households: 2005 to present. Retrieved from www.census.gov/data/tables/time-series/demo/same-sex-couples/ssc-house-characteristics.html.

U.S. Census Bureau. 2018a. Table 8: Projected size of the native and foreign-born population: Main projections series for the United States, 2017-2060. Retrieved from www.census.gov/data/tables/2017/demo/popproj/2017-summary-tables.html.

U.S. Census Bureau. 2018b. Quick facts: United States. Retrieved from www.census.gov/quickfacts/fact/table/US/PST045217.

U.S. Department of Education. 2016. *Office of Elementary and Secondary Education, Consolidated State Performance Report, 2010–11 through 2013–14.*

U.S. Department of Education. 2017a. Consolidated state performance report, 2010–11 through 2015–16. Office of Elementary and Secondary Education.

U.S. Department of Education. 2017b. The condition of education 2017. National Center for Education Statistics. NCES 2017-144.

U.S. Department of Education, Office for Civil Rights. 2014a. Data snapshot: Teacher equity. Washington, DC. Retrieved from www2.ed.gov/about/offices/list/ocr/docs/crdc-teacher-equity-snapshot.pdf.

U.S. Department of Education, Office for Civil Rights. 2014b. Data snapshot: School discipline. Washington, DC. Retrieved from http://ocrdata.ed.gov/Downloads/CRDC-School-Discipline-Snapshot.pdf.

U.S. Department of Education, Office for Civil Rights. 2015. Guidance on the voluntary use of race to achieve diversity and avoid racial isolation in elementary and secondary schools. Washington, DC.

U.S. Department of Health and Human Services. 2010. *Healthy people 2020.* Retrieved from www.healthypeople.gov/2020/topicsobjectives2020/overview.aspx?topicid=12.

U.S. Department of Health and Human Services. 2016. Health, United States, 2015. Hyattsville, MD. Retrieved from www.cdc.gov/nchs/data/hus/hus15.pdf#015.

U.S. Department of Housing and Urban Development. 2013. Housing discrimination against racial and ethnic minorities, 2012. Washington, DC. Retrieved from www.huduser.gov/portal/publications/fairhsg/hsg_discrimination_2012.html.

U.S. Department of Housing and Urban Development. 2017. The 2017 Annual Homeless Assessment Report (AHAR) to Congress. Retrieved from www.hudexchange.info/resources/documents/2017-AHAR-Part-1.pdf.

U.S. Department of Justice. 2016. About domestic violence. Retrieved from www.ovw.usdoj.gov/domviolence.htm.

U.S. Department of Justice, Federal Bureau of Investigation. 2017a. Crime in the United States: 2016. https://ucr.fbi.gov/crime-in-the-u.s/2016/crime-in-the-u.s.-2016.

U.S. Department of Justice, Federal Bureau of Investigation. 2017b. 2016 hate crime statistics. https://ucr.fbi.gov/hate-crime/2016/hate-crime.

U.S. Department of State. 2016. Saudi Arabia: Country reports on human rights practices for 2015. Retrieved from www.state.gov/j/drl/rls/hrrpt/humanrightsreport/index.htm?year=2015&dlid=252945.

U.S. Equal Employment Opportunity Commission. 2016. Sexual harassment. Retrieved from www.eeoc.gov/laws/types/sexual_ harassment.cfm.

U.S. Government Accountability Office. 2016. Most large profitable U.S. corporations paid tax but effective tax rates differed significantly from the statutory rate. Retrieved from www.gao.gov/assets/680/675844.pdf.

U.S. Government Accountability Office. 2018. K-12 education: Discipline disparities for black students, boys, and students with disabilities. GAO-18-253. Retrieved from https://www.gao.gov/assets/700/690828.pdf.

U.S. Senate Permanent Subcommittee on Investigations. 2011. *Wall Street and the financial crisis.* April 13. Washington, DC. Retrieved from http://hsgac.senate.gov/public/_files/ financial_crisis/financialcrisisreport.pdf.

Ugochukwu, Chioma. 2008. Cultural resistance and resilience amid imported TV programming in Nigeria. *Africa Today* 55 (1): 35–58.

UN Department of Economic and Social Affairs. 2017. The world's cities in 2016. Retrieved from www.un.org/en/development/desa/population/publications/pdf/urbanization/the_worlds_cities_in_2016_data_booklet.pdf.

UN Department of Economic and Social Affairs, Population Division. 2017a. World population prospects: The 2017 revision. Retrieved from www.un.org/development/desa/publications/world-population-prospects-the-2017-revision.html.

UN Department of Economic and Social Affairs, Population Division. 2017b. The end of high fertility is near. Retrieved from https://esa.un.org/unpd/wpp/Publications/Files/PopFacts_2017-3_The-end-of-high-fertility.pdf.

UN Department of Economic and Social Affairs, Population Division. 2017c. International migration report, 2017. Retrieved from www.un.org/en/development/desa/population/migration/publications/migrationreport/index.shtml.

UN Development Programme. 2015. *Human Development Report: 2015.* Retrieved from http://hdr.undp.org/sites/default/files/2015_human_development_report.pdf.

UN Office on Drugs and Crime. 2016. Global report on trafficking in persons, 2016. Retrieved from https://www.unodc.org/documents/data-and-analysis/glotip/2016_Global_Report_on_Trafficking_in_Persons.pdf.

UN Population Fund. 2008. State of the world's population, 2007. Retrieved from www.unfpa.org/swp/2007/presskit/pdf/sowp2007_eng.pdf.

Underwood, Anne, and Jerry Adler. 2005. When cultures clash. *Newsweek,* April 25, pp. 68–72.

UNESCO (United Nations Educational, Scientific, and Cultural Organization). 2015. Re-shaping cultural policies. http://unesdoc.unesco.org/.

UNESCO. 2016a. Culture and development. Retrieved from www.unesco.org/new/en/culture/themes/culture-and-development/.

UNESCO. 2016b. *The globalization of cultural trade: A shift in consumption.* Montreal, Quebec, Canada: UNESCO Institute for Statistics. Retrieved from www.uis.unesco.org/culture/Documents/international-flows-cultural-goods-report-en.pdf.

UNESCO. 2016c. *Diversity in the film industry.* Montreal, Quebec, Canada: UNESCO Institute for Statistics. Retrieved from www.uis.unesco.org/culture/Documents/ip29-diversity-film-data-2016-en.pdf.

UNESCO. 2017. Accountability in education: Meeting our commitments. *Global Education Monitoring Report* 18. Paris: UNESCO.

UNESCO Institute for Statistics. 2017, September. Literacy rates continue to rise from one generation to the next. FS/2017/LIT/45.

UNFPA (United Nations Fund for Population Activities). 2016. Universal access to reproductive health: Progress and challenges. New York. Retrieved from www.unfpa.org/sites/default/files/pub-pdf/UNFPA_Reproductive_Paper_20160120_online.pdf.

UN-Habitat. 2016. Housing & slum upgrading. Retrieved from http://unhabitat.org/urban-themes/housing-slum-upgrading/.

UNHCR (United Nations High Commissioner for Refugees). 2016. Refugee crisis in Europe. Retrieved from www.unrefugees.org/where-we-work/refugee-crisis-in-europe/.

UNHCR (United Nations High Commissioner for Refugees). 2018a. Syria emergency. Retrieved from www.unhcr.org/en-us/syria-emergency.html.

UNHCR (United Nations High Commissioner for Refugees). 2018b. Global trends: Forced displacement in 2017. Retrieved from www.unhcr.org/globaltrends2017/.

UNICEF (United Nations Children's Fund). 2014. The state of the world's children 2015. Retrieved from www.unicef.org/publications/files/SOWC_2015_Summary_and_Tables.pdf.

UNICEF (United Nations Children's Fund). 2015. Committing to child survival: A promise renewed. Retrieved from www.apromiserenewed.org/wp-content/uploads/2015/09/APR_2015_8_Sep_15.pdf.

Unionstats.com. 2018. Union membership and coverage database from the CPS.

Unitarian Universalist Association of Congregations. 2013. Existence of a higher power in Unitarian Universalism. Retrieved from www.uua.org/beliefs/welcome/higherpower/index.shtml.

United Nations. 2015. The world's women 2015: Trends and statistics. United Nations Department of Economic and Social Affairs. Retrieved from http://unstats.un.org/unsd/gender/downloads/WorldsWomen2015_report.pdf.

United Nations. 2016. Background information on sexual violence used as a tool of war. Retrieved from www.un.org/en/preventgenocide/rwanda/about/bgsexualviolence.shtml.

United Nations. 2018. Sustainable development goals. Retrieved from www.un.org/sustainabledevelopment/poverty/.

United Nations Development Programme. 2016. *Human development report 2016: Human development for everyone.* New York, NY: UNDP.

United Nations Environment Programme. 2016. Rate of environmental damage increasing across the planet but there is still time to reverse worst impacts if governments act now, UNEP assessment says. Retrieved from http://unep.org/newscentre/Default.aspx?DocumentID=27074&ArticleID=36180&l=en.

Unnever, James D., and Francis T. Cullen. 2007. The racial divide in support for the death penalty. Does white racism matter? *Social Forces* 85 (3): 1281–301.

Unnever, James D., and Francis T. Cullen. 2010. Racial-ethnic intolerance and support for capital punishment: A cross-national comparison. *Criminology* 48 (3): 831–64.

Upton, Rachel, and Courtney Tanenbaum. 2014, September. The role of historically black colleges and universities as pathway providers: Institutional pathways to the STEM PhD among black students. American Institutes for Research. Issue Brief, Broadening Participation in STEM Graduate Education.

Urban, Wayne J., and Jennings L. Wagoner Jr. 2009. *American education: A history,* 4th ed. New York: Routledge.

Urbatsch, Robert. 2014. *Families' values: How parents, siblings, and children affect political attitudes.* New York: Oxford University Press.

Vaidhyanathan, Siva. 2018. *Antisocial media: How Facebook disconnects us and undermines democracy.* New York: Oxford University Press.

Vaisse, Justin. 2004. *Veiled meaning: The French law banning religious symbols in public schools.* Washington, DC: Brookings Institution.

Valkenburg, Patti M., and Jessica Taylor Piotrowski. 2017. *Plugged in: How media attract and affect youth.* New Haven, CT: Yale University Press.

Valkenburg, Patti M., Jochen Peter, and Joseph B. Walther. 2016. Media effects: Theory and research. *Annual Review of Psychology* 67: 315–38.

Vallas, Steven Peter. 2007. Theorizing teamwork under contemporary capitalism. *Research in* the *Sociology of Work* 16: 3–24.

van Eeden-Moorefield, Brad, April L. Few-Demo, Kristen Benson, Jacqueline Bible, and Shannon Lummer. 2018. A content analysis of LGBT research in top family journals 2000–2015. *Journal of Family Issues* 39 (5): 1374–95.

van Gennep, Arnold. (1909) 1961. *The rites of passage,* trans. Monika B. Vizedom and Gabrielle L. Caffee. Chicago: University of Chicago Press.

Van Houtte, Mieke, Jannick Demanet, and Peter Stevens. 2013. Curriculum Tracking and Teacher Evaluations of Individual Students: Selection, Adjustment, or Labeling? *Social Psychology of Education* 16 (3): 329–52.

van Reijmersdal, Eva A., Sophie C. Boerman, Moniek Buijzen, and Esther Rozendaal. 2017. This is advertising! Effects of disclosing television brand placement on adolescents. *Journal of Youth and Adolescence* 46: 328–42.

Vander Wal, Jillon S. 2012. Unhealthy weight control behaviors among adolescents. *Journal of Health Psychology* 17 (1): 110–20.

Vanoutrive, Thomas. 2016. Don't think of them as roads. Think of them as road transport markets: Congestion pricing as a neoliberal political project. *Progress in Planning.* doi:10.1016/j.progress.2016.04.001

Vargas, Robert. 2016. *Wounded city: Violent turf wars in a Chicago barrio.* New York: Oxford University Press.

Vartabedian, Ralph, and Ken Bensinger. 2010. Toyota's structure may be an issue. *Los Angeles Times,* February 23, p. A1.

Vaughan, Diane. 1996. *The* Challenger *launch decision.* Chicago: University of Chicago Press.

Vaughan, Diane. 2003. History as cause: *Columbia* and *Challenger. Report, Columbia Accident Investigation Board,* vol. 1, ch. 8.

Vaught, Charles, and David L. Smith. 2003. Incorporation and mechanical solidarity in an underground coal mine. In *The cultural study of work,* ed. Douglas Harper and Helene M. Lawson, pp. 96–115. Lanham, MD: Rowman & Littlefield.

Vaznis, James. 2017. Report: Half of Boston's school buildings in "fair" condition. Retrieved from www.bostonglobe.com/metro/2017/03/01/city-report-sizes-school-repair-needs/ZmkLxbxu0h3PbdjtMwFJZL/story.html.

Veblen, Thorstein. (1899) 1973. *The theory of the leisure class.* Boston: Houghton Mifflin.

Vedantam, Shankar. 2005. See no bias. *Washington Post Magazine,* January 23, pp. 12–17, 38.

Verhoeven, Piet. 2016. The co-production of business news and its effects: The corporate framing mediation-moderation model. *Public Relations Review.* Online preview. doi:10.1016/j.pubrev.2016.03.006

Verrier, Richard. 2009. MPAA stops disclosing average costs of making and marketing movies. Retrieved from http://articles.latimes.com/2009/apr/01/business/fi-cotown-mpaa1.

Vertigans, Stephen. 2013. *The sociology of terrorism: People, places and processes.* New York: Routledge.

Vertovec, Steven. 2009. *Transnationalism.* New York: Routledge.

Vespa, Jonathan, David M. Armstrong, and Lauren Medina. 2018. Demographic turning points for the United States: Population projections for 2020 to 2060. Retrieved from www.census.gov/content/dam/Census/library/publications/2018/demo/P25_1144.pdf.

Vespa, Jonathan, Jamie M. Lewis, and Rose M. Kreider. 2013. America's families and living arrangements: 2012. U.S. Census Bureau. August. Retrieved from www.census.gov/prod/2013pubs/p20-570.pdf.

Vigil, Tammy R., and H. Denis Wu. 2015. Facebook users' engagement and perceived life satisfaction. *Media and Communication* 3 (1): 5–16.

Vine, David. 2015. *Base nation: How US military bases abroad harm America and the world.* New York: Metropolitan Books.

Voas, David and Mark Chaves. 2016. Is the United States a counterexample to the secularization thesis? *American Journal of Sociology* 121 (5): 1517–56.

Voas, David, and Fenella Fleischmann. 2012. Islam moves west: Religious change in the first and second generations. *Annual Review of Sociology* 38: 525–45.

Vogel, Steve. 2007. *The Pentagon: A history.* New York: Random House.

Volz, Dustin. 2015. U.S. regulators reject push for "do not track" internet rules. Retrieved from www.reuters.com/article/usa-tech-tracking/u-s-regulators-reject-push-for-do-not-track-internet-rules-idUSL1N1311XW20151106.

von Clausewitz, Carl. (1832) 1976. *On war,* ed. and trans. Michael Howard and Peter Paret. Princeton, NJ: Princeton University Press.

Wade, Ann, and Tanya Beran. 2011. Cyberbullying: The new era of bullying. *Canadian Journal of Social Psychology* 26 (1): 44–61.

Wagenheim, Kal, and Olga Jimenez De Wagenheim. 2013. *The Puerto Ricans.* Princeton, NJ: Marcus Wiener.

Wajcman, Judy. 2008. Life in the fast lane? Toward a sociology of technology and time. *British Journal of Sociology* 59 (1): 59–77.

Wajcman, Judy. 2015. *Pressed for time: The acceleration of life in digital capitalism.* Chicago: University of Chicago Press.

Wakefield, Sara, and Christopher Uggen. 2010. Incarceration and stratification. *Annual Review of Sociology* 36: 387–406.

Wald, Kenneth D., and Allison Calhoun-Brown. 2014. *Religion and politics in the United States.* New York: Rowman & Littlefield.

Walker, Edward T. 2014. *Grassroots for hire: Public affairs consultants in American democracy.* New York: Cambridge University Press.

Walker, Edward T., 2015. Beyond the rhetoric of the "sharing economy." *Contexts* 14 (1): 15–17.

Walker, Edward T. and Christopher M. Rea. 2014. The political mobilization of firms and industries. *Annual Review of Sociology* 40: 281–304.

Walker, Gordon. 2012. *Environmental justice: Concepts, evidence, and politics.* New York: Routledge.

Walker, Kent. 2017. Four steps we're taking today to fight terrorism online. Retrieved from https://blog.google/topics/google-europe/four-steps-were-taking-today-fight-online-terror/.

Walker, Pat, ed. 1979. *Between labor and capital.* Boston: South End Press.

Wallerstein, Immanuel. 1974. *The modern world-system.* New York: Academic Press.

Wallerstein, Immanuel. 1979. *The capitalist world-economy.* New York: Cambridge University Press.

Wallerstein, Immanuel, Carlos Aguirre Rojas, and Charles C. Lemert. 2012. *Uncertain worlds: World-systems analysis in changing times.* New York: Taylor and Francis.

Walters, Mikel L., Jieru Chen, and Matthew J. Breiding. 2013. The National Intimate Partner and Sexual Violence Survey (NISVS): 2010 Findings on victimization by sexual orientation. Atlanta, GA: Centers for Disease Control and Prevention. Retrieved from www.cdc.gov/violenceprevention/pdf/nisvs_sofindings.pdf.

Wang, Tova Andrea. 2012. *The politics of voter suppression.* Ithaca, NY: Cornell University Press.

Wang, Wendy. 2015. Interracial marriage: Who is "marrying out"? Washington, DC: Pew Research Center. Retrieved from www. pewresearch.org/fact-tank/2015/06/12/interracial-marriage-who-is-marrying-out/.

Wang, Wendy, and Kim Parker. 2014. Record share of Americans have never married. Washington, DC: Pew Research Center. Retrieved from www.pewsocialtrends.org/2014/09/24/record-share-of-americans-have-never-married/.

Ward, Brian W., James M. Dahlhamer, Adena M. Galinsky, and Sarah S. Joestl. 2014. Sexual orientation and health among U.S. adults: National Health Interview Survey, 2013. *National Health Statistics Reports* 77 (July 15). Retrieved from www.cdc.gov/nchs/data/nhsr/nhsr077.pdf.

Ward, L. Monique, and Jennifer Stevens Aubrey. 2017. *Watching gender: How stereotypes in movies and on TV impact kids' development.* San Francisco, CA: Common Sense Media. Retrieved from www.commonsensemedia.org/sites/default/files/uploads/pdfs/2017_commonsense_watchinggender_fullreport_0620.pdf.

Warde, Alan. 2015. The sociology of consumption: Its recent development. *Annual Review of Sociology* 41: 117–34.

Warde, Alan. 2017. *Consumption: A sociological analysis.* New York: Palgrave Macmillan.

Warner, Kris. 2013. The decline of unionization in the United States: Some lessons from Canada. *Labor Studies Journal* 38: 110–38.

Warner, Michael, Jonathan VanAntwerpen, and Craig Calhoun, eds. 2010. *Varieties of secularism in a secular age.* Cambridge, MA: Harvard University Press.

Warren, Wendy. 2016. *New England Bound: Slavery and Colonization in Early America.* New York: Norton.

Waskul, Dennis D., and Justin A. Martin. 2010. Now the orgy is over. *Symbolic Interaction* 33 (2): 297–318.

Watts, Duncan. 2004. The "new" science of networks. *Annual Review of Sociology* 30: 243–70.

Watts, Jacqueline H. 2015. *Gender, health and healthcare: Women's and men's experience of health and working in healthcare roles.* New York: Routledge.

We Are Social. 2018. Global digital report. Retrieved from https://wearesocial.com/sg/blog/2018/01/global-digital-report-2018.

Weber, Max. (1905) 1958. *The Protestant ethic and the spirit of capitalism,* trans. Talcott Parsons. New York: Scribner.

Weber, Max. (1915) 1946a. Religious rejections of the world and their directions. In *From Max Weber: Essays in sociology,* ed. H. H. Gerth and C. Wright Mills, pp. 323–59. New York: Oxford University Press.

Weber, Max. (1915) 1946b. The social psychology of world religions. In *From Max Weber: Essays in sociology,* ed. Hans Gerth and C. Wright Mills, pp. 267–301. New York: Oxford University Press.

Weber, Max. (1919) 1946a. Politics as a vocation. In *From Max Weber: Essays in sociology,* ed. H. H. Gerth and C. Wright Mills, pp. 77–128. New York: Oxford University Press.

Weber, Max. (1919) 1946b. Science as a vocation. In *From Max Weber: Essays in sociology,* ed. H. H. Gerth and C. Wright Mills, pp. 129–56. New York: Oxford University Press.

Weber, Max. (1922) 1978. *Economy and society,* ed. Guenther Rother and Claus Wittich. Berkeley: University of California Press.

Weber, Max. (1949) 2011. *Methodology of social sciences,* trans. Edward A. Shils and Henry A. Finch. New Brunswick, NJ: Transaction.

Weber, Max. 1946. *From Max Weber: Essays in sociology,* trans. Hans Gerth and C. Wright Mills. New York: Oxford University Press.

Weiner, Rachel. 2013. Black voters turned out at higher rate than white voters in 2012 and 2008. *Washington Post,* April 29. Retrieved from www.washingtonpost.com/blogs/the-fix/wp/2013/04/29/black-turnout-was-higher-than-white-turnout-in-2012-and-2008/.

Weinstein, Jay. 2010. *Social change.* Lanham, MD: Rowman & Littlefield.

Weiss, Gregory L., and Lynne E. Lonnquist. 2015. *Sociology of health, healing, and illness.* New York: Routledge.

Weitz, Rose. 2017. *The sociology of health, illness, and health care: A critical approach.* Boston: Cengage.

Wellman, Barry, and Scot Wortley. 1990. Different strokes from different folks: Community ties and social support. *American Journal of Sociology* 96 (3): 558–88.

Welzel, Christian, and Ronald Inglehart. 2010. Agency, values, and well-being: A human development model. *Social Indicators Research* 97: 43–63.

Wesch, David. 2009. YouTube and you: Experiences of self-awareness in the context collapse of the recording webcam. *Explorations in Media Ecology* 8 (2): 19–34.

West, Candace, and Don H. Zimmerman. 1987. Doing gender. *Gender & Society* 1 (2): 125–51.

Western, Bruce. 2007. *Punishment and inequality in America.* New York: Russell Sage Foundation.

White, Peter B., Dragana Vidovic, Belén González, Kristian Skrede Gleditsch, and David E. Cunningham. 2015. Nonviolence as a weapon of the resourceful: From claims to tactics in mobilization. *Mobilization: An International Quarterly* 20 (4): 471–91.

Whitehouse, Kaja. 2016. JPMorgan CEO gets 35% pay raise to $27M amid cutbacks. *USA Today,* January 22. Retrieved from www.usatoday.com/story/money/2016/01/21/jpmorgan-ceo-gets-pay-raise-35-27m/79132018/.

Whiteley, Paul. 2016. Four reasons why the polls got the U.S. election result so wrong. Retrieved from www.newsweek.com/polls-2016-us-elections-trump-potus-hillary-clinton-520291.

Whyte, William Foote. (1943) 1993. *Street corner society,* 4th ed. Chicago: University of Chicago Press.

Wike, Richard, Bruce Stokes, Jacob Poushter, and Janell Fetterolf. 2017. U.S. image suffers as publics around world question Trump's leadership. Washington, DC: Pew Research Center. www.pewglobal.org/2017/06/26/u-s-image-suffers-as-publics-around-world-question-trumps-leadership/.

Wiley, Stephanie A., and Finn-Aage Esbensen. 2016. The effect of police contact: Does official intervention result in deviance amplification? *Crime & Delinquency* 62 (3): 283–307.

Wilk, Richard. 2016. Consuming ourselves to death. In *Reflecting on America: Anthropological views of U.S. culture,* 2nd ed., ed. Clare L. Boulanger, pp. 29–39. New York: Routledge.

Wilkerson, Isabel. 2010. *The warmth of other suns: The epic story of America's Great Migration.* New York: Vintage.

Williams, Krissah. 2005. In hip-hop, making name-dropping pay. *Washington Post,* August 29, pp. D1, D9.

Williams, Robin M. 1970. *American society: A sociological interpretation.* New York: Knopf.

Willis, Paul. 1977. *Learning to labor.* New York: Columbia University Press.

Wilson, Clint C., II, Félix Gutiérrez, and Lena M. Chao. 2013. *Racism, sexism, and the media.* Thousand Oaks, CA: Sage.

Wilson, James Q. 2002. *The marriage problem.* New York: Harper.

Wilson, William Julius. 1980. *The declining significance of race.* Chicago: University of Chicago Press.

Wilson, William Julius. 1996. *When work disappears: The world of the new urban poor.* New York: Knopf.

Wilson, William Julius. 2016. Black youths, joblessness, and the other side of "Black Lives Matter." *Ethnic and Racial Studies* 39 (8): 1450–57.

Wilson, William Julius. 2017. Race, class, politics, and the disappearance of work: A rejoinder. *Ethnic and Racial Studies* 40 (9): 1502–07.

Wimmer, Andreas, and Kevin Lewis. 2010. Beyond and below racial homophily: ERG models of a friendship network documented on Facebook. *American Journal of Sociology* 116 (2): 583–642.

Wingfield, Adia Harvey. 2015. Are some emotions marked "whites only"?: Racialized feeling rules in professional workplaces. In *Working in America: Continuity, conflict, and change in a new economic era,* 4th ed., ed. Amy S. Wharton, pp. 201–15. New York: Taylor & Francis.

Wolfe, Alan. 2005. *The transformation of American religion.* Chicago: University of Chicago Press.

Wolff, Edward. 2017. Household wealth trends in the United States, 1962 to 2016: Has the middle class wealth recovered?" Cambridge, MA: National Bureau of Economic Research. Working Paper 24085. www.nber.org/papers/w24085.

Wolff, Edward N. 2014. Household wealth trends in the United States, 1962–2013: What happened over the Great Recession? Working Paper 20733. National Bureau of Economic Research. Retrieved from www.nber.org/papers/w20733.pdf.

Women's Media Center. 2015. The status of women in the US media, 2015. Retrieved from http://wmc.3cdn.net/83bf6082a319460eb1_hsrm680x2.pdf.

Women's Media Center. 2017. The status of women in the U.S. media, 2017. Retrieved from www.womensmediacenter.com/assets/site/reports/the-status-of-women-in-u.s.-media-2017/10c550d19ef9f3688f_mlbres2jd.pdf.

Women's Prison Association. 2015. Foreword: Women's Prison Association biannual review for years 2014–2015. New York.

Wong, Edward. 2013. Air pollution linked to 1.2 million premature deaths in China. *New York Times,* April 1. Retrieved from www.nytimes.com/2013/04/02/world/asia/air-pollution-linked-to-1-2-million-deaths-in-china.html?_r=0.

Woolley, Samuel C. and Philip N. Howard. 2017. Computational propaganda worldwide: Executive summary. Working Paper 2017.11. Oxford, UK: Project on Computational Propaganda. comprop.oii.ox.ac.uk.

World Bank. 2016. World development indicators. http://data.worldbank.org/indicator/SP.DYN.LE00.IN.

World Bank. 2018. World Bank country and lending groups. Retrieved from https://datahelpdesk.worldbank.org/knowledgebase/articles/906519-world-bank-country-and-lending-groups.

World Bank Database. 2014. Retrieved from http://data.worldbank.org/indicator/NY.GNP.PCAP.PP.CD/countries.

World Health Organization. 2013. Global and regional estimates of violence against women: Prevalence and health effects of intimate partner violence and non-partner sexual violence. Retrieved from http://apps.who.int/iris/bitstream/10665/85239/1/9789241564625_eng.pdf.

World Health Organization. 2016a. Female genital mutilation. Retrieved from www.who.int/mediacentre/factsheets/fs241/en/.

World Health Organization. 2016b. Male circumcision for HIV prevention. Retrieved from www.who.int/hiv/topics/malecircumcision/en/.

World Health Organization. 2016c. *Preventing disease through healthy environments.* Geneva, Switzerland. Retrieved from http://apps.who.int/iris/bitstream/10665/204585/1/9789241565196_eng.pdf.

World Health Organization. 2016d. *World health statistics 2016.* Geneva, Switzerland. Retrieved from http://apps.who.int/gho/data/view.main.182?lang=en.

World Inequality Database. 2018. http://wid.world/data/.

World Internet Stats. 2018. Internet usage statistics. www.internetworldstats.com/stats.htm.

World Values Survey. 2010–2014. Wave 6. OFFICIAL AGGREGATE v.20150418. World Values Survey Association. Aggregate File Producer: Asep/JDS, Madrid SPAIN. Retrieved from www.worldvaluessurvey.org/.

Worldwatch Institute. 2006. *State of the world, 2006.* New York: Norton.

Wray, John. 2010. Lives: Acquired taste. *New York Times Magazine,* February 25, p. 50.

Wright, Daniel, Gail Self, and Chris Justice. 2000. Memory conformity: Exploring misinformation effects when presented by another person. *British Journal of Psychology* 91: 189–202.

Wright, Dwayne Kwaysee, and Liliana M. Garces. 2018. Understanding the controversy around race-based affirmative action in American higher education. In *Controversies on campus: Debating the issues confronting American universities in the 21st century,* ed. Joy Blanchard, pp. 3–21. Santa Barbara, CA: Praeger.

Wright, Erik Olin. 1985. *Classes.* London: Verso Press.

Wrong, Dennis. 1979. *Power: Its forms, bases and uses.* New York: Oxford University Press.

Wuthnow, Robert. 2008. The sociological study of values. *Sociological Forum* 23 (June): 333–43.

Yang, Chia-chen, and B. Bradford Brown. 2015. Online self-presentation on Facebook and self development during the college transition. *Journal of Youth and Adolescence* 45 (2): 402–16.

Yavorsky, Jill E., Claire M. Kamp Dush, and Sarah J. Schoppe-Sullivan. 2015. The production of inequality: The gender division of labor across the transition to parenthood. *Journal of Marriage and Family* 77 (3): 662–79.

Yglesias, Matthew. 2018. The Parkland conspiracy theories, explained. Retrieved from www.vox.com/policy-and-politics/2018/2/22/17036018/parkland-conspiracy-theories.

Yoon, InJeong. 2016. Why is it not just a joke? Analysis of Internet memes associated with racism and hidden ideology of colorblindness. *Journal of Cultural Research in Art Education* 33: 92.

Yukl, G., H. Kim, and C. Falbe. 1996. Antecedents of influence outcomes. *Journal of Applied Psychology* 81: 309–17.

Zacharek, Stephanie, Eliana Dockterman, and Haley Sweetland Edwards. 2017. The silence breakers. Retrieved from http://time.com/time-person-of-the-year-2017-silence-breakers/.

Zaimov, Stoyan. 2013. Pope Francis condemns big business idolatry, global economy for high unemployment. *The Christian Post*, September 24. Retrieved from www.christianpost.com/news/pope-francis-condemns-big-business-idolatry-global-economy-for-high-unemployment-105202/.

Zappos. 2016. Quick stats and FAQ—updated 1/15/16. Retrieved from www.zappos.com/wow/super-cloud-teal-offer-faq.

Zeisler, Andi. 2016. *We were feminists once: From Riot Grrrl to CoverGirl®, the buying and selling of a political movement.* New York: Public Affairs/Perseus.

Zickuhr, Kathryn. 2013. Who's not online and why. Washington, DC: Pew Research Center. www.pewinternet.org/files/old-media//Files/Reports/2013/PIP_Offline%20adults_092513_PDF.pdf.

Zimmerman, Jonathan. 2002. *Whose America? Culture Wars in the Public Schools. Cambridge:* Harvard University Press.

Zimmerman, Jonathan, and Emily Robertson. 2017. *The case for contention: Teaching controversial issues in American schools.* Chicago: University of Chicago Press.

Zollmann, Florian. 2017. Bringing propaganda back into news media studies. *Critical Sociology* 1-17, 0896920517731134.

Zukin, Sharon, and Jennifer Smith Maguire. 2004. Consumers and consumption. *Annual Review of Sociology,* 30: 173–97.

Zweig, Michael. 2011. *The working class majority.* Ithaca, NY: Cornell University Press.

Name Index

Italicized page numbers indicate material in tables, figures, and maps.

C

D

E

M

T

U

V

Subject Index

Italicized page numbers indicate material in tables, figures, and maps.

C

F

G

H

I

S

T

U

V

W

X

Y

Z

Applying Sociological Theory

Sociological theory is discussed and applied in every chapter of *Experience Sociology*. Listed here is a sample of places in the text where theory is applied, loosely organized around the broad sociological perspectives with which theories are sometimes associated. The numbers in parentheses indicate the chapters in which the topics appear.